T0189547

Lecture Notes in Computer Science 12396

More information about this series at http://www.springer.com/series/7407

Igor Farkaš · Paolo Masulli ·
Stefan Wermter (Eds.)

Artificial Neural Networks and Machine Learning – ICANN 2020

29th International Conference on Artificial Neural Networks
Bratislava, Slovakia, September 15–18, 2020
Proceedings, Part I

Springer

Editors
Igor Farkaš (iD)
Department of Applied Informatics
Comenius University in Bratislava
Bratislava, Slovakia

Stefan Wermter (iD)
Department of Informatics
University of Hamburg
Hamburg, Germany

Paolo Masulli (iD)
Department of Applied Mathematics
and Computer Science
Technical University of Denmark
Kgs. Lyngby, Denmark

ISSN 0302-9743   ISSN 1611-3349 (electronic)
Lecture Notes in Computer Science
ISBN 978-3-030-61608-3   ISBN 978-3-030-61609-0 (eBook)
https://doi.org/10.1007/978-3-030-61609-0

LNCS Sublibrary: SL1 – Theoretical Computer Science and General Issues

This Springer imprint is published by the registered company Springer Nature Switzerland AG
The registered company address is: Gewerbestrasse 11, 6330 Cham, Switzerland

Preface

Research on artificial neural networks has progressed over decades, in recent years being fueled especially by deep learning that has proven to be data-greedy but efficient in solving various, mostly supervised tasks. Applications of artificial neural networks, especially related to artificial intelligence, influence our lives, reaching new horizons. Examples range from autonomous car driving, virtual assistants, and decision support systems, to healthcare data analytics, financial forecasting, and smart devices in our homes, just to name a few. These developments, however, also provide challenges, which were not imaginable previously, e.g., verification to prevent manipulation of voice, videos, or people's opinions during elections.

The International Conference on Artificial Neural Networks (ICANN) is the annual flagship conference of the European Neural Network Society (ENNS). This year, the special situation due to the COVID-19 pandemic influenced the planning of this conference in an unprecedented way. Based on the restrictions to travel and gatherings, as well as forecasts for the following months, it was not appropriate to decide for a large gathering such as ICANN to take place as a physical event in September 2020. Therefore, after a lot of consideration and discussions, the Organizing Committee, together with the Executive Committee of ENNS decided to postpone the physical meeting of ICANN 2020 and schedule next year's ICANN in September 2021 in Bratislava, Slovakia, since we also believe that a physical meeting has so many advantages compared to a virtual one.

Nevertheless, we decided to assist and do justice to the authors by disseminating their current work already completed for this year, running the paper selection and review process so that the successful submissions could appear online. Following a long-standing successful collaboration, the proceedings of ICANN are published as volumes within Springer's *Lecture Notes in Computer Science* series. The response to this year's call for papers resulted in an impressive number of 381 article submissions, of which almost all were long papers. After the official announcement that the conference would be postponed, 21 authors decided to withdraw their papers. The paper selection and review process that followed was decided during the online meeting of the Bratislava organizing team and the ENNS Executive Committee. The 20 Program Committee (PC) members agreed to review the long papers in stages. Stage one involved the review of 249 papers, of which 188 papers were selected for a stage-two review by independent reviewers. The majority of PC members had doctoral degrees (85%) and 70% of them were also professors. At the stage-two review, in total, 154 reviewers participated in the process, all having filled in an online questionnaire focusing on their areas of expertise, which significantly helped the general chair to properly assign papers to them. The reviewers were assigned one to three articles, but each article received three reports by the PC and reviewers, and these served as a major source for the final decision.

In total, 142 articles were accepted for the proceedings and the authors were requested to submit final versions. The acceptance rate was hence 37% when calculated from all initial submissions, or 57% when calculated from the initial papers selected for stage-two reviews. A list of PC members and reviewers, who agreed to publish their names, is included in these proceedings. With these procedures we tried to keep the quality of the proceedings high, while still having a critical mass of contributions reflecting the progress of the field. Overall, we hope that these proceedings will contribute to the dissemination of new results by the neural network community during these challenging times and that we can again have a physical ICANN in 2021.

We greatly appreciate the PC members and the reviewers for their invaluable work.

September 2020   Igor Farkaš
                                                       Paolo Masulli
                                                      Stefan Wermter

Organization

General Chairs

Igor Farkaš — Comenius University in Bratislava, Slovakia
L'ubica Beňušková — Comenius University in Bratislava, Slovakia

Organizing Committee Chairs

Kristína Malinovská — Comenius University in Bratislava, Slovakia
Alessandra Lintas — ENNS Lausanne, Switzerland

Honorary Chairs

Stefan Wermter — University of Hamburg, Germany
Věra Kůrková — Czech Academy of Sciences, Czech Republic

Program Committee

L'ubica Beňušková — Comenius University in Bratislava, Slovakia
Jérémie Cabessa — Panthéon-Assas University Paris II, France
Wlodek Duch — Nicolaus Copernicus University, Poland
Igor Farkaš — Comenius University in Bratislava, Slovakia
Juraj Holas — Comenius University in Bratislava, Slovakia
Věra Kůrková — Czech Academy of Sciences, Czech Republic
Tomáš Kuzma — Comenius University in Bratislava, Slovakia
Alessandra Lintas — University of Lausanne, Switzerland
Kristína Malinovská — Comenius University in Bratislava, Slovakia
Paolo Masulli — Technical University of Denmark, Denmark
Alessio Micheli — University of Pisa, Italy
Sebastian Otte — University of Tübingen, Germany
Jaakko Peltonen — University of Tampere, Finland
Antonio J. Pons — University of Barcelona, Spain
Martin Takáč — Comenius University in Bratislava, Slovakia
Igor V. Tetko — Technical University Munich, Germany
Matúš Tuna — Comenius University in Bratislava, Slovakia
Alessandro E. P. Villa — University of Lausanne, Switzerland
Roseli Wedemann — Rio de Janeiro State University, Brazil
Stefan Wermter — University of Hamburg, Germany

Communication Chair

Paolo Masulli   ENNS, Technical University of Denmark, Denmark

Reviewers

Argimiro Arratia   Polytechnic University of Catalonia, Spain
Andrá Artelt   Bielefeld University, Germany
Miguel Atencia   Universidad de Malaga, Spain
Cristian Axenie   Huawei German Research Center, Germany
Fatemeh Azimi   TU Kaiserslautern, Germany
Jatin Bedi   BITS Pilani, India
L'ubica Beňušková   Comenius University in Bratislava, Slovakia
Bernhard Bermeitinger   Universität St. Gallen, Switzerland
Yann Bernard   Inria, France
Jyostna Devi Bodapati   Indian Institute of Technology Madras, India
Nicolas Bougie   National Institute of Informatics, Japan
Evgeny Burnaev   Skoltech, Russia
Rüdiger Busche   Osnabrück University, Germany
Jérémie Cabessa   Panthéon-Assas University Paris II, France
Hugo Eduardo Camacho   Universidad Autónoma de Tamaulipas, Mexico
Antonio Candelieri   University of Milano-Bicocca, Italy
Siyu Cao   Beijing Jiaotong University, China
Antonio Carta   University of Pisa, Italy
Nico Cavalcanti   UFPE, Brazil
Gavneet Singh Chadha   South Westphalia University of Applied Sciences,
                                 Germany
Shengjia Chen   Guangxi Normal University, China
Alessandro Di Nuovo   Sheffield Hallam University, UK
Tayssir Doghri   INRS, Canada
Haizhou Du   Shanghai University of Electric Power, China
Wlodzislaw Duch   Nicolaus Copernicus University, Poland
Ola Engkvist   AstraZeneca, Sweden
Manfred Eppe   University of Hamburg, Germany
Yuchun Fang   Shanghai University, China
Igor Farkaš   Comenius University in Bratislava, Slovakia
Oliver Gallitz   Technische Hochschule Ingolstadt, Germany
Jochen Garcke   University of Bonn, Germany
Dominik Geissler   Relayr GmbH, Germany
Claudio Giorgio   Catholic University of Milan, Italy
  Giancaterino
Francesco Giannini   University of Siena, Italy
Kathrin Grosse   CISPA Helmholtz Center for Information Security,
                                 Germany
Philipp Grüning   University of Lübeck, Germany
Michael Guckert   Technische Hochschule Mittelhessen, Germany

An Luo	South China University of Technology, China
Thomas Lymburn	The University of Western Australia, Australia
Kleanthis Malialis	University of Cyprus, Cyprus
Kristína Malinovská	Comenius University in Bratislava, Slovakia
Fragkiskos Malliaros	CentraleSupélec, France
Gilles Marcou	University of Strasbourg, France
Michael Marino	Universität Osnabrück, Germany
Paolo Masulli	Technical University of Denmark, Denmark
Guillaume Matheron	Institut des Systèmes Intelligents et de Robotique, France
Alessio Micheli	University of Pisa, Italy
Florian Mirus	BMW Group, Germany
Roman Neruda	Institute of Computer Science, ASCR, Czech Republic
Hasna Njah	University of Sfax, Tunisia
Mihaela Oprea	Petroleum-Gas University of Ploiesti, Romania
Christoph Ostrau	Bielefeld University, Germany
Sebastian Otte	University of Tübingen, Germany
Hyeyoung Park	Kyungpook National University Daegu Campus, South Korea
Jaakko Peltonen	Tampere University, Finland
Daniele Perlo	University of Turin, Italy
Vincenzo Piuri	University of Milan, Italy
Antonio Javier Pons Rivero	Universitat Politècnica de Catalunya, Spain
Mike Preuss	Universiteit Leiden, The Netherlands
Miloš Prágr	Czech Technical University, FEE, Czech Republic
Yili Qu	Sun Yat-Sen University, China
Laya Rafiee	Concordia University, Canada
Rajkumar Ramamurthy	Fraunhofer IAIS, Germany
Zuzana Rošťáková	Slovak Academy of Sciences, Slovakia
Frank Röder	University of Hamburg, Germany
Jun Sang	Chongqing University, China
Anindya Sarkar	Indian Institute of Technology, India
Yikemaiti Sataer	Southeast University, China
Simone Scardapane	Sapienza University of Rome, Italy
Jochen Schmidt	Rosenheim University of Applied Sciences, Germany
Cedric Schockaert	Paul Wurth Geprolux S.A., Luxembourg
Friedhelm Schwenker	University of Ulm, Germany
Andreas Sedlmeier	LMU Munich, Germany
Gabriela Šejnová	Czech Technical University in Prague, Czech Republic
Alexandru Serban	Radboud University, The Netherlands
Linlin Shen	Shenzhen University, China
Shashwat Shukla	Indian Institute of Technology Bombay, India
Caio Silva	Universidade Federal de Pernambuco, Brazil
Aleksander Smywiński-Pohl	AGH University of Science and Technology, Poland
Pouya Soltani Zarrin	IHP, Germany

Miguel Soriano	Institute for Cross-Disciplinary Physics and Complex Systems, Spain
Lea Steffen	FZI Research Center for Information Technology, Germany
Michael Stettler	University of Tübingen, Germany
Ruxandra Stoean	University of Craiova, Romania
Jérémie Sublime	ISEP, France
Chanchal Suman	IIT Patna, India
Xiaoqi Sun	Shanghai University, China
Alexander Sutherland	University of Hamburg, Germany
Zaneta Swiderska-Chadaj	Warsaw University of Technology, Poland
Rudolf Szadkowski	Czech Technical University in Prague, Czech Republic
Philippe Thomas	Université de Lorraine, France
Shiro Takagi	The University of Tokyo, Japan
Martin Takáč	Comenius University, Slovakia
Max Talanov	Kazan Federal University, Russia
Enzo Tartaglione	Università degli Studi Torino, Italy
Igor Tetko	Helmholtz Zentrum München, Germany
Juan-Manuel Torres-Moreno	Université d'Avignon, France
Jochen Triesch	Frankfurt Institute for Advanced Studies, Germany
Matúš Tuna	Comenius University in Bratislava, Slovakia
Takaya Ueda	Ritsumeikan University, Japan
Sagar Verma	CentraleSupélec, France
Ricardo Vigário	Universidade NOVA de Lisboa, Portugal
Alessandro E. P. Villa	University of Lausanne, Switzerland
Paolo Viviani	Noesis Solutions NV, Belgium
Shuo Wang	Monash University and CSIRO, Australia
Huiling Wang	Tampere University, Finland
Xing Wang	Ningxia University, China
Zhe Wang	Soochow University, China
Roseli Wedemann	Rio de Janeiro State University, Brazil
Baole Wei	Chinese Academy of Sciences, China
Feng Wei	York University, Canada
Yingcan Wei	The University of Hong Kong, Hong Kong
Martin Georg Weiß	Regensburg University of Applied Sciences, Germany
Thomas Wennekers	Plymouth University, UK
Marc Wenninger	Rosenheim Technical University of Applied Sciences, Germany
Stefan Wermter	University of Hamburg, Germany
John Wilmes	Brandeis University, USA
Christoph Windheuser	ThoughtWorks Inc., Germany
Moritz Wolter	University of Bonn, Germany
Changmin Wu	Ecole Polytechnique, France
Takaharu Yaguchi	Kobe University, Japan
Tsoy Yury	Solidware, South Korea

Yuchen Zheng   Kyushu University, Japan
Meng Zhou   Shanghai Jiao Tong University, China
Congcong Zhu   Shanghai University, China
Andrea Zugarini   University of Florence, Italy
Adrian De Wynter   Amazon Alexa, USA
Zhao Jiapeng   Chinese Academy of Sciences, China
Tessa Van Der Heiden BMW Group, Germany
Tadeusz Wieczorek   Silesian University of Technology, Poland

Contents – Part I

Cognitive Models

Convolutional Neural Networks and Kernel Methods

Deep Learning Applications I

Deep Learning Applications II

Explainable Methods

Few-Shot Learning

Generative Adversarial Network

Generative and Graph Models

Hybrid Neural-Symbolic Architectures

Image Processing

Medical Image Processing

Recurrent Neural Networks

Contents – Part II

Neural Network Theory and Information Theoretic Learning

Normalization and Regularization Methods

Reinforcement Learning I

Reinforcement Learning II

Reinforcement Learning III

Reservoir Computing

Robotics and Neural Models of Perception and Action

Sentiment Classification

Text Understanding I

Text Understanding II

Unsupervised Learning

Adversarial Machine Learning

On the Security Relevance of Initial Weights in Deep Neural Networks

Kathrin Grosse[1,2($\boxtimes$)], Thomas A. Trost[2,3], Marius Mosbach[2,3],
Michael Backes[1], and Dietrich Klakow[2,3]

[1] CISPA Helmholtz Center for Information Security, Saarbrücken, Germany
kathrin.grosse@cispa.saarland
[2] Saarland University, SIC, Saarbrücken, Germany
[3] Spoken Language Systems (LSV), Saarbrücken, Germany

Abstract. Recently, a weight-based attack on stochastic gradient descent inducing overfitting has been proposed. We show that the threat is broader: A task-independent permutation on the initial weights suffices to limit the achieved accuracy to for example 50% on the Fashion MNIST dataset from initially more than 90%. These findings are supported on MNIST and CIFAR. We formally confirm that the attack succeeds with high likelihood and does not depend on the data. Empirically, weight statistics and loss appear unsuspicious, making it hard to detect the attack if the user is not aware. Our paper is thus a call for action to acknowledge the importance of the initial weights in deep learning.

Keywords: Adversarial machine learning · Security · Initializations

1 Introduction

One of many security concerns about machine learning (ML) [4] is the threat of *poisoning*: The attacker manipulates the training data to alter the resulting classifier's accuracy [3,20,21,25,26]. Recent work tailored poisoning to deep neural networks [18,20,34] or targeted the untrained, initial weights [18].

Training and in particular initialization of deep neural networks is still based on heuristics, such as breaking symmetries in the network, and avoiding that gradients vanish or explode [2,23]. State of the art approaches rely on the idea that given a random initialization, the variance of weights is particularly important [9,10] and determines the dynamics of the networks [13,24]. In accordance with this, weights are nowadays usually simply drawn from some zero-centered (and maybe cut-off) Gaussian distribution with appropriate variance [7], while the biases are often set to a constant. The order of the weights is typically not considered, so an adversarial (or simply unlucky) permutation with particularly bad properties has a good chance of being overseen, if the user is caught unaware.

Contributions. We propose a data-independent-training attack on neural networks that underlines the importance of the initial weights. Specifically, we show

K. Grosse and T. A. Trost—Equal contribution.

© Springer Nature Switzerland AG 2020
I. Farkaš et al. (Eds.): ICANN 2020, LNCS 12396, pp. 3–14, 2020.
https://doi.org/10.1007/978-3-030-61609-0_1

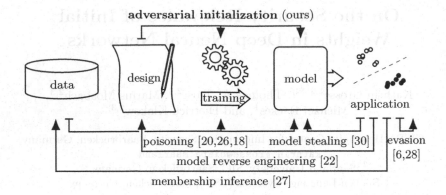

Fig. 1. An overview of attacks on Machine Learning.

ways to permute initial weights before training (such that all statistics are preserved and seem inconspicuous) that effectively reduce the network capacity, implying decreased accuracy and increased training time. More concretely, on the MNIST benchmark, where benign accuracy is easily >98%, the attacker is able to limit the accuracy to 50%. On Fashion MNIST, she reduces the accuracy from >90% to slightly more than 50%. For CIFAR, the accuracy of our simple LeNet [17] model is reduced from 65% to 50%.

Related Work. We give an overview over attacks on ML in Fig. 1. Closest to our work, yet orthogonal, is poisoning for deep learning. These attacks cause misclassification of individual points [34] or introduce backdoors [20,26,29]. Such a backdoor pattern is small, yet tricks the model into reliably outputting an attacker-chosen class. All these approaches rely on altering the training data. Also orthogonally, Cheney et al. [5] investigate adversarial weight perturbations at test time (not at training time of the initial weights). In general, benign hardware failures during training have been studied as well [31].

Liu et al. [18], however, target the weights of an SGD-trained model which consecutively over-fits the data. There are several differences to our contribution: (1) our attacks are independent of the optimizer and other hyper-parameters, and (2) the damage of decreased accuracy is more severe than overfitting. Furthermore, (3) our attack is also more stealthy, as the statistics of the original weights are preserved, and (4) our attacks take place *before* training.

2   Adversarial Initialization

We introduce attacks that alter the initial weights of a neural network. The goal of the attacker is to decrease accuracy drastically, or to increase training time. Ideally, this is done in a stealthy way: the victim should not spot the attack.

Before we discuss specifics and the generalization of our attacks, we motivate our approach by discussing its most basic version. The following equation represents two consecutive layers in a fully connected feed-forward network with weight matrices $\mathbf{A} \in \mathbb{R}^{m \times n}$ and $\mathbf{B} \in \mathbb{R}^{\ell \times m}$, corresponding biases $\mathbf{a} \in \mathbb{R}^m$ as well as $\mathbf{b} \in \mathbb{R}^\ell$, and ReLU activation functions

$$\mathbf{y} = \text{ReLU} \left(\mathbf{B} \, \text{ReLU}(\mathbf{A}\mathbf{x} + \mathbf{a}) + \mathbf{b} \right). \tag{1}$$

This vulnerable structure or similar vulnerable structures (like two consecutive convolutional layers) can be found in a plethora of typical DNN architectures. We assume that the neurons are represented as column vectors. The formulation for a row vector is completely analogous. We further assume that the components of $\mathbf{x}$ are positive. This corresponds to the standard normalization of the input data between 0 and 1. For input vectors $\mathbf{x}$ resulting from the application of previous layers it is often reasonable to expect an approximately normal distribution with the same characteristics for all components of $\mathbf{x}$. This assumption is (particularly) valid for wide previous layers with randomly distributed weights because the sum of many independent random variables is an approximately normally distributed random variable due to the central limit theorem [24].

The idea behind our approach is to make many components of $\mathbf{y}$ vanish with high probability and is best illustrated by means of the sketches in Eq. 2 and Eq. 3. The components of the matrices and vectors are depicted as little squares. Darker colors mean larger values. In addition, hatched squares indicate components with a high probability of being zero.

In matrix $\mathbf{A}$, the largest components of the original matrix are distributed in the lower $(1 - r_A)m$ rows. $r_A \in \{\frac{1}{m}, \frac{2}{m}, ..., 1\}$ controls the fraction of rows that are filled with the "small" values. The small and often negative components are randomly distributed in the upper $r_A m$ rows. The products of these negative rows with the positive $\mathbf{x}$ are likely negative. If the bias $\mathbf{a}$ is not too large, the resulting vector has many zeros in the upper rows due to the ReLU-cutoff.

$$\text{ReLU} \left(\begin{bmatrix} \\ \\ \end{bmatrix}_{\text{matrix } \mathbf{A}} \begin{bmatrix} \\ \end{bmatrix}_{\mathbf{x}} + \mathbf{a} \right) = \begin{bmatrix} \\ \end{bmatrix} \tag{2}$$

Next, a similar approach can be used with matrix $\mathbf{B}$ to eliminate the remaining positive components. Let r_B control the fraction of "small" columns of $\mathbf{B}$.

$$\text{ReLU} \left(\begin{bmatrix} \\ \\ \end{bmatrix}_{\text{matrix } \mathbf{B}} \begin{bmatrix} \\ \end{bmatrix} + \mathbf{b} \right) = \begin{bmatrix} \\ \end{bmatrix}_{\mathbf{y}} \tag{3}$$

In summary, we concentrate the positive contributions in a few places and "cross" **A** and **B** in order to annihilate them. For the typical case of weights drawn from a zero mean distribution, $r_A = r_B = \frac{1}{2}$ effectively kills all the neurons and makes training impossible.

The probability for obtaining a matrix like **A** in Eq. 2 by chance is very small and given by $((r_A mn)!((1-r_A)mn)!)/(mn)!$.

With the general idea of our attack in mind, we can now discuss specifics. A complete blockade of the entire network obviously contradicts the idea of stealthiness because at least some learning is expected by the user. The prototypical attack must thus be "weakened" in a controlled manner to be stealthy.

Soft Knockout Attack. The first way of controlling the network capacity is by varying r_A and r_B in such a way that some but not all of the neurons have some non-vanishing probability of being non-zero. This is achieved by choosing $r_A < 1/2$ or $r_B < 1/2$, respectively $r_A \gg 1/2$ or $r_B \gg 1/2$.

Shift Attack. As an alternative, we can choose $r_A = r_B = 1/2$ and shift the columns of **B** periodically by s positions. In a fully connected network, this corresponds to s active neurons, yielding specific control over capacity.

We formalize both algorithms a long version of this paper [8]. The attack's **computational complexity** is linear in the number of components of the matrices because one pass over them is sufficient for the split into large and small weights.

2.1 Statistical Analysis of Adversarial Initialization

The matrices which are permuted in the above attacks are initialized randomly. To establish that we can expect to observe a sufficiently large fraction of negative weights, we proceed with a formal analysis of the statistics of the attacks. The goal is to give estimates of the probabilities of deactivating certain neurons by means of malicious initialization in the above sense. We investigate how the layer size, the variance of the weights and the magnitude of the biases influence our attack and show that the input data is indeed not important for its success. For clarity, we consider the case of two fully connected layers as presented as the prototype of our attack. Thus, our architecture is described by the formula $\mathbf{y} = \mathrm{ReLU}\left(\mathbf{B}\,\mathrm{ReLU}(\mathbf{A}\mathbf{x}+\mathbf{a})+\mathbf{b}\right)$. Note that the analysis of this case is not merely relevant for two-layer networks. For the attack it does not matter whether the two layers are part of a bigger network or not and whether they are the first layers or somewhere in between other layers, as long as they interrupt the data flow by deactivating neurons. Additionally, the analysis of the two fully connected layers basically carries over to convolutions, shifting and soft knockout attack because the corresponding parameters can be adapted to all cases.

Statistics of Adversarial Weights. As groundwork for the subsequent discussion, we first look at the statistics of the components of the block matrices **A** in Eq. 2, where the randomly sampled components are split into two sets of large respectively small values. In particular, we are interested in the mean values $\mu_{A,S}$ and $\mu_{A,L}$ as well as the variances $\sigma^2_{A,S}$ and $\sigma^2_{A,L}$ of the components of the two blocks of $\mathbf{A}$, depending on the parameter r_A that determines the size of the split. The subscript A denotes matrix $\mathbf{A}$, so that we can distinguish the values from those for $\mathbf{B}$ (from Eq. 3) for which the respective values can be calculated in a completely analogous way. The quantities that refer to the block of *small* values have the subscript S and the respective quantities for the block of *large* values are sub-scripted with L. We later need the means and variances for estimating the probability of knocking out neurons.

We focus on the most relevant case of components that are drawn from a normal distribution with mean μ_A and variance σ^2_A, now without the subscripts S or L because we refer to the unsplit values. The distribution of the weights in the "small values" block of $\mathbf{A}$ can then be approximated as a normal distribution that is cut off (i.e. zero for all values greater than some c) depending on the parameter r_A in such a way that the respective part of the original distribution covers the fraction r_A of the overall probability mass. Formalizing this, the value of the cut-off-parameter c is obtained by solving the equation

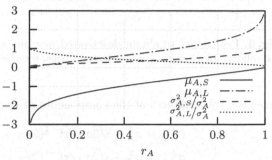

Fig. 2. Mean and variance of the weights in the "small values" respectively "large values" blocks of $\mathbf{A}$.

$$r_A = \int_{-\infty}^{c} \frac{1}{\sqrt{2\pi}\sigma_A} \exp\left(-\frac{z^2}{2\sigma_A^2}\right) dz \tag{4}$$

for c. We obtain $c = \sqrt{2}\sigma_A \, \mathrm{erf}^{-1}(2r_A - 1)$, where erf^{-1} is the inverse error function. As a result, we get the following probability density distribution for the weights of the "small values" block of $\mathbf{A}$:

$$f_{A,S}(z) = \begin{cases} \frac{1}{\sqrt{2\pi}\sigma_A r_A} \exp\left(-\frac{z^2}{2\sigma_A^2}\right) & \text{for } z < c, \\ 0 & \text{else.} \end{cases} \tag{5}$$

The density $f_{A,L}$ for the "large values" block is found accordingly.

Before proceeding, we introduce the shorthand notation

$$g(r) := \sqrt{\pi} \exp\left(\left(\mathrm{erf}^{-1}(2r - 1)\right)^2\right), \tag{6}$$

which will prove useful for presenting the results in a more succinct form. From Eq. 5 a straightforward integration yields

$$\mu_{A,S} = -\frac{\sigma_A}{\sqrt{2}r_A g(r_A)}, \quad \mu_{A,L} = \frac{\sigma_A}{\sqrt{2}(1 - r_A)g(r_A)}. \tag{7}$$

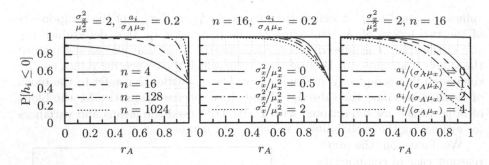

Fig. 3. Probability to obtain deactivated neurons after the first layer, depending on the relative block size r_A and selected values for the other parameters.

Likewise, the variances of the components of the blocks are:

$$\sigma_{A,S}^2 = \sigma_A^2 + \sqrt{2}\sigma_A \operatorname{erf}^{-1}(2r_A - 1)\mu_{A,S} - \mu_{A,S}^2 \tag{8a}$$

$$\sigma_{A,L}^2 = \sigma_A^2 + \sqrt{2}\sigma_A \operatorname{erf}^{-1}(2r_A - 1)\mu_{A,L} - \mu_{A,L}^2 \tag{8b}$$

The means and variances are plotted in Fig. 2. Here, $\mu_{A,S}$ is always negative while $\mu_{A,L}$ is always positive because there is always an imbalance between positive and negative values. Large or small values of r_A make the statistics of the larger block look like those of the original matrix $\mathbf{A}$, while the few values in the small block have a mean with large absolute value and small variance.

First Layer. With these results in mind, we are ready to analyze the effect of the first layer of Eq. 1 with a weight matrix $\mathbf{A}$ that is split according to Eq. 2 and a bias $\mathbf{a}$. With the convenient definition $\mathbf{h} = \mathbf{A}\mathbf{x} + \mathbf{a}$ we can estimate the expected value $\mu_{h,i} := \mathrm{E}[h_i]$ of the components of $\mathbf{h}$ given random inputs and fixed weights and biases. We define the expected values $\mu_x := \mathrm{E}[x_i]$ (for any i, see below) as well as $\mu_{A,i} := \mathrm{E}[A_{i:}]$ and get

$$\mu_{h,i} = \sum_{j=1}^n A_{ij} \mathrm{E}[x_j] + a_i \approx n\mu_x \frac{1}{n} \sum_{j=1}^n A_{ij} + a_i \approx n\mu_x \mu_{A,i} \tag{9}$$

The first approximation is based on the premise that the components of $\mathbf{x}$ are approximately equally distributed while the second approximation gets better with increasing n. The assumption of equal distributions is particularly justified if the first layer of our model is not the first layer of the network because in that case input differences are evened out by forming sums with random weights in the previous layers. If $\mathbf{x}$ is actually the input layer, we can of course not always guarantee a particular distribution of its components. Nevertheless, given typical datasets, it is still reasonable to assume similar distributions for a sufficiently large part of the features so that the approximation is meaningful.

Under the same assumptions and with the variance $\sigma_{A,i}^2$ of the elements of the i-th row of $\mathbf{A}$ as well as the variance σ_x^2 of the components of $\mathbf{x}$, together with the premise that the components of $\mathbf{A}$ and those of $\mathbf{x}$ are statistically independent, we obtain:

$$\mathrm{E}[h_i^2] \approx \mathrm{E}[x]^2 n(n-1)\mu_{A,i}^2 + 2a_i n \,\mathrm{E}[x]\,\mathrm{E}[A_{i:}] + \mathrm{E}[x^2]n(\sigma_{A,i}^2 + \mu_{A,i}^2) + a_i^2 \quad (10)$$

With that, we get the variance of h_i:

$$\sigma_{h,i}^2 := \mathrm{E}[h_i^2] - \mathrm{E}[h_i]^2 \approx n\left(\mu_{A,i}^2\sigma_x^2 + \sigma_{A,i}^2\sigma_x^2 + \sigma_{A,i}^2\mu_x^2\right) \quad (11)$$

As we assume n to be large enough for our approximations to be reasonable, we can apply the central limit theorem that tells us that h_i will approximately follow a normal distribution $\mathcal{N}(\mu_{h,i}, \sigma_{h,i}^2)$. Because of this, Eq. 9 and Eq. 11 completely determine the distribution of h_i and the probability for h_i to be smaller than or equal to zero is readily estimated as

$$\mathrm{P}[h_i \leq 0] = \int_{-\infty}^{0} \mathcal{N}(h; \mu_{h,i}, \sigma_{h,i}^2)dh = \frac{1}{2} - \frac{1}{2}\,\mathrm{erf}\left(\frac{\mu_{h,i}}{\sigma_{h,i}\sqrt{2}}\right). \quad (12)$$

For normally distributed weights, Eq. 9 and Eq. 11 can be calculated on the basis of our previous results for the statistics of $\mathbf{A}$, given in Eq. 7 and Eq. 8. Under our assumptions, the row index i matters only in so far that it either belongs to the (hopefully) deactivated neurons or to the other block. We find that $\mu_{h,s}/\sigma_{h,s}$ equals

$$\frac{\frac{2}{\sqrt{n}}\left(\frac{a_i}{\sigma_A\mu_x}\right)r_A g(r_A) - \sqrt{\frac{n}{2}}}{\sqrt{\left(r_A^2\, g(r_A)^2 - r_A\,\mathrm{erf}^{-1}(2r_A - 1)g(r_A)\right)\left(\frac{\sigma_x^2}{\mu_x^2} + 1\right) - \frac{1}{2}}}. \quad (13a)$$

The analogous expression for $\mu_{h,L}/\sigma_{h,L}$ with $\bar{r}_A = 1 - r_A$ is

$$\frac{\frac{2}{\sqrt{n}}\left(\frac{a_i}{\sigma_A\mu_x}\right)\bar{r}_A g(r_A) + \sqrt{\frac{n}{2}}}{\sqrt{\left(\bar{r}_A^2\, g(r_A)^2 + \bar{r}_A\,\mathrm{erf}^{-1}(2r_A - 1)g(r_A)\right)\left(\frac{\sigma_x^2}{\mu_x^2} + 1\right) - \frac{1}{2}}}. \quad (13b)$$

Together with Eq. 12 we obtain estimations for the probabilities of switching off neurons after the first layer. The behavior depends on three dimensionless[1] parameters that are given due to the setup: The input dimension n, the ratio $a_i/\sigma_A\mu_x$ that corresponds to the relative importance of the bias and σ_x^2/μ_x^2, which can roughly be described as a measure of sharpness of the input distribution. The influence of these parameters can be observed in Fig. 3. As expected, a significant positive bias deteriorates the probability; nevertheless it must be unusually high to have a significant effect. For large n, the probabilities are more distinct because the statistics get sharper. The characteristics of the input data, on the other hand, do not play a big role, as it can be seen in the second diagram. Note that the variance of the weights does not directly influence the probabilities.

---

[1] Here, "dimensionless" stems from physics and related disciplines, where similar quantities are used to describe and classify complex systems in a unit-independent way.

Overall we can conclude that the chances of deactivating neurons is indeed high for realistic choices of parameters and that the characteristics of the input data hardly influence the system.

Second Layer. The statistical analysis of the effect of the second layer is very similar to that of the first layer, just significantly more complex in terms of the length of the expressions and cases that have to be distinguished. As there is not much to learn from that, we leave out the details of the respective computation and simply remark that after the second layer neurons are indeed deactivated with a high probability for realistic parameters.

3 Empirical Evaluation

We evaluate the previously derived attacks. We first detail the setting, datasets and architectures and explain how we illustrate findings.

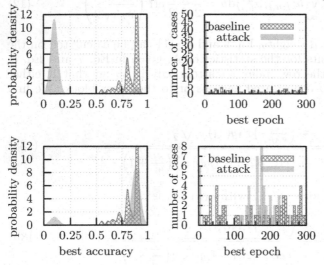

Setting. We deploy the attacks on a range of datasets, including MNIST [17], Fashion MNIST [32] and CIFAR10 [14]. We evaluate two different kinds of architectures, fully connected networks and convolutional networks. All our fully connected networks contain $n/2$ neurons in the first hidden layer, where n is the number of features. The second hidden layer has 49 neurons for the two MNIST tasks. As an example for a convolutional architecture, we use LeNet on CIFAR.

Fig. 4. The soft knockout attack allows little control over final accuracy: Fashion-MNIST, fully connected network, $r = 0.25$ (upper) versus $r = 0.2$ (lower).

All networks are initialized with He initializer [11] and constant bias. The fully connected networks are trained for 300 epochs on both MNIST variants. LeNet is trained for 200 epochs. We optimize the nets with the Adam optimizer with a learning rate of 0.001. However, in a long version of this paper, we show that initializer, optimizer, learning rate and even activation function do not affect vulnerability.

Presentation of Results. We are interested in how our attacks affect the probability to get a well performing network after training. Towards this end, we mainly consider two quantities: the best accuracy that is reached during training and the epoch in which it has been reached. We approximate both distributions by evaluating a sample of 50 networks with different seeds for the random initializer.[2] We plot the smoothed probability density function over the best test accuracies during training and the epochs at which this accuracy was observed. While we use Gaussian kernel density estimation for the former, the latter is depicted using histograms. Both distributions are compared to a baseline derived from a sample of 50 clean networks with the same 50 random seeds.

Knockout Attack. In this attack, we control the size of the split between small and large values of the weight matrices in order not to knock out all the neurons at once. The experiments show that this gives little control over performance: On fully connected networks, when $r > 0.3$ training fails entirely. when $r \leq 0.2$ the network achieves normal accuracy (however needs more of epochs). As soon as the networks have some non-vanishing chance of updating the weights (which is the idea of a soft knockout),

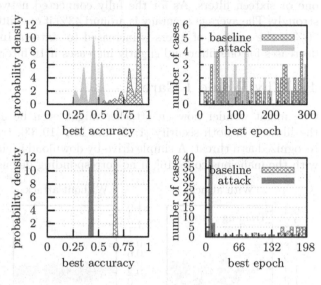

Fig. 5. The shift attack on Fashion MNIST (upper) and CIFAR10 (lower). In both cases, shift is set to eight, for the convolutional network on CIFAR, we apply the shift to one filter.

they can recover from the bad initialization.

We plot the results on Fashion-MNIST for $r = 0.2$ and $r = 0.25$ in Fig. 4. A parameter $r > 0.3$ leads to complete failure to learn: all accuracies are equivalent to guessing. Networks that perform with random guess accuracy usually perform best in their first iteration, and do not improve during training. This is visible as well for $r = 0.25$. We picked Fashion-MNIST to illustrate this, although it occurs in general. For slightly lower $r = 0.2$, however, most seeds achieve baseline accuracy, where training time increases on average.

Shift Attack. This attack gives more fine-grained control over the network. In fully connected networks, the shift parameter is equivalent to the number of active neurons. Our experiments show that a number of 10 (MNIST)/12 (Fashion MNIST) neurons suffices to learn the task with unchanged accuracy. We set the shift of 4 and 8 on MNIST and Fashion MNIST (see Fig. 5). In

---

[2] We keep the same 50 seeds in all experiments for comparability. However, due to effects from parallelization on GPUs, the accuracy might differ by up to 2% for seemingly identical setups.

both cases, the maximal accuracy is around 50%, but the network still learns. On Fashion-MNIST, training time increases by around 50 epochs. This is less clear for MNIST, where several networks are failing, and achieve their best (random guess) accuracy in epoch one.

The results of convolutional networks on CIFAR10 are in Fig. 5. We apply a shift of eight (more plots are in a long version of this paper) and apply it to one or sixteen filters. As for the fully connected networks, accuracy decreases strongly. The average accuracy is around 43% if one filter is affected and around 50% if the number of filters is increased to sixteen. Intriguingly, training time decreases for one filter and slightly increases if 16 filters are targeted.

4   Why Would I Care?

One might wonder how an attacker might even be able to alter the code of the library. In both security [1,15] and ML [19,33], trust in libraries has been recognized as a threat. A simple drive-by download is enough to infect a machine with the malicious code [16], if no corresponding defense is in place [12].

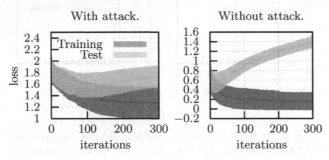

Furthermore, one might ask whether a user would actually fall for such an easy-to-fix attack as maliciously permuted weights. We argue that this hinges on the user's awareness of the attack and that current debugging routines hardly take initialization into account.

Fig. 6. Loss during training on Fashion MNIST (fully connected network, shift is 4). Along with the achievable accuracy, the scale of the loss is unknown to the victim.

In order to underpin this statement, we carry out a study on www.stackoverflow.com and www.stackexchange.com, popular and typical Q&A sites for programming-related issues. We browse the replies to questions concerning neural network failure and check whether people would discover our attack based on this advice (the full study can be found in a long version of this paper [8]). In a nutshell, for the specific setting the attack causes, in 115 relevant questions, the majority of the answers either point out a bug (32.2%), concern the data (31.3%), or suggest altering the model (30.4%). In only 3.5% (i.e. four) of the cases the suggestions hint at initializations or information flow. However, in three of these cases, the model is described as not learning at all, or the loss is severely diverging. For our attack, the loss does not look that suspicious, as can be seen in Fig. 6. This leaves *one* answer that would actually point into the direction of our attack for the symptoms it causes: "*Gradient check your implementation with a small batch of data and be aware of the pitfalls*" This is still far from a direct hint—we conclude that there is a lack of awareness on the importance of the initial weights.

5   Conclusion

We show that the threat of adversarial initialization goes far beyond previously known attacks that induced overfitting. A permutation of the initial weight matrices before training suffices to limit the victim's accuracy <50% on the MNIST benchmark, where benign accuracy is easily >98%. On Fashion MNIST, the attacker limits the accuracy from >90% to around 50%. Furthermore, the loss looks unsuspicious, and a user, given current knowledge, will not discover the source of the bad performance. In addition to these empirical results, we formally derive statistical evidence that the attacks succeed for standard initializations and are independent of the input distribution and the task at hand.

Acknowledgments. This work was supported by the German Federal Ministry of Education and Research (BMBF) through funding for the project CISPA_AutSec (FKZ: 16KIS0753). Marius Mosbach acknowledges partial support by the German Research Foundation (DFG) as part of SFB 1102.

References

1. Backes, M., Bugiel, S., Derr, E.: Reliable third-party library detection in android and its security applications. In: CCS. pp. 356–367. ACM (2016)
2. Bengio, Y., Simard, P., Frasconi, P.: Learning long-term dependencies with gradient descent is difficult. IEEE Trans. Neural Netw. **5**(2), 157–166 (1994)
3. Biggio, B., Nelson, B., Laskov, P.: Poisoning attacks against support vector machines. In: ICML (2012)
4. Biggio, B., Roli, F.: Wild patterns: ten years after the rise of adversarial machine learning. Pattern Recogn. **84**, 317–331 (2018)
5. Cheney, N., Schrimpf, M., Kreiman, G.: On the robustness of convolutional neural networks to internal architecture and weight perturbations. arXiv preprint arXiv:1703.08245 (2017)
6. Dalvi, N., Domingos, P., Mausam, Sanghai, S., Verma, D.: Adversarial classification. In: KDD. pp. 99–108 (2004)
7. Giryes, R., Sapiro, G., Bronstein, A.M.: Deep neural networks with random gaussian weights: a universal classification strategy? IEEE Trans. Signal Process. **64**(13), 3444–3457 (2016)
8. Grosse, K., Trost, T.A., Mosbach, M., Backes, M., Klakow, D.: On the security relevance of initial weights in deep neural networks. arXiv preprint arXiv:1902.03020 (2019)
9. Hanin, B.: Which neural net architectures give rise to exploding and vanishing gradients? pp. 580–589 (2018)
10. Hanin, B., Rolnick, D.: How to start training: the effect of initialization and architecture. In: NeurIPS, pp. 569–579 (2018)
11. He, K., Zhang, X., Ren, S., Sun, J.: Delving deep into rectifiers: surpassing human-level performance on imagenet classification. In: ICCV. pp. 1026–1034 (2015)
12. Javed, A., Burnap, P., Rana, O.: Prediction of drive-by download attacks on twitter. Inf. Process. Manage. **56**(3), 1133–1145 (2019)
13. Kadmon, J., Sompolinsky, H.: Transition to chaos in random neuronal networks. Phys. Rev. X **5**, 041030 (2015)

14. Krizhevsky, A., Hinton, G.: Learning multiple layers of features from tiny images. Technical Report, Citeseer (2009)
15. Lauinger, T., Chaabane, A., Arshad, S., Robertson, W., Wilson, C., Kirda, E.: Thou shalt not depend on me: analysing the use of outdated javascript libraries on the web. In: NDSS (2017)
16. Le, V.L., Welch, I., Gao, X., Komisarczuk, P.: Anatomy of drive-by download attack. In: Eleventh Australasian Information Security Conference, AISC 2013, Adelaide, Australia, February 2013. pp. 49–58 (2013)
17. LeCun, Y., Bottou, L., Bengio, Y., Haffner, P.: Gradient-based learning applied to document recognition. Proc. IEEE **86**(11), 2278–2324 (1998)
18. Liu, S., Papailiopoulos, D., Achlioptas, D.: Bad global minima exist and sgd can reach them. In: ICML (2019)
19. Liu, Y., Wei, L., Luo, B., Xu, Q.: Fault injection attack on deep neural network. In: Proceedings of the 36th International Conference on Computer-Aided Design. pp. 131–138. IEEE Press (2017)
20. Liu, Y., Ma, S., Aafer, Y., Lee, W., Zhai, J., Wang, W., Zhang, X.: Trojaning attack on neural networks. In: NDSS (2018)
21. Mei, S., Zhu, X.: Using machine teaching to identify optimal training-set attacks on machine learners. In: AAAI. pp. 2871–2877 (2015)
22. Oh, S.J., Augustin, M., Fritz, M., Schiele, B.: Towards reverse-engineering black-box neural networks. In: ICLR (2018)
23. Pascanu, R., Mikolov, T., Bengio, Y.: On the difficulty of training recurrent neural networks. In: ICML. pp. 1310–1318 (2013)
24. Poole, B., Lahiri, S., Raghu, M., Sohl-Dickstein, J., Ganguli, S.: Exponential expressivity in deep neural networks through transient chaos pp. 3360–3368 (2016)
25. Rubinstein, B.I., et al.: Antidote: understanding and defending against poisoning of anomaly detectors. In: ACM SIGCOMM Conference on Internet Measurement (2009)
26. Shafahi, A., et al.: Poison frogs! targeted clean-label poisoning attacks on neural networks. NeurIPS pp. 6106–6116 (2018)
27. Shokri, R., Stronati, M., Song, C., Shmatikov, V.: Membership inference attacks against machine learning models pp. 3–18 (2017)
28. Szegedy, C., et al.: Intriguing properties of neural networks. In: ICLR (2014)
29. Tan, T.J.L., Shokri, R.: Bypassing backdoor detection algorithms in deep learning. arXiv preprint arXiv:1905.13409 (2019)
30. Tramèr, F., Zhang, F., Juels, A., Reiter, M.K., Ristenpart, T.: Stealing machine learning models via prediction apis. In: USENIX Security. pp. 601–618 (2016)
31. Vialatte, J.C., Leduc-Primeau, F.: A Study of Deep Learning Robustness Against Computation Failures. ArXiv e-prints (2017)
32. Xiao, H., Rasul, K., Vollgraf, R.: Fashion-mnist: a novel image dataset for bench-marking machine learning algorithms. arXiv preprint arXiv:1708.07747 (2017)
33. Xiao, Q., Li, K., Zhang, D., Xu, W.: Security risks in deep learning implementations. In: IEEE S&P Workshops. pp. 123–128 (2018)
34. Zhu, C., Huang, W.R., Li, H., Taylor, G., Studer, C., Goldstein, T.: Transferable clean-label poisoning attacks on deep neural nets. In: ICML. pp. 7614–7623 (2019)

Fractal Residual Network for Face Image Super-Resolution

Yuchun Fang(✉)⦿, Qicai Ran, and Yifan Li

School of Computer Engineering and Science, Shanghai University,
Shanghai 200436, China
{ycfang,haddy}@shu.edu.cn, yvanlee@t.shu.edu.cn

Abstract. Recently, many Convolutional Neural Network (CNN) algorithms have been proposed for image super-resolution, but most of them aim at architecture or natural scene images. In this paper, we propose a new fractal residual network model for face image super-resolution, which is very useful in the domain of surveillance and security. The architecture of the proposed model is composed of multi-branches. Each branch is incrementally cascaded with multiple self-similar residual blocks, which makes the branch appears as a fractal structure. Such a structure makes it possible to learn both global residual and local residual sufficiently. We propose a multi-scale progressive training strategy to enlarge the image size and make the training feasible. We propose to combine the loss of face attributes and face structure to refine the super-resolution results. Meanwhile, adversarial training is introduced to generate details. The results of our proposed model outperform other benchmark methods in qualitative and quantitative analysis.

Keywords: Face super-resolution · Generative adversarial networks · Fractal block

1 Introduction

Human faces play an essential role in our social life. Face analysis has been widely used in related fields such as online transactions, face unlocking, and mobile payment. However, due to the diversity of the way to collect face image, many factors such as deformation, blur, and noise are often encountered in imaging, resulting in quality degraded face images. In order to achieve the necessary quality requirements of face analysis applications such as criminal investigation in security [1], face super-resolution technology is particularly important to improve resolution, sharpness, and information content for face images.

The previous studies [2,3] only used the deep learning based method to reconstruct the low resolution face images, but the facial details were ignored, resulting the disappear of the face details. Other researches [4,5] only used one single prior

The work is supported by the National Natural Science Foundation of China under Grant No.: 61976132 and the National Natural Science Foundation of Shanghai under Grant No.: 19ZR1419200.

© Springer Nature Switzerland AG 2020
I. Farkaš et al. (Eds.): ICANN 2020, LNCS 12396, pp. 15–26, 2020.
https://doi.org/10.1007/978-3-030-61609-0_2

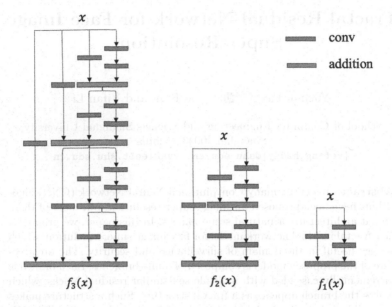

Fig. 1. Illustration of the fractal residual block structure.

knowledge of the face for image reconstruction. The previous studies only use a specific magnification for training, and some important information was often lost.

In order to create a more realistic face reconstruction, it is essential to incorporate both local and global information. Inspired by the self-similarity of the fractal structure, we innovatively propose a new network cell, called fractal residual block (FRB) structure, as shown in Fig. 1. The general residual blocks are nested into a self-similar fractal structure. Such a structure makes it possible to integrate image details in multiple layers. Using the proposed fractal residual block as the basic modules, we propose a new face super-resolution model named Fractal-SRGAN, as shown in Fig. 2. The proposed fractal residual block can incorporate information on multiple resolutions and annotate the prior structure of face appearance. It is often difficult to learn large scale super-resolution mapping directly by a single step. In order to improve the training efficiency and reduce the training difficulty of the model, inspired by the work of Lap-SRN [6], we introduce the Laplace pyramid into the model. The implementation of Fractal-SRGAN involves adversarial learning to enhance the reconstruction and progressive generation mechanism to improve training efficiency. We carried out verification experiments on benchmark face datasets. The experimental results show that the proposed model has an excellent performance in the face image super-resolution task. Extension tests on the Mini-ImageNet dataset also validate the effectiveness of the proposed model.

The major contributions of our work are summarized as follows.

- We creatively propose the fractal residual block, which serves to integrate both local and global information in more sufficient layers of details.
- We actively introduce the priori knowledge of face structure and facial attributes by introducing the face structure loss and the face attribute loss, which assists the model to generate more accurate results.
- In the process of model training, we introduce the Laplacian pyramid and adopt progressive training to improve the training efficiency.

2 Related Work

Generally, face image super-resolution refers to the process of recovering high-resolution face images from low-resolution face images. The research on face image super-resolution can be classified as three types, i.e., interpolation-based methods [7–9], reconstruction-based method [10–12] and learning-based methods [3,4,13,14]. The previous two types of methods are usually hard to adapt to large amplification coefficients [15], while the learning-based methods are promising in handling various amplification coefficients.

Compared with the traditional learning-based methods, deep learning methods have distinct advantages in the reconstruction results and efficiency, and various CNN models have been designed to tackle super-resolution problems. Recently, Dong et al. [2] proposed the SRCNN to introduce the convolutional neural network (CNN) for super-resolution reconstruction. Kim et al. [4] proposed VDSR to emphasize the reconstruction residuals between low-resolution images and high-resolution images. Legid et al. [3] propose the SRGAN that utilize adversarial learning to generate details and avoid image flatness in super-resolution.

To generalized the learning-based super-resolution method for face images, a promising direction is to combine the prior information such as the edge loss or the artifacts of face appearance. Yang et al. [5] designed a face super-resolution algorithm based on edge priori information enhancement. Lim et al. [14] proposed the EDSR model on a modified SRResNet architecture and obtained improved PSNR results. Chen et al. [13] proposed to use facial structure prior information to assist facial image super-resolution.

3 Method

Our super-resolution network is essentially a generative adversarial network. It contains two main structures: a generator and a discriminator. In the generator, the input image firstly goes through several FRB modules to extract the feature maps, then goes through an upsampling layer to get a super-resolution result. Several combinations of such FRBs-upsampling form our progressive learning network. Furthermore, our FRB module can adopt the principle of self-similarity to get the image feature information of the previous network layer. Using the FRB module makes it possible for our model to complete the task of image super-resolution with higher magnification. In the discriminator, we add the face attribute and face structure feature to obtain more detailed facial reconstruction results.

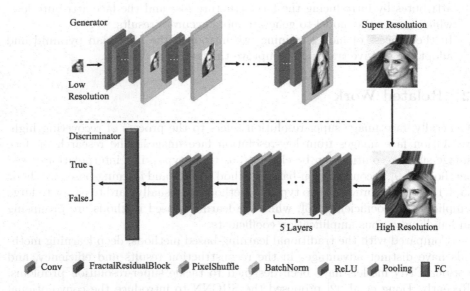

Fig. 2. The framework of the proposed FractalSRGAN model. The LR images firstly go through several FRB modules, then LR images are upsampled by the pixelShuffle module. Through this progressive training, our model generates more accurate SR images. The generated SR images and the HR images pass through the discriminator network to evaluate the quality of the generated SR images.

3.1   Fractal Residual Block

High-resolution images and low-resolution images have structural similarities in features. To utilize such information, we design the fractal residual block. An implementation instance is illustrated in Fig. 3. The feedforward calculation of the FRB module can be mathematically computed according to Eq. (1).

$$
\begin{aligned}
f_1(x) &= C(C(x)) + C(x) \\
f_2(x) &= C(x) + f_1(f_1(x)) \\
y = f_3(x) &= C(x) + f_2(f_2(x))
\end{aligned}
\tag{1}
$$

where x and y are the input FB_{n-1} and output FB_n, and the function $C(x)$ represents a convolution function.

Residual networks can effectively lighten the difficulty of training in deep neural networks through global residual learning, so we also use the global residual learning module in our network branch. Besides, deep networks with too many layers may experience performance degradation issues. The reason may be that many image details are lost after so many layers. In order to solve this problem, we introduce an enhanced residual unit structure called multipath local residual learning module, where the identity branch not only delivers rich image detail to the subsequent network layer but also help with gradient flow. The main difference between global residual learning module and local residual learning module is that the local residual learning module executes in the layer of each branch, while the global residual learning module performs between the input and output images, the fractal residual block has multiple local residual learning modules but only one global residual learning module.

As is shown in the Fig. 3, where $F_1(x)$ is the local residual learning module of $F_2(x)$ and $F_2(x)$ is the local residual learning module of $F_3(x)$, And so on. The fractal residual block used in Fig. 2 is the structure of $F_3(x)$. So we called the model FractalSRGAN, our method without adversarial loss is so called FractalSRNet.

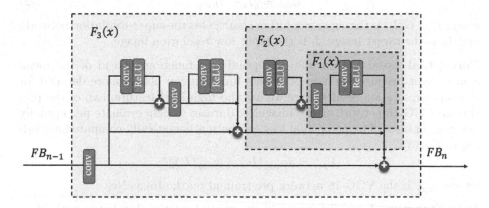

Fig. 3. Implementation instance of the fractal residual block.

3.2 Generator Network

Compared with those direct reconstruction methods, progressive methods can provide better quality for higher magnification factors and lower parameters by sharing information between each super-resolution branch. As is shown in the top half of the Fig. 2, our generator network is a progressive structure, with each layer consisting of three fractal residual blocks and one deconvolution layer.

3.3 Discriminator Network

As is shown in the lower part of the Fig. 2, unlike the previous face super-resolution [13], in order to force the super-resolution network to encode the face attribute information, we add the face attribute and face structure feature to the discriminator network. The discriminator judges the picture true and false, at the same time, can distinguish the input face image, whether a new generated picture or an original photo. Provide face attribute constraint information for super-resolution results to improve the quality of super-resolution images.

3.4 Training Objective

In order to preserve the input picture's face structure and property, our object function combines reconstruction loss L_{rec}, perceptual loss L_{per}, face structure loss L_{fan}, face attribute loss L_{attr} and adversarial loss L_{adv}.

Reconstruction Loss: Since the upsampled HR image's content should be similar to the input LR image's content, we use the Euclidean distance to force this similarity, and the reconstruction loss can be mathematically computed according to Eq. (2).

$$L_{rec} = \|I_s - I_h\|_2^2 \tag{2}$$

where $I_s = G(I_l)$ is the super-resolution result, G is the super-resolution network, and I_h is the target image, I_l is the input low resolution image.

Perceptual Loss: We use the perceptual loss function instead of the mean square error because the perceptual loss function can obtain more detailed for the super-resolution results. Here we use the high-level feature map of the pre-trained VGG-16 network on the ImageNet dataset to help evaluate perceptually relevant features. The perceptual loss can be mathematically computed according to Eq. (3).

$$L_{per} = \|\phi_{vgg}(I_h) - \phi_{vgg}(I_s)\|_2^2 \tag{3}$$

where ϕ_{vgg} is the VGG-16 network pre-trained on the ImageNet.

Face Structure Loss: To constrain the spatial relationship between the face component and its visibility, we use a face alignment network to constrain the face component. The face structure loss can be mathematically computed according to Eq. (4).

$$L_{fan} = \|\phi_{fan}(I_h) - \phi_{fan}(I_s)\|_2^2 \tag{4}$$

where ϕ_{fan} is the face alignment network FAN [16].

Face Attribute Loss: Each low-resolution facial image may be mapped to many high-resolution facial pictures in the process of high resolution. In order to reduce the ambiguity in the super-resolution process, we propose the face attribute constraint. The face attribute loss can be mathematically computed according to Eq. (5).

$$L_{attr} = \Sigma_{i=1}^N(a_h^{(i)}log(a_s^{(i)}) + (1 - a_h^{(i)})log(1 - a_s^{(i)})) \tag{5}$$

where $a_h^{(i)}$ represents the i-th attribute in the N-dimensional face attribute vector of the target image and the $a_s^{(i)}$ represents the i-th face attribute prediction probability result of the super-resolution image.

Adversarial Loss: GAN exhibits tremendous power in image super-resolution tasks [3], which produces realistic images with better visual effects than depth models based on pixel-by-pixel reconstruction loss. The main idea is to use a discriminant network to distinguish between super-resolution images and real high-resolution images. The adversarial loss can be mathematically computed according to Eq. (6).

$$
\begin{aligned}
L_{adv} &= \min_{G} \max_{D} L(G, D) \\
&= \mathbb{E}_{I_h \sim P_{data}(I_h)} \left[log D(I_h | I_l) \right] \\
&\quad + \mathbb{E}_{I_s \sim P_{data}(I_s)} \left[log(1 - D(G(I_s | I_l))) \right]
\end{aligned}
\tag{6}
$$

where D represents the discriminator network.

Our model performs end-to-end training through the above equations. The final loss function can be mathematically computed according to Eq. (7).

$$
\begin{aligned}
L_{total} &= L_{rec} + \lambda_{per} L_{per} + \lambda_{fan} L_{fan} \\
&\quad + \lambda_{attr} L_{attr} + \lambda_{adv} L_{adv}
\end{aligned}
\tag{7}
$$

where λ is the different parameters between different loss terms.

4   Experiments

4.1   Datasets

We perform face super-resolution experiments on two commonly used human face datasets: the Helen dataset [17] and the CelebA dataset [18], and one sub-dataset of ImageNet named Mini-ImageNet [19]. There are 202,599 individuals in CelebA and 2,330 individuals in Helen, while in the Mini-ImageNet, there are 60,000 colour images with 100 classes, each having 600 examples. During the training phase, we follow the standard protocol, use CelebA's large training set (162,770 images) for training, and using CelebA's validation set (19,867 images) for verification. In the testing phase, we evaluate 19,962 test set images in the CelebA dataset, and Helen's 330 test set images and Mini-ImageNet's 12000 test set to ensure that there were no overlapping images during the training and testing phases.

4.2   Parameter Setting

Model Parameter. The model is trained by the Adam optimizer, setting the initial learning rate to 0.0002, and we empirically set the two parameters of the Adam optimizer $\beta_1 = 0.9$, $\beta_2 = 0.999$. The batch size is set to 32 due to memory limitations. As for the coefficient of the loss function, we choose as follows: $\lambda_{per} = 0.005$, $\lambda_{fan} = 0.003$, $\lambda_{attr} = 0.003$, $\lambda_{adv} = 0.003$. In the progressive training phase, we use three FRB modules in front of each PixelShuffle layer, and each such structure was able to carry out a super-resolution image with double amplification. Finally, we conduct our experiment with a factor of 8 magnification.

Training Settings. We take a 134 by 134 pixel size face area in the center of the image and adjust it to 128 by 128 using the bicubic interpolation without any pre-alignment. The bicubic interpolation method is also used to obtain a 16×16 pixel size low-resolution image as input. The output image size of all methods is 128 by 128 pixel size.

Data enhancement. Data enhancement is a crucial way to generate sufficient training samples and improve the generalization capabilities of the model. We roughly crop the training image based on their facial area. We amplify the training set by randomly cropping the image and flipping it horizontally.

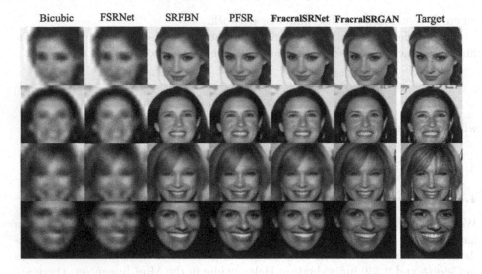

Bicubic   FSRNet   SRFBN   PFSR   FracraISRNet   FracraISRGAN   Target

Fig. 4. Qualitative comparison with the most advanced super-resolution methods. The first 3 samples are from the CelebA dataset and the last sample is from the Helen dataset. Super resolution scale factor is 8.

We compare the proposed method with several other mainstream super-resolution methods, including the face super-resolution algorithm FSRNet [13], PFSR [20] and SRFBN [21]. For a fair comparison, we reproduce the above algorithm and train the above model using the same training data. For all of the above methods, we use the default parameters provided by the author for training and prediction. We use an eight super-resolution scale factor to compare our algorithms with others.

4.3 Qualitative Comparison

As is shown in Fig. 4, the first three samples are from the CelebA dataset, and the last one is from the Helen dataset. The super-resolution results of the algorithms above on the CelebA and Helen datasets are shown.

It can be observed that the FSRNet [13] algorithm cannot fully generate real facial details, and the super-resolution face is still blurred, just better than the bicubic interpolation. SRFBN [21] can super-resolution images directly with an eight magnification factor and enhance face detail by feedback learning. Our methods (the FractalSRNet and the FractalSRGAN) and PFSR [20] both reconstructed the facial details, showing that the face image prior information helps to improve the texture information of the restored image further. Super-resolution results after using adversarial loss are more realistic and closer to natural images.

Table 1. Quantitative comparisons using different network structures for x8 super-resolution results of PSNR, SSIM and FID

	Dataset	Bicubic	FSRNet [13]	SRFBN [21]	PFSR [20]	FractalSR-Net(ours)	FractalSR-GAN(ours)
PSNR	Helen	19.16	22.14	23.65	24.32	**25.27**	24.50
	CelebA	23.24	23.73	24.12	25.73	**26.91**	25.92
	Mini-ImageNet	21.92	23.26	23.14	25.49	**26.39**	25.71
SSIM	Helen	0.4587	0.6123	0.6600	0.6720	**0.7150**	0.6792
	CelebA	0.5263	0.6757	0.6850	0.7307	**0.7797**	0.7453
	Mini-ImageNet	0.4556	0.5956	0.5797	0.5856	**0.6789**	0.6243
FID	Helen	157.81	87.81	80.95	53.49	54.74	**36.45**
	CelebA	130.73	86.09	58.52	47.87	52.73	**33.37**
	Mini-ImageNet	105.15	84.45	87.37	66.78	56.76	**38.52**

4.4 Quantitative Analysis

We quantitatively evaluate the performance of all methods across the entire test data set, employing average PSNR, SSIM, and FID scores.

Table 1 show that our approach achieves superior performance compared to other methods, and our super-resolution approach surpasses the most advanced face super-resolution methods in PSNR, SSIM, and FID standards. On the CelebA dataset, the PSNR value is increased by 1.18 dB, and the SSIM value is increased by 0.049, and the FID score is increased by 14.5 over the PFSR [20] method. On Helen dataset, our PSNR results outperformed the PFSR method by 0.95 dB, and the SSIM value increased by 0.043, and the FID score is increased by 17.04. On the Mini-ImageNet dataset, our PSNR results outperformed the second-best method by 0.9 dB, and the SSIM value increased by 0.0933, and the FID score is increased by 28.26.

4.5 Ablation Study

In order to illustrate the performance of each part of the proposed fractal residual block, we implement ablation study by using the $f_1(x)$ structure, $f_2(x)$ structure and $f_3(x)$ structure shown in Fig. 1 as the FRB module respectively for experimental comparison. In addition, we also carry out experiments on the model without using the residual block and gave the experimental results. From the evaluation scores in Table 2, we prove that using the $f_3(x)$ struct as the residual block serves to improve the performance of the model noticeably.

Table 2. Ablation study of the proposed fractal residual block on the validation set of CelebA. The results of PSNR and SSIM score show that the $f_3(x)$ struct is better than the others.

Ablation	Dataset:CelebA		
	PSNR	SSIM	FID
Without-residuals	22.17	0.6731	87.58
$f_1(x)$-structure	24.76	0.7242	58.92
$f_2(x)$-structure	25.49	0.7376	52.56
$f_3(x)$(proposed)	**25.92**	**0.7453**	**33.37**

4.6   User Study

Evaluating the model based on PSNR and SSIM may cause the model to lose the necessary high-frequency information, making the final result too smooth. Because the evaluation indicators are sometimes inconsistent with the subjective evaluation of human observers, we design a user study to compare and evaluate the FractalSRNet and FractalSRGAN methods. We invite six volunteers to participate in our experiment. The experiment is done as follows: we use the trained model to generate the super-resolution image using the CelebA dataset.

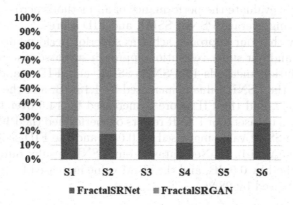

Fig. 5. The result of user study to compare the performance results of the two proposed methods, the FractalSRNet and the FractalSRGAN, from the perspective of human eyes. We invited 6 participants, denoted as S1, S2,..., S6, and each performed 50 experiments. The horizontal axis represents the label of participants in the experiment, and the vertical axis represents the percentage of the better results between the two compared algorithms chosen by each participant.

Each participant selects the best image from two randomly selected models at a time, and each participant performs 50 experiments, totaling 300 samples. As can be seen from Fig. 5, the image generated by FractalSRGAN using adversarial loss is better in most samples. Although the use of adversarial loss reduces the PSNR and SSIM measures, it improves the super-resolution similarity.

5 Conclusion

We propose a super-resolution algorithm based on the Generative Adversarial Network combined with face attribute information and face structure information to parse tiny low-resolution face images. We not only use image pixel-level and feature-level similarity constraints but also use facial structure information and face attribute information estimated by LR input images. Combined with the pyramid network structure, it can generate more accurate multi-scale high-resolution images, surpassing existing models, and achieving better performance. For future work, we plan to use more prior knowledge, such as face segmentation feature maps, for better performance.

References

1. Nasrollahi, K., Moeslund, T.B.: Super-resolution: a comprehensive survey. Mach. Vis. Appl. **25**(6), 1423–1468 (2014). https://doi.org/10.1007/s00138-014-0623-4
2. Chao, D., Chen, C.L., Kaiming, H., Xiaoou, T.: Image super-resolution using deep convolutional networks. IEEE Trans. Pattern Anal. Mach. Intell. **38**(2), 295–307 (2015)
3. Christian, L., et al.: Photo-realistic single image super-resolution using a generative adversarial network. In: Proceedings of the IEEE Conference on Computer Vision and Pattern Recognition, pp. 4681–4690 (2017)
4. Jiwon, K., Jung, K.L., Kyoung, M.L.: Accurate image super-resolution using very deep convolutional networks. In: Proceedings of the IEEE Conference on Computer Vision and Pattern Recognition, pp. 1646–1654 (2016)
5. Yang, W., et al.: Deep edge guided recurrent residual learning for image super-resolution. IEEE Trans. Image Process. **26**(12), 5895–5907 (2017)
6. Wei-Sheng, L., Jia-Bin, H., Narendra, A., Ming-Hsuan, Y.: Deep laplacian pyramid networks for fast and accurate super-resolution. In: Proceedings of the IEEE Conference on Computer Vision and Pattern Recognition, pp. 624–632 (2017)
7. Duchon, C.E.: Lanczos filtering in one and two dimensions. J. Appl. Meteor. **18**(8), 1016–1022 (1979)
8. Zhang, L., Xiaolin, W.: An edge-guided image interpolation algorithm via directional filtering and data fusion. IEEE Trans. Image Process. **15**(8), 2226–2238 (2006)
9. Kim, K.I., Kwon, Y.: Single-image super-resolution using sparse regression and natural image prior. IEEE Trans. Pattern Anal. Mach. Intell. **32**(6), 1127–1133 (2010)
10. Elad, M., Feuer, A.: Restoration of a single superresolution image from several blurred, noisy, and undersampled measured images. IEEE Trans. Image Process. **6**(12), 1646–1658 (1997)

11. Hu, H., Lisimachos, P.K.: An image super-resolution algorithm for different error levels per frame. IEEE Trans. Image Process. **15**(3), 592–603 (2006)
12. Zhang, K., Gao, X., Tao, D., Li, X.: Single image super-resolution with non-local means and steering kernel regression. IEEE Trans. Image Process. **21**(11), 4544–4556 (2012)
13. Yu, C., Ying, T., Xiaoming, L., Chunhua, S., Jian, Y.: FSRNET: end-to-end learning face super-resolution with facial priors. In: Proceedings of the IEEE Conference on Computer Vision and Pattern Recognition, pp. 2492–2501 (2018)
14. Bee, L., Sanghyun, S., Heewon, K., Seungjun, N., Kyoung, M.L.: Enhanced deep residual networks for single image super-resolution. In: Proceedings of the IEEE Conference on Computer Vision and Pattern Recognition Workshops, pp. 136–144 (2017)
15. Baker, S., Kanade, T.: Limits on super-resolution and how to break them. IEEE Trans. Pattern Anal. Mach. Intell. **9**, 1167–1183 (2002)
16. Adrian, B., Georgios, T.: Super-fan: integrated facial landmark localization and super-resolution of real-world low resolution faces in arbitrary poses with gans. In: Proceedings of the IEEE Conference on Computer Vision and Pattern Recognition, pp. 109–117 (2018)
17. Le, V., Brandt, J., Lin, Z., Bourdev, L., Huang, T.S.: Interactive facial feature localization. In: Fitzgibbon, A., Lazebnik, S., Perona, P., Sato, Y., Schmid, C. (eds.) ECCV 2012. LNCS, vol. 7574, pp. 679–692. Springer, Heidelberg (2012). https://doi.org/10.1007/978-3-642-33712-3_49
18. Ziwei, L., Ping, L., Xiaogang, W., Xiaoou, T.: Deep learning face attributes in the wild. In: Proceedings of the IEEE International Conference on Computer Vision, pp. 3730–3738 (2015)
19. Oriol , V., et al.: Matching networks for one shot learning. In: Advances in Neural Information Processing Systems, pp. 3630–3638 (2016)
20. Deokyun, K., Minseon, K., Gihyun, K., Dae-Shik, K.: Progressive face super-resolution via attention to facial landmark. arXiv preprint arXiv:1908.08239 (2019)
21. Zhen, L., Jinglei, Y., Zheng, L., Xiaomin, Y., Gwanggil, J., Wei, W.: Feedback network for image super-resolution. In: Proceedings of the IEEE Conference on Computer Vision and Pattern Recognition, pp. 3867–3876 (2019)

From Imbalanced Classification to Supervised Outlier Detection Problems: Adversarially Trained Auto Encoders

Max Lübbering[1(✉)], Rajkumar Ramamurthy[1], Michael Gebauer[2],
Thiago Bell[1], Rafet Sifa[1], and Christian Bauckhage[1]

[1] Fraunhofer IAIS, Sankt Augustin, Germany
{max.luebbering,rajkumar.ramamurthy,thiago.bell,rafet.sifa,
christian.bauckhage}@iais.fraunhofer.de
[2] PriceWaterhouseCoopers GmbH, Berlin, Germany

Abstract. Imbalanced datasets pose severe challenges in training well performing classifiers. This problem is also prevalent in the domain of outlier detection since outliers occur infrequently and are generally treated as minorities. One simple yet powerful approach is to use autoencoders which are trained on majority samples and then to classify samples based on the reconstruction loss. However, this approach fails to classify samples whenever reconstruction errors of minorities overlap with that of majorities. To overcome this limitation, we propose an adversarial loss function that maximizes the loss of minorities while minimizing the loss for majorities. This way, we obtain a well-separated reconstruction error distribution that facilitates classification. We show that this approach is robust in a wide variety of settings, such as imbalanced data classification or outlier- and novelty detection.

Keywords: Autoencoder · Outlier detection · Imbalanced datasets · Adversarial training

1 Introduction

Machine learning methods have achieved state-of-the-art results in various domains such as computer vision, natural language processing, and speech recognition. Despite their success, standard methods and algorithms mostly assume that the number of training examples pertaining to different categories is roughly equal. However, in real-world scenarios, the distribution of categories is rather skewed, with some group of data (majority class samples) occurring more frequently than others (minority class samples), leading to the *imbalanced dataset problem* [23]. These problems are common in medical diagnosis [33], fraud detection [36,37], image classification [20,26], etc.

The imbalanced data problem poses several challenges. First, it has significant effects on the performance of classifiers [4,33]. Secondly, the skewed distribution in data induces a bias in learning algorithms towards predicting only

© Springer Nature Switzerland AG 2020
I. Farkaš et al. (Eds.): ICANN 2020, LNCS 12396, pp. 27–38, 2020.
https://doi.org/10.1007/978-3-030-61609-0_3

the majority group, which is a known problem of *fairness and bias* [34]. From a data mining perspective, the minority class is more crucial in many applications, e.g., detection of seizures, arrhythmia. Due to the limited availability of training samples for these events, classifiers may fail to detect these rare patterns.

A plethora of approaches for handling imbalanced datasets have been proposed, which falls under two main categories. *Data-level methods* focus on balancing the skewed data distribution either by under-sampling of the majority samples [5] or, more commonly, by over-sampling of minority samples [8]. On the other hand, *Algorithm-level methods* focus on modifying the learning algorithm directly to facilitate the learning of minority samples by adjusting the decision threshold [29], assigning different costs [27] for minority samples and to apply anomaly detection methods [22, 31, 40] using autoencoders or support vector machines, to learn one class of examples and use reconstruction errors to distinguish the minority and majority samples.

Methods for handling imbalance are very closely related to outlier detection problems when looking at the one-class solution or thresholding [14, 21, 28]. The relatedness stems from the similarity in characteristics for both machine learning problems. Firstly, outliers are generally a minority in a dataset. Secondly, they are generated by a different underlying mechanism than the majority class, which also applies for a minority class in a supervised setting [10, 18, 45]. Furthermore, outlier detection is generally seen as an unsupervised problem, which distinguishes it from the imbalanced data problem the most. It becomes a supervised problem if data is labeled as "normal" and "abnormal" in training set to detect outliers in the test data. This is referred to as *supervised outlier detection* or *classification based anomaly detection*, which one of its subproblems is dataset imbalance [1, 7].

In this work, we are concerned with such a setting and therefore decided to devise solutions that can be applied to both supervised outlier detection and imbalanced dataset problems. In particular, we focus on the autoencoder approach and using reconstruction error as an informative feature for classification. Typically, only majority samples are used for fitting the autoencoder, which is referred as one-class autoencoders (OCA). However, this approach becomes ineffective when the majority and minority samples overlap in the feature space of the AE or minority samples are learned in later epochs by the AE [3]. In this case, the corresponding loss distributions also overlap and therefore prevent us from accurate discrimination. To address this limitation, we propose an adversarial style of training autoencoders. The main idea is, instead of training the autoencoders to minimize only the reconstruction loss for majority samples, they can also be trained to maximize the loss for minorities, thereby enriching the reconstruction error signal for classification.

Therefore, our main contributions are as follows: (i) We introduce *adversarially trained autoencoders* (ATA) for imbalanced classification, as well as, supervised outlier and novelty detection problems. (ii) We empirically show that ATA outperforms two baselines, namely OCA and a multilayer perceptron (MLP), in terms of AUC and F1 score. (iii) While the baselines show task dependent performances, ATA provides high robustness across all three tasks.

2   Related Work

Early autoencoder like networks for outlier detection have been introduced by Hawkins et al. as replicator networks [19]. These networks have been used further in a one-class fashion [6,11]. Autoencoders showed to generalize better than principal component analysis, reconstruct easily non-linear relations and perform better in higher dimensions than support vector machines. In the past years multiple approaches for outlier detection involving autoencoders have been introduced [9,21,39]. The most prominent ones are robust deep autoencoders, which isolate outliers during training by using a modified loss function [44].

For treating class imbalance autoencoders have been recently used to modify input features to improve classification performance [35] and showed significant improvements, which makes them a good candidate for imbalanced dataset problems. In contrast, our model focus on producing separable reconstruction scores for the majority and minority. Therefore we employ an adversarial training style, which changes the direction of the gradient for the minority class. This training is fundamentally different from adversarial autoencoders, since we modify the gradients of the autoencoder. Adversarial autoencoders use an arbitrary prior to learn a posterior distribution for the hidden state vector, resulting in a generative model for the decoder part [32]. In our case, the term refers to adversarial examples, which are originally used to improve model robustness [16].

3   Autoencoders for Anomaly Detection

Our ATA proposal builds upon the autoencoder architecture. These networks are a special kind of feed-forward neural network, in that they have a significant hidden contraction layer, the so called encoding layer and map an input vector $\mathbf{x} \in \mathbb{R}^d$ to itself. During training, an autoencoder minimizes the reconstruction loss w.r.t. its weights θ. Typically the mean squared error (MSE) is selected as a reconstruction loss, which is defined as

$$L_r(\mathbf{x}, \mathbf{x}') = \frac{1}{d} \sum_{i=1}^{d} (x_i - x_i')^2. \tag{1}$$

In the context of outlier detection and more generally of imbalanced datasets, AEs are usually trained unsupervised under the assumption that on average the reconstruction error for a minority sample $\mathbf{x}_{m^-}$ is higher than for a majority sample $\mathbf{x}_{m^+}$ given that no oversampling of the minority class was applied [11,19]. To predict the class (minority m^-, majority m^+) of a sample $\mathbf{x}$, the reconstruction error $L_r(\mathbf{x}, \mathbf{x}')$ can be thresholded by

$$y(\mathbf{x}, \mathbf{x}') = \begin{cases} m^-, & L_r(\mathbf{x}, \mathbf{x}') \geq \beta \\ m^+, & \text{otherwise,} \end{cases} \tag{2}$$

where parameter β is the predefined threshold optimized e.g., for F1 score [2,10]. In practice, one class autoencoders (OCAs) are trained solely on the majority class in a semi-supervised fashion, thus actively minimizing loss L_r only for the majority class [6,11,12]. Both unsupervised autoencoders and the semi-supervised OCA, only work under the premise of $L_r(\mathbf{x}_{m-}, \mathbf{x}'_{m-}) \gg L_r(\mathbf{x}_{m+}, \mathbf{x}'_{m+})$. This assumption is rather strong and only works if the majority and minority samples are uncorrelated in feature space. Only then, reconstruction error distributions of majorities and minorities are well separated allowing for a well-chosen threshold β.

4 Adversarially Trained Autoencoders

In this work, we introduce *adversarially trained autoencoders* (ATA), a novel approach that builds upon OCA's idea of leveraging the reconstruction loss as an expressive feature for classification. While architecturally similar, we propose a new training style that additionally incorporates minority samples, making this a supervised classifier. ATA targets to resolve OCA's aforementioned deficiency of working poorly in imbalanced classification scenarios and MLP's deficiency concerning novelty and outlier detection tasks, by introducing an adversarial loss function specifically engineered to deliver robust results in each of these domains.

This loss function not only minimizes the reconstruction loss for majority samples, but also maximizes the loss for minority samples as defined by

$$L_{adv}(\mathbf{x}, \mathbf{x}', t) = \begin{cases} L_r(\mathbf{x}, \mathbf{x}') \cdot 0, & L_r \in [\mathrm{l},\, \mathrm{u}] \quad \wedge \quad t \in minority \\ L_r(\mathbf{x}, \mathbf{x}'), & L_r(\mathbf{x}, \mathbf{x}') > u \quad \vee \quad t \in majority \\ -\alpha L_r(\mathbf{x}, \mathbf{x}'), & \text{otherwise.} \end{cases} \quad (3)$$

While the loss for majority samples, i.e. target $t \in majority$, is calculated as the plain reconstruction loss, the reconstruction loss for minority samples is adapted in ways depending on its magnitude. Our objective is to maximize the minority reconstruction loss until it falls within the pre-defined range $[l \in \mathbb{R}, u \in \mathbb{R}]$, thus effectively clipping the maximum loss of minority samples. If a minority sample's loss already falls within this range, then we clear out its gradient by multiplying the loss with 0 (first case). If the loss value is above the range, we minimize it, as we do for the majority samples (second case). If the loss is below range $[l, u]$, the loss is multiplied by the negation of the minority weighting factor $\alpha \in \mathbb{R}^+$. While not immediately apparent, negation of the loss function corresponds to flipping the gradient as stated by Theorem 1. With this adversarial approach, then it becomes easy to find a threshold afterwards that discriminates the samples efficiently. We refer to the autoencoder trained in this fashion as an *adversarially trained autoencoder* (ATA).

Theorem 1. *The gradient $\nabla_\theta L_{adv}$ for minority samples acts in opposing directions to keep the loss of minority samples in the defined bin $[l, u]$.*

Proof. Let $X = \{\mathbf{x}_1, \ldots, \mathbf{x}_n\}$ be a set of n samples, where each sample $\mathbf{x}_i \in \mathbb{R}^d$. The corresponding targets are denoted by the set $t = \{t_1, \ldots, t_n\}$. Each target

$t_i \in \{m^+, m^-\}$, where minorities are denoted by m^- and majorities by m^+. The autoencoder network $f_\theta : x \mapsto f_\theta(x)$ parameterized by weights θ reconstructs a sample $\mathbf{x}_i$.

Then, the gradient of the overall loss L_{tot} computes to

$$\nabla_\theta L_{tot}(\boldsymbol{\theta}, x, t) = \nabla_\theta \sum_{i=0}^{n-1} L_{adv}(f_\theta(\mathbf{x}_i), t_i) \tag{4}$$

$$= \nabla_\theta \Bigg(\underbrace{\sum_{\{i | t_i \in m^+\}} L_r(f_\theta(\mathbf{x}_i), t_i)}_{\text{majority rec. loss}} + \underbrace{\sum_{\{i | t_i \in m^-\}} L_{adv}(f_\theta(\mathbf{x}_i), t_i)}_{\text{minority rec. loss } L_{m^-}} \Bigg).$$

$$\tag{5}$$

The gradient for the minority reconstruction loss, which is the second addend, can thus be expressed by

$$s_1 = \{i | t_i \in m^- \wedge L_r(f_\theta(x_i), t_i) \in [l, u]\} \tag{6}$$

$$s_2 = \{i | t_i \in m^- \wedge L_r(f_\theta(x_i), t_i) < l\} \tag{7}$$

$$s_3 = \{i | t_i \in m^- \wedge L_r(f_\theta(x_i), t_i) > u\} \tag{8}$$

$$\nabla_\theta L_{m^-}(\boldsymbol{\theta}, x, t) = \nabla_\theta \Bigg(\sum_{s_3} L_r(f_\theta(x_i), t_i) \Bigg) \tag{9}$$

$$+ 0 \cdot \nabla_\theta \Bigg(\sum_{s_1} L_r(f_\theta(x_i), t_i) \Bigg)$$

$$- \alpha \nabla_\theta \Bigg(\sum_{s_2} L_r(f_\theta(x_i), t_i) \Bigg) \square$$

The complete training algorithm is presented in Algorithm 1. The procedure L_{adv} is a direct implementation of Eq. 3. The training routine for a single epoch is implemented in the procedure $TRAIN\_EPOCH$. The dataset is split into batches. While iterating over the batches, a batch's samples X are reconstructed by the autoencoder f_θ as denoted by reconstructions $\tilde{X}$. Then, the respective losses L_{adv} are computed from the samples and reconstructions. Finally, the gradient of L_{adv} is calculated w.r.t. the network parameters θ by backpropagation and parameters θ are updated using gradient descent. Once the network is trained, the classification threshold β is found through brute-force line by trying out different threshold values and selecting the one, which has the highest F1 score on the validation set.

In summary, the intuition behind our adversarial loss function is to minimize the loss L_r of majority samples as done by OCA for outlier and novelty detection. However, this approach immediately fails, when the loss of minority samples is mistakenly minimized as well. This is a common issue for instance when minority and majority samples are highly correlated in feature space. The loss maximization of L_{adv} successfully addresses this issue by enforcing loss maximization of minority

Algorithm 1. Adversarial Training of ATA

Input: sample $\mathbf{x}$, reconstruction $\mathbf{x}'$, **Input:** Sample set X, Target set t, Batch size b, Auto
target t, minority weighting factor α, encoder f with parameters θ, lr λ
minority loss range $[l, u]$ **procedure** TRAIN_EPOCH$(X, t, b, f_\theta, \lambda)$

procedure $L_{adv}(\mathbf{x}, \mathbf{x}', t, \alpha, l, u)$
  $L_r \leftarrow \frac{1}{n}\sum_{i=1}^{n}(\mathbf{x}_i - \mathbf{x}'_i)^2$
  if t is *minority* **then**
$$L \leftarrow \begin{cases} L_r \cdot 0, & L_r \in [l, u] \\ L_r, & L_r > u \\ -\alpha L_r, & \text{otherwise} \end{cases}$$
  end if
  return L
end procedure

  Generate *batches* from X each of size b
  for each $\tilde{X}, \tilde{t} \in batches$ **do**   ▷ for each batch
    $\tilde{X}' \leftarrow \{f_\theta(\tilde{\mathbf{x}}_i) \mid \forall \tilde{\mathbf{x}}_i \in \tilde{X}\}$ ▷ forward pass
    $L \leftarrow \{\}$ ▷ initialize batch loss
    for $i \leftarrow 0, b$ **do**
      $L \leftarrow L \cup \{L_{adv}(\tilde{\mathbf{x}}_i, \tilde{\mathbf{x}}'_i, \tilde{t}_i)\}$ ▷ sample loss
    end for
    Calc. gradient $\mathbf{g} \leftarrow \nabla_\theta (\sum_{i=0}^{b} L_i)$ ▷ backprop
    $\theta \leftarrow \theta - \lambda \mathbf{g}$ ▷ gradient update step
  end for
end procedure

samples. Of course, there is a limit to it, when samples are virtually indistinguishable, causing any machine learning approach inherently to fail.

5   Experiments and Results

In this section, we discuss the experiments and performance of our approaches on different datasets, which have been selected to individually represent one of the previously described aspects of imbalanced classification, as well as supervised outlier and novelty detection. The models are evaluated with respect to the two metrics AUC (*area under curve*) of receiver operating characteristics and F1 score. The AUC metric corresponds to evaluating a model at all possible thresholds, resulting in a score that is independent of thresholds. Thus, this metric is highly compelling for outlier and novelty detection, as a concrete threshold is generally chosen based on the use case. To evaluate the models for imbalanced classification problems, macro F1 score is used for evaluation. In the following sections, we first introduce the datasets separately and subsequently evaluate the model performance on each dataset.

5.1   Datasets

For imbalanced classification, we selected three prominent benchmark datasets, namely Reuters dataset[1], Arrhythmia dataset[2] and ATIS dataset[3]. Similarly, for outlier detection and novelty detection, the KDD dataset[4] is a commonly adopted dataset. Following other researcher's work, we derived four sub-datasets from KDD, giving us in total of 7 datasets to benchmark our algorithms against. Since our algorithm deals with binary classification tasks, each dataset is binarized into the classes *minority* and *majority* as shown in Table 1. With respect to preprocessing, textual datasets are vectorized using Glove word embeddings

---

[1] http://www.daviddlewis.com/resources/testcollections/reuters21578/.
[2] http://archive.ics.uci.edu/ml/datasets/Arrhythmia.
[3] http://www.ai.sri.com/natural-language/projects/arpa-sls/atis.html.
[4] https://www.unb.ca/cic/datasets/nsl.html.

Table 1. Datasets and their subdatasets: majority and minority frequencies for train, validation and test split

Dataset	Type	Majority	Minority	Subclass share	Train		Val		Test	
					#N	#P	#N	#P	#N	#P
KDD	Outlier imbal.	NORMAL	U2R, R2L	All	47122	745	20221	302	9711	2236
	Outlier bal.	NORMAL	U2R, R2L, DOS, PROBE	All	47122	41059	20221	17571	9711	9083
	Novelty imbal.	NORMAL	U2R, R2L	None	47122	745	20221	302	9711	716
	Novelty bal.	NORMAL	U2R, R2L, DOS, PROBE	None	47122	41059	20221	17571	9711	3750
Reuters	Imbal	EARN, ACQ, TRADE, INTEREST MONEY-FX, MONEY-SUPPLY	RESERVES	All	3613	25	1609	12	2051	12
ATIS	Imbal	FLIGHT	QUANT, AIRFARE, ABBR GSERVICE, REST, APORT ALINE, CITY, F_NO, F_TIME G_FARE, F_AIRFARE DIST, AIRCRAFT, CAPA	All	3173	1101	423	149	424	162
ARR	Imbal	NORMAL	OTHERS (15 classes)	All	122	31	62	15	61	15

[38] pooled to obtain document representation, thus providing a 100-dimensional dense vector. Additionally, categorical features are converted to one-hot encoded vectors, and real-valued features are z-transformed.

Reuters Dataset: This dataset is a standard benchmark for multi-labeled document classification [24,42] and outlier detection [25]. The task is to classify a given document into a total of 90 categories. The distribution of labels is very skewed, making this a suitable candidate for imbalanced classification benchmarking. To convert this to an imbalanced binary dataset and to be without multiple labels per document, we only consider documents that belong to only one category.

ATIS Dataset: The *ATIS Spoken Language Systems Pilot Corpus* contains transcribed queries against the air travel information system (ATIS), which provides flight-related information to passengers. Each query has been assigned exactly one of 17 possible classes. Due to its imbalanced nature, the dataset is utilized to benchmark the algorithms for imbalanced classification.

ARR Dataset: The ARR dataset is an imbalanced dataset containing 16 categories of heart arrhythmia. The small size of the dataset makes it more challenging than the previous datasets.

KDD Dataset: Due to the low prevalence of network intrusions and their distinction to normal network communication, the KDD dataset is used as a standard dataset for outlier and novelty detection, as in [13,15,17,21]. While the original KDD dataset had multiple shortcomings such as redundant samples and information leakage, the improved version has fixed this inherent issues [41], which we use in our work. The KDD dataset contains 126-dimensional samples of five classes, where samples of class *NORMAL* reflect regular connections, and the remaining ones are intrusions. Each intrusion class has multiple subclasses, which are either present in all dataset splits or just limited to train/validation split; therefore, the dataset can be used in both outlier and novelty detection settings. To this end, we derive four subsets, varying with respect to outlier/novelty detection and imbalanced/balanced, as shown in Table 1.

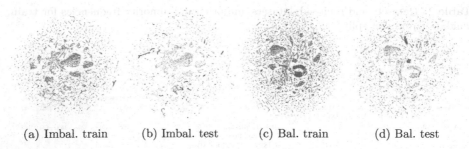

(a) Imbal. train   (b) Imbal. test   (c) Bal. train   (d) Bal. test

Fig. 1. KDD dataset: Visualization of the train and test splits after reducing the dimensionality to a 2D plane using UMAP. Outlier samples are highlighted in red, inliers in blue and novelties in green. Figure a) and Fig. b) show the clustering of the imbalanced datasets, while Fig. c) and Fig. d) show the clustering for the balanced datasets. Note that, as per definition, novelties only appear in the test set, whereas outliers appear in both (Color figure online).

Table 2. Macro AUC and F1 scores of the best ATA, MLP and OCA models on the seven datasets. It is observed ATA outperforms baseline methods in most of the tasks, depicting its robustness

Models	Imbalanced						Outlier				Novelty			
	ATIS		REU		ARR		KDD OI		KDD OB		KDD NI		KDD NB	
	AUC	F1	AUC	F1	AUC	F1	AUC	F1	AUC	F1	AUC	F1	AUC	F1
ATA	99.07%	95.77%s	99.80%	97.76%	92.26%	88.17%	97.36%	86.73%	97.10%	89.26%	82.34%	57.18%	92.11%	70.86%
MLP	99.00%	94.64%	99.82%	97.34%	89.46%	89.38%	93.93%	78.22%	93.96%	89.06%	61.54%	55.68%	89.31%	73.45%
OCA	86.17%	74.51%	85.42%	71.26%	80.65%	75.30%	92.75%	83.88%	95.68%	90.60%	80.48%	70.83%	93.15%	84.93%

UMAP Visualization: To visualize the aspects of the datasets, we used the dimensionality reduction technique UMAP to visualize the data points on a 2-D plane. Figure 2 (a), (b) and (c) shows the plot for Reuters, ATIS and ARR datasets, respectively. It depicts varying levels of cohesion, indicating their nature of imbalancedness. Similarly, Fig. 1 (a), (b) shows the imbalanced train and test splits and similarly (c) and (d) shows the splits for balanced datasets. Note, that only the test sets contain novelties. The inliers, outliers, and novelties are colored in blue, red, and green, respectively. It is observed that outliers generally tend to produce clusters, whereas novelties do not form clusters and also do not appear in any of the outlier clusters.

5.2   Results

To benchmark our ATA approach, we consider the baselines of MLP and OCA as they are standard approaches in tackling imbalanced and outlier detection tasks, respectively. For a fair comparison, we keep the model complexity roughly similar. The MLP has a single hidden layer of size 50 with sigmoid activations and an output layer with one neuron. The autoencoder of OCA and ATA models has a single hidden layer of size 50 with also sigmoid activations. Note, weights of AE are not tied as we did not witness any significant performance differences.

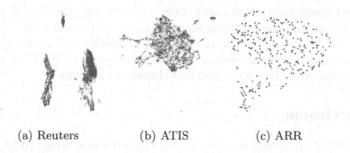

(a) Reuters   (b) ATIS   (c) ARR

Fig. 2. Visualization of the Reuters, ATIS and arrhythmia dataset after projecting the samples onto a two dimensional plain using *Uniform Manifold Approximation and Projection* (UMAP) for dimensionality reduction. Minorities samples are highlighted in red, majorities in blue (Color figure online).

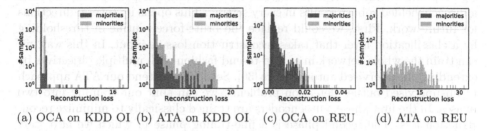

(a) OCA on KDD OI (b) ATA on KDD OI (c) OCA on REU (d) ATA on REU

Fig. 3. Loss histograms of the best OCA models and ATA models on the Reuters and KDD OI datasets.

Further, we applied a weight decay of $1e^{-4}$ to all of the models to prevent overfitting and exploding of gradients. For the MLP and ATA, we allowed for balanced sampling of each class, which for OCA is by design not applicable. The models are trained using Adadelta [43]. We performed a formal grid search of hyperparameters concerning learning rate, balanced sampling, and outlier weighting factor and bin range. For each MLP, OCA, and ATA, we select the model based on the AUC score on the validation set.

Table 2 summarizes the performance of selected best models on each dataset. By comparing the AUC scores, we observe that ATA outperforms each baseline in 6 out of 7 tasks. Another important observation is that MLP and OCA excel in different types of tasks. While MLP is strong on imbalanced classification tasks, its performance degrades on outlier and novelty detection tasks. Whereas, OCA excels on outlier/novelty detection but performs much worse on imbalanced classification tasks. This task dependent performance degradation is not prevalent for ATA. In fact, not only does ATA outperform MLP on imbalanced classification and perform equally with OCA on novelty tasks, it also clearly outperforms both baselines on the intermediate outlier detection task.

Therefore, our results clearly indicate that ATA approach is robust in all settings of imbalanced classification and supervised outlier detection, even in supervised novelty detection tasks. This is due to the adversarial autoencoder training for minimizing and maximizing the reconstruction losses. As captured in Fig. 3, ATA provides a clear separation of majority and minority loss distributions irrespective of the task at hand. This property of ATA makes it overall a highly compelling tool for supervised classification tasks.

6   Conclusion

In this work, we proposed an adversarially trained autoencoder (ATA) for outlier and novelty detection. Maximizing the reconstruction loss for majorities while minimizing that of minorities, resulted in models that beat our two baselines, a multilayer perceptron and one-class autoencoders, on settings of imbalanced and supervised outlier detection. While each baseline works only in a limited setting, e.g., repetitive clusters in train and test for the multilayer perceptron, the ATA approach yielded robust results in every setting. This opens up several directions for future work; First, we could replace the brute-force routine of thresholding by a classification layer that takes reconstruction loss as input. In this way, we can train the whole network in an end-to-end fashion with multiple objectives by extending on supervised autoencoders [30]. Second, to extend our ATA approach to unsupervised outlier detection problems, we can split our training into two phases. In the first phase, autoencoders are trained classically to minimize reconstruction loss. The second phase is a fine-tuning phase in which we also start maximizing the reconstruction loss for potential anomalies, which are samples with higher reconstruction errors.

References

1. Aggarwal, C.C.: Outlier Analysis. Data Mining, pp. 237–263. Springer, Cham (2015). https://doi.org/10.1007/978-3-319-14142-8_8
2. An, J., Cho, S.: Variational autoencoder based anomaly detection using reconstruction probability. Special Lect. IE **2**(1), 1–18 (2015)
3. Laura, B., Michael, P., Bernd, B.: Robust anomaly detection in images using adversarial autoencoders. In: Proceedings of Joint European Conference on Machine Learning and Knowledge Discovery in Databases (2019)
4. Buda, M., Maki, A., Mazurowski, M.A.: A systematic study of the class imbalance problem in convolutional neural networks. Neural Netw. **106**, 249–259 (2018)
5. Cardie, C., Howe, N.: Improving minority class prediction using case-specific feature weights (1997)
6. Raghavendra, C., Aditya, K.M., Sanjay, C.: Anomaly Detection using One-Class Neural Networks. arXiv preprint arXiv:1802.06360 (2018)
7. Varun, C., Arindam, B., Vipin, K.: Anomaly detection: a survey. ACM Comput. Surv. **41**(3), 1–58 (2009)
8. Chawla, N.V., Bowyer, K.W., Hall, L.O., Kegelmeyer, W.P.: SMOTE: synthetic minority over-sampling technique. J. Artif. Intell. Res. **16**, 321–357 (2002)
9. Jinghui, C., Saket, S., Charu, A., Deepak, T.: Outlier detection with autoencoder ensembles. In: Proceedings of the SIAM International Conference on Data Mining (2017)

10. Yong, S.C., Yong, H.T.: Abnormal event detection in videos using spatiotemporal autoencoder. In: Proceedings of International Symposium on Neural Network (2017)
11. Dau, H.A., Ciesielski, V., Song, A.: Anomaly detection using replicator neural networks trained on examples of one class. In: Dick, G., et al. (eds.) SEAL 2014. LNCS, vol. 8886, pp. 311–322. Springer, Cham (2014). https://doi.org/10.1007/978-3-319-13563-2_27
12. Hoang, A.D., Vic, C., Andy, S.: Anomaly detection using replicator neural networks trained on examples of one class. In: Proceedings of the 10th International Conference on Simulated Evolution and Learning (2014)
13. Abhishek, D., Meet, P., Vaibhav, S., Rudra, M., Mahesh, S.: Benchmarking datasets for anomaly-based network intrusion detection: KDD CUP 99 alternatives. In: Proceedings of 3rd International Conference on Computing, Communication and Security (ICCCS) (2018)
14. Haimonti, D., Chris, G., Kirk, B., Hillol, K.: Distributed top-k outlier detection from astronomy catalogs using the demac system. In: Proceedings of the 2007 SIAM International Conference on Data Mining (2007)
15. Gogoi, P., Borah, B., Bhattacharyya, D.K., Kalita, J.K.: Outlier identification using symmetric neighborhoods. Procedia Technol. **6**, 239–246 (2012)
16. Ian, J.G., Jonathon, S., Christian, S.: Explaining and harnessing Adversarial Examples. arXiv preprint arXiv:1412.6572 (2014)
17. Ville, H., Ismo, K., Pasi, F.: Outlier detection using k-nearest neighbour graph. In: Proceedings of the 17th International Conference on Pattern Recognition, vol. 3 (2004)
18. Douglas, M.H.: Identification of Outliers. Springer, Berlin (1980)
19. Simon, H., Hongxing, H., Graham, W., Rohan, B.: Outlier detection using replicator neural networks. In: Proceedings of International Conference on Data Warehousing and Knowledge Discovery (2002)
20. Chen, H., Yining, L., Chen, C.L., Xiaoou, T.: Learning deep representation for imbalanced classification. In: Proceedings of Conference on Computer Vision and Pattern Recognition (2016)
21. Ishii, Y., Takanashi, M.: Low-cost unsupervised outlier detection by autoencoders with robust estimation. J. Inf. Process. **27**, 335–339 (2019)
22. Nathalie, J., Catherine, M., Mark, G., et al.: A novelty detection approach to classification. In: Proceedings of International Joint Conference on Artificial Intelligence (1995)
23. Japkowicz, N., Stephen, S.: The class imbalance problem: a systematic study. Intell. Data Anal. **6**(5), 429–449 (2002)
24. Thorsten, J.: Text categorization with support vector machines: learning with many relevant features. In: Proceedings of European Conference on Machine Learning (1998)
25. Ramakrishnan, K., Hyenkyun, W., Charu, C.A., Haesun, P.: Outlier detection for text data. In: Proceedings of International Conference on Data Mining (2017)
26. Kubat, M., Holte, R.C., Matwin, S.: Machine learning for the detection of oil spills in satellite radar image. Mach. Learn. **30**, 195–215 (1988)
27. Matjaz, K., Igor, K., et al.: Cost-sensitive learning with neural networks. In: Proceedings of European Conference on Artificial Intelligence (1998)
28. Longin, J.L., Aleksandar, L., Dragoljub, P.: Outlier detection with kernel density functions. In: Proceedings of International Workshop on Machine Learning and Data Mining in Pattern Recognition (2007)

29. Steve, L., Ian, B., Andrew, B., Ah Chung, T., Giles, C.L.: Neural network classification and prior class probabilities. In: Neural Networks: Tricks of the Trade (1998)
30. Lei, L., Andrew, P., Martha, W.: Supervised autoencoders: improving generalization performance with unsupervised regularizers. In: Proceedings of Neural Information Processing Systems (2018)
31. Hyoung-joo, L., Sungzoon, C.: The novelty detection approach for different degrees of class imbalance. In: Proceedings of International Conference on Neural Information processing (2006)
32. Alireza, M.,, Jonathon, S., Navdeep, J., Ian, G., Brendan, F.: Adversarial Autoencoders. arXiv preprint arXiv:1511.05644 (2015)
33. Mazurowski, M.A., Habas, P.A., Zurada, J.M., Lo, J.Y., Baker, J.A., Tourassi, G.D.: Training neural network classifiers for medical decision making: the effects of imbalanced datasets on classification performance. Neural Networks **21**(2–3), 427–436 (2008)
34. Ninareh, M., Fred, M., Nripsuta, S., Kristina, L., Aram, G.: A survey on Bias and Fairness in Machine Learning. arXiv preprint arXiv:1908.09635 (2019)
35. Ng, W.W., Zeng, G., Zhang, J., Yeung, D.S., Pedrycz, W.: Dual autoencoders features for imbalance classification problem. Pattern Recogn. **60**, 875–889 (2016)
36. Olszewski, D.: A probabilistic approach to fraud detection in telecommunications. Knowl.-Based Syst. **26**, 246–258 (2012)
37. Panigrahi, S., Kundu, A., Sural, S., Majumdar, A.K.: Credit card fraud detection: A fusion approach using Dempster-theory and Bayesian learning. Information Fusion **10**(4), 354–363 (2009)
38. Jeffrey, P., Richard, S., Christopher, D.M.: Glove: global vectors for word representation. In: Proceedings of Conference on Empirical Methods in Natural Language Processing (EMNLP), (2014)
39. Hamed, S., Carlotta, D., Bardh, P., Giovanni, S.: Unsupervised Boosting-based Autoencoder Ensembles for Outlier Detection. arXiv preprint arXiv:1910.09754, 2019
40. Scholkopf, B., Smola, A.J.: Learning with Kernels: Support Vector Machines. Optimization, and Beyond, Regularization (2001)
41. Tavallaee, M., Bagheri, E., Lu, W., Ghorbani, A.A.: A detailed analysis of the KDD CUP 99 data set. In: 2009 IEEE Symposium on Computational Intelligence for Security and Defense Applications (2009)
42. Yang, Y., Liu, X.: A re-examination of text categorization methods. In: Proceedings of International Conference on Research and Development in Information, Retrieval (1999)
43. Matthew, D.Z.A.: An Adaptive Learning Rate Method. arXiv preprint arXiv:1212.5701 (2012)
44. Zhou, C., Paffenroth, R.C.: Anomaly detection with robust deep autoencoders. In: Proceedings of the 23rd ACM SIGKDD International Conference on Knowledge Discovery and Data Mining (2017)
45. Junyi, Z., Jinliang, Z., Ping, J.: Credit Card Fraud Detection Using Autoencoder Neural Network. arXiv preprint arXiv:1908.11553 (2019)

Generating Adversarial Texts
for Recurrent Neural Networks

Chang Liu[1]([✉]) [iD], Wang Lin[2], and Zhengfeng Yang[1]

[1] Software Engineering Institute, East China Normal University, Shanghai, China
cliu@stu.ecnu.edu.cn, zfyang@sei.ecnu.edu.cn
[2] School of Information Science and Technology, Zhejiang Sci-Tech University,
Hangzhou, China
linwang@zstu.edu.cn

Abstract. Adversarial examples have received increasing attention
recently due to their significant values in evaluating and improving the
robustness of deep neural networks. Existing adversarial attack algorithms have achieved good result for most images. However, those algorithms cannot be directly applied to texts as the text data is discrete in
nature. In this paper, we extend two state-of-the-art attack algorithms,
PGD and C&W, to craft adversarial text examples for RNN-based models. For Extend-PGD attack, it identifies the words that are important for
classification by computing the Jacobian matrix of the classifier, to effectively generate adversarial text examples. For Extend-C&W attack, it
utilizes $\mathcal{L}_1$ regularization to minimize the alteration of the original input
text. We conduct comparison experiments on two recurrent neural networks trained for classifying texts in two real-world datasets. Experimental results show that our Extend-PGD and Extend-C&W attack algorithms have advantages of attack success rate and semantics-preserving
ability, respectively.

Keywords: Adversarial text · Recurrent neural network · PGD ·
C&W

1 Introduction

Deep neural networks (DNNs) have recently achieved remarkable success in various tasks such as classification, regression and decision making. However, DNNs
have been found to be vulnerable to adversarial examples, which are generated by adding small unperceivable perturbations to legitimate inputs. Szegedy
et al. [19] first evaluated DNNs used for image classification with small generated perturbations on the input images. They found that the image classifier
were fooled with high probability, but human judgment is not affected. Goodfellow et al. [4] proposed a fast generation method which popularized this research
topic. Followed their works, many research efforts have been made on generating adversarial examples. However, majority of the prior works in this field are
targeted at DNNs for image or audio classification, the text classification DNNs
are seriously underestimated.

© Springer Nature Switzerland AG 2020
I. Farkaš et al. (Eds.): ICANN 2020, LNCS 12396, pp. 39–51, 2020.
https://doi.org/10.1007/978-3-030-61609-0_4

The textual data consists of discrete characters, which cannot be directly processed by the classifier. Small perturbations to the input text, such as modifying a character in a word can be easily detected by human observers and spell check. Meanwhile, the replacement of words may change the semantics of the original sentence. For these reasons, it is nontrivial to generate adversarial examples for text data.

Recently, some attack algorithms are proposed to generate adversarial texts. TextFool [9] was a FGSM-based attack method that generated adversaries for both *white-box* attack and *black box* attack. The authors designed three strategies (i.e., *insertion, modification* and *removal*) to perturb the items. However, insert or remove some words may change the semantic and syntactic of the original texts. In the work of [3], the authors directly adapted gradient-based methods in image field to text field to search for adversaries in embedding space. Then reconstructed the adversarial texts combined with nearest neighbor search algorithm. However, these methods are tied heavily on the size and quality of the embedding space. Moreover, most of the generated adversarial texts seem strange to the reader. Li et al. [8] proposed an attack framework to generate adversarial texts in both *black-box* and *white-box* settings. And the provided *white-box* attack adopting gradient-based methods.

Original Text (label = Negative)	Original Text (label = Negative)
This is an example of why the majority of action films are the same. Generic and boring, there's really nothing worth watching here. A complete waste of the then barely-tapped talents of Ice-T and Ice Cube, who've each proven many times over that they are capable of acting, and acting well.	This is an example of why the majority of action films are the same. Generic and boring, there's really nothing worth watching here. A complete waste of the then barely-tapped talents of Ice-T and Ice Cube, who've each proven many times over that they are capable of acting, and acting well.

Adversarial Text (label = Positive)	Adversarial Text (label = Positive)
This is an example of why the majority of action films are the smae. Geneirc and boirng, there's really nothnig worth watching hree. A complete watse of the then barely-tapped talents of Ice-T and Ice Cube, who've each proven many times over that they are capalbe of acting, and acting well.	This is an example of why the majority of action films are the same. Ordinary and frivolous, there's really nothing worth seeing here. A complete lose of the then barely-tapped talents of Ice-T and Ice Cube, who've each proven many times over that they are capable of acting, and acting excellently.

     (a) DeepWordBug   (b) Extend-PGD

Fig. 1. Adversarial examples generated by DeepWordBug and Extend-PGD. Modified words are highlighted in red (Color figure online)

In this paper, we propose two methods that can effectively generate semantic-preserving adversarial texts. The coherence of the sentence cannot be guaranteed due to the insertion or deletion of words in the input text. Our main strategy is to modify as few words as possible in the input text. We extend PGD and

C&W attacks that have been shown to achieve sound performance on image to text data. In the Extend-PGD attack, we first compute the Jacobian matrix of the classifier to evaluate which words are important. Then modify these words via adding imperceptible perturbations, the generated adversarial sentences are semantically and syntactically similar to the original texts. More specifically, the perturbations are generated by PGD attack. Based on C&W attack, we introduce $\mathcal{L}_1$ norm distance metric to limit the number of perturbed words. Adversarial texts generated by the extended attack method can successfully deceive the classifier to make wrong predictions. As illustrated in Fig. 1, the adversarial text generated by our Extend-PGD is visually and semantically similar to the original one. Figure 1(a) shows the adversarial text generated by DeepWordBug has more modifications and can be detected by spell check.

Contributions. (i) We propose Extend-PGD, a framework that can effectively generate adversarial texts, by modifying the words that are important for classification. (ii) We suggest Extend-C&W, a framework that can generate semantic-preserving adversarial texts, by introducing $\mathcal{L}_1$ regularization to minimize the alteration of the original input text.

2   Background

To facilitate our discussion of adversarial example crafting in Sect. 3, we first demonstrate the definition of adversarial text for ease of understanding. Then we present a brief overview of recurrent neural networks.

Adversarial Text. Given a well-trained neural network classifier $f : \mathbb{X} \to \mathbb{Y}$, which maps from input text set to label set. For a legitimate input text $\mathbf{x} = (x_1, x_2, x_3, \cdots, x_n)$, the number of words in $\mathbf{x}$ is n. Adding small perturbations to text input can confuse the trained model to misclassify [2]. The perturbed version of $\mathbf{x}$ is defined as adversarial text, $\mathbf{x}' = (x_1', x_2', x_3', \cdots, x_n')$. Besides fooling the classifier, an effective adversarial text cannot draw human readers' attention. Moreover, the adversarial text should preserve semantic similarity from original text and human readers can easily classify it correctly [9]. Formally, an adversarial example is defined as [4]:

$$\mathbf{x}' = \mathbf{x} + \triangle\mathbf{x}, \; \|\triangle\mathbf{x}\|_p < \varepsilon,$$
$$\mathbf{x} \in \mathbb{X}, \; f(\mathbf{x}) = y, \tag{1}$$
$$f(\mathbf{x}') \neq y \; or \; f(\mathbf{x}') = t$$

Here $\triangle\mathbf{x}$ is the perturbations that we can make to the original text. The scalar ε restricts the strength of the perturbations. Generally, for $\triangle\mathbf{x} = \mathbf{x}' - \mathbf{x}$, the $\mathcal{L}_p$ norm is defined as

$$\|\triangle\mathbf{x}\|_p = \sqrt[p]{\sum_{i=1}^{n} |\mathbf{x}_i' - \mathbf{x}_i|^p} \tag{2}$$

There are typically three distance metrics $\mathcal{L}_\infty$, $\mathcal{L}_2$, $\mathcal{L}_0$. According to different methods of generating adversarial examples, it can be divided into targeted attacks ($f(\mathbf{x}') = t$) and untargeted attacks ($f(\mathbf{x}') \neq f(\mathbf{x})$).

Recurrent Neural Networks. Recurrent Neural Networks (RNNs) are proposed to model the sequence data [18]. The most important feature of RNNs is that in addition to the links between neurons in different layers, there are also links between neurons in the same layer. These specificities result in the existence of cycles in the model's computation graph, which can capture the sequential dependencies among items of a sequence. However, the gradient vanishing and gradient explosion issues can make basic RNNs hard to learn the nonlinear relationship of long spans.

To handle the problem of long-term dependence, Hochreiter et al. [6] proposed a variant of vanilla RNN called Long Short-Term Memory (LSTM) network. LSTM networks also can solve complex long time lag tasks that have never been solved by basic RNNs. Due to the use of LSTM, recurrent neural networks work tremendously well on a large variety of problems including sentiment analysis [13], machine translation [10] and speech recognition [5].

3   Attack Design

In this section, we present two attack methods to generate adversarial text examples for RNN-based models.

3.1   Extend PGD Method

Madry et al. [12] proposed a novel attack method named Project Gradient Descent (PGD). It starts with a random point in the allowed norm ball and applies FGSM multiple times with a small step size. If the perturbation exceeds the space of radius ϵ, it will be projected to the "ball". The perturbation process can be expressed as:

$$\mathbf{x}^{t+1} = \text{Proj}_{\mathbf{x}+S}(\mathbf{x}^t + \alpha \text{sgn}(\nabla_\mathbf{x} L(\mathbf{x}^t, \mathbf{y}))) \tag{3}$$

Here $\mathbf{x}^t$ denotes the perturbed text at the tth iteration, $S = \{r \in \mathbb{R}^d : \|r\|_2 \leq \epsilon\}$ is the constraint space of perturbation, α is the step size.

PGD is optimized for the $\mathcal{L}_\infty$ distance metric, it can perturb all the words in the input text. Therefore, the generated adversarial sentence may be detected by human observers and drastically alter the semantics of the original text. We extend this attack method and propose new strategies to generate adversarial texts which are close to the original. Different from PGD perturbs all the items in the input text, our Extend-PGD only perturbs a few words in the original text. Specifically, we first find the words that have great influence on the classification. Then modify these words each at a time according to the influence value. The steps of our Extend-PGD are as follows.

Algorithm 1. Extend-PGD algorithm

Input: original text $\mathbf{x}$ and its true label $\mathbf{y}$, classifier f, step size α, radius ϵ, attack iteration I, maximum number of words allowed to change m.

Output: adversarial text $\mathbf{x}'$

1: Initialize: $\mathbf{x}' \leftarrow Random_{start}$, $n_{iter} \leftarrow 0$.
2: **for** word x_i in $\mathbf{x}$ **do**
3:    Compute $J_{f_{(i,j)}}$ according Eq.5;
4: **end for**
5: $L_{istorder} \leftarrow Sort(x_1, x_2, x_3, \cdots, x_n)$;
6: **while** $f(\mathbf{x}') == y$ **do**
7:    Select a word x_k in $L_{istorder}$
8:    **for** i = 1 to I **do**
9:        $\mathbf{x}^{i+1} = \text{Proj}_{\mathbf{x}+S}(\mathbf{x}^i + mask_k(\alpha sgn(\nabla_{\mathbf{x}}L(\mathbf{x}^i, \mathbf{y}))))$
10:    **end for**
11:    $n_{iter} \leftarrow n_{iter} + 1$
12:    **if** $n_{iter} > m$ **then**
13:        Return None
14:    **end if**
15: **end while**
16: **return** $\mathbf{x}'$

Step 1: Find Important Words. The first step is to compute the Jacobian matrix of the classifier f to find out the words that have great impact on the classification results. Given the input $\mathbf{x} = (x_1, x_2, x_3, \cdots, x_n)$, x_i is the ith word of the text, the matrix is calculated as follows

$$J_{f(\mathbf{x})} = \frac{\partial f(\mathbf{x})}{\partial \mathbf{x}} = \left[\frac{\partial f(\mathbf{x})_j}{\partial x_i} \right]_{i \in 1...n, j \in 1...m} \tag{4}$$

where m denotes the number of classes in $\mathbb{Y}$, and $f(\cdot)$ represents the function learned by the neural network after training. The influence of word x_i is computed as

$$J_{f(i,y)} = \frac{\partial f(\mathbf{x})_j}{\partial x_i} \tag{5}$$

By sorting the words in reverse order according to the influence value, we can find which words are important and should be changed to create adversarial examples.

Step 2: Generate Perturbations. To preserve the semantics of the text, we propose to change the original words slightly. There are two kinds of perturbations can be used, word-level perturbation and character-level perturbation. Since modifying characters of the word can be perceived by human observers and spell checker, we choose to replace the words in the text. According to the order in step 1, we perturb one word in the original text at a time. The word-based perturbation process is illustrated as:

$$\mathbf{x}^{t+1} = \text{Proj}_{\mathbf{x}+S}(\mathbf{x}^t + mask(\alpha sgn(\nabla_{\mathbf{x}}L(\mathbf{x}^t, \mathbf{y})))) \tag{6}$$

where $mask(\alpha sgn(\nabla_{\mathbf{x}} L(\mathbf{x}^t, \mathbf{y})))$ is the perturbation added to the word at the $t + 1^{th}$ iteration. The details of Extend-PGD attack are summarized in Algorithm 1.

3.2 Extend Carlini and Wagner Attack

Carlini and Wagner [1] proposed three targeted adversarial attacks to generate adversarial examples (C&W attack). They are tailored to different distance metrics, $\mathcal{L}_\infty$, $\mathcal{L}_2$ and $\mathcal{L}_0$. For example, the $\mathcal{L}_2$ attack finds adversarial examples that have low distortion in the $\mathcal{L}_2$ metric. Given a clean example $\mathbf{x}$, a target class t, and it searches for adversarial example that solves the following optimization problem

$$\min_{\mathbf{x}'} \quad \left\| \tfrac{1}{2}(tanh(\mathbf{x}') + 1) - \mathbf{x} \right\|_2^2 + c \cdot g(\tfrac{1}{2}(tanh(\mathbf{x}') + 1)) \qquad (7)$$

here $g(\cdot)$ defined as

$$g(\mathbf{x}') = \max(\max\{Z(\mathbf{x}')_i : i \neq t\} - Z(\mathbf{x}')_t, -\kappa) \qquad (8)$$

where $Z(\mathbf{x})$ is the logits before the softmax layer, κ can adjust the confidence that the adversarial instance is misclassified as class t. The constant c is hyperparameter that chose by binary search from [0.01, 100]. This attack algorithm generates the minimal adversarial perturbation that can successfully fool both distilled and undistilled neural networks.

However, the optimization-based C&W attack creates dense perturbation for a given input. This dense perturbation can easily change the structure and semantics of sentences. Therefore, sparse attacks are preferred in our work. $\mathcal{L}_1$ norm regularization is widely used for promoting sparsity in the perturbation and encourages sparse attack. Inspired by this, we propose to find an optimal adversarial example by solving the following optimization problem

$$\min_{\mathbf{x}'} \quad \lambda \left\| \mathbf{x}' - \mathbf{x} \right\|_1 + c \cdot g(\mathbf{x}') \qquad (9)$$

where $g(\cdot)$ is illustrated in Eq. 8, κ is set to 0 to generate adversarial text with small perturbations and $\lambda > 0$ is the $\mathcal{L}_1$ regularization parameter. The loss function is similar to the one in C&W, aiming to fool the model to classify $\mathbf{x}'$ into the target label t. Similar to [1], we use Adam [7] optimization algorithm to find adversarial examples. The procedure of our Extend-C&W is summarized in Algorithm 2.

Algorithm 2. Extend-C&W algorithm

Input: original text $\mathbf{x}$ and an adversarial label y_t, classifier f, learning rate γ, attack iteration I, $\mathcal{L}_1$ regularization parameter λ, maximum number of words allowed to change m.

Output: adversarial text $\mathbf{x}'$

1: Initialize: $\mathbf{x}' \leftarrow \mathbf{x}$, $bestl1 \leftarrow m$, $bestattack \leftarrow 0$.
2: **for** i=0 to I **do**
3:    $\mathbf{x}'_{i+1} \leftarrow Adam(\gamma, L(\mathbf{x}'_i, \lambda))$, $L(\cdot)$ is the loss function of Eq.9
4:    $l1 = \left\| \mathbf{x}'_{i+1} - \mathbf{x} \right\|_1$
5:    $y_{i+1} = f(\mathbf{x}'_{i+1})$
6:    **if** $y_{i+1} = y_t$ **and** $l1 < bestl1$ **then**
7:       $bestattack = \mathbf{x}'_{i+1}$, $bestl1 = l1$
8:    **end if**
9: **end for**
10: $\mathbf{x}' = bestattack$
11: **return** $\mathbf{x}'$

---

4 Experiment

To evaluate the effectiveness of our attack methods, we conduct experiments on a sentiment analysis task and a spam detection task. For the Extend-PGD attack, we run $I = 15$ iterations of project gradient descent with radius $\epsilon = 0.5$. To find successful adversarial examples, we choose the optimal step size $\alpha \in [0.05, 0.08]$ for different models and datasets. For the Extend-C&W attack, we perform 9 binary search steps over c (starting from 0.001) and run $I = 10000$ iterations of gradient descent with the initial learning rate $\gamma = 0.01$ for each step.

In this section, we analyze the performance of the proposed methods for generating adversarial examples. We start with our experimental setup, then we analyze and discuss the possible causes of the results.

4.1 Experimental Setup

Datasets. We conduct our experiments on two popular datasets: IMDB [11] and Enron Spam [14]. The IMDB dataset has been divided into training set and testing set, each part is composed of 12500 positive reviews and 12500 negative reviews. The dataset has an average length of 216 words. In our experiment, 20% of the training set is used as a validation set. Enron Spam dataset consists of 3672 ham emails and 1500 spam emails. It is a subset of the original Enron Spam Dataset and has an average length of 149 words. We divide this dataset into three parts, 70% as the training set, 20% as the validation set and 10% as the test set. Particularly, the adversarial texts are generated on the test sets.

Targeted Models. In this work, we focus on recurrent neural network architectures. To fairly compare with other methods, we performed experiments on models described in previous work [2]. The first model consists of input layer, embedding layer, an LSTM layer with 100 hidden units and a fully connected layer. The second model consists of input layer, embedding layer, a bi-directional LSTM layer with 100 hidden nodes and a fully connected layer. In embedding layer, all words within the raw input will be embedded to 300-dimensional vectors through the pre-trained Glove [17] word embeddings. If the word does not exist in the vocabulary, it will be mapped to the *"unknown"* embedding vector. Each model is trained for sentiment analysis task and spam detection task.

Baseline Methods. We implemented three baseline methods for generating adversarial texts and compared our methods with them. (i) **FGSM:** Gong et al. [3] applied FGSM to generate adversaries in the text embedding space, then reconstructing the adversarial texts via nearest neighbor search to ensure the effectiveness. (ii) **DeepFool:** Moosavi-Dezfooli et al. [15] proposed Deep-Fool for iteratively compute the perturbation. In the work of [3], this method was also used to search for adversarial examples in the word embedding space. (iii) **DeepWordBug:** Gao et al. [2] proposed a novel algorithm DeepWordBug (WordBug for short). This method develops a scoring strategy to calculate the importance score of each word and select top-m words to perturb. The authors adopted four modification strategies such as, replacing a letter in the word with a random character, exchanging the order of two letters in the word, deleting and inserting a letter in the word.

Perturbation Metrics. In our experiment, we use two metrics proposed in previous work to measure the quality of adversarial texts. (i) **Edit Distance:** It is a way to measure how dissimilar two sentences are according to minimum changes from one sentence to another. There are different definitions of edit distance. which use different string operations [8]. As our strategy is to replace words in text, we use *Number of changes* to simply measure the edits. (ii) **Cosine Similarity:** It is a method for measuring semantic similarity based on word vector. First, we need to encode clean text and adversarial text to k-dimensional vectors. In our experiment, we use Sent2Vec [16] to encode sentences into high dimensional vectors. Then we can calculate the cosine value of the angle between two vectors. The cosine similarity of two k-dimensional vectors $\mathbf{p}$ and $\mathbf{q}$ is defined as

$$S(\mathbf{p}, \mathbf{q}) = \frac{\mathbf{p} \cdot \mathbf{q}}{||\mathbf{p} \cdot \mathbf{q}||} = \frac{\sum_{i=1}^{k} p_i \times q_i}{\sqrt{\sum_{i=1}^{k}(p_i)^2} \times \sqrt{\sum_{i=1}^{k}(qi)^2}} \tag{10}$$

Under Euclidean space, the similarity between two vectors has a positive correlation with their cosine value.

4.2   Evaluation

Figures 2 and 3 show the relations between edit distance and the classification accuracy on adversarial examples. Figure 2 indicates the classification accuracy on the IMDB dataset. Figure 3 shows the experimental results on the Enron Spam dataset. The definition of model accuracy on avadjust dataset is the accuracy of the text classifier based on neural networks. Thus, the lower accuracy on generated adversarial examples, the better performance the attack method is.

From Fig. 2, we can see that all targeted models work well on the original dataset. The model accuracy is close to the state-of-the-art results on these datasets. When the number of modified words is set to 5 and 10, the five attack methods have small difference. But when the number of modifications is set to 20, 25 and 30, the results are quite different. The Extend-PGD and WordBug have notably higher attack success rate than Extend-C&W, FGSM and DeepFool. As all the sentences are padded to a fixed length of 300, we consider the 25-changes of the original text as effective. For the LSTM model, adversarial texts generated by WordBug reduced the classification accuracy from 88.91% to 34.60%. And adversarial examples generated by Extend-PGD managed to reduce the model accuracy from 88.91% to 25.07%. Adversaries generated by FGSM, DeepFool and Extend-C&W have similar model accuracy, around 61%. For the Bi-LSTM model, adversarial examples generated by Extend-PGD and WordBug reduce the model accuracy from 88.57% to 23.81% and from 88.57% to 25.8%. Adversarial texts generated by the other attack methods reduce the classification accuracy from 88.57% to around 60%.

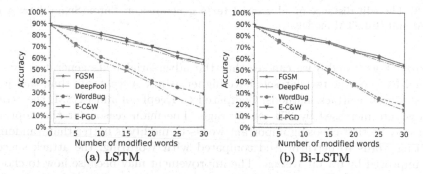

(a) LSTM   (b) Bi-LSTM

Fig. 2. The edit distance of adversarial texts generated on IMDB dataset for LSTM and Bi-LSTM models.

Figure 3 indicates that all the targeted models work well without perturbation. As shown in Fig. 3(a), our Extend-PGD performs significantly better than other attack methods on the Enron Spam dataset for different edit distances. When the number of modified words is set to 5, 10 and 15, WordBug, Extend-C&W, DeepFool and FGSM have small difference. However, when the number of modified words is set to 20, the model accuracy on adversarial examples generated by WordBug drop greatly. It can be seen from Fig. 3(b) that when the number of modified words is set to 5, all the attack methods have small difference. The Extend-PGD and WordBug perform better than Extend-C&W, DeepFool and FGSM attacks under other settings. Similar to [2], we consider modifying 20 words per review as valid. For the LSTM model, the adversarial examples generated by Extend-PGD and WordBug respectively reduce the model accuracy from 98.93% to 29.54% and from 98.93% to 41.79%. Adversaries generated by Extend-C&W, DeepFool and FGSM can reduce the model accuracy from 98.93% to around 64%. For the Bi-LSTM model, adversarial texts generated by Extend-C&W, DeepFool and FGSM reduce the classification accuracy from 98.88% to around 66%. Adversarial examples generated by Extend-PGD and WordBug can reduce the model accuracy from 98.88% to 30.04% and from 98.88% to 35.96%.

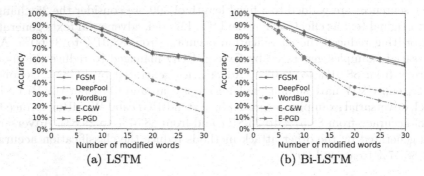

(a) LSTM   (b) Bi-LSTM

Fig. 3. The edit distance of adversarial texts generated on Enron Spam dataset for LSTM and Bi-LSTM models.

From Figs. 2 and 3 we can see that the adversarial texts generated by our Extend-PGD on the two datasets have higher attack success rate than that generated by other attack methods. Compared to DeepFool and FGSM, the attack success rate increased by 37% on average. The main reason for the improvement may be that choosing important words to modify is better than randomly selecting words to perturb. And compared with WordBug, the attack success rate improved by 6% on average. The improvement may because how to choose important word and how to modify these words both have influence on the classification results.

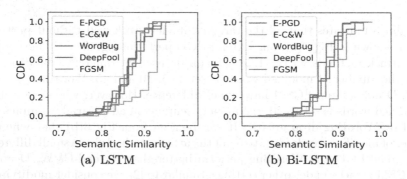

(a) LSTM   (b) Bi-LSTM

Fig. 4. The utility of adversarial texts generated on IMDB dataset for LSTM and Bi-LSTM models.

The similarity between original texts and adversarial texts generated by Extend-PGD, Extend-C&W and baseline methods are shown in Figs. 4 and 5. As most of the adversarial texts preserve more than 0.7 semantic similarity, the X axis starts from 0.7 to clearly reveal the distribution of semantic similarity. From Fig. 4 and 5, we can see that the adversarial texts generated by our attack algorithms preserve good utility in terms of vector-level. Specifically, Fig. 4(a) shows almost 75% adversarial texts generated by Extend-PGD preserve semantic similarity in a range of [0.84, 0.92]. And almost 80% adversarial examples generated by Extend-C&W preserve at least 0.89 semantic similarity of the original texts. Also, 80% adversarial texts generated by WordBug preserve semantic similarity in a range of [0.84, 0.9]. Most of the adversarial samples generated by FGSM and DeepFool preserve semantic similarity in a range of [0.82, 0.9]. Figure 5(a) shows majority of the adversarial examples generated by Extend-PGD preserve more than 0.86 semantic similarity. Almost 95% of adversarial texts generated by Extend-C&W preserve at least 0.88 semantic similarity. Most of adversarial texts generated by WordBug preserve semantic similarity in a range of [0.85, 0.89]. The semantics of adversarial texts generated by DeepFool are similar to the one generated by FGSM.

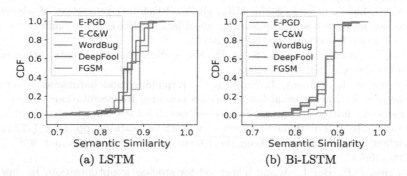

Fig. 5. The utility of adversarial texts generated on Enron Spam dataset for LSTM and Bi-LSTM models.

From Fig. 4 and 5, we can see adversarial texts generated by Extend-C&W are more semantically similar to the original texts than that generated by other attack algorithms. This is mainly because Extend-C&W adds small perturbations to the input word vectors and some of the perturbed vectors are projected to original words via *Nearest Neighbor Search*. Therefore, the Extend-C&W only achieves low success rate and the valid adversarial texts preserve utility.

5   Conclusion

In this paper, we have extended and adapted two powerful algorithms in image domain to text domain, then compare them with other state-of-the-art attack methods. Adversarial examples generated by Extend-PGD can reduce the model accuracy from about 80–90% to 20–30%. We also find an interesting result that the attack success rate of our Extend-C&W method is only about 40%. There may be two causes to the low success rate. The perturbation generated by Extend-C&W is quasi-imperceptible. On the other hand, the words changed by perturbation are randomly selected. While the modified word vectors may be projected to the original words during reconstructing.

We hope our work light some spark for other researchers. In the future, we would like to investigate adversarial examples of different datasets in natural language domain and experiment with more text classification architectures.

References

1. Carlini, N., Wagner, D.A.: Towards evaluating the robustness of neural networks. In: IEEE Symposium on Security and Privacy, pp. 39–57 (2017)
2. Gao, J., Lanchantin, J., Soffa, M.L., Qi, Y.: Black-box generation of adversarial text sequences to evade deep learning classifiers. In: IEEE Symposium on Security and Privacy Workshops, pp. 50–56 (2018)
3. Gong, Z., Wang, W., Li, B., Song, D., Ku, W.S.: Adversarial texts with gradient methods. arXiv:1801.07175 (2018)
4. Goodfellow, I.J., Shlens, J., Szegedy, C.: Explaining and harnessing adversarial examples. In: International Conference on Learning Representations (2015)
5. Graves, A., Jaitly, N.: Towards end-to-end speech recognition with recurrent neural networks. In: International Conference on Machine Learning, pp. 1764–1772 (2014)
6. Hochreiter, S., Schmolze, J.: Long short-term memory. Neural Comput. **9**(8), 1735–1780 (1997)
7. Kingma, D.P., Ba, J.: Adam: a method for stochastic optimization. In: International Conference on Learning Representations (2015)
8. Li, J., Ji, S., Du, T., Li, B., Wang, T.: TextBugger: generating adversarial text against real-world applications. In: Network and Distributed System Security Symposium (2018)
9. Liang, B., Li, H., Su, M., Bian, P., Li, X., Shi, W.: Deep text classification can be fooled. In: IJCAI, pp. 4208–4215 (2018)
10. Liu, S., Yang, N., Li, M., Zhou, M.: A recursive recurrent neural network for statistical machine translation. In: ACL, pp. 1491–1500 (2014)
11. Maas, A.L., Daly, R.E., Pham, P.T., Huang, D., Ng, A.Y., Potts, C.: Learning word vectors for sentiment analysis. In: ACL, pp. 142–150 (2011)
12. Madry, A., Makelov, A., Schmidt, L., Tsipras, D., Vladu, A.: Towards deep learning models resistant to adversarial attacks. In: ICLR (2018)
13. Mesnil, G., Mikolov, T., Ranzato, M.A., Bengio, Y.: Ensemble of generative and discriminative techniques for sentiment analysis of movie reviews. In: ICLR (2015)
14. Metsis, V., Androutsopoulos, I., Paliouras, G.: Spam fitering with naive bayes-which naive bayes? CEAS **17**, 28–69 (2006)

15. Moosavi-Dezfooli, S., Fawzi, A., Frossard, P.: DeepFool: a simple and accurate method to fool deep neural networks. In: IEEE Conference on Computer Vision and Pattern Recognition, pp. 2574–2582 (2016)
16. Pagliardini, M., Gupta, P., Jaggi, M.: Unsupervised learning of sentence embeddings using compositional n-gram features. In: NAACL: Human Language Technologies, pp. 528–540 (2018)
17. Pennington, J., Socher, R., Manning, C.: GloVe: global vectors for word representation. In: Empirical Methods in Natural Language Processing (2014)
18. Rumelhart, D.E., Hinton, G.E., Williams, R.J.: Learning representations by back-propagating errors. Cogn. Model. **14**(2) (1988)
19. Szegedy, C., et al.: Intriguing properties of neural networks. arXiv:1312.6199 (2014)

Enforcing Linearity in DNN Succours Robustness and Adversarial Image Generation

Anindya Sarkar[✉] and Raghu Iyengar

Indian Institute of Technology, Hyderabad, India
anindyasarkar.ece@gmail.com, raghu.sesha@gmail.com

Abstract. Recent studies on the adversarial vulnerability of neural networks have shown that models trained with the objective of minimizing an upper bound on the worst-case loss over all possible adversarial perturbations improve robustness against adversarial attacks. Beside exploiting adversarial training framework, we show that by enforcing a Deep Neural Network (DNN) to be linear in transformed input and feature space improves robustness significantly. We also demonstrate that by augmenting the objective function with Local Lipschitz regularizer boost robustness of the model further. Our method outperforms most sophisticated adversarial training methods and achieves state of the art adversarial accuracy on MNIST, CIFAR10 and SVHN dataset. We also propose a novel adversarial image generation method by leveraging Inverse Representation Learning and Linearity aspect of an adversarially trained deep neural network classifier.

1 Introduction

Despite the successes of deep learning [7] in wide ranges of computer vision tasks [6,11,12], it is well known that neural networks are not robust. In particular, it has been shown that the addition of small but carefully crafted human imperceptible deviations to the input, called adversarial perturbations, can cause the neural network to make incorrect predictions with high confidence [3,8]. The existence of adversarial examples pose a severe security threat to the practical deployment of deep learning models, particularly in safety critical systems, such as health-care, autonomous driving [15] etc.

Starting with the seminal work [8], there has been extensive work in the area of crafting new adversarial perturbations. These work can be broadly classified in two categories: (i) finding strategies to defend against adversarial inputs [9,17]; (ii) new attack methods that are stronger and can break the proposed defense mechanism [13].

Most of the defense strategies proposed in the literature are targeted towards a specific adversary, and as such they are easily broken by stronger adversaries [1,18]. [13] proposed robust optimization technique, which overcome this problem by finding the worst case adversarial examples at each training step and adding them

© Springer Nature Switzerland AG 2020
I. Farkaš et al. (Eds.): ICANN 2020, LNCS 12396, pp. 52–64, 2020.
https://doi.org/10.1007/978-3-030-61609-0_5

to the training data. While the resulting models show strong empirical evidence that they are robust against many attacks, we cannot yet guarantee that a different adversary cannot find inputs that cause the model to predict incorrectly. In fact, [16] observed a phenomenon that motivates why Projected Gradient Descent (PGD) - the technique at the core of Madry et al.'s method - does not always find the worst-case attack. This finding initiates the desideratum to explore more efficient strategy to enforce on the model for improving Robustness, beside exploiting adversarial training framework as developed by [13].

We list the main contributions of our work below:

- We design a model which progressively generalize a linear classifier, enforced via our regularization method **Linearity Constraint Regularization**.
- Our trained model achieve **state of the art adversarial accuracy** compared to other adversarial training approaches which aims to improve robustness against PGD attack on MNIST, CIFAR10 and SVHN datasets.
- Our proposed model contains almost half number of parameters compared to the models used by other baseline methods and still able to achieve state of the art adversarial accuracy on different benchmark.
- We also propose a two step iterative technique for **generating adversarial image** by leveraging **Inverse Representation Learning** and **Linearity** aspect of our adversarially trained model. We show that our proposed adversarial image generation method is well generalized and can act as adversary to other deep neural network classifiers also.

2   Background and Related Work

In this section, we briefly discuss about adversarial attack problem formulation in classification framework and then describe Projected Gradient Descent (PGD) [13] adversarial attack which we use as a baseline in our paper.

The goal of an adversarial attack is to find out minimum perturbation δ in the input space x (i.e. input pixels for an image) that results in the change of class prediction by the network ψ. Mathematically, we can write this as follows:

$$\operatorname*{argmin}_{\delta} \, ||\delta||_{p\text{-}norm} \quad s.t \;\; \psi_k(x + \delta; \theta) \geq \psi_{k'}(x; \theta)$$

Here, $\psi_{k'}$ and ψ_k represents the classifier output component corresponding to the true class and any other class except the true class respectively. θ denotes the parameters of the classifier ψ. Input and output are represented as x and y respectively and the objective function as $J(\theta, x, y)$.

The magnitude of adversarial perturbation is constrained by a $p\text{-}norm$ where $p\text{-}norm \in \{0, 2, \infty\}$ to ensure that the adversarially perturbed example x_{adv} is close to the original sample. Below, we pose this as an optimization problem:

$$x_{adv} = \operatorname*{argmax}_{x'} \, J(\theta, x', y) \quad s.t. ||x' - x||_{p\text{-}norm} < \epsilon \tag{1}$$

Projected Gradient Descent [13] is an iterative method to generate perturbed output using Fast Gradient Sign Method (FGSM) [8] confined to bounded perturbation space S and can be formulated as follows:

$$x^{i+1} = Proj_{x+S} \left(x^i + \alpha \operatorname{sgn} \left(\nabla_x J(\theta, x^i, y) \right) \right) \tag{2}$$

Here x^i represents perturbed sample at i-th iteration.

In general, there are mainly two types of adversarial attacks, white box and black box attacks. In white box attack, adversary has complete knowledge of the network and its parameters. While in Black box attack there is no information available about network architecture or parameters. Numerous works have been proposed to defend against such adversarial attacks. [2,4,10] showed different defense strategies to improve the robustness of deep neural networks. Unfortunately, [1] find that all these defense policies use obfuscated gradients, a kind of gradient masking, that leads to false sense of security in defense against adversarial examples and provides a limited improvement in robustness. [1] also observes Adversarial training is the only defense which significantly increases robustness to adversarial examples within the threat model.

Hence, we focus on adversarial training framework which allows to defend against adversarial attack by training neural networks on adversarial images that are generated on-the-fly during training. Adversarial training constitutes the current state of the art in adversarial robustness against white-box attacks. In this work we aim to improve model robustness further by leveraging adversarial training framework.

[20] proposed a network architecture (termed as FDT) that comprises of denoising blocks at the intermediate hidden layers which aims to remove noise from the features in latent layers introduced due to adversarial perturbation, in turn increases the adversarial robustness of the model. [14] observes that latent layers of an adversarially trained model is not robust and proposed a technique to perform adversarial training of latent layer (termed as LAT) in conjunction with adversarial training of the full network which aims at increasing the adversarial robustness of the model. In this paper we have shown improvements in adversarial accuracy as well as clean accuracy over these aforementioned methods.

3   Neural Network Architecture and Training Objective Function

In this section, we briefly discuss our proposed network architecture and training objective. As depicted in Fig. 1 , our network architecture consists of two separate branches: Concept and Significance branch. Concept branch consists of series of stacked residual convolution block of ResNet18 architecture along with global average pooling and two parallel components: fully connected layer and series of up-Convolution layers. Significance branch consists of series of stacked residual convolution block of ResNet18 architecture along with global average pooling and fully connected combined with reshape layer.

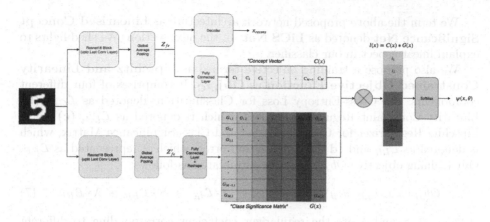

Fig. 1. Network architecture of our proposed neural network classifier LiCS Net.

x_0 is fed as input to Concept branch to output "Concept Vector" $C(x)$ from fully connected layer and reconstructed image x_{recons} from series of up-convolution layer. x_0 is also fed as input to Significance branch to produce "Class Significance Matrix" $G(x)$, a 2-Dimensional Matrix as output. Finally, we multiply "Concept Vector" $C(x)$ with "Class Significance Matrix" $G(x)$, which forms the logit vector $l(x)$ and apply the softmax function to produce class probabilities of the classifier ψ.

Let's assume, Concept branch of our network is defined by a sequence of transformations h_k for each of its K layers. For an input x_0 (which we represent as C_0), we can formulate the operation performed by the Concept branch of our architecture as below:

$$C_K = h_k(C_{k-1}) \quad \text{for } k = 1, ..., K \tag{3}$$

Here "Concept Vector" $C_K \in \mathbb{R}^M$, where M represents the number of different concepts, we want to capture from underlying data distribution.

Similarly we assume, Significance branch of the network is defined by a sequence of transformations f_k for each of its K layers. We can formulate the operation performed by the Significance branch of our architecture with same input x_0 (which we represent as G_0) as below:

$$G_K = f_k(G_{k-1}) \quad \text{for } k = 1, ..., K \tag{4}$$

Here "Class Significance Matrix" $G_K \in \mathbb{R}^{M*N}$, where, N and M represents number of classes and concepts respectively.

We define logit vector l as product of Concept vector C_K and Class Significance Matrix G_K. We formulate the logit vector l and output of classifier ψ as follows:

$$l(x, \theta) = C_K(x, \theta) \cdot G_K(x, \theta) \tag{5}$$

$$\psi(x, \theta) = Softmax\left(l(x, \theta)\right) \tag{6}$$

We term the above proposed network architecture as **Linearised Concept Significance Net** denoted as **LiCS Net**. In the next section, We shed lights to explain linear aspect in our classifier.

We also propose a training objective termed as **Lipschitz and Linearity Constrained Objective Function** as $\mathbf{Obj_{L^2C}}$. It comprises of four different components: **(a)** Cross-Entropy Loss for Classification, denoted as $\mathcal{L}_{CE}$, **(b)** Linearity Constraint Regularization loss, which is denoted as $\mathcal{L}_{LC}$, **(c)** Local Lipschitz Regularizer for Concept Vector and Class Significance Matrix, which is denoted as $\mathcal{L}_{LR}$ and **(d)** Reconstruction error, which is represented as $\mathcal{L}_{RE}$. Our training objective Obj_{L^2C} can be formulated as follows:

$$Obj_{L^2C}(x, x_{adv}, \theta, y) = \alpha \cdot \mathcal{L}_{CE} + \beta \cdot \mathcal{L}_{LC} + \gamma \cdot \mathcal{L}_{LR} + \lambda \cdot \mathcal{L}_{RE} \quad (7)$$

Here α, β, γ and λ are the regularizer coefficient corresponding to different component of our objective function.

We briefly discuss about different component of the objective function.

(a) **Cross-Entropy loss** is defined as follows:

$$\mathcal{L}_{CE} = \sum_{c=1}^{N} (y_{true} \cdot log(y_{pred})) \ where \ y_{pred} = \psi(x_{adv}, \theta) \quad (8)$$

Here c represents class index, N denotes number of classes, y_{true} holds ground-truth class label score. y_{pred} hold class probability scores when an adversarial image x_{adv} is being fed through the classifier.

For the remainder of this section, x_{adv} refers to the generated adversarial image from its corresponding true image x by following Eq. 2. Note that ground-truth label is same for both x_{adv} and x.

(b) **Linearity Constraint Regularization loss** is defined as follows:

$$\mathcal{L}_{LC} = \left\| \frac{\partial l(x_{adv}, \theta)}{\partial C_K(x_{adv}, \theta)} - G_K(x_{adv}, \theta) \right\|_2 \quad (9)$$

Here $\| \cdot \|_2$ represents the $l2\text{-}norm$ of a given vector. We are enforcing the logit vector $l(x_{adv}, \theta)$ to behave as a linear classifier with "Concept Vector" C_K as the input and "Class Significance Matrix" G_K as the parameters or weights of that linear classifier.

Intuitively, a linear classifier can be defined as $L(x, W) = W^T \cdot x$, where x is input and W captures significance of each input features for the classification task. Comparing Eq. 5 with linear classifier L, we hypothesize C_K encodes the transformed input features like x and G_K encodes the significance weight factor for concept features same as W.

(c) **Local Lipschitz Regularizer for Concept Vector and Class Significance Matrix** is defined based on the concept of "Lipschitz constant". Let's assume a function $\phi(x)$ having Lipschitz Constant value of L_Φ. Below equation holds true for all Δ.

$$\|\phi(x + \Delta) - \phi(x)\| \leq L_\Phi \cdot \|\Delta\| \quad (10)$$

Hence, we argue that a lower Lipschitz constant ensures that the function's output for its corresponding perturbed input is not significantly different and it can be used to improve the adversarial robustness of a classifier.

The Lipschitz constant of our network ψ has an upper bound defined by the product of Lipschitz constant of its sub-networks: Concept and Significance branch. We can formulate this as follows:

$$L_\psi \leq L_{sub_C} \cdot L_{sub_G} \tag{11}$$

Here L_{sub_C} and L_{sub_G} are the Lipschitz constant of the sub network Concept branch and Significance branch respectively.

To achieve a robust classifier, we aim to improve robustness of its subnetworks using Local Lipschitz Regularizer for Concept Vector and Class Significance Matrix, which is formulated as follows:

$$\mathcal{L}_{LR} = \beta_1 \cdot ||C_K(x,\theta) - C_K(x_{adv},\theta)||_2 + \beta_2 \cdot ||G_K(x,\theta) - G_K(x_{adv},\theta)||_2 \tag{12}$$

Here, $C_K(x,\theta)$ and $G_K(x,\theta)$ are Concept vector and Class Significance Matrix respectively when a true image is passed through our network. Similarly, $C_K(x_{adv},\theta)$ and $G_K(x_{adv},\theta)$ are Concept vector and Class Significance Matrix respectively when the corresponding adversarial image is passed through the network. β_1 and β_2 are the regularization coefficients.

Note that, we enforce invariability of Concept vector C_K and Class Significance matrix G_K to the model for an original image x and its corresponding adversarial image x_{adv} through Local Lipschitz Regularizer.

(d) **Reconstruction error** is defined as follows:

$$\mathcal{L}_{RE} = ||x_{adv} - x_{recons}||_2 \tag{13}$$

where x_{adv} is an adversarial image and x_{recons} is the reconstructed image at last up-convolution layer of the Concept branch of our network.

4   Adversarial Image Generation

In this section, we propose adversarial image generation method which consists of two iterative steps stated as follows: **(i)** Find minimum perturbation of Concept Vector $C(x,\theta)$ which guarantees to fool the classifier by exploiting "linearity" aspect of the classifier. **(ii)** Using the perturbed concept vector from step (i), generate an equivalent perturbation in image space (i.e. image pixels) by leveraging inverse representation which fools the classifier.

We elaborate above steps of adversarial image generation method below:

Step (i): We represent the i-th component of logit vector defined in Eq. 5 as:

$$l^i(x,\theta) = C_K(x,\theta) \cdot G_K^i(x,\theta) \tag{14}$$

Here $G_K^i(x,\theta)$ is the i-th column of Class Significance Matrix which encodes the significance weight factor of concepts for the i-th class.

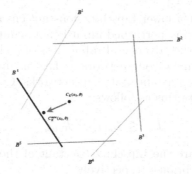

Fig. 2. Depicts the optimal shift of concept vector towards the normal direction of the nearest class decision boundary plane in order to change the classifier prediction.

Let 's assume for a given image x_0, the network produces a Concept Vector C_K, and the ground truth class label corresponding to image x_0 is $\tilde{i}$. Now, the minimum perturbation (δ) required in Concept Vector to fool the classifier can be formulated as follows:

$$\underset{\delta}{\mathrm{argmin}} \, ||\delta||_2 \quad s.t. \quad (C_K(x_0, \theta) + \delta) \cdot G_K^i(x_0, \theta) \geq (C_K(x_0, \theta) + \delta) \cdot G_K^{\tilde{i}}(x_0, \theta)$$

In the above relation, "i" represents the class index and $i \neq \tilde{i}$ must satisfy. Now, we can re-arrange and write above equation as follows:

$$\delta \leq \frac{C_K(x_0, \theta) \cdot (G_K^i(x_0, \theta) - G_K^{\tilde{i}}(x_0, \theta))}{G_K^{\tilde{i}}(x_0, \theta) - G_K^i(x_0, \theta)} \tag{15}$$

Using Eq. 5 into Eq. 15, we write this as follows:

$$\delta \leq \frac{l^i(x_0, \theta) - l^{\tilde{i}}(x_0, \theta)}{G_K^{\tilde{i}}(x_0, \theta) - G_K^i(x_0, \theta)} \tag{16}$$

As shown in Fig. 2, Concept vector is represented as a point in M dimensional concept space. We decide to perturb the Concept vector $C_K(x_0, \theta)$ towards the linear decision boundary of a target class i^t, which satisfy the following relation:

$$i^t = \underset{i \neq \tilde{i}}{\mathrm{argmin}} \frac{|l^i(x_0, \theta) - l^{\tilde{i}}(x_0, \theta)|}{||G_K^{\tilde{i}}(x_0, \theta) - G_K^i(x_0, \theta)||_2} \tag{17}$$

Here, i^t is the target class index, which has the decision boundary nearest to the Concept vector $C_K(x_0, \theta)$ compared to decision boundary of any other class in terms of $|| \, . \, ||_2$ norm.

We then shift the Concept vector $C_K(x_0, \theta)$ in the direction normal to the i^t linear decision boundary surface. As shown in Fig. 2, the movement of Concept vector is represented by a red arrow and the linear decision boundary of the target class i^t is depicted as B^t. Mathematically, we represent the direction of the optimal shift (δ^*) of the concept vector $C_K(x_0, \theta)$ as follows:

$$\delta^* = \frac{|l^{i^t}(x_0, \theta) - l^{\tilde{i}}(x_0, \theta)|}{||G_K^{i^t}(x_0, \theta) - G_K^{\tilde{i}}(x_0, \theta)||_2^2} \cdot (\nabla(l^{i^t}) - \nabla(l^{\tilde{i}})) \tag{18}$$

Hence, we obtain a new perturbed concept vector $C_K^{new}(x_0, \theta)$, by adding the optimal shift to the actual value of concept vector $C_K(x_0, \theta)$. We represents this as follows:

$$C_K^{new}(x_0, \theta) = C_K(x_0, \theta) + \delta^* \tag{19}$$

We perform this whole process iteratively, until the perturbed concept vector change the classifier's true prediction. We denote the final perturbed concept vector as $C_K^{perturb}(x_0, \theta)$ which obeys below condition:

$$C_K^{perturb}(x_0, \theta) \cdot G_K^i(x_0, \theta) \geq C_K(x_0, \theta) \cdot G_K^{\tilde{i}}(x_0, \theta)$$
$$s.t. \ i \neq \tilde{i} \tag{20}$$

Step (ii): From step (i), we obtain a final perturbed concept vector $C_K^{perturb}(x_0, \theta)$ which guarantees to change the classifier's prediction. Now the main question is "How do we generate the adversarial image $(x_{adv}^{perturb})$ which corresponds to the final Perturbed Concept vector $C_K^{perturb}(x_0, \theta)$?".

As illustrated in [5], the Representation vector of a given input x are the activations of the penultimate layer of the network. [5] also illustrate that adversarially trained model produces similar Representation vectors for semantically similar images. For a given input, Concept vector generated from the Concept branch of our network LiCS Net is analogous to Representation vector.

We have used "Inverse Representation" [5,19] method to generate adversarial image $x_{adv}^{perturb}$ which corresponds to the final Perturbed Concept vector $C_K^{perturb}(x_0, \theta)$, starting from the true input image x_0 and its corresponding Concept vector $C_K(x_0, \theta)$. We can pose this method as an optimization problem detailed in Algorithm 1.

Algorithm 1: Pseudo-code of Step (ii)

Input: True Image x_0, Perturbed Concept Vector $C_K^{perturb}(x_0, \theta)$, LiCS Net
Classifier ψ_{LiCS}
Output: Adversarial Image $x_{adv}^{perturb}$
1 Initialise $x_{adv} = x_0$
2 Set $C_K^{target} = C_K^{perturb}(x_0, \theta)$
3 **while**
argmax $\psi_{LiCS}(x_{adv}, \theta) \neq$ argmax $\psi_{LiCS}(x_0, \theta)$
do
(i) $x_{adv} = x_{adv} - \nabla_{x_{adv}}||C_K^{target} - C_K(x_{adv}, \theta)||$
(ii) if $||x_{adv} - x_0||_{2\text{-}norm} \geq \epsilon$
then, $x_{adv} = Proj_{x_0 + S}(x_{adv})$
4 Adversarial Image, $x_{adv}^{perturb} = x_{adv}$

We term above proposed algorithm as **Adversarial Image Generation using Linearity and Inverse Representation as AIG$_{LiIR}$**.

In Fig. 3, we depicted few adversarial images generated by our proposed method AIG_{LiIR}. Such adversarial image guarantees to fool white box threat model. For example, in the case of CIFAR10, generated adversarial images by AIG_{LiIR} method are being classified by our proposed LiCS Net as *Bird* and *Deer* whereas its corresponding true level are *Airplane* and *Horse*.

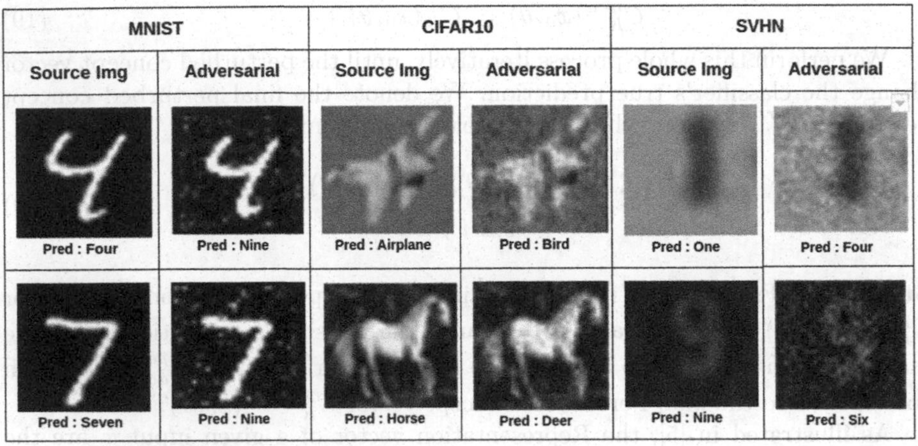

MNIST		CIFAR10		SVHN	
Source Img	Adversarial	Source Img	Adversarial	Source Img	Adversarial
Pred : Four	Pred : Nine	Pred : Airplane	Pred : Bird	Pred : One	Pred : Four
Pred : Seven	Pred : Nine	Pred : Horse	Pred : Deer	Pred : Nine	Pred : Six

Fig. 3. Depicts few sample pairs of source image and its corresponding adversarial image generated by our proposed AIG_{LiIR} method.

Moreover with evident results provided in next section, we claim that our adversarial image generation method AIG_{LiIR} is very effective in fooling various deep neural network designed for classification task.

5   Experiments and Results

In this section, we briefly discuss our experimental findings to analyze the robustness of our proposed network LiCS Net. We have performed experiment to show the "Transferability" of the adversarial images generated by our method AIG$_{LiIR}$. We also discuss findings on the effectiveness of Linearity Constraint and Local Lipschitz Regularizer in our objective function Obj_{L^2C} to improve adversarial robustness. The samples are constructed using PGD adversarial perturbations as proposed in [13] for adversarial training. For the remainder of this section, we refer an adversarially trained model as a model which is trained using PGD adversarial examples [13]. Clean and Adversarial accuracy are defined as a accuracy of a network over original images and over the adversarial images generated from the test dataset respectively. Higher adversarial accuracy implies more robust network. To test the efficacy of our proposed training method, we perform experiments

Table 1. Comparison of Adversarial accuracy and Clean accuracy for CIFAR10, SVHN and MNIST datasets acheieved by different adversarial training techniques

Dataset	Adversarial training techniques	Architecture used	No. of parameters used	Adversarial accuracy	Clean accuracy
CIFAR10	AT	WRN 28-10	36M	47.12%	87.27%
	FDT	WRN 28-10	36M	46.99%	87.31%
	LAT	WRN 28-10	36M	53.84%	87.80%
	CSAT	**LiCS Net**	**21M**	**56.77%**	**87.65%**
SVHN	AT	WRN 28-10	36M	54.58%	91.88%
	FDT	WRN 28-10	36M	54.69%	92.45%
	LAT	WRN 28-10	36M	60.23%	91.65%
	CSAT	**LiCS Net**	**21M**	**61.37%**	**95.11%**
MNIST	AT	WRN 28-10	36M	95.53%	98.49%
	FDT	WRN 28-10	36M	95.72%	98.41%
	LAT	WRN 28-10	36M	96.41%	98.98%
	CSAT	**LiCS Net**	**21M**	**98.68%**	**99.46%**

over CIFAR10, SVHN and MNIST dataset. For fairness, we compare our method against three different fine-tuned techniques applied in adversarial training framework. These are Adversarial Training (AT) [13], Feature Denoising Training (FDT) [20] and Latent adversarial Training (LAT) [14].

5.1 Evaluation Using Adversarial Accuracy

We adversarially train LiCS Net using Obj_{L^2C} training objective and denote this as Concept-Significance Adversarial Training (CSAT). In order to compare CSAT with other adversarial training techniques we use PGD.

PGD Configuration: The configuration of PGD adversarial perturbation varies for different datasets. For MNIST dataset, we restrict the maximum amount of per pixel perturbation as 0.3 (in the pixel scale of 0 to 1 range) and we choose 40 steps of PGD iterations with step size of 2/255. For CIFAR10 and SVHN dataset, we restrict the maximum amount of per pixel perturbation as 8.0 (in the pixel scale of 0 to 255 range) and we choose 10 steps of PGD iterations with step size of 2/255.

Concept-Significance Adversarial Training (CSAT) vs Others: Table 1 reports the adversarial accuracy comparison between CSAT and other adversarial training techniques. Note that we choose dimension of concept vector as 10 and the dimension of class significance matrix as 10×10. Note that CSAT requires almost half number of parameters compared to other baseline methods.

5.2 Transferability of Generated Adversarial Samples

Training on adversarial samples has been shown as one of the best method to improve robustness of a classifier [13,14,17]. We denote AIG_{CSPGD} as the

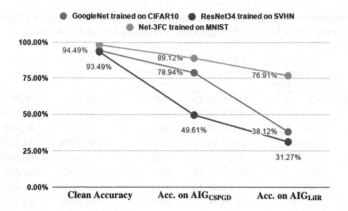

Fig. 4. Depicts the comparison between clean accuracy and adversarial accuracy evaluated on samples generated by AIG_{CSPGD} and AIG_{LiLR} method.

adversarial image generation method to generate adversarial samples using PGD adversarial perturbations [13] on our trained network LiCS Net using our objective function Obj_{L^2C}. In previous section, we proposed our adversarial image generation method AIG_{LiIR} to generate adversarial samples using our trained network LiCS Net.

We evaluate adversarial accuracy of different standard pre-trained models such as GoogleNet (trained on CIFAR10), ResNet34 (trained on SVHN) and custom Net-3FC (trained on MNIST) on adversarial samples generated using AIG_{LiIR} and AIG_{CSPGD} method and compare with their respective clean test accuracy. Note that custom Net-3FC consists of 3 fully connected layers along with Relu activation and softmax function.

AIG$_{LiIR}$ vs AIG$_{CSPGD}$: As evident in Fig. 4, For classifiers GoogleNet, ResNet34 and custom Net-3FC, we observe significant drop in accuracy on adversarial samples generated using AIG_{CSPGD} and AIG_{LiIR} method, in comparison to their clean accuracy. For example in case of ResNet34, drop in accuracy on adversarial samples generated using AIG_{LiIR} method is 18.34% more than drop in accuracy on adversarial samples generated using AIG_{CSPGD} in comparison with clean accuracy on SVHN dataset.

These experimental finding suggests adversarial samples generated using AIG_{LiIR} act as a better adversary to various network architectures such as GoogleNet, Resnet34 and custom Net-3FC which shows the "transferability" of these adversarial samples.

5.3   Ablation Study

Architecture: We have used our proposed network LiCS Net for ablation experiments on our objective function as stated in Eq. 7. We kept all the hyperparameters same for different experiments of ablation study. We evaluated adversarial accuracy of our network LiCS Net trained with base objective function (termed as Obj_{BASE}) which consists of cross-entropy and reconstruction loss and used it as our baseline adversarial accuracy for ablation study.

Linearity Constraint vs Local Lipschitz Regularizer: As evident from Table 2, adversarial accuracy improves in both the cases when base training objective is augmented with Linearity Constraint Regularizer (termed as $Obj_{BASE+LCR}$) and also when Obj_{BASE} is augmented with Local Lipschitz Regularizer (termed as $Obj_{BASE+LLR}$) compared to the baseline adversarial accuracy. Experimental findings suggests that the regularization impact of Linearity Constraint is much more effective compared to Local Lipschitz Regularization to improve model robustness. Note that we achieve state of the art adversarial accuracy when Obj_{BASE} is augmented with both Linearity Constraint and Local Lipschitz Regulariser.

Table 2. Depicts adversarial accuracy comparison of our model LiCS Net trained using different objective functions on various datasets

Training Obj.	Adv. Accuracy		
	CIFAR10	SVHN	MNIST
$Obj_{\mathbf{BASE}}$	47.02%	54.17%	93.14%
$Obj_{\mathbf{BASE+LLR}}$	49.75%	55.70%	95.39%
$Obj_{\mathbf{BASE+LCR}}$	54.39%	60.61%	98.06%
$Obj_{\mathbf{L^2C}}$	**56.77%**	**61.37%**	**98.68%**

6   Conclusion

We observe that adversarial training method is the de-facto method to improve model robustness. We propose **LiCS Net** which achieves state of the art adversarial accuracy trained with our proposed objective function on the MNIST, CIFAR10 and SVHN datasets along with the improvement in normal accuracy. We also propose an Adversarial Image Generation method **AIG$_{\mathbf{LiIR}}$** that exploits Linearity Constraint and Inverse Representation learning to construct adversarial examples. We performed several experiments to exhibit the robustness and transferability of the adversarial samples generated by our Adversarial Image Generation method across different networks. Through our research, we shed lights on the impact of linearity on robustness. We hope, our findings will inspire discovery of new adversarial defenses and attacks and, offers a significant pathway for new developments in adversarial machine learning.

References

1. Athalye, A., Carlini, N., Wagner, D.A.: Obfuscated gradients give a false sense of security: circumventing defenses to adversarial examples. CoRR, abs/1802.00420 (2018)

2. Buckman, J., Roy, A., Raffel, C., Goodfellow, I.: Thermometer encoding: one hot way to resist adversarial examples (2018)
3. Carlini, N., Wagner, D.A.: Towards evaluating the robustness of neural networks. CoRR, abs/1608.04644 (2016)
4. Cisse, M., Bojanowski, P., Grave, E., Dauphin, Y., Usunier, N.: Parseval networks: improving robustness to adversarial examples. arXiv preprint arXiv:1704.08847 (2017)
5. Engstrom, L., Ilyas, A., Santurkar, S., Tsipras, D., Tran, B., Madry, A.: Learning perceptually-aligned representations via adversarial robustness. CoRR, abs/1906.00945 (2019)
6. Girshick, R., Donahue, J., Darrell, T., Malik, J.: Rich feature hierarchies for accurate object detection and semantic segmentation. In: Proceedings of the IEEE Conference on Computer Vision and Pattern Recognition, pp. 580–587 (2014)
7. Goodfellow, I., Bengio, Y., Courville, A.: Deep Learning. MIT Press, Cambridge (2016)
8. Goodfellow, I.J., Shlens, J., Szegedy, C.: Explaining and harnessing adversarial examples. CoRR, abs/1412.6572 (2014)
9. Goodfellow, I.J., Shlens, J., Szegedy, C.: Explaining and harnessing adversarial examples. arXiv preprint arXiv:1412.6572 (2014)
10. Guo, C., Rana, M., Cissé, M., van der Maaten, L.: Countering adversarial images using input transformations. CoRR, abs/1711.00117 (2017)
11. He, K., Gkioxari, G., Dollár, P., Girshick, R.B.: Mask R-CNN. CoRR, abs/1703.06870 (2017)
12. He, K., Zhang, X., Ren, S., Sun, J.: Deep residual learning for image recognition. In: Proceedings of the IEEE Conference on Computer Vision and Pattern Recognition, pp. 770–778 (2016)
13. Madry, A., Makelov, A., Schmidt, L., Tsipras, D., Vladu, A.: Towards deep learning models resistant to adversarial attacks. ArXiv, abs/1706.06083 (2017)
14. Sinha, A., Singh, M., Kumari, N., Krishnamurthy, B., Machiraju, H., Balasubramanian, V.N.: Harnessing the vulnerability of latent layers in adversarially trained models. CoRR, abs/1905.05186 (2019)
15. Sitawarin, C., Bhagoji, A.N., Mosenia, A., Chiang, M., Mittal, P.: DARTS: deceiving autonomous cars with toxic signs. CoRR, abs/1802.06430 (2018)
16. Tjeng, V., Tedrake, R.: Verifying neural networks with mixed integer programming. CoRR, abs/1711.07356 (2017)
17. Tramèr, F., Kurakin, A., Papernot, N., Goodfellow, I.J., Boneh, D., McDaniel, P.D.: Ensemble adversarial training: attacks and defenses. ArXiv, abs/1705.07204 (2017)
18. Uesato, J., O'Donoghue, B., van den Oord, A., Kohli, P.: Adversarial risk and the dangers of evaluating against weak attacks. CoRR, abs/1802.05666 (2018)
19. Ulyanov, D., Vedaldi, A., Lempitsky, V.: Deep image prior. In: Proceedings of the IEEE Conference on Computer Vision and Pattern Recognition, pp. 9446–9454 (2018)
20. Xie, C., Wu, Y., van der Maaten, L., Yuille, A.L., He, K.: Feature denoising for improving adversarial robustness. CoRR, abs/1812.03411 (2018)

Computational Analysis of Robustness in Neural Network Classifiers

Iveta Bečková[✉], Štefan Pócoš, and Igor Farkaš

Faculty of Mathematics, Physics and Informatics, Comenius University in Bratislava,
Mlynská dolina, 84248 Bratislava, Slovakia
kiwicko@gmail.com

Abstract. Neural networks, especially deep architectures, have proven excellent tools in solving various tasks, including classification. However, they are susceptible to adversarial inputs, which are similar to original ones, but yield incorrect classifications, often with high confidence. This reveals the lack of robustness in these models. In this paper, we try to shed light on this problem by analyzing the behavior of two types of trained neural networks: fully connected and convolutional, using MNIST, Fashion MNIST, SVHN and CIFAR10 datasets. All networks use a logistic activation function whose steepness we manipulate to study its effect on network robustness. We also generated adversarial examples with FGSM method and by perturbing those pixels that fool the network most effectively. Our experiments reveal a trade-off between accuracy and robustness of the networks, where models with a logistic function approaching a threshold function (very steep slope) appear to be more robust against adversarial inputs.

Keywords: Robustness · Logistic sigmoid · Pixel attack

1 Introduction

Neural networks (especially with deep architectures) have demonstrated excellent performance in various complex machine learning tasks such as image classification, speech recognition, or natural language processing [1]. At the same time, neural networks in general are due to their multilayer nonlinear structure not transparent and so it is hard to understand their behavior. Therefore, a lot of effort has been dedicated to uncovering their function [6]. In addition, it was discovered that solutions they provide are surprisingly not robust, and that they can be fooled with carefully crafted images called adversarials, which are similar to original ones. The notion of adversarial images was introduced in [14], where it was shown that even small perturbations of input can lead to misclassification with a high confidence. It is even possible to fool the classifier with single pixel attacks as demonstrated in [12]. There exist multiple ways to generate these adversarial inputs and it is applicable not only for images but many other kinds of neural network as for example voice recognition [16].

© Springer Nature Switzerland AG 2020
I. Farkaš et al. (Eds.): ICANN 2020, LNCS 12396, pp. 65–76, 2020.
https://doi.org/10.1007/978-3-030-61609-0_6

Thus the ability of a network to resist adversarial attacks (robustness) became a major concern. Several papers already proposed methods how to alleviate the problem. For instance, enforcing compactness in the learned features of a convolutional neural network by modifying the loss function was observed to enhance robustness [9]. Alternatively, a modified version of conditional GAN network was used to generate boundary samples with true labels near the decision boundary of a pre-trained classifier, and these were added to the pre-trained classifier as data augmentation to make the decision boundary more robust [13]. Other papers have focused on the relationship between robustness and model accuracy. In [8] this opposing relationship is more formally explored and shown how the evoked tension between the two properties impacts the accuracy of models.

Related line of research has focused on looking at internal representations and their relation to model performance. In our recent work, we analyzed trained deep neural network classifiers in terms of learned representations (and their properties) and confirmed that there exist qualitatively different, but quantitatively similar (with similar testing errors) solutions to the complex classification problems, depending on activation functions used in the hidden layers [4]. One of these standard activations is the logistic function whose effect is investigated here, but in the context of robustness.

In the following, we provide our pilot results on the analysis of the robustness and its relation to accuracy of the trained relatively simple feedforward networks. We introduce four image datasets and the models used (Sect. 2), methods of analysis of trained models (Sect. 3), their results (Sect. 4), and conclusion (Sect. 5).

2   Data and Models

We used four well-known datasets, with increasing levels of complexity, namely MNIST, Fashion-MNIST, SVHN and CIFAR10, to be able to better track the analysis.

The MNIST database is a set of 28×28 pixel grayscale images corresponding to ten classes. It is made of centered, upright hand-written digits on black background, with 60000 samples in the training set and 10000 in the testing set. Since MNIST is one of the most basic datasets for image classification, one does not require a deep convolutional network to classify the images with satisfying accuracy [5].

Fashion MNIST (referred to as F-MNIST) is a dataset created due to overuse of MNIST. It consists of 28×28 pixel grayscale images, where each of them belongs to one of ten classes describing clothing or accessory. Training set (50000 samples) and testing set (10000 samples) make up all 60000 samples of the dataset [15].

The SVHN (Street View House Numbers) database consists of 32×32 pixel RGB images of house numbers, each image centered on one digit, thus belonging to one of ten classes. We used ~73000 images for training and ~26000 for testing [7].

CIFAR10 provides variety of 32×32 pixel RGB images, belonging to one of ten classes representing an animal or a vehicle. The number of images included in training and testing sets are 50000 and 10000 respectively [3].

For easier datasets (MNIST and F-MNIST) we use a multilayer perceptron with a single hidden layer containing 256 neurons with a logistic sigmoid activation function and softmax outputs. An architecture for SVHN and CIFAR10 classification is depicted in Fig. 1. To optimize the learning process we use Adam optimizer and cross entropy loss. The training length of models is set to 100 epochs for MNIST and F-MNIST and 50 epochs for SVHN and CIFAR10. All models are trained with a batch size 64 and their properties are evaluated after each epoch.

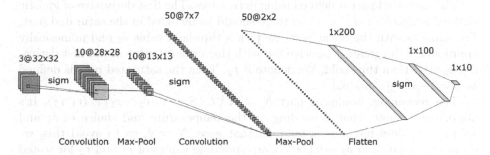

Fig. 1. SVHN and CIFAR10 classifier architecture (plotted using NN-SVG tool).

3 Methods of Analysis

In our computational analysis we monitored the distribution of neuron's activation values during training and computed the gradient of the loss function with respect to the input. To make the monitoring of the neuron activation levels more understandable, we quantized these into three regimes. We expected to find a relation between these regimes and the network robustness, evaluated by generating adversarial examples using two different methods.

3.1 Quantized Activation Levels

We investigated the effect of temperature T in the logistic sigmoid defined as

$$f(net) = \frac{1}{1 + \exp(-net/T)} \tag{1}$$

By modifying the value of T one can adjust the slope at $net = 0$, thus affecting the distribution of function values. We considered $T = \{1/64, 1/32, \ldots, 4, 16\}$ for MNIST and F-MNIST datasets and $T = \{1/8, 1/4, \ldots, 4, 8\}$ for SVHN and CIFAR10, since these temperatures allowed to train the models with higher accuracy. Using values beyond these ranges in many cases led to significant drop of network performance.

To test how the choice of temperature affects the activations of hidden neurons, we divide *net* values of neurons on the last hidden layer, which is a set of real numbers $\mathcal{R}$ into three disjoint regions – linear, nonlinear and saturated, dependent on T. We define the linear part as follows: first we calculate the tangent line of the logistic sigmoid at $net = 0$. Since the first derivative is symmetrical and monotonous for $net \in [0, \infty)$, with an increasing (or decreasing) net, the value $f(net)$ moves away from (closer to) this line. We choose a threshold δ_1 and numerically approximate the smallest $net > 0$, for which the Euclidean distance of $(net, f(net))$ from this tangent line is larger than δ_1. Let's denote it r_1. Then the linear part is $L = [-r_1, r_1]$.

The saturated part is defined using derivatives. The first derivative of logistic sigmoid is zero for $net = \pm\infty$, so these should be included in the saturated part. The same as with the linear part, we pick a threshold value δ_2 and numerically approximate the greatest positive net with the absolute value of the first derivative greater than threshold. We denote it r_2. Then the saturated part is defined as $S = (-\infty, r_2] \cup [r_2, \infty)$.

The remaining, nonlinear part $N = \mathcal{R} \setminus L \setminus S = (-r_2, -r_1) \cup (r_1, r_2)$. It's important to note, that depending on the temperature and choice of δ_1 and δ_2, $r_2 > r_1$ does not always hold. In that case, $N = \emptyset$, so to avoid this, we choose $\delta_1 = 0.05$ and $\delta_2 = 0.0005$. Corresponding values of r_1 and r_2 for tested temperatures are shown in Fig. 2.

Then, we define the operation of a tested network in the respective regime as a fraction of *net* values occurred in that region.

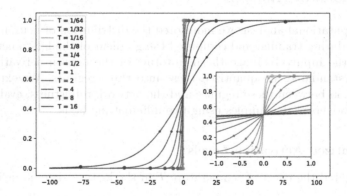

Fig. 2. Logistic sigmoid $f(net)$ with various temperatures. The larger dots denote $\pm r_2$, and smaller ones $\pm r_1$. These dots delineate the three different activity regions used in analysis.

3.2   Robustness

For testing the robustness we use fast gradient sign method (FGSM) described in [2], which works as follows. First, the gradient of loss function with respect to input image is calculated. This gradient shows such a local change of each pixel of input image that the loss of network increases the most. Second, the attack itself is executed by adding the sign of the corresponding gradient multiplied by a small factor ϵ to each input pixel. For creating adversarial examples we mainly use $\epsilon = 0.1$ for each sample from the testing sets. Then the class robustness is defined as $1-$ fraction of adversarial inputs created from samples belonging to the given class that are classified incorrectly. Finally, network robustness is evaluated as an average robustness over all classes. This is the most frequent way to analyze the network robustness and is used in many applications such as [11]. On the other hand, there exist more complex definitions of robustness, that mainly involve measuring the strength of perturbation. Some examples can be found in [9,13]. Since we generate the adversarial examples with a given magnitude of perturbation, we stick to the most basic but effective evaluation of robustness.

In the FGSM attack, the original input image is changed by adding the sign of a gradient of the loss function with respect to the input. Thus the magnitude of change is the same for each pixel (except for pixels whose values in adversarials would exceed $[0,1]$; these are trimmed). This does not take into account the magnitude of gradients, or differences among pixels. Some sources [10] suggest the use of fast gradient value method (FGVM) that does not incorporate the sign. We decided to use FGSM but we also analyzed the values of gradients by computing $G(x_i) = \sum_{n=1,m=1}^{N,M} |\frac{\partial L}{\partial x_i(n,m)}|/(N.M)$, i.e. the arithmetic mean of absolute values of partial derivatives of the loss function L with respect to individual pixels (in case of SVHN and CIFAR10 also for individual channels).

3.3   Pixel Attack

Another way to generate adversarial examples besides FGSM (which adds minimal perturbation to all pixels) is to seek such (greater) perturbations of only a few pixels so that the modified input would not be classified correctly. An important step here is the pixel selection. In order to select those, which cause the biggest change in the output probabilities, we look at the gradients mentioned above. We sort the pixels by absolute values of the corresponding gradients. If we choose top n pixels, there is a chance for misclassification. Naturally, the higher n implies the bigger chance to misclassify the input, but as we show, in many cases even one pixel can do the trick. Therefore, using the same definition of class robustness as above, we get another measure of model's robustness just by changing the way of generating the adversarials.

4   Experiments

We managed to train all our models with up to 98%, 90%, 92% and 65% testing accuracy on MNIST, F-MNIST, SVHN and CIFAR10 respectively. In some cases (mainly for CIFAR10) the accuracy could have been significantly improved by using a more sophisticated architecture and training methods, but for subsequent analysis of robustness the given accuracy was satisfactory. In all four datasets, the models with extreme temperatures (too high or too low) were the most difficult to train, as shown in Fig. 3. Large values of T yield too small gradients, and too small T leads to zero gradients except $net \approx 0$ where they are enormous. Under these extreme circumstances the hardest task for a given network is to start the learning procedure.

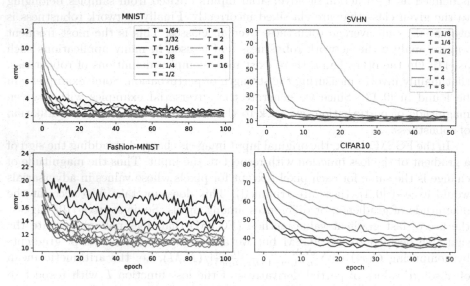

Fig. 3. Learning curves for all four datasets using selected temperatures. Figures on either side use the same temperatures, shown in upper figure.

4.1 Quantized Activation Levels

After each epoch of training we analyzed our model's properties. All of the trained networks show similar behavior. Linearity drastically drops with decreasing temperature. In these areas high level of saturation is detected. Detailed caption of these properties is shown in Fig. 4.

All the figures, quite consistent for all four datasets, reveal the dynamics of gradual transitions between respective operation modes during learning. For most values of T, the network gradually spends less time in the linear and non-linear modes (albeit the baseline for the latter is significantly higher), and more time in the saturation mode. All transitions highly depend on T. In case of MNIST, these transitions are quite smooth, probably due to lower task complexity.

Figure 5 shows how FGSM robustness evolves during training, evaluated for fixed $\epsilon = 0.1$. One can notice that all of the trained classifiers on four datasets are more robust when using lower sigmoid temperatures and less robust for high

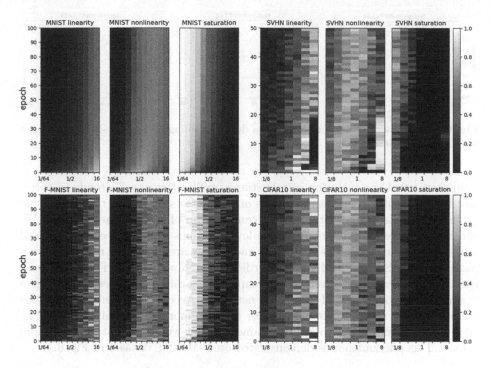

Fig. 4. Operation in the three modes during training for all datasets and various values of T (on x-axis). Consistent gradual shift of the dominant regime is observed in all cases, in terms of gradual transition from linear and nonlinear modes towards the saturation mode.

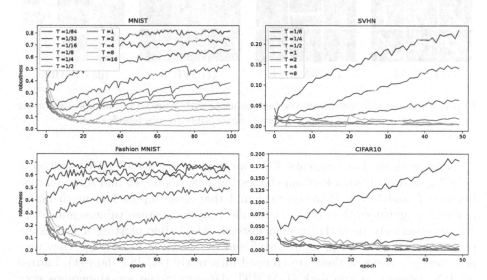

Fig. 5. Development of network robustness during training on all datasets. The same pattern is visible in all cases.

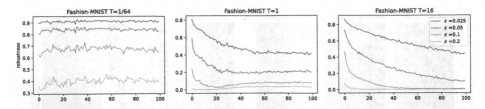

Fig. 6. Development of network robustness during training on Fashion-MNIST dataset evaluated for different values of ϵ.

temperatures. Also, evolution of robustness profiles (for any T) tends to correlate with that of the saturation modes in all datasets, implying that increasing robustness is associated with growing contribution of the saturation mode. We can also observe vast difference in the level of robustness between feedforward and convolutional networks. CIFAR10 and SVHN are much less robust in comparison to MNIST and F-MNIST, regardless the temperature and network accuracy. We also generated adversarial examples using different values of ϵ and then evaluated the robustness of individual networks. According to our expectations we consistently see that the higher ϵ we use, the more successful the attack is. Also it is still clear that networks trained with lower temperatures are more robust. This phenomenon is demonstrated on F-MNIST dataset in Fig. 6.

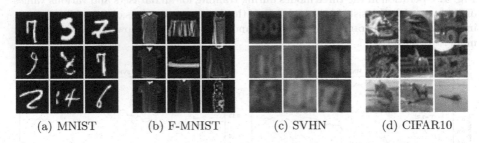

(a) MNIST   (b) F-MNIST   (c) SVHN   (d) CIFAR10

Fig. 7. Examples of images from the four datasets with large $G(x_i)$, all obtained using models with $T = 1$. These images are more susceptible to misclassification.

Next, we looked at gradients. First we tried to average $G(x_i)$ (described in Sect. 3.2) across all samples from the testing sets, hoping to find some relation between T and $G(x_i)$. However, we found that some inputs had much higher gradient magnitudes than others, thus affecting the average value significantly. So, we eventually used the median instead. Also, after plotting a few examples of these high gradient inputs, we found (as shown in Fig. 7) that they were not "pretty". Some of them are cropped incorrectly (MNIST dataset), blurred (SVHN dataset), or too dark (F-MNIST dataset). Some are ambiguous even to humans. Therefore, we also looked at the correlation coefficient between the output confidence of the correct class (given by the activation value of the repre-

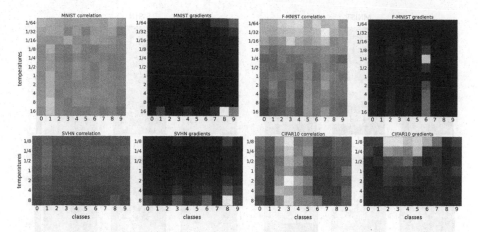

Fig. 8. Class-specific medians of input gradients $G(x_i)$ and the correlation coefficients between $G(x_i)$ and the target class confidence. All pictures showing correlations are in the range $[-1, 0]$. Figures showing gradient magnitudes are in range $[0, 0.0002]$ for MNIST, $[0, 0.2]$ for Fashion-MNIST, $[0, 0.04]$ for SVHN and $[0, 0.15]$ for SVHN. All ranges are scaled from black to white.

senting output neuron) and the input gradient $G(x_i)$ to find out if these inputs are indeed for our models hard to classify correctly.

Figure 8 depicts how the median values of $G(x_i)$ depend on T and an input class. It seems that the network has generally higher gradients when it is trained with too big or too small temperatures, exception being networks trained on Fashion-MNIST, where gradients depend more on input class than T. The correlation between median of $G(x_i)$ and the correct class confidence is similar in all datasets (strong and negative), significant at $p < .001$ in almost all cases (exception being the class 3 in CIFAR10 dataset). This means that inputs with greater gradients are more likely to be classified incorrectly.

4.2 Pixel Attack

We conducted the search for perturbations changing up to 3 pixels in case of MNIST and F-MNIST images, and up to 2 pixels in SVHN and CIFAR10 images. After selecting the pixels for perturbation, we sought all combinations until the adversarial input was found (or not). For simplicity we tried to change each pixel to the lowest and highest value, i.e. 0 and 1, respectively. After running through the test set, we evaluated the percentage of images for which we found at least one perturbation that caused misclassification. It holds that the lower the percentage, the more robust is the network.

Pixel attack on SVHN and CIFAR10 images is slightly different because of 3 color channels. In this case, the arithmetic mean of absolute values of gradients was computed for each pixel, as we get 3 gradients per pixel, each for one of the color channels. Pixel attack then consists of perturbation of three times more

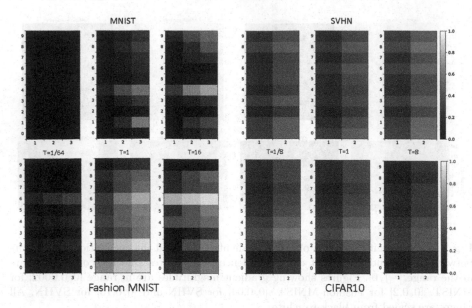

Fig. 9. Success of pixel attack for different classes and all four datasets for different T. Columns correspond to the number of perturbed pixels and rows to class index. The lower the temperature, the less likely it is to generate successful perturbation resulting in misclassification. Relative robustness remains the same for all temperatures. We see that in MNIST and F-MNIST, different classes yield different robustness, while in SVHN and CIFAR10 dataset, they are more equal.

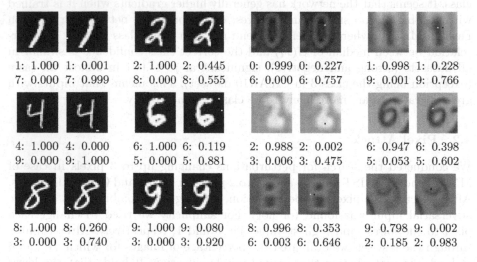

Fig. 10. Visualization of input images (from MNIST and SVHN datasets), classified correctly and adversarials created by altering only two pixels (for $T = 1$). Below the individual images is shown the network confidence (after softmax) for correct classification as well as for the winner class of the corresponding adversarial input. Interestingly, even the perturbed pixels at the boundaries (outside the digits) can evoke successful adversarials as seen in case of MNIST digits.

values. Results depicted in Fig. 9 reveal high similarity between pixel attack and FGSM robustness, since the higher the temperature, the less robust is the network, except for F-MNIST dataset. Figure 10 shows a few examples on two selected datasets of original and perturbed images, along with network's output confidences. One can notice that perturbation of even two pixels may cause misclassification with a high confidence score.

5 Conclusion

We looked at potential factors affecting the robustness which has been revealed as a general problem of end-to-end trained neural network classifiers. This gradient-based approach apparently does not induce any stability of categories during learning, despite the finding that hidden layers tend to learn features with a growing abstraction that eventually enable correct classification on novel data. In our computational experiments, we found many significant differences among classifiers for various temperatures, most crucial being the ability to train and solve the task satisfactorily, which is lost for too extreme temperatures. The speed of training is also altered, with greater temperatures converging more slowly. That also implies the difference in the network's linearity/saturation.

Probably the most interesting result is that two different methods of evaluating robustness both showed that lower temperatures lead to higher robustness of the models. On the other hand, shallow and simple feed-forward network yielded much higher level of robustness than a convolutional network. Another important finding are the inter-class differences in robustness, but the similarity of robustness for different temperatures. Our analysis of input gradients discovered some similarities even between MNIST and SVHN dataset classes. There was a strong negative correlation between the magnitude of input gradients and the network output confidence of the correct class, suggesting that by evaluating input gradients one can select inputs that are likely to be classified incorrectly. These findings might be informative for the training methods that could lead to increased robustness of the networks against adversarial inputs.

Acknowledgement. This work was supported by projects VEGA 1/0796/18 and KEGA 042UK-4/2019. We thank anonymous reviewers for useful comments.

References

1. Deng, L., Yu, D.: Deep learning: methods and applications. Found. Trends Signal Process. **7**(3–4), 197–387 (2014). https://doi.org/10.1561/2000000039
2. Goodfellow, I.J., Shlens, J., Szegedy, C.: Explaining and harnessing adversarial examples (2014). http://arxiv.org/abs/1412.6572
3. Krizhevsky, A.: Learning multiple layers of features from tiny images. Technical report TR-2009, University of Toronto (2009)
4. Kuzma, T., Farkaš, I.: Computational analysis of learned representations in deep neural network classifiers. In: IEEE International Joint Conference on Neural Networks (IJCNN) (2018)

5. LeCun, Y., Cortes, C., Burges, C.: The MNIST database of handwritten digits (2010). http://yann.lecun.com/exdb/mnist/
6. Montavon, G., Samek, W., Müller, K.R.: Methods for interpreting and understanding deep neural networks. Digit. Signal Proc. **73**, 1–15 (2018). https://doi.org/10.1016/j.dsp.2017.10.011
7. Netzer, Y., Wang, T., Coates, A., Bissacco, A., Wu, B., Ng, A.Y.: Reading digits in natural images with unsupervised feature learning. In: NIPS Workshop on Deep Learning and Unsupervised Feature Learning (2011)
8. Papernot, N., McDaniel, P.D., Sinha, A., Wellman, M.P.: Towards the science of security and privacy in machine learning (2016). http://arxiv.org/abs/1611.03814
9. Ranjan, R., Sankaranarayanan, S., Castillo, C.D., Chellappa, R.: Improving network robustness against adversarial attacks with compact convolution. CoRR (2017). http://arxiv.org/abs/1712.00699
10. Rozsa, A., Rudd, E., Boult, T.: Adversarial diversity and hard positive generation. In: IEEE Conference on Computer Vision and Pattern Recognition Workshops (CVPRW), pp. 410–417 (2016). https://doi.org/10.1109/CVPRW.2016.58
11. Schott, L., Rauber, J., Brendel, W., Bethge, M.: Robust perception through analysis by synthesis. CoRR (2018). http://arxiv.org/abs/1805.09190
12. Su, J., Vargas, D.V., Kouichi, S.: One pixel attack for fooling deep neural networks. IEEE Trans. Evol. Comput. **23**(5), 828–841 (2019). https://doi.org/10.1109/TEVC.2019.2890858
13. Sun, K., Zhu, Z., Lin, Z.: Enhancing the robustness of deep neural networks by boundary conditional GAN (2019). http://arxiv.org/abs/1902.11029
14. Szegedy, C., et al.: Intriguing properties of neural networks. In: International Conference on Learning Representations (2014). http://arxiv.org/abs/1312.6199
15. Xiao, H., Rasul, K., Vollgraf, R.: Fashion-MNIST: a novel image dataset for benchmarking machine learning algorithms (2017). https://arxiv.org/abs/1708.07747
16. Zhang, G., Yan, C., Ji, X., Zhang, T., Zhang, T., Xu, W.: DolphinAttack: inaudible voice commands. In: Proceedings of the ACM SIGSAC Conference on Computer and Communications Security, pp. 103–117 (2017)

Bioinformatics and Biosignal Analysis

Convolutional Neural Networks with Reusable Full-Dimension-Long Layers for Feature Selection and Classification of Motor Imagery in EEG Signals

Mikhail Tokovarov[✉] [iD]

Lublin University of Technology, Nadbystrzycka 38D, 20-618 Lublin, Poland
m.tokovarov@pollub.pl

Abstract. In the present article the author addresses the task of classification of motor imagery in EEG signals by proposing innovative architecture of neural network. Despite all the successes of deep learning, neural networks of significant depth could not ensure better performance compared to shallow architectures. The approach presented in the article employs this idea, making use of yet shallower, but productive architecture. The main idea of the proposed architecture is based on three points: full-dimension-long 'valid' convolutions, dense connections - combination of layer's input and output and layer reuse. Another aspect addressed in the paper is related to interpretable machine learning. Interpretability is extremely important in medicine, where decisions must be taken on the basis of solid arguments and clear reasons. Being shallow, the architecture could be used for feature selection by interpreting the layers' weights, which allows understanding of the knowledge about the data cumulated in the network's layers. The approach, based on a fuzzy measure, allows using Choquet integral to aggregate the knowledge generated in the layer weights and understanding which features (EEG electrodes) provide the most essential information. The approach allows lowering feature number from 64 to 14 with an insignificant drop of accuracy (less than a percentage point).

Keywords: Motor imagery · Feature selection · Convolutional neural network · Reusable convolutions

1 Introduction

While analyzing EEG signals, researchers discovered an effect appearing when an examined person was imaging hand movements without even actually performing them [7]. The effect was called motor imagery and attracted serious attention of researchers. Further research revealed, that one of the fields, where motor imagery could be used in therapy purposes, was post-stroke rehabilitation, helping patients to recover faster [2, 4].

© Springer Nature Switzerland AG 2020
I. Farkaš et al. (Eds.): ICANN 2020, LNCS 12396, pp. 79–91, 2020.
https://doi.org/10.1007/978-3-030-61609-0_7

Another field, where motor imagery presents interest, is brain computer interface (BCI): it could potentially become a source of control signals for brain computer interfaces, able to help severely disabled people in communication and rehabilitation [14].

The author of the present research proposes a novel model which can solve the task of subject-independent classification with a high level of accuracy.

The structure of the model also allows to interpret the contribution of each EEG electrode, thus performing feature selection and ensuring interpretability of the model. The proposed method of feature selection allows to significantly decrease the number of electrodes: down to 14 from 64 electrodes by the cost of slightly lower accuracy (less than a percentage point). The method of network interpretation based on fuzzy integral calculation is also proposed, so it does not simply compute the weighed sum of all filters, but takes into account their interactions, expressed by the language of set theory.

2 Related Work

Recent years have brought rapid development of machine learning, and, more specifically, its subset - deep learning. Motor imagery classification is no exception and many studies involving deep models have appeared. Various types of deep learning models were tested: deep feed forward networks with dense layers, using separate feature extraction techniques [3], convolutional neural networks, ensuring feature extraction without standalone feature extraction methods [16], recurrent neural network, addressing the sequent nature of EEG signals [17].

Despite all the successes of deep learning models, shallow models have proven to be more effective for EEG signal processing [16], so the proposed model is shallow as well.

One of the advantages, that convolution layers provide lies in the fact, that they do not require feature extraction methods, since feature extraction is performed by the convolutional layers themselves. This approach is called end-to-end processing. Its main advantage is no need of feature extraction, filtering and other kinds of preprocessing [18, 19].

As for feature selection, researchers present various approaches to feature selection in EEG signals: Fisher ranking methods [9], the approaches based on differential evolution [1]. The authors of [12] proposed the method of feature selection based on application of convolutional network filter weights, but no fuzzy measure was introduced, so the weights were simply averaged. Another novelty of the architecture in question is the method of its interpretation and feature selection by means of fuzzy aggregation.

3 Materials and Methods

3.1 Dataset Description

In order to test the performance of the proposed architecture one of the largest publicly available motor imagery signal datasets was used [15]. The dataset contains the samples of EEG signals of 109 volunteers. The recordings were gathered in accordance with 64 electrode 10-10 montage standard. The sampling frequency was equal to 160 Hz.

The present research is focused on developing an architecture allowing to distinguish between two types of motor imagery: imaging left- or right-hand movement. Similarly to the research [5], signals of 4 persons were rejected due to the fact that they contained steady state signal in many motor imagery cues [20]. Each of 105 participants provided 21 observations of each type of motor imagery, which in total gave 4410 observations.

3.2 Proposed Architecture Description

The main idea of the proposed architecture is based on three main points:

- full length 'valid' convolutions,
- reusable layers,
- dense layer connections, i.e. combining input and output of the layer.

Convolutional networks used in image processing have comparatively small filters [6]. As for EEG, this approach proves to be insufficient, so researchers choose longer filters [5, 16, 20]. After preliminary tests it was discovered that introducing longer convolution filters leads to higher accuracy. The present research goes even further and makes use of factorized convolutions analyzing the whole correspondent dimensions.

Figure 1 presents the idea of full length valid convolutions.

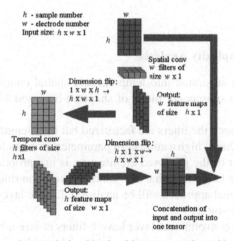

Fig. 1. Full length convolution block with concatenation of input and output

One of the key ideas of the research was to introduce a block consisting of two sequent convolution layers: spatial and temporal convolutions having the same length as the corresponding input's dimension. In order to obtain the output of the same shape as the input the following filters are applied to the h-by-w-by-1 input:

- w filters of shape w-by-1, which are applied in order to extract spatial features,
- h filters of shape h-by-1, being trained to capture the temporal features.

As the result of 'valid' application of the first (spatial) convolution to a h-by-w-by-1 input, an h-by-1-by-w tensor is obtained. In order to obtain a tensor with shapes h-by-w-by-1, a dimension flip is carried out. The output is fed to the temporal convolution layer. The result of the temporal convolution is also flipped back to shapes h-by-w-by-1. An output tensor of extracted features is concatenated with the input tensor.

Another solution based on repeated use of full-dimension convolution block was introduced. This approach was first presented in [10]. In order to make repeated application of the convolution block possible, a compressing 1-by-1 convolution (denoted as (1) in Fig. 2) is applied.

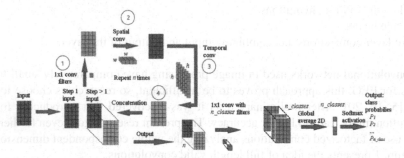

Fig. 2. Complete diagram of the proposed architecture

3.3 Computing Complexity Analysis

The filters are usually separated into temporal and spatial components [5, 16]. This approach employs two subsequent filters of shapes n-by-1 and 1-by-m instead of one n-by-m filter.

In the present research the filters are factorized but their length equals to the corresponding dimension. Due to high a number of parameters in every layer it may seem that the computational cost of the proposed architecture is inappropriately high. Actually, this is not the case, due to the fact, that the 'valid' convolution rule is used.

Firstly, a conventional approach will be analyzed. Let the layer input be denoted as I and its size be h-by-w-by-d.

Let the considered convolutional layer have k filters of size n-by-1 and 1-by-m.

Many packages implementing convolutional models employ cross-correlation function instead of convolution [6]. Discrete cross correlation of multichannel input (I) and convolutional filter (f) for the output pixel (i, j) of the output feature map can be expressed as follows:

$$(I \star f)_{i,j} = \sum_{p=0}^{n-1} \sum_{q=o}^{m-1} \sum_{z=1}^{d} I^*_{i+p,j+q,z} \cdot f_{i+1,j+1,z} + b \tag{1}$$

Where b is the filter's bias and I^* denotes the input padded with zeros in order to implement 'same' rule convolution, i.e. to ensure the output shapes equal to the input shapes.

From formula (1) the number of operations per output pixel (N_{same}^{op}) can be obtained in the following way:

$$N_{same}^{op} = 2 \cdot n \cdot m \cdot d \tag{2}$$

In the case if factorized convolutions are used, (2) can be written as for temporal and spatial convolutions in the following way:

$$N_{same}^{op-time} = 2 \cdot n \cdot d \tag{3}$$

$$N_{same}^{op-space} = 2 \cdot m \cdot k \tag{4}$$

Where k is the number of filters, and thus, the depth of the output of both layers.

Taking into consideration the fact that the output shape is equal to the input shape, one can obtain the total number of operations per one input tensor (N_{same}^{total}):

$$N_{same}^{total} = \left(N_{same}^{op-time} + N_{same}^{op-space} \right) \cdot h \cdot w \cdot k + 2 \cdot N_{same}^{act} \tag{5}$$

$$N_{same}^{total} = \left(N_{same}^{op-time} + N_{same}^{op-space} \right) \cdot h \cdot w \cdot k + 2 \cdot h \cdot w \cdot k$$
$$= \left(N_{same}^{op-time} + N_{same}^{op-space} + 2 \right) \cdot h \cdot w \cdot k$$

Where N_{same}^{act} is the number of the activation function application, which is equal to the output shape. The activation is applied twice: for the spatial and temporal convolution.

As for the proposed method, the number of operations per output pixel is expressed in the following way:

$$N_{valid}^{op-time} = 2 \cdot h \tag{6}$$

$$N_{valid}^{op-space} = 2 \cdot w \tag{7}$$

The depth of the input is guaranteed to be equal to 1 by the application of 1-by-1 convolutional layer with 1 filter, so the depth is not presented in (6), (7) and (8). The total number of operations for the proposed method is expressed as follows:

$$N_{valid}^{total} = \left(N_{valid}^{op-time} + N_{valid}^{op-space} \right) \cdot h \cdot w + 2 \cdot N_{valid}^{act}$$

$$N_{valid}^{total} = \left(N_{valid}^{op-time} + N_{valid}^{op-space} \right) \cdot h \cdot w + 2 \cdot h \cdot w$$
$$= \left(N_{valid}^{op-time} + N_{valid}^{op-space} + 2 \right) \cdot h \cdot w \tag{8}$$

In order to compare the complexities, divide (5) by (8):

$$\frac{N_{same}^{total}}{N_{valid}^{total}} = \frac{\left(N_{same}^{op-time} + N_{same}^{op-space} + 2 \right) \cdot k}{N_{valid}^{op-time} + N_{valid}^{op-space} + 2} = \frac{(2 \cdot n \cdot d + 2 \cdot m \cdot k + 2) \cdot k}{h + w + 2} \tag{9}$$

On the basis of [5] it was assumed that $d = 1$ and the 'valid' rule for the spatial convolution, decreased its output size by w times (due to the fact that the spatial filter has the size of 1-by-w). We thus obtain the following:

$$\frac{N_{same}^{total}}{N_{valid}^{total}} = \frac{\left(2 \cdot n + 1 + \frac{2 \cdot w \cdot k + 1}{w}\right) \cdot k}{2 \cdot h + 2 \cdot w + 2} \tag{10}$$

Using values from [5] in (10) for comparison one can obtain:

$$\frac{N_{same}^{total}}{N_{valid}^{total}} = \frac{\left(2 \cdot 30 + 1 + \frac{2 \cdot 64 \cdot 40 + 1}{64}\right) \cdot 40}{2 \cdot 480 + 2 \cdot 64 + 2} \approx \frac{5640}{1090} \approx 5.17$$

Being approximately 5 times faster (per one repeat), the proposed convolution block can be used repeatedly without causing increase of computational load compared to conventional convolutional layers.

3.4 Regularization and Data Augmentation

The overall number of observations in the dataset is equal to 4410, which is not very high for a convolution network, prone to overfitting in the case of a small dataset [6]. For data augmentation and overcoming overfitting, two measures were taken:

- adding normally distributed noise to the input and intermediate feature maps,
- randomly shifting the start of the analyzed signal segment, presented in Fig. 3. The shift value was generated uniformly from [−m_shift, m_shift].

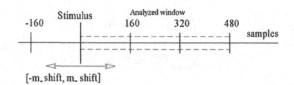

Fig. 3. Data augmentation by means of window random shift

3.5 Interpretation of Feature Maps

Being shallow, the network does not behave as a black box. The fact, that the spatial filters cover the whole electrode set means, that every weight in a spatial filter corresponds to the importance, the specific electrode has in the output of the filter.

Only the feature maps computed for the net input were analyzed, as they contain the information that was obtained directly from the input EEG signal, thus reflecting the electrode importance directly. Figure 4 shows the output of spatial convolution layer. The columns of the output tensor correspond to the output of the spatial convolution filter.

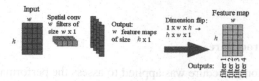

Fig. 4. Output of spatial convolution layer

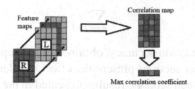

Fig. 5. Obtaining correlation map from feature maps

The coefficients of Pearson correlation between the elements of the feature map and class predictions were chosen to be fuzzy measures of the filters' relevance (Fig. 5). It can be thought of as the measure of consistent behavior of a filter, i.e. that it generates lower values for class 0 and higher values for class 1, or vice versa. Maximal absolute correlation coefficients were considered, since for assessing filters' relevance it was not the sign of correlation coefficient, what was important, but the strength of correlation.

The obtained maximal values of filter correlation coefficients $\{C_n\}$, $n = 1, 2, ...,$ can be thought of as the values of fuzzy measure over the set of convolutional filters [13].

After obtaining $\{C_n\}$, being the fuzzy measures of the filters' importance, aggregation of the electrode weights can be performed by application of Choquet integral [13]:

$$w(e_j) = \sum_{i=1}^{m} \left[w_i(e_j) - w_{i+1}(e_j) \right] \cdot g(A_i) \tag{11}$$

where:

$w(e_j)$ - aggregated weight of the j-th electrode;

$w_i(e_j)$ - weight of the j-th electrode in the i-th filter, the weights have to be arranged to produce nonincreasing sequence [13];

$g(A_i)$ - fuzzy measure of subset of first i weights $w_i(e_j)$.

The values of $g(A_i)$ for j-th electrode, can be obtained by the following formula:

$$g(A_i) = \begin{cases} C_1^j, & i = 1 \\ g(A_{i-1}) + C_i^j + \lambda \cdot g(A_{i-1}) \cdot C_i^j, & i > 1 \end{cases} \tag{12}$$

Coefficient λ describing the interaction can be obtained by following formula [13]:

$$1 + \lambda = \prod_{i=1}^{m} (1 + \lambda g_i) \tag{13}$$

Thus, in order to find the value of λ, the roots of the m-degree polynomial have to be found. For the considered case, the degree of polynomial is equal to 64, so direct computing of polynomial roots is too computationally expensive and even not reasonable, as only one root is needed. The root was obtained by Newton-Raphson method.

4 Experiment

4.1 Experiment Procedure

5-fold cross-validation procedure was applied to assess the performance of the model.

Repeat number needed for stable result was found on the basis of partial mean accuracy:

$$Acc_i^{part} = \sum_{j=1}^{i} Acc_j \tag{14}$$

where Acc_j is the cross validation accuracy, obtained in j-th repetition. Number of repetitions was set to 30. Further sections present the effect of selected hyperparameters on accuracy. Differences between separate results presented in the chapter are not high, but fine tuning of hyperparameters allows improving accuracy from 82.33% to 83.26%.

4.2 Activation Function Influence

Several activation functions were examined. The results are presented in Table 1.

Table 1. Accuracies obtained for various activation functions

Activation function	Mean (acc), %
relu	82.33
selu	82.93
tanh	**83.06**

Interestingly, the best performance was obtained with the use of the tanh activation function, so it was used for further experiments.

4.3 Reuse Number Influence

Table 2 contains the values of parameters and accuracies achieved for various reuse numbers.

Table 2. Comparison of accuracy values obtained for various number of repeated convolution block application

Reuse number	Mean (acc), %
1	0.8306
2	**0.8326**
3	0.8315
4	0.8307

The application convolution block repeated twice allows to improve the accuracy by 0.21 percentage point, further increase of repeat number leads to lower accuracy, so the repeat number equal to 2 was chosen for further experiments.

4.4 Dense Connection Influence

In order to investigate the influence of dense connections on the accuracy, the experiment with the network without dense connections was conducted. Table 3 contains the results achieved for the architecture without use of dense connection.

Table 3. Accuracy obtained for the architecture without dense connections.

Dense connection	Mean (acc), %
No	83.08
Yes	**83.26**

4.5 Influence of Multiple Block Application

The tests of deeper architecture were conducted. The deeper architecture was made of sequentially repeated convolutional blocks presented in Sect. 3.2. The results are presented in Table 4.

Table 4. Accuracy obtained for the architectures with various numbers of convolutional blocks.

Conv. block number	Mean (acc), %
1	**83.26**
2	83.05
3	82.95

5 Feature Selection by Analysis of Activation Maps

The method presented in the Sect. 3.5 allows to explain and interpret the weights of spatial convolutions. It also allows to find the most relevant electrodes, thus permitting to perform feature selection. The experiment was conducted in the following way:

1. the network was trained with the training dataset;
2. the procedure of feature selection described in Sect. 3.5 was performed;
3. the training set was modified, only selected electrodes were used;

4. a new model was created and trained on the modified dataset;
5. the performance of the trained model was assessed by applying the test dataset modified in a way similar to the training dataset: only selected electrodes were taken into account.

The procedure was conducted three times (runs): selecting 14, 32 and 48 electrodes. Every run included 30 repetitions. The set of weights, associated with correspondent electrodes was obtained in each repetition. The sets were averaged. Figure 6 presents the heatmaps of the electrode weights obtained with the proposed method. The weights were mapped to 2D structure in accordance with 10-10 EEG montage system.

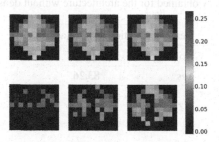

Fig. 6. Heatmaps of the electrode weights obtained in three runs. Top: all electrodes shown. Bottom: only selected electrodes (with first 14, 32, 48 highest weights) shown.

Accuracies obtained for each number of electrodes are presented in Table 5. The proposed procedure of feature selection allows obtaining similarly high results (less than a percentage point difference) for the limited electrode set.

Table 5. Accuracy for various numbers of selected features.

Selected electrode number	Mean (acc), %
14	82.34
32	82.9
48	83.16
64	83.26

6 Discussion and Conclusion

The paper presents the novel architecture of convolutional neural networks, dedicated to classification of motor imagery in EEG signals. The architecture combines the ideas proved to be promising in the areas outside neuroscience, e.g.: convolutional filter reuse and dense connections. The present paper presents the first example of application of reusable filters for classifying motor imagery. The positive influence of this approach was shown in the Sect. 4.3.

Dense connections proved to be a promising approach as well.

As for making the network deeper, it did not provide any improvement and, on the contrary, led to decrease of classification accuracy, and made computations slower.

Table 6 contains the comparison of the accuracies presented in the published papers. The accuracies were achieved in the same conditions as the method proposed in the present paper, i.e.:

- Physionet benchmark dataset,
- 3-second long signal segments analyzed,
- 105 participants. Many papers present high results obtained for a significantly limited subset of Physionet benchmark dataset. Only the papers, where the analysis of at least a 105-person dataset is presented, are taken into account.

Table 6. Comparison of achieved accuracies.

Paper	Mean (acc), %
[20]	82.43
[8]	80.1
[5]	80.05
[18]	74.71
[11]	70.6
Present research	83.26

As it was shown in Sect. 3.3, despite the long filters applied, proposed architecture has low computational complexity, even compared to shallow model, presented in [5].

Another innovation proposed in the present paper was a feature selection method which allowed to find the electrodes, providing the most valuable information, allowing to achieve high classification accuracy even with a limited electrode set. The measure of an electrode's importance was obtained on the basis of Choquet integral, which made possible effective aggregation of the data cumulated in in the network filters, ensuring clear representation of the knowledge regarding the electrode's importance. Constructing fuzzy measures on the basis of correlation coefficients is the approach which can be easily understood and interpreted.

Table 7 presents the classification accuracies achieved by applying a limited set of electrodes in the present paper and in other papers published in recent years.

The results in the table show, that even with a very limited set of electrodes the proposed method of feature selection can ensure sufficient classification accuracy, which is higher compared to the results presented in the literature. It is worth noting that in the proposed method the electrodes are selected on the basis of a clearly understandable measure, which takes into account the "consistency" of the filters' behavior, contrary to

Table 7. Comparison of achieved accuracies for limited electrode set

Paper	Electrode number	Mean (acc), %
[8]	14	80.05
[5]	14	76.66
[20]	19	81.95
	38	81.86
Present research	14	**82.34**

approaches presented in other research, such as selecting the electrodes on the basis of empirical observations stating that specific electrodes are related to motor imagery more closely than the others or simple averaging of the electrode weights across all filters of the trained convolutional network. The first approach is too general, as EEG signals are known to be highly subject specific. That is why data driven method presented in the paper allows achieve higher performance. As for the latter approach, not all the filters of the trained network become trained for extracting valuable for classification features to the same degree, due to that reason the approach based on simple averaging will lead to poorer performance of classification model.

The proposed approach of feature selection by network weights interpretation can be used not only for EEG signal processing, but also within any other field where multidimensional data are analyzed.

The author hopes that the present research makes real impact in the field of machine learning and EEG signal processing and, in order to encourage further research in the field, makes the source code publicly available on the github platform upon the paper publication. The code can be found under the following link: https://github.com/mtokov arov/cnn_reuse_full_dim_fs.git.

References

1. Baig, M.Z., Aslam, N., Shum, H.P., Zhang, L.: Differential evolution algorithm as a tool for optimal feature subset selection in motor imagery EEG. Expert Syst. Appl. **90**, 184–195 (2017)
2. Belkofer, C.M., Konopka, L.M.: Conducting art therapy research using quantitative EEG measures. Art Ther. **25**(2), 56–63 (2008)
3. Chai, R., Ling, S.H., Hunter, G.P., Nguyen, H.T.: Mental non-motor imagery tasks classifi- cations of brain computer interface for wheelchair commands using genetic algorithm-based neural network. In The 2012 International Joint Conference on Neural Networks (IJCNN), pp. 1–7. IEEE (2012)
4. Dijkerman, H.C., Ietswaart, M., Johnston, M., MacWalter, R.S.: Does motor imagery training improve hand function in chronic stroke patients? A pilot study. Clin. Rehabil. **18**(5), 538–549 (2004)
5. Dose, H., Møller, J.S., Puthusserypady, S., Iversen, H.K.: A deep learning MI-EEG classifica- tion MODEL for BCIs. 2018 In: 26th European Signal Processing Conference, pp. 1690–1693. IEEE (2018)

6. Goodfellow, I., Bengio, Y., Courville, A.: Deep Learning. MIT Press, Cambridge (2016)
7. Ikeda, A., Lüders, H.O., Burgess, R.C., Shibasaki, H.: Movement-related potentials recorded from supplementary motor area and primary motor area: role of supplementary motor area in voluntary movements. Brain 115(4), 1017–1043 (1992)
8. Kim, Y., Ryu, J., Kim, K.K., Took, C.C., Mandic, D.P., Park, C.: Motor imagery classification using mu and beta rhythms of EEG with strong uncorrelating transform based complex common spatial patterns. Comput. Intell. Neurosci. (2016)
9. Kirar, J.S., Agrawal, R.K.: Relevant feature selection from a combination of spectral-temporal and spatial features for classification of motor imagery EEG. J. Med. Syst. 42(5), 78 (2018)
10. Köpüklü, O., Babaee, M., Hörmann, S., Rigoll, G. Convolutional Neural networks with layer reuse. In: proceedings of 2019 IEEE International Conference on Image Processing (ICIP), pp. 345–349 (2019)
11. Netzer, E., Frid, A., Feldman, D.: Real-time EEG classification via coresets for BCI applications. Eng. Appl. Artif. Intell. 89, 103455 (2020)
12. Mzurikwao, D., Ang, C.S., Samuel, O.W., Asogbon, M.G., Li, X., Li, G.: Efficient channel selection approach for motor imaginary classification based on convolutional neural network. In: 2018 IEEE International Conference on Cyborg and Bionic Systems (CBS), pp. 418–421 (2018)
13. Pedrycz, W., Gomide, F.: An Introduction to Fuzzy Sets: Analysis and Design. Mit Press, Cambridge (1998)
14. Pfurtscheller, G., et al.: Current trends in Graz brain-computer interface (BCI) research. IEEE Trans. Rehabil. Eng. 8(2), 216–219 (2000)
15. Schalk, G., McFarland, D.J., Hinterberger, T., Birbaumer, N., Wolpaw, J.R.: BCI2000: a general-purpose brain-computer interface (BCI) system. IEEE Trans. Biomed. Eng. 51(6), 1034–1043 (2004)
16. Schirrmeister, R.T., et al.: Deep learning with convolutional neural networks for EEG decoding and visualization. Hum. Brain Mapp. 38(11), 5391–5420 (2017)
17. Wang, P., Jiang, A., Liu, X., Shang, J., Zhang, L.: LSTM-based EEG classification in motor imagery tasks. IEEE Trans. Neural Syst. Rehabil. Eng. 26(11), 2086–2095 (2018)
18. Zhang, D., Chen, K., Jian, D., Yao, L.: Motor imagery classification via temporal attention cues of graph embedded EEG signals. IEEE J. Biomed. Health Inf., 2570–2579 (2020)
19. Zhang, D., Yao, L., Chen, K., Wang, S., Chang, X., Liu, Y.: Making sense of spatio-temporal preserving representations for EEG-based human intention recognition. IEEE Trans. Cybern., 3033–3044 (2019)
20. Wang, X., Hersche, M., Tömekce, B., Kaya, B., Magno, M., Benini, L.: An accurate EEGNet-based motor-imagery brain-computer interface for low-power edge computing. arXiv preprint arXiv:2004.00077 (2020)

Compressing Genomic Sequences
by Using Deep Learning

Wenwen Cui, Zhaoyang Yu, Zhuangzhuang Liu, Gang Wang,
and Xiaoguang Liu[✉]

College of CS, TJ Key Lab of NDST, Nankai University, Tianjin, China
{cuiww,yuzz,liuzhuangzhuang,wgzwp,liuxg}@nbjl.nankai.edu.cn

Abstract. Huge amount of genomic sequences have been generated with the development of high-throughput sequencing technologies, which brings challenges to data storage, processing, and transmission. Standard compression tools designed for English text are not able to compress genomic sequences well, so an effective dedicated method is needed urgently. In this paper, we propose a genomic sequence compression algorithm based on a deep learning model and an arithmetic encoder. The deep learning model is structured as a convolutional layer followed by an attention-based bi-directional long short-term memory network, which predicts the probabilities of the next base in a sequence. The arithmetic encoder employs the probabilities to compress the sequence. We evaluate the proposed algorithm with various compression approaches, including a state-of-the-art genomic sequence compression algorithm DeepDNA, on several real-world data sets. The results show that the proposed algorithm can converge stably and achieves the best compression performance which is even up to 3.7 times better than DeepDNA. Furthermore, we conduct ablation experiments to verify the effectiveness and necessity of each part in the model and implement the visualization of attention weight matrix to present different importance of various hidden states for final prediction. The source code for the model is available in Github (https://github.com/viviancui59/Compressing-Genomic-Sequences).

Keywords: Genomic sequence compression · Deep learning · Arithmetic coding

1 Introduction

Due to the development of high-throughput sequencing technologies, the cost of sequencing has gradually decreased and the amount of genomic sequences has increased explosively [3]. Both researchers and doctors can gain the scientific knowledge of genomic sequences information, thereby promoting the development of biological science, as well as the therapy and diagnosis of patients.

This work is partially supported by National Science Foundation of China (61872201, 61702521, U1833114) and Science and Technology Development Plan of Tianjin (18ZXZNGX00140, 18ZXZNGX00200).

I. Farkaš et al. (Eds.): ICANN 2020, LNCS 12396, pp. 92–104, 2020.
https://doi.org/10.1007/978-3-030-61609-0_8

But the storage, processing and transmission of genomic sequences data have become major challenges [17]. Data compression can not only reduce the size of data storage, but also reduce the cost of processing and the time of transmission, which makes it become one of key ways to alleviate these problems [3].

A genomic sequence mainly consists of four nucleotides that is adenine (A), cytosine (C), guanine (G), and thymine (T). There are also many unknown nucleotides in genomic sequences which are generally represented by N [16]. General compression algorithms are designed dedicatedly for English text compression and they are not able to get an ideal compression performance for genomic sequences [1], in which the regularities are very small. The standard compression tools such as **compress**, **gzip** and **bzip2** have poor compression ratios [2]. Besides, the content of genomic sequences are different from general random text sequences, and the characteristics of sequences need to be taken into account for better compression, such as exact repeat, approximate repeat of a sub-string and complementary palindromes that may occur many times in a given genome sequence [1]. Furthermore, the probabilities of these base occurrence are not so different and inappropriate compression methods will decrease the speed of decompression, both making genomic sequence compression become a tough task [15,20]. Consequently, the compression of genomic sequence has become an important challenge and a specific method is needed urgently.

Arithmetic coding, a lossless data compression method, can minimize the redundancy of information and is optimal within one bit of the Shannon limit of $log_2 1/P(x)$ bits, where $P(x)$ is the probability of the entire input sequence x. However, its compression ratio depends almost entirely on the predictor [14], which is the key to high-quality compression. Recently, deep learning has developed as one of the most promising prediction methods. In particular, Recurrent Neural Networks (RNNs) have been widely used to deal with sequence data, such as the tasks of text, audio sequence prediction, and language translation, which are able to extract better structured information from vast amounts of sequences and find dependent relationship between contexts.

In this paper, we propose an effective genomic sequence compression algorithm combining a deep learning model comprising Convolutional Neural Network (CNN) and attention-based Bi-directional Long Short-Term Memory Networks (BiLSTM), and an arithmetic encoder. In summary, the contributions of this article are as follows:

- We introduce a deep learning model that automatically learns and captures features of genomic sequences to predict the probability of the each base at the next position.
- We use CNN to exact the local features of the sequences and use BiLSTM to learn the long-term dependence features of sequences as well as the characteristics of palindromes, considering both forward and backward directions.
- We exploit an attention mechanism to learn the importance of the hidden states and features provided by the BiLSTM for global situation. Higher weights are given to more important features to estimate the final probability more accurately.

– We conduct experiments based on several real-world genomic data sets and demonstrate the superior performance of the proposed approach for compressing genomic sequences. Ablation experiments verify the effectiveness of each part of the model and the visualization of attention weight matrix shows the various importance of hidden states and features of sequences for the probability estimation.

The rest of the paper is organized as follows: Sect. 2 discusses related work. Section 3 presents the overview of the proposed algorithm. Section 4 details the experimental settings and analyzes the results of experiments, and we conclude in Sect. 5.

2 Related Work

In this section, we report some main studies on genomic sequences compression, and divide them into two categories which are traditional methods and learning-based methods, according to whether deep learning methods are used. To compress genomic sequences, the former detects exact repeats or approximate repeats , while the latter resorts to deep learning technologies.

Traditional Methods. Biocompress [9] was the first genomic sequence compression algorithm, which detects exact and palindromes repeats in DNA sequence through an antomaton and encodes the lengths and positions of their earliest occurrences through Fibonacci encoding. The extension version, Biocompress-2 algorithm [10] uses a Markov model of order-2 to encode when there is non-repeat region. Besides, other algorithms exploit approximate repeats to encode sequences, such as GenCompress proposed by Chen et al. [5]. The followed DNA-Compress algorithm [6] searches all approximate repeats in the first phase and uses the Ziv and Lempel compression algorithm to encode them in the second phase. Behzadi and Le Fessant proposed DNAPack [2] which uses dynamic programming to find better repeats, achieving better average compression ratios.

In addition, some studies provide the probability of next symbol to the arithmetic coder in various ways. XM introduced by Cao et.al [4], applies Bayesian averaging of a mixture of experts to provide the probability, including an order-1 Markov, an order-2 Markov, and a copy expert. Although it gains better compression performance, it is not suitable for long sequences. MFCompress [18] uses single finite-context models for encoding the header text, as well as multiple competing finite-context models for encoding the main stream of the DNA sequences, but its main problem is memory limitation.

Learning-based Methods. Deep learning approaches such as CNN can be applied for predicting various biological targets through genomic sequences [19,22]. Inspired by DeepZip [8], Wang et al. [21] introduced DeepDNA for the human mitochondrial genomes compression. It relies on CNN to extract the local features and LSTM to capture the long-term dependence of the sequences to provide the probability for compression. Since only approximately 0.1% of 3GB human genome is specific [7], so DeepDNA shows excellent performance compared with **gzip**. But it does not consider the importance of chunks of sequences for the probability estimation of next base. Nor does it consider the feature of global sequences, such as complementary palindromes.

We improve DeepDNA by proposing a compression algorithm using deep learning based on local and global features of genomic sequences, including palindromes, approximate repeats and exact repeats.

3 Proposed Algorithm

The overview of our algorithm is illustrated in Fig. 1, including the following two main parts: a deep learning model to estimate probability of next base and an arithmetic encoder to encode this base. The process of compression is follows. A sliding window of a genomic sequence as the input is transformed into vectors in the pre-processing stage. Then the CNN and attention-based BiLSTM are used to extract the local and global features respectively. Through the fully connected layer and softmax layer on the top, we obtain a vector of the probabilities of bases. The probabilities are send to arithmetic encoder to obtain the final compressed data.

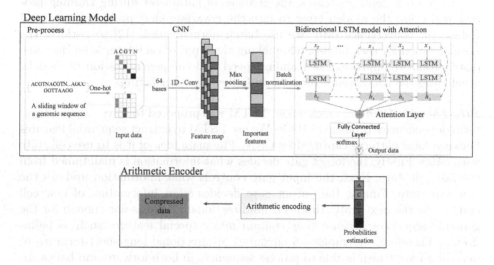

Fig. 1. The overview of proposed algorithm.

3.1 Deep Learning Model

Pre-processing. After inputting a sliding window of length n to the model, each base in it is firstly processed through one-hot encoding and represented by a 5-dimensional vector $x_i \in \mathbb{R}^5$, where i is the i-th base in the sliding window. Each dimension represents one kind of base, and the dimension corresponding to the current base is set to 1 while the other dimensions are set to 0. For example, we transform a A into $\{1, 0, 0, 0, 0\}$ and a C into $\{0, 1, 0, 0, 0\}$. So the sequences can be denoted by a set of vectors finally.

CNN. In this stage, the input set of n vectors of the sliding window $\mathbf{x}$ is processed by the weight-sharing strategy of filters to capture simple local patterns through a convolution unit. The exact repeated patterns have the same features, and the approximate repeated patterns have similar features. The calculation process of a convolution unit is represented by

$$z_{i,f}(\mathbf{x}) = \sigma(W_f \widehat{x}_i + b_f) \tag{1}$$

where $z_{i,f}(\mathbf{x})$ gives the feature map of filter f for the i-th base of $\mathbf{x}$, W_f is the parameters matrix of filter f for the feature map, $\widehat{x}_i = [x_i, x_{i+1}, ..., x_{i+k-1}]$ denotes the concatenation of the vectors for k bases from the i-th base to the $i + k - 1$-th base of input $\mathbf{x}$, b_f is a shared value of filter f for bias, and $\sigma(\cdot)$ is a non-linear activation function.

The max-pooling operation is taken for each feature map to select the most important features by choosing the max value in each block. Meanwhile, the size of the output is reduced by one third in the proposed model, reducing the complexity of computation.

As network depth increases, the changes of parameter during training process will cause the hidden layer to face the covariate shift problem that could reduce the convergence rate. We use batch normalization [12] to perform the normalization for each mini-batch, making the input of each layer keep the same distribution. It improves the training speed and the generalization of models, accelerates the convergence process, and alleviates over-fitting.

BiLSTM with Attention mechanism. LSTM was proposed to solve existing long-term dependencies problem of RNN. We use LSTM to extract sequential features between local patterns captured by CNN. The main idea of it is to use cell state with gates. Firstly, the forget gate decides what information is maintained from the last cell state. Next, the input gate controls what information updates the new cell state. Finally, the output gate decides what information of new cell state to be the next state. However, unidirectional LSTM is not enough for the genomic sequences because they contain many special features such as palindrome. Therefore, we employ an advanced bi-directional long short-term memory(BiLSTM), which is able to process sequences in both forward and backward directions for better capturing the long dependence in genomic sequences.

We use $\overrightarrow{h}$ and $\overleftarrow{h}$ to represent the hidden state of forward and backward direction respectively. The output of the t-th hidden state is a list of two directions of hidden states that can be represented as $h_t = \left[\overrightarrow{h_t}, \overleftarrow{h_t}\right]$. Due to the occurrence of approximate repeats in genomic sequences, various hidden states contribute differently to probability estimation. Therefore, we apply an attention mechanism to learn the importance of various parts automatically, which improves the performance of prediction and overall compression ratio.

Assuming that the LSTM layer produces m hidden states h_t, $t = 1, 2, ..., m$, and a score u_t is calculated by Eq. (2) to evaluate the importance for each hidden state.

$$u_t = \sigma(W^T h_t + b) \tag{2}$$

where W^T is the parameter vector and b is the bias. Finally, the softmax function α_t given by Eq. (3) is used to calculate the weighted average coefficient of score u_t, and the output of attention mechanism o is the sum of the products of hidden states and theirs scores, which is shown in Eq. (4).

$$\alpha_t = \frac{\exp(u_t)}{\sum_{t=1}^{m} \exp(u_t)} \tag{3}$$

$$o = \sum_{t=1}^{m} \alpha_t h_t \tag{4}$$

3.2 Arithmetic Coder

Arithmetic coding maps the data to be encoded, that is the gene sequence, to a decimal between the interval $[0, 1]$. The concrete algorithm is described in Algorithm 1. $level_{low}$ and $level_{high}$ represent the lower and upper boundaries of the current interval. $delta$ represents the length of the interval. $base.level_{low}$ and $base.level_{high}$ represent the lower and upper boundaries of the coding interval for each base respectively. When coding, starting from the initial interval $[0, 1]$, the current interval is divided into multiple sub-intervals according to the probability of the bases (A, C, G, T, N). Then, select the corresponding sub-interval according to the current input base and use this sub-interval as the current interval for the next coding step. Repeat this process until all bases are encoded. Finally, assign a unique decimal from the final sub-interval as the encoding result of the gene sequence.

Algorithm 1. Arithmetic Encoding

Input: The base table $dict = \{A, C, G, T, N\}$, the probability P of five bases in $dict$
    and the gene sequence Seq
Output: a decimal

1: $level_{low}, inter \leftarrow 0$
2: $level_{high}, delta \leftarrow 1$
3: **for** base in $dict$ **do**
4:     $base.level_{low} \leftarrow inter$
5:     $base.level_{high} \leftarrow inter + P_{base}$
6:     $inter \leftarrow base.level_{high}$
7: **end for**
8: **for** base in Seq **do**
9:     $delta \leftarrow level_{high} - level_{low}$
10:    $level_{high} \leftarrow level_{low} + delta *$ $base.level_{high}$
11:    $level_{low} \leftarrow level_{low} + delta *$ $base.level_{low}$
12: **end for**
13: **return** a random decimal between $level_{low}$ and $level_{high}$

Algorithm 2. Arithmetic Decoding

Input: The base table $dict = \{A, C, G, T, N\}$, the probability P of five bases in $dict$,
the encoded decimal d and the length of compressed sequence len
Output: the gene sequence Seq

1: $inter \leftarrow 0$
2: $num \leftarrow 1$
3: **for** base in $dict$ **do**
4:    $base.level_{low} \leftarrow inter$
5:    $base.level_{high} \leftarrow inter + P_{base}$
6:    $inter \leftarrow base.level_{high}$
7: **end for**
8: **while** $num \leq len$ **do**

9:    find the base $base$ whose interval covers d
10:    append $base$ to Seq
11:    $delta \leftarrow base.level_{high} - base.level_{low}$

12:    $d \leftarrow (d - base.level_{low})/delta$
13:    $num \leftarrow num + 1$
14: **end while**
15: **return** the gene sequence Seq

The process of decoding which is described in Algorithm 2 is equivalent to the inverse operation of the encoding process. When decoding, only one decimal is entered. First, divide the initial interval $[0, 1]$ according to the probability of bases. Second, observe which sub-interval the input decimal is in and output the corresponding base. Third, select this sub-interval and divide it continually. Repeat this process until all bases of the gene sequence are decoded.

4   Experiments and Evaluation

4.1   Data Sets and Baselines

The effectiveness of proposed algorithm is evaluated through several data sets, including 2851 mitochondrial sequences of various fishes species and 745 mitochondrial sequences of various bird species downloaded from National Center for Biotechnology Information[1], 303 transcriptome sequences of ray-finned fishes used in [11] and 1000 human mitochondrial sequences obtained from DeepDNA [21] respectively. We use 70% of each data set for training, 20% for validation, and the rest of 10% for testing. The statistics of data sets are summarized in Table 1.

Table 1. The statistics of data sets

Data sets	Bases	Sequences	Size (KB)	Proportion				
				A	C	G	T	N
Fishes	5	2851	53336	29.28%	27.86%	16.37%	26.48%	0.0024%
Birds	5	745	12703	30.44%	31.22%	14.35%	23.95%	0.04%
Human	4	1000	16532	30.90%	31.25%	13.15%	24.70%	
Ray-finned fishes	5	305	169385	14%	17%	17%	12%	40%

[1] https://www.ncbi.nlm.nih.gov/.

Based on these data sets, we compare the performance of proposed algorithm with (a) **Gzip** and **7-zip**, classic standard compression tools, (b) **MFCompress**: a traditional and state-of-the-art compression algorithm, which can compress multi-fasta files, and (c) **DeepDNA**, a learning-based method, which applies deep learning methods, i.e. CNN and LSTM, for compressing genomes.

4.2   Configurations of Our Deep Learning Model

We set the sliding window size to be 64, the number of filters of CNN layer to be 1024 and the size of the convolution unit to be 24 with step of 1. For max-pooling layer, the size of the window is 3 with the same size of step. The dimension of LSTM is set to be 256, which makes BiLSTM to be 512 dimensions for each hidden state. We train the deep learning model until it converges.

The loss function in the training process based on cross entropy. The smaller the value of loss function is, the better the model's performance manifests. And we use a optimizer in [13] to directly minimize the loss function with a mini-batch size of 128. The learning rate is set to 0.0001 at the beginning and changes adaptively by the optimizer during the training process. The size of the model weights is only 11.8MB. We explore more innovations in the model structure to achieve superior compression performance rather than just stacking parameters and the experimental results are shown in Sect. 4.3. So our model can be used in various sequences with a wider application prospect.

4.3   Experimental Results and Analysis

Compression Performance. Table 2 presents the results of the experiment comparing the proposed algorithm with the baselines based on the data sets, in terms of bpb (bit per base).

Table 2. Compression performance of various methods (bpb)

Methods	Name	Fishes	Birds	Human	Ray-finned fishes
Traditional	Gzip	2.4968	2.47	2.519	1.69
	7-zip	1.2628	1.1692	0.0929	**0.6698**
	MFCompress	1.42	1.364	1.5572	1.1155
learning-based	DeepDNA	1.3591	1.363	0.0548	1.4693
	Proposed algorithm	**0.7036**	**0.6655**	**0.01456**	0.8193

From Table 2, the following observations can be made. First, The proposed algorithm beats all the traditional or learning-based methods on Fishes, Birds and Human data sets. That is because the proposed algorithm can learn more complicated patterns from the sequences to be utilized in compression. Second, the learning-based methods achieve even greater advantages over the traditional methods on the Humans data set, since it has a higher genetic similarity than other data sets. Meanwhile, the performance of the proposed method outperforms DeepDNA's, even up to 3.7 times. Third, the traditional methods perform better on the data set of Ray-finned fishes than the learning-based method DeepDNA. The 7-zip achieves the best result of 0.6698, because this data set contains many continuous 'N' bases, fitting in the mechanism of traditional compression algorithm. However, the proposed algorithm obtains the performance that is next to 7-zip closely.

Comparison with DeepDNA. Learning-based methods can mine the potential connections of genetic information more intelligently meeting the compression needs, so we compare learning ability of the deep learning model in our proposed algorithm with another learning-based method DeepDNA. From the results of experiments in Table 2, our algorithm performance better than DeepDNA on all data sets. Due to the limitation of space, we only display the results on Fishes data. To verify its convergence, we plot the average loss of validation set after each epoch in the training process in Fig. 2. We can see that the average loss of our model steadily decreases as traing processes while the loss of DeepDNA increases after epoch 1 and the loss of subsequent epochs fluctuates up and down repeatedly, which shows that our model gradually converges and learns the features of sequences better than DeepDNA during the training process.

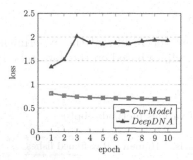 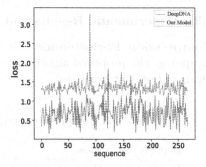

Fig. 2. The average loss of validation set during training.

Fig. 3. The test loss of our model compared with DeepDNA

We then calculate the loss of all sequences in the test data sets as shown in Fig. 3 to verify the efficiency of the proposed model. Each sample of the horizontal axis represents a complete genomic sequence and the vertical axis shows its average loss. As the figure shown, for each sample (281 in total), the loss of our model is lower obviously than that of DeepDNA.

Since the average loss of a sequence is susceptible to the extreme loss of some slide windows in the sequence, so we randomly select a sequence whose ID is NC_011180.1 in the test set and plot the average loss of every ten consecutive sliding windows for further exploration and illustration. The result is shown

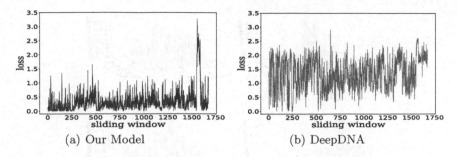

(a) Our Model   (b) DeepDNA

Fig. 4. Average loss of ten consecutive sliding windows in sequence NC_011180.1.

in Fig. 4. We can see that the values of loss fluctuation are relatively smooth between samples, which are in 0-0.5 in general from Fig. 4 (a) while in 0.5-2 for DeepDNA in Fig. 4 (b). The average loss of this sequence is 0.35 when using our model and 1.33 when using DeepDNA.

Ablation Experiments. We also conduct ablation experiments that delete or replace one part of our model to verify their importance based on training, validation, and test data sets respectively. The results are shown in Table 3, in which **Without CNN** means removing the CNN layer and the max-pooling layer, **Without BiLSTM** means replacing the BiLSTM with a unidirectional LSTM, **Without Attention** means removing the top-layer attention mechanism of the model and **Complete Model** denotes the one combining all the parts. Except for the removed parts, the remaining parts of these models are consistent with those in the complete model.

Table 3. Results of ablation experiments

Model	Training	Validation	Test
Without CNN	0.6978 + 15.2%	0.7232 + 3.5 %	0.7137 + 1.4 %
Without BiLSTM	0.6710 + 10.8%	0.7321 + 4.8 %	0.7320 + 4.0 %
Without Attention	**0.5964−1.4%**	0.7107 + 1.7 %	0.7174 + 1.9 %
Complete Model	0.6053	**0.6982**	**0.7036**

As shown in the table, each part of our model is indispensable. Although **Complete Model** is 1.4% worse than **Without Attention** on the training set, it has the best performance on both the validation set and the test set and outperforms other models up to 4.8% and 4% respectively. In addition, the results of **Without BiLSTM** show that bi-directional LSTM is able to capture long-term dependency and learn the special features such as complementary palindromes much better in the genomic sequences.

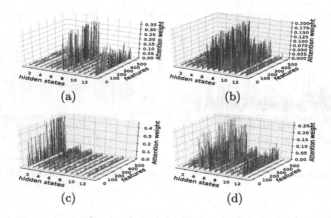

Fig. 5. The attention weights in four sliding windows

Visualizing Attention. For LSTM network without attention mechanism, each hidden state has the same weight of the final feature representation or is merely based on the last hidden state. However, various hidden states contribute to the final prediction differently. The attention mechanism automatically learns the importance of hidden states to assign higher weights for more important ones. To better interpret the attention mechanism, as shown in Fig. 5, we visualize the attention weight matrix of four randomly selected sliding windows and there are 512 features being generated in each hidden state. Different colored bars display the different ranges of the weight values of high-level features learned by BiLSTM.

We can observe that the seventh hidden state and the last hidden state are assigned higher weights in Fig. 5 (a), while the first hidden state has a higher weight in Fig. 5 (c), and there is the same regularity in (b) and (d). What's more, it can be seen that the contributions of 512 features in each hidden state are different, too. So the learned varieties of weight values promoting the accuracy for the final prediction, indicting the effectiveness of attention mechanism.

5   Conclusion

Facing the challenges of genomic sequences compression, we propose an algorithm including a deep learning model and arithmetic encoder. The deep learning model consists of CNN, BiLSTM and attention mechanism that learns the characteristics of the genomic sequences to estimate the probability needed in the arithmetic encoder for compression. Also, we conduct experiments on various data sets, indicating the proposed algorithm outperforms the learning-based method DeepDNA and traditional compression methods. At the same time, additional ablation experiments prove the importance of each part of the proposed algorithm and the visualization of attention weights shows various importance of hidden states to the final prediction.

In the future, we intend to input pure sequences and additional information of them, such as the species of sequence or any other properties to the algorithm. It may help reduce the redundancy of genomic sequences for better compression.

References

1. Bakr, N.S., Sharawi, A.A., et al.: DNA lossless compression algorithms. Am. J. Bioinf. Res. **3**(3), 72–81 (2013)
2. Behzadi, B., Le Fessant, F.: DNA compression challenge revisited: a dynamic programming approach. In: Apostolico, A., Crochemore, M., Park, K. (eds.) CPM 2005. LNCS, vol. 3537, pp. 190–200. Springer, Heidelberg (2005). https://doi.org/10.1007/11496656_17
3. Berger, B., Peng, J., Singh, M.: Computational solutions for omics data. Nat. Rev. Genet. **14**(5), 333 (2013)
4. Cao, M.D., Dix, T.I., Allison, L., Mears, C.: A simple statistical algorithm for biological sequence compression. In: 2007 Data Compression Conference (DCC 2007), pp. 43–52. IEEE (2007)
5. Chen, X., Kwong, S., Li, M.: A compression algorithm for DNA sequences and its applications in genome comparison. Genome Inform. **10**, 51–61 (1999)
6. Chen, X., Li, M., Ma, B., Tromp, J.: Dnacompress: fast and effective DNA sequence compression. Bioinformatics **18**(12), 1696–1698 (2002)
7. Deorowicz, S., Grabowski, S.: Robust relative compression of genomes with random access. Bioinformatics **27**(21), 2979–2986 (2011)
8. Goyal, M., Tatwawadi, K., Chandak, S., Ochoa, I.: Deepzip: lossless data compression using recurrent neural networks. arXiv preprint arXiv:1811.08162 (2018)
9. Grumbach, S., Tahi, F.: Compression of DNA sequences. In: Proceedings of DCC93: Data Compression Conference, pp. 340–350. IEEE (1993)
10. Grumbach, S., Tahi, F.: A new challenge for compression algorithms: genetic sequences. Inf. Process. Manage. **30**(6), 875–886 (1994)
11. Hughes, L.C., et al.: Comprehensive phylogeny of ray-finned fishes (Actinopterygii) based on transcriptomic and genomic data. Proc. Natl. Acad. Sci. **115**(24), 6249–6254 (2018)
12. Ioffe, S., Szegedy, C.: Batch normalization: accelerating deep network training by reducing internal covariate shift. In: International Conference on Machine Learning, pp. 448–456 (2015)
13. Kingma, D.P., Ba, J.: Adam: a method for stochastic optimization. arXiv preprint arXiv:1412.6980 (2014)
14. Mahoney, M.V.: Fast text compression with neural networks. In: FLAIRS Conference, pp. 230–234 (2000)
15. Matsumoto, T., Sadakane, K., Imai, H.: Biological sequence compression algorithms. Genome Inf. **11**, 43–52 (2000)
16. Mishra, K.N., Aaggarwal, A., Abdelhadi, E., Srivastava, D.: An efficient horizontal and vertical method for online DNA sequence compression. Int. J. Comput. Appl. **3**(1), 39–46 (2010)
17. Muir, P., et al.: The real cost of sequencing: scaling computation to keep pace with data generation. Genome Biol. **17**(1), 53 (2016)
18. Pinho, A.J., Pratas, D.: Mfcompress: a compression tool for fasta and multi-fasta data. Bioinformatics **30**(1), 117–118 (2013)

19. Quang, D., Xie, X.: DanQ: a hybrid convolutional and recurrent deep neural network for quantifying the function of DNA sequences. Nucleic Acids Res. **44**(11), e107–e107 (2016)
20. Sato, H., Yoshioka, T., Konagaya, A., Toyoda, T.: DNA data compression in the post genome era. Genome Inform. **12**, 512–514 (2001)
21. Wang, R., et al.: Deepdna: a hybrid convolutional and recurrent neural network for compressing human mitochondrial genomes. In: 2018 IEEE International Conference on Bioinformatics and Biomedicine (BIBM), pp. 270–274. IEEE (2018)
22. Zhou, J., Troyanskaya, O.G.: Predicting effects of noncoding variants with deep learning-based sequence model. Nat. Methods **12**(10), 931 (2015)

Learning Tn5 Sequence Bias
from ATAC-seq on Naked Chromatin

Meshal Ansari[1,2], David S. Fischer[1], and Fabian J. Theis[1,3(✉)]

[1] Institute of Computational Biology, Helmholtz Zentrum München,
85764 Munich, Germany
fabian.theis@helmholtz-muenchen.de
[2] Comprehensive Pneumology Center (CPC) / Institute of Lung Biology and Disease
(ILBD), Helmholtz Zentrum München, Member of the German Center for Lung
Research (DZL), 85764 Munich, Germany
[3] Department of Mathematics, Technische Universität München,
85748 Munich, Germany

Abstract. Technological advances in the last decade resulted in an
explosion of biological data. Sequencing methods in particular provide
large-scale data sets as resource for incorporation of machine learning in
the biological field. By measuring DNA accessibility for instance, enzymatic hypersensitivity assays facilitate identification of regions of open
chromatin in the genome, marking potential locations of regulatory elements. ATAC-seq is the primary method of choice to determine these
footprints. It allows measurements on the cellular level, complementing the recent progress in single cell transcriptomics. However, as the
method-specific enzymes tend to bind preferentially to certain sequences,
the accessibility profile is confounded by binding specificity. The inference of open chromatin should be adjusted for this bias [1].
To enable such corrections, we built a deep learning model that learns
the sequence specificity of ATAC-seq's enzyme Tn5 on naked DNA. We
found binding preferences and demonstrate that cleavage patterns specific to Tn5 can successfully be discovered by the means of convolutional
neural networks. Such models can be combined with accessibility analysis
in the future in order to predict bias on new sequences and furthermore
provide a better picture of the regulatory landscape of the genome.

Keywords: Single-cell ATAC-seq · Convolutional neural networks ·
Deep learning · Sequence preference bias · Regulatory element
discovery

1 Introduction

It is still not completely understood how heterogeneity can arise from identical nucleotide sequences. Epigenetic modification like DNA phosphorylation
and histone alterations are implicated in additionally regulating gene expression
without inducing changes in the nucleotide sequence, representing one association between variants in genome regions and phenotypic variation. Characterizing transcription factor binding sites across the genome and identifying the

© Springer Nature Switzerland AG 2020
I. Farkaš et al. (Eds.): ICANN 2020, LNCS 12396, pp. 105–114, 2020.
https://doi.org/10.1007/978-3-030-61609-0_9

positions of regulatory elements that can increase or decrease the transcription rates will further our understanding of gene regulation. These modifications can only take place as DNA and RNA binding proteins access the genome. Enzymatic hypersensitivity assays allow to measure the chromatin accessibility to the transcription machinery and identify relevant DNA sites. They are useful tools for building a genome-wide landscape of epigenetic regulatory structures.

Interestingly, many epigenetic events have been linked to non-coding RNA. However, the functional description and interpretation of non-coding variants is still lacking [2]. Since *deep learning* methods are able to learn functional relationships from data without having to explicitly define them beforehand, these approaches can overcome the still limited description of non-coding regions. They are in particular suited to learn sequence specificity from experimental data and have been applied for detection of transcription factors in nucleotide sequences [3,4]. Here, we build a deep learning model based on neural networks for the purpose of gaining insights on enzyme-specific sequence preferences.

1.1 Assay for Transposase Accessible Chromatin Using Sequencing

Chromatin is found in eukaryotic cells and has a main function of packaging DNA into a more compact form in order to prevent DNA damage. It is also involved in regulation of gene expression and DNA replication, as it controls the density of the DNA at different cell cycle states by its structural changes. It has been shown that there is a certain heterogeneity in not only the gene expression patterns but also the chromatin structure across different cell types, indicating differences in accessibility of the genome to the transcription machinery based on cellular profiles [5].

In recent years more and more single-cell sequencing methods have been introduced, empowering researchers to pinpoint changes at the highest resolution. One approach to study chromatin accessibility is the Assay for Transposase Accessible Chromatin using sequencing (ATAC-seq) described by Buenrostro *et al.* [6]. A basic scheme of this method is outlined in Fig. 1.

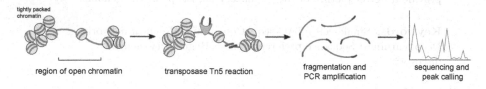

tightly packed chromatin

region of open chromatin   transposase Tn5 reaction   fragmentation and PCR amplification   sequencing and peak calling

Fig. 1. Tn5 transposase in ATAC-seq integrates sequencing adapters into sites of open chromatin. A transposition to less accessible regions is less likely due to steric hindrances. In contrast to previous methods which consist of multiple steps and long incubation times, the assay of scATAC-seq requires far smaller number of sample cells and involves only two steps: Tn5 insertion and PCR. Finally peak calling and footprinting is performed after high-throughput sequencing.

ATAC-seq is based on Tn5 transposase's ability to access open regions of the DNA. Transposases are enzymes that bind transposons, cut them out of the region and catalyse their movement across the genome. The hyperactive Tn5 transposase used in this assay cuts and simultaneously ligates synthetic sequencing adapters into the accessible sites. By tagging these sites the characterization and quantification of open genome regions even after high-throughput sequencing is enabled.

Single-cell ATAC-seq provides a genome-wide map of the sequence accessibility. This picture of the regulatory landscape can be further used to explore multiple questions, e.g. quantification of these changes across different populations. Based on position and length distribution of the adapter insertions, one can gain insight to nucleosome positions in regulatory regions and the interplay of genomic sites with DNA binding factors [7].

The sequence specificities of Tn5 are still poorly understood. Computational DNA footprinting is frequently used to investigate associated regions of DNA binding proteins. Sequence signatures that are obtained by footprinting methods can be distorted by preferences specific to the enzyme used in the assay and should be considered when interpreting the signals. There have been efforts made in correcting for these artefacts in ATAC-seq by incorporating Hidden Markov Models [8] or via mathematical models *e.g.* scaling experimental data by the ratio of expected insertion events for a sequence window to the observed occurrences [1]. We evaluated whether we can identify a binding bias and aim to learn potential cleavage preferences of Tn5 by applying deep learning algorithms.

1.2   Convolutional Neural Networks in Genomics

One prominently applied approach to capture certain structures of interest in biological sequences are neural networks. During the learning phase the connections between the neurons are refined and relevant features in the data can be extracted without the need to manually define them beforehand.

Although these are a powerful machine learning tool, they do not scale well with increasing data size and carry the risk of overfitting when adjusting to minimal details of the image. Instead it is reasonable to focus on certain patterns. *Convolutional* neural networks are specifically developed for this application. Inspired by an animal's visual cortex and its receptive field, a region of a single sensory neuron in which a stimulus can affect the behaviour of the neuron, the connections between neurons mirror this region. Each neuron is assigned to a local region of the image which it processes [9].

Compared to a fully connected network, additional filters in form of so-called *convolutional layers* are applied in order to reduce dimensions. By this a certain window of the size of the predefined receptive field is slid over the input image. During this sliding the values located in the window are combined into one single number which is then propagated to the next layer [10,11].

In the context of biology, the first convolutional layer can be thought of as a motif scanner resembling position weight matrices PWMs. During convolution each filter searches for its specific motif while sliding along a biological sequence.

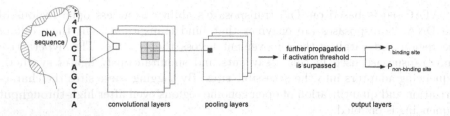

Fig. 2. Characteristic structure of a CNN constituted of multiple layers. Convolution layers combine input values (*e.g.* biological sequences). Pooling layers are employed to further reduce the dimensions. An activation function is applied before passing the signal to the fully connected layers, where the score for each category of interest is calculated and returned via output neurons [10].

These networks are perfectly suited to detect motifs in sequence windows and thus enable binding classification and motif discovery. By adding even more convolutional layers and abstracting the model further, additional information like the spatial interaction between the initial detectors' output as well as local sequence context can be captured [4,11].

2   Materials and Methods

To detect the transposase's sequence bias in ATAC-seq experiments, it was important to consider a data set resulting from ATAC-seq performed on "naked" DNA, *i.e.* DNA that was purified such that no other molecules as proteins, lipids, *etc.* were associated to it. It has been shown previously that the probability of a cleavage event by the Tn5 transposase is higher in DNA stretc.hes void of nucleosomes or proteins attached [1,12]. Particularly in the case of scATAC-seq where genomic accessibility is in question, such purified DNA lessens the confounding effect introduced via binding preferences of the assay's Tn5.

Moreover, clearer results on the cleavage bias are obtained as it avoids capturing molecular profiles that arise due to protein/DNA interaction.

We fetched a data set from GEO (accession number GSM1550786) [13] which contains the result of a scATAC-seq assay performed on FACS sorted germ cells of *Mus musculus*. The data set consists of positions with known transposition events and the read density at corresponding coordinates in the genome. The procedure as to how they were extracted is outlined in Fig. 3. Briefly, the 46 base pair sequences centered at each signal peak were selected as positive sequences. To create the corresponding negative counterpart with similar properties, windows of length 46 which did not have a read overlapping should be considered.

Therefore, the negative set was chosen such that it mirrors the size and the GC contents of the sequences in the positive set and preferably contains sequences across the whole chromosome. Finally, in order to focus on sequences with strongest signal, the 100 000 sequence windows with the highest read count

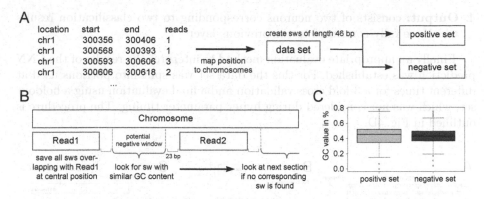

Fig. 3. (A) Creation of a data set from scATAC-seq experiment on naked DNA on sorted mouse germ cells, given as `.bedGraph` file. (B) The positive set was created as follows: A window of length 46 base pairs (bp) was slid over the sequence. If the center position overlaps with a read, save the current sequence window (sw) and assign the value of the original read. Creation of negative set: For each sequence in the positive set, search in a certain range for a sw with similar GC content ($\pm$ 0.1). The range is defined as region between reads, to ensure that no transposition event happened. If none is found, continue search in next possible range. If the chromosome's end is reached, jump to its start and continue search. (C) Both positive and negative test sets show the same GC content distribution in order to avoid sequence bias.

values are selected as base training input for the model. The sequences were converted to a one hot encoded representation as multidimensional arrays (*tensors*, see Fig. 4A). The generation of the CNN models was done via the python package keras due to its comprehensible and simple way of translating the desired CNN architecture into machine-readable format [14].

For the purpose of identifying transposition sites of transposase Tn5, we designed a shallow CNN. The architecture was inspired by models that predict transcription factor binding based on CHIPseq data. One of the first approaches to apply deep learning for identification of protein binding sites was DeepBind [3]. By using a CNN with a single convolutional layer the model can learn sequence specificities of DNA- and RNA-binding proteins from raw genomic sequences and detect known motifs. Based on an appropriate architecture such neural networks tend to outperform prevailing simpler models. The `DeepBind` model consists of following layers:

1. **Convolution:** one dimensional convolution over 4-channel input. Can be interpreted as a motif scan in the context of biological sequences
2. **Rectification:** take output of the first layer and propagate maximal value. Applies activation threshold for a certain motif at every position. If a motif's score at a position passes the threshold, the score is propagated
3. **Max Pooling:** reduce input matrix to a vector with length = number of motif detectors by retaining the maximal score per detector

4. **Output:** consists of two neurons corresponding to two classification results which are fully connected to the previous layer

Finally an appropriate evaluation method to interpret the results of the CNN prediction was established. For this the data set was split into portions used at different times for a 3-fold cross validation and a final evaluation using a holdout set, which was not considered during hyper parameter tuning. The procedure is outlined in Fig. 4D.

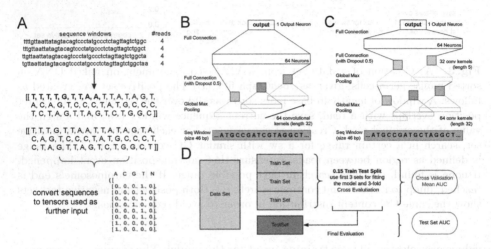

Fig. 4. (A) Conversion of genomic sequence using one hot encoding. Tensors have dimension of *number of sequences × window length × nucleotides*, in this case 100 000 × 46 × 5. (B) Architecture of model 1 (shallow model). The first layer consists of 64 convolutional kernels that transform its output using rectified linear unit as activation function. The propagated output is further condensed by the global max pooling layer, as only the maximal value of its corresponding convolutional layer is propagated to the fully connected layer. (C) Architecture of model 2 (deeper model): The main difference to the first model is the additional convolution layer of size 5. (D) Evaluation method for CNN prediction. In a first step a forth of the data set was put aside (holdout set). A 3-fold cross validation was performed, in each iteration the remaining portion of the data set was split such that 85% of the sequences were used for training and 15% for evaluation as test set. The final evaluation of the model was performed on the hold-out set. In each data split an equal amount of positive and negative sequences was ensured.

3   Results

Since `DeepBind`'s application differs from what we aim for, some adjustments in layer sizes and number of neurons were made. It has been shown that increasing the number of convolutional kernels can improve the performance of motif-based tasks [11]. We therefore expanded our initial shallow model by adding a second convolutional layer (deeper model). The architectures are presented in Fig. 4.

In order to find the most appropriate properties for the models, different combinations of adjustable parameters of *keras* were compared in a grid hyper parameter search. The optimization was done on 10,000 sequences (excluding the holdout set) as a run of all combinations on the whole set proved to be too time consuming. The results can be seen in Fig. 5. The available optimization functions consist of *stochastic gradient descent, RMSprop, adagrad, adadelta, adam* and *adamax* and the loss functions tested were *binary crossentropy, mean absolute error, mean squared error, mean squared logarithmic error* and *poisson*. Likewise different lengths of filters [3, 5, 16, 24, 32] and number of filters [16, 32, 64, 86, 100] were tested for their accuracy. Due to the increase in computation time with larger number of filters, 64 filters with a length of 24 were chosen, indicating sufficient enough accuracy as shown in Fig. 6A.

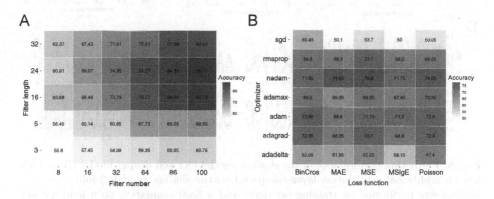

Fig. 5. Overview of parameter optimization. Test accuracy obtained by grid parameter search using 10,000 training sequences. Results for different (A) filter length and filter number combinations and (B) optimization and loss function combinations.

The hyper parameter search was executed on the shallow model. The resulting parameters were then re-applied on the deeper model, with slight adjustments. In contrast to the first model, the deeper one uses 64 filters of length 32 in a first convolutional layer, and additionally 32 of length 5 in a second convolutional layer. For both models *adam* was adopted as optimizer and *poisson* as loss function. The activation function was constantly kept as `rectified linear unit` due to its prominent use in comparable methods.

After deciding on these parameters, the evaluation as described in 4D was executed for both models separately. Their performances are presented in Fig. 6A and B. In both parts of the evaluation the deeper model with an additional convolutional layer containing short filters achieved better accuracy.

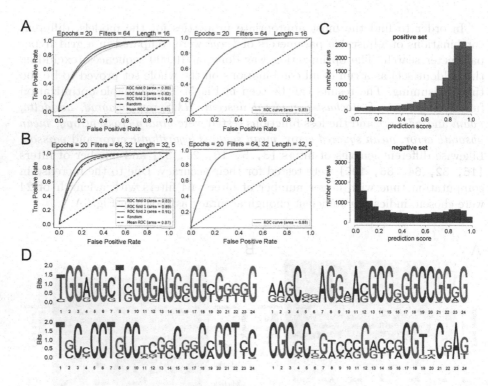

Fig. 6. Prediction performance of the shallow model (A) and deeper model (B), which has an additional convolution layer compared to the shallow model. 3-fold cross validation was performed on training set (left) and a final evaluation on a hold-out set (right). (C) Bar plots showing prediction score distribution separately for sequences that originated from either positive (upper) or negative set (bottom). (D) Examples of the generated set of sequence logos based on extracted weights of shallow model. Size of the motif filter was chosen as 24, leading to logos of the same length. Relative sizes of letters indicate the contribution of a nucleotide at given position to the associated weight in the convolutional layer.

To further examine whether the score returned for an input sequence can be used as a measure to how reliable the prediction is, Fig. 6C shows a distribution of scores returned for sequences from the hold-out set. Indeed for a vast majority of cases a high score was output if a transposition was observed in the sequence and a low score if not. This indicates that the significant signal could be captured by the established convolutional network.

The associated motifs in the genomic sequence that were learnt during training of model one can be extracted via the *keras* architecture. Applying the methods described by Basset *et al.* [4] the position weight matrix for each kernel in the first convolutional layer could be reconstructed be accessing its learnt weights respectively. These were further used to generate the corresponding sequence logos, part of the results are shown in Fig. 6D.

4   Discussion

It is essential to assess changes in the regulatory element landscape in pathological conditions to further grasp altered mechanisms in disease. Due to researchers' still limited knowledge of these regions it is hard to distinguish functional stretches from non-functional ones. Compared to coding regions no encoded genes can be detected which typically guide the functional interpretation of the sequence. Machine learning approaches enable to use these genome regions as input and find underlying patterns intrinsic to regulatory elements and enable the extension of known functional loci into the still mostly undescribed genomic regions. Modification of chromatin accessibility is one of the explorable aspects which can be measured thanks to the advances in recent profiling techniques. The regions of open chromatin are considerably variable across different cell types. Differentially open elements like enhancers, promoter etc. can have a vast effect on a cell's signature and therefore their analysis adds further insight to transcriptomics.

Like previously described the individual binding preferences of the enzymes used in the techniques can influence the peak distribution and aggravate the interpretation of results [1]. Considering these confounding factors and correcting for them is essential for meaningful biological analysis.

We show that convolutional neural networks provide a powerful tool that can catch motifs that are predominantly bound to by the ATAC-seq assay's transposase Tn5. These captured preferences on purified DNA can be used to improve the confounded observations in new ATAC-seq experiments and enable to understand the underlying biology behind accessible regions of the genome untarnished by technical artefacts.

Based on this outcome there are many directions that are worth looking into in more detail. The results presented were obtained using mouse germ cell lines. Still, as there is perceivable heterogeneity across different cell types, it might be interesting to consider these during training and bias correction in order to streamline the results more.

References

1. Martins, A.L., et al.: Universal correction of enzymatic sequence bias reveals molecular signatures of protein/DNA interactions. Nucleic Acids Res. **46**(2), e9 (2018). https://doi.org/10.1093/nar/gkx1053
2. Costa, FF.: Non-coding RNAs, epigenetics and complexity. Gene **410**(1), 9–17 (2008). https://doi.org/10.1016/j.gene.2007.12.008
3. Alipanahi, B., et al.: Predicting the sequence specificities of DNA- and RNA-binding proteins by deep learning. Nat. Biotechnol. **33**, 831–838 (2015). https://doi.org/10.1038/nbt.3300
4. Kelley, D.R., Snoek, J., Rinn, J.L.: Basset: learning the regulatory code of the accessible genome with deep convolutional neural networks. Genome Res. **26**(7), 990–999 (2016). https://doi.org/10.1101/gr.200535.115

5. Natarajan, A., Yardimci, G.G., Sheffield, N.C., Crawford, G.E., Ohler, U.: Predicting cell-type-specific gene expression from regions of open chromatin. Genome Res. **22**(9), 1711–1722 (2012). https://doi.org/10.1101/gr.135129.111

6. Buenrostro, J.D., Giresi, P.G., Zaba, L.C., Chang, H.Y., Greenleaf, W.J.: Transposition of native chromatin for fast and sensitive epigenomic profiling of open chromatin, DNA-binding proteins and nucleosome position. Nat. Methods **10**(12), 1213–1218 (2013). https://doi.org/10.1038/nmeth.2688

7. Buenrostro, J., et al.: Single-cell chromatin accessibility reveals principles of regulatory variation. Nature **523**, 486–490 (2015). https://doi.org/10.1038/nature14590

8. Li, Z., Schulz, M.H., Look, T., Begemann, M., Zenke, M., Costa, I.G.: Identification of transcription factor binding sites using ATAC-seq. Genome Biol. **20**(1), 45 (2019). https://doi.org/10.1186/s13059-019-1642-2

9. Angermueller, C., Pärnamaa, T., Parts, L., Stegle, O.: Deep learning for computational biology. Mol. Syst. Biol. **12**(7), 878 (2016). https://doi.org/10.15252/msb.20156651

10. A Guide to Convolutional Neural Networks. https://adeshpande3.github.io/A-Beginner's-Guide-To-Understanding-Convolutional-Neural-Networks/. Accessed 30 Apr 2020

11. Zeng, H., Edwards, M.D., Liu, G., Gifford, D.K.: Convolutional neural network architectures for predicting DNA-protein binding. Bioinformatics **32**(12), 121–127 (2016). https://doi.org/10.1093/bioinformatics/btw255

12. Picelli, S., Björklund, A.K., Reinius, B., Sagasser, S., Winberg, G., Sandberg, R.: Tn5 transposase and tagmentation procedures for massively scaled sequencing projects. Genome Res. **24**(12), 2033–2040 (2014). https://doi.org/10.1101/gr.177881.114

13. Pastor, W.A., Stroud, H., Nee, K., et al.: MORC1 represses transposable elements in the mouse male germline. Nat. Commun. **5**, 5795 (2014). https://doi.org/10.1038/ncomms6795

14. Chollet, F. et al.: Keras. https://keras.io

Tucker Tensor Decomposition
of Multi-session EEG Data

Zuzana Rošťáková$^{(\boxtimes)}$, Roman Rosipal, and Saman Seifpour

Institute of Measurement Science, Slovak Academy of Sciences,
Dúbravská cesta 9, 841 04 Bratislava, Slovakia
zuzana.rostakova@savba.sk

Abstract. The Tucker model is a tensor decomposition method for multi-way data analysis. However, its application in the area of multi-channel electroencephalogram (EEG) is rare and often without detailed electrophysiological interpretation of the obtained results. In this work, we apply the Tucker model to a set of multi-channel EEG data recorded over several separate sessions of motor imagery training. We consider a three-way and four-way version of the model and investigate its effect when applied to multi-session data. We discuss the advantages and disadvantages of both Tucker model approaches.

Keywords: Multi-channel electroencephalogram · Sensorimotor rhythms · Tucker model

1 Introduction

A compact and physiologically interpretable representation and analysis of electroencephalographic (EEG) data represent a challenging task. An important part of EEG analysis is the detection of latent sources of rhythmic activity in the time-varying EEG spectrum. For this purpose, the frequency decomposition of EEG signals, like the fast Fourier (FFT) or wavelet transform (WT), is often used. The time modality is often represented by a sequence of short EEG windows at which the frequency decomposition is applied. Finally, because EEG is often recorded at multiple electrodes, the third important modality is space, represented by different montages of EEG electrodes on the scalp. Other modalities often associated with EEG data analysis are the separation of subjects into different groups (male vs female, healthy vs patient, etc.) or experiments with a set of, in time separated, recorded sessions (different days, blocks of trials, etc.), to name a few. Therefore, the arrangement of EEG data into a multi-way array (a tensor) and application of the proper multi-way array decomposition method represents a natural way to analyse EEG data [3,7].

This contrasts with a set of traditional methods, for example, the principal component analysis (PCA) or independent component analysis (ICA), which operates on a two-way array where different modalities are concatenated into a single-mode (frequency and space or time and space, etc.).

© Springer Nature Switzerland AG 2020
I. Farkaš et al. (Eds.): ICANN 2020, LNCS 12396, pp. 115–126, 2020.
https://doi.org/10.1007/978-3-030-61609-0_10

The most frequently used tensor decomposition methods are the parallel factor analysis (PARAFAC) [5] and the Tucker model [12]. In both models, a multi-way array is decomposed into a set of interpretable matrices representing latent sources of variability present in data.

In the study, we focus on the tensor decomposition of EEG data with the aim of detection, monitoring, and analysis of latent sensorimotor EEG rhythms activated during motor imagery-based neurofeedback training of patients with hemiplegia due to a stroke.

We already successfully demonstrated the usefulness of PARAFAC when applied to multi-channel EEG data [9, 10]. However, in these studies, each subject and each training session data were analysed separately, and the subject-specific PARAFAC latent factors, common across all training sessions, were detected in a semi-automatic way by using a combined data clustering and visual inspection approach. Therefore, it is reasonable to ask if these common latent factors, referred to as 'atoms', could be extracted by analysing the combined data pooled across all training sessions and in one step. Note, in our experimental design, a session represents motor imagery-based training on a separate day.

Following the previous detailed analysis of identified EEG rhythms across days and subjects [9], we hypothesise, that simultaneous analysis of all training sessions may lead to the direct detection of subject-specific atoms, which would closely match the ones extracted using a single session approach. To do this, it turns to be natural to rearrange EEG data into a four-way tensor representing time, space, frequency, and session modes. However, the training sessions do not share common patterns in the time domain, because the number of motor imagery tasks and the subject's performance varies across days. In other words, the value representing a session needs to be considered as a qualitative, not quantitative, variable in the four-way tensor arrangement. This also leads to the second form of data representation where data across the time mode are concatenated and create one large three-way tensor.[1]

In this study, we discuss the advantages and disadvantages of the two approaches and validate their performance to detect subject-specific motor imagery related EEG rhythms of two patients with hemiplegia.

Our preliminary study showed that the Tucker model can produce a more compact representation of data than PARAFAC [11]. Interpretation of the four-way PARAFAC would be difficult when applied to data collected across different sessions. This is because the PARAFAC model assumes the same number of components in each mode. To adequately model variability of the time activation of a given atom across different sessions, it would be required to set the number of components in the PARAFAC model to be several times higher than the number of sessions. This would lead to an unnecessarily complex model with difficult interpretability of the extracted components. On the other hand, a flexible Tucker model with appropriate restrictions is applicable also in the case of multi-session recordings. Therefore, in this study, we focus on the Tucker model only,

---

[1] This approach can be interpreted as an unfolding of a four-way tensor [2].

and we validate and compare our results with subject-specific atoms previously obtained by applying PARAFAC to each session separately.

2   Data

Multi-channel EEG data of two patients with right-hand hemiplegia recorded over twenty-four and eight motor imagery-based neurorehabilitation training sessions with the robotic splint were used in the study [8]. During the training blocks, a trained technician recorded EEG continuously using 12 active Ag/AgCl electrodes embedded in an elastic fabric cap (g.GAMMAcap; g.tec medical engineering, Schiedlberg, Austria). The technician placed the electrode cap on the participant's head according to the manufacturer's instructions, attaching six active EEG left-side scalp electrodes (FC3, C1, C3, C5, CP3, and O1), six active right-side electrodes (FC4, C2, C4, C6, CP4, and A2), one reference electrode (A1), and one ground electrode (AFz). Later, for signal processing, we used the signal from the A2 electrode to re-reference all EEG recordings to the average earlobe [(A1+ A2)/2] signal. A 16-channel g.USBamp system (g.tec medical engineering), with the sampling rate 128 Hz served to record all EEG signals.

We performed initial analyses using the BrainVision Analyzer 2 software (Brain Products, GmbH). This involved automatic artifact detection with criteria of maximally allowed voltage step $50\,\mu V/ms$, lowest allowed activity in intervals of 100 ms set to $0.5\,\mu V$, and maximally allowed difference of voltages in intervals of 20 ms set to $50\,\mu V$. If any of the first two criteria were met, the interval preceding and following the detected artifact by 150 ms was marked as bad. In the case of the third criterion, this interval was set to 50 ms. Next, using the same software, a trained technician visually inspected EEG data and detected artifacts. The technician manually marked periods with undetected artifacts and removed artifact markers wrongly assigned automatically. This included the detection and removal of ocular artifacts.

The EEG signal was then segmented into two-second time windows with 250 ms of overlap. For each time window, the oscillatory component of the amplitude spectrum was estimated by the irregular resampling auto-spectral analysis (IRASA) [13]. Possible negative spectral densities of the oscillatory part estimate were set to zero and a value of one was added before performing the logarithmic transformation with a base of ten. Obtained logarithmic spectral data in the frequency range of 4 to 25 Hz and with the 0.5 Hz frequency resolution were re-arranged into:

i) a four-way tensor $\mathbb{X}_{(4)} \in \mathbb{R}_+^{I_1 \times I_2 \times I_3 \times I_4}$ (*time* × *electrodes* × *frequencies* × *sessions*)
ii) three-way tensors $\mathbb{Y}_l \in \mathbb{R}_+^{I_1 \times I_2 \times I_3}, l = 1, \ldots, I_4$ (*time* × *electrodes* × *frequencies*), which were concatenated across the first mode into the final three-way tensor $\mathbb{X}_{(3)} \in \mathbb{R}_+^{I_1 I_4 \times I_2 \times I_3}$.

The tensors $\mathbb{X}_{(4)}$ and $\mathbb{X}_{(3)}$ were centred across the first mode. To detect a subject-specific oscillatory activity, the tensors were constructed and analysed for each subject separately.

3   Methods

The N-way Tucker model [12] decomposes an N-way tensor $\mathbb{X} \in \mathbb{R}^{I_1 \times I_2 \times \cdots \times I_N}$ into matrices $A^{(n)} \in \mathbb{R}^{I_n \times J_n}, n = 1, \ldots, N$ and a core tensor $\mathbb{G} \in \mathbb{R}^{J_1 \times J_2 \times \cdots \times J_N}$

$$X_{i_1, i_2, \ldots, i_N} = \sum_{k=1}^{N} \sum_{j_k=1}^{J_k} g_{j_1, j_2, \ldots, j_n} a_{i_1 j_1}^{(1)} a_{i_2 j_2}^{(2)} \cdots a_{i_N j_N}^{(N)} + e_{i_1, i_2, \ldots, i_N} \tag{1}$$

by minimising the sum of squared residuals.[2] The tensor

$$\mathbb{E} = (e_{i_1, i_2, \ldots, i_N})_{\substack{i_k = 1, \ldots, I_k \\ k = 1, \ldots, N}} \in \mathbb{R}^{I_1 \times I_2 \times \cdots \times I_N}$$

represents the noise term. The factor matrices $A^{(n)}, n = 1, \ldots, N$ are constrained to have normalised columns.

In the study, we consider a four-way Tucker model (next denoted as Tucker4D) for $\mathbb{X}_{(4)}$ and a three-way Tucker model (Tucker3D) for the tensor $\mathbb{X}_{(3)}$. In both cases, the factor matrices $A^{(1)}, A^{(2)}, A^{(3)}$ represent *time scores* (TS), *spatial signatures* (SS) and *frequency signatures* (FS), respectively. An atom's activation in time is represented by a single or a linear combination of TS with weights equal to the corresponding elements of G.

In Tucker4D, the matrix $A^{(4)}$ characterises the presence of atoms across sessions. However, as highlighted in the Introduction section, sessions do not share common patterns in the time domain. In other words, atoms sharing the same FS and SS should follow their own time scores for different sessions. Consequently, $A^{(4)}$ should be a fixed matrix with a diagonal structure. However, due to the unit norm assumption of the matrix columns, $A^{(4)}$ is considered as an $(I_4 \times I_4)$-dimensional identity matrix.

To improve the stability and interpretability of the Tucker decomposition, it is recommended to constrain the solution following the character of the analysed data [6]. Due to the fact that our data represent a positive log_{10}-transformed oscillatory part of the amplitude spectrum, we assumed the matrices $A^{(2)}, A^{(3)}$ to be non-negative. Because we focus on extracting sources of narrow-band oscillations, the columns of $A^{(3)}$ were constrained to be unimodal. Following our previous studies [9,11], the matrix $A^{(1)}$ in Tucker3D was set to be non-negative. For Tucker4D, we considered two alternatives for $A^{(1)}$ – non-negativity and orthogonality. In the following text, these two versions of Tucker4D are denoted as Tucker4D_N and Tucker4D_O.

In [11], we observed an improvement in the physiological interpretation and stability of the Tucker model decomposition with the non-negative constraint on elements of the core tensor $\mathbb{G}$. This was true in comparison to the model with an unconstrained $\mathbb{G}$ structure. Following this result, we set the core tensor $\mathbb{G}$ to be non-negative in all Tucker3D and Tucker4D model variants also in this study.

---

[2] The PARAFAC model also follows the formula (1), but with the assumption of the same number of factors in each mode ($J_1 = \cdots = J_N = J$) and a super–diagonal structure of $\mathbb{G}$.

Two stable SS patterns representing EEG oscillatory sources in the left or right hemisphere were observed in [11]. Therefore, in the current study, the number of SS was also set to two ($J_2 = 2$). We varied the number of frequency signatures (J_3) between 8 and 11. Also, following our previous experience and results [11], the number of TS was varied between J_3 and $2 * J_3$. This follows the observation that the majority of atoms in the left and right hemisphere often show different time activation.

The variation of these parameters leads to a set of solutions (runs). Instead of choosing one final Tucker model for a subject, we investigated all solutions whose core consistency diagnostics (CCD) [1] was greater than 0.5. When validating solutions of the Tucker3D and Tucker4D models we focused on the

- comparison of time, spatial and frequency characteristics of atoms obtained from the models
- maximum number of factors necessary to adequately describe data structure variability
- presence of stable atoms across solutions and their comparison with the subject-specific atoms already known from applying the PARAFAC model to each training session separately.

4   Results

An example of the Tucker3D model with 16 TS and 8 FS is depicted in Fig. 1. The model detected eight oscillatory rhythms with the peak frequencies at 6.5, 8, 9.5, 11, 13, 14.5, 16.5, and 19.5 Hz (Fig. 1, first row). Spatial signatures represent the location of these oscillatory EEG sources either in the left or right hemisphere (Fig. 1, first and second row, two right plots). The core tensor $\mathbb{G}$ slices represent the relationship between SS and TS for a given atom (Fig. 1, second row, left). For example, the time activation of the left 8 Hz EEG rhythm across all sessions corresponds to the 6th TS. For the right hemisphere, it is the 10th TS.

The interpretation and visualisation of the Tucker4D model is similar, however, in this case, $\mathbb{G}$ represents a four-way core tensor.

For both subjects, the core tensor $\mathbb{G}$ of the Tucker3D and Tucker4D_N models showed a sparse structure. For Subject 1 this is depicted in Fig. 1 (second row) and Fig. 2 (top and middle rows). Consequently, the time activation of the extracted atoms is equal to one TS (a column of $A^{(1)}$) or to a linear combination of a few of them. However, their interpretation differs between three- and four-way models. For Tucker3D, the time scores are vectors with the length $I_1 * I_4$ and they represent the time activation across all sessions, but for Tucker4D_N they characterise only one session.

Due to the sparse structure of $\mathbb{G}$, the optimal number of time scores for the Tucker3D model is approximately $J_2 * J_3 = 2 * J_3$. But for Tucker4D_N it is $J_2 * J_3 * k, k \approx J_4$. However, in this study, we considered J_1 to be at most $2 * J_3$, and therefore the Tucker4D_N model did not have enough TS to adequately describe data structure variability. Consequently, the model shows a significantly higher mean squared error (MSE) in comparison to Tucker3D,

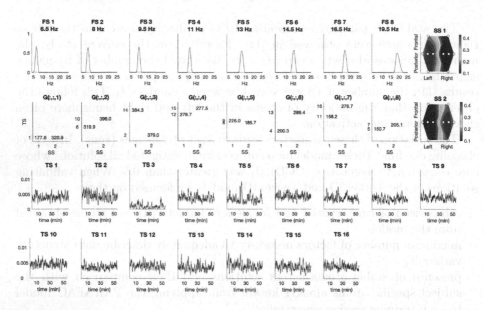

Fig. 1. Subject 1. An example of the Tucker3D model with eight frequency signatures (FS, first row), two spatial signatures (SS, first and second row, two right plots) and 16 time scores (TS, third and fourth row). Non-zero elements in slices of the core tensor $\mathbb{G}$ for a given FS are depicted in the second row on the left (Color figure online).

but also when compared with the Tucker4D_O model (Fig. 3). Naturally, an improvement can be achieved by increasing the number of TS, but this would be at the cost of longer computation time, numerical and convergence problems as well as leading to higher complexity of the model.[3] Therefore, we conclude that the Tucker4D_N model may not be appropriate when used in the studied multi-session EEG recording scenario and was not further analysed.

In contrast to Tucker3D and Tucker4D_N, the core tensor $\mathbb{G}$ after the convergence turned to be dense in the case of the Tucker4D_O models (Fig. 2, bottom). In the Tucker4D_O model, the columns of $A^{(1)}$ form an orthogonal basis and can not be interpreted directly. More attention needs to be paid to each particular linear combination of the $A^{(1)}$ columns representing the final time activation of an atom in a given session.

A comparison of time activation of 8 Hz right hemisphere oscillatory atom for a randomly chosen session and solution of the Tucker4D_O and Tucker3D models is depicted in Fig. 4a. The observed differences between curves are due to different constraints applied to $A^{(1)}$ in each of the two models. However, and most importantly, the dynamic of both curves is very similar. Because the overall dynamic profiles of time scores, and not their absolute values are in our focus,

---

[3] For Subject 1, fixing the number of FS to eight and SS to two, the Tucker4D_N model with eighty TS shows MSE approximately of the same value as the Tucker4D_O model with sixteen TS.

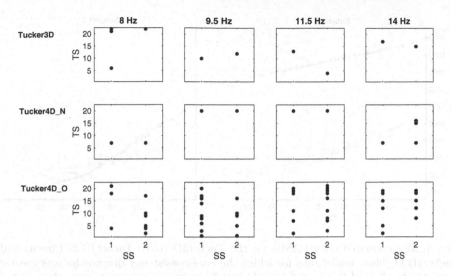

Fig. 2. Subject 1. Slices of the core tensor $\mathbb{G}$ for oscillatory atoms with the peak frequencies at 8, 9.5, 11.5, and 14 Hz of the Tucker3D (top row), Tucker4D_N (second row) and Tucker4D_O (third row) models. Slices over the first session are depicted in the case of the Tucker4D_N and Tucker4D_O models. The Tucker3D and both variants of the Tucker4D model were run with 22 time scores (TS), 2 space signatures (SS) and 11 frequency signatures (FS). Only the non-zero elements of the core tensor $\mathbb{G}$ slices are depicted (black circles).

we can conclude that both versions of the Tucker model led to comparable time activation profiles.

Spatial signatures from all solutions (runs with different parameter settings) of the Tucker3D and Tucker4D_O models are depicted in Fig. 4b. Similarly to [11], SS represent the spatial distribution of the oscillatory EEG activity either in the left or right hemisphere. We observed high stability of these SS across all runs and models.

Finally, we investigated the detectability and stability of FS across different runs. For this purpose, DBSCAN [4], a density-based clustering method, was applied to FS solutions of both Tucker3D and Tucker4D_O models.

For Subject 1, the dominant clusters of FS of the Tucker3D and Tucker4D_O models represent EEG oscillatory activity with the peak frequencies at 8, 9.5, 11.5, 14, and 15.5 Hz (Fig. 5a, middle, and bottom) and are consistent with FS of the subject-specific atoms already detected by PARAFAC applied to each training session separately (Fig. 5a, top).

The difference between considered approaches occurred only for rhythms with higher frequencies (in the range of 17 to 19 Hz). The Tucker4D_O model FS form a cluster with the peak frequency at 17.5 Hz, which is consistent with the PARAFAC results, but the corresponding Tucker3D model cluster indicates a slight shift of the peak frequency of this atom to 16.5 Hz. The rhythm with the peak frequency close to 19 Hz was detected in several runs of the two

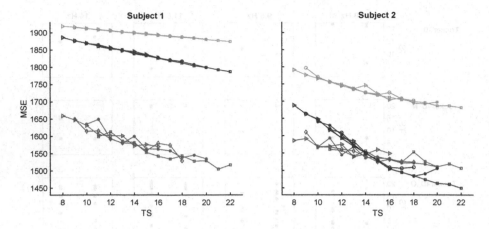

Fig. 3. Mean squared error (MSE) for the Tucker3D (red), Tucker4D_N (green) and Tucker4D_O (blue) model runs for which the core consistency diagnostics was greater than 0.5. In all models, the number of spatial signatures was set to two, the number J_3 of frequency signatures was set to 8 (▷), 9 (◇), 10 (*) or 11 (□) and the number of time scores (TS) varied between J_3 and $2 * J_3$ (Color figure online).

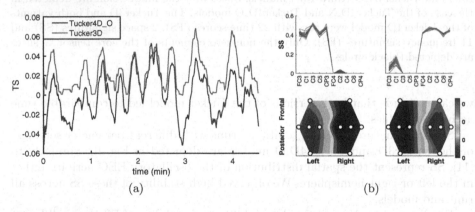

Fig. 4. Subject 1. (a) Time scores (TS) for 8 Hz oscillatory EEG activity in the right hemisphere for a randomly chosen solution of the Tucker4D_O (blue) and Tucker3D (red) models. (b) *Top*: Spatial signatures (SS) from all runs of the Tucker4D_O and Tucker3D models representing spatial distribution of the oscillatory EEG activity in the left and right hemisphere over the sensorimotor cortex. *Bottom*: scalp topographic map of the average of SS depicted in the top plot. (Color figure online)

models (Fig. 1), but a stable cluster was identified neither in Tucker3D nor in Tucker4D_O.

Subject 2 specific atoms detected by PARAFAC show the peak frequencies at 8, 9.5, 11, 13.5, 16, and 17 Hz. The dominant clusters of FS for both Tucker4D_O and Tucker3D indicate the peak frequencies at 7.5, 9-9.5, 11, and 13-13.5 Hz (Fig. 5b).

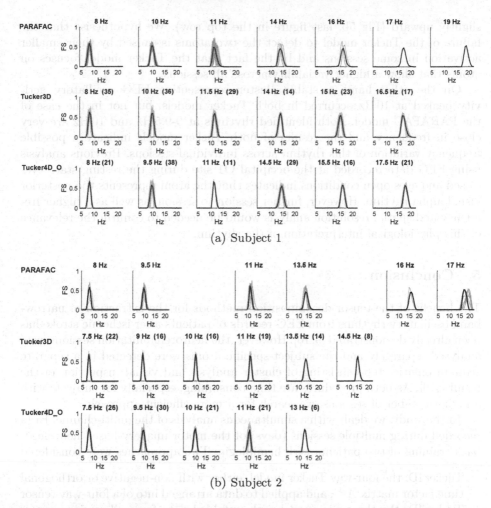

(a) Subject 1

(b) Subject 2

Fig. 5. Frequency signatures (FS) of the atoms detected by the DBSCAN cluster analysis. For each subject, the PARAFAC (top row), Tucker3D (middle row), and Tucker4D_O (bottom row) solutions are depicted. The grey curves represent cluster elements for the Tucker models (individual solutions), the cluster representative (black bold curve) was computed as an average of all solutions. In the title of each subplot, the number of elements in each cluster is depicted in parenthesis. For PARAFAC, the cluster analysis was applied within each session separately. Cluster representatives for each session are depicted in green, the black bold curve represents their average (Color figure online).

The rhythms at 16 and 17 Hz formed stable clusters neither in Tucker3D nor in Tucker4D_O. However, when looking at the results of PARAFAC and cluster analysis applied to each session separately (Fig. 5b), the atom with the peak frequency 16 Hz was present only in five of the eight sessions. The 17 Hz atom was also not stable, and for several sessions its peak frequency was shifted slightly upward (Fig. 5b, last figure in the top row). We hypothesise that the failure of the Tucker model to detect the two atoms is caused by their smaller activation in some sessions and by the fact that the Tucker model focuses on atoms that show a higher variability across all sessions.

On the other hand, a stable cluster representing EEG oscillatory activity peaked at 10 Hz occurred in both Tucker models, but not in the case of the PARAFAC model. Both identified rhythms at 9-9.5 Hz and 10 Hz are very close in frequency and the results of both Tucker models indicate a possible frequency variation of this rhythm across individual sessions. Previous analysis using EEG data recorded at the occipital O1 site during the resting state eyes closed and eyes open conditions indicates that the atom represents the posterior visual alpha rhythm. However, further session to session, as well as a higher frequency and spatial resolution analysis would be needed to confirm the relevance of this physiological interpretation of the rhythm.

5   Conclusion

The benefit of the tensor decomposition methods for the extraction of narrow-band oscillatory rhythms from EEG records of patients after ischemic stroke has been already demonstrated [9,10]. However, the neurorehabilitation sessions were analysed separately and the subject-specific atoms were detected in a separate semi-automatic step consisting of cluster analysis and visual inspection of the results [10]. As both procedures are time-consuming, especially for subjects with a higher number of sessions, we search for a more efficient approach.

In the study, we dealt with a simultaneous analysis of the multi-channel EEG recorded during multiple sessions (days) of the motor imagery-based neurofeed-back training of two patients with hemiplegia. Two approaches were considered

- Tucker4D: the four-way Tucker model, either with non-negative or orthogonal time factor matrix $A^{(1)}$, and applied to data arranged into of a four-way tensor
- Tucker3D: the three-way model with unfolded data from all sessions across the time mode resulting in one large three-way tensor.

The benefit of the Tucker3D model in comparison to PARAFAC was already demonstrated in [11]. However, we observed a practical disadvantage of the model. The Tucker model algorithm is based on the Kronecker products [2]. For tensors with one mode of a large size, the Kronecker product matrices are large in size and they can require up to several GB of computer memory. Therefore, an appropriate optimisation of the algorithm may be needed if the number of analysed sessions grows. To address this problem, in this study, we also investigated the Tucker4D model, where the memory allocation is reduced.

For Tucker4D_N, the assumption of the non-negative time scores matrix $A^{(1)}$ showed to be inappropriate. The model showed significantly higher MSE than the Tucker3D and Tucker4D_O models. An improvement can be achieved by increasing the number of components to a multiple of the number of sessions. However, that leads to an unnecessarily complex model and possible numerical problems. Better results were observed for the alternative four-way Tucker4D_O model in which the columns of $A^{(1)}$ formed an orthogonal basis. In this case, the number of time scores was chosen to be at most $2 * J_3$. Using the estimated elements of the core tensor $\mathbb{G}$, the weighted linear combinations of the $A^{(1)}$ columns then represent the final time activation for an arbitrary atom.

The Tucker3D and Tucker4D_O models produced consistent results when validating obtained spatial and frequency signatures, as well as time scores. But what is more important, in both cases we were able to detect stable atoms which were consistent with the subject-specific atoms already detected by a combination of the PARAFAC model and a cluster analysis applied to each training session separately [10,11]. This was especially true for slower frequency rhythms (7 to 15 Hz), which are in the focus of the studied motor imagery related changes of EEG oscillatory activity.

We can conclude that both approaches showed comparable and adequate results when applied to the simultaneous analysis of multi-session recordings of multi-channel EEG. When the subject-specific atom extraction is in the focus, they provide a time-saving alternative to the tensor decomposition applied to each session separately.

Acknowledgment. This research was supported by the Slovak Research and Development Agency (grant APVV-16-0202) and by the VEGA grant 2/0081/19.

References

1. Bro, R., Kiers, H.A.L.: A new efficient method for determining the number of components in PARAFAC models. J. Chemom. **17**(5), 274–286 (2003). https://doi.org/10.1002/cem.801
2. Cichocki, A., Zdunek, R., Phan, A.H., Amari, S.I.: Nonnegative Matrix and Tensor Factorizations: Applications to Exploratory Multi-way Data Analysis and Blind Source Separation. Wiley, New York (2009). https://doi.org/10.1002/9780470747278
3. Cong, F., Lin, Q.H., Kuang, L.D., Gong, X.F., Astikainen, P., Ristaniemi, T.: Tensor decomposition of EEG signals: a brief review. J. Neurosci. Methods **248**, 56–69 (2015). https://doi.org/10.1016/j.jneumeth.2015.03.018
4. Ester, M., Kriegel, H.P., Sander, J., Xu, X.: A density-based algorithm for discovering clusters in large spatial databases with noise. In: Proceedings of the Second International Conference on Knowledge Discovery and Data Mining (KDD-96), pp. 226–231. AAAI Press (1996)
5. Harshman, R.A.: Foundations of the PARAFAC procedure: models and conditions for an "explanatory" multimodal factor analysis. In: UCLA Working Papers in Phonetics, vol. 16, no. 1 (1970)
6. Kiers, H.A.L.: Recent developments in three-mode factor analysis: constrained three-mode factor analysis and core rotations. In: Hayashi, C., Yajima, K., Bock, H.H., Ohsumi, N., Tanaka, Y., Baba, Y. (eds.) Data Science, Classification, and Related Methods. STUDIES CLASS, pp. 563–574. Springer, Tokyo (1998). https://doi.org/10.1007/978-4-431-65950-1_62

7. Miwakeichi, F., Martınez-Montes, E., Valdés-Sosa, P.A., Nishiyama, N., Mizuhara, H., Yamaguchi, Y.: Decomposing EEG data into space-time-frequency components using Parallel Factor Analysis. NeuroImage **22**(3), 1035–1045 (2004). https://doi.org/10.1016/j.neuroimage.2004.03.039

8. Rosipal, R., Porubcová, N., Cimrová, B., Farkaš, I.: Neurorehabilitation training based on mental imagery of movement (using a robotic splint) (2017). http://aiolos.um.savba.sk/~roman/rrLab/projects.html

9. Rosipal, R., Porubcová, N., Barančok, P., Cimrová, B., Farkaš, I., Trejo, L.J.: Effects of mirror-box therapy on modulation of sensorimotor EEG oscillatory rhythms: a single-case longitudinal study. J. Neurophysiol. **121**(2), 620–633 (2019). https://doi.org/10.1152/jn.00599.2018

10. Rošťáková, Z., Rosipal, R.: Three-way analysis of multichannel EEG data using the PARAFAC and Tucker models. In: 12th International Conference on Measurement, Smolenice, Slovakia, pp. 127–130 (2019). https://doi.org/10.23919/MEASUREMENT47340.2019.8780005

11. Rošťáková, Z., Rosipal, R., Seifpour, S., Trejo, L.J.: A comparison of non-negative Tucker decomposition and parallel factor analysis for identification and measurement of human EEG rhythms. Meas. Sci. Rev. **20**(3), 126–138 (2020). https://doi.org/10.2478/msr-2020-0015

12. Tucker, L.R.: Some mathematical notes on three-mode factor analysis. Psychometrika **31**(3), 279–311 (1966). https://doi.org/10.1007/BF02289464

13. Wen, H., Liu, Z.: Separating fractal and oscillatory components in the power spectrum of neurophysiological signal. Brain Topogr. **29**(1), 13–26 (2015). https://doi.org/10.1007/s10548-015-0448-0

Reactive Hand Movements from Arm Kinematics and EMG Signals Based on Hierarchical Gaussian Process Dynamical Models

Nick Taubert[1][(✉)], Jesse St. Amand[1], Prerana Kumar[1], Leonardo Gizzi[2], and Martin A. Giese[1]

[1] Section Computational Sensomotorics, Department of Cognitive Neurology, University Clinic Tübingen, CIN, HIH and University of Tübingen, Otfried-Müller-Str. 25, 72076 Tübingen, Germany
{nick.taubert,jesse.st-amand,martin.giese}@uni-tuebingen.de
[2] Institute for Modelling and Simulation of Biomechanical Systems, Chair for Continuum Biomechanics and Mechanobiology, University of Stuttgart, Stuttgart, Germany
leonardo.gizzi@mechbau.uni-stuttgart.de

Abstract. The prediction of finger kinematics from EMG signals is a difficult problem due to the high level of noise in recorded biological signals. In order to improve the quality of such predictions, we propose a Bayesian inference architecture that enables the combination of multiple sources of sensory information with an accurate and flexible model for the online prediction of high-dimensional kinematics. Our method integrates hierarchical Gaussian process latent variable models (GP-LVMs) for nonlinear dimension reduction with Gaussian process dynamical models (GPDMs) to represent movement dynamics in latent space. Using several additional approximations, we make the resulting sophisticated inference architecture real-time capable. Our results demonstrate that the prediction of hand kinematics can be substantially improved by inclusion of information from the online-measured arm kinematics, and by exploiting learned online generative models of finger kinematics. The proposed architecture provides a highly flexible framework for the integration of accurate generative models with high-dimensional motion in real-time inference and control problems.

Keywords: EMG · Decoding · Kinematics · Gaussian process · Dimension reduction

1 Introduction

Dynamical systems have been used extensively to model human motion [8, 18]. For example, networks of coupled dynamic movement primitives or 'central pattern generators' have been shown to describe coordinated motor patterns [14]. Applications in computer graphics and robotics have resulted in powerful methods for

© Springer Nature Switzerland AG 2020
I. Farkaš et al. (Eds.): ICANN 2020, LNCS 12396, pp. 127–140, 2020.
https://doi.org/10.1007/978-3-030-61609-0_11

modeling complex, high-dimensional, coordinated human motion. These models may be exploited in the context of prosthesis control applications, where often the available control signals (e.g. from electromyography (EMG)) are too low-dimensional or noisy to ensure accurate decoding of the desired actuator motion.

As a theoretical framework for this integration of neural signal decoding and synthesizing human motion, we propose probabilistic graphical models [1]. These models provide a highly flexible, systematic framework for modular model construction and realizing inference on arbitrary variables in such models. However, complex graphical models, due to the computational complexity of this inference, often do not easily transfer to online control applications or the online generation of human motion. Neither do many of the common methods for the offline synthesis of human motion, e.g. by motion capture and subsequent filtering or interpolation between stored trajectories [4], transfer easily to online synthesis applications. Based on a combination of GP-LVMs [22] with GPDMs [33], we propose here an implementation of a hierarchical probabilistic graphical model that is suitable for real-time inference. We exploit this architecture to estimate hand kinematics from EMG signals by a learned generative model of hand-arm coordination, with support by real-time kinematic data from the arm. This inferred hand motion can be used in the control of a hand orthosis for patients with unhindered arms, but impaired grasping abilities (e.g. due to stroke) [3].

2   Background

The industry standards and the typical benchmarks in research for online hand and arm myocontrol comprise the two-electrode "conventional control" approaches, co-contraction control (CC) and slope control (SC) [16]. Both require users to make targeted muscle contractions for switching between two single degrees of freedom (DOF) modes of control—operating a wrist rotation and opening/closing the hand. Users often consider these systems to be unintuitive compared to natural hand and arm function, difficult to use in everyday life, and to be fatiguing [11,16]. Other approaches exploiting classification and multiple DOFs regression methods have been shown to produce better results with the same hardware [16]. More advanced techniques have effectively employed methods of auto-encoding for dimensionality reduction [31], have utilized biomechanical models for imposing realistic system constraints [10,28], or have incorporated proprioceptive feedback or direct cortical feedback into sensory-motor brain areas [12]. Here, we explore the use of generative hierarchical Gaussian process models for establishing control by non-invasive EMG signals, augmented by predictive signals derived from the measurement of additional arm kinematic signals.

Probabilistic models for human motion have been used extensively in computer graphics for the synthesis of character motion [7], and for the editing and interpolation of motion styles [2,17,19]. Many of these techniques result in offline models that cannot react to online control inputs, while simple online control schemes often are not accurate enough to convey the exact motion characteristics.

GP-LVMs have been used for kinematic modeling and motion interpolation [15], inverse kinematics [24], and for the learning of low-dimensional dynamical models [34].

Gaussian processes (GPs) can be interpreted as probabilistic neural networks with a particular prior on the weights and biases in the limit of infinitely many hidden units [26]. The GP-LVM have been extended by latent dynamics in [33], resulting in an architecture that has been termed the Gaussian process dynamical model (GPDM). Due to its probabilistic nature, this model is well equipped to handle the variability of natural motion data, and it is possible to model full-body human motion with just one GPDM [29,30,33]. Here, we use a combination of GP-LVMs and GPDM to build a hierarchical GPDM with goal/style-content separation for modeling the kinematics of coordinated hand and arm movements. To achieve real-time performance, we approximate computationally costly inference steps by learning a fast, approximate inverse of our generative model with GP, which we refer to as *back-projection*. This way of making inference tractable was inspired by the Helmholtz Machine [9], which also learns an explicit inversion of a generative model.

3   Model Components

Our model architecture is shown in Fig. 1a. It is composed of a hierarchical combination of GP-LVMs, and a top level that is implemented by a GPDM-like dynamical layer.

3.1   GP-LVMs

In a GP-LVM, each point $\mathbf{y}_n$ of a high dimensional data set $\mathbf{Y} = [\mathbf{y}_1, \ldots, \mathbf{y}_N]^{\mathrm{T}} \in \Re^{N \times D}$ is represented by a corresponding, uncertain instance $\mathbf{x}_n$ of low dimensional latent variables $\mathbf{X} = [\mathbf{x}_1, \ldots, \mathbf{x}_N]^{\mathrm{T}} \in \Re^{N \times Q}$, where N is the length of the data set, D the dimension of the data space, and Q the dimension of the latent space. The mapping between the latent space and the components of the data is defined by a (typically nonlinear) function $f(\mathbf{x})$ that is drawn from a Gaussian process (with $\mathbf{y} = [y_1, \ldots, y_D]^{\mathrm{T}}$):

$$y_d = f_d(\mathbf{x}) + \varepsilon_d, \qquad f_d(\mathbf{x}) \sim GP(0, k_{\mathbf{f}}(\mathbf{x}, \mathbf{x}')) \tag{1}$$

where ε_d is white noise of the data, and $f_d(\mathbf{x})$ is drawn from a GP prior with zero mean function and kernel function $k_{\mathbf{f}}(\mathbf{x}, \mathbf{x}')$. We used composite kernel functions (see Eq. 14, 15, 18) which were composed of a radial basis function (RBF) and a linear kernel [27]:

$$k_{\mathrm{RBF}}(\mathbf{x}, \mathbf{x}') = \gamma_1 \exp\left(-\frac{\gamma_2}{2}|\mathbf{x} - \mathbf{x}'|^2\right) \tag{2}$$

$$k_{\mathrm{lin}}(\mathbf{x}, \mathbf{x}') = \gamma_3 \mathbf{x}^{\mathrm{T}} \mathbf{x}' \tag{3}$$

The RBF kernel models local structure in the data and has an inverse width γ_2. The linear kernel allows linear extrapolation and interpolation between data points. The other γ_i are positive weights.

We learned the parameters of the GP-LVMs by determining the latent variables that maximize their log-posterior, exploiting a scaled conjugate gradient (SCG) algorithm [22]. The evaluation of the log-posterior involves the inversion of a $N \times N$ kernel matrix $\mathbf{K_{ff}}$ which results from computing the kernel at every pair of latent points. This inversion has computational complexity $O(N^3)$ which is prohibitive for large data-sets, such as our motion capture recordings.

3.2 Sparse Aproximation

We solved this problem by a sparse approximation approach [6]. For this purpose, the noise free function value set $\mathbf{F} = [\mathbf{f}_1, \ldots, \mathbf{f}_N]^T$, where $\mathbf{f}_d = f_d(\mathbf{x})$ with $\mathbf{f} = [\mathbf{f}_1, \ldots, \mathbf{f}_D]^T$, is approximated by selection of a small set of $M \ll N$ pseudo-points $\mathbf{U} = [\mathbf{u}_1, \ldots, \mathbf{u}_M]^T$. It is assumed that training and test points of the Gaussian process are approximately conditionally independent, if conditioned on their pseudo-points. Under this assumption, the GP prior can be approximated as follows:

$$q(\mathbf{f}|\boldsymbol{\theta}) = \int p(\mathbf{f}|\mathbf{u}, \boldsymbol{\theta})p(\mathbf{u}|\boldsymbol{\theta})\,\mathrm{d}\mathbf{u}, \tag{4}$$

where $\boldsymbol{\theta}$ are the model hyperparameters and $p(\mathbf{u}|\boldsymbol{\theta})$ is the GP prior over $\mathbf{u}$. The conditional relationship between $\mathbf{u}$ and $\mathbf{f}$ is fundamental for this equation. With the GP priors $p(\mathbf{f}|\boldsymbol{\theta})$ and $p(\mathbf{u}|\boldsymbol{\theta})$ it is possible to derive from their joint probability the conditional dependency. This leads to the result $p(\mathbf{f}|\mathbf{u}, \boldsymbol{\theta}) = \mathcal{N}(\mathbf{f}; \mathbf{K_{fu}K_{uu}^{-1}u}, \mathbf{D_{ff}})$ where $\mathbf{D_{ff}} = \mathbf{K_{ff}} - \mathbf{Q_{ff}}$ and $\mathbf{Q_{ff}} = \mathbf{K_{fu}K_{uu}^{-1}K_{uf}}$. The constructed matrices correspond to the covariance function evaluations at the pseudo-point input locations $\{[\mathbf{x_u}]_m\}_{m=1}^M$, i.e. $[\mathbf{K_{uu}}]_{m,m'} = k_{\mathbf{f}}([\mathbf{x_u}]_m, [\mathbf{x_u}]_{m'})$ and similarly covariance function evaluations between pseudo-point input and data locations $[\mathbf{K_{fu}}]_{n,m} = k_{\mathbf{f}}(\mathbf{x}_n, [\mathbf{x_u}]_m)$. Unfortunately, even this equation is still cubic in terms of its computational complexity. However, the matrices of $p(\mathbf{f}|\mathbf{u}, \boldsymbol{\theta})$ can be approximated by simpler forms, resulting in computationally tractable distributions with $q(\mathbf{f}|\mathbf{u}, \boldsymbol{\theta}) \approx p(\mathbf{f}|\mathbf{u}, \boldsymbol{\theta})$ [5]. We chose a subset of pseudo-inputs which parameterize the GP prior through the Deterministic Training Conditional (DTC) approximation [20] in order to ensure real-time capability for prediction and to render our approach feasible for larger data sets,

$$q(\mathbf{f}|\mathbf{u}, \boldsymbol{\theta}) = \mathcal{N}(\mathbf{f}|\mathbf{K_{fu}K_{uu}^{-1}u}, \mathbf{0}). \tag{5}$$

This approximation assumes that $f(\mathbf{x})$ is fully determined by the pseudo-point inputs and reduces the computational cost to $O(M^2 N)$ during learning. The prior $q(\mathbf{f}|\boldsymbol{\theta})$ with DTC approximation can be combined with the likelihood $p(\mathbf{y}_d|\mathbf{f}_d, \boldsymbol{\theta}) = \mathcal{N}(\mathbf{y}_d|\mathbf{f}_d, \gamma_4^{-1}\mathbf{I})$:

$$p(\mathbf{Y}|\theta) = \prod_{d=1}^{D} \int p(\mathbf{y}_{:,d}|\mathbf{f}_{:,d}, \boldsymbol{\theta})q(\mathbf{f}_{:,d}|\boldsymbol{\theta})\,\mathrm{d}\mathbf{f}_d \tag{6}$$

$$= \prod_{d=1}^{D} \mathcal{N}(\mathbf{y}_{:,d}|\mathbf{0}, \mathbf{K_{fu}K_{uu}^{-1}K_{uf}} + \gamma_4^{-1}\mathbf{I}). \tag{7}$$

where γ_4 is the noise precision into which any Gaussian observation noise can be absorbed and $\mathbf{y}_{:,d}, \mathbf{f}_{:,d}$ are the vectors for the dth dimension of $\mathbf{Y}$ and $\mathbf{F}$. Combined with priors $p(\mathbf{X})$ and $p(\boldsymbol{\theta})$ we got the log-marginal, reformulated with matrix inversion lemma [20] for $O(M^2 N)$:

$$\mathcal{L} = -\frac{D(N-M)}{2} \ln 2\pi - \frac{\gamma_4}{2} \mathrm{tr}(\mathbf{Y}\mathbf{Y}^T) \frac{D}{2} \ln |\mathbf{K}_{uu}^{-1}| + \frac{D}{2} \ln |\mathbf{A}| \qquad (8)$$

$$-\frac{\gamma_4}{2} \mathrm{tr}(\mathbf{A}^{-1}\mathbf{K}_{uf}\mathbf{Y}\mathbf{Y}^T\mathbf{K}_{fu}) - \frac{1}{2}\sum_{n=1}^{N} \mathbf{x}_n^T \mathbf{x}_n - \sum_j \ln \gamma_j, \qquad (9)$$

with $\mathbf{A} = \gamma_4^{-1}\mathbf{K}_{uu} - \mathbf{K}_{uf}\mathbf{K}_{fu}$. This implies that the computation time depends only on the number of pseudo- and test inputs, which enables real-time performance.

For the prior function of new test data $p(\tilde{\mathbf{Y}}|\boldsymbol{\theta})$, we followed the same derivations as in Eqs. (4)–(7), replacing $\mathbf{f}$ with test function values $\tilde{\mathbf{f}}$, assumed conditional independence between $\tilde{\mathbf{f}}$ and $\mathbf{f}$. With the joint probability of the new GP priors $p(\mathbf{Y}|\boldsymbol{\theta})$ and $p(\tilde{\mathbf{Y}}|\boldsymbol{\theta})$, a posterior distribution $p(\tilde{\mathbf{y}}|\mathbf{Y}, \mathbf{X}, \mathbf{x}_*, \boldsymbol{\theta})$ for the prediction of new test outputs $\tilde{\mathbf{y}}$ with given test inputs $\mathbf{x}_*$ can be derived [21],

$$\tilde{\mathbf{y}} \sim \mathcal{N}(\mu(\mathbf{x}_*), \sigma(\mathbf{x}_*)), \qquad (10)$$

where

$$\mu(\mathbf{x}_*) = \mathbf{K}_{*u}\mathbf{A}^{-1}\mathbf{K}_{uf}\mathbf{Y}, \qquad (11)$$

$$\sigma(\mathbf{x}_*) = \mathbf{K}_{**} - \mathbf{K}_{*u}(\mathbf{K}_{uu} - \mathbf{A}^{-1})\mathbf{K}_{*u}^T, \qquad (12)$$

where $\mathbf{K}_{**}$ is the kernel function evaluated at the test inputs, $\mathbf{K}_{*u}$ is the kernel function evaluated at the test and pseudo-point inputs.

3.3 GPDM

In order to model the dynamics of our data in the latent space—that which is given by the temporal evolution of the columns of the inferred input matrix $\mathbf{X}$, we used a Gausian Process Dynamical Model (GPDM) [33]. This is a GP-LVM with autoregressive dynamics for the hidden variables $\mathbf{x}_n$. These dynamics are given by a nonlinear auto-regressive model of the form:

$$\mathbf{x}_n = f_{\mathbf{x}}(\mathbf{x}_{n-1}, \ldots, \mathbf{x}_{n-z}) + \xi, \qquad (13)$$

where z is the order of the dynamics (we used $z = 2$), and where $f_{\mathbf{x}}(\cdot)$ is also drawn from a Gaussian process prior with the associated kernel function:

$$k_{\mathrm{dyn}}([\mathbf{x}_{n-1}, \mathbf{x}_{n-2}], [\mathbf{x}_{\eta-1}, \mathbf{x}_{\eta-2}])$$
$$= \gamma_5 \exp\left(-\frac{\gamma_6}{2}|\mathbf{x}_{n-1} - \mathbf{x}_{\eta-1}|^2 - \frac{\gamma_7}{2}|\mathbf{x}_{n-2} - \mathbf{x}_{\eta-2}|^2\right) \qquad (14)$$
$$+ \gamma_8 \mathbf{x}_{n-1}^T \mathbf{x}_{\eta-1} + \gamma_9 \mathbf{x}_{n-2}^T \mathbf{x}_{\eta-2}.$$

This is again a combination of non-linear and linear kernel functions. This autoregressive model defines a Markov chain and generalizes a hidden Markov model (HMM) [25] in a non-linear way.

4   Hierarchical Model Architecture

For the representation of goal-dependent hand movements, we devised a hierarchical model that consists of GP-LVMs for successive dimension reduction, and of a GPDM in the highest layer for the representation of the dynamics in the latent space (cf. Fig. 1a). The model is composed of three layers, which were learned jointly. Learning includes both the bottom-up and top-down contributions at each hierarchy level.

The proposed model can be run in two different modes: (i) As a *fully generative model*, where the complete hand-arm kinematics is generated online, dependent on an external variable that controls the goal position; (ii) as a *partially generative model*, where the goal position is inferred online from measured arm kinematics and/or EMG signals. In this case these variables are treated as observed nodes in the graphical model, and the other variables are inferred

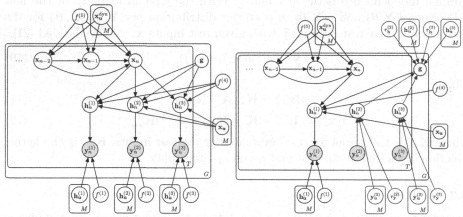

a) Graphical model of the hierarchical GPDM.   b) Back-projection of the hierarchical GPDM.

Fig. 1. *Hierarchical probabilistic model.* **(a)** Three data structures $\mathbf{Y}^{(i)}, i \in \{1,2,3\}$ including the arm kinematic data, the hand kinematic data, and the EMG data are represented by sparse GP-LVMs, each over T trials and G goal positions. Each data structure is mapped by a prior mapping function $f^{(i)}(\cdot)$ drawn from a GP prior with a lower-dimensional latent variable $\mathbf{h}^{(i)}$. For each a set M pseudo-input variables $\mathbf{h}_u^{(i)}$ are specified for sparse approximation. The dimensionality of the variables $\mathbf{h}^{(i)}$ on the middle level of the model is further reduced by a sparse GP-LVM in the same way, with the hidden state variables $\mathbf{x}$, the corresponding inducing variables $\mathbf{x}_u^{(i)}$, and the style variable $\mathbf{g}$. The temporal evolution of the hidden state variables $\mathbf{x}_n$ is modeled with second order dynamics using a GPDM also drawn from a GP prior $f^{(5)}$. Corresponding inducing variables for the sparse representation are signified by $\mathbf{x}_u^{\mathrm{dyn}}$. **(b)** Back-projection mapping (blue) from data space of $\mathbf{y}^{(j)}, j \in \{2,3\}$ to the latent spaces $\mathbf{h}^{(j)}$, using sparse GP regressions with prior functions $r_{\mathbf{y}}^{(j)}$ and the pseudo-inputs $\mathbf{y}_u^{(j)}$. Similarly, a back-projection from $\mathbf{h}^{(j)}$ to $\mathbf{g}$ is computed with the function prior $r_{\mathbf{h}}^{(j)}$ and pseudo-input $\mathbf{h}_u^{(j)}$. (Color figure online)

by Bayesian model inversion. For the separation of style and content [32], style referring here to the goal position, we introduced a specific goal/style variable **g** that captures specifically the goal position, which either is pre-specified in the fully generative mode, or inferred in the partially generative mode.

4.1 Individual Layers

Bottom Layer. The bottom layer of our model represents the observed kinematic data of the hand, the kinematic velocity data of the arm, and the EMG data as matrices $\mathbf{Y}^{(i)}, i \in \{1; 2; 3\}$. The dimensionality of each of these data sets is reduced by a sparse GP-LVM with the same sample size ($N^{(i)} = 1440$), but different dimensionalities of the data vectors ($D_{\mathbf{y}}^{(1)} = 63, D_{\mathbf{y}}^{(2)} = 15, D_{\mathbf{y}}^{(3)} = 28$). For each data type, a separate set of mapping functions is used with their own GP prior $f^{(i)}(\cdot)$ to map the latent variables $\mathbf{h}^{(i)}$ onto the corresponding data vectors, according to Eq. (1). The dimensionalities of the hidden variable vectors are $Q_{\mathbf{h}}^{(1)} = 10$, $Q_{\mathbf{h}}^{(2)} = 4$, and $Q_{\mathbf{h}}^{(3)} = 15$. The kernel functions in this layer are given by a linear combination of the RBF and the linear kernel functions defined in Eqs. (2), (3) to capture the nonlinearity of the data and support smooth blending between styles:

$$k_{\mathbf{f}}^{(i)}(\mathbf{h}^{(i)}, \mathbf{h}'^{(i)}) = k_{\mathrm{rbf}}(\mathbf{h}^{(i)}, \mathbf{h}'^{(i)}) + k_{\mathrm{lin}}(\mathbf{h}^{(i)}, \mathbf{h}'^{(i)}). \tag{15}$$

Intermediate Layer. For further dimensionality reduction, an additional sparse GP-LVM was introduced that maps from the latent variable $\mathbf{x}$ ($Q_{\mathbf{x}} = 2$) onto the concatenation of the variables $\mathbf{h}^{(i)}$. We assume that $\mathbf{h}^{(i)}$ is represented in the same latent space across trials, number of goals, and time steps.

A key assumption in our approach is that the goal positions can be modeled by a separate 'style variable' **g**. During the learning of the model parameters, we separate the motion content, i.e. the basic shape of the trajectories, from this motion style variable, using a factorial representation. For the partially generative model, we infer the style variable **g** online from the measured EMG and kinematic data of the arm. To promote such a factorization of the latent variables in terms of motion content and style dimensions, we applied *back-constraints* during learning [23]. This method constrains the hidden space variable to a low-dimensional manifold in a way that ensures that close points in the data space remain close in the latent space. Adjusting the gradient steps during optimization, we enforced the components of **x** to lie on a circular manifold for all styles that are given by the functions z_1 and z_2 [30]:

$$x_{n,1} = z_1([\mathbf{h}^{(1)}, \mathbf{h}^{(2)}, \mathbf{h}^{(3)}]_n, \phi_n) = \sum_{\tau=1}^{N} c_{\tau,1} k_{\mathrm{rbf}}(\cos(\phi_n), \cos(\phi_\tau)) \tag{16}$$

$$x_{n,2} = z_2([\mathbf{h}^{(1)}, \mathbf{h}^{(2)}, \mathbf{h}^{(3)}]_n, \phi_n) = \sum_{\tau=1}^{N} c_{\tau,2} k_{\mathrm{rbf}}(\sin(\phi_n), \sin(\phi_\tau)) \tag{17}$$

The variable ϕ_n specifies the motion phase, and the coefficients $c_{\tau,i}$ were chosen to ensure that the latent points lie (approximately) on a circle for all motion 'styles'.

The motion style variable $\mathbf{g}$, which specifies the reaching goal, was initially specified using 1-of-K encodings [1], each goal being specified by a (eight-dimensional) unit vector (goal 1: $\mathbf{g}_1$, goal 2: $\mathbf{g}_2$, etc.) which will also be optimized. In order to blend linearly between the behaviors for the different goals, we used a linear kernel for the 'style' dimensions. The composite kernel function for the middle layer of our model was thus given by (Eqs. (2), (3)):

$$k_{\mathbf{h}}([\mathbf{x}, \mathbf{g}], [\mathbf{x}', \mathbf{g}']) = k_{\mathrm{lin}}(\mathbf{g}, \mathbf{g}')k_{\mathrm{rbf}}(\mathbf{x}, \mathbf{x}') + k_{\mathrm{lin}}(\mathbf{x}, \mathbf{x}'). \qquad (18)$$

Similar to the multi-factor model [32], the multiplication of style and latent position act similarly to a logical 'AND' operation. The resulting kernel matrix links each goal point to a pair of latent points.

Top Layer. The top layer represents the temporal evolution of $\mathbf{x}_n$, i.e. the underlying dynamics. We used a second-order GPDM, which allowed us to model the dynamical dependencies on velocity and acceleration of $\mathbf{X}$. The evolution function for $\mathbf{x}_n$ is given by Eq. (13). We drew the function $f_{\mathbf{x}}(\cdot)$ from a GP with the kernel given in Eq. (14), where we learned the model with multiple motion sequences (T trials for G goals, see Fig. 1a), assuming they are i.i.d. samples from the complete model.

In order to accelerate the inference of the partially generative model, we introduced an explicit learning of the back-projections from the hidden variables $\mathbf{h}^{(2)}$ and $\mathbf{h}^{(3)}$ that represent the EMG and the arm kinematics to the variable $\mathbf{h}^{(1)}$ that represents the hand kinematics. These mappings were again represented by sparsely approximated Gaussian process regressions with the function priors $r_{\mathbf{y}}^{(j)}$, $j \in \{2, 3\}$ (blue elements in Fig. 1b):

$$\mathbf{h}^{(j)} = r_{\mathbf{y}}^{(j)}(\mathbf{y}^{(j)}) + \boldsymbol{\epsilon}^{(j)}, \quad r_{\mathbf{y}}^{(j)}(\mathbf{y}^{(j)}) \sim GP(\mathbf{0}, k_{\mathrm{back}}^{(j)}(\mathbf{y}^{(j)}, \mathbf{y}'^{(i)})), \qquad (19)$$

The kernel was given by $k_{\mathrm{back}}^{(j)}(\mathbf{y}^{(j)}, \mathbf{y}'^{(i)}) = k_{\mathrm{rbf}}^{(j)}(\mathbf{y}^{(j)}, \mathbf{y}'^{(i)}) + k_{\mathrm{lin}}^{(j)}(\mathbf{y}^{(j)}, \mathbf{y}'^{(i)})$, and $\boldsymbol{\epsilon}^{(j)}$ is Gaussian noise. As for a usual GP regression, only the kernel parameters are optimized during this step, while the latent variables for both layers were kept fixed. In an equivalent way, we introduced explicit back-projections for the second layer to predict the style variable $\mathbf{g}$.

4.2   Motion Generation and Prediction

In the fully generative mode, our model, after training, predicts the hand kinematics (and also the arm kinematics and EMG signals) from a defined goal position. In the partially generative mode, it generates the hand kinematics from the arm kinematics and/or the EMG signals, estimating the likely goal position $\mathbf{g}$ from the available input data, while exploiting the back-projections for fast inference.

In both cases, the top dynamic layer ensures the generation of smooth hand motion. Given the states for the previous time steps, the GPDM predicts a novel state according to Eq. (10):

$$\tilde{\mathbf{x}}_n \cong \mu_{\mathbf{x}}([\tilde{\mathbf{x}}_{n-1}, \tilde{\mathbf{x}}_{n-2}]). \tag{20}$$

In the fully generative mode, the predicted state is propagated down the hierarchy to predict the original data components $\tilde{\mathbf{y}}_n^{(i)}$ according to the relationships:

$$\tilde{\mathbf{h}}_n^{(i)} \cong \mu_{\mathbf{h}}([\tilde{\mathbf{x}}_n, \mathbf{g}_*]), \tag{21}$$
$$\tilde{\mathbf{y}}_n^{(i)} \cong \mu_{\mathbf{y}}(\tilde{\mathbf{h}}_n^{(i)}). \tag{22}$$

The functions $\mu_i(.)$ are following from the posteriors of the individual layers. The goal information is added through the variable $\mathbf{g}_*$ in this equation, for which values can be chosen that interpolate between the training goals' vectors, resulting in continuously interpolated intermediate goal positions.

In the partially generative mode, the goal vector $\mathbf{g}$ is predicted from the measurements $\mathbf{y}_*^{(j)}$, $j \in \{2, 3\}$, through the back-projections, according to the relationships:

$$\tilde{\mathbf{h}}_n^{(j)} \cong \mu_{\mathbf{h}}(\mathbf{y}_*^{(j)}) \tag{23}$$
$$\tilde{\mathbf{g}} \cong \mu_{\mathbf{g}}^{(j)}(\tilde{\mathbf{h}}_n^{(j)}) \tag{24}$$

For the models with two predictive variables $\tilde{\mathbf{h}}_n^{(j)}$, the estimates were combined using a maximum a posteriori framework. The style vector estimate is then combined with the predicted state $\tilde{\mathbf{x}}_n$ from the dynamics and projected down to predict the hand kinematics $\tilde{\mathbf{y}}_n^{(1)}$ according to:

$$\tilde{\mathbf{h}}_n^{(1)} \cong \mu_{\mathbf{h}}([\tilde{\mathbf{x}}_n, \tilde{\mathbf{g}}]), \tag{25}$$
$$\tilde{\mathbf{y}}_n^{(1)} \cong \mu_{\mathbf{y}}(\tilde{\mathbf{h}}_n^{(1)}). \tag{26}$$

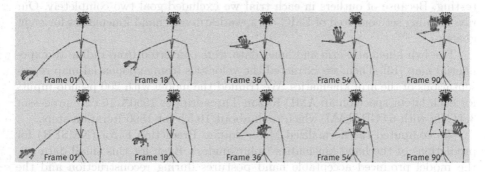

Fig. 2. *Frames from animations illustrating the results.* Prediction examples of hand and finger orientations over time for goal 1 (top row) and goal 09 (bottom row). Predicted hand kinematics are shown in red, and the corresponding ground truth data are in blue. (Color figure online)

5 Results

5.1 Data Set

In order to test the performance of our approach, we applied it to a data set with grasping movements that included kinematic data from the arm and the hand, and HD-sEMG data from 3 high-density 8×8 surface electrode arrays (OT Bioelettronica) placed around the forearm, and from 16 bipolar sEMG electrodes on the larger muscles of the upper arm, shoulder, chest, and back. EMG recordings were done with an OT Bioelettronica Quattrocento 400 channel desktop amplifier (OTBioelettronica, Torino, IT) and three EMG pre-amplifiers. Samples were taken at 2,848 Hz, with an amplification gain of 150 V/V, and an online bandpass filter between 10 900 Hz. MOCAP recordings were conducted through VICON Nexus version 2.8 using eight VICON infrared cameras at 256.41 Hz.

Reaching movements were performed by a healthy, left-handed, adult male (39 years old, 178 cm tall, 82 kg) with no prior record of neuromuscular disease. Grasped objects were mounted on a vertical panel in the form of a rectangular 3×3 grid with a distance of 25 cm between the objects. All movements started from a resting position next to the hip.

EMG signals were processed by digital band-pass filtering between 20–450 Hz with a fourth-order Butterworth filter. A second-order Butterworth filter was applied as a band-stop filter between 49–51 Hz to remove power line interference. The signals were full-wave rectified and processed with a low-pass, second-order Butterworth filter 10 Hz to extract the linear envelope.

5.2 Model Evaluation

We applied our method to infer the hand kinematics (63 DOFs) from either the arm kinematics (velocities) (15 DOF), the EMG signals, or from both (see Fig. 2). In total, we learned 16 motion trajectories. Due to outliers in the EMG data, we selected only two trials per goal for learning and one trial per goal for testing. Because of outliers in each trial we excluded goal two completely. Our raw training set consisted of EMG data, and arm and hand kinematics for eight goals.

The bvh kinematic arm and hand data were converted from radian to exponential map [13]. Then, we extracted the velocities from exponential map representations of the arm kinematics. We trained the model with 200 pseudo-inputs for each latent space on an AMD Ryzon Threadripper 1950X 16 core processor 3.4 GHz with 64 GB RAM, which took about 10.5 h for 1500 iteration steps.

We computed the normalized Mean Square Prediction Error (NMSPR) for predictions of the hand kinematics (joint angles). Even for this small data set, the model produced acceptable hand postures during reconstruction and the NMSPRs for the hand kinematics were smaller for predictions from the arm kinematics than for predictions from the EMG. Combining the prediction from EMG and arm kinematics reduced the prediction error substantially compared to the prediction from EMG alone.

Table 1. *Normalized Mean Square Prediction Error (NMSPR) for hand kinematics and goal position.* Prediction from arm velocities results in the smallest prediction error.

Hand NMSPR				Goal NMSPR			
Goals	EMG + Velocity	EMG	Velocity	Goals	EMG + Velocity	EMG	Velocity
Goal 01	0.2425	0.2549	0.2472	Goal 01	0.3317	0.2885	0.3377
Goal 03	0.2380	0.2852	0.2477	Goal 03	0.2964	0.3150	0.2578
Goal 04	0.3692	0.4450	0.2795	Goal 04	0.3682	0.4302	0.2860
Goal 05	0.3368	0.3851	0.3109	Goal 05	0.2488	0.4081	0.3458
Goal 06	0.2865	0.3657	0.2436	Goal 06	0.3463	0.4081	0.2631
Goal 07	0.3701	0.4206	0.3191	Goal 07	0.3508	0.4874	0.3563
Goal 08	0.3920	0.4153	0.2992	Goal 08	0.4040	0.4813	0.3170
Goal 09	0.2120	0.2091	0.1802	Goal 09	0.2864	0.2561	0.1918
Average	0.3059	0.3476	**0.2659**	Average	0.3291	0.3844	**0.2944**

We also analyzed the classification of the goal from the last 20 stimulus frames based on the latent space variable g. The predicted classification was determined by the largest element of the inferred variable, which corresponds to the most likely class. The right part of Table 1 shows the NMSPR for the resulting predicted vectorial binary classification vectors relative to the ground truth, which is given by the true classes defined by the individual goals. Also for this measure, classification is best from the arm kinematics, and including the arm kinematics in the prediction improves accuracy compared to predictions derived from EMG alone.

An additional important point is that the proposed algorithm achieves *real-time performance* for online prediction of the hand kinematics. Running the algorithm on the same computer used for optimization, the prediction time per frame was on average about 23.74 ms.

6   Conclusion

Combining several methods from Bayesian unsupervised learning and inference, we have devised a new real-time-capable method for the simulation of reactive hand movements controlled by EMG. The high flexibility of the underlying inference framework was exploited to combine the EMG with additional kinematic data from the arm. Our model successfully predicted hand positions relative to the goal objects and reproduced hand kinematics with acceptable accuracy. Predictions derived from arm kinematics were more accurate for the tested data set than were the reconstructions from EMG. In addition, the accuracy of the reconstruction from EMG could be significantly improved by adding information from arm kinematics. The superiority of arm kinematics might be a consequence of our data set, which did not include transitions between different grip types, or supination movements. Such a variation in the dataset might give predictive power to the forearm HD-sEMG signals, enabling the disambiguation of movements that cannot be derived from the arm kinematics alone.

Despite the sophistication of the underlying probabilistic model, we have demonstrated that the algorithm is real-time-capable on a standard hardware. To our knowledge, underlying, advanced statistical methods such as GPDMs or inference on hierarchical GP-LVMs have never been tested and prepared for real-time applications. In our implementations real-time capability could be achieved by inclusion of several additional approximations, such as explicit back-projections and sparse approximations.

Future work will extend such architectures by applying variational optimization with better approximation methods to enable deep architectures with increased scalability. This will enable testing of these algorithms on much bigger data sets. Furthermore, we plan to implement the architecture with GPU computing for faster learning and inference.

Acknowledgments. The authors thank the International Max Planck Research School for Intelligent Systems (IMPRS-IS) for supporting Jesse St. Amand. We would also like to thank Albert Mukovskiy for his invaluable insight and code regarding the pre-processing of our EMG and kinematic data. This research was funded through HFSP RGP0036/2016, BMBF FKZ 01GQ1704, KONSENS-NHE BW Stiftung NEU007/1, DFG GZ: KA 1258/15-1, ERC 2019-SyGRELEVANCE-856495.

References

1. Bishop, C.M.: Pattern Recognition and Machine Learning. Springer, New York (2007)
2. Brand, M., Hertzmann, A.: Style machines. In: Proceedings of the SIGGRAPH 2000, pp. 183–192 (2000)
3. Brokaw, E., Black, I., Holley, R., Lum, P.: Hand spring operated movement enhancer (handsome): a portable, passive hand exoskeleton for stroke rehabilitation. IEEE Trans. Neural Syst. Rehabil. Eng. **19**, 391–399 (2011)
4. Bruderlin, A., Williams, L.: Motion signal processing. In: Proceedings of the SIGGRAPH 1995, pp. 97–104. ACM (1995)
5. Bui, T.D.: Efficient Deterministic Approximate Bayesian Inference for Gaussian Process models, September 2017
6. Quiñonero Candela, J., Rasmussen, C.E.: A unifying view of sparse approximate Gaussian process regression. J. Mach. Learn. Res. **6**, 1939–1959 (2005)
7. Chai, J., Hodgins, J.K.: Performance animation from low-dimensional control signals. ACM Trans. Graph. **24**(3), 686–696 (2005)
8. Churchland, M., et al.: Neural population dynamics during reaching. Nature **487**, 51–6 (2012)
9. Dayan, P., Hinton, G., Neal, R., Zemel, R.: The Helmholtz machine. Neural Comput. **7**, 1022–1037 (1995)
10. Farina, D., et al.: Man/machine interface based on the discharge timings of spinal motor neurons after targeted muscle reinnervation. Nature Biomed. Eng. **1**, 0025 (2017)
11. Franzke, A., et al.: Users' and therapists' perceptions of myoelectric multi-function upper limb prostheses with conventional and pattern recognition control. PLOS ONE **14**, e0220899 (2019)

12. Ganzer, P.D., et al.: Restoring the sense of touch using a sensorimotor demulti-plexing neural interface. Cell **181**, 1–11 (2020)
13. Grassia, F.S.: Practical parameterization of rotations using the exponential map. J. Graph. Tools **3**(3), 29–48 (1998)
14. Grillner, S., Wallen, P.: Central pattern generators for locomotion, with special reference to vertebrates. Ann. Rev. Neurosci. **8**(1), 233–261 (1985)
15. Grochow, K., Martin, S.L., Hertzmann, A., Popovic, Z.: Style-based inverse kine-matics. ACM Trans. Graph. **23**(3), 522–531 (2004)
16. Hahne, J.M., Schweisfurth, M.A., Koppe, M., Farina, D.: Simultaneous control of multiple functions of bionic hand prostheses: performance and robustness in end users. Sci. Robot. **3**(19) (2018). https://robotics.sciencemag.org/content/3/19/eaat3630
17. Ikemoto, L., Arikan, O., Forsyth, D.A.: Generalizing motion edits with Gaussian processes. ACM Trans. Graph. **28**(1), 1:1–1:12 (2009)
18. Jeka, J., Kelso, S.: Manipulating symmetry in the coordination dynamics of human movement. J. Exp. Psychol. Hum. Perception Perform. **21**, 360–74 (1995)
19. Lau, M., Bar-Joseph, Z., Kuffner, J.: Modeling spatial and temporal variation in motion data. ACM Trans. Graph. **28**(5), 171 (2009)
20. Lawrence, N.: Learning for larger datasets with the Gaussian process latent variable model. J. Mach. Learn. Res. Proceedings Track **2**, 243–250 (2007)
21. Lawrence, N.D.: Large scale learning with the Gaussian process latent variable model. Technical report cs-06-05, University of Sheffield (2006)
22. Lawrence, N.D., Moore, A.J.: Hierarchical Gaussian process latent variable models. In: Proceedings of ICML, pp. 481–488. Omnipress (2007)
23. Lawrence, N.D., Court, R., Science, C.: Local distance preservation in the GP-LVM through back constraints. In: ICML, pp. 513–520 (2006)
24. Levine, S., Wang, J.M., Haraux, A., Popović, Z., Koltun, V.: Continuous character control with low-dimensional embeddings. ACM Trans. Graph. **31**(4), 1–10 (2012)
25. Li, X., Parizeau, M., Plamondon, R.: Training hidden Markov models with multiple observations-a combinatorial method. IEEE Trans. Pattern Anal. Mach. Intell. **22**(4), 371–377 (2000)
26. Neal, R.: Bayesian Learning for Neural Networks. Ph.D. thesis, Department of Computer Science, University of Toronto (1994)
27. Rasmussen, C.E., Williams, C.K.I.: Gaussian processes for machine learning. J. Am. Stat. Assoc. **103**, 429–429 (2008)
28. Sartori, M., Durandau, G., Dosen, S., Farina, D.: Robust simultaneous myoelec-tric control of multiple degrees of freedom in wrist-hand prostheses by real-time neuromusculoskeletal modeling. J. Neural Eng. **15**(6) (2018)
29. Taubert, N., Endres, D., Christensen, A., Giese, M.A.: Shaking hands in latent space. In: Bach, J., Edelkamp, S. (eds.) KI 2011. LNCS (LNAI), vol. 7006, pp. 330–334. Springer, Heidelberg (2011). https://doi.org/10.1007/978-3-642-24455-1_32
30. Urtasun, R., Fleet, D.J., Lawrence, N.D.: Modeling human locomotion with topo-logically constrained latent variable models (2007). Workshop on Human Motion: Understanding, Modeling, Capture and Animation
31. Vujaklija, I., Shalchyan, V., Kamavuako, E., Jiang, N., Marateb, H., Farina, D.: Online mapping of EMG signals into kinematics by autoencoding. J. Neuroeng. Rehabil. **15**(1), 21 (2018)
32. Wang, J.M., Fleet, D.J., Hertzmann, A.: Multifactor Gaussian process models for style-content separation. In: Proceedings of ICML (2007)

33. Wang, J.M., Fleet, D.J., Hertzmann, A.: Gaussian process dynamical models for human motion. IEEE Trans. Pattern Anal. Mach. Intell. **30**(2), 283–298 (2008)
34. Ye, Y., Liu, C.K.: Synthesis of responsive motion using a dynamic model. Comput. Graph. Forum **29**(2), 555–562 (2010)

Cognitive Models

Investigating Efficient Learning and Compositionality in Generative LSTM Networks

Sarah Fabi$^{(\boxtimes)}$, Sebastian Otte, Jonas Gregor Wiese, and Martin V. Butz

Neuro-Cognitive Modeling Group, Eberhard Karls University Tübingen,
Tübingen, Germany
sarah.fabi@uni-tuebingen.de

Abstract. When comparing human with artificial intelligence, one major difference is apparent: Humans can generalize very broadly from sparse data sets because they are able to recombine and reintegrate data components in compositional manners. To investigate differences in efficient learning, Joshua B. Tenenbaum and colleagues developed the character challenge: First an algorithm is trained in generating handwritten characters. In a next step, one version of a new type of character is presented. An efficient learning algorithm is expected to be able to re-generate this new character, to identify similar versions of this character, to generate new variants of it, and to create completely new character types. In the past, the character challenge was only met by complex algorithms that were provided with stochastic primitives. Here, we tackle the challenge without providing primitives. We apply a minimal recurrent neural network (RNN) model with one feedforward layer and one LSTM layer and train it to generate sequential handwritten character trajectories from one-hot encoded inputs. To manage the re-generation of untrained characters when presented with only one example of them, we introduce a one-shot inference mechanism: the gradient signal is back-propagated to the feedforward layer weights only, leaving the LSTM layer untouched. We show that our model is able to meet the character challenge by recombining previously learned dynamic substructures, which are visible in the hidden LSTM states. Making use of the compositional abilities of RNNs in this way might be an important step towards bridging the gap between human and artificial intelligence.

Keywords: Generative RNN · LSTMs · Efficient learning · Compositionality · Character challenge

1 Introduction

Despite numerous recent success stories with Deep Learning (DL) [10] including game playing as well as image and speech recognition, over the last years various limitations in DL have been uncovered. One important issue lies in the fact that DL algorithms lack mechanisms that lead to the development of hierarchical, generative structures in a natural way [11]. Current DL algorithms essentially

© Springer Nature Switzerland AG 2020
I. Farkaš et al. (Eds.): ICANN 2020, LNCS 12396, pp. 143–154, 2020.
https://doi.org/10.1007/978-3-030-61609-0_12

learn correlations between features on a flat plane. When dealing with hierarchical problems, approximations are applied, which are often incorrect and do not generalize well. As a result, DL algorithms are still easily fooled [12] and are not particularly or naturally noise-robust [2].

Following the same line of reasoning, Lake and colleagues [6] stated that Recurrent Neural Networks (RNNs) do not develop compositional representations. That is, they are not able to parse an object or event into its components and flexibly recombine them in novel ways, making generalization hard, especially when training and test sets differ significantly. A related phenomenon was also analyzed by Otte and colleagues [13], showing that the compositional disentanglement of superimposed dynamics is only possible when additional inductive learning biases of modularization and error distribution are added to the standard backpropagation through time weight adaptation mechanism in RNNs.

In the light of these current DL deficiencies, one may state that there exist two different kinds of artificial intelligence (AI) systems: ones that are inspired by human cognition and ones that are not. Current DL techniques are mostly of the second type. Accordingly, Marcus [11] and Lake et al. [9] propose that in order to overcome the flaws of current DL systems, researchers should apply human cognition as a model for AI systems. Marcus [11] advises against using findings of the human brain, since the insights of neuroscience are not yet advanced enough. He even assumes that we will need advanced AI systems to understand the human brain in the future. In his view, cognitive science and developmental psychology are more promising models than neuroscience, since they already provide helpful insights into human intelligence.

In line with this argument, Hassabis et al. [3], Lake et al. [6], and Marcus [11] identify several key areas of cognition, in which human intelligence still outperforms artificial intelligence. These include intuitive physics and folk psychology, imagination, reasoning, and planning, as well as learning efficiency. Here we focus on imagination and efficient learning.

Humans have mental models, which enable the anticipation of future outcomes based on experiences. As a result, actions can be chosen in explicitly goal-directed manners. Moreover, imaginations are compositional in nature, that is, we are able to recombine previous experiences in innovative but meaningful manners. Hassabis and colleagues [3] pose the challenge that DL algorithms should be enhanced such that generative models of the environment are developed that allow compositional, simulation-based planning – ideally without handcrafting strong priors into the DL network architecture.

Another main superiority of human compared to artificial intelligence is efficient learning [3]: Humans but not DL algorithms generalize very broadly from a sparse amount of data [3,9]. The resulting rich conceptual representations can then be applied to a wide range of tasks, like parsing an object into its components or generating new examples of a concept. They even allow the creative generation of novel concepts by putting components together in a new but somewhat meaningful manner [3]. This ability to re-combine structures in a compositional manner is a very important ingredient of efficient human learning and productivity because a finite number of conceptual primitives can be recombined into a mere infinite number of instances. Lake et al. [9] argue that this enables the brain to think an infinite number of thoughts and understand an infinite number of sentences.

To investigate efficiency differences between human and artificial learning, Lake et al. [7] developed the *character challenge*. It investigates one-shot classification and generation of handwritten characters. Those are well-suited for investigation because they are two-dimensional, clearly separated from the background, and unoccluded [9]. The character challenge consists of the following tasks, combining several fundamental AI challenges [4]:

   i. Free generation of characters (after a single example)
  ii. Generation of new samples of a concept (after a single example)
 iii. Identifying novel instances of a concept (after a single example)
 iv. Generation of whole new concepts (after single examples of some concepts)

Lake and colleagues [7] applied Bayesian program learning (BPL), representing concepts as stochastic programs to achieve results in machines that are comparably efficient to those generated by humans. Structure sharing across concepts was accomplished by re-using the components of stochastic motor primitives. The motor primitives were handcrafted and provided as priors to the BPL architecture.

Following the demand of Hassabis et al. [3] to build simple models without handcrafted priors by the experimenter, in this paper, we aim at building a generative neural network model that faces the character challenge without providing handcrafted motor primitives. As a result, we are addressing efficient learning with respect to the character challenge, investigating to which extent imagination, planning, and compositional encodings and recombination abilities develop. In particular, this paper introduces a generative RNN architecture that integrates the request for simulation-based planning, thereby managing the character challenge without prior information about stochastic primitives. We show that our recurrent LSTM network, when trained on some characters, becomes able to recombine previously learned dynamical substructures when facing the task of generating untrained characters, of which only one variant is presented. With such compositional structures at hand, the network is not only able to re-generate those untrained characters, but it is also able to create new examples of a particular type of character and even totally new ones. Moreover, we show that the network is able to recognize similar variants of a (potentially just recently learned) character.

2   Data and Model

Handwritten characters of the Latin alphabet were collected from 10 subjects, obtaining 440 samples per character in total. Each character trajectory was a sequence of a variable amount of time steps with two positional features that

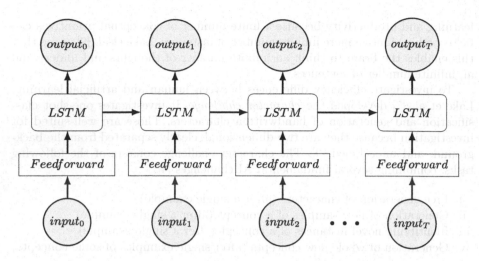

Fig. 1. Model architecture: At every time step, the one-hot encoded input of length 26 is processed in a first fully-connected feed-forward layer with 100 neurons, followed by one recurrent LSTM layer with 100 units, which generates the output trajectory (change in x and y direction, pressure, and stroke for every time step). During the one-shot inference mechanism, only the weights into the feedforward layer were adapted (blue). (Color figure online)

indicated the relative change in position in x and y direction, one feature representing the pressure with which the character was written and one representing the onset of a stroke. The labels, which served as the input, consisted of one-hot encoded input vectors with length 26 for every time step. The first 50% of the characters of the alphabet (a–m) were used to train the network, whereas only one variant of the remaining untrained characters (n–z) each was presented to the network during the different character challenge tasks.

The model architecture is shown in Fig. 1. The input is the one-hot encoded vector of length 26 for every time step, which is first processed in a fully-connected feedforward layer of 100 neurons, followed by one LSTM layer of 100 units, resulting in the output of pressure, stroke, and the relative change in x and y direction for every time step, which constitute the trajectory over time. As we will see below, the fully-connected feedforward layer is highly useful when intending to recombine attractor dynamics in the RNN layer to quickly learn to generate untrained characters. In preliminary experiments, the size of the architecture has been proven to be a good trade-off between model complexity and the quality of the generated outputs.

The model's weight parameters were trained for $500k$ training steps. We applied the mean squared error (MSE) loss function for training the model. For gradient computation, we used Backpropagation Through Time [14]. The weights of the network were optimized with Adam [5] using default parameters (learning rate of 0.001, $\beta_1 = 0.9$ and $\beta_2 = 0.999$).

After training, when presented with an untrained character trajectory and an unknown one-hot encoded label, the model generated a character trajectory that did, of course, not match the target trajectory. To probe the ability to freely generate new characters with only one example, we implemented the following *one-shot inference* mechanism. The gradient signals of the loss function were again propagated backwards through time. However, only the weights into the feedforward layer were adapted. The weights of the LSTM layer were not adapted at all. This iterative process was repeated 13,000 times with a learning rate of 0.001. As a result, the feedforward layer activities can be tuned such that the constant input activity flowing into the LSTM structure systematically activates those dynamic attractors and attractor successions that are best-suited to generate the novel character. From a cognitive perspective, this iterative inference process may be viewed as an imagination phase, in which the network essentially infers how to redraw the presented trajectory.

3   Experiments

In our experiments, we address the aforementioned four points of the character challenge. After learning, we probe if the network can re-generate a character, when presented with one example of a novel character, whether it can reliably identify such a novel character correctly as one particular novel type of character, and whether it can generate new variations of that novel character. Moreover, we probe if the network can generate completely new but related characters after being confronted with single examples of some new characters and we further analyse the hidden LSTM states. Remember, that we applied varying human handwritten trajectories that are not always easily readable. Hence, it might be difficult to recognize some of the (realistically) generated letters by the model, too.

3.1   Free Generation of Characters (After a Single Example)

Training against multiple training samples per character leads to a character model that generates one variant per character, essentially producing the mean of the encoded character concept. When presented with untrained inputs, the model is obviously not able to generate the correct trajectories (cf. Fig. 2, red trajectories). But by means of our one-shot inference mechanism, our RNN architecture is indeed able to re-generate different untrained character trajectories (cf. Fig. 2, blue trajectories). Note that we do not provide or explicitly train our RNN architecture to encode basic motion primitives, that is sub-trajectories, as was done in [7]. Instead, our architecture has developed such sub-trajectories implicitly in its LSTM layer. As a result, it is able to compose the trajectory components it needs to generate the target trajectory by selective activation via the inferred, constant feed-forward layer activities, providing first hints that our architecture develops compositional, generative structures.

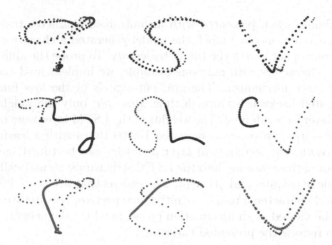

Fig. 2. Top: Three examples of re-generated trajectories after applying our one-shot inference mechanism (blue) given single examples of untrained characters (green), when applied in our character generation network architecture that was previously trained on other characters. Middle: Generated trajectories from unknown one-hot input vectors of the trained model without the one-shot inference mechanism (red). Bottom: Generated trajectories after the one-shot inference mechanism was applied to an untrained model (orange). (Color figure online)

In contrast, an untrained model of the same architecture is not able to re-generate the characters via our one-shot inference mechanism, as shown in orange in Fig. 2. The only exception for which the re-generated character looked similar to the original one in the untrained case was the 'v' – probably because of its simplicity. Even for this 'v', the shape is less edged than in the original version. These results confirm that the training of other characters is indeed crucial, presumably because it fosters the development of character sub-trajectories that can be flexibly adapted and recombined to generate other characters of the alphabet.

The importance of backpropagating the gradient onto the weights into the feedforward layer is further substantiated by the fact that similar attempts without the feedforward layer, like backpropagating the gradient onto constant one-hot mixture input vectors, have not been successful.

3.2   Generation of New Samples of a Concept (After Single Example)

Next, we evaluate if the network architecture is able to generate new samples of a character that was learned from one single example presented to the model via our one-shot inference mechanism. After the adaptation of the weight vector into the feed-forward layer, we then added normally distributed noise ($M = 0$, $0.009 \leq SD \leq 0.07$) to the input label with 26 dimensions at every time step, allowing the network to create new instances of the presented target character.

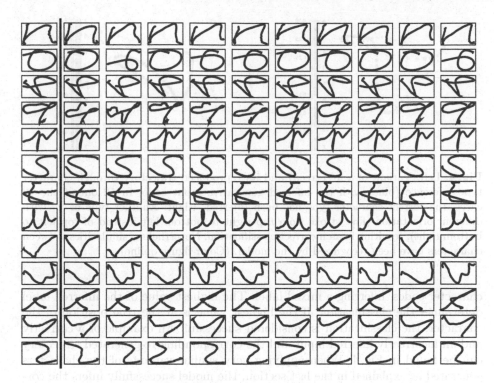

Fig. 3. The first column displays the re-generated character via one-shot inference, followed by generated variants via the addition of normally distributed noise to the inputs.

The generated variants shown in Fig. 3 confirm that the network is indeed able to generate similar character variants.

3.3 Identifying Novel Instances of a Concept (After Single Example)

The next task of the character challenge is to distinguish a novel instance of an untrained character from other characters. We thus present the trained model first with one instance each for each untrained character (i.e. characters n–z), applying our one-shot inference mechanism with a distinct one-hot encoded input for each untrained character. We then probe character type inference when confronted with a similar instance of one of those novel characters. During character type inference we do not provide any label (one-hot encoded) information, that is, we start with a zero vector of length 26 as the input vector. We then backpropagate the gradient from the L2 loss onto that input vector, enforcing constant values for every time step. This iterative inference process is repeated $1k$ times with a learning rate of 0.01 for every character. As a consequence of this setup, the model is allowed to recombine the information of previously learned

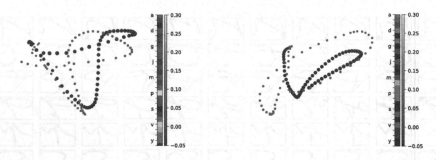

Fig. 4. Left: Variant of a 'p' (green) and its reproduced trajectory through character type inference (blue) with the inferred generative input code. In 12 out of the 13 cases, the correct character type has been inferred. Right: Another type of 'p' with different orientation (first stroke from top right to bottom left instead of top left to bottom right), resulting in an incorrect classification. Nevertheless, similarities between characters have been recognized by the model. (Color figure online)

character codes, inferring a mixed label. The highest value of the inferred label determines the classification. If the highest value is at the true position of the character, the classification is considered successful. An example of a correctly and an incorrectly inferred input and the corresponding re-generated trajectory can be found in Fig. 4. When applying very similar variants of the characters generated as explained in the last section, the model successfully infers the correct class in 12 out of the 13 cases. When using dissimilar variants of characters (for example print and script versions), the model is not able to determine the class reliably, which is not surprising because it has been shown only either one or the other variant. Nevertheless, the inferred inputs show that the system can detect similarities, since the correctly inferred 'p' on the left in Fig. 4 shares some components with a 'v', leading to an input vector that has high values both at the 'p' and the 'v' position. Even for the incorrectly classified 'p' on the right, the high values at the 'n', 'o', 'p', 'q', and 'd' positions seem reasonable given their shared components.

3.4   Generation of Entirely New Concepts (After Single Examples of Some Concepts)

Finally, we investigate whether the system is able to generate novel characters in a somewhat innovative manner, ideally generating characters that do not exist but that nonetheless look like plausible characters. We realize this aspect by investigating the effects of blending two characters. Again, we use the trained model with the feedforward layer input weights for the characters n–z optimized via one-shot inference. We present the resulting model with blending input vectors with two non-zero values that sum up to one. In a sense, this input vector instructs the model to generate a trajectory that expresses a compromise between two character trajectories, mixing and blending sub-trajectories of each character. Figure 5 shows that our network trajectory indeed generates innovative character blendings. The observable smooth blending transitions from one

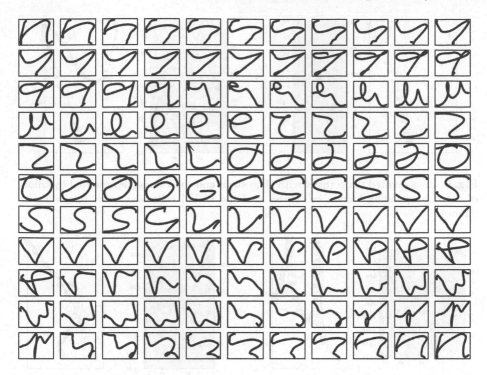

Fig. 5. Blending of single examples of untrained characters in ten steps. The second column shows blendings of 90% of the first and 10% of the second character, the third column 80% of first and 20% of second character and so on. Note that blending for trained characters (a - m) looks conceptually similar.

character to the other underline the compositional recurrent codes that developed in the LSTM layer. A video that illustrates the blending between different characters can be found here: https://youtu.be/VyqdUxrCRXY

3.5 Analysis of Hidden LSTM States

To shed more light on the nature of the encodings that have developed in the hidden LSTM cell states, we further analyzed the neural activities while generating particular character trajectories. Hidden neural cell state activities c of the LSTM layer and the corresponding trajectories are plotted in Fig. 6. Although only exemplarily, the analysis confirms that similar sub-dynamics unfold when similar sub-trajectories are generated: For the character 'v', the downward (approx. steps 1–16) and upward (approx. steps 21–37) strokes reveal distinct but partially stable patterns in the LSTM cell states. Most interestingly, a closely related pattern can be detected for the first part of the trajectory of the character 'y' (approx. steps 2–30), essentially drawing a similar 'v' shaped sub-trajectory.

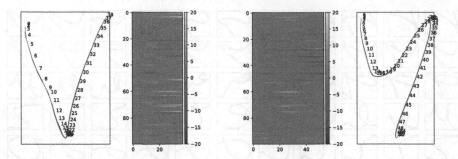

Fig. 6. Re-generated trajectories with time steps and the values (represented by color) of the corresponding hidden cell states c of the LSTM cells over time. (Color figure online)

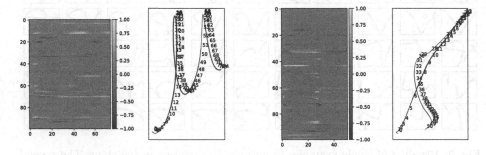

Fig. 7. Re-generated trajectories with time steps and the values (represented by color) of the corresponding hidden states h of the LSTM cells over time. (Color figure online)

Figure 7 shows some exemplary hidden states h of the LSTM layer. When generating the character 'u' a pattern repetition can be detected for the two upwards-downwards motions. For the character 'x', distinct diagonal upwards, jump, and cross-diagonal downwards patters are visible in the hidden states.

4 Conclusion

In a review on the models having attempted to solve the character challenge until 2019, Lake and colleagues [8] stated that except for the one-shot classification task, there has not been a lot of progress on the other tasks. They expressed their hopes that 'researchers will take up the challenge of incorporating compositionality and causality into more neurally-grounded architectures'. The current paper provides important insights regarding efficient learning, the emergence of compositional encodings and recombinations thereof, and the integration of a type of imagination and planning into RNNs.

Our generative feed-forward-LSTM model, combined with a one-shot inference mechanism, was able to meet the character challenge. Deep learning methods are usually bottom-up methods that need a large number of training examples. Lake and colleagues [7] applied a top-down approach by giving their program information about the existence of components, like strokes, half-circles and so on. Our approach was able to re-generate unseen character trajectories over time from just one example of a novel character, without providing any a priori structured motor primitives. This indicates that the system combined the knowledge of previously learned characters in an innovative manner to generate untrained characters, providing evidence that LSTM networks can indeed (i) partition time-series data implicitly into components, which encode sub-trajectories, and (ii) recombine them in a compositional manner to efficiently learn new characters.

The network and inference mechanisms were furthermore able to classify different variants of a character as belonging to the same one, as long as the presented trajectory variants were closely related. However, when the network was presented, for example, with a print 't', it was not able to classify the trajectory of a script 't' – which starts at the bottom and continues upward instead of starting at the top, continuing downward. This makes sense conceptually because our model encodes the motor trajectory in a recurrent, generative manner. It does not encode the actual image of the character that was generated. As a consequence, it classifies trajectory similarities, not image similarities. This corresponds to the fact that humans may classify both a script and a print 't' as the character 't' but indeed need to invoke very different motor programs when generating the one or the other, and switching between both styles comes with effort. Accordingly, one-shot classification is only possible for similar trajectory variants with the presented method. In the future, we intend to enhance our model with an encoder-decoder-oriented convolutional module, which may indeed interact with our trajectory generation module and the one-hot encoded classification layer, which we used as input to our generative architecture.

A further interesting result is that by using the learned components from the known characters, the model generated new examples of a particular type of character and even novel but plausibly looking character trajectories by blending previously seen ones in a somewhat innovative, smooth manner. Additionally, the visualization of recurrent hidden states showed similar patterns for characters that share similar sub-trajectories, providing interesting insights regarding the explainability of LSTMs, indicating the emergence of compositional dynamic attractor patterns within LSTM's hidden states. Further analyses should be conducted to shed additional light on the nature of these dynamic patterns.

Overall, these results provide strong evidence that LSTM networks tend to develop kinds of compositional encodings, which may be reused to generate untrained, but related trajectories in fast and innovative manners. Such combinatorial generalization abilities are of course not restricted to letter trajectories, but can be applied to all time series patterns. They are of major significance, since they seem to be a key ingredient of human intelligence, which is why AI researchers have been interested in combinatorial abilities since the origins of AI [1]. The awareness and utilization of these compositional abilities of RNNs will hopefully inspire future research and may be an essential aspect towards bridging the gap between human and machine intelligence.

Acknowledgements. The results of this work were produced with the help of the GPU cluster of the BMBF funded project Training Center for Machine Learning (TCML) at the Eberhard Karls Universität Tübingen, administered by the Cognitive Systems group. We especially thank Maximus Mutschler who is responsible for the maintenance of the cluster.

References

1. Battaglia, P.W., et al.: Relational inductive biases, deep learning, and graph networks. arXiv preprint arXiv:1806.01261 (2018)
2. Geirhos, R., Temme, C.R.M., Rauber, J., Schütt, H.H., Bethge, M., Wichmann, F.A.: Generalisation in humans and deep neural networks. In: Advances in Neural Information Processing Systems (NeurIPS), pp. 7538–7550. Curran Associates, Inc. (2018)
3. Hassabis, D., Kumaran, D., Summerfield, C., Botvinick, M.: Neuroscience-inspired artificial intelligence. Neuron **95**(2), 245–258 (2017)
4. Hofstadter, D.: Metamagical Themas: Questing for the Essence of Mind and Pattern. Basic Books, New York (1985)
5. Kingma, D.P., Ba, J.L.: Adam: a method for stochastic optimization. In: 3rd International Conference for Learning Representations (2015)
6. Lake, B., Baroni, M.: Still not systematic after all these years: On the compositional skills of sequence-to-sequence recurrent networks. arXiv preprint arXiv:1711.00350 (2018)
7. Lake, B.M., Salakhutdinov, R., Tenenbaum, J.B.: Human-level concept learning through probabilistic program induction. Science **350**(6266), 1332–1338 (2015)
8. Lake, B.M., Salakhutdinov, R., Tenenbaum, J.B.: The Omniglot challenge: a 3-year progress report. Curr. Opin. Behav. Sci. **29**, 97–104 (2019)
9. Lake, B.M., Ullman, T.D., Tenenbaum, J.B., Gershman, S.J.: Building machines that learn and think like people. Behav. Brain Sci. **40**, e253 (2017)
10. LeCun, Y., Bengio, Y., Hinton, G.: Deep learning. Nature **521**, 436–444 (2015)
11. Marcus, G.: Deep learning: A critical appraisal. arXiv preprint arXiv:1801.00631 (2018)
12. Nguyen, A., Yosinski, J., Clune, J.: Deep neural networks are easily fooled: high confidence predictions for unrecognizable images. In: IEEE Conference on Computer Vision and Pattern Recognition, pp. 427–436 (2015)
13. Otte, S., Rubisch, P., Butz, M.V.: Gradient-based learning of compositional dynamics with modular RNNs. In: Tetko, I.V., Kurková, V., Karpov, P., Theis, F. (eds.) ICANN 2019. LNCS, vol. 11727, pp. 484–496. Springer, Cham (2019). https://doi.org/10.1007/978-3-030-30487-4_38
14. Werbos, P.J.: Backpropagation through time: what it does and how to do it. In: Proceedings of the IEEE, pp. 1550–1560 (1990)

Fostering Event Compression Using Gated Surprise

Dania Humaidan[ID], Sebastian Otte[ID], and Martin V. Butz[✉][ID]

University of Tuebingen - Neuro-Cognitive Modeling Group,
Sand 14, 72076 Tuebingen, Germany
martin.butz@uni-tuebingen.de

Abstract. Our brain receives a dynamically changing stream of senso-rimotor data. Yet, we perceive a rather organized world, which we segment into and perceive as events. Computational theories of cognitive science on event-predictive cognition suggest that our brain forms generative, event-predictive models by segmenting sensorimotor data into suitable chunks of contextual experiences. Here, we introduce a hierarchical, surprise-gated recurrent neural network architecture, which models this process and develops compact compressions of distinct event-like contexts. The architecture contains a contextual LSTM layer, which develops generative compressions of ongoing and subsequent contexts. These compressions are passed to a GRU-like layer, which uses surprise signals to update its recurrent latent state. The latent state is passed on to another LSTM layer, which processes actual dynamic sensory flow in the light of the provided latent, contextual compression signals. Our model develops distinct event compressions and achieves the best performance on multiple event processing tasks. The architecture may be very useful for the further development of resource-efficient learning, hierarchical model-based reinforcement learning, as well as the development of artificial event-predictive cognition and intelligence.

Keywords: Event cognition · Surprise · Event segmentation

1 Introduction

The way our brain perceives information and organizes it remains an open question. It appears that we have a tendency to perceive, interpret, and thus understand our sensorimotor data streams in the form of events. The so-called Event Segmentation Theory (EST) [23] suggests that we utilize temporary increases in prediction errors for segmenting the stream of sensorimotor information into separable events [8]. As a result, compact event encodings develop.

M.V. Butz—Funding from the DFG Cluster of Excellence "Machine Learning: New Perspectives for Science", EXC 2064/1, project number 390727645 is acknowledged. Moreover, we thank the International Max Planck Research School for Intelligent Systems (IMPRS-IS) for supporting Dania Humaidan.

© Springer Nature Switzerland AG 2020
I. Farkaš et al. (Eds.): ICANN 2020, LNCS 12396, pp. 155–167, 2020.
https://doi.org/10.1007/978-3-030-61609-0_13

Event encodings certainly do not develop for their own sake or for the mere sake of representing sensorimotor information, though. Rather, it appears that event encodings are very useful for memorizing events and event successions, as well as for enabling effective hierarchical reinforcement learning [3], amongst other benefits [4]. Indeed it appears that our brain prepares for upcoming events in the prefrontal cortex [21]. Moreover, the whole midline default network [20] seems to actively maintain a push-pull relationship between externally-generated stimulations and internally-generated imaginations, including retrospective reflections and prospective anticipations.

We have previously modeled such processes with REPRISE – a retrospective and prospective inference scheme [5, 6] – showing promising planning and event-inference abilities. However, the retrospective inference mechanism is also rather computationally expensive; plus, a more constant representation of the event is desired. Here, we introduce a complementary surprise-processing modular architecture, which may support the event-inference abilities of REPRISE and the development of event-predictive compressions in general. We show that when contextual information is selectively routed into a predictive processing layer via gated recurrent unit (GRU)-like [7] switching-gates, suitable event compressions are learned via standard back-propagation through time. As a result, the architecture can generate and switch between distinct functional operations.

After providing background on related event processing mechanisms in humans and neural models, we introduce our surprise-processing modular architecture. We evaluate our system exemplarily on a set of simple function prediction tasks, where the lower-layer network needs to predict function value outputs given inputs and contextual information. Meanwhile, deeper layers learn to distinguish different functional mappings, compressing the individual functions into event-like encodings. In the near future, we hope to scale this system to more challenging real-world tasks and to enhance the architecture such that upcoming surprise signals and consequent event switches are anticipated as well.

2   Related Work

The ability to distinguish different contexts was previously tested in humans [18, 23, 24]. Segmenting these events was suggested to make use of the prediction failures to update the internal model and suggest that a new event has begun. Loschky and colleagues [13] showed a group of participants selected parts of a film. They showed that when the clip could be put within a larger context, the participant had more systematic eye movements. Baldassano and colleagues [2] showed that the participants had consistently different brain activity patterns for different ongoing contexts (flying from the airport and eating at a restaurant). Pettijohn and colleagues have shown that increasing the number of event boundaries can have a positive effect on memory [16].

From the computational aspect, the usage of prediction error to predict the next stimulus was presented in the work of Reynolds and colleagues [17] who used a feed forward network in combination with a recurrent neural network module, memory cells, and a gating mechanism. This model was later extended with a reinforcement learning (RL) agent that controls the gating mechanism with a learned policy [15]. Successfully segmenting the information stream into understandable units was also attempted with reservoir computing [1]. It was shown that this mechanism can be sufficient to identify event boundaries. However, it did not develop a hierarchical structure that is believed to be present when considering action production and goal directed behaviors [11].

[12] offers a background survey and a general hierarchical framework for neuro-robotic systems (NRS). In this framework, the processing of the perceptual information happens in a high level cognition layer whose output passes via middle to a lower level execution layer, which includes the sensory feedback between the agent and the surrounding environment. An interesting hierarchical structure for spatial cognition was presented in the work of Martinet and colleagues [14]. Their presented model showed how interrelated brain areas can interact to learn how to navigate towards a target by investigating different policies to find the optimal one. However, this structure focused on a certain maze and only used the size of the reward at the goal location to make decisions.

Another important aspect of forming loosely hierarchical structured event compressions lies in the prediction of event boundaries. Indeed, it was shown that having background knowledge about the ongoing activities while an event unfolds can help to predict when the current event might end [9]. This means that the developing event-generative compression structure may develop deeper knowledge about the currently unfolding event. Amongst other things, such structures may develop event boundary anticipating encodings, which, when activated, predict initially unpredictable event changes.

3   Surprise-Processing Modular Architecture

We present a hierarchical surprise-gated recurrent neural network architecture. The system simulates the flow of contextual information from a deep layer, which prepares the processing of upcoming events developing event-compressing encodings. These encodings are used to modify the processing of the lower-level sensor- or sensorimotor-processing layer. In between, a GRU-like gating layer controls when novel context modifying signals are passed on to the lower-level layer and when the old signal should be kept. As a result, the lower-level layer is generating predictions context-dependently, effectively learning to distinguish different events.

3.1   The Structure

The proposed structure is composed of a contextual recurrent neural network layer, implemented using a long short-term memory (LSTM) network (called LSTMc) [10], which is responsible for generating an event compression that is representing the currently ongoing or next upcoming context. While a simple recurrent neural network (RNN) is also well-suited for time series prediction, it will not maintain the long-term temporal dependency. This contextual information is fed into a middle layer, which is implemented by a GRU-like gate [7]. The gate decides how much of

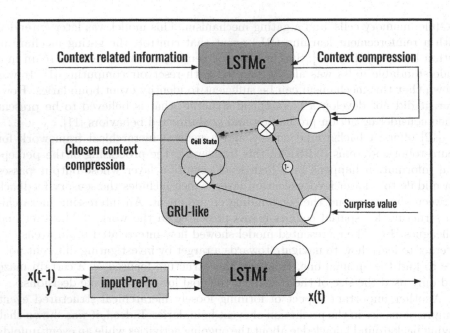

Fig. 1. The hierarchical structure composed of a deep contextual layer (LSTMc), a GRU-like gating layer and a low-level function processing layer (LSTMf). Additionally, we added an MLP to preprocess the function input (inputPrePro).

the novel contextual information in proportion to the previous contextual information will be passed on to the lower level layer based on the received surprise value, which represents an increased prediction error. This lower level function processing layer, which is also implemented by an LSTM, predicts a function value (LSTMf). The function input is preprocessed using a multilayer perceptron (MLP) unit (inputPrePro), before being provided to LSTMf. The structure is shown in Fig. 1. Note that the dotted lines denote unweighted inputs.

The decision about the current context is taken at the GRU-like top down gating layer. When a new event begins, LSTMf will produce erroneous predictions as the function switched. As a result, this correspondingly large surprise value, representing the unexpectedly high prediction error [5], may be provided to the gating layer. A surprise signal can thus be used to manipulate the update gate of a GRU layer, receiving and passing on new contextual information from LSTMc surprise-dependently. If the context has not changed, then the gate stays closed, and the same old event compression is provided as the contextual information to the LSTMf layer.

3.2 The Switch GRU

The used GRU structure was adapted to act as a switch to decide when (i) to keep the gate closed, in which case the already saved context compression from the previous time step will be maintained and passed on, or (ii) to open the gate, in which case the new context generated by LSTMc will flow in. To perform this task, the update gate at the GRU is modified to be unweighted, with its input being the surprise signal. The combined gate is now getting the new context compression from LSTMc and the hidden cell state (context compression of the previous time step) inputs. The reset gate is removed as it has no role here. The output of the this layer can be expressed as:

$$cell\_state_t = (\sigma(sur) * cell\_state_{t-1}) + ((1 - \sigma(sur)) * \sigma(LSTMc\_output)) \quad (1)$$

4 Experiments and Results

For evaluation purposes, we used an example of a time series that includes four functions $f_e(x, y)$ representing four different contexts or events e. Converting this into a continuous time series, the previous function output is used as the first function input at the following time step t, that is, $x_t = f_e(x_{t-1}, y_{t-1})$. Meanwhile, function inputs y_t are generated independently and uniformly distributed between -1 and 1. Function switches occurred uniformly randomly every 5 to 12 times steps. The four functions are:

1. An addition function (add): $f_{add}(x, y) = 0.9x + y$,
2. A sine function (sin): $f_{sin}(x, y) = x + sin(\pi y)$,
3. A subtraction function (sub): $f_{sub}(x, y) = 0.9x - y$,
4. A constant function (con): $f_{con}(x, y) = x$.

4.1 Single Network Experiments

As an upper error baseline, we first evaluated the performance of a single LSTM layer or a two-layer perceptron (MLP), which receives x and y as input and is trained to learn $f_e(x, y)$ without providing any direct information about e. Next, as a lower error baseline, we evaluate the performance of the two networks when we augment the input with a one-hot vector denoting the ongoing event. Finally, to make the problem harder again and enforce the anticipation of an event switch, we switched the event information at a time point uniformly randomly earlier than the actual next scheduled event switch, but at least two time steps after the last event switch. This was done to simulate the idea of preparing for the next event switch before it actually happens. In addition, we distinguish between runs in which the consecutive functions were in the same order and runs in which the next function type $e \in \{add, sub, con, sin\}$ is randomly chosen each time.

The used LSTM network had 10 hidden units and the MLP had two hidden layers each with 50 units. The weights of the networks were updated at a fixed rate every 20 time steps. We used a learning rate of 10^{-4} and trained every network for 2 000 epochs each with 2 000 steps. Finally, we tested every network for 150 test iterations. Reported performance results are averaged over ten differently initialized networks.

The results are shown in Table 1. As expected, worst performance is obtained when the network does not receive any context-related information, while best

Table 1. Average training error in single LSTM and MLP layer experiments.

Experiment	LSTM		MLP	
	Avg. error	Stdev.	Avg. error	Stdev.
No CI provided	0.2670	0.0272	0.4180	0.0016
CI provided with fixed function order	0.0533	0.0292	0.0098	0.0011
CI provided with random function order	0.0551	0.0215	0.0139	0.0022
CI provided but switched earlier	0.1947	0.0134	0.3180	0.0012

performance is achieved when context information is provided. When the order of the successive functions is randomized, performance only slightly degrades. When the context information switches earlier than the actual function, performance degrades, yielding an average error between the case when no context information is provided and when context information is provided perfectly in tune with the actual context switches.

When comparing the performance of the LSTM with the MLP, several observations can be made. First, when no context information or ill-tuned context information is provided, LSTM outperforms the MLP. This is most likely the case because the LSTM can in principle infer the function that currently applies by analyzing the successive input signals. As a result, it appears to decrease its prediction error via its recurrent information processing ability. On the other hand, when perfect context information is provided, the MLP learns to approximate the function even better than the LSTM module, indicating that the MLP can play out its full capacity, while the recurrent connections are somewhat prohibiting better performance with the LSTM module.

4.2 Full Network Experiments

Next, we performed the experiments using the introduced surprise-processing modular neural architecture. We evaluated the structure by testing four cases:

- The gate is always closed: The GRU-like layer output is constantly zero (approximately corresponding to the upper error baseline).
- The gate is always open: The GRU-like layer output is continuously controlled by the new context compression from LSTMc.
- The gate is only open at context switches: The GRU-like layer output maintains the context prediction generated by LSTMc when the context is switched.
- The gate is gradually open at context switches: The GRU-like layer switches its context output more smoothly.

Note that the fourth scenario is meant to probe whether a gradual surprise signal, i.e., a set of discrete surprise values, can help to predict the switches between the contexts in a smoother manner. The gate in this case turns from being closed, to being half-open, to being fully opened, and back to half-open and closed.

Table 2. Average training prediction error and average distance between the centers of the clusters formed by the context compressions' values in different gate states. The lowest average error and largest average distances are marked in bold.

Gate status	Avg. error	Stdev. error	Compared clusters	Avg. distance	Stdev. distance
Always closed	0.280	0.059	Any	0.0	0.0
Always open	0.206	0.014	Add Sin	0.28	0.17
			Add Sub	1.22	0.42
			Add Const	0.64	0.19
			Sin Sub	1.27	0.34
			Sin Const	0.70	0.24
			Sub Const	0.7	0.26
Only open at switch	**0.059**	0.017	Add Sin	**0.69**	0.15
			Add Sub	**3.12**	0.42
			Add Const	**1.46**	0.27
			Sin Sub	**2.59**	0.47
			Sin Const	0.92	0.17
			Sub Const	**1.72**	0.4
Gradually opened	0.083	0.030	Add Sin	0.61	0.17
			Add Sub	2.17	0.69
			Add Const	1.35	0.56
			Sin Sub	1.81	0.39
			Sin Const	**1.00**	0.20
			Sub Const	0.82	0.31

Final test errors – again averaged over ten independently randomly weight-initialized networks - are shown in Table 2. The results show that the best results are obtained by keeping the gate closed while the same context is progressing, and only opening it when a new event starts. As expected, the worst performance is achieved when the gate is always closed. Note also that the performance only slightly improves when the gate is always open, indicating that the architecture cannot detect the event switches on its own. Gradually opening and closing the gate slightly degrades the performance in comparison to when the gate is only open at the actual switch. When considering the differences in the compression codes that are passed down to LSTMf in the different events, the largest distances are generated by the network when the GRU-like update gate is open at the switch, only, thus indicating that it generated the most distinct compressions for the four function events.

Figure 2 shows the development of the average prediction error and its standard deviation with respect to the best performing network setup, that is, the one where the gate only opens as the switches. As can be seen, the error first plateaus at a level of 0.4, which approximately corresponds to an identity mapping. It then rather reliably appears to find the gradient towards distinguishing the four functions over the subsequent training epochs, thus converging to an error level that corresponds to the lower-error boundary of the single-layer LSTM network with perfect context information (cf. Table 1).

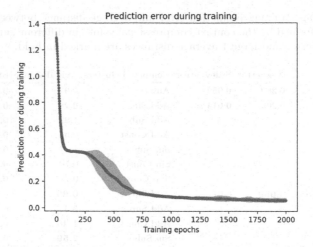

Fig. 2. Prediction error average and standard deviation during training over ten differently initialized networks. Gate is only open at the switches.

All the above-mentioned results were obtained using a fixed weight update frequency of 20 time steps, backpropagating the error 20 time steps into the past. Table 3 shows the effect when the update frequency is changed. In this case, the gradually changing surprise signal provides better results because in some of the runs, the network with the gate open at the context switch only fails to find the gradient down to the 0.05 error niveau. The gradual opening and closing effectively increases the error flow into LSTMc, increasing the likelihood of convergence. Thus, in the future a gradual change from weak, smooth surprise signals to strong and progressively more punctual surprise signals should be investigated further. Indeed such a surprise signal can be expected when derived from LSTMf during learning [5].

Please remember that in the experiments above the context switch provided to LSTMc switches earlier than the actual function event switch. As a result, LSTMc can prepare for the switch but should only pass the information down when the event switch is actually happening. This is accomplished by the GRU-like module. Instead, when the surprise signal is provided to LSTMc and the

Table 3. Average training prediction error while using different weight update frequency settings.

Weight update frequency	Fixed at 35		Random 20–50		Random 10–30	
	Avg. error	Stdev. error	Avg. error	Stdev. error	Avg. error	Stdev. error
Always closed	0.365	0.070	0.428	0.083	0.345	0.078
Always open	0.270	0.071	0.224	0.022	0.206	0.018
Open at context switch	0.200	0.142	0.318	0.122	0.166	0.149
Gradually opened	**0.106**	0.077	**0.103**	0.041	**0.070**	0.013

Table 4. Average prediction error when (i) the surprise signal is fed to LSTMc, whereby the GRU-like gate is always open (Surp. to LSTMc), (ii) the context information is provided to LSTMc exactly in tune with the function event (In-tune CI to LSTMc), and when an MLPf is used instead of an LSTMf (MLPf).

Input to LSTMc/Gate status	Surp. to LSTMc		In-tune CI to LSTMc		MLPf	
	Avg. error	Stdev.	Avg. error	Stdev.	Avg. error	Stdev.
0/Always closed	0.2515	0.0678	0.310	0.080	0.4213	0.00164
1/Always open	0.2280	0.0198	0.066	0.040	0.4215	0.00123
1 at c.s./open at c.s	0.1031	0.0555	0.055	0.019	0.4211	0.00165

GRU-like gate is always open, the error less reliably drops to the 0.05 niveau, as shown in Table 4. On the other hand, when the contextual information was provided exactly in tune with the currently ongoing event to LSTMc – opening the gate only at the switches still yielded a slightly better performance than when the gate was always open (cf. Table 4).

It is also worth mentioning that when we ran the architecture with an MLP (an MLPf module) as the function processing layer (instead of LSTMf), the error stayed on an average of 0.42, without any difference between the gating mechanisms (cf. Table 4). It thus appears that the gradient information from LSTMf is more suitable to foster the development of distinct contextual codes.

Finally, we took a closer look at the event-encoding compressions generated by the contextual layer and passed on by the GRU-like layer. Figure 3 shows the context compression vector values produced by the deep context layer over time. Figure 4 shows the outputs of the GRU-like gating layer. We can see stable compressions when the gate is only open at the switches. When the gate is always open, the context also switches systematically but much more gradually and thus less suitably.

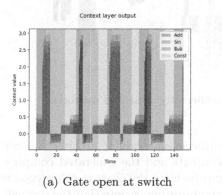
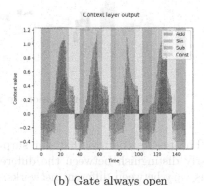

(a) Gate open at switch   (b) Gate always open

Fig. 3. Context compressions produced by the context layer. Background colors indicate the different contexts.

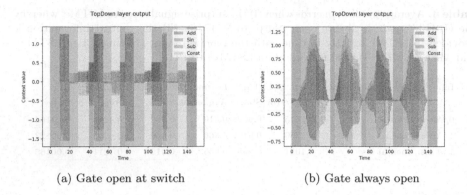

(a) Gate open at switch   (b) Gate always open

Fig. 4. Context compressions produced by the GRU-like gating layer. Background colors indicate the different contexts. Note that as the gate was still closed during the first event in (a), context values are still on zero.

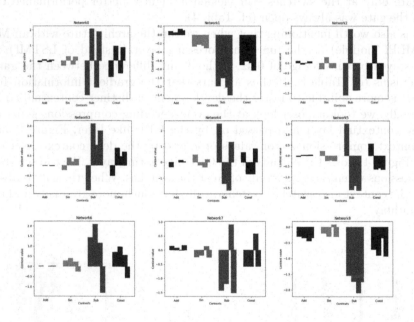

Fig. 5. Context compressions in nine differently initialized networks.

The results confirm that our surprise-processing modular architecture can clearly distinguish between the different contexts and the generated compressions vary between different networks. Figure 5 shows the context compressions for nine differently initialized networks. It is interesting to note that the context-respective code for increasing is always close to zero, which is because the data always started with the increasing function at the beginning of an epoch and a network reset to zero activities. Moreover, it can be noted that, albeit clearly different, the constant function code lies somewhat in between the code for increasing and the code for decreasing. Finally, the sine function compression is distinct but also somewhat in between the increasing and constant function code (except for that in the lower right graph). Further investigations with larger networks are pending to evaluate whether the sine function may be predictable more exactly with larger networks and whether the compression code from the GRU-like layer for the sine function may become more distinct from the others in that case.

5   Discussion

Motivated by recent theories on event-predictive cognition [4,22,23], this paper has investigated how dedicated neural modules can be biased towards reliably developing event-predictive compressions. We have introduced a surprise-processing modular neural network architecture, which contains a deep contextual layer that learns to generate suitable event-encoding compressions. These compressions are selectively passed through a GRU-like top-down layer, depending on current estimates of surprise. If the surprise is low, then the old compression is used. On the other hand, the larger the current surprise, the more the current context compression is adapted and passed onto the function processing layer, effectively invoking an event transition. As a result, the function processing layer predicts subsequent function values dependent on the currently active, compressed, top-down event-predictive signal.

Our surprise-processing modular architecture was able to generate best predictive performance when the GRU-like gating structures was opened only at or surrounding the event switch, mimicking the processing of a surprise signal. When the upcoming context information is provided in advance, the deep context layer does not only consider the currently ongoing event, but it also prepares the processing of the next one. The prepared transition, however, should only be passed down to the function processing layer when a new event actually starts. Elsewhere, event-triggered learning was proposed for control, such that the system requests new information and the model is updated only when learning is actually needed [19]. Our structure shows that even when the context layer receives always the information regarding the actual ongoing event, the gate may still open only at the context switch, since this is the time point when new information must be passed onto the event dynamics processing layer. As a result, the same prediction accuracy is achieved more resource-efficiently.

In future work, we will integrate surprise estimates from the LSTMf module directly (cf. [5]). Moreover, we will enhance the architecture further to enable it to predict event boundaries, which initially can be identified by surprise signals [9]. Combinations with retrospective and prospective inference, as implemented in REPRISE, may yield faster and more reliable event compressions. Finally, we plan to scale up the mechanism to more challenging problems, including robot control, object and tool usage, as well as language grounding.

References

1. Asabuki, T., Hiratani, N., Fukai, T.: Interactive reservoir computing for chunking information streams. PLOS Comput. Biol. **14**(10), e1006400 (2018)
2. Baldassano, C., Hasson, U., Norman, K.A.: Representation of real-world event schemas during narrative perception. J. Neurosci. Off. J. Soc. Neurosci. **38**(45), 9689–9699 (2018)
3. Botvinick, M., Niv, Y., Barto, A.C.: Hierarchically organized behavior and its neural foundations: a reinforcement learning perspective. Cognition **113**(3), 262–280 (2009)
4. Butz, M.V.: Towards a unified sub-symbolic computational theory of cognition. Front. Psychol. **7**(925) (2016)
5. Butz, M.V., Bilkey, D., Humaidan, D., Knott, A., Otte, S.: Learning, planning, and control in a monolithic neural event inference architecture. Neural Netw. **117**, 135–144 (2019)
6. Butz, M.V., Menge, T., Humaidan, D., Otte, S.: Inferring event-predictive goal-directed object manipulations in REPRISE. In: Tetko, I.V., Kurková, V., Karpov, P., Theis, F. (eds.) ICANN 2019. LNCS, vol. 11727, pp. 639–653. Springer, Cham (2019). https://doi.org/10.1007/978-3-030-30487-4_49
7. Chung, J., Gülçehre, Ç., Cho, K., Bengio, Y.: Empirical evaluation of gated recurrent neural networks on sequence modeling. CoRR abs/1412.3555 (2014)
8. Franklin, N.T., Norman, K.A., Ranganath, C., Zacks, J.M., Gershman, S.J.: Structured event memory: a neuro-symbolic model of event cognition. bioRxiv, p. 541607 (February 2019)
9. Hard, B.M., Meyer, M., Baldwin, D.: Attention reorganizes as structure is detected in dynamic action. Mem. Cogn. **47**(1), 17–32 (2019)
10. Hochreiter, S., Schmidhuber, J.: Long short-term memory. Neural Comput. **9**, 1735–1780 (1997)
11. Koechlin, E., Ody, C., Kouneiher, F.: The architecture of cognitive control in the human prefrontal cortex. Science **302**(5648), 1181–1185 (2003)
12. Li, J., Li, Z., Chen, F., Bicchi, A., Sun, Y., Fukuda, T.: Combined sensing, cognition, learning, and control for developing future neuro-robotics systems: a survey. IEEE Trans. Cogn. Develop. Syst. **11**(2), 148–161 (2019)
13. Loschky, L.C., Larson, A.M., Magliano, J.P., Smith, T.J.: What would jaws do? The tyranny of film and the relationship between gaze and higher-level narrative film comprehension. PLOS One **10**(11), e0142474 (2015)
14. Martinet, L.E., Sheynikhovich, D., Benchenane, K., Arleo, A.: Spatial learning and action planning in a prefrontal cortical network model. PLOS Comput. Biol. **7**(5), e1002045 (2011)
15. Metcalf, K., Leake, D.: Modeling unsupervised event segmentation: learning event boundaries from prediction errors, p. 6 (2017)
16. Pettijohn, K.A., Thompson, A.N., Tamplin, A.K., Krawietz, S.A., Radvansky, G.A.: Event boundaries and memory improvement. Cognition **148**, 136–144 (2016)
17. Reynolds, J.R., Zacks, J.M., Braver, T.S.: A computational model of event segmentation from perceptual prediction. Cogn. Sci. **31**(4), 613–643 (2007)
18. Serrano, A., Sitzmann, V., Ruiz-Borau, J., Wetzstein, G., Gutierrez, D., Masia, B.: Movie editing and cognitive event segmentation in virtual reality video. ACM Trans. Graph. **36**(4), 1–12 (2017)
19. Solowjow, F., Baumann, D., Garcke, J., Trimpe, S.: Event-triggered learning for resource-efficient networked control. In: 2018 Annual American Control Conference (ACC), pp. 6506–6512 (June 2018). arXiv: 1803.01802

20. Stawarczyk, D., Bezdeck, M.A., Zacks, J.M.: Event representaion and predictive processing: The role of the midline default network core. Topics in Cognitive Science (2019)

21. Tanji, J., Hoshi, E.: Behavioral planning in the prefrontal cortex. Curr. Opin. Neurobiol. **11**(2), 164–170 (2001)

22. Zacks, J.M.: Event perception and memory. Annu. Rev. Psychol. **71**(1), 165–191 (2020)

23. Zacks, J.M., Swallow, K.M.: Event segmentation. Curr. Dir. Psychol. Sci. **16**(2), 80–84 (2007)

24. Zhao, J., Hahn, U., Osherson, D.: Perception and identification of random events. J. Exp. Psychol. Hum. Percept. Perform. **40**(4), 1358–1371 (2014)

Physiologically-Inspired Neural Circuits for the Recognition of Dynamic Faces

Michael Stettler[1,2](✉), Nick Taubert[1], Tahereh Azizpour[1], Ramona Siebert[1], Silvia Spadacenta[1], Peter Dicke[1], Peter Thier[1], and Martin A. Giese[1]

[1] Section for Computational Sensomotorics, Department of Cognitive Neurology, Centre for Integrative Neuroscience and Hertie Institute for Clinical Brain Research, University Clinic Tübingen, Tübingen, Germany
michael.stettler@cin.uni-tuebingen.de, martin.giese@uni-tuebingen.de
[2] International Max Planck Research School for Intelligent Systems, Tübingen, Germany

Abstract. Dynamic faces are essential for the communication of humans and non-human primates. However, the exact neural circuits of their processing remain unclear. Based on previous models for cortical neural processes involved for social recognition (of static faces and dynamic bodies), we propose two alternative neural models for the recognition of dynamic faces: (i) an example-based mechanism that encodes dynamic facial expressions as sequences of learned keyframes using a recurrent neural network (RNN), and (ii) a norm-based mechanism, relying on neurons that represent differences between the actual facial shape and the neutral facial pose. We tested both models exploiting highly controlled facial monkey expressions, generated using a photo-realistic monkey avatar that was controlled by motion capture data from monkeys. We found that both models account for the recognition of normal and temporally reversed facial expressions from videos. However, if tested with expression morphs, and with expressions of reduced strength, both models made quite different prediction, the norm-based model showing an almost linear variation of the neuron activities with the expression strength and the morphing level for cross-expression morphs, while the example based model did not generalize well to such stimuli. These predictions can be tested easily in electrophysiological experiments, exploiting the developed stimulus set.

Keywords: Dynamic facial expressions · Recognition · Neural network model · Norm-referenced encoding · Visual cortex

1 Introduction

Dynamic facial expressions are central for the social communication of humans and non-human primates. In spite of this importance, the underlying detailed local neural circuits remain unclear. Single cells responding to dynamic facial expressions have been investigated so far only in very few studies in the superior temporal sulcus (STS) [1,2], and the amygdala [3]. Advances in the technology

© Springer Nature Switzerland AG 2020
I. Farkaš et al. (Eds.): ICANN 2020, LNCS 12396, pp. 168–179, 2020.
https://doi.org/10.1007/978-3-030-61609-0_14

for stimulus generation, e.g. the use of highly controlled dynamic avatars, in combination with the simultaneous recording of large numbers of neurons promise to clarify the underlying mechanisms. For the guidance of such experiments it seems useful to develop theoretical hypotheses about possible underlying neural computations and circuit structures for the recognition of dynamic faces.

We propose here two alternative models for the recognition of dynamic faces. Both models are derived from previous neural models that have provided good agreement with electrophysiological data from single-cell recordings in visual areas, either on the recognition of face identity in area IT [4,5] or for the representation of head actions in area F5 of the macaque monkey [6,7]. From these previous models we derive two alternative mechanisms for the recognition of dynamic facial expressions. We test these models with a highly controlled stimulus set of monkey facial expressions. We demonstrate that both models are feasible and derive predictions that can be used to distinguish the two models in electrophysiological experiments.

After a brief review of related work, we introduce in the following the model architectures and our simulation studies, followed by a discussion of implications for electrophysiological experiments.

2 Related Work

Most physiologically-inspired models on the processing of faces investigate the recognition of static faces (e.g. [8]). Biologically-inspired models have been proposed for the recognition of dynamic bodies [9–11]. It seems likely that computational principles might shared between the processing of different social stimulus classes. Beyond this, a variety of conceptual models have been developed in psychology and the functional imaging literature, e.g. the separate processing of static and dynamic aspects of faces [12], or the idea of a face space [13] and a norm-referenced encoding of static faces relative to an average face (review see [14]). This work sets important general constraints for the modelling, but does not provide ideas about specific neural circuits. Dominant approaches on dynamic face processing in computer vision are based on deep recurrent neural networks [15], but typically not related to details of the brain.

3 Model Architectures

Our model mimics the basic architecture of the visual pathway, from the retina up to higher-levels that contain neurons that are selective for dynamic facial expressions. Figure 1A shows an overview of the model architecture. In the following, we first describe the mid-level feature extraction hierarchy, which is identical for both model versions. Then we discuss separately for the two models the circuits including the face-selective neurons that implement different computational principles.

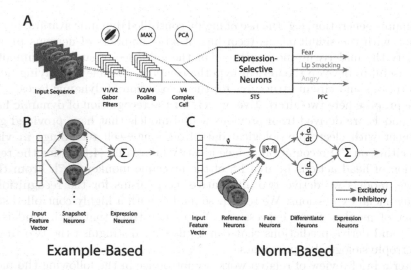

Fig. 1. Model architectures. (A) Mid-level feature extraction hierarchy (common to both models). (B) Example-based circuit, and (C) Norm-based circuit for the recognition of one dynamic expression.

3.1 Shape Feature Extraction Hierarchy

The first levels of our model hierarchy extract mid-level form features, similar to neurons area V4 in the macaque visual cortex. While more sophisticated models have been proposed for this part of the visual pathway (e.g. [16]), we applied here a highly simplified implementation that was sufficient for our stimuli since we wanted to focus on higher-level face-selective circuits, whose behavior is to some degree invariant against the chosen mid-level feature dictionary that is used as input. The feature extraction hierarchy of our model can be easily exchanged against more elaborate models from the literature. Our feature extraction hierarchy consists of 3 layers. The face region in our stimulus movies was down-sampled 200×200 pixels and converted to gray level for further processing.

First Layer. The first layer consists of even and uneven Gabor filters with 8 different orientations, and 3 different spatial scales that differed by $\sqrt{2}$. A constant was subtracted from these filter functions to make them mean-free. Filter responses for the three spatial scales were computed on rectangular grids with 49, 69, and 97 points spaced equally along the sides of the image region. This layer models orientation-selective neurons such as V1 simple cells [17].

Second Layer. The second layer models V1 complex cells and makes the responses of the first layer partially position- and spatial phase-invariant. For this purpose, the thresholded responses of the even and the uneven Gabor filters with the same orientation preference and spatial scale were pooled within a spatial region (receptive field) using a maximum operation. The receptive fields of these pooling neurons comprised 3 neurons in the previous layer (respectively one for the largest spatial scale). The receptive fields centers of the pooling neurons were again positioned in quadratic grids with 15, 10 and 14 grid points for the three spatial scales.

Third Layer. The third layer of our model extracts informative mid-level features, combining a simple heuristic feature selecting algorithm with a Principal Components Analysis (PCA). These two steps can be implemented by a sparsely connected simple linear feed-forward neural network. For feature selection, we simply computed the standard deviation over all input signals from the previous layer (after thresholding) over our training set. Only those features were retained for which this variability measure exceeded a certain threshold. This eliminated uninformative features that are zero or constant over the training set. In total we retained 17% of the original features.

The vector of the selected features was then subject to a PCA analysis. The activity of the selected features was projected to a subspace that corresponds to 97% of the total variance for the training set. The resulting (thresholded) PCA features provide the input to the expression-selective neurons that form the next layer of our model.

3.2   Expression-Selective Neurons

The next layers of the model were implemented in two different ways, implementing two different computational principles. The first mechanism is based on the recognition of temporal sequences of learned snapshots from face movies by a recurrent neural network (RNN), referred to as *example-based* mechanism. The second mechanism is based on the concept of norm-referenced encoding, as discovered in the context of the representation of static images of faces [14]. The dynamic face is encoded by neurons that represent the difference between the actual face picture and a norm picture, in this case the shape of a neutral face. The details of the two implementation are described in the following.

Example-Based Model. For this model the recognition is accomplished by using a RNN that detects temporal sequences of learned keyframes from facial expressions (Fig. 1B). This type of mechanism has been shown to reproduce data from cortical neurons during the recognition of body actions (e.g. [7,9]). It has been shown to reproduce activity data from action selective neurons in the STS and in premotor cortex.

Expressions were represented by a total of 50 keyframes. The structure of the example-based encoding circuit for one expression is shown in Fig. 1B. The output from the previous layer, signified as vector $\mathbf{z}$, is providing input to Radial Basis Function units (RBFs) that were trained by setting their centers to the vectors $\mathbf{z}_n^p$ for the individual expression frames of expression p. The actual outputs of these neurons are then given by: $f_k^p = \exp((|\mathbf{z} - \mathbf{z}_k^p|^2/(2\sigma^2))$. (For sufficient selectivity to distinguish temporally distant keyframes we chose $\sigma = 0.1$.). The outputs of the RBFs were thresholded with a linear threshold function.

The output signals of the RBFs were used as input of a recurrent neural network, or discretely approximated neural field [18], that obeys the dynamics:

$$\tau \dot{u}_n^p(t) = -u_n^p(t) + \sum_m w(n - m)[u_m^p(t)]_+ + s_n^p(t) - h - w_c I_c^p(t) \qquad (1)$$

The activity $u_n^p(t)$ is the activity of the neuron in the RNN that encodes keyframe n of the facial expression type p. The resting level constant was $h = 1$, and the time constant $\tau = 5$ (using an Euler approximation). The lateral interaction was asymmetric, inducing a network dynamics that is sequence selective. It was given by the function $w(n) = A \exp(-(n - C)^2 / (2\sigma_{\text{ker}}^2)) - B$ with the parameters $A = 1$, $B = 0.5$, and $C = 3.5$. A cross inhibition term leads to competition between the neural subnetworks that encode different expressions. It was defined by the equation: $I_c^p(t) = \sum_{' \neq n}[\mathbf{u}_m^{p'}(t)]_+$ with the cross-inhibition weight $w_c = 0.5$.

The input signals $s_n^p(t)$ was computed from the output signals of the RBF units that recognize the key frames of expression p. These can be described by the vector $\mathbf{b}^p = [b_1^p, \ldots, b_{50}^p]^T$ for the actual time step. The components of this vector were smoothed along the neuron axis using a Gaussian filter with a width (standard deviation) of 2 neurons.

The neurons in this RNN are called *snapshot neurons* in the following. They are expression-selective and fire phasically during the evolution of the expressions. In addition, they are sequence-selective, i.e. they fire less strongly if the same keyframe is presented as part of temporally inverted sequence.

The thresholded output signals of the snapshot neurons belonging to the same expression are integrated by an *expression neuron* that computes the maximum over all snapshot neuron outputs (cf. Fig. 1B). These neurons have a time constant $\tau_v = 4$, so that their outputs can be describe by the dynamics:

$$\tau_v \dot{v}_p(t) = -v_p(t) + \sum_n [u_n^p(t)]_+ \qquad (2)$$

The expressions neuron thus fire continuously during the evolution of the corresponding expression p, but only weakly during the other ones.

Norm–Based Model. The second mechanism for the recognition of dynamic expressions is inspired by results on the norm-referenced encoding of face identity by cortical neurons in area IT [4]. We have proposed before a neural model that accounts for these electrophysiological results on the norm-referenced encoding [5]. We demonstrate here that the same principles can be extended to account for the recognition of dynamic facial expressions.

The circuit for norm-based encoding is shown in Fig. 1C. The idea of norm-referenced encoding is to represent the shape of faces in terms of differences relative to a reference face, where we assume that this is the shape of a neutral expression. In our model postulates a special class of Reference Neurons that represent the output feature vector $\mathbf{z}_0^p$ from the mid-level feature hierarchy for a neutral face picture (e.g. at the beginning of the movies). Representations of this pattern could be established by learning or robust averaging, for example exploiting the fact that the neutral expression is much more frequent than the intermediate keyframes of dynamic expressions. The prediction from this mechanism is thus the existence of a sub-population of neurons that represent the neutral expression in terms of its multi-dimensional feature vector. The output activities of these neurons is signified by the reference vector $\mathbf{r} = \mathbf{z}_0^p$.

A physiologically plausible way for the encoding of the vectorial difference $\mathbf{d}(t) = \mathbf{z}(t) - \mathbf{r}$ between the actual feature input $\mathbf{z}(t)$ and the reference vector $\mathbf{r}$ can be based on neurons with the tuning function:

$$f_p = \|\mathbf{d}\| \left(\frac{\frac{\mathbf{d}^T}{\|\mathbf{d}\|}\mathbf{n}_p + 1}{2} \right)^{\nu} \tag{3}$$

This expression defines the output activity of a directionally tuned neuron whose maximum firing rate depends linearly on the norm of the difference vector $\mathbf{d}$. The unit vector $\mathbf{n}_p$ defines the preferred direction of the neuron in a multi-dimensional space. The term in the parenthesis is a direction tuning function that is maximal if the difference vector is aligned with this preferred direction $\mathbf{n}_p$. The positive parameter ν determines the width of the direction tuning in multi-dimensional space. As shown by [5], using $\nu = 1$ results in reasonable fits of neural data from area IT. In this special case if $\|.\|$ signifies the 1-norm, this tuning function can be implemented by a simple two-layer network with linear rectifying units:

$$f_p = 0.5 \left(\mathbf{1} + \mathbf{n}_p\right)^T [\mathbf{d}]_+ + 0.5(\mathbf{1} - \mathbf{n}_p)^T [-\mathbf{d}]_+ \tag{4}$$

It has been shown in [5] that the tuning fits the properties of face-selective neurons in area IT. We call this type of neuron *face neuron* in our model. The activity of these neurons is expression-selective and increases towards the frame with the maximum expression strength. However, these neurons also respond to static pictures of faces.

A very simple way to generate from the responses $f_p(t)$ responses that are selective for dynamically changing expressions is to add a simple output network that consists of *differentiator neurons* that respond phasically to increasing or decreasing changes of the activity $f_p(t)$, and to sum the output signals from these neurons to obtain the *expression neuron* output: $v_p(t) = \frac{df_p}{dt} + \frac{d(-f_p)}{dt}$ (cf. Fig. 1C). In fact, such differentiating neurons have been observed and the dependence of this behavior on channel dynamics has been analyzed in detail (e.g. [19]).

4   Results

In the following, we describe briefly the applied stimulus set, and then show a number of simulation results that show that both models are suitable to classify dynamic facial expressions, while they result in fundamentally different prediction of the behavior of single neurons, especially for morphed stimuli.

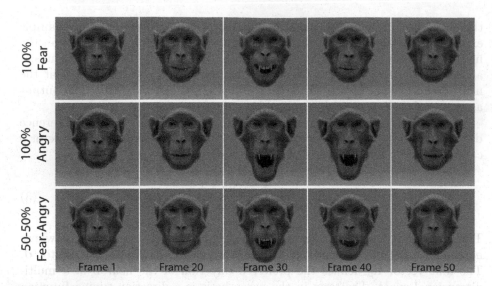

Fig. 2. Monkey Avatar Head. Movies of the three training expressions Fear, Lip Smacking and Angry, and morph (50%–50%) between Fear and Angry.

4.1 Stimulus Generation

In order to test our model we developed a novel highly-realistic monkey head model that was animated using motion capture data from monkeys. The head model was based on an MRI scan of a monkey. The resulting surface mesh model was regularized and optimized for animation. A sophisticated multi-channel texture model for the skin and fur animation were added. The face motion was based on motion capture (VICON), exploiting 43 markers that were placed on the face of a rhesus monkey that executed different facial expressions. By interaction with an experimenter, three expressions (prototypes) were recorded: Fear, Lip Smacking and a Threat/Angry expression (Fig. 2). Exploiting a muscle-like deformable ribbon structure, the motion capture data was transferred to the face mesh, resulting in highly realistic face motion. A recent study shows that the generated facial expressions are perceived by animals as almost as realistic as videos of real monkey expressions, placing the method on the 'good side' of the uncanny valley [22].

In addition to the original expression, we generated morphs between them exploiting a Bayesian motion morphing algorithm [20]. In addition, expressions with reduced strength were generated by morphing the original expression with a neutral facial expressions. This allowed us to study the behavior of the models for gradual variations between the expressions, and for expressions with reduced strength. Expressions always started with neutral, evolved to a maximally expressive frame, and went back to the neutral face. Natural durations of the expressions were between 2 and 3s. All expressions were time-normalized to 50 frames for our analysis of the model. For the experiments reported here, we used the prototype expressions, and expressions with reduced strength that included 25-50-75-100% of each prototype. In addition, morphs between the expressions Fear and Angry with contributions of 0-25-50-75-100% of the Fear prototype were generated.

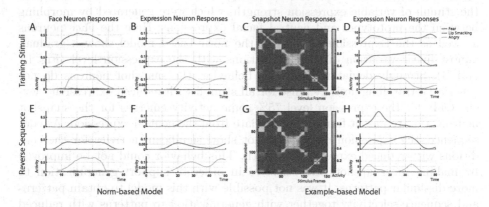

Fig. 3. Activity of model neurons. Presentation of the prototypical expressions: Fear, Lip Smacking and Angry expressions. Upper panels shows data for the original, and the lower panels the reversely played expression movies. Norm-based model: (A, E) Face neurons, and (B, F) Expression Neurons. Example-based model: (C, G) Snapshot neurons, and (D, H) Expression Neurons.

4.2   Simulation Results

We first tested whether the models can classify the prototypical expressions that were used for training correctly. Figure 3A shows the responses of the face neurons that are selective for individual expressions. They show a bell-shaped increase and decrease of activity that is selective for the encoded expression. Panel B shows the response of the corresponding expression neurons, which is also selective for the individual expressions. Opposed to the face neurons, these neurons remain silent during the presentation of static pictures showing the extreme frames of the expressions. Panels C and D show the responses for the example-based model. The activity of the snapshot neurons for the three test expressions is shown in Fig. 3C. Only the frames of the learned expression cause a travelling pulse solution in the corresponding part of the RNN, while the neurons remain silent for the other test patterns. This induces a high selectivity of the responses of the corresponding expression neurons (panel D).

We tested the model also with temporally reversed face sequences in order to investigate the sequence selectivity. The results are shown in Fig. 3E–H. Due to the high temporal symmetry of facial expressions (backwards-played expressions look very similar, but not identical to forward-played expressions), the responses of the face neurons in the norm-based model and also the one of the expression neurons are very similar the responses in panels A-D. Most prominently, the responses of the snapshot neurons show now a travelling pulse that runs in opposite direction. The small differences between forward and backwards movie result in slightly lower amplitudes of the expression neuron responses, especially for the example-based model (panel H), but interestingly also for the norm-based model.

Interesting differential predictions emerged when the models were tested with the stimuli of variable expression strength, which were generated by morphing between the prototypes and neutral facial expressions. Here the Face neurons as well as the Expression neurons in the norm-based model show a gradual, almost linear variation of their activations with the expression level (Fig. 4A and B). Strongly deviating from this behavior, the snapshot neurons do not generate a travelling activity pulse for all stimuli with reduced expressivity levels. Only for the expression level 75% some activity emerges for the snapshot neurons that represent frames that deviate from the neutral expression. As consequence, the expression neurons do not show significant activity for the conditions with reduced expression strength. This behavior could not be improved by making the snapshots less selective in order to support generalization to more dissimilar patterns. It was not possible with this model to obtain pattern- and sequence-selectivity together with generalization to patterns with reduced expression strength.

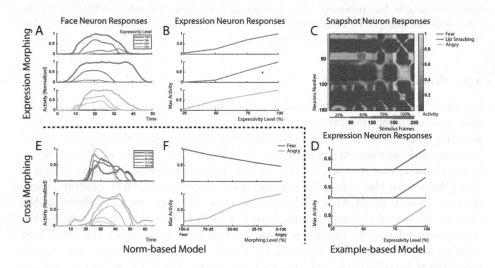

Fig. 4. Upper panels: Neuron activities for stimuli with different expressivity levels (25-50-75-100%). Lower panels: Neuron activities for cross-expression morphs of the neurons of the norm-based model. (A) Normalised activity of Face neurons, and (B) maximum activity of Expression neurons as function of the expressivity level for the norm-based model. (C) Normalised activities of snapshot neurons, and (D) maximum activity of Expression neurons in example-based model. (E) Normalised activity of Face neurons, and (F) maximum activity of Expression neurons as function of the morph level form morphs between Fear and Angry expressions.

The norm-based model showed also very smooth an gradual generalization between different expressions. This is shown in Fig. 4E–F that shows the responses of the Face and the Expression neurons for morphs between the Fear and the Angry expression. Both neuron types show a very smooth change of their activity with the morph level, which is antagonistic for the neurons with selectivity for the two expressions. Also in this case, the example-based model failed to show generalization to stimuli with intermediate morph levels (not shown).

5 Conclusions

Based on previous models that are grounded in electrophysiological data, we have proposed two alternative mechanisms for the processing of dynamic facial expressions. Both mechanisms are consistent with physiological data from other cortical structures that process social stimuli, static faces and dynamic bodies. Both models were able to recognize monkey expressions from movies. Also the recognition of reversed movies of facial expressions could be accounted for by both models. Testing the models with morphed expressions, and expressions with reduced expression strength, however, resulted in fundamentally different predictions. The norm-based model showed smooth and almost linear variation of the activity patterns with the expression strength and the morph level, while the example-based model had problems to generalize to such morphed patterns. In addition, the models make specific predictions about the activity dynamics of the different postulated neuron classes. For example, an example-based mechanism predicts a traveling pulse of activity, as observed e.g. in premotor cortex [6]. The norm-based mechanism predicts a linear tuning of the activity with the distance from the neutral reference pattern in morphing space for the Face neurons, etc.

Obviously, the proposed models are only a very simple proof-of-concept demonstration of the discussed encoding principles that need a much more thorough investigation. First, the initial stages of the models have to be replaced by more powerful deep recognition networks that result in mid-level feature dictionaries that make recognition more robust against variations in lighting, texture, etc. Second, the proposed encoding principles have to be tested on much larger sets of dynamic face stimuli, including specifically human facial expressions, to test whether the proposed coding principles can be extended to more challenging recognition problems. Only this will allow to verify whether the proposed norm-based encoding has computational advantages to the more common example-based encoding that underlies many popular RNN-based technical solutions. In addition, such extended models need to be tested against optic flow-based recognition models [21]. Predictions from such models then can be tested against the measured behavior of recorded dynamic face-selective neurons. Even it its present simple form, however, our model makes some interesting predictions that can help to guide the search for the tuning properties of neurons in areas (patches) with neurons that are selective for dynamic facial expressions. Likewise, the developed stimulus sets will likely be useful to characterize the computational properties of such neurons.

Acknowledgements. This work was supported by HFSP RGP0036/2016 and EC CogIMon H2020 ICT-23-2014/644727. It was also supported by BMBF FKZ 01GQ1704, BW-Stiftung NEU007/1 KONSENS-NHE, ERC 2019-SyG-RELEVANCE-856495 and the Deutsche Forschungsgesellschaft Grant TH425/12-2. NVIDIA Corp.

References

1. Barraclough, N.E., Perrett, D.I.: From single cells to social perception. Philos. Trans. R. Soc. B: Biol. Sci. **366**(1571), 1739–1752 (2011)
2. Ghazanfar, A.A., Chandrasekaran, C., Morrill, R.J.: Dynamic, rhythmic facial expressions and the superior temporal sulcus of macaque monkeys: implications for the evolution of audiovisual speech. Eur. J. Neurosci. **31**(10), 1807–1817 (2010)
3. Mosher, C.P., Zimmerman, P.E., Gothard, K.M.: Neurons in the monkey amygdala detect eye contact during naturalistic social interactions. Curr. Biol. **24**(20), 2459–2464 (2014)
4. Leopold, D.A., Bondar, I.V., Giese, M.A.: Norm-based face encoding by single neurons in the monkey inferotemporal cortex. Nature **442**(7102), 572–575 (2006)
5. Giese, M.A., Leopold, D.A.: Physiologically inspired neural model for the encoding of face spaces. Neurocomputing **65**, 93–101 (2005)
6. Caggiano, V., Fleischer, F., Pomper, J.K., Giese, M.A., Thier, P.: Mirror neurons in monkey premotor area F5 show tuning for critical features of visual causality perception. Curr. Biol. **26**(22), 3077–3082 (2016)
7. Fleischer, F., Caggiano, V., Thier, P., Giese, M.A.: Physiologically inspired model for the visual recognition of transitive hand actions. J. Neurosci. **33**(15), 6563–6580 (2013)
8. Serre, T., Wolf, L., Bileschi, S., Riesenhuber, M., Poggio, T.: Robust object recognition with cortex-like mechanisms. IEEE Trans. Pattern Anal. Mach. Intell. **29**(3), 411–426 (2007)
9. Giese, M.A., Poggio, T.: Neural mechanisms for the recognition of biological movements. Nat. Rev. Neurosci. **4**(3), 179–192 (2003)
10. Lange, J., Lappe, M.: A model of biological motion perception from configural form cues. J. Neurosci. **26**(11), 2894–2906 (2006)
11. Jhuang, H., Serre, T., Wolf, L., Poggio, T.: A biologically inspired system for action recognition. In: 2007 IEEE 11th International Conference on Computer Vision, pp. 1–8. IEEE (2007)
12. Haxby, J.V., Hoffman, E.A., Gobbini, M.I.: The distributed human neural system for face perception. Trends Cogn. Sci. **4**(6), 223–233 (2000)
13. Valentine, T., Lewis, M.B., Hills, P.J.: Face-space: a unifying concept in face recognition research. Q. J. Exp. Psychol. **69**(10), 1996–2019 (2016)
14. Leopold, D.A., Rhodes, G.: A comparative view of face perception. J. Comp. Psychol. **124**(3), 233 (2010)
15. Li, S., Deng, W.: Deep facial expression recognition: a survey. IEEE Trans. Affect. Comput. (2020)
16. Schrimpf, M., et al.: Brain-score: which artificial neural network for object recognition is most brain-like? BioRxiv, p. 407007 (2018)
17. Jones, J.P., Palmer, L.A.: The two-dimensional spatial structure of simple receptive fields in cat striate cortex. J. Neurophysiol. **58**(6), 1187–1211 (1987)
18. Amari, S.: Dynamics of pattern formation in lateral-inhibition type neural fields. Biol. Cybern. **27**(2), 77–87 (1977)

19. Ratté, S., Lankarany, M., Rho, Y.-A., Patterson, A., Prescott, S.A.: Subthreshold membrane currents confer distinct tuning properties that enable neurons to encode the integral or derivative of their input. Front. Cell. Neurosci. **8**, 452 (2015)
20. Taubert, N., Christensen, A., Endres, D., Giese, M.A.: Online simulation of emotional interactive behaviors with hierarchical Gaussian process dynamical models. In: Proceedings of the ACM Symposium on Applied Perception, pp. 25–32 (2012)
21. Barron, J.L., Fleet, D.J., Beauchemin, S.S.: Performance of optical flow techniques. Int. J. Comput. Vis. **12**(1), 43–77 (1994)
22. Siebert, R., Taubert, N., Spadacenta, S., Dicke, P.W., Giese, M.A., Thier, P.: A naturalistic dynamic monkey head avatar elicits species-typical reactions and overcomes the uncanny valley. Eneuro **7**(4) (2020)

Hierarchical Modeling with Neurodynamical Agglomerative Analysis

Michael Marino[1(✉)], Georg Schröter[1], Gunther Heidemann[1],
and Joachim Hertzberg[1,2]

[1] Universität Osnabrück, Wachsbleiche 27, 49090 Osnabrück, Germany
{mimarino,gschroeter,gunther.heidemann,
joachim.hertzberg}@uni-osnabrueck.de
[2] DFKI Laboratory Niedersachsen, Plan-Based Robot Control Department,
Berghoffstr. 11, 49090 Osnabrück, Germany

Abstract. We propose a new analysis technique for neural networks, Neurodynamical Agglomerative Analysis (NAA), an analysis pipeline designed to compare class representations within a given neural network model. The proposed pipeline results in a hierarchy of class relationships implied by the network representation, i.e. a semantic hierarchy analogous to a human-made ontological view of the relevant classes. We use networks pretrained on the ImageNet benchmark dataset to infer semantic hierarchies and show the similarity to human-made semantic hierarchies by comparing them with the WordNet ontology. Further, we show using MNIST training experiments that class relationships extracted using NAA appear to be invariant to random weight initializations, tending toward equivalent class relationships across network initializations in sufficiently parameterized networks.

Keywords: Neural network theory · Deep learning · Cognitive models

1 Introduction

The problem of how to analyze neural network models has been an increasingly important focus as the efficacy of deep networks continues to be demonstrated in many applications. This is a unique aspect of solving problems using structured feedback systems such as machine learning models, where the designer's task is to design a system that will exhibit certain properties upon being restructured by feedback according to update rules (e.g. stochastic gradient descent), as opposed to designing a solution via a robust understanding of relevant first principles.

Analyzing a very high-dimensional model evokes the classic problem of dimensionality reduction, or determining how to simplify a model with potentially millions of variables into something meaningful to a human being. The choice of what aspects of the model to focus on and how to bring meaningful information to the forefront is non-trivial in this case. One would ascertain

Funded by the Deutsche Forschungsgemeinschaft (DFG, German Research Foundation) - GRK 2340.

very different information about the network from a technique that focuses on analyzing which regions of the input are most significant to the output, such as Relevance Propagation [1], than by using an approach focused on evaluating model dimensionality and latent similarity, such as SVCCA [2].

In this paper we introduce Neurodynamical Agglomerative Analysis (NAA), an analysis model that takes as input a collection of network activations sorted according to input classes, and outputs a hierarchy of network clusters that gives insight into the class relationships in the hidden representation. The goal of this analysis pipeline is to allow designers to convert a network model of seemingly random activations and transform them into a hierarchical graphical model that can give insight into how the network models classes with respect to one another, and which classes are most well-differentiated by the model. This way of analyzing neural networks opens the door to new ways of considering issues such as class imbalance and error analysis in the context of training. Further, since up until now most supervised deep neural network models are not developed with any consideration for higher-order class relationships, a computationally efficient and intuitive way to analyze the implied class relationships naturally begs the question of how one would approach enforcing arbitrary relationships into machine learning methods, thus introducing a key aspect of top-down reasoning into bottom-up models.

The proposed model considers the cross-correlation matrix of network activations for a given class as a lower dimensional encoding of the neural relationships that have been developed at a particular layer. We then take the generalized cosine of the correlation matrices as a similarity metric between the class representations and use the matrix defined by these class similarities in order to compare network representations using both agglomerative clustering and the generalized cosine between the similarity matrices themselves. Training experiments with the MNIST [3] dataset show that class relationships exhibit invariance to random initialization, tending toward a particular state as training progresses. Underparameterized networks exhibit dynamic relationships with higher class similarities that never reach a steady state. Additionally, NAA was used to derive class hierarchies based on the ImageNet [4] dataset which were compared to the WordNet [5] ground-truth ontology in order to consider how this notion of similarity relates to a human-made one.

2 Related Work

As the interest in neural networks has increased over the last decade, analysis techniques for deep networks have become an increasing focus in the field. In [1], Bach et al. develop Relevance Propagation, a method to visualize the contributions single pixels make to output predictions by calculating the extent to which an individual pixel impacted the model in choosing or not choosing a particular output class. This analysis method visualizes the saliency of input pixels via a heat map that enables a human to view which regions of an image contributed most to the output.

In [6], Li et al. explored to what extent invariant features are learned from different random initializations by computing the within-net and between-net correlation of network activations. They then inferred corresponding feature maps by sorting the feature maps according to their between-net correlation values, as well as looking for higher level correspondences among features via spectral clustering on within-net correlation matrices. Their model collects a matrix composed of vectorized activations across the entire dataset from each layer and treats each layer of each input instance as a separate feature in the analysis model, thus it effectively compares similar and dissimilar features at the level of individual feature maps of individual input instances. This can be a prohibitively high level of granularity in the case of deep neural networks, as insight still must be gained via the inspection of individual features. In contrast, NAA generates a correlation matrix of activations across a particular class and compares averaged class representations, as well as performing agglomerative clustering on output classes in a bottom-up fashion. In essence, we trade feature-level granularity for hierarchy-level granularity with respect to the class structure.

Another recent work using a similar approach is SVCCA [2], which forms matrices of network activations across a dataset and then performs canonical correlation analysis [7] on filtered approximations of the activation matrices via singular value decomposition. Raghu et al. show relationships between SVCCA and network parameterization that are used to develop networks that use the parameter space more efficiently.

Our method differs from SVCCA in a similar way as it does to [1] and [6]. SVCCA compares representations across architectures for a given dataset by evaluating the correlation values of maximally-correlated subspaces of features across network representations. In contrast, we compare the network to itself using the generalized cosine of correlation matrices across classes at a given layer to evaluate how well-oriented the correlation matrices are with respect to one another, and therefore how similar the class representations are. Unlike SVCCA, our method is only invariant to global rotations in the feature subspace. Intuitively, this means that our method does not allow for flexible neural correspondences in its notion of representational similarity.

The idea to use the generalized cosine of the cross-correlation matrices was inspired by [8], in which Jaeger similarly uses the generalized cosine between cross-correlation matrices as a similarity metric for Excited Network Dynamics in Echo State Networks. Jaeger shows that, in some cases, evaluating the similarity of the conceptor matrices he defines produces a better correspondence to a human notion of similarity than do the raw matrices.

3   Methods

3.1   Dimensionality Reduction for Analysis

Dimensionality reduction is often brought up in the context of computational feasibility, but many scientific methods can be viewed in terms of dimensionality reduction. For example, representing a collection of data as a probability distribution could be seen as representing a vast collection of data points by a few parameters.

The dimensionality reduction approach used by NAA is to take the cross-correlation matrix of network activations, it being considered in this sense a low-dimensional representation for the network "dynamics". Given a set of neural activation vectors specific to class c in layer l, $Z_{c,l} = \{z_1, \ldots, z_m\}$, where z_k represents the activations on the kth datapoint, and is of dimensionality n, defined by the amount of output neurons at a given layer. The cross-correlation matrix, R is defined according to

$$r_{ij} = E[z_i z_j] \tag{1}$$

where, in this case, z_i and z_j represent the ith and j^{th} (scalar) activations in a given vector, respectively, and $E[z_i z_j]$ is the expectation over the product of scalar neural activations z_i and z_j. The cross-correlation matrix is a way of assessing the "neurodynamics" of the network, used here in an analogical sense, in that, although there is no time variable in the convolutional networks in consideration per se, we are using the way neurons would vary together in a dynamical sense as being a low-dimensional representation of the network's class representations. The analysis pipeline can also be generally applied to any data composed of vectors of network activations. The cross-correlation matrix can be estimated for a dataset according to

$$R = \frac{1}{n} Z Z^T. \tag{2}$$

3.2   Generalized Cosine for Assessing Neurodynamical Similarity

Definition. Singular Value Decomposition (SVD) is a common tool that forms the basis of dimensionality reduction techniques such as Principle Component Analysis as well as being used for applications such as solving homogeneous linear equations. The Singular Value Decomposition of a real, symmetric matrix R is defined as

$$SVD(R) = U \Sigma U^T \tag{3}$$

where U is a unitary matrix composed of the eigenvectors of R, and Σ is a diagonal matrix composed of the eigenvalues of R. This decomposition defines a hyperellipsoid, with axes oriented according to the unitary basis defined by U and radii corresponding to the diagonal entries of Σ. A generalized cosine [8] between two such hyperellipsoids is defined according to

$$cos^2(R_i, R_j) = \frac{\left\| \Sigma_i^{1/2} U_i' U_j \Sigma_j^{1/2} \right\|^2}{\left\| diag\left\{ \Sigma_i \right\} \right\| \left\| diag\left\{ \Sigma_j \right\} \right\|} \tag{4}$$

where $diag\{\Sigma\}$ is the vectorized diagonal entries of Σ and $\|\cdot\|$ represents the Frobenius norm, or the L^2 vector norm. The relationship in (4) defines a similarity metric between two matrices and in this case is used for comparing two class representations of a given layer of a neural network.

Computational Optimization and Implementation. Calculating the generalized cosine defined in (4) requires performing singular value decomposition on the matrix, which would require $\mathcal{O}(n^3)$ computation time, where n is the dimensionality of the square matrix, R, or dimensionality of the layer of interest in our case. However, an equivalent relationship can be derived that avoids the SVD step by using the trace of matrix products, resulting in the equivalent formula

$$cos^2(R_i, R_j) = \frac{Tr\{R_i R_j\}}{\sqrt{Tr\{R_i R_i\} Tr\{R_j R_j\}}} \tag{5}$$

which brings the computational cost of calculating the similarity metric down to $\mathcal{O}(n^2)$, since for the trace of matrix products only the diagonal elements are required.

Proof. The numerator of (4) can be simplified utilizing the following properties of the trace product and Frobenius norm

$$\left\| A \right\|^2 = Tr\{A^T A\} \tag{6}$$

$$Tr\{AB\} = Tr\{BA\} \tag{7}$$

along with the property that

$$U^T = U^{-1} \tag{8}$$

for any unitary matrix U. In order to derive the relationship in (5) we exploit the fact that the trace of matrix products is invariant with respect to cycling the matrices being multiplied, in accordance with (7), as well as the fact that $UU^T = I$, the identity matrix. Thus, using the relationship in Eq. (6) we can redefine a formula equivalent to the numerator of (4) as follows -

$$\left\| \Sigma_i^{1/2} U_i^T U_j \Sigma_j^{1/2} \right\|^2 = Tr\left\{ (\Sigma_i^{1/2} U_i^T U_j \Sigma_j^{1/2})^T \Sigma_i^{1/2} U_i^T U_j \Sigma_j^{1/2} \right\}$$

$$= Tr\left\{ (U_i \Sigma_i U_i^T)(U_j \Sigma_j U_j^T) \right\}$$

$$= Tr\left\{ R_i R_j \right\}$$

Similarly, since Σ is a diagonal matrix, the factors in the denominator can be expressed as

$$\left\|diag\left\{\Sigma_i\right\}\right\|^2 = \left\|\Sigma_i\right\|^2$$
$$= Tr\left\{\Sigma_i^T \Sigma_i\right\}$$
$$= Tr\left\{U_i \Sigma_i U_i^T U_i \Sigma_i U_i^T\right\}$$
$$= Tr\left\{R_i R_i\right\}$$

and so a similarity metric equivalent to the generalized cosine defined in (4) can be formed according to (5) which brings the computational complexity of our metric from $\mathcal{O}(n^3)$ to $\mathcal{O}(n^2)$. The similarity defined in (5) is then used to construct a distance matrix, D, according to

$$d_{ij} = 1 - s_{ij} \tag{9}$$

where (i, j) refers to classes i and j, respectively. The class similarities $s_{ij} = cos^2(R_i, R_j)$ are used to build a similarity matrix, S, which is used to compare different network representations. Thus, D defines the distance matrix which can be used to generate a hierarchy of network classes via agglomerative clustering, as in Sect. 4.1, or the similarity matrices can be used to compare entire representations by taking the generalized cosine between the similarity matrices calculated from different models, as in Sect. 4.2.

3.3 Agglomerative Clustering

Agglomerative clustering is a hierarchical clustering method, which merges points one at a time in a greedy fashion until there is only one supercluster remaining. In this case we are concerned with a sort of mean representation of the clusters formed by similar classes, so the merging rule we chose was to take the averaging method which takes the distance between two clusters u and v according to [9]

$$d(u, v) = \frac{1}{|u| * |v|} \sum_{ij} d(u[i], v[j]) \tag{10}$$

where $|u|$ and $|v|$ represent the cardinalities of clusters u and v. Linkage calculations were done using the scikit-learn library [10]. Neural network training and data collection was done using tensorflow 2.0 with data processing performed in Python 3.6.

4   Experimental Results and Discussion

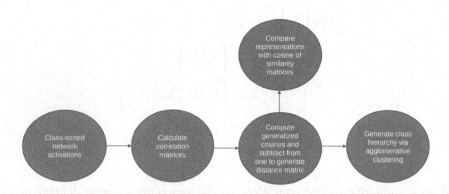

Fig. 1. Method Overview - This flow diagram represents the analysis methods used in Sects. 4.1 and 4.2. In both experiments, network activations from hidden layers are sorted by class membership to calculate correlation matrices. Class similarities are then calculated using the generalized cosine between the correlation matrices and converted to distances by subtracting from one. In Sect. 4.1, agglomerative clustering is performed on the distance matrix, resulting in a class hierarchy implied by the hidden representation at a given layer. In Sect. 4.2, different network representations are compared by performing the generalized cosine metric on the similarity matrices themselves.

4.1   Comparing Network Models with the WordNet Ontology

In order to compare some trained hierarchies with a more human-minded view of the world, we performed NAA on the VGG16 [11], Resnet50 [12], and Inception V3 [13] architectures pretrained on the ImageNet [4] benchmark dataset, the class structure of which is conveniently based on the WordNet [5] ontology. By treating the resulting clusters as a sort of classification problem, we can get an idea of the similarity with human-made ontologies. That is, for each supercluster in the WordNet subtree, we find the closest matching cluster in the agglomerative hierarchy by searching for the cluster with the closest F1 score. The results can be seen in Fig. 2. Comparing the trees is done in this way due to limitations of standard graph distance measures, which generally assume a well-defined superclass structure. In order to show that these correspondences are not merely a matter of random chance, the results were compared with the resulting clustering when the distance matrix was randomly permuted. This randomized baseline ensures the distribution of distance values is identical to the experimental distribution, while showing that the correspondences between the results and WordNet are not a result of random chance.

Figure 2(a) shows the distribution of F1 scores resulting from the fully connected layers of VGG16 and Fig. 2(b) shows the distribution resulting from the

permuted distance matrix. Only classes from the WordNet ontology with at least
15 true class members were included in the analysis in order to eliminate bias
introduced by including groups with low member counts.

The clusters with the top-10 and bottom-10 F1 scores for the final hidden
layers of all three architectures can be seen in Tables 1 and 2, respectively. The
significant overlap in both top and bottom scoring clusters in the VGG16 and
Resnet50 architectures may indicate an invariance even across architectures,
although the significant difference between the InceptionV3 results indicates this
would not be true across all architectures.

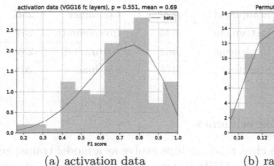
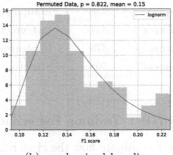

(a) activation data   (b) randomized baseline

Fig. 2. Results from performing agglomerative clustering on the fully connected layers
of the VGG16 architecture trained on the ImageNet dataset; 2(a) normalized histogram
with the best fit distribution of resulting similarities from both fully connected layers
of the VGG16 architecture; 2(b) normalized histogram with the best fit distribution
resulting from clustering the permuted distance matrix

Table 1. Top-10 F1 score results from searching NAA hierarchy of the final fully connected layer in VGG16, Resnet50, and InceptionV3 for best match to each superclass in
the WordNet ground-truth hierarchy; note the significant overlap in groupings between
VGG16 and Resnet50

VGG		Resnet50		InceptionV3	
Class	F1 score	Class	F1 score	Class	F1 score
Bird	1.00	Bird	1.00	Snake	.941
Snake	1.00	Dog	.967	Primate	.923
Dog	.992	Mammal	.962	Artifact	.743
Primate	.976	Dom. animal	.953	Diapsid	.708
Dom. animal	.971	Placental	.952	Wading bird	.692
Canine	.944	Primate	.950	Fruit	.667
Artifact	.939	Artifact	.946	Plant part	.667
Aquatic bird	.917	Canine	.937	Terrier	.667
Diapsid	.848	Snake	.903	Repr. structure	.667
Carnivore	.848	Carnivore	.887	Plant organ	.667

Table 2. Bottom-10 F1 score results, as in Table 1

VGG		Resnet50		InceptionV3	
Class	F1 score	Class	F1 score	Class	F1 score
Protective cov.	.200	Protective cov.	.188	Prot. covering	.171
Machine	.273	Machine	.273	Structure	.176
Working dog	.405	Furnishing	.341	Equipment	.213
Device	.427	Furniture	.345	Matter	.214
Equipment	.444	Working dog	.390	Vehicle	.231
Instrument	.444	Device	.408	Conveyance	.244
Furniture	.448	Equipment	.429	Container	.256
Furnishing	.457	Instrument	.444	Invertebrate	.257
Structure	.479	Implement	.464	Arthropod	.259
Implement	.508	Structure	.471	Machine	.261

4.2 MNIST Training Experiments

In order to evaluate how the class relationships evolve as a model trains, generic CNNs were trained to classify the MNIST dataset [3]. The number of convolutional layers were varied from 1 to 2, with channel depth varying from 2 to 8. The number of fully connected layers was set at 2, each layer having between 2 and 16 nodes. ReLu activations were used for all hidden layers. Distances relative to digits 6 for two example networks can be seen in Fig. 3, as well as the minimum distance across all digits which appears to be a good indicator of validation accuracy. Accuracy and loss plots are included in Figs. 3(c) and (d) for comparison. The heat maps indicate training epoch, with the darkest line corresponding to epoch 100.

As can be seen by comparing the plots in Fig. 3, the relationships in the underparameterized network are relatively unstable, varying significantly across training epochs compared with the relational stability exhibited in the sufficiently parameterized networks in Fig. 3(b). In general, sufficiently parameterized networks showed stable class relationships and increased minimum distances while underparameterized network relationships oscillated back and forth through training and often reflected a lack of effective delineation between classes.

Comparing Representations Across Networks. One useful component of other analysis methods that has not been addressed is the ability to compare across networks. As mentioned previously, our method is not invariant to rotations in the feature subspace and so using the relationship defined in (2) in order to compare across networks would require a step to make the R matrices of the same dimensionality as well as likely being a poor method to evaluate relationships since it does not allow for flexible neural correspondences. However, we can compare representations in different layers by calculating the generalized cosine

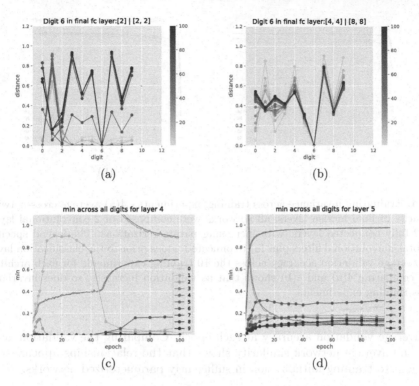

Fig. 3. NAA results on the final hidden layer across training for CNNs with 1–2 convolutional layers and two fully connected layers with varying degrees of parameterization; 3(a) and 3(b) class distances relative to digit 6 plotted across training for 2 sample networks, parameterization increasing from left to right(network parameterization shown above plot); 3(c) and 3(d) minimum distances across all digits for the respective networks for the same layer, with accuracy and loss curves plotted in red and blue for reference (Color figure online)

between the similarity matrices themselves, each being a symmetric matrix in $\mathbb{R}^n$, where n is the dimensionality of the classification layer. We therefore define the similarity between two network representations i and j at layers l_i and l_j analogous to (5) using the cosine between S_{l_i} and S_{l_j}, where S_{l_i} and S_{l_j} represent the class similarity matrices at layer l_i in network representation i and S_{l_j} defined similarly for network j.

Figure 4 shows the results from comparing network representations across training experiments. The figure shows experiments where the number of parameters in networks consisting of one to two convolutional layers and two fully connected layers were gradually increased in order to evaluate cross-training invariance as the level of parameterization increases. Each configuration was used to train 10 different models with the same architecture, which were then compared as described above. Figure 4(a) shows the average similarity of the final fully connected layers at different points in training, while Fig. 4(b) shows

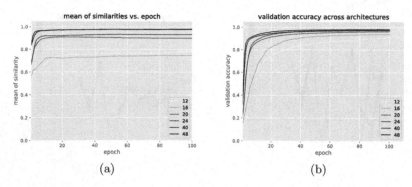

(a)   (b)

Fig. 4. Evaluating invariance across training experiments - 4(a) average cross-network similarity of final hidden layers; all networks were composed of 2 convolutional layers and 2 fully connected layers, with increasing parameterizations. The legend specifies the total convolutional filters plus fully connected nodes prior to the classification layer; 4(b) average validation accuracy across the 10 training experiments for each architecture; comparing 4(a) and 4(b) shows that as validation increases, so does invariance across training experiments.

the average validation accuracy at each epoch. Comparing the validation accuracy and average network similarity shows that the relationships appear to be invariant to training initialization in sufficiently parameterized networks.

5   Summary

In this work, we introduced Neurodynamical Agglomerative Analysis, a hierarchical analysis pipeline that takes as input a subset of network activations sorted by class and layer, and outputs an agglomerative hierarchy of output classes based on the generalized cosine of cross-correlation matrices as a similarity metric.

Using the ImageNet benchmark dataset, we showed the extent to which this similarity corresponds to a human-made view of the world in some architectures, likely corresponding to the extent to which class delineation relates to textural similarity. Further, by comparing the resulting hierarchies across different well-known architectures, we showed that some relationships in NAA may even be invariant across some architectures based on similarities between results for VGG16 and Resnet50 architectures, as well as that this invariance would not be global since there were significant differences apparent in the InceptionV3 architecture.

Using MNIST training experiments, we also showed how some class relationships in NAA evolve over training in networks to varying degrees of parameterization. Preliminary analysis shows underparameterized networks exhibit more erratic relationships between classes while overparameterized networks tend toward more or less steady-state relationships over time. This steady-state relationship appears to also be relatively invariant to training initializations, showing that this type of analysis may be a step in the direction of uncovering properties of the network that are invariant across training experiments. Future work with these insights will include further exploration into how invariant these relationships are, as well as how the relationships in the correlation space relate to class-delineated error analysis. Additionally, in order to add another dimension of experimental variation, methods of embedding arbitrary hierarchies into the correlation space will be explored.

References

1. Bach, S., et al.: On pixel-wise explanations for non-linear classifier decisions by layer-wise relevance propagation. PLoS ONE **10**(7), e0130140 (2015)
2. Raghu, M., et al.: SVCCA: singular vector canonical correlation analysis for deep learning dynamics and interpretability. In: Advances in Neural Information Processing Systems (2017)
3. Deng, L.: The MNIST database of handwritten digit images for machine learning research [best of the web]. IEEE Signal Process. Mag. **29**(6), 141–142 (2012)
4. Deng, J., et al.: ImageNet: a large-scale hierarchical image database. In: 2009 IEEE Conference on Computer Vision and Pattern Recognition. IEEE (2009)
5. Fellbaum, C.: WordNet. In: Poli, R., Healy, M., Kameas, A. (eds.) Theory and Applications of Ontology: Computer Applications, pp. 231–243. Springer, Dordrecht (2010). https://doi.org/10.1007/978-90-481-8847-5_10
6. Li, Y., et al.: Convergent learning: do different neural networks learn the same representations?. In: FE@ NIPS (2015)
7. Hardoon, D.R., Szedmak, S., Shawe-Taylor, J.: Canonical correlation analysis: an overview with application to learning methods. Neural Comput. **16**(12), 2639–2664 (2004)
8. Jaeger, H.: Controlling recurrent neural networks by conceptors. arXiv preprint arXiv:1403.3369 (2014)
9. Müllner, D.: Modern hierarchical, agglomerative clustering algorithms. arXiv preprint arXiv:1109.2378 (2011)
10. Pedregosa, F., et al.: Scikit-learn: machine learning in Python. J. Mach. Learn. Res. **12**(Oct), 2825–2830 (2011)
11. Simonyan, K., Zisserman, A.: Very deep convolutional networks for large-scale image recognition. arXiv preprint arXiv:1409.1556 (2014)
12. He, K., et al.: Deep residual learning for image recognition. In: Proceedings of the IEEE Conference on Computer Vision and Pattern Recognition (2016)
13. Szegedy, C., et al.: Going deeper with convolutions. In: Proceedings of the IEEE Conference on Computer Vision and Pattern Recognition (2015)

Convolutional Neural Networks and Kernel Methods

Deep and Wide Neural Networks
Covariance Estimation

Argimiro Arratia[1]($\boxtimes$), Alejandra Cabaña[2], and José Rafael León[3]

[1] Computer Science, Polytechnical University of Catalunya, Barcelona, Spain
argimiro@cs.upc.edu
[2] Department of Mathematics, Universidad Autónoma de Barcelona,
Barcelona, Spain
AnaAlejandra.Cabana@uab.cat
[3] IMERL, Universidad de La República, Montevideo, Uruguay
rlramos@fing.edu.uy

Abstract. It has been recently shown that a deep neural network with
i.i.d. random parameters is equivalent to a Gaussian process in the limit
of infinite network width. The Gaussian process associated to the neural
network is fully described by a recursive covariance kernel determined
by the architecture of the network, and which is expressed in terms of
expectation. We give a numerically workable analytic expression of the
neural network recursive covariance based on Hermite polynomials. We
give explicit forms of this recursive covariance for the cases of neural
networks with activation function the Heaviside, ReLU and sigmoid.

Keywords: Deep neural networks · Gaussian process · Kernels ·
Hermite polynomials

1 Introduction

The connection between deep feed forward neural networks with i.i.d. random
parameters and Gaussian processes has recently been formalised from two different
perspectives. Following on work by Neal [9], who showed the equivalence in computation of Gaussian processes and one layer neural (random) networks in the limit
of infinite width, Lee et al. [6] and Matthews et al. [7] extended this equivalence
(independently and simultaneously submitting their work to the same conference
venue), for multiple layers networks (with i.i.d. random weights and biases at each
layer) and Gaussian processes. The main tool in these model equivalence results
is some suitable version of the Central Limit Theorem (CLT). The crux of their
argument is the way the hidden layers widths are taken to infinity. Lee et al. [6]

A. Arratia—Supported by grant TIN2017-89244-R from MINECO (Ministerio de
Economía, Industria y Competitividad) and the recognition 2017SGR-856 (MACDA)
from AGAUR (Generalitat de Catalunya).
A. Cabaña—Supported by grant RTI2018-096072-B-I00D Ministerio de Ciencia, Inno-
vación y Universidades.

I. Farkaš et al. (Eds.): ICANN 2020, LNCS 12396, pp. 195–206, 2020.
https://doi.org/10.1007/978-3-030-61609-0_16

make the hidden layers widths grow to infinity *in succession*: by making the width of layer μ grow arbitrarily large while keeping the width of layer $\mu + 1$ fixed, this guarantees that the input to layer $\mu + 1$ coming from layer μ is already governed by a Gaussian process, and the result is attained by an application of a classical Lindeberg-Lévy CLT. On the other hand, Matthews et al. [7] consider that hidden layers grow their widths *simultaneously*. This assumption permits for all the layers to have different widths, and can be considered as a more natural tuning method of deep neural networks in practice. However, their proof of the equivalence with GP is more involved as it requires a version of the CLT suitable for *interchangeable sequences* [2]. We will outline the main ideas of Matthews et al. result as shown in their extended paper [8].

The outcome of both works is that the found correspondence implies that over the class of infinitely wide neural networks, "an i.i.d prior over weights and biases can be replaced with a corresponding GP prior over functions, and this substitution enables exact Bayesian inference for neural networks regression" [6]. The regression problem then boils down to building the corresponding covariance matrices that govern the GPs, over the training and test sets. Our contribution is to give a general and effective analytic expression to compute these covariance matrices based on Hermite polynomials.

2   Gaussian Processes

A stochastic process is a collection of random variables $\{Y(\boldsymbol{x}) : \boldsymbol{x} \in \mathcal{X}\}$ indexed by a set $\mathcal{X}$. We consider $\mathcal{X} = \mathbb{R}^d$, so that d is the number of inputs. A stochastic process is specified by giving the probability distribution for every finite subset of its variables in a consistent manner.

We now present the particular case of a Gaussian process. Our exposition follows the contents in the textbook [11], where the reader can get more details. A Gaussian process (GP) $\{f(\boldsymbol{x}) : \boldsymbol{x} \in \mathcal{X}\}$ is a stochastic process, any finite subset of its variables having a *joint Gaussian distribution*. A GP is completely determined by its mean and its covariance or kernel function $m(\boldsymbol{x}) = \mathbb{E}[f(\boldsymbol{x})]$ and $k(\boldsymbol{x}, \boldsymbol{x}') = \mathbb{E}[(f(\boldsymbol{x}) - m(\boldsymbol{x}))(f(\boldsymbol{x}') - m(\boldsymbol{x}'))]$; although, in practice it is often assumed a zero mean function: $m(\boldsymbol{x}) = 0$.

Given a (training) set of observations $(X, \boldsymbol{y}) = \{(\boldsymbol{x}_i, y_i) : i = 1, \ldots, n\}$, each $\boldsymbol{x}_i$ is d-dimensional input vector, y_i is output. To find the relation between inputs and outputs with a Gaussian process regression, one assumes $y_i = f(\boldsymbol{x}_i) + \epsilon_i$ where $f(\boldsymbol{x})$ is a GP with kernel $k(\boldsymbol{x}, \boldsymbol{x})$ and $\epsilon_i \sim \mathcal{N}(0, \sigma_n^2)$ are i.i.d. random variables representing the noise in the data. In Gaussian process regression one starts from a prior Gaussian process to impose initial knowledge about function f, and then combines this with the observed data points $(X, \boldsymbol{y})$ to obtain a posterior distribution on the observations (a Bayesian method). Mathematically, this boils down to conditioning a joint distribution on the observations.

For a sample $(X, \boldsymbol{f}) = \{(\boldsymbol{x}_i, f_i) : i = 1, \ldots, n\}$ generated from $f(\boldsymbol{x})$, we then have $\boldsymbol{f} \sim \mathbf{N}(0, K(X, X))$, where $K(X, X)$ is the covariance matrix from kernel $k(x, x')$:

$$K(X,X) = \begin{pmatrix} k(\boldsymbol{x}_1,\boldsymbol{x}_1) & \cdots & k(\boldsymbol{x}_1,\boldsymbol{x}_n) \\ k(\boldsymbol{x}_2,\boldsymbol{x}_1) & \cdots & k(\boldsymbol{x}_2,\boldsymbol{x}_n) \\ \vdots & \vdots & \vdots \\ k(\boldsymbol{x}_n,\boldsymbol{x}_1) & \cdots & k(\boldsymbol{x}_n,\boldsymbol{x}_n) \end{pmatrix}$$

Consider a $n_* \times d$ matrix X_* of n_* test inputs, each of dimension d, and let f_* be the corresponding (unknown) vector of function values. Then the joint distribution of training outputs $\boldsymbol{y}$ (from observations $(X,\boldsymbol{y})$) and function values $\boldsymbol{f}_*$ is

$$\begin{bmatrix} \boldsymbol{y} \\ \boldsymbol{f}_* \end{bmatrix} = \mathbf{N}\left(0, \begin{bmatrix} K(X,X) + \sigma_n^2 I & K(X,X_*) \\ K(X_*,X) & K(X_*,X_*) \end{bmatrix}\right) \tag{1}$$

To evaluate the GP posterior in the test inputs X_* and training $(X,\boldsymbol{y})$, the joint distribution (1) is conditioned on the observations $\boldsymbol{y}$,

$$\boldsymbol{f}_*|X_*,X,\boldsymbol{y} \sim \mathbf{N}(K(X_*,X)[K(X,X) + \sigma_n^2 I]^{-1}\boldsymbol{y},$$
$$K(X_*,X_*) - K(X_*,X)[K(X,X) + \sigma_n^2 I]^{-1}K(X,X_*)) \tag{2}$$

Point predictions correspond to the mean of this distribution:

$$\bar{\boldsymbol{f}}_* = \mathbb{E}[\boldsymbol{f}_*|X_*,X,\boldsymbol{y}] = K(X_*,X)[K(X,X) + \sigma_n^2 I]^{-1}\boldsymbol{y}$$

and its covariance

$$cov(\boldsymbol{f}_*) = K(X_*,X_*) - K(X_*,X)[K(X,X) + \sigma_n^2 I]^{-1}K(X,X_*) \tag{3}$$

There are many choices for kernel functions, the necessary condition for any of them is that the defined covariance matrix $K(X,X)$ must be positive definite. In this work we are concerned in obtaining an effective expression for the kernel of the Gaussian process underlying a Deep Neural Network in terms of its activation function.

3 Deep Neural Networks

We adapt the description of wide deep neural networks (WDNet) of Matthews et al. [7] and summarise their proof that the output of the WDNet defines a GP indexed by the inputs $\mathcal{X} = \mathbb{R}^d$ [7,8]. This is necessary for understanding the general form of the kernel associated to the process.

For a deep (fully connected) neural network of D layers, $D > 1$, each labelled by $\mu = 1,\ldots,D$, we assume that the weights of the network at each layer form a matrix of independent random elements $W^{(\mu)} = (w_{i,j}^{(\mu)})_{H_\mu \times H_{\mu-1}}$, with $w_{i,j}^{(\mu)} \sim \mathbf{N}(0, C_w^{(\mu)})$, and the random bias are also mean zero Gaussian vectors $b_i^{(\mu)}$ independent of the matrix terms and i.i.d. with variance equal to $C_b^{(\mu)}$, where $i = 1,\ldots,H_\mu$ and $j = 1,\ldots,H_{\mu-1}$. We set $H_0 = M$, so that there are M inputs to the network. We assume there is one activation function ϕ for all the layers of the network. The output for the first layer can be expressed by the formula

$$f_i^{(1)}(\boldsymbol{x}) = \sum_{j=1}^{H_0} w_{i,j}^{(1)} x_j + b_i^{(1)}, \; i = 1, 2, \ldots H_1.$$

In vectorial notation this is expressed as $\mathbf{f}^{(1)}(\boldsymbol{x}) = W^{(1)}\boldsymbol{x} + \mathbf{b}^{(1)}$, and the analysis of the dimension gives $\mathbf{f}^{(1)}(\boldsymbol{x}) \in \mathbb{R}^{H_1}$. If our network has only one layer ($D = 1$), we get the output by using the recursion

$$g_i^{(1)}(\boldsymbol{x}) = \phi(f_i^{(1)}(\boldsymbol{x}))$$
$$f_i^{(2)}(\boldsymbol{x}) = \sum_{j=1}^{H_1} w_{i,j}^{(2)} g_i^{(1)}(\boldsymbol{x}) + b_i^{(2)}.$$

which in vectorial notation amounts to

$$g^{(1)}(\boldsymbol{x}) = \tilde{\phi}(f^{(1)}(\boldsymbol{x}))$$
$$f^{(2)}(\boldsymbol{x}) = W^{(2)} g^{(1)}(\boldsymbol{x}) + \mathbf{b}^{(2)}.$$

where $\tilde{\phi}(\mathbf{z}) = (\phi(z_1), \ldots, \phi(z_{H_1}))$, and $\mathbf{z} \in \mathbb{R}^{H_1}$. If there are D layers the recursion can be written as

$$g^{(\mu)}(\boldsymbol{x}) = \tilde{\phi}(f^{(\mu)}(\boldsymbol{x}))$$
$$f^{(\mu+1)}(\boldsymbol{x}) = W^{(\mu+1)} g^{(\mu)}(\boldsymbol{x}) + \mathbf{b}^{(\mu+1)}.$$

And the final output is the vector $f^{(D+1)}(\boldsymbol{x})$.

We are interested in studying the asymptotic behavior of a sequence of networks, such for each $n \in \mathbb{N}$, the width for each layer is $H_\mu(n)$ and it is assumed that $H_\mu(n) \to \infty$ as $n \to \infty$, *simultaneously*. The random matrices $W^{(\mu)}$ can be represented using $\mathbf{N}(0, 1)$ random variables. So, if $Z^{(\mu)}$ are matrices of standard Gaussian r.v. and defining $C_W^{(\mu)} = \frac{\hat{C}_W^{(\mu)}}{H_\mu(n)}$, it holds

$$g^{(\mu)}(\boldsymbol{x}) = \tilde{\phi}(f^{(\mu)}(\boldsymbol{x}))$$
$$f^{(\mu+1)}(\boldsymbol{x}) = \sqrt{\frac{\hat{C}_W^{(\mu+1)}}{H_\mu(n)}} Z^{(\mu+1)} g^{(\mu)}(\boldsymbol{x}) + \mathbf{b}^{(\mu+1)}.$$

Let us remark that conditioning by the random vector $g^{(\mu)}(\boldsymbol{x})$ the conditional distribution of the above r.v. is a zero mean Gaussian vector with covariance matrix given by

$$\left(\frac{\hat{C}_W^{(\mu+1)}}{H_\mu(n)} ||g^{(\mu)}(\boldsymbol{x})||^2 + C_b^{(\mu+1)} \right) I_{H_\mu \times H_\mu},$$

where $I_{H_\mu \times H_\mu}$ denotes the identity matrix in $\mathbb{R}^{H_\mu} \times \mathbb{R}^{H_\mu}$.

In the sequel we will define the statistics of interest as a sum of random vectors. Let us consider the infinite real sequence $\chi = (x[i])_{i=1}^{\infty}$ and set $\mathcal{L}$ a finite set of tuples of indexes $\mathcal{L} \subset \chi \times \mathbb{N}$. Then an element of this set can be written as $((x[j_1],\ldots,x[j_M]),i) = (x_{j_1 j_2,\ldots j_M},i) = (x_{J_M},i) \in \mathcal{L}$. For each $n \in \mathbb{N}$ the following finite sum can be defined

$$T^{(\mu)}(\mathcal{L},\alpha)(n) = \sum_{(x_{J_M},i)\in\mathcal{L}} \alpha^{(x_{J_M},i)}\big[f_i^{(\mu)}(x_{J_M})(n) - b_i^{(\mu)}\big]$$

$$= \sum_{(x_{J_M},i)\in\mathcal{L}} \alpha^{(x_{J_M},i)}\sqrt{\frac{\hat{C}_W^{(\mu)}}{H_{\mu-1}(n)}} \sum_{j=1}^{H_{\mu-1}(n)} \varepsilon_{i,j} g_j^{(\mu-1)}(x_{J_M})$$

$$= \sqrt{\frac{\hat{C}_W^{(\mu)}}{H_{\mu-1}(n)}} \sum_{j=1}^{H_{\mu-1}(n)} \sum_{(x_{J_M},i)\in\mathcal{L}} \alpha^{(x_{J_M},i)} g_j^{(\mu-1)}(x_{J_M})\varepsilon_{i,j}. \quad (4)$$

Consider the vector $(\gamma_1^{(\mu)}(\mathcal{L},\alpha)(n),\ldots,\gamma_{H_{\mu-1}(n)}^{(\mu)}(\mathcal{L},\alpha)(n))$. Each one of the coordinates say γ_j, is one the summands in (4),

$$\gamma_j^{(\mu)}(\mathcal{L},\alpha)(n) = \sum_{(x_{J_M},i)\in\mathcal{L}} \alpha^{(x_{J_M},i)} g_j^{(\mu-1)}(x_{J_M})\varepsilon_{i,j},$$

where

$$g_j^{(\mu-1)}(x_{J_M}) = \phi\Big(\sqrt{\frac{\hat{C}_W^{(\mu-1)}}{H_{\mu-2}(n)}} \sum_{k=1}^{H_{\mu-2}(n)} \varepsilon_{j,k} g_k^{(\mu-2)}(x_{J_M}) + b_j\Big).$$

Conditioning with respect to the random variables $g_k^{(\mu-2)}(x_{J_M})$, for $k = 1, \ldots,$ $H_{\mu-2}(n)$, the $g_j^{(\mu-1)}(x_{J_M})$ result independent and i.i.d. As a consequence the same holds true for the random variables $\gamma_j^{(\mu)}(\mathcal{L},\alpha)(n)$. By de Finetti Theorem [4, Theorem 1.1. p 25] these variables are interchangeable.

Matthews et al. [8] introduce another key notation. Let us denote as $|\mathcal{L}|$ the cardinal of the set $\mathcal{L}$, and consider an enumeration of this set that we will index by defining $\{(1),\ldots,(|\mathcal{L}|)\}$. In this form it can be written $(x_{J_M},i) = (x(\ell),(\ell))$ for some $(\ell) \in \{(1),\ldots,(|\mathcal{L}|)\}$. Thus we have

$$\gamma_j^{(\mu)}(\mathcal{L},\alpha)(n) = \sum_{\ell=1}^{|\mathcal{L}|} \alpha_{(\ell)} g_j^{(\mu-1)}(x(\ell))\varepsilon_{(\ell),j}. \quad (5)$$

This expression can be interpreted as the scalar product $\langle \alpha, g_j^{\mu-1}\rangle$ of the vectors: $\alpha = (\alpha_{(1)}\ldots,\alpha_{(\mathcal{L})})$ and $g_j^{\mu-1} = (g_j^{(\mu-1)}(x(1))\varepsilon_{(1),j},\ldots,g_j^{(\mu-1)}(x((|\mathcal{L}|))\varepsilon_{(|\mathcal{L}|)),j})$.

All these definitions imply that for proving the weak convergence of the last vector it is sufficient, using the Cramer-Wold device, to show that the sum (5) is weakly convergent for each α. It remains to verify that the sequence of random variables $\gamma_j^{(\mu)}(\mathcal{L},\alpha)(n)$, for $j = 1,\ldots,H_{\mu-1}(n)$ satisfy the hypothesis of the

Central Limit Theorem for interchangeable random variables. This is proven in detail in [8]. We are here interested in the computation of the first two moments.

By conditioning with respect to the σ-algebra $\mathcal{F}_{\mu-2}(x_{J_M})$ generated by the random variables $g_k^{(\mu-2)}(x_{J_M})$, for $k = 1, \ldots, H_{\mu-2}(n)$, one has $\mathbb{E}[\gamma_j^{(\mu)}(\mathcal{L}, \alpha)(n)] = 0$ and also by conditional independence $\mathbb{E}[\gamma_j^{(\mu)}(\mathcal{L}, \alpha)(n)\gamma_{j'}^{(\mu)}(\mathcal{L}, \alpha)(n)] = 0$, whenever $j \neq j'$. The computation for the variance is more involved. Indeed, one has

$$
\begin{aligned}
\mathbb{E}[(\gamma_j^{(\mu)}(\mathcal{L}, \alpha)(n))^2] &= \sum_{\ell=1}^{|\mathcal{L}|} \alpha_{(\ell)}^2 \mathbb{E}[(g_j^{(\mu-1)}(x(\ell)))^2 \varepsilon_{(\ell),j}^2] \\
&= \sum_{\ell=1}^{|\mathcal{L}|} \alpha_{(\ell)}^2 \mathbb{E}[\mathbb{E}[(g_j^{(\mu-1)}(x(\ell)))^2 \varepsilon_{(\ell),j}^2 | \mathcal{F}_{\mu-2}(x(\ell))]] \\
&= \sum_{\ell=1}^{|\mathcal{L}|} \alpha_{(\ell)}^2 \mathbb{E}[(g_j^{(\mu-1)}(x(\ell)))^2] \\
&= \sum_{\ell=1}^{|\mathcal{L}|} \alpha_{(\ell)}^2 \mathbb{E}[\phi^2(\sqrt{\frac{\hat{C}_W^{(\mu-1)}}{H_{\mu-2}(n)}} \sum_{k=1}^{H_{\mu-2}(n)} \varepsilon_{j,k} g_k^{(\mu-2)}(x(\ell)) + b_j)].
\end{aligned}
$$

This last expression can be used to compute by recurrence the limit variance. Let us begin with the first recursion where the input is a set of vectors $x(\ell)$. Then

$$
\begin{aligned}
\gamma_j^{(2)}(\mathcal{L}, \alpha)(n) &= \sum_{\ell=1}^{|\mathcal{L}|} \alpha_{(\ell)} g_j^{(1)}(x(\ell)) \varepsilon_{(\ell),j} \\
&= \sum_{\ell=1}^{|\mathcal{L}|} \alpha_{(\ell)} \phi(\sqrt{\frac{\hat{C}_W^{(0)}}{M}} \sum_{k=1}^{H_0(n)} \varepsilon_{j,k} x_k(\ell) + b_j).
\end{aligned}
$$

The input has always the same dimension that we have set as M. Thus we know that the r.v. $\sqrt{\frac{\hat{C}_W^{(0)}}{M}} \sum_{k=1}^{M} \varepsilon_{j,k} x_k(\ell) + b_j$ is a Gaussian with zero mean and variance equal to $\frac{\hat{C}_W^{(0)}}{M} \sum_{k=1}^{M} x_k^2(\ell) + C_b$. Thus

$$\mathbb{E}[(\gamma_j^{(2)}(\mathcal{L}, \alpha)(n))^2]$$

$$= \sum_{\ell=1}^{|\mathcal{L}|} \sum_{\ell'=1}^{|\mathcal{L}|} \alpha_{(\ell)} \alpha_{(\ell')} \mathbb{E}[\phi(\sqrt{\frac{\hat{C}_W^{(0)}}{M}} \sum_{k=1}^{M} \varepsilon_{j,k} x_k(\ell) + b_j) \phi(\sqrt{\frac{\hat{C}_W^{(0)}}{M}} \sum_{k=1}^{M} \varepsilon_{j,k} x_k(\ell') + b_j)]$$

Let us note that all the random variables $\gamma_j^{(2)}(\mathcal{L}, \alpha)(n)$ give the same result. Then it is enough to compute $\mathbb{E}[(\gamma_1^{(2)}(\mathcal{L}, \alpha)(n))^2]$. Hence we obtain

$$\mathbb{E}[(\mathcal{T}^{(2))}(\mathcal{L},\alpha)(n))^2]$$

$$= \frac{\hat{C}_W^{(2)}}{H_1(n)} \sum_{\ell=1}^{|\mathcal{L}|} \sum_{\ell'=1}^{|\mathcal{L}|} \alpha_{(\ell)}\alpha_{(\ell')}\mathbb{E}[\phi(\sqrt{\frac{\hat{C}_W^{(0)}}{M}} \sum_{k=1}^{M} \varepsilon_{1,k}x_k(\ell) + b_1)\phi(\sqrt{\frac{\hat{C}_W^{(0)}}{M}} \sum_{k=1}^{M} \varepsilon_{1,k}x_k(\ell') + b_1)]$$

$$= \frac{\hat{C}_W^{(2)}}{H_1(n)} \sum_{\ell=1}^{|\mathcal{L}|} \sum_{\ell'=1}^{|\mathcal{L}|} \alpha_{(\ell)}\alpha_{(\ell')}\mathcal{K}(x(\ell), x(\ell')).$$

Moreover we can give another step in the above computation by using the Hermite polynomials tools.

4 Hermite Polynomials

We consider the Hermite polynomials defined by the formula

$$H_n(x) = (-1)^n \left[\frac{d^n}{dx^n}(e^{-\frac{1}{2}x^2})\right] e^{\frac{1}{2}x^2}. \tag{6}$$

It is well known that these polynomials conform a complete and orthogonal set for $\mathbb{L}^2(\mathbb{R}, \varphi(x)dx)$, where φ is the density of the Gaussian standard. Moreover $||H_n||^2 = n!$ [10, Ch. 8].

Other properties of Hermite polynomials that we need in this work are:

$$H_n(x) = n! \sum_{j=0}^{\lfloor \frac{n}{2} \rfloor} \frac{(-1)^j}{2^j j!(n-2j)!} x^{n-2j}, \quad n > 0; \ H_0(x) = 1; \tag{7}$$

$$H_{2k-1}(0) = 0 \quad \text{for } k > 0 \tag{8}$$

$$H_{2k}(0) = (-1)^k(2k-1)!! = (-1)^k \prod_{s=1}^{k}(2s-1) \quad \text{for } k > 0 \tag{9}$$

Furthermore, if X, Y are two jointly Gaussian random variables with variance 1 and correlation ρ, the following relation, known as the Mehler's formula, holds

$$\mathbb{E}[H_n(X)H_m(Y)] = \delta_{n,m}n!\rho^n.$$

Suppose now that F and G are two functions belonging to $\mathbb{L}^2(\mathbb{R}, \varphi(x)dx)$. Thus the following expansion in quadratic mean holds for F

$$F(x) = \sum_{n=0}^{\infty} \hat{F}_n H_n(x), \quad \text{where} \quad \hat{F}_n = \frac{1}{n!} \int_{\mathbb{R}} F(x)H_n(x)\varphi(x)dx \tag{10}$$

and $||F||^2 = \sum_{n=1}^{\infty} \hat{F}_n^2 n!$. A similar expansion holds for G.

By using Mehler's formula and the $\mathbb{L}^2$ convergence we obtain the following formula

$$\mathbb{E}[F(X)G(Y)] = \sum_{n=0}^{\infty} \hat{F}_n \hat{G}_n n!\rho^n. \tag{11}$$

We have then

$$\mathbb{E}\left[\phi\left(\sqrt{\frac{\hat{C}_W^{(0)}}{M}}\sum_{k=1}^{M}\varepsilon_{1,k}x_k(\ell)+b_1\right)\phi\left(\sqrt{\frac{\hat{C}_W^{(0)}}{M}}\sum_{k=1}^{M}\varepsilon_{1,k}x_k(\ell')+b_1\right)\right]$$

$$= \mathbb{E}[\phi(\sigma(\boldsymbol{x}(\ell))X(\boldsymbol{x}(\ell)))\phi(\sigma(\boldsymbol{x}(\ell'))Y(\boldsymbol{x}(\ell')))]. \tag{12}$$

Here $\sigma(\boldsymbol{x}(\ell))^2 = \frac{\hat{C}_W^{(0)}}{M}\sum_{k=1}^{M}x_k^2(\ell) + C_b$, $\sigma(\boldsymbol{x}(\ell'))^2 = \frac{\hat{C}_W^{(0)}}{M}\sum_{k=1}^{M}x_k^2(\ell') + C_b$ and

$$(X(\boldsymbol{x}(\ell))), Y(\boldsymbol{x}(\ell')))) = \mathbf{N}\left(\mathbf{0}, \begin{bmatrix} 1 & \rho(\boldsymbol{x}(\ell),\boldsymbol{x}(\ell')) \\ \rho(\boldsymbol{x}(\ell),\boldsymbol{x}(\ell')) & 1 \end{bmatrix}\right),$$

where

$$\rho(\boldsymbol{x}(\ell),\boldsymbol{x}(\ell')) = \frac{\frac{\hat{C}_W^{(0)}}{M}\sum_{k=1}^{M}x_k(\ell)x_k(\ell') + C_b}{\sigma(\boldsymbol{x}(\ell))\sigma(\boldsymbol{x}(\ell'))}$$

$$= \frac{\frac{\hat{C}_W^{(0)}}{M}\langle\boldsymbol{x}(\ell),\boldsymbol{x}(\ell')\rangle + C_b}{(\frac{\hat{C}_W^{(0)}}{M}||\boldsymbol{x}(\ell)||^2 + C_b)^{\frac{1}{2}}(\frac{\hat{C}_W^{(0)}}{M}||\boldsymbol{x}(\ell')||^2 + C_b)^{\frac{1}{2}}}. \tag{13}$$

This formula says that correlation only depends on the scalar product of the inputs and on their norms. Summing all up, we can compute the associated kernel. Let us define the following coefficients

$$\hat{\phi}_n(\sigma) = \frac{1}{n!}\int_{\mathbb{R}}\phi(\sigma x)H_n(x)\varphi(x)dx. \tag{14}$$

In such a form we get

$$\mathbb{E}[\phi(\sigma(\boldsymbol{x}(\ell))X(\boldsymbol{x}(\ell)))\phi(\sigma(\boldsymbol{x}(\ell'))Y(\boldsymbol{x}(\ell')))]$$

$$= \sum_{n=0}^{\infty}\hat{\phi}_n(\sigma(\boldsymbol{x}(\ell)))\hat{\phi}_n(\sigma(\boldsymbol{x}(\ell')))n!(\rho(\boldsymbol{x}(\ell),\boldsymbol{x}(\ell')))^n. \tag{15}$$

5   The Recurrence Kernel for Deep Network

The previous form of the covariance of the GP underlying a 1-layer network (Eq. (15)) can be naturally extended to multiple layer networks as follows. For $\mu = 1, \ldots, D$,

$$K^{(\mu)}(\boldsymbol{x}(\ell),\boldsymbol{x}(\ell')) =$$

$$\mathbb{E}[\phi((K^{(\mu-1)}(\boldsymbol{x}(\ell),\boldsymbol{x}(\ell)))^{1/2})X^{(\mu-1)}(\boldsymbol{x}(\ell)))\phi((K^{(\mu-1)}(\boldsymbol{x}(\ell'),\boldsymbol{x}(\ell')))^{1/2})Y^{(\mu-1)}(\boldsymbol{x}(\ell')))]$$

$$= \sum_{n=0}^{\infty}\hat{\phi}_n((K^{(\mu-1)}(\boldsymbol{x}(\ell),\boldsymbol{x}(\ell)))^{1/2})\hat{\phi}_n((K^{(\mu-1)}(\boldsymbol{x}(\ell'),\boldsymbol{x}(\ell')))^{1/2})n!(\rho_{\boldsymbol{x},\boldsymbol{x}'}^{(\mu-1)})^n$$

$$\tag{16}$$

where

$$\rho_{x,x'}^{(\mu)} = \frac{K^{(\mu)}(x(\ell), x(\ell'))}{(K^{(\mu)}(x(\ell), x(\ell)))^{1/2}(K^{(\mu)}(x(\ell'), x(\ell')))^{1/2}} \tag{17}$$

and

$$\hat{\phi}_n(\sigma) = \frac{1}{n!}\int_{\mathbb{R}} \phi(\sigma x)H_n(x)\varphi(x)dx \tag{18}$$

The initial step is

$$K^{(0)}(x(\ell), x(\ell')) = \frac{C_W^{(0)}}{M}\langle x(\ell), x(\ell')\rangle + C_b \tag{19}$$

and consequently $\rho_{x,x'}^{(0)} = \rho(x(\ell), x(\ell'))$ (see Eq. 13).

And as before, the random variables

$$(X^{(\mu)}(x(\ell)), Y^{(\mu)}(x(\ell'))) = N\left(0, \begin{bmatrix} 1 & \rho_{x,x'}^{(\mu)} \\ \rho_{x,x'}^{(\mu)} & 1 \end{bmatrix}\right).$$

6 Examples of Activation Functions

1. Homogeneous Functions. Consider $C_b^{(0)} = 0$, and that $\phi(\lambda x) = \lambda^m \phi(x)$, that is the function is homogeneous of degree m. We obtain
$\mathbb{E}[\phi(\sigma(x(\ell))X(x(\ell)))\phi(\sigma(x(\ell'))Y(x(\ell')))]$

$$= \sigma^m(x(\ell))\sigma^m(x(\ell)) \sum_{n=0}^{\infty} \hat{\phi}_n^2 n! \cos^n(x(\ell), x(\ell')).$$

Similarly if $C_b^{(0)} \neq 0$,
$\mathbb{E}[\phi(\sigma(x(\ell))X(x(\ell)))\phi(\sigma(x(\ell'))Y(x(\ell')))]$

$$= \sigma^m(x(\ell))\sigma^m(x(\ell')) \sum_{n=0}^{\infty} \hat{\phi}_n^2 n!(\rho(x(\ell), x(\ell')))^n.$$

2. Functions of the form $\phi^{(r)}(x) = \Theta(x)x^r$. Important examples are the functions $\phi^{(r)}(x) = \Theta(x)x^r$, where $r = 0, 1, 2, 3$, and Θ is the Heaviside function. These functions are all homogenous with degree r.

For the case $r = 0$, we get for $n = 0$, $\hat{\phi}_0^{(0)} = \frac{1}{2}$, and for $n \geq 1$

$$\hat{\phi}_n^{(0)} = \frac{1}{n!}\int_0^{\infty} H_n(x)\varphi(x)dx = \frac{(-1)^n}{\sqrt{2\pi}n!}\int_0^{\infty} \frac{d^n}{dx^n}(e^{-\frac{1}{2}x^2})dx = \frac{1}{\sqrt{2\pi}}\frac{H_{n-1}(0)}{n!}.$$

Thus, we have a kernel corresponding to a 1-layer network with activation function the Heaviside

$$\mathbb{E}[\phi^{(0)}(\sigma(\boldsymbol{x}(\ell))X(\boldsymbol{x}(\ell)))\phi^{(0)}(\sigma(\boldsymbol{x}(\ell'))Y(\boldsymbol{x}(\ell')))]$$

$$= \frac{1}{4} + \frac{1}{2\pi}\sum_{n=1}^{\infty}\frac{H_{n-1}^2(0)}{n!}(\rho(\boldsymbol{x}(\ell),\boldsymbol{x}(\ell')))^n = \frac{1}{4} + \frac{1}{2\pi}\sum_{k=0}^{\infty}\frac{H_{2k}^2(0)}{(2k+1)!}(\rho(\boldsymbol{x}(\ell),\boldsymbol{x}(\ell')))^{2k+1}.$$

Observe that for a deep network with $D > 1$ layers and the Heaviside as activation function, the recursive kernel given by Eqs. (16)–(19) is for each layer $\mu = 1,\ldots,D$,

$$K^{(\mu)}(\boldsymbol{x}(\ell),\boldsymbol{x}(\ell')) = \sum_{n=0}^{\infty}(\hat{\phi}_n^{(0)})^2 n!(\rho_{\boldsymbol{x},\boldsymbol{x}'}^{(\mu-1)})^n \tag{20}$$

$$= \frac{1}{4} + \frac{1}{2\pi}\sum_{k=0}^{\infty}\frac{H_{2k}^2(0)}{(2k+1)!}(\rho_{\boldsymbol{x},\boldsymbol{x}'}^{(\mu-1)})^{2k+1}$$

$$= \frac{1}{4} + \frac{1}{2\pi}\rho_{\boldsymbol{x},\boldsymbol{x}'}^{(\mu-1)} + \frac{1}{2\pi}\sum_{k=1}^{\infty}\frac{1}{2k+1}\prod_{s=1}^{k}\left(\frac{2s-1}{2s}\right)(\rho_{\boldsymbol{x},\boldsymbol{x}'}^{(\mu-1)})^{2k+1}$$

where $\rho_{\boldsymbol{x},\boldsymbol{x}'}^{(\mu-1)}$ and the initial kernel $K^{(0)}$ are given by Eqs. (17) and (19), and we use property (9) to simplify the Hermite polynomials at 0.

The case for $r = 1$ is resolved with similar calculations (we omit details for lack of space) and to obtain the kernel for a neural network with ReLU as activation function:

$$\mathbb{E}[\phi^{(1)}(\sigma(\boldsymbol{x}(\ell))X(\boldsymbol{x}(\ell)))\phi^{(1)}(\sigma(\boldsymbol{x}(\ell'))Y(\boldsymbol{x}(\ell')))] =$$

$$\sigma(\boldsymbol{x}(\ell))\sigma(\boldsymbol{x}(\ell'))\left(\frac{1}{4\pi} + \frac{1}{4}\rho(\boldsymbol{x}(\ell),\boldsymbol{x}(\ell')) + \frac{1}{2\pi}\sum_{k=0}^{\infty}\frac{H_{2k}^2(0)}{(2k+2)!}(\rho(\boldsymbol{x}(\ell),\boldsymbol{x}(\ell')))^{2k+2}\right). \tag{21}$$

3. The *erf* activation function. Consider the activation function

$$\phi(x) = \int_{-x}^{x}e^{-t^2/2}dt = \sqrt{2\pi}(2\Phi(x) - 1) \tag{22}$$

where $\Phi(x)$ is the distribution function of the standard Gaussian. This function is very similar in its values to $\tanh(x)$ with an appropriate scaling. Then it can be shown that the coefficients $\hat{\phi}_n$ of the expansion of covariance in Hermite polynomials (Eq. (15)) are such that $\hat{\phi}_{2k} = 0$, and

$$\hat{\phi}_{2k+1} = \frac{1}{2^{k-1/2}(2k+1)}\sum_{j=0}^{k}\frac{(-1)^j(2k-2j)!!}{j!(2k-2j-1)!!}$$

for $k = 1,2,\ldots$. In particular, $\hat{\phi}_0 = 0, \hat{\phi}_1 = \sqrt{2}, \hat{\phi}_2 = 0, \hat{\phi}_3 = \sqrt{2}/12$.

7   Experiments

As a proof of concept we report results on both classification and regression problems with: a (deep) 3-layers neural network, and a Gaussian process driven by a recurrence kernel of 3-layers and activation function the Heaviside (Eq. (20)). For computing with the GP we use only 30 terms of the Hermite approximation for the covariance function. Since the Hermite coefficients in this case are independent of inputs, we hard-wired their values in a look-up table. This improves computation speed notably. The recurrent kernel is programmed in C++ and wired to R with Rcpp [3] to be used with the function kernlab::gausspr, which builds the Gaussian regression [5]. This allows for a quick and lazy programming for demonstration purposes, albeit not the most efficient.

Example 1 (Classification). We use the white wine data set from the UCI Machine Learning data repository. The goal is to predict wine *quality* (integer values ranging from 3 to 9), considering 11 independent variables (fixed acidity, volatile acidity, citric acid, residual sugar, chlorides, free sulfur dioxide, total sulfur dioxide, density, pH, sulphates, and alcohol). We turn this into a binary classification task to predict whether a wine is of *good* quality (value 6 and above) or not. The dataset comprises 4,898 rows, from which we randomly select 75% (3,674 rows) for training and the remain for testing.

The GP resolved the task with an accuracy of 75.2% with no tuning; the 3-layer neural network had an accuracy of 76.4% tuning size and decay with 10-fold cross-validation. Additionally we applied model averaging over a 1-layer neural network; that is, the same neural network model is fitted using different random number seeds, and all the resulting models are used for prediction by averaging their scores and then translating these averages to predicted classes. 10-fold cross-validation was also used to fine tune size. The accuracy attained by this model on the predictions was of 79.9%.

Example 2 (Regression). We have a dataset of monthly prices of the *Standard and Poor's 500 Index* (SP500) from 1900 to 2012, and the task is to predict next month price using as information up to 3 lags of the price history. Again we partition the data in 75% for training and the rest for testing. The evaluation measure we use is the normalize residual mean square error (NRMSE), from which we can extract the percentage of outperforming direct sample mean (as $(1 - NRMSE) * 100$). The GP with the 3-layers recurrence kernel outperformed direct sample mean by 93.8%; the neural network achieved a 94.7%.

Notwithstanding the similarities in predictive power, with regards to regression the Gaussian process has the added advantage of providing interpretability to the model.

References

1. Goodfellow, I., Bengio, Y., Courville, A.: Deep Learning. The MIT Press, Cambridge (2016)
2. Blum, J.R., Chernoff, H., Rosenblatt, M., Teicher, H.: Central limit theorems for interchangeable processes. Canad. J. Math. **10**, 222–229 (1958)
3. Eddelbuettel, D., Romain Francois, R.: RCPP: Seamless R and C++ Integration. J. Stat. Softw. **40**(8), 1–18 (2011)
4. Kallenberg, O.: Probabilistic Symmetries and Invariance Principles. Springer Series Probability and Applications. Springer, Heidelberg (2005). https://doi.org/10.1007/0-387-28861-9
5. Karatzoglou, A., Smola, A., Hornik, K., Zeileis, A.: kernlab - an S4 package for kernel methods in R. J. Stat. Softw. **11**(9), 1–20 (2004)
6. Lee, J., Bahri, Y., Novak, R., Schoenholz, S.S., Pennington, J., Sohl-Dickstein, J.: Deep neural networks as Gaussian processes. In: International Conference on Learning Representations, vol. 4 (2018)
7. de G. Matthews, A.G., Hron, J., Rowland, M., Turner, R.E., Ghahramani, Z.: Gaussian process behaviour in wide deep neural networks. In: International Conference on Learning Representations, vol. 4 (2018)
8. de G. Matthews, A.G., Hron, J., Rowland, M., Turner, R.E., Ghahramani, Z.: Gaussian process behaviour in wide deep neural networks. arXiv:1804.11271 (2018)
9. Neal, R.M.: Bayesian learning for neural networks. Ph.D. Thesis, Department of Computer Science, University of Toronto (1994)
10. Peccati, G., Taqqu, M.: Wiener Chaos, Moments, Cumulants and Diagrams. Bocconi & Springer (2011)
11. Rasmussen, C.E., Williams, C.K.I.: Gaussian Processes for Machine Learning, vol. 1. MIT Press, Cambridge (2006)

Monotone Deep Spectrum Kernels

Ivano Lauriola[1,2](✉) [iD] and Fabio Aiolli[1] [iD]

[1] Department of Mathematics, University of Padova,
Via Trieste 63, 35121 Padova, Italy
`ivano.lauriola@phd.unipd.it, aiolli@math.unipd.it`
[2] Fondazione Bruno Kessler, Via Sommarive 18, 38123 Trento, Italy

Abstract. A recent result in the literature states that polynomial and conjunctive features can be hierarchically organized and described by different kernels of increasing expressiveness (or complexity). Additionally, the optimal combination of those kernels through a Multiple Kernel Learning approach produces effective and robust deep kernels. In this paper, we extend this approach to structured data, showing an adaptation of classical spectrum kernels, here named monotone spectrum kernels, reflecting a hierarchical feature space of sub-structures of increasing complexity. Finally, we show that (i) our kernels adaptation does not differ significantly from classical spectrum kernels, and (ii) the optimal combination achieves better results than the single spectrum kernel.

Keywords: Multiple Kernel Learning · Deep learning · Spectrum kernel

1 Introduction

The benefits of deep representations have been widely exposed in the recent literature, especially in the context of neural networks, where deep architectures are monopolizing the majority of applications, replacing shallow solutions. An emerging challenge in kernel learning is to transpose the concepts and pillars of deep neural networks to build effective deep kernels [4]. To this end, different definitions and frameworks to learn deep kernels have been recently proposed.

As a first example, authors in [9] combined the structural properties of deep architectures with the non-parametric flexibility of kernel methods by transforming the inputs of a base kernel with a deep architecture, and then leveraging local kernel interpolation. Differently, Cho et al. [2] analyzed deep kernels defined as successive embeddings of a mapping function ϕ, that is $k(\boldsymbol{x}, \boldsymbol{z}) = \langle \phi(\phi(\dots \phi(\boldsymbol{x}))), \phi(\phi(\dots \phi(\boldsymbol{z}))) \rangle$, showing remarkable theoretical and practical results. More recently, authors in [4] focused on deep polynomial kernels, with form $k^{(d)}(\boldsymbol{x}, \boldsymbol{z}) = \langle \boldsymbol{x}, \boldsymbol{z} \rangle^d$, and their linear combinations. Specifically, they showed that polynomial features can be hierarchically organized and grouped by their complexity. The intuition behind that work is that a feature describing a monomial of degree 4 is more complex than a feature describing a monomial of degree 3. Additionally, the different layers of the hierarchy of features can be described with homogeneous polynomial kernels of different degrees.

© Springer Nature Switzerland AG 2020
I. Farkaš et al. (Eds.): ICANN 2020, LNCS 12396, pp. 207–219, 2020.
https://doi.org/10.1007/978-3-030-61609-0_17

The same authors proposed a theoretical framework to develop deep kernels through this hierarchy by learning the optimal combination of polynomial kernels via Multiple Kernel Learning [5] (MKL).

However, homogeneous polynomials are not the only kernel functions able to group and to describe features of increasing complexity (or expressiveness). The same concepts can be applied to different kernel functions. For instance, authors in [6] applied the same framework to conjunctive kernels of increasing complexity, whose feature space consists of conjunctions of input variables of a specified arity. However, things get more complicated when dealing with structured data, where the features represent the frequency of sub-structures (e.g. sub-strings, sub-trees...). Authors in [1] applied the framework to graph kernels, showing a grouping strategy (i.e. complexity) that depends on the dimension of the sub-structures, i.e. the graph g_1 is more complex than g_2 if g_1 contains g_2. However, only empirical results have been exposed in that work, showing the hierarchy of graph kernels and conjecturing that they have increasing complexity.

In this paper, we extend the aforementioned methodology, focusing on structured data and string kernels. Specifically, we propose an extension of the popular spectrum string kernel, here named monotone spectrum kernel, and we show theoretical properties regarding its complexity. Moreover, we analyze deep combinations of monotone spectrum kernels learned via MKL, showing remarkable results in terms of accuracy and robustness to overfitting.

2   Background

Kernel methods are a set of machine learning algorithms widely used to solve classification, regression and clustering problems. These methods rely on a modular architecture which comprises two elements, a general purpose optimization engine, and the kernel [8]. The kernel is a semidefinite positive function $k : \mathcal{X} \times \mathcal{X} \rightarrow \mathbb{R}$ that defines the similarity between pairs of inputs through their dot-products in an implicit feature space $\mathcal{K}$, i.e. $k(x, z) = \langle \phi(x), \phi(z) \rangle$. The embedding function $\phi : \mathcal{X} \rightarrow \mathcal{K}$ maps data from the input space $\mathcal{X}$ to the kernel space $\mathcal{K}$. The kernel allows us to solve tasks with different data-types and structures, such as graphs, trees, and sequences or strings.

2.1   Multiple Kernel Learning

Usually, the kernel function is selected a priori by using a validation procedure, electing the most performant kernel from a pool of possibilities. Recently, the literature showed mechanisms to directly learn the kernel function from data. One of the most popular kernel learning approaches is Multiple Kernel Learning [5] (MKL), which learns the kernel as a combination of multiple base (or weak) kernels. In this work, linear non-negative combinations of base kernels are considered, with form:

$$k_{\mu}(x, z) = \sum_{r} \mu_r k_r(x, z), \ \|\mu\|_1 = 1 \wedge \mu_r \geq 0,$$

where k_r is the r-th base kernel and μ is the weights vector parametrizing the combination. Two MKL algorithms are used in this work, that are EasyMKL [4] and GRAM [6]. The former is a time and memory efficient MKL algorithm that optimizes the margin between classes. The latter finds the kernels combination that maximizes the margin between classes while minimizing the radius of the Minimum Enclosing Ball (MEB) simultaneously. The MEB is the minimum enclosing hyper-spere containing data in the kernel space. However, both of these algorithms only provide the kernels combination. On top of that, a kernel machine, such as the popular SVM, is trained with the resulting combined kernel and it is used to perform classification.

2.2 Complexity of a Kernel Function

The expressiveness (or complexity) of a kernel function can be defined as the number of dichotomies that can be realized by a linear separator in that feature space. This value can be effectively captured by the rank of the kernel matrix [4]. However, the computation of the rank is expensive since it requires the decomposition of the kernel matrix. In order to alleviate the computational effort, authors in [4] proposed an alternative complexity measure, the Spectral Ratio, that is strictly related to the rank of the matrix and it can be easily computed as the ratio between the trace and the Frobenius norm of the kernel matrix:

$$\mathcal{C}(\boldsymbol{K}) = \frac{\|\boldsymbol{K}\|_T}{\|\boldsymbol{K}\|_F} = \frac{\sum_i \boldsymbol{K}_{i,i}}{\sqrt{\sum_{i,j} \boldsymbol{K}_{i,j}^2}}.$$

Let k_r and k_s be two kernel functions. The kernel k_r is said to be more general (i.e. less complex) than k_s when $\mathcal{C}(\boldsymbol{K}_r^X) \leq \mathcal{C}(\boldsymbol{K}_s^X)$ for any possible dataset $\boldsymbol{X}$, where $\boldsymbol{K}^X$ is the kernel matrix computed on $\boldsymbol{X}$. We also use the notation $k_r \geq_G k_s$. When dealing with normalized kernels $\tilde{k}(\boldsymbol{x}, \boldsymbol{z}) = \frac{k(\boldsymbol{x}, \boldsymbol{z})}{\sqrt{k(\boldsymbol{x}, \boldsymbol{x}) k(\boldsymbol{z}, \boldsymbol{z})}}$, the trace of the associated kernel matrix $\tilde{\boldsymbol{K}}$ is fixed, and spectral ratio can be simplified $\mathcal{C}(\tilde{\boldsymbol{K}}) = \frac{l}{\|\tilde{\boldsymbol{K}}\|_F}$, where l is the number of input examples.

In this case, it is possible to show that $\tilde{k}_r \geq_G \tilde{k}_s$ holds if for any possible pair of examples $(\boldsymbol{x}, \boldsymbol{z})$ we have that $\tilde{k}_r(\boldsymbol{x}, \boldsymbol{z})^2 \geq \tilde{k}_s(\boldsymbol{x}, \boldsymbol{z})^2$ [7], or equivalently:

$$\frac{k_r(\boldsymbol{x}, \boldsymbol{z})^2}{k_r(\boldsymbol{x}, \boldsymbol{x}) k_r(\boldsymbol{z}, \boldsymbol{z})} \geq \frac{k_s(\boldsymbol{x}, \boldsymbol{z})^2}{k_s(\boldsymbol{x}, \boldsymbol{x}) k_s(\boldsymbol{z}, \boldsymbol{z})} \tag{1}$$

2.3 Spectrum Kernel

Let Σ be the set of possible symbols, Σ^p be the set of strings (or sequences) of length p, and $\Sigma^* = \bigcup_p \Sigma^p$ be the set of strings of arbitrary length. The feature space (or embedding) of the p-Spectrum kernel [8] $\phi_p^s : \Sigma^* \to \mathbb{Z}_+^{|\Sigma^p|}$ counts the occurrences of any possible contiguous sub-sequence of length p in a string $\boldsymbol{x}$. The feature indexed by the sub-sequence u is defined as

$\phi_{p,(u)}^s(\boldsymbol{x}) = |\{(v_1, v_2) : \boldsymbol{x} = v_1 u v_2\}|$, $u \in \Sigma^p$, where $v_1 u v_2$ denotes the con-catenation of strings v_1, u, and v_2. The p-spectrum kernel is defined as the dot-product between p-spectrum embeddings, that is

$$k_p^s(\boldsymbol{x}, \boldsymbol{z}) = \langle \phi_p^s(\boldsymbol{x}), \phi_p^s(\boldsymbol{z}) \rangle = \sum_{u \in \Sigma^p} \phi_{p,(u)}^s(\boldsymbol{x}) \cdot \phi_{p,(u)}^s(\boldsymbol{z}).$$

In order to simplify the notation, we use $\boldsymbol{x}_p$ as the p-spectrum embedding of the string $\boldsymbol{x}$, whereas $\boldsymbol{x}_{p,(u)}, u \in \Sigma^p$ identifies the u-th feature, i.e. the number of occurrences of the sub-string u in $\boldsymbol{x}$. Finally, $|\boldsymbol{x}|$ denotes the length of $\boldsymbol{x}$.

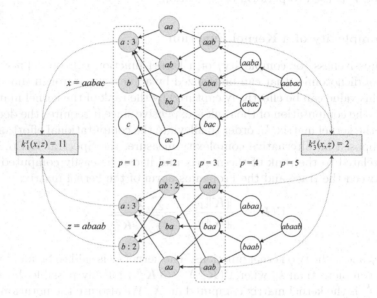

Fig. 1. The graph shows the active spectrum features (with count if greater than 1) of different length for two strings $\boldsymbol{x}$ and $\boldsymbol{z}$. The orange circles identify the shared sub-structures. The spectrum kernel of length 1 and 3 is also computed and exposed. The arrows show the dependencies between features.

An example of spectrum computation is described in Fig. 1, where the input sequences *aabac* and *abaab* share two sub-structures of length 3, that are *aab* and *aba*. The spectrum representation is based on local information provided by sub-structures rather than spatial dependencies, and the same sub-string gives the same information when appearing either as prefix or as suffix of a given string. The spectrum kernel has some nice properties here summarized:

Number of Substructures. Each feature of the p-spectrum embedding reflects the number of occurrences of a certain sub-string u of length p in $\boldsymbol{x}$. The number of possible sub-strings of length p extractable from $\boldsymbol{x}$ is bounded by its length and p, i.e. $\|\boldsymbol{x}_p\|_1 = |\boldsymbol{x}| - p + 1$ if $p \le |\boldsymbol{x}|$ else 0. For instance, given the sequence *aabc*, we can extract only 3 sub-strings of length 2, that are *aa*, *ab*, and *bc*.

Hierarchical Feature Space. The spectrum embedding of length $p + 1$ is developed on the top of the spectrum embedding of length p, and their active features can be hierarchically described by a simple *implication rule*. The presence of the feature $x_{p+1,(c_1 v c_2)}$ implies that $x_{p,(c_1 v)}$ and $x_{p,(v c_2)}$ have to be active. In case of multiple occurrences of the same sub-structure, $x_{p+1,(c_1 v c_2)} \leq \min\{x_{p,(c_1 v)}, x_{p,(v c_2)}\}$ holds.

3   Monotone Spectrum Kernel

Here, we introduce the *monotone* spectrum kernel, that is a variant of the classical spectrum kernel with an additional property, i.e. the monotonicity. The monotone spectrum embedding encodes sub-structures together with their occurrence (or relative positions) in the input string. In practice, if a sub-string u occurs 3 times in x, we have 3 different active binary monotone spectrum features, where the first feature is univocally associated to the first occurrence of u, in x and so on.

Formally, the feature space of the monotone p-spectrum kernel consists of boolean features indexed by pairs $(u, t) \in \Sigma^p \times \mathbb{Z}_+$ and defined as $\phi^{\hat{s}}_{p,(u,t)}(x) = [\![\phi^s_{p,(u)}(x) \geq t]\!]$, where u is the sub-string of length p, and t is its relative position, i.e. the occurrence ID of u in x. Intuitively, each p-spectrum feature u builds a sub-vector of virtually infinite[1] dimensions in the monotone p-spectrum embedding, whose first $\phi^s_{p,(u)}(x)$ components are 1 and the remaining are 0. The monotone p-spectrum embedding consists of the concatenation of all of these vectors. See Fig. 2 for a graphical explanation of the difference between p-spectrum and monotone p-spectrum embeddings. Trivially, the monotone p-spectrum kernel is defined as the dot product of the monotone p-spectrum embeddings, that is $k^{\hat{s}}_p(x, z) = \langle \phi^{\hat{s}}_p(x), \phi^{\hat{s}}_p(z) \rangle$. To simplify the notation, we use $\hat{x}_p$ to identify the binary p-spectrum embedding of the string x, and $\hat{x}_{p,(u,t)}$ its (u, t)-th feature.

The number of sub-structures of the p-spectrum kernel and its monotone extension is the same, and also in this case $\|\hat{x}_p\|_1 = |x| - p + 1$ if $p \leq |x|$, 0 else.

The difference between the spectrum kernel and its monotone version may be also described from a computational point of view, where a pairwise minimum operation replaces the classical dot-product between spectrum embeddings:

$$k^s_p(x, z) = \sum_{u \in \Sigma^p} x_{p,(u)} \cdot z_{p,(u)}; \quad k^{\hat{s}}_p(x, z) = \sum_{u \in \Sigma^p} \min\{x_{p,(u)}, z_{p,(u)}\}$$

In this paper, we also consider a further variation of the spectrum kernel, named binary spectrum kernel. Unlike the classical spectrum, the binary spectrum kernel only checks if a certain sub-structure occurs or not in the input string, without taking its frequency into account. Similarly to the previous equations, the binary spectrum kernel can be computed as $k^s_{p[bin]}(x, z) = \sum_{u \in \Sigma^p} x_{p,(u)} \wedge z_{p,(u)}$.

---

[1] This value is practically bounded by the length of the longer string in the dataset.

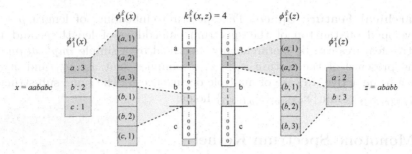

Fig. 2. The transformation from 1-spectrum to monotone 1-spectrum. The value of the monotone kernel computation is also exposed.

4 Complexity of Monotone Spectrum Kernels

In this section we describe how the hierarchical features organization affects the complexity of the normalized monotone spectrum kernel. Specifically, we show that the complexity is monotone with the length p.

Theorem 1. *The normalized monotone p-spectrum kernel has monotonically increasing expressiveness with respect to the value of p, that is $k_p^{\hat{s}} \geq_G k_{p+1}^{\hat{s}}$.*

Proof. With the results stated in Sect. 2.2, we just need to show that

$$\tilde{k}_{p+1}^{\hat{s}}(\boldsymbol{x}, \boldsymbol{z})^2 = \frac{k_{p+1}^{\hat{s}}(\boldsymbol{x}, \boldsymbol{z})^2}{k_{p+1}^{\hat{s}}(\boldsymbol{x}, \boldsymbol{x})k_{p+1}^{\hat{s}}(\boldsymbol{z}, \boldsymbol{z})} \leq \frac{k_p^{\hat{s}}(\boldsymbol{x}, \boldsymbol{z})^2}{k_p^{\hat{s}}(\boldsymbol{x}, \boldsymbol{x})k_p^{\hat{s}}(\boldsymbol{z}, \boldsymbol{z})} = \tilde{k}_p^{\hat{s}}(\boldsymbol{x}, \boldsymbol{z})^2 \qquad (2)$$

for any possible $\boldsymbol{x}, \boldsymbol{z} \in \Sigma^*$. The value of the monotone p-spectrum kernel identifies the exact number of shared sub-structures of length p between two strings $\boldsymbol{x}$ and $\boldsymbol{z}$. Let $\mathcal{S}_p^{(\boldsymbol{x},\boldsymbol{z})} \subset \Sigma^p \times \mathbb{Z}_+$ be the set of active monotone p-spectrum features shared between $\boldsymbol{x}$ and $\boldsymbol{z}$, $|\mathcal{S}_p^{(\boldsymbol{x},\boldsymbol{z})}| = k_p^{\hat{s}}(\boldsymbol{x}, \boldsymbol{z})$.

According to the implication rule described in the previous section, each active feature $(c_l v c_r, \cdot) \in \mathcal{S}_{p+1}^{(\boldsymbol{x},\boldsymbol{z})}$ implies that there are two active features of length p, namely $(c_l v, \cdot)$ and $(v c_r, \cdot) \in \mathcal{S}_p^{(\boldsymbol{x},\boldsymbol{z})}$ with certain relative positions. At the same time, each monotone p-spectrum feature $(v, \cdot) \in \mathcal{S}_p^{(\boldsymbol{x},\boldsymbol{z})}$ may cooperate to build at most two features at the next level $(p + 1)$, that are $(v c_r, \cdot)$ and $(c_l v, \cdot) \in \mathcal{S}_{p+1}^{(\boldsymbol{x},\boldsymbol{z})}$. The main consequence of this feature dependency is that $|\mathcal{S}_p^{(\boldsymbol{x},\boldsymbol{z})}| \not< |\mathcal{S}_{p+1}^{(\boldsymbol{x},\boldsymbol{z})}|$. This behavior is described in Fig. 3, where arrows describe the generation of features. Note that, in case of non-monotone spectrum kernels, you may have a higher number of arrows entering a node due to multiple occurrences of the same sub-structure.

Additionally, The number of shared sub-structures decreases with p, i.e.

$$|\mathcal{S}_p^{(\boldsymbol{x},\boldsymbol{z})}| > |\mathcal{S}_{p+1}^{(\boldsymbol{x},\boldsymbol{z})}| \text{ when } |\mathcal{S}_p^{(\boldsymbol{x},\boldsymbol{z})}| > 0.$$

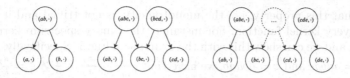

Fig. 3. Examples of features dependencies between monotone spectrum layers.

Assume that $|\mathcal{S}_p^{(x,z)}| = |\mathcal{S}_{p+1}^{(x,z)}|$, this means that each monotone p-spectrum feature cooperates to build exactly 2 distinct $p+1$ features. This scenario is described in Fig. 4, where $(v_j, t_j) \in \mathcal{S}_{p+1}^{(x,z)}$ and $(v'_j, t'_j) \in \mathcal{S}_p^{(x,z)}$. This solution assumes that the sub-structure v'_1 appears two times in the shared sequence with the same relative position t'_1. This scenario is infeasible because in case of multiple occurrences of v'_1, the monotone spectrum kernel generates multiple features with different (and univoke) relative positions t'_1 and t'_2. Thus, we need an additional extra feature, (v'_{m+1}, t'_{m+1}) to build the right part of (v_m, t_m).

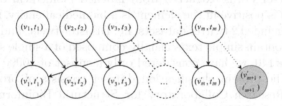

Fig. 4. Example of dependencies. The feature (v_m, t_m) cannot be derived from (v'_1, t'_1) as it occurs on a different (and infeasible) position.

In other words, the set $\mathcal{S}_p^{(x,z)}$ contains at least one additional element than $\mathcal{S}_{p+1}^{(x,z)}$, and thus $k_p^{\hat{s}}(x, z) - k_{p+1}^{\hat{s}}(x, z) \geq 1$. Additionally, due to the binary nature of the monotone spectrum embeddings we have that:

$$k_{p+1}^{\hat{s}}(x, x) = \langle \hat{x}_{p+1}, \hat{x}_{p+1} \rangle = \|\hat{x}_{p+1}\|_2^2 = \|\hat{x}_{p+1}\|_1 = \|\hat{x}_p\|_1 - 1 = k_p^{\hat{s}}(x, x) - 1.$$

With the two results stated above, we have that

$$\frac{k_{p+1}^{\hat{s}}(x, z)}{k_{p+1}^{\hat{s}}(x, x)} \leq \frac{k_p^{\hat{s}}(x, z) - 1}{k_p^{\hat{s}}(x, x) - 1} \leq \frac{k_p^{\hat{s}}(x, z)}{k_p^{\hat{s}}(x, x)}$$

The second inequality is always true since $k_p^{\hat{s}}(x, x) \geq k_p^{\hat{s}}(x, z)$ due to the boolean construction. The same procedure is clearly valid for z, i.e. $\frac{k_p^{\hat{s}}(x,z)}{k_p^{\hat{s}}(z,z)} \geq \frac{k_{p+1}^{\hat{s}}(x,z)}{k_{p+1}^{\hat{s}}(z,z)}$. Having said that, we can easily prove the Inequality 2:

$$\tilde{k}_{p+1}^{\hat{s}}(x, z)^2 = \frac{k_{p+1}^{\hat{s}}(x, z)}{k_{p+1}^{\hat{s}}(x, x)} \cdot \frac{k_{p+1}^{\hat{s}}(x, z)}{k_{p+1}^{\hat{s}}(z, z)} \leq \frac{k_p^{\hat{s}}(x, z)}{k_p^{\hat{s}}(x, x)} \cdot \frac{k_p^{\hat{s}}(x, z)}{k_p^{\hat{s}}(z, z)} = \tilde{k}_p^{\hat{s}}(x, z)^2 \quad \blacksquare$$

Note that this property, i.e. the monotonicity, is not trivial and it does not apply to every kernel function. For instance, the binary spectrum kernel is not monotone, and we can show this with the example in Fig. 1. Specifically, given the strings $x = aabac$ and $z = abaab$, we have that $\frac{k^s_{1[bin]}(x,z)}{k^s_{1[bin]}(x,x)} = \frac{2}{3} \not\geq \frac{3}{4} = \frac{k^s_{2[bin]}(x,z)}{k^s_{2[bin]}(x,x)}$.

5   Empirical Evaluation

A wide empirical assessment has been carried out to evaluate (i) the performances of deep kernels defined as a combination of base spectrums, and (ii) the difference between spectrum variations, including the classical spectrum kernel, the monotone spectrum kernel, and the binary spectrum kernel.

Several sequence classification datasets with different characteristics have been used in this work, including 4 biomedical token classification datasets, 2 Tweet (sentences) classification corpora, and 1 protein classification task. The biomedical token classification datasets consist of extremely short sequences composed of one or two terms. These datasets have been artificially generated and they consist of words extracted from labelled biomedical documents [3][2]. The binary label is positive iff the element is a biomedical entity, negative otherwise[3]. We have included 2 twitter datasets, i.e. Disaster-tweet, and Sentiment140. These datasets contain simple texts usually composed of a single sentence. In the case of Sentiment140, we have considered only a subset of 10000 examples with binary labels. The protein classification dataset consists of protein sequences retrieved from Research Collaboratory for Structural Bioinformatics (RCSB) Protein Data Bank (PDB). In this work, only the two majority classes have been used. Twitter and protein datasets are available in the Kaggle repository.

Datasets also consist of different dictionaries and set of characters. Tweets and biomedical entities rely on common alphabetical character sets, whereas protein sequences are composed of simplified dictionaries consisting of a few symbols, making the spectrum representations denser. The detailed description of the datasets is available in Table 1.

The spectrum kernel and its variants have been separately analyzed and evaluated by using different methods, including the SVM and MKL combinations. These methods and baselines are:

SVM: this simple baseline consists of a SVM classifier with a single spectrum-based kernel of length d as input. This method allows us to understand the empirical difference between kernels and to provide a baseline for kernels combination methods.

EasyMKL: multiple spectrum kernels (or the binary or monotone variant) from length 1 to d have been combined with EasyMKL [4].

GRAM: multiple spectrum kernels from length 1 to d have been combined with GRAM [6].

---

[2] https://github.com/cambridgeltl/MTL-Bioinformatics-2016.

[3] Note that this task is different from classical Named Entity Recognition, where the whole sentence is simultaneously observed.

Table 1. Datasets description

Dataset	Examples	Length	$|\Sigma|$
BioNLP13PC-cc	2295	$6.9_{\pm 4.4}$	55
BioNLP13PC-chemical	12708	$8.6_{\pm 7.0}$	77
BioNLP13CG-species	2216	$5.1_{\pm 2.2}$	63
BioNLP13CG-cc	2470	$5.7_{\pm 2.7}$	52
Disaster-tweet	7613	$101.0_{\pm 33.8}$	122
Sentiment140	10000	$73.8_{\pm 36.4}$	171
Structural Protein Seq	20553	$311.2_{\pm 192.2}$	25

Datasets have been randomly split into training (60%), validation (20%) and test (20%) sets. The hyper-parameters have been selected by observing the performance in validation. These hyper-parameters are $C \in \{10^i, i : -4 \ldots 4\}$ value for the SVM and $\lambda \in \{0, 0.1, \ldots, 1\}$ for EasyMKL. The value d, that defines the length of the kernel, or the maximum length in the case of MKL solutions, has not been selected with a validation procedure. On the contrary, we prefer to observe the empirical results by varying this value from 1 to 10. In the case of MKL solutions, an identity kernel matrix has been included in the combination. We remind that MKL algorithms only deal with the kernels combination. After the kernel learning phase, a SVM has been used to solve the task with the resulting kernel. The training procedure has been repeated 5 times with 5 different training, validation, and test splits (the same for each method), and the results computed on the test sets have been averaged. The main results are exposed in Fig. 5 and Fig. 6.

The figures emphasize two main results, that are the similarity amongst different spectrum variants and the superiority of deep combined kernels. The single spectrum-based kernels achieve almost the same AUC scores on several datasets, with a few exceptions when using low p values. This result is expected and reasonable. The spectrum-based kernels, i.e. the simple spectrum, the monotone, and the binary version, only differ each other when there are multiple occurrences of the same sub-structures. If there are no repeated sub-structures, then the value of those kernels is the same. This aspect heavily affects entity recognition tasks, which contain extremely short sequences built on a huge dictionary (see Table 1). Concerning the protein dataset, we observed an interesting boost of the monotone kernel with low degrees, where the probability of having shared sub-structures is high. On the other hand, the figures clearly show the dominance of the kernels combinations against single spectrums. The two MKL algorithms, i.e. EasyMKL and GRAM, achieve comparable results with a few small exceptions. Moreover, the combinations achieve better results in AUC, and they are able to drastically reduce the overfitting, usually observed with single kernel solutions. To better understand this aspect, Fig. 7 shows the combination weights learned by EasyMKL (we omit GRAM for simplicity) when dealing with spectrum and monotone spectrum kernels for a few datasets.

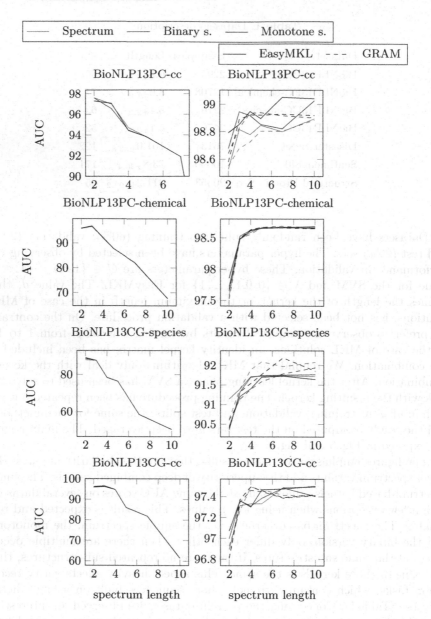

Fig. 5. Average AUC scores computed on the test sets. Left: single spectrum-based kernels with SVM; right: kernels combination with EasyMKL and GRAM.

What is striking from the figure, is the ability of the algorithm to select the optimal combination weights for a given task. In the case of biomedical datasets consisting of short sequences, general kernels (i.e. kernels with low complexity)

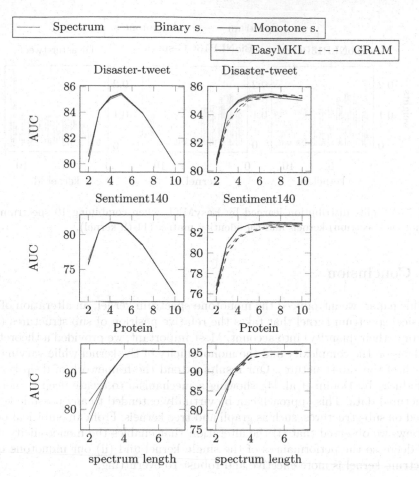

Fig. 6. Average AUC scores computed on the test sets. Left: single spectrum-based kernels with SVM; right: kernels combination with EasyMKL and GRAM.

receive the highest weights as they are expressive enough to encode the useful information. Differently, Disaster-tweet, which consists of longer texts, requires larger sub-structures and complex kernels. Not surprisingly, there is only a small difference between the two kernels. Note that this solution is conceptually different from the *blended* spectrum kernel (see [8] pp. 350), that assigns a decay factor to each spectrum $\sum_d \lambda^d k_d^s(x, z)$ selected with a validation procedure. Here, we automatically learn the combination.

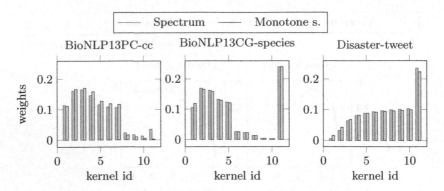

Fig. 7. Weights distribution learned by EasyMKL when combining 10 spectrum (or monotone spectrum) kernels and the identity matrix (11-th kernel).

6   Conclusion

In this paper, we introduced the monotone spectrum kernel, an alteration of the classical spectrum kernel that takes the relative position of sub-structures (and not only their quantity) into account. Most important, we provided a theoretical analysis on the complexity and the monotonicity of the kernel while varying the length of the sub-structures. Our results extend the framework of deep kernels introduced by Donini et al. [4], showing a mechanism to create deep kernels on structured data. This approach can be virtually extended to any possible kernel based on sub-structures, such as graph and tree kernels. From an empirical point of view, we observed that (i) the alteration that enables the monotonicity does not decrease the performances of the single kernel and (ii) our monotone deep spectrum kernel is more effective and robust to overfitting.

References

1. Aiolli, F., Donini, M., Navarin, N., Sperduti, A.: Multiple graph-kernel learning. In: Symposium Series on Computational Intelligence, pp. 1607–1614. IEEE (2015)
2. Cho, Y., Saul, L.K.: Kernel methods for deep learning. In: Advances in Neural Information Processing Systems, pp. 342–350 (2009)
3. Crichton, G., Pyysalo, S., Chiu, B., Korhonen, A.: A neural network multi-task learning approach to biomedical named entity recognition. BMC Bioinform. **18**(1), 368 (2017)
4. Donini, M., Aiolli, F.: Learning deep kernels in the space of dot product polynomials. Mach. Learn. **106**, 1245–1269 (2016). https://doi.org/10.1007/s10994-016-5590-8
5. Gönen, M., Alpaydin, E.: Multiple kernel learning algorithms. J. Mach. Learn. Res. **12**(64), 2211–2268 (2011)
6. Lauriola, I., Polato, M., Aiolli, F.: Radius-margin ratio optimization for dot-product Boolean Kernel learning. In: Lintas, A., Rovetta, S., Verschure, P.F.M.J., Villa, A.E.P. (eds.) ICANN 2017. LNCS, vol. 10614, pp. 183–191. Springer, Cham (2017). https://doi.org/10.1007/978-3-319-68612-7_21

7. Polato, M., Aiolli, F.: Boolean Kernels for collaborative filtering in top-n item recommendation. Neurocomputing **286**, 214–225 (2018)
8. Shawe-Taylor, J., Cristianini, N., et al.: Kernel Methods for Pattern Analysis. Cambridge University Press, Cambridge (2004)
9. Wilson, A.G., Hu, Z., Salakhutdinov, R., Xing, E.P.: Deep kernel learning. In: Artificial Intelligence and Statistics, pp. 370–378 (2016)

Permutation Learning in Convolutional Neural Networks for Time-Series Analysis

Gavneet Singh Chadha[1]([⊠]) [iD], Jinwoo Kim[1], Andreas Schwung[1], and Steven X. Ding[2]

[1] South Westphalia University of Applied Sciences, Soest, Germany
{chadha.gavneetsingh,kim.jinwoo,schwung.andreas}@fh-swf.de
[2] University of Duisburg-Essen, Duisburg, Germany
steven.ding@uni-due.de
https://www4.fh-swf.de/cms/fat/

Abstract. This study proposes a novel module in the convolutional neural networks (CNN) framework named permutation layer. With the new layer, we are particularly targeting time-series tasks where 2-dimensional CNN kernel loses its ability to capture the spatially co-related features. Multivariate time-series analysis consists of stacked input channels without considering the order of the channels resulting in an unsorted "2D-image". 2D convolution kernels are not efficient at capturing features from these distorted as the time-series lacks spatial information between the sensor channels. To overcome this weakness, we propose learnable permutation layers as an extension of vanilla convolution layers which allow to interchange different sensor channels such that sensor channels with similar information content are brought together to enable a more effective 2D convolution operation. We test the approach on a benchmark time-series classification task and report the superior performance and applicability of the proposed method.

Keywords: Permutation learning · Time-series analysis · Convolutional neural networks.

1 Introduction

Convolutional neural networks (CNN) [1] are known to provide superior performance not only in image recognition tasks but also in speech recognition, natural language processing and time-series analysis [2]. time-series analysis is especially an important part of the current "Industrial Internet of Things" [3] era. Therefore, efficient condition monitoring (CM) with time-series analysis has gained a lot of traction in the research community [4,5]. The input space for multivariate CM time-series analysis consists of individual sensor channels from which the data is recorded over time. Hence, each sensor channel values changes just over the time axis and not in the spatial dimension which is usually the case in images. However, we can create a virtual 2D image by stacking the 1D sensor channels column-wise, constituting the second dimension where the row-wise dimension

© Springer Nature Switzerland AG 2020
I. Farkaš et al. (Eds.): ICANN 2020, LNCS 12396, pp. 220–231, 2020.
https://doi.org/10.1007/978-3-030-61609-0_18

is time. CNNs have been be applied to multivariate time-series analysis in [5,6] wherein the most universal way is to convolve a kernel with an input sequence over just the time dimension, resulting in 1D convolutions. Since the size of a 1D convolution kernel is directly proportional to the number of sensor channels, if the number of sensor channels is high, the size of each convolution kernel in a layer drastically increases. This in turn, hinders one of the prime strengths of CNNs, its weight sharing capacity [7].

Hence, in this paper we propose to use the standard 2D convolution kernels which have led to tremendous success for in computer vision tasks [8,9], also for time-series analysis. The standard 2D convolutional layers use various learnable convolutional kernels to effectively learn spatially distributed features in the input domain i.e. height and width of an image. This approach holds under the assumption that such spatial relationships are available in the input domain, which is in general not the case in time-series data. Therefore, at the first thought, this renders the use of 2D convolutions meaningless for time-series data. However, if sensor channels have some spatial relationship, for e.g. due to the underlying physics of the process, a 2D convolution operation can be meaningful, provided that related sensor channels are spatially close to each other. This is however, not usually possible since a deeper knowledge about the relationship between the channels is missing, and they are concatenated randomly. Furthermore, for different time-series applications, different spatial relationships are required. Hence, we claim that the successful application of CNNs for time-series analysis demands for another learnable mechanism which optimizes the ordering of the input channels increasing the spatial relations among them.

Consequently, we propose the permutation layer (PL) for CNNs, a novel layer structure which facilitates the learning of a meaningful spatial relationship of input channels for time-series analysis. PL is based on a binary permutation matrix (PM) which transforms the input receptive field resulting in a permutation of the channels. The binary PM is made end-to-end learnable by applying soft binarization using sigmoidal activations for the parameters as well as a corresponding layer-wise cost function employing the barrier method. We also propose a generalization of the PM to contain arbitrary values in the interval $[0,1]$. We propose to apply multiple channels of the PL at the input sequence which helps in extracting multiple relevant spatial relationships of the input channels. Thereafter, the standard convolution operation extracts the relevant features for the final classification. The proposed PL is tested on the benchmark Tennessee Eastman (TE) dataset for time-series classification.

The rest of the paper is organized as follows. In Sect. 2 related literature on permutation learning is described. Section 3 introduces the basics of CNN for time-series analysis. Section 4 explains the proposed PL and its end-end training. Section 5 reports the experimental results from the CNN architectures on the benchmark Tennessee Eastman problem followed by a short conclusion in Sect. 6.

2   Related Work

In this section, we describe the existing literature related to permutation learning. Since it is computationally expensive to consider all the permutation matrices, the stochastic approach for identifying permutation matrix as a *doubly stochastic matrix* (DSM) [10], which characterizes the permutation matrices that belong to the set of Birkhoff polytope β_N [11] of dimension N, reduces the heavy computation for optimization. Some approaches utilizing the DSM are introduced here. Cruz et al. [12] describe the problem of visual permutation learning where a permutation matrix is learned to reorder an image from a random sequence in which the image is divided. The supervised permutation learning task is setup as a bi-level optimization problem, where the target permutation matrix is known for each image sequence. Also, [12] use the Sinkhorn normalization to solve for the doubly stochastic nature of the permutation matrix. Mena et al. [11] propose a similar use of the Sinkhorn operator which normalizes the rows and columns of the permutation matrix iteratively. They also show that the hard choice of a permutation matrix can be obtained as a limit of the Sinkhorn operator. Helmbold et al. [13] propose a Loss matrix which summarizes the distribution of loss over all the possible permutations. This additional expected loss of the whole sequence minus the total loss of the best permutation for the whole sequence, helps in finding a provable minimum worst-case loss. On the contrary to the literature above, we don't consider the permutation matrix learning task as a supervised learning task since the target permutation matrix is unknown for each sequence length in a time-series. We frame it as an auxiliary task which comprehends the supervised classification task. Furthermore, we use the log-barrier method for the constrained optimization task of the permutation matrix which is, according to the authors, missing in the literature.

3   Convolutional Neural Networks for Time-Series Analysis

In this section, we revisit the application of CNNs to time-series analysis formally including the input data representation and the different aspects of the channel-wise permutation operation. We consider multivariate a time-series signal $\{x_t\}_{t=1}^{T}$ with $x \in \mathbb{R}^n$, n the number of sensor channels and T the length of the time-series. N such time-series signals make up a complete dataset. Each of these N time-series signals might also be equipped with outputs $\{y_b\}_{b=1}^{N}$ which can be either class labels, i.e. $y \in \mathbb{Z}^m$ or continuous variables, i.e. $y \in \mathbb{R}^m$ with m the output dimension.

To use the time-series for computations in CNNs we have to recast it into a 2D-format which can be naturally achieved by stacking the time-series data sensor channel wise having the channel number $i = 1 \ldots n$ and the time $t = 1 \ldots T$ as the two dimensions. For process datasets, where a continuous sampling from each of sensor occurs, usually a sliding window approach is used wherein the individual sequences are created by shifting the 2D-input image by a certain step size over the input dataset [4]. Formally, the 2D operation is defined as

$$h_{ij} = (X * K)_{ij} = \sum_{f=0}^{n_k-1} \sum_{h=0}^{n_k-1} X_{i+f,j+h} K_{i+f,j+h}, \tag{1}$$

where h_{ij} denotes the output of the $(i,j)^{th}$ receptive field in the input, $X_{i+f,j+h}$ are the elements in the receptive field of the input image or sequence, $K_{i+f,j+h}$ is the convolution kernel and n_k the weight kernel size or the receptive field size. Therefore, the size of each convolution kernel $K \in \mathbb{R}^{n_k \times n_k}$.

To overcome the issue of non-existent spatial dependency, previous studies [14,15] have performed time-series classification using 1D-convolution operation. In 1D-convolution, the convolution kernel ranges over the entire sensor channel size, i.e. the size of each convolution yields $n_k \times n$ where n_k denotes the kernel size in time direction. Formally, the 1D operation is defined as

$$h_i = (X * K)_i = \sum_{f=0}^{n_k-1} \sum_{h=0}^{n-1} X_{i+f} K_{i+f}, \tag{2}$$

where h_i denotes the output of the $(i)^{th}$ receptive field in the input, X_{i+f} are the elements in the receptive field of input sequence, K_{i+f} is the convolution kernel. Therefore, the size of each convolution kernel $K \in \mathbb{R}^{n_k \times n}$ which makes the kernel size increase correspondingly to the increase in channel size. For multivariate time-series analysis, this hinders the efficiency of CNNs with regard to its weight sharing capabilities. Therefore, the aim is to incorporate spatial dependency in the time-series, so that standard 2D-convolutions with their efficient weight sharing capabilities can be applied to for time-series classification. An example of learning a permutation is shown below where an arbitrary sequence $\{a_{ij}\}$ of 5×5 undergoes a permutation as following

$$\begin{pmatrix} a_{11} & a_{12} & a_{13} & a_{14} & a_{15} \\ a_{21} & a_{22} & a_{23} & a_{24} & a_{25} \\ a_{31} & a_{32} & a_{33} & a_{34} & a_{35} \\ a_{41} & a_{42} & a_{43} & a_{44} & a_{45} \\ a_{51} & a_{52} & a_{53} & a_{54} & a_{55} \end{pmatrix} \begin{pmatrix} 0 & 1 & 0 & 0 & 0 \\ 0 & 0 & 1 & 0 & 0 \\ 1 & 0 & 0 & 0 & 0 \\ 0 & 0 & 0 & 0 & 1 \\ 0 & 0 & 0 & 1 & 0 \end{pmatrix} = \begin{pmatrix} a_{13} & a_{11} & a_{12} & a_{15} & a_{14} \\ a_{23} & a_{21} & a_{22} & a_{25} & a_{24} \\ a_{33} & a_{31} & a_{32} & a_{35} & a_{34} \\ a_{43} & a_{41} & a_{42} & a_{45} & a_{44} \\ a_{53} & a_{51} & a_{52} & a_{55} & a_{54} \end{pmatrix}.$$

The PM is an $n \times n$ doubly stochastic matrix consisting of only 1 and 0. For our case, the permutation between the columns is needed, which is accomplished by applying the right multiplication to the original sequence.

4   Permutation Layer

This section introduces the permutation layer and its end-to-end training. We assume to have a multivariate time-series of dimension n. Then, each $PM \in \mathbb{R}^{n \times n}$ corresponding to a permutation $(\pi(1), \ldots, \pi(n))$ of sensor channels $1 \ldots n$ can be written as

$$PM_\pi = (pm_{ij}) \in \mathbb{R}^{n \times n} \tag{3}$$

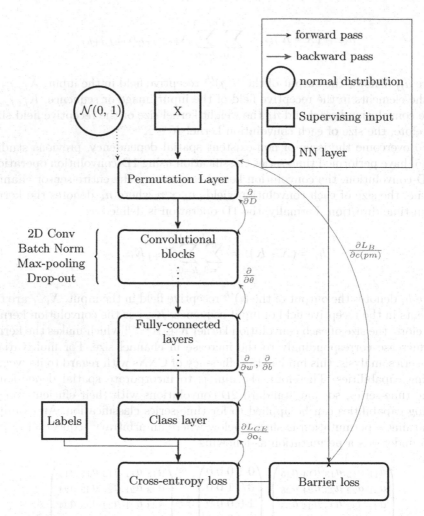

Fig. 1. Diagram of PCNN structure where θ is the parameters of the CNN and $c(pm)$ is the barrier constraints of PL.

with

$$pm_{ij} = \begin{cases} 1, & \text{if } \pi(i) = j \\ 0, & \text{else.} \end{cases} \tag{4}$$

The above constraints can be written more compact. Letting $pm_i \in \{0,1\}^n$ denote the ith row and $pm_j \in \{0,1\}^n$ denote the jth column of PM we impose constraints to PM to ensure that each row and column has exactly one entry equal to one as

$$\begin{aligned} c_i(x) &= 1 - pm_i^T \cdot \mathbf{1} \\ c_j(x) &= 1 - pm_j \cdot \mathbf{1} \end{aligned} \tag{5}$$

where $c_i(x)$, $c_j(x)$ denote the constraint in row and column respectively and $\mathbf{1}$ denotes an all-one vector. Then, designating the layer input x_i we obtain the permuted input by right-multiplication with PM, i.e.

$$x_o = x_i \cdot PM. \tag{6}$$

We propose a permutation layer where a number of permutations are obtained, and all the obtained permutations are fed into a consequent convolution layer which are responsible for extracting features from these new data-transformation.

4.1   Training of Permutation Layer

The end-to-end training to the permutation matrices pm_{ij} results in optimizing binary variables which makes the learning problem combinatoric and does not directly allow for end-to-end training. To circumvent this, we follow a similar approach as in [16] in that we define continuous vectors $\tilde{PM} \in \mathbb{R}^{n \times n}$ which are run through a sigmoidal activation function, i.e. we define

$$PM = \sigma(\tilde{PM}). \tag{7}$$

Using this reparameterization, the entries of the permutation matrix are bounded to the interval $[0, 1]$ and due to the characteristics of the sigmoid function will tend to its boundaries as training proceeds. Using the above reparameterization the training is done on the set of network parameters θ consisting of the kernel weights of the convolution kernels and the permutation matrices PM using stochastic gradient descent on the cross entropy loss. However, we have to consider the additional constraints on the parameters PM as given in Eq. (5) which impose hard constraints. There hard constraints can be circumvented with the constrained optimization methods.

In general, various approaches exist to incorporate hard constraints in stochastic gradient descent algorithms, namely barrier functions, projection methods and active set methods [17]. In this work we propose to use the log barrier functions in addition to the standard cross-entropy loss for classification to incorporate the constraints of Eq. (5). Hence, we add the barrier loss function $L_B PM$ which combines all constraints of the PM yielding

$$L(\theta, PM) = L_{CE}(\theta, PM) + \alpha \cdot L_B(PM), \tag{8}$$

where $L_{CE}(\theta, PM)$ denote the cross entropy loss and $\alpha > 0$ is a parameter to balance both cost functions for the constraints handling. The barrier function chosen in this study is a quadratic logarithmic

$$L_B(c_i(x)) = \sum_{i=1}^{m} \left(\mu \ln(1 + \frac{c_i(x)}{\mu}) \right)^2, \qquad (9)$$

where $c_i(x)$ denote the constraints and μ is the barrier parameter to set barrier regions. The constraints are set to the vector-wise summation domain so that the permutation characteristics take place during the training.

The overall architecture of the proposed model is illustrated in Fig. 1 where the PL is arbitrarily initialized by the standard normal distribution with zero mean and unit as standard deviation, followed by a set of convolution and fully connected layers. Important to note here is in the backward pass, the gradient from barrier loss is directly fed to the permutation since the other parameters have no effect on the barrier loss. In this way, the gradients update the parameters θ and the PM of the complete network for better classification and also permutation at the same time. The training process therefore, updates the PL not only for minimizing the classification loss, but also restrains the PL so that it keeps its doubly stochastic permutation characteristics.

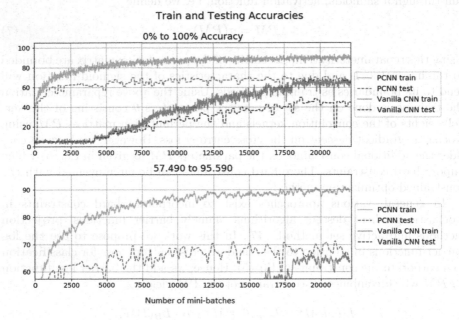

Fig. 2. Training and Testing Accuracy for the complete training along with a zoomed in version of PCNN and Vanilla CNN

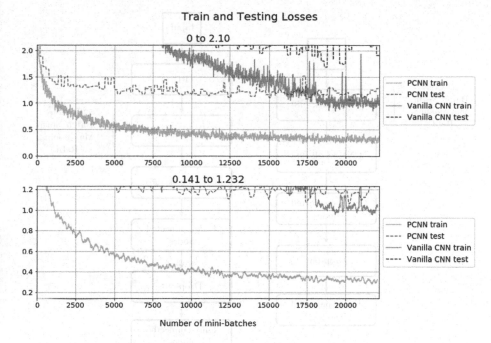

Fig. 3. Training and Testing Loss for the complete training along with a zoomed in version of PCNN and Vanilla CNN

5 Experimental Results

In this section, we provide a thorough comparison of the proposed PL network structures on time-series classification task. To this end, we employ the well known industrial benchmark TE process [18] which has been widely used in literature [19] to evaluate its fault classification performance. The dataset consists of 52 variables used for monitoring or control of the industrial process. 21 fault cases have been explained in [18] with the non-faulty case will serve the labels for the classification task. The dataset from [20] consists of 5,250,000 samples for training and 10,080,000 samples for testing. Although there are more testing samples as training, the number of training samples per class is the same. Therefore, no data balancing techniques have been used. The structure of the network used is illustrated in Fig. 4 where two CNN blocks and two fully-connected layers are used. The channel size of the first block is set as 48, and the second block as 96. Operations of 2d-convolution, Batch Normalization [21], max-pooling and ReLu activation [22] are set in order within a CNN block. The dropout [23] of probability 0.3 is set in between fully-connected layers to avoid over-fitting of the network. The structure of the Permutation CNN (PCNN) is set by adding the PL before the first CNN block as shown in Fig. 4. The Adam [24] optimizer with default parameters ($\mu = 10^{-3}$, $\beta_1 = 0.9$, $\beta_2 = 0.999$, $\epsilon = 10^{-8}$, $\lambda = 0$) was used for 50 training epochs. For simplicity, the number of PM were chosen

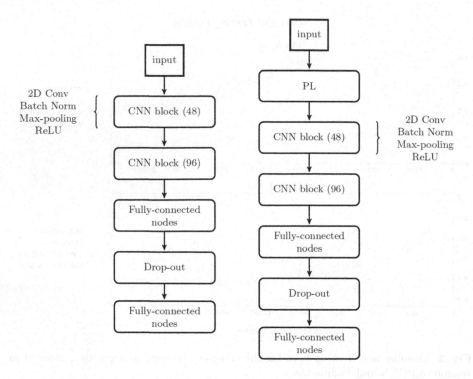

Fig. 4. Network structures of vanilla CNN (left) and Permutation CNN (right).

among $\{10,20,30\}$ and the sequence length $T = 52$. The barrier coefficient, μ was chosen from $\{0.005, 0.0003\}$. The overall plots of training and testing accuracy and loss in the PCNN and the vanilla CNN are shown in Fig. 2 and Fig. 3 respectively. The bottom part of each of the figures shows a zoomed in version to better distinguish among the architectures. A probable reason for the low accuracy of the vanilla CNN in the early part of the training can be attributed to not being able to model spatial dependency in the input without the permutation layer. The training progress shows that the PCNN consistently and considerably outperforms the vanilla CNN architecture in terms of training and testing accuracy with the final test accuracy of 65% and 42% respectively. This shows that the PL has learnt to find spatial dependencies among the different sensor channels.

Since the final accuracy with multi-class classification was not optimal, we tested for binary classification for each of the fault cases. The binary fault detection approach is usually used in literature [25]. Therefore, 20 individual PCNN were trained for the 20 fault cases for detecting the fault and the normal operating condition. Since the task is much simpler, a smaller CNN with 30 and 48 convolution channels were used for this binary classification task. All the other hyperparameters remained the same as described above. The resulting testing accuracy is shown in Table 1 where except fault case 15, the PCNN outperforms the vanilla CNN. Interesting to note here is that the smaller vanilla CNN could not differentiate among the two classes at all, performing only at random choice i.e. at 50 % for binary classification in all the fault cases. This phenomenon highlights again the weakness of 2d convolution for where there is no spatial dependency in the input.

Table 1. Binary Fault detection Accuracy for PCNN and Vanilla CNN

Fault Case	Test Accuracy % PCNN	Test Accuracy % Vanilla CNN
1	100.0	49.99
2	100.0	49.99
3	50.32	49.99
4	100.0	49.99
5	93.06	49.99
6	100.0	49.99
7	99.53	49.99
8	100	49.99
9	50.24	49.99
10	71.83	49.99
11	91.73	49.99
12	100	49.99
13	99.69	49.99
14	92.53	49.99
15	49.45	49.99
16	92.94	49.99
17	99.99	49.99
18	100	49.99
19	87.84	49.99
20	99.91	49.99
Overall	86.19	49.99

6 Conclusion

We presented permutation layer as a built in module into the training of convolutional neural networks. Their main purpose is to lower the problem of non-spatial relations in time-series data which are inherently assumed when training 2D CNNs. Learning permutations of the input channels allows to bring channels with meaningful relations into a spatial order which can more efficiently be analyzed by CNNs. We provide experimental evidence by testing the proposed method on a benchmark fault detection dataset underlining its practical applicability. The results prove the inherent weakness of vanilla 2d CNN for time-series analysis, especially on the benchmark Tennessee Eastman dataset. However, in conjunction with the proposed permutation layer, the CNN model was successful in capturing the spatial dependency among the sensor channels. In future work, we will explore the possibilities of using other permutation methods as a baseline for the comparison with the proposed method.

References

1. LeCun, Y., et al.: Handwritten digit recognition with a back-propagation network. In: Advances in Neural Information Processing Systems, pp. 396–404 (1990)
2. Bai, S., Kolter, J.Z., Koltun, V.: An empirical evaluation of generic convolutional and recurrent networks for sequence modeling. arXiv preprint arXiv:1803.01271 (2018)
3. Da Li, X., He, W., Li, S.: Internet of things in industries: a survey. IEEE Trans. Industr. Inf. **10**(4), 2233–2243 (2014)
4. Chadha, G.S., Krishnamoorthy, M., Schwung, A.: Time series based fault detection in industrial processes using convolutional neural networks. In: 45th Annual Conference of the IEEE Industrial Electronics Society, IECON 2019, vol. 1, pp. 173–178 (2019)
5. Jiang, G., et al.: Multiscale convolutional neural networks for fault diagnosis of wind turbine gearbox. IEEE Trans. Industr. Electron. **66**(4), 3196–3207 (2019)
6. Ince, T., et al.: Real-time motor fault detection by 1-D convolutional neural networks. IEEE Trans. Industr. Electron. **63**(11), 7067–7075 (2016). https://doi.org/10.1109/TIE.2016.2582729. ISSN: 0278-0046
7. Goodfellow, I., Bengio, Y., Courville, A.: Deep Learning. MIT Press, Cambridge (2016)
8. Krizhevsky, A., Sutskever, I., Hinton, G.E.: Imagenet classification with deep convolutional neural networks. In: Advances in Neural Information Processing Systems, pp. 1097–1105 (2012)
9. Redmon, J., et al.: You only look once: unified, real-time object detection. In: The IEEE Conference on Computer Vision and Pattern Recognition (CVPR) (2016)
10. Marshall, A.W., Olkin, I., Arnold, B.C.: Doubly stochastic matrices. Inequalities: Theory of Majorization and Its Applications. SSS, pp. 29–77. Springer, New York (2010). https://doi.org/10.1007/978-0-387-68276-1_2
11. Mena, G., et al.: Learning latent permutations with Gumbel-Sinkhorn networks. In: International Conference on Learning Representations (2018). https://openreview.net/forum?id=Byt3oJ-0W
12. Cruz, R.S., et al.: Visual permutation learning. IEEE Trans. Pattern Anal. Mach. Intell. **41**(12), 3100–3114 (2019). https://doi.org/10.1109/tpami.2018.2873701
13. Helmbold, D.P., Warmuth, M.K.: Learning permutations with exponential weights. J. Mach. Learn. Res. **10**, 1705–1736 (2009). ISSN: 1532-4435. http://dl.acm.org/citation.cfm?id=1577069.1755841
14. Yang, J., et al.: Deep convolutional neural networks on multichannel time series for human activity recognition. In: IJCAI, vol. 15, pp. 3995–4001 (2015)
15. Liu, C.-L., Hsaio, W.-H., Tu, Y.-C.: Time series classification with multivariate convolutional neural network. IEEE Trans. Industr. Electron. **66**(6), 4788–4797 (2019). https://doi.org/10.1109/TIE.2018.2864702. ISSN: 0278-0046
16. Trask, A., et al.: Neural arithmetic logic units. In: Advances in Neural Information Processing Systems, pp. 8035–8044 (2018)

17. Boyd, S.P., Vandenberghe, L.: Convex Optimization. Cambridge University Press, Cambridge (2004)
18. Downs, J.J., Vogel, E.F.: A plant-wide industrial process control problem. Comput. Chem. Eng. **17**(3), 245–255 (1993)
19. Park, P., et al.: Fault detection and diagnosis using combined autoencoder and long short-term memory network. Sensors **19**(21), 4612 (2019)
20. Rieth, C.A., et al.: Additional Tennessee Eastman Process Simulation Data for Anomaly Detection Evaluation (2017). https://doi.org/10.7910/dvn/6c3jr1
21. Ioffe, S., Szegedy, C.: Batch normalization: accelerating deep network training by reducing internal covariate shift. In: Proceedings of the 32nd International Conference on International Conference on Machine Learning, ICML 2015, vol. 37, pp. 448–456. JMLR.org (2015)
22. Glorot, X., Bordes, A., Bengio, Y.: Deep sparse rectifier neural networks. In: AISTATS, vol. 15, p. 275 (2011)
23. Srivastava, N., et al.: Dropout: a simple way to prevent neural networks from overfitting. J. Mach. Learn. Res. **15**(1), 1929–1958 (2014)
24. Kingma, D.P., Ba, J.: Adam: a method for stochastic optimization. arXiv e-prints (2014). arXiv:1412.6980
25. Iqbal, R., et al.: Fault detection and isolation in industrial processes using deep learning approaches. IEEE Trans. Industr. Inf. **15**(5), 3077–3084 (2019). https://doi.org/10.1109/TII.2019.2902274

Deep Learning Applications I

Deep Learning Applications I

GTFNet: Ground Truth Fitting Network for Crowd Counting

Jinghan Tan[1,2], Jun Sang[1,2(✉)], Zhili Xiang[1,2], Ying Shi[1,2], and Xiaofeng Xia[1,2]

[1] Key Laboratory of Dependable Service Computing in Cyber Physical
Society of Ministry of Education, Chongqing University, Chongqing 400044, China
jsang@cqu.edu.cn

[2] School of Big Data and Software Engineering, Chongqing University, Chongqing 401331,
China

Abstract. Crowd counting aims to estimate the number of pedestrians in a single image. Current crowd counting methods usually obtain counting results by integrating density maps. However, the label density map generated by the Gaussian kernel cannot accurately map the ground truth in the corresponding crowd image, thereby affecting the final counting result. In this paper, a ground truth fitting network called GTFNet was proposed, which aims to generate estimated density maps which can fit the ground truth better. Firstly, the VGG network combined with the dilated convolutional layers was used as the backbone network of GTFNet to extract hierarchical features. The multi-level features were concatenated to achieve compensation for information loss caused by pooling operations, which may assist the network to obtain texture information and spatial information. Secondly, the regional consistency loss function was designed to obtain the mapping results of the estimated density map and the label density map at different region levels. During the training process, the region-level dynamic weights were designed to assign a suitable region fitting range for the network, which can effectively reduce the impact of label errors on the estimated density maps. Finally, our proposed GTFNet was evaluated upon three crowd counting datasets (ShanghaiTech, UCF_CC_50 and UCF-QRNF). The experimental results demonstrated that the proposed GTFNet achieved excellent overall performance on all these datasets.

Keywords: Crowd counting · Ground truth · Regional consistency · Dynamic weights

1 Introduction

The monitoring of crowd density is of great significance due to the rapid growth of the world population and the acceleration of urbanization [1, 2]. However, the crowd counting task is extremely challenging due to the low resolution and high crowd density of crowd images, and the problems of lighting, camera angle of view, and head scale changes.

© Springer Nature Switzerland AG 2020
I. Farkaš et al. (Eds.): ICANN 2020, LNCS 12396, pp. 235–246, 2020.
https://doi.org/10.1007/978-3-030-61609-0_19

The early crowd counting methods were usually based on the traditional machine learning, which detect each pedestrian in the scene by using a sliding window [3–8].

In recent years, CNN-based crowd counting methods have performed well in the crowd counting task. Such method that generates the corresponding crowd density map by CNN and integrates it to get the crowd number is also the most mainstream in the crowd counting task [9–13]. The density map can reflect the distribution of population density in the single image, and provide the location information of each object, which is more practical for density monitoring. Li et al. [14] proposed a network called CSRNet, which used the first ten layers of the pre-trained VGG-16 [15] with strong feature extraction and transfer learning capabilities as a front-end network, and used dilated convolution [16] as a back-end network to maintain spatial information. Jiang et al. [17] proposes a trellis encoder-decoder network named TEDNet, which incorporates multiple decoding paths. The network architecture uses skip connection to get accurate counting and density map in high-density crowd scenes. In addition, to compensate the limited MSE loss, a spatial abstraction loss (SAL) was defined. SAL divides the density map into three abstraction levels by cascading max pooling layers with down-sampling strides. The pixel values at each abstraction level represent the abstract mappings of receptive fields with different sizes in the original estimated density map. Finally, by computing MSE on each abstraction level, supplement the pixel-wise MSE loss with patch wise supervision.

Since CSRNet was proposed, many crowd counting researchers have used the first 10 layers of pre-trained VGG-16 [15] as the front-end network in their networks and achieved good counting results. However, there still exist some significant shortcomings. We performed visual experiments on the features extracted from some intermediate layers of VGG backbone network (as shown in Fig. 1). It can be noticed that with the deeper network, although the network may obtain more accurate spatial semantic information to successfully distinguish the crowd from background noise, due to three pooling operations, many detailed texture information was lost, which may affect the quality of the estimated density map. Therefore, from the perspective of network architecture, the feature information of each level should be fully obtained to generate the estimated density maps to fit the ground truth better.

In addition, in the view of loss function, most researchers usually used the traditional Euclidean loss to train the network and only focused on difference of point pixel value between the estimated map and the true density map [6, 13, 14]. However, the label density map generated by the Gaussian kernel based on the head center coordinates is not accurate. It seems that, there is no need to have the estimated density map fit the label pixel by pixel.

Based on the above two points, in this paper, we proposed a novel method called GTFNet to generate density maps which may fit the ground truth better for crowd counting. We connected three dilated convolutional layers after the first 10 layers of pre-trained VGG-16 [15] as the feature map extractor to extract detailed texture features and spatial semantic features, and designed a feature concatenate block to cascade the extracted feature information. Meanwhile, inspired by TEDNet [17], the region consistency loss (RCL) was designed to solve pixel-wise isolation and independence. In addition, the dynamic weights for each region-level of RCL were designed, so that the estimated density map can fit both the edge region and the dense region of the ground truth.

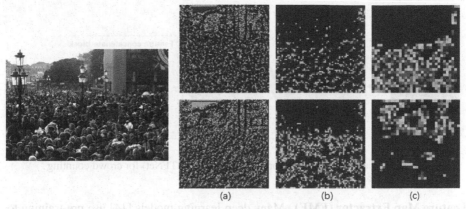

(a)   (b)   (c)

Fig. 1. Features of different VGG blocks. (a) represents the two feature maps selected from the output of BLOCK 2. (b) represents the two feature maps selected from the output of BLOCK 3. (c) represents the two feature maps selected from the output of BLOCK 4.

In summary, the main contributions of this paper are as follows:

- We proposed a new network architecture to fuse detailed texture information and spatial semantic information in crowd images and generate high-quality density map.
- We designed a novel training loss, which assigns different task indicators to the training process by assigning dynamic weights to each region-level loss, achieving a high-precision fitting of the estimated density map to the ground truth, and then obtaining accurate counting results.
- The proposed approach achieved well-performance on ShanghaiTech (Part A and Part B), UCF-QNRF and UCF CC 50 datasets.

2 The Proposed GTFNet

The motivation of the proposed method is to generate the estimated density maps to fit the ground truth better. In this section, the architecture of the proposed GTFNet (Fig. 2) was discussed in detail. Also, a new subscale pixel region consistency loss was introduced, which can obtain more accurate sub-scale region distribution information by comparing the difference between the estimated value and the ground truth of the multi-scale pixel region, so that the estimated density map can fit both the edge region and the dense region of the ground truth.

2.1 Architecture of GTFNet

The proposed GTFNet consists of feature map extractor (FME) and feature concatenate block (FCB). Firstly, the crowd images are feed into FME to extract the shallow texture information and the deep semantic information. Then, the extracted hierarchical information is fused by FCB. Finally, the output of FCB is passed to a simple convolution with $1 \times 1 \times 1$ kernel to generate the density map. We adopt all 3×3 filters in the network [15], which may reduce the training parameters with the same receptive field.

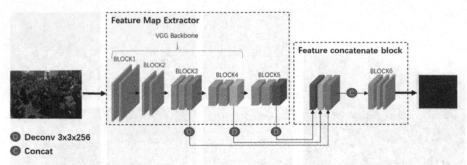

Fig. 2. The architecture of the proposed network (GTFNet) for crowd counting

Feature Map Extractor (FME). Many deep learning models [14] use pre-training to avoid over-fitting. Due to the superior feature extraction performance of the VGG-16 [15] on crowd counting tasks, following CSRNet [14], we keep the first ten layers of per-trained VGG-16 [15] to be our backbone network. Because the dilated convolution [16] can enlarge the receptive field without loss of resolution, in order to obtain more semantic features, we added three dilated convolutional layers with 3×3 kernel, 512 channels and 2 dilated rates at the back end of VGG backbone. Our feature map extractor consists of Block 1–5 as shown in Fig. 2.

Feature Concatenate Block (FCB). Yosinski et al. [20] revealed that the features learned by the first few layers of the neural network are task-independent texture features, and as the network deepening, the features learned by each layer will gradually be transformed into spatial semantic features closely related to the task. Hence, in order to compensate for the loss of features caused by the pooling operation and avoid too many basic features from affecting the learning task, so that the network can obtain not only texture features but also spatial semantic features, we fused the features of Block3–5. Features of each block are feed into a deconvolutional layer deconv3 $\times$ 3 $\times$ 256 and output the same size as Block3, and then the hierarchical features are directly concatenated. Finally, the concatenated feature maps are feed into Block6 with conv3 $\times$ 3 $\times$ 256, conv3 $\times$ 3$\times$ 128, conv3 $\times$ 3$\times$ 64 and a simple convolution with $1 \times 1 \times 1$ kernel to generate the density map. The ablation experiments in Sect. 5.3 demonstrated that the FCB we proposed can improve the performance.

2.2 Loss Function

Counting result are related to the quality of density map. As discussed above, CNN-based crowd counting label density maps have a large number of errors, and the loss functions commonly used in current methods [13, 14, 17, 19] cannot effectively fit the ground truth, which affect the quality of the density maps. In this paper, we designed a new crowd counting loss function to effectively improve the goodness of fit of the estimated density maps and the ground truth.

MAE Loss. There are some outliers in the crowd count data set, such as overexposed or underexposed of some heads. MSE loss amplifies the distance between the estimated value and the true value by square calculation, so it gives a large penalty to the output that deviates from the observed value, which may affect the generalization ability of the network. MAE loss is more robust to these outliers, thus we choose MAE loss as the basic loss function, which is defined as follows:

$$L_1 = \frac{1}{N} \sum_{i=1}^{N} \left\| D(X_i; \theta) - D_i^{GT} \right\|_1, \tag{1}$$

where N is the number of images in the batch, $D(X_i; \theta)$ is the estimated density map for training image X_i with parameters θ, D_i^{GT} is the ground truth density map for X_i. We chose MAE loss at each pixel scale level.

Region Consistency Loss (RCL). The common Euclidean loss function or the mean absolute error loss function represent pixel-wise isolation and independence. As described in TEDNet [17], loss functions at multiple receptive field levels can effectively enhance the correlation among pixels and constraint the consistency of multi-pixel region. Based on TEDNet, we defined the region consistency loss (RCL). RCL consists of MAE loss at multiple subscale region levels. The subscale region levels were divided by average pooling on estimated density maps with different sized pooling kernel, and the single pixel value in each region level denotes the mean of different pixel ranges of the estimated density map. The pooling kernels we adopted are 1×1, 2×2 and 4×4. Finally, by calculating the MAE loss of each region level, the difference between different pixel levels of the estimated density map and the real density map is mapped. The computation of RCL is formalized as:

$$L_{rc} = \frac{1}{N} \sum_{i=1}^{N} \sum_{s=1}^{S} W_s \times S \times \left\| P_{avg}(D(X_i; \theta), S) - 16 \times P_{avg}(D_i^{GT}, 4S) \right\|_1, \tag{2}$$

where S is the pooling kernel size of average pooling on estimated density map, W_s is the weight of loss at each pixel level, P_{avg} is average pooling operation. Because the network undergoes two subsampling, the width and height of the real density map is four times of the estimated density map, and the size of the pooling kernel used in the real density map is $4S$.

Region-Level Dynamic Weights. During the crowd counting training process, the network needs to obtain the crowd location information firstly, and then identify each head in the crowd to count.

We believe that, the point pixel loss function is more effective in segmenting the crowd from the background. Therefore, we choose the pixel-level MAE loss as the dominant at the initial stage of training to accurately divide the crowd and noise. The global consistency between the estimated map and the ground truth is maintained through pixel-level fitting.

However, because of the influence of lighting and occlusion, features of head are inapparent and contradict with the label. In addition, the data set is manually labeled, there are errors in the center of the labeled heads, and the Gaussian kernel estimates the size of the head as a circular. Thereby, some pixel region within the estimated frame are misidentified. We believe that the goodness of fit of the pixel-by-pixel fitting as the loss function is meaningless for the region with high perspective and complex textures, and the goodness of fit, which fits from large-scale region (large pooling kernel size), can map the error of estimated map and ground truth effectively. Thus, the weight of loss with lager receptive field (pooling kernel 2×2 and 4×4) are gradually increased during training. According to the experiments, the weight set values for different pixel level are shown in Table 1.

Table 1. The values of weight Ws for different pixel levels according to training process. W_1 represents the weight of MAE loss between the generated density maps and the true density maps. W_2 represents the weight of loss MAE loss of the density map with 2×2 down-sampling. W_4 represents the weight of loss MAE loss of the density map with 4×4 down-sampling. T_i represents the weight update according to number of training epochs.

Weight	Epoch				
	$[0, T_1)$	$[T_1, T_2)$	$[T_2, T_3)$	$[T_3, T_4)$	$[T_4, \infty)$
W_1	0.8	0.6	0.4	0.2	0.1
W_2	0.1	0.2	0.3	0.4	0.3
W_4	0.1	0.2	0.3	0.4	0.6

3 Experiments and Results

3.1 Training Details

Following [13], we adopted the geometry-adaptive Gaussian kernel to generate density map. The geometry-adaptive Gaussian kernel is defined as follow:

$$D^{GT} = \sum_{i=1}^{N} \delta(x - x_i) \times G_{\sigma i}(x), \tag{3}$$

where $\sigma_i = \beta \overline{d_i}$, x is the position of pixel and N is the number of head annotations in the image. For each targeted object x_i in the ground truth δ, use $\overline{d_i}$ to indicate the average distance of k nearest neighbors. Then convolve $\delta(x - x_i)$ with a Gaussian kernel with parameter σ_i. Following [14], we set $\beta = 0.3$, $k = 3$, and used the same data augmentation method.

In the training procedure, the first 10 layers of pre-trained VGG-16 [15] and a new block with three convolutional layers were applied as the front-end feature extractor, while three deconvolutional layers and three convolutional layers were applied as the feature concatenate block. All new layers were initialized from a Gaussian distribution with zero mean and 0.01 standard deviation. For faster convergence than stochastic gradient descent with momentum, Adam optimizer was used to train with learning rate of 1e-6 and decreased by a factor of 0.9 every 10 K iterations. The network was trained with batch size of 5. And then an ablation study of ShanghaiTech Part A dataset [13] is conducted to analyze the weight update of our loss function (shown in Table 2). Our method was implemented on the Pytorch [21] framework.

Table 2. Region-level dynamic weights update according to number of training epochs

	Number of training epochs		
	A	B	C
T_1	10	20	40
T_2	20	40	80
T_3	30	60	120
T_4	40	80	160

3.2 Evaluation Metrics

We adopted the MAE and the MSE to evaluate the performance of our network. These two metrics are defined as follows:

$$MAE = \frac{1}{N} \sum_{i=1}^{N} \left| C_i - C_i^{GT} \right|, \tag{4}$$

$$MSE = \sqrt{\frac{1}{N} \sum_{i=1}^{N} \left| C_i - C_i^{GT} \right|^2}, \tag{5}$$

where N is the number of images in test set, C_i represents the estimated count while C_i^{GT} is the ground truth count.

3.3 Ablation Experiments

In this section, we conduct ablation experiments on ShanghaiTech Part A [13] and the loss function layout is analyzed.

Loss Function. Region consistency loss is divided into three levels by three different sized average pooling kernels (i.e. $1 \times 1, 2 \times 2, 4 \times 4$). We test each loss level separately and compare the static weight with the dynamic weights we designed. Experimental results are presented in Table 3 and proved that dynamic weights can get more accurate counting results and GTFNet B achieves the lowest error.

Table 3. Comparison of region consistency loss on ShanghaiTech Part A [13]

Method	MAE	MSE
Normal MSE	69.9	117.4
$W_1 \equiv 1, W_{2,3} \equiv 0$	62.9	106.1
$W_2 \equiv 1, W_{1,3} \equiv 0$	61.8	104.6
$W_3 \equiv 1, W_{1,2} \equiv 0$	60.6	101.9
$W_S \cong 1/3$	60.3	100.9
GTFNet A	60.2	100.8
GTFNet B	**58.8**	**99.6**
GTFNet C	59.0	100.2

Network Architecture. GTFNet consists of feature map extractor, feature concatenate block and region consistency loss. In order to verify their effectiveness, we add component in turn for experiments. As the comparison result illustrated in Table 4, feature concatenate block shows excellent performance in crowd counting tasks and region consistency loss proposed by us can effectively improve the counting accuracy.

Table 4. Estimation errors for different components of our proposed network on ShanghaiTech Part A [13]

Method	MAE	MSE
FME	71.9	117.2
FME + FCB	69.9	117.4
FME + FCB + RCL	**58.8**	**99.6**

3.4 Counting Accuracy

We evaluate our GTFNet on four publicly available crowd counting datasets: ShanghaiTech [13], UCF-QNRF [19] and UCF_CC_50 [18]. As shown in Table 5.

Table 5. Estimation errors on ShanghaiTech [13], UCF_CC_50 [18] and UCF-QNRF [19] datasets

	ShanghaiTech A		ShanghaiTech B		UCF_CC_50		UCF-QNRF	
Method	MAE	MSE	MAE	MSE	MAE	MSE	MAE	MSE
MCNN [13]	110.2	173.2	26.4	41.3	377.6	509.1	277	426
CSRNet [14]	68.2	115.0	10.6	16.0	266.1	397.5	–	–
SANet [22]	67.0	104.5	8.4	13.6	258.4	334.9	–	–
Idrees et al. [19]	–	–	–	–	–	–	132	191
SFCN [23]	64.8	107.5	7.6	13.0	**214.2**	318.2	102	**171.4**
TEDNet [17]	64.2	109.1	8.2	12.8	249.4	354.5	113	188
ADCrowdNet [24]	63.2	**98.9**	7.7	12.9	257.1	363.5	–	–
PACNN [25]	62.4	102.0	7.6	11.8	241.7	320.7	–	–
Ours	**58.8**	99.6	**6.9**	**11.2**	230.6	**307.5**	**101**	181

ShanghaiTech Dataset [13]. The ShanghaiTech crowd dataset is the dataset with the largest number of people. It consists of two parts: A and B. Part A consists of 482 randomly selected crowd images from the Internet, and part B includes 716 crowd images obtained from downtown Shanghai. We evaluate our method and compare it to other five recent works [13, 14, 17, 19, 21–24] and results are shown in Table 5. It indicates that our method achieves good performance on both Part A and Part B datasets, the MAE in Part A is improved by 5.6% and the MAE in Part B is also delivers 9.2% lower. Several examples of our approach are presented in Fig. 3.

UCF_CC_50 Dataset [18]. The UCF_CC_50 dataset includes a variety of scenes with various densities and different visual angle distortions. It contains a total of 50 images of different resolutions, with an average of 1280 people per image. 63075 people were tagged throughout the dataset. The number of individuals ranges from 94 to 4543. Table 5 shows the experiment result of MAE and MSE compared with other approaches. we achieve an improvement of 3.4% in terms of the MSE metric.

UCF-QNRF Dataset [19]. UCF-QNRF dataset is a new and the largest crowd dataset for evaluating crowd counting and localization methods. The dataset has larger resolution images, more complex background interference and more diverse perspectives. UCF-QNRF dataset is more challenging than other datasets. The GTFNet obtains the good performance with 1% MAE improvement. several examples of our approach are presented in Fig. 3.

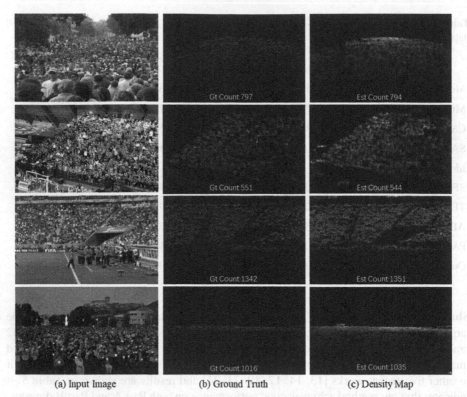

| (a) Input Image | (b) Ground Truth | (c) Density Map |

Fig. 3. An illustration of estimated density maps and crowd counts generated by proposed GTFNet. Row 1 and 2 are examples from ShanghaiTech part A. Row 3 and 4 are examples from UCF-QNRF.

4 Conclusions

In this paper, we proposed a new crowd counting method called GTFNet generate estimated density maps to fits ground truth better. Networks architecture have stronger feature extraction capabilities by fusing hierarchical features. We further introduced a novel loss to reduce the impact of label errors and improve crowd counting accuracy. Experiments demonstrated that GTFNet achieves the excellent performance with other state-of-the-art approaches.

Acknowledgements. This work was supported by National Natural Science Foundation of China (No. 61971073).

References

1. Beibei, Z.: Crowd analysis: a survey. Mach. Vis. Appl. **19**(5–6), 345–357 (2008)
2. Teng, L.: Crowded scene analysis: a survey. IEEE Trans. Circuits Syst. Video Technol. **25**(3), 367–386 (2015)

3. Dalal, N.: Histograms of oriented gradients for human detection. In: 2005 IEEE Computer Society Conference on Computer Vision and Pattern Recognition (CVPR'05), vol. 1, pp. 886–893. IEEE (2005)
4. Felzenszwalb, P.F.: Object detection with discriminatively trained part-based models. IEEE Trans. Pattern Anal. Mach. Intell. **32**(9), 1627–1645 (2009)
5. Zhao, T.: Segmentation and tracking of multiple humans in crowded environments. IEEE Trans. Pattern Anal. Mach. Intell. **30**(7), 1198–1211 (2008)
6. Rodriguez, M.: Density-aware person detection and tracking in crowds. In: 2011 International Conference on Computer Vision, pp. 2423–2430. IEEE (2011)
7. Wang, M.: Automatic adaptation of a generic pedestrian detector to a specific traffic scene. In: 2011 IEEE Conference on Computer Vision and Pattern Recognition (CVPR'11), vol. 7, pp. 3401–3408. IEEE (2011)
8. Wu, B.: Detection of multiple, partially occluded humans in a single image by bayesian combination of edgelet part detectors. In: Tenth IEEE International Conference on Computer Vision (ICCV'05), vol. 1, pp. 90–97. IEEE (2005)
9. Zhang, C.: Cross-scene crowd counting via deep convolutional neural networks. In: Proceedings of the IEEE Conference on Computer Vision and Pattern Recognition, pp. 833–841. IEEE (2015)
10. Szegedy, C.: Going deeper with convolutions. In: Proceedings of the IEEE Conference on Computer Vision and Pattern Recognition, pp. 1–9. IEEE (2015)
11. Szegedy, C.: Rethinking the inception architecture for computer vision. In: Proceedings of the IEEE Conference on Computer Vision and Pattern Recognition, pp. 2818–2826. IEEE (2016)
12. He, K.: Deep residual learning for image recognition. In: Proceedings of the IEEE Conference on Computer Vision and Pattern Recognition, pp. 770–778. IEEE (2016)
13. Zhang, Y.: Single-image crowd counting via multi-column convolutional neural network. In: Proceedings of the IEEE Conference on Computer Vision and Pattern Recognition, pp. 589–597. IEEE (2016)
14. Li, Y.: Csrnet: dilated convolutional neural networks for understanding the highly congested scenes. In: Proceedings of the IEEE Conference on Computer Vision and Pattern Recognition, pp. 1091–1100. IEEE (2018)
15. Simonyan, A.: Very deep convolutional networks for large-scale image recognition (2014). arXiv preprint arXiv:1409.1556
16. Yu, F.: Dilated residual networks. In: Proceedings of the IEEE Conference on Computer Vision and Pattern Recognition, pp. 472–480. IEEE (2017)
17. Jiang, X.: Crowd counting and density estimation by trellis encoder-decoder networks. In: Proceedings of the IEEE Conference on Computer Vision and Pattern Recognition, pp. 6133–6142. IEEE (2019)
18. Idrees, H.: Multi-source multi-scale counting in extremely dense crowd images. In: Proceedings of the IEEE Conference on Computer Vision and Pattern Recognition, pp. 2547–2554. IEEE (2013)
19. Idrees, H., et al.: Composition Loss for Counting, Density Map Estimation and Localization in Dense Crowds. In: Ferrari, V., Hebert, M., Sminchisescu, C., Weiss, Y. (eds.) ECCV 2018. LNCS, vol. 11206, pp. 544–559. Springer, Cham (2018). https://doi.org/10.1007/978-3-030-01216-8_33
20. Yosinski, J.: How transferable are features in deep neural networks? In: Advances in Neural Information Processing Systems, pp. 3320–3328. MIT Press (2014)
21. Paszke, A., Gross, S., Chintala, S., Chanan, G.: Pytorch: tensors and dynamic neural networks in python with strong gpu acceleration. PyTorch: tensors and dynamic neural networks in Python with strong GPU acceleration 6 (2017)

22. Cao, X., Wang, Z., Zhao, Y., Su, F.: Scale aggregation network for accurate and efficient crowd counting. In: Ferrari, V., Hebert, M., Sminchisescu, C., Weiss, Y. (eds.) ECCV 2018. LNCS, vol. 11209, pp. 757–773. Springer, Cham (2018). https://doi.org/10.1007/978-3-030-01228-1_45

23. Wang, Q.: Learning from synthetic data for crowd counting in the wild. In: Proceedings of the IEEE Conference on Computer Vision and Pattern Recognition, pp. 8198–8207. IEEE (2019)

24. Liu, N.: Adcrowdnet: an attention-injective deformable convolutional network for crowd understanding. In: Proceedings of the IEEE Conference on Computer Vision and Pattern Recognition, pp. 3225–3234. IEEE (2019)

25. Shi, M.: Perspective-aware CNN for crowd counting (2018)

Evaluation of Deep Learning Methods for Bone Suppression from Dual Energy Chest Radiography

Ilyas Sirazitdinov[1], Konstantin Kubrak[1], Semen Kiselev[1(✉)],
Alexey Tolkachev[1], Maksym Kholiavchenko[1], and Bulat Ibragimov[1,2]

[1] Innopolis University, Innopolis, Russia
{ilyas.sirazitdinov,konstantin.kubrak,s.kiselev,alexey.tolkachev,
maksym.kholiavchenko,bulat.ibragimov}@innopolis.ru
[2] University of Copenhagen, Copenhagen, Denmark

Abstract. Bone suppression in chest x-rays is an important processing step that can often improve visual detection of lung pathologies hidden under ribs or clavicle shadows. Current diagnostic imaging protocol does not include hardware-based bone suppression, hence the need for a software-based solution. This paper evaluates various deep learning models adapted for bone suppression task, namely, we implemented several state-of-the-art deep learning architectures: convolution autoencoder, U-net, FPN, cGAN; augmented them with domain-specific denoising techniques, such as wavelet decomposition, with the aim to identify the optimal solution for chest x-ray analysis. Our results show that wavelet decomposition does not improve the rib suppression, "skip connections" modification outperforms baseline autoencoder approach with and without the usage of the wavelet decomposition, the residual models are trained faster than plain models and achieve higher validation scores.

Keywords: Bone suppression · Bone shadow exclusion · Chest x-ray · Convolutional neural networks · Deep learning

1 Introduction

Chest x-ray (CXR) remains the most common medical imaging modality and is routinely utilized to diagnose various lung pathologies. Due to the projective nature of x-rays, ribs and clavicles are superimposed over lung fields and can potentially obstruct lung pathologies. For example, it has been estimated that up to 22% of missed lung cancer lesions were partially obstructed by the clavicles [12]. Bone shadow elimination is a problem of removing the visual presence of bones on x-ray images followed by reconstruction of the residual soft-tissue structure. Loog et al. [8] showed that the radiograph contrast of bone structures

This research was supported by the Russian Science Foundation under Grant No. 18-71-10072.
I. Sirazitdinov and K. Kubrak—Equal contribution
I. Sirazitdinov—Currently with Philips Research, Skolkovo, Russia.

© Springer Nature Switzerland AG 2020
I. Farkaš et al. (Eds.): ICANN 2020, LNCS 12396, pp. 247–257, 2020.
https://doi.org/10.1007/978-3-030-61609-0_20

decreases more than that of lung nodules making the nodules more distinguishable and hence improving the performance of automatic lung cancer detection. Nowadays, the most widely used hardware method for obtaining the soft-tissue image is the dual-energy subtraction (DES) technique. The single-shot or double-shot DES obtains low-energy x-ray and high-energy x-ray with visually suppressed bones on the image. Both single-shot and double-shot DES have major drawbacks. The single-shot DES has a limitation in energy separation and produces noisy images, and the double-shot DES requires the exposure to higher doses of radiation and can produce visual defects due to the patient motions between the x-ray shots. To avoid the problems of DES and eliminate the need for new hardware in diagnostic chest imaging, several software bone exclusion methods were proposed. Early work addressed rib suppression as a blind source separation problem and based their research on the idea of the explicit bone signal subtraction [2,10]. Recent progress in the bone elimination task is caused by deep learning approaches, that either treated bone structures as noise and proposed different denoising techniques or formulated the task as the image-to-image translation problem. Gusarev et al. [4] utilized the convolution denoising autoencoder and compared various training configurations on rib suppression. Yang et al. [15] proposed an idea of the iterative refinement in a multi-resolution setting in a gradient domain, where the resulting bone image was obtained after 2-d integration. Chen et al. [3] utilized a Haar wavelet decomposition combined with a two-level convolutional neural network (CNN) to leverage coarse-to-fine bone image reconstruction. In contrast to direct optimization of defined loss functions, Oh et al. [9] proposed the adversarial approach and revealed its superiority in a wavelet domain. There is however no systematic comparison of the various type bone suppression methods. Current research effort aims to investigate modern deep learning denoising approaches and evaluate their applicability to the bone elimination task, namely, we implemented discriminative and generative state-of-the-art models and evaluated their performance on different settings.

2   Methodology

2.1   Dataset

Data for the experiments was kindly provided by Gusarev et al. [4]. The dataset consists of 35 double-shot DES image pairs, each containing an initial CXR image and corresponding DES soft-tissue image. Images from ChestX-ray-14 dataset were used in order to perform visual analysis of the obtained models [14].

2.2   Data Preprocessing

The double-shot DES images are usually partially misaligned due to motion artifacts, e.g. patient breathing. To compensate for such misalignment, low energy diagnostic CXR were first non-rigidly registered to DES soft-tissue images. The registration was performed using B-splines with mutual information criterion.

After registration, the inter-CXR alignment measured in terms of structure similarity (SSIM, Eq. 1) increased from 0.8744 to 0.9131. Figure 1, where each image is a subtraction of a DES image from clinical CXR, illustrates the benefit of the alignment: while sharp textures of the left and the right images indicate shift between images, the middle smooth image shows better alignment. This initial registration is needed to correctly evaluate the results of rib suppression. Due to the fact that evaluation metrics of image restoration are based on a pixelwise difference, shift artifacts may result in a high error rate even for perfectly suppressed images.

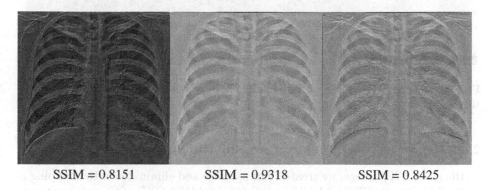

SSIM = 0.8151   SSIM = 0.9318   SSIM = 0.8425

Fig. 1. The impact of registration on the quality of visual representation of radiographs: soft tissue image before registration (left) and after registration (middle). The right image is a subtraction of artificially shifted diagnostic CXR image after registration.

2.3   Wavelet Domain

Wavelet decomposition is one of the steps commonly utilized for rib suppression as it helps to highlight rib edges [3,9]. At the same time, convolutional neural network utilized in our work for rib suppression does not require wavelet decomposition of the input. We therefore implemented and compared both rib suppression using only diagnostic CXRs and using wavelet decomposition of CXRs. Following previous works, we adopted Haar wavelet transform and decomposed CXRs into 4 components: sub-sampled original image and vertical, horizontal and diagonal details feature images. The Haar wavelets are defined as a square-shape step function and their convolution with the target image results in highlighting image edges at different orientations. The results of wavelet decomposition are shown in Fig. 2, for low-dose and DES CXRs, for a randomly selected patient.

Fig. 2. 4-channel wavelet decomposition of a chest x-ray and corresponding DES soft-tissue image

2.4   Neural Network Architectures for Rib Suppression

In the given CXR image, we treated ribs as noise and eliminated it by mapping a "noisy" diagnostic CXR with ribs to the denoised DES CXR of the same patient. In this work, we implemented and modified a number of state-of-the-art network architectures to solve the described-above CXR denoising problem. In particular, we implemented and compared: a) a convolutional denoising autoencoder [4]; b) U-net architecture [11]; c) Feature pyramid network (FPN) architecture [7]; and d) generative adversarial network-based (GAN) solution [6]. Following [4], we considered the denoising autoencoder as a baseline model. The autoencoder is designed to first compress the input to a smaller space and then decompress the compression results to the original image space. As a result, the autoencoder preserves only valuable information about the input, while losing the noise, which is defined as ribs during autoencoder training. The U-net was originally designed in 2015 as a solution for image segmentation task and introduced the "skip connections" concept. The key idea is the following: the output of each transposed convolution layer in the decoder is concatenated with the output of the convolution layer of the encoder with the same size in order to be jointly convolved by additional filters. The "skip connections" idea improves the standard autoencoder in a number of ways: it addresses the "vanishing gradient" problem and helps to preserve small details of the original image. The feature pyramid network (FPN) was introduced in 2017 as a solution for object detection and instance segmentation tasks. The main contribution of the work was joint processing of high-level and low-level features: semantically strong features are upsampled and jointly filtered with semantically weak features to obtain the final result. The decoder part is also augmented with features obtained during encoding via lateral connections. In our work, we additionally extended proposed architectures with residual connections that reduce the risks of vanishing gradients and consequently improve network performance. For objective comparison of autoencoders, U-nets, and FPNs we used identical encoding parts of the networks: 5×5 convolutions (double 3×3 convolutions to preserve the same receptive field for ResNet) followed by 2 × 2 convolutions for the downsampling, regular denoising autoencoder used tied encoder-decoder weights, residual autoencoder used independent weights, starting features number (16) was doubled after each downsampling. Two versions of each network were implemented having diagnostic CXRs (last ReLu activation) or wavelet decomposition of diagnostic CXRs (last linear activation) as the network input. The problem of rib suppression on CXR can be reformulated as the problem of the generation of the soft-tissue CXR that is maximally similar to the distribution of reference soft-tissue CXR. Such reformulation allows us to utilize GAN - a specific type of neural network for the generation of realistic samples according to certain criteria. GANs consist of a generator network that serves to produce a rib-suppressed CXR from the corresponding diagnostic CXR, and a discriminator network that assesses the quality of the generator results knowing the distribution of reference soft-tissue CXRs. By discarding the results of the generator, the discriminator trains it to produce the rib-suppressed CXRs of better similarity to the soft-tissue CXRs distribution. The U-net architecture was selected to be the generator, while the discriminator was defined as a patch-wise PatchGAN classifier [6] with a receptive field of 70 pixels. The PatchGAN proved to be effective for various problems including recovering obscured images and converting thermal images to RGB images [6].

2.5 Loss Functions and Performance Metrics

Three loss functions most-commonly utilized for denoising networks training were applied, namely, mean squared error (MSE), mean absolute error (MAE) and multi-scale structure similarity loss (MS-SSIM, multi-scale case of Eq. 1).

$$SSIM(x, y) = \frac{(2\mu_x\mu_y + c_1)(2\sigma_{xy} + c_2)}{(\mu_x^2 + \mu_y^2 + c_1)(\sigma_x^2 + \sigma_y^2 + c_2)} \tag{1}$$

MSE was used on the first epoch to provide starting weights initialization. Following [16], we selected a weighted combination of MAE and MS-SSIM as a primary loss function. During the initial experiments, it was noticed that the higher contribution of MS-SSIM led to better results yet slower convergence. To account for this observation and train network efficiently, the weight of MS-SSIM was gradually increased at every training epoch. For the experiments that include GAN training, we used the conventional combination of the discriminator objective and MAE loss functions (Eq. 2), where λ is a custom parameter.

$$L_{cGAN} = \log(D(\hat{I}, I)) + \log(1 - D(\hat{I}, G(\hat{I}, I))) + \lambda MAE(\hat{I}, I) \tag{2}$$

Values of λ can tune the appearance of rib-suppressed CXRs by balancing sharpness (lower values of λ) and the absence of image artifacts (higher values of λ).

The efficiency of models was evaluated in terms of Scaled MAE (sMAE, Eq. 3),

$$sMAE(I, \hat{I}) = \sqrt{\frac{1}{mn} \sum_{i=0}^{m-1} \sum_{j=0}^{n-1} \frac{|I(i,j) - \hat{I}(i,j)|}{I_{max} - I_{min}}} \qquad (3)$$

peak signal-to-noise ratio (PSNR, Eq. 4),

$$PSNR(I, \hat{I}) = 20 * \log_{10} \frac{I_{max}}{\sqrt{MSE(I, \hat{I})}} \qquad (4)$$

SSIM index (Eq. 1), where I of size (m, n) is a ground-truth soft-tissue image, $\hat{I}$ is a prediction of the model, x is from I, y is from $\hat{I}$ are local neighborhood pixels of images, μ is the average, σ^2 the variance, σ_{xy} is the covariance, $c1 = (k_1 L)^2$, $c2 = (k_2 L)^2$ are variables are used for stabilizing weak denominator, L – the dynamic range of pixel values (255 for our case), $k_1 = 0.01$ and $k_2 = 0.03$ by default.

3   Results

The dataset of diagnostic CXR and the corresponding soft-tissue CXRs was split into train, validation, and test subsets with 24, 4 and 7 samples accordingly. Each diagnostic image in the validation and test subsets was augmented 99 times with soft transformations that resulted in 400 and 700 images in validation and test sets correspondingly. For training data, we applied a hard set of random augmentations where for each image the following transformations were applied: Contrast Limited Adaptive Histogram Equalization with contrast limit from 1 to 2 and application probability equal to 0.5; either Gaussian noise with variance range for noise from 10 to 50, application probability equal to 0.417 or image blurring with the random-sized kernel with the size of the side ranging from 3 to 7, application probability equal to 0.083; the horizontal flip of an image with application probability equal to 0.5; image shift within the range of 5% with application probability equal to 0.5; image scaling within the range of 40% with application probability equal to 0.5; image rotation within the range of 20 degrees with application probability equal to 0.5; either adjustment of brightness and contrast within the ranges of 40% with application probability equal to 0.25 or gamma correction on an image with power within the range from 0.8 to 1.2 and application probability equal to 0.25; either grid distortion within the range of 40% with application probability equal to 0.25 or elastic image deformation with Gaussian filter parameter set to 60 and application probability equal to 0.25. [1, 13] Selection from any range in image transformations was done in a uniform manner, padding was set to reflect mode without the repetition of border pixels. For all models except cGAN, we used Adam optimizer for training, with betas set to default values of (0.9, 0.999) respectively, and an initial learning rate set to 10^{-3}. We reduced the learning rate by factor 10 after 75th and 90th epochs.

Each model was trained for 100 epochs with a batch size of 12. In order to train an adversarial framework, we utilized a slightly modified procedure, which was the same for both Generator and Discriminator networks. In particular, we used Adam optimizer, with betas set to values of (0.5, 0.999) respectively, and an initial learning rate set to $2 * 10^{-4}$. We trained for 100 epochs using an initial learning rate, and starting with the 101st epoch the learning rate was linearly decreased to zero during 100 more epochs.

Table 1. The comparison of the models applied to rib suppression problem, * denotes residual-based models

Model	CXR domain			Wavelet domain		
	sMAE	PSNR	SSIM	sMAE	PSNR	SSIM
A.enc	1.439	34.05	0.9507	1.783	32.06	0.8958
FPN	1.408	**34.32**	0.9549	1.636	33.16	0.9132
U-net	**1.394**	34.30	**0.9556**	**1.593**	**33.45**	0.9209
A.enc*	1.412	34.22	0.9536	1.693	32.86	0.9149
FPN*	1.399	34.30	0.9552	1.791	31.66	**0.9389**
U-net*	1.459	34.10	0.9488	1.618	33.35	0.9203
cGAN	1.810	32.58	0.9025	3.560	27.43	0.8611

Table 1 shows the comparison of the models used in the study. Table 1 demonstrates that, wavelet decomposition did not improve the rib suppression and that skip-connections modification outperformed baseline autoencoder approach in both settings. Figure 3 illustrates the learning curves of discriminative models providing the evidence that residual models were trained faster than plain models and achieved higher validation scores.

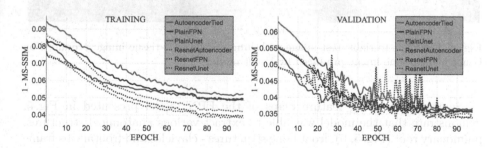

Fig. 3. Learning curves of models trained on diagnostic CXRs

4   Discussion

In this paper, we evaluated various rib suppression techniques in search of methods suitable to be trained on labeled datasets. We also investigated if adding Haar wavelet decomposition helps the neural network during rib suppression on CXR, and did not find any evidence of that. This result can be attributed to the fact that the wavelet decomposition is a convolution operation, and it, therefore, may be parametrized by the first convolution layer of the neural networks. So the explicit domain change results in additional wavelet, and inverse wavelet transforms operations where the error might accumulate. Thus we can conclude that the applicability of the wavelet decomposition needs to be further investigated. According to Table 1, models that utilized skip and lateral connection ideas, i.e. U-net and FPN, outperformed denoising autoencoder approach, which may indicate that important image details disappear during encoder part of the autoencoders. Figure 3 shows that residual models achieved lower training and validation loss values, while the holdout results (Table 1) were comparable with plain models. Figure 4 illustrates the challenging case where the round-shaped low-contrast nodule finding was hidden under the rib. Despite the bone shadow overlapping, the suppression model (U-net) successfully eliminated bone shadows and did not seriously distort the finding. Moreover, it can be observed that the nodule is more visible on a suppressed image than on diagnostic CXR.

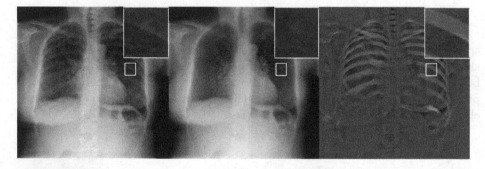

Fig. 4. From left to right: test image with lung nodule, soft-tissue image produced by U-net model, bone image produced by U-net model

Semantically-strong feature maps of the FPN model presented in Fig. 5, demonstrate that the model was able to extract various anatomical structures: pulmonary root (Fig. 5, b), front bone structures - clavicles and frontal ribs frame (Fig. 5, c), rear ribs shadow (Fig. 5, d, h) and inter-ribs soft-tissue space (Fig. 5, e, f, g, i). In other words, rib suppression required recognition of surrounding anatomical structures, potentially, with the aim to preserve or to eliminate them. Experiments with cGAN showed that the generator produces unintended artifacts on suppressed images that in turn affected performance metrics. Figure 6 shows the artifacts that were observed during validation. These artifacts might

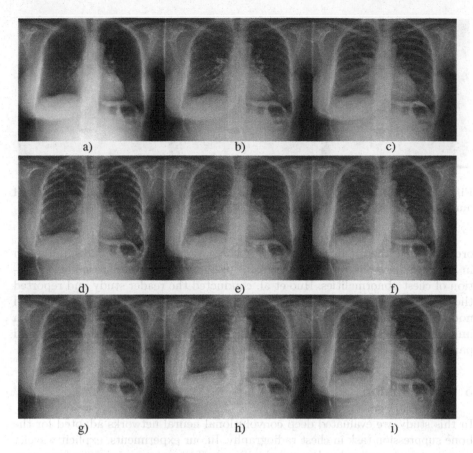

Fig. 5. Feature maps from the last layer of FPN model

have been caused by PatchGAN discriminator since the patches without any bone structures might be indistinguishable for it. Upon careful analysis of all kinds of the artifacts that appeared in our experiments we concluded that while these image distortions brought highly noticeable change in the output image, they were not obstructive to the clinical inference since most of them appeared on non-lung image fragments. As a further improvement of the GAN approach, we consider the technical task of accurate search of hyper-parameters that may help to minimize the artifact appearance. In general, Generative Adversarial Networks are prone to introduce unintended image details and proved themselves in the tasks of image creation and image completion. In contrast, the task of bone suppression does not imply any generation of new image details. It implies the removal of bone silhouettes in the image preserving all the possible information about soft tissue, at the same time not introducing any information which was not originally contained in the X-ray image. As a result, we methodologically consider mostly non-adversarial approaches to be implemented in the future in

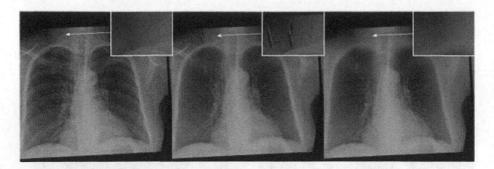

Fig. 6. Input CXR (left), generator output (middle), and target image (right) used during the validation of cGAN

order to solve the discussed problem. A software approach to bone suppression in chest radiographs finds its successful application in computer-aided detection of chest abnormalities. Huo et al. conducted the reader study and reported the significant improvement in sensitivity of radiologists detecting CT-confirmed nodules and pneumothorax [5], which confirms that the current work will be an important base for any researcher investigating the field of X-ray processing and particularly bone suppression in chest radiographs.

5   Conclusion

In this study, we evaluated deep convolutional neural networks adapted for the bone suppression task in chest radiography. In our experiments, explicit wavelet domain transfer proved to have no significant effect on suppression performance. The experiments showed that more complex discriminative models that utilized skip-connections resulted in the best overall bone elimination performance. Moreover, visual analysis of learned features showed that models were able to distinguish anatomical structures, which may indicate reasonable feature extraction and processing.

References

1. Buslaev, A., Iglovikov, V.I., Khvedchenya, E., Parinov, A., Druzhinin, M., Kalinin, A.A.: Albumentations: fast and flexible image augmentations. Information **11**(2) (2020). https://doi.org/10.3390/info11020125. https://www.mdpi.com/2078-2489/11/2/125
2. Chan, T.H., Ma, W.K., Chi, C.Y., Wang, Y.: A convex analysis framework for blind separation of nonnegative sources. IEEE Trans. Signal Process. TSP **56**, 5120–5134 (2008). https://doi.org/10.1109/TSP.2008.928937
3. Chen, Y., et al.: Bone suppression of chest radiographs with cascaded convolutional networks in wavelet domain. IEEE Access **7**, 8346–8357 (2019)

4. Gusarev, M., Kuleev, R., Khan, A., Rivera, A.R., Khattak, A.M.: Deep learning models for bone suppression in chest radiographs. In: 2017 IEEE Conference on Computational Intelligence in Bioinformatics and Computational Biology (CIBCB), pp. 1–7. IEEE (2017)
5. Huo, Z., et al.: Bone suppression technique for chest radiographs, February 2014. https://doi.org/10.1117/12.2043754
6. Isola, P., Zhu, J.Y., Zhou, T., Efros, A.A.: Image-to-image translation with conditional adversarial networks. In: Proceedings of the IEEE Conference on Computer Vision and Pattern Recognition, pp. 1125–1134 (2017)
7. Lin, T.Y., Dollár, P., Girshick, R., He, K., Hariharan, B., Belongie, S.: Feature pyramid networks for object detection. In: Proceedings of the IEEE Conference on Computer Vision and Pattern Recognition, pp. 2117–2125 (2017)
8. Loog, M., van Ginneken, B., Schilham, A.M.: Filter learning: application to suppression of bony structures from chest radiographs. Medical Image Anal. 10(6), 826–840 (2006)
9. Oh, D.Y., Yun, I.D.: Learning bone suppression from dual energy chest x-rays using adversarial networks. arXiv preprint arXiv:1811.02628 (2018)
10. Rasheed, T., Ahmed, B., Khan, M., Bettayeb, M., Lee, S., Kim, T.S.: Rib suppression in frontal chest radiographs: a blind source separation approach. In: 2007 9th International Symposium on Signal Processing and its Applications, ISSPA 2007, Proceedings, pp. 1–4, March 2007. https://doi.org/10.1109/ISSPA.2007.4555516
11. Ronneberger, O., Fischer, P., Brox, T.: U-Net: convolutional networks for biomedical image segmentation. In: Navab, N., Hornegger, J., Wells, W.M., Frangi, A.F. (eds.) MICCAI 2015. LNCS, vol. 9351, pp. 234–241. Springer, Cham (2015). https://doi.org/10.1007/978-3-319-24574-4_28
12. Shah, P.K., et al.: Missed non-small cell lung cancer: radiographic findings of potentially resectable lesions evident only in retrospect. Radiology 226(1), 235–241 (2003)
13. Simard, P.Y., Steinkraus, D., Platt, J.C.: Best practices for convolutional neural networks applied to visual document analysis. In: Seventh International Conference on Document Analysis and Recognition. Proceedings, pp. 958–963 (2003)
14. Wang, X., Peng, Y., Lu, L., Lu, Z., Bagheri, M., Summers, R.M.: ChestX-Ray8: hospital-scale chest x-ray database and benchmarks on weakly-supervised classification and localization of common thorax diseases. In: 2017 IEEE Conference on Computer Vision and Pattern Recognition (CVPR), pp. 3462–3471. IEEE (2017)
15. Yang, W., et al.: Cascade of multi-scale convolutional neural networks for bone suppression of chest radiographs in gradient domain. Medical Image Anal. 35, 421–433 (2017)
16. Zhao, H., Gallo, O., Frosio, I., Kautz, J.: Loss functions for neural networks for image processing. arXiv preprint arXiv:1511.08861 (2015)

Multi-person Absolute 3D Human Pose Estimation with Weak Depth Supervision

Márton Véges[(✉)] and András Lőrincz

Eotvos Lorand University, Budapest, Hungary
{vegesm,lorincz}@inf.elte.hu

Abstract. In 3D human pose estimation one of the biggest problems is the lack of large, diverse datasets. This is especially true for multi-person 3D pose estimation, where, to our knowledge, there are only machine generated annotations available for training. To mitigate this issue, we introduce a network that can be trained with additional RGB-D images in a weakly supervised fashion. Due to the existence of cheap sensors, videos with depth maps are widely available, and our method can exploit a large, unannotated dataset. Our algorithm is a monocular, multi-person, absolute pose estimator. We evaluate the algorithm on several benchmarks, showing a consistent improvement in error rates. Also, our model achieves state-of-the-art results on the MuPoTS-3D dataset by a considerable margin. Our code will be publicly available (https://github.com/vegesm/wdspose).

1 Introduction

While the initial focus in 3D pose estimation was on single pose estimators [6,10,18,19,25,40], recently multi-pose methods also started to appear [4,21,31,38]. Usually, in single-pose detection the problem is simplified to relative pose prediction, that is, joint coordinates are estimated relative to a root joint. However, in a multi-pose setting this could be insufficient for downstream tasks. For instance, to detect proximity, locations are needed as well. The combined prediction of the relative pose and the location of the person is called absolute pose estimation [31]. Here, the coordinates of the joints are predicted in a coordinate system relative to the camera, instead of the hip.

The largest obstacle in 3D pose estimation is the lack of large, diverse datasets. Annotations require special equipment, thus large 3D pose datasets are restricted to a studio setting [12,28]. This is especially true for multi-pose estimation, where, to our knowledge, the only non-synthetic multi-pose 3D database for training is Panoptic [13], and it only has approximate 3D joint coordinates.

To overcome this issue, various methods using different kind of auxiliary datasets were proposed: 2D pose datasets [40], synthetic poses [34] or 3D poses generated from multi-view cameras [14]. In our work, we focus on RGB-D videos. Videos with depth maps have advantages. First, it is not required to manually annotate additional data, unlike 2D pose datasets. Second, RGB-D videos can

I. Farkaš et al. (Eds.): ICANN 2020, LNCS 12396, pp. 258–270, 2020.
https://doi.org/10.1007/978-3-030-61609-0_21

be recorded with a single camera, while multi-camera setups require special hardware with synchronization. The accessibility of the Kinect resulted in a multitude of RGB-D datasets taken in diverse environments [7]. Specifically, we use Panoptic [13] as a weak supervisory signal.

However, depth maps do not provide an accurate representation of the 3D body joint location. Keypoints are easily occluded by other objects, or by the person him/herself. To solve the problem of occlusion we propose a pose decoder network that reconstructs the depth map at the joint locations. Then, the output of the network can be compared with the ground truth depth and the errors backpropagated.

To summarize, we propose a method that exploits RGB-D datasets to improve absolute 3D pose estimation. The RGB-D datasets do not require further annotations, only camera calibration matrices are needed. We tested our method on the Panoptic and MuPo-TS datasets, improving previous results and achieving state-of-the-art results in absolute pose estimation.

2 Related Work

3D Pose Estimation. Although various approaches were used for 3D pose estimation, such as dictionary based methods [24,39] or conditional random fields [2], recently state-of-the-art results are dominated by deep learning based algorithms [16,18,23,26,30,34]. Methods include regressing 3D joints directly [16], using volumeric heatmaps [23] or including soft-argmax layers [30].

A common approach is to split the 3D estimation into two steps: first estimating 2D joint coordinates with an off-the-shelf pose detector, then lifting the 2D coordinates into 3D [6,15,18,32]. In [32], an equivariant network is built to decrease the overfitting to cameras in the training set. Li and Lee [15] predict a distribution for each joint instead of a point estimation to produce uncertainty estimations.

Weak- and Semi-supervised Approaches. The lack of diverse datasets for 3D pose estimation led to interest in weak- and self-supervised approaches. For instance, depthwise ordinal ranking of joints helps training [22]. Datasets with 2D annotations can be used as well, via a reprojection loss [40]. Another approach is to add adversarial losses. Drover *et al.* [5] backproject rotated poses into 2D and regularize them with a discriminator trained on real 2D poses.

Additionally, multi-camera setup can effectively decrease the required amount of training data [14,25]. Kocabas *et al.* [14] uses epipolar geometry to generate 3D ground truth data from unannotated multi-view images.

Absolute Pose Estimation. Unlike the above approaches, absolute pose estimation predicts not only the root-relative pose, but the location of the person as well. One approach is to find an optimal translation that minimizes the reprojection error [19,37] to 2D. However, this needs the 2D pose to be estimated along the 3D pose. Additionally, the prediction is done in a separate stage preventing end-to-end training. Moon *et al.* [21] predicts the location of the root

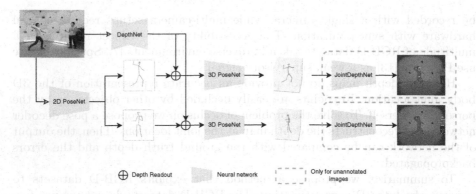

Fig. 1. The network architecture. The input image is fed to the 2D PoseNet and DepthNet. The 2D PoseNet detects humans on the picture and also returns the keypoint coordinates in pixel space. DepthNet estimates the depth for each pixel. Then the 2D pose and predicted depth are combined by reading out the predicted depth at the 2D joint locations. The 3D PoseNet predicts 3D poses from the concatenated 2D pose and depth features. The 3D estimation is performed for all poses separately. If the image does not have 3D pose annotation, the JointDepthNet estimates the depth at each joint on the ground-truth depth map (note that this is different from the depth of the joint because of occlusions).

joint directly, using a separate network. In contrast, in the method of [31], the location prediction and relative pose estimation share the same network.

Using Depth in Pose Estimation. While using depth maps as additional data is largely unexplored in 3D pose estimation, it is popular in hand joint prediction [3,33,36]. In [3] the authors directly estimate the depth map from the predicted 3D coordinates. The estimation error is used as an additional regularizer.

Our work is closest to [3]. However, we do not predict a full depth map, rather just depth at individual points. This results in a smaller network and faster training.

3   Method

The problem of absolute pose estimation can be formalized as follows: the algorithm must predict the $P_j^{3D} \in \mathbb{R}^3, 1 \leq j \leq J$ joint coordinates, where J is the number of joints. The P_j^{3D} points are in a camera-centered coordinate system where depth is perpendicular to the camera plane and the x and y axes align with the image edges.

3.1   Overview

Our method is a multi-person, monocular estimator that takes single images as input. We use RGB-D images as additional training examples, providing

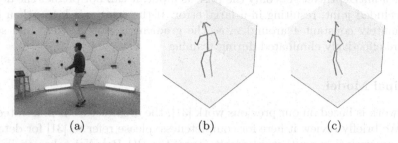

(a)   (b)   (c)

Fig. 2. Reconstructing a skeleton from the depth map under heavy self-occlusion. a) Original image. b) Ground-truth 3D pose, from a different angle. c) Pose created by using ground-truth 2D coordinates and the depth from the depth images. Note how the (orange) right leg and arm are incorrect since the person is sideways on the image. Best viewed in color. (Color figure online)

weak supervision. That is, we have two datasets: $\mathcal{D} = \{(I_1, P_1^{3D}), (I_2, P_2^{3D}), \ldots\}$, images with 3D pose annotations and $\mathcal{D}^* = \{(I_1, D_1), (I_2, D_2), \ldots\}$, images with pixelwise depth maps. On training images that have pose annotations, the prediction error can be calculated easily. For images from $\mathcal{D}^*$, one option would be to simply reconstruct the skeleton from the depth map and compare our prediction with that. However, due to self-occlusions and occlusion by other objects, the reconstructed skeleton would be noisy (see Fig. 2).

To solve this problem, we take a reverse approach: instead of comparing our predicted skeleton to a reconstructed one, we transform the predicted skeleton further, calculating the values of the depth map at the joint locations (see Fig. 1 for the architecture). We introduce a network called *JointDepthNet* that takes as input the predicted 3D pose $\hat{P}^{3D}$ and outputs the value of the depth map at every joint j, denoted by D_j^P. It is important to note that D_j^P is not the z coordinate of the 3D pose in the camera coordinate system, but the depth detected by the depth sensor at the 2D position of joint j. To get the 2D locations of D_j^P we use the output of the 2D PoseNet (see Sect. 3.3).

3.2   Handling Occlusions with Robust Loss

While JointDepthNet can resolve self-occlusions, it can not detect occlusion caused by the environment as it receives only the pose as input.

We use the Geman–McClure robust loss function [8] to overcome the large errors in the loss due to occlusions. The function is defined as:

$$\rho(x) = \frac{x^2}{x^2 + \alpha},$$

where α is a parameter. The function is close to x^2/α around zero and converges to constant 1 for large numbers.

Since JointDepthNet gets only the pose as input, it can not predict the depth at an occluded joint, resulting in a large error. If the error x is large, then ρ is approximately constant 1 around x, so the gradient is close to zero and such errors are effectively eliminated during training.

3.3   Final Model

Our network is based on our previous work [31], the architecture is illustrated in Fig. 1. We briefly review it here for completeness, please refer to [31] for details.

The network is a multi-stage architecture: the *2D PoseNet* takes an image as input, and detects and predicts all the $P_{(i)}^{2D}$ 2D poses on the image, while *DepthNet* predicts a single pixelwise depth map D. Then, for each pose $P_{(i)}^{2D}$, the depth at the joint locations are read out from D and concatenated to the calibration matrix normalized $P_{(i)}^{2D}$. The normalization is needed by the model to handle different focal lengths and viewing angles. The concatenated vector is passed to the *3D PoseNet* that predicts the 3D poses $P_{(i)}^{3D}$. If the input image does not have a pose annotation, then $P_{(i)}^{3D}$ is given to the JointDepthNet that resolves occlusions and outputs the $D_{j,(i)}^{P}$, $1 \leq j \leq J$ depth values (see Sect. 3.1).

JointDepthNet is run only for unannotated images during training. In inference and for images with pose annotations it is ignored.

For pose annotated images, the loss is the L1 loss, for unannotated images it is the Geman–McClure loss. The total loss is then:

$$L = \sum_{I \in \mathcal{D}} L_1\left(\hat{P}_{(i)}^{3D}, P_{(i)}^{3D}\right) + \lambda \sum_{I \in \mathcal{D}^*} \sum_{j=1}^{J} \rho\left(\hat{D}_{j,(i)}^{P} - D_{j,(i)}^{P}\right),$$

where λ is a weight, $\hat{P}_{(i)}^{3D}$ are the predicted poses, and $\hat{D}_{j,(i)}^{P}$ are the predicted depths at each joint j.

One difference compared to [31] is that instead of Batch Normalization layers [11] we used Layer Normalization [1]. We have found that normalizing over the entire batch while mixing two datasets led to suboptimal results, since the characteristics of the two databases were different. When normalizing each training example separately, the performance of the network increased, see Table 5.

4   Experiments

4.1   Datasets

MuPoTS-3D. We conducted experiments on the MuPoTS-3D database [20]. It is a multi-person dataset having both indoor and outdoor videos. In the standard protocol, the training set is the MuCo-3DHP dataset [20] that contains synthetic images, composited from frames in the MPI-INF-3DHP [19] database. We have created 150k images, each containing 4 persons. The training and test set are quite different so it is a good measurement of in-the-wild robustness.

In addition to the raw annotations, the MuCo-3DHP and MuPoTS-3D databases contain normalized skeletons. The normalization process rescales the skeleton from the hip such that the knee to neck distance becomes a fixed value. Prior work uses either one or the other skeleton, we evaluate our method on both annotations for completeness. Note that using unnormalized skeletons for absolute pose estimation is more principled. Normalized poses were proposed for the relative pose estimation task where only the orientation and angles of limbs are relevant. In contrast, in absolute pose estimation the location of the joints is important too. Applying a hip-centered scaling on the skeleton leaves the hip in the correct position, while all the other joints are moved to an incorrect location.

Panoptic. We also performed experiments on the Panoptic dataset [13]. The dataset consists of multiple RGB-D videos, recorded by Kinect sensors, from multiple viewpoints.

Since there is no standard training/test set defined, we selected one session as test and another as validation. The test/validation split contained the recordings of all the RGB-D cameras for the selected session.

4.2 Evaluation Metrics

Table 1. Relative-3DPCK on the MuPoTS-3D dataset (normalized skeletons). Comparison with previous work that uses normalized coordinates (see text for details). Each column corresponds to a video sequence. Higher values are better. Our results are competitive to the state-of-the-art.

Method	S1	S2	S3	S4	S5	S6	S7	S8	S9	S10	S11	S12	S13	S14	S15	S16	S17	S18	S19	S20	Avg.
Comparing every pose																					
Rogez [26]	67.7	49.8	53.4	59.1	67.5	22.8	43.7	49.9	31.1	78.1	50.2	51.0	51.6	49.3	56.2	66.5	65.2	62.9	66.1	59.1	53.8
Mehta [20]	81.0	60.9	64.4	63.0	69.1	30.3	65.0	59.6	64.1	83.9	68.0	68.6	62.3	59.2	70.1	80.0	79.6	67.3	66.6	67.2	66.0
Rogez [27]	87.3	61.9	67.9	74.6	78.8	48.9	58.3	59.7	78.1	89.5	69.2	73.8	66.2	56.0	74.1	82.1	78.1	72.6	73.1	61.0	70.6
Moon [21]	94.4	77.5	79.0	81.9	85.3	72.8	81.9	75.7	90.2	90.4	79.2	79.9	75.1	72.7	81.1	89.9	89.6	81.8	81.7	76.2	81.8
Ours	89.5	75.9	85.2	83.9	85.0	73.4	83.6	58.7	65.1	90.4	76.8	81.9	67.0	55.9	80.8	90.6	90.0	81.1	81.1	68.6	78.2
Comparing detected poses only																					
Rogez [26]	69.1	67.3	54.6	61.7	74.5	25.2	48.4	63.3	69.0	78.1	53.8	52.2	60.5	60.9	59.1	70.5	76.0	70.0	77.1	81.4	62.4
Mehta [20]	81.0	65.3	64.6	63.9	75.0	30.3	65.1	61.1	64.1	83.9	72.4	69.9	71.0	72.9	71.3	83.6	79.6	73.5	78.9	90.9	70.8
Rogez [27]	88.0	73.3	67.9	74.6	81.8	50.1	60.6	60.8	78.2	89.5	70.8	74.4	72.8	64.5	74.2	84.9	85.2	78.4	75.8	74.4	74.0
Moon [21]	94.4	78.6	79.0	82.1	86.6	72.8	81.9	75.8	90.2	90.4	79.4	79.9	75.3	81.0	81.0	90.7	89.6	83.1	81.7	77.3	82.5
Ours	89.5	81.6	85.9	84.4	90.5	73.5	85.5	68.9	65.1	90.4	79.1	82.6	72.7	68.1	81.0	94.0	90.4	87.4	90.4	92.6	82.7

Different works use different evaluation metrics for absolute pose estimation. For completeness we evaluate our method on all of them. We shortly review these below:

A-MPJPE or Absolute Mean per Joint Position Error [31]. It is the Euclidean distance between the ground-truth and predicted joints, averaged over all poses and joints. The metric has the drawback that it does not take into account undetected poses. We present it in mm in our results.

Table 2. Absolute-3DPCK on the MuPoTS-3D dataset (normalized skeletons). Comparison with previous work that uses normalized coordinates (see text for details). Each column corresponds to a video sequence. Higher values are better. We achieve state-of-the-art results both for detected poses and all poses.

Method	S1	S2	S3	S4	S5	S6	S7	S8	S9	S10	S11	S12	S13	S14	S15	S16	S17	S18	S19	S20	Avg.
Comparing every pose																					
Moon [21]	59.5	44.7	51.4	46.0	52.2	27.4	23.7	26.4	39.1	23.6	18.3	14.9	38.2	26.5	36.8	23.4	14.4	19.7	18.8	25.1	31.5
Ours	50.4	33.4	52.8	27.5	53.7	31.4	22.6	33.5	38.3	56.5	24.4	35.5	45.5	34.9	49.3	23.2	32.0	30.7	26.3	43.8	37.3
Comparing detected poses only																					
Moon [21]	59.5	45.3	51.4	46.2	53.0	27.4	23.7	26.4	39.1	23.6	18.3	14.9	38.2	29.5	36.8	23.6	14.4	20.0	18.8	25.4	31.8
Ours	50.4	35.9	53.3	27.7	57.2	31.4	23.1	39.3	38.3	56.5	25.2	35.8	49.3	42.5	49.4	24.1	32.1	33.1	29.3	59.2	39.6

R-MPJPE or Relative Mean per Joint Position Error [12,31]. It is the same as A-MPJPE but with root joints moved to the ground-truth location. The metric is often referred as MPJPE in other work. Presented in mm everywhere.

A-3DPCK or Absolute 3D Percentage of Correct Keypoints [21]. It is the percentage of keypoints where the prediction error is less then 15 cm. If a pose is not detected, then the prediction error is defined as infinite thus it does not contribute to the metric. In contrast to A-MPJPE, the metric is sensitive to undetected poses.

R-3DPCK or Relative 3D Percentage of Correct Keypoints [20,21], commonly referred as 3DPCK. Same as A-3DPCK but with root joints moved to the ground-truth position. It is the standard metric for relative pose estimation on the MuPo-TS dataset. Similarly to A-3DPCK, it takes into account undetected poses.

4.3 Implementation Details

Our network architecture is based on [31]. For the 2D PoseNet we selected the state-of-the-art HR-Net pose estimator [29] with Mask-RCNN [9] as the human bounding-box detector; for DepthNet, following [31], we used MegaDepth [17]. The 3D PoseNet consists of two residual blocks, each having two fully connected layers of 1024 neurons. The dense layers are followed by a Layer Normalization, Dropout and ReLU activation layers. The JointDepthNet has the same structure, having two residual blocks. The dropout rate was 0.5. We normalized the poses to have standard deviation of 1 and zero mean before training and split it to relative pose and root joint localization. See [31] for details. JointDepthNet predicts D_i^P for only 14 joints that we found to be stable, these are the wrists, elbows, shoulders, hips, knees and elbows.

The 3D PoseNet and JointDepthNet were trained jointly, using Adam with a learning rate of 0.001. Every four epoch, the learning rate was multiplied by a factor of 0.96. Half of a mini-batch contained images with pose annotations and the other half contained images with depth map only. The network was trained for 100 epochs.

During training, we applied image augmentation by randomly zooming into the images, while camera intrinsics remained unchanged. This augmentation was performed both for images in $\mathcal{D}$ and $\mathcal{D}^*$, while the target depth maps and poses were appropriately scaled. With this setup, zooming corresponds to moving the poses closer or further away from the camera. We found that this step is essential, otherwise the network overfits to the y locations in the training set.

5 Results

5.1 Quantitative Results

We evaluated our model quantitatively on the MuPoTS-3D and Panoptic datasets.

On MuPoTS-3D, we trained our model on the MuCo and on Panoptic datasets jointly, using only depth maps from the latter (*Ours* in the results). Previous work either used the raw unnormalized, or height-normalized coordinates (see Sect. 4.1 for details).

The absolute pose estimation results on normalized coordinates are shown in Table 2. The A-3DPCK metric can be calculated on all poses or only on the detected ones. The latter is useful to asses the pose estimation performance, while the former also takes into account the detection performance. On all poses, our model achieved 37.3%, which is 5.8% larger than the previous state of the art. This corresponds to a 18.4% relative increase in the metric. On detected poses only, we improved A-3DPCK by 7.8% (24.5% relatively). Our model remains competitive with the state-of-the-art in the relative pose prediction metrics (Table 1).

Table 3 compares our method to prior work using unnormalized coordinates on MuPoTS-3D. The authors of [31] evaluated their method using the MPJPE metrics. Our method decreases the A-MPJPE and R-MPJPE error by 37 mm and 12 mm (12.6% and 10% relatively). Moreover, our model's detection rate is also higher (93% vs 91%).

Table 3. Results on the MuPoTS-3D dataset (unnormalized skeletons). Comparison with previous work that uses unnormalized coordinates (see text for details). Metrics are calculated on detected poses only. MPJPE errors are in mm.

	A-MPJPE ↓	R-MPJPE ↓	A-3DPCK ↑	R-3DPCK ↑	Det. Rate ↑
LCR-Net [26]	–	146	–	–	86%
Mehta et al. [20]	–	132	–	–	93%
Veges et al. [31]	292	120	30.1	–	91%
Ours	**255**	**108**	**35.9**	**78.7**	**93%**

Finally, we evaluate our algorithm on the Panoptic dataset. The database contains both depth maps and 3D pose annotations, thus we split the training set in two parts, one part uses only pose annotations, the other only depth maps.

Table 4. Results on the Panoptic dataset. *Ours w/o JDN* is our network without JointDepthNet, using only frames with pose annotations. Evaluating on detected poses only. MPJPE errors are in mm. Ties are not marked in bold. To our knowledge, no other work predicts absolute poses on Panoptic.

	Fine-tuned	A-MPJPE ↓	A-3DPCK ↑	R-MPJPE ↓	R-3DPCK ↑
Ours w/o JDN	No	151	60.6	**67.4**	95.2
Ours	No	**147**	**62.5**	67.6	95.2
Ours w/o JDN	Yes	144	64.1	**62.2**	**96.6**
Ours	Yes	**134**	**68.8**	62.3	96.5

The results are shown in Table 4. The weak supervision improves both A-MPJPE and A-3DPCK, while the relative metrics remain unchanged or change slightly.

The 3D pose estimator has a depth estimator component. Since we have depth images in the Panoptic dataset, it is natural to investigate, whether fine-tuning the DepthNet on images from $\mathcal{D}^*$ negates the improvement from JointDepthNet. We performed this experiment (Fine-tuned: Yes in Table 4). Results show that the weak supervision still improves the performance, in fact with larger margin than without fine-tuning.

5.2 Qualitative Results

Fig. 3. Qualitative results on MuPoTS-3D. Top row contains random images from the top 10 percentile, medium row contains those from the middle 10 percentile and bottom row from the worst 10 percentile. Green skeletons are the ground truth poses, blue ones are our predictions. Note that not every person in an image has ground truth annotation. (Color figure online)

We present example outputs of our model in Fig. 3. Each row shows random examples from the best, median and worse deciles. A common failure case of our model are non-standing poses (in he middle of the bottom row).

5.3 Ablation Studies

We investigate the effectiveness of our JointDepthNet in Table 5. We trained our network without JointDepthNet, only using full supervision. Our weak supervision improves on the absolute metrics. However, on relative metrics they remain unchanged. This finding is consistent on other databases, see Table 4. We attribute this to two facts. First, depth images hold information only for visible joints, so the root-relative location of an occluded joint can be guessed only with a high uncertainty. On the other hand, even if large part of the body is occluded, the absolute distance from the camera can still be deduced. Second, the relative error of the Kinect is different in the two tasks. The depth sensor of the Kinect has an error of 1–2 cm [35]. The z coordinate of a relative pose varies mostly between -50 cm and 50 cm in the MuPoTS-3D dataset, while the absolute depth is between 200 cm and 700 cm. That is, the error of the Kinect in proportion to the target value is 4–14 times larger for relative pose estimation than for absolute pose estimation.

We also show the effect of Layer Normalization vs Batch Normalization. When using Batch Normalization instead of Layer Normalization, the performance drops considerably in all metrics.

Table 5. Ablation studies. We turned off features of our network separately. All results are on MuPoTS-3D, using unnormalized coordinates. 3DPCK is calculated on detected poses.

	A-MPJPE ↓	A-3DPCK ↑	R-MPJPE ↓	R-3DPCK ↑
BatchNorm vs LayerNorm	288	28.1	114	75.2
w/o JDN	264	33.0	108	78.7
Full model	255	35.9	108	78.7

6 Conclusion and Future Work

We proposed a multi-person absolute pose estimation algorithm that can utilize unannotated RGB-D datasets. The inclusion of depth images improved absolute pose metrics over two datasets. We also achieved new state-of-the-art results on the MuPoTS-3D dataset in absolute pose estimation, beating previous best results by a large margin. However, the weak supervision did not affect the relative pose estimation results. We attribute this to self-occlusion and measurement errors.

In future work, larger RGB-D datasets can be explored. In our work we used only the Panoptic dataset but creating a large, unified database of RGB-D images with human poses could bring further improvements.

Acknowledgment. MV received support from the European Union and co-financed by the European Social Fund (EFOP-3.6.3-16-2017-00002). AL was supported by the National Research, Development and Innovation Fund of Hungary via the Thematic Excellence Programme funding scheme under Project no. ED_18-1-2019-0030 titled Application-specific highly reliable IT solutions.

References

1. Ba, J.L., Kiros, J.R., Hinton, G.E.: Layer normalization. arXiv preprint, arXiv:1607.06450 (2016)
2. Belagiannis, V., Amin, S., Andriluka, M., Schiele, B., Navab, N., Ilic, S.: 3D pictorial structures for multiple human pose estimation. In: CVPR, pp. 1669–1676, June 2014
3. Cai, Y., Ge, L., Cai, J., Yuan, J.: Weakly-supervised 3D hand pose estimation from monocular RGB images. In: Ferrari, V., Hebert, M., Sminchisescu, C., Weiss, Y. (eds.) ECCV 2018. LNCS, vol. 11210, pp. 678–694. Springer, Cham (2018). https://doi.org/10.1007/978-3-030-01231-1_41
4. Dabral, R., Gundavarapu, N.B., Mitra, R., Sharma, A., Ramakrishnan, G., Jain, A.: Multi-person 3D human pose estimation from monocular images. In: 3DV (2019)
5. Drover, D., Mv, R., Chen, C.H., Agrawal, A., Tyagi, A., Huynh, C.P.: Can 3D pose be learned from 2D projections alone? In: ECCV Workshops, pp. 78–94 (2019)
6. Fang, H.S., Xu, Y., Wang, W., Liu, X., Zhu, S.C.: Learning pose grammar to encode human body configuration for 3D pose estimation. In: AAAI (2018)
7. Firman, M.: RGBD datasets: past, present and future. In: CVPR Workshops, June 2016
8. Geman, S., McClure, D.E.: Statistical methods for tomographic image reconstruction. Bull. Int. Stat. Inst. **52**(4), 5–21 (1987)
9. He, K., Gkioxari, G., Dollar, P., Girshick, R.: Mask R-CNN. In: ICCV, October 2017
10. Hossain, M.R.I., Little, J.J.: Exploiting temporal information for 3D pose estimation (2017)
11. Ioffe, S., Szegedy, C.: Batch normalization: accelerating deep network training by reducing internal covariate shift. In: ICML, pp. 448–456 (2015)
12. Ionescu, C., Papava, D., Olaru, V., Sminchisescu, C.: Human3.6m: large scale datasets and predictive methods for 3D human sensing in natural environments. TPAMI **36**(7), 1325–1339 (2014)
13. Joo, H., et al.: Panoptic studio: a massively multiview system for social motion capture. In: ICCV (2015)
14. Kocabas, M., Karagoz, S., Akbas, E.: Self-supervised learning of 3D human pose using multi-view geometry. In: CVPR, June 2019
15. Li, C., Lee, G.H.: Generating multiple hypotheses for 3D human pose estimation with mixture density network. In: CVPR, June 2019

16. Li, S., Chan, A.B.: 3D human pose estimation from monocular images with deep convolutional neural network. In: Cremers, D., Reid, I., Saito, H., Yang, M.-H. (eds.) ACCV 2014. LNCS, vol. 9004, pp. 332–347. Springer, Cham (2015). https://doi.org/10.1007/978-3-319-16808-1_23

17. Li, Z., Snavely, N.: Megadepth: learning single-view depth prediction from internet photos. In: CVPR (2018)

18. Martinez, J., Hossain, R., Romero, J., Little, J.J.: A simple yet effective baseline for 3D human pose estimation. In: ICCV, pp. 2659–2668 (2017)

19. Mehta, D., et al.: Monocular 3D human pose estimation in the wild using improved CNN supervision. In: 3DV, pp. 506–516 (2017)

20. Mehta, D., et al.: Single-shot multi-person 3D pose estimation from monocular RGB. In: 3DV, September 2018

21. Moon, G., Chang, J.Y., Lee, K.M.: Towards 3D human pose estimation in the wild: a weakly-supervised approach. In: ICCV, October 2019

22. Pavlakos, G., Zhou, X., Daniilidis, K.: Ordinal depth supervision for 3D human pose estimation. In: CVPR (2018)

23. Pavlakos, G., Zhou, X., Derpanis, K.G., Daniilidis, K.: Coarse-to-fine volumetric prediction for single-image 3D human pose. In: CVPR, pp. 1263–1272 (2017)

24. Ramakrishna, V., Kanade, T., Sheikh, Y.: Reconstructing 3D human pose from 2D image landmarks. In: Fitzgibbon, A., Lazebnik, S., Perona, P., Sato, Y., Schmid, C. (eds.) ECCV 2012. LNCS, vol. 7575, pp. 573–586. Springer, Heidelberg (2012). https://doi.org/10.1007/978-3-642-33765-9_41

25. Rhodin, H., Salzmann, M., Fua, P.: Unsupervised geometry-aware representation for 3D human pose estimation. In: ECCV (2018)

26. Rogez, G., Weinzaepfel, P., Schmid, C.: LCR-Net: localization-classification-regression for human pose. In: CVPR, pp. 1216–1224, July 2017

27. Rogez, G., Weinzaepfel, P., Schmid, C.: LCR-Net++: multi-person 2D and 3D pose detection in natural images. TPAMI 42(5), 1146–1161 (2019)

28. Sigal, L., Balan, A.O., Black, M.J.: HumanEva: synchronized video and motion capture dataset and baseline algorithm for evaluation of articulated human motion. IJCV 87(1), 4 (2009)

29. Sun, K., Xiao, B., Liu, D., Wang, J.: Deep high-resolution representation learning for human pose estimation. In: CVPR (2019)

30. Sun, X., Xiao, B., Liang, S., Wei, Y.: Integral human pose regression. In: ECCV, pp. 529–545, September 2018

31. Véges, M., Lőrincz, A.: Absolute human pose estimation with depth prediction network. In: IJCNN, pp. 1–7, July 2019

32. Véges, M., Varga, V., Lőrincz, A.: 3D human pose estimation with siamese equivariant embedding. Neurocomputing 339, 194–201 (2019)

33. Wan, C., Probst, T., Gool, L.V., Yao, A.: Self-supervised 3D hand pose estimation through training by fitting. In: CVPR, pp. 10853–10862 (2019)

34. Wang, L., et al.: Generalizing monocular 3D human pose estimation in the wild. In: ICCV Workshops, October 2019

35. Wasenmüller, O., Stricker, D.: Comparison of Kinect V1 and V2 depth images in terms of accuracy and precision. In: Chen, C.-S., Lu, J., Ma, K.-K. (eds.) ACCV 2016. LNCS, vol. 10117, pp. 34–45. Springer, Cham (2017). https://doi.org/10.1007/978-3-319-54427-4_3

36. Yuan, S., Stenger, B., Kim, T.K.: RGB-based 3D hand pose estimation via privileged learning with depth images (2018)

37. Zanfir, A., Marinoiu, E., Sminchisescu, C.: Monocular 3D pose and shape estimation of multiple people in natural scenes the importance of multiple scene constraints. In: CVPR, pp. 2148–2157 (2018)
38. Zanfir, A., Marinoiu, E., Zanfir, M., Popa, A.I., Sminchisescu, C.: Deep network for the integrated 3D sensing of multiple people in natural images. In: NIPS, pp. 8410–8419 (2018)
39. Zhou, X., Leonardos, S., Hu, X., Daniilidis, K.: 3D shape estimation from 2D landmarks: a convex relaxation approach. In: CVPR, pp. 4447–4455 (2015)
40. Zhou, X., Huang, Q., Sun, X., Xue, X., Wei, Y.: Towards 3D human pose estimation in the wild: a weakly-supervised approach. In: ICCV, pp. 398–407, October 2017

Solar Power Forecasting Based on Pattern Sequence Similarity and Meta-learning

Yang Lin[1(✉)], Irena Koprinska[1(✉)], Mashud Rana[2], and Alicia Troncoso[3]

[1] School of Computer Science, University of Sydney, Sydney, NSW, Australia
ylin4015@uni.sydney.edu.au, irena.koprinska@sydney.edu.au
[2] Data61, CSIRO, Sydney, Australia
mdmashud.rana@data61.csiro.au
[3] Data Science and Big Data Lab, University Pablo de Olavide, Seville, Spain
atrolor@upo.es

Abstract. We consider the task of simultaneously predicting the solar power output for the next day at half-hourly intervals using data from three related time series: solar, weather and weather forecast. We propose PSF3, a novel pattern sequence forecasting approach, an extension of the standard PSF algorithm, which uses all three time series for clustering, pattern sequence extraction and matching. We evaluate its performance on two Australian datasets from different climate zones; the results show that PSF3 is more accurate than the other PSF methods. We also investigate if a dynamic meta-learning ensemble combining the two best methods, PSF3 and a neural network, can further improve the results. We propose a new weighting strategy for combining the predictions of the ensemble members and compare it with other strategies. The overall most accurate prediction model is the meta-learning ensemble with the proposed weighting strategy.

Keywords: Solar power forecasting · Pattern sequence similarity forecasting · Neural networks · Meta-learning ensemble

1 Introduction

Renewable energy production and utilization is rapidly growing, providing numerous economic, environmental and social benefits. This is encouraged by government policies, with many countries setting renewable energy targets. Solar energy produced by photovoltaic (PV) systems is one of the most promising renewable options. However, unlike traditional energy sources such as gas, oil and coal, solar energy is variable as it is weather-dependent. This makes its integration into the electricity grid more difficult and requires forecasting of the generated solar power, to balance supply and demand during power dispatching and to ensure the stability and efficient operation of the electricity grid.

Both statistical and machine learning methods have been applied for solar power forecasting. Linear regression, exponential smoothing and auto-regressive

© Springer Nature Switzerland AG 2020
I. Farkaš et al. (Eds.): ICANN 2020, LNCS 12396, pp. 271–283, 2020.
https://doi.org/10.1007/978-3-030-61609-0_22

moving average are classical statistical methods for modelling time series data [1]. Previous studies [2,3] have shown that they are promising for solar power forecasting especially when a single time series is available, but have limitations for modelling noisy and nonlinear time series [4]. Machine learning methods such as Neural Networks (NNs) [2,3,5,6], nearest neighbour [2,3] and support vector regression [7], have also been applied and often shown to provide more accurate predictions than statistical methods.

Recently, the application of Pattern Sequence-based Forecasting (PSF) [8] methods has been studied for solar power forecasting [9–11]. PSF assigns a cluster label to each day and then uses a nearest neighbour approach to find sequences of days which are similar to the target sequence. One of PSF's distinct characteristics is that it predicts all values for the next day simultaneously (e.g. all half-hourly PV values for the next day), as opposed to predicting them iteratively, as most of the other methods. While the standard PSF algorithm uses only one time series (the time series of interest, PV data), two PSF extensions using multiple related time series (weather and weather forecast data) have been proposed in [9] and evaluated for solar power forecasting. The results showed that both PSF1 and PSF2 were more accurate than the standard PSF. However, there is still an opportunity for further improvement, since even the best performing PSF2 method does not fully utilize all three available data sources for constructing the pattern sequences. In this paper, we propose PSF3, a new pattern sequence forecasting algorithm, which utilizes multiple related time series for clustering, sequence extraction and pattern matching.

In addition, we investigate if a dynamic meta-learning ensemble, combining PSF3 and NN, can further improve the performance. Motivated by [12], we employ meta-learners to predict the errors of the ensemble members for the new day and assign higher weights to the more accurate ones. However, unlike [12] which combines ensemble members of the same type (NNs) and generates diversity by using random examples and feature sampling, we create a heterogeneous ensemble combining the predictions of PSF3 and NN, to generate natural diversity, and we also utilize data from multiple data sources (PV, weather and weather forecast) not only PV data. In addition, we propose a new weighting strategy, which increases the difference in contribution between the most and least accurate ensemble members, and show the effectiveness of this strategy.

In summary, the contributions of this paper are as follows:

1. We propose PSF3, a novel pattern sequence forecasting approach, which uses all three related time series (PV, weather and weather forecast) for pattern sequence extraction, matching and forecasting. We evaluate the performance of PSF3 on two Australian datasets, from different climate zones, each containing data for two years from three different sources. Our results show that PSF3 outperformed the other PSF methods.
2. We investigate if a dynamic meta-learning ensemble (MLE), combining PSF3 and NN, can further improve the results. We propose a new log weighting strategy for combining the ensemble member predictions and show its effectiveness compared to linear and softmax strategies. The most accurate

prediction model was the meta-learning ensemble with the log weighting strategy, outperforming the single methods it combines, all other PSF methods and a persistence baseline model used for comparison.

2 Task and Data

We consider the task of simultaneously predicting the PV power output for the next day at half-hourly intervals. Given: (1) a time series of PV power output up to day d: $PV = [PV_1, ..., PV_d]$, where PV_i is a vector of half-hourly PV power output for day i, (2) a time series of weather vectors for the same days: $W = [W_1, ..., W_d]$, where W_i is a weather vector for day i, and (3) a weather forecast vector for the next day $d+1$: WF_{d+1}, our goal is to forecast PV_{d+1}, the half-hourly PV power output for day $d+1$.

2.1 Data Sources and Feature Sets

We collected data from two Australian PV plants located in different climate zones: humid subtropical (Brisbane) and hot desert (Alice Springs). The two datasets are referred as the University of Queensland (UQ) and Sanyo, and contain both PV and weather data. The data sources and extracted features for each dataset are shown in Table 1 and Table 2 respectively.

Solar PV Data. The PV data for the UQ dataset was collected from a rooftop PV plant located at the University of Queensland in Brisbane[1]. The Sanyo dataset was collected from the Sanyo PV plant in Alice Springs[2]. Both datasets contain data for two years - from 1 January 2015 to 31 December 2016 (731 days).

Weather Data. The weather data for the UQ dataset was collected from the Australian Bureau of Meteorology[3]. There are three sets of weather features - W1, W2 and WF, see Table 1 and Table 2.

W1 includes the full set of collected weather features - 14 for the UQ dataset and 10 for the Sanyo dataset. The 10 features are common for both datasets but UQ contains four additional features (daily rainfall, daily sunshine hours and cloudiness at 9 am and 3 pm) which were not available for Sanyo.

W2 is a subset of W1 and includes only 4 features for the UQ dataset and 3 features for the Sanyo dataset. These features are frequently used in weather forecasts and are available from meteorological bureaus.

The weather forecast feature set WF is obtained by adding 20% Gaussian noise to the W2 data. This is done since the weather forecasts were not available retrospectively for previous years. When making predictions for the days from the test set, the WF set replaces W2 as the weather forecast for these days.

---

[1] https://solar-energy.uq.edu.au/.

[2] http://dkasolarcentre.com.au/source/alice-springs/dka-m4-b-phase.

[3] https://www.bom.gov.au/climate/data/.

Table 1. UQ dataset - data sources and feature sets

Data source	Feature set	Description
PV data	PV∈ $\Re^{731\times20}$	Daily: half-hourly solar power from 7 am to 5 pm
Weather data 1	W1∈ $\Re^{731\times14}$	(1–6) Daily: min temperature, max temperature, rainfall, sunshine hours, max wind gust and average solar irradiance; (7–14) At 9 am and 3 pm: temperature, relative humidity, cloudiness and wind speed
Weather data 2	W2∈ $\Re^{731\times4}$	Daily: min temperature, max temperature, rainfall and solar irradiance. W2 is a subset of W1
Weather forecast data	WF∈ $\Re^{731\times4}$	Daily: min temperature, max temperature, rainfall and average solar irradiance

Table 2. Sanyo dataset - data sources and feature sets

Data source	Feature set	Description
PV data	PV∈ $\Re^{731\times20}$	Daily: half-hourly solar power from 7 am to 5 pm
Weather data 1	W1∈ $\Re^{731\times10}$	(1–4) Daily: min temperature, max temperature, max wind gust and average solar irradiance; (5–10) At 9 am and 3 pm: temperature, relative humidity and wind speed
Weather data 2	W2∈ $\Re^{731\times3}$	Daily: min temperature, max temperature and solar irradiance. W2 is a subset of W1
Weather forecast data	WF∈ $\Re^{731\times3}$	Daily: min temperature, max temperature and average solar irradiance

2.2   Data Pre-processing

The raw PV data was measured at 1-min intervals for the UQ dataset and 5-min intervals for the Sanyo dataset and was aggregated to 30-min intervals by taking the average value of every 30-min interval. There was a small percentage of missing values - for the UQ dataset: 0.82% in the PV power and 0.02% in the weather data; for the Sanyo dataset: 1.98% in the PV power and 4.85% in the weather data. These missing values were replaced as in [13] by a nearest neighbour method, applied firstly to the weather data and then to the PV data. Both the PV and weather data were normalised between 0 and 1.

3   Pattern Sequence Forecasting Methods: PSF, PSF1 and PSF2

PSF [8] utilizes a single data source for clustering and sequence matching - the time series of interest, which is the PV data in our case. It uses k-means to cluster the days in the training data based on their PV vectors into k_1 clusters with labels $C_1, ..., C_{k_1}$. To make a prediction for a new day $d+1$, PSF extracts a target sequence of w consecutive days, starting from the previous day and going backwards. This sequence of cluster labels is matched with the previous days to find the set of equal sequences ES. The final prediction is obtained by averaging the PV vectors of the post-sequence days for each sequence in ES.

PSF1 [9] is an extension of PSF, which utilizes the W2 data for clustering and sequence matching. It clusters the training set days based on the W2 data into k_2 clusters with labels $C_1, ..., C_{k_2}$. To make a prediction for a new day $d+1$, PSF1 firstly obtains the cluster label for this day using its WF vector. It then extracts a target sequence of cluster labels for w consecutive days from day $d+1$ backwards and including $d+1$, matches this sequence with the previous days and finds a set of equal sequences ES. The final prediction is obtained by taking the average of the PV vectors of the last days for each sequence in ES.

PSF2 [9] is an extension of PSF utilizing two of the related time sequences for clustering and pattern matching - W1 and W2. It clusters the days from the training set using W1 (k_1 clusters with labels $C_1, ..., C_{k_1}$) and W2 (k_2 clusters with labels $K_1, ..., K_{k_2}$). The prediction for the new day $d+1$ is computed as follows. A target sequence of cluster labels for w consecutive days from day d backwards and including day d is extracted based on W1 and matched to find the set of equal sequences ES. The cluster label K_x for day $d+1$ is obtained based on WF. Then, the cluster label of the post-sequence day for all sequences in ES is checked and if it is not K_x, these sequences are excluded from ES. The final prediction for $d+1$ is formed by taking the average of the post-sequence days for all sequences in ES.

In summary, in PSF and PSF1 the clustering, sequence extraction and pattern matching are done using only one of the related time series, while PSF2 uses two of them. The proposed PSF3 algorithm builds upon PSF2, but utilizes all three related time series (PV, W1 and W2) for clustering, sequence extraction and pattern matching. We investigate if this approach improves performance.

4   Proposed Methods

4.1   Pattern Sequence Forecasting: PSF3

PSF3 is an extension of PSF, which utilizes all related time series (PV, weather and weather forecast) in the clustering, pattern extraction and matching phases.

PSF3 firstly employs the k-means algorithm to cluster the days from the training data separately based on their PV, W1 and W2 vectors. Specifically, it clusters the days (i) based on the W1 weather data in k_1 clusters with labels

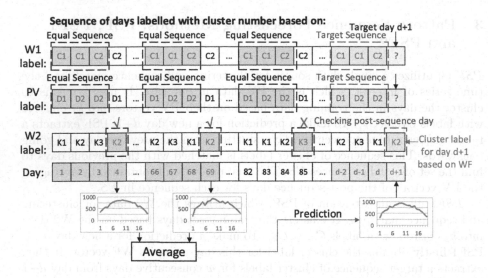

Fig. 1. The proposed PSF3 method

$C_1, ..., C_{k_1}$, (ii) based on the PV data in k_2 clusters with labels $D_1, ..., D_{k_2}$ and (iii) based on the W2 weather forecast data in k_3 clusters with labels $K_1, ..., K_{k_3}$, as shown in Fig. 1. Hence, each day from the training data is assigned three cluster labels, one for each of the three clusterings.

To make a prediction for a new day $d+1$ from the test set, PSF3 firstly assigns cluster labels to the previous days if they were not part of the training set. This is done by comparing these days with the cluster centroids and assigning them to the cluster of the closest centroid, for each data source separately. Then, the prediction for the new day $d+1$ is computed using the following steps:

1. A target sequence of w consecutive days from day d backwards, including day d, is extracted based on the W1 weather data. This sequence consists of the cluster labels. It is matched with the previous days to find the set of equal sequences ES.
2. The same process is repeated for the PV data - a target sequence of w consecutive days from day d backwards, including day d, is extracted based on the PV data and matched to find the set of equal sequences ES_{PV}.
3. The sequences included in ES and ES_{PV} are compared, to find a subset for which both the W1 and PV cluster label sequence matches. The non-matching sequences are excluded from ES. Only ES is used for further analysis, and not ES_{PV}.
4. The cluster label K_x for day $d+1$ is obtained based on the weather forecast data.
5. The cluster label of the post-sequence day for each sequences in ES is checked and if it is not K_x, these sequences are excluded from ES.
6. The final prediction of the PV power for day $d+1$ is obtained by taking the average of the PV powers of the post-sequence days for all sequences in ES.

For example, in Fig. 1, the PV power prediction for day $d+1$ will be the average of the PV vectors for days 4 and 69. Note that day 85 is not included in the final prediction - the sequence ending with day 84 matches the target sequence in terms of both W1 and PV, but the post-sequence days do not match in terms of W2 - the cluster label of day 85 is K_3, while the cluster label of day $d+1$ is K_2, i.e. the matching condition in step 5 is not satisfied.

The window size w and the number of clusters $k1$, $k2$ and $k3$ are hyperparameters of the PSF3 algorithm, selected using 12-fold cross-validation with grid search as described in Sect. 5.

4.2 Meta-Learning Ensemble: MLE

We also investigate if a dynamic meta-learning ensemble can further improve the performance of PSF3. The motivation behind dynamic ensembles is that the different ensemble members have different areas of expertise and as the time series changes over time, the accuracy of the ensemble members also changes. By using a suitable criterion, we can select the most appropriate weighted combination of ensemble members for the new example.

A meta-learning ensemble (called EN-meta), combining only NNs and employing random example and random feature sampling, was used in [12], demonstrating good performance for univariate solar power forecasting (PV data only). In this paper, we propose to build a heterogeneous ensemble combining the predictions of the two best single models - PSF3 and NN. PSF3 and NN are representatives of different machine learning paradigms. Heterogeneous ensembles have been shown to perform well in various applications [12,14,15], by providing natural diversity and complementary expertise. Another important difference with EN-Meta [12] and the other ensemble methods [14,15], is that we utilize data from different data sources and related time series (PV, weather and weather forecast), not only univariate data (PV).

The main idea of our Meta-Learning Ensemble (MLE) is to predict the error of each ensemble member for the new day and based of this error to determine the contribution of the ensemble member in the final prediction.

Building MLE involves three steps: 1) training ensemble members, 2) training meta-learners, 3) calculating the weights of the ensemble members for the new day and predicting the new day.

Training Ensemble Members. The first step is training the ensemble members, PSF3 and NN, to predict the PV power for the next day. PSF3 performs clustering separately on the PV, W1 and W2 data and then pattern matching, see Sect. 4.1. NN also uses all three data sources but directly, without clustering, to build a prediction model. It constructs training data as follows: the feature vector consists of the PV and W1 weather data for day d and the weather forecast data W2 for the next day $d+1$: $[\text{PV}_d; \text{W1}_d; \text{W2}_{d+1}]$, and the associated target output is the PV vector for the next day: PV_{d+1}.

Training Meta-learners. The second step is training the meta-learners. There is one meta-learner for each ensemble member and we used NN models as meta-learners. Each meta-learner takes the same input as above ($[PV_d; W1_d; W2_{d+1}]$), but learns to predict the error of its corresponding ensemble member (PSF3 or NN) for the next day. We used the Mean Absolute Error (MAE) as an error. For example, the meta-learner for the NN ensemble member ML_{NN} will have as an input $[PV_d; W1_d; W2_{d+1}]$ and as a target output MAE_{d+1} of the NN ensemble member. Similarly, the meta-learner of the PSF3 ensemble member ML_{PSF3} will take the same input but learn to predict MAE_{d+1} of the PSF3 ensemble member. To create a training set for a meta-learner, we first obtain the predictions of its corresponding ensemble member for all training examples and then calculate the MAEs, which are the target outputs.

Weight Calculation and Final Prediction. The third step involves calculating the weights of the ensemble members for the new day by converting the predicted errors into weights and calculating the final weighted average prediction.

The rationale behind MLE is that different ensemble members have different areas of expertise and their performance changes over time. It assumes that the error of an ensemble member could be predicted based on its past performance and uses this error to weight the contributions of ensemble members when making the final prediction - the ensemble members which are predicted to be more accurate will be given higher weights.

Two weight calculation strategies were investigated in [12]: linear and softmax nonlinear. The linear strategy decreases the weight of an ensemble member linearly as its error increases:

$$w_i^{d+1} = \frac{1 - e_{norm,i}^{d+1}}{\sum_{j=1}^{S}(1 - e_{norm,j}^{d+1})}$$

where w_i^{d+1} is the weight of ensemble member E_i for predicting day $d + 1$, $e_{norm,i}^{d+1}$ is the predicted error of E_i by its corresponding meta-learner, normalized between 0 and 1, and S is the number of ensemble members.

The nonlinear strategy in [12] computes a softmax function of the negative of the predicted error:

$$w_i^{d+1} = \frac{exp(-e_i^{d+1})}{\sum_{j=1}^{S} exp(-e_j^{d+1})} = softmax(-e_i^{d+1})$$

where e_i^{d+1} is the predicted error of E_i by its corresponding meta-learner and exp denotes the exponential function.

The use of $1 - e_{norm,i}^{d+1}$ and $- e_i^{d+1}$ above is necessary for the inverse relationship between forecasting error and weight (lower errors resulting in higher weights and vice versa), and the denominator ensures the weights of all ensemble members sum to 1.

We propose a new nonlinear weight calculation strategy, the log weighting, where the weights are calculated as follows:

$$w_i^{d+1} = \frac{ln(\frac{e_i^{d+1}}{\sum_{m=1}^{S} e_m^{d+1}})^{-1}}{\sum_{j=1}^{S} ln(\frac{e_j^{d+1}}{\sum_{m=1}^{S} e_m^{d+1}})^{-1}}$$

In summary, we take the natural logarithm of the inverse of the ensemble member error, normalised over all ensemble members. The denominator ensures that the weights of all ensemble members sum to 1.

Compared to the linear and softmax strategies, the log strategy increases the difference between the weights of the more accurate and less accurate ensemble members. Hence, it increases the contribution of the most accurate ensemble members and decreases the contribution of the less accurate ones in the final prediction.

5   Experimental Setup

All prediction models were implemented in Python 3.6 using scikit-learn 0.22.1 and Keras 2.3.1 libraries. For both datasets, the PV power and corresponding weather data were split into two equal subsets: training and validation (the first year) and test (the second year). Cross-validation with grid search was used for tuning of the hyperparameters as described below.

Table 3. Hyperparameters for the PSF models

UQ dataset		Sanyo dataset	
Method	Hyperparameters	Method	Hyperparameters
PSF	$k_1 = 2, w = 2$	PSF	$k_1 = 2, w = 1$
PSF1	$k_1 = 2, w = 2$	PSF1	$k_1 = 2, w = 2$
PSF2	$k_1 = 2, k_2 = 2, w = 1$	PSF2	$k_1 = 2, k_2 = 2, w = 2$
PSF3	$k_1 = 2, k_2 = 2, k_3 = 2, w = 1$	PSF3	$k_1 = 2, k_2 = 2, k_3 = 2, w = 1$

5.1   Tuning of Hyperparameters

For the PSF models, the first year was used to determine the hyperparameters (number of clusters k_1, k_2 and k_3, and sequence size w) by using 12-fold cross-validation with grid search, consistent with the original PSF algorithm [8]. The grid search for w included values from 1 to 5. The best number of clusters was selected by varying k_1, k_2 and k_3 from 1 to 10 and evaluating three cluster quality indexes (Silhouette, Dunn and Davies-Bouldin) as described in [9]. The selected best hyperparameters are listed in Table 3.

For the NN models, the tuning of the hyperparameters was done using 5-fold cross-validation with grid search on the first year data. The training algorithm was the mini-batch gradient descent with Adam optimization. The tunable hyperparameters and options considered were: hidden layer size: 1 layer with 25, 30, 35 and 40 neurons, 2 layers with 25 and 20, 30 and 20, 35 and 25, 40 and 30 neurons; learning rate: 0.0005, 0.001, 0.003, 0.005, 0.01, 0.1 and 0.3; L2 regularization λ: 0.0005, 0.0008, 0.001 and 0.0015; batch size: 64 and 256, and fixed number of epochs 900. The activation functions were ReLu for the hidden layers and linear for the output layer, and the weight initialization mode was set to normal. The selected hyperparameters for the NN models based on the cross-validation performance are listed in Table 4. After the best parameters were selected, a new NN model is built using the whole first year data and then evaluated on the test set.

For the NN meta-learners, we followed the same procedure as above but used early stopping instead of the maximum number of epochs. The selected hyperparameters are also listed in Table 4.

Table 4. Hyperparameters for the NN models

Model	Hidden layer size	Learning rate	L2 λ	Batch size	Epochs
NN (UQ dataset)	[25]	0.0005	0.0015	64	900
NN (Sanyo dataset)	[35, 25]	0.001	0.0015	64	900
NN meta-learner (UQ dataset)	[25]	0.0015	0.0001	64	505
NN meta-learner (Sanyo dataset)	[35]	0.001	0.0015	64	103

5.2   Baseline and Evaluation Measures

As a baseline for comparison, we developed a persistence prediction model B_{per}. It simply predicts the PV power output of the previous day as the PV power output for the next day, i.e. $\hat{PV}_{d+1} = PV_d$.

To evaluate the performance on the test set, we used the MAE and the Root Mean Squared Error (RMSE).

6   Results and Discussion

Table 5 shows the MAE and RMSE results of all models for UQ and Sanyo datasets. The main results can be summarized as follows:

- The proposed PSF3 is the most accurate PSF method, followed by PSF2, PSF1 and PSF. This shows the effectiveness of the proposed pattern matching algorithm, utilising all available data sources.

Table 5. Accuracy of all models

Method	UQ dataset		Sanyo dataset	
	MAE (kW)	RMSE (kW)	MAE (kW)	RMSE (kW)
B_{per}	124.80	184.29	0.75	1.25
PSF	117.15	149.77	0.77	1.07
PSF1	115.55	147.72	0.70	0.98
PSF2	109.89	141.50	0.69	0.98
PSF3	106.11	138.39	0.65	0.95
NN	81.23	115.76	0.49	0.74
MLE (linear)	81.26	111.47	0.51	0.74
MLE (softmax)	81.09	**109.73**	0.52	0.76
MLE (log)	**78.67**	110.74	**0.48**	**0.72**

- The accuracy ranking of the other PSF methods (PSF2, PSF1 and PSF) is consistent with [9], confirming that the extensions PSF1 and PSF2 outperformed the standard PSF algorithm.
- From the single models, NN is the most accurate model, outperforming all PSF models. This finding is also consistent with [9]. Unlike the PSF models, NN does not require clustering and pattern matching; it uses directly the data from the three sources to construct a feature vector and build a prediction model. Compared to the PSF models, however, it requires significantly more time for training and parameter tuning.
- The overall most accurate prediction model is MLE (log), the proposed meta-learning ensemble with the log weighting strategy. This shows the benefit of combining the two best models, NN and PSF3, using meta-learning and the advantage of using the log weighting strategy.
- All three ensemble models are considerably more accurate than the PSF methods in all cases but only the ensemble MLE (log) was consistently more accurate than NN on both datasets. This again shows the advantage of using log weighting strategy to increase the influence of the more accurate ensemble members, compared to the linear and softmax strategies.
- All models outperform the persistence baseline B_{per}, except for one case - PSF on the Sanyo dataset for MAE.
- We further analysed the performance of the best models, PSF3 and NN, by comparing the characteristics of the days for which they performed well. NN is better than PSF3 at forecasting days with slightly higher PV power and temperature on both datasets, and days with higher humidity for the Sanyo dataset.

7   Conclusions

We considered the task of simultaneously predicting the PV solar power for the next day at half-hourly intervals using data from three related time series:

PV, weather and weather forecast. We proposed PSF3, a novel pattern sequence forecasting approach, an extension of the standard PSF algorithm, which uses all three time series for clustering, pattern sequence extraction and matching. We evaluated its performance on two Australian datasets, from different climate zones (humid subtropical and hot desert), each containing data for two years. Our results show that PSF3 was more accurate than the other PSF methods. We also investigated if a dynamic meta-learning ensemble combining the two best methods, PSF3 and NN, can further improve the results. For this ensemble, we proposed and evaluated a new log weighting strategy for combining the predictions of the ensemble members and showed that it was more effective than linear and softmax strategies. The overall most accurate prediction model was the meta-learning ensemble with the proposed weighting strategy; it outperformed both PSF3 and NN, the other PSF models and the persistence baseline.

References

1. Trull, Ó., García-Díaz, J.C., Troncoso, A.: Application of discrete-interval moving seasonalities to Spanish electricity demand forecasting during Easter. Energies **12**, 1083 (2019)
2. Pedro, H.T., Coimbra, C.F.: Assessment of forecasting techniques for solar power production with no exogenous inputs. Sol. Energy **86**, 2017–2028 (2012)
3. Chu, Y., Urquhart, B., Gohari, S.M., Pedro, H.T., Kleissl, J., Coimbra, C.F.: Short-term reforecasting of power output from a 48 MWe solar PV plant. Sol. Energy **112**, 68–77 (2015)
4. Inman, R.H., Pedro, H.T., Coimbra, C.F.: Solar forecasting methods for renewable energy integration. Prog. Energy Combust. Sci. **39**, 535–576 (2013)
5. Rana, M., Koprinska, I., Agelidis, V.: Forecasting solar power generated by grid connected PV systems using ensembles of neural networks. In: International Joint Conference on Neural Networks (IJCNN) (2015)
6. Chen, C., Duan, S., Cai, T., Liu, B.: Online 24-h solar power forecasting based on weather type classification using artificial neural networks. Sol. Energy **85**, 2856–2870 (2011)
7. Rana, M., Koprinska, I., Agelidis, V.G.: 2D-interval forecasts for solar power production. Sol. Energy **122**, 191–203 (2015)
8. Martínez-Álvarez, F., Troncoso, A., Riquelme, J.C., Aguilar Ruiz, J.S.: Energy time series forecasting based on pattern sequence similarity. IEEE Trans. Knowl. Data Eng. **23**, 1230–1243 (2011)
9. Wang, Z., Koprinska, I., Rana, M.: Solar power forecasting using pattern sequences. In: Proceedings of the International Conference on Artificial Neural Networks (ICANN) (2017)
10. Torres, J., Troncoso, A., Koprinska, I., Wang, Z., Martínez-Álvarez, F.: Big data solar power forecasting based on deep learning and multiple data sources. Expert Syst. **36**, e12394 (2019)
11. Lin, Y., Koprinska, I., Rana, M., Troncoso, A.: Pattern sequence neural network for solar power forecasting. In: Proceedings of the International Conference on Neural Information Processing (ICONIP) (2019)
12. Wang, Z., Koprinska, I.: Solar power forecasting using dynamic meta-learning ensemble of neural networks. In: Proceedings of the International Conference on Artificial Neural Networks and Machine Learning (ICANN) (2018)

13. Wang, Z., Koprinska, I.: Solar power prediction with data source weighted nearest neighbors. In: Proceedings of the International Joint Conference on Neural Networks (IJCNN) (2017)
14. Cerqueira, V., Torgo, L., Pinto, F., Soares, C.: Arbitrated ensembles for time series forecasting. In: Proceedings of the European Conference on Machine Learning and Principles of Knowledge Discovery in Databases (ECML-PKDD) (2017)
15. Galicia, A., Talavera-Llames, R., Troncoso, A., Koprinska, I., Martínez-Álvarez, F.: Multi-step forecasting for big data time series based on ensemble learning. Knowl.-Based Syst. **163**, 830–841 (2019)

Analysis and Prediction of Deforming 3D Shapes Using Oriented Bounding Boxes and LSTM Autoencoders

Sara Hahner[1]([⊠]), Rodrigo Iza-Teran[1], and Jochen Garcke[1,2][iD]

[1] Fraunhofer Center for Machine Learning and SCAI, Sankt Augustin, Germany
{sara.hahner,rodrigo.iza-teran,jochen.garcke}@scai.fraunhofer.de
[2] Institut für Numerische Simulation, Universität Bonn, Bonn, Germany

Abstract. For sequences of complex 3D shapes in time we present a general approach to detect patterns for their analysis and to predict the deformation by making use of structural components of the complex shape. We incorporate long short-term memory (LSTM) layers into an autoencoder to create low dimensional representations that allow the detection of patterns in the data and additionally detect the temporal dynamics in the deformation behavior. This is achieved with two decoders, one for reconstruction and one for prediction of future time steps of the sequence. In a preprocessing step the components of the studied object are converted to oriented bounding boxes which capture the impact of plastic deformation and allow reducing the dimensionality of the data describing the structure. The architecture is tested on the results of 196 car crash simulations of a model with 133 different components, where material properties are varied. In the latent representation we can detect patterns in the plastic deformation for the different components. The predicted bounding boxes give an estimate of the final simulation result and their quality is improved in comparison to different baselines.

Keywords: LSTM autoencoder · 3D shape deformation analysis · CAE analysis · 3D time series

1 Introduction

Deforming 3D shapes that can be subdivided into components can be found in many different areas, for example crash analysis, structure, and material testing, or moving humans and animals that can be subdivided into body parts. The data can be especially challenging since it has a temporal and a spatial dimension that have to be considered jointly. In particular, we consider shape data from Computer Aided Engineering (CAE), where numerical simulations play a vital role in the development of products, as they enable simpler, faster, and more cost-effective investigations of systems. If the 3D shape is complex, the detection of patterns in the deformation, called deformation modes in CAE (Fig. 1), speeds up the analysis.

© Springer Nature Switzerland AG 2020
I. Farkaš et al. (Eds.): ICANN 2020, LNCS 12396, pp. 284–296, 2020.
https://doi.org/10.1007/978-3-030-61609-0_23

Mode A:  Mode B:

Fig. 1. Deformation modes of left front beams in the example car model.

While deformation modes are dependent on model parameters, their behavior is accessible, albeit tediously, upon manifestation when having access to the completed simulation run. In practice this detection of deformation modes is based on error-prone supervision of a non-trivial, hand-selected subset of nodes in critical components.

In general, simulation results contain abundant features and are therefore high dimensional and unwieldy, which makes comparative analysis difficult. Intuitively, the sampled points describing the component are highly correlated, not only in space but also over time. This redundancy in the data invites further analysis via feature learning, reducing unimportant information in space as well as time and thus dimensionality. The low dimensional features capture distinguishing characteristics to detect the deformation modes. As soon as the deformation of a component is attributed to a deformation mode, there is little variance regarding its further course in the simulation. This motivates the in-situ detection, that is during the simulation, of deformation modes; we can then interrupt the simulation and anticipate targeted changes to the model parameters.

For the in-situ analysis of deforming shapes, we propose the application of an LSTM autoencoder trained on a component-wise shape representation by oriented bounding boxes instead of directly on the 3D data points (or meshes) describing the shapes. Motivated by an architecture with two decoders that stems from unsupervised video prediction [26], we choose a composite LSTM autoencoder that is specialized on handling time sequences and can both reconstruct the input and predict the future time steps of a sequence. It creates an additional low dimensional hidden or latent representation which after successful training represents the features of the input time sequences and allows its reconstruction and prediction. In this case the features encode the distinctive characteristics of the component's deformation. Figure 2 illustrates the process.

The research goals can be summarized as a) the definition of a distinguishing and simple shape representation for structural components of a complex model, b) the in-situ detection of patterns in the deformation behavior, and c) the in-situ prediction of structural component positions at future time steps.

Further on in Sect. 2, we give an introduction to simulation data, which we choose as example data, its characteristics and limitations. In Sect. 3, we present oriented bounding boxes, the selected shape representation for structural components, followed by the definition of the LSTM autoencoder in Sect. 4. In Sect. 5, we discuss related work on machine learning for simulations. Results on a car crash simulation are presented in Sect. 6.

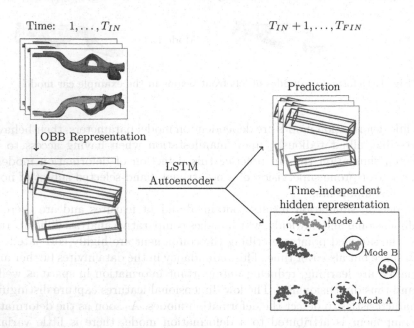

Fig. 2. Analysis and prediction of deforming shapes. Preprocess the first T_{IN} time steps of simulation data by oriented bounding boxes, apply an LSTM autoencoder which predicts the future time steps and creates a hidden representation representing the deformation over time. Finally, the deformation modes from Fig. 1 can be detected in the hidden representations.

2   Simulation Data and Their Characteristics

As an example for a deforming shape over time, we consider 3D (surface) meshes, which are decomposed into structural components. A numerical simulation approximately computes the deformation of the underlying object on the basis of physical relations. For each simulation, model, material, or environment parameters might be varied as well as the geometry of components or their connections. The output of a simulation are the positions of the mesh points at different times and point-wise values of physical quantities. While a large variety of deformation processes is observed per component, they result in a small number of meaningful patterns, called deformation modes. In Fig. 1 two distinct deformation modes of two structural components during a car crash can be observed.

Car crash simulations are a complex example. The mesh sizes for the car models can be large, the number and diversity of the input parameters is high and the behavior is nonlinear. Furthermore, the calculations need to have a high degree of precision, because the evaluation of the passenger's safety is based on the simulation outputs, i.e. plastic deformation, strain, and rupture. The stored simulations nowadays contain detailed information for up to two hundred time steps and more than ten million nodes. Due to the large computational costs of one simulation, for one model there are generally less than 500 different runs.

From simulation run to simulation run the input parameters are modified to achieve the design goals, e.g. crash safety, weight, or performance. In the beginning, the goal is the broad understanding of deformation behavior by applying major changes to the model. In later design stages a fine tuning is done and tests address some issues that have not been captured in early stages. We present an approach that analyzes the whole car as a multi-body object under dynamic deformation. Therefore, it is applied at an early design stage where the broad deformation behavior and component interaction has to be understood.

Challenges in the Analysis. Because of the high data complexity, the relatively low number of samples, and fatal consequences of wrong results on the passenger's safety, many data analysis methods cannot be applied directly. Furthermore, a full prediction of the complex simulation results, including detailed deformation or strains, only based on the input parameters is error prone and critical for the purpose of precise parameter selections and the understanding of detailed physical behavior. Existing methods create a surrogate model given some input parameters, see e.g. [27]. Others show how deformation modes depend on input parameters by using visualizations in low dimensional representations without defining an explicit surrogate model [15,30].

We do not want to base our analysis on input parameters, but present a more general approach that concentrates on general deformation behavior. By applying an in-situ analysis and an estimation of the deformation in the future time steps, we provide information that allows a faster selection of new model parameters in the development process.

Different mesh resolutions or changes in the geometry of two different models lead to a correspondence problem. The 3D surface meshes cannot be compared point-wise anymore requiring the use of shape representations of the meshes, that capture the differences between different modes of deformation (Fig. 1). However, semantic design rules apply for the car model's components as is the case for most man-made models. Car wheels, the seats, and beams are all of similar shape for different car models, which can be inferred once the general form and dimension are known, especially when analyzing broad characteristics in the early design stages. Because of these semantic rules, the model's components can be approximated by their optimal bounding boxes which capture their translation, rotation, and scale.

3   Preprocessing by Oriented Bounding Boxes

We preprocess every structural component by determining an oriented bounding box for each time step. For that, we consider the set of points $\mathcal{X}$ describing the selected component. The oriented bounding box is then defined by

Definition 1. *Given a finite set of N points $\mathcal{X} = \{X_i \mid i = 1, ..., N\} \subset \mathbb{R}^3$, the optimal oriented bounding box (OBB) is defined as the arbitrarily oriented cuboid, or rectangular parallelepiped, of minimal volume enclosing $\mathcal{X}$.*

Each OBB is uniquely defined by its center $\mathbf{X} \in \mathbb{R}^3$, its rotation $R \in SO(3, \mathbb{R})$, and its extensions $\mathbf{\Delta} \in \mathbb{R}^3$, where $SO(3, \mathbb{R}) = \{R \in \mathbb{R}^{3\times3} \mid R^T R = I_d = RR^T, det(R) = 1\}$ are all the orthogonal and real 3-by-3-matrices. Given the definition, the optimal oriented bounding box is the solution to a constrained optimization problem

$$\begin{aligned} \min_{\substack{\mathbf{\Delta}, \mathbf{X} \in \mathbb{R}^3 \\ R \in SO(3, \mathbb{R})}} \quad & \prod_{k=1}^{d} \mathbf{\Delta}_k \\ \text{s.t.} \quad & -\tfrac{1}{2}\mathbf{\Delta} \leq RX_i - \mathbf{X} \leq \tfrac{1}{2}\mathbf{\Delta} \ \forall i = 1, \dots, N \end{aligned} \tag{1}$$

The matrix R rotates the standard coordinate system of $\mathbb{R}^3$, such that the bounding box is axis aligned in the rotated reference frame.

We employ the HYBBRID algorithm [4] to approximate the boxes, since the exact algorithm has cubic runtime in the number of points in the convex hull of $\mathcal{X}$ [21]. Also, the quality of the approximation by fast principal component analysis (PCA) based algorithms is limited [6]. However, we need the oriented bounding boxes to fit tightly, which is why we adapted the HYBBRID algorithm for the OBB approximations of time sequences.

Adapted HYBBRID Algorithm. A redefinition of (1) as in [4] allows the problem's analysis as an unconstrained optimization over $SO(3, \mathbb{R})$

$$\min_{R \in SO(3, \mathbb{R})} f(R),$$

where $f(R)$ is the volume of the axis aligned bounding box of the point set $\mathcal{X}$ rotated by R. Since the function is not differentiable, a derivative-free algorithm combining global search by a genetic algorithm [8,14] (exploration) and local search by the Nelder-Mead simplex algorithm [20] (exploitation) to find the rotation matrix $R^* \in SO(3, \mathbb{R})$ that minimizes f is introduced in [4], where a detailed description of the algorithm can be found.

By utilizing the best rotation matrix from the previous time step of the same component, we can give a good initial guess to the algorithm. This improves the quality of the approximations and reduces the runtime by 30% in comparison to the original HYBBRID algorithm.

Information Retrieval from OBBs. The oriented bounding boxes further allow consideration of translation, rotation, and scale of the car components individually. The rigid transform of a component, composed of its translation and rotation, is normally estimated using a few fixed reference points for each component [28] and might be subtracted from the total deformation for analysis. Nevertheless, the quality of this rigid transform estimation depends highly on the hand selected reference points. When utilizing oriented bounding boxes the use of reference points is not necessary any more, since the HYBBRID algorithm outputs the rotation matrix R^*. This allows detecting interesting characteristics in the components' deformations that are not translation or rotation based.

4   LSTM Autoencoders

Autoencoders are a widely used type of neural network for unsupervised learning. They learn low dimensional characteristic features of the input that allow its recreation as well as possible. Therefore, the hidden or low dimensional representations should show the most relevant aspects of the data and classification tasks can generally be solved better in the low dimensional space. Autoencoders stand out against other dimension reduction approaches, because the encoder enables quick evaluation and description of the manifold, on which the hidden representations lie [9]. Therefore, a new data point's embedding does not have to be obtained by interpolation.

Since in the case of simulation data we are always handling time sequences, we implemented an autoencoder as in [26], using long short-term memory (LSTM) layers [11,13] in the encoder and decoder. LSTM are a type of recurrent neural networks (RNN) [24] that apply parameter sharing over time and thus reduce the number of trainable weights. By this means, we can analyze the deformation process of a structural component over time, because the information from all the input time steps is summarized into one hidden representation taking advantage of the temporal correspondences in the data.

Because we want to analyze the time sequences in-situ, we not only recreate the input, but also predict the future time steps by implementing a second decoder [26], as illustrated in Fig. 3. The prediction gives a first estimate of the simulation result. Furthermore, the low dimensional embedding is expected to be more significant with respect to the detection of deformation modes in future time steps, since the low dimensional features are also trained to predict future deformation.

We take advantage of the good generalization performance of autoencoders and train an LSTM autoencoder that can handle all the differently shaped components and generalizes their deformation behavior represented by oriented bounding boxes.

Therefore, we separately feed the oriented bounding boxes of each structural component for the first T_{IN} time steps to the autoencoder. As outputs, the autoencoder produces a hidden representation $h_{T_{IN}}$ and a reconstruction of the input sequence $S_{reconstruct}$. Since we implement two decoders, we also obtain a prediction $S_{predict}$, as illustrated in Fig. 3. We chose to use only one LSTM layer for each en-/decoder, to minimize the number of trainable weights and impede overfitting. Depending on the size of the training set, an increase in the number of layers might improve the prediction and representation results.

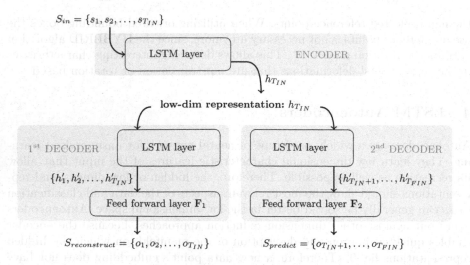

Fig. 3. LSTM autoencoder. The last hidden vector $h_{T_{in}}$ of the encoder layer is utilized as the low dimensional representation, which is input to all the LSTM units of the decoders. By applying time independent feed forward layers to the hidden vectors $h'_{\bullet}$ of each decoder, their size is reduced and the output sequences $S_{reconstruct}$ and $S_{predict}$ are created. The weights of the LSTM layers and $\mathbf{F}_{\bullet}$ are time independent.

5   Related Work

The analysis of car crash simulations has been studied with different machine learning techniques. For example, [1,2,10,32] base their analysis on the finished simulation runs, whereas we focus on in-situ analysis of car crash simulations.

Other recent works study analysis and prediction of car crash simulation data with machine learning under different problem definitions than in this work, for example the estimation of the result given the input parameters [12] or plausibility checks [25]. For a recent overview on the combination of machine learning and simulation see [23].

There are alternatives to oriented bounding boxes as low dimensional shape representations for 3D objects. The authors of [15] construct low dimensional shape representations via a projection of mesh data onto an eigenbasis stemming from a discrete Laplace Beltrami Operator. The data is then represented by the spectral coefficients. We have chosen a simpler representation, that can also be applied to point clouds and allows a faster training.

The majority of works about neural networks for geometries extend convolutional neural networks on non-euclidean shapes, including graphs and manifolds. The works in [3,17,19] present extensions of neural networks via the computation of local patches. Nevertheless, the networks are applied to the 3D meshes directly and are computationally expensive, when applied for every time step and component of complex models.

Table 1. Structure of the composite LSTM autoencoder with two decoders for reconstruction and prediction. The bullets • reference the corresponding batch size.

Layer	Output shape	Param	Connected to
Input	$(\bullet, T_{IN}, 24)$	0	
LSTM 1	$(\bullet, 24)$	4704	Input
Repeat Vector 1	$(\bullet, T_{IN}, 24)$	0	LSTM 1
Repeat Vector 2	$(\bullet, T_{FIN} - T_{IN}, 24)$	0	LSTM 1
LSTM 2	$(\bullet, T_{IN}, 256)$	287744	Repeat Vector 1
LSTM 3	$(\bullet, T_{FIN} - T_{IN}, 256)$	287744	Repeat Vector 2
Fully Connected 1	$(\bullet, T_{IN}, 24)$	6168	LSTM 2
Fully Connected 2	$(\bullet, T_{FIN} - T_{IN}, 24)$	6168	LSTM 3

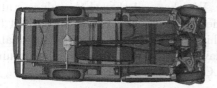 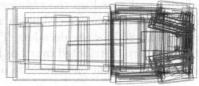

Fig. 4. Snapshot and bounding box representation of the example car model at $T_{IN} = 12$ (bottom view). The four beams from Fig. 2 are colored.

Based on the shape deformation representation by [7], recent works studied generative modeling of meshes for 3D animation sequences via bidirectional LSTM network [22] or variational autoencoder [29]. The shape representation yields good results, however, it solves an optimization problem at each vertex and requires identical connectivity over time. The architectures are tested on models of humans with considerably fewer nodes, which is why computational issues seem likely for the vertex-wise optimization problem.

6 Experiments

We evaluated the introduced approach on a frontal crash simulation of a Chevrolet C2500 pick-up truck[1]. The data set consists of $n_{simulations} = 196$ completed simulations[2] of a front crash (see Fig. 4), using the same truck, but with different material characteristics, which is a similar setup to [2]. For 9 components (the front and side beams and the bumper parts) the sheet thickness has been varied while keeping the geometry unchanged. From every simulation we select $T_{FIN} = 31$ equally distributed time steps and use $T_{IN} = 12$ time steps for the input to the in-situ analysis, which is applied to 133 structural components

---

[1] From NCAC http://web.archive.org/web/*/www.ncac.gwu.edu/vml/models.html.

[2] Computed with LS-DYNa http://www.lstc.com/products/ls-dyna.

represented by oriented bounding boxes. That means, when detecting a bad simulation run after T_{IN} of T_{FIN} time steps the design engineer can save 60% of the simulation time. The impact at $T_{IN} = 12$ is visualized in Fig. 4. At this time most of the deformation and energy absorption took place in the so-called crumble zone at the front of the car.

The data is normalized to zero mean for each of the three dimensions and standard deviation one over all the dimensions. Using all 133 components from 100 training samples we train the network[3] for 150 epochs with adaptive learning rate optimization algorithm [16]. We minimize the mean squared error between true and estimated bounding boxes over time, summing up the error for reconstruction and prediction decoder as well as for the components. The remaining 96 simulations are testing samples.

Because of the limited number of training samples, we tried to minimize the number of hidden neurons while maintaining the quality, to reduce the possibility of overfitting and speed up the training. We observed that the result is stable with respect to the number of hidden neurons, which we finally set to 24 for the encoder and 256 for the decoders. This leads to a total of 592,528 trainable weights, which are distributed over the layers as listed in Table 1. The training has a runtime of 36 s for one epoch on a CPU with 16 cores.

6.1 Prediction of Components' Deformations During a Crash Test

The predicted oriented bounding boxes give an estimate after T_{IN} time steps for the result of simulation S afterwards. For comparison, we define two baselines using a nearest neighbor search, where the prediction of S is estimated by the future time steps of another simulation S', which is either the corresponding simulation for the nearest neighbor of S in the input sequences or in the input parameter space. We compare the results by their mean squared error which is also used for training. Note that an interpolation has not been chosen for comparison, because interpolated rectangular boxes can have any possible shape.

The prediction error of our method is 38% lower than a prediction based on nearest neighbor search in the input parameter space and 16% lower than a prediction using the nearest neighbor of the training input sequences, see Table 2. We also compare the LSTM composite autoencoder to a simple RNN composite autoencoder, to evaluate the use of the LSTM layers in comparison to a different network architecture. When using the same number of hidden weights for the simple RNN layer in the encoder and the decoders, the prediction error is higher than for the LSTM autoencoder. This indicates, that the LSTM layers better detect the temporal correspondence in the time sequences. Additionally, the results depending on random initial weights are stable, which is demonstrated by the low standard deviation of the error.

We observe an improvement in the orthogonality between the faces of the rectangular boxes over time for both the prediction and reconstruction output of the LSTM layers. The LSTM layers recognize the conditions on the rectangular

---

[3] Implemented in Keras [5], no peephole connections.

Table 2. Mean Squared Errors ($\times 10^{-4}$) on testing samples for different prediction methods applied to oriented bounding boxes. For methods depending on random initialization, mean and standard deviation of 5 training runs are listed.

Method	Test-MSE	STD
Nearest neighbor in parameter space	13.34	–
Nearest neighbor in input sequences	6.13	–
Composite RNN autoencoder	5.80	0.095
Composite LSTM autoencoder	5.14	0.127

shape and implicitly enforce it in every output time step. Note, the network generalizes well to the highly different sizes and shapes of 133 different structural components, whose oriented bounding boxes are illustrated in Fig. 4.

6.2   Clustering of the Deformation Behavior

The LSTM autoencoder does not only output a prediction, but also a hidden low dimensional representation. It captures the most prominent and distinguishing features of the data, because only based on those the prediction and reconstruction are calculated. Its size corresponds to the number of hidden neurons in the encoder. Hence, our network reduces the size of the $24 \times T_{IN}$-dimensional input to 24. The hidden representation summarizes the deformation over time, which is why we obtain one hidden representation for the whole sequence of each structural component and simulation.

In the case of car crash simulations we are especially interested in patterns in the plastic deformation to detect plastic strain and material failure. Therefore, we add an additional preprocessing step for the analysis of deformation behavior. We subtract the rigid movement of the oriented bounding boxes, that means we translate the oriented bounding boxes to the origin and rotate them to the standard coordinate system (see Sect. 3). In that way only the plastic deformation and strain are studied, but not induced effects in the rigid transform.

For a subset of components we visualize the 24-dimensional hidden representations in two dimensions with the t-SNE dimension reduction algorithm [18]. Figure 2 illustrates the embedding for the four frontal beams. We notice that the deformation mode from Fig. 1 is clearly manifesting in the hidden representations of the left frontal beams.

When observing the hidden representations of other components, we can detect the pattern corresponding to the deformation mode from Fig. 1 in other structural components, whose plastic deformation is seemingly influenced by the behavior of the left frontal beams. Even though the interaction between structural components is not fed to the network, the components that are affected by the mode can be identified in Fig. 5.

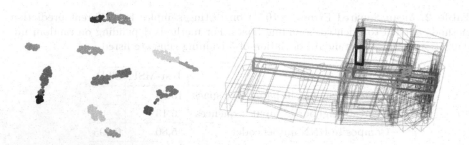

Fig. 5. Embedded hidden representations for all simulations and seven structural components, that manifest the deformation modes from Fig. 1. The two different patterns for each of the selected structural components are illustrated in the same color with different intensity, the corresponding component on the right in the matching color.

7   Conclusion

We have presented a general approach for in-situ analysis and prediction of deforming 3D shapes by subdividing them into structural components. The simple shape representation makes an analysis of complex models feasible and allows the detection of coarse deformation patterns. The method is applied successfully to a car crash simulation, estimates the final position of the boxes to a higher quality than other methods, and speeds up the selection of new simulation parameters without having to wait for the final results of large simulations.

Although we have selected a relatively simple shape representation, the patterns can be reliably detected. In future work, we plan to compare and combine the approach with other low dimensional shape representations and investigate other application scenarios, in particular in engineering. Apart from simulation data, our approach has more application areas, including the analysis and prediction of the movement of deformable articulated shapes, to which [31] gives an overview. The authors present data sets for human motion and pose analysis, on which the introduced approach can also be applied.

References

1. Bohn, B., Garcke, J., Griebel, M.: A sparse grid based method for generative dimensionality reduction of high-dimensional data. J. Comput. Phys. **309**, 1–17 (2016)
2. Bohn, B., et al.: Analysis of car crash simulation data with nonlinear machine learning methods. Procedia Comput. Sci. **18**, 621–630 (2013)
3. Bronstein, M.M., Bruna, J., LeCun, Y., Szlam, A., Vandergheynst, P.: Geometric deep learning: going beyond euclidean data. IEEE Signal Process. Mag. **34**(4), 18–42 (2017)
4. Chang, C.T., Gorissen, B., Melchior, S.: Fast oriented bounding box optimization on the rotation group $SO(3, \mathbb{R})$. ACM TOG **30**(5), 122 (2011)
5. Chollet, F., et al.: Keras (2015). https://keras.io

6. Dimitrov, D., Knauer, C., Kriegel, K., Rote, G.: Bounds on the quality of the PCA bounding boxes. Comput. Geom. **42**(8), 772–789 (2009)
7. Gao, L., Lai, Y.K., Yang, J., Ling-Xiao, Z., Xia, S., Kobbelt, L.: Sparse data driven mesh deformation. IEEE Trans. Vis. Comput. Graph. 1 (2019). https://doi.org/10.1109/TVCG.2019.2941200
8. Goldberg, D.E.: Genetic Algorithms in Search, Optimization and Machine Learning. Addison-Wesley Longman Publishing Co., Inc., Boston (1989)
9. Goodfellow, I., Bengio, Y., Courville, A.: Deep Learning. MIT Press, Cambridge (2016)
10. Graening, L., Sendhoff, B.: Shape mining: a holistic data mining approach for engineering design. Adv. Eng. Inform. **28**(2), 166–185 (2014)
11. Graves, A.: Generating sequences with recurrent neural networks. arXiv:1308.0850 (2013)
12. Guennec, Y.L., Brunet, J.P., Daim, F.Z., Chau, M., Tourbier, Y.: A parametric and non-intrusive reduced order model of car crash simulation. Comput. Methods Appl. Mech. Eng. **338**, 186–207 (2018)
13. Hochreiter, S., Schmidhuber, J.: Long short-term memory. Neural Comput. **9**(8), 1735–1780 (1997)
14. Holland, J.H.: Adaptation in Natural and Artificial Systems. University of Michigan Press, Ann Arbor (1975). Second edition (1992)
15. Iza-Teran, R., Garcke, J.: A geometrical method for low-dimensional representations of simulations. SIAM/ASA J. Uncertain. Quantif. **7**(2), 472–496 (2019)
16. Kingma, D.P., Ba, J.: Adam: a method for stochastic optimization. In: ICLR (2015). arXiv:1412.6980
17. Litany, O., Remez, T., Rodola, E., Bronstein, A., Bronstein, M.: Deep functional maps: structured prediction for dense shape correspondence. In: Proceedings of the IEEE International Conference on Computer Vision, pp. 5659–5667 (2017)
18. van der Maaten, L., Hinton, G.: Visualizing data using t-SNE. J. Mach. Learn. Res. **9**, 2579–2605 (2008)
19. Monti, F., Boscaini, D., Masci, J., Rodola, E., Svoboda, J., Bronstein, M.M.: Geometric deep learning on graphs and manifolds using mixture model CNNs. In: CVPR, pp. 5115–5124 (2017)
20. Nelder, J.A., Mead, R.: A simplex method for function minimization. Comput. J. **7**(4), 308–313 (1965)
21. O'Rourke, J.: Finding minimal enclosing boxes. Int. J. Comput. Inf. Sci. **14**(3), 183–199 (1985)
22. Qiao, Y.L., Gao, L., Lai, Y.K., Xia, S.: Learning bidirectional LSTM networks for synthesizing 3D mesh animation sequences. arXiv:1810.02042 (2018)
23. von Rueden, L., Mayer, S., Sifa, R., Bauckhage, C., Garcke, J.: Combining machine learning and simulation to a hybrid modelling approach: current and future directions. In: Berthold, M.R., Feelders, A., Krempl, G. (eds.) IDA 2020. LNCS, vol. 12080, pp. 548–560. Springer, Cham (2020). https://doi.org/10.1007/978-3-030-44584-3_43
24. Rumelhart, D.E., Hinton, G.E., Williams, R.J.: Learning representations by back-propagating errors. Nature **323**, 533–536 (1986)
25. Sprügel, T., Schröppel, T., Wartzack, S.: Generic approach to plausibility checks for structural mechanics with deep learning. In: DS 87-1 Proceedings of the 21st International Conference on Engineering Design, vol. 1, pp. 299–308 (2017)
26. Srivastava, N., Mansimov, E., Salakhudinov, R.: Unsupervised learning of video representations using LSTMs. In: ICML, Lille, France, vol. 37, pp. 843–852 (2015)

27. Steffes-lai, D.: Approximation Methods for High Dimensional Simulation Results-Parameter Sensitivity Analysis and Propagation of Variations for Process Chains. Logos Verlag Berlin GmbH (2014)
28. Söderkvist, I., Wedin, P.Å.: On condition numbers and algorithms for determining a rigid body movement. BIT Numer. Math. **34**(3), 424–436 (1994)
29. Tan, Q., Gao, L., Lai, Y.K., Xia, S.: Variational autoencoders for deforming 3D mesh models. In: CVPR, pp. 5841–5850 (2018)
30. Thole, C.A., Nikitina, L., Nikitin, I., Clees, T.: Advanced mode analysis for crash simulation results. In: Proceedings of 9th LS-DYNA Forum (2010)
31. Wan, J., Escalera, S., Perales, F.J., Kittler, J.: Articulated motion and deformable objects. Pattern Recogn. **79**, 55–64 (2018)
32. Zhao, Z., Xianlong, J., Cao, Y., Wang, J.: Data mining application on crash simulation data of occupant restraint system. Expert Syst. Appl. **37**, 5788–5794 (2010)

Deep Learning Applications II

Deep Learning Applications II

Novel Sketch-Based 3D Model Retrieval via Cross-domain Feature Clustering and Matching

Kai Gao[1], Jian Zhang[1], Chen Li[1], Changbo Wang[1], Gaoqi He[1(✉)], and Hong Qin[2]

[1] East China Normal University, Shanghai, China
gqhe@cs.ecnu.edu.cn
[2] Stony Brook University (SUNY at Stony Brook), Stony Brook, USA

Abstract. To date, with the rapid advancement of scanning hardware and CAD software, we are facing technically challenging on how to search and find a desired model from a huge shape repository in a fast and accurate way in this bigdata digital era. Sketch-based 3D model retrieval is a flexible and user-friendly approach to tackling the existing challenges. In this paper, we articulate a novel way for model retrieval by means of sketching and building a 3D model retrieval framework based on deep learning. The central idea is to dynamically adjust the distance between the learned features of sketch and model in the encoded latent space through the utility of several deep neural networks. In the pre-processing phase, we convert all models in the shape database from meshes to point clouds because of its lightweight and simplicity. We first utilize two deep neural networks for classification to generate embeddings of both input sketch and point cloud. Then, these embeddings are fed into our clustering deep neural network to dynamically adjust the distance between encodings of the sketch domain and the model domain. The application of the sketch embedding to the retrieval similarity measurement could continue to improve the performance of our framework by re-mapping the distance between encodings from both domains. In order to evaluate the performance of our novel approach, we test our framework on standard datasets and compare it with other state-of-the-art methods. Experimental results have validated the effectiveness, robustness, and accuracy of our novel method.

Keywords: Shape retrieval · Feature description · Feature clustering and matching · Latent space embedding

1 Introduction

3D modeling is of fundamental significance to computer graphics and geometry processing and analysis, and 3D models are ubiquitous in CAD/CAM, computer games, digital entertainment, virtual reality, healthcare industry, etc.

© Springer Nature Switzerland AG 2020
I. Farkaš et al. (Eds.): ICANN 2020, LNCS 12396, pp. 299–311, 2020.
https://doi.org/10.1007/978-3-030-61609-0_24

The number of models has been growing rapidly in recent decades because of the development of both 3D modeling software and 3D scanning hardware. However, constructing a brand new 3D model remains costly and laborious, so it is very important to reuse the already available 3D models to the largest extent. There is an urgent problem that it is difficult to quickly find what designers/users want from a gigantic number of models in a shape repository, and this paper's central theme is on 3D model retrieval.

The main challenge of 3D model retrieval is how to precisely calculate the distance between the input and all candidate models from the desired database. In recent years, many research endeavors have been devoted to overcoming the challenge by using text, sketch, or even 3D geometry. Whereas, model retrieval by keyword is not able to rank models in a specific category for which users must look through all candidates one by one. Retrieval by a 3D object [6] is a straightforward way to solve the 3D model retrieval problem, but users would need to find an appropriate input model and it may fall into a chicken-and-egg problem. Some researchers retrieve models by matching sketch and (parallel and/or perspective) projection of shape geometry, however, the performance of matching mostly depends on the best view projection [24]. It is also a difficult problem on how to select the best view projection for every model.

Compared with the existing methods briefly mentioned above, directly matching the sketch and the candidate models (without resorting to any type of projections) possesses certain advantages like storage saving and no information loss. Furthermore, users do not need to spend time learning how to draw a sketch [8]. Despite these merits, how to measure the feature difference between a sketch and 3D candidate models remains challenging as they are from completely different domains. The key to tackle this problem is to first make features in each individual domain as discriminative as possible. Then, creating a shared feature space where features from the sketch domain and the model domain consistent [5] is equally important.

In this paper, we leverage available works from the classification deep learning networks to generate a feature embedding space for sketch and model respectively as the feature embeddings from two disjoint domains are intuitively and intrinsically discriminative. Then, we use another clustering network to understand these features for increasing the distance between corresponding encoders that belong to different categories and decreasing the distance between encoders that belong to the same class. Moreover, the discriminative information produced by the classification network is also used to enhance the performance of retrieval during online-query, and our extensive experimental results show the new approach improves the preciseness of our framework. Our contributions are as follows:

- We propose to learn feature clustering and matching for 3D model retrieval. Our framework will encode features of sketches and models into one feature space and automatically adjust the feature distance between them.
- We design an effective loss function to dynamically adjust the feature distribution in the cross domain. Features that belong to the same category

will be clustered, and at the same time features from different classes will be separated far apart.

- Applying the classification result of the sketch into measurement in the online query phase can promote the performance of the retrieval framework. It adaptively reduces the distance between features that belong to the same class based on the newly-adjusted feature distribution.

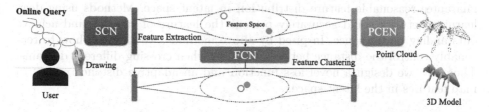

Fig. 1. The pipeline of online-query stage of our 3D model retrieval framework. We firstly convert all models from mesh to point cloud and use PCEN to extract features (the green rectangle) from them. SCN processes the sketch from the user and converts it into a embedding (the blue rectangle). After processing by FCN, the distance between these new embeddings (red rectangle with blue inside and the red rectangle with green inside) are closer. (Color figure online)

2   Related Works

Sketch-Based 3D Model Retrieval. Sketch-based 3D model retrieval attracts researchers around the world. Kang et al. [7] designed a novel way that uses jointboost classiffier and conditional random field (CRF) to segment the sketch and projection images into different semantic components. After that, they matched models by corresponding components. Wang et al. [21] used a collaborative recommendation method to improve the performance of retrieval. They created a shape descriptor called histogram of orientation angular distribution (HOAD) for extracting features from the sketch and designed a self-learning recommendation system. Li et al. [13] devised a novel composite feature for sketch. There were 16 different encoding schemas for every 2×2 region in an image. They used these features to match the sketch and the view of model. Liu et al. [14] proposed a method via supervised multi-view feature learning. These traditional retrieval methods use descriptors or mathematical algorithms, which may bring inaccuracy or time-consuming. The advent of deep learning technology gives researchers another choice to solve the problem.

Deep Learning Based 3D Model Retrieval. A lot of deep learning based methods are proposed to solve 3D model retrieval problem. Su et al. [19] designed a network called MVCNN, which learns from multi-views of model. They compared the similarity between two models by the output of MVCNN.

Wang et al. [20] used Siamese networks to process predefined viewpoints of models and achieve good performance. Bai et al. [1] devised a two-layers coding framework with high time efficiency. The first layer focuses on encoding features around interest points and the second layer encodes these features for comparison. However, aforementioned methods use rendered views which causes unnecessary waste of storage. Instead of using views of model, Xie et al. [23] designed a deep shape descriptor with the discriminative auto-encoder, which is insensitive to geometric structure variations. Dai et al. [5] proposed a framework which can guarantee reasonable feature distribution in latent space. Methods using deep learning network could accurately present the feature of samples and achieve outstanding performance. Inspired by above methods, we focus on how to reasonably control the distance between features when crossing different domains. Therefore, we design a novel loss function and an adaptive distance metric to map features in the latent space.

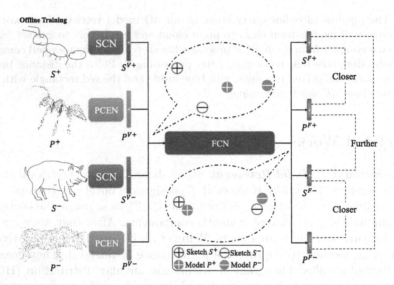

Fig. 2. The pipeline of offline-training stage of our 3D model retrieval framework. We select four types of data: the sketch S^+ and the point cloud P^+ from same category; the sketch S^- and the point cloud P^- from another category. Firstly, we feed these samples into SCN and PCEN. Then, FCN can automatically adjust the distance between them.

3   Our Approach

We design a novel approach to retrieve 3D models with a sketch image. There are two stages in our approach, i.e. online-query (see Fig. 1) and offline-training (see Fig. 2). We firstly convert all 3D models from mesh to point cloud. The point cloud is regarded as the process unit of the model in our approach. Additionally, there are three networks in our framework: sketch classification network (SCN), point cloud encoding network (PCEN) and feature clustering network (FCN). We use SCN and PCEN to construct initiatory distribution of features. Based on that, FCN is trained to re-adjust the distance between these features in one latent space. The output of FCN can be used in online-query stage.

3.1   Online-Query

In order to scientifically evaluate the similarity between two samples in retrieval mission, a similarity or distance has to be clarified. Assume that there is a sketch S uploaded from the user and candidate point clouds $\{P_i\}$. S^F and $\{P_i^F\}$ are the output of FCN. Before ranking 3D models according to the similarity, we use the learned classification embeddings to further adjust the distance metric D:

$$D_i = ||S^F - P_i^F||_1 \times (1 - \Delta_i), \tag{1}$$

where *support factor* Δ is calculated from the output of SCN with feeding S. It equals the possibility of S belongs to the category of P_i. If Δ_i is relatively large, D_i would be much smaller than the case that Δ_i is not used. Otherwise, D_i would be much larger. Moreover, our framework intentionally increases the distance between every feature for which Δ can affect more if $||S^F - P_i^F||_1$ is relatively large. The usage of Δ improves the performance of our retrieval framework (see Sect. 5 for details). Once the final distance is calculated, the user will receive the candidate model list which is generated by sorting $\{D_i\}$ in ascending order.

3.2   Offline-Training

The preparation progress of our retrieval framework is shown in Fig. 2. The overall training procedure of offline-training can be described as following steps: 1. Train SCN and PCEN with labeled sketches and point clouds; 2. Prepare four types of data, randomly picked sketches $\{S_i\}$ and point clouds $\{P_i\}$ from same category; randomly picked sketches $\{S_j\}$ and point clouds $\{P_j\}$ that belongs to another class; 3. These samples are processed by SCN and PCEN and results of them are fed into FCN; 4. Train FCN with L_{FCN}. All configurations of networks can be found in Sect. 4.

This stage improves the ability of our framework to map features from both domains. SCN and PCEN firstly construct the discriminative distribution of features in each domain. Then, features are remapped by FCN, which automatically adjusts the distance between them.

SCN and PCEN. The critical purpose of these networks is to create unique encoding for each sample. We use a larger convolution kernel size at the beginning layer of SCN in order to obtain more comprehensive information of sketch. Additionally, PCEN uses a simple structure in order to reduce the time of preprocessing and the requirement of hardware. Moreover, due to the clustering ability of the classification network, features in each domain are discriminative. It reduces the difficulty of training FCN.

FCN. FCN is designed to gather the embeddings from same class closer as well as separate embeddings that belong to the different class in the feature space. Inspired by Rendle et al. [17] and Chen et al. [3], we construct an effective loss function L_{FCN}, which is designed to adjust the distance between features. L_{FCN} will help to achieve two goals: 1. The features should be discriminative in each domain; 2. The features should be consistent when cross domains [5]. Additionally, L_{FCN} is made up of three components, which are L_S, L_P and L_{intra} as follows:

$$L_{FCN} = \alpha \times L_S + \beta \times L_P + \gamma \times L_{intra}, \tag{2}$$

$$L_S = \sum_{i,j}^{N}[\epsilon - \sigma(S_i^V \cdot P_i^V - S_i^V \cdot P_j^V)], \tag{3}$$

$$L_P = \sum_{i,j}^{N}[\epsilon - \sigma(P_j^V \cdot S_j^V - P_j^V \cdot S_i^V)], \tag{4}$$

$$L_{intra} = \sum_{i,j}^{N}[\epsilon + \sigma(S_i^V \cdot S_j^V + P_i^V \cdot P_j^V)], \tag{5}$$

where i, j are the indices of samples from two different categories, N is the number of samples, α, β, γ and ϵ are hyper-parameters, S^V or P^V indicates the output of SCN or PCEN. The function $\sigma(x)$ is the logistic sigmoid:

$$\sigma(x) = \frac{1}{1 + e^{-x}}. \tag{6}$$

The distance of features from both domains is automatically adjusted by L_S and L_P. L_{intra} enlarges the distance of features in order to cooperate with *support factor*. Our framework can accurately match sketch and model based on the adjusted distribution. The visualized distribution of features from both domains can be found in Sect. 5.1.

4   Implementation Details

SCN Configuration. The structure of SCN is shown in Fig. 3 and the dimension of the output layer would be modified corresponding to the number of categories in the database.

PCEN Configuration. PCEN is mainly modified from PointNet [16] and the structure is shown in Fig. 4. The dimension of the output layer would be modified corresponding to the number of categories in the database and the number of sample points during converting is 1024.

FCN Configuration. FCN is made up of three fully-connected layers. The dimension of the input layer would be modified corresponding to the number of categories in the database. The structure of three layers is configured as follows:

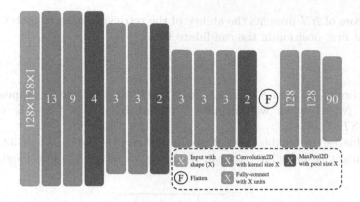

Fig. 3. Structure of SCN.

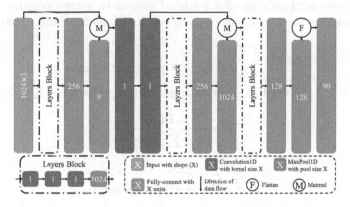

Fig. 4. Structure of PCEN.

the first layer uses 128 units; the second and third layers use 64 units; all layers use activation function *relu*. The value of $\alpha, \beta, \gamma, \epsilon$ in L_{FCN} is 0.4, 0.4, 0.2, 2.0, respectively.

Evaluation Metrics. In order to reasonably evaluate our retrieval framework, we use standard metrics to measure our proposed method, i.e. prediction-recall curve, nearest neighbor (NN), first-tier (FT), second-tier (ST), e-measure (E), discounted cumulative gain (DCG) and mean average precision (mAP). Let L denote the number of models return to the user, N denote the number of relative models in whole database, $r(i)$ denote the number of relative models in i returned candidates, respectively. Metrics above can be described as follows:

$$Prediction = \frac{r(L)}{L}, \tag{7}$$

$$Recall = \frac{r(L)}{N}. \tag{8}$$

The score of NN presents the ability of the retrieval engine to match positive samples at first position in the candidate list.

$$NN = r(1). \tag{9}$$

The score of FT and ST present how many positive samples appear in top K. $K = N - 1$ when we calculate FT and $K = 2 \times (N - 1)$ when we calculate ST.

E evaluates the combination of prediction and recall when $L = 32$ because the user might be more interested in the query results in the first page.

$$E = \frac{2}{\frac{1}{Prediction} + \frac{1}{Recall}}. \tag{10}$$

DCG presents the ability of a retrieval system to gather positive results in the front because the user might concern results in the front more than those in the end.

$$DCG_k = \begin{cases} G_1 & k = 1 \\ DCG_{k-1} + \frac{G_k}{log_2(k)} & otherwise \end{cases}, \tag{11}$$

where $G_k = 1$ if the result is positive at position k, otherwise $G_k = 0$.

$$DCG = \frac{DCG_k}{1 + \sum_{j=2}^{N} \frac{1}{log_2(j)}}. \tag{12}$$

$$mAP = \frac{1}{N} \times \sum_{i=1}^{N} \frac{i}{position(i)}. \tag{13}$$

5   Evaluation and Discussion

In this section, we evaluate the performance of our 3D model retrieval framework on standard datasets. Some examples of retrieval results are shown in Fig. 6. All experiments are conducted on a PC with Intel i7-6700 CPU, Nvidia GTX-1060 3 GB GPU and 8 GB RAM. The average time of a single query is about 6×10^{-2} second.

5.1   Feature Distribution

In Sect. 3.2, we introduce the conception and composition of L_{FCN}. To inspect the functionality of it, we use PCA to reduce dimensions of features from both domains to two-dimension space and visualize them in Fig. 5. Features directly generated by SCN and PCEN mostly gather together, which leads to the cluttered feature distribution that is not suitable for tackling matching problem. After processing by FCN, features from the sketch domain and the model domain are separated. The feature distribution is more discriminative and consistent than the original one.

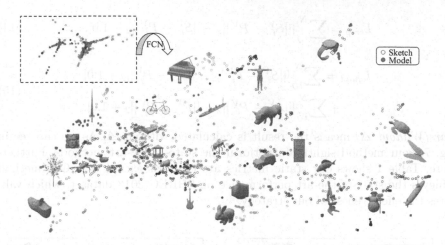

Fig. 5. The visualized distribution of features from the sketch domain and the model domain on the SHREC 2013 dataset. Colours present categories.

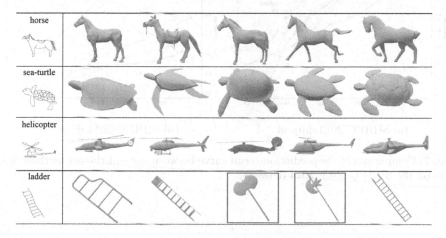

Fig. 6. Some examples of retrieval results of our 3D model retrieval framework on SHREC 2013 dataset. Wrong retrieved models are marked with the blue rectangles.

5.2   Retrieval on SHREC 2013 Dataset

SHREC 2013 dataset [10] contains 1,814 models and 7,200 sketches, which are grouped into 90 categories. Some examples of retrieval results from our framework are shown in Fig. 6. We compare our proposed method with DPSML [9], Semantic [15], DCA [2], DCHML [4] and CF [13] on the SEREC 2013 dataset. Moreover, we also test two different loss in our method to validate the performance of our loss is better than original: *Ours(RefTrip)* [18] and *Ours(RefQuad)* [3]. The loss functions used by *Ours(RefTrip)* and *Ours(RefQuad)* can be summarized as follows:

$$L_{trip} = \sum_{i,j}^{N}[||S_i^V - P_i^V||_2 - ||S_i^V - P_j^V||_2 + 1.0], \tag{14}$$

$$L_{quad} = \sum_{i,j}^{N}[||S_i^V - P_i^V||_2 - ||S_i^V - P_j^V||_2 + 1.0]$$
$$+ \sum_{i,j}^{N}[||S_i^V - P_i^V||_2 - ||P_i^V - P_j^V||_2 + 1.0]. \tag{15}$$

Ours(Without Δ) means the result is calculated without Δ. As we can see in Fig. 7a, our method sightly outperform the state-of-the-art methods. Furthermore, Table 1 shows our static metrics are the best except *NN*. Our method achieves the state-of-the-art performance on SHREC 2013 dataset, which validates the effectiveness of our strategy.

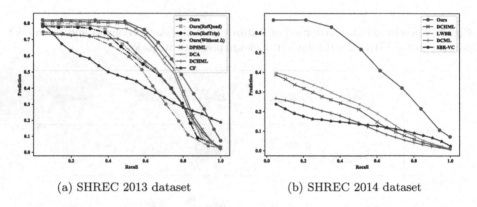

(a) SHREC 2013 dataset   (b) SHREC 2014 dataset

Fig. 7. Comparison of the prediction-recall curve between state-of-the-art methods and ours on the SHREC 2013, 2014 datasets.

5.3   Retrieval on SHREC 2014 Dataset

SHREC 2014 dataset [12] contains 13,680 sketches and 8,987 models in total, grouped into 171 classes. We compare our framework with DCHML [4], LWBR [22], DCML [5] and SBR-VC [11] on this dataset. As we can see in Fig. 7b, our method could significantly outperform aforementioned methods. Moreover, for all evaluation metrics, our method could outperform the above methods as Table 2 shows. Furthermore, the improvement of our method is obvious, about more than 40% in average compared to the best reported method DCHML [4].

Table 1. Summary of performance metrics between state-of-the-art methods and ours on the SHREC 2013 dataset.

	NN	FT	ST	E	DCG	mAP
Ours	0.818	**0.841**	**0.891**	**0.589**	**0.900**	**0.857**
Ours(RefQuad)	0.796	0.800	0.862	0.539	0.899	0.811
Ours(RefTrip)	0.779	0.786	0.849	0.545	0.857	0.798
Ours(Without Δ)	0.712	0.733	0.816	0.503	0.822	0.741
DPSML [9]	0.819	0.834	0.875	0.415	0.892	0.857
Semantic [15]	**0.823**	0.828	0.860	0.403	0.884	0.843
DCA [2]	0.783	0.796	0.829	0.376	0.856	0.813
DCHML [4]	0.730	0.715	0.773	0.368	0.816	0.744
CF [13]	0.342	0.348	0.419	0.361	0.563	0.362

Table 2. Summary of performance metrics between state-of-the-art methods and ours on the SHREC 2014 dataset.

	NN	FT	ST	E	DCG	mAP
Ours	**0.664**	**0.697**	**0.799**	**0.499**	**0.871**	**0.747**
DCHML [4]	0.403	0.329	0.394	0.201	0.554	0.336
LWBR [22]	0.403	0.378	0.455	0.236	0.581	0.401
DCML [5]	0.272	0.275	0.345	0.171	0.498	0.286
SBR-VC [11]	0.198	0.118	0.180	0.104	0.391	0.131

6   Conclusion and Future Work

In this paper, we have proposed a novel sketch-based 3D model retrieval framework via cross-domain feature clustering and matching. Instead of matching the sketch and the projection of candidate models, we directly extract features from the sketches and models. Furthermore, we designed an effective loss for sketch-based 3D model retrieval to organize features from both domains. The final query result is generated by adaptively reducing the distance between features in the latent space. We evaluated our method on the two standard datasets. The experimental results show our strategy can reasonably cluster features in the latent space and improve the accuracy of retrieval. In the future, it would be worth of new research investigating how to fit new data without re-training networks as it is uneconomic to always re-train networks in new applications for practical use. Moreover, we intend to design a new descriptor that could better represent the model and the sketch for improved performance. The descriptor should possess the ability of extracting semantic, higher-level, or even knowledge information, such as visual segmentation and functionality information, from candidate samples in the respective database.

Acknowledgements. This paper is partially supported by the National Natural Science Foundation of China (61532002 and 61672237), the Natural Science Foundation of Shanghai (19ZR1415800), the Science Popularization Foundation of Shanghai (19DZ2301100) and the National Science Foundation of USA (IIS-1715985 and IIS-1812606). The authors wish to thank constructive comments from all the reviewers.

References

1. Bai, X., Bai, S., Zhu, Z., Latecki, L.J.: 3D shape matching via two layer coding. IEEE PAMI **37**(12), 2361–2373 (2015)
2. Chen, J., Fang, Y.: Deep cross-modality adaptation via semantics preserving adversarial learning for sketch-based 3D shape retrieval. In: ECCV, pp. 624–640 (2018)
3. Chen, W., Chen, X., Zhang, J., Huang, K.: Beyond triplet loss: a deep quadruplet network for person re-identification. In: IEEE CVPR, pp. 1320–1329 (2017)
4. Dai, G., Xie, J., Fang, Y.: Deep correlated holistic metric learning for sketch-based 3D shape retrieval. IEEE TIP **27**(7), 3374–3386 (2018)
5. Dai, G., Xie, J., Zhu, F., Fang, Y.: Deep correlated metric learning for sketch-based 3D shape retrieval. In: AAAI, pp. 4002–4008 (2017)
6. Funkhouser, T.A., et al.: A search engine for 3D models. ACM TOG **22**(1), 83–105 (2003)
7. Kang, Y., Xu, C., Lin, S., Xu, S., Luo, X., Chen, Q.: Component segmentation of sketches used in 3D model retrieval. In: SIGGRAPH, p. 64:1 (2015)
8. Lei, H., Luo, G., Li, Y., Liu, J., Ye, J.: Sketch-based 3D model retrieval using attributes. IJGHPC **10**(3), 60–75 (2018)
9. Lei, Y., Zhou, Z., Zhang, P., Guo, Y., Ma, Z., Liu, L.: Deep point-to-subspace metric learning for sketch-based 3D shape retrieval. PR **96**, 106981 (2019)
10. Li, B., et al.: Shrec'13 track: large scale sketch-based 3D shape retrieval. In: 3DOR, pp. 89–96 (2013)
11. Li, B., Lu, Y., Johan, H., Fares, R.: Sketch-based 3D model retrieval utilizing adaptive view clustering and semantic information. MTA **76**(24), 26603–26631 (2017)
12. Li, B., et al.: Extended large scale sketch-based 3D shape retrieval. In: 3DOR, pp. 121–130 (2014)
13. Li, Y., Lei, H., Lin, S., Luo, G.: A new sketch-based 3D model retrieval method by using composite features. MTA **77**(2), 2921–2944 (2018)
14. Liu, A., Shi, Y., Nie, W., Su, Y.: View-based 3D model retrieval via supervised multi-view feature learning. MTA **77**(3), 3229–3243 (2018)
15. Qi, A., Song, Y., Xiang, T.: Semantic embedding for sketch-based 3D shape retrieval. In: BMVC, p. 43 (2018)
16. Qi, C.R., Su, H., Mo, K., Guibas, L.J.: Pointnet: deep learning on point sets for 3D classification and segmentation. In: IEEE CVPR, pp. 77–85 (2017)
17. Rendle, S., Freudenthaler, C., Gantner, Z., Schmidt-Thieme, L.: BPR: Bayesian personalized ranking from implicit feedback. In: UAI, pp. 452–461 (2009)
18. Schroff, F., Kalenichenko, D., Philbin, J.: Facenet: a unified embedding for face recognition and clustering. In: IEEE CVPR, pp. 815–823 (2015)
19. Su, H., Maji, S., Kalogerakis, E., Learned-Miller, E.G.: Multi-view convolutional neural networks for 3D shape recognition. In: IEEE ICCV, pp. 945–953 (2015)
20. Wang, F., Kang, L., Li, Y.: Sketch-based 3D shape retrieval using convolutional neural networks. In: IEEE CVPR, pp. 1875–1883 (2015)

21. Wang, F., Lin, S., Wu, H., Wang, R., Luo, X.: Data-driven method for sketch-based 3D shape retrieval based on user similar draw-style recommendation. In: SIGGRAPH, p. 34 (2016)
22. Xie, J., Dai, G., Zhu, F., Fang, Y.: Learning barycentric representations of 3D shapes for sketch-based 3D shape retrieval. In: IEEE CVPR, pp. 3615–3623 (2017)
23. Xie, J., Fang, Y., Zhu, F., Wong, E.K.: Deepshape: deep learned shape descriptor for 3D shape matching and retrieval. In: IEEE CVPR, pp. 1275–1283 (2015)
24. Yasseen, Z., Verroust-Blondet, A., Nasri, A.H.: View selection for sketch-based 3D model retrieval using visual part shape description. TVC **33**(5), 565–583 (2017)

Multi-objective Cuckoo Algorithm for Mobile Devices Network Architecture Search

Nan Zhang, Jianzong Wang$^{(\boxtimes)}$, Jian Yang, Xiaoyang Qu, and Jing Xiao

Ping An Technology (Shenzhen) Co., Ltd., Shenzhen, China
jzwang@188.com

Abstract. The network architecture search technique is nowadays becoming the next generation paradigm of architectural engineering, which could free experts from trials and errors while achieving state-of-the-art performances in lots of applications such as image classification and language modeling. It is immensely crucial for deploying deep networks on a wide range of mobile devices with limited computing resources to provide more flexible service. In this paper, a novel multi-objective oriented algorithm called MOCS-Net for mobile devices network architecture search is proposed. In particular, the search space is compact and flexible which leverages good virtues from efficient mobile CNNs and is block-wise constructed by different stacked blocks. Moreover, an enhanced multi-objective cuckoo algorithm is incorporated, in which mutation is achieved by Lévy flights which are performed at the block level. Experimental results suggest that MOCS-Net could find competitive neural architectures on ImageNet with a better trade-off among various competing objectives compared with other state-of-the-art methods. Meanwhile, these results show the effectiveness of proposed MOCS-Net and the promise to further the use of MOCS-Net in various deep-learning paradigms.

Keywords: Multi objective · Deep learning · Neural architecture search · Cuckoo search

1 Introduction

Deep neural networks nowadays have been widely applied in image recognition, speech recognition, language modeling, and many other applications. However, the deeper and larger models require more computing resources in spite of their better performance. It is difficult to enable real-world deployment of these state-of-the-art but large models on resource-constrained platforms such as mobile or embedded devices. To address this issue, mobile CNN models with less expensive operations and shallower networks, such as depth-wise convolution [8] and group convolution [21] have been developed. Even so, it is still challenging to balance accuracy and resource-efficiency for designing a resource-constrained

© Springer Nature Switzerland AG 2020
I. Farkaš et al. (Eds.): ICANN 2020, LNCS 12396, pp. 312–324, 2020.
https://doi.org/10.1007/978-3-030-61609-0_25

mobile model. In fact, it is a time-consuming process even for an expert who has profound domain knowledge to design appropriate networks because of various combinations of different kernel sizes and filter numbers in each layer of networks. Besides, most of the real-world deployments of models require the balance of the performance and hardware resources such as power consumption, available memory, available FLOPs, latency constraints, and etc. And it is hard to achieve the best trade-off among these multiple and conflicting objectives. In addition, the optimal network for different devices is different because of different latencies of the same operation on different devices. In other words, design different architectures case-by-case is scarcely possible in reality.

Neural architecture search (NAS) technique, which explores automating the process of designing network architectures, has achieved state-of-the-art performances in applications such as image classification and language modeling. In essence, the NAS technique consists of three main components, i.e. search space, search strategy, and performance estimation strategy. The search space consists of all possible candidate architectures which might be discovered. In early work, a relatively simple search space is defined as chain-structured neural networks [2]. Later on, the more complex search space is designed as multi-branch neural networks that incorporate additional layer types and multiple branches and skip connections [6,14]. For reducing the size of the search space, the search space is designed by repeating the same structure called cell or block [23]. Recently, an efficient and flexible search space composed of different blocks is explored [18]. Search strategy is used to search for the best architecture from the search space, such as evolutionary methods [11], reinforcement learning (RL) [1], and gradient-based methods [12]. RL methods can achieve state-of-the-art performances [15], but they are computationally expensive which usually require thousands of GPU days to find good networks. Gradient-based optimization could efficiently identify the promising architecture from a complex search space, along with reducing the time cost by orders of magnitude. However, gradient-based methods focus on the single objective of minimizing an error metric on a task and cannot be easily adapted to handle multiple conflicting objectives. Luckily, evolutionary methods could be successfully applied in both single-objective [14] and multi-objective NAS [13], in which network representation and mutation are kernels and need to be well designed.

To address the aforementioned problems, we propose a novel multi-objective NAS approach based on the cuckoo search algorithm called MOCS-Net. The contributions can be summarized as follows:

1. Designing a compact and flexible search space. Specifically, a block-wise search space with efficient mobile CNNs is designed, which overcomes the disadvantages of simply composing the same block throughout an entire network. It is significant in mobile device deployment. For further improvement of efficiency, the training process of the hyper network is one-shot and the weights of each candidate architecture are shared.
2. Employing the cuckoo algorithm to the multi-objective NAS. Concretely, an enhanced multi-objective cuckoo algorithm, which incorporates the fast

non-dominated sorting approach and the diversity preservation, is employed to seek for best trade-off architectures. Furthermore, the mutation is achieved by Lévy flights.

3. Verifying the effectiveness of MOCS-Net on the image classification task with ImageNet [5] via maximizing the classification accuracy and minimizing the inference latency, the number of parameters, and the number of floating-point operations (FLOPs). Numerical results show that MOCS-Net could find out a set of architectures that are significantly much superior to hand-crafted methods and are competitive with other state-of-the-art NAS methods. Additionally, the results also demonstrate the efficacy and potential of MOCS-Net, which explores the search space efficiently and requires less computational time than other competing methods.

2   Related Work

2.1   Single-Objective Oriented NAS

Roughly speaking, the majority of early NAS methods can fall into this category since the validation accuracy of these models is single. Basically, they could be divided into three groups according to the search strategy: reinforcement learning (RL), evolutionary algorithm (EA), and gradient-based approaches. The main idea behind RL is training a recurrent neural network controller which could generate networks. The accuracies of these generated models on a validation dataset are used as rewards for the controller [22]. Thus, better networks could be created by the controller via learning from experience over time. However, these RL approaches may be subject to bad convergence, especially when scaling is involved. EA methods search for optimal networks from the evolutionary population with mutation and crossover. The Gordian knot of the EA-based NAS is the architecture representation. Recently, individual architectures are encoded as a graph in [15], which refers to the DNA. And [11] proposes a hierarchical architecture representation method that has several motifs at different levels of hierarchy. Different from RL and EA methods that search over a discrete set of candidate architectures, the gradient-based method is applied to the continuous search space, which could be optimized with validation performance by gradient descent. The search space is extended to continuous by assigning continuous weights to the candidate operations. The gradient-based NAS achieves outstanding results as well as greatly reduces the computation resources [12]. Even so, the application of these approaches in practice is limited due to their focuses on the sole objective.

2.2   Multi-objective Oriented NAS

Deploying neural models in a wide range of settings naturally requires a multi-objective perspective. MONAS [9] is an approach for multi-objective NAS based on reinforcement learning, in which a linear combination of validation accuracy and average energy cost of the target model is used as reward functions. Mnas-Net [17], which utilizes a novel factorized hierarchical search space and reinforcement learning to find good trade-off models between accuracy and latency, is proposed for automated mobile NAS. In MnasNet, the reward is customized as the weighted product of accuracy and latency, which an easy but suboptimal strategy. Meanwhile, the multi-objective NAS based on evolution algorithms has been widely explored as well. LEMONADE [6] is a multi-objective evolutionary algorithm, which leverages good virtues from the Lamarckian inheritance mechanism to speed up the training. NSGA-Net [13] utilizes the non-dominated sorting genetic algorithm II (NSGA-II) to deal with the trade-off of NAS between classification error and computational complexity, which has more effective and efficient exploration in the search space. Similar to RL-based NAS, gradient-based NAS could be easily realized by incorporating the latency to the loss function. For instance, FBNet [18] is a differentiable NAS framework based on the gradient to handle the automated design of the hardware-aware model, where the search space is defined as a layer-wise stochastic supernet. The loss function in training this supernet is latency-aware, which is the weighted product of cross-entropy loss and the actual target device latency. DenseNAS [7] proposes a novel differentiable NAS method in which the search space is composed of densely connected blocks with different width and spatial resolution. Differently, the loss function is defined as the weighted sum of cross-entropy loss and latency-based regularization.

3   Proposed Approach

3.1   Problem Formulation

Generally speaking, the goal of multi-objective NAS is to find the model having the best trade-off among multiple and conflicting objectives. Specifically, there are four indexes, including classification accuracy, inference latency, the number of parameters and FLOPs, as optimization objectives in this work. Mathematically, this multi-objective optimization problem could be represented as follows,

$$\min_{m \in S} \quad objs(m)$$

$$\text{where} \quad objs(m) = \{(-accuary(m), latency(m), \quad\quad (1)$$
$$FLOPs(m), params(m)) \,|\, m \in S\}$$

where m is a certain model from the search space S, and the purpose is to maximize the accuracy of this model evaluated on benchmarks while minimizing its inference latency, FLOPS and number of parameters. Similar to FBNet [18] and ProxylessNAS [3], the latency of a network is the sum of the latency of each operation which is measured independently on the target device and recorded on a lookup table.

On account of the competition and confliction of these objectives, there is no single solution that could optimize each objective simultaneously without any concession. In such an optimization problem, a feasible solution x_1 is said to dominate another solution x_2 if and only if no objective of solution x_1 is worse than solution x_2 and at least one objective is more superior. A solution is called Pareto optimal if there is no other solutions that dominate it. The set of Pareto optimal solutions is often defined as the Pareto front. In a sense, the NAS could be regarded as a multi-objective optimization problem as well. The goal of this work is to find an architecture on the Pareto front in the search space S.

3.2   Search Space

In many studies, a common approach to define a search space is to design a few complex cells and then repeatedly stack the same cells. And architecture search aims to find a well-performance cell structure. However, complicated and fragmented cells usually have high latency when deploying to mobile CPUs. Besides, cells at different layers may have different influences on the accuracy and latency of the overall network even though they are the same here. In consideration of both accuracy and latency, the diversity of cells is permitted in some works. Likewise, it is allowed in this work that architectures could be different in different blocks via searching operations and connections of each block separately to achieve both high accuracy and lower latency.

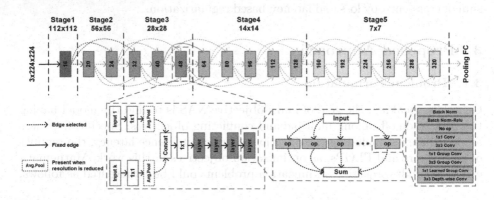

Fig. 1. Diagram of the search space designed in this paper. Solid lines indicate present components in every architecture while dashed lines indicate optional components.

In general, the search space in this work is block-wise which is constructed by different blocks. As shown in Fig. 1, the search space is composed of several connected blocks with different input resolutions and filter sizes. Each block will be connected with several subsequent blocks. And the input to a given block will be one output of the three most recent previous blocks. Since earlier stages of a model usually process larger amounts of data and thus have a much higher impact on inference latency than later stages, the input resolution in each block will decrease gradually while the filter size will increase corresponding. Meanwhile, this hyper network could be partitioned into several stages according to the different filter sizes and the same input resolution. Earlier stages will have a relatively small growing stride of the filter size but later stages will have larger ones. For example, the input resolution in stage 3 is 28×28 and the growing stride of the filter size is 8, but they will change to 7×7 and 32, respectively, in stage 5.

In each block, different inputs been followed by a 1×1 convolution are concatenated together. Once the resolution decreased, the average pooling will be applied. After that, there is the concatenation which will be always followed by a 1×1 convolution as well. Then, the result will be input to the next several stacked layers. It is worth noting that this hyper network will obtain all different inputs which are concatenated together at training time. Nevertheless, the network containing any combination of the incoming connections could be simulated by zeroing out or removing the other incoming connections from the trained hyper network. In this way, the size of the search space grows linearly only concerning the number of incoming skip-connections.

All candidate operations are included in each layer, the results of which will be added up. Similarly, some of these operations will be zeroed out or removed from the network during the evaluation process. The hyper network utilizes hand-crafted efficient operations to take advantage of human prior knowledge for designing efficient CNNs like group convolution, learned group convolution and depth-wise convolution. Besides, batch normalization, batch normalization ReLU and no operation are available operations in layers as well. Although each operation might be one of nine candidates, we could also emulate a layer containing a certain operation via removing other operations from the network without retraining weights.

3.3   Search Algorithm

Cuckoo search is a relatively new nature-inspired metaheuristic algorithms developed by [19] based on the brood parasitism of cuckoos, which has many advantages such as fast convergence, diversity in distribution of solutions, exploitation as well as exploration. In the original multi-objective cuckoo search algorithm (MOCS) [20], there are following three ideal assumptions: (1) Each cuckoo will lay K eggs at a time and dumps it in a randomly selected nest; (2) The best nests with high-quality eggs will carry over to the next generations; (3) Each nest will be abandoned with a probability $p_a \in (0,1)$ and a new nest with K eggs will be built. In our multi-objective NAS problem, each nest represents a network, multiple eggs in the nest represents the multiple objectives of the network.

Lévy Flights: Lévy flights play an important role in both exploration and exploitation in cuckoo search. Lévy flights essentially provide a random walk while the random step length is drawn from a Lévy distribution. The Lévy distribution requires a large probability to fall in the place where the value is

---

Algorithm 1. Mutation

Input: Current nest $nest_i^t$
Output: New cuckoo $nest_i^{t+1}$

1: Let $n = 1$, $S = \text{Lévy}(\beta)$
2: **while** $n < S$ or $n < \text{len}(nest_i^t)$ **do**
3:     $nest_i^{t+1} = \text{Replace}(nest_i^{t+1}, nest_{\text{random}}^t)$
4:     $n = n + 1$
5: **end while**
6: **return** $nest_i^{t+1}$

---

relatively small, and a small probability to fall in the place where the value is relatively large. One of the most efficient yet straightforward ways of applying Lévy flights is the so-called Mantegna's algorithm. In Mantegna's algorithm, the step length S is calculated by

$$S = \frac{u}{|v|^{\frac{1}{\beta}}} \tag{2}$$

where u and v are random values which are drawn from normal distributions, i.e.

$$u \sim \mathcal{N}(0, \sigma_u^2), \qquad v \sim \mathcal{N}(0, \sigma_v^2) \tag{3}$$

$$\sigma_u = \left[\frac{\Gamma(\beta + 1) \sin(\frac{\pi\beta}{2})}{\Gamma(\frac{\beta+1}{2})\beta 2^{(\frac{\beta-1}{2})}} \right]^{\frac{1}{\beta}}, \quad \sigma_v = 1 \tag{4}$$

Here Γ is the standard Gamma function, β is the variance which controls distribution by $\beta \in [1,2]$ and considered to be 1.5 here, σ_u is the standard deviation which is used to calculate the step size of the random walk. Some studies have shown that Lévy flights can maximize the efficiency of searching in an uncertain space.

Mutation by Lévy Flights: The Lévy flights are utilized to generate new cuckoos (different network architectures), which will enhance the diversity of the population and the ability to escape from local optimums. Lévy flights guarantee a reasonable balance between local and global evolution. The search space in this work is stacked different blocks with different input resolutions and filter sizes. The mutation of the current network is achieved by replacing with the block having the same filter size from other networks, and the number of the replaced blocks is determined by the step length S of Lévy flight. For example, if $S = 3$ and the current network has more than 3 blocks, then the new network is generated by replacing 3 blocks of current network. The pseudo-code of mutation is presented in Algorithm 1, where $nest_i^t$ represents the ith nest in tth generation and $nest_i^{t+1}$ is the next generation at current position. $\text{Replace}(nest_i^t, nest_{\text{best}}^t)$ is a function that can randomly replace a block of $nest_i^t$ with the one of randomly selected $nest_{\text{random}}^t$.

Discovery: The cuckoo eggs that are lodged with every nest can be discovered with a probability p_a, which causes these nests will be abandoned and new nests with K eggs will be built. The cuckoo eggs that have not been found remain as they are to keep the number of the population. Some random changes can be used to generate diversity,

$$nest_i^{t+1} = \begin{cases} nest_i^t & \text{if} \quad rand < p_a \\ \text{change}(nest_i^t) & \text{if} \quad rand > p_a \end{cases} \tag{5}$$

where $\text{change}(nest_i^t)$ is a function that built new nest $nest_i^{t+1}$ near the abandoned nest $nest_i^t$ and $rand$ is a random number in $[0, 1]$. This process is implemented by enabling or disabling incoming connections of a block and randomly modifying an operation of all layers in this block. Notice that only one block will be selected in each generation.

Sort the Population: To reduce computational complexity of considering K eggs for each cuckoo, we use the fast non-dominated sorting approach and the crowding distance to sort the population, which is useful in the evolutionary multi-objective optimization such as NSGAII [4].

The proposed multi-objective cuckoo search can be summarized in Algorithm 2. Initialize the algorithm parameters consisting of the discovering probability p_a, the number of *population* P, and the maximum number of iterations C as the stopping criterion. Particularly, *population* set is initialized by trained architectures that selected from the search space randomly with the same probability. The update *population* in each generation will be recorded in *history*. Repeat the above procedures until the number of iterations is greater than C. And the Pareto optimal front will be chosen from the *history*.

Algorithm 2. Multi-objective cuckoo search algorithm

Parameter: discovering probability p_a, maximum of iterations C

1: Generate an initial *population* of n host nests (*model*) and each with K eggs (*objects*)
2: Evaluate and sort the *population*
3: **while** next generation$<$C **do**
4:    Keep the best $N/2$ elites of the *population* and generate N new child nests from elites by mutation
5:    Combine the parent and child nests and sort the $2N$ nests
6:    Keep the best N as new generation
7:    Build N new *nest* randomly with the discovery probability p_a
8:    Sort the $2N$ nests and keep the best N as new generation
9: **end while**
10: **return** The Pareto optimal front from *population*

---

4 Experiments

4.1 Setup and Implementation Details

Dataset: Generally speaking, the experiment conducted on large tasks like ImageNet is time and resource consuming. Some previous researches use small proxy tasks such as CIFAR-10 to verify the effect of promising models. Then the architectures are transferred to ImageNet by modification on the number of repeated cells. However, those small proxy tasks probably do not work because the structure of each block in our work is different. The other two approaches of searching architecture on the ImageNet are sampling fewer data and setting fewer training steps. In this paper, we randomly sample 20% data from the ImageNet as the validation dataset. and the remaining part is used for training. The original validation dataset of ImageNet is only used for testing the final searched architecture. The search process runs only 10 epoches in total.

Hyper-Parameters: To finish training our model, we also need to determine some hyper-parameters, i.e. parameters in the training process and the cuckoo search algorithm. Detailed hyper-parameters are shown in Table 1.

Table 1. Values of hyper-parameters

Item	Value	Item	Value
batch size	16	optimizer	Adam
epoch	10	population	100
dropout	0.5	generation	20
learning rate	0.001–0.00001	probability (p_a)	0.5

Training Hyper Network: The hyper network is a standard huge neural network that contained all candidate networks in search space. The specific architecture could be emulated by zeroing out the other options such as inputs and operations that no need for retraining weights at evaluation time. Actually, removing any component even an unimportant one from the network may lead to reduced accuracy of predictions and reduced correlations between the hyper network and the stand-alone model. To avoid this issue, path dropout is added in training. Besides, the learning rate is a linear schedule.

Model Selection and Retraining: Once the hyper network is trained, the cuckoo search algorithm will be employed to select the best trade-off architectures. The performance of each architecture could be evaluated on a hold-out validation set by sharing the weights of the hyper network. After completing the search, the selected Pareto optimal architectures will be retrained from scratch with tuned hyper parameters as a post-processing step.

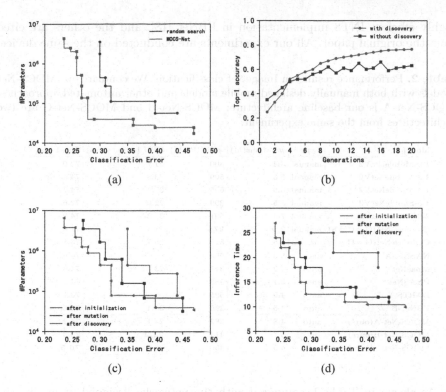

Fig. 2. (a) Pareto frontiers comparison between random search and MOCS-Net.(b) Generational comparison of the offspring network architectures with and without discovery process. (c) and (d) Pareto frontiers comparison with each stage of MOCS-Net.

4.2 Result

The trade-off frontier comparison with MOCS-Net and random search is presented in Fig. 2(a), which shows that MOCS-Net could find a much better set of network architectures compared to random search. After analyzing the benefits of the two main stages of MOCS-Net, i.e. mutation and discovery, Fig. 2(b) shows the top-1 accuracy of two main stages through the different generations of the population. Both stages are conducive to the discovery of better models over the generations while the discovery balances the global and local search to ensure the monotonic increase of the metrics. The progress of MOCS-Net in the objective-space is visualized in Fig. 2(c) and 2(d), clearly showing the Pareto frontiers obtained by various stages of the search gradually improve.

The results of our model on ImageNet classification compared with some state-of-the-art efficient models that designed automatically or manually are shown in Table 2. The metrics we concerned are parameter size, FLOP count, latency and top-1 accuracy, of which we cite latency measured using Caffe2 with highly efficient INT8 implementation in FBNet [18], and the others are cited from the original paper. All our experiments are conducted on the same device.

Table 2. Performance results on ImageNet classification. We compare our MOCS-Net models with both manually designed mobile models and other automated approaches. MOCS-Net-A is our baseline architecture; MOCS-Net-B and MOCS-Net-C are two architectures from the same experiment.

Model	Type	#Params(M)	#FLOPs(M)	CPU Latency(ms)	Top-1 acc(%)
1.0-MobileNetV2	manual	3.4	300	21.7	72.0
1.3-MobileNetV2	manual	5.3	509	33.8	74.4
1.4-MobileNetV2	manual	6.9	585	37.4	74.7
1.5-ShuffleNetV2	manual	3.5	299	22.0	72.6
2.0-ShuffleNetV2	manual	7.4	591	33.3	74.9
ConsenseNet($G = C = 8$)	manual	**2.9**	**274**	28.4	71.0
ConsenseNet($G = C = 4$)	manual	4.8	529	28.7	73.8
NASNet-A	auto	5.3	564	–	74.0
MnasNet	auto	4.2	317	23.7	74.0
PNASNet	auto	5.1	588	–	74.2
DARTS	auto	4.9	595	–	73.1
FBNet-B	auto	4.5	295	23.1	74.1
MOCS-Net-A(ours)	auto	4.8	383	24.1	74.2
MOCS-Net-B(ours)	auto	5.7	414	**21.2**	75.3
MOCS-Net-C(ours)	auto	6.5	456	26.6	**76.5**

As shown in Table 2, compared with the networks designed manually, the proposed MOCS-Net architectures achieve significantly outstanding accuracy. MOCS-Net-C achieves 76.5% top-1 accuracy, better than 1.4-MobileNetV2 [16] (+1.8%) with lower latency (−10.8 ms, relative 28.9%). MOCS-Net-B achieves 75.3% top-1 accuracy with 21.2 ms latency and 5.7M parameters/414M FLOPs, which means higher accuracy, a lot fewer FLOPs and lower latency comparing with NASNet-A [23], PNASNet [10] and DARTS [12].

5   Conclusion

In this paper, a novel resource-efficient model automated designing approach called MOCS-Net for mobile devices is proposed, which aims to search for Pareto optimal architectures among various competing objectives. MOCS-Net leverages virtues from both the cuckoo algorithm and the neural architecture search technique. Specifically, a compact and flexible search space with efficient mobile CNNs is designed which is suitable for mobile device deployment. The search space is block-wise which is constructed by different blocks rather than the same ones. For improvement of efficiency, the hyper network is one-shot trained and each candidate architecture could share weights. Moreover, an enhanced multi-objective cuckoo search algorithm that incorporates the fast non-dominated sorting approach and diversity preservation is employed to search for the best trade-off architectures. Thereinto, the mutation is achieved by Lévy flights which are performed at the block level.

Experimental results on ImageNet suggest that MOCS-Net could find out competitive neural architectures with a better trade-off among various competing objectives compared with other state-of-the-art methods. Apparently, the networks found by MOCS-Net have significantly outstanding accuracy compared with manually designed networks. Further, MOCS-Net also has higher accuracy and a lot fewer FLOPs and lower latency in the comparison with other NAS methods including NASNet-A, PNASNet, and DARTS. Additionally, the search process of MOCS-Net takes about 4 GPU days which is much faster than most NAS methods. These results demonstrate the effectiveness of our proposed MOCS-Net and the promise to further use of MOCS-Net in various deep-learning paradigms.

Acknowledgement. This paper is supported by National Key Research and Development Program of China under grant No. 2018YFB1003500, No. 2018YFB0204400 and No. 2017YFB1401202. Corresponding author is Jianzong Wang from Ping An Technology (Shenzhen) Co., Ltd.

References

1. Baker, B., Gupta, O., Naik, N., Raskar, R.: Designing neural network architectures using reinforcement learning. In: 5th International Conference on Learning Representations, April 2017
2. Cai, H., Chen, T., Zhang, W., Yu, Y., Wang, J.: Efficient architecture search by network transformation. In: Proceedings of the Thirty-Second AAAI Conference on Artificial Intelligence, pp. 2787–2794 (2018)
3. Cai, H., Zhu, L., Han, S.: ProxylessNAS: direct neural architecture search on target task and hardware. In: 7th International Conference on Learning Representations, May 2019
4. Deb, K., Pratap, A., Agarwal, S., Meyarivan, T.: A fast and elitist multiobjective genetic algorithm: NSGA-II. IEEE Trans. Evol. Comput. **6**(2), 182–197 (2002)
5. Deng, J., Dong, W., Socher, R., Li, L.J., Li, K., Fei-Fei, L.: Imagenet: a large-scale hierarchical image database. In: 2009 IEEE Conference on Computer Vision and Pattern Recognition, pp. 248–255. IEEE (2009)
6. Elsken, T., Metzen, J.H., Hutter, F.: Efficient multi-objective neural architecture search via Lamarckian evolution. In: 7th International Conference on Learning Representations, May 2019
7. Fang, J., Sun, Y., Zhang, Q., Li, Y., Liu, W., Wang, X.: Densely connected search space for more flexible neural architecture search. arXiv preprint arXiv:1906.09607 (2019)
8. Howard, A.G., et al.: Mobilenets: efficient convolutional neural networks for mobile vision applications. arXiv preprint arXiv:1704.04861 (2017)
9. Hsu, C.H., et al.: Monas: multi-objective neural architecture search using reinforcement learning. arXiv preprint arXiv:1806.10332 (2018)
10. Liu, C., et al.: Progressive neural architecture search. In: Proceedings of the European Conference on Computer Vision (ECCV), pp. 19–34 (2018)
11. Liu, H., Simonyan, K., Vinyals, O., Fernando, C., Kavukcuoglu, K.: Hierarchical representations for efficient architecture search. In: 6th International Conference on Learning Representations, May 2018

12. Liu, H., Simonyan, K., Yang, Y.: DARTS: differentiable architecture search. In: 7th International Conference on Learning Representations, May 2019
13. Lu, Z., et al.: NSGA-Net: neural architecture search using multi-objective genetic algorithm. In: Proceedings of the Genetic and Evolutionary Computation Conference, pp. 419–427. ACM (2019)
14. Real, E., Aggarwal, A., Huang, Y., Le, Q.V.: Regularized evolution for image classifier architecture search. In: Proceedings of the Thirty-Third AAAI Conference on Artificial Intelligence, pp. 4780–4789 (2019)
15. Real, E., et al.: Large-scale evolution of image classifiers. In: Proceedings of the 34th International Conference on Machine Learning, vol. 70, pp. 2902–2911 (2017)
16. Sandler, M., Howard, A., Zhu, M., Zhmoginov, A., Chen, L.C.: Mobilenetv 2: Inverted residuals and linear bottlenecks. In: Proceedings of the IEEE Conference on Computer Vision and Pattern Recognition, pp. 4510–4520 (2018)
17. Tan, M., et al.: Mnasnet: platform-aware neural architecture search for mobile. In: Proceedings of the IEEE Conference on Computer Vision and Pattern Recognition, pp. 2820–2828 (2019)
18. Wu, B., et al.: Fbnet: hardware-aware efficient convnet design via differentiable neural architecture search. In: Proceedings of the IEEE Conference on Computer Vision and Pattern Recognition, pp. 10734–10742 (2019)
19. Yang, X.S., Deb, S.: Cuckoo search via Lévy flights. In: 2009 World Congress on Nature & Biologically Inspired Computing (NaBIC), pp. 210–214. IEEE (2009)
20. Yang, X.S., Deb, S.: Multiobjective cuckoo search for design optimization. Comput. Oper. Res. 40(6), 1616–1624 (2013)
21. Zhang, X., Zhou, X., Lin, M., Sun, J.: Shufflenet: an extremely efficient convolutional neural network for mobile devices. In: Proceedings of the IEEE Conference on Computer Vision and Pattern Recognition, pp. 6848–6856 (2018)
22. Zoph, B., Le, Q.V.: Neural architecture search with reinforcement learning. In: 5th International Conference on Learning Representations, April 2017
23. Zoph, B., Vasudevan, V., Shlens, J., Le, Q.V.: Learning transferable architectures for scalable image recognition. In: Proceedings of the IEEE Conference on Computer Vision and Pattern Recognition, pp. 8697–8710 (2018)

DeepED: A Deep Learning Framework for Estimating Evolutionary Distances

Zhuangzhuang Liu, Mingming Ren, Zhiheng Niu, Gang Wang$^{(\boxtimes)}$, and Xiaoguang Liu$^{(\boxtimes)}$

College of Computer Science, Nankai University, Tianjin, China
{liuzhuangzhuang,rmingming,nzh,wgzwp,liuxg}@nbjl.nankai.edu.cn

Abstract. Evolutionary distances refer to the number of substitutions per site in two aligned nucleotide or amino acid sequences, which reflect divergence time and are much significant for phylogenetic inferences. In the past several decades, lots of molecular evolution models have been proposed for evolutionary distance estimation. Most of these models are designed under more or less assumptions and some assumptions are in good agreement with some real-world data but not all. To relax these assumptions and improve accuracies in evolutionary distance estimation, this paper proposes a framework containing Deep Neural Networks (DNNs), called DeepED (Deep learning method to estimate Evolutionary Distances), to estimate evolutionary distances for aligned DNA sequence pairs. The purposely designed structure in this framework enables it to handle long and variable length sequences as well as to find important segments in a sequence. The models of the network are trained with reliable data from real world which includes highly credible phylogenetic inferences. Experimental results demonstrate that DeepED models achieve a accuracy up to 0.98 (R-Squared), which outperforms traditional methods.

Keywords: Evolutionary distance · Deep learning · Molecular evolution · Convolutional neural networks

1 Introduction

Evolutionary distances are significant for divergence time estimation and phylogenetic inferences. Traditional methods of evolutionary distance estimation are designed under some assumptions and based on one or more mathematical models such as a Markov process [1]. These traditional methods can not perform well on all data and sometimes the researchers must take the time to figure out the best method for specific data [2,3].

This work is partially supported by National Science Foundation of China (U1833114, 61872201, 61702521) and Science and Technology Development Plan of Tianjin (18ZXZNGX00140, 18ZXZNGX00200).
Z. Liu and M. Ren—These authors contributed equally to this work.

© Springer Nature Switzerland AG 2020
I. Farkaš et al. (Eds.): ICANN 2020, LNCS 12396, pp. 325–336, 2020.
https://doi.org/10.1007/978-3-030-61609-0_26

This work aims to lighten over-reliance on assumptions and to improve accuracies in evolutionary distance estimation by designing a framework based on deep neural networks. The framework is called DeepED, and an overview of it is illustrated in Fig. 1. The networks in the framework are convolutional neural networks [4], i.e. CNNs, consisting of two subnetworks, the dist-net and the weight-net, detailed in Sect. 3.1. A technique similar to attention mechanism [5,6] is applied in the weight-net. One-hot encoding is used to encode DNA sequences and sliding window method to handle long and variable length sequences. The datasets for training the network models are from the results of highly credible phylogenetic inferences, including lots of extra support, e.g., sufficient fossil calibrations and wide recognition. Experimental results show the effectiveness of the framework. The major contributions of the work are summarized as follows:

- A framework based on deep neural networks for evolutionary distance estimation.
- Verification of the effectiveness of the proposed framework by experiments on real-world data.
- An efficient implementation and some optimizations for training the network models.

The remainder of this paper is organized as follows. Section 2 discusses related work. The details of our proposed framework are illustrated in Sect. 3. Then in Sect. 4, the experimental results and respective analysis are presented. Finally, Sect. 5 concludes this paper.

2   Related Work

A lot of methods to estimate evolutionary distances have been proposed for decades. The oldest and simplest method, p-distance merely treats the proportion of different sites between the two nucleotide sequences as the evolutionary distance. However, it is well known that more than once substitution (multiple hits) may occur at a site in evolutionary history, and for this reason, p-distance usually underestimates evolutionary distances. Jukes-Cantor distance [1] attempts to correct the bias caused by multiple hits, in which Markov models are firstly introduced into evolutionary distance estimation. The formula of Jukes-Cantor distance is:

$$d = -\frac{3}{4} \ln\left(1 - \frac{4}{3}p\right) \tag{1}$$

where p is the result given by p-distance and d is the corrected distance. Obviously, Jukes-Cantor distance is invalid when $p > 0.75$, which means it can not calculate the distance of a sequence pair with more than 75% different sites.

The both aforementioned methods assume that four nucleotides, i.e. adenine (A), cytosine (C), guanine (G), and thymine (T), are substituted with an equal rate, but this assumption is not in line with the facts observed in real data. In real-world DNA sequences, the frequencies of the four nucleotides are not always 0.25. Unequal substitution rates among four nucleotides are firstly taken account

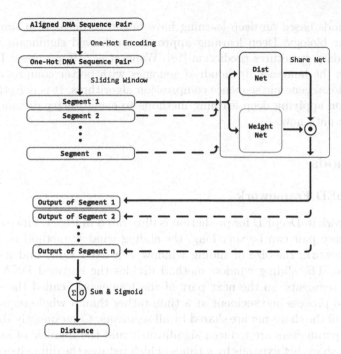

Fig. 1. Overview of the proposed framework for prediction.

into the estimation by Tajima-Nei distance [7], based on a more complicated model that allows 4 nucleotides have different proportions when the substitution process reaches equilibrium. Kimura 2-parameter distance [8] differentiates two types of substitutions, i.e. transitional substitutions and transversional substitutions, due to the former occur much more often than the latter in real-world data. Tamura 3-parameter distance [9] relies on a model which focuses on the GC content for the reason that the proportions of nucleotides G and C differ in DNA sequences, not always around 0.5.

All of the above methods assume substitution rates across sites are equal, that is, all sites are treated equally. Gamma distance [10,11] relaxes this assumption and holds a view that substitution rates across sites satisfy a gamma distribution. It is often used in conjunction with the other methods mentioned above. A number of similar methods have been proposed. Most of them are based on various assumptions and proven in practice that their performance varies from data to data, and consequently some methods to select the best evolutionary distance method for specific data were proposed [2,3].

Deep neural networks are popular machine learning methods nowadays, which have been widely used in computer vision [4,12,13], natural language processing [4,14,15] and many other fields, significantly surpassing the performance of some traditional methods. At the same time, deep neural networks are also general methods which are proven in theory that deep neural networks have the ability to fit arbitrary functions with arbitrary precision [16,17]. In recent years, methods based on deep learning have begun to be used in some studies of molecular biology. Deep learning approaches achieved significant results in RNA secondary structures prediction [18]. Wang *et al.* [19] proposed DeepDNA to compress the human mitochondrial genomes with better compression ratios than traditional genomic sequence compression algorithms. It is regrettable that no studies on applying deep learning methods to evolutionary distance estimation appear until now.

3   Methods

3.1   DeepED Framework

The framework in DeepED for prediction is illustrated in Fig. 1. Since an aligned DNA sequence pair can be very long, the sliding window method is used here. In the framework, the size of sliding window is a fixed value and its stride is half the size. The sliding window method divides the encoded DNA sequence pair into n segments, so the next part of the framework, called the share-net, only need to process one segment at a time rather than a whole sequence. The parameters of the share-net are shared by all segments. Consequently the amount of network parameters are reduced significantly and the number of samples for training the share-net expands by n times, which reduces the difficulty of training the models. Furthermore, the sliding window method enables the framework to accept variable-length sequences.

As shown in the framework, the share-net consists of two subnetworks, the dist-net and the weight-net. The internal structures of the two are shown in Table 1. Both of them take a segment of the DNA sequence pair as input, but the dist-net outputs a value related to the distance from the segment while the weight-net outputs a weight value ranging from 0 to 1, which means the contribution of the segment to the evolutionary distance among all segments. The output of the share-net is the product of the outputs of the dist-net and the weight-net. The designing of the weight-net is inspired by attention mechanism in neural networks for tasks of computer vision and natural language processing, which prompts neural networks to focus on some important areas of data and ignore other areas. In this work, attention mechanism helps the framework achieve performance and improve its interpretability. In the sequel, the weight-net is expected to output relatively high weights for the segments which are important for the distance of a whole sequence pair. In the final part of the framework, the outputs of the share-net of all segments are summed and then a sigmoid function is used to limit the predictive value of distance to $[0, 1]$.

The dist-net is a classic convolutional neural network with four convolutional layers connecting to three fully connected layers. 2D convolution and 1D convolution are used successively to adapt to different shapes of layer inputs and average-pooling with size of 2 is used to perform downsampling after every two convolutional layers. Practice shows that the configurations of the first two convolutional layers are critical for the performance of the dist-net.

Table 1. Configuration of the layers in the two subnetworks.

Dist-net	Weight-net
1 × 1 conv_2d, 32	1 × 1 conv_2d, 32
6 × 2 conv_2d, 32	3 × 3 conv_2d, 32
average_pool 2	average_pool 4
3 conv_1d, 64	5 conv_1d, 64
3 conv_1d, 64	5 conv_1d, 64
average_pool 2	average_pool 4
fc 1024	global average pooling
fc 128	1 conv_1d, 1
fc 1	softmax(across segments)

The weight-net is a fully convolutional network [20], i.e., all layers in it are convolutional layers. With more convolutions than the dist-net, it is designed to extract features at different levels to differentiate the importances of different segments for distance estimation. The final output of the weight-net, namely the weight for each segment, is generated by a softmax operating across all segments.

3.2   Datasets Building

An important thing before training the deep neural networks is to convert aligned DNA sequences to appropriate digital representations. One-hot encoding is an efficient way for processing DNA sequences, which has been widely used in previous work about applications of machine learning in molecular biology. One-hot encoding is a kind of binary representation for category features, which uses n-bit binary number to encode n categories and embeds the features to the Euclidean space and therefore encodes characters in DNA sequences without bias.

One-hot encoding is still used in our work, however, differing from some previous work in which only the four types of nucleotides A, C, G and T are encoded, the gap and missing in a sequence are also included here. In most aligned DNA sequences from real world, there are not only A, C, G and T in sequences but also pervasive gap and missing for a variety of reasons. To utilize these real-world data in the work, the gap and missing in aligned DNA sequences must be taken into account. Discarding gap and missing leads to very bad performance, which was shown in an early framework. With A, C, G, T, gap and missing, there are six categories of characters in an aligned DNA sequence.

Aiming to output evolutionary distances directly, the network model is a supervised regression model, thus a sample here is composed of feature x and label y. In this work, the feature x is an encoded DNA sequence pair, and the label y is the evolutionary distance of the sequence pair. All the evolutionary distances of sequence pairs are extracted from the phylogenetic trees included in the two datasets described above and are treated as the ground truth.

A single DNA sequence will be encoded into a $6 \times n\_site$ matrix, here n_site is the length of sequences. Consequently a sequence pair is encoded into two such matrices like an image with a width of n_site, height of 6 and channel of 2. That is to say, a sequence pair are encoded into an image-like format with two channels as the feature x. Due to the great success of deep learning especially convolutional neural networks in the field of computer vision, the way that a DNA sequence pair is converted into the format of an image makes it convenient to use some successful deep learning techniques from computer vision off the shelf.

A dataset containing m DNA sequences will generate m^2 samples after processed since there are m^2 sequences pairs. An example to illustrate the details of this procedure: supposing a tiny dataset only contains two DNA sequences denoted as a and b, four samples will be generated, i.e., (a, a), (a, b), (b, a), (b, b), and note that none of them are redundancy. A sample with two identical sequences such as (a, a) or (b, b) is valid, and its label y is set to be zero. And (a, b) and (b, a) are treated as two different samples even they share the same label y. As described above, in a sample (a, b), the information of sequence a is placed in the first channel, and the information of sequence b in the second channel. The situation of sample (b, a) is the opposite. Training with the samples such as (a, a) or (b, b) makes the network models output a close to zero distance when it handles two slightly different sequences, which is consistent with most traditional methods. Meanwhile, the samples with the same label y such as (a, b) and (b, a) help the network models ignore the order of two sequences in a pair, which follows the time reversible theory in evolutionary distance estimation.

When a dataset is split into the training set and the test set, it should be guaranteed that any two samples such as (a, b) and (b, a) must be divided into the same set. In other words, it is impossible that sample (a, b) is in the training set and sample (b, a) in the test set. Otherwise the network models would cause fake good predictions on samples in the test set. In the case that the models are trained with sample (a, b) in the training set and overfitting happens, the models remember the label of sample (a, b) and then easily give the same prediction on sample (b, a) in the test set which seems to be a misleading good result. Dividing sample (a, b) and sample (b, a) into the same set prevents this risk.

3.3   Training and Optimization

As predicting of distance is a supervised regression task, the Huber loss [21] is selected for the loss of the whole network. Compared with the squared error loss which is used more often in regression tasks, the Huber loss is not susceptible to outliers in the samples especially those with large distances, which adds more robust to the training of DeepED models and improves the accuracies on samples with small distances.

We choose tensorflow platform to build DeepED framework. To improve efficiency in the training phase, some techniques are used. Since the original sequences are usually very long and one-hot encoding makes them even bigger, the size of a single sample is quite large. Building static samples on disk is almost impossible since those samples would occupy extremely huge storage space. In addition, feeding huge samples is inefficient for training network models, because transferring samples with huge size from disk to GPU memory severely hurts the performance. For this problem and considering the characteristics of platform, the deep learning platform we use, we adopt a dynamic sample generating strategy. In this strategy, the original sequences are loaded in memory only once before the training process starts. When a sample is requested in a training epoch, the generator assembles the two sequences into a sequence pair, performs one-hot encoding on it, and then feeds it to the training process. Moreover, one-hot encoding is part of the tensorflow graph and implemented by the tensorflow builtin operating, so it is quite efficient.

The optimizer of the network training is Adam [22] with an adaptive learning rate. The Xavier initializer [23] helps the network models start training at a good parameter initialization. L_2 regularization also used to reduce the risk of overfitting and to maintain stability of training.

4   Experiments

4.1   Datasets Introduction

Two datasets are used in the experiments of this work. The first dataset is a relatively new and credible phylogenetic inference about living primates [24], which was constructed in 2009. In the inference of its phylogenetic tree, 54 nuclear genes were used and the final length of sequences is 34927bp after aligned by MAFFT software [25]. This dataset contains 191 nuclear DNA sequences from different taxa, in which 186 nuclear DNA sequences are from primates in 61 genera covering around 90% diversity of living primates. BEAST software [26] was used by the authors to estimate the phylogeny with GTR+I+G model of DNA substitution. At the same time, nine widely recognized fossil calibration points were used for correction in the inference. In the final phylogenetic tree, 88% of the nodes have a bootstrap value over 90%, and the phylogenetic tree is in line with lots of previous hypothesis and inferences. The authors claimed that this dataset solved the problem of insufficient data in primates phylogenetic inference and a strong phylogenetic tree about living primates was constructed via their inference and correction.

The second dataset is about phylogenetic inference of ray-finned fishes' genomes [27], which was constructed in 2018. There are 305 genome-scale DNA sequences in this dataset, and the length of the aligned sequences is 555288bp. The software used for its phylogenetic inference is ASTRAL-II [28] and the selected substitution model is GTR+G. Compared with the first dataset, up to 34 fossil calibration points were used more widely in this inference. In the final phylogenetic tree, the nodes with 100% bootstrap values occupy over 80% of the total.

As mentioned above, both of the two datasets chosen in this work have high accuracies, and are not just the results of any models or algorithms, in which the phylogenetic trees were very carefully verified and corrected. Training with

Table 2. Information of the two datasets.

Information	Dataset	
	Primates	Ray-finned fishes
Building date	2009	2018
Number of taxa	191	305
Sequence length	34927	555288
Substitution model	GTR+I+G	GTR+G
Fossil calibration	9	34

such datasets of high quality helps the network models give better evolutionary distances of DNA sequence pairs than traditional methods. The details of the two datasets are listed in Table 2.

4.2 Models Training

There are 191 and 305 sequences in the two datasets, Primates and Ray-finned fishes respectively, thus the number of samples generated by the first dataset is $191^2 = 36481$ and the second is $305^2 = 93025$. After one-hot encoded, the samples of each dataset are split into the training set and the test set by 4:1 randomly under the restriction described in Sect. 3.2.

Due to different distance scales of the two datasets, merging the two datasets into one and using it to training models would cause much instability. Consequently, we train models based on the two training sets independently. The size of sliding window in DeepED framework is set to 1000, and then two models based on the two training sets are trained for 10 epochs and 35 epochs respectively to minimize training losses.

4.3 Accuracies Evaluation

Two models of DeepED are obtained after training the two datasets independently. Distances of sequence pairs in the test sets of the two datasets are predicted by our models as well as calculated by a series of traditional evolutionary distance estimation methods as baselines.

SMAPE (Symmetric Mean Absolute Percentage Error) and R-Squared (Coefficient of Determination) are chosen as metrics to measure and compare the accuracies between the results of DeepED models and the traditional methods. We use a toolkit provided by the software Mega 7.0 [29] to calculate the evolutionary distances of pairwise DNA sequences using traditional methods.

Five traditional methods, p-distance, jukes-cantor distance, tajima-nei distance, Kimura 2-parameter distance and Tamura 3-parameter distance, are applied to the test sets with proper configures as baselines. Table 3 shows the accuracies of DeepED models as well as the baselines. Obviously, the accuracies of DeepED models is significantly higher than the five traditional methods

Table 3. Accuracies on test sets using the DeepED models and traditional methods.

Method	Accuracy			
	Primates		Ray-finned fishes	
	SMAPE	R-Squared	SMAPE	R-Squared
P-dist	0.0067	0.8639	0.0559	−1.3245
Jukes-cantor	0.0023	0.9534	0.0103	0.5729
Tajima-nei	0.0023	0.9539	0.0101	0.5801
Kimura-2	0.0022	0.9557	0.0092	0.6164
Tamura-3	0.0021	0.9565	0.0090	0.6231
DeepED	**0.0009**	**0.9820**	**0.0022**	**0.9089**

under the both metrics on the two test sets. Especially in the test set of Ray-finned fishes, the accuracies of DeepED models exceeds the baselines by a large margin. High accuracies of DeepED models on test sets indicate that DeepED models have learned evolutionary distances from pairwise DNA sequences. As mentioned above, a large number of fossil calibrations were used to the phylogenetic inference of Ray-finned fishes dataset, thus we hold a view that DeepED models learns more reliable evolutionary distances than traditional methods so they perform better on such datasets.

We use a new dataset about Hemiptera [30] to demonstrate the generalization performance of the two models. As shown in Table 4, although the accuracies of the two models on Hemiptera dataset are lower than accuracies on their own test sets, the two models still show high accuracies (model based on Primates have higher accuracies than all traditional methods). This indicates a certain degree of generalization performance of DeepED models.

Table 4. Accuracies on Hemiptera dataset using the two DeepED models and traditional methods

Method	Accuracy	
	SMAPE	R-Squared
P-dist	0.0176	0.8214
Jukes-cantor	0.0047	0.9043
Tajima-nei	0.0043	0.9137
Kimura-2	0.0032	0.9258
Tamura-3	0.0031	0.9215
DeepED(Primates)	**0.0019**	**0.9514**
DeepED(Ray-finned fishes)	**0.0083**	**0.8089**

4.4 Weights Analysis

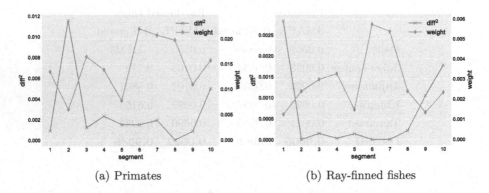

(a) Primates   (b) Ray-finned fishes

Fig. 2. Squared differences between the segment distances and the whole sequence distance (calculated using Tamura-3 distance) as well as the segment weights given by the weight-net, for the two test sets.

The weight-net in the framework is expected to measure the importances of segments of a sequence pair for the prediction of the distance of the whole sequence pair. To illustrated the effectiveness of the weight-net, a sequence pair is taken randomly from each test set and ten consecutive segments are selected. We calculate the Tamura-3 distances of these segments and the whole sequences, and then the squared difference between each segment distance and the corresponding whole sequence distance is calculated as shown in Fig. 2. The weights of these segments given by the weight-net are also shown in Fig. 2. On the overall datasets, the Pearson correlation coefficient between the squared differences and the weights are -0.5628(Primates) and -0.5493(Ray-finned fishes).

There is a clear negative correlation between the squared differences and the weights, and as a preliminary analysis, it shows that the weight-net will assign a higher weight for a segment with a closer distance to the distance of the whole sequence pair. Furthermore, it is observed that there are more gap and missing characters in some segments with lower weights, which reveals that some segments with higher weights probably contain some gene fragments pivotal for evolution.

5 Conclusions

This paper presents a framework based on deep learning networks, called DeepED, to estimate evolutionary distances, which can accept long and variable length DNA sequences. We propose a way to encode aligned DNA sequences and a convolutional network which is trained with real world data and is proven efficient. Attention mechanism is used to find the important parts of a sequence pair for evolutionary distance estimation. Experiments demonstrate that the

DeepED models outperform traditional evolutionary distance estimation methods in accuracy.

In future work, more extensive and high-quality real world data will be collected to improve and verify the effectiveness of the framework. With sufficient data for training, the DeepED framework promises a generic model to estimate evolutionary distances for various data.

Acknowledgements. This work is partially supported by National Science Foundation of China (61872201, 61702521, U1833114) and Science and Technology Development Plan of Tianjin (18ZXZNGX00140, 18ZXZNGX00200).

References

1. Jukes, T.H., Cantor, C.R., et al.: Evolution of protein molecules. Mamm. Protein Metab. **3**(21), 132 (1969)
2. Posada, D., Crandall, K.A.: Selecting the best-fit model of nucleotide substitution. Syst. Biol. **50**(4), 580–601 (2001)
3. Cunningham, C.W., Zhu, H., Hillis, D.M.: Best-fit maximum-likelihood models for phylogenetic inference: empirical tests with known phylogenies. Evolution **52**(4), 978–987 (1998)
4. LeCun, Y., Bengio, Y., Hinton, G.: Deep learning. Nature **521**(7553), 436–444 (2015)
5. Xu, K., et al.: Show, attend and tell: neural image caption generation with visual attention. In: International Conference on Machine Learning, pp. 2048–2057 (2015)
6. Vaswani, A., et al.: Attention is all you need. In: Advances in Neural Information Processing Systems, pp. 5998–6008 (2017)
7. Tajima, F., Nei, M.: Estimation of evolutionary distance between nucleotide sequences. Mol. Biol. Evol. **1**(3), 269–285 (1984)
8. Kimura, M.: A simple method for estimating evolutionary rates of base substitutions through comparative studies of nucleotide sequences. J. Mol. Evol. **16**(2), 111–120 (1980)
9. Tamura, K.: Estimation of the number of nucleotide substitutions when there are strong transition-transversion and G+ C-content biases. Mol. Biol. Evol. **9**(4), 678–687 (1992)
10. Waddell, P.J., Steel, M.A.: General time reversible distances with unequal rates across sites (1996)
11. Zhang, J., Xun, G.: Correlation between the substitution rate and rate variation among sites in protein evolution. Genetics **149**(3), 1615–1625 (1998)
12. Simonyan, K., Zisserman, A.: Very deep convolutional networks for large-scale image recognition. arXiv preprint arXiv:1409.1556 (2014)
13. He, K., Zhang, X., Ren, S., Sun, J.: Deep residual learning for image recognition. In: Proceedings of the IEEE Conference on Computer Vision and Pattern Recognition, pp. 770–778 (2016)
14. Collobert, R., Weston, J.: A unified architecture for natural language processing: deep neural networks with multitask learning. In: Proceedings of the 25th International Conference on Machine Learning, pp. 160–167 (2008)
15. Devlin, J., Chang, M.W., Lee, K., Toutanova, K.: Bert: pre-training of deep bidirectional transformers for language understanding. arXiv preprint arXiv:1810.04805 (2018)

16. Hornik, K., Stinchcombe, M., White, H., et al.: Multilayer feedforward networks are universal approximators. Neural Netw. **2**(5), 359–366 (1989)
17. Park, J., Sandberg, I.W.: Universal approximation using radial-basis-function networks. Neural Comput. **3**(2), 246–257 (1991)
18. Zhang, H., et al.: A new method of RNA secondary structure prediction based on convolutional neural network and dynamic programming. Front. Genet. **10**, 467 (2019)
19. Wang, R., et al.: Deepdna: a hybrid convolutional and recurrent neural network for compressing human mitochondrial genomes. In: 2018 IEEE International Conference on Bioinformatics and Biomedicine (BIBM), pp. 270–274. IEEE (2018)
20. Long, J., Shelhamer, E., Darrell, T.: Fully convolutional networks for semantic segmentation. In: Proceedings of the IEEE Conference on Computer Vision and Pattern Recognition, pp. 3431–3440 (2015)
21. Huber, P.J.: Robust estimation of a location parameter. In: Kotz, S., Johnson, N.L. (eds.) Breakthroughs in Statistics, pp. 492–518. Springer, New York (1992). https://doi.org/10.1007/978-1-4612-4380-9_35
22. Kingma, D.P., Ba, J.: Adam: a method for stochastic optimization. arXiv preprint arXiv:1412.6980 (2014)
23. Glorot, X., Bengio, Y.: Understanding the difficulty of training deep feedforward neural networks. In: Proceedings of the Thirteenth International Conference on Artificial Intelligence and Statistics, pp. 249–256 (2010)
24. Perelman, P., et al.: A molecular phylogeny of living primates. PLoS Genet. **7**(3), e1001342 (2011)
25. Katoh, K., Standley, D.M.: MAFFT multiple sequence alignment software version 7: improvements in performance and usability. Mol. Biol. Evol. **30**(4), 772–780 (2013)
26. Bouckaert, R., et al.: Beast 2: a software platform for Bayesian evolutionary analysis. PLoS Comput. Biol. **10**(4), e1003537 (2014)
27. Hughes, L.C., et al.: Comprehensive phylogeny of ray-finned fishes (Actinopterygii) based on transcriptomic and genomic data. Proc. Natl. Acad. Sci. **115**(24), 6249–6254 (2018)
28. Mirarab, S., Warnow, T.: ASTRAL-II: coalescent-based species tree estimation with many hundreds of taxa and thousands of genes. Bioinformatics **31**(12), i44–i52 (2015)
29. Kumar, S., Stecher, G., Tamura, K.: Mega7: molecular evolutionary genetics analysis version 7.0 for bigger datasets. Mol. Biol. Evol. **33**(7), 1870–1874 (2016)
30. Song, N., Liang, A.-P., Bu, C.-P.: A molecular phylogeny of hemiptera inferred from mitochondrial genome sequences. PLoS ONE **7**(11), e48778 (2012)

Interpretable Machine Learning Structure for an Early Prediction of Lane Changes

Oliver Gallitz[1]([✉]) [iD], Oliver De Candido[2] [iD], Michael Botsch[1] [iD], Ron Melz[3],
and Wolfgang Utschick[2] [iD]

[1] Technische Hochschule Ingolstadt, 85049 Ingolstadt, Germany
oliver.gallitz@thi.de
[2] Technical University of Munich, 80333 Munich, Germany
[3] Audi AG, 85049 Ingolstadt, Germany

Abstract. This paper proposes an interpretable machine learning structure for the task of lane change intention prediction, based on multivariate time series data. A Mixture-of-Experts architecture is adapted to simultaneously predict lane change directions and the time-to-lane-change. To facilitate reproducibility, the approach is demonstrated on a publicly available dataset of German highway scenarios. Recurrent networks for time series classification using Gated Recurrent Units and Long-Short-Term Memory cells, as well as convolution neural networks serve as comparison references. The interpretability of the results is shown by extracting the rule sets of the underlying classification and regression trees, which are grown using data-adaptive interpretable features. The proposed method outperforms the reference methods in false alarm behavior while displaying a state-of-the-art early detection performance.

Keywords: Interpretability · Early prediction · Autonomous driving

1 Introduction

The society around Explainable Artificial Intelligence (XAI) [10,18,20] aims to open the often-cited "Black Box" of Deep Neural Networks (DNN) through interpretable methods. Interpretability can therefore be considered one of the major keys to make Machine Learning (ML) validatable, since its goal is to provide understandable and traceable statements even for potential non-experts in ML. In the field of driving, ML is still very sparsely used in safety critical applications, since the majority of existing XAI approaches help to deliver explanations of passed actions, but lack the ability to evaluate the safety of ML algorithms pre-use, a property also termed as *intrinsic interpretability*. The task of lane change intention prediction is considered safety critical, as it might directly affect driving commands. Intention prediction functions can shift the planning horizon from

Funded by Audi AG.

reactive maneuvers to being able to predict upcoming actions multiple seconds ahead of time. Early planned maneuvers enable safe and comfortable driving.

The contribution of this paper is an ML system for the task of early prediction on multivariate time series (MTS). The main components of the proposed system are (A) multiple sets of data-adaptive interpretable features that are generated based on DNNs [8] and (B) a Mixture-of-Experts (MoE) structure consisting of intrinsically interpretable classification and regression trees. The MoE structure is thereby configured to optimize the individual experts for pre-specified time regions. The developed approach is compared to three reference networks to examine the advantages in performance and interpretability. Early prediction is a prevalent task in autonomous driving. Hence, the proposed approach has several possible applications, of which lane change prediction will serve as prominent example. The rest of this section will introduce the techniques and related publications. Section 3 will explain the classification and regression networks in detail. The interpretability of the results is demonstrated in Sect. 4. The performance of the network is compared and discussed in Sect. 5, followed by a discussion of the results in Sect. 6.

1.1 Related Work

Early classification methods for MTS are typically applied, when the prediction horizon of a classification task is not known in advance. Typical applications that have a time-sensitive nature and benefit from early classification include the fields of medical anomaly detection, predictive maintenance and intention prediction for autonomous driving functions. Within these topics, several methods have been proposed in order to classify time series with a maximized prediction horizon while preserving classification accuracy. A common approach for time series classification is the use of shapelets, which can be defined as class-representative sequences [24]. Recent publications also take MTS into account [11,15]. Shapelets, as subsequences of time series data, inherit interpretability from the input data, hence several publications claim the extraction of interpretable features [16,22]. The claim of interpretability is limited to the feature space and does not hold for downstream multi-layer networks. Algorithms that possess this property are termed *interpretable methods* and provide a comprehensive understanding of the learning algorithm as a whole, including its inputs and results. Methods that offer *post-hoc interpretability* require an active inference of the network in order to reason why a decision was made. One of those methods is the Layer-wise Relevance Propagation (LRP) [1]. Its purpose is to generate explanations of a network output in the input space by following a set of local propagation rules backwards through the network. In contrast, *intrinsic interpretability* for ML algorithms is defined as the ability to comprehend a classifier or regressor without preceding inference. Classic ML approaches, such as decision trees (DTs) [4] or linear models, have this property as a natural consequence of their structural simplicity [9]. Since this work contributes towards *Validation by Design*, a project aiming towards the validation of ML algorithms, the proposed method not only has to achieve high accuracy values, but has to provide full intrinsic interpretability.

The prediction horizon for intention predictions is usually highly varying. An evasive lane change maneuver cannot be classified until shortly before, while consciously planned maneuvers can be classified multiple seconds in advance. In order to cover the full time range, a single classifier will have to find globally shared features throughout the whole observation length. A resulting trade-off is the negligence of under-represented scenarios. With the MoE [13], a technique following the *divide-et-impera* principle has been proposed. An MoE structure consists of multiple expert networks, that were each trained to perform well within one segment of the overall input space. A meta network is then optimized as a gating mechanism to find the best expert for a given input sample. Within the topic of MoE, the segmentation of the input space into pre-specified subspaces, as it will be used within this paper, is known as *Mixture of Explicitly Localized Experts* (MELE) [3]. MoE is a classic method in ML, but remains relevant today by introducing DNN experts and its ability to achieve state-of-the-art performances on suitable tasks [2,7]. In [19], an MoE structure has been used to predict lane change trajectories by classifying the maneuver through a random forest and subsequently calculating the trajectory by means of class-specific experts. The benefits of splitting dynamic- and vehicle constellation-based features for highway maneuver classification has been proposed by [21]. Network interpretability and the evolution of relevant features through time, that play an essential role in this publication, have not been considered in these approaches.

1.2   Dataset of Real-Life Lane Changes

The highD Dataset of highway scenarios [14] has become one of the reference datasets for evaluating driver behavior. It consists of several hours of drone footage from six different locations in Germany, processed through an object detection and tracking algorithm. From this dataset, all lane changes that were observed for at least $T_{\mathrm{LC,min}} = 6.52s$ before the lane change are extracted. The timestep t_0, at which a lane change is detected, is defined as the intersection between any lane marking and the geometric center of an object. The extracted sequences are split into training and test set in the ratio 80/20. The dataset is normalized and balanced. The balancing process discards random samples of overrepresented classes. The labels are assigned as

$$k = \{LCL, LCR, NoLC\}, \tag{1}$$

where LCL denotes a lane change to the left, LCR a lane change to the right and $NoLC$ no lane change. Within the dataset, the m-th scenario describes an MTS

$$\boldsymbol{X}^m \in \mathbb{R}^{F \times T}, \tag{2}$$

with F features along T discrete timesteps. Every feature f is an interpretable physical property such as distances to surrounding vehicles or velocity and acceleration values of the EGO vehicle.

2 Reference Methods

In this publication, we chose three different state-of-the-art networks as reference methods. However, all compared reference methods are uninterpretable, multi hidden layer structures and can therefore only be utilized as performance reference. Recurrent Neural Networks (RNNs) are considered to be the state-of-the-art network types for time series classification. Among the most prominent representatives of RNNs are the Long-Short-Term Memory (LSTM)[12] networks, as well as Gated Recurrent Units (GRUs)[5]. Both of these recurrent structures introduce additional trainable parameters to store the information of the preceding layers, known as *Gates*. In [6], a combined classification and regression using multitask networks with LSTM cells are examined. The application is a lane change intention prediction with an estimated TLC for the ego vehicle, using internal vehicle data and eye tracking. A comparable classifier with a GRU layer as recurrent structure is proposed in [23]. GRU cells have less hidden parameters than LSTM cells, hence they perform better in smaller datasets. The learning target is a two-fold regression for the TLC and the time to lane change completion. A modification in the output layer of this network enables the classification of lane change directions. Both methods achieve strong prediction performances for the task of lane change prediction and will be used as recurrent reference methods. Next to the popularity of RNNs, Convolutional Neural Networks (CNNs) are proven to be highly capable of time series classification tasks [17,25]. A convolutional neural network for time series classification and regression will therefore also be part of the reference methods.

3 Expert Classifiers and Regression Network

The main idea of MoE, as explained in Sect. 1, is to achieve a better classification performance by splitting the input space and learning an expert classifier for each split. The following sections will explain the generation of the training data, as well as the inner structure of the DNNs for the initial training, preceding the interpretability conversion. The global layout of the MoE structure for regression and classification of the lane change intentions is shown in Fig. 1. In this figure, X_{SW}^m denotes the input, a fixed-length segment of a dataset sample X^m as introduced in (2), starting at position SW. The outputs for classification and TLC regression are denoted as y_{cl} and y_{reg}, respectively.

The lane change sequences extracted from the original dataset have a common length of $T_{\mathrm{LC,min}}$. For the proposed MoE structure, splits along the time dimension of these sequences are performed to obtain the expert training sets. Figure 2 visualizes a lane change sample with the features along the ordinate and the time dimension with the expert splits along the abscissa. These splits are based on the hypothesis, that the relevant features to classify lane changes are considerably different between short- and long-term experts, e.g. $E1$ and $E5$. Additionally, this splitting method facilitates the double assignment of the TLC regressor as meta network of an MoE structure as depicted in Fig. 1.

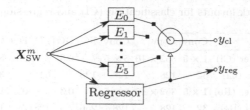

Fig. 1. Layout of the MoE structure.

Each expert subset contains multiple positions of a fixed-length moving window. Window positions may overlap between two expert regions and are assigned to the subset of the expert closer to t_0. For this publication, a time window length $\triangle t = 1s$ is chosen. A time window position (a) at $t = 3s$ defines a subsequence X_{3s}^m that is assigned to expert E_3. The earliest subsequence (b) of a sample, associated with expert E_5, ranges from $5.52s$ to $6.52s$.

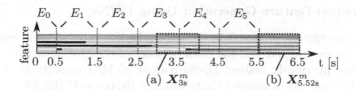

Fig. 2. Full sample with expert splits.

The regressor has to be able to estimate the TLC over the full range of the dataset. To achieve this goal, the training set of the regressor contains time windows from all positions along the sample, labeled with the position index. All samples of the *NoLC* class are explicitly excluded from this training, since no TLC value can be assigned.

3.1 Network Design

Before their conversion into interpretable structures, the networks for classification and regression share a common layout through the convolutional layers (Conv) and start to diverge in the fully connected (FC) layers. In between the FC layers, dropout (DO) is applied. Table 1 lists both network designs. Since the regression network is trained with samples across the full time, a much larger dataset than the individual experts, an increase in dimensionality for the FC layers turned out to be beneficial for the performance.

The gating mechanism of the meta classifier is a winner-takes-it-all strategy, assigning one responsible expert to perform the classification. Responsibility is assigned by comparing the regression result with the range of each expert, which corresponds to its individual training set as denoted in Fig. 2.

Table 1. Network layouts for classification (Cl) and regression networks (Re).

	Conv	Conv	Conv	FC	DO	FC	DO	Output
Parameter (Cl)	1×5	352×10	5×5	/	0.3	/	0.2	Softmax
Channels (Cl)	32	128	128	128	/	64	/	3
Parameter (Re)	1×5	352×10	5×5	/	0.3	/	0.3	Linear
Channels (Re)	32	128	128	256	/	128	/	1

4   Generation of Interpretable Structures

This paper seeks to generate an intrinsically interpretable classification and regression. In Sect. 3, multiple deep networks are trained in an MoE structure. Each of these networks contains multiple hidden layers and is therefore non-interpretable. The chosen network layouts however prepare the MoE structure for a conversion into capable interpretable classifiers.

4.1   Enriched Feature Generation Using DNNs

Following the process proposed in [8], data-adaptive interpretable features are generated for each expert and the meta network of the MoE structure. The first layers of the previously trained DNNs consist of 1D convolutions, leading to expert-individual sets of learned Finite Impulse Response (FIR) filters. The outputs of this layer therefore describe filtered representations of physical properties and can subsequently still be considered interpretable. In this latent space, LRP highlights salient regions, which are extracted as feature subsets. Additionally, a complementary set of features termed *smart features* is constructed from the salient regions. For this publication, the generated smart features are the gradient, minimum and maximum, as well as the signal energy of each detected salient region. The subsets of filtered input features and the generated smart features are combined to enriched datasets, which are individual for each expert e, as well as the regressor. An input sample to the structure X_{SW}^{m} as depicted in Fig. 1 will therefore be mapped to E different enriched representations $X_{\mathrm{SW},e}^{\prime m}$ for the experts and one representation $X_{\mathrm{SW},r}^{\prime m}$ for the regressor.

4.2   Interpretation of Predictions

In order to demonstrate the established interpretability, one randomly chosen sample from the test set is visualized at two timesteps before the lane change in Fig. 3 and Fig. 4. In the referenced figures, the text box refers to the observed vehicle, whose lane change is to be predicted by the presented MoE method. The top row denotes the TLC regression ground truth t, as well as the prediction t_{pred}. The bottom row denotes the ground truth class k for the lane change classification and the prediction k_{pred}. The results can be interpreted by extracting the decision rules underlying both constellations from its corresponding expert

DTs, as seen in Table 2. The table rows describe the subsequent features chosen for the splits until a classification is made. Note, that the physical features of input X_{SW}^{m} have multiple filtered representations within $X_{\mathrm{SW},e}^{\prime m}$.

In Fig. 3, the regressor shows some deviation from ground truth, but correctly determined expert E_5 for the classification. Constellations from the test set that end up in this leaf of E_5 can be identified as middle-lane scenarios with a slow leading vehicle in front of the observed object. The lane change direction is decided upon by the speed difference to the leading vehicle on the right lane. Table 2 (right) illustrates the decision process for the same scenario, but closer to the lane change as depicted in Fig. 4. Expert E_2 is correctly assigned. By that point in time, the vast majority of scenarios show clear indications of a lane change. Therefore, the decision path mainly consists of splits based on lateral movement and the distance to the lane marking, and does not consider the surrounding vehicles as much as expert E_5.

Fig. 3. Lane change scenario, $t = 5.48s$ before a lane change to the left.

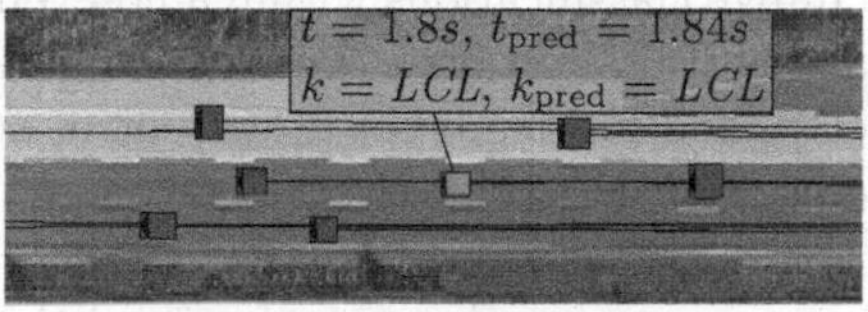

Fig. 4. Lane change scenario, $t = 1.8s$ before a lane change to the left.

Table 2. Decision processes of the constellations in Fig. 3 (left) and Fig. 4 (right). The column *Input Ft.* refers to the physical features from X_{SW}^{m}, the columns *Smart Ft.* and *FIR* refer to the enriched representations $X_{\mathrm{SW},e}^{\prime m}$.

Split	Input Ft.	Smart Ft.	FIR	Split	Input Ft.	Smart Ft.	FIR
1	d_{RearLeft}	Minimum	1	1	d_{MarkLeft}	Maximum	11
2	$d_{\mathrm{SameFront}}$	Gradient	21	2	$d_{\mathrm{RearRight}}$	Maximum	17
3	$d_{\mathrm{SameFront}}$	Gradient	8	3	a_y	*none*	11
4	$d_{\mathrm{RearRight}}$	Minimum	26	4	d_{MarkLeft}	Minimum	11
5	$d_{\mathrm{SameFront}}$	Minimum	21	5	a_y	Gradient	11
6	a_x	Gradient	15	6	a_y	Gradient	11
7	$d_{\mathrm{RightFront}}$	Gradient	21				

5   Experimental Results

Common methods to compare model performances are typically based on confusion matrices and derived measures. The well-known F-score however only has limited informative value on the classification performance for time series datasets, since the scoring relies on single-frame comparisons between prediction and label. A dataset with M samples, each containing N_{TW} time window positions yields $M \times N_{TW}$ independent entries in the confusion matrix with no temporal relations. This publication aims to retain the temporal information in the evaluation of a learned classifier. The earliness of a reliable prediction and the amount of false alarms are therefore used as suitable and application-oriented measures.

Within the application of lane change prediction, like in most prediction tasks, the set of classes contains a no-event class. This class does not have a specific t_0 associated with a predictable action. Since lane changes are rarely occurring events as compared to lane following, i.e. samples that are labeled *NoLC*, an imbalanced dataset would contain a large majority no-event class samples. It is essential to appropriately show the tendency of a classifier to produce false alarms, which are defined as a sequence of at least n_{min} identical lane change classifications within a no-event sample. Vice versa, this smoothing operation also affects true positive detections, since any decision has to be robustly classified for the defined amount of subsequent timesteps. The parameter n_{min} corresponds to time t through

$$t_{min} = \frac{n_{min}}{f_s}, \tag{3}$$

where $f_s = 25$ Hz is the sampling frequency of the dataset. Fig. 5 indicates the amount of false alarms within the subset of *NoLC* samples. The MoE approach shows strong fluctuations when the smoothing parameter n_{min} is chosen small. Recurrent structures can play out their main strength here, as the preceding states are taken into account for each new decision. Therefore, the smoothing factor benefits the MoE approach more than the compared references. In order to achieve a fair comparison, several points of interest are identified for the classification of lane change samples in the test set. Table 3 presents the comparison of reliable prediction times for the MoE and the CNN (a, d), the MoE and the GRU Network (b, e), as well as the MoE and the LSTM network (c, f). The time of reliable prediction t_{rel} denotes the point in time, where a correctly classified sample is not reclassified until t_0. In (a),(b) and (c), each comparison is generated with n_{min} only applied to the MoE Structure, which is adjusted to match the false alarm rates of the compared approaches. For the corresponding reference methods, the parameter $n_{min} = 1$. Note, that a single *NoLC* sample may contain multiple false alarms, especially when n_{min} is set low. This setting puts the focus on the earliness of a reliable prediction. Since an increase of n_{min} buys a better false alarm behavior at the cost of a decreasing t_{rel}, all reference approaches show a slightly earlier mean reliable prediction time μ_{trel} than the MoE approach while displaying comparable false alarm rates.

A high false alarm rate has negative impact on driving safety and comfort. A lane change detection might continuously instigate braking maneuvers to leave space for other vehicles if the false alarm rate is too high. The results in Fig. 6 are generated with $n_{min} = 28$ for all methods, which is the parameter setting for

Table 3. Comparison of the MoE structure with reference methods.

Reference Method (RM)	(a) CNN	(b) GRU	(c) LSTM	(d) CNN	(e) GRU	(f) LSTM
False Alarms MoE	572	572	356	0	0	0
False Alarms RM	649	520	348	62	95	103
n_{min} MoE	5	5	6	28	28	28
n_{min} RM	1	1	1	28	28	28
μ_{trel} MoE	4.86	4.86	4.82	3.44	3.44	3.44
μ_{trel} RM	4.91	4.96	4.87	3.89	3.91	3.84

MoE to show no false alarms in the test set. As Table 3 (d), (e) and (f) show, the mean reliable prediction time μ_{trel} for MoE has decreased more than those of the compared methods. The reason for this behavior can be explained by short discontinuities of length $t_{disc} < t_{min}$ within sequences of correct classifications in the early stage of upcoming lane changes. These discontinuities do not trigger reclassifications and are therefore smoothed out once a classification is made, but prevent the initial classification if long robust sequences n_{min} are required. The parameter setting for MoE in Fig. 6 offers a fully interpretable classification with a very low false alarm rate. A lane change is reliably detected on average $3.44s$ in advance. The reference methods offer longer reliable prediction durations, but at the cost of significantly more false alarms during lane following.

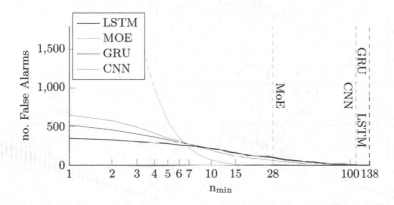

Fig. 5. False alarms over n_{min}. Vertical lines indicate n_{min} for zero false alarms with the respective method.

A comparison of the regression performance has to differentiate between early- and late-stage errors. All methods were trained on the same regression dataset, which is described in Sect. 3.1. Figure 7 displays box plots for the TLC regression of the methods MoE (a), CNN (b), GRU (c) and LSTM (d). For this illustration, t_{gt} denotes the ground truth and t_{pred} the predicted value. The whiskers cover 95% of the data, rendering the upper and lower 2.5% as outliers.

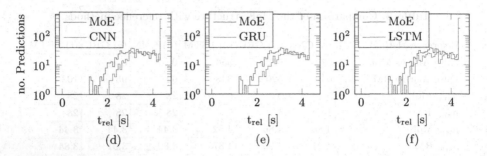

Fig. 6. Histograms of reliable predictions at time t_{rel} before lane change, referring to the results in Table 3.

The ground truth is depicted as gray line for reference. The LSTM network, despite having the largest spread between the quantiles, shows the best ability to keep the median close to the ground truth even for larger values. The proposed MoE approach has a slightly larger distribution than the uninterpretable GRU and CNN networks, particularly visible for values $t_{gt} > 3s$. All compared networks show high regression accuracy for values $t_{gt} < 3s$, which is essential for safety critical predictions.

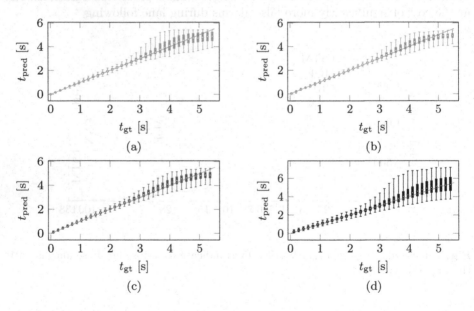

Fig. 7. Box plots of TLC predictions.

6   Discussion and Conclusion

The proposed approach applied an MoE methodology to an intention prediction task. By splitting up the input space it could be shown, that the extracted interpretable classifiers generate human-understandable decision processes. It could further be shown, that the proposed MoE structure outperforms compared methods by means of a low false alarm rate, if a trade-off in earliness of the prediction can be accepted. During function development, an individual priorization of these factors will have to be made. An extension of this work will examine alternative intrinsically interpretable classifiers, seeking to further increase the earliness of reliable predictions.

References

1. Bach, S., Binder, A., Montavon, G., Klauschen, F., Müller, K.R., Samek, W.: On pixel-wise explanations for non-linear classifier decisions by layer-wise relevance propagation. PLoS ONE **10**(7) (2015). https://doi.org/10.1371/journal.pone.0130140
2. Baldacchino, T., Cross, E.J., Worden, K., Rowson, J.: Variational Bayesian mixture of experts models and sensitivity analysis for nonlinear dynamical systems. Mech. Syst. Signal Process. **66-67**, 178–200 (2016). https://doi.org/10.1016/j.ymssp.2015.05.009. http://www.sciencedirect.com/science/article/pii/S0888327015002307
3. Tang, B., Heywood, M.I., Shepherd, M.: Input partitioning to mixture of experts. In: Proceedings of the 2002 International Joint Conference on Neural Networks, IJCNN 2002 (Cat. No. 02CH37290), vol. 1, pp. 227–232 (2002). https://doi.org/10.1109/IJCNN.2002.1005474
4. Breiman, L.: Classification and regression trees. The Wadsworth statistics/probability series, Wadsworth International Group and Wadsworth & Brooks/Cole and Wadsworth & Brooks/Cole Advanced Books & Software, Belmont, Calif. and Pacific Grove, Calif. and Pacific Grove, Calif. and Monterey, Calif. (1984)
5. Cho, K., et al.: Learning phrase representations using RNN encoder-decoder for statistical machine translation. In: Moschitti, A., Pang, B., Daelemans, W. (eds.) Proceedings of the 2014 Conference on Empirical Methods in Natural Language Processing (EMNLP), pp. 1724–1734. Association for Computational Linguistics, Stroudsburg (2014). https://doi.org/10.3115/v1/D14-1179
6. Dang, H.Q., Furnkranz, J., Biedermann, A., Hoepfl, M.: Time-to-lane-change prediction with deep learning. In: IEEE ITSC 2017, pp. 1–7. IEEE, Piscataway (2017). https://doi.org/10.1109/ITSC.2017.8317674
7. Ebrahimpour, R., Kabir, E., Esteky, H., Yousefi, M.R.: A mixture of multilayer perceptron experts network for modeling face/nonface recognition in cortical face processing regions. Intell. Autom. Soft Comput. **14**(2), 151–162 (2008). https://doi.org/10.1080/10798587.2008.10642988
8. Gallitz, O., de Candido, O., Botsch, M., Utschick, W.: Interpretable feature generation using deep neural networks and its application to lane change detection. In: The 2019 IEEE Intelligent Transportation Systems Conference - ITSC, pp. 3405–3411. IEEE, Piscataway (2019). https://doi.org/10.1109/ITSC.2019.8917524

9. Guidotti, R., Monreale, A., Ruggieri, S., Turini, F., Giannotti, F., Pedreschi, D.: A survey of methods for explaining black box models. ACM Comput. Surv. **51**(5), 1–42 (2019). https://doi.org/10.1145/3236009

10. Gunning, D.: Explainable artificial intelligence (XAI). Defense Advanced Research Projects Agency (DARPA), nd Web (2017)

11. He, G., Duan, Y., Peng, R., Jing, X., Qian, T., Wang, L.: Early classification multivariate time series. Neurocomputing **149**, 777–787 (2015). https://doi.org/10.1016/j.neucom.2014.07.056. http://www.sciencedirect.com/science/article/pii/S092523121401008X

12. Hochreiter, S., Schmidhuber, J.: Long short-term memory. Neural Comput. **9**(8), 1735–1780 (1997). https://doi.org/10.1162/neco.1997.9.8.1735

13. Jacobs, R.A., Jordan, M.I., Nowlan, S.J., Hinton, G.E.: Adaptive mixtures of local experts. Neural Comput. **3**(1), 79–87 (1991). https://doi.org/10.1162/neco.1991.3.1.79

14. Krajewski, R., Bock, J., Kloeker, L., Eckstein, L.: The highd dataset: a drone dataset of naturalistic vehicle trajectories on German highways for validation of highly automated driving systems. In: 2018 IEEE Intelligent Transportation Systems Conference, pp. 2118–2125. IEEE, Piscataway (2018). https://doi.org/10.1109/ITSC.2018.8569552

15. Lin, Y.-F., Chen, H.-H., Tseng, V.S., Pei, J.: Reliable early classification on multivariate time series with numerical and categorical attributes. In: Cao, T., Lim, E.-P., Zhou, Z.-H., Ho, T.-B., Cheung, D., Motoda, H. (eds.) PAKDD 2015. LNCS (LNAI), vol. 9077, pp. 199–211. Springer, Cham (2015). https://doi.org/10.1007/978-3-319-18038-0_16

16. Ghalwash, M.F., Obradovic, Z.: Early classification of multivariate temporal observations by extraction of interpretable shapelets. BMC Bioinform. **13**(1), 1–12 (2012). https://doi.org/10.1186/1471-2105-13-195

17. Sadouk, L.: CNN approaches for time series classification. In: Ngan, C.K. (ed.) Time Series Analysis - Data, Methods, and Applications. IntechOpen (2019). https://doi.org/10.5772/intechopen.81170

18. Samek, W., Wiegand, T., Müller, K.R.: Explainable artificial intelligence: understanding, visualizing and interpreting deep learning models (2017). http://arxiv.org/pdf/1708.08296v1

19. Schlechtriemen, J., Wirthmueller, F., Wedel, A., Breuel, G., Kuhnert, K.D.: When will it change the lane? A probabilistic regression approach for rarely occurring events. In: 2015 IEEE Intelligent Vehicles Symposium (IV), pp. 1373–1379 (2015)

20. van Lent, F.: An explainable artificial intelligence system for small-unit tactical behavior. In: Proceedings of the 16th Conference on Innovative Applications of Artificial Intelligence, pp. 900–907 (2004)

21. Wissing, C., Nattermann, T., Glander, K.H., Hass, C., Bertram, T.: Lane change prediction by combining movement and situation based probabilities. IFAC-PapersOnLine **50**(1), 3554–3559 (2017). https://doi.org/10.1016/j.ifacol.2017.08.960

22. Xing, Z., Pei, J., Yu, P.S., Wang, K.: Extracting interpretable features for early classification on time series. In: Liu, B., Liu, H., Clifton, C.W., Washio, T., Kamath, C. (eds.) Proceedings of the 2011 SIAM International Conference on Data Mining, pp. 247–258. Society for Industrial and Applied Mathematics, Philadelphia (2011). https://doi.org/10.1137/1.9781611972818.22

23. Yan, Z., Yang, K., Wang, Z., Yang, B., Kaizuka, T., Nakano, K.: Time to lane change and completion prediction based on gated recurrent unit network. In: 2019 IEEE Intelligent Vehicles Symposium (IV), pp. 102–107. IEEE, Piscataway (2019). https://doi.org/10.1109/IVS.2019.8813838

24. Ye, L., Keogh, E.: Time series shapelets. In: Elder, J., Fogelman, F.S., Flach, P., Zaki, M. (eds.) KDD 2009, p. 947. ACM, New York (2009). https://doi.org/10.1145/1557019.1557122

25. Zheng, Y., Liu, Q., Chen, E., Ge, Y., Zhao, J.L.: Exploiting multi-channels deep convolutional neural networks for multivariate time series classification. Front. Comput. Sci. **10**(1), 96–112 (2016). https://doi.org/10.1007/s11704-015-4478-2

Explainable Methods

Convex Density Constraints for Computing Plausible Counterfactual Explanations

André Artelt[✉] and Barbara Hammer

CITEC - Cognitive Interaction Technology, Bielefeld University,
33619 Bielefeld, Germany
{aartelt,bhammer}@techfak.uni-bielefeld.de

Abstract. The increasing deployment of machine learning as well as legal regulations such as EU's GDPR cause a need for user-friendly explanations of decisions proposed by machine learning models. Counterfactual explanations are considered as one of the most popular techniques to explain a specific decision of a model. While the computation of "arbitrary" counterfactual explanations is well studied, it is still an open research problem how to efficiently compute plausible and feasible counterfactual explanations. We build upon recent work and propose and study a formal definition of plausible counterfactual explanations. In particular, we investigate how to use density estimators for enforcing plausibility and feasibility of counterfactual explanations. For the purpose of efficient computations, we propose convex density constraints that ensure that the resulting counterfactual is located in a region of the data space of high density.

Keywords: XAI · Counterfactual explanations · Transparency & interpretability

1 Introduction

As research on machine learning (ML) is making more and more progress and ML models constitute state-of-the-art approaches in domains such as machine translation, image and text classification, we observe an increased deployment of ML technology in practice [12,16,32]. At the same time, ML models are vulnerable to unexpected behavior such as adversarial attacks [29] and behavior which is regarded as unfair by humans [21], hence a large amount of the decision making process offered by ML is not fully understood by humans. As a consequence of this fact and due to legal regulations like EU's GDPR [23], transparency and interpretability of ML models becomes more and more relevant. Therefore, there is a need for tools that make ML models transparent in the sense that we

We gratefully acknowledge funding from the VW-Foundation for the project *IMPACT* funded in the frame of the funding line *AI and its Implications for Future Society*.

I. Farkaš et al. (Eds.): ICANN 2020, LNCS 12396, pp. 353–365, 2020.
https://doi.org/10.1007/978-3-030-61609-0_28

can explain the decision making process of a model. Accordingly, we observe an increase of research in the area of explainable AI (XAI) [11,15,28,30].

Over time, researchers developed a diverse set of methods for explaining ML models [15,22]: Model-agnostic methods [15,25] are not tailored to a particular model or representation, hence they are (in theory) applicable to any different types of ML models; in the extreme "truly" model-agnostic methods do not need access to the training data or model internals but they regard the model as a black-box. There exists a variety of different model-agnostic approaches, including feature interaction methods [13], feature importance methods [9], partial dependency plots [34] and local methods that approximates the model locally by an explainable model [14,26]. This group of technologies relies on feature importance ranking or similar to express decisions of a given model. A different class of explanations relies on examples that explain a prediction by a (set of) data points [2]. Prototypes & criticisms [17] and influential instances [18] are instances of such example-based explanations.

One popular instance of example-based explanations, often realized as black-box scheme, are counterfactual explanations [22,31]. A counterfactual explanation states a change to the original input that leads to a different prediction of a given ML model. This type of explanation is considered as particularly intuitive, because it tells the user what to do in order to achieve a desired goal [22,31]. Despite the huge variety of different - equally important - types of explanations, we limit ourselves to counterfactual explanations in this contribution. Counterfactual explanations can be phrased as a constrained optimization problem, aiming for minimizing the change which results in a different output. Depending on the specific setting, this optimization problem is solved by either gradient-based schemes or, in particular in agnostic settings, by black-box solvers. Thereby, approaches which rely on the specific form of the given classifier can lead to much more efficient computation schemes, as demonstrated in [6].

Yet, stated in its simplest form, counterfactuals are very similar to adversarial examples, since there are no guarantees that the resulting counterfactual is plausible and feasible in the data domain. As a consequence, the absence of such constraints often leads to counterfactual explanations that are not plausible [8,19,24] - an observation that we will also confirm in this work.

In this work, we aim for an extension of counterfactual explanation schemes which restricts possible explanations to plausible regions of the data space. More specifically, we propose and study a formal definition of plausible counterfactual explanations and propose a modeling framework, which phrases such constraints in convex form, such that they can efficiently be integrated into optimization schemes, preserving uniqueness of solutions or efficiency if this is valid for the constrained version.

2   Definition and Related Work

We briefly review existing work on enforcing plausibility of counterfactual explanations (Definition 1). In the context of ML models, counterfactual explanations are formalized as follows:

Definition 1 (Counterfactual explanation [31]). *Assume a prediction function h is given. Computing a counterfactual $x' \in \mathbb{R}^d$ for a given input $x \in \mathbb{R}^d$ is phrased as the following optimization problem:*

$$\underset{x' \in \mathbb{R}^d}{\arg\min} \; \ell\big(h(x'), y^c\big) + C \cdot \theta(x', x) \tag{1}$$

where $\ell(\cdot, \cdot)$ denotes a loss function, y^c the requested prediction, and $\theta(\cdot, \cdot)$ a penalty term for deviations of x' from the original input x. $C > 0$ denotes the regularization strength.

Two common regularizations are the weighted Manhattan distance and the Mahalanobis distance. The weighted Manhattan distance is defined as:

$$\theta(x', x) = \sum_j \alpha_j \cdot |(x)_j - (x')_j| \tag{2}$$

where $\alpha_j > 0$ denote feature-wise weights. The Mahalanobis distance is defined as:

$$\theta(x', x) = (x - x')^\top \Omega (x - x') \tag{3}$$

where Ω denotes a s.psd. matrix.

In general, x' is arbitrary, hence possibly implausible. A variety of approaches aims for a restriction of the domain to plausible patterns only. The authors of [24] propose to compute a path of intermediate counterfactuals that lead to the final counterfactual. The idea is to provide the user with a set of intermediate goals that finally lead to the desired goal - it might be easier to "go into the direction" of the final goal step by step instead of accomplishing it in a single step. In order to compute such a path of intermediate counterfactuals, different strategies for constructing a graph on the training data set are proposed - including the query point. In this graph, two samples are connected by a weighted edge if they are "sufficiently close to each other" - e.g. based on density estimation. The path of intermediate counterfactuals is then computed as the shortest path between the query point and a point that has the requested label - this data point is the final counterfactual. Therefore, the final counterfactual as well as all intermediate counterfactuals are elements of the training data set, which ensures that all counterfactuals are plausible and feasible. However, the limitation to samples from the training set can be seen as a major drawback of this method, in particular for sparsely populated data spaces.

A slightly modified version of Eq. (1) was proposed in [19]. The authors suggest that the original formalization Eq. (1) does not take into account that the counterfactual should lie on the data manifold which would enforce plausibility. Therefore, they propose to add two additional terms to the original objective in Eq. (1), which should be simultaneously optimized: The distance between the counterfactual x' and the reconstructed version of it that has been computed by using a pretrained autoencoder, and the distance between the encoding of the counterfactual x' and the mean encoding of training samples that belong to the requested class y^c. The first term is supposed to ensure that the counterfactual

x' lies on the data manifold and thus is a plausible data instance. The second term is supposed to accelerate the solver for computing the solution of the final optimization problem. We think that this is a very promising approach - However, the objective itself still behaves like "a heuristic" because, like the original Eq. (1), there are no guarantees that the resulting counterfactual is plausible/feasible or even valid at all - one would have to do an extensive hyperparameter tuning of the objective. Furthermore, the need of a working autoencoder can be considered as another bottleneck because building high quality and stable autoencoders can be quite challenging if only very little data are available - in particular if the autoencoder is modeled by deep neural networks. Lastly, due to the non-convexity of the autoencoder and the model itself, the resulting optimization problem is highly non-convex and thus difficult to solve.

Somehow similar to [19], the authors of [20] propose to use GANs and VAEs for creating realistic images. Although they do not talk explicitly about counterfactuals - they want to compute contrastive explanations [8] which are similar to counterfactuals in the sense that in both cases we want to find a minimal change that leads to a specific prediction (although we have a second objective in constrastive explanations).

The authors of [5] propose a convex modeling framework for efficiently computing counterfactual explanations of different ML models. They propose to turn the optimization problem Eq. (1) into a constraint optimization problem:

$$\arg\min_{x' \in \mathbb{R}^d} \theta(x', x) \quad \text{s.t.} \quad h(x') = y^c \tag{4}$$

By exploiting model specific structures, they are able to turn Eq. (4) into a convex program for many different ML models. The benefits of this modeling are that convex programs can be solved very efficiently [7], additional convex constraints can be added without changing the complexity of the problem, feasibility - does a solution (counterfactual), under a given set of constraints, exist? - can be verified easily. By adding additional constraints we can ensure that the counterfactual is plausible/feasible in the specific data domain. However, manually constructing plausibility constraints can be very time consuming and requires solid domain knowledge which might not be available. These approaches yield promising approaches, yet their greatest disadvantage is the potentially high computational load of the induced optimization problem. Here, we will take a different avenue by phrasing the condition of plausibility as a convex constraint.

Our contribution builds on our prior work [5], which phrases counterfactual computation in terms of efficient constrained optimization problems for many popular classifiers. Besides a formal definition of plausible counterfactuals, we propose convex density constraints that can be built from a given data set automatically and efficiently. These constraints ensure that the density of the resulting counterfactual is lower bounded by a predefined/requested threshold. Due to space constraints, all proofs and derivations can be found in an extended version on arXiv[1].

---

[1] https://arxiv.org/abs/2002.04862.

3   Plausible Counterfactual Explanations

3.1   Computation of Plausible Counterfactual Explanations

For the purpose of enforcing plausibility of counterfactuals, we propose to add a target specific density constraint to Eq. (4):

$$\arg\min_{x' \in \mathbb{R}^d} \theta(x', x) \tag{5a}$$

$$\text{s.t. } h(x') = y^c \tag{5b}$$

$$\hat{p}_y(x') \geq \delta \tag{5c}$$

where $\hat{p}_y(\cdot)$ denotes a class dependent density estimator. There exists a variety of different density estimators that estimate the density based on training samples.

A popular choice, when it comes to estimate densities from training data, is a kernel density estimator (KDE): $\hat{p}_{\text{KDE}}(x) = \sum_i \alpha_i k(x, x_i)$ where $k(\cdot, \cdot)$ denotes a suitable kernel function, x_i denotes the i-th sample in the training data set and $\alpha_i > 0$ denotes the weighting of the i-th sample. However, in case of non-linear kernels (e.g. Gaussian kernel) the resulting density estimator is highly non-convex and does not induce an efficient optimization problem.

In a Gaussian mixture model (GMM) the density is modeled as a mixture of multivariate normal distributions. The density under a GMM with m components is defined as:

$$\hat{p}_{\text{GMM}}(x) = \sum_{j=1}^{m} \pi_j \mathcal{N}(x \mid \mu_j, \Sigma_j) \tag{6}$$

where π_j denotes the prior probability of the j-th component, μ_j and Σ_j denote the mean and covariance of the j-th component. Although a GMM is much simpler (has fewer components/parameters) than a KDE, it still does not induce convex constraints for Eq. (5c).

Here we propose to approximate the density of a GMM Eq. (6) by a component wise maximum:

$$\hat{p}(x) = \max_j \left(\hat{p}_j(x) \right) \tag{7}$$

where

$$\hat{p}_j(x) = \pi_j \mathcal{N}(x \mid \mu_j, \Sigma_j) \tag{8}$$

By construction, the approximation Eq. (7) is always a lower bound of the true GMM density Eq. (6). The inequality constraint of a single component Eq. (8)

$$\hat{p}_j(x) = \pi_j \mathcal{N}(x \mid \mu_j, \Sigma_j) \geq \delta \tag{9}$$

can be rewritten as a convex quadratic constraint:

$$(x - \mu_j)^\top \Sigma_j^{-1}(x - \mu_j) + c_j \leq \delta' \tag{10}$$

where

$$c_j = -2\log(\pi_j) + d\log(2\pi) - \log\left(\det(\Sigma_j^{-1})\right) \qquad \delta' = -2\log(\delta) \tag{11}$$

By making use of the approximation Eq. (7), the original constraint Eq. (5c) becomes:

$$\min_j \left((\boldsymbol{x}' - \boldsymbol{\mu}_j)^\top \boldsymbol{\Sigma}_j^{-1}(\boldsymbol{x}' - \boldsymbol{\mu}_j) + c_j \right) \leq \delta' \tag{12}$$

Although Eq. (12) is still non-convex, we can turn it into a set of convex constraints by observing the following:

Let $\boldsymbol{x}'_*$ be a solution of Eq. (5) where we substituted Eq. (5c) by Eq. (12). Then it holds that: $\exists j \in \{1, \ldots, m\} : (\boldsymbol{x}'_* - \boldsymbol{\mu}_j)^\top \boldsymbol{\Sigma}_j^{-1}(\boldsymbol{x}'_* - \boldsymbol{\mu}_j) + c_j \leq \delta'$. Note that there might exists more than one j for which Eq. (9) holds. Because we do not know for which j Eq. (9) holds, we simply try all possible $j \in \{1, \ldots, m\}$ and select the counterfactual $\boldsymbol{x}'$ that yields the smallest value of the objective Eq. (5a). Depending on $h(\cdot)$ it can happen that Eq. (5) is not feasible for all j. Because each constraint Eq. (9) can be rewritten as a convex quadratic constraint, the final optimization problem Eq. (5) becomes convex iff the objective Eq.(5a) and (if necessary) the prediction constraint Eq. (5b) are convex. The Manhattan distance as well as the Mahalanobis distance as regularizers $\theta(\cdot, \cdot)$ together with common ML models - like GLMs, linear SVM, LDA, matrix LVQ, decision tree, etc. - yield convex programs [5] that can be solved efficiently [7].

3.2 A Formal Approach

We aim for a formal description of plausible counterfactuals as modeled in Eq. (5). We assume a classification setting with an underlying generating process $\Psi = (\mathcal{X}, \mathcal{Y}, p)$ where the measurable set $\mathcal{X}$ denotes the data domain, the discrete and finite set $\mathcal{Y}$ denotes the set of possible labels and $p : \mathcal{X} \times \mathcal{Y} \mapsto \mathbb{R}_+$ denotes the joint density - we assume that $\{\boldsymbol{x} \in \mathcal{X} \mid p(\boldsymbol{x}, y) \geq \delta\}$ is closed for all $\delta > 0, y \in \mathcal{Y}$. Furthermore, let $\theta : \mathcal{X} \times \mathcal{X} \mapsto \mathbb{R}_+$ be a distance metric on $\mathcal{X}$. Following Eq. (4), we propose to define a *plausible counterfactual* according to Definition 2.

Definition 2 (δ-plausible counterfactual). *Let $h : \mathcal{X} \mapsto \mathcal{Y}$ be a classifier. We call a counterfactual explanation $(\boldsymbol{x}', y^c)$ of a particular sample $\boldsymbol{x} \in \mathcal{X}$ δ-plausible iff the following holds:*

$$\boldsymbol{x}' = \underset{\boldsymbol{x}' \in \mathcal{X}}{\arg\min} \; \theta(\boldsymbol{x}', \boldsymbol{x}) \quad s.t. \; h(\boldsymbol{x}') = y^c \wedge p(\boldsymbol{x}', y^c) \geq \delta \tag{13}$$

where $\delta > 0$ denotes a minimum density at which we consider a sample plausible. Note that we state the definition of an δ-plausible counterfactual as an optimization problem Eq. (13) which makes the definition particular appealing from a practical perspective. Next, in Theorem 1 we state under what conditions δ-plausible counterfactuals do not depend on the classifier.

Theorem 1 (Model free δ-plausible counterfactuals under zero risk classifiers). *Let $\mathcal{H}$ be the set of all classifiers $h : \mathcal{X} \mapsto \mathcal{Y}$ that have zero risk on the generating process Ψ - that is: $h \in \mathcal{H} \Leftrightarrow \underset{\boldsymbol{x}, y \sim p}{\mathbb{E}} [\mathbb{1}(h(\boldsymbol{x}) \neq y)] = 0$. Then the* *following holds* $\forall h \in \mathcal{H}, (\boldsymbol{x}, y^c) \in \mathcal{X} \times \mathcal{Y} \setminus \{y\}$:

$$\underset{\boldsymbol{x}' \in \mathcal{X}}{\arg\min} \; \theta(\boldsymbol{x}', \boldsymbol{x}) \; s.t. \; h(\boldsymbol{x}') = y^c \wedge p(\boldsymbol{x}', y^c) \geq \delta$$

$$\Leftrightarrow \underset{\boldsymbol{x}' \in \mathcal{X}}{\arg\min} \; \theta(\boldsymbol{x}', \boldsymbol{x}) \; s.t. \; p(\boldsymbol{x}', y^c) \geq \delta \tag{14}$$

Note that Theorem 1 states that in the case of perfect classifiers, δ-plausible counterfactuals become independent from the specific classifiers - thus we can compute the δ-plausible counterfactuals solely in the data domain without taking the classifiers into account. However, in practice we usually do not have a perfect classifier because either the class wise densities are overlapping or the classifier itself can not model a zero risk decision boundary. Therefore, we state a weaker version of Theorem 1 in Theorem 2, in which we assume that a classifiers h is locally δ-sufficient perfect at a sample $(\boldsymbol{x}, y)$ (Definition 3) - that is: the classifier h classifies the sample $\boldsymbol{x}$ as y, which is consistent with the ground truth induced by the generating process Ψ, and the decision boundary does not "cut to deep" into the closest parts of high density regions of the other classes.

Definition 3 (Locally δ-sufficient perfect classifier). *Let* $h : \mathcal{X} \mapsto \mathcal{Y}$ *be a classifier and denote the set of all* $\boldsymbol{x} \in \mathcal{X}$ *that have a class dependent density of at least* δ *by* $\mathcal{X}_\delta(y^c)$ *- that is:* $\mathcal{X}_\delta(y) = \{\boldsymbol{x} \in \mathcal{X} \mid p(\boldsymbol{x}, y) \geq \delta\}$. *We call* h *locally δ-sufficient perfect at a sample* $(\boldsymbol{x}, y) \in \mathcal{X} \times \mathcal{Y}$ *iff the following holds:*

$$h(\boldsymbol{x}) = \underset{y_i \in \mathcal{Y}}{\arg\max} \, p(\boldsymbol{x}, y_i) = y \wedge h(\boldsymbol{x}_*) = y^c \; \forall y^c \in \mathcal{Y} \setminus \{y\}, \; \boldsymbol{x}_* = \underset{z \in \mathcal{X}_\delta(y^c)}{\arg\min} \, \theta(\boldsymbol{z}, \boldsymbol{x})$$

$$\tag{15}$$

Theorem 2 (Model free δ-plausible counterfactual under locally δ-sufficient perfect classifiers). *Let* $\mathcal{H}(\boldsymbol{x}, y)$ *be the set of locally δ-sufficient perfect classifiers (Definition 3) at a sample* $(\boldsymbol{x}, y) \in \mathcal{X} \times \mathcal{Y}$. *Then the following holds* $\forall h \in \mathcal{H}(\boldsymbol{x}, y), (\boldsymbol{x}, y^c) \in \mathcal{X} \times \mathcal{Y} \setminus \{y\}$:

$$\underset{\boldsymbol{x}' \subset \mathcal{X}}{\arg\min} \; \theta(\boldsymbol{x}', \boldsymbol{x}) \; s.t. \; h(\boldsymbol{x}') = y^c \wedge p(\boldsymbol{x}', y^c) \geq \delta$$

$$\Leftrightarrow \underset{\boldsymbol{x}' \in \mathcal{X}}{\arg\min} \; \theta(\boldsymbol{x}', \boldsymbol{x}) \; s.t. \; p(\boldsymbol{x}', y^c) \geq \delta \tag{16}$$

Note that Theorem 2 states that for a set of classifiers that are locally δ-sufficient perfect at a sample $(\boldsymbol{x}, y) \in \mathcal{X} \times \mathcal{Y}$ (Definition 3), the δ-plausible counterfactuals of this particular sample $\boldsymbol{x}$ are exactly the same for all classifiers in this set. Because we only assume locally δ-sufficient perfectness of the classifier, Theorem 2 is very appealing for practice because tells us when we can drop the classification constraint and thus simplify the optimization problem Eq. (13).

In practice, when the true density (or a density estimation) is not available, one could try to check for locally δ-sufficient perfectness at a given sample $\boldsymbol{x}$ by checking if the "closest" training samples (incl. samples from different classes) around $\boldsymbol{x}$ are classified correctly.

4   Experiments

We perform experiments on several data sets[2] for empirically evaluating our proposed density constraints Eq. (12). We use the "Breast Cancer Wisconsin (Diagnostic) Data Set" [33], the "Iris Plants Data Set" [10], the "Wine Data Set" [27], the "Boston Housing Data Set" [1][3] and the "Optical Recognition of Handwritten Digits Data Set" [3]. We repeat the following procedure in a 4-fold cross validation: First, we fit class dependent KDE (we use the Gaussian kernel) and a GMM to the training data set - where we use a 5-fold cross validation grid search for hyperparameter tuning. Next, we fit a classifier (either a softmax regression or decision tree) to the training data set. For each sample in the test set, we compute two counterfactuals (both with the same but random target class) - one counterfactual without any additional density/plausibility constraints and another counterfactual with our proposed density constraint Eq. (10). We set the density threshold δ from Eq. (9) to the median density Eq. (7) of the training samples under the approximated GMM of the target class y^c. To enforce sparsity, we use the Manhattan distance as a regularizer $\theta(\cdot, \cdot)$. Finally, we compute the Manhattan distance to the original sample and the log-density of both counterfactuals under the KDE. We use the KDE instead of the GMM because our proposed density constraint is an approximation of the GMM which itself can be interpreted as an approximation of the KDE. In order to increase the accuracy of the classifiers and density estimators, we apply a PCA to the breast cancer data set (5 components), the house prices data set (10 components), the wine data set (8 components) and the digits data set (40 components). Since the PCA transformation is affine, it can be easily integrated into our convex programs - so that we can still compute counterfactuals in the original space.

   The results of the experiments are listed in Table 1. We observe that our proposed density constraint consistently yields counterfactuals that have a higher density than the counterfactuals without any additional density/plausibility constraints - whereby we only observe a minor increase in computation time (e.g. from 30 ms to 70 ms per sample). However, the distance to the original sample is much higher for the "more plausible" counterfactuals than for arbitrary (e.g. closest) counterfactuals. This seems reasonable because one would expect that samples from a different class look quite differently. In addition, we observe that the distances of the counterfactuals to the original samples on the Iris data set and Digits data set are more or less the same for both models, whereas the opposite is true for the wine, breast cancer and house prices data sets. This observation can be explained by the hypothesis that in the case of Iris and digits data set, both models learned a locally δ-sufficient perfect classifier (Definition 3) at most samples - then Theorem 2 explains our observation. Conversely, this

---

[2] https://github.com/andreArtelt/ConvexDensityConstraintsForPlausibleCounter factuals.

[3] We turn it into a binary classification problem by setting the target to 1 if the price is greater or equal to 20k$.

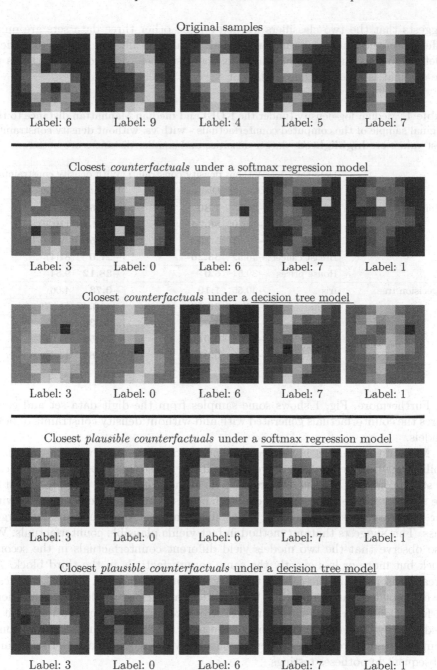

Fig. 1. Samples from the digit data set. *First block:* Original samples. *Second block:* Counterfactuals generated without any density/plausibility constraints. *Third block:* Counterfactuals generated with our proposed density constraint. The corresponding labels are shown below each image - note that the shown labels of the counterfactuals are the requested labels.

suggests that the two classifiers learned on the other three data sets are quite different in the sense that they are not all locally δ-sufficient perfect classifiers (Definition 3) at most samples - hence, the distances of the counterfactuals to the original samples are quite different.

Table 1. Median log-density (under the KDE) and median Manhattan distance to the original sample of the computed counterfactuals - with vs. without density constraints. Best values are **highlighted** - larger densities and smaller distances are better.

	Data set	Without density constraints		With density constraints	
		Density	Distance	Density	Distance
Softmax regresssion	Iris	−34.55	**1.80**	**−0.75**	4.06
	Digits	−164.03	**36.74**	**−112.40**	110.10
	Wine	−82.31	**5.19**	**−37.58**	49.59
	Breast cancer	−46.52	**33.26**	**−27.0**	81.47
	House prices	−39.51	**5.0**	**−38.12**	9.54
Decision tree	Iris	−40.55	**1.19**	**−0.73**	4.06
	Digits	−170.25	**36.69**	**−110.48**	114.78
	Wine	−102.44	**3.92**	**−34.38**	66.92
	Breast cancer	−43.44	**0.01**	**−25.55**	22.27
	House prices	−40.49	**0.01**	**−37.84**	14.92

Furthermore, Fig. 1 shows some samples from the digit data set and compares the counterfactuals generated with and without density constraints of both models.

Most of the samples in the second block - counterfactuals without any plausibility constraints - look like adversarials in the sense that the original label can be still recognized but the requested label can not be inferred. However, most of the samples in the third block - counterfactuals that have been computed with our proposed density constraint - look like samples from the requested target class. This suggests that our method in fact yields plausible counterfactuals. We also observe that the two models yield different counterfactuals in the second block but more or less exactly the same counterfactuals in the third block. As already discussed in the case of the very similar distances in Table 1, this can be explained by assuming that both models are (close to) locally δ-sufficient perfect (Definition 3) at most samples, which confirms the observations as it is predicted by Theorem 2. However, please note that a visual inspection of some samples does not replace a proper evaluation by doing an expert user study and subsequent hypotheses testings.

5   Discussion and Conclusion

In this work, we proposed and studied a formal definition of plausible counterfactual explanations. In this definition we proposed to add density constraints to the optimization problem for computing counterfactual explanations to ensure that the resulting counterfactual is plausible in the given data domain. For practical purposes, we proposed convex approximations of a Gaussian mixture model to get tractable density constraints. These constraints give rise to convex optimization problems for computing plausible counterfactual explanations many common models like linear models and decision trees. In addition, these constraints allow to specify a lower bound on the density of the resulting counterfactual that is guaranteed to be full filled. Finally, we empirically evaluated our proposed methods on several data sets and observe that our method consistently yields counterfactual explanations that are located in high density regions. A visual inspection of samples from the digits data set suggests that in fact our method seems to yield plausible counterfactuals.

As future work, we plan to conduct a proper user study where humans judge the plausibility of generated counterfactual explanations - counterfactuals generated with and without density constrains. Furthermore, we want to explore density estimators for high dimensional data as well as density constraints for computing counterfactual explanations of more complex models - in particular non-linear models (e.g. Deep neural networks). Lastly, our source code will be released as part of our open-source toolbox CEML [4], a Python toolbox for computing counterfactual explanations of ML models, so that our proposed method can be easily used by practitioners.

References

1. Boston housing data set (1978). https://archive.ics.uci.edu/ml/datasets/Housing
2. Aamodt, A., Plaza, E.: Case-based reasoning: foundational issues, methodological variations, and system approaches. AI Commun. **7**(1), 39–59 (1994)
3. Alpaydin, E., Kaynak, C.: Optical recognition of handwritten digits data set (1998). https://archive.ics.uci.edu/ml/datasets/Optical+Recognition+of+Handwritten+Digits
4. Artelt, A.: Ceml: counterfactuals for explaining machine learning models - a python toolbox (2019). https://www.github.com/andreArtelt/ceml
5. Artelt, A., Hammer, B.: On the computation of counterfactual explanations - a survey. CoRR abs/1911.07749 (2019). http://arxiv.org/abs/1911.07749
6. Artelt, A., Hammer, B.: Efficient computation of counterfactual explanations of LVQ models. In: Verleysen, M. (ed.) Proceedings of the 28th European Symposium on Artificial Neural Networks, Computational Intelligence and Machine Learning (ESANN 2020) (2020, accepted)
7. Boyd, S., Vandenberghe, L.: Convex Optimization. Cambridge University Press, New York (2004)
8. Dhurandhar, A., et al.: Explanations based on the missing: towards contrastive explanations with pertinent negatives. In: Advances in Neural Information Processing Systems 31: Annual Conference on Neural Information Processing Systems 2018, NeurIPS 2018, Montréal, Canada, 3–8 December 2018, pp. 590–601 (2018)
9. Fisher, A., Rudin, C., Dominici, F.: All Models are Wrong but many are Useful: Variable Importance for Black-Box, Proprietary, or Misspecified Prediction Models, using Model Class Reliance. arXiv e-prints arXiv:1801.01489, January 2018

10. Fisher, R.A.: The use of multiple measurements in taxonomic problems. Ann. Eugenics **7**(Part II), 179–188 (1936)
11. Gilpin, L.H., Bau, D., Yuan, B.Z., Bajwa, A., Specter, M., Kagal, L.: Explaining explanations: an overview of interpretability of machine learning. In: 5th IEEE International Conference on Data Science and Advanced Analytics, DSAA 2018, Turin, Italy, 1–3 October 2018, pp. 80–89 (2018). https://doi.org/10.1109/DSAA.2018.00018
12. Goel, S., Rao, J.M., Shroff, R.: Precinct or prejudice? Understanding racial disparities in New York city's stop-and-frisk policy (2016)
13. Greenwell, B.M., Boehmke, B.C., McCarthy, A.J.: A simple and effective model-based variable importance measure. CoRR abs/1805.04755 (2018). http://arxiv.org/abs/1805.04755
14. Guidotti, R., Monreale, A., Ruggieri, S., Pedreschi, D., Turini, F., Giannotti, F.: Local rule-based explanations of black box decision systems. CoRR abs/1805.10820 (2018). http://arxiv.org/abs/1805.10820
15. Guidotti, R., Monreale, A., Ruggieri, S., Turini, F., Giannotti, F., Pedreschi, D.: A survey of methods for explaining black box models. ACM Comput. Surv. **51**(5), 93:1–93:42 (2018). https://doi.org/10.1145/3236009
16. Khandani, A.E., Kim, A.J., Lo, A.: Consumer credit-risk models via machine-learning algorithms. J. Bank. Finance **34**(11), 2767–2787 (2010). https://EconPapers.repec.org/RePEc:eee:jbfina:v:34:y:2010:i:11:p:2767-2787
17. Kim, B., Koyejo, O., Khanna, R.: Examples are not enough, learn to criticize! criticism for interpretability. In: Advances in Neural Information Processing Systems 29: Annual Conference on Neural Information Processing Systems 2016, Barcelona, Spain, 5–10 December 2016, pp. 2280–2288 (2016). http://papers.nips.cc/paper/6300-examples-are-not-enough-learn-to-criticize-criticism-for-interpretability
18. Koh, P.W., Liang, P.: Understanding black-box predictions via influence functions. In: Proceedings of the 34th International Conference on Machine Learning, ICML 2017, Sydney, NSW, Australia, 6–11 August 2017, pp. 1885–1894 (2017). http://proceedings.mlr.press/v70/koh17a.html
19. Looveren, A.V., Klaise, J.: Interpretable counterfactual explanations guided by prototypes. CoRR abs/1907.02584 (2019). http://arxiv.org/abs/1907.02584
20. Luss, R., Chen, P., Dhurandhar, A., Sattigeri, P., Shanmugam, K., Tu, C.: Generating contrastive explanations with monotonic attribute functions. CoRR abs/1905.12698 (2019). http://arxiv.org/abs/1905.12698
21. Mehrabi, N., Morstatter, F., Saxena, N., Lerman, K., Galstyan, A.: A survey on bias and fairness in machine learning. CoRR abs/1908.09635 (2019). http://arxiv.org/abs/1908.09635
22. Molnar, C.: Interpretable Machine Learning (2019). https://christophm.github.io/interpretable-ml-book/
23. Regulation (EU) 2016/679 of the European parliament and of the council of 27 April 2016 on the protection of natural persons with regard to the processing of personal data and on the free movement of such data, and repealing directive 95/46/EC (general data protection regulation) (2016). https://eur-lex.europa.eu/eli/reg/2016/679/oj
24. Poyiadzi, R., Sokol, K., Santos-Rodriguez, R., Bie, T.D., Flach, P.A.: FACE: feasible and actionable counterfactual explanations. CoRR abs/1909.09369 (2019). http://arxiv.org/abs/1909.09369
25. Ribeiro, M.T., Singh, S., Guestrin, C.: Model-agnostic interpretability of machine learning. In: ICML Workshop on Human Interpretability in Machine Learning (WHI) (2016)

26. Ribeiro, M.T., Singh, S., Guestrin, C.: "Why should i trust you?": explaining the predictions of any classifier. In: Proceedings of the 22nd ACM SIGKDD International Conference on Knowledge Discovery and Data Mining, KDD 2016, pp. 1135–1144. ACM, New York (2016). https://doi.org/10.1145/2939672.2939778

27. Aeberhard, S., Coomans, D., de Vel, O.: Comparison of classifiers in high dimensional settings. Technical report no. 92-02 (1992)

28. Samek, W., Wiegand, T., Müller, K.: Explainable artificial intelligence: understanding, visualizing and interpreting deep learning models. CoRR abs/1708.08296 (2017). http://arxiv.org/abs/1708.08296

29. Szegedy, C., et al.: Intriguing properties of neural networks. In: 2nd International Conference on Learning Representations, ICLR 2014, Banff, AB, Canada, 14–16 April 2014, Conference Track Proceedings (2014)

30. Tjoa, E., Guan, C.: A survey on explainable artificial intelligence (XAI): towards medical XAI. CoRR abs/1907.07374 (2019). http://arxiv.org/abs/1907.07374

31. Wachter, S., Mittelstadt, B.D., Russell, C.: Counterfactual explanations without opening the black box: automated decisions and the GDPR. CoRR abs/1711.00399 (2017). http://arxiv.org/abs/1711.00399

32. Waddell, K.: How algorithms can bring down minorities' credit scores. The Atlantic (2016)

33. Wolberg, W.H., Street, W.N., Mangasarian, O.L.: Breast cancer wisconsin (diagnostic) data set (1995). https://archive.ics.uci.edu/ml/datasets/Breast+Cancer+Wisconsin+(Diagnostic)

34. Zhao, Q., Hastie, T.: Causal interpretations of black-box models. J. Bus. Econ. Stat. 1–19 (2019). https://doi.org/10.1080/07350015.2019.1624293

Identifying Critical States by the Action-Based Variance of Expected Return

Izumi Karino$^{(\boxtimes)}$, Yoshiyuki Ohmura , and Yasuo Kuniyoshi

The University of Tokyo, 7-3-1 Hongo, Bunkyo-ku, Tokyo 113-8656, Japan
{karino,ohmura,kuniyosh}@isi.imi.i.u-tokyo.ac.jp

Abstract. The balance of exploration and exploitation plays a crucial role in accelerating reinforcement learning (RL). To deploy an RL agent in human society, its explainability is also essential. However, basic RL approaches have difficulties in deciding when to choose exploitation as well as in extracting useful points for a brief explanation of its operation. One reason for the difficulties is that these approaches treat all states the same way. Here, we show that identifying critical states and treating them specially is commonly beneficial to both problems. These critical states are the states at which the action selection changes the potential of success and failure dramatically. We propose to identify the critical states using the variance in the Q-function for the actions and to perform exploitation with high probability on the identified states. These simple methods accelerate RL in a grid world with cliffs and two baseline tasks of deep RL. Our results also demonstrate that the identified critical states are intuitively interpretable regarding the crucial nature of the action selection. Furthermore, our analysis of the relationship between the timing of the identification of especially critical states and the rapid progress of learning suggests there are a few especially critical states that have important information for accelerating RL rapidly.

Keywords: Critical state · Reinforcement learning · Exploration · Explainability

1   Introduction

Balancing exploration and exploitation is essential for accelerating reinforcement learning (RL) [22]. The explainability of an RL agent is also necessary when considering its application to human society. In both of these problems, identifying a few critical states at which action selection dramatically changes the potential of success or failure would be beneficial. These critical states are states that should be exploited and would be useful points for a brief explanation. Previous work demonstrated that critical states are both useful for designing humanoid motion and related to human recognition [11].

However, basic RL approaches do not try to detect specific states and treat all states in the same way. The basic approach to balancing exploration and

© Springer Nature Switzerland AG 2020
I. Farkaš et al. (Eds.): ICANN 2020, LNCS 12396, pp. 366–378, 2020.
https://doi.org/10.1007/978-3-030-61609-0_29

exploitation is to add a stochastic perturbation to the policy in any state in the same manner using ϵ-greedy or stochastic policy, when considering application to continuous state space. Some methods give additional rewards to rarely experienced states to bias the learning towards exploration [1,15], but they also added a stochastic perturbation in any state in the same manner. This approach has difficulty exploring in an environment where some state-action pairs change future success and failure dramatically. This approach makes it difficult to choose the required actions for limited transitions to successful state space. For example, an environment might include a narrow path between cliffs through which the agent has to pass to reach a goal, or a state where the agent has to take specific action not to fall into the inescapable region due to torque limits.

Critical states contain important information that helps humans understand success and failure [11]. To the best of our knowledge, no work has tried to detect such critical states autonomously. Some studies have translated the entire policy by decomposing it into simple interpretable policies [12,20]. However, translated policies are expressed as complex combinations of simple policies and are difficult to understand. Therefore, instead of explaining everything, extracting a few critical states that have essential information regarding success and failure is useful for creating an easily understandable explanation.

Bottleneck detection is related to critical state detection in that it captures special states. To the best of our knowledge, a bottleneck is not defined by the action selection [5,13,16]. However, critical states should be defined by action selection to detect the states where specific actions are essential for success.

In this paper, we propose a method to identify critical states by the variance in the Q-function of actions and an exploration method that chooses exploitation with high probability at identified critical states. We showed this simple method accelerates RL in a toy problem and two baseline tasks of deep RL. We also demonstrate that the identification method extracts states that are intuitively interpretable as critical states and can be useful for a brief explanation of where is the critical point to achieve a task. Furthermore, an analysis of the relationship between the timing of the identification of especially critical states and the rapid progress of learning suggests there are a few especially critical states that have important information that accelerates RL rapidly.

2 Identification of Critical States

2.1 Related Work: Bottleneck Detection

With respect to the identification of special states, critical state detection is related to the notion of bottleneck detection, which is used to locate subgoals in hierarchical RL. Many studies defined bottleneck states based on state visitation frequency, that was, as ones visited frequently when connecting different state spaces [17,19], the border states of graph theory-based clustering [9,18], states visited frequently in successful trajectories but not in unsuccessful ones [13], and states at which it was easy to predict the transition [8]. However, these methods can detect states that are not critical for the success of the task. They might detect states at which the agent can return back to a successful state space by retracing its path even after taking incorrect actions. Another method defined bottlenecks based on the difference in the optimal action at the same state for a set of tasks [5]. Unfortunately, this method highly depends on the given set of tasks, cannot be applied to a single task, and might classify almost all states as bottlenecks if the given tasks have few optimal actions in common.

2.2   Formulation of a Critical State

Success and failure in RL are defined according to its return. The critical states at which the action selection changes the potential for future success and failure dramatically correspond to the states where the variance in the return is dramatically decreased by the action selection. We define state importance (SI) as reduction in the variance of the return caused by action selection and define critical states as states that have an SI that exceeds a threshold. This formulation can distinguish the states that are sensitive to action selection and does not depend on a given set of tasks. We consider the standard Markov decision process in RL. From the definition of the SI, we can calculate the SI by

$$\text{SI}(s) = \text{Var}_{p(cr|s)}[CR] - \mathbb{E}_{p(a|s)}[\text{Var}_{p(cr|s,a)}[CR]] \tag{1}$$

$$= \text{Var}_{\int p(a|s)p(cr|s,a)da}[CR] - \mathbb{E}_{p(a|s)}[\text{Var}_{p(cr|s,a)}[CR]] \tag{2}$$

$$= \text{Var}_{p(a|s)}[\mathbb{E}_{p(cr|s,a)}[CR]] + \mathbb{E}_{p(a|s)}[\text{Var}_{p(cr|s,a)}[CR]]$$
$$\qquad\qquad - \mathbb{E}_{p(a|s)}[\text{Var}_{p(cr|s,a)}[CR]] \tag{3}$$

$$= \text{Var}_{p(a|s)}[\mathbb{E}_{p(cr|s,a)}[CR]], \tag{4}$$

where cr denotes the return as an abbreviation of cumulative reward, s and a denote the state and action, respectively. We considered that the agent selected action a based on a distribution $p(a|s)$ at state s and selected the actions to take at the following states based on the current policy π. With this setup and the following definition of the Q-function:

$$\text{SI}(s) = \text{Var}_{p(a|s)}[Q^{\pi}(s, a)]. \tag{5}$$

We used a uniform distribution as $p(a|s)$ to consider the changes in return of all actions at the current state. We can calculate the SI without estimating the complex distributions of return $p(cr|s)$ and $p(cr|s, a)$.

We regard the states whose SI is greater than a threshold as critical states. We set this threshold by assuming critical states make up $100q\%$ of all states. To calculate the threshold, we first calculate the SIs of all states, if possible. If the state space is too large to calculate the SIs of all states, we calculate the SIs of recently visited states instead. Then, we set the threshold that separates the upper $100q\%$ of SIs from the lower SIs. We used a ratio of critical states of $q = 0.1$ in all the subsequent experiments.

2.3   Exploration with Exploitation on Critical States

We propose an exploration method that chooses exploitation with a high probability of k on the identified critical states and chooses an action based on any exploration method in other situations. This method increases exploration in the areas where the agent can transit with only a limited set of actions and decreases the likelihood of less promising exploration. We choose exploration at the identified critical state with a small probability because the estimated exploitation during learning could still be wrong. We used an exploitation probability of $k = 0.95$ in all the experiments.

3   Experiments

3.1   Cliff Maze Environment

We employed the cliff maze environment, shown on the left of Fig. 1, as the test environment. This environment includes a clear critical state at which action selection divides future success and failure dramatically. A cliff is located in all cells of the center column of the maze except at the center cell. The states are the 121 discrete addresses on the map. The initial state is the upper left corner, and the goal state is the lower right corner. The actions consist of four discrete actions: up, down, left, and right. The agent receives a reward of +1 at the goal state and −1 at the cliff states. An episode terminates when the agent visits either a cliff or the goal. The state between the two cliffs should be the most critical state. We evaluated the proposed identification method of the critical states and the exploration performance, which was evaluated by the number of steps required for the agent to learn the optimal shortest path.

The agent learned the Q-function via Q-learning [21]. The Q-function was updated every episode sequentially from the end of trajectory with a learning rate of 0.3. We evaluated the exploration performance of the proposed method by comparing the proposed method (based on ϵ-greedy) with the simple ϵ-greedy method. The proposed method chooses exploitation if the current state is a critical state with high probability of k and chooses a random action with low probability $1 - k$ depending on the current state. If the current state is not a critical state, this method selects action as ϵ-greedy does with exploration ratio ϵ'. We controlled the exploration ratio ϵ' using the following equation so that the exploitation probabilities of both the methods were as similar as possible.

$$\epsilon' = \frac{\epsilon - (1 - k)q}{1 - q}. \tag{6}$$

This control means that exploitation at a critical state is essential rather than randomly taking exploitation with certain probability regardless of the state. The exploration ratio ϵ of ϵ-greedy was annealed linearly from 0.905 at the initial step to 0.005 at the final 100k-th step. The exploration ratio ϵ' of the proposed method was correspondingly decayed from 1.0 to 0.0. We conducted 100 experiments each with both methods with different random seeds.

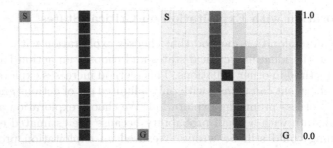

Fig. 1. Cliff maze and SIs. Left: The cliff maze environment has cliffs in the center column in all cells except for the center cell. The initial state is the upper-left corner cell, and the goal state is the lower-right corner cell. The agent receives a reward of +1 when it reaches the goal state and a reward of −1 when it reaches a cliff state. An episode terminates when the agent visits the goal state or a cliff state. Right: SIs of each cell in the cliff maze. The values are normalized to [0, 1].

The right part of the Fig. 1 shows the SI calculated after a 100k-step exploration. The SI was maximum at the state between the two cliffs. Intuitively, this state is a critical state, where the action selection divides the potential for success and failure dramatically. Table 1 shows the mean and standard deviation of the steps required to learn the shortest path. The proposed method reduced the median number of required steps by about 71% and the mean by about 68% compared to the simple ϵ-greedy method. To analyze the results, we used the Wilcoxon rank-sum test, and the p value was 5×10^{-13}. Its result shows that the proposed method significantly reduces the number of exploration steps required to learn the optimal shortest path in the cliff maze.

Table 1. Number of exploration steps required to learn the optimal shortest path.

Method	p value ($N = 100$)	Median	Mean	Std
ϵ-greedy	–	22815	26789	19907
Proposed	5×10^{-13}	6450	8468	6443

3.2 Scalability to Large State-Action Space

We evaluated the proposed method on two baseline tasks of deep RL to confirm whether it could scale up to high-dimensional complex tasks. The statistical significance of the mean of the acquired return was calculated with a Bayes regression of the time-series model, as defined in the Appendix. We show the results for a ratio of critical states $q = 0.1$ below, since changing the ratio q from 0.05 to 0.5 did not make a significant difference in the results.

Large Discrete Space. We used the Arcade Learning Environment Atari2600 Breakout [2] as an example of a high-dimensional discrete space task. The agent learned the Q-function with the deep Q-network (DQN) [14]. The comparison procedure was the same as that in the experiment of Sect. 3.1 except that we linearly annealed ϵ from 0.905 at the initial step to 0.005 at the final 2,000k-th step. We calculated the threshold of the SI every 1,000 steps with the 1,000 most recently visited states because it is difficult to calculate the SI of all the states in the large state space. We evaluated the return after every 1,000 steps of exploration by choosing exploitation from the initial state to the end of the episode.

The hyperparameter settings were as follows. The environment setting was the same as that of [14] except that we did not use flickering reduction and we normalized each pixel to the range [0, 1]. We approximated Q-function with a convolutional neural network (CNN). The CNN had three convolutional layers with size (32× 32, 8, 4), (64 × 64, 4, 2), and (64 × 64, 3, 1) with rectified linear unit (ReLU) activation. The elements in the brackets correspond to (filter size, channel, stride). A fully-connected layer of unit size 256 with ReLU activation followed the last convolutional layer. A linear output layer followed this layer with a single output for each action. We used the target network [14] as the prior work. The target network was updated every 500 steps, and the Q-function was updated every four steps after 1,000 steps. The size of the replay buffer was 10^4, the discount factor was 0.99, and the batch size was 64. We used the Adam optimizer [10] and clipped the gradient when the L2 norm of the gradient of the DQN loss function exceeded 10. We initialized the weights using Xavier initialization [4] and the biases to zero.

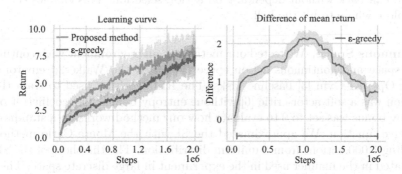

Fig. 2. Learning curve in the Breakout task. Returns are the average of the ten most recent evaluations to smooth the curve for visibility. Left: Each colored line and shading corresponds to the mean and standard deviation of the average return at each evaluation, respectively. Right: The line and shading correspond to mean and 95% credibility interval of the estimated difference of the return from the proposed method at each step, respectively. The horizontal line at the bottom indicates the interval over which the 95% credibility interval is greater than 0. The sample size is 25 for each method.

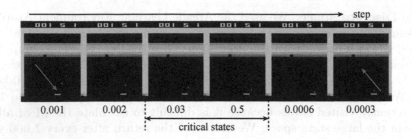

Fig. 3. Critical states identified in the Breakout task. The numbers correspond to the SIs. The arrow indicates the direction the ball is moving to.

The left part of Fig. 2 shows the change in the acquired return during learning. The right part of Fig. 2 shows the mean and the 95% credibility interval of the difference of mean return between the proposed method and ϵ-greedy method. The difference in the mean return was greater than 0 from the 50k-th step to the final 2000k-th step. A statistical difference existed in the latter 97.5% steps, at least in the sense of Bayes regression under our modeling (detailed modeling is shown in the Appendix). This result shows that the proposed method acquired a higher return in fewer exploration steps in the latter 97.5% of the learning process than ϵ-greedy. Figure 3 shows part of a fully exploited trajectory and the identified critical states. The agent could identify critical states at which the action selection is critical. At these critical states, the agent must move the plate toward the ball. Otherwise, the ball will fall. The fifth frame is not a critical state because it has already been determined that the agent can hit the ball back without depending on action selection. This enables the agent to explore where to hit the ball.

Continuous Space. We tested our method in an environment with continuous state space and continuous action space. We used the Walker2d environment of the OpenAI Gym [3] baseline tasks. The RL algorithm used to train the Q-function was a soft actor-critic [6] without entropy bonus. The coefficient of the entropy bonus was set to 0 to evaluate how our method works on a standard RL objective function. We approximated the SI with the Monte Carlo method by sampling 1,000 actions from a uniform distribution. The threshold of the SI was calculated in the manner used in the experiment in large discrete space. The proposed method chooses exploitation with high probability of k and chooses action based on a stochastic policy in other situations. We compared the exploration performance of the proposed method to two methods. One of the methods is called Default, and chooses action based on a stochastic policy at all states. The other one is EExploitation, which chooses exploitation with probability e and uses a stochastic policy with a low probability of $1-e$. We controlled the exploitation ratio e so that exploitation probabilities of both the proposed method and EExploitation were as similar as possible. This control means that exploitation at a critical state is essential rather than randomly taking exploitation with certain probability regardless of the state. The exploitation ratio e was set to $e = qk$. We evaluated the return every 1,000 steps of exploration by choosing exploitation from the initial state to the end of the episode.

The hyperparameter settings were as follows. We used neural networks to approximate the Q-function, V-function, and policy. The Q-function and V-function and the policy had two fully-connected layers of unit size 100 with ReLU activations. The output layers of the Q-function and V-function networks were linear layers that output a scalar value. The policy was modeled as a Gaussian mixture model (GMM) with four components. The output layer of the policy network outputted the four means, log standard deviations, and log mixture weights. The log standard deviations and the log mixture weights were clipped in the ranges of $[-5, 2]$ and $[-10,]$, respectively. To limit the action in its range, a sampled action from the GMM passed through a tanh function and then was multiplied by its range. L2 regularization was applied to the policy parameters. We initialized all the weights of neural networks using Xavier initialization [4] and all the biases to zero. The size of the replay buffer was 10^6, the discount factor was 0.99, and the batch size was 128. We used the Adam optimizer [10]. We updated the networks every 1,000 steps.

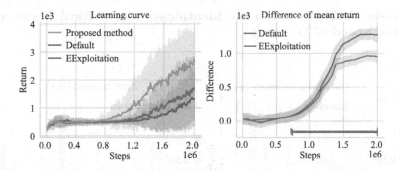

Fig. 4. Learning curve in the Walker2d task. Returns were averaged over the ten most recent evaluations to smooth the curve for visibility. Left: The colored line and shading correspond to the mean and standard deviation of the averaged return at each evaluation, respectively. Right: The lines and shading correspond to the means and 95% credibility intervals of the estimated difference of the return from the proposed method at each step, respectively. Each horizontal line at the bottom indicates the interval where 95% interval is greater than zero. The sample size is 25 for each method.

The left part of Fig. 4 shows the trend of the return acquired through learning. The right part of Fig. 4 shows the mean and the 95% credibility interval of the difference in the mean returns of the proposed method and each of the other methods. The difference of the mean return was greater than 0 from the 720k-th step to the final 2000k-th step for Default, and from the 740k-th step to the final 2000k-th step for EExploitation. A statistical difference existed in the latter 63% steps, at least in the sense of Bayes regression under the modeling

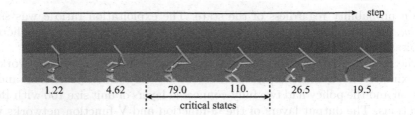

Fig. 5. Critical states identified in the Walker2d task. The numbers correspond to the SIs. The arrows indicate contact force.

(the detailed model is given in Appendix). This result shows that the proposed method acquired a higher return with fewer exploration steps in the latter 63% of the learning process. Figure 5 shows a part of a fully exploited trajectory and the identified critical states. The agent could identify critical states at which the action selection was critical. The agent had to lift the body by pushing the ground with one leg while it lifted and moved forward with the other leg. Otherwise it would stumble and fall.

3.3 Relationship Between the Identification of Critical States and the Speed of Learning

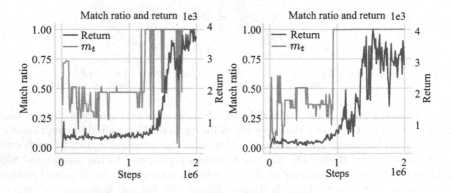

Fig. 6. Two examples of the match ratio. Here, m_t corresponds to the maximum match ratio of the top-ten critical states between the t-th step and the final step.

We analyzed the relationship between the timing of the identification of the especially critical states and the rapid progress of learning in the Walker2d task. The analysis process was as follows. The parameters of the Q-function at each t step and all states visited by the agent over the entire training were saved. We calculated the SI of all of the states with the saved Q-function's parameters. We regarded states whose SI values were in the top ten as especially critical states.

We calculated the minimum Euclidean distance d_t between the top-ten critical states of the final step and those of the t-th step, assuming that the SIs at the final step were correct. We calculated the d_t from the 1k-th step to the 2000k-th step in 10k step intervals. We calculated the match ratio m_t at each step t as $m_t = 1.0 - d_t/d_{\max}$, where $d_{\max}$ is the maximum value in d_t. The value of match ratio m_t becomes closer to 1 as at least one of the top-ten critical states of t step become closer to those of the final step.

Figure 6 shows two examples of the relationship between the timing of the identification of the top-ten critical states and the progress of learning. The return curves rapidly rose shortly after the agent begins to identify the top-ten critical states. This phenomenon might be interpreted as the agents "got the knack of" the task. This tendency was observed in some but not all agents. This result suggests there are a few critical states that had important information for accelerating RL rapidly.

4   Conclusion

In this paper, we assumed that the critical states at which the action selection dramatically changes the potential for future success and failure are useful for both exploring environments that include such states and extracting useful information for explaining the RL agent's operation. We calculated the critical states using the variance of the Q-function for the actions. We proposed to choose exploitation with high probability at the critical states for efficient exploration. The results show that the proposed method increases the performance of exploration and the identified states are intuitively critical for success. An analysis of the relationship between the timing of the identification of especially critical states and the rapid progress of learning suggests there are a few especially critical states that have important information for accelerating RL rapidly.

One limitation of our proposed method is that it does not increase the performance of exploration in environments with no critical states, where it does not decrease the performance significantly. Exploitation at falsely detected critical states is not critical for future success in such environments. In addition, this approach does not greatly increase the possibility of being trapped in local optima because it does not aim to reach critical states but just chooses exploitation when the visited state is a critical state. We decided the ratio of critical states q to use to set the threshold and the exploitation ratio k in advance. These values could be decided automatically during learning using the uncertainty of the Q-function with a Bayesian method. The proposed identification method extracted useful contents for a brief explanation, but their interpretation was constructed by a human. A method to construct a brief explanation using the identified critical states is future work.

Acknowledgments. This paper is based partly on results obtained from a project commissioned by the New Energy and Industrial Technology Development Organization (NEDO), and partly on results obtained from research activity in Chair for

Frontier AI Education, School of Information Science and Technology, The University of Tokyo.

Appendix

Calculation of the Statistical Difference of Two Learning Dynamics.
A statistical test to confirm the difference between algorithms is necessary for deep RL, because large fluctuations in performance have been observed even as a result of different random seeds [7]. We cannot evaluate the exploration steps required to learn the optimal solution because the optimal solution is difficult to define in a large state space. A statistical test has been performed on the difference of the mean of return at a certain step [7], but this makes determining the evaluation points arbitrary. In addition, independently treating each timestep does not properly handle the data because the return curve is time-series data. In this paper, we used Bayesian regression for the return curves by modeling them as random walks depending on one previous evaluation step. We consider there to be a statistical difference when the 95% credibility interval of the time series of the average difference of returns between the proposed method and each method exceeds 0. We model the return curve by

$$\mu[t] \sim \mathcal{N}(\mu[t-1], \sigma_\mu) \tag{7}$$
$$\delta_X[t] \sim Cauchy(\delta_X[t-1], \sigma_X) \tag{8}$$
$$R_{\text{Proposed}}[t] \sim \mathcal{N}(\mu[t], \sigma_R) \tag{9}$$
$$R_X[t] \sim \mathcal{N}(\mu[t] - \delta_X[t], \sigma_R). \tag{10}$$

We suppose that return of the proposed method $R_{\text{Proposed}}[t]$ is observed from the true value $\mu[t]$ with observation noise σ_R. This observation noise is caused by evaluating only several episodes instead of evaluating all possible trajectories. We assume that the return of a comparison method $R_X[t]$ has fluctuation $\delta_X[t]$ from $\mu[t]$, and that observation noise σ_R has been added. Here, $\mu[t]$ is modeled as a random walk with a normal distribution depending on the previous evaluation step with a variance of σ_μ. In addition, $\delta_X[t]$ is modeled as a random walk with a Cauchy distribution depending on the previous evaluation step with a parameter of σ_μ so that large fluctuations can be handled robustly. The statistical difference $\delta_X[t]$ was calculated by estimating the posterior with a Markov chain Monte Carlo (MCMC) method. We modeled the priors of all variables as a no-information uniform prior and initialized the first MCMC sample of $\mu[t]$ by the mean return of the proposed method at each evaluation step t.

References

1. Bellemare, M., Srinivasan, S., Ostrovski, G., Schaul, T., Saxton, D., Munos, R.: Unifying count-based exploration and intrinsic motivation. In: Advances in Neural Information Processing Systems, pp. 1471–1479 (2016)

2. Bellemare, M.G., Naddaf, Y., Veness, J., Bowling, M.: The arcade learning environment: an evaluation platform for general agents. J. Artif. Intell. Res. **47**, 253–279 (2013)
3. Brockman, G., et al.: Openai gym (2016)
4. Glorot, X., Bengio, Y.: Understanding the difficulty of training deep feedforward neural networks. In: Proceedings of the Thirteenth International Conference on Artificial Intelligence and Statistics, vol. 9, pp. 249–256. PMLR, 13–15 May 2010
5. Goyal, A., et al.: Transfer and exploration via the information bottleneck. In: International Conference on Learning Representations (2019)
6. Haarnoja, T., Zhou, A., Abbeel, P., Levine, S.: Soft actor-critic: off-policy maximum entropy deep reinforcement learning with a stochastic actor. In: Proceedings of the 35th International Conference on Machine Learning, vol. 80, pp. 1861–1870. PMLR, 10–15 July 2018
7. Henderson, P., Islam, R., Bachman, P., Pineau, J., Precup, D., Meger, D.: Deep reinforcement learning that matters. In: Thirty-Second AAAI Conference on Artificial Intelligence (2018)
8. Jayaraman, D., Ebert, F., Efros, A., Levine, S.: Time-agnostic prediction: predicting predictable video frames. In: International Conference on Learning Representations (2019)
9. Kazemitabar, S.J., Beigy, H.: Using strongly connected components as a basis for autonomous skill acquisition in reinforcement learning. In: Yu, W., He, H., Zhang, N. (eds.) ISNN 2009. LNCS, vol. 5551, pp. 794–803. Springer, Heidelberg (2009). https://doi.org/10.1007/978-3-642-01507-6_89
10. Kingma, D.P., Ba, J.: Adam: a method for stochastic optimization. In: 3rd International Conference on Learning Representations, San Diego, CA, USA, 7–9 May 2015. Conference Track Proceedings (2015)
11. Kuniyoshi, Y., Ohmura, Y., Terada, K., Nagakubo, A., Eitoku, S., Yamamoto, T.: Embodied basis of invariant features in execution and perception of whole-body dynamic actions–knacks and focuses of roll-and-rise motion. Robot. Auton. Syst. **48**(4), 189–201 (2004)
12. Liu, G., Schulte, O., Zhu, W., Li, Q.: Toward interpretable deep reinforcement learning with linear model U-trees. In: Berlingerio, M., Bonchi, F., Gärtner, T., Hurley, N., Ifrim, G. (eds.) ECML PKDD 2018. LNCS (LNAI), vol. 11052, pp. 414–429. Springer, Cham (2019). https://doi.org/10.1007/978-3-030-10928-8_25
13. McGovern, A., Barto, A.G.: Automatic discovery of subgoals in reinforcement learning using diverse density. In: Proceedings of the Eighteenth International Conference on Machine Learning, pp. 361–368 (2001)
14. Mnih, V., et al.: Human-level control through deep reinforcement learning. Nature **518**(7540), 529–533 (2015)
15. Pathak, D., Agrawal, P., Efros, A.A., Darrell, T.: Curiosity-driven exploration by self-supervised prediction. In: International Conference on Machine Learning (ICML), vol. 2017 (2017)
16. Şimşek, Ö., Barto, A.G.: Using relative novelty to identify useful temporal abstractions in reinforcement learning. In: Proceedings of the Twenty-First International Conference on Machine Learning, p. 95. ACM (2004)
17. Şimşek, Ö., Barto, A.G.: Skill characterization based on betweenness. In: Advances in Neural Information Processing Systems, pp. 1497–1504 (2009)
18. Şimşek, Ö., Wolfe, A.P., Barto, A.G.: Identifying useful subgoals in reinforcement learning by local graph partitioning. In: Proceedings of the 22nd International Conference on Machine Learning, pp. 816–823. ACM (2005)

19. Stolle, M., Precup, D.: Learning options in reinforcement learning. In: Koenig, S., Holte, R.C. (eds.) SARA 2002. LNCS (LNAI), vol. 2371, pp. 212–223. Springer, Heidelberg (2002). https://doi.org/10.1007/3-540-45622-8_16
20. Verma, A., Murali, V., Singh, R., Kohli, P., Chaudhuri, S.: Programmatically interpretable reinforcement learning. In: Proceedings of the 35th International Conference on Machine Learning, vol. 80, pp. 5045–5054. PMLR, 10–15 July 2018
21. Watkins, C.J., Dayan, P.: Machine learning. Q-learning 8(3–4), 279–292 (1992). https://doi.org/10.1007/BF00992698
22. Witten, I.H.: The apparent conflict between estimation and control–a survey of the two-armed bandit problem. J. Franklin Inst. 301(1–2), 161–189 (1976)

Explaining Concept Drift by Mean of Direction

Fabian Hinder$^{(\boxtimes)}$, Johannes Kummert, and Barbara Hammer

Cognitive Interaction Technology (CITEC), Bielefeld University,
Inspiration 1, 33619 Bielefeld, Germany
{fhinder,jkummert,bhammer}@techfak.uni-bielefeld.de

Abstract. The notion of concept drift refers to the phenomenon that the distribution, which is underlying the observed data, changes over time; as a consequence machine learning models may become inaccurate and need adjustment. In this paper we present a novel method to describe concept drift as a whole by means of flows, i.e. the change of direction and magnitude of particles drawn according to the distribution over time. This problem is of importance in the context of monitoring technical devices and systems, since it allows us to adapt models according to the expected drift, and it enables an inspection of the most prominent features where drift manifests itself. The purpose of this paper is to establish a formal definition of this problem and to present a first, yet simple linear method as a proof of concept. Interestingly, we show that a natural choice in terms of normalized expected linear change constitutes the canonical solution for a linear modeling under mild assumptions, which generalizes expected differences on the one hand and expected direction on the other. This first, global linear approach can be extended to a more fine grained method using common localization techniques. We demonstrate the usefulness of our approach by applying it to theoretical and real world data.

Keywords: Concept drift · Online learning · Learning with drift · Explanation of data

1 Introduction

One fundamental assumption in classical machine learning is the fact that observed data are i.i.d. according to some unknown probability P_X, i.e. the data generating process is stationary. Yet, this assumption is often violated as soon as machine learning faces real world problems: models are subject to seasonal changes, changed demands of individual costumers, ageing of sensors, etc. In such settings, life-long model adaptation rather than classical batch learning is required for optimal performance. Since drift, i.e. the fact that data is no

We gratefully acknowledge funding by the BMBF under grant number 01 IS 18041 A.

© Springer Nature Switzerland AG 2020
I. Farkaš et al. (Eds.): ICANN 2020, LNCS 12396, pp. 379–390, 2020.
https://doi.org/10.1007/978-3-030-61609-0_30

longer identically distributed, is a major issue in many real-world applications of machine learning, many attempts were made to deal with this setting [3].

Depending on the domain of data and application, the presence of drift is modelled in different ways. As an example, covariate shift refers to the situation of training and test set having different marginal distributions [7]. Learning for data streams extends this setting to an unlimited (but usually countable) stream of observed data, mostly in supervised learning scenarios [5]. Here, one distinguishes between virtual and real drift, i.e. non-stationarity of the marginal distribution only or also the posterior. Learning technologies for such situations often rely on windowing techniques, and adapt the model based on the characteristics of the data in an observed time window. Active methods explicitly detect drift, usually referring to drift of the classification error, and trigger model adaptation this way, while passive methods continuously adjust the model [3].

Interestingly, a majority of approaches deal with supervised scenarios, aiming for a small interleaved train-test error; this is accompanied by first approaches to identify particularly relevant features where drift occurs [10], and a large number of methods aim for a detection of drift, an identification of change points in given data sets, or a characterization of overarching types of drift [1,6]. However, non of those methods aim for a description of the observed drift by means of a characterization of the change of the underlying process as a whole. A first approach, which seeks to provide an explainable inspection of drift by highlighting the features with most variance, is presented in [10]; yet this is restricted to an inspection of drift in single features. The purpose of our contribution is to formalize the problem to describe observed drift in an explicit form, such that an informed monitoring of the process and an adaptation of models in regards to observed drift becomes possible. Besides a mathematical characterization and its investigation, we provide an algorithm, provided the form of drift is restricted to a linear form, and we show its efficiency in benchmarks.

This paper is organized as follows: In the first part of Sect. 2 we describe the setup of our problem and give a formal definition (see Definition 1). In Sects. 2.1 and 2.2 we derive three approaches to instantiate this modeling with specific functional forms and we investigate their mutual relation. In Sects. 2.3 and 2.4 we explain how the approaches can be realized. In the second part we apply the resulting algorithms for several benchmark data sets (see Sect. 3). Due to lack of space, all proofs are omitted in this contribution.

2 Describing Drift by Means of a Change Function

In the classical batch setup of machine learning one considers a generative process P_X, i.e. a probability measure, on $\mathbb{R}^d$. In this context one views the realizations of i.i.d. random variables $X_1, ..., X_n$ as samples. Depending on the objective, learning algorithms try to infer the data distribution based on these samples or, in the supervised setting, a posterior distribution. We will not distinguish these settings and only consider distributions in general, this way subsuming the notion of both, real drift and virtual drift.

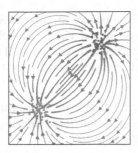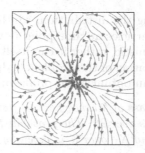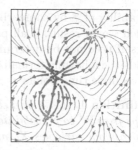

Fig. 1. Simple example flows; sample points are displayed (p_{t_0} blue, p_{t_1} yellow); the displayed directions describe underlying dynamics, which would explain the observed data points at the two consecutive time points. (Color figure online)

Many processes in real-world applications are online with data x_i arriving consecutively as drawn from a possibly changing distribution, hence it is reasonable to incorporate temporal aspects. One prominent way to do so is to consider an index set $\mathcal{T}$, representing time, and a collection of probability measures p_t on $\mathbb{R}^d$ indexed over $\mathcal{T}$, which describe the underlying probability at time point t and which may change over time [5]. In the following we investigate the relationship of those p_t. Drift refers to the fact that p_t is different for different time points t, i.e. $\exists t_0, t_1 \in \mathcal{T} : p_{t_0} \neq p_{t_1}$. A relevant problem is to explain and model drift, i.e. characterize the way in which probabilities p_t differ. We take the stance that the underlying generating process corresponds to a collection of particles moving through space. We are interested in characterizing the movement of these particles. For deterministic motion, the resulting flow describes the ongoing drift. For non-deterministic behavior, one can analyse the probability of a location for a particle at two consecutive time points. Figure 1 illustrates this idea.

We aim for an estimation of such flows. Further requirements are, that the solution is continuous w.r.t. the considered distribution and that it can efficiently be computed based on empirical distributions, i.e. it needs to be efficient w.r.t computational complexity as well as the required amount of data. Further, we aim for a method which can work for data x_i which are drawn independently according to p_i and no alignment of consecutive samples is given, as well as time series data, for which consecutive samples x_i and x_{i+1} are dependent and aligned to each other.

As before, $\mathcal{T}$ will be our time-index set. We consider a $\mathcal{T}$-indexed stochastic process X_t over a probability space $(\Omega, \mathcal{F}, \mathbb{P})$; the probability law of X_t at some $t_0 \in \mathcal{T}$ is denoted $\mathbb{P}_{X_{t_0}}$, and it holds $\mathbb{P}_{X_t} = p_t$ for all $t \in \mathcal{T}$. We assume a discrete time, i.e. $\mathcal{T} \subset \mathbb{N}$. This allows us to reduce the problem by solving it for two consecutive time points, which we model as $\mathcal{T} = \{0, 1\}$ for simplicity.

Assume that we can track particles in these two consecutive time steps. The idea behind the optimal-flow-problem is to find a map $f \in \mathfrak{F}$ that captures the information where a particle will go in the next step. We can measure the suitability of f by comparing the distribution, which we observe at time 1, and which would result, if all particles at time point 0 were moved via f. Thereby, f itself need not be deterministic, rather it can itself induce a distribution. This yields the following formalization of the problem of drift characterization for two consecutive time points as an optimization problem:

Definition 1. *Let $\mathfrak{F}$ be a class of Markov kernels from $\mathbb{R}^d$ to $\mathbb{R}^d$, i.e. measurable maps from $\mathbb{R}^d$ to probabilities over $\mathbb{R}^d$. The probabilistic optimal-flow-problem for two random variables X_0 and X_1 over $\mathfrak{F}$ is given by the objective*

$$\operatorname*{argmin}_{f \in \mathfrak{F}} D_{KL}(\mathbb{P}_{X_1} \| \mathbb{E}[f(X_0)]), \tag{1}$$

where D_{KL} denotes the Kullback-Leibler divergence.

Provided we restrict to a set of deterministic functions $\mathfrak{F} \subset L^1(\mathbb{R}^d, \mathbb{R}^d)$ the analogous problem is called the deterministic optimal-flow-problem, which is defined by the objective

$$\operatorname*{argmin}_{f \in \mathfrak{F}} D_{KL}(\mathbb{P}_{X_1} \| \mathbb{P}_{f(X_0)}). \tag{2}$$

Note that the deterministic optimal-flow-problem is a special case of the probabilistic optimal-flow-problem: a deterministic flow can be modeled as $f_{\text{prob}}(x) = \delta_{f_{\text{det}}(x)}$, where δ_x denotes the Dirac measure concentrated on x.

This general problem is computationally infeasible, unless the functional form of the flow is further restricted. Here, we restrict the functional form to a global transition function, i.e. we choose $\mathfrak{F} = \{x \mapsto x + \tau | \tau \in \mathbb{R}^d\}$ as a reasonable and particular intuitive first step. Furthermore, we assume for the moment that we deal with *aligned data*, i.e. pairs of consecutive data points are samples from a probability distribution over $\mathbb{R}^d \times \mathbb{R}^d$. These assumptions reduce the optimization problem to the construction of a mapping

$$D : \mathbf{P}(\mathbb{R}^d \times \mathbb{R}^d) \to \mathbb{R}^d, \tag{3}$$

which, given a set of pairs of points from two consecutive time steps, estimates the most likely translation underlying the observed drift. Here $\mathbf{P}$ denotes the set of all probability measures. We will see that this restricted form yields algorithmic solutions, which are efficient w.r.t. computation time and required training data. We impose two further assumptions:

(i) D should be continuous with respect to a suitable topology on $\mathbf{P}(\mathbb{R}^d \times \mathbb{R}^d)$. Since the empirical estimate should converge to the value of the real distribution, it is reasonable to choose the topology of weak convergence or weak*-topology interpreting it as a subspace of the space of all bounded, signed measures; recall that the weak*-topology is induced by the Wasserstein metric for probability distributions in this case.

(ii) If the process is concentrated on x_0 and on x_1, respectively, for the two consecutive time steps, then the translation vector $\overrightarrow{x_0 x_1}$ should be recovered up to scaling.

This yields the following definition:

Definition 2. *Let d be finite. A direction detection is a continuous mapping*

$$D : \mathbf{P}(\mathbb{R}^d \times \mathbb{R}^d) \to \mathbb{R}^d, \tag{4}$$

where $\mathbf{P}(\mathbb{R}^d \times \mathbb{R}^d)$ *is equipped with the topology of weak convergence of measures, and the following condition is imposed: for all* $x_0, x_1 \in \mathbb{R}^d$ *there exists* $\lambda > 0$ *such that*

$$D(\delta_{(x_0,x_1)}) = \lambda \cdot (x_1 - x_0). \tag{5}$$

We say that a direction detection is linear if D *is a linear map, i.e. for all* $P, Q \in \mathbf{P}(\mathbb{R}^d \times \mathbb{R}^d)$ *and* $\lambda \in [0,1]$ *it holds*

$$D(\lambda P + (1 - \lambda)Q) = \lambda D(P) + (1 - \lambda)D(Q). \tag{6}$$

It is computationally demanding to estimate the Kullback–Leibler divergence of continuous random variables with general distribution. Therefore, we aim for a surrogate method which can rely on popular estimation techniques (see Sect. 3). In the following, we construct a family of (linear) direction detections.

2.1 Mean of Normalized Translations

For the moment, we assume aligned data, i.e. consecutive pairs x_i, x_{i+1} sampled according to $P_{(X_0,X_1)}$. One natural candidate for a direction detection is offered by the mean translation vector of such pairs. This yields the following definition:

Definition 3. *The mean translation direction is defined as*

$$D_\infty(\mathbb{P}_{(X_0,X_1)}) := \mathbb{E}[X_1 - X_0] \tag{7}$$

If X_0 and X_1 are independent normally distributed random variables, this yields the analytic solution of optimal flow:

Theorem 1. *Assume that* $X_0 \sim \mathcal{N}(\mu_0, \Sigma_0)$ *and* $X_1 \sim \mathcal{N}(\mu_1, \Sigma_1)$ *are independent random variables. Then it holds*

$$D_\infty(\mathbb{P}_{(X_0,X_1)}) = \underset{\tau \in \mathbb{R}^d}{\operatorname{argmin}} D_{KL}(\mathbb{P}_{X_1} \| \mathbb{P}_{X_0+\tau}). \tag{8}$$

where $\mathbb{P}_X$ *refers to the probability distribution of random variable* X.

In general, however, the mean translation is not a direction detection, as can be seen in the following example:

Remark 1. Consider the case $d = 1$ with $P_n = \delta_0 \times ((1 - n^{-1})\delta_0 + n^{-1}\delta_n)$ where δ_n is the Dirac distribution at position n. For $(X_0^{(n)}, X_1^{(n)}) \sim P_n$ it holds

$$\mathbb{E}[X_1^{(n)} - X_0^{(n)}] = ((1 - n^{-1})0 + n^{-1}n) - 0 = 1 \tag{9}$$

for all $n \in \mathbb{N}$. On the other hand, it holds for $P = \delta_0 \times \delta_0$

$$\|P_n - P\| = \|(1 - n^{-1})\delta_0 \times \delta_0 + n^{-1}\delta_0 \times \delta_n - ((1 - n^{-1}) + n^{-1})\delta_0 \times \delta_0\| \quad (10)$$

$$= n^{-1}\|\delta_0 \times \delta_n - \delta_0 \times \delta_0\| \quad (11)$$

$$\leq 2n^{-1} \xrightarrow{n \to \infty} 0, \quad (12)$$

where $\| \cdot \|$ denotes the total variation norm. It therefore follows that $P_n \to P$ in total variation and hence in the weak*-topology. For $(X_0, X_1) \sim P$ it holds

$$\mathbb{E}[X_1 - X_0] = 0 - 0 = 0 \neq 1 = \mathbb{E}[X_1^{(n)} - X_0^{(n)}], \quad (13)$$

hence the expected difference is not continuous w.r.t. the weak*-topology.

This problem regarding the mean translation direction is caused by the fact that the identity function, which is used in the expectation, is not bounded; for bounded functions, mathematical guarantees on the continuity hold. Therefore, we normalize the translation vector, whereby a small positive constant avoids a singularity at $x_0 = x_1$.

Definition 4. *For fixed $\varepsilon > 0$ we define the normalized translation direction as*

$$D_\varepsilon(\mathbb{P}_{(X_0,X_1)}) := \mathbb{E}\left[\frac{X_1 - X_0}{\|X_1 - X_0\|_2 + \varepsilon}\right]. \quad (14)$$

This definition yields a valid direction detection:

Theorem 2. *For every $\varepsilon > 0$, the form D_ε is a linear direction detection.*

Further, this form approximates the mean translation direction for large ε:

Theorem 3. *Let X_0, X_1 be $\mathbb{R}^d$-valued random variables, with finite mean and variance. Then it holds pointwise convergence*

$$\varepsilon \cdot D_\varepsilon(\mathbb{P}_{X_0,X_1}) \to D_\infty(\mathbb{P}_{X_0,X_1}) \qquad \text{as } \varepsilon \to \infty. \quad (15)$$

Note that the normalized translation direction can be estimated given pairs of data points sampled from the underlying distribution. Before considering unpaired data, we have a look at the limit behavior of this direction detection for small values ε.

2.2   Optimal Alignment

An alternative, intuitive estimation is based on the idea to find the direction that aligns best with the observed ones; this leads to the following definition:

Definition 5. *The optimal alignment direction is defined as*

$$D_0(\mathbb{P}_{(X_0,X_1)}) := \operatorname*{argmax}_{w \in \mathbb{R}^d, \|w\|=1} \mathbb{E}[\cos \angle(w, \overrightarrow{X_0 X_1})] \quad (16)$$

The optimal alignment direction is not a valid direction detection, as demonstrated in the following example:

Remark 2. Consider the case $d = 1$. Since $\delta_x \times \delta_y = \delta_{(x,y)}$ and $d_{W_1}(\delta_x, \delta_y) = \|x - y\|$, where d_{W_1} denotes the Wasserstein 1-metric, it follows that

$$d_{W_1}(\delta_0 \times \delta_{-\varepsilon}, \delta_0 \times \delta_{+\varepsilon}) = 2|\varepsilon| \xrightarrow{\varepsilon \to 0} 0. \tag{17}$$

However, for all $\varepsilon > 0$ it holds

$$D_0(\delta_0 \times \delta_\varepsilon) = 1 \tag{18}$$
$$D_0(\delta_0 \times \delta_{-\varepsilon}) = -1. \tag{19}$$

This implies that D_0 is not continuous.

Yet, the optimal alignment direction results as a limit case of the normalized translation direction:

Theorem 4. *Let X_0, X_1 be $\mathbb{R}^d$-valued random variables, with finite mean and variance. Then it holds pointwise convergence*

$$D_\varepsilon(\mathbb{P}_{X_0,X_1}) \to D_0(\mathbb{P}_{X_0,X_1}) \qquad \text{as } \varepsilon \to 0. \tag{20}$$

Theorems 2 and 4 may be interpreted as the fact that normalized translation direction interpolates between mean translation direction and optimal alignment direction. As shown in Remark 1 and Remark 2, mean translation direction is sensitive in the case of large drift whereas optimal alignment direction is sensitive to small drift. Hence the choice of ε constitutes a relevant hyper-parameter for the robustness of the method.

We illustrate this behavior in Fig. 2. X_0 is distributed according to a zero centered normal distribution and X_1 is distributed according to a mixture of two normal distributions, one centered at $\mu = (0, 15)$ with a high probability of occurrence and one centered at $\mu = (5000, 0)$ with low probability of occurrence. For small ε, D_ε chooses the direction, which is induced by the part of X_1 with high density. For large ε, D_ε points towards the distant part of X_1, since large values dominate the expectation. In practice, estimation of drift directions should therefore be based on a suitable ε.

2.3   Handling Unaligned Data

So far we have considered the estimation of drift directions for paired data. Now we will discuss the case where we only know the marginal distributions of X_0 and X_1 without an explicit alignment of observed points in pairs. Hence we are now looking for a map

$$D^s : \mathbf{P}(\mathbb{R}^d) \times \mathbf{P}(\mathbb{R}^d) \to \mathbb{R}^d. \tag{21}$$

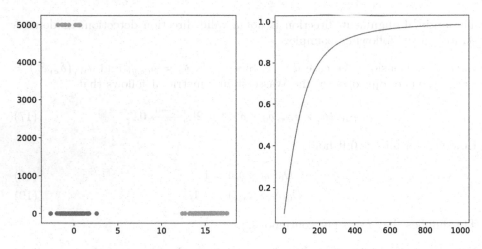

Fig. 2. Left: distribution at 0 (blue) and at 1 (yellow); Right: x-component of D_ε (normalized to length 1) for different values of ε (Color figure online)

As before, we impose the condition that D^s is continuous, where we equip $\mathbf{P}(\mathbb{R}^d)$ with the weak*-topology. As a consequence of this choice, we can naturally identify $\mathbf{P}(\mathbb{R}^d) \times \mathbf{P}(\mathbb{R}^d)$ with a subspace of $\mathbf{P}(\mathbb{R}^d \times \mathbb{R}^d)$, hence the following definition provides a valid choice:

$$D_\varepsilon^s(\mathbb{P}_{X_0}, \mathbb{P}_{X_1}) := D_\varepsilon(\mathbb{P}_{X_0} \times \mathbb{P}_{X_1}), \tag{22}$$

where $\mathbb{P}_{X_0} \times \mathbb{P}_{X_1}$ denotes the product measure. Note that the association problem becomes trivial if either the first or the second component is concentrated on one point, i.e. it is distributed according to a Dirac-measure. In these cases the above definition of D_ε^s constitutes the only consistent choice. Since Dirac-measures constitute a dense subspace of $\mathbf{P}(\mathbb{R}^d)$, it immediately follows that this choice of D_ε^s is the only possible extension to a continuous mapping D^s if we additionally assume it to be linear in both of its arguments. As before, an empirical estimation of D_ε^s on the base of all products of given samples from $\mathbb{P}_{X_0}$ and $\mathbb{P}_{X_1}$ is immediate.

2.4 Estimating Translation Length

So far we have focused on an estimation of an optimal translation direction. We can extend this to an estimation of a suitable length of the optimal translation. For this purpose, we project all data points onto the one-dimensional subspace spanned by the vector obtained via the direction detection. Then, the length of the translation can be estimated by the expectation along this projection:

$$\mathbb{E}\left[\langle D(\mathbb{P}_{(X_0, X_1)}), X_1 - X_0 \rangle\right]. \tag{23}$$

3   Experiments

We apply our method to theoretical data with known ground truth and real world data sets. For all data sets, we assume that no alignment of consecutive points is given. We evaluate the performance of the proposed direction estimation by displaying the extracted drift. Albeit we can compare to the known drift for theoretical data, we compare these presentations to the visualizations obtained by using the *drift magnitude* [10] for the real-world data. In addition, we compute the error, which arises, when comparing the distribution of observed data and the distribution of data predicted by our method. This error is measured by Kullback-Leibler divergence using a k-nearest neighbour approach [9]. We refer to this quantity as D_{KL}-error. As a second quantitative evaluation, we investigate the capability of the estimated shift to be used in transfer learning. More precisely, we document the relative error of a regressor for the original and the shifted data: (err = $MSE_{reference}/MSE_{shifted}$); this is referred to as transfer error. The results are summarized in Table 1.

Theoretical Data: To demonstrate how our method can be used to characterize and visualize drift, we apply it to a simple, theoretical data set, which is displayed, together with the results of the direction detection, in Fig. 3. The data set consists of a series of normal distributions with the same variance, where means are moving along a spiral, i.e. $\mu_t = (\sin(t), \cos(t))$; it is possible to reconstruct this drift exactly as can be seen in Fig. 3.

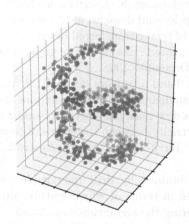 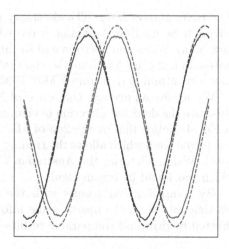

Fig. 3. Left: normal distribution with mean moving along a spiral curve (time is displayed on Z-axis); Right: components of normalized translation direction (solid line) and (shifted) sinus and cosinus wave (dashed line)

Table 1. Resulting errors for real world data sets

Data set	D_{KL}-error	Transfer error (larger is better)
Electricity market	5.3	1.2
Weather	0.3	9.4
Forest covertype	3.9	1.5

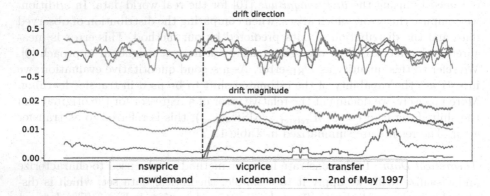

Fig. 4. Top: Components of normalized translation direction applied to electricity market data set (window length 1000). Bottom: drift magnitude applied to electricity market data set

Electricity Market Data: The electricity market data set [8] describes electricity pricing in South-East Australia. It records the price and demand in the states of New South Wales and Victoria and the amount of power transferred between the states. In our considerations the class label is ignored. Examples are generated for every 30 min period from 7 May 1996 to 5 December 1998.

We achieve an average D_{KL}-error of 5.3 ± 4.0 and a transfer error of 1.2. We illustrate the detected direction of change by visualizing the feature components in Fig. 4. Notice that at the 2nd of May 1997 a new national electricity market was introduced, which allows the trading of electricity between the states of New South Wales, Victoria, the Australian Capital Territory, and South Australia, which was found by our method.

By comparing our results with the ones obtained by drift magnitude we see that we obtain the nearby same information in terms of which features are effected by drift and comparable results comparing the significance of change.

Weather Data. The weather data set [4] contains an extensive range of 50 years (1949–1999) of weather data, gathered by the U.S. National Oceanic and Atmospheric Administration at Offutt Air Force Base in Bellevue, Nebraska. It contains daily measurements of various features (temperature, pressure, wind speed, etc.) and indicators for precipitation and other weather-related events. We illus-

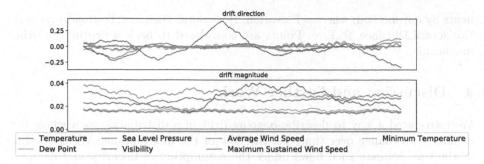

Fig. 5. Top: Components of normalized translation direction applied on weather data (window length 1500) Bottom: drift magnitude applied to weather data

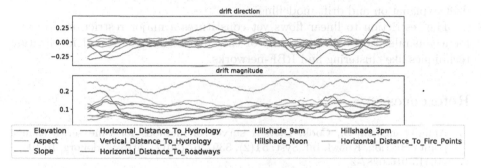

Fig. 6. Top: Components of normalized translation direction applied on forest cover type data set (window length 500) Bottom: drift magnitude applied to forest cover type data set

trate the results of the drift components in Fig. 5. We achieve an average D_{KL}-error of 0.3 ± 0.2 and a transfer error of 9.4.

By comparing our results with the drift magnitude we see that Visibility and Maximum Sustained Wind Speed are considered to change drastically by both methods, Sea Level Pressure is considered as drifting only by our method while Average Wind Speed seems to have stronger drift if we consider drift magnitude. The remaining features are comparable for both methods.

Forest Covertype Data. The forest covertype data set [2] consists of cartographic variables such as elevation, slope, soil type, etc. of 30×30 meter cells to different forest cover types. Only forests with minimal human-caused disturbances were used, so that resulting forest cover types are more a result of ecological processes. We normalize the data component-wise to $[0, 1]$. We illustrate the results in Fig. 6. We achieve an average D_{KL}-error of 3.9 ± 1.9 and transfer error of 1.5.

By comparing our results with the drift magnitude we see that all features are drifting. However drift magnitude identifies Aspect as the most relevant component while our method identifies Elevation, Horizontal_Distance_To_Roadways and Horizontal_Distance_To_Fire_Points as the most relevant components. Aspect is identified as one of the more relevant components by our method, whereas Elevation, Horizontal_Distance_To_Roadways and Horizontal_Distance_To_Fire_ Points are considered to be less drifting by drift magnitude.

4   Discussion and Further Work

We introduced a way to describe ongoing drift of a distribution as a whole by means of its change over time, i.e. the flow of the distributions. We created a method to estimate such flows under the assumption of linearity and demonstrated its relation to intuitive expected directions or change of expectations, respectively. We demonstrated the behavior in several examples, and the empirical results demonstrate that this constitutes a promising approach as regards drift explanation and drift modelling.

The restriction to linear flows yet constitutes a major restriction. We aim for a generalization based on ideas of the Fréchet derivative and localization techniques like clustering and RBF-networks.

References

1. Aminikhanghahi, S., Cook, D.J.: A survey of methods for time series change point detection. Knowl. Inf. Syst. **51**(2), 339–367 (2017). https://doi.org/10.1007/s10115-016-0987-z
2. Blackard, J.A., Dean, D.J., Anderson, C.W.: Covertype data set (1998). https://archive.ics.uci.edu/ml/datasets/Covertype
3. Ditzler, G., Roveri, M., Alippi, C., Polikar, R.: Learning in nonstationary environments: a survey. IEEE Comput. Int. Mag. **10**(4), 12–25 (2015). https://doi.org/10.1109/MCI.2015.2471196
4. Elwell, R., Polikar, R.: Incremental learning of concept drift in nonstationary environments. IEEE Trans. Neural Netw. **22**(10), 1517–1531 (2011). https://doi.org/10.1109/TNN.2011.2160459
5. Gama, J.A., Žliobaitė, I., Bifet, A., Pechenizkiy, M., Bouchachia, A.: A survey on concept drift adaptation. ACM Comput. Surv. **46**(4), 44:1–44:37 (2014). https://doi.org/10.1145/2523813
6. Goldenberg, I., Webb, G.I.: Survey of distance measures for quantifying concept drift and shift in numeric data. Knowl. Inf. Syst. **60**(2), 591–615 (2018). https://doi.org/10.1007/s10115-018-1257-z
7. Gretton, A., Smola, A., Huang, J., Schmittfull, M., Borgwardt, K., Schölkopf, B.: Covariate Shift and Local Learning by Distribution Matching, pp. 131–160. MIT Press, Cambridge (2009)
8. Harries, M., Cse-tr, U.N., Wales, N.S.: Splice-2 comparative evaluation: electricity pricing. Technical report (1999)
9. Wang, Q., Kulkarni, S.R., Verdu, S.: Divergence estimation for multidimensional densities via k-nearest-neighbor distances. IEEE Trans. Inf. Theory **55**(5), 2392–2405 (2009). https://doi.org/10.1109/TIT.2009.2016060
10. Webb, G.I., Lee, L.K., Petitjean, F., Goethals, B.: Understanding concept drift. CoRR abs/1704.00362 (2017). http://arxiv.org/abs/1704.00362

Few-Shot Learning

Context Adaptive Metric Model for Meta-learning

Zhe Wang and Fanzhang Li[✉]

Provincial Key Laboratory for Computer Information Processing Technology,
Soochow University, Suzhou 215006, China
zhewang.wi@qq.com, lfzh@suda.edu.cn

Abstract. The metric-based meta-learning is effective to solve few-shot problems. Generally, a metric model learns a task-agnostic embedding function, maps instances to a low-dimensional embedding space, then classifies unlabeled examples by similarity comparison. However, different classification tasks have individual discriminative characteristics, and previous approaches are constrained to use a single set of features for all possible tasks. In this work, we introduce a Context Adaptive Metric Model (CAMM), which has adaptive ability to extract key features and can be used for most metric models. Our extension consists of two parts: Context parameter module and Self-evaluation module. The context is interpreted as a task representation that modulates the behavior of feature extractor. CAMM fine-tunes context parameters via Self-evaluation module to generate task-specific embedding functions. We demonstrate that our approach is competitive with recent state-of-the-art systems, improves performance considerably (4%–6% relative) over baselines on mini-imagenet benchmark. Our code is publicly available at https://github.com/Jorewang/CAMM.

Keywords: Context adaptive · Metric model · Meta-learning · Few-shot learning

1 Introduction

Meta-learning [3,5,25] can be expressed as a *learning to learn* process. Traditional learning algorithms can perform well on one task, but they do not work well when applied to other tasks. The meta-learning algorithm [11,28] improves some aspects of the recent learning algorithm through the meta-knowledge learned from prior tasks, so the meta-learning algorithm can flexibly adapt to different tasks.

This work is supported by the National Key R&D Program of China (2018YFA0701700; 2018YFA0701701), and the National Natural Science Foundation of China under Grant No. 61902269.

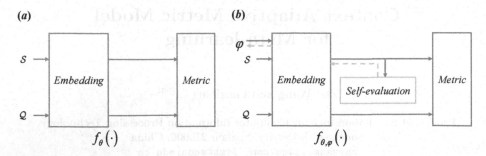

Fig. 1. (*a*) In previous methods, the embedding function f_θ uses a fixed set of comparison features for all possible tasks (as θ is fixed after training), without associating the task-specific information. (*b*) The proposed Context Adaptive Metric Model $f_{\theta,\varphi}$ uses task-specific context φ to dynamically modulate the behavior of the feature extractor.

Few-shot learning [6,13,18,20,26] is one of the main problems to be solved in meta-learning. The goal of few-shot learning is to classify unseen data instances (query examples) into a set of new categories, given just a small number of labeled instances (support examples) in each class. Recent learning algorithms, especially deep learning, often result in poor performance when learning with limited data. However, observing the human learning process, we found that humans can deal with data-less situations well, and can quickly learn a new concept or skill from prior knowledge. For example, after observing one or several pictures of cats and dogs, a child can correctly distinguish them; a child who has never seen a zebra can recognize it by describing to him the similarities and differences between a zebra and a horse.

To this end, metric-based meta-learning has emerged as a promising approach in tackling this challenge, which learn to represent image data in an appropriate feature space and use a distance metric to predict image labels. The distance function directly compute a distance between the embeddings of the query images and support images for classification. Assuming a common embedding space implies that this model should extract all necessary discriminative features, and visual features discovered from training tasks are also effective for target tasks.

Intuitively, such approaches do suffer from limitations. Suppose we have two simple visual classification tasks: identifying "ants or elephants" and identifying "horses or zebras". The key characteristics of these two tasks are size and color, respectively. For the second task, the size is not a discernible feature. Hence, the optimal model needs to extract all distinguishable features for possible tasks, which is challenging with the model design. Even if the model can extract enough features, it is often the case that the distinguishable features for one task could be irrelevant and noise to others.

In this work, we propose a context-adaptive extension that incorporates adaptive capability into metric models. Figure 1 illustrates our approach and previous methods at a high level. The component has two parts: Context parameter module and Self-evaluation module. Our model adopts the same interleaved training procedure as MAML [9] to simulate fast adaptation. The model learns task-specific context parameter by performing one or several gradient steps through the self-evaluation module, thereby modulates the model to extract distinguishable features suitable for different tasks. On the standard dataset, CAMM has achieved superior performance. Compared with the baseline, the average accuracy is improved by 5.8% in 5-way 1-shot classification and 4% in 5-shot.

1.1   Background

In meta-learning problems [8], we assume there exists a task distribution $\mathcal{P}(\mathcal{T})$, and the learning goal is to make the model f fit this distribution. The training data for meta-learning is organized into many subsets, which called tasks. An *n-way k-shot p-query* classification task contains a small number of examples, partly as $\mathcal{D}^s$(support set) and others $\mathcal{D}^q$(query set). Each task is generated by uniformly sampling n classes and k training examples, p testing examples per class:

$$\mathcal{D}^s = \{(x,y)_m\}_{m=1}^{n*k}, \quad \mathcal{D}^q = \{(x,y)_m\}_{m=1}^{n*p} \tag{1}$$

Each time we sample a batch of tasks $\mathcal{T}^{train}$ from $\mathcal{P}(\mathcal{T})$ during the meta-train phase. For each task $\mathcal{T}_i^{train}$, model learns from support instances and tests on query instances to get the loss. Formally, f is learnt to minimize the averaged error over those sampled tasks:

$$f^* = \arg\min_f \mathbb{E}_{\mathcal{T}^{train}} \sum_{(x,y)\in\mathcal{D}^q} \mathcal{L}(f(x;\mathcal{D}^s),y) \tag{2}$$

In meta-test phase, we randomly sample a sufficient number of tasks $\mathcal{T}^{test}$ from $\mathcal{P}(\mathcal{T})$, where $\mathcal{T}^{test}\cap\mathcal{T}^{train}\cap\mathcal{T}^{valid} = \emptyset$. We test the meta-trained model by using the average performance of the model learned from the corresponding support examples of each task.

Briefly, metric-based methods [15,30] learn a general embedding function E, mapping d-dimensional input $x \in X \subseteq \mathbb{R}^d$ to p-dimensional embedding space $y \in Y \subseteq \mathbb{R}^p$, usually $d \gg p$. We predict the classification result by comparing the query to each of the support sample. Such models consist of three main components: (1) Function f: map support instances $x^s \subseteq \mathbb{R}^d$ to $y^s \subseteq \mathbb{R}^p$. (2) Function g: map query instances $x^q \subseteq \mathbb{R}^d$ to $y^q \subseteq \mathbb{R}^p$. (3) Metric measure m: calculate the similarity among the vectors in embedding space.

1.2   Summary of Contributions

Fast Adaptation in Metric Models: To our knowledge, this is the first study to combine two types meta-learning methods(metric-based and optimization-based) to address the limitations of previous metric models. We apply an interleaved training procedure to the metric model to achieve fast adaptation.

Context Conditioning: We add extra context parameters to the base feature extractor, which is interpreted as a task embedding. Optimized context modulates model to extract distinguishable feature sets suitable for different tasks.

Self-evaluation: Self-evaluation module is a learnable label-free loss function that determines whether the embedded support set is discriminative in metric space. We use it to fine-tune context parameters via one or several gradient updates(only use two updates in experiments).

2   Related Work

The existing meta-learning methods can be roughly categorized into three categories: (a) model-based, (b) optimization-based, and (c) metric-based.

The **model-based** methods are based on a model designed specifically for fast learning, which updates its parameters rapidly with a few training steps and labeled data. Ravi *et al.* [21] propose an LSTM meta-learner to learn optimization algorithms for few-shot problems, which can learn the parameter update rules to speed up the convergence of classifier model. MetaNet [16] allows neural networks to dynamically learn new tasks or concepts from a single example for continuous learning. Based on the idea of Turing Machine NTMs, MANN [24] uses a neural network with external storage to solve the few-shot problems. MANN has the ability to long-term and short-term memory for fast coding of new information.

The second category of work are **optimization-based** solutions, which aims at effectively adapting model parameters to new tasks in the few-shot regime. In Model-agnostic Meta-learning, Finn *et al.* [9] propose the idea of fast adaptation for the first time. MAML uses an interleaved training procedure, comprised of inner loop and outer loop. The inner loop only performs a few gradient updates to simulate the fast adaptation process. Then, in the outer loop, model parameters from before the inner loop update are updated to reduce the expected loss across tasks after the inner loop update on the individual tasks. Finally, MAML learns an optimal model initialization. Nichol *et al.* [17] point out that the second-order gradient calculation of MAML can be approximately replaced by addition and subtraction operations on first-order gradients, which makes the algorithm less computation and memory consumption.

The **metric-based** methods focus on learning a deep representation with a metric in feature space. Matching network [29] uses bidirectional LSTM as support set mapping, LSTM with attention mechanism as query set mapping, and cosine distance as metric method. The attention mechanism can comprehensively consider the similarity between query and support instances. Prototypical network [26] regards the mean of feature embeddings as prototype points of individual classes, and replace cosine similarity with Euclidean distance which is a Bregman divergence. Unlike other methods, Relation network [27] uses a learnable convolutional neural network instead of a non-parametric distance function as the similarity measure. It improves model performance by learning a more complex and accurate similarity measure.

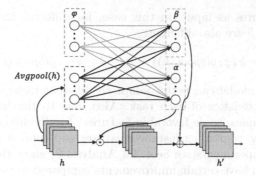

Fig. 2. Illustration of the context parameter module. We set the context parameters φ as extra inputs of the model. Combining context and sample features as input, it generates scaling and bias through a linear transformation.

3   Model Description

3.1   Context Parameter Module

We add context parameters to original metric models, so the embedding function $f_{\theta,\varphi}$ is controlled by two parts: context parameters φ and base parameters θ.

Base parameters θ are obtained through meta-training and fixed when applying to target tasks; Context parameters φ are task-specific and adapted with one or several gradient updates in the inner loop. In practice, we set context parameters as extra input, and they affect the base model through FiLM layers. Perez *et al.* [19] propose Feature-wise Linear Modulation, which adaptively affects the output of convolutional layers by applying an affine transformation to feature maps. Specifically, FiLM learns functions k and t that encode input x to generate scaling coefficients α and bias coefficients β corresponding to each channel:

$$\alpha = k\left(x\right) + 1, \quad \beta = t\left(x\right) \tag{3}$$

Then it applies α and β to feature maps h to generate new transformed feature maps h':

$$h' = \alpha \odot h + \beta \tag{4}$$

Figure 2 schematically illustrates our context module. For the input information x_i, we consider the following two cases:

Only-Context Feature. Context parameters are used as FiLM layer inputs. For different tasks, updated context parameters φ are unique, so the conditioning layer generates specific α and β. For different instances in a task, model uses the same α and β.

Mixed-Context and Instance Features. We consider both instance-related information and task-related information. Concretely, we take the output of feature maps after global average pooling as instance features, then concat context and instance features as input. In this case, for different instances in a task, coefficients α and β are also different:

$$\alpha = k\left(\varphi, glbpool\left(h\right)\right) + 1, \quad \beta = t\left(\varphi, glbpool\left(h\right)\right) \tag{5}$$

With context, model can better adapt to different tasks and highlight discriminative characteristics of each task. Also, due to the limitation of available support examples, some favorable features of individual examples may be ignored. Intuitively, combining instance features and context parameters is the optimal choice. Experiments(see Sect. 4.3 Analysis 2) show that the above two input settings both have certain improvements compared to the benchmark, and Mixed-features is indeed better than Only-context, both in 1-shot and 5-shot tasks.

3.2   Self-evaluation Module

In the inner loop, when only the support set is available, we need a label-free loss function to compute the loss. Manually designing such a loss function is challenging, often only yielding loss functions that might work in one setting but not in another.

To this end, we use the self-evaluation module C_w as a label-free loss function, which is parameterized as a neural network and the w is meta-trained across tasks. With evaluation contents of the support set, self-evaluation module outputs a loss value, which indicates the compatibility between the current embedding function to the target task.

The performance of C_w is unsurprisingly dependent on the quality of critic features F it is given access to. In this work, we consider the following three statistical parts: *embedded support example, mean and variance of embedded support examples with the same class, mean and variance of all embedded support examples*:

$$F_i = \{f\left(x_i\right), \mathbb{E}\left[f\left(\mathcal{D}_n^s\right)\right], \mathbb{D}\left[f\left(\mathcal{D}_n^s\right)\right], \mathbb{E}\left[f\left(\mathcal{D}^s\right)\right], \mathbb{D}\left[f\left(\mathcal{D}^s\right)\right]\};$$
$$where(x, y)_i \in \mathcal{D}^s, y_i = n \tag{6}$$

By comparing above contents, C_w judges whether the features extracted by embedding function are suitable for current task. Experiments (see Sect. 4.3 Analysis 4) show that the meta-trained C_w does have this self-evaluation ability. C_w makes embedded support examples with the same label closer in the embedding space, and embedding vectors of different types are more distinguishable.

3.3   How to Learn

The complete algorithm is described in Algorithm 1. We denote $f_{\theta,\varphi}$ as embedding function and m as the Euclidean distance. During each meta-train iteration, a batch task set $\mathcal{T}^{train}$ containing N tasks is sampled from the task distribution $\mathcal{P}\left(\mathcal{T}\right)$. For each task $\mathcal{T}_i \in \mathcal{T}^{train}$, $\mathcal{D}_i^s$ represents the support set, where $\mathcal{D}_{i,n}^s$ is the support set belonging to class n, and $\mathcal{D}_i^q$ represents the query set.

Algorithm 1. Training strategy of Context Adaptive Metric Model

---

Require: Distribution over tasks $\mathcal{P}(\mathcal{T})$, every task is *n-way k-shot p-query*.
Require: Embedding model $f_{\theta,\varphi}$ with θ initialized randomly and $\varphi_0 = 0$, self-evaluation function C_w with w initialized randomly, metric function m.
Require: inner loop learning rate λ, steps s; outer loop learning rate γ.
1: **while** not done **do**
2:     Sample batch of tasks $\mathcal{T}^{train} = \{\mathcal{T}_i\}_{i=1}^{N}$ where $\mathcal{T}_i \sim \mathcal{P}(\mathcal{T})$
3:     **for** i in range(N) **do**
4:         $\mathcal{T}_i = \{\mathcal{D}_i^s, \mathcal{D}_i^q\}, \quad \varphi_0 = 0$
5:         **for** j in range(s) **do**
6:             $F = \{f_{\theta,\varphi}(x), f_{\theta,\varphi}(\mathcal{D}_{i,n}^s), f_{\theta,\varphi}(\mathcal{D}_i^s)\}$
7:             $\varphi_{j+1} = \varphi_j - \lambda\nabla_\varphi \frac{1}{n*k} \sum\limits_{x \in \mathcal{D}_i^s} C_w(F)$
8:         **end for**
9:         $c_n = \frac{1}{k} \sum\limits_{x \in \mathcal{D}_{i,n}^s} f_{\theta,\varphi_s}(x)$
10:        $\mathcal{L}_{out} = \mathcal{L}_{out} + \frac{1}{n*p} \sum\limits_{(x,y) \in \mathcal{D}_i^q} \mathcal{L}_{\mathcal{T}_i}(m(f_{\theta,\varphi_s}(x), c), y)$
11:    **end for**
12:    $\theta \leftarrow \theta - \frac{\gamma}{N}\nabla_\theta \mathcal{L}_{out}$
13:    $w \leftarrow w - \frac{\gamma}{N}\nabla_w \mathcal{L}_{out}$
14: **end while**

Before the inner loop update, we first initialize context parameters φ to 0, which implies that the context does not affect the CNN output before adaptation. In the inner loop, model $f_{\theta,\varphi}$ uses $\mathcal{D}_i^s$ to generate the support set embeddings and then integrates the required evaluation contents(see Sect. 3.2) into F:

$$F = \{f_{\theta,\varphi}(x), f_{\theta,\varphi}(\mathcal{D}_{i,n}^s), f_{\theta,\varphi}(\mathcal{D}_i^s)\} \tag{7}$$

Given each support example criticizing information F, the self-evaluation module C_w computes the average loss. Then we learn the task-specific context parameters φ_i via one or several gradient updates:

$$\varphi_i = \varphi - \lambda\nabla_\varphi \frac{1}{n*k} \sum_{x \in \mathcal{D}_i^s} C_w(F) \tag{8}$$

For the meta-update in the outer loop, with the optimized context parameters φ_i, model f_{θ,φ_i} maps $\mathcal{D}_i^s$ and $\mathcal{D}_i^q$ to task-specific embedding space. Then class prototypes c_n are computed as the mean of embedded support examples for each class:

$$c_n = \frac{1}{k} \sum_{x \in \mathcal{D}_{i,n}^s} f_{\theta,\varphi_i}(x) \tag{9}$$

Every query embedding is compared with class prototypes to get predicted labels through m. Then the prediction and true label are used to compute the cross-entropy loss $\mathcal{L}_{\mathcal{T}_i}$ for this task. Finally, we calculate the average loss of sampled batch tasks and update parameters θ and w via backpropagation:

$$\theta_i = \theta - \gamma \nabla_\theta \frac{1}{N} \sum_{\mathcal{T}_i \in \mathcal{T}^{train}} \frac{1}{n*p} \sum_{(x,y) \in \mathcal{D}_i^q} \mathcal{L}_{\mathcal{T}_i} \left(m \left(f_{\theta,\varphi_i} (x) , c \right) , y \right) \qquad (10)$$

$$w_i = w - \gamma \nabla_w \frac{1}{N} \sum_{\mathcal{T}_i \in \mathcal{T}^{train}} \frac{1}{n*p} \sum_{(x,y) \in \mathcal{D}_i^q} \mathcal{L}_{\mathcal{T}_i} \left(m \left(f_{\theta,\varphi_i} (x) , c \right) , y \right) \qquad (11)$$

3.4   Architecture

We employ a four-layer convolution structure as the backbone feature extractor f, which is the same architecture used in Prototypical network, MAML, etc. [9,26,27,31]. Each convolutional block comprises a 64-filter 3×3 convolution, a batch normalization layer, a ReLU activation function, and a 2×2 maxpool layer. We add the context conditioning layer after batch normalization layer of each convolution block. The context undergoes a linear transformation to obtain α and β. We also test the case of nonlinear transformation with one hidden layer. We find that it results in similar performance(see Sect. 4.3 Analysis 3).

The self-evaluation module C_w uses a three-layer convolution structure with the same block as f and finally attaches a single-node fully-connected layer to output the loss. For $3 \times 84 \times 84$ input instances, the embedding function outputs a 1600-dimensional embedding vector, and then resized to $1 \times 40 \times 40$ feature maps. We concatenate the evaluation information at channel dimension into F.

4   Experiments

In this chapter, Sect. 4.1 introduces the relevant experiment settings. Section 4.2 shows the main experimental results. In Sect. 4.3, we conduct ablation studies to analyze the following four issues: (1) Whether context adaptation in CAMM actually improves the task-agnostic embeddings? (2) Compare two different input settings for the context module. (3) Whether a more complex context module is better? (4) How context adaptation qualitatively improves the performance of embedding function?

4.1   Experimental Setups

Dataset. The mini-imagenet dataset was first proposed by Vinyal [7,22,29], which has 100 classes, each class has 600 images. We follow Ravi's [21] settings to split this dataset into three parts: a train set of 64 classes for meta-train, a validation set of 16 classes for meta-validation, and a test set of 20 classes for meta-test.

Evaluation Protocols. Previous approaches [9,26,27,29,31] evaluate models on 600 tasks randomly sampled from the test set. To further reduce the evaluation error, we evaluate our approach with 1000 sampled tasks.

Pre-train. In the meta-train phase, we need to optimize embedding function and self-evaluation module at the same time. To better decouple these two parts and speed up the model training process, we apply a pre-train as suggested in papers [20,23]. The pre-trained weight θ' is used as initialization of θ in the embedding function $f_{\theta,\varphi}$.

Model Setups. As 100 parameters are sufficient to represent different tasks for mini-imagenet, we use 100 context parameters. Our models were trained using 2 gradient steps in the inner loop and evaluated using 2 gradient steps at test time. We started with an inner loop learning rate of 0.1 and the Adam optimizer [10] with the standard learning rate of 0.001 for the outer loop. As the backbone network has been pre-trained, we scale the learning rate for those sets of parameters by 0.1. We use a meta batch-size of 2 tasks for 1-shot and 5-shot training. All models are trained for 30000 iterations.

Table 1. Few-shot classification accuracies on mini-imagenet.

Model	5-way 1-shot	5-way 5-shot
Model-based		
Meta-LSTM [21]	43.44 ± 0.77%	60.60 ± 0.71%
Meta-SGD [12]	50.47 ± 1.87%	64.03 ± 0.94%
MM-Net [4]	53.37 ± 0.48%	66.97 ± 0.35%
Optimization-based		
MAML [9]	48.70 ± 1.75%	63.15 ± 0.91%
Reptile [17]	48.21 ± 0.69%	66.00 ± 0.62%
CAVIA [31]	51.82 ± 0.65%	65.85 ± 0.55%
MAML++ [1]	52.15 ± 0.26%	68.32 ± 0.44%
MAML++ with SCA [2]	54.24 ± 0.99%	71.85 ± 0.53%
Metrics-based		
Matching network [29]	43.56 + 0.84%	55.31 + 0.73%
Relation network [27]	50.44 ± 0.82%	65.32 ± 0.70%
Prototypical network (**Baseline**) [26]	49.42 ± 0.78%	68.20 ± 0.66%
Ours: CAMM	**55.22 ± 0.66%**	**72.16 ± 0.51%**

4.2   Main Result

The prototypical network [26] achieves state-of-art performance among metric models. Therefore, we use prototypical network as the benchmark model and add our context adaptive framework. The compared models are all based on same four-convolution architecture. As shown in Table 1, CAMM is far superior to the benchmark model, and has been increased by 5.8% and 4% in 1-shot and 5-shot experiments. Compared with other approaches, our method has also been greatly improved.

Table 2. Ablation study results. (*a*) Whether the context adaptation improves performance. (*b*) Compare two different input settings. (*c*) Whether a more complex context module is better.

	Ablation condition	5-way 1-shot	5-way 5-shot
(a)	Pre-adaptation	49.1	69.7
	Post-adaptation	55.0	71.8
(b)	Only-context	52.1	70.2
	Mixed-features	55.0	71.8
(c)	Linear	54.8	72.2
	Nonlinear	54.5	72.0

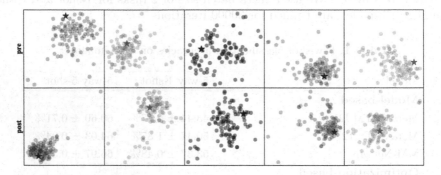

Fig. 3. A t-SNE visualization of support(star) and query(dot) embeddings for each class. **first row:** context pre-adaptation. **second row:** context post-adaptation. Interestingly, we found that the context adaptation step has the tendency of pushing the query points to the clutter, support points to the true prototypes.

4.3   Ablation Studies and Analysis

Analysis 1: Whether context adaptation in CAMM actually improves the task-agnostic embeddings? To investigate this issue, We show the few-shot classification results on test set using pre- and post-adaptation context parameters. Table 2 shows that with the task-specific context, both 1-shot and 5-shot classifications improve.

Analysis 2: Compare two different input settings for the context module. In Sect. 3.1, we considered two input cases for the context module. Table 2 shows that using Mixed-features performs better both in 1-shot and 5-shot experiments. We guess that with the context modulation, the feature extractor is easier to ignore favorable features of individual examples, especially when support set is smaller(1-shot case). So these characteristics not be selected as comparative features.

Analysis 3: Whether a more complex context module is better? We perform ablation study to test CAMM with hidden layers in the context parameter module, which increases the complexity of scaling and bias generator. Empirically, Table 2 shows that it results in similar performance when using nonlinear transformation. So linear transformations are sufficient to encode context for generating scaling and bias.

Analysis 4: How context adaptation qualitatively improves the performance of embedding function? We randomly sample a 5-way 1-shot 100-query task and use t-SNE [14] to visualize the embedding vectors of each class(use embedding functions before and after the context adaptation). Figure 3 implies that embedding function with post-adaptation context extracts better discriminative features. We found that query points change from scattered state to a more clustered state(e.g. red, green and purple), and support points are closer to the center of query points so that they can better serve as class prototypes. The figure has qualitatively shown that our approach is effective.

5 Conclusions and Future Work

Previous metric models all learn a general embedding function, which cannot extract the optimal distinguishable visual knowledge for target tasks. We propose a context adaptive metric model to increase the adaptation ability for previous methods. We use the context as task representation, so the context adaptation process corresponds to the task recognition process. The context quickly adapts to new tasks via only a few gradients updates. Our model achieves state-of-art performance on the benchmark dataset. For metric-based methods, there might be two future improvements: one is to design more effective algorithms to extend the adaptive ability; The other is to improve the feature extraction capability of deep learning models.

References

1. Antoniou, A., Edwards, H., Storkey, A.: How to train your MAML. arXiv preprint arXiv:1810.09502 (2018)
2. Antoniou, A., Storkey, A.: Learning to learn by self-critique. arXiv preprint arXiv:1905.10295 (2019)
3. Biggs, J.B.: The role of metalearning in study processes. Br. J. Educ. Psychol. **55**(3), 185–212 (1985)
4. Cai, Q., Pan, Y., Yao, T., Yan, C., Mei, T.: Memory matching networks for one-shot image recognition. In: Proceedings of the IEEE Conference on Computer Vision and Pattern Recognition, pp. 4080–4088 (2018)
5. Caruana, R.: Learning many related tasks at the same time with backpropagation. In: Advances in Neural Information Processing Systems, pp. 657–664 (1995)
6. Chen, W.Y., Liu, Y.C., Kira, Z., Wang, Y.C., Huang, J.B.: A closer look at few-shot classification. In: International Conference on Learning Representations (2019)
7. Deng, J., Dong, W., Socher, R., Li, L.J., Li, K., Fei-Fei, L.: Imagenet: a large-scale hierarchical image database. In: 2009 IEEE Conference on Computer Vision and Pattern Recognition, pp. 248–255. IEEE (2009)

8. Finn, C.: Learning to Learn with Gradients. Ph.D. thesis, UC Berkeley (2018)
9. Finn, C., Abbeel, P., Levine, S.: Model-agnostic meta-learning for fast adaptation of deep networks. In: Proceedings of the 34th International Conference on Machine Learning, vol. 70, pp. 1126–1135. JMLR. org (2017)
10. Kingma, D.P., Ba, J.: Adam: A method for stochastic optimization. arXiv preprint arXiv:1412.6980 (2014)
11. Lemke, C., Budka, M., Gabrys, B.: Metalearning: a survey of trends and technologies. Artif. Intell. Rev. **44**(1), 117–130 (2013). https://doi.org/10.1007/s10462-013-9406-y
12. Li, Z., Zhou, F., Chen, F., Li, H.: Meta-sgd: Learning to learn quickly for few-shot learning. arXiv preprint arXiv:1707.09835 (2017)
13. Liu, Y., et al.: Learning to propagate labels: Transductive propagation network for few-shot learning. arXiv preprint arXiv:1805.10002 (2018)
14. Maaten, L.v.d., Hinton, G.: Visualizing data using T-SNE. J. Mach. Learn. Res. **9**(Nov), 2579–2605 (2008)
15. Mensink, T., Verbeek, J., Perronnin, F., Csurka, G.: Metric learning for large scale image classification: generalizing to new classes at near-zero cost. In: Fitzgibbon, A., Lazebnik, S., Perona, P., Sato, Y., Schmid, C. (eds.) ECCV 2012. LNCS, vol. 7573, pp. 488–501. Springer, Heidelberg (2012). https://doi.org/10.1007/978-3-642-33709-3_35
16. Munkhdalai, T., Yu, H.: Meta networks. In: Proceedings of the 34th International Conference on Machine Learning, vol. 70, pp. 2554–2563. JMLR. org (2017)
17. Nichol, A., Achiam, J., Schulman, J.: On first-order meta-learning algorithms. arXiv preprint arXiv:1803.02999 (2018)
18. Oreshkin, B., López, P.R., Lacoste, A.: TADAM: task dependent adaptive metric for improved few-shot learning. In: Advances in Neural Information Processing Systems, pp. 721–731 (2018)
19. Perez, E., Strub, F., De Vries, H., Dumoulin, V., Courville, A.: Film: visual reasoning with a general conditioning layer. In: Thirty-Second AAAI Conference on Artificial Intelligence (2018)
20. Qiao, S., Liu, C., Shen, W., Yuille, A.L.: Few-shot image recognition by predicting parameters from activations. In: Proceedings of the IEEE Conference on Computer Vision and Pattern Recognition, pp. 7229–7238 (2018)
21. Ravi, S., Larochelle, H.: Optimization as a model for few-shot learning. In: In International Conference on Learning Representations (ICLR) (2017)
22. Russakovsky, O., et al.: ImageNet large scale visual recognition challenge. Int. J. Comput. Vis. **115**(3), 211–252 (2015)
23. Rusu, A.A., et al.: Meta-learning with latent embedding optimization. arXiv preprint arXiv:1807.05960 (2018)
24. Santoro, A., Bartunov, S., Botvinick, M., Wierstra, D., Lillicrap, T.: Meta-learning with memory-augmented neural networks. In: International Conference on Machine Learning, pp. 1842–1850 (2016)
25. Schmidhuber, J.: Evolutionary principles in self-referential learning, or on learning how to learn: the meta-meta-... hook. Ph.D. thesis, Technische Universität München (1987)
26. Snell, J., Swersky, K., Zemel, R.: Prototypical networks for few-shot learning. In: Advances in Neural Information Processing Systems, pp. 4077–4087 (2017)
27. Sung, F., Yang, Y., Zhang, L., Xiang, T., Torr, P.H., Hospedales, T.M.: Learning to compare: Relation network for few-shot learning. In: Proceedings of the IEEE Conference on Computer Vision and Pattern Recognition, pp. 1199–1208 (2018)

28. Vilalta, R., Drissi, Y.: A perspective view and survey of meta-learning. Artif. Intell. Rev. **18**(2), 77–95 (2002)
29. Vinyals, O., Blundell, C., Lillicrap, T., Wierstra, D., et al.: Matching networks for one shot learning. In: Advances in Neural Information Processing Systems, pp. 3630–3638 (2016)
30. Wang, Y., Yao, Q.: Few-shot learning: a survey. arXiv preprint arXiv:1904.05046 (2019)
31. Zintgraf, L.M., Shiarlis, K., Kurin, V., Hofmann, K., Whiteson, S.: Fast context adaptation via meta-learning. In: Thirty-sixth International Conference on Machine Learning (ICML 2019) (2019)

Ensemble-Based Deep Metric Learning
for Few-Shot Learning

Meng Zhou, Yaoyi Li, and Hongtao Lu[✉]

Department of Computer Science and Engineering, Shanghai Jiao Tong University,
Shanghai 200240, People's Republic of China
{zhoumeng,dsamuel,htlu}@sjtu.edu.cn

Abstract. Overfitting is an inherent problem in few-shot learning. Ensemble learning integrates multiple machine learning models to improve the overall prediction ability on limited data and hence alleviates the problem of overfitting effectively. Therefore, we apply the idea of ensemble learning to few-shot learning to improve the accuracy of few-shot classification. Metric learning is an important means to solve the problem of few-shot classification. In this paper, we propose ensemble-based deep metric learning (EBDM) for few-shot learning, which is trained end-to-end from scratch. We split the feature extraction network into two parts: the shared part and exclusive part. The shared part is the lower layers of the feature extraction network and is shared across ensemble members to reduce the number of parameters. The exclusive part is the higher layers of the feature extraction network and is exclusive to each individual learner. The coupling of the two parts naturally forces any diversity between the ensemble members to be concentrated on the deeper, unshared layers. We can obtain different features from the exclusive parts and then use these different features to compute diverse metrics. Combining these multiple metrics together will generate a more accurate ensemble metric. This ensemble metric can be used to assign labels to images of new classes with a higher accuracy. Our work leads to a simple, effective, and efficient framework for few-shot classification. The experimental results show that our approach attains superior performance, with the largest improvement of 4.85% in classification accuracy over related competitive baselines.

Keywords: Ensemble · Few-shot learning · Metric learning

1 Introduction

Deep learning has seen tremendous success in computer vision, speech recognition and natural language processing tasks [9]. However, learning the enormous number of parameters of these supervised learning models typically needs to

---

H. Lu—Also with MoE Key Lab of Articial Intelligence, AI Institute, Shanghai Jiao Tong University.

I. Farkaš et al. (Eds.): ICANN 2020, LNCS 12396, pp. 406–418, 2020.
https://doi.org/10.1007/978-3-030-61609-0_32

iterate lots of times on huge amounts of labeled training examples and data is expensive to obtain. Therefore, the study of few-shot learning [25] is of great significance, which is a sub-field of machine learning. Few-shot learning may work on three main paradigms: learning a hyper network to produce a learner for the current task [8], mapping the samples into a learned metric space [22,25] and the network optimization or initialization [1,4,18].

The goal of machine learning is to minimize the expected risk and empirical risk is usually used to estimate the expected risk, so the goal of machine learning becomes to minimize the empirical risk. In few-shot learning, very limited data causes the empirical risk minimization is no longer reliable. That is to say, few-shot learning naturally has serious overfitting problem. There are a few related works at present, and most methods solve this problem from the perspective of probability. BMAML [12] introduced Bayesian inference and Chaser loss into MAML which can access the uncertainty to alleviate the overfitting problem in meta-learning. PLATIPUS [5] incorporates a parameter distribution which is trained via a variational lower bound into MAML and thus can sample multiple potential models for a new task to deal with the core issue of task ambiguity.

Ensemble is a widely used technique of combining multiple weak models to produce a strong model, which will improve the performance by a significant margin and effectively alleviate the problem of overfitting. Generally speaking, ensemble method will have a lower error rate than any of its component classifiers because the disagreements will cancel out. This advantage is more prominent when the data is limited, which is exactly the condition for few-shot learning. Therefore, we apply the idea of ensemble learning to few-shot learning to improve the accuracy of few-shot classification.

Following the work of metric-learning based approaches for few-shot classification, we propose a new framework based on ensemble metric for few-shot learning, abbreviated as EBDM. We divide the feature extraction module into shared part (lower layers of the network) and exclusive part (higher layers of the network). The two key points for ensemble method to achieve a high performance are the diversity among ensemble members and the high performance of each ensemble member. To ensure the diversity among ensemble units, each ensemble member has its own exclusive feature extraction module and the shared feature extraction module is shared among the ensemble units. The shared part is designed to extract the low-level features shared among each individual learners. The exclusive part is initialized using different random seed to ensure the diversity among the learned features. Multiple diverse metrics can be computed from different features and then we integrate these diverse metrics to obtain an ensemble metric. This ensemble metric can measure the distance between samples and their prototypes more accurately.

Our main contributions can be summarized as follows:

– To the best of our knowledge, we are the first one that applies the technique of ensemble learning to solve the problem of few-shot learning.

- We propose a new framework based on ensemble metric for few-shot learning which can be combined with any metric and improves the performance of few-shot classification significantly.
- Our experimental results reveal that the proposed method is able to match previous state-of-the-art few-shot learning methods on most tasks of several few-shot learning benchmarks.

2   Related Work

Few-shot learning has become an increasingly popular research direction in recent years. Most proposed methods to solve the problems of few-shot learning can be divided into two types: meta-learning based approaches and metric-learning based approaches.

Meta-learning Based Approaches. Meta-learning aims to learn meta knowledge from various tasks and apply these knowledge in new tasks. HyperNet [8] aims to learn a model to produce the parameters of the network for a new task automatically. MM-Net [3] construct a Contextual Learner to learn the network parameters for the unlabelled images using CNNs augmented with memory. The work of DynamicNet [7] train a shared embedding network using the whole training set in the first stage and learn a classification weight generator for the new tasks in the second stage. GNN [6] uses Graph Neural Network, essentially an extension of CNN in non-Euclidean space, to explore the spacial distribution of similar tasks. MAML [4] initialize the network's parameters to an average position which is close to all the tasks so that the network can adapt to new tasks quickly with limited data. PLATIPUS [5] incorporates model distribution which is trained by the variational lower bound with MAML. The key challenge of task ambiguity for few-shot learning can be solved by sampling a model for a new task from the model distribution. BMAML [12] introduced Bayesian inference into MAML which can access the uncertainty to solve the overfitting problem in few-shot learning. This method combined gradient descent-based meta-learning methods with non-parametric variational inference in a probabilistic framework. LEO [20] maps the original high dimensional parameter space to a low dimensional parameter space and performs MAML on it, which will solve the problem that it is hard to perform fast adaptation of MAML in the high-dimensional parameter space. MetaLSTM [18] uses LSTM as an optimizer and treats the model parameters as its hidden state. The method proposed in [1] also uses LSTM to simulate optimizer, but unlike MetaLSTM, it takes the current gradient as input and outputs an increment of the parameters. [24] train a meta-learner to generate a better loss function for current task. Memory-augmented models [17,21] are trained across tasks to utilize the past experience and thus can generalize on novel concepts rapidly with small training data without forgetting the ones learned previously.

Metric-Learning Based Approaches. These methods aim to learn a transferable feature embedding and obtain a distribution based on distances between two images computed using it. SiameseNet [13] aims to learn discriminative representations which can be generalized to unseen classes. MatchingNet [25] uses cosine distance to compute the similarity between two images and applies attention mechanism to assign weights to each image in support set. ProtoNet [22] uses the cluster centroids to represent each class in query set and euclidean distance to compute the distance between two images. RelationNet [23] uses a network to learn a more effective metric function. DN4 [15] learns the optimal deep local descriptors for the image-to-class measure and then conducts k-nearest neighbor search on them. [2] aims to learn a shared feature embedding function on the base classes and use ridge regression to deal with novel classes. [16] performs classification in all the spatial locations not global average pooling at the end. CTM [14] fuses information from all classes inside one task to generate an attention projector, which will project extracted features onto more discriminative dimensions and then concatenate them on these dimensions.

3 Methodology

3.1 Problem Statement

In the task of few-shot classification, we have two datasets sharing the same label space: support set S and query set Q. We call the target few-shot problem N-way K-shot when each of the N unique classes contains K labelled samples in support set.

The goal of few-shot classification is to learn a classifier with the support set S only, which can be used to classify each sample in the query set Q correctly. Episode-based training proposed in [25] is an effective way to make use of the training set by mimicking the few-shot learning setting. In each training iteration, an episode is formed by randomly selecting N classes from the training set with $K + W$ labelled samples for each class, of which K for support set S and W for query set Q. While at test time, the learned model can be further fine-tuned using the support set and tested on the query set.

3.2 Model Description

The core idea of our approach is to extract multiple diverse features and then compute the distance in these features. Finally, we obtain a more accurate distance by integrating these distances of different features. The feature extraction module is divided into two parts: shared feature extraction module and exclusive feature extraction module. Shared feature extraction module is shared among the ensemble members and each ensemble member has its own exclusive feature extraction module which are initialized using different random seed. Thus, the exclusive feature embedding function changes the intermediate feature map extracted by the shared part and generates diverse features in the end. We can obtain an ultimate distance metric by combining the metrics computed on these different features and the ultimate distance can measure the distance between two images more accurately.

Our model is composed of three modules: feature extraction module, metric module, and metric ensemble module, as shown in Fig. 1. Given an image as input, the feature extraction module outputs M different embedding feature vectors. Metric module $D(\cdot)$ computes the similarity between two images in each of the features. Ensemble module $E(\cdot)$ integrates base distances to obtain the ultimate distance.

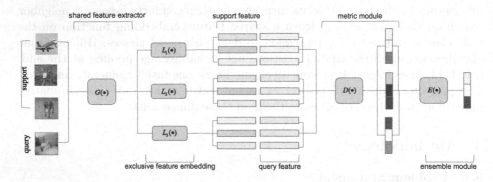

Fig. 1. Architecture of our few-shot learning model taking 3-way 1-shot classification for instance. Feature extraction module consists of shared feature extractor $G(\cdot)$ and exclusive feature embedding $L(\cdot)$. Shared feature extractor $G(\cdot)$ is used to learn the low-level features shared among each ensemble members. Exclusive feature embedding module is initialized using different manual seed and generates different features based on the output from global feature extractor $G(\cdot)$. Metric module $D(\cdot)$ is to compute the base distances between two images in different features. Ensemble module $E(\cdot)$ is to compute the ultimate distance based on M base distances.

Feature Extraction Module. The advantages and disadvantages of ensembles and single models are complementary. Ensembles collect as much high-value information from multiple instances of base learner as possible. However, single models need to adjust their parameters carefully to achieve excellent performance. The ensemble model will introduce a large number of redundant parameters on a large probability, causing the model to expand and the training time to increase dramatically. The hierarchy structure of CNN is a good choice for the ensemble method. The lower layers can extract shared features to reduce parameters and higher layers are owned by each individual learner to ensure the diversity.

We assume a CNN architecture as:

$$F(x) = h_l(h_{l-1}(\cdots(h_1(x)))) \tag{1}$$

We divide the layers into higher and lower parts with a branching point at i, $G(\cdot)$ includes $h_1, \cdots, h_i$ and $L(\cdot)$ includes $h_{i+1}, \cdots, h_l$. We call $G(\cdot)$ the shared feature extractor and $L(\cdot)$ the exclusive feature embedding function with respect to the output of each function. $G(\cdot)$ is shared among ensemble members and each individual learner has its own exclusive feature embedding function $L(\cdot)$. Given an image x as input, the embedding function $B_m(x)$ for the learner m is defined as the following:

$$B_m(x) = L_m(G(x)) \tag{2}$$

By sharing weights in the shared feature extractor, each weight is updated by the multiple sources of supervision from each exclusive embedding function and thus the extracted low-level feature has a stronger generalization ability. Each ensemble member consisting of shared feature extractor and exclusive feature embedding can be viewed as an independent network. This tree structure makes full use of the characteristics of CNN, which not only reduces the amount of parameters but also ensures the diversity to satisfy the key points of ensemble method.

Few-Shot Classification. We denote support set $\mathcal{S} = \{(x_1, y_1), \cdots, (x_N, y_N)\}$ where x_i is the image and $y_i \in \{1, \cdots, k\}$ is the corresponding label. $\mathcal{S}_k$ represents the set of examples labeled with class k. The prototype of class k in m-th feature:

$$C_{m,k} = \frac{1}{|\mathcal{S}_k|} \sum_{(x_i, y_i) \subset \mathcal{S}_k} B_m(x_i) \tag{3}$$

For a query point x, the base distance to the prototype k in m-th feature:

$$d_m(x, k) = D(B_m(x), C_{m,k}) \tag{4}$$

The m-th feature produces a distribution over classes based on a softmax over the m-th base distance:

$$p_m(y = k|x) = \frac{\exp(-d_m(x, k))}{\sum_{k'} \exp(-d_m(x, k'))} \tag{5}$$

The prediction result for x of learner m is:

$$\hat{y} = \arg\max_k p_m(y = k|x) \tag{6}$$

We can obtain the ultimate distance by integrating the base distances:

$$d(x, k) = E(d_1(x, k), \cdots, d_M(x, k)) = \frac{1}{M} \sum_{m=1}^{M} d_m(x, k) \tag{7}$$

A distribution over classes based on a softmax over the ultimate distances can be generated:

$$p(y = k|x) = \frac{\exp(-d(x, k))}{\sum_{k'} \exp(-d(x, k'))} \tag{8}$$

The prediction result of distribution $p(y = k|x)$ is more accurate than distribution $p_m(y = k|x)$ of any single learner. Therefore, the ultimate prediction result for query point x is:

$$\hat{y} = \arg\max_k p(y = k|x) \tag{9}$$

Objective Function. In the training stage of few-shot classification, we are given a support set S as mentioned in previous section and a query set $Q = \{(x_1, y_1), \cdots, (x_V, y_V)\}$. Our model can be trained using two ways: directly optimizing for model averaging and optimizing ensemble member independently.

Generally speaking, the prediction result of an ensemble model is typically performed by averaging the output of the member learners, thus it is natural to optimize the model by the loss computed from the mean of all ensemble members's output. For a query point x, we can obtain the ultimate distance $d(x, k)$ by averaging all the base distances. And then a distribution $p(y = k|x)$ over classes based on a softmax over the ultimate distance can be generated. Our objective function is the negative log-probability $p(y = k|x)$ of the true class k, which is defined as following:

$$
\begin{aligned}
J_{mean}(Q) &= -\frac{1}{V} \sum_{x \in Q} \log p(y = k|x) \\
&= \frac{1}{V} \sum_{x \in Q} \left[d(x, k) + \log \sum_{k'} \exp(-d(x, k')) \right]
\end{aligned}
\tag{10}
$$

The essence of the ensemble method is that multiple diverse models cancel disagreement to improve prediction accuracy. To guarantee the diversity, each ensemble unit should be optimized independently. For a query point x, we can obtain the multiple different metrics $d_m(x, k)$ from multiple ensemble members. And then the distribution $p_m(y = k|x)$ over classes based on a softmax over the distance computed by each ensemble member can be generated. Our objective function is the sum of the negative log-probability $p_m(y = k|x)$ of the true class k for each ensemble unit, which is defined as following:

$$
\begin{aligned}
J_{ind}(Q) &= \sum_{m=1}^{M} -\frac{1}{V} \sum_{x \in Q} \log p_m(y = k|x) \\
&= \sum_{m=1}^{M} \frac{1}{V} \sum_{x \in Q} \left[d_m(x, k) + \log \sum_{k'} \exp(-d_m(x, k')) \right]
\end{aligned}
\tag{11}
$$

Directly optimizing the mean of the ensemble member output eliminates diversity when the gradient is back propagated from ensemble. Perform averaging on the outputs of each ensemble unit:

$$
E(d_1, d_2, \cdots, d_M) = \frac{1}{M} \sum_{m=1}^{M} d_m
\tag{12}
$$

Assume the final loss is J and the derivative of J with respect to d_i:

$$
\frac{\partial J}{\partial d_m} = \frac{\partial J}{\partial E} \frac{\partial E}{\partial d_m} = \frac{\partial J}{\partial E} \frac{1}{M}
\tag{13}
$$

This expression has nothing to do with m, thus the gradients back propagated to each ensemble member are identical. The averaging operation cause the responsibility for mistake is shared by each ensemble member, which reduce the diversity of gradients. Optimizing each ensemble member individually ensure the varrying gradient based on its own performance is back propagated to each learner, which ensures the diversity among ensemble members. Therefore, optimizing each ensemble member individually performs better.

4 Experiments

4.1 Datasets

miniImageNet. miniImageNet, originally proposed by [18], is a standard dataset for few-shot classification. It contains 100 classes sampled from ILSVRC-12, each having 600 colour images resized to 84×84. The dataset is split into training set, validation set and testing set with 64 classes, 16 classes and 20 classes respectively [18]. The label space of these three sets is disjoint each other.

tieredImageNet. tieredImageNet, proposed by [19], is also a subset of ILSVRC-12. Unlike miniImagenet, tieredImageNet is organized as a hierarchical structure and contains more classes and samples. The classes in tieredImageNet are grouped into higher-level categories and the higher-level categories are divided into training, validation and testing categories.

4.2 Implementation Details

Feature Extraction Module. The backbone for our experiments consists of four convolutional layers. We use two different kinds of feature extraction module. The first one uses the first two layers of convolution as our shared feature extractor $G(\cdot)$ and the last two layers as our exclusive feature embedding function $L(\cdot)$, denoted as "arc1". The second one uses the first three convolution layers as shared feature extractor $G(\cdot)$ and the last one layers as our exclusive feature embedding function $L(\cdot)$, denoted as "arc2".

Metric Module. We perform our experiments using two kinds of distance metric function: euclidean distance (EBDM-Euc) and a deep nonlinear distance (EBDM-DD). Deep distance consists of two convolutional blocks and two fully-connected layers. We conduct 5-way 1-shot and 5-way 5-shot classification in our experiments.

4.3 Results

Comparison with Baselines. The metrics used in ProtoNet and RelationNet are euclidean distance and deep distance respectively, so we take them as our baselines. We compare our methods with various state-of-the-art methods for few-shot learning on miniImageNet and tieredImageNet. Besides, we explore the effect of the number of ensemble members in our ensemble model. The comparison results are reported in Table 1 and Table 2.

ProtoNet in original paper [22] performs 30-way classification in 1-shot and 20-way in 5-shot during the meta-training stage and it is re-implemented with the same setting as meta-testing in [15]. Therefore, we reference the results in [15] with the same setting as us for a fair comparison. The experimental results show that our model achieves a higher accuracy than the baseline regardless of the number of ensemble members. The greater the number of integrated units, the higher the accuracy. However, when the number of ensemble units exceeds 5, increasing the number of heads does not significantly improve the performance, but will increase the amount of calculation.

On miniImageNet, our model is 2.92% lower than previous best method in 5-way 1-shot task and comparable with previous state-of-the-art in 5-way 5-shot task. Nevertheless, our method is a general framework that can be combined with any few-shot learning algorithm based on metric learning. On tieredImageNet, our model achieves the new state-of-the-art in both settings. We also can see that the performance of individual learners in our ensemble model is better than corresponding single learner significantly. Thus our model can not only improve the overall accuracy but also the accuracy of each ensemble member. Besides, our model has a higher variance in 5-way 1-shot task.

Table 1. Few-shot classification accuracy on miniImageNet with 95% confidence intervals. "†": Results reported by the original work. "∗": Results re-implemented by other work in the same setting for a fair comparison.

Methods		1-shot	5-shot
MatchingNet [25]		46.6%	60.0%
MetaLSTM [1]		$43.44 \pm 0.77\%$	$60.60 \pm 0.71\%$
MAML [4]		$48.70 \pm 1.84\%$	$63.11 \pm 0.92\%$
MM-Net [3]		$53.37 \pm 0.48\%$	$66.97 \pm 0.35\%$
DynamicNet [7]		$\mathbf{55.45 \pm 0.89\%}$	$70.13 \pm 0.68\%$
GNN [6]		$49.34 \pm 0.85\%$	$63.25 \pm 0.81\%$
EGNN [11]		–	66.85%
TAML [10]		$49.33 \pm 1.8\%$	$66.05 \pm 0.85\%$
LR-D2 [2]		$51.9 \pm 0.2\%$	$68.7 \pm 0.2\%$
Meta-MinibatchProx [26]		$50.77 \pm 0.90\%$	$67.43 \pm 0.89\%$
ProtoNet† [22]		$49.42 \pm 0.78\%$	$68.20 \pm 0.66\%$
RelationNet [23]		$50.44 \pm 0.82\%$	$65.32 \pm 0.70\%$
ProtoNet∗ [15]		$48.45 \pm 0.96\%$	$66.53 \pm 0.51\%$
EBDM-Euc	2 heads	$49.96 \pm 1.00\%$	$68.30 \pm 0.83\%$
	3 heads	$50.49 \pm 1.00\%$	$69.14 \pm 0.84\%$
	5 heads	$52.53 \pm 1.01\%$	$69.64 \pm 0.77\%$
EBDM-DD	2 heads	$51.42 \pm 1.07\%$	$67.99 \pm 0.81\%$
	3 heads	$52.56 \pm 1.10\%$	$68.74 \pm 0.80\%$
	5 heads	$53.08 \pm 1.05\%$	$\mathbf{70.17 \pm 0.79\%}$

Table 2. Few-shot classification accuracy on tieredImageNet with 95% confidence intervals. "*": Results re-implemented in the same setting for a fair comparison. "Average" represents the mean accuracy of each ensemble member.

Methods		1-shot	5-shot
EGNN [11]		–	70.98%
Meta-MinibatchProx [26]		$50.14 \pm 0.92\%$	$68.30 \pm 0.91\%$
MAML* [4]		$46.84 \pm 1.39\%$	$64.12 \pm 1.13\%$
ProtoNet* [22]		$49.75 \pm 1.24\%$	$68.20 \pm 1.00\%$
EBDM-Euc	3 heads	$\mathbf{51.22 \pm 1.11\%}$	$\mathbf{72.24 \pm 0.89\%}$
	1-st head	$50.04 \pm 1.11\%$	$71.07 \pm 0.89\%$
	2-nd head	$50.29 \pm 1.11\%$	$71.28 \pm 0.89\%$
	3-rd head	$50.52 \pm 1.11\%$	$70.84 \pm 0.89\%$
	Average	$50.28 \pm 1.11\%$	$71.06 \pm 0.89\%$

Table 3. Comparison of 3 heads EBDM-Euc with different loss on miniImageNet. "Average" represents the average of the accuracy of the three learners.

		Ensemble	First head	Second head	Third head	Average
1-shot	With J_{ind}	$50.49 \pm 1.00\%$	$48.92 \pm 1.00\%$	$49.24 \pm 1.00\%$	$48.96 \pm 1.00\%$	49.04%
	With J_{mean}	$49.64 \pm 0.99\%$	$35.62 \pm 0.99\%$	$43.45 \pm 0.99\%$	$35.28 \pm 0.99\%$	38.12%
5-shot	With J_{ind}	$69.65 \pm 0.78\%$	$66.78 \pm 0.78\%$	$66.70 \pm 0.78\%$	$67.19 \pm 0.78\%$	66.89%
	With J_{mean}	$67.22 \pm 0.77\%$	$55.12 \pm 0.77\%$	$58.61 \pm 0.77\%$	$49.92 \pm 0.77\%$	54.55%

Effects of Objective Functions. To prove that optimizing the ensemble members individually performs better than optimizing the mean of ensemble members output, we conduct experiments with these two objective functions on miniImageNet using euclidean distance. The comparison results are reported in Table 3. The advantages of optimizing with objective function J_{ind} over using objective function J_{mean} is not obvious on 5-way 1-shot task, but is prominent on 5-way 5-shot task. So the experimental results have confirmed our assertion. The accuracy of each ensemble member optimized with J_{ind} is significantly higher than optimized with J_{mean}. This fact indicates that our model can not only improve the overall accuracy but also the accuracy of each ensemble member when each ensemble member is optimized independently.

Effects of the Architecture for Feature Extractor. We study the sensitivity of our model to the architecture of feature extractor on miniImageNet with 3 heads ensemble. The experimental results are shown in Table 4. Our model using arc1 performs slightly better than arc2 in the 5-way 1-shot task and significantly higher in 5-way 5-shot task. This shows that arc1 is better than arc2. In both structures, the difference between the accuracy of each ensemble member and the overall is not very large compared to using the objective function J_{mean} in

Table 4. Comparison of 3 heads EBDM-Euc with different architecture of feature extraction module on miniImageNet. "Average" represents the average of the accuracy of the three learners.

		Ensemble	First head	Second head	Third head	Average
1-shot	With arc1	50.49 ± 1.00%	48.92 ± 1.00%	49.24 ± 1.00%	48.96 ± 1.00%	49.04%
	With arc2	50.38 ± 1.08%	50.04 ± 1.08%	50.21 ± 1.08%	49.79 ± 1.08%	50.01%
5-shot	With arc1	69.65 ± 0.78%	66.78 ± 0.78%	66.70 ± 0.78%	67.19 ± 0.78%	66.89%
	With arc2	66.51 ± 0.85%	65.75 ± 0.85%	65.65 ± 0.85%	65.83 ± 0.85%	65.74%

the Table 3. This again shows that optimizing each learner individually in our model can improve the prediction accuracy of each ensemble member.

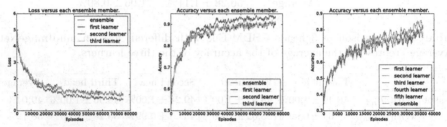

(a) The loss of each individual learner for EBDM-Euc on 5-way 5-shot task.

(b) The accuracy of each individual learner for EBDM-Euc on 5-way 5-shot task.

(c) The accuracy of each individual learner for EBDM-DD on 5-way 1-shot task.

Fig. 2. Accuracy and loss while varrying episodes on miniImageNet in different settings.

Convergence afig:convnalysis. Figure 2a and Fig. 2b show the training loss and accuracy of each ensemble member for 3-heads EBDM-Euc varrying with episodes on the 5-way 5-shot task of miniImageNet respectively. Figure2c shows the training accuracy of each ensemble member for 5-heads EBDM-DD on the 5-way 1-shot task of miniImageNet while varrying episodes. The few-shot classification accuracy or the loss on training set of each ensemble member is very close and the ensemble accuracy is higher than ensemble member.

5   Conclusion

In this paper, we propose a novel few-shot learning method. There are a few key contributions in this work. Firstly, we introduce ensemble learning to few-shot learning which improves the classification accuracy significantly. Secondly, we propose an efficient and flexible framework based on ensemble metric for few-shot learning, which can be combined with diverse metrics. Thirdly, we explored the effect of different objective functions on performance of our model. The experimental results show that the performance of optimizing each ensemble member individually is better than optimizing the mean for the output of the ensemble members. Finally, we analyzed the sensitivity of our model to the structure of the feature extraction module and experimental results show that our proposed method can achieve better results on both architectures. In the future, we would like to move forward to apply the idea of ensemble learning to other few-shot learning methods, such as MAML and HyperNet.

Acknowledgement. This paper is supported by NSFC (No.61772330, 61533012, 61876109), the pre-research project (No.61403120201), Shanghai Key Laboratory of Crime Scene Evidence (2017XCWZK01) and the Interdisciplinary Program of Shanghai Jiao Tong University (YG2019QNA09).

References

1. Andrychowicz, M., Denil, M.: learning to learn by gradient descent by gradient descent. In: Advances in Neural Information Processing Systems (2016)
2. Bertinetto, L.: Meta-learning with differentiable closed-form solvers. In: International Conference on Learning Representations (2019)
3. Cai, Q., Pan, Y., Yao, T., Yan: Memory matching networks for one-shot image recognition. In: Proceedings of the IEEE Conference on Computer Vision and Pattern Recognition (2018)
4. Finn, C., Abbeel, P.: Model-agnostic meta-learning for fast adaptation of deep networks. In: Proceedings of the 34th International Conference on Machine Learning, vol. 70 (2017)
5. Finn, C., Xu, K.: Probabilistic model-agnostic meta-learning. In: Advances in Neural Information Processing Systems (2018)
6. Garcia, V.: Few-Shot Learning With Graph Neural Networks (2017)
7. Gidaris, S.: Dynamic few-shot visual learning without forgetting. In: Proceedings of the IEEE Conference on Computer Vision and Pattern Recognition (2018)
8. Ha, D., Dai, A.: Hypernetworks. arXiv preprint arXiv:1609.09106 (2016)
9. Hinton, G.: Deep neural networks for acoustic modeling in speech recognition. IEEE Sig. Process. Mag. **29**, 82–97 (2012)
10. Jamal, M.A.: Task-agnostic meta-learning for few-shot learning. CoRR abs/1805.07722 (2018)
11. Kim, J., Kim, T.: Edge-labeling graph neural network for few-shot learning. CoRR abs/1905.01436 (2019)
12. Kim, T., Yoon: Bayesian model-agnostic meta-learning. arXiv preprint arXiv:1806.03836 (2018)
13. Koch, G., Zemel, R.: Siamese neural networks for one-shot image recognition. In: ICML Deep Learning Workshop (2015)
14. Li, H., Eigen, D.: Finding task-relevant features for few-shot learning by category traversal. CoRR abs/1905.11116 (2019)
15. Li, W., Wang, L.: Revisiting local descriptor based image-to-class measure for few-shot learning. In: Proceedings of the IEEE Conference on Computer Vision and Pattern Recognition (2019)
16. Lifchitz, Y., Avrithis, Y.: Dense classification and implanting for few-shot learning. CoRR abs/1903.05050 (2019)

17. Munkhdalai, T., Yu, H.: Meta networks. In: Proceedings of the 34th International Conference on Machine Learning, vol. 70 (2017)
18. Ravi, S., Larochelle, H.: Optimization as a Model for Few-shot Learning (2016)
19. Ren, M.: Meta-learning for semi-supervised few-shot classification. arXiv preprint arXiv:1803.00676 (2018)
20. Rusu, A.A., Rao, D.: Meta-learning with latent embedding optimization. arXiv preprint arXiv:1807.05960 (2018)
21. Santoro, A., Bartunov, S.: Meta-learning with memory-augmented neural networks. In: International Conference on Machine Learning (2016)
22. Snell, J., Swersky, K.: Prototypical networks for few-shot learning. In: Advances in Neural Information Processing Systems (2017)
23. Sung, F., Yang, Y., Zhang, L.: Learning to compare: relation network for few-shot learning. In: Proceedings of the IEEE Conference on Computer Vision and Pattern Recognition (2018)
24. Sung, F., Zhang, L.: Learning to learn: meta-critic networks for sample efficient learning. arXiv preprint arXiv:1706.09529 (2017)
25. Vinyals, O., Blundell, C.: Matching networks for one shot learning. In: Advances in Neural Information Processing Systems (2016)
26. Zhou, P., Yuan. X.: Efficient meta learning via minibatch proximal update. In: Advances in Neural Information Processing Systems, vol. 32 (2019)

More Attentional Local Descriptors for Few-Shot Learning

Hui Li[ID], Liu Yang[✉][ID], and Fei Gao[ID]

College of Intelligence and Computing, Tianjin University, Tianjin 300350, China
{li_hui1998,yangliuyl,g_f}@tju.edu.cn

Abstract. Learning from a few examples remains a key challenge for many computer vision tasks. Few-shot learning is proposed to tackle this problem. It aims to learn a classifier to classify images when each class contains only few samples with supervised information in image classification. So far, existing methods have achieved considerable progress, which use fully connected layer or global average pooling as the final classification method. However, due to the lack of samples, global feature may no longer be useful. In contrast, the local feature is more conductive to few-shot learning, but inevitably there will be some noises. In the meanwhile, inspired by human visual systems, the attention mechanism can obtain more valuable information and be widely used in various areas. Therefore, in this paper, we propose a method called More Attentional Deep Nearest Neighbor Neural Network (MADN4 in short) that combines the local descriptors with attention mechanism and is trained end-to-end from scratch. The experimental results on four benchmark datasets demonstrate the superior capability of our method.

Keywords: Few-shot learning · Local · Attention

1 Introduction

In recent years, deep neural networks have demonstrated their usefulness in supervised learning tasks. However, training these tasks requires a great deal of labeled data to achieve a good performance, which restricts the problems they can be applied to. If data with supervised information is hard to acquire due to privacy issues, neural network would suffer from the problem of data over-fitting and the performance would be poor. In contrast, humans are able to recognize an object category easily from only few examples. Inspired by such an ability, researchers also hope that machine learning models can mimic the behavior to construct classifiers that can rapidly generalize to new tasks with little samples.

The research on this subject is usually termed few-shot learning. And researchers have proposed a lot of efficient methods. The mainstream methods can be roughly divided into three categories, including meta-learning based method [2,7,17,20–22], data augmentation method [4,6,10,23,28] and metric-learning based method [8,13,15,16,24–26]. The first kind of method employs

© Springer Nature Switzerland AG 2020
I. Farkaš et al. (Eds.): ICANN 2020, LNCS 12396, pp. 419–430, 2020.
https://doi.org/10.1007/978-3-030-61609-0_33

meta-learning strategies to train a meta-learner for generalizing new few-shot tasks. Besides, the major obstacle of learning good classifiers in few-shot learning is the lack of training data. To mitigate this drawback, a nature method is to expand the data, which is the idea of the second kind of method. The last kind of method aims at learning a similarity space in which the learning is valid.

The key challenge of few-shot learning is how to utilize insufficient data to learn a better representation. In computer vision, the attention mechanism has been widely used for object detection and image classification. It not only tells where to focus, but also improves the representation by focusing on useful features and suppressing useless ones. Therefore, we can employ attention mechanism into the research of few-shot learning to improve the performance further.

In few-shot learning, traditional global information is probably not useful when only few examples are available for each class. But local information becomes increasingly important. As Naive-Bayes Nearest-Neighbor (NBNN) method described in [3], image-level representation may lose discriminative information. Besides, using fully connected layer or global average pooling in the final layer of network and having only few samples can both aggravate this loss. Not only that, if we use image-to-image measure, the local representation still has bad results. Instead, an image-to-class measure is more generalized than an image-to-image measure. Hence a method named DN4 that takes local descriptors based image-to-class measure is proposed by [15]. Specifically, all local descriptors from a class are put in one pool. And the image-to-class measure is calculated via a k-nearest neighbor search over local descriptors, that is, for each local descriptor in each query image, to search for its k-nearest neighbors in each class pool. If a class has many samples, the calculation of measure is very huge and difficult. In this case, because the number of samples in few-shot learning is small, it can make the calculation more convenient. However, we find that if the local descriptors are extracted directly from a general network, they will be noisy. It is very possible to use irrelevant features to search for their k-nearest neighbors, which greatly affects the classification performance. So we want to use more related features to search for their k-nearest neighbors. At the same time, we try to have more relevant features in each class pool, so that we can get more similar features when searching for k-nearest neighbors. These improvements to reduce the impact of noises on the performance of DN4 can be achieved by attention mechanism.

Therefore, in this paper, we propose an approach named More Attentional Deep Nearest Neighbor Neural Network (MADN4 in short) that it combines the local descriptors with attention mechanism. Specifically, we embed Convolutional Block Attention Module (CBAM in short) [30] into the process of extracting local descriptors. The CBAM can be viewed as a plug-and-play module to provide more representative and discriminative features. When given an intermediate feature map, this lightweight yet effective module infers it one by one according to the channel and spatial dimensions. In final, we will get a new feature map, and its size remains unchanged. In our experiments, the results are more better than DN4 and other state-of-the-art methods.

The paper is organized as follows: Sect. 2 reviews related work in the filed of few-shot learning and application of attention mechanism. Section 3 describes our MADN4 model. Section 4 shows the experimental results and demonstrates the effectiveness of our method. Finally, Sect. 5 gives the conclusion.

2 Related Work

2.1 Few-Shot Learning

So far, there have been many methods for solving few-shot learning problems. They can be roughly divided into three categories.

Meta-learning Based Method. Meta-learning can also be called "learn to learn". In this kind of method, there are two learners. One is the meta-learner which gains experience from many tasks and learns a strategy finally, the other is the learner which learns to classify new classes under the guidance of this meta-learner. There are three branches for this kind of method. The first branch is memory based meta-learning, i.e., MANN [22], SNAIL [17]. Next branch is parameter prediction based meta-learning, i.e., feed-forward one-shot learners [2], parameter predictor [20]. The last branch is optimization based meta-learning, i.e., Meta-Learner LSTM [21], MAML [7]. Compared to other methods, it is very difficult to train the complicated memory-addressing architecture for meta-learning based method [18].

Data Augmentation Method. Due to the limited number of samples, it is essential to expand the number of samples. There are some representative methods, such as learning a network of synthesizing samples [23], employing GAN [9] and its variants, using extra semantic vector or attribute [4,6], as well as learning how to hallucinate more training data [10,28]. Data augmentation method can be combined with other types of methods to enhance the performance of few-shot learning together.

Metric-learning Based Method. This kind of method aims to find a great metric space. In other words, it models the distance distribution between samples, and makes the same kind of sample close and the different kind of sample far away. Siamese Network [13], Matching Network [26] and Prototype Network [24] all adopt fixed measure. And some approaches to consider the relation between support set and the query image are also proposed, i.e., Relation Network [25] and the application of GNN [8]. Both dense classification [16] and DN4 [15] indicate the importance of local features in few-shot learning. Metric-learning based method has no complicated network architecture and shows good universality.

2.2   Attention Mechanism

Over the last few years, attention mechanism has become one of the most popular tools in deep learning since it was proposed in [19]. It is similar to the human visual mechanism, which tends to focus on some more discriminative information and ignore irrelevant information.

In few-shot learning, some methods mentioned above [17,26] more or less employ attention mechanism. Besides, some researchers have proposed to combine it with previous work, such as SARN [12]. And various new methods have been proposed by other researches, including the methods of using semantic information to guide visual attention features [5,27], Cross Attention Network [11], as well as Dual Attention Network [31] using spatial attention and task attention.

Our method is motivated by attentive mechanism. In particular, in our paper, we embed an attentive module called CBAM [30] into our network framework.

3   The Proposed MADN4 Method

3.1   Problem Background

In few-shot learning, we have three datasets: a training set, a support set and a query set. The training set has a large of labeled and seen samples. It can also be called an auxiliary set to learn transferable knowledge, which enables us to achieve better few-shot learning on the support set and thus classify the query set more successfully. We denote the training set as $D = (\mathbf{X}, \mathbf{Y}) = (\mathbf{x}_i, y_i)_{i=1}^{N}$. Note that $\mathbf{x}_i$ denotes the image, and y_i denotes the corresponding label. And we denote the support set as $S = (\mathbf{X}', \mathbf{Y}') = (\mathbf{x}_i', y_i')_{i=1}^{N'}$. If the support set contains C unique classes and K labeled examples, the problem is called C-way K-shot. When given a query set, our goal is to classify each query image into one of C classes of support set. Generally speaking, the label space of the training set and support/query set is disjoint: $\mathbf{Y} \cap \mathbf{Y}' = \emptyset$, and the number of samples in the training set is far more than that in the support/query set: $N \gg N'$.

In order to make better use of training set, episode training mechanism [26] has been proved to be an effective way. Specifically, in the process of training, many episodes will be constructed to train the classification model. In each episode, we randomly select C classes from the training set, then randomly choose K labeled examples for per class as the sample set and non-repetitive examples as the testing set. In other words, the division of the sample/testing set imitates the support/query set that will be encountered at predicting time.

3.2   Model

Since the local descriptors extracted by a simple network have some noises, in our paper, we combine local descriptors with attention mechanism to improve the representation and thus enhance the classification performance. The specific model is described as follows.

As illustrated in Fig. 1, the network architecture includes two modules. One is the Feature Extraction Module embedded with the attention module, which is used to extract features from support set and query set. The other is the Measure Module, which is used to select which class in the support set is closest to that of the query image.

Feature Extraction Module. In this module, our spotlight is the combination of the local descriptors with the attention module. We can extract the local descriptors via any convolutional neural network. For fair comparison with other baselines, we still adopt a common network architecture. It includes four convolutional blocks and each block has a 64 filter 3×3 convolutional layer followed by a batch normalization layer and a Leaky ReLU layer. And it adds a 2×2 max-pooling layer after the first two blocks. On the contrary, the latter two blocks have no max-pooling layer. It is worth pointing out that we only extract local descriptors, which means the network does not have fully connected layer. We call the network as *Conv-64F*.

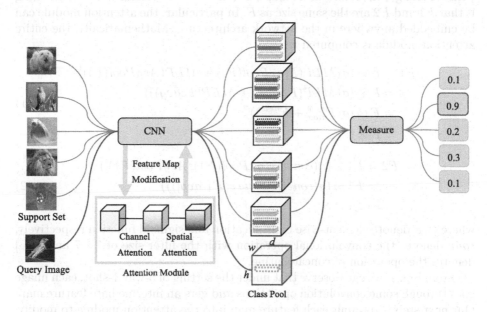

Fig. 1. The illustration of the MADN4 under the setting of 5-way 1-shot for few-shot learning. This framework combines local descriptors extracted from any CNN with attention module. After getting more attentional local descriptors, the following operation is computing the similarity between a query image and each class from support set.

In this network, we embed the attention module after the first two blocks, it contains channel attention module and spatial attention module. The channel attention focuses on 'what' is significant for an image. Concretely, given an intermediate feature map $F \in \mathbb{R}^{C \times W \times H}$, we use max-pooling and avg-pooling simultaneously and get two pooled feature maps called F_max and F_avg. So far, avg-pooling is a commonly used method. However, max-pooling can obtain different information compared to the avg-pooling. Therefore, the combination of two ways is better for the performance. Then, we input F_max and F_avg into a shared MLP with one hidden layer, and get two new feature maps named F_{max}^{new} and F_{avg}^{new}. After that, we add both using element-wise summation. For this output, we use a sigmoid function to obtain the final channel attention coefficient $C \in \mathbb{R}^{C \times 1 \times 1}$. Next, we multiply C with F and obtain a new feature map $F1 \in \mathbb{R}^{C \times W \times H}$. Different from the channel attention, the spatial attention focuses on 'where' is more valuable part, which is a complement to channel attention. We carry out max-pooling and avg-pooling along the channel direction for $F1$ firstly, and get two feature maps called $F1\_max$ and $F1\_avg$. Both are concatenated and convolved by a normal convolutional layer, producing a spatial attention map. Finally, like channel attention module, we use a sigmoid function to obtain the final spatial attention coefficient $S \in \mathbb{R}^{1 \times W \times H}$. Then we multiply S with $F1$ and get the final feature map $F2 \in \mathbb{R}^{C \times W \times H}$. What is worth mentioning is that $F1$ and $F2$ are the same size as F. In particular, the attention module can be embedded anywhere in the network architecture. Mathematically, the entire attention module is computed as:

$$
\begin{aligned}
F1 &= F \otimes (\sigma(MLP(MaxPool(F)) + MLP(AvgPool(F)))) \\
&= F \otimes (\sigma(MLP(F\_max) + MLP(F\_avg))) \\
&= F \otimes (\sigma(F_{max}^{new} + F_{avg}^{new})) \\
&= F \otimes C
\end{aligned} \tag{1}
$$

$$
\begin{aligned}
F2 &= F1 \otimes (\sigma(conv([MaxPool(F1); AvgPool(F1)]))) \\
&= F1 \otimes (\sigma(conv([F1\_max; F1\_avg]))) \\
&= F1 \otimes S,
\end{aligned} \tag{2}
$$

where $\otimes$, σ denote element-wise multiplication and sigmoid function respectively, $conv$ denotes the convolutional operation with the filter size of 7×7 and $[\cdot \ ; \ \cdot]$ denotes the operation of concatenating.

From Fig. 1, we can observe that under the setting of 5-way 1-shot, each image goes through some convolution operations and gets an intermediate feature map. Our next step is to input each feature map into the attention module to modify. Then the attention module output a new feature map with more discriminative information, and it remains keeping the same size as the initial feature map. In the end, we get $h \times w$ d-dimensional local descriptors for each class. Concretely, h, w, d denote the height, width and depth of the feature map respectively. We put these local descriptors from a class into one pool. In particular, if the setting is 5-way 5-shot, each image will get $h \times w$ local descriptors similarly, and each class will get $5 \times h \times w$ local descriptors. What putting in the pool is all

$5 \times h \times w$ local descriptors. Certainly, the operation of query image is the same as that of support set.

Algorithm 1: The process of a training episode for our MADN4. N_C, N_S, N_T, N_{TT} denote the number of classes per episode, the number of samples in the sample set and testing set per class, the total number of samples in the testing set, respectively. Φ denotes the *Conv-64F* embedded with CBAM. RANDOMSAMPLE(A,B) denotes a set of B elements selected randomly from the set A, without replacement.

Input: Training set $D = (\mathbf{x}_i, y_i)_{i=1}^N$, where $y_i \in \{1, ..., M\}$. And the elements that $y_i = p$ of D make up a subset named D_p. And hyperparameter k.

```
 1  V ← RANDOMSAMPLE({1,...,M},N_C)          ▷ select class indices for episode
 2  for p in {1,...,N_C} do
 3  │   S_p ← RANDOMSAMPLE(D_{V_p},N_S)                      ▷ select sample set
 4  │   T_p ← RANDOMSAMPLE(D_{V_p}\S_p,N_T)                  ▷ select testing set
 5  │   for a in {1,...,N_S} do
 6  │   │   F_m ← Φ(sample)              ▷ extract local descriptors (feature map)
 7  │   │   Pool[p] ← all local descriptors (that is F_m) from a class
 8  │   end
 9  end
10  for b in {1,...,N_{TT}} do
11  │   F_m ← Φ(sample)                ▷ extract local descriptors (feature map)
12  │   L ← a set of all local descriptors (that is F_m) from a query image
13  │   m ← the total number of elements in L
14  │   for c in {1,...,N_C} do
15  │   │   Sum[c] ← 0
16  │   │   for e in {1,...,m} do
17  │   │   │   J ← a set of k-nearest neighbors of L[e] found from Pool[c])
18  │   │   │   for f in {1,...,k} do
19  │   │   │   │   Sum[c] ← Sum[c] + cos(L[e],J[f])
20  │   │   │   │                          ▷ calculate the cosine similarity
21  │   │   │   end
22  │   │   end
23  │   end
24  │   get the predicted value for each query image
25  end
26  Calculate loss and update network
```

Measure Module. After extracting the more important local descriptors, we can input them into Measure Module. In this module, we calculate the distance between a query image and each class through k-NN. For each local descriptor, we search its k-nearest neighbors in a class and calculate the cosine similarity between it and its k-nearest neighbors. Finally, we sum the $h \times w \times k$ similarities and take the result as the final similarity.

Note the Feature Extraction Module and Measure Module are a whole. Accordingly, we can train it in an end-to-end way. The pseudo code of MADN4 for a training episode is outlined in Algorithm 1.

4 Experiments

In our experiments, we evaluate our approach on a universal miniImageNet dataset and three datasets used for fine-grained classification. All the experiments are implemented on PyTorch. The details are shown below.

4.1 Dataset

The following is a brief description of the four datasets.

miniImageNet. The dataset is a subset of ImageNet and is proposed originally by [26]. It consists of 60,000 colour images of 84×84 pixels, with 100 classes and each class has 600 examples. According to the split introduced by [21], we take 64, 16 and 20 classes for training, validation and testing, respectively.

StanfordDogs. The StanfordDogs dataset [1] is a fine-grained classification data set for dogs. It contains 120 breeds of dogs and a total of 20,580 images. Similarly, we take 70, 20 and 30 classes for training, validation and testing, respectively.

StanfordCars. The StanfordCars dataset [14] is a fine-grained classification data set for cars. It contains 196 classes of cars and a total of 16,185 images. We take 130, 17 and 49 classes for training, validation and testing, respectively.

CUB-200. The CUB-200 [29] is a fine-grained classification data set for birds. It has two versions, CUB 200-2010 and CUB 200-2011. Their difference is the volume of data. We take CUB 200-2010 that contains 200 bird species and 6033 images, and adopt 130, 20 and 50 classes for training, validation and testing, respectively.

Note that in order to match the miniImageNet, we resize the fine-grained datasets to 84×84 pixels.

4.2 Training

Setting. We conduct 5-way 1-shot and 5-way 5-shot classification to follow general setting used by most existing few-shot learning work. To be specific, in the training phase, we adopt episode training mechanism and construct 300,000 episodes. And we use the Adam optimizer with $\beta_1 = 0.5$ and $\beta_2 = 0.9$ for training. Moreover, the learning rate for the optimizer is 0.001 and we reduce it by half of each 100,000 episodes. When testing, we randomly sample 600 episodes from the test set, and the top-1 accuracy results are reported with 95% confidence intervals.

In our experiments, k of k-nearest neighbors is a hyperparameter. As for the miniImageNet dataset, we still adopt $k = 3$. On account of the specificity of fine-grained tasks, we set $k = 1$. Besides, we embed the attention module behind the second layer of the *Conv-64F*.

Baselines. To verify the merit of our MADN4, we compare against various state-of-the-art methods for few-shot learning, including metric-learning based methods such as Matching Network [26], Prototypical Network [24], GNN [8], Relational Network [25], SARN [12], DN4 [15] and meta-learning based methods such as Meta-Learner LSTM [21], SNAIL [17], MAML [7].

Since our MADN4 belongs to the metric-learning branch, it is mainly compared with the metric-learning based methods. Meanwhile, to make comparison with the meta-learning based methods, we report their results based on the *Conv-32F*, a structure similar to *Conv-64F* but with 32 filters per convolutional layer.

Table 1. Mean accuracy (%) of our MADN4 and other methods on miniImageNet few-shot task, with 95% confidence intervals. The second column indicates the embedding network for this method, and the third column refers to the type of this method.

Model	Network	Type	5-way Acc (%)	
			1-shot	5-shot
Matching Net [26]	*Conv-64F*	Metric	43.56 ± 0.84	55.31 ± 0.73
Prototypical Net [24]	*Conv-64F*	Metric	49.42 ± 0.78	68.20 ± 0.66
GNN [8]	*Conv-256F*	Metric	50.33 ± 0.36	66.41 ± 0.63
Relational Net [25]	*Conv-64F*	Metric	50.44 ± 0.82	65.32 ± 0.70
DN4 ($k = 3$) [15]	*Conv-64F*	Metric	51.24 ± 0.74	71.02 ± 0.64
SARN [12]	*Conv-64F*	Metric	51.62 ± 0.31	66.16 ± 0.51
Meta-Learner LSTM [21]	*Conv-32F*	Meta	43.44 ± 0.77	60.60 ± 0.71
SNAIL [17]	*Conv-32F*	Meta	45.10	55.20
MAML [7]	*Conv-32F*	Meta	48.70 ± 1.84	63.11 ± 0.92
MADN4 ($k = 3$)	*Conv-64F*	Metric	$\mathbf{53.20 \pm 0.52}$	$\mathbf{71.66 \pm 0.47}$

Table 2. Mean accuracy (%) of our MADN4 and other methods on fine-grained few-shot task based on the *Conv-64F* network, with 95% confidence intervals.

Model	5-way Acc (%)					
	CUB-200		StanfordDogs		StanfordCars	
	1-shot	5-shot	1-shot	5-shot	1-shot	5-shot
Matching Net* [26]	45.30 ± 1.03	59.50 ± 1.01	35.80 ± 0.99	47.50 ± 1.03	34.80 ± 0.98	44.70 ± 1.03
Prototypical Net* [24]	37.36 ± 1.00	45.28 ± 1.03	37.59 ± 1.00	48.19 ± 1.03	40.90 ± 1.01	52.93 ± 1.03
GNN* [8]	51.83 ± 0.98	63.69 ± 0.94	46.98 ± 0.98	62.27 ± 0.95	55.85 ± 0.97	71.25 ± 0.89
DN4 ($k = 1$) [15]	46.84 ± 0.81	74.92 ± 0.64	45.41 ± 0.76	63.51 ± 0.62	59.84 ± 0.80	88.65 ± 0.44
MADN4 ($k = 1$)	$\mathbf{57.11 \pm 0.70}$	$\mathbf{77.83 \pm 0.40}$	$\mathbf{50.42 \pm 0.27}$	$\mathbf{70.75 \pm 0.47}$	$\mathbf{62.89 \pm 0.50}$	$\mathbf{89.25 \pm 0.34}$

428 H. Li et al.

4.3 Results

miniImageNet. The miniImageNet dataset is usually used to conduct few-shot classification. The results of this dataset under the settings of 5-way 1-shot and 5-way 5-shot are summarized in Table 1, and the hyperparameter k is 3. From Table 1, we can see the accuracy under the setting of 5-way 1-shot is roughly 53.20%, outperforming the previous result of 51.24% conducted by DN4 [15]. Similarly, compared with other state-of-the-art methods, our MADN4 also has some improvement. For the 5-way 5-shot classification, the attention module still works even though the effect of the improvement is not obvious.

Fine-Grained Datasets. We also conduct experiments on three fine-grained datasets, i.e., StanfordDogs, StanfordCars and CUB-200. Table 2 shows the results under the settings of 5-way 1-shot and 5-way 5-shot, which also reveal our new approach is better than previous works. And * results reported by [15] and they denote the results of re-training in the same setting.

5 Conclusion

In this paper, we propose a method named MADN4 that combines local descriptors with attention mechanism for few-shot learning. At first, the local descriptors may be more suitable for few-shot learning, rather than the global representation. But the extracted local descriptors may have some noises. Therefore, a lightweight attention module is incorporated into the DN4 to improve the extracted features. MADN4 can learn more discriminative local descriptors in an end-to-end manner. We also confirm that the proposed MADN4 is superior to the state-of-the-art methods according to the experiments on miniImageNet and fine-grained datasets.

Acknowledgements. This work is supported in part by the National Natural Science Foundation of China under Grant 61732011 and Grant 61702358, in part by the Beijing Natural Science Foundation under Grant Z180006, in part by the Key Scientific and Technological Support Project of Tianjin Key Research and Development Program under Grant 18YFZCGX00390, and in part by the Tianjin Science and Technology Plan Project under Grant 19ZXZNGX00050.

References

1. Aditya, K., Nityananda, J., Bangpeng, Y., Li, F.: Novel dataset for fine-grained image categorization. In: Proceedings of the First Workshop on Fine-Grained Visual Categorization, IEEE Conference on Computer Vision and Pattern Recognition. IEEE, Springs, USA (2011)
2. Bertinetto, L., Henriques, J.F., Valmadre, J., Torr, P., Vedaldi, A.: Learning feed-forward one-shot learners. In: Advances in neural information processing systems, pp. 523–531 (2016)

3. Boiman, O., Shechtman, E., Irani, M.: In defense of nearest-neighbor based image classification. In: 2008 IEEE Conference on Computer Vision and Pattern Recognition, pp. 1–8. IEEE (2008). https://doi.org/10.1109/CVPR.2008.4587598

4. Chen, Z., Fu, Y., Zhang, Y., Jiang, Y.G., Xue, X., Sigal, L.: Semantic feature augmentation in few-shot learning. arXiv preprint arXiv:1804.05298 (2018)

5. Chu, W.H., Wang, Y.C.F.: Learning semantics-guided visual attention for few-shot image classification. In: 2018 25th IEEE International Conference on Image Processing (ICIP), pp. 2979–2983. IEEE (2018). https://doi.org/10.1109/ICIP.2018.8451350

6. Dixit, M., Kwitt, R., Niethammer, M., Vasconcelos, N.: AGA: attribute-guided augmentation. In: Proceedings of the IEEE Conference on Computer Vision and Pattern Recognition, pp. 7455–7463 (2017). https://doi.org/10.1109/CVPR.2017.355

7. Finn, C., Abbeel, P., Levine, S.: Model-agnostic meta-learning for fast adaptation of deep networks. In: Proceedings of the 34th International Conference on Machine Learning-Volume 70, pp. 1126–1135. JMLR. org (2017)

8. Garcia, V., Bruna, J.: Few-shot learning with graph neural networks. arXiv preprint arXiv:1711.04043 (2017)

9. Goodfellow, I., et al..: Generative adversarial nets. In: Advances in Neural Information Processing Systems, pp. 2672–2680 (2014)

10. Hariharan, B., Girshick, R.: Low-shot visual recognition by shrinking and hallucinating features. In: Proceedings of the IEEE International Conference on Computer Vision, pp. 3018–3027 (2017). https://doi.org/10.1109/ICCV.2017.328

11. Hou, R., Chang, H., Bingpeng, M., Shan, S., Chen, X.: Cross attention network for few-shot classification. In: Advances in Neural Information Processing Systems, pp. 4005–4016 (2019)

12. Hui, B., Zhu, P., Hu, Q., Wang, Q.: Self-attention relation network for few-shot learning. In: 2019 IEEE International Conference on Multimedia & Expo Workshops (ICMEW), pp. 198–203. IEEE (2019). https://doi.org/10.1109/ICMEW.2019.00041

13. Koch, G., Zemel, R., Salakhutdinov, R.: Siamese neural networks for one-shot image recognition. In: ICML deep learning workshop, vol. 2. Lille (2015)

14. Krause, J., Stark, M., Deng, J., Fei-Fei, L.: 3D object representations for fine-grained categorization. In: Proceedings of the IEEE International Conference on Computer Vision Workshops, pp. 554–561 (2013). https://doi.org/10.1109/ICCVW.2013.77

15. Li, W., Wang, L., Xu, J., Huo, J., Gao, Y., Luo, J.: Revisiting local descriptor based image-to-class measure for few-shot learning. In: Proceedings of the IEEE Conference on Computer Vision and Pattern Recognition, pp. 7260–7268 (2019). https://doi.org/10.1109/cvpr.2019.00743

16. Lifchitz, Y., Avrithis, Y., Picard, S., Bursuc, A.: Dense classification and implanting for few-shot learning. In: Proceedings of the IEEE Conference on Computer Vision and Pattern Recognition, pp. 9258–9267 (2019). https://doi.org/10.1109/CVPR.2019.00948

17. Mishra, N., Rohaninejad, M., Chen, X., Abbeel, P.: A simple neural attentive meta-learner. arXiv preprint arXiv:1707.03141 (2017)

18. Mishra, N., Rohaninejad, M., Chen, X., Abbeel, P.: A simple neural attentive meta-learner. In: ICLR (2018)

19. Mnih, V., Heess, N., Graves, A., et al.: Recurrent models of visual attention. In: Advances in neural information processing systems, pp. 2204–2212 (2014)

20. Qiao, S., Liu, C., Shen, W., Yuille, A.L.: Few-shot image recognition by predicting parameters from activations. In: Proceedings of the IEEE Conference on Computer Vision and Pattern Recognition, pp. 7229–7238 (2018). https://doi.org/10.1109/CVPR.2018.00755
21. Sachin, R., Hugo, L.: Optimization as a model for few-shot learning. In: ICLR (2017)
22. Santoro, A., Bartunov, S., Botvinick, M., Wierstra, D., Lillicrap, T.: Meta-learning with memory-augmented neural networks. In: International conference on machine learning, pp. 1842–1850 (2016)
23. Schwartz, E., : Delta-encoder: an effective sample synthesis method for few-shot object recognition. In: Advances in Neural Information Processing Systems, pp. 2845–2855 (2018)
24. Snell, J., Swersky, K., Zemel, R.: Prototypical networks for few-shot learning. In: Advances in Neural Information Processing Systems, pp. 4077–4087 (2017)
25. Sung, F., Yang, Y., Zhang, L., Xiang, T., Torr, P.H., Hospedales, T.M.: Learning to compare: relation network for few-shot learning. In: Proceedings of the IEEE Conference on Computer Vision and Pattern Recognition, pp. 1199–1208 (2018). https://doi.org/10.1109/CVPR.2018.00131
26. Vinyals, O., Blundell, C., Lillicrap, T., Wierstra, D., et al.: Matching networks for one shot learning. In: Advances in Neural Information Processing Systems, pp. 3630–3638 (2016)
27. Wang, P., Liu, L., Shen, C., Huang, Z., van den Hengel, A., Tao Shen, H.: Multi-attention network for one shot learning. In: Proceedings of the IEEE Conference on Computer Vision and Pattern Recognition, pp. 2721–2729 (2017). https://doi.org/10.1109/CVPR.2017.658
28. Wang, Y.X., Girshick, R., Hebert, M., Hariharan, B.: Low-shot learning from imaginary data. In: Proceedings of the IEEE Conference on Computer Vision and Pattern Recognition, pp. 7278–7286 (2018). https://doi.org/10.1109/CVPR.2018.00760
29. Welinder, P., et al..: Caltech-ucsd birds 200 (2010)
30. Woo, S., Park, J., Lee, J.Y., So Kweon, I.: CBAM: convolutional block attention module. In: Proceedings of the European Conference on Computer Vision (ECCV), pp. 3–19 (2018). https://doi.org/10.1007/978-3-030-01234-2_1
31. Yan, S., Zhang, S., He, X., et al.: A dual attention network with semantic embedding for few-shot learning. In: Proceedings of the AAAI Conference on Artificial Intelligence, vol. 33, pp. 9079–9086 (2019)

Implementation of Siamese-Based Few-Shot Learning Algorithms for the Distinction of COPD and Asthma Subjects

Pouya Soltani Zarrin[1](✉) and Christian Wenger[1,2]

[1] IHP–Leibniz-Institut fuer innovative Mikroelektronik,
15236 Frankfurt (Oder), Germany
soltani@ihp-microelectronics.com
[2] BTU Cottbus-Senftenberg, 01968 Cottbus, Germany

Abstract. This paper investigates the practicality of applying brain-inspired Few-Shot Learning (FSL) algorithms for addressing shortcomings of Machine Learning (ML) methods in medicine with limited data availability. As a proof of concept, the application of ML for the detection of Chronic Obstructive Pulmonary Disease (COPD) patients was investigated. The complexities associated with the distinction of COPD and asthma patients and the lack of sufficient training data for asthma subjects impair the performance of conventional ML models for the recognition of COPD. Therefore, the objective of this study was to implement FSL methods for the distinction of COPD and asthma subjects with a few available data points. The proposed FSL models in this work were capable of recognizing asthma and COPD patients with 100% accuracy, demonstrating the feasibility of the approach for applications such as medicine with insufficient data availability.

Keywords: Few-shot learning · Siamese networks · COPD–asthma distinction · Zero-shot learning · Precision diagnostic · Machine learning in medicine

1 Introduction

Artificial Intelligence (AI), with its galloping progress, has revolutionized various aspects of our data-driven world [1]. A broad spectrum of AI's applications has been introduced in recent years, covering many aspects of science from robotics to medicine [1]. The astonishing performance of AI-oriented Machine Learning (ML) methods for exceeding human capabilities in medical recognition and classification tasks has already been demonstrated [2]. However, the significant dependence of these methods, especially deep learning, on the availability of a vast training dataset has hindered their far-reaching application in many areas of medicine with limited data availability [3]. A training dataset in this scope

© Springer Nature Switzerland AG 2020
I. Farkaš et al. (Eds.): ICANN 2020, LNCS 12396, pp. 431–440, 2020.
https://doi.org/10.1007/978-3-030-61609-0_34

is defined as properly-labeled data points which can be used for training ML-based models. Some of the causes behind the scarcity of ML-friendly datasets in medicine include, but are not limited to, the following: First, incomplete, incorrect, inaccurate, and heterogeneous nature of old medical records, due to the inconsistency in their acquisition methods and vocabulary, degrade their labeling and usability for ML. In addition, generating ground-truth labels is generally an expensive and time-consuming process, which has been neglected until recently. Second, the AI-oriented data collection for various medical applications, especially rare diseases or novel treatments, is still at its infancy. For instance, genetic engineering, drug discovery, or surgical robotics are exemplary domains where extensive data collections are still required for the enhancement of their performances [4–7]. Third, different standardization methods, ethical concerns, and strict privacy regulations have hindered the data sharing in medicine, further restricting their availability. Last but not least, data acquisitions through invasive and complex medical operations is extremely challenging, if not impossible, thus restricting the size of the available data in this realm [3]. The intracranial electrode placement for the prediction and management of the drug-resistant epilepsy is an example of this kind, where very few data points are available due to safety concerns [8,9]. The lack of sufficient data for training ML models for the mentioned applications not only limits their performance and accuracy but also questions their generalizability to a larger population of patients or medical cases [3,9]. Patient-to-patient variability is a challenging concern for the development of medical–diagnostic solutions in personal healthcare [10]. As an example, the discussed epileptic seizure management setup requires the implantation of numerous electrodes within a patient's skull for the monitoring of the brain's electrical activities. However, the exact location of the implanted electrodes, the number of functioning–active electrode channels after the operation, and the specific area of a patient's brain where the excessive electrical discharges occur make the developed ML models for this application strongly patient specific [9]. This is significantly problematic for the development of a generalizable healthcare solution for the management of epilepsy. Furthermore, despite the availability of vast sources of epilepsy data from canine, with a similar seizure mechanism to human, generalization of the developed models based on the canine data to the human is still hampered. Similarly, ML models developed for the diagnostic classification of Chronic Obstructive Pulmonary Disease (COPD) patients from Healthy Controls (HC) suffer from generalization to a broader group of respiratory disease such as asthma [11,12]. Patients suffering from asthma or COPD develop similar symptoms due to the analogous mechanism of the diseases and a significant overlap between them, causing diagnostic complexities [13,14]. On the other hand, the lack of sufficient training data is a significant hurdle for improving the performance of the developed ML models for the COPD detection [11,12]. Therefore, due to the lack of data availability, ML-models need to be re-trained from scratch to provide a comparable performance for every individual patient or disease case in spite of an identical task. This is a significant drawback of these models for real-world applications, where rapid adaptation and learning is essential [15]. Examples of these applications include autonomous driving, surgical robotics, medical mechatronics, personalized medicine, precision diagnostic, etc., where online learning of a ML-enabled system with the least possible computation for the interaction with external circumstances is crucially important. Therefore, implementation of novel brain-inspired meta-learning algorithms such as few-shot learning, possibly on neuromorphic platforms, could be a solution for the real-world learning and rapid adaptations with fewer data points [15].

Few-shot Learning (FSL), a novel ML method, falls under a broader umbrella term known as meta-learning which aims for bridging the gap between AI and human-like learning by learning the meta information of classes–tasks rather than merely the data [15,16]. Therefore, by using prior–meta knowledge, FSL can rapidly learn from fewer data points and can better generalize a model to new tasks with the least supervision [15]. As a result, FSL could possibly relieve the burden of collecting large-scale labelled-data for medical applications [15]. Since FSL denotes learning out of a few data points per class, upon the availability of only one example per class the method would be called as one-shot learning, while zero-shot learning represents a scenario where no data points are available for learning a new class of inputs. Siamese networks are among the most popular and simple models used in FSL algorithms with potential applications in areas such as disease diagnosis, object tracking, one-shot robotic imitation, visual navigation, and drug discovery [17].

The objective of this work was to implement siamese-based zero-shot, one-shot, and five-shot learning models for the distinction of COPD subjects from asthma, with a few available data points. Differentiation of COPD patients from asthma, at an early stage of the disease, is significantly important from a medical perspective for the efficiency of the treatment [13]. However, due to the lack of sufficient data from asthma subjects, the classification performance of conventional methods is significantly limited. As a result, implementation of the FSL-based approaches for the distinction of COPD patients from asthma can possibly address the generalization problem with the current available ML models for this application. Therefore, in the continuum, the practicality of applying FSL methods for enhancing the performance of ML models in applications such as medicine—with limited availability of large-scale, high-quality, and correctly labelled training data—will be investigated.

2   Methods

The open access Exasens dataset, available at the UCI machine learning repository (https://archive.ics.uci.edu/ml/datasets/Exasens), was used in this study for the classification and distinction of saliva samples of COPD and asthma patients, as well as Healthy Controls (HC). This novel dataset contains information on hundred saliva samples collected from four groups of respiratory patients including: COPD (40 samples), HC (40 samples), asthma (10 samples), and respiratory infected subjects without COPD or asthma (10 samples), as shown in Fig. 1 [11]. The attributes of the dataset used for the classification of subjects include demographic information of patients (age, gender, and smoking status) as well as the dielectric properties of the characterized saliva samples for every class [18,19]. Despite the high performance of classifiers for the segregation of COPD and HC samples, simultaneous classification of all three classes of COPD, HC, and asthma led to a deficient accuracy of 55%, due to the extremely small-size of the asthma population. Therefore, the FSL method was applied for the distinction of COPD and asthma subjects to make the developed COPD diagnosis models further resilient against adversarial samples like asthma, thus making the ML-based classification of COPD more reliable and valuable for real-world applications. Prior to analytics, the analog values of these four attributes were thresholded and converted into 23 binary bits (Gender (1), smoking status (3), age (9), dielectric (10)), as shown in Fig. 1. Binarization of the attributes of this small-sized dataset has shown to reduce overfitting and noise, and to improve the performance of ML tools for the classification of COPD and HC samples [11]. In addition, considering the small size of the investigated dataset, 5-fold cross-validation method was implemented for the evaluation of models, thus preventing overfitting and providing reliable and generalizable results. After data preparations, as the first step, an Artificial Neural Network (ANN), with one hidden-layer and one read-out layer, was developed for the classification of COPD and HC samples, as shown in Fig. 2 (left). The hidden-layer consisted of four neurons with a rectified linear unit activation function, while the read-out layer determined the two possible classes using softmax. A dropout of 20% was implemented on the hidden-layer for the overfitting prevention. Adam optimization algorithm, with a 0.0001 learning rate, and a cross entropy error function were used for training and optimizing the network parameters. The compiled network was trained for 4000 epochs and a 5-fold cross-validation was applied for the network performance evaluations. After training the initial ANN classifier, the network structure without the readout layer (up to the output of the hidden-layer) was used as an embedding function for extracting the feature vectors of input samples, determining their unique footprints. Next, this feature-extracting network (embedding function) was integrated into a siamese architecture for the recognition of identical input pairs, as shown in Fig. 2 (right). A Euclidean distance function was used as an energy function to calculate the similarities between the feature vectors of the input pairs. Subsequently, a contrastive loss function, with a margin value of one, was used for training the siamese network and minimizing the calculated Euclidean error. For training the developed siamese network, two datasets of genuine and imposite pairs were prepared. The genuine dataset included 20 pairs of COPD–COPD samples, while the imposite dataset consisted of 20 pairs of COPD–HC samples. The data were fed into the siamese network for 1000 training epochs and a 5-fold cross-validation was performed for assessing the model performance. After the successful distinction of genuine COPD inputs from the imposite input pairs, the model was used in a zero-shot learning scheme to distinguish COPD subjects from asthma, as demonstrated in Fig. 3. Through this approach, the feature vector of a test input was extracted and compared to the feature vector of the class of COPD using

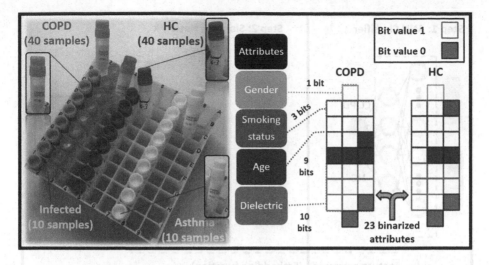

Fig. 1. Four groups of saliva samples available within the Exasens dataset.

the Euclidean error function. In case of a smaller than margin distance of the feature vector of the test input, it was determined as a COPD sample, while inputs with greater margin distances belonged to the adversarial samples class (either asthma or infected). However, to improve the recognition performance of the model and to make it more resilient against other adversarial inputs like infected, the developed siamese network was re-trained for an additional 500 epochs using one and five COPD–asthma imposite pairs (along with COPD–COPD genuine pairs) for one- and five-shot learning schemes, respectively, as shown in Fig. 4. Similar procedure, as for the zero-shot learning testing, was performed for evaluating the performance of the one- and five-shot learning models for distinguishing asthma subjects from COPD. The data preparations and ML implementations were performed on the JupyterLab environment using Keras 2.2.5 and Scikit-learn 0.22 libraries of Python [20]. The metrics and data used in this study are publicly available at https://github.com/Pouya-SZ/SFSL_MED.

3   Results and Discussions

The initial ANN classifier, developed for the classification of COPD and HC patients, provided an average accuracy of 95% for the 5-fold cross-validations, thus making it an adequate embedding function for extracting the feature vectors of input pairs. The modeled siamese network was capable of distinguishing the genuine input pairs of COPD–COPD from the imposite pairs of COPD–HC with 100% average accuracy for the 5-fold cross-validations, thus accurately comparing their feature vectors encoded through the pre-trained embedding function. The high performance of the siamese network made the accurate distinction of COPD and asthma samples through FSL schemes possible, as presented in

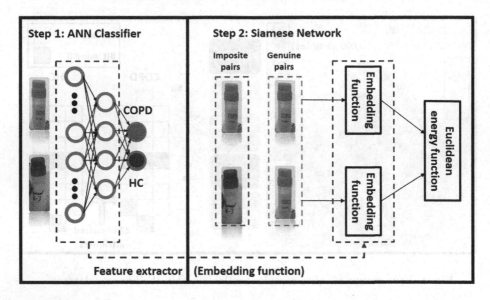

Fig. 2. Required steps for developing a classifier (left) and a siamese network (right).

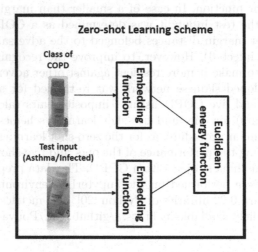

Fig. 3. Zero-shot Learning Scheme for the recognition of asthma vs. COPD.

Table 1. Although all of the zero-, one-, and five-shot learning schemes provided remarkable performance for the distinction of COPD and asthma samples, the incapability of the zero-shot learning approach for distinguishing different adversarial inputs such as asthma and infected was considered the main drawback of this method from the medical perspective. However, its remarkable performance of 100% accuracy for distinguishing asthma and COPD samples, without any training, indicates its significant importance for medical applications with no available training data. On the other hand, Table 1 presents similar accuracies

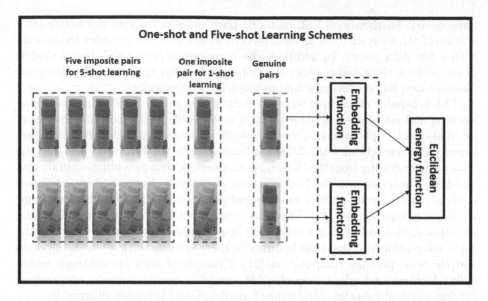

Fig. 4. One-shot and five-shot Learning schemes for training–evaluations.

of 100% for both one- and five-shot learning schemes. Apart from their high recognition capabilities, the one-shot and five-shot learning approaches are further resilient for the reliable distinction of COPD and asthma subjects upon the introduction of other adversarial inputs like infected subjects. As reported in Table 1, in contrast to the zero-shot learning, one-shot and five-shot learning methods were capable of distinguishing asthma and infected samples with 80% accuracies. Although the FSL models presented promising results for the recognition of asthma subjects with no prior knowledge or training, due to the small size of the scrutinized asthma dataset, we consider this work as a proof of concept, requiring further investigations in the future for comprehensive conclusions.

Generalizability to a larger population, as the main limitation with any ML study on a small-sized novel dataset, is a fundamental concern for this study, demanding extensive investigations. Nonetheless, to the best of our knowledge, there is no other comprehensive dataset available up to date on the COPD and asthma samples, which can be used for training and evaluating the introduced FSL models in this work. Therefore, we consider our study as a stepping stone to future studies in the field, while endorsing the necessity for further data collections.

The results discussed in this work demonstrated the practicality of applying FSL methods for addressing the shortcomings of ML models in applications like medicine with a few or none available data points. By taking advantage of brain-inspired algorithms such as FSL, it is possible not only to enhance the performance of conventional ML models, but also to make them further resilient against adversarial inputs. In addition, through meta-learning approaches like FSL, training ML models from scratch for every individual patient or disease is unnecessary. Furthermore, FSL methods pave the way towards the better integration of ML tools with old medical records as well as novel–complex treatments with a few data points. In addition, the main advantage of FSL-based models in medicine is their better generalization to a broader spectrum of patients or disease cases, while offering a human-like learning possibility.

FSL is capable of learning with fewer data points, thus facilitating the online learning and adaptation of ML-equipped systems like neuromorphic processors for real-world applications. The energy-efficient neuromorphic processors are expected to revolutionize the ML-based medicine in the future by bringing the data post-processing from the backend onto the chip, thus providing accurate and real-time predictions on the health status of patients. Neuromorphic-equipped medical devices better protect users' sensitive medical data without cloud communication requirements [12]. Therefore, implementation of novel meta learning algorithms, such as few-shot learning, on neuromorphic platforms will enable the rapid adaptation and real-time learning in these systems with a few data points and the least possible computation [21]. Example of such applications, where online learning and adaptation of a ML model is crucial, include autonomous driving, surgical robotics, personalized medicine, and precision diagnostic.

In the future, integration of the proposed FSL tools with the epileptic seizure prediction models will enable the better generalization of these models to a larger population of patients. In addition, the employment of canine-based models for the human epilepsy managements will be possible. Furthermore, integration of these models into the kafka framework facilitates the management of ML pipelines through data streams in a user friendly environment, which is the next step of this work [22]. Moreover, the final goal of this work is to develop and deploy siamese-based FSL techniques on a neuromorphic platform for the on-chip prediction of epileptic seizure using smart healthcare wearables.

Table 1. Results of zero-, one-, and five-shot learning schemes for the distinction of asthma samples from COPD and infected.

	Zero-shot	One-shot	Five-shot
COPD vs. Asthma	100%	100%	100%
Asthma vs. Infected	NA	80%	80%

4 Conclusions

In this work, the practicality of applying few-shot learning algorithms for addressing the shortcomings of ML models in medical applications with limited data availability was investigated. Siamese-based zero-, one-, and five-shot learning models were developed for the distinction of COPD and asthma subjects. The developed models provided high performance for the recognition of asthma samples, while making the ML-based diagnosis of COPD more resilient against adversarial inputs. Implementation of the proposed FSL models in other medical applications with limited data availability will address the generalization issues of the most ML models in this realm. The brain-inspired few-shot learning could possibly address AI's problems in medicine caused due to the lack of sufficient training data. Therefore, implementation of FSL algorithms for the epileptic seizure prediction with fewer data is the next goal of this study.

Acknowledgement. The authors acknowledge IHP GmbH and the Federal Ministry for Education and Research (BMBF) of Germany for funding this work. The authors thank the BioMaterialBank Nord (BMB Nord) for the collection of saliva samples and FZ Borstel-Leibniz Lung Center, especially Niels Roeckendor, for their precious help with the biological and medical aspects of the work. Special thanks to the staff at CerCo–CNRS and Toulouse Mind and Brain Institute, especially Timothée Masquelier, for their valuable support.

References

1. LeCun, Y., Bengio, Y., Hinton, G.: Deep learning. Nature **521**, 436–444 (2015). https://doi.org/10.1038/nature14539
2. Fogel, A.L., Kvedar, J.C.: Artificial intelligence powers digital medicine. NPJ Digit. Med. **1**, 1–4 (2018). https://doi.org/10.1038/s41746-017-0012-2
3. Ching, T., et al.: Opportunities and obstacles for deep learning in biology and medicine. J. Roy. Soc. Interface **15**, 141 (2018). https://doi.org/10.1098/rsif.2017. 0387
4. Zarrin, P.S., Escoto, A., Xu, R., Naish, M.D., Patel, R.V., Trejos, A.L.: Development of an optical fiber-based sensor for grasping and axial force sensing. In: IEEE Conference on Robotics and Automation (ICRA), Singapore, pp. 939–944 (2017). https://doi.org/10.1109/ICRA.2017.7989114
5. Zeiaee, A., Soltani-Zarrin, R., Jayasuriya, S., Langari, R.: A uniform control for tracking and point stabilization of differential drive robots subject to hard input constraints. In: Dynamic Systems and Control Conference, Ohio, USA, vol. 57243, p. V001T04A005 (2015). https://doi.org/10.1115/DSCC2015-9925
6. Soltani-Zarrin, R., Zeiaee, A., Langari, R., Robson, N.: Reference path generation for upper-arm exoskeletons considering scapulohumeral rhythms. In: International Conference on Rehabilitation Robotics (ICORR), London, UK, pp. 753–758 (2017). https://doi.org/10.1109/ICORR.2017.8009338
7. Zarrin, P.S., Escoto, A., Xu, R., Naish, M.D., Patel, R.V., Trejos, A.L.: Development of a 2-DOF sensorized surgical grasper for grasping and axial force measurements. IEEE Sens. J. **18**, 2816–2826 (2018). https://doi.org/10.1109/JSEN.2018. 2805327
8. Kiral-Kornek, I.: Epileptic seizure prediction using big data and deep learning: toward a mobile system. EBioMedicine **27**, 103–111 (2018). https://doi.org/10. 1016/j.ebiom.2017.11.032
9. Zarrin, P.S., Zimmer, R., Wenger, C., Masquelier, T.: Epileptic seizure detection using a neuromorphic-compatible deep spiking neural network. In: Rojas, I., Valenzuela, O., Rojas, F., Herrera, L.J., Ortuño, F. (eds.) IWBBIO 2020. LNCS, vol. 12108, pp. 389–394. Springer, Cham (2020). https://doi.org/10.1007/978-3-030-45385-5_34
10. Prabhu, V.U.: Few-Shot Learning for Dermatological Disease Diagnosis. Georgia Institute of Technology (2019)

11. Zarrin, P.S., Roeckendorf, N., Wenger, C.: In-vitro classification of saliva samples of COPD patients and healthy controls using machine learning tools. IEEE Access **8**, 168053–168060 (2020). https://doi.org/10.1109/ACCESS.2020.3023971

12. Soltani Zarrin, P., Wenger, C.: Pattern recognition for COPD diagnostics using an artificial neural network and its potential integration on hardware-based neuromorphic platforms. In: Tetko, I.V., Kůrková, V., Karpov, P., Theis, F. (eds.) ICANN 2019. LNCS, vol. 11731, pp. 284–288. Springer, Cham (2019). https://doi.org/10.1007/978-3-030-30493-5_29

13. Barnes, P.J.: Mechanisms in COPD: differences from asthma. Chest **117**, 10S–14S (2000). https://doi.org/10.1378/chest.117.2_suppl.10S

14. Postma, D.S., Rabe, K.F.: The asthma-COPD overlap syndrome. N. Engl. J. Med. **373**, 1241–1249 (2015). https://doi.org/10.1056/NEJMra1411863

15. Wang, Y., Kwok, J., Ni, L.M., Yao, Q.: Generalizing from a few examples: a survey on few-shot learning. ACM Comput. Surv. (CSUR) **53**, 1–34 (2019). https://doi.org/10.1145/3386252

16. Santoro, A., Bartunov, S., Botvinick, M., Wierstra, D., Lillicrap, T.: Meta-learning with memory-augmented neural networks. In: International Conference on Machine Learning, vol. 11, pp. 1842–1850 (2016)

17. Altae-Tran, H., Ramsundar, B., Pappu, A.S., Pande, V.: Low data drug discovery with one-shot learning. ACS Central Sci. **3**, 283–293 (2017). https://doi.org/10.1021/acscentsci.6b00367

18. Soltani Zarrin, P., Ibne Jamal, F., Roeckendorf, N., Wenger, C.: Development of a portable dielectric biosensor for rapid detection of viscosity variations and its in vitro evaluations using saliva samples of COPD patients and healthy control. Healthcare **7**, 11 (2019). https://doi.org/10.3390/healthcare7010011

19. Soltani Zarrin, P., Jamal, F.I., Guha, S., Wessel, J., Kissinger, D., Wenger, C.: Design and fabrication of a BiCMOS dielectric sensor for viscosity measurements: a possible solution for early detection of COPD. Biosensors **8**, 78 (2018). https://doi.org/10.3390/bios8030078

20. Pedregosa, F.: Scikit-learn: machine learning in Python. J. Mach. Learn. Res. **12**, 2825–2830 (2011)

21. Stewart, K., Neftci, E., Orchard, G: On-chip Few-shot Learning with Surrogate Gradient Descent on a Neuromorphic Processor. arXiv:1910.04972 (2019). https://doi.org/10.1109/AICAS48895.2020.9073948

22. Martín, C., Langendoerfer, P., Zarrin, P.S., Díaz, M. and Rubio, B: Kafka-ML: connecting the data stream with ML/AI frameworks. arXiv preprint (2020). https://arxiv.org/abs/2006.04105

Few-Shot Learning for Medical Image Classification

Aihua Cai, Wenxin Hu$^{(\boxtimes)}$, and Jun Zheng

East China Normal University, Shanghai, China
cah0231@163.com, {wxhu,jzheng}@cc.ecnu.edu.cn

Abstract. Rapid and accurate classification of medical images plays an important role in medical diagnosis. Nowadays, for medical image classification, there are some methods based on machine learning, deep learning and transfer learning. However, these methods may be time-consuming and not suitable for small datasets. Based on these limitations, we propose a novel method which combines few-shot learning method and attention mechanism. Our method takes end-to-end learning to solve the problem of artificial feature extraction in machine learning and few-shot learning method is especially to fulfill small datasets tasks, which means it performs better than traditional deep learning. In addition, our method can make full use of spatial and channel information which enhances the representation of models. Furthermore, we adopt 1×1 convolution to enhance the interactions of cross channel information. Then we apply the model to the medical dataset Brain Tumor and compare it with the transfer learning method and Dual Path Network. Our method achieves an accuracy of 92.44%, which is better than the above methods.

Keywords: Medical image classification · Few-shot learning · Attention mechanism · Transfer learning

1 Introduction

The classification of medical images such as tumor types is important for the diagnosis and subsequent treatment of diseases. However, classifying medical images with similar structures manually is a difficult and challenging task that requires a lot of time for experienced experts. In order to improve the efficiency and accuracy of classification, researchers propose plenty of methods, such as machine learning [8], deep learning [14] and transfer learning [7]. However, these methods have some shortcomings. As the most important step in machine learning, feature extraction requires experts to spend much time determining the features. Deep learning is more suitable for huge datasets, which means the small amount and unbalanced categories problems will limit the efficiency of deep models. Transfer learning can use a pre-trained model to address the problems of small datasets, while there is a great difference between natural and medical images. So we need to explore new methods to solve these problems.

© Springer Nature Switzerland AG 2020
I. Farkaš et al. (Eds.): ICANN 2020, LNCS 12396, pp. 441–452, 2020.
https://doi.org/10.1007/978-3-030-61609-0_35

The emergence of few-shot learning provides new directions for medical image classification tasks. The few-shot learning [17,18] is proposed to solve the problem of overfitting and aims to recognize novel categories from very few labeled examples. To this day, it has also produced a variety of effective models and algorithms. The main methods are meta-learning [12], metric-based [20], data-augmented [5], semantic-based [19], and so on. The baseline used in the paper is Prototypical Network [17] which is based on metric learning. This model is outstanding in the classification of small samples, but there is still the problem that spatial and channel information is not considered in feature extraction. Due to the noise in the medical image, the features that contribute to the classification results should be found more accurately.

Based on this deficiency, we improve the original model. In the embedding module, we extract features through several convolution operations. After extracting many features, we consider "what" is meaningful in the image and "where" is an informative part of the classification task. So we add an attention module into the embedding module. Inspired by *Network in Network* [13], we add 1×1 convolution into the convolutional blocks to enhance the interactions of cross channel information. In this way, we can improve feature representations and suppress more useless information. The use of few-shot learning methods can effectively address the problem of overfitting. We conduct a series of comparative experiments to validate the effectiveness of our methods. At last, the results show that compared with pre-trained models, our model is more effective.

The main contributions of this paper can be summarized as follows:

1. We propose to add the attention mechanism into the network, which helps model extract features from spatial and channels simultaneously. Through the experiments, we find different placements of attention mechanism share different results. When the Convolutional Block Attention Module(CBAM) is put between the last two convolutional blocks, the result is the best.
2. We propose to add 1×1 convolution into the convolutional blocks. This operation can enhance the interactions of cross channel information and the results outperform the prior one.
3. We apply few-shot learning methods to the field of medical image classification to solve the problem of small datasets and achieve good results.

The rest of the paper is organized as follows: we first introduce the related work about methods to solve medical image classification in Sect. 2. Then we describe our methods in detail in Sect. 3. In Sect. 4, we mainly present our datasets, experimental setup and results. Finally, in Sect. 5, we conclude our work and indicate future directions.

2 Related Work

2.1 Method Based on Machine Learning

In the medical field, doctors need to judge the type of tumors according to CT or MRI images [8]. However, it costs much time and energy of doctors and experts that they need to identify the location of tumors, compare the location and shape, make more accurate judgment and conclusion. In the beginning, researchers adopt machine learning methods, which involve data preprocessing, image segmentation, feature extraction, selection and classification. Before feature extraction, experts are required to select a series of features for calculation, which can be gray value, texture features, etc. Due to too many features, feature selection is also required. From these processes, we can see that these features for classification are very important and these processes have great flexibility and complexity, so it may lead to the result is not ideal, unstable and has weak generation. These methods cannot apply to several datasets well.

2.2 Method Based on Deep Learning

Unlike machine learning, deep learning does not require manual feature extraction. The image can be directly classified without image segmentation because most methods are end-to-end which greatly save time and energy. Deep learning is also widely used in the medical field, from image segmentation to recognition to classification. [11] classified diabetic retinopathy images by combining Inception-v3, ResNet152 [9] and Inception-ResNet-v2, which achieved great results. [23] proposed the siamese-like structure and used two pictures as input to learn their correlation to help classify. [3] proposed an improved capsule network to classify brain tumor types. Through a large number of experiments, deep learning has been proved to be effective in processing medical images. However, at present, most deep learning methods extract features through convolution operation. Convolution operation can extract information such as edges and textures of images, but spatial and channel information cannot be used well.

2.3 Method Based on Transfer Learning

There are still some problems in the application of deep learning to the medical field, mainly due to the small medical datasets. Since the datasets are small, it is probable to be overfitting when applying deep learning models. In view of the small amount of data, researchers proposed to use transfer learning methods. Most models are trained on big datasets such as ImageNet and use medical datasets to fine-tune some layers of the model so that the model can better adapt to medical datasets [21]. However, there are also some papers question whether the effect of transferring the pre-trained model learned on ImageNet to the medical dataset is good and experiments have proved that the use of a smaller and simpler model can achieve comparable results as the use of pre-trained models.

2.4 Method Based on Few-Shot Learning

Few-shot learning [15] is also applied to fulfill the task of medical image classification. [14] proposed an AffinityNet, which used the k-Nearest-Neighbor attention pooling layer to extract abstract local features. This model based on semi-supervised few-shot learning shows great performance on disease type prediction.

[6] used Siamese Network, one of the classical network in few-shot learning, to retrieve images in medical datasets. [16] applied Triplet Network, which was improved by Siamese Network, to accomplish brain imaging modality recognition. So far, few cases use few-shot learning to solve the problem of medical image classification and the method above mainly uses CNN to extract features which can not find discriminative features to help classify.

3   Methodology

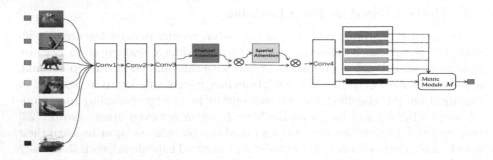

Fig. 1. The overview architecture of our method.

3.1   Overview

In this paper, we propose a novel method to solve the medical image classification task. As the original convolutional block can only extract the basic information and it focuses on the whole image, while the features of medical images are usually much noisier and heterogeneous, we choose Prototypical Network and improve it with the attention mechanism. With this improvement, our model can pay more attention to the part that contributes to the classification. The specific structure is demonstrated in Fig. 1. When the sample is mapped to the feature space, we mainly use an embedding function $f(x)$, which is a neural network, and it is composed of four convolutional blocks as shown in Fig. 2. Since the convolution operation can only extract partial edge, texture, direction and other information, we use the attention mechanism to increase the representation ability of the model. We add spatial and channel attention module between the third and fourth convolutional blocks respectively to extract the spatial and channel information of the image. Furthermore, we adopt 1×1 convolution kernels in the convolutional block. This convolution can greatly increase the nonlinear characteristics and deepen the network without losing the resolution. Next, we will introduce the basic model.

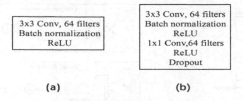

(a)   **(b)**

Fig. 2. Two types of convolutional blocks used in the experiment. (a) is the classical one which is widely used in few-shot learning models. (b) is the modified convolutional blocks, which is added 1×1 convolution kernel and dropout.

3.2 Prototypical Network

Prototypical Network is a classical model in few-shot learning. It was proposed by [17] in 2017, and was mainly used to solve the problem of overfitting in few-shot datasets. It projects the sample into the feature space, where the homogeneous samples are closer together and the heterogeneous samples are farther apart. In the Prototypical Network, the prototype is obtained by calculating the mean value of the features from the same class. In the subsequent testing process, the distance between the test sample and each prototype is calculated to see which prototype is close to it. The class is decided by which class the prototype belonging to. As in Fig. 1, we present a 5-way 1-shot condition. The input is 5 images from 5 classes, so we do not calculate the mean of every embedding value. When we use 5-way 5-shot, we need to calculate the mean of embedding values as a prototype. Our method is based on the Prototypical Network and then we will introduce the attention mechanism.

3.3 Attention Mechanism

CBAM was proposed by [22] in 2018. The main purpose is to increase the representation ability of models through the attention mechanism. It considers the information in channels and spatial. In the channel attention module, it can generate a channel attention map and it mainly mines "what" is meaningful in the input image. In the spatial attention module, it uses the information on the relationship in feature space to explore "where" is important. Especially in medical fields, doctors determine the type of tumor mainly from the position, size, or color in medical images. Therefore, it is very important to explore the spatial and channel information in medical images.

3.4 Network Architecture

The model based on metric learning includes two components, one is the embedding module and the other is the classifier. The image x_i from support set and the image x_j from query set are fed into the embedding module respectively and obtain their feature maps $f(x_i)$ and $f(x_j)$. Then the feature map will be input

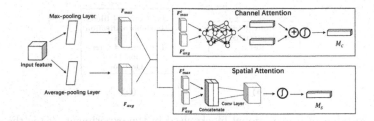

Fig. 3. CBAM module

into the classifier to calculate the distance between them. The classifier in Proto-typical Network is Euclidean distance. In prior works, four convolutional blocks are utilized for embedding modules, which can be seen in Fig. 2(a). Every block contains 64 filters 3×3 convolution, batch normalization and a ReLU nonlinearity layer. We also conduct experiments with the modified convolutional blocks (Fig. 2(b)). It differs in that we add 1×1 convolution and dropout. By adding these two operations we can further enhance the representation of models and the effect of dropout is to reduce the number of intermediate features and reduce redundancy. Between convolutional blocks, there is a 2×2 max-pooling layer. The CBAM module is shown in Fig. 3. According to the conclusions in [22], we choose to place the module in a sequential arrangement and put the spatial attention behind the channel attention. The two modules are both use max-pooling and average-pooling. In channel attention module, max-pooling and average-pooling are first adopted to generate respect features F_{max}^c and F_{avg}^c and then put them into a shared network. After that, we merge the output feature vectors through element-wise summation. Finally, the sigmoid function is used to calculate the channel attention M_c in the following formula:

$$M_c = \sigma(MLP(F_{avg}^c) + MLP(F_{max}^c)) \tag{1}$$

where σ denotes the sigmoid function, MLP is a shared network with a hidden layer.

In spatial attention module, after max-pooling and average-pooling, we do concatenate operation to generate feature descriptors. Then we apply a convolution layer to generate a spatial attention map M_s. The whole process can be described by the following formula:

$$M_s = \sigma(Conv([F_{avg}^s; F_{max}^s])) \tag{2}$$

where σ denotes the sigmoid function, $Conv$ represents a convolution operation, $[;]$ means the concatenation operation.

4   Experiments

4.1   Datasets and Preprocessing

The brain tumor dataset [1] consists of three types: meningioma, glioma and pituitary tumor, which is shown in Fig. 4. The number of these three brain tumor images is 708, 1426 and 930, which is quite different, so we need to do data augmentation. We rotate these images at 90, 180 and 270 degrees. We also add Gaussian noise and Salt-Pepper noise to images to enhance the robustness of the model. Finally, the amount of data can reach 2832, 2852, 2790, which achieves the class balance generally. All images are 512×512.

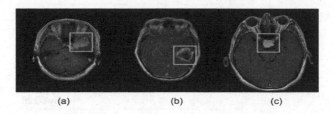

     (a)   (b)   (c)

Fig. 4. (a) Meningioma, (b) Glioma, (c) Pituitary tumor. Tumors are localized inside a red rectangle.

4.2 Experimental Settings and Training Details

In the following experiments, we adopt Adam as the optimizer for model training and the initial learning rate is 10^{-3}. The number of training and testing episodes per epoch is 100. The batch size is 8. The number of epochs to train is 100. To alleviate overfitting, we also adopt dropout and the value is 0.5. The dimensionality of hidden layers is 64.

    In the few-shot learning, episode training strategy is widely used. We use 5-way 20-shot with 20 query images for each class in the training episode. Firstly, we sample 5 classes in the training set and then sample 20 images from these 5 classes. The 20 query image is selected from the rest images of the 5 classes. Finally, the $5 \times 20 + 5 \times 20 = 200$ images compose a training episode. The training and testing conditions are the same. In our experiments, there are only three classes, so we have to use prior knowledge to train the model. We use other medical datasets [2] to augment the class of training set, while the dataset is not very similar to the brain tumor dataset, then we combine 1500 images each class in the brain tumor dataset to help fine-tune the model. We considered that if we involve the images of novel classes at the beginning of the training, it would make the model more suitable to solve the existing classification problem.

4.3 The Effect of Adding CBAM Module

In Sect. 3, we discuss the CBAM module can exploit the information from channel and spatial to strengthen the representation ability. In this section, we conduct several experiments to validate this idea. Some network architectures can be seen in Table 1. P1 is the network that uses four convolutional blocks (Fig. 2(a)) and P2 is the network that we add a CBAM module between the third and fourth

Table 1. The network architectures used in the experiment

Name	P1	P2	P3	P4
Input	Brain Tumor Dataset: 512 × 512 gray-scale images			
Network architecture	conv3-64	conv3-64	conv3-64 conv1-128	conv3-64 conv1-128
	maxpool: 2 × 2			
	conv3-64	conv3-64	conv3-64 conv1-128	conv3-64 conv1-128
	maxpool: 2 × 2			
	conv3-64	conv3-64	conv3-64 conv1-128	conv3-64 conv1-128
	conv3-64	CBAM	CBAM	conv3-64 conv1-128
		conv3-64	conv3-64 conv1-128	
	Flatten			
Results	83.27%	87.35%	**92.44%**	89.48%

convolutional blocks. From their results, we can see that P2 is better than P1 by an increased accuracy of 4%.

To further investigate the effect of CBAM, we try to add the CBAM module between different convolutional blocks. Such as P2, CBAM is added between the third and fourth blocks. We also try to put it in other places. Through the experiment, we find that different locations and numbers of CBAM modules generate different results. The results are shown in Table 2. In the experiment, it is found that 4 convolutional blocks are more effective than 3 or 5 convolutional blocks. Placing the CBAM module between the third and fourth convolutional blocks (Number 2 in Table 2) is better than others. Using several CBAM modules (Number 5 in Table 2) is no better than using a single module.

Table 2. Comparison with different placements of CBAM modules

Number	Method	Accuracy
1	3_CNN_12_CBAM	62.24%
2	4_CNN_34_CBAM	**87.35%**
3	4_CNN_23_CBAM	77.06%
4	4_CNN_12_CBAM	70.40%
5	4_CNN_2CBAM	79.26%
6	5_CNN_45_CBAM	68.73%

Different convolutional blocks convey different information, the lower convolutional blocks extract low-level features, the upper extract high-level features.

And the closer to the lower layer, the vaguer the information CBAM extracts, the less contribution to the classification task. The higher convolutional blocks, especially the third and fourth convolutional block, extract more specific and useful information. And these convolutional blocks contribute more to classification tasks. Therefore, the CBAM module placed between the last two convolutional blocks performs best. The information extracted using three convolutional blocks cannot accomplish classification, so it is the least effective. The above experiments also show that different placements are very important for the results.

4.4   The Effect of Adding 1×1 Convolution Kernel

In this part, we conduct a series of experiments to validate the effect of adding 1×1 convolutions. In Table 1, P3 and P4 are used to compare the effectiveness. When we compare P1 with P4, we can find that adding 1×1 convolution is definitely effective and it performs better than P2. We use 1×1 convolution and it can increase nonlinear characteristics without losing resolution. It can also reduce dimension and increase dimension. In P3 and P4, we change the number of output channels to strengthen the information interaction between channels.

So we add both CBAM and 1×1 convolution into the model which is shown as P3. Figure 5(a) is the confusion matrix of P2 and Fig. 5(b) is the confusion matrix of P3. During the test process, we use 3240 images. From the confusion

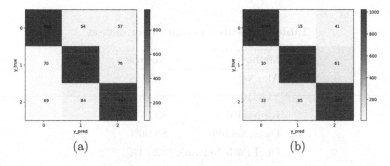

(a)   (b)

Fig. 5. Two types of convolutional blocks used in the experiment. (a) is the classical one which is widely used in few-shot learning. (b) is the modified convolutional blocks, which is added 1×1 convolution kernel and dropout.

Table 3. Classification performance of the proposed method on brain tumor dataset. The values in parentheses are the results of adding the 1×1 convolution kernel and CBAM module. The values outside parentheses are the results of adding CBAM module.

Type	Accuracy	Precision	Recall	F1-score
Meningioma	0.90(**0.95**)	0.87(**0.96**)	0.90(**0.95**)	0.89(**0.95**)
Glioma	0.86(**0.93**)	0.87(**0.91**)	0.86(**0.93**)	0.87(**0.92**)
Pituitary tumor	0.86(**0.89**)	0.87(**0.90**)	0.86(**0.89**)	0.87(**0.90**)

matrixes, we can easily calculate the accuracy, precision, recall and f1-score, which is list in Table 3. From the table, we can see that the effect of the model is greatly improved after the addition of 1×1 convolution, thus further demonstrating that information interaction between channels is very useful for image classification.

4.5   Comparison of Different Methods

In the experiment, we compare the transfer learning method with our method. We use AlexNet, VGG16, ResNet101 [9] and DenseNet169 [10] pre-trained models which are modified with the last classification layer.

The results are presented in Table 4. We use the Prototypical Network to train and test on the brain tumor dataset and achieve the accuracy of 92.44%. The experimental results show that compared to models with pre-trained, our method has obvious advantages. The parameters of the pre-trained models are usually trained on the ImageNet dataset, while the natural images on ImageNet are quite different from the medical images, which often lead to unsatisfactory results. The performance of Dual Path Network [4] which combines ResNeXt and DenseNet is also not good and we find that when the embedding module is modified to ResNet, DenseNet or other deeper networks, the results are not ideal, which may be caused by the characteristics of the medical image itself. Therefore, our method performs better than these deeper networks.

Table 4. Results on brain tumor dataset

Method	Accuracy
AlexNet	79.80%
VGG16	82.08%
ResNet101	82.57%
DenseNet169	83.06%
Dual Path Network	82.74%
Our method	**92.44%**

5   Conclusion

In this paper, we adopt the few-shot learning model to solve the problem of medical image classification. We concretely choose Prototypical Network because this approach is far simpler and more efficient than other meta-learning approaches. We improve it and add a CBAM module based on the attention mechanism and 1×1 convolution kernel into the embedding module, which greatly strengthens the presentation ability of the model. We perform several comparative experiments on the brain tumor dataset. The results prove that these combinations are applicable to the classification of medical images. As the interpretability of models and results is very important, in future studies, we will continue to explore the interpretability of the model to explain why different positions of CBAM have different effects on the final results. In our method, we use Euclidean distance to calculate the distance between the prototype and query image and we will try other distance measures for further study.

Acknowledgments. We thank all viewers who provided the thoughtful and constructive comments on this paper. This research is funded by Shanghai Key Laboratory of Multidimensional Information Processing, East China Normal University, Shanghai 200241, China. The computation is supported by ECNU Multifunctional Platform for Innovation (001).

References

1. Brain tumor. https://figshare.com/articles/brain_tumor_dataset/1512427
2. OCT and Chest X-Ray. https://data.mendeley.com/datasets/rscbjbr9sj/2
3. Afshar, P., Plataniotis, K.N., Mohammadi, A.: Capsule networks for brain tumor classification based on MRI images and coarse tumor boundaries. In: IEEE International Conference on Acoustics, Speech and Signal Processing, ICASSP 2019, Brighton, United Kingdom, 12–17 May 2019, pp. 1368–1372. IEEE (2019)
4. Chen, Y., Li, J., Xiao, H., Jin, X., Yan, S., Feng, J.: Dual path networks. In: Guyon, I., et al. (eds.) Advances in Neural Information Processing Systems 30: Annual Conference on Neural Information Processing Systems 2017, Long Beach, CA, USA, 4–9 December 2017, pp. 4467–4475 (2017)
5. Chen, Z., Fu, Y., Wang, Y., Ma, L., Liu, W., Hebert, M.: Image deformation meta-networks for one-shot learning. In: IEEE Conference on Computer Vision and Pattern Recognition, CVPR 2019, Long Beach, CA, USA, 16–20 June 2019, pp. 8680–8689. Computer Vision Foundation/IEEE (2019)
6. Chung, Y., Weng, W.: Learning deep representations of medical images using Siamese CNNs with application to content-based image retrieval. CoRR abs/1711.08490 (2017)
7. Deepak, S., Ameer, P.M.: Brain tumor classification using deep CNN features via transfer learning. Comput. Biol. Med. **111**, 103345 (2019)
8. García-Floriano, A., Ferreira-Santiago, Á., Camacho-Nieto, O., Yáñez-Márquez, C.: A machine learning approach to medical image classification: detecting age-related macular degeneration in fundus images. Comput. Electr. Eng. **75**, 218–229 (2019)
9. He, K., Zhang, X., Ren, S., Sun, J.: Deep residual learning for image recognition. In: 2016 IEEE Conference on Computer Vision and Pattern Recognition, CVPR 2016, Las Vegas, NV, USA, 27–30 June 2016, pp. 770–778. IEEE Computer Society (2016)
10. Huang, G., Liu, Z., van der Maaten, L., Weinberger, K.Q.: Densely connected convolutional networks. In: 2017 IEEE Conference on Computer Vision and Pattern Recognition, CVPR 2017, Honolulu, HI, USA, 21–26 July 2017, pp. 2261–2269. IEEE Computer Society (2017)
11. Jiang, H., Yang, K., Gao, M., Zhang, D., Ma, H., Qian, W.: An interpretable ensemble deep learning model for diabetic retinopathy disease classification. In: Conference of the IEEE Engineering in Medicine and Biology Society, EMBC 2019, Berlin, Germany, 23–27 July 2019, pp. 2045–2048 (2019)

12. Kim, J., Kim, T., Kim, S., Yoo, C.D.: Edge-labeling graph neural network for few-shot learning. In: IEEE Conference on Computer Vision and Pattern Recognition, CVPR 2019, Long Beach, CA, USA, 16–20 June 2019, pp. 11–20. Computer Vision Foundation/IEEE (2019)

13. Lin, M., Chen, Q., Yan, S.: Network in network. In: Bengio, Y., LeCun, Y. (eds.) 2nd International Conference on Learning Representations, ICLR 2014, Banff, AB, Canada, 14–16 April 2014, Conference Track Proceedings (2014)

14. Ma, T., Zhang, A.: Affinitynet: semi-supervised few-shot learning for disease type prediction. In: The Thirty-Third AAAI Conference on Artificial Intelligence, AAAI 2019, The Thirty-First Innovative Applications of Artificial Intelligence Conference, IAAI 2019, The Ninth AAAI Symposium on Educational Advances in Artificial Intelligence, EAAI 2019, Honolulu, Hawaii, USA, 27 January–1 February 2019, pp. 1069–1076. AAAI Press (2019)

15. Munkhdalai, T., Yu, H.: Meta networks. In: Proceedings of the 34th International Conference on Machine Learning, ICML 2017, Sydney, NSW, Australia, 6–11 August 2017, pp. 2554–2563 (2017)

16. Puch, S., Sánchez, I., Rowe, M.: Few-shot learning with deep triplet networks for brain imaging modality recognition (2019)

17. Snell, J., Swersky, K., Zemel, R.S.: Prototypical networks for few-shot learning. In: Guyon, I., von Luxburg, U., Bengio, S., Wallach, H.M., Fergus, R., Vishwanathan, S.V.N., Garnett, R. (eds.) Advances in Neural Information Processing Systems 30: Annual Conference on Neural Information Processing Systems 2017, Long Beach, CA, USA, 4–9 December 2017, pp. 4077–4087 (2017)

18. Sung, F., Yang, Y., Zhang, L., Xiang, T., Torr, P.H.S., Hospedales, T.M.: Learning to compare: relation network for few-shot learning. In: 2018 IEEE Conference on Computer Vision and Pattern Recognition, CVPR 2018, Salt Lake City, UT, USA, 18–22 June 2018, pp. 1199–1208. IEEE Computer Society (2018)

19. Wang, X., Yu, F., Wang, R., Darrell, T., Gonzalez, J.E.: Tafe-net: task-aware feature embeddings for low shot learning. In: IEEE Conference on Computer Vision and Pattern Recognition, CVPR 2019, Long Beach, CA, USA, 16–20 June 2019, pp. 1831–1840. Computer Vision Foundation/IEEE (2019)

20. Wang, X., Hua, Y., Kodirov, E., Hu, G., Garnier, R., Robertson, N.M.: Ranked list loss for deep metric learning. In: IEEE Conference on Computer Vision and Pattern Recognition, CVPR 2019, Long Beach, CA, USA, 16–20 June 2019, pp. 5207–5216. Computer Vision Foundation/IEEE (2019)

21. Wong, K.C.L., Moradi, M., Wu, J.T., Syeda-Mahmood, T.F.: Identifying disease-free chest x-ray images with deep transfer learning. CoRR abs/1904.01654 (2019). http://arxiv.org/abs/1904.01654

22. Woo, S., Park, J., Lee, J.-Y., Kweon, I.S.: CBAM: convolutional block attention module. In: Ferrari, V., Hebert, M., Sminchisescu, C., Weiss, Y. (eds.) ECCV 2018. LNCS, vol. 11211, pp. 3–19. Springer, Cham (2018). https://doi.org/10.1007/978-3-030-01234-2_1

23. Zeng, X., Chen, H., Luo, Y., Ye, W.B.: Automated diabetic retinopathy detection based on binocular siamese-like convolutional neural network. IEEE Access 7, 30744–30753 (2019)

Generative Adversarial Network

Adversarial Defense via Attention-Based Randomized Smoothing

Xiao Xu[1], Shiyu Feng[1], Zheng Wang[1,2], Lizhe Xie[3,4], and Yining Hu[1,2(✉)]

[1] School of Cyber Science and Engineering, Southeast University, Nanjing, China
hyn.list@seu.edu.cn
[2] Jiangsu Provincial Key Laboratory of Computer Network Technology,
Nanjing, China
[3] Jiangsu Key Laboratory of Oral Diseases, Nanjing Medical University,
Nanjing, China
[4] Institute of Stomatology, Nanjing Medical University, Nanjing, China

Abstract. Recent works have shown the effectiveness of randomized smoothing in adversarial defense. This paper presents a new understanding of randomized smoothing. Features that are vulnerable to noise are not conducive to the prediction of model under adversarial perturbations. An enhanced defense called Attention-based Randomized Smoothing (ARS) is proposed. Based on smoothed classifier, ARS designs a mixed attention module, which helps model merge smoothed feature with original feature and pay more attention to robust feature. The advantages of ARS are manifested in four ways: 1) Superior performance on both clean and adversarial samples. 2) Without pre-processing in inference. 3) Explicable attention map. 4) Compatible with other defense methods. Experiment results demonstrate that ARS achieves the state-of-the-art defense against adversarial attacks on MNIST and CIFAR-10 datasets, outperforming Salman's defense when the attacks are limited to a maximum norm.

Keywords: Adversarial defence · Attention mechanism · Neural network

1 Introduction

In recent years, convolutional neural network (CNN) has been extensively deployed to computer vision tasks, particularly visual classification problems. However, Nguyen et al. [1] pointed out that CNN is sometimes vulnerable to subtle input perturbations. The samples with certain perturbations which result in false recognition are called adversarial samples.

Many researches have been proposed against adversarial attacks, among which randomized smoothing has been paid universal attention as a scalable technique. Randomized smoothing transforms any classifier (e.g. a neural network) into a new smoothed classifier by adding random perturbations to the

© Springer Nature Switzerland AG 2020
I. Farkaš et al. (Eds.): ICANN 2020, LNCS 12396, pp. 455–466, 2020.
https://doi.org/10.1007/978-3-030-61609-0_36

input, which called smoothed images. Cohen et al. [2] proved a tight robustness guarantee in L2 norm for smoothing. Salman et al. [3] combined randomized smoothing with adversarial training, which substantially improves the effect of randomized smoothing as an enhanced defense.

Recently, Ilyas et al. [4] demonstrated that adversarial examples can be directly attributed to the presence of non-robust features that are highly predictive, yet brittle and incomprehensible to humans. Meanwhile, visual attention is used to explain which region of image feature is responsible for the network's decision. Wu et al. [5] and Goodman et al. [6] proposed to introduce restrictions to attention map, which has been verified to help classifiers focus on robust features and enhance robust of model. Goodman et al. [6] suggests that the final decision of a network is highly correlated with visual attention.

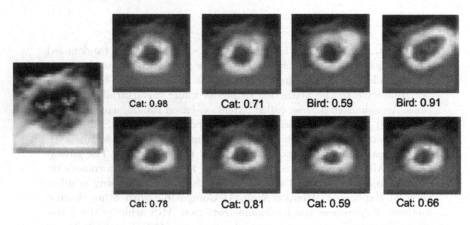

Fig. 1. Visual attention of images under perturbations from standard classifier (top row) and smoothed classifier (bottom row). In each row, we show original image's attention map, two random smoothed images' attention maps and adversarial image's attention map. Below the attention map shows the predicted object label and confidence score.

We obtain the attention map using Grad-CAM [7] and compare the changes of attention maps caused by perturbations from adversarial sample and smoothed sample, which is shown in Fig. 1. The influence of perturbations can be summarized as: (1) With different perturbations, the trend of change on attention map is almost the same, which verifies the existence of non-robust features that are sensitive to perturbations and not conducive to the prediction of model. (2) Adversarial perturbations may increase the possibility that final prediction being determined by non-robust features. (3) Perturbations on smoothed images randomly affect the proportion of non-robust features in all image information. Inference could be made according to the points above: Randomized smoothing regularizes model to focus on robust features and ignore the non-robust ones, thus guarantees the robustness of the model.

Another point should be stressed. From experimental data [3], we notice that randomized smoothing have some weaknesses. (1) Useful features are not completely considered, hence the accuracy of the model is poor in the case of limited perturbations. (2) Randomized smoothing is too sensitive to hyper parameter, which is adverse to the generalization of the model.

Considering the inference above, Attention-based Randomized Smoothing (ARS) is proposed to encourage model to pay more attention to the robust features while maintaining focus on other useful features. Based on smoothed classifier, ARS designs a mixed attention module and merges smoothed feature with original feature to enhance attention on robust and useful features.

The main contributions of this study are as follows:

(1) We conduct a comprehensive analysis to the classification task from the perspective of attention, giving a new understanding of adversarial sample and the effectiveness of randomized smoothing.
(2) Based on randomized smoothing, a novel attention-based adversarial defense method is proposed to enhance attention on robust and useful features. Qualitative and quantitative results on MNIST and CIFAR-10 datasets demonstrate its superiority in adversarial defense.
(3) Attention map for prediction of various defense methods are shown, intuitively explaining the superiority of ARS.

2   Related Work

In general, defenses against adversarial attacks mainly focus on three aspects: training process, network architecture and pre-processing of input examples.

Adversarial training [8] defends against adversarial perturbations by training networks on adversarial images. Such methods explicitly prevent model from learning features that are useful but non-robust. Kurakin et al. [9] proposed to train on a mixture of clean and adversarial examples to maintain model accuracy on clean images. Rony et al. [10] proposed Decoupling Direction and Norm (DDN) attack to speed up the process of adversarial training.

In terms of network architecture, the most relevant work is Adversarial Logit Pairing (ALP) [11], encouraging logits for pairs of examples to be similar. Goodman et al. [6] further suggested both attention map and logits for pairs of examples to be similar.

Pre-processing methods are with best transferring ability. Such methods generally reduce adversarial perturbations by pre-processing of the input. For example, Xie et al. [12] randomly shifted the input and Mustafa et al. [13] denoised adversarial samples by reconstructing images through a super-resolution network, so as to increase adversarial robustness. Cohen et al. [2] introduced random noise at training, which is so called randomized smoothing and proved a tight robustness guarantee in L2 norm for smoothing. However, none of the above approaches focuses on effects of pre-processing on feature and attention map.

The proposed work is an attempt to improve the robustness of classifier according to the correlation between the perturbation and feature.

3   Attention-Oriented Data Analysis

3.1   Robust and Non-robust Features

Ilyas et al. [4] considered a feature f ρ-useful (Metric of Correlation) if it is correlated with the true label y in expectation under a given distribution D, as follows:

$$E_{(x,y) \sim D} [y \cdot f(x)] \geqslant \rho \tag{1}$$

f is taken as a robust feature, when under adversarial perturbations σ (for some specified set of valid perturbations Δ), f remains γ-useful ($\gamma > 0$, Positive correlate with true label), which can be formulated as:

$$E_{(x,y) \sim D} \left[\inf_{\sigma \in \Delta(x)} y \cdot f_{rob}(x + \sigma) \right] \geqslant \gamma \tag{2}$$

Since accurate robust features are unknown, we define robust features broadly from the correlation with perturbation. As shown in Fig. 1, the model accuracy is negatively correlated with the change of attention. Therefore, we distinguish robust and non-robust features according to the sensitivity of features to perturbations. We take f as robust features f_{rob}, which cause small changes on attention map under perturbations, satisfying that:

$$|CAM(f_{rob}(x + \sigma)) - CAM(f_{rob}(x))| < \varepsilon \ \ where \ \varepsilon \propto 1/\rho \tag{3}$$

where CAM represents attention map. Similarly, we define f as non-robust features f_{non}, which are vulnerable to perturbations. Non-robust features are not conducive to the prediction of model under perturbations, as follows:

$$E_{(x,y) \sim D} [y \cdot f_{non}(x + \sigma)] < 0 < E_{(x,y) \sim D} [y \cdot f_{non}(x)] \tag{4}$$

3.2   Randomized Smoothing

Randomized smoothing transforms a classifier F (e.g. a neural network) into a new smoothed classifier G by introducing random perturbations σ to the input. The smoothed classifier G assigns the class, which is most likely to be returned by F, to a query point x under isotropic Gaussian noise perturbations. This means $g(x)$ returns the class c whose decision region has the largest measure under the distribution. Randomized smoothing can be formulated as:

$$G(x) = \arg \max_{c \in y} \mathbb{P} \{F[f(x + \sigma)] = c\} \, where \, \sigma \sim N(0, \delta^2 I) \tag{5}$$

For samples with perturbations, both $f_{rob}(x + \sigma)$ and $f_{non}(x + \sigma)$ exists. According to (2) and (4), $f_{rob}(x + \sigma)$ is more useful than $f_{non}(x + \sigma)$ for model to make correct decision, which can be formulated as:

$$P \{F[f_{rob}(x + \sigma)] = y\} > P \{F[f_{non}(x + \sigma)] = y\} \tag{6}$$

In the training process, the stability of the model will rely more on robust features rather than unreliable non-robust features for samples with noise perturbations, which means model pay more attention to robust features. The effectiveness of randomized smoothing is explained intuitively from the perspective of attention.

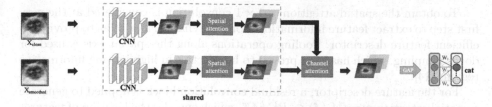

Fig. 2. Overall pipeline of ARS during training

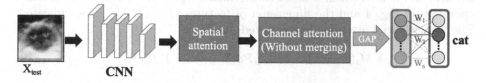

Fig. 3. Inference stage of ARS

4   Attention-Based Randomized Smoothing

From the perspective of attention, we explore empirical defense on the basis of randomized smoothing, so as to achieve the best defense ability. Our goal is to increase representation capability using attention mechanism, that is: focusing on robust and useful features. We propose Attention-based Randomized Smoothing (ARS) to extract robust features and merge with clean image features so as to directly increase the weight of robust features meanwhile retain the attention to useful features. Figure 2 shows the overall pipeline of our method. The overall training process can be summarized as:

$$f' = M_s(f) \otimes f \tag{7}$$

$$f'' = M_c[f'(x), f'(x+\sigma)] \otimes [f'(x), f'(x+\sigma)] \tag{8}$$

where $\otimes$ denotes element-wise multiplication. f, f' are original and refined features respectively. M_s, M_c represent spatial attention module and channel attention module. Figure 4 and Fig. 5 depicts the computation process of each attention map. The objective function can be formulated as:

$$g(x) = \arg\max_{c \in y} \mathbb{P}\left\{F[f''(x, x+\sigma)] = c\right\} \quad where \, \sigma \sim N(0, \delta^2 I) \tag{9}$$

Attention mechanism enhances attention to robust features in order to improve the representation of interests under noise. The attention module is described in detail as follows.

4.1   Spatial Attention Module

We generate a spatial attention module by utilizing the inter-spatial relationship of features. Based on smoothed classifier, the spatial attention module focuses on 'where' the robust part to avoid the disturbance caused by perturbations.

To obtain the spatial attention, a 1×1 convolution is considered at the very first step to extract feature information along the channel axis so as to provide an efficient feature descriptor. Pooling operations along the spatial axis is used for down-sampling, which has been proven to be effective in highlighting informative regions [14].

For the feature descriptor, a residual convolution block is applied to generate a spatial attention map $M_s(f) \in R^{1 \times h \times w}$, which encodes the location of features that needs to emphasize or suppress. A residual structure that merges the original features and refined features is set as the final output. We describe the detailed operation in Fig. 4 and the dimension of features ($f \in R^{c \times h \times w}$) is indicated. The whole spatial attention is computed as:

$$M_s(F) = Block(AvgPool(conv1 \times 1(f(x))))$$ (10)

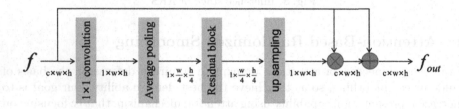

Fig. 4. Computation process of spatial attention module

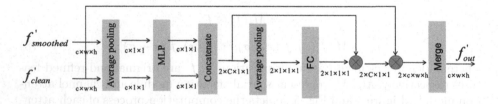

Fig. 5. Computation process of channel attention module

4.2 Channel Attention Module

We produce a channel attention module by exploiting the inter-channel relationship of features and correlation between smoothed and original features for prediction. As each feature map is considered as a feature detector [14], channel attention focuses on 'what' is important given an input image.

We first combine spatial information of original feature map and corresponding smoothed feature map by using global average pooling (GAP), generating two different spatial context descriptors: $f'(x)$ and $f'(x+\sigma)$, which denote features of original inputs and inputs with perturbations respectively. Both descriptors are then forwarded to a shared network to produce channel attention map $M_c \in R^{c\times1\times1}$. The shared network is composed of multi-layer perceptron (MLP) with one hidden layer, which is useful to reduce parameter overhead. Then we concatenate feature vectors of smoothed and original images as a two-channel vector $\in R^{2\times1\times1\times1}$, which is forwarded to a fully connected (FC) layer to learn the correlation and importance index of smoothed and original features for prediction. After model has learned the importance index of feature descriptors, we merge the output feature vectors using element-wise summation. The detailed operation is illustrated in Fig. 5. Thus, the whole channel attention is computed as:

$$M_c(F) = c_1 * MLP\left\{AvgPool[f'(x)]\right\} + c_2 * MLP\left\{AvgPool[f'(x+\sigma)]\right\} \quad (11)$$

where c_1, c_2 denotes the correlation and importance index of smoothed and original features learned by a fully connected layer.

Other than advantages for exploiting the inter-channel relationship, channel attention effectively increase the weight of robust and useful features on attention by merging smoothed and original features, formulated as:

$$P\left\{F\left[c_1 * f(x+\sigma) + c_2 * f(x) = c\right]\right\} \quad (12)$$
$$= P\left\{F\left[(c_1 + c_2) * f_{rob} + c_1 * f_{non}(x+\sigma) + c_2 * f_{non}(x)\right]\right\}$$

where f_{rob} and $f_{non}(x)$ remains γ-useful($\gamma > 0$), while $f_{non}(x+\sigma)$ is t-useful ($t < 0$)

In summary, compared with randomized smoothing, ARS not only encourages model to focus on robust features f_{rob} that cause little change on attention map, but also enhances the attention to useful features $f_{non}(x)$, which is helpful in maintaining the accuracy of model on clean image. The overhead of parameters and computation is negligible in most cases because of our exquisite design. When model has been trained, it has the ability to recognize robust features without pre-processing and feature fusion as shown in Fig. 3, which will be further verified in the experiment.

5   Experiment

5.1   Experimental Setting

The proposed Attention-based Randomized Smoothing (ARS) can be applied with different convolutional networks. In this study, we train model using the same architectures and adversarial training as Rony et al. [10]: a small CNN for MNIST, a Wide ResNet (WRN) 28-10 for CIFAR-10 and Decoupling Direction and Norm (DDN) for adversarial training.

In this paper, we consider gray-box attack setting which means both original network and defense method are known. [6] The backend prediction model is the same architectures as us with different implementations of the state-of-the-art defense methods, such as DDN_ADV [10], SMOOTHADV [3] and AT+ALP [6].

5.2   Results and Discussion

Here, we present our main results with ARS on CIFAR-10 and MNIST datasets. Refer to related previous work, we choose different adversarial attacks and L2 radius of perturbations to evaluate the robustness of the model.

Projected Gradient Descent (PGD) [8], C&W [15] and DeepFool [16] are selected as attack methods for evaluating models. Among them, PGD is gradient-based attacks. C&W and DeepFool are optimization-based attacks. Table. 1 shows the evaluation results of different attacks under L2 norm (maximum perturbation $\epsilon = 128/256 = 0.5$ for CIFAR-10 and $\epsilon = 2$ for MNIST). Our ARS outperforms the state-of-the-art in adversarial robustness against highly challenging attacks. For example, under strong 100-iteration PGD gray-box attacks, the accuracy for prior art is 65.5% and 43.3%, while our proposed ARS reaches 67.3% and 46.2% respectively. We test the spatial attention module of ARS separately. The results demonstrate that combining attention mechanism with randomized smoothing is helpful for improving robustness. For example, using SMOOTHADV as the base method under PGD, the accuracy is 64.1% and 32.7% and that of ours is 66.2% and 44.1%.

The level of perturbations is proportional to the maximum perturbation ϵ, which leads to more significant adversarial attack effects. To further evaluate the robustness of model against adversarial attack, We explore the changes of performance of defense methods under different L2 radius of perturbations. As shown in Fig. 6, the defense performance of ARS is relatively stable, and it remains the best when attacks are limited to a maximum norm of $\epsilon = 1.5$.

Generally, ARS achieves superior performance on CIFAR-10 and MNIST datasets. Furthermore, ARS performs much better than SMOOTHADV on MNIST dataset.

Table 1. Defense performance comparison with other advanced defenses under different adversarial attacks.

	CIFAR10				MNIST			
	Clean	PGD	Deepfool	C&W	Clean	PGD	Deepfool	C&W
NO DEFENCE	**94.9**	1.5	17.1	2.0	**99.6**	9.3	16.4	10.8
DDN_AT [10]	87.9	63.1	69.9	65.9	99.4	39.7	65.0	45.2
AT+ALP [6]	87.0	65.5	71.2	68.5	99.4	43.3	69.5	61.8
SMOOTHADV [3]	79.9	64.1	73.1	65.5	99.1	32.7	63.5	44.9
ARS (spatial)	81.2	66.2	72.3	67.1	99.3	44.1	69.1	60.9
ARS	87.9	**67.3**	**73.5**	**70.4**	99.5	**46.2**	**71.4**	**62.2**

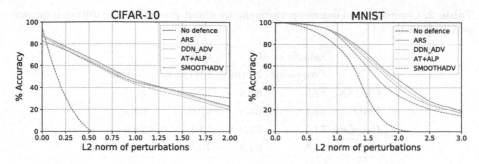

Fig. 6. Robustness of models on CIFAR-10 (left) and MNIST (right): impact on accuracy as we increase the maximum perturbation ϵ.

5.3 Comparison to Randomized Smoothing

Referring to the experiment of Salman et al. [3], we set up three experiments on CIFAR-10 dataset to comprehensively compare ARS with randomized smoothing.

We compare the empirical defense performance of ARS, single randomized smoothing [2] and SMOOTHADV [3] under PGD with different maximum perturbation ϵ on CIFAR-10 dataset. Figure 7 (left) shows the results of evaluation. The ARS shows best performance when the attacks are limited to a maximum norm of $\epsilon = 1.5$.

Then, we conduct hyper parameter sensitivity analysis. Referring to Salman et al. [3], randomized smoothing is sensitive to hyper parameter δ, which controls the level of gaussian noise introduced to input during training. Figure 7 (right) shows the results of evaluation under PGD attacks with different maximum perturbation on CIFAR-10.

In the inference stage, we take two ways to test images: one is normal ($\delta = 0$) and the other is pre-processing ($\delta = 0.25$). Table 2 is the results.

To sum up, for both SMOOTHADV and ARS, large parameter δ works better with large perturbations, which means the model pay more attention to robust features and lose useful features. The differences between ARS and randomized smoothing (SMOOTHADV) are as follows:

(1) Compared with randomized smoothing, ARS is not sensitive to hyper parameter δ. For example, under PGD ($\epsilon = 0.25$) attack, when the value of δ is 0.12 and 0.5, ARS achieves 78.0% and 76.7% accuracy, and random smoothing achieved 74% and 67.0% accuracy, which is shown in Fig. 7.
(2) In the inference stage, pre-processing has less influence on ARS, which is observed from Table 2.

In conclusion, the performance of ARS is much better than randomized smoothing when the attacks are limited to a maximum norm. Moreover, ARS has a broader application, because it does not need pre-processing in inference and is relatively insensitive to hyper parameter δ.

Table 2. Comparison of defense performance without pre-processing during inference on CIFAR-10.

	Salman et al.		Ours	
	Processing	Normal	Processing	Normal
CLEAN	82.9	81.6	87.2	87.9
PGD	64.1	63.8	67.0	67.3
Deepfool	73.1	72.9	73.1	73.5
C&W	65.5	64.3	70.5	70.4

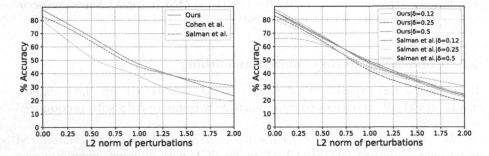

Fig. 7. Comparison of random smoothing methods on CIFAR-10 under PGD attacks with different maximum perturbation. (Left) Upper envelopes of accuracies over all experiments. (Right) Accuracies of one representative model per δ.

5.4   Visualization of Attention Map Evolution

ARS is expected to enable network to make prediction based on robust and useful features. Figure 8 is the visualization of attention maps from different models on adversarial image.

According to Fig. 8, conclusions could be made as follows:

(1) Adversarial pertubations result in the center deviation of the model's attention and misclassification, which can be observed from adversarial images.

(2) The defense methods generally cause the shrinkage of attention areas on adversarial images, which verifies that all defense models possess constrain on attention map while improving robustness against adversarial attack.

(3) The proposed ARS shows best performance according to confidence score for the correct object class. The attention map of ARS not only effectively pays attention to the correct area representing robust features, but also retains enough attention to useful features, which is effective in preventing center deviation of model's attention and improving accuracy.

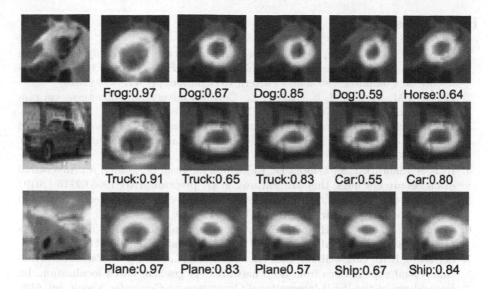

Fig. 8. Attention maps of adversarial images from models implemented by different methods (From left to right columns: Baseline, DDN_ADV, AT+ALP, SMOOTHADV and Our ARS). Below each attention map shows the predicted object label and the corresponding confidence score.

6 Conclusion

In this paper, we analyse the influence of perturbations on features, which presents a new understanding of randomized smoothing from the perspective of attention. Features that vulnerable to noise are not conducive to the prediction of model under adversarial perturbations. Besides, data in Table 1 reminds us that the randomized smoothing shows poor performance in clean image, the reason for that is randomized smoothing encourages model to focus on robust features ignoring other useful features, leading to the decrease of the accuracy of the model on clean image.

We propose enhanced defense using attention mechanism called Attention-based Randomized Smoothing (ARS) to encourage model focusing on robust and useful features. The attention map of ARS show more attention on key areas while maintaining focus on other useful features, which is helpful to avoid misclassification.

Our ARS achieves the state-of-the-art defense on CIFAR-10 and MNIST datasets against different highly challenging attacks. Compared with randomized smoothing methods, the superiority of the proposed method is verified on both clean and adversarial samples. Moreover, ARS does not require pre-processing in inference and is not sensitive to hyper parameter δ.

References

1. Nguyen A., Yosinski, J., Clune, J.: Deep neural networks are easily fooled: high confidence predictions for unrecognizable images. In: Proceedings of the IEEE Conference on Computer Vision and Pattern Recognition, pp. 427–436 (2015)
2. Cohen, J.M., Rosenfeld, E., Kolter, Z.: Certified adversarial robustness via randomized smoothing. arXiv preprint arXiv:1902.02918 (2019)
3. Salman, H., et al.: Provably robust deep learning via adversarially trained smoothed classifiers. In: Advances in Neural Information Processing Systems, pp. 11289–11300 (2019)
4. Ilyas, A., Santurkar, S., Tsipras, D., Engstrom, L., Tran, B., Madry, A.: Adversarial examples are not bugs, they are features. arXiv preprint arXiv:1905.02175 (2019)
5. Wu, S., et al.: Attention, please! adversarial defense via attention rectification and preservation. arXiv preprint arXiv:1811.09831 (2018)
6. Goodman, D., Li, X., Huan, J., Wei, T.: Improving adversarial robustness via attention and adversarial logit pairing. arXiv preprint arXiv:1908.11435 (2019)
7. Selvaraju, R.R., Cogswell, M., Das, A., Vedantam, R., Parikh, D., Batra, D.: Gradcam: visual explanations from deep networks via gradient-based localization. In: Proceedings of the IEEE International Conference on Computer Vision, pp. 618–626 (2017)
8. Madry, A., Makelov, A., Schmidt, L., Tsipras, D., Vladu, A.: Towards deep learning models resistant to adversarial attacks. arXiv preprint arXiv:1706.06083 (2017)
9. Kurakin, A., Goodfellow, I., Bengio, S.: Adversarial machine learning at scale. arXiv preprint arXiv:1611.01236 (2016)
10. Rony, J., Hafemann, L.G., Oliveira, L.S., Ayed, I.B., Sabourin, R., Granger, E.: Decoupling direction and norm for efficient gradient-based l2 adversarial attacks and defenses. In: Proceedings of the IEEE Conference on Computer Vision and Pattern Recognition, pp. 4322–4330 (2019)
11. Kannan, H., Kurakin, A., Goodfellow, I.: Adversarial logit pairing. arXiv preprint arXiv:1803.06373 (2018)
12. Xie, C., Wang, J., Zhang, Z., Ren, Z., Yuille, A.: Mitigating adversarial effects through randomization. arXiv preprint arXiv:1711.01991 (2017)
13. Mustafa, A., Khan, S.H., Hayat, M., Shen, J., Shao, L.: Image super-resolution as a defense against adversarial attacks. arXiv preprint arXiv:1901.01677 (2019)
14. Woo, S., Park, J., Lee, J.-Y., Kweon, I.S.: CBAM: convolutional block attention module. In: Proceedings of the European Conference on Computer Vision (ECCV), pp. 3–19 (2018)
15. Carlini, N., Wagner, D.: Towards evaluating the robustness of neural networks. In: 2017 IEEE Symposium on Security and Privacy (SP), pp. 39–57. IEEE (2017)
16. Moosavi-Dezfooli, S.-M., Fawzi, A., Frossard, P.: DeepFool: a simple and accurate method to fool deep neural networks. In: Proceedings of the IEEE Conference on Computer Vision and Pattern Recognition, pp. 2574–2582 (2016)

Learning to Learn from Mistakes: Robust Optimization for Adversarial Noise

Alex Serban[1(✉)], Erik Poll[1], and Joost Visser[2]

[1] Radboud University, Nijmegen, The Netherlands
a.serban@cs.ru.nl
[2] Leiden University, Leiden, The Netherlands

Abstract. Sensitivity to adversarial noise hinders deployment of machine learning algorithms in security-critical applications. Although many adversarial defenses have been proposed, robustness to adversarial noise remains an open problem. The most compelling defense, adversarial training, requires a substantial increase in processing time and it has been shown to overfit on the training data. In this paper, we aim to overcome these limitations by training robust models in low data regimes and transfer adversarial knowledge between different models. We train a meta-optimizer which learns to robustly optimize a model using adversarial examples and is able to transfer the knowledge learned to new models, without the need to generate new adversarial examples. Experimental results show the meta-optimizer is consistent across different architectures and data sets, suggesting it is possible to automatically patch adversarial vulnerabilities.

Keywords: Adversarial examples · Meta learning · Machine learning

1 Introduction

Machine learning (ML) algorithms exhibit low robustness against intentionally crafted perturbations [8] or high invariance for distinct inputs [12]. From a security standpoint this means an attacker can craft inputs that look similar but cause ML algorithms to misbehave or find distinct inputs that give the same result. From a safety standpoint, this means that ML algorithms are not robust against perturbations close to an input or are inflexible to changes in the operational environment.

Creating defenses (or finding robust counterparts for ML models) has received increased attention, in particular in the field of adversarial examples. Although many defenses have been proposed, with the most notable results using formal methods to guarantee robustness [10] most solutions overfit on the training data and behave poorly against data outside this distribution [20,30]. Theoretical investigations suggest these results are expected because training robust models requires more data [6], more computational resources [3] or accepting a trade off

© Springer Nature Switzerland AG 2020
I. Farkaš et al. (Eds.): ICANN 2020, LNCS 12396, pp. 467–478, 2020.
https://doi.org/10.1007/978-3-030-61609-0_37

between accuracy and robustness [24]. Moreover, solutions to one vulnerability have a negative impact on others [11].

On a different path, designing ML algorithms capable to rapidly adapt to changes in the operational environment, to adapt to distribution shifts or capable to learn from few samples is an active research field. Particularly, the field of meta-learning investigate optimization algorithms learned from scratch for faster training [1], with less resources [19] and capable of rapid adaptation [7].

In this paper, we show that meta-learning algorithms can be used to extract knowledge from a model's vulnerability to adversarial examples and transfer it to new models. We train a meta-optimizer to learn how to robustly optimize other models using adversarial training. Later, when asked to optimize new models without seeing adversarial examples, the trained meta-optimizer can do it robustly. This process is analogous to learning a regularization term for adversarial examples, instead of manually designing one. The experimental results suggest a broader horizon, in which algorithms learn how to automatically repair or treat vulnerabilities without explicit human design.

The rest of the paper is organized as follows. In Sect. 2 we introduce prerequisites and related work. Section 3 formalizes meta-learning and the adversarial training problems and gives implementation details. Section 4 presents experimental results on two distinct data sets, followed by a discussion in Sect. 5 and conclusions in Sect. 6.

2   Background and Related Work

We focus on the task of supervised classification, i.e. given a set of inputs from the input space $\mathcal{X}$ and a set of labels from the space $\mathcal{Y}$ a ML algorithm attempts to find a mapping from $f : \mathcal{X} \rightarrow \mathcal{Y}$ which minimizes the number of misclassified inputs. We assume that $\mathcal{X}$ is a metric space such that a distance function $d(\cdot)$ between two points of the space exists. The error made by a prediction $f(\boldsymbol{x}) = \hat{y}$ when the true label is y is measured by a loss function $l : \mathcal{Y} \times \mathcal{Y} \rightarrow \mathbb{R}$ with non-negative values when the labels are different and zero otherwise. $f(\cdot)$ is defined over a hypothesis space $\mathcal{F}$ which encompasses any mapping from $\mathcal{X}$ to $\mathcal{Y}$ and can take any form – e.g. a linear function or a neural network. Through learning, a ML algorithm selects $f^*(\cdot)$ from $\mathcal{F}$ such that the expected empirical loss on a training set $\mathcal{S}$ consisting of pairs of samples $(\boldsymbol{x}_i, y_i) \sim \mathcal{Z} = \mathcal{X} \times \mathcal{Y}$ is minimal.

A robust solution to the minimization problem above involves immunizing it against uncertainties in the input space. In the adversarial examples setting, uncertainties are modeled in the space around an input $\boldsymbol{x}_u : \mathcal{U}_{\boldsymbol{x}} = \{\boldsymbol{x} | d(\boldsymbol{x}, \boldsymbol{x}_c) \leq \epsilon\}$, where $d(\cdot)$ is a distance function defined on the metric space $\mathcal{X}$. The robust counterpart of the learning problem is defined as:

$$f = \arg\min_{f \in \mathcal{F}} \mathbb{E}_{(\boldsymbol{x},y) \sim \mathcal{S}} [\max_{\boldsymbol{x}_u \in \mathcal{U}_{\boldsymbol{x}}} l(f(\boldsymbol{x}_u), y)], \tag{1}$$

where $\boldsymbol{x}_u$ is a realization of $\boldsymbol{x}$ in the uncertainty set described by $d(\cdot)$. A common distance function used in the field of adversarial examples is the l_p-norm.

Arguably, this metric can not capture task-specific semantic information, but it is suitable for comparative benchmarks. Moreover, the lack of robust p-norm solutions for complex tasks makes it hard to believe that other notions of robustness can lead to better results [4]. In this paper we use the l_∞-norm distance.

Finding models robust to adversarial examples is an open question, spanning two research directions: (1) finding solutions robust to an upper bound on the perturbation size ϵ (i.e. no perturbation higher than ϵ can cause a misclassification) [8,16] and (2) finding lower bounds on robustness (i.e. no adversarial example can be found in a space around an input) [17,26].

Notable results are obtained by solving the inner maximization problem from Eq. (1) with projected gradient descent (PGD) [16], by training with over-approximations of the input [17] or extensively searching for spaces where no adversarial examples can be found using exact solvers [13]. In all cases, the benchmarks show overfitting on the training distribution and can be bypassed by samples outside it [30].

Until recently, solving the outer minimization objective from Eq. (1) relied on static, hand designed algorithms, such as stochastic gradient descent or ADAM. This line of research is driven by the no free lunch theorem of optimization which states that, on average, in combinatorial optimization no algorithm can do better than a random strategy; suggesting that designing specific algorithms for a class of problems is the only way to improve performance.

Recent advancements in the field of meta-learning have taken a different approach, posing the problem of algorithm design dynamically and modeling it with neural networks [1] or as a reinforcement learning (RL) problem [14]. In both cases, the algorithms show empirically faster convergence and the ability to adapt to different tasks.

For example, in [1] the hand designed update rules are replaced with a parameterized function modeled with a recurrent neural network (RNN). During training, both the *optimizer* and the *optimizee* parameters are adjusted. The algorithm design now becomes a learning problem, allowing to specify constraints through data examples. The method has roots in previous research [22], where initial RNNs were designed to update their own weights. The results of backpropagation from one network were only later fed to a second network which learns to update the first [28]. Andrychowicz et al. build on previous work using a different learning architecture. Similarly, [19] used this paradigm to train neural networks in a few shot regime and [21] augmented it with memory networks. Meta-learning has also shown promising results in designing algorithms for fast adaptation using gradient information [7].

Instead of using RNNs, [14] formulate the optimization problem as a RL problem where the reward signal represents successful minimization and train an agent using guided policy search. Later, the authors refine their method for training neural networks [15]. In both cases the agent learns to optimize faster than hand designed algorithms and exhibits better stability.

Recent research in adversarial examples has also tackled the need to decrease training resources by either accumulating perturbations [23,27] or by restricting back-propagation to some layers of the model [29]. While the latter method requires forward and backward passes, the former reduces the need to do backward passes in order to generate adversarial examples. And not to abstract or transfer information from adversarial training.

3   Learning to Optimize Robustly

Meta-learning frames the learning problem at two levels: acquiring higher level (meta) information about the optimization landscape and applying it to optimize one task. In this paper, we are interested to learn robust update rules and transfer this knowledge to new tasks without additional constraints. We focus on training robust ML models through adversarial training, which is one of the most effective defenses against upper bounded adversarial examples [16]. Because generating adversarial examples during training is time consuming, especially for iterative procedures and can only provide robustness for the inputs used during training [30], through meta-learning we learn to optimize robustly without explicit regularization terms and transfer the knowledge to new tasks, without the need to generate new adversarial examples.

At a high level, adversarial training discourages *local* sensitive behavior – in the vicinity of each input in the training set – by guiding the model to behave constantly in regions surrounding the training data. The regions are defined by a chosen uncertainty set (as in Eq. (1)). This procedure is equivalent to adding a prior that defines local constancy, for each model we want to train. In most cases, specifying this prior is not trivial and requires the design of new regularization methods [18], new loss functions [26] or new training procedures [17]. In this paper we take a different approach and try to learn a regularization term automatically, using meta-learning. During the meta-knowledge acquisition phase, the meta-optimizer learns to perform the updates robustly using adversarial training. Later, the knowledge acquired is transferred to new models using the meta-optimizer to train new models, without generating adversarial examples. In the next paragraphs we describe the meta-optimizer, some implementation details and the adversarial training procedure.

Learning to Optimize. The classification function defined in Sect. 2, $f(\cdot)$, is parametrized by a set of parameters θ. Upon seeing new data, we update the parameters in order to minimize the prediction errors. The update consists in moving one step in the opposite direction of the gradient:

$$\theta_{t+1} = \theta_t - \eta \nabla_{\theta_t} l(\cdot), \tag{2}$$

where η (the learning rate) determines the size of the step. Different choices of η or ways to automatically adapt it results in different optimization algorithms such as stochastic gradient descent or ADAM.

In order to avoid overfitting or impose additional constraints such as constancy around inputs, it is common to add a regularization term to the loss function which will be back-propagated and reflected on all parameter updates.

Instead of looking for regularization terms manually, we use a method to automatically learn robust update steps with regularization included.

As discussed in Sect. 2, a parameterized update rule has been previously represented with a RNN [1,19] or as a RL problem [14]. In this paper, we follow an approach similar to [1] and model the update rule with a RNN with long short-term memory (LSTM) cells:

$$\theta_t = \theta_{t-1} + c_t,$$

where :

$$c_t = f_t c_{t-1} + i_{t-1}\tilde{c}_t, \tag{3}$$

is the output of an LSTM network m with input $\nabla_{\theta_t}(l(\cdot))$:

$$\begin{bmatrix} c_t \\ h_{t+1} \end{bmatrix} = m(\nabla_t, h_t, \phi), \tag{4}$$

and ϕ are the LSTM's parameters.

In [19], the authors consider each term in Eq. (3) equivalent to each term in Eq. (2) – e.g. $f_t = 1$, $c_{t-1} = \theta_t$ – and disentangle the internal state of the LSTM, h_t, with special terms for individual updates of f_t and i_t. This type of inductive bias brings benefits in some cases and will be further discussed in Sect. 5. However, in this paper we try to avoid such biases whenever possible.

Parameters Sharing and Gradient Preprocessing. In order to limit the number of parameters of the optimizer, we follow a procedure similar to [1,19] in which for each parameter of the function we want to optimize, $\theta_{i:n}$, we keep an equivalent internal state of the optimizer, $h_{i:n}$, but share the weights ϕ between all states. This procedure allows a more compact optimizer to be used and makes the update rule dependent only on its respective past representation, thus being able to simulate hand designed optimization features such as momentum.

Moreover, since gradient coordinates can take very distinct values, we apply a common normalization step in which the gradients are scaled and the information about their magnitude and their direction is separated:

$$\nabla \rightarrow \begin{cases} \left(\frac{\log(|\nabla|)}{p}, \text{sign}(\nabla) \right) & \text{if } |\nabla| \geq e^{-p} \\ (-1, e^p \nabla) & \text{otherwise.} \end{cases} \tag{5}$$

We experiment with different values for p by grid search and observe that increasing the size of p yields better results when the perturbations are larger. However, for consistency, we use $p = 10$ for all experiments.

The meta-optimizer's parameters are updated using an equivalent to Eq. (2). Since its inputs are based on the gradient information of the function to be optimized (also called the optimizee) the updates will require second order information about it (taking the gradient of the gradient). This information is commonly used for meta-learning – e.g. in [7,25] – and will be further discussed in Sect. 5. However, in this paper only first order information is used, corresponding to limiting the propagation of the optimizer's gradient on the optimizee parameters (or stopping the gradient flow in the computational graph).

Adversarial Training. Adversarial training is still one of the most effective defenses against adversarial examples. This procedure is equivalent to adding a regularization term to the loss function of the optimizee, corresponding to:

$$\tilde{l}(\cdot) = \alpha l(\boldsymbol{\theta}, \boldsymbol{x}, y) + (1 - \alpha)l(\boldsymbol{\theta}, \boldsymbol{x}', y), \tag{6}$$

where $\boldsymbol{x}'$ is an adversarial example generated from input $\boldsymbol{x}$ and α is a parameter which controls the contribution of the adversarial loss. In some cases adversarial training is performed using only the adversarial loss, corresponding to $\alpha = 0$ in Eq. (6), e.g. when training with the worst adversarial loss as in Eq. (1).

Several methods to generate adversarial examples have been proposed, ranging from fast, less precise, attacks [8] to strong, adaptive attacks [5]. However, due to processing constraints, only some algorithms are used in adversarial training: the fast gradient sign method (FGSM) attack – which moves one step in the direction of the gradient – and the PGD attack – which approximates the uncertainty set $\mathcal{U}_x$ running several steps of the FGSM and projecting the outcomes on the norm ball surrounding an input, defined by ϵ.

In this paper, we use both FGSM and PGD during the meta-learning phase to generate adversarial examples and incorporate them in the training procedure. Formally, the FGSM attack is defined as:

$$\boldsymbol{x}' = \boldsymbol{x} + \epsilon \operatorname{sign}(\nabla_x l(\boldsymbol{\theta}, \boldsymbol{x}, y)). \tag{7}$$

The term ϵ controls the size of the perturbation added in order to cause a misclassification. We are aware that defenses against FGSM attacks sometimes lead to a false sense of protection and to gradient masking [2], however, we remind that hereby the goal is to reduce the data needed to train robust models and increase the generalization outside the training distribution.

The PGD attack is defined as follows:

$$\boldsymbol{x}' = \prod_n (\boldsymbol{x}' + \epsilon \operatorname{sign}(\nabla_x l(\boldsymbol{\theta}, \boldsymbol{x}, y))). \tag{8}$$

If the number of iteration suffices to approximate the space we want to provide robustness to, training with adversarial examples generated with this method should protect against any perturbation in the space defined by ϵ. In order to obtain better approximations, we can increase the iteration number, n. However, this comes at increased computational costs.

4   Results

In all experiments the optimizer consists of a two-layer LSTM network with a hidden state size of 20. We compare the results on training two types of neural networks on two distinct data sets with the adaptive optimizer ADAM.

We focus on two experiments related to training neural networks, as in prior work on meta-learning [1,14,15,19]. More experiments with minimizing other functions – e.g. logistic regression – and an integration with the Clever-hans framework are available in the project's repository, which can be found at https://github.com/NullConvergence/Learning2LearnAdv. In all cases, an optimizer is trained using normal and adversarial examples on a data set and tested by training a robust optimizee without generating adversarial examples. Several perturbation sizes are analyzed, as introduced below.

4.1   MNIST

We begin by training a small, fully connected, neural network with 20 units and ReLU activation on the MNIST data set. The perturbations take different values in the set $\epsilon \in \{0.05, 0.1, 0.2, 0.3\}$ for both attacks introduced earlier (Eq. (7) and Eq. (8)). We experiment with different learning rates by grid search and find the best to be 0.001 for the meta-optimizer. Training is performed using the common cross entropy loss function, with a batch size of 128. We shuffle the training data set (consisting of 60.000 examples) and divide in two parts equally: the first is used to train a meta-optimizer using both normal data and adversarial examples and the second is used to test its performance while training with normal data and testing with perturbed data. Each experiment ran for 100 steps and the average results are illustrated in Figs. 1 and 2. All experiments are done using $\alpha = 0.5$ in Eq. (6) during training and $\alpha = 0.0$ during the meta-optimizer transfer phase, as first introduced in [8]. In addition to ADAM's performance compared to the meta-optimizer, we evaluate the performance of the meta-optimizer during training and the performance of training a meta-optimizer using $\alpha = 1$ and testing with $\alpha = 0$ (L2L and Transfer-NOT labels in Figs. 1 and 2). Figure 1 illustrates the results from generating adversarial examples using the FGSM method (Eq. (7)). The loss functions start from approximately the same value because the networks are always initialized with the same values.

In all cases, the meta-optimizer is able to transfer the information learned during training and has comparable performance to ADAM (in some cases per-forming better). We remind that during testing the optimizer uses normal data, but the plots are generated by feeding adversarial perturbed data to the opti-mizee. This implies that the meta-optimizer proposes update rules which lead to smooth surfaces around the tested inputs. Moreover, it is able to learn a robust regularization term during training and transfer it to new tasks without the need to generate new data. Also, the trained meta-optimizer exhibits more stable behavior. This brings evidence that adversarial training leads to more interpretable gradients [24].

When the optimizer is trained only with normal examples, but used to opti-mize the model using adversarial examples – Transfer-NOT label in Fig. 1 – its performance decrease significantly. This implies that a meta-optimizer is domain specific and does not have the general behavior of ADAM, an observations which will be further discussed in Sect. 5.

In Fig. 2 we illustrate the results from running similar experiments, but gen-erate adversarial examples using the PGD method from Eq. (8). Training with PGD is generally performed only using the perturbed examples (corresponding

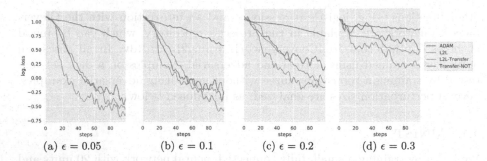

(a) $\epsilon = 0.05$ (b) $\epsilon = 0.1$ (c) $\epsilon = 0.2$ (d) $\epsilon = 0.3$

Fig. 1. The loss landscape when training a neural network on the MNIST data set, perturbed with FGSM and different perturbation sizes (ϵ). The meta-optimizer is trained with adversarial examples – label L2L – transferred to a scenario where training is performed with normal and adversarial data, but tested with adversarial examples – label L2L-Transfer – and compared with a meta-optimizer trained with normal data and transferred to adversarial settings – label Transfer-NOT – and with ADAM. Best seen in color. (Color figure online)

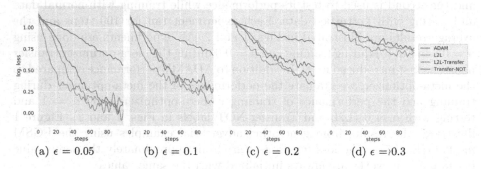

(a) $\epsilon = 0.05$ (b) $\epsilon = 0.1$ (c) $\epsilon = 0.2$ (d) $\epsilon = 0.3$

Fig. 2. The loss landscape when training a neural network on the MNIST data set perturbed with the PGD method and different perturbation sizes (ϵ). The legend is detailed in the caption of Fig. 1.

to $\alpha = 0$ in Eq. (6)), as in the original paper [16]. We take a similar approach in this paper.

The results are consistent with the FGSM method, although the gap between ADAM and the transferred meta-optimizer is smaller. A constant decrease in performance is also observed, possibly corresponding to the decrease in performance specific to adversarial training [24]. Nevertheless, the results are consistent and bring evidence that the meta-optimizer is able to learn robust update rules.

4.2   CIFAR-10

We present the results from training a model using both convolution and fully connected layers on the CIFAR-10 data set. The network consists of three convolutional layers with kernel size 3, a fully connected layer with 32 hidden units

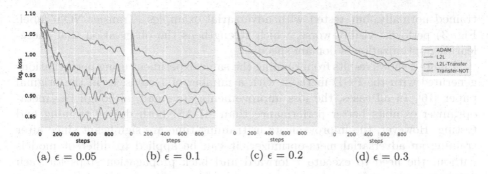

(a) $\epsilon = 0.05$ (b) $\epsilon = 0.1$ (c) $\epsilon = 0.2$ (d) $\epsilon = 0.3$

Fig. 3. The loss landscape when training a neural network on the CIFAR-10 data set, perturbed with the FGSM method and different perturbation sizes (ϵ). The legend is detailed in the caption of Fig. 1.

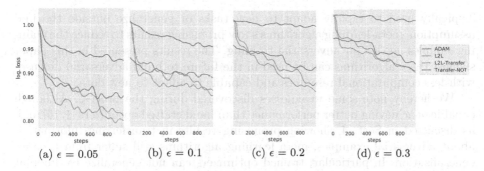

(a) $\epsilon = 0.05$ (b) $\epsilon = 0.1$ (c) $\epsilon = 0.2$ (d) $\epsilon = 0.3$

Fig. 4. The loss landscape when optimizing a neural network on the CIFAR-10 data set, perturbed with PGD and different perturbation sizes (ϵ). The legend is detailed in the caption of Fig. 1.

and a logits layer of size 10. All activation functions are ReLU, the loss is cross-entropy and batch normalization is used in the convolutional layers. The meta-optimizer is trained using a learning rate of 0.001 determined through grid search.

Since there are striking differences between the convolution and the linear layer, we use two sets of parameters for the meta-optimizer – one for optimizing all convolutional layers and one for the linear layers. Moreover, since the CIFAR-10 problem is more difficult, we train the optimizee for 1000 steps and present the results in Fig. 3 for perturbations generated with FGSM and in Fig. 4 for perturbations generated with PGD. The evaluation was performed as earlier, using 2-fold cross validation for training a meta-optimizer in adversarial settings and transfer it to training a model in normal settings which is tested with adversarial examples.

We observe that in the case of FGSM, the transferred meta-optimizer (label L2L-Transfer, Fig. 3) exhibits similar behavior as in the MNIST experiments: it has similar and sometimes better performance than ADAM. We remind that, in this case, no adversarial examples are used during training. The meta-optimizer trained normally, but tested with adversarial examples (Transfer-NOT label, Fig. 3) performs visibly worse, which strengthens the observation that meta-learning optimization is domain specific.

Figure 4 shows results from running the same experiment using perturbations generated with the PGD method, with a number of 7 steps, as in the original paper [16]. In all cases, the loss improvements are small, although the meta-optimizer exhibits better performance than ADAM both during training and testing. However, the improvements in training time are significant since after training an adversarial meta-optimizer, it can be applied to different models without the need to execute 7 forward and back propagation steps for each batch of data.

5   Discussion

Typically used to rapidly adapt to new tasks or generalize outside the i.i.d assumption, meta-learning algorithms show promising results to reduce the training samples needed for adversarial training. The results presented in this paper suggest these algorithms can be used in the future to build adversarial defenses with less computational resources and capable to adapt to new data.

We hereby note some weaknesses discovered during the process. Although capable of achieving better performance than hand crafted optimizers [1, 15] and, as discussed in Sect. 4, showing promising results in transferring information about adversarial examples, meta learning algorithms still suffer from broader generalization. In particular, trained optimizers can not generalize to different activation functions, or between architectures with noticeable differences [25]. This means that an optimizer trained for ReLU can not be used for sigmoid (or other) activation functions. Moreover, if the meta-optimizer is not trained with specific data that will be later used, it does not exhibit general behavior. For example, if the meta-optimizer does not use any adversarial examples during training, but it encounters such examples during testing, it faces difficulties. This behavior is illustrated in the figures above with the label Transfer-NOT.

Second order information (taking the gradient of the gradient, as introduced in Sect. 3) was not used in this paper. As shown in [25], this information can help the meta-optimizer better generalize and induce more stable behavior. However, it also introduces more complexity. Analyzing the trade-off between the optimizer's complexity and its ability to learn and transfer knowledge related to adversarial vulnerabilities is left for future work.

6   Conclusions and Future Research

We introduce a method to learn how to optimize ML models robust to adversarial examples, in low data regimes. Instead of specifying custom regularization terms, they are learned automatically by an adaptive optimizer. Acquiring meta information about the optimization landscape under adversarial constraints allows the optimizer to reuse it for new tasks.

For future research, we propose to train the meta-optimizer concomitantly with different perturbation types – e.g. l_1, l_2-norm – and test if the optimizer can learn to robustly optimize under all constraints. Other perturbations, such as naturally occurring perturbations [9] can also be included. Another research direction is to use the meta-optimizer to refine a trained model and evaluate if it is possible to robustly regularize it with less data.

References

1. Andrychowicz, M., et al.: Learning to learn by gradient descent by gradient descent. In: NeurIPS, pp. 3981–3989 (2016)
2. Athalye, A., Carlini, N., Wagner, D.: Obfuscated gradients give a false sense of security: circumventing defenses to adversarial examples. In: ICML (2018)
3. Bubeck, S., Price, E., Razenshteyn, I.: Adversarial examples from computational constraints. arXiv:1805.10204 (2018)
4. Carlini, N., et al.: On evaluating adversarial robustness. arXiv:1902.06705 (2019). http://arxiv.org/abs/1902.06705
5. Carlini, N., Wagner, D.: Towards evaluating the robustness of neural networks. In: 2017 IEEE Symposium on Security and Privacy (S&P), pp. 39–57. IEEE (2017)
6. Cullina, D., Bhagoji, A.N., Mittal, P.: PAC-learning in the presence of evasion adversaries. arXiv:1806.01471 (2018)
7. Finn, C., Abbeel, P., Levine, S.: Model-agnostic meta-learning for fast adaptation of deep networks. In: ICML, pp. 1126–1135 (2017)
8. Goodfellow, I.J., Shlens, J., Szegedy, C.: Explaining and harnessing adversarial examples. arXiv:1412.6572 (2014)
9. Hendrycks, D., Dietterich, T.: Benchmarking neural network robustness to common corruptions and perturbations. In: ICLR (2019)
10. Huang, X., et al.: Safety and trustworthiness of deep neural networks: a survey. arXiv:1812.08342 (2018)
11. Jacobsen, J.H., Behrmann, J., Carlini, N., Florian Tramer, N.: Exploiting excessive invariance caused by norm-bounded adversarial robustness. In: ICLR (2019)
12. Jacobsen, J.H., Behrmann, J., Zemel, R., Bethge, M.: Excessive invariance causes adversarial vulnerability. In: ICLR (2019)
13. Katz, G., Barrett, C., Dill, D.L., Julian, K., Kochenderfer, M.J.: Reluplex: an efficient SMT solver for verifying deep neural networks. In: Majumdar, R., Kunčak, V. (eds.) CAV 2017. LNCS, vol. 10426, pp. 97–117. Springer, Cham (2017). https://doi.org/10.1007/978-3-319-63387-9_5
14. Li, K., Malik, J.: Learning to optimize. arXiv:1606.01885 (2016)
15. Li, K., Malik, J.: Learning to optimize neural nets. arXiv:1703.00441 (2017)
16. Madry, A., Makelov, A., Schmidt, L., Tsipras, D., Vladu, A.: Towards deep learning models resistant to adversarial attacks. In: ICLR (2018)
17. Mirman, M., Gehr, T., Vechev, M.: Differentiable abstract interpretation for provably robust neural networks. In: ICML (2018)
18. Miyato, T., Maeda, S.I., Koyama, M., Nakae, K., Ishii, S.: Distributional smoothing with virtual adversarial training. arXiv:1507.00677 (2015)
19. Ravi, S., Larochelle, H.: Optimization as a model for few-shot learning. In: ICLR (2017)
20. Rice, L., Wong, E., Kolter, J.Z.: Overfitting in adversarially robust deep learning. arXiv preprint arXiv:2002.11569 (2020)

21. Santoro, A., Bartunov, S., Botvinick, M., Wierstra, D., Lillicrap, T.: Meta-learning with memory-augmented neural networks. In: ICML, pp. 1842–1850 (2016)
22. Schmidhuber, J.: A neural network that embeds its own meta-levels. In: ICNN, pp. 407–412. IEEE (1993)
23. Shafahi, A., et al.: Adversarial training for free! arXiv:1904.12843 (2019)
24. Tsipras, D., Santurkar, S., Engstrom, L., Turner, A., Madry, A.: There is no free lunch in adversarial robustness (but there are unexpected benefits). arXiv:1805.12152 (2018)
25. Wichrowska, O., et al.: Learned optimizers that scale and generalize. In: ICML, pp. 3751–3760 (2017)
26. Wong, E., Kolter, J.Z.: Provable defenses against adversarial examples via the convex outer adversarial polytope. In: ICML (2018)
27. Wong, E., Rice, L., Kolter, J.Z.: Fast is better than free: Revisiting adversarial training. arXiv preprint arXiv:2001.03994 (2020)
28. Younger, A.S., Hochreiter, S., Conwell, P.R.: Meta-learning with backpropagation. In: IJCNN, vol. 3. IEEE (2001)
29. Zhang, D., Zhang, T., Lu, Y., Zhu, Z., Dong, B.: You only propagate once: accelerating adversarial training via maximal principle. arXiv:1905.00877 (2019)
30. Zhang, H., Chen, H., Song, Z., Boning, D., Dhillon, I.S., Hsieh, C.J.: The limitations of adversarial training and the blind-spot attack. In: ICLR (2019)

Unsupervised Anomaly Detection with a GAN Augmented Autoencoder

Laya Rafiee[✉] and Thomas Fevens

Concordia University, Montréal, QC, Canada
{laya.rafiee,thomas.fevens}@concordia.ca

Abstract. Anomaly detection is a task of identifying samples that differ from the training data distribution. There are several studies that employ generative adversarial networks (GANs) as the main tool to detect anomalies using the rich contextual information that GANs provide. We propose an unsupervised GAN-based model combined with an autoencoder to detect the anomalies. Then we use the latent information obtained from the autoencoder, the internal representation of the discriminator, and visual information of the generator to assign an anomaly score to samples. This anomaly score is used to discriminate anomalous samples from normal samples. The model was evaluated on benchmark datasets such as MNIST and CIFAR10 plus on a specific domain of medical images of a public Leukemia dataset. The model achieved state-of-the-art performance in comparison with its counterparts in almost all of the experiments.

Keywords: Anomaly detection · Generative adversarial network · Autoencoder

1 Introduction

Anomaly detection is an interesting task which is investigated in several areas such as fraud detection [7], network intrusion [16], and computer vision [18]. The problem is defined as finding samples in the test distribution which are not close to what has been observed during training. Such an approach can be utilized to train models which are able to distinguish one class among the others (cats versus other pets) as well as a tool to capture unknown anomalies, e.g., within the process of disease detection, benefiting the lack of known anomalies and limited labeled data.

Generative adversarial networks (GANs) [8] consist of two deep neural networks competing against each other leading to a rich contextual representation of the training data [20]. Image generation in different domains such as natural images [8,11,20] and medical images [9], image-to-image translation [10,29], and text-to-image translation [3,21,27] are among successful works which benefited from the power of GAN models. Even though GANs can model data distributions quite well, in order to take advantage of a GAN for anomaly detection we

© Springer Nature Switzerland AG 2020
I. Farkaš et al. (Eds.): ICANN 2020, LNCS 12396, pp. 479–490, 2020.
https://doi.org/10.1007/978-3-030-61609-0_38

need to find a corresponding latent representation of a given image. Therefore, in current approaches, either an optimization strategy to find a latent representation of the test image [22] or augmenting the vanilla GAN with other modules (e.g., BiGAN [25]) should be used.

In this study, we present a simpler, yet effective, unsupervised anomaly detection model which consists of an autoencoder and a vanilla GAN. We consider an anomaly score, the distance of the generated image from the original image, as an indicator of anomaly. The anomaly score presented in this study differs from the scores in [22,25] in a sense that it exploits the learned representation of the autoencoder used by our model as an extra feature to discriminate anomalous samples. The proposed model was evaluated on MNIST and CIFAR10 and outperformed its counterparts. As a specific case, to showcase the model's ability on a small-sized dataset, an evaluation on a public Acute Lymphoblastic Leukemia (ALL) dataset [14] has been done. The experiments demonstrate our model's ability to nearly always outperform its counterparts on all three different datasets. The code is available under https://github.com/LayaaRS/Unsupervised-Anomaly-Detection-with-a-GAN-Augmented-Autoencoder.

2   Related Work

There are many studies which mainly rely on classical machine learning (ML) approaches such as one-class support vector machines (SVMs) [23], and clustering [24] to detect anomalies in the context of images. Rather than pure classical ML approaches, there is also some work presented as a combination of classical ML and deep learning models. One-class SVM combined with deep belief networks (DBNs) [6] and k-means clustering on top of the features extracted with an autoencoder [2] are known as successful hybrid models. Apart from the hybrid approaches, there is a series of works that solely rely on the representation power of deep learning approaches. Variational autoencoder [1] and autoencoder [28] were used to show deep models could be designed to detect anomalies.

More recent studies leveraged GANs to obtain the desired representations. However, finding these meaningful representations of the normal images distribution is challenging. One of the very first attempts using GAN was AnoGAN [22], a vanilla GAN followed by a heavy optimization process during inference time. Instead of a vanilla GAN, a BiGAN model [25] and a modified BiGAN model [26] were proposed to alleviate the extensive and time-consuming process of inference. A detailed explanation of each of these GAN-based models is presented in Sect. 3. Analogous to the three former works we introduce an unsupervised GAN-based model, specifically a GAN combined with an autoencoder, to find the latent representation of the given image with the purpose of reducing inference time and at the same time improving the performance.

3   Anomaly Detection

In order to take advantage of a GAN to detect anomalies, two steps are required: the first step is to find the corresponding latent representation of a given image, and the second step is to define an anomaly score based on the difference of the learned representations of the given image and the generated image from GAN.

In the following, we briefly review the three previously introduced GAN-based models and their differences with respect to the two above-mentioned steps. Then, our proposed GAN-based model will be explained in more detail.

3.1   AnoGAN

AnoGAN [22] was the first attempt to use a GAN to detect anomalies. They showed that even a vanilla GAN which is sufficiently trained on a normal data distribution can be useful in detecting anomalous samples in the test data. The reason behind this is that, given a well-trained GAN on the normal data distribution, the model is capable of generating only images close to this distribution.

During inference, AnoGAN generates a new sample from a random noise, then repeatedly optimizes the noise and regenerates the new sample in order to find the closest generated image to the input test image. This process requires extremely high number of iterations of generating samples and optimization of the noise. As the result, the model suffers from a very slow inference process which makes it impractical in the cases where computational resources are limited.

In order to measure the difference between the generated image from the optimized noise and the given image, they used a scoring function to assign an anomaly score to the test samples to estimate how far they are from the training distribution. The scoring function assigns a high anomaly score for anomalous images that are far from the normal data distribution.

3.2   Efficient-GAN

To alleviate the issue of the extensive inference process of AnoGAN, Zenati et al. [25] presented "Efficient GAN-based anomaly detection", an unsupervised model based on a bidirectional generative adversarial networks (BiGAN) model [4,5] to accelerate the inference procedure. For simplicity, we will refer to their model as Efficient-GAN.

A BiGAN is an adversarial model which consists of a generator, discriminator, and an encoder. Unlike a vanilla GAN, the discriminator of the BiGAN receives an input pair of an image and its corresponding latent representation. A pair of a generated image $G(z)$ and a random noise z from the generator or a pair of an input image x and its encoded representation of $E(x)$ from the encoder are the inputs to the discriminator. This is done with the expectation that in an ideal training setting the generated image of the generator will be the same as the input image to the encoder, with the same scenario for the latent representations.

To detect anomalies, Zenati et al. [25] utilized a similar scoring function idea of measuring anomalies as presented by Schlegl et al. [22].

3.3   ALAD

Adversarially Learned Anomaly Detection (ALAD) [26] is inspired mainly by the idea of using BiGANs to detect anomalies. They modified the BiGAN so that it has three discriminators instead of one where each of them is responsible for receiving an input pair. The discriminator D_{zz} is responsible for handling the latent representations, D_{xx} is responsible for the input image x, and D_{xz} is the same as the discriminator used in BiGAN. They presented a new anomaly score based on the L_1 reconstruction error in the feature space:

$$A(x) = \|f_{xx}(x, x) - f_{xx}(x, G(E(x)))\|_1 \tag{1}$$

where $G(E(x))$ is the image generated by the generator G given the encoded representation of input image x created by the encoder E, and f_{xx} is defined as the activation of the layer before the logits in the D_{xx} network for the given pair of input samples. In an ideal setting with a well-trained model, it will assign higher values to anomalous images while normal images receive smaller scores.

3.4   Our Anomaly Detection Model

Similar to the previous GAN-based models, we propose an unsupervised model to detect anomalies using adversarial training. We present a new unsupervised model consists of a GAN combined with an autoencoder (see Fig. 1). Our model uses shared weights for both the decoder of the autoencoder and the generator of the GAN to keep the autoencoder within the same distribution as the GAN. In this way, we make sure we can find the corresponding latent representation of a given image during inference time in the learned distribution of our GAN.

The model is only trained on the normal data distribution. Therefore, given an anomalous image at the inference stage, the latent representation generated by the encoder would be close to the normal image representation the model trained on. As the result, the generated image of the generator would not be

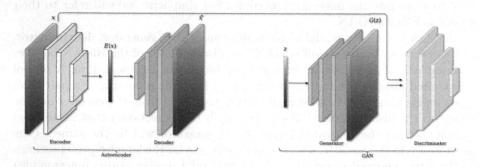

Fig. 1. Our proposed anomaly detection model, autoencoder in the left and GAN in the right, are shown. The decoder of the autoencoder and the generator of the GAN share their weights.

similar to the input image. Hence, measuring the dissimilarity between the generated images and the input images would allow us to indicate anomalies.

To train the generator G and the discriminator D of the GAN model, we use a similar objective function to that presented in [8].

$$\min_G \max_D V(D, G) = \mathbb{E}_{x \sim p_{data}(x)}[\log D(x)] + \mathbb{E}_{z \sim p_z(z)}[\log(1 - D(G(z)))] \quad (2)$$

where $p_{data}(x)$ is the distribution of the training data which in our case includes all normal images and $p_z(z)$ is the random noise distribution. Similar to [8] we decided to maximize $\log D(G(z))$ rather than minimize $\log(1 - D(G(z)))$ to prevent the generator from saturating in early training stages.

We use the mean squared error (MSE) reconstruction loss function to train the autoencoder AE, $L_{AE} = \|x - G(E(x))\|^2$ where $E(x)$ is the encoded representation of an input image x produced by encoder E.

We train our model exclusively on normal images to learn only the distribution of the normal data. To distinguish normal samples from anomalous samples during inference time, we propose a modified version of the anomaly score function presented in [22].

$$A(x) = \lambda L_D(x) + (1 - \lambda)L_R(x) \quad (3)$$

The scoring function introduced by [22], shown in Eq. 3, consists of two components: discrimination loss and residual loss along with a hyperparameter λ to control the contribution of these two losses in the anomaly score. The discrimination loss, $L_D(x)$ given in Eq. 4, is defined to be the difference between the intermediate representation $(f(\cdot))$ of an input image x and the intermediate representation of the generated sample from the corresponding latent representation.

$$L_D(x) = \sum |f_D(x) - f_D(G(E(x)))| \quad (4)$$

Conversely, the residual loss, $L_R(x)$ given in Eq. 5, is introduced to measure the visual dissimilarity between a real image and its corresponding generated image.

$$L_R(x) = \sum |x - G(E(x))| \quad (5)$$

To take advantage of the representation learned by the encoder module of the autoencoder, we add a new term of latent loss to Eq. 3 and present a new anomaly scoring function, given in Eq. 6. The effect of latent loss is controlled by the parameter β.

$$A(x) = \lambda L_D(x) + (1 - \lambda)L_R(x) + \beta L_L(x) \quad (6)$$

The latent loss, L_L (Eq. 7), is defined as a measurement of the distance between the latent representation of an input image x and the latent representation of its corresponding decoded image $G(E(x))$ where both latent representations come from the encoder.

$$L_L(x) = \sum |E(x) - E(G(E(x)))| \quad (7)$$

Similar to the previously mentioned GAN-based models, when the model learns the true distribution of normal data, it will assign a higher anomaly score to anomalous samples as opposed to the score for the normal samples.

4   Datasets

We considered MNIST [15] and CIFAR10 [13] as the two benchmark datasets to compare the anomaly detection power of our model with previous work. In order to evaluate the performance of our model in case of an inadequate number of training samples, which is often the case in medical applications, we also considered a public Acute Lymphoblastic Leukemia (ALL) dataset [14] with only 260 images.

4.1   MNIST and CIFAR10

Both the MNIST (60,000 training and 10,000 test) and CIFAR10 (50,000 training and 10,000 test) have 10 classes. Each of the classes can be identified as either normal or anomalous. In this way, we will have two different strategies to form the datasets: a) *1 versus 9* where one of the classes is chosen as the anomalous class while the rest of them represent the normal samples. b) *9 versus 1* where one of the classes is chosen as the normal class while the rest of them form the anomalous samples. As the result, we can have 20 different datasets from each of MNIST and CIFAR10 with a total of 40 datasets.

For both the above-mentioned datasets, our unsupervised model is only trained on the normal images of the training data while the whole test data plus the anomalous class is used to evaluate the model's ability to detect anomalies.

4.2   ALL Dataset

For the special task of anomaly detection on medical data, we consider using Acute Lymphoblastic Leukemia (ALL) dataset with 260 samples, 130 images for each class of normal and anomalous. 100 samples from the normal class are used for the training, 20 samples as validation set, and the rest of 140 samples including both normal and anomalous samples are considered for the inference. The validation set in ALL dataset is chosen only for the sake of threshold. Since the results in Sect. 5.2 are reported in different performance metrics, a threshold is needed to discriminate samples based on their obtained anomaly score.

5   Experiments and Results

We trained our model on all three datasets (MNIST, CIFAR10, and ALL). In order to compare the performance of our model with the previously proposed GAN-based models, we implemented Efficient-GAN [25], ALAD [26], and AnoGAN [22]. We trained Efficient-GAN and ALAD on all of the above-mentioned datasets, however, due to the extremely long inference phase of AnoGAN (see Sect. 5.2), we only trained it on the ALL dataset.

In order to have a fair comparison in our experiments on the ALL dataset, we used similar hyper-parameters for all three GAN-based models as we used for our model. However, it wasn't possible in all cases. For example, ALAD model

Table 1. The number of layers of our model for MNIST, CIFAR10 and ALL datasets; the generator of the GAN and decoder of autoencoder are the same.

Module	ALL			MNIST			CIFAR10		
	Conv	Deconv	Linear	Conv	Deconv	Linear	Conv	Deconv	Linear
Encoder	6	–	1	3	–	1	4	–	–
Generator/Decoder	1	8	–	–	3	2	–	4	–
Discriminator	6	–	1	3	–	2	3	–	1

uses three discriminators whereas our model has only one. In the case of MNIST and CIFAR10 datasets, we tried to keep our model's hyper-parameters close to those presented in [25] and [26] (see Table 1).

For the experiment on the ALL dataset, each of the four GAN-based models trained for 1000 epochs on the normal images with a learning rate of $1e-4$, and dropout ratio of 0.2 for the encoder and discriminator. The batch size is set to 16, and the latent size is 200. The models trained on MNIST and CIFAR10 datasets for at most 25 epochs, batch size of 64, and learning rate of $1e-4$. The latent sizes 200 and 100 were used for MNIST and CIFAR10 respectively. In all experiments, models are optimized using the ADAM [12] optimizer.

For the inference process on our model, we used different values of β determined as the amount of the contribution of latent loss in our anomaly score function. We used $\beta = 1$ for CIFAR10, $\beta = 0.5$ for MNIST, and a smaller value of $\beta = 0.1$ on the ALL dataset.

5.1   Experimental Setup

Residual Loss Versus Discrimination Loss. The anomaly score function used in [22] and [25] consists of two components, discrimination loss and residual loss as shown in Eq. 3. Since λ is responsible for the contribution of each of those losses, it has a significant impact on the performance of Efficient-GAN, AnoGAN, as well as our model. In order to measure the impact of λ, we evaluated the area under the ROC curve (AUC) for different values of λ in the range of $[0,1]$ for the

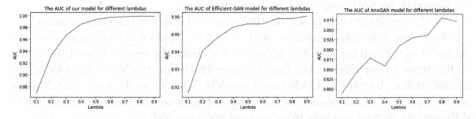

Fig. 2. The effect of λ on the performance of Efficient-GAN, AnoGAN and our model.

Table 2. The performance of AnoGAN, Efficient-GAN, ALAD and our model on ALL dataset. We set λ as 0.8, 0.9, and 0.8 for AnoGAN, Efficient-GAN, and our model respectively. In this and following tables, the ᵀ sign shows the result obtained from our implementation. ($\pm$ std. dev.)

Model	Sensitivity	Specificity	f1-measure	Accuracy	AUC
AnoGANᵀ	0.7308 ± 0.254	0.7444 ± 0.164	0.7919 ± 0.203	0.7334 ± 0.236	0.7571 ± 0.241
Efficient-GANᵀ	0.7154 ± 0.229	**0.9889 ± 0.016**	0.8107 ± 0.165	0.7667 ± 0.183	0.8723 ± 0.137
ALADᵀ	0.9461 ± 0.016	0.750 ± 0.057	0.8852 ± 0.016	0.8609 ± 0.022	0.7988 ± 0.048
Ours	**0.9615 ± 0.029**	0.9222 ± 0.041	**0.9713 ± 0.011**	**0.9542 ± 0.016**	**0.9893 ± 0.010**

three mentioned models on the ALL dataset (see Fig. 2). For these experiments, we considered the value of 0.1 for β in our modified anomaly score function.

As we can see, all the models achieve their higher performance with a higher contribution of discrimination loss. It can be inferred that the internal representation of the discriminator is more informative than the visual information of the images when it comes to distinguishing between the normal and anomalous images.

Random Initialization. GANs are notorious for their unstable behaviour during training. Different architectures, different hyperparameters, computational resources, and even random initialization can lead GANs to exhibit instability [17]. In order to compare the models from the instability behaviour point of view, we trained each model with three different random initializations. All the reported results in this study are computed as an average on the three runs.

5.2   Experimental Results

ALL Dataset. Table 2 shows the detailed results of the four GAN-based models on the ALL dataset. It can be observed from the table that our model outperformed the other three GAN-based models on almost all performance metrics by a large margin. From the sensitivity point of view, ours performs best followed closely by ALAD and then more distantly Efficient-GAN whereas for the specificity metric Efficient-GAN shows higher performance followed closely by Ours and then more distantly ALAD. Overall, our model showed very high and stable performance on both sensitivity and specificity.

As the results reveal, based on the ranges of standard deviation, AnoGAN exhibits very unstable behaviour with different random initializations on the ALL dataset. From the stability point of view, both the results from Table 2 and ROC curves of our model from Fig. 3 demonstrate the stability behaviour of our model unlike the typical GAN-based models. The anomaly score distribution shown on Fig. 3 of our model on ALL dataset express the model's capability to differentiate normal samples from anomalous quite well.

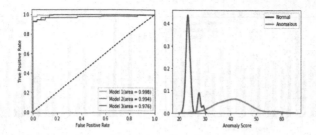

Fig. 3. Comparison of our model with three different random initializations; on the left, ROC curves of our models with different initials, and on the right anomaly score distribution of our best model are depicted.

Table 3. The AUC of Efficient-GAN, ALAD and our model on MNIST and CIFAR10 datasets with *1 versus 9* and *9 versus 1* strategies. The symbol * represents results reported from original paper. (± std. dev.)

Model	1 versus 9		9 versus 1	
	MNIST	CIFAR10	MNIST	CIFAR10
Efficient-GAN[T]	0.509 ± 0.116	0.515 ± 0.064	0.604 ± 0.096	0.506 ± 0.053
ALAD[T]	**0.572** ± 0.140	0.516 ± 0.086	0.607 ± 0.112	0.607 ± 0.120*
Ours	0.557 ± 0.075	**0.555** ± 0.082	**0.693** ± 0.129	**0.611** ± 0.088

MNIST and CIFAR10. For these datasets, two series of experiments have been done on Efficient-GAN, ALAD and our model to compare the effectiveness of each of these models for the task of anomaly detection. Table 3 demonstrates the AUC of each of the models on MNIST and CIFAR10 with *1 versus 9* strategy. Table 3 shows the average AUC on all classes of MNIST and CIFAR10 on three runs. As can be seen, our model performs quite well in comparison with the other two GAN-based models on CIFAR10 while ALAD performs better on MNIST. Table 3 also presents a comparison of performance between Efficient-GAN, ALAD, and our model on MNIST and CIFAR10 with the *9 versus 1* strategy. Again, our model performs quite well in comparison with the other two GAN-based models on MNIST and CIFAR10. Individual performance of each of the classes of MNIST and CIFAR10 can be found in Fig. 4.

Inference Time Comparison. In most of machine learning tasks, the inference time has a big impact on choosing the most suitable model for the desired task. Therefore to compare all of the models discussed in this study from the inference time perspective, we evaluated their running times during inference process on the ALL dataset. These measurements were done using Python 3.7 with PyTorch [19] library on a GeForce GTX 1080 Ti GPU. In the experiment for AnoGAN, the model iterates 500 times for each input test image to find the noise (z) generating the closest image to the input image. Table 4 shows the inference time of each of the models on the ALL test set with a total of 160 images. As

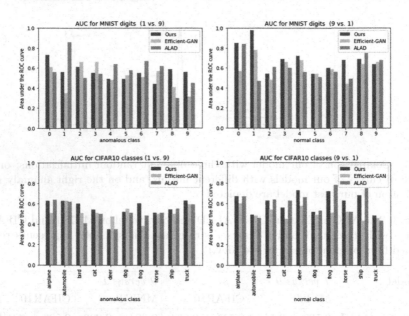

Fig. 4. The performance of models on MNIST and CIFAR10 for each label.

Table 4. GAN-based models and their corresponding inference time on the Acute Lymphoblastic Leukemia (ALL) dataset; the size of input image is (3, 220, 220) and the random noise has dimensionality of 200.

Models	Number of parameters			Inference time (ms)
	Encoder	Generator/Decoder	Discriminator	
AnoGAN[T]	–	2,450,307	5,159,170	13110.47
Efficient-GAN[T]	5,874,352	1,906,240	7,024,929	3.33
ALAD[T]	5,771,752	1,906,240	7,814,915	3.85
Ours	8,716,888	2,450,307	5,159,170	2.90

the table shows, our model has a slightly lower inference time in comparison with Efficient-GAN, and ALAD, while the improvement is more notable as compared to AnoGAN.

Latent Loss Impact. In order to evaluate the effectiveness of our proposed anomaly score with its counterparts in [22] and [25], we evaluated the performance of our model on MNIST and CIFAR10 with and without latent loss. The results in Table 5 demonstrate the benefit of adding latent loss in anomaly score to identify anomalies. Except the experiments on MNIST dataset using *1 versus 9* strategy, the impact of using latent loss were quite significant.

Table 5. The AUC of our model on MNIST and CIFAR10 datasets with and without latent loss. (± std. dev.)

Model	CIFAR10 *(9 vs. 1)*	CIFAR10 *(1 vs. 9)*	MNIST *(9 vs. 1)*	MNIST *(1 vs. 9)*
Without latent loss	0.569 ± 0.107	0.502 ± 0.084	0.670 ± 0.114	0.547 ± 0.099
With latent loss	**0.611 ± 0.088**	**0.555 ± 0.082**	**0.693 ± 0.129**	**0.557 ± 0.075**

6 Conclusion

In this study, we proposed a simple and yet effective unsupervised GAN-based model which consists of a GAN and an autoencoder to detect anomalies. The proposed model is accompanied by a new anomaly score function that benefits from the learned features obtained from its autoencoder. We further evaluated our model on MNIST, CIFAR10, and public Acute Lymphoblastic Leukemia (ALL) datasets. Our proposed model outperformed its counterparts in nearly every experiment and it showed more stable behaviour in comparison with other GAN-based models. Our model is capable of identifying anomalies in MNIST, CIFAR10, and ALL datasets with a very fast inference procedure. In particular, its performance on the ALL dataset demonstrates our model's capability of working on small-sized datasets. Although our model achieved quite promising results on almost all of the datasets there is still room for improvement of its performance on more complicated datasets like CIFAR10. Therefore, further studies may investigate considering other anomaly score functions and model architectures to fill this gap.

References

1. An, J., Cho, S.: Variational autoencoder based anomaly detection using reconstruction probability. Spec. Lect. IE **2**(1), 1–18 (2015)
2. Aytekin, C., Ni, X., Cricri, F., Aksu, E.: Clustering and unsupervised anomaly detection with l_2 normalized deep auto-encoder representations. In: Proceedings of IJCNN, pp. 1–6. IEEE (2018)
3. Dash, A., Gamboa, J.C.B., Ahmed, S., Liwicki, M., Afzal, M.Z.: TAC-GAN-text conditioned auxiliary classifier generative adversarial network. arXiv preprint arXiv:1703.06412 (2017)
4. Donahue, J., Krähenbühl, P., Darrell, T.: Adversarial feature learning. In: Proceedings of ICLR (2017)
5. Dumoulin, V., et al.: Adversarially learned inference. In: Proceedings of ICLR (2017)
6. Erfani, S.M., Rajasegarar, S., Karunasekera, S., Leckie, C.: High-dimensional and large-scale anomaly detection using a linear one-class SVM with deep learning. Pattern Recogn. **58**, 121–134 (2016)
7. Fawcett, T., Provost, F.: Adaptive fraud detection. Data Min. Knowl. Disc. **1**(3), 291–316 (1997)
8. Goodfellow, I., et al.: Generative adversarial nets. In: Proceedings of NIPS, pp. 2672–2680 (2014)

9. Han, C., et al.: GAN-based synthetic brain MR image generation. In: Proceedings of ISBI, pp. 734–738. IEEE (2018)
10. Isola, P., Zhu, J.Y., Zhou, T., Efros, A.A.: Image-to-image translation with conditional adversarial networks. In: Proceedings of CVPR, pp. 1125–1134 (2017)
11. Karras, T., Laine, S., Aila, T.: A style-based generator architecture for generative adversarial networks. In: Proceedings of CVPR, pp. 4401–4410 (2019)
12. Kingma, D.P., Ba, J.: Adam: A method for stochastic optimization. In: Proceedings of ICLR, San Diego, CA, May 2015
13. Krizhevsky, A.: Learning multiple layers of features from tiny images. Master's thesis, Computer Science Department, University of Toronto (2009)
14. Labati, R.D., Piuri, V., Scotti, F.: All-IDB: The acute lymphoblastic leukemia image database for image processing. In: Proceedings of ICIP, pp. 2045–2048. IEEE (2011)
15. Lecun, Y., Bottou, L., Bengio, Y., Haffner, P.: Gradient-based learning applied to document recognition. Proc. IEEE **86**(11), 2278–2324 (1998)
16. Leung, K., Leckie, C.: Unsupervised anomaly detection in network intrusion detection using clusters. In: Proceedings of the 28h Australasian conference on Computer Science, vol. 38, pp. 333–342 (2005)
17. Lucic, M., Kurach, K., Michalski, M., Gelly, S., Bousquet, O.: Are GANs created equal? A large-scale study. In: Proceedings of NIPS, pp. 700–709 (2018)
18. Mahadevan, V., Li, W., Bhalodia, V., Vasconcelos, N.: Anomaly detection in crowded scenes. In: Proceedings of CVPR, pp. 1975–1981 (2010)
19. Paszke, A., Gross, S., Massa, F., et al.: PyTorch: an imperative style, high-performance deep learning library. In: Wallach, H., Larochelle, H., et al. (eds.) Advances in Neural Information Processing Systems, vol. 32, pp. 8024–8035. Curran Associates, Inc. (2019)
20. Radford, A., Metz, L., Chintala, S.: Unsupervised representation learning with deep convolutional generative adversarial networks. In: Proceedings of ICLR (2016)
21. Reed, S.E., Akata, Z., Mohan, S., Tenka, S., Schiele, B., Lee, H.: Learning what and where to draw. In: Proceedings of NIPS, pp. 217–225 (2016)
22. Schlegl, T., Seeböck, P., Waldstein, S.M., Schmidt-Erfurth, U., Langs, G.: Unsupervised anomaly detection with generative adversarial networks to guide marker discovery. In: Niethammer, M., et al. (eds.) IPMI 2017. LNCS, vol. 10265, pp. 146–157. Springer, Cham (2017). https://doi.org/10.1007/978-3-319-59050-9_12
23. Tax, D.M., Duin, R.P.: Support vector data description. Mach. Learn. **54**(1), 45–66 (2004)
24. Xiong, L., Póczos, B., Schneider, J.G.: Group anomaly detection using flexible genre models. In: Proceedings of NIPS, pp. 1071–1079 (2011)
25. Zenati, H., Foo, C.S., Lecouat, B., Manek, G., Chandrasekhar, V.R.: Efficient GAN-based anomaly detection. arXiv preprint arXiv:1802.06222 (2018)
26. Zenati, H., Romain, M., Foo, C.S., Lecouat, B., Chandrasekhar, V.: Adversarially learned anomaly detection. In: 2018 IEEE International Conference on Data Mining (ICDM), pp. 727–736. IEEE (2018)
27. Zhang, H., et al.: StackGAN: text to photo-realistic image synthesis with stacked generative adversarial networks. In: Proceedings of ICCV, pp. 5907–5915 (2017)
28. Zhou, C., Paffenroth, R.C.: Anomaly detection with robust deep autoencoders. In: Proceedings of the 23rd ACM SIGKDD International Conference on Knowledge Discovery and Data Mining, pp. 665–674. ACM (2017)
29. Zhu, J.Y., Park, T., Isola, P., Efros, A.A.: Unpaired image-to-image translation using cycle-consistent adversarial networks. In: Proceedings of ICCV, pp. 2223–2232 (2017)

An Efficient Blurring-Reconstruction Model to Defend Against Adversarial Attacks

Wen Zhou[1,2], Liming Wang[1(✉)], and Yaohao Zheng[1,2]

[1] Institute of Information Engineering, Chinese Academy of Sciences, Beijing, China
{zhouwen,wangliming,zhengyaohao}@iie.ac.cn
[2] School of Cyber Security, University of Chinese Academy of Sciences,
Beijing, China

Abstract. Although deep neural networks have been widely applied in many fields, they can be easily fooled by adversarial examples which are generated by adding imperceptible perturbations to natural images. Intuitively, traditional denoising methods can be used to remove the added noise but the original useful information is eliminated inevitably when denoising. Inspired by image super-resolution, we propose a novel blurring-reconstruction method to defend against adversarial attacks which consists of two period, blurring and reconstruction. When blurring, the improved bilateral filter, which we call it Other Channels Assisted Bilateral Filter (OCABF), is firstly used to remove the perturbations, followed by a bilinear interpolation based downsampling to resize the image into a quarter size. Then, in the reconstruction period, we design a deep super-resolution neural network called SrDefense-Net to recover the natural details. It enlarges the downsampled image after blurring to the same size as the original one and complements the lost information. Plenty of experiments show that the proposed method outperforms the state-of-the-art defense methods as well as less training images demanded.

Keywords: Defense against adversarial examples · Image reconstruction · Bilateral filter

1 Introduction

With the development of deep neural networks (DNNs), they have played a more and more significant role in a large amount of fields, such as object detection, speech recognition, sentiment analysis. But even the most advanced DNNs are still struggling against adversarial examples. Take image recognition tasks for example, when carefully crafted perturbations which are imperceptible for humans are added to clean images, DNNs can output incorrect classification results with high confidence [1,2]. Adversarial examples are also proved to have transferability [2], that is, the adversarial images specifically designed for one

© Springer Nature Switzerland AG 2020
I. Farkaš et al. (Eds.): ICANN 2020, LNCS 12396, pp. 491–503, 2020.
https://doi.org/10.1007/978-3-030-61609-0_39

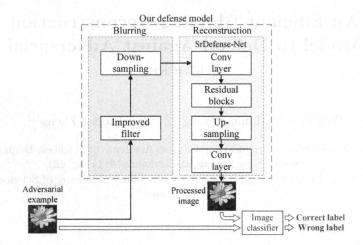

Fig. 1. The overall structure of the proposed method. When blurring, input is first filtered and then downsampled. The right reconstruction part is SrDefense-Net, whose goal is to reconstruct the image as well as complement the lost useful information.

classifier can also attack others successfully. It's a serious hidden danger for deep models and this phenomenon has attracted extensive attention of researchers.

There are plenty of efforts [3] dedicated to preventing adversarial examples, which can be roughly classified into the following three categories: 1) Modifying the training dataset to improve the robustness of neural networks. Adversarial training [1,2] is known as a typical representation which improves the model's defensive performance by adding adversarial examples to the training set and retraining the classification model. 2) Modifying the neural network to defend against adversarial attacks. For example, gradient masking [4] penalizes the gradient of loss function with respect to the inputs to increase the robustness of DNNs. 3) Transforming the input to remove the perturbations before feeding them into the classifier. ComDefend [5] uses an autoencoder-like structure to remove adversarial perturbations, compresses the input with ComCNN and reconstructs the clean image with RecCNN.

The first kind of methods requires the information of adversarial examples, which is not always available. The second kind of methods sometimes even needs to modify the classifier, which is obviously not realistic. And both of the two methods are restricted by computing power since they need to retrain the model. As for the third methods, how to eliminate noise while keep the information of original image in the same time is a sticking point. Commonly, when removing the perturbations, the original information is removed as well, resulting in low quality images, which makes it more difficult to classify. What if we can recover the image , just like turn a low-resolution image into a high-resolution one?

Inspired by this, we focus on input transformation based defense methods and develop a blurring-reconstruction structure as shown in Fig. 1. Our defense model has two phases, blurring and reconstruction. First, inputs are feed into a highly efficient improved filter called Other Channels Assisted Bilateral Filter (OCABF) to obtain smoothed images. In order to further remove the perturbations, we then carry out a downsampling operation to discard more adversarial information. Second, for reconstruction process, we use a deep super-resolution (SR) network to recover clean images. Inspired by SRGAN [6], we design a simpler but effective deep super-resolution network named as SrDefense-Net, of which the main component is residual blocks with identity mapping. Extensive experiments show that our method can effectively defend against typical attacks and exceeds state-of-the-art methods. We summarize our contributions as follows:

- We observe that the attack algorithms seem to try to increase the gradient of two adjacent pixels in an image by generating perturbations in opposite direction, which makes it become a kind of high frequency noise.
- Based on the above observations, we propose an advanced defense method based on blurring-reconstruction structure. Image blurring is used to smooth the inputs in a filtering-downsampling manner. And a more complicated DNN called SrDefense-Net is used to complete the image reconstruction.
- Our experiments show that our approach exceeds many advanced methods. And the advantage of our method is that it only needs to be trained with a few clean images. Also, we don't need to retrain the original classifier.

2 Related Work

2.1 Adversarial Attacks

Several well-known attack methods have been proposed in the literature. Szegedy et al. [1] first demonstrate the existence of adversarial examples. They show that adding certain imperceptible perturbations which maximize the prediction error to an image can cause the network to misclassify. Goodfellow et al. [2] propose a method to effectively generate adversarial images called Fast Gradient Sign Method (FGSM) by adding perturbations in the gradient direction of the loss function. FGSM calculates the gradient only once. Basic Iterative Method (BIM) [7] is an improved iterative version of FGSM. Dong et al. [8] introduce momentum into the calculation process of FGSM and propose Momentum Iterative Fast Gradient Sign Method (MI-FGSM).

Deepfool [9] searches the added perturbations that cause the image to cross the boundary of the polyhedron which is obtained by linearizing the boundaries of image space. Carlini and Wagner [10] design Carlini and Wagner attack (C&W) which contains three versions of attacks, using L_0, L_2 and L_∞ norm. C&W is an optimization-based attack whose optimization goal consists of two main items: the prediction result and the distance between the adversarial example and the clean image.

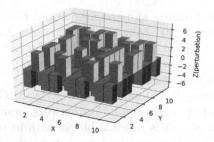

Fig. 2. Part of the perturbations of an adversarial example in one channel generated by FGSM with $L_\infty = 4$. (X, Y) denotes index of the pixel, Z denotes the generated perturbation at corresponding position.

2.2   Defense Methods

An intuitive defense method is adversarial training [1,2], which is to add adversarial images to the training set. Ensemble adversarial training [11] augments training data with adversarial examples transferred from other models. Defensive distillation [12], proposed by Papernot et al., is developed from the research of Hinton et al. [13]. It trains an initial DNN from the original training samples to obtain a probability distribution of training data, then uses it to retrain the original model. Their work shows that defensive distillation can reduce effectiveness of sample creation. Guo et al. [14] study a variety of input transformation methods to counter adversarial images and find that Total Variance Minimization (TVM) [15] is a very effective method in practice. Pixel deflection [16] defends against attacks by transforming the inputs. It replaces some pixels in the image with randomly sampled pixels within the neighborhood of that pixel, then performs wavelet transform based denoising. ComDefend [5] is also an input transformation method. It has an autoencoder-like structure, which contains a compression CNN and a reconstruction CNN. Experiments in [5] show that it outperforms many state-of-the-art defense methods including High-Level Representation Guided Denoiser (HGD) [17].

3   Blurring-Reconstruction Model

3.1   Motivation

We study the adversarial noise which uses L_∞ norm to restrict the perturbations. What interests us is that most of the two adjacent pixels have opposite perturbations as showed in Fig. 2. For example, if the generated perturbation for a pixel is a positive number, its adjacent pixels are more likely to have negative ones. In this way, the attackers increase the gap between two adjacent pixels, bringing high frequency component to original clean images. Trying to eliminate these perturbations by learning the features of the perturbations through complicated DNNs may not be worth the effort. On the contrary, we can eliminate the perturbations by simply smoothing the adversarial examples.

In view of the feature mentioned above, we design a blurring-reconstruction defense model as shown in Fig. 1. First, when blurring, rather than designing a DNN, a relatively simple and training-free smoothing filter OCABF is used to remove the redundant information. In order to further wipe off the adversarial noise, we then down sample the filtered images. Second, to complement the image information that was discarded in blurring phase, we design a deep super-resolution network called SrDefense-Net which supplements the details. SrDefense-Net not only ensures the image quality, but also improves the performance of our defense model.

3.2   Improved Bilateral Filter Based Blurring

In order to get rid of the perturbations in the input, we first design a relatively simple but effective method in our architecture. We use a bilateral filter to denoise images which can be expressed as:

$$
g(i,j) = \frac{\sum_{k,l} f(k,l) w(i,j,k,l)}{\sum_{k,l} w(i,j,k,l)}. \tag{1}
$$

$g(i,j)$ denotes the pixel value at position (i,j) after filtering. (k,l) is the neighboring pixel of (i,j) in the filtering window and $f(k,l)$ denotes the pixel value at position (k,l) of original image. $w(i,j,k,l)$ represents the weight of the neighboring pixel, and it can be expressed as follows:

$$
w(i,j,k,l) = d(i,j,k,l) \times r(i,j,k,l). \tag{2}
$$

The domain function $d(i,j,k,l)$ is used to illustrate the contribution of neighboring pixels to the weight $w(i,j,k,l)$ according to spatial closeness, and the range function $r(i,j,k,l)$ represents the contribution of them to $w(i,j,k,l)$ according to value difference. They can be expressed as:

$$
d(i,j,k,l) = \exp\left(-\frac{(i-k)^2 + (j-l)^2}{2\sigma_d^2}\right), \tag{3}
$$

$$
r(i,j,k,l) = \exp\left(-\frac{\|f(i,j) - f(k,l)\|^2}{2\sigma_r^2}\right). \tag{4}
$$

σ_d and σ_r are hyperparameters which control the strength of the domain and range information respectively.

When dealing with RGB images, one way is to apply smoothing to the red, green, and blue channels separately. However, the intensity profiles across the edge in three color channels are in general different. Using the information of only one channel may result in fuzzy band edges. To better preserve edges, we add edge information of other channels to correct the filtering result of current channel and propose an improved bilateral filter called Other Channels Assisted

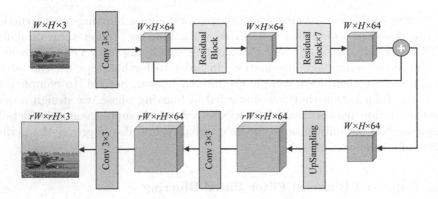

Fig. 3. The structure of SrDefense-Net. r is the scaling factor and it is set to 2.

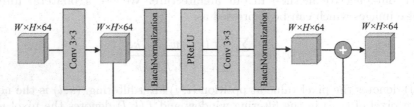

Fig. 4. The detail of the residual block. It's the major component of our SrDefense-Net.

Bilateral Filter (OCABF). When filtering each channel m, the weight of OCABF can be expressed as:

$$w_m(i, j, k, l) = \exp\left(-\frac{(i - k)^2 + (j - l)^2}{2\sigma_d^2} - \sum_c \frac{\lambda \|f_c(i, j) - f_c(k, l)\|^2}{2\sigma_r^2} \right), \quad (5)$$

where $m \in \{R, G, B\}$ and m represents the current filtered channel. $c \in \{R, G, B\}$ and $f_c(i, j)$ represents pixel value of the image at (i, j) on channel c. And λ can be expressed as:

$$\lambda = \begin{cases} \alpha, & if \quad c = m \\ \beta, & otherwise \end{cases}, \quad (6)$$

where α and β respectively indicate weights of current channel and other channels, and $\alpha + 2\beta = 1$.

To further remove adversarial perturbations, the filtered image is then down sampled. We use the bilinear interpolation algorithm to achieve downsampling. When downsampling, we can take random sampling rate to introduce randomness to further resist white-box attacks. Let $0 < p \leq q \leq 1$, sampling rate S is random sampled from uniform distribution $U(p, q)$. Due to the random sampling, it's almost impossible for the attackers to perform white-box attacks.

3.3 SrDefense-Net Based Reconstruction

We take a direct approach to get rid of the adversarial noise, while we also violently remove some effective information of the input image, reducing the classification accuracy. So it's necessary to reconstruct the images after blurring. Super-resolution network can complete the details of the image and transfer low-resolution input into high-resolution one.

In order to learn the distribution of natural samples to restore the images, we design a deep reconstruction network called SrDefense-Net which is inspired by the generator network of SRGAN [6]. SrDefense-Net is a super-resolution network, it learns the distribution of natural images, completes the image details, and gives high-resolution outputs.

The overall structure of SrDefense-Net is shown in Fig. 3. The input images first go through a convolutional layer consisting of 64 filters of size $3 \times 3 \times 3$, then pass through 8 residual blocks. Finally, the feature maps are upsampled to enlarge the size of the input and the number of channels is changed back to 3. Since the input of SrDefense-Net is downsampled from the original image, the output of SrDefense-Net is consistent with the original images in size. Figure 4 shows the structure of each residual block with an identity mapping from the beginning of the block to the end of the block.

4 Experiments

4.1 Experiment Setup

Training Data. We train SrDefense-Net with classic super-resolution datasets. The training set we use is [18,19], which is comprised of 91 images, and the validation set is [20,21] with a total of 19 images. Each image is divided into four 64×64 patches as labels, and four 32×32 low-resolution patches that are obtained by downsampling the corresponding patches are as input. We chose the common pixel-level mean square error (MSE) as the loss function. Compared to other approaches, our method needs a relatively small dataset and don't require the information of adversarial examples, but can also achieve outstanding results.

Test Set and Attack Methods. To evaluate the proposed method, we test our model with around 1000 ImageNet images from NIPS 2017 competition on defense against adversarial attacks [22]. Deep neural networks, such as ResNet-50 [23] and Inception-v3 [24], have high classification accuracy on these image samples. When generating adversarial examples, we use different attack methods, including FGSM [2], BIM [7], MI-FGSM [8], Deepfool [9] and C&W [10] to get adversarial images with different sizes of perturbations, and L_∞ norm is used to measure the perturbations.

4.2 Against Gray-Box Attacks

In this section, we show the experimental results of various defense methods on gray-box attacks. Here gray-box attacks indicate that attackers know all of the

Table 1. The comparison of defense effects against different attacks obtained by our method and other defenses. Here we omit the percent signs (%) of the data.

Defense	Clean	FGSM $L_\infty = 2/4/7$	BIM $L_\infty = 2/4/7$	Deepfool $L_\infty = 2/4/7$	C&W $L_\infty = 2/4/7$
ND	95.4	23.7/22.1/23.0	13.5/7.0/2.0	3.8/4.5/6.0	4.1/4.9/6.1
TVM	86.6	63.9/51.5/43.8	73.1/65.9/55.4	71.5/60.2/45.9	71.9/61.8/50.0
PD	**91.0**	50.7/35.9/29.7	75.2/52.6/28.3	63.6/34.1/19.6	68.3/38.2/21.7
CD	77.4	67.2/60.9/55.5	73.6/67.1/58.5	72.1/66.7/61.8	72.7/67.8/61.7
Ours	84.6	**76.0/71.3/62.6**	**79.3/76.8/73.7**	**78.8/75.3/70.9**	**78.6/75.8/72.1**

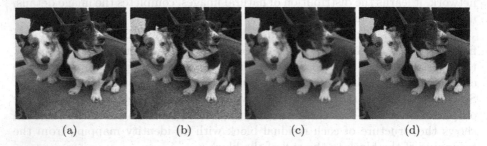

(a)   (b)   (c)   (d)

Fig. 5. Visualization of the results in different phases of our blurring-reconstruction model. Picture (a), (b), (c) and (d) respectively represent original image, adversarial example, adversarial example after blurring and finally reconstructed result.

information about the classifier, but the attackers do not know the information about defense model.

Comparison with State-of-the-Art Methods. In Table 1, we present classification accuracy obtained using our proposed method and compare it with other state-of-the-art defense methods including TVM [14], pixel deflection (PD) [16] and ComDefend (CD) [5]. And "ND" means there is no defense. We use Inception-v3 [24] as the classifier. The kernel size of our OCABF is 35 and hyperparameters σ_d, σ_r, α and β are separately set to 44, 18.5, 0.28, 0.36, which are the general results that we search out. And the downsampling rate is set to 0.5.

Our experiments in Table 1 show that our method has better defense effect against multiple kinds of attacks with different sizes of perturbations. Especially, compared with pixel deflection and TVM, whose performance decline palpably when the attack intensity is large, our method has a stable performance when the perturbations increase. Similar to ComDefend, an important advantage of our method is that it doesn't require attack information for training. And as mentioned in Sect. 4.1, we only need to train our model in a relatively small dataset. What's more, when processing an image, the average time of ComDefend is 0.419 s and the average time of our method is 0.294 s. The reason is that although the numbers of network layers of SrDefense-Net and ComDefend are close, SrDefense-Net processes an image much smaller than the original image

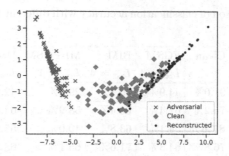

Fig. 6. The principal component analysis of high level features obtained from clean images, adversarial examples and finally reconstructed adversarial images

due to the downsampling, which makes it more efficient. In addition, when dealing with large-scale images like images in ImageNet, ComDefend need to divide each into patches of size 32×32, process each patch and put them together in the end, making the final output images have clear stitching traces. Our method processes a complete image directly and get clear results with the same size as the original one. So our method is more practical.

To more intuitively demonstrate the effect of our model, as shown in Fig. 5, we visually illustrate the adversarial images processed by blurring and reconstruction. All the settings are the same with Table 1 except $L_\infty = 11$. Here we set L_∞ to 11 in order to give a more obvious contrast. It can be seen clearly that there is a significant noise in the input adversarial examples compared to the clean image. After filtering and downsampling, perturbations are successfully removed and the edges of image are preserved. But part of the useful information is eliminated as well and the image becomes a low-resolution one, that is the reason why we need a SR network to reconstruct it. Finally our SrDefense-Net complements image details, strengthens the edges, and gives a clear output.

To further study the images processed by our defense model, we use Principal Component Analysis (PCA) to analyze high-level features of 100 images obtained by DNNs as showed in Fig. 6. The green points denote original clean images, the red points represent corresponding adversarial examples and the black points denote the adversarial examples processed by our method. Adversarial examples and clean images cluster in different areas with clear boundary. Obviously, our method pull adversarial examples back to the natural distribution and make them away from the adversarial region. Thus, our blurring-reconstruction method indeed restore the adversarial examples to legitimate images and have significant defense effect against attacks.

Effect of Filtering. When selecting different filters, the defense effect is shown in Table 2. We chose five filters for blurring phase, including Gaussian filter, median filter, wavelet-transform based filter, bilateral filter, and OCABF (ours). Hyperparameters used in the two bilateral filters are the same as above. The hyperparameters of other filters are the optimal results from grid searches.

Table 2. The comparison of classification accuracy with different filters in our structure

Filters	Clean	FGSM $L_\infty = 4$	BIM $L_\infty = 4$	MI-FGSM $L_\infty = 4$	Deepfool $L_\infty = 4$	C&W $L_\infty = 4$
No filter	91.0%	44.9%	59.1%	29.2%	42.8%	47.0%
Gaussian	75.2%	61.4%	66.4%	58.9%	64.3%	65.0%
Median	**87.6%**	54.1%	63.8%	40.0%	55.9%	58.5%
Wavelet	76.8%	64.3%	71.6%	65.1%	68.5%	69.7%
Bilateral	83.5%	70.9%	76.5%	71.0%	75.0%	**76.1%**
OCABF (ours)	84.6%	**71.3%**	**76.8%**	**71.5%**	**75.3%**	75.8%

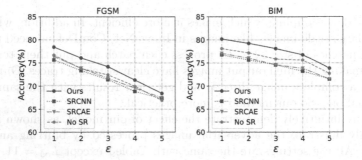

Fig. 7. Defense results of using different super-resolution network on attacks of FGSM and BIM. "No SR" means that it doesn't use super-resolution network.

Performance of the two bilateral filters significantly outperforms that of the other filters and they can effectively remove adversarial noise. And our OCABF has a better defense effect against different attacks. When filtering, filters like Gaussian filter mainly consider the spatial relationship between pixels, thus the edge may be smoothed and only obtain a blurred image. Bilateral filter and OCABF not only consider the relationship of pixels in spatial distance, but also take the pixel value similarity into account. Furthermore, when OCABF filters one channel of the image, it effectively combines the edge information of other channels, so it can better retain the edges and get a clearer output.

Effect of Super-Resolution Reconstruction. We explore the influence of different super-resolution network on classification performance as showed in Fig. 7. Its horizontal ordinate represents different perturbations. The settings of adversarial examples and blurring part are consistent with Sect. 4.2. We compare our SrDefense-Net with other two models: deep convolutional neural network for super-resolution (SRCNN) [25] and convolutional autoencoders for image restoration (SRCAE) [26].

For different attacks, the tendency of accuracy are consistent when adopting different super-resolution networks. And our SrDefense-Net is superior to the other two models. It's worth noting that the result of not applying SR model is better than that of using the other two models. The other two SR models can't fully learn the distribution of natural images. Using them for super-resolution may cause the results to deviate from the distribution of original images, resulting in worse results. This shows that our model can guide the image to the natural distribution and restore clean image. Compared with other inputs transformation methods, because of SrDefense-Net, our model can not only effectively defend against attacks, but also get high-resolution results.

5 Conclusion

In this paper, we propose a blurring-reconstruction method to defend against the adversarial examples. Our insight is that adversarial perturbations can be treated as a kind of high frequency noise. It may not be worth removing the noise by using complex supervised method, such as DNNs. So we use a filter to deal with it. To further remove noise, we use downsampling to change the image into a quarter size. In order to complete the information lost in blurring period, we design the SrDefense-Net to supplement the details and restore original images. The experimental results show that our method can effectively defend against various types of adversarial attacks. In the future, we can turn the blurring part into network layers and make our model become an end-to-end structure.

Acknowledgement. This work is supported by National Research and Development Program of China (No. 2017YFB1010004).

References

1. Szegedy, C., Zaremba, W., Sutskever, I., et al.: Intriguing properties of neural networks. arXiv preprint arXiv:1312.6199 (2013)
2. Goodfellow, I.J., Shlens, J., Szegedy, C.: Explaining and harnessing adversarial examples. arXiv preprint arXiv:1412.6572 (2015)
3. Akhtar, N., Mian, A.S.: Threat of adversarial attacks on deep learning in computer vision: a survey. IEEE Access **6**, 14410–14430 (2018). https://doi.org/10.1109/access.2018.2807385
4. Ross, A.S., Doshi-Velez, F.: Improving the adversarial robustness and interpretability of deep neural networks by regularizing their input gradients. In: Proceedings of the Thirty-Second AAAI Conference on Artificial Intelligence (AAAI), pp. 1660–1669 (2018)
5. Jia, X., Wei, X., Cao, X., Foroosh, H.: ComDefend: an efficient image compression model to defend adversarial examples. In: IEEE Conference on Computer Vision and Pattern Recognition (CVPR), pp. 6084–6092 (2019). https://doi.org/10.1109/cvpr.2019.00624

6. Ledig, C., et al.: Photo-realistic single image super-resolution using a generative adversarial network. In: 2017 IEEE Conference on Computer Vision and Pattern Recognition (CVPR), pp. 105–114 (2017). https://doi.org/10.1109/cvpr.2017.19
7. Kurakin, A., Goodfellow, I.J., Bengio, S.: Adversarial examples in the physical world. arXiv preprint arXiv:1607.02533 (2017)
8. Dong, Y., Liao, F., Pang, T., et al.: Boosting adversarial attacks with momentum. In: 2018 IEEE Conference on Computer Vision and Pattern Recognition (CVPR). pp. 9185–9193 (2018). https://doi.org/10.1109/cvpr.2018.00957
9. Moosavi-Dezfooli, S., Fawzi, A., Frossard, P.: DeepFool: a simple and accurate method to fool deep neural networks. In: 2016 IEEE Conference on Computer Vision and Pattern Recognition (CVPR), pp. 2574–2582 (2016). https://doi.org/10.1109/cvpr.2016.282
10. Carlini, N., Wagner, D.A.: Towards evaluating the robustness of neural networks. In: 2017 IEEE Symposium on Security and Privacy (SP), pp. 39–57 (2017). https://doi.org/10.1109/sp.2017.49
11. Tramèr, F., Kurakin, A., Papernot, N., et al.: Ensemble adversarial training: attacks and defenses. arXiv preprint arXiv:1705.07204 (2018)
12. Papernot, N., McDaniel, P.D., Wu, X., Jha, S., Swami, A.: Distillation as a defense to adversarial perturbations against deep neural networks. In: IEEE Symposium on Security and Privacy (SP), pp. 582–597 (2016). https://doi.org/10.1109/sp.2016.41
13. Hinton, G.E., Vinyals, O., Dean, J.: Distilling the knowledge in a neural network. CoRR abs/1503.02531 (2015)
14. Guo, C., Rana, M., Cissé, M., van der Maaten, L.: Countering adversarial images using input transformations. arXiv preprint arXiv:1711.00117 (2018)
15. Rudin, L.I., Osher, S., Fatemi, E.: Nonlinear total variation based noise removal algorithms. Phys. D **60**(1–4), 259–268 (1992). https://doi.org/10.1016/0167-2789(92)90242-f
16. Prakash, A., Moran, N., Garber, S., et al.: Deflecting adversarial attacks with pixel deflection. In: 2018 IEEE Conference on Computer Vision and Pattern Recognition (CVPR), pp. 8571–8580 (2018). https://doi.org/10.1109/cvpr.2018.00894
17. Liao, F., Liang, M., Dong, Y., Pang, T., Hu, X., Zhu, J.: Defense against adversarial attacks using high-level representation guided denoiser. In: 2018 IEEE Conference on Computer Vision and Pattern Recognition (CVPR), pp. 1778–1787 (2018). https://doi.org/10.1109/cvpr.2018.00191
18. Timofte, R., Smet, V.D., Gool, L.V.: Anchored neighborhood regression for fast example-based super-resolution. In: 2013 IEEE International Conference on Computer Vision (ICCV), pp. 1920–1927 (2013). https://doi.org/10.1109/iccv.2013.241
19. Yang, J., Wright, J., Huang, T.S., Ma, Y.: Image super-resolution via sparse representation. IEEE Trans. Image Process. **19**(11), 2861–2873 (2010). https://doi.org/10.1109/tip.2010.2050625
20. Bevilacqua, M., Roumy, A., Guillemot, C., Alberi-Morel, M.: Low-complexity single-image super-resolution based on nonnegative neighbor embedding. In: British Machine Vision Conference (BMVC), pp. 1–10 (2012). https://doi.org/10.5244/c.26.135
21. Zeyde, R., Elad, M., et al.: On single image scale-up using sparse-representations. In: Curves and Surfaces - 7th International Conference, pp. 711–730 (2010)
22. Kurakin, A., Goodfellow, I.J., Bengio, S., et al.: Adversarial attacks and defences competition. CoRR abs/1804.00097 (2018)
23. He, K., Zhang, X., Ren, S., Sun, J.: Deep residual learning for image recognition. In: 2016 IEEE Conference on Computer Vision and Pattern Recognition (CVPR), pp. 770–778 (2016). https://doi.org/10.1109/cvpr.2016.90

24. Szegedy, C., Vanhoucke, V., Ioffe, S., Shlens, J., Wojna, Z.: Rethinking the inception architecture for computer vision. In: 2016 IEEE Conference on Computer Vision and Pattern Recognition (CVPR), pp. 2818–2826 (2016). https://doi.org/10.1109/cvpr.2016.308
25. Dong, C., Loy, C.C., He, K., Tang, X.: Image super-resolution using deep convolutional networks. IEEE Trans. Pattern Anal. Mach. Intell. **38**(2), 295–307 (2016). https://doi.org/10.1109/tpami.2015.2439281
26. Mao, X., Shen, C., Yang, Y.: Image restoration using convolutional auto-encoders with symmetric skip connections. CoRR abs/1606.08921 (2016)

EdgeAugment: Data Augmentation by Fusing and Filling Edge Maps

Bangfeng Xia[1], Yueling Zhang[1(✉)], Weiting Chen[1], Xiangfeng Wang[1],
and Jiangtao Wang[1,2(✉)]

[1] School of CS and SE, East China Normal University,
3663, North Zhongshan Rd, Shanghai, China
51184501064@stu.ecnu.edu.cn, {ylzhang,jtwang}@sei.ecnu.edu.cn
[2] National Trusted Embedded Software Engineering Technology Research Center,
1006, Jinsha Jiang Rd, Shanghai, China

Abstract. Data augmentation is an effective technique for improving the accuracy of network. However, current data augmentation can not generate more diverse training data. In this article, we overcome this problem by proposing a novel form of data augmentation to fuse and fill different edge maps. The edge fusion augmentation pipeline consists of four parts. We first use the Sobel operator to extract the edge maps from the training images. Then a simple integrated strategy is used to integrate the edge maps extracted from different images. After that we use an edge fuse GAN (Generative Adversarial Network) to fuse the integrated edge maps to synthesize new edge maps. Finally, an edge filling GAN is used to fill the edge maps to generate new training images. This augmentation pipeline can augment data effectively by making full use of the features from training set. We verified our edge fusion augmentation pipeline on different datasets combining with different edge integrated strategies. Experimental results illustrate a superior performance of our pipeline comparing to the existing work. Moreover, as far as we know, we are the first using GAN to augment data by fusing and filling feature from multiple edge maps.

Keywords: Data augmentation · Adversarial generation networks · Deep learning · Convolution neural network

1 Introduction

Deep convolution neural network [12] has made a series of breakthroughs in many tasks, such as image classification, object detection, and image segmentation. The performance of deep learning network has exceeded human recognition capabilities in many scenarios. So far, the machine learning and computer vision community have focused on how to build better network architectures [9]. However, the excellent performance of the deep learning model requires sufficient training data. In fact, it is difficult or costly to collect enough training data in many fields. For example, industrial defect detection is an important application

© Springer Nature Switzerland AG 2020
I. Farkaš et al. (Eds.): ICANN 2020, LNCS 12396, pp. 504–516, 2020.
https://doi.org/10.1007/978-3-030-61609-0_40

of deep learning. In this field, it is easy to collect a large number of normal images during production, but the number of defect images we can obtain is limited [23]. This phenomenon causes the classifier to perform poorly in defect detection. Therefore, it is important to improve the performance of the model by data augmentation when the amount of training data is insufficient.

The data augmentation aims to generate more training data based on limited training data to improve the accuracy of the deep learning model. In fact, data augmentation has been widely used in model training which can teach the model about variety of the data domain [4]. Rotating, scaling, and randomly cropping the image are the most commonly used label-invariant data augmentation methods which can generate training images that are consistent with the original image label. A lot of related work has proved that using label-invariant geometric changes to augment the data is a helpful method to increase the generalization ability of model [12,24].

With the development of Adversarial Generation Networks [6], it has shown a strong generating capability in the image generating field. Isola et al. [10] proposed the Pix2Pix network which generate images similar to the training set based on mask labels or sketch images. Inspired by such image transformation network [10,19], we can adjust the mask or sketch images and then use the transformation network to generate more training data.

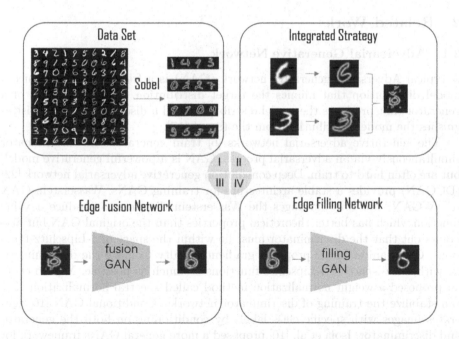

Fig. 1. The overview of our proposed method. We first use the Sobel operator to extract gradient images from the limited dataset (I) and use a simple integrated strategy to integrate the different edge maps (II). Then we use an GAN to fuse the integrated edge maps to synthesize additional edge map (III). Finally, an edge image filling GAN is used to fill the edge map to new training image (IV).

In this paper, we propose a novel data augmentation method, which we call edge fusion data augmentation (see Fig. 1). We first use the Sobel operator to extract edge map for each image in the dataset and then use a simple integrated strategy to combine different edge maps. After that, an edge fusion GAN is used to fuse simple combined edge maps to synthesize new edge maps. Finally, we use an edge image filling GAN to fill the edge maps to generate new training images. By our novel edge fusion augmentation pipeline, we can make full use of the important edge features in limited training data to synthesize more training images by integrating edge features from different images.

To summarize, our primary contributions can be summarized as follows. Firstly, we propose a novel data augmentation pipeline which can merge and make full use of edge features in training data. Secondly, we present several edge combination strategies which can integrate different edge features efficiently. Thirdly, to the best of our knowledge, we are the first using GAN to augment data by fusing and filling feature from different edge maps.

This paper is organized as follows. In Sect. 2, we cover some related works about Generative Adversarial Networks and Data Augmentation. Section 3 specifies our data augmentation pipeline for data augmentation, including simple edge integrated strategies, edge fusion and filling pipeline. Lastly, a series of experiments are presented in Sect. 4 followed by a conclusion in Sect. 5.

2 Related Work

2.1 Adversarial Generative Network

A typical Adversarial generative network (GAN) is a framework to produce a model distribution that mimics the target distribution. GAN is consists of a generator that produces the model distribution and a discriminator that distinguishes the model distribution from the target [17].

The generative adversarial networks [6] train generator and discriminator simultaneously via an adversarial process. GAN is a powerful generative model, but are often hard to train. Deep convolution generative adversarial network [22] (DCGAN) provides a stable architecture for training GANs. Wasserstein GAN [1] (WGAN) not only leverages the Wasserstein distance to produce a value function which has better theoretical properties than the original GAN but also points out that the discriminator must lie within the space of 1-Lipschitz functions. Gulrajani et al. [7] proposed gradient penalty to make the discriminator lie within the space of 1-Lipschitz functions as much as possible. Miyato et al. [8] proposed a weight normalization method called spectral normalization that can stabilize the training of discriminator networks. Conditional GAN [16] generates images with specific class labels by conditioning on both the generator and discriminator. Isola et al. [10] proposed a more general GANs framework for image-to-image mappings which achieved impressive results on inpainting, future state prediction, style transfer and super resolution [14,21]. These works have optimized the network structure of GANs, made the training of GANs easier, and provided various excellent GAN frameworks for image-to-image maps.

2.2   Data Augmentation

Since data augmentation was used in training deep learning networks [12], this method has been widely used to augment training data when training data is limited. In fact, data augmentation can teach the model what is invariant in the transform. So, some intra-class transform always used to generate more training data, [11] like random cropping, image mirroring and color shifting. Cubuk et al. [4] uses reinforcement learning to obtain an intra-class transform change strategy that maximizes the generalization ability of the target model. The intra-class transform is characterized by calculating efficiently and implementing easily, but the biggest limitation of this method is that it cannot integrate features from different images to generate more diverse training images.

Recently, there is making great progress with using the GAN model to improve the deep network performance with limited training samples. Frid-Adar et al. [5] synthesizes liver lesion images by using GAN and uses CNN for liver lesion classification. Bowles et al. [3] uses the GAN to augment the data for brain image segmentation. Wang et al. [25] uses GAN to improve the accuracy when he trains a model for plate recognition with a carefully designed pipeline. They both use unconditional GAN in data augmentation, so we cannot directly intervene the image generation process. Bailo et al. [2] proposes an efficient system that generates red blood cell images via incorporating conditional GAN and synthetic segmentation mask. This method can control images generated by GAN and achieved good results on the blood cell dataset, but the method of generating blood cell mask label is difficult to use in other datasets.

3   Proposed Approach

As far as we know, we are the first introducing edge maps to augment training data. Edge map is characterised by simpleness but informativeness. So we creatively synthesize new training images by fusing and filling different edge maps which are extracted from training data by Sobel operator. In detail, the edge fuse data augmentation pipeline mainly composed of four stages. We first use the Sobel operator to extract edges map for training images. Then simple edge integrated strategies are used to integrate edge maps which are extracted from different images. After that we use the edge fusion GAN to fuse the integrated edge map. Finally, we synthesize new training images by the edge filling GAN to fill fusion edge maps. The graphical visualization of the whole pipeline is shown in Fig. 1.

In order to use edge fusion-filling pipeline for data augmentation, we need an edge fusion network with great ability to encode and decode images, and an edge filling network which requires more detailed texture in the generated images.

These requirements narrow our search space considerably. We chose the approach of Isola et al. [10] as our edge fusion network and chose the approach of Park et al. [20] as our filling network. In this section we will introduce the details about our novel edge combination strategy and the edge fusion-filling pipeline we proposed.

Fig. 2. Block randomly integrated

Fig. 3. Multiple edge maps concatenate

3.1   Edge Extraction and Combination Strategy

An important purpose of data augmentation is to provide more information for model to improve its stability. We innovatively focus on the edge maps of image to augment the data by gradually fusing the features from different images. We use edge integrated strategies to integrate different edge maps. These integrated edge maps retains features from original images after integrated. Detail is we have a limited image data set I_{limit}. For each image $I_i \sim I_{limit}$, we use the Sobel operator to compute the gradient edge map E_i and get an edge set E_{limit}. Then integrated edge maps E_{int} can be got by using edge integrated strategy from E_{limit}. We mainly introduce and use following three kinds of strategies in the experiment according to different dataset. The strategies are block randomly integrated strategy, multiple edge maps concatenate strategy and mask label integrated strategy.

1. Block randomly integrated strategy:
   We first sample two images I_1, I_2 from I_{limit}. Then Sobel operator was used to extract edge gradient maps E_1, E_2. After that, Edge map E_i be divided into n * n blocks and we randomly select t (t $< n^2/2$) blocks from one map and fill them into another to gain a integrated edge map E_{int}. This process is shown in Fig. 2.
2. Multiple edge maps concatenate strategy:
   We compute edge gradient maps E_1, E_2, $E_3...E_n$ by applying the Sobel operator to images I_1, I_2, $I_3...I_n$. Then we only keep a part of pixels in each image E_i and concatenate them in the direction of the image channel. The integrated process is shown in Fig. 3.
3. Mask label integrated strategy:
   We sample edge maps and mask labels (E_1, M_1), (E_2, M_2) from dataset. Then we can extract interested regions r_{ex} based on the mask labels M_1 from one map E_1 and replace the target area in another edge maps E_2. Mask label will make the combination result more efficiently. The process is shown in Fig. 4.

We can extract and integrate edge features from different image by applying integrated strategy. In this way, we can make full use of important edge features in the data set and further use the edge fusion and filling network to synthesize images in the next stage.

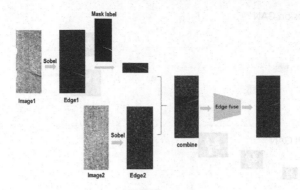

Fig. 4. Integrated base on mask label

3.2   Edge Fusion and Filling Pipeline

Edge fusion and filling pipeline employs an edge fusion GAN to fuse integrated edge map E_{int} and employs an edge filling GAN to fill edge maps E_{fuse} after fusion (Detailed in Fig. 5). In detail, E_{int} is obtained after using simple integrated strategy. Then we can further use the edge fusion GAN to fuse elements in E_{int} and obtain a edge map E_{fuse}. The edge fusion GAN consists of a generator and a discriminator (Fig. 5(a)). The structure about the generator is similar to Unet [24] which has the good performance in feature encoder and decoder.

The loss function about the edge fusion GAN is shown in Eq. 1. The G_1 and D_1 represents generator and discriminator in fusion GAN. E_{int} represents the simple integrated edge maps. c represents the target class.

$$L_f = \min_G \max_D \mathbb{E}_{x \sim E_{limit}}[log(D_1(x,c))] + \mathbb{E}_{z \sim E_{int}}[log(1 - D_1(G_1(z,c)))] \quad (1)$$

Edge filling GAN is used to further fill the E_{fuse} to synthesize training images I_{fill}. As shown in Fig. 5(b). We chose the Gau GAN [20] as our filling network which uses a conditional normalization layer that modulates the activation using input conditional map through a spatially adaptive. This structure has been shown can significantly improve the detailed texture of the generated images. In addition, target class is added to both generator and projection discriminator.

The loss function of the edge filling GAN is shown in Eq. 2. G_2 represents the generator and D_2 represents the discriminator. E_{fuse} represents the fused edge map and E_{limit} represents the edge maps that extracts from I_{limit} by using Sobel operator. In addition, c represents target class and z samples from a normal distribution.

$$L_c = \min_G \max_D \mathbb{E}_{x \sim I_{limit}}[log(D_2(x))] + \mathbb{E}_{e \sim E_{fuse}, z \sim Z}[log(1 - D_2(G_2(e,z,c)))] \quad (2)$$

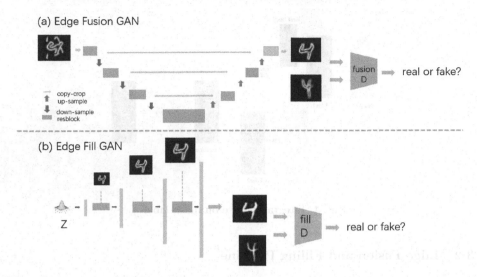

Fig. 5. Structure of fusion GAN and filling GAN. The generator of fusion GAN uses a structure similar to Unet [24] (a). The SPAED structure [20] is used in filling GAN to fill the edge image (b). Projection discriminator [18] is both used in (a) and (b).

4   Experiments

We validate our edge fusion data augmentation method on three different datasets which are Mnist [13], Fashion-Mnist [26] and Kolektor [23] dataset. Kolektor is one of the industrial datasets which is characterized by the number of normal images are much larger than defect images. As far as we know, we are the first to balance the number of normal images and defect images by adding defect features to normal images and fusing them.

We extract a part of images from dataset to construct several limited datasets and evaluate the target model's performance on each dataset. In detail, we first train and evaluate target models based on limited datasets. After that, we augment limited datasets by using edge fusion data augmentation pipeline. Finally, the target model is evaluated after augmented. The loss function we used is Hinge loss [15] which shows helpful for GAN training. We evaluate the target model's performance by using different augmentation methods like label-invariant transform, our edge-fusion augmentation and both at the same time. In all experiments, we use a learning rate of $1e^{-4}$ and the Adam optimizer (momentum β_1 = 0.9, β_2 = 0.999). All the experiments are conducted on NVIDIA Geforce with two 8 GB 1080 GPUs.

4.1   Augment on Mnist and Fashion-Mnist

The Mnist dataset was first introduced by LeCun et al. [13] which is comprised of 10-class handwritten digits and the training data includes 50,000 training images.

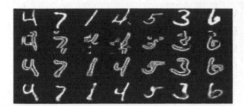

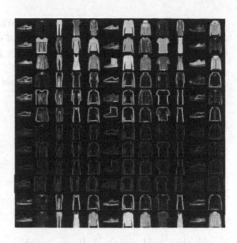

Fig. 6. Mnist: the first line is the training data, the second line are integrated edge maps, the third line is the output of the edge fusion GAN, and the fourth line is the images after filling

Fig. 7. Fashion-Mnist: Row 1–3 are training data. Row 4–6 are corresponding edge maps. Row 7–9 sample from row 4–6. Row 10 is the edge map concatenate on the channel, Row 11 is the edge map after the edge fusion network fused, and the row 12 is the result after filling.

Fashion MNIST is a direct drop-in replacement for the original MNIST dataset but with more complex classes with higher variability. Fashion MNIST consists of grayscale images of 70, 000 fashion products from 10 categories including 60, 000 images in training set has and 10, 000 images in test set [26]. We randomly extracted 500, 1000, 1500 images from Mnist and randomly extracted 1000, 2000, 5000 images from the Fashion-Mnist to construct several limited datasets. After that we use the target model we selected is Resnet [9] which was widely used and the residual module in Resnet has been used in various works. ResNet18 as our target model in this experiment is enough. We use the block randomly integrated strategy on Mnist to get edge features from different images in order to increase the variation of digital and use multiple edge maps concatenate strategy on Fashion-Mnist which is beneficial to increase the clothing's pattern. Integrated strategy are shown in Fig. 2 and Fig. 3. The target class we chose to fuse and fill in Mnist is the class which providing more blocks.

The process of edge fusion data augmentation is shown in Fig. 6 and Fig. 7. The process of the pipeline shows that the fusion GAN can naturally merge integrated edge maps to synthesize new target class edge maps. So, new training image can be generated after filling. Table 1 demonstrates the quantitative results with different amount and different dataset used as training instances. For instance, "OI" column represents results where the network is only trained with original images (OI). "Aug" and "fuse" represent results where training set is composed of real images with label invariable augmentations and real images mixed with fusion image respectively. The label invariable augmentation includes

Table 1. Quantitative evaluation on various tasks. Column names respectively represent different datasets used for training of the networks: original images (OI), label invariable augmentations (aug), edge fuse pipeline (fuse).

Dataset	Limited dataset	OI	Aug	Fuse	Aug+fuse
Mnist	M_{500}	0.858	0.926	0.914	0.946
	M_{1000}	0.933	0.962	0.964	0.973
	M_{1500}	0.963	0.972	0.977	0.982
Fashion-Mnist	F_{1000}	0.804	0.817	0.814	0.821
	F_{2000}	0.832	0.848	0.852	0.854
	F_{5000}	0.867	0.879	0.883	0.885

horizontal and vertical flips, brightness change, contrast normalization, and rotates randomly within 15°. The "aug"+"fuse" means we use label invariable augmentation and fuse pipeline simultaneously. Resnet18 is a powerful model capable of reaching a high accuracy of 0.858, 0.933 and 0.963 in each Mnist limited dataset by utilizing real data exclusively without any augmentations. Label invariable augmentation helps to boost performance about 6.84%, 2.9% and 0.92%. The model's accuracy increases by 5.63%, 3.1% and 1.39% with our fuse augmentation pipeline. Lastly, the accuracy can be further improved when we use our pipeline with label invariable augmentation. Similar results can be observed on Fashion-Mnist. To sum up, this experiment implies that the performance of target network will significantly increased by using our edge fusion augmentation pipeline to augment training data.

Fig. 8. The images of the top line are defect images. The second line images are mask labels, the third are normal images and the fourth are edge maps after fused. The bottom line are the new training images after filled.

4.2   Augment on Kolektor Surface-Defect Dataset

Industry is an important application field of deep learning which can significantly improve the efficient and quality during the industrial process. Compared with Mnist and Fashion-Mnist, Kolektor is a dataset for the field of industrial inspection and is collected from actual industrial process. This dataset is characteristic by the number of normal image is exceedingly more than the defect images. In fact, this dataset consists of 399 commutator surface images in total. 347 of them are normal images without defects, 52 of them are defective images containing cracks. We balance the defect image and normal images by using our edge fusion augmentation pipeline to fuse the cracks from defect images to normal images in order to generate new negative images.

The target model we evaluate is proposed by Kolektor et al. [23]. This model is a segmentation-based deep-learning architecture designed for the detection and segmentation of surface anomalies. This model is demonstrated state-of-the-art on Kolektor. We use mask label integrated strategy in this experiment because each image in dataset has mask label and we can get the crack's location by it. The process of edge fusion data augmentation is shown in Fig. 8. We use mask label integrated strategy to integrate edge maps which are from normal edge maps and defect edge maps. After that, edge fusion GAN and edge filling GAN are used to fuse integrated edge maps and fill fused edge maps to synthesize new defect images. We divide the Kolektor into a training set and a test set according to 4:6. The training data have 20 defect images and 138 normal images after division. We randomly extracted 5, 10, and 20 defect images from training data and keep the number of normal images unchanged to construct three limited datasets D_1, D_2, D_3. The amount's disparity about normal and defect images simulates industrial processes scenario. We evaluate the model's performance before and after our edge fuse augmentation. It is more reasonable to use the recall rate to evaluate the model's performance when there is a large disparity between the amount of positive and negative images and we treated defect image as positive. The experimental results are shown in histogram Fig. 9. The target model is capable of reaching accuracy of 0.73, 0.78 and 0.90 on each limited

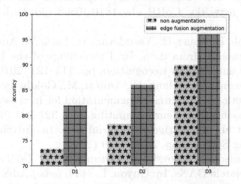

Fig. 9. Comparison of model accuracy under the Kolektor dataset

dataset. The model's accuracy reaches to 0.82, 0.87 and 0.96 after augmenting by our novel pipeline. This experiment shows that our method can improve the model's performance by fusing and generating images to balance the amount of positive images and negative images.

5   Conclusion

In this paper, we propose a novel edge fuse data augmentation pipeline to synthesize training images by combining Sobel operator and Conditional Generative Adversarial Networks. Compared to the existing work, our method can make use of the features in the limited dataset and increase diversity of training images. What's more, We validate our data augmentation pipeline on industry filed. The result shows that our pipeline can be much beneficial to the performance of the network by fusing positive and negative images. To sum up, based on the experiments we performed, make full use of image's edge maps to augment data deserves more attention.

Acknowledgement. This work was supported by National Key Research and Development Program of China (No. 2018YFB2101300), Shanghai Natural Science Foundation (Grant No. 18ZR1411400) and the National Trusted Embedded Software Engineering Technology Research Center (East China Normal University). We benefit a lot from the Research on algorithms for large-scale structural Optimization problems driven by Machine Learning [2019–2022, 19ZR141420].

References

1. Arjovsky, M., Chintala, S., Bottou, L.: Wasserstein GAN. arXiv preprint arXiv:1701.07875 (2017)
2. Bailo, O., Ham, D., Min Shin, Y.: Red blood cell image generation for data augmentation using conditional generative adversarial networks. In: Proceedings of the IEEE Conference on Computer Vision and Pattern Recognition Workshops, pp. 0–0 (2019)
3. Bowles, C., et al.: GAN augmentation: Augmenting training data using generative adversarial networks. CoRR abs/1810.10863 (2018). http://arxiv.org/abs/1810.10863
4. Cubuk, E.D., Zoph, B., Mane, D., Vasudevan, V., Le, Q.V.: AutoAugment: learning augmentation strategies from data. In: Proceedings of the IEEE Conference on Computer Vision and Pattern Recognition, pp. 113–123 (2019)
5. Frid-Adar, M., Diamant, I., Klang, E., Amitai, M., Goldberger, J., Greenspan, H.: Gan-based synthetic medical image augmentation for increased CNN performance in liver lesion classification. Neurocomputing **321**, 321–331 (2018)
6. Goodfellow, I., et al.: Generative adversarial nets. In: Advances in Neural Information Processing Systems, pp. 2672–2680 (2014)
7. Gulrajani, I., Ahmed, F., Arjovsky, M., Dumoulin, V., Courville, A.C.: Improved training of Wasserstein GANs. In: Guyon, I., et al. (eds.) Advances in Neural Information Processing Systems, vol. 30, pp. 5767–5777. Curran Associates, Inc. (2017). http://papers.nips.cc/paper/7159-improved-training-of-wasserstein-gans.pdf

8. Gulrajani, I., Ahmed, F., Arjovsky, M., Dumoulin, V., Courville, A.C.: Improved training of Wasserstein GANs. In: Advances in Neural Information Processing Systems, pp. 5767–5777 (2017)

9. He, K., Zhang, X., Ren, S., Jian, S.: Deep residual learning for image recognition. In: 2016 IEEE Conference on Computer Vision and Pattern Recognition (CVPR) (2016)

10. Isola, P., Zhu, J.Y., Zhou, T., Efros, A.A.: Image-to-image translation with conditional adversarial networks. In: Proceedings of the IEEE Conference on Computer Vision and Pattern Recognition, pp. 1125–1134 (2017)

11. Jackson, P.T., Atapour-Abarghouei, A., Bonner, S., Breckon, T., Obara, B.: Style augmentation: data augmentation via style randomization. arXiv preprint arXiv:1809.05375, pp. 1–13 (2018)

12. Krizhevsky, A., Sutskever, I., Hinton, G.E.: ImageNet classification with deep convolutional neural networks. In: Pereira, F., Burges, C.J.C., Bottou, L., Weinberger, K.Q. (eds.) Advances in Neural Information Processing Systems, vol. 25, pp. 1097–1105. Curran Associates, Inc. (2012). http://papers.nips.cc/paper/4824-imagenet-classification-with-deep-convolutional-neural-networks.pdf

13. LeCun, Y., Bottou, L., Bengio, Y., Haffner, P.: Gradient-based learning applied to document recognition. Proc. IEEE 86(11), 2278–2324 (1998)

14. Ledig, C., et al.: Photo-realistic single image super-resolution using a generative adversarial network. In: Proceedings of the IEEE Conference on Computer Vision and Pattern Recognition, pp. 4681–4690 (2017)

15. Lim, J.H., Ye, J.C.: Geometric GAN. arXiv preprint arXiv:1705.02894 (2017)

16. Mirza, M., Osindero, S.: Conditional generative adversarial nets. CoRR abs/1411.1784 (2014). http://arxiv.org/abs/1411.1784

17. Miyato, T., Kataoka, T., Koyama, M., Yoshida, Y.: Spectral normalization for generative adversarial networks. CoRR abs/1802.05957 (2018). http://arxiv.org/abs/1802.05957

18. Miyato, T., Koyama, M.: CGANs with projection discriminator. CoRR abs/1802.05637 (2018). http://arxiv.org/abs/1802.05637

19. Nazeri, K., Ng, E., Joseph, T., Qureshi, F.Z., Ebrahimi, M.: EdgeConnect: generative image inpainting with adversarial edge learning. arXiv Computer Vision and Pattern Recognition (2019)

20. Park, T., Liu, M.Y., Wang, T.C., Zhu, J.Y.: Semantic image synthesis with spatially-adaptive normalization. In: Proceedings of the IEEE Conference on Computer Vision and Pattern Recognition, pp. 2337–2346 (2019)

21. Pathak, D., Krahenbuhl, P., Donahue, J., Darrell, T., Efros, A.A.: Context encoders: feature learning by inpainting. In: Proceedings of the IEEE Conference on Computer Vision and Pattern Recognition, pp. 2536–2544 (2016)

22. Radford, A., Metz, L., Chintala, S.: Unsupervised representation learning with deep convolutional generative adversarial networks. arXiv preprint arXiv:1511.06434 (2015)

23. Ren, R., Hung, T., Tan, K.C.: A generic deep-learning-based approach for automated surface inspection. IEEE Trans. Cybern. 48(3), 929–940 (2018)

24. Ronneberger, O., Fischer, P., Brox, T.: U-net: convolutional networks for biomedical image segmentation. In: Navab, N., Hornegger, J., Wells, W.M., Frangi, A.F. (eds.) MICCAI 2015. LNCS, vol. 9351, pp. 234–241. Springer, Cham (2015). https://doi.org/10.1007/978-3-319-24574-4_28

25. Wang, X., You, M., Shen, C.: Adversarial generation of training examples for vehicle license plate recognition. CoRR abs/1707.03124 (2017). http://arxiv.org/abs/1707.03124
26. Xiao, H., Rasul, K., Vollgraf, R.: Fashion-MNIST: a novel image dataset for benchmarking machine learning algorithms. CoRR abs/1708.07747 (2017). http://arxiv.org/abs/1708.07747

Face Anti-spoofing with a Noise-Attention Network Using Color-Channel Difference Images

Yuanyuan Ren[1,2], Yongjian Hu[1,2(✉)], Beibei Liu[1,2], Yixiang Xie[2], and Yufei Wang[2]

[1] South China University of Technology, Guangzhou 510640, Guangdong, China
eeyjhu@scut.edu.cn
[2] Sino-Singapore International Joint Research Institute, Guangzhou 510700, Guangdong, China

Abstract. The wide deployment of face recognition systems has raised serious concern on its security level. One of the most prominent threats is the presentation attack, which attempts to fool the system in the absence of the real person. In this article, we propose a way of identifying the spoof face by using spoofing noise. Since the spoofing noise is brought into the spoof image when an adversary uses some tricks to fool the face recognition system, it consists of imagining device noise and is affected by the spoofing environments. We think it is a clue against fake face. We first address how to use color channel difference images to enhance the spoofing noise, and then introduce a self-adapting attention framework named Noise-Attention Network to learn the end-to-end spoofing-features. Experiments on benchmarks including CASIA-FASD, MSU-MFSD and Idiap Replay-Attack demonstrate the effectiveness of the proposed method. It can yield results comparable with other current methods but has better robustness.

Keywords: Face anti-spoofing · Color-channel difference images · Spoofing noise · Neural network

1 Introduction

Due to the variety of spoof types and picture qualities, face anti-spoofing is a great challenge and draws much attention in recent years. Face spoofing detection can be considered as a binary image classification problem. Most prior works rely on handcrafted features such as Local Binary Pattern (LBP) [1,26], face motion feature [23,24], Histogram of Oriented Gradient(HOG) [28,29], and Speed-up Robust Feature(SURF) [25]. Classifier such as support vector machines (SVM)

Supported in part by Sino-Singapore International Joint Research Institute (No. 206-A017023, No. 206-A018001), and Science and Technology Foundation of Guangzhou Huangpu Development District under Grant 201902010028.

I. Farkaš et al. (Eds.): ICANN 2020, LNCS 12396, pp. 517–526, 2020.
https://doi.org/10.1007/978-3-030-61609-0_41

is used to differentiate the details between live faces and spoof samples. There are also some works looking for solutions in alterative color spaces such as HSV and YCbCr [2].

Recently, it is found that deep learning based approaches [4,5,14,15,18,27] generally perform better than those based on handcrafted features in terms of accuracy. In [4], local texture features as well as depth features are extracted via CNN from the face images and fused for face spoofing detection. In [5], the LSTM-CNN (Long Short-Term Memory units with Convolutional Neural Network) architecture was proved to be effective for video face spoofing detection. Most existing CNN based spoofing detection algorithms extract features directly from the RGB image. However, public face anti-spoofing datasets are often not large and only contain a limited number of subjects. Besides, positive and negative samples are imbalanced. As a result, detection models are not well trained. They often have good performance in intra-dataset testing but poor performance in cross-dataset testing.

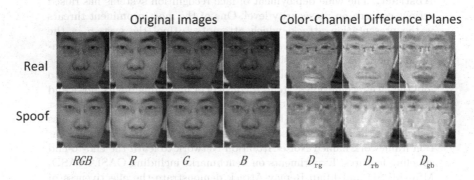

Fig. 1. Comparison between real and spoof images. In sequence, the left four columns show the original color versions and the R, G, B channels. The right three columns demonstrate the three color-channel difference images, namely D_{r-g}, D_{r-b} and D_{g-b}.

A spoof face may be a printed photo paper (i.e., print attack), a digital image/video (i.e., replay attack), or a 3D mask and facial cosmetic makeup. It can be viewed as a re-rendering of the live image but with some "special" noise from the spoof medium and the environment [6]. Such noise only belongs to spoof images and does not exist in live images. Since the spoof medium and the environment may change each time during spoofing, the spoofing noise is difficult to be peeled off from the spoof image.

Motivated by [6], this work discusses how to use this special noise as the distinctive feature to identify the spoof face. To better extract it, we choose to use color channel difference images rather than RGB images as the input data so that image content is effectively weaken due to subtraction operation between color-channel images (see Fig. 1). We then design an attention-aware network to enhance this special noise and extract its features. Experiments on benchmarks including CASIA-FASD, MSU-MFSD and Idiap Replay-Attack demonstrate the

effectiveness of the proposed method. It can yield results comparable with other
current methods but has better robustness.

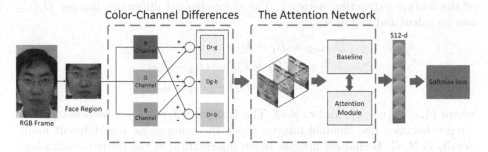

Fig. 2. Framework of the proposed face spoofing detection approach. The first part is
to obtain the color-channel difference images and the second part is an attention-aware
network to enhance this special noise and extract its features.

2 Methodology

The flow chart of the proposed method is shown in Fig. 2. There are two major
stages, namely, building normalized color-channel difference images for spoofing
noise enhancement and designing a noise-attention network for spoof feature
extraction.

2.1 The Color-Channel Difference Images

The framework of the proposed method is shown in Fig. 2. We first discuss the
components of image noise. Assume a noiseless face image as O, and a face image
as J. During imaging process, the physical and electronic noise from camera
pipeline as well as quantization noise is brought into J. Let N_0 refer to the sum
of the above noise components. If someone fools the face recognition system, the
spoof medium and the environment would bring the additional spoofing noise
Z into J. Since $O + N_0$ refers to a live face, we let $I = O + N_0$ for simplicity.
Consequently, a face image can be represented by

$$J = O + N_0 + Z = I + Z. \tag{1}$$

If $Z = 0$, J is a live face; otherwise, it is a fake face. In practice, an image is
read in RGB format. So we have three color channel images:

$$J_c = I_c + Z_c, c \in \{r, g, b\}. \tag{2}$$

The subscripts r, g, b represent red, green, and blue components, respectively. As
stated before, the spoofing noise is an important clue for face spoofing detection.

It can be easily observed from Fig. 1 that the color-channel subtraction operation can suppress image content on the color-channel images and enhance the presence of spoofing noise. Based on this, we attempt to construct the input data of the feature extraction network. The color-channel difference images D_{c1-c2} can be calculated as follows.

$$
\begin{aligned}
D_{c1-c2} &= J_{c1} - J_{c2} \\
&= (I_{c1} + Z_{c1}) - (I_{c2} + Z_{c2}) \\
&= (I_{c1} - I_{c2}) + (Z_{c1} - Z_{c2}).
\end{aligned} \tag{3}
$$

where $c1, c2 \in \{r, g, b\}$, and $c1 \neq c2$. The first item $I_{c1} - I_{c2}$ represents the difference between two channel images. Since the same scene has different image details in R, G, B channel-images, much information of the scene is redundant, and thus, the image content is greatly reduced after subtraction. On the contrary, the spoofing noise comes from different spoof media and environments. Degradation due to spoofing is versatile, complex, and subtle. It consists of 2-stage degradation: one from the spoof medium (e.g., paper and digital screen), and the other from the interaction of the spoof medium with the imaging environment. Each stage includes a large number of variations, such as medium type, illumination, non-rigid deformation and sensor types. Combination of these variations makes the overall degradation varies greatly [6]. As a result, it is almost impossible to model the spoofing noise. In this article, we simply regard it as a combination of random noise components. So the subtraction operation between Z_{c1} and Z_{c2} can not weaken their strength. This is the core basis for our spoof noise enhancement scheme. To speed up the training, we normalize the three color-channel difference images as follows.

$$
D_{du} = \frac{D_d - min(D_d)}{max(D_d) - min(D_d)}, d \in \{r - g, g - b, r - b\} \tag{4}
$$

2.2 The Network Architecture

In this section, we introduce our attention framework for spoof feature extraction: NANet. Attention mechanism [7–9, 21, 22] has been widely used in the field of computer vision and the performance of deep learning algorithms. The proposed noise-attention network consists of two parts: a CNN backbone and the attention module. We use the ResNet-18 [10] as our baseline. The overall framework of our noise-attention network is illustrated in Fig. 3. The proposed attention modules are placed at every ResNet-block of the baseline. With such design, we can realize the multi-level feature attention simultaneously.

The detail of the attention module is shown in Fig. 3. We first introduce the attention mechanism. Given a convolution feature map of the color-channel difference images as input, the attention module infers the attention map T. Our attention process can be summarized as:

$$
T = (M(F) + 1) \otimes F \tag{5}
$$

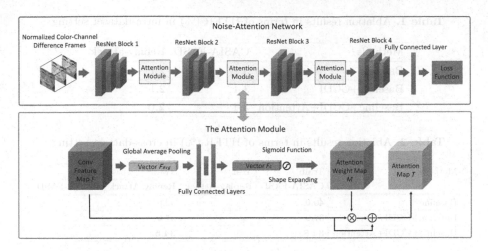

Fig. 3. Diagram of the noise-attention network. The proposed attention modules are set at every ResNet-block of our baseline. As illustrated, the attention module utilizes average-pooling output with shared a group of fully connected layers. And then the attention weight map is generated by a sigmoid activation function.

Where $M(F)$ means learning the attention weight map M from convolution feature map F, and $\otimes$ denotes element-wise multiplication. Via the element-wise multiplication operation, the attention values are broadcasted into all pixels of the convolution feature map accordingly. Meanwhile, via sigmoid activation function, the attention weight map is normalized to the range of (0, 1). Such attention method can reinforce the crucial content while suppressing the irrelevant information of the convolution feature map. The attention map T is the final refined output of the attention module, which includes lots of spoof-related content.

The structure of the attention module is shown in Fig. 3. It aims to learn the weight relationship among different channels for attention source. First of all, to aggregate the feature map in each channel, we employ a global average pooling layer on the feature map F to produce a vector, F_{avg}. It softly encodes different global information in each channel, which includes average-pooled information of input feature map. And then, the three fully connected layers (FCs) are employed to optimize the attention-values across channels from the vector F_{avg}, formulated as $FCS(\cdot)$ and generate an optimized vector F_c. Finally, a batch normalization (BN) layer and a shape expanding layer are used to adjust the scale of the F_c and create the attention weight map $M(F)$:

$$M(F) = \sigma(FCS(AvgPool(F))) = \sigma(W_1(W_0(F_{avg}))) \tag{6}$$

where W_0 and W_1 mean the FCs weights of $FCS(\cdot)$. Notation σ means using sigmoid activation function.

Table 1. Ablation results in terms of HTER (%) in intra-dataset setting.

Methods	CASIA-FASD	Replay-attack
Baseline	3.2	2.1
Baseline+CCDI	3.4	2.1
Baseline+CCDI+Attention	**3.1**	**2.0**

Table 2. Ablation results in terms of HTER (%) in cross-dataset setting.

Methods	Train	Test	Train	Test
	CASIA-FASD	Replay-Attack	Replay-Attack	CASIA-FASD
Baseline	40.0		52.6	
Baseline+CCDI	37.9		37.6	
Baseline+CCDI+Attention	34.8		**34.5**	

3 Experiments

3.1 Datasets and Experimental Setting

We validate our approach through extensive experiments on three public datasets: CASIA-FASD [3], MSU-MFSD [20] and Idiap Replay-Attack [1].

CASIA – FASD. This video face anti-spoofing dataset contains 600 videos from 50 subjects. The training set contains 20 subjects and the test set contains 30 subjects. Presentation attack types include warped photo attack, cut photo attack, and video attack. Three different imaging qualities are provided, i.e., low quality, normal quality, and high quality.

MSU – MFSD. This video face anti-spoofing dataset contains 280 video clips of photo and video attack attempts of 35 subjects. Three types of spoof attacks are provided, high-resolution replay video attacks using an iPad Air screen, mobile phone replay video attacks using an iPhone 5 S screen, and printed photo attacks using an A3 paper with fully-occupied printed photo.

Idiap Replay – Attack. This video face anti-spoofing dataset contains 1200 videos from 50 subjects. The training set contains 15 subjects, while the development set contains 15 subjects and the test set contains 20 subjects. Presentation attack types include print photo attack, iPad display attack, and mobile video attack. Two different illumination conditions are provided, i.e., controlled and adverse.

Implementation Details. The dimension of input image is 224×224. At training step, we use Adam optimizer and set the learning rate as 0.0001 and weight decay as 0.0005.

Evaluation Metrics. The Half Total Error Rate (HTER) is half of the sum of the False Rejection Rate (FRR) and the False Acceptance Rate (FAR). It is often used for evaluating detection performance of a spoofing recognition system. Both False Acceptance Rate (FAR) and False Rejection Rate (FRR) depend on a threshold τ, which is calculated from the development set on CASIA-FASD, MSU-MFSD or Idiap Replay-Attack datasets in our experiments.

3.2 Experimental Results

Performance of the Proposed Method: To assess the effectiveness and the generalization capability of the proposed method, we have performed two evaluations on both intra-dataset testing and cross-dataset testing. Note that the intra-dataset testing was carried out on both CASIA-FASD (C for short), MSU-MFSD (M for short) and Idiap Replay-Attack (I for short) datasets.

The experimental results of the ablation study are shown in Table 1 and Table 2. Notation CCDI denotes using the color-channel difference images for model training. Attention denotes using the attention module.

Table 3. Performance comparison with the state-of-the-art methods in terms of HTER (%).

Methods	Train	Test	Train	Test	Train	Test	Train	Test
	C	I	I	C	I	M	M	I
LBP [1]	47.0		39.6		45.8		45.5	
LBP-TOP [11]	49.7		60.0		47.7		46.5	
Motion [11]	50.2		47.9		–		–	
Motion-mag [16]	50.1		47.0		–		–	
Spectral cubes [17]	34.4		50.0		–		–	
CNN [18]	48.5		45.5		48.6		37.1	
Deep-learning [14]	48.2		45.4		–		–	
Color-LBP [2]	37.9		35.4		**33.0**		44.8	
Attention-Resnet [13]	36.2		34.7		–		–	
Auxiliary [12]	**27.6**		**28.4**		–		–	
Frame difference [19]	50.3		42.6		38.0		48.0	
NANet (ours)	34.8		34.5		35.7		**36.2**	

From Table 1 and Table 2, we can observe that: (1) The ablation experiment between Baseline and Baseline+CCDI confirms the effectiveness of the color-channel difference images for face anti-spoofing. Compared with original images, the color-channel difference images have a better performance. The experimental results in Table 2 prove that using the color-channel difference images for feature extraction can achieve a robust generalization ability. (2) The results show the performance of the proposed noise-attention network NANet. Compared with the baseline, the final model has a better performance. It also demonstrates that the proposed attention network is effective for feature extraction.

Comparison with the State-of-the-Art Methods: Table 3 presents the comparisons with state-of-the-art methods. The experiment is set in cross-dataset scenarios on CASIA-FASD (C for short), MSU-MFSD (M for short) and Idiap Replay-Attack (I for short). It is observed that our method has satisfactory results of 34.8%, 34.5%, 35.7% and 36.2% in terms of HTER in the cross-dataset setting. It yields results comparable with those of other current methods but has better robustness of the generalization ability facing with a face image from an unknown domain. Note that the accuracy of work [12] is better than our method. However, [12] uses more auxiliary information (i.e., depth map and rPPG) than our method. In addition, our approach performs as well as [13] that is based on two separate ResNet-18 networks with a two-input structure. Compared with the method of [13], our network is lighter and has smaller number of parameters.

4   Conclusion

In this article, we introduced a way of identifying the spoof face by utilizing spoofing noise. We first proposed a novel method named the color-channel difference images to enhance the spoofing noise. And then, a self-adapting attention framework named Noise-Attention Network was designed for spoof feature extraction. Finally, we evaluated the proposed method on multiple widely-used face anti-spoofing datasets.

References

1. Zinelabidine B., Jukka K., Abdenour H.: Face anti-spoofing based on color texture analysis. In: International Conference on Image Processing (ICIP), pp. 2636–2640. IEEE, Quebec City (2015)
2. Boulkenafet, Z., Komulainen, J., Hadid, A.: Face anti-spoofing based on color texture analysis. In: 2015 IEEE International Conference on Image Processing (ICIP), pp. 2636–2640. IEEE, Quebec City (2015)
3. Zhang, Z., Yan, J., Liu, S., Lei, Z., Yi, D., Li, S.Z.: A face anti-spoofing database with diverse attacks. In: 2012 5th IAPR International Conference on Biometrics (ICB), pp. 26–31. IEEE, New Delhi (2012)
4. Atoum, Y., Liu, Y., Jourabloo, A., Liu, X.: Face anti-spoofing using patch and depth-based CNNs. In: 2017 IEEE International Joint Conference on Biometrics (IJCB), pp. 319–328. IEEE, Denver (2017)
5. Xu, Z., Li, S., Deng, W.: Learning temporal features using LSTM-CNN architecture for face anti-spoofing. In: 2015 3rd IAPR Asian Conference on Pattern Recognition (ACPR), pp. 141–145. IEEE, Kuala Lumpur (2015)
6. Jourabloo, A., Liu, Y., Liu, X.: Face de-spoofing: anti-spoofing via noise modeling. In: Ferrari, V., Hebert, M., Sminchisescu, C., Weiss, Y. (eds.) ECCV 2018. LNCS, vol. 11217, pp. 297–315. Springer, Cham (2018). https://doi.org/10.1007/978-3-030-01261-8_18

7. Park, J., Woo, S., Lee, J., Kweon, I.: BAM: bottleneck attention module. In: Proceedings of British Machine Vision Conference (BMVC), Newcastle, UK, p. 147 (2018)
8. Ma, B., Wang, X., Zhang, H., Li, F., Dan, J.: CBAM-GAN: generative adversarial networks based on convolutional block attention module. In: Sun, X., Pan, Z., Bertino, E. (eds.) ICAIS 2019. LNCS, vol. 11632, pp. 227–236. Springer, Cham (2019). https://doi.org/10.1007/978-3-030-24274-9_20
9. Klein, T., Nabi, M.: Attention is (not) all you need for commonsense reasoning. arXiv preprint arXiv:1905.13497(2019)
10. He, K., Zhang, X., Ren, S., Sun, J.: Deep residual learning for image recognition. In: Proceedings of the IEEE Conference on Computer Vision and Pattern Recognition, pp. 770–778. IEEE, Las Vegas (2016)
11. de Freitas Pereira, T., Anjos, A., De Martino, J. M., Marcel, S.: Can face anti-spoofing countermeasures work in a real world scenarion. In: 2013 International Conference on Biometrics (ICB), pp. 1–8. IEEE, Madrid (2013)
12. Liu, Y., Jourabloo, A., Liu, X.: Learning deep models for face anti-spoofing: binary or auxiliary supervision. In: Proceedings of the IEEE Conference on Computer Vision and Pattern Recognition, pp. 389–398. IEEE, Salt Lake City (2018)
13. Chen, H., Hu, G., Lei, Z., Chen, Y., Robertson, N.M., Li, S.Z.: Attention-based two-stream convolutional networks for face spoofing detection. IEEE Trans. Inf. Forensics Secur. 15, 578–593 (2019)
14. Menotti, D., et al.: Deep representations for iris, face, and fingerprint spoofing detection. IEEE Trans. Inf. Forensics Secur. 10(4), 864–879 (2015)
15. Lucena, O., Junior, A., Moia, V., et al.: Transfer learning using convolutional neural networks for face anti-spoofing. Proceedings of the 14th International Conference on Image Analysis and Recognition (ICIAR), Montreal, Canada, pp. 27–34 (2017)
16. Li, H., Li, W., Cao, H., Wang, S., Huang, F., Kot, A.C.: Unsupervised domain adaptation for face anti-spooing. IEEE Trans. Inf. Forensics Secur. 13, 1794–1809 (2018)
17. Pinto, A., Pedrini, H., Schwartz, W.R., Rocha, A.: Face spoofing detection through visual codebooks of spectral temporal cubes. IEEE Trans. Image Process 24, 4726–4740 (2015)
18. Yang, J., Lei, Z., Li, S.Z.: Learn convolutional neural network for face anti-spoofing. CoRR, vol. abs/1408.5601, August 2018. http://arxiv.org/abs/1408.5601
19. Benlamoudi, A., Aiadi, K.E., Ouafi, A., et al.: Face antispoofing based on frame difference and multilevel representation. J. Electron. Imaging 26(4), 043007 (2017)
20. Di, W., Hu, H., Jain, A.K.: Face spoof detection with image distortion analysis. IEEE Trans. Inf. Forensics Secur. 10(4), 746–761 (2015)
21. Sutskever, I., Vinyals, O., Le, Q.V.: Sequence to sequence learning with neural networks. In: Proceedings of the Advances in Neural Information Processing Systems (NIPS), Montreal, Canada, pp. 3104–3112 (2014)
22. Luong, M.T., Pham, H., Manning, C.D.: Effective approaches to attention-based neural machine translation. In: Proceedings of the Conference on Empirical Methods in Natural Language Processing(EMNLP), Lisbon, Portugal, pp. 17–21 (2015)
23. Sun, L., Pan, G., Wu, Z., Lao, S.: Blinking-based live face detection using conditional random fields. In: Lee, S.-W., Li, S.Z. (eds.) ICB 2007. LNCS, vol. 4642, pp. 252–260. Springer, Heidelberg (2007). https://doi.org/10.1007/978-3-540-74549-5_27
24. Pan, G., Sun, L., Wu, Z., et al.: Eyeblink-based anti-spoofing in face recognition from a generic webcamera. In: Proceedings of the 2007 IEEE 11th International Conference on Computer Vision, Rio de Janeiro, Brazil, pp. 1–8. IEEE (2007)

25. Gragnaniello, D., Poggi, G., Sansone, C., et al.: An investigation of local descriptors for biometric spoofing detection. IEEE Trans. Inf. Forensics Secur. **10**(4), 849–863 (2015)

26. Mirjalili, V., Ross, A.: Soft biometric privacy: retaining biometric utility of face images while perturbing gender. In: 2017 IEEE International Conference on Biometrics (IJCB), pp. 564–573. IEEE, CO, USA (2017)

27. Li, H., He, P., Wang, S., et al.: Learning generalized deep feature representation for face anti-spoofing. IEEE Trans. Inf. Forensics Secur. **13**, 2639–2652 (2018)

28. Komulainen, J., Hadid, A., Pietikainen, M.: Context based face anti-spoofing. In: IEEE Sixth International Conference on Biometrics: Theory, Applications and Systems, Arlington, US, pp. 1–8 (2013)

29. Yang, J., Lei, Z., Liao, S., Li, S.Z.: Face liveness detection with component dependent descriptor. In: IEEE International Conference on Biometrics, Madrid, Spain, pp. 1–6 (2013)

Generative and Graph Models

Variational Autoencoder with Global- and Medium Timescale Auxiliaries for Emotion Recognition from Speech

Hussam Almotlak[✉], Cornelius Weber[✉], Leyuan Qu[✉], and Stefan Wermter[✉]

Departent of Informatics, Knowledge Technology, University of Hamburg, Hamburg, Germany
{8almotla,weber,qu,wermter}@informatik.uni-hamburg.de
https://www.inf.uni-hamburg.de/en/inst/ab/wtm/

Abstract. Unsupervised learning is based on the idea of self-organization to find hidden patterns and features in the data without the need for labels. Variational autoencoders (VAEs) are generative unsupervised learning models that create low-dimensional representations of the input data and learn by regenerating the same input from that representation. Recently, VAEs were used to extract representations from audio data, which possess not only content-dependent information but also speaker-dependent information such as gender, health status, and speaker ID. VAEs with two timescale variables were then introduced to disentangle these two kinds of information from each other. Our approach introduces a third, i.e. medium timescale into a VAE. So instead of having only a global and a local timescale variable, this model holds a global, a medium, and a local variable. We tested the model on three downstream applications: speaker identification, gender classification, and emotion recognition, where each hidden representation performed better on some specific tasks than the other hidden representations. Speaker ID and gender were best reported by the global variable, while emotion was best extracted when using the medium. Our model achieves excellent results exceeding state-of-the-art models on speaker identification and emotion regression from audio.

Keywords: Unsupervised learning · Feature extraction · Variational autoencoders · VAE with auxiliary variables · Multi-timescale neural network · Speaker identification · Emotion recognition

1 Introduction

Autoencoders have shown an obvious ability to capture the essential features in the data and reduce its dimensionality [4]. They are also, with their non-linear

Supported by Novatec Consulting GmbH, Dieselstrasse 18/1, D-70771 Leinfelden Echterdingen and by the German Research Foundation (DFG) under the transregio Crossmodal Learning TRR-169.

I. Farkaš et al. (Eds.): ICANN 2020, LNCS 12396, pp. 529–540, 2020.
https://doi.org/10.1007/978-3-030-61609-0_42

behavior, preferred for dimensionality reduction over other linear methods such as principal component analysis (PCA) when the data is very high dimensional.

Lately, much effort has been made on the processing of static data like images, and less on the processing of sequential data like audio and videos [12]. Sequential data typically holds instantaneous as well as long-term information. The longterm information in the speech describes specific characteristics from the voice. Some of these characteristics do not change with time, such as health status, age, gender, and speaker ID. Others could change with time like the emotion. This work pays attention to both kinds and aims to preprocess speech data for the first time with a VAE with two auxiliary variables and then uses its low dimensional representations as input to three downstream applications: speaker identification, gender classification, and emotion recognition. It is also the first time to use emotion recognition as a downstream application of a VAE.

The design of the model has the purpose of disentangling between these two kinds of long-term characteristics and also the instantaneous content of information using an auxiliary variable for each. After deriving the mathematical model for a VAE with two auxiliary variables starting with the standard evidence lower bound (ELBO) used for VAEs, results on testing the model will be displayed.

2   Related Work

Over the last years, many architectures were introduced that aim to extract low-dimensional useful representations from high-dimensional data such as images and audio data. An architecture based on variational autoencoders was developed to process audio data [2]. It used only one latent variable and was trained on a small dataset consisting of only 123 utterances in Spanish. The model did deliver slightly better results than the RBM (Restricted Boltzmann Machine), but not good enough for a downstream task.

Later, a model was developed to distinguish global from local timescale speech characteristics in audio data [12]. Its design is based on extending the variational autoencoder with an auxiliary variable h for capturing the global timescale features. This method created an architecture with four probability density distributions. The new architecture consists of the following subnetworks:

1. Global timescale network: takes as input the preprocessed speech audio data and outputs a global latent variable h, which represents information extracted from an entire input-sequence.
2. Local time-scale network: takes as input a concatenation between the sameinput to the global time-scale network and its output. Its output is the local latent variable z. These two networks form unitedly the encoder.
3. The decoder network: takes the local latent variable to predict the nextspeech frame or make a reconstruction on the same input.
4. The predictor network: processes the local latent variable z to extract information from the global time-scale latent variable h hidden inside the local variable z. Its output is the global timescale variable h.

The model was trained and tested on the LibriSpeech dataset [7] (see Sect. 5.1). The performance of this model is compared with the performance of other models in Sect. 6.1. The model has shown excellent results of recognizing the gender of the speaker as well as making speaker identification.

A byte-level language model based on recurrent neural networks (RNNs) was introduced to perform sentiment analysis [11]. Radford et al. aimed to use a simple recurrent neural network (1 layer with 4096 neurons) to get a sufficiently high-level representation of language data with disentangled features. Amazon reviews were used to train and test the model. The learning process was achieved by feeding the network one character (1 byte) and asking it to predict the next one. That means that the new representation of the input is not the output of the network. It is, however, the hidden states. The model has shown good results on sentiment analysis but was not tested on other downstream applications that we are interested in, such as speaker identification and gender classification.

A predictive model was developed for the same goal of learning useful representations from high-dimensional data like images and speech [6]. It was called Contrastive Predictive Coding (CPC), which uses a probabilistic contrastive loss function to finetune the network parameters. For audio speech data, the model was tested on the same LibriSpeech dataset for speaker identification.

3   Proposed Model

Deriving the Mathematical Model. A variational autoencoder solves the problem of discontinuity in the latent space of autoencoders with variational inference, which results in a continuous latent space. Each of the two networks (the encoder and the decoder) is represented as a statistical model in Bayes formula:

$$p(z|x) = \frac{p(x|z) \cdot p(z)}{p(x)}$$

where $p(x)$ is the likelihood of generating the data x, $p(z|x)$ represents the encoder and $p(x|z)$ represents the decoder. Using the latent variable z, we could define a probabilistic model that could learn the distribution of the data x by defining the likelihood $p(x)$, using the tractable components $p(x|z)$ and $p(z)$, as:

$$p(x) = \int p(x, z)dz$$

In this equation we could add another component $\frac{p(z)}{p(z)}$ which does not change it, assuming that $p(z) \neq 0$:

$$p(x) = \int \frac{p(x, z)}{p(z)} \cdot p(z)dz$$

Now we apply logarithm on both sides, and then Jensens inequality rule on the logarithm and the integral on the second side of the equation to set a lower bound on $log[p(x)]$:

$$log[p(x)] \geq E_{p(z)}[log[\frac{p(x, z)}{p(z)}]]$$

$p(z)$ is the prior of z which is a wide distribution with vast areas that are not important for the data distribution, so we replace it by the posterior $p(z|x)$, but calculating the posterior requires components that we even need for our equation, so we approximate it with a function $q(z|x)$. This function can be calculated with a neural network. Now we need to add another term to the equation to ensure that $q(z|x)$ will approximate $p(z|x)$ with a tiny error. For that, we can use the Kullback Leibler divergence (KL). The KL divergence determines how different two distributions are from each other, and it is given for $q(x)$ and $p(x)$ as $KL(q(x) \parallel p(x)) = \int q(x) \cdot log[\frac{q(x)}{p(x)}]\, dx$, by adding this term to the last equation:

$$log[p(x)] \geq E_{q(z|x)}[log[\frac{p(x,z)}{q(z|x)}]] + KL[q(z|x) \parallel p(z|x)]$$

$$\geq E_{q(z|x)}[log[p(x,z)]] + H[q(z|x)] + KL[q(z|x) \parallel p(z|x)]$$

where $H[q(z|x)]$ is the entropy given by: $H[q(z|x)] = -\int q(z|x) \cdot log[q(z|x)]\, dz$. In a similar approach, we consider now the existence of another two sources of information, h and m, which leads to:

$$p(x) = \int \int \int p(x,h,m,z)\, dh\, dm\, dz$$

Now we would multiply and divide with the joint probability of the latent variables $p(h,m,z)$. This probability represents the prior probability which means, that there are many values that do not matter for the desired data distribution x. So we take the posterior instead of the prior probability as it was done before when we took $p(z|x)$ instead of $p(z)$. As for $p(z|x)$, $p(h,m,z|x)$ is impossible to calculate, so we take a similar function $q(h,m,z|x)$ generated by a neural network. The KL divergence term will be ignored since it is not very important for the cost function. That leaves us with:

$$p(x) = \int \int \int p(x,h,m,z) \cdot \frac{q(h,m,z|x)}{q(h,m,z|x)}\, dh\, dm\, dz$$

$$= E_{q(h,m,z|x)}[\frac{p(x,h,m,z)}{q(h,m,z|x)}]$$

Now we take the logarithm of both sides as before and apply the Jensen rule after that:

$$log[p(x)] \geq E_{q(h,m,z|x)}log[\frac{p(x,h,m,z)}{q(h,m,z|x)}]$$

$$\geq E_{q(h,m,z|x)}log[p(m|h,z,x)]$$

$$+ E_{q(h,m,z|x)}log[p(h|z,x)] + E_{q(h,m,z|x)}log[p(x|z)]$$

$$+ E_{q(h,m,z|x)}log[p(z)] - E_{q(h,m,z|x)}log[q(z|h,m,x)]$$

$$- E_{q(h,m,z|x)}log[q(m|h,x)] - E_{q(h,m,z|x)}log[q(h|x)]$$

(1)

$$- E_{q(h,m,z|x)} log[q(z|h, m, x)] = - \int q(h, m, z|x) \cdot log[q(z|h, m, x)]$$

$$= - \int q(z|h, m, x) \cdot q(h, m|x) \cdot log[q(z|h, m, x)] \qquad (2)$$

$$= E_{q(h,m|x)} H[q(z|h, m, x)]$$

$$- E_{q(h,m,z|x)} log[q(m|h, x)] = - \int q(h, m|x) \cdot log[q(m|h, x)]$$

$$= - \int q(m|h, x) \cdot q(h|x) \cdot log[q(m|h, x)] \qquad (3)$$

$$= E_{q(h|x)} H[q(m|h, x)]$$

$$-E_{q(h,m,z|x)} log[q(h|x)] = -E_{q(h|x)} log[q(h|x)] = H[q(h|x)] \qquad (4)$$

By replacing (2), (3) and (4) in (1) and removing variables that do not have an effect on the distribution and introducing hyperparameters α, β, and γ, we get:

$$log[p(x)] \geq E_{q(z|x)} log[p(x|z)]$$
$$+ \alpha(\ E_{q(h|x)} log[p(z)] + E_{q(h,m|x)} H[q(z|h, m, x)])$$
$$+ \beta(\ E_{q(h,z|x)} log[p(m|h, z, x)] + E_{q(h|x)} H[q(m|h, x)]) \qquad (5)$$
$$+ \gamma(\ E_{q(z|x)} log[p(h|z, x)] + H[q(h|x)])$$

This is the final equation for the cost function of a variational autoencoder with two auxiliary variables. The three hyperparameters work as regularization terms on the KL divergence [12].

4   Proposed Architecture

The model introduced in this work is based on the equation of the variational lower bound of an Aux-VAE with two auxiliary variables. There are six different probability distributions, each of which can be modeled using neural networks as shown in Fig. 1. These distributions are as follow:

1. $P(h|x)$ represents the global timescale network, which is modeled as follows: Three blocks, each consists of a convolutional layer with kernel size three and Tanh as an activation function, as well as a batch normalization layer. Followed by a convolutional layer with kernel size one. The stride value is one for all convolutional layers. A global average pooling layer GAP follows to encode global features from the input. The output of GAP is then turned into a normal distribution h with a mean and a standard deviation.

2. $P(m|h, x)$: represents the medium time-scale network, which has the same first three blocks as $p(h|x)$ and then a convolutional layer with kernel size one. After that, instead of applying only one global average pooling on the whole output, the average pooling is applied on a medium duration (1 s) of the output. That makes it possible to encode features in a way different from

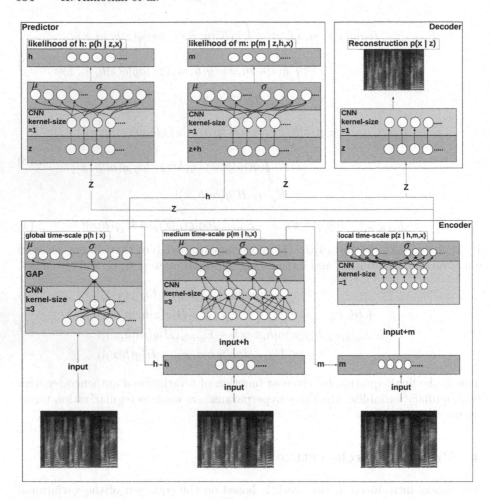

Fig. 1. The structure of the network. The same input goes into the three subnetworks of the encoder. The output of the decoder is the same as its input. Over each subnetwork, the distribution which it represents is written as label.

both the global and the local time-scale networks, an encoding between both. The output of the GAP is turned into a normal distribution called m. This network takes as input a concatenation between the same input as before and a random sample from the distribution h.

3. $P(z|h, m, x)$: represents the local time-scale network. It is modeled by a CNN, which consists of three convolutional layers with kernel size one and batch normalization layers. The Output of the CNN is turned into a normal distribution z. This network takes as input a concatenation between the same input to the last two networks and a random sample from the distribution m.

4. $P(x|z)$: represents the reconstruction network for the input x using the latent variable z. It is also modeled by a CNN with four convolutional layers with kernel size one and batch normalization layers. It takes as input a random sample from the distribution z and reconstructs x from it.

5. $P(m|h, z, x)$: represents the reconstruction network for m using h, z, and x, which is implemented inside z. This network is a CNN of three convolutional layers with kernel size one and batch normalization layers. It takes as input a concatenation between a random sample from h and a random sample from z to output the distribution m.

6. $P(h|z, x)$: represents the reconstruction network for h using z and x, which is implemented inside z. This network is a CNN of two convolutional layers with kernel size one and batch normalization layers. It takes as input a random sample from z and outputs the distribution h.

The first three networks model the encoder, while the forth network models the decoder. The later two networks model the predictor, which predicts the globaland medium-timescale variables from the lcoal-timescale varible.

5 Datasets and Training

5.1 Datasets

LibriSpeech is a corpus of read English speech containing about 1000 h of speech derived from audiobooks and sampled at a rate of 16 kHz. It comprises many subsets such as train-clean-100, which was used in this work for speaker identification and gender recognition. This subset contains 100 h of audio data taken from 251 speakers (126 males and 125 females). The dataset was used very often to train and test models on speaker identification, as in [12] and [6].

One-Minute-Gradual (OMG). Emotion Dataset is a dataset consisting of about 8 h of emotional monolog youtube videos. The videos were separated based on utterances and individual utterances were labeled separately by humans. The labels are the arousal and the valence of the utterance as well as the overall utterance-level emotion. The used emotions are anger, disgust, fear, happy, neutral, sad, and surprise [1].

5.2 Preprocessing and Training

Preprocessing. The main goal here is to reach an effective spectrogram from the audios to be used as input for the variational autoencoder. We found experimentally that a Mel-spectrogram with 140 frequencies achieves these requirements.

Training. The model was trained first for 40 epochs on the LibriSpeech dataset for speaker identification, and after that, 40 epochs on the OMG-Emotion dataset to perform emotion regression with the following hyperparameters for both training processes: Learning rate = 0.0001, batch size = 32 and adam as an optimizer. The hyperparameters of the loss function α, β and γ were determined empirically and set to 0.01.

6   Experiments

6.1   Speaker Identification and Gender Classification

Speaker identification is basically a classification task, where the model takes an audio speech record as input and outputs the label of the speaker. Recently, it was often used as a downstream task to assess how powerful unsupervised-learned representations are. Since the goal of this work is proving the effectiveness of the learned representations by the multi-timescale Aux-VAE proposed in this work, speaker identification and gender classification are essential tasks to compare among the results of the three learned representations by the model, and also with results from previous works. The first step is training the VAE to learn how to extract the representations and then using them as input to a linear classifier. The same procedure was made and the same LibriSpeech dataset was used by [12] for training the Aux-VAE and by [6] for training the CPC.

Table 1. Speaker ID accuracy results compared with previous works on the LibriSpeech dataset; h denotes the global variable, m denotes the medium variable, and z denotes the local variable.

Model	Accuracy
Aux-VAE; h [12]	95.3
Aux-VAE; z [12]	98.1
CPC [6]	97.4
Supervised [6]	98.5
VAE with two auxiliaries; h	**99.86 ± 0.05**
VAE with two auxiliaries; m	98.30 ± 0.20
VAE with two auxiliaries; z	99.68 ± 0.08

As we see in Table 1, the accuracy results of our multi-timescale Aux-VAE using each the global and the local time-scale variables have outperformed the results of both the AuxVAE and the CPC and also the supervised model that was mentioned in [6]. The accuracy results on gender classification are also excellent: global = 97.66%, medium = 96.34%, and local = 98.14%. We can see as well that the global time-scale variable has outperformed the medium variable on both classification tasks, which supports the fact that the global latent variable learns features that are related to the speaker identity better than the medium variable. The local timescale variable was also better than the medium, which was expected because the local latent variable takes as a part of its input a sample from the medium variable, which in his turn takes as a part of its input a sample from the global variable. With that, the local latent variable was able to capture some features by its composed input that the medium variable has missed.

6.2   Visualizing the Latent Spaces Using T-Distributed Stochastic Neighbor Embedding (t-SNE)

T-SNE is an algorithm developed for visualizing multidimensional data, based on the idea of dimensionality reduction. We will use t-SNE plots as in [12] to visualize the latent variables of the VAE and to get an optical feeling of how good they perform. First, the latent representations were acquired for each audio speech record of 8 different speakers with equal gender separation (four females and four males). Each audio record is now a multidimensional data point (512 dimensions). T-SNE was then used to reduce the dimensions to only two for a 2D plot. The speakers from the LibriSpeech dataset were also used in [12] for visualizing the global variable of the Aux-VAE. The clustering and separation between different speakers and genders is here clearer than in [12].

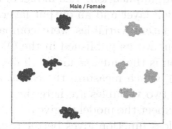
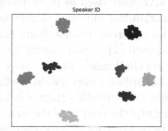

Fig. 2. A plot from the global latent space; the left figure shows the separation between male and female; the right one shows different speakers as the data from each speaker come together to form a separable cluster.

Visualizing the global time-scale variable in Fig. 2, we can see the perfect separation between the two genders, where only drawing one line would be enough to separate the classes. We also see a perfect separation among the speakers; data points of each speaker has made their own cluster.

Visualizing the medium time-scale variable shows that the separation between the two genders is not as perfect as in Fig. 2, where a single line would have been enough to separate the two classes. The visualization also shows a good separation between the speakers. Such results are expected since the results of the speaker identification in Sect. 6.1 were also excellent.

6.3   Emotion Recognition

Each emotion or affective experience can be expressed using at least two properties: arousal, which is a measurement between pleasant and unpleasant, and

Table 2. CCC values of arousal and valence when using the different latent variables. In the first column, the downstream model was trained with MSE. In the second column, the downstream model was trained with CCC; h denotes the global variable, m denotes the medium variable, and z denotes the local one.

Property; Variable	MSE training	CCC training
Arousal; h	0.14668	0.33457
Arousal; m	**0.30027**	**0.3531**
Arousal; z	0.26032	0.32033
Valence; h	0.30452	0.34355
Valence; m	**0.36961**	**0.37399**
Valence; z	0.30650	0.36010

valence, which is a measurement between quiet and active [5]. So instead of fitting a model to classify different emotions such as happy, angry, and sad, we have a downstream application for predicting these two values using a regression model. As in Sect. 6.1 the learned representations of a trained multi-timescale Aux-VAE were used as input to this downstream application. The model of this application has only two dense-layers, one hidden layer and an output layer.

The different results from using different latent variables were compared among each other and among results of previous works published in the OMG-Emotion challenge[1]. The measure of comparison is the same as in the challenge, the Concordance correlation coefficient (CCC), which measures the correlation between two variables (larger is better). These two variables are here the annotations and the output of the model (what we expect the model to give as output and its real output). Since choosing the right loss function gives better results, two different losses were used for training to see which one delivers better results on CCC. First, the model was trained to minimize the mean square error (MSE) between its output and the labels and then using the resulting model to calculate CCC values. Second, the model was trained to maximize CCC directly. From Table 2, we can notice that the CCC value got better on all latent variables and for both arousal and valence when using the CCC as a loss function. Also, we notice instantly that the medium variable is the best among the three in terms of predicting the value of both arousal and valence.

We see also that the CCC values obtained from the medium variable are better than the baseline and all other models that are based on audio for training and testing (see Table 3).

6.4   Gender and Emotion Transformation

These tasks were performed by feeding the global variable (for gender transformation) or the medium variable (for emotion transformation) different input

---

[1] https://www2.informatik.uni-hamburg.de/wtm/omgchallenges/omg_emotion2018_results2018.html.

Table 3. Compares the CCC value on arousal and valence of previous works with m.

Model	Arousal	Valence
AudEERING [13]	0.2925419226	0.361123256087
ExCouple [9]	0.182249525233	0.211179832035
Peng et al. [8]	0.1879	0.256
Deng et al. [3]	0.273	0.266
Pereira et al. [10]	0.17	0.16
Baseline [1]	0.15	0.21
Medium variable m	**0.36961**	**0.37399**

from the others so that the global or the medium encodes the high-level characteristics of a speaker (from opposite gender or other emotion) and give them to the local variable. It can then build a new z distribution for the reconstruction process on the input x. As an example, a gender transformation from male to female was performed. That means the global variable took as input speech data from a female, while the local and medium variables took speech data from a male. The results can be heard in the git repository^2 under "experiments/reconstructions". Gender transformation was performed before using an Aux-VAE with one auxiliary variable [12]. In Fig. 3, we can notice that the content of the audio is still the same, but the fundamental frequency was raised a little bit with some changes. Content of the audio is still the same, but the fundamental frequency was raised a little bit with some changes.

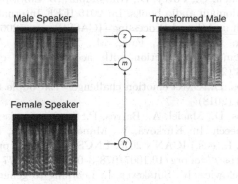

Fig. 3. Transforming the Mel spectrogram of a male using the global characteristics of a female speaker.

---

^{2} https://github.com/Hussam-Almotlak/voice_analysis.

7   Conclusion

We have developed an Aux-VAE, which includes beside the global variable h also an additional medium variable m. We tested the model on audio speech data, where the architecture worked as a multi-timescale model. The experiments have shown that the global variable h is better than the medium m on speaker identification and gender classification, while m is better than h on emotion regression. Our model has also exceeded the state-of-the-art on speaker identification, and emotion regression from speech.

References

1. Barros, P., Churamani, N., Lakomkin, E., Sequeira, H., Sutherland, A., Wermter, S.: The OMG-emotion behavior dataset. In: 2018 International Joint Conference on Neural Networks (IJCNN), pp. 1408–1414. IEEE (2018). https://doi.org/10.1109/IJCNN.2018.8489099
2. Blaauw, M., Bonada, J.: Modeling and transforming speech using variational autoencoders. In: INTERSPEECH, pp. 1770–1774 (2016)
3. Deng, D., Zhou, Y., Pi, J., Shi, B.E.: Multimodal utterance-level affect analysis using visual, audio and text features. arXiv preprint arXiv:1805.00625 (2018)
4. Hsu, W.N., Zhang, Y., Glass, J.: Learning latent representations for speech generation and transformation. arXiv preprint arXiv:1704.04222 (2017)
5. Kuppens, P., Tuerlinckx, F., Russell, J.A., Barrett, L.F.: The relation between valence and arousal in subjective experience. Psychol. Bull. **139**(4), 917 (2013)
6. Oord, A.v.d., Li, Y., Vinyals, O.: Representation learning with contrastive predictive coding. arXiv preprint arXiv:1807.03748 (2018)
7. Panayotov, V., Chen, G., Povey, D., Khudanpur, S.: LibriSpeech: an ASR corpus based on public domain audio books. In: 2015 IEEE International Conference on Acoustics, Speech and Signal Processing (ICASSP), pp. 5206–5210. IEEE (2015)
8. Peng, S., Zhang, L., Ban, Y., Fang, M., Winkler, S.: A deep network for arousal-valence emotion prediction with acoustic-visual cues. arXiv preprint arXiv:1805.00638 (2018)
9. Pereira, I., Santos, D.: OMG emotion challenge - ExCouple team. arXiv preprint arXiv:1805.01576 (2018)
10. Pereira, I., Santos, D., Maciel, A., Barros, P.: Semi-supervised model for emotion recognition in speech. In: Kůrková, V., Manolopoulos, Y., Hammer, B., Iliadis, L., Maglogiannis, I. (eds.) ICANN 2018. LNCS, vol. 11139, pp. 791–800. Springer, Cham (2018). https://doi.org/10.1007/978-3-030-01418-6_77
11. Radford, A., Jozefowicz, R., Sutskever, I.: Learning to generate reviews and discovering sentiment. arXiv preprint arXiv:1704.01444 (2017)
12. Springenberg, S., Lakomkin, E., Weber, C., Wermter, S.: Predictive auxiliary variational autoencoder for representation learning of global speech characteristics. In: Proceedings of INTERSPEECH 2019, pp. 934–938 (2019)
13. Triantafyllopoulos, A., Sagha, H., Eyben, F., Schuller, B.: audEERING's approach to the one-minute-gradual emotion challenge. arXiv preprint arXiv:1805.01222 (2018)

Improved Classification Based on Deep Belief Networks

Jaehoon Koo[iD] and Diego Klabjan[✉]

Northwestern University, Evanston, IL 60208, USA
jh.koo@u.northwestern.edu, d-klabjan@northwestern.edu

Abstract. For better classification, generative models are used to initialize the model and extract features before training a classifier. Typically, separate unsupervised and supervised learning problems are solved. Generative restricted Boltzmann machines and deep belief networks are widely used for unsupervised learning. We developed several supervised models based on deep belief networks in order to improve this two-phase strategy. Modifying the loss function to account for expectation with respect to the underlying generative model, introducing weight bounds, and multi-level programming are all applied in model development. The proposed models capture both unsupervised and supervised objectives effectively. The computational study verifies that our models perform better than the two-phase training approach. In addition, we conduct an ablation study to examine how a different part of our model and a different mix of training samples affect the performance of our models.

Keywords: Classification · Deep belief networks · Deep learning.

1 Introduction

A Restricted Boltzmann machine (RBM), an energy-based model to define an input distribution, is widely used to extract latent features before classification. Such an approach combines unsupervised learning for feature modeling and supervised learning for classification. Two training steps are needed. The first step, called pre-training, is to model features used for classification. This can be done by training a RBM that captures the distribution of input. The second step, called fine-tuning, is to train a separate classifier based on the features from the first step [1]. This two-phase training approach for classification can be also used for deep networks. Deep belief networks (DBN) are built with stacked RBMs, and trained in a layer-wise manner [2]. Two-phase training based on a deep network consists of DBN and a classifier on top of it.

The two-phase training strategy has three possible problems. 1) It requires two training processes; one for training RBMs and one for training a classifier. 2) It is not guaranteed that the modeled features in the first step are useful in the classification phase since they are obtained independently of the classification task. 3) It can be difficult to decide which classifier to use. Therefore, there

© Springer Nature Switzerland AG 2020
I. Farkaš et al. (Eds.): ICANN 2020, LNCS 12396, pp. 541–552, 2020.
https://doi.org/10.1007/978-3-030-61609-0_43

is a need for a method that can conduct feature modeling and classification concurrently [1].

To resolve these problems, recent papers suggest transforming RBMs to a model that can deal with both unsupervised and supervised learning. Since a RBM can calculate the joint and conditional probabilities, the suggested prior models combine a generative and discriminative RBM. Consequently, this hybrid discriminative RBM is trained concurrently for both objectives by summing the two contributions [1,3]. In a similar way, a self-contained RBM for classification is developed by applying the free-energy function based approximation to RBM, which is used for a supervised learning method, reinforcement learning [4]. However, these approaches are limited to transforming RBM that is a shallow network.

In this study, we develop alternative models to solve a classification problem based on DBN. Viewing the two-phase training as two separate optimization problems, we apply optimization modeling techniques in developing our models. Our first approach is to design new objective functions. We design an expected loss function based on $p(h|x)$ built by DBN and the loss function of the classifier. Second, we introduce constraints that bound the DBN weights in the feed-forward phase. The constraints ensure that extracted features are good representations of the input during model training. Third, we apply bilevel programming to the two-phase training method. The bilevel model has a loss function of the classifier in its objective function but it constrains the DBN values to the optimal to phase-1. This model searches possible optimal solutions for the classification objective only where DBN objective solutions are optimal.

Our main contributions are several classification models combining DBN and a loss function in a coherent way. In the computational study we verify that the suggested models perform better than the two-phase method.

2 Literature Review

The two-phase training strategy is applied to many classification tasks on different types of data. Two-phase training with RBM and support vector machine (SVM) is explored in classification tasks on images, documents, and network intrusion data [5–8]. Replacing SVM with logistic regression is explored in [9,10]. Gehler *et al.* [11] use the 1-nearest neighborhood classifier with RBM to solve a document classification task. Hinton and Salakhutdinov [2] suggest a DBN consisting of stacked RBMs that is trained in a layer-wise manner. A two-phase method using DBNs and deep neural networks is used to solve various classification problems such as image and text recognition [2,12,13]. Recently, this approach is applied to motor imagery classification in the area of brain-computer interface [14], biomedical research, classification of Cytochrome P450 1A2 inhibitors and non-inhibitors [15], web spam classification that detects web pages deliberately created to manipulate search rankings [16], and human emotion recognition that classifies physiological signals such as "happy", "relaxed", "disgust", "sad", and "neutral" [17]. All these papers rely on two distinct phases, while our models assume a holistic view of both aspects.

Many studies are conducted to improve the problems of two-phase training. Most of the research is focused on transforming RBMs so that the modified model can achieve generative and discriminative objectives at the same time. Schmah *et al.* [18] propose a discriminative RBM method, and subsequently classification is done in the manner of a Bayes classifier. However, this method cannot capture the relationship between the classes since the RBM for each class is trained separately. Larochelle *et al.* [1,3] propose a self-contained discriminative RBM framework where the objective function consists of the generative learning objective $p(x, y)$, and the discriminative learning objective, $p(y|x)$. Both distributions are derived from RBM. Similarly, a self-contained discriminative RBM method for classification is proposed [4]. The free-energy function based approximation is applied in the development of this method, which is initially suggested for reinforcement learning. This prior paper relies on the RBM conditional probability, while we handle general loss functions. Our models also hinge on completely different principles.

3 Background

Restricted Boltzmann Machines. RBM is an energy-based probabilistic model, which is a restricted version of Boltzmann machines (BM) that is a log-linear Markov Random Field. It has visible nodes x corresponding to input and hidden nodes h matching the latent features. The joint distribution of the visible nodes $x \in \mathbb{R}^J$ and hidden variable $h \in \mathbb{R}^I$ is defined as

$$p(x, h) = \frac{1}{Z} e^{-E(x,h)}, \; E(x, h) = -hWx - ch - bx$$

where $W \in \mathbb{R}^{I \times J}$, $b \in \mathbb{R}^J$, and $c \in \mathbb{R}^I$ are the model parameters, and Z is the partition function. Since units in a layer are independent in RBM, we have the following form of conditional distributions:

$$p(h|x) = \prod_{i=1}^{I} p(h_i|x), \; p(x|h) = \prod_{j=1}^{J} p(x_j|h).$$

For binary units where $x \in \{0, 1\}^J$ and $h \in \{0, 1\}^I$, we can write $p(h_i = 1|x) = \sigma(c_i + W_i x)$ and $p(x_j = 1|h) = \sigma(b_j + W_j x)$ where $\sigma()$ is the sigmoid function. In this manner RBM with binary units is an unsupervised neural network with a sigmoid activation function. The model calibration of RBM can be done by minimizing negative log-likelihood through gradient descent. RBM takes advantage of having the above conditional probabilities which enable to obtain model samples easier through a Gibbs sampling method. Contrastive divergence (CD) makes Gibbs sampling even simpler: 1) start a Markov chain with training samples, and 2) stop to obtain samples after k steps. It is shown that CD with a few steps performs effectively [19,20].

Deep Belief Networks. DBN is a generative graphical model consisting of stacked RBMs. Based on its deep structure DBN can capture a hierarchical representation of input data. Hinton *et al.* (2006) introduced DBN with a training algorithm that greedily trains one layer at a time. Given visible unit x and ℓ hidden layers the joint distribution is defined as [19,21]

$$p(x, h^1, \cdots, h^\ell) = p(h^{\ell-1}, h^\ell) \left(\prod_{k=1}^{\ell-2} p(h^k | h^{k+1}) \right) p(x | h^1).$$

Since each layer of DBN is constructed as RBM, training each layer of DBN is the same as training a RBM.

Classification is conducted by initializing a network through DBN training [12,21]. A two-phase training can be done sequentially by: 1) pre-training, unsupervised learning of stacked RBM in a layer-wise manner, and 2) fine-tuning, supervised learning with a classifier. Each phase requires solving an optimization problem. Given training dataset $D = \{(x^{(1)}, y^{(1)}), \ldots, (x^{(|D|)}, y^{(|D|)})\}$ with input x and label y, the pre-training phase solves the following optimization problem at each layer k

$$\min_{\theta_k} \quad \frac{1}{|D|} \sum_{i=1}^{|D|} \left[-log\, p(x_k^{(i)}; \theta_k) \right]$$

where $\theta_k = (W_k, b_k, c_k)$ is the RBM model parameter that denotes weights, visible bias, and hidden bias in the energy function, and $x_k^{(i)}$ is visible input to layer k corresponding to input $x^{(i)}$. Note that in layer-wise updating manner we need to solve ℓ of the problems from the bottom to the top hidden layer. For the fine-tuning phase we solve the following optimization problem

$$\min_{\phi} \quad \frac{1}{|D|} \sum_{i=1}^{|D|} \left[\mathcal{L}(\phi; y^{(i)}, h(x^{(i)})) \right] \tag{1}$$

where $\mathcal{L}()$ is a loss function, h denotes the final hidden features at layer ℓ, and ϕ denotes the parameters of the classifier. Here for simplicity we write $h(x^{(i)}) = h(x_\ell^{(i)})$. When combining DBN and a feed-forward neural networks (FFN) with sigmoid activation, all the weights and hidden bias parameters among input and hidden layers are shared for both training phases. Therefore, in this case we initialize FFN by training DBN.

4 Proposed Models

We model an expected loss function for classification. Considering classification of two phase method is conducted on hidden space, the probability distribution of the hidden variables obtained by DBN is used in the proposed models. The two-phase method provides information about modeling parameters after each phase is trained. Constraints based on the information are suggested to prevent the model parameters from deviating far from good representation of input. Optimal solution set for unsupervised objective of the two-phase method is good candidate solutions for the second phase. Bilevel model has the set to find optimal solutions for the phase-2 objective so that it conducts the two-phase training in one-shot. We call our models combined models.

DBN Fitting Plus Loss Model. We start with a naive model of summing pre-training and fine-tuning objectives. This model conducts the two-phase training strategy simultaneously; however, we need to add one more hyperparameter ρ to balance the impact of both objectives. The model (DBN+Loss) is defined as

$$\min_{\theta_L, \theta_{DBN}} \mathbb{E}_{\mathbf{y}, \mathbf{x}}[\mathcal{L}(\theta_L; \mathbf{y}, h(\mathbf{x}))] + \rho \, \mathbb{E}_{\mathbf{x}}[- \log p(\mathbf{x}; \theta_{DBN})]$$

and empirically based on training samples D,

$$\min_{\theta_L, \theta_{DBN}} \frac{1}{|D|} \sum_{i=1}^{|D|} \left[\mathcal{L}(\theta_L; y^{(i)}, h(x^{(i)})) - \rho \log p(x^{(i)}; \theta_{DBN}) \right] \tag{2}$$

where θ_L, θ_{DBN} are the underlying parameters. Note that $\theta_L = \phi$ from (1) and $\theta_{DBN} = (\theta_k)_{k=1}$. This model has already been proposed if the classification loss function is based on the RBM conditional distribution [1,3].

Expected Loss Model with DBN Boxing. We first design an expected loss model based on conditional distribution $p(h|x)$ obtained by DBN. This model conducts classification on the hidden space. Since it minimizes the expected loss, it should be more robust and thus it should yield better accuracy on data not observed. The mathematical model that minimizes the expected loss function is defined as

$$\min_{\theta_L, \theta_{DBN}} \mathbb{E}_{\mathbf{y}, \mathbf{h}|\mathbf{x}}[\mathcal{L}(\theta_L; \mathbf{y}, h(\theta_{DBN}; \mathbf{x}))]$$

and empirically based on training samples D,

$$\min_{\theta_L, \theta_{DBN}} \frac{1}{|D|} \sum_{i=1}^{|D|} \left[\sum_h p(h|x^{(i)}) \mathcal{L}(\theta_L; y^{(i)}, h(\theta_{DBN}; x^{(i)})) \right].$$

With notation $h(\theta_{DBN}; x^{(i)}) = h(x^{(i)})$ we explicitly show the dependency of h on θ_{DBN}. We modify the expected loss model by introducing a constraint that sets bounds on DBN related parameters with respect to their optimal values. This model has two benefits. First, the model keeps a good representation of input by constraining parameters fitted in the unsupervised manner. Also, the constraint regularizes the model parameters by preventing them from blowing up while being updated. Given training samples D the mathematical form of the model (EL-DBN) reads

$$\min_{\theta_L, \theta_{DBN}} \frac{1}{|D|} \sum_{i=1}^{|D|} \left[\sum_h p(h|x^{(i)}) \mathcal{L}(\theta_L; y^{(i)}, h(\theta_{DBN}; x^{(i)})) \right]$$
$$\text{s.t.} \quad |\theta_{DBN} - \theta_{DBN}^*| \le \delta$$

where θ_{DBN}^* are the optimal DBN parameters and δ is a hyperparameter. This model needs a pre-training phase to obtain the DBN fitted parameters.

Expected Loss Model with DBN Classification Boxing. Similar to the DBN boxing model, this expected loss model has a constraint that the DBN parameters are bounded by their optimal values at the end of both phases. This model regularizes parameters with those that are fitted in both the unsupervised and supervised manner. Therefore, it can achieve better accuracy even though we need an additional training to the two-phase trainings. Given training samples D the model (EL-DBNOPT) reads

$$\min_{\theta_L, \theta_{DBN}} \frac{1}{|D|} \sum_{i=1}^{|D|} \left[\sum_h p(h|x^{(i)}) \mathcal{L}(\theta_L; y^{(i)}, h(\theta_{DBN}; x^{(i)})) \right] \qquad (3)$$

$$\text{s.t.} \quad |\theta_{DBN} - \theta_{DBNOPT}^*| \le \delta$$

where θ_{DBNOPT}^* are the optimal values of DBN parameters after two-phase training and δ is a hyperparameter.

Feed-Forward Network with DBN Boxing. We also propose a model based on boxing constraints where FFN is constrained by DBN output. The mathematical model (FFN-DBN) based on training samples D is

$$\min_{\theta_L, \theta_{DBN}} \frac{1}{|D|} \sum_{i=1}^{|D|} \left[\mathcal{L}(\theta_L; y^{(i)}, h(\theta_{DBN}; x^{(i)})) \right] \qquad (4)$$

$$\text{s.t.} \quad |\theta_{DBN} - \theta_{DBN}^*| \le \delta.$$

Feed-forward Network with DBN Classification Boxing. Given training samples D this model (FFN-DBNOPT), which is a mixture of (3) and (4), reads

$$\min_{\theta_L, \theta_{DBN}} \frac{1}{|D|} \sum_{i=1}^{|D|} \left[\mathcal{L}(\theta_L; y^{(i)}, h(\theta_{DBN}; x^{(i)})) \right]$$

$$\text{s.t.} \quad |\theta_{DBN} - \theta_{DBNOPT}^*| \le \delta.$$

Bilevel Model. We also apply bilevel programming to the two-phase training method. This model searches optimal solutions to minimize the loss function of the classifier only where DBN objective solutions are optimal. Possible candidates for optimal solutions of the first level objective function are optimal solutions of the second level objective function. This model (BL) reads

$$\min_{\theta_L, \theta_{DBN}^*} \mathbb{E}_{\mathbf{y}, \mathbf{x}}[\mathcal{L}(\theta_L; \mathbf{y}, h(\theta_{DBN}^*; \mathbf{x}))]$$

$$\text{s.t.} \quad \theta_{DBN}^* = \arg\min_{\theta_{DBN}} \mathbb{E}_{\mathbf{x}}[-\log p(\mathbf{x}; \theta_{DBN})]$$

and empirically based on training samples,

$$\min_{\theta_L, \theta_{DBN}^*} \frac{1}{|D|} \sum_{i=1}^{|D|} \left[\mathcal{L}(\theta_L; y^{(i)}, h(\theta_{DBN}^*; x^{(i)})) \right]$$

$$\text{s.t.} \quad \theta_{DBN}^* = \arg\min_{\theta_{DBN}} \frac{1}{|D|} \sum_{i=1}^{|D|} \left[-log\, p(x^{(i)}; \theta_{DBN}) \right].$$

One of the solution approaches to bilevel programming is to apply Karush-Kuhn-Tucker (KKT) conditions to the lower level problem. After applying KKT to the lower level, we obtain

$$\min_{\theta_L, \theta_{DBN}^*} \quad \mathbb{E}_{\mathbf{y},\mathbf{x}}[\mathcal{L}(\theta_L; \mathbf{y}, h(\theta_{DBN}^*; \mathbf{x}))]$$

$$\text{s.t.} \quad \nabla_{\theta_{DBN}} \mathbb{E}_{\mathbf{x}}[-log\, p(\mathbf{x}; \theta_{DBN})|_{\theta_{DBN}^*}] = 0.$$

Furthermore, we transform this constrained problem to an unconstrained problem with a quadratic penalty function:

$$\min_{\theta_L, \theta_{DBN}^*} \mathbb{E}_{\mathbf{y},\mathbf{x}}[\mathcal{L}(\theta_L; \mathbf{y}, h(\theta_{DBN}^*; \mathbf{x}))] + \frac{\mu}{2}||\nabla_{\theta_{DBN}} \mathbb{E}_{\mathbf{x}}[-log\, p(\mathbf{x}; \theta_{DBN})]|_{\theta_{DBN}^*}||^2$$

$$(5)$$

where μ is a hyperparameter. The gradient of the objective function is derived in the appendix.

5   Computational Study

To evaluate the proposed models classification tasks on three datasets are conducted: the KDD'99 network intrusion dataset (NI)[1], the isolated letter speech recognition dataset (ISOLET)[2], and a collection of newswire articles (Reuters)[3]. The experimental results of the proposed models on these datasets are compared to the results of the two-phase method.

In FFNs, we use the sigmoid function in the hidden layers and the softmax function in the output layer, and negative log-likelihood is used as the loss function. We select the hyperparameters based on the settings used in [22], which are fine-tuned. We first implement the two-phase method with DBNs of 1, 2, 3 and 4 hidden layers to find the best configuration for each dataset, and then apply the best configuration to the proposed models.

Implementations are done in Theano using GeForce GTX TITAN X. We use the mini-batch gradient descent method to solve the optimization problems for each model. To calculate the gradients of each objective function of the models Theano's built-in functions, 'theano.tensor.grad,' is used. We denote the two-phase approach as 2-Phase.

---

[1] kdd.ics.uci.edu/databases/kddcup99/kddcup99.html.
[2] archive.ics.uci.edu/ml/datasets/ISOLET.
[3] archive.ics.uci.edu/ml/datasets/reuters-21578+text+categorization+collection.

5.1   Network Intrusion

The classification task on NI is to distinguish between normal and bad connections given the related network connection information. The preprocessed dataset consists of 41 input features and 5 classes, and 4,898,431 examples for training and 311,029 examples for testing. The experiments are conducted on 20%, 30%, and 40% subsets of the whole training set, which are obtained by stratified random sampling. We use the following hyperparameters. Each layer has 15 hidden units and is trained for 100 epochs with learning rate 0.01 during pre-training, and the whole network is trained for 500 epochs with learning rate 0.1 during fine-tuning. The mini-batch size is 1,000, and ρ in the DBN+Loss and μ in the BL model are diminishing during epochs.

On NI the best structure of 2-Phase is 41-15-15-5 for all three datasets, and so we compare it to the proposed models with the same sized networks. We compute the means of the classification errors and their standard deviations for each model averaged over 5 random runs. In each table, we stress in bold the best three models with ties broken by standard deviation. Table 1 shows the experimental results of the proposed models with the same network as the best 2-Phase. BL performs the best in all datasets, achieving the lowest mean classification error without the pre-training step. The difference in the classification error between our best model, BL, and 2-Phase is statistically significant as the p-values are 0.03, 0.01, and 0.03 for 20%, 30%, and 40% datasets, respectively. This shows that the model being trained concurrently for unsupervised and supervised purpose can achieve better accuracy than the two-phase method. Furthermore, both EL-DBNOPT and FFN-DBNOPT yield similar to, or lower mean error rates than 2-Phase in all of the three subsets.

5.2   ISOLET

The classification on ISOLET is to predict which letter-name is spoken among the 26 English alphabets given 617 input features of the related signal processing information. The dataset consists of 5,600 for training, 638 for validation, and 1,559 samples for testing. We use the following hyperparameters. Each layer has 1,000 hidden units and is trained for 100 epochs with learning rate 0.005 during pre-training, and the whole network is trained for 300 epochs with learning rate 0.1 during fine-tuning. The mini-batch size is 20, and ρ in the DBN+Loss and μ in the BL model are diminishing during epochs.

In this experiment the shallow network performs better than the deep network; 617-1000-26 is the best structure for 2-Phase. One possible reason for this is that the training set does not include many samples. EL models perform well on this dataset. EL-DBNOPT achieves the best mean classification error, tied with FFN-DBNOPT. With the same training effort, EL-DBN achieves a lower mean classification error and smaller standard deviation than the two-phase method, 2-Phase. Considering a relatively small sample size of ISOLET, EL shows that it yields better accuracy on unseen data as it minimizes the expected loss, i.e., it generalizes better. In this data set, p-value is 0.07 for the difference in the classification error between our best model, FFN-DBNOPT, and 2-Phase.

Table 1. Classification errors with respect to the best DBN structure

	NI					
	20% dataset		30% dataset		40% dataset	
	Mean	Sd.	Mean	Sd.	Mean	Sd.
2-Phase	8.14%	0.12%	8.18%	0.12%	8.06%	0.02%
DBN+Loss	**8.07%**	**0.06%**	**8.13%**	**0.09%**	**8.05%**	**0.05%**
EL-DBN	8.30%	0.09%	8.27%	0.07%	8.29%	0.14%
EL-DBNOPT	8.14%	0.14%	8.15%	0.15%	8.08%	0.10%
FFN-DBN	8.17%	0.09%	8.20%	0.08%	8.07%	0.11%
FFN-DBNOPT	**8.07%**	**0.12%**	**8.12%**	**0.11%**	**7.95%**	**0.11%**
BL	**7.93%**	**0.09%**	**7.90%**	**0.11%**	**7.89%**	**0.10%**

	ISOLET		Reuters	
	Mean	Sd.	Mean	Sd.
2-Phase	3.94%	0.22%	10.09%	0.16%
DBN+Loss	4.38%	0.20%	**9.77%**	**0.15%**
EL-DBN	**3.91%**	**0.18%**	15.83%	0.12%
EL-DBNOPT	**3.75%**	**0.14%**	**9.65%**	**0.18%**
FFN-DBN	3.94%	0.19%	10.09%	0.13%
FFN-DBNOPT	**3.75%**	**0.13%**	**9.60%**	**0.25%**
BL	4.43%	0.18%	9.79%	0.18%

5.3 Reuters

Reuters is a public dataset of newswire articles, used to predict 52 news categories given 2,000 input features of the most common words. The dataset consists of 6,532 samples for training and validation, and 2,568 samples for testing. We use the following hyperparameters. Each layer has 500 hidden units and is trained for 100 epochs with learning rate 0.1 during pre-training, and the whole network is trained for 500 epochs with learning rate 0.1 during fine-tuning. The mini-batch size is 50, and ρ in the DBN+Loss and μ in the BL model are decreased during epochs.

On this dataset, 2000-500-52 is the best structure for 2-Phase; the shallow network performs better than the deep network. As we pointed out in ISOLET, a small training set is one possible reason for this. As Table 1 shows, FFN-DBNOPT achieves the best mean classification error. It is statistically significant as p-value is 0.01 for the difference in the classification error between our best model, FFN-DBNOPT, and 2-Phase. We find that our combined models, BL and DBN+Loss, obtain better test accuracy than 2-Phase.

5.4 Ablation Study

We conduct an ablation study in order to understand various aspects of our models. First, we study which part of our models is the most influential in classification accuracy. Second, we study how the size of training data affects the performance of our models.

Hybrid 2-Phase and Combined Model. In this ablation study, we examine which part of our networks contributes the most to classification accuracy if some parts of the network are trained based on 2-Phase and the other part by a combined model. We conduct ablation experiments by freezing layer-wise. For a network with three hidden layers, one case is to freeze a hidden layer with weights from 2-Phase while the rest is trained by a combined model; and the other case is to freeze any two hidden layers by 2-Phase weights and the rest is trained by a combined model. In this study, we use NI (40% training set) since its best model structure has more than two hidden layers. Figure 1 shows classification errors on the test set. We find that freezing the top hidden layer obtains higher classification accuracy than freezing the lower layers. We conclude that lower hidden layers in our networks contribute to performance more than higher layers.

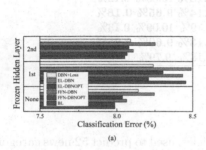 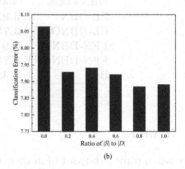

(a)   (b)

Fig. 1. Experimental results for (a) hybrid 2-Phase and combined model and (b) the impact of samples

Impact of Samples. We also conduct an ablation study to understand if our models are affected by the size of training samples. We select the NI dataset as it has the largest set of training samples, and conduct the ablation study on our best model, BL, for this dataset. In order to carry out a meaningful ablation study with respect to the effect of samples on BL, we formulate a model by combining BL and 2-Phase and training on all samples, but one portion of samples is subject to BL while the remaining samples use 2-Phase. Formally, given training dataset $D = S \cup \bar{S}$, our ablation model reads

$$\min \quad \frac{1}{|S|} \sum_{i \in |S|} \mathcal{J}_{\mathrm{BL}}^i + \frac{1}{|\bar{S}|} \sum_{i \in |\bar{S}|} \mathcal{L}_{\text{2-Phase}}^i$$

where $\mathcal{J}_{\mathrm{BL}}$ denotes the loss function of BL as defined in (5), and $\mathcal{L}_{\text{2-Phase}}$ denotes the loss function of 2-Phase. Model weights are shared by both models. We use the same setting of hyperparameters as in Sect. 5.1. We conduct experiments on different sizes of S and $\bar{S}$, and each experiment uses five random runs to create each S by sampling from training set. Figure 1 shows test accuracy on different sizes of S. Note that $\frac{|S|}{|D|} = 0$ corresponds to pure 2-Phase while $\frac{|S|}{|D|} = 1$ means using solely BL on all samples. We observe that as we increase the size of S, the classification error on test decreases. In addition, we find that test error drops sharply once the BL is actually introduced (ratio = 0.2). We conclude that the impact of BL is very pronounced. Even if BL is used only a small fraction of samples (while the remaining samples are treated by 2-Phase), it improves the performance significantly.

From both studies, we conclude that using a combined model only a subset of a network or samples has a significant benefit.

6 Conclusion

DBN+Loss performs better than two-phase training 2-Phase in two instances. Aggregating two unsupervised and supervised objectives is effective. Second, the models with DBN boxing, EL-DBN and FFN-DBN, do not perform better than 2-Phase in almost all datasets. Regularizing the model parameters with unsupervised learning is not so effective in solving a supervised learning problem. Third, the models with DBN classification boxing, EL-DBNOPT and FFN-DBNOPT, perform better than 2-Phase in almost all of the experiments. FFN-DBNOPT is consistently one of the best three performers in all instances. This shows that classification accuracy can be improved by regularizing the model parameters with the values trained for unsupervised and supervised purpose. One drawback of this approach is that one more training phase to the two-phase approach is necessary. Last, BL shows that one-step training can achieve a better performance than two-phase training.

References

1. Larochelle, H., Mandel, M., Pascanu, R., Bengio, Y.: Learning algorithms for the classification restricted Boltzmann machine. J. Mach. Learn. Res. **13**, 643 669 (2012)
2. Hinton, G.E., Salakhutdinov, R.R.: Reducing the dimensionality of data with neural networks. Science **313**(5786), 504–507 (2006)
3. Larochelle, H., Bengio, Y.: Classification using discriminative restricted Boltzmann machines. In: International Conference on Machine Learning (ICML), Helsinki, Finland, vol. 25, pp. 536–543 (2008)
4. Elfwing, S., Uchibe, E., Doya, K.: Expected energy-based restricted Boltzmann machine for classification. Neural Networks **64**, 29–38 (2015)
5. Dahl, G.E., Adams, R.P., Larochelle, H.: Training restricted Boltzmann machines on word observations. In: International Conference on Machine Learning (ICML), Edinburgh, Scotland, UK, vol. 29, pp. 679–686 (2012)
6. Norouzi, M., Ranjbar, M., Mori, G.: Stacks of convolutional restricted Boltzmann machines for shift-invariant feature learning. In: IEEE Computer Society Conference on Computer Vision and Pattern Recognition Workshops (CVPR), Miami, FL, USA, pp. 2735–2742 (2009)

7. Salama, M.A., Eid, H.F., Ramadan, R.A., Darwish, A., Hassanien, A.E.: Hybrid intelligent intrusion detection scheme. Adv. Intell. Soft Comput. **96**, 293–303 (2011)
8. Xing, E.P., Yan, R., Hauptmann, A.G.: Mining associated text and images with dual-wing Harmoniums. In: Conference on Uncertainty in Artificial Intelligence (UAI), vol. 21, Edinburgh, Scotland, pp. 633–641 (2005)
9. Cho, K., Ilin, A., Raiko, T.: Improved learning algorithms for restricted Boltzmann machines. In: Artificial Neural Networks and Machine Learning (ICANN), vol. 21. Springer, Heidelberg (2011)
10. Mccallum, A., Pal, C., Druck, G., Wang, X.: Multi-conditional learning: generative/discriminative training for clustering and classification. In: National Conference on Artificial Intelligence (AAAI), vol. 21, pp. 433–439 (2006)
11. Gehler, P.V., Holub, A. D., Welling, M.: The rate adapting poisson (RAP) model for information retrieval and object recognition. In: International Conference on Machine Learning (ICML), Pittsburgh, PA, USA, vol. 23, pp. 337–344 (2006)
12. Bengio, Y., Lamblin, P.: Greedy layer-wise training of deep networks. In: Advances in Neural Information Processing Systems (NeurIPS), vol. 20, pp. 153–160. MIT Press (2007)
13. Sarikaya, R., Hinton, G.E., Deoras, A.: Application of deep belief networks for natural language understanding. IEEE/ACM Trans. Audio Speech Lang. Process. **22**(4), 778–784 (2014)
14. Lu, N., Li, T., Ren, X., Miao, H.: A deep learning scheme for motor imagery classification based on restricted Boltzmann machines. IEEE Trans. Neural Syst. Rehabil. Eng. **25**, 566–576 (2017)
15. Yu, L., Shi, X., Shengwei, T.: Classification of cytochrome P450 1A2 of inhibitors and noninhibitors based on deep belief network. Int. J. Comput. Intell. Appl. **16**, 1750002 (2017)
16. Li, Y., Nie, X., Huang, R.: Web spam classification method based on deep belief networks. Expert Syst. Appl. **96**(1), 261–270 (2018)
17. Hassan, M.M., Alam, G.R., Uddin, Z., Huda, S., Almogren, A., Fortino, G.: Human emotion recognition using deep belief network architecture. Inf. Fusion **51**, 10–18 (2019)
18. Schmah, T., Hinton, G.E., Zemel, R.S., Small, S.L., Strother, S.: Generative versus discriminative training of RBMs for classification of fMRI images. In: Advances in Neural Information Processing Systems (NeurIPS), vol. 21, pp. 1409–1416. Curran Associates Inc. (2009)
19. Bengio, Y.: Learning deep architectures for AI. Found. Trends Mach. Learn. **2**(1), 1–127 (2009)
20. Hinton, G.E.: Training products of experts by minimizing contrastive divergence. Neural Comput. **14**(8), 1771–1800 (2002)
21. Hinton, G.E., Osindero, S., Teh, Y.W.: A fast learning algorithm for deep belief nets. Neural Comput. **18**(7), 1527–54 (2006)
22. Wang, B., Klabjan, D.: Regularization for unsupervised deep neural nets. In: National Conference on Artificial Intelligence (AAAI), vol. 31, pp. 2681–2687 (2017)

Temporal Anomaly Detection by Deep Generative Models with Applications to Biological Data

Takaya Ueda[✉][iD], Yukako Tohsato[iD], and Ikuko Nishikawa[iD]

Ritsumeikan University, Kyoto, Shiga, Japan
is0203xf@ed.ritsumei.ac.jp

Abstract. An approach to anomaly detection is to use a partly disentangled representation of the latent space of a generative model. In this study, generative adversarial networks (GAN) are used as the normal data generator, and an additional encoder is trained to map data to the latent space. Then, a data anomaly can be detected by a reconstruction error and a position in the latent space. If the latent space is disentangled (in a sense that some latent variables are interpretable and can characterize the data), the anomaly is also characterized by the mapped position in the latent space. The present study proposes a method to characterize temporal anomalies in time series using Causal InfoGAN, proposed by Kurutach et al., to disentangle a state space of the dynamics of time-series data. Temporal anomalies are quantified by the transitions in the acquired state space. The proposed method is applied to four-dimensional biological dataset: morphological data of a genetically manipulated embryo. Computer experiments are conducted on three-dimensional data of the cell (nuclear) division dynamics in early embryonic development of *C. elegans*, which lead to the detection of morphological and temporal anomalies caused by the knockdown of lethal genes.

Keywords: Unsupervised anomaly detection · Generative model · Disentangled representation · Causal InfoGAN · Encoder · Time series data · Biological dynamic data

1   Introduction

Anomaly detection can be implemented by modeling the probability distribution of "normal" data and detecting the outliers that have a low probability. If both normal and abnormal data distributions are well-defined, anomaly detection is an instance of two-class classification. However, in most situations, all possible varieties of abnormal data are not known in advance, while the normal data distribution can be defined. Therefore, a generative model for the normal distribution can be effectively used to detect abnormal data with unsupervised training.

Supported by JSPS KAKENHI Grant Number 19K12164.

Variational autoencoder (VAE) [6] and generative adversarial networks (GAN) [2] are two well-known generative models based on neural networks. The data distribution is expressed by a probability distribution in a lower-dimensional latent space of those generators.

The first model, VAE, is composed of an encoder and a decoder. The encoder part is trained to map a data distribution to an arbitrary distribution in a latent space, while the decoder part is trained to reconstruct an input data from its mapped point in the latent space. Therefore, if training data are sampled from a normal data distribution, the acquired latent space contains all necessary features to reconstruct any normal data. Further, an abnormality cannot be expressed in the latent space. Thus, an abnormal data can be detected by a large reconstruction error, or by a large deviation from the normal distribution in the latent space.

The second model, GAN, is composed of a generator and a discriminator. The generator is trained to acquire a map from a latent space to a data space in an adversarial way against the discriminator. Therefore, if the training data are sampled from a normal data distribution, the acquired latent space can generate any normal data but cannot generate an abnormal data. Thus, an abnormal data is discriminated as a sample without a corresponding point in the latent space.

The following approaches were proposed to search for the optimal corresponding point in the latent space for each data with a minimum reconstruction error. AnoGAN proposed by Schlegl et al. [13] updates a point in the latent space to decrease the reconstruction error between the original data and generated data. ALAD proposed by Zenati et al. [17], or f-AnoGAN [12] as a modification of AnoGAN, adds an encoder to be attached to the generator. Then, the abnormality is detected by the reconstruction error.

The above approach can be extended to the temporal anomaly detection. For the time-series data, a recurrent neural network can be used for VAE and GAN. For example, GGM-VAE proposed by Guo et al. [3] implemented a gated recurrent unit (GRU) for an encoder and a decoder in VAE. Li et al. [9] used a long short-term memory (LSTM) unit for a generator and a discriminator in GAN. The temporal anomaly is mainly discriminated by the reconstruction error at each time step.

If input data are well reconstructed, then each data is represented by the corresponding point in the latent space, and an outlying position can also be used for anomaly detection. Furthermore, if any interpretable latent variable is obtained in the latent space, its value can be used to characterize and quantify the anomaly. As an original approach to obtain such disentangled representation of the latent space, Chen et al. proposed InfoGAN [1], where some latent variables are trained to express independent features of the data (such as thickness, tilt, and class of a handwritten character) by maximizing mutual information between the variables and the generated data. Moreover, Causal InfoGAN [7] extended the approach aiming to extract a subspace of a latent space as a state space, which expresses inherent dynamics of time-series data. The state space is obtained by the InfoGAN framework, where the generator is trained to generate a pair of samples at two successive time steps, and the time development is express as a transition rule in the state space.

The present study proposes temporal anomaly detection in time-series data based on the disentangled representation for the time development by Causal InfoGAN. Moreover, a temporal anomaly is quantified using the obtained state space. First, a generator is trained by normal time-series data. Then, an encoder is attached to the obtained generator. The encoder is trained to map an input data to a point in the latent space, optimizing the reconstruction error [14, 15]. Then, the time development of time-series data is expressed by the trajectory in the state space, and the temporal anomaly is detected and quantified by the abnormal trajectory.

The rest of this paper is organized as follows. Section 2 describes the existing approach of Causal InfoGAN. Section 3 presents our encoder-based model of anomaly detection. Section 4 presents the application of the proposed method and the anomaly score to biological data. Phenotype anomalies, including morphological and temporal anomalies during the cell division process, are characterized for each embryo of C. elegans, where a particular lethal gene is knocked down.

Our original contributions are summarized as follows:

- Anomalies are detected and quantified by the position in the latent space, owing to the disentangled representation, not by the reconstruction error as the most existing methods.
- Temporal anomalies are quantified by the normal dynamics acquired in a disentangled state space based on Causal InfoGAN.
- Phenotype anomalies in the biological system are quantified as the first approach using deep neural networks for four-dimensional biological data.

2 Disentangled Representation by Causal InfoGAN

This section describes related work. Specifically, GAN by Goodfellow ey al. [2], InfoGAN by Chen et al. [1], and Causal InfoGAN by Kurutach et al. [7] are described as the basis of our method from Sect. 3.

GAN is a deep generative model that acquires distribution $P(\mathbf{x})$ of data $\mathbf{x}$. Data generator G is a map from a low-dimensional latent variable $\mathbf{z} \sim P(\mathbf{z})$ to a data point. Discriminator D is trained to output the probability ratio of whether data $\mathbf{x}$ is sampled from the real data distribution $P(\mathbf{x})$ or generated as $G(\mathbf{z})$. The correct label is given only to D, and G learns distribution $P(\mathbf{x})$ by deceiving D. The objective function for training both networks is given by

$$\min_{G} \max_{D} V(G, D) = \mathbb{E}_{\mathbf{x} \sim P(\mathbf{x})}[\log D(\mathbf{x})] + \mathbb{E}_{\mathbf{z} \sim P(\mathbf{z})}[\log (1 - D(G(\mathbf{z})))] \ . \quad (1)$$

After the training, stochastic variable $\mathbf{z}$, which is used as a latent input variable of G, obtains the necessary features to generate data $\mathbf{x}$. If element z_i of i-th dimension possesses any interpretable feature of the data, it is useful to characterize or control generated data $\mathbf{x}$. Therefore, the acquisition of such disentangled representation is important in the generative model.

InfoGAN [1] is a direct approach to make some latent variables interpretable. The latent space is decomposed into an interpretable subspace $\mathbf{s}$ and the others $\mathbf{z}$, and the mutual information between $\mathbf{s}$ and a generated data $\mathbf{x}$ from $(\mathbf{z}, \mathbf{s})$ by G is an additional objective function, which should be maximized during the GAN training. Then, each s_i becomes correlated with any observable feature of generated data $\mathbf{x} = G(\mathbf{z}, \mathbf{s})$. During the training, auxiliary probability distribution $Q(\mathbf{s}|\mathbf{x})$ of $\mathbf{s}$ conditioned by generated data $\mathbf{x}$ is introduced as the maximization target. As a result, the objective function for training three networks (G, D, and Q) is given by

$$\min_{G,Q} \max_{D} V(G, D, Q) - \lambda \mathbb{E}_{\mathbf{s}\sim P(\mathbf{s}), \mathbf{z}\sim P(\mathbf{z}), \mathbf{x}\sim G(\mathbf{z},\mathbf{s})} [\log Q(\mathbf{s}|\mathbf{x})] \ . \tag{2}$$

In a similar approach, Causal InfoGAN [7] (CIGAN) aims to obtain a subspace, denoted a state space, which represents the inherent dynamics of time-series data. Generator G in CIGAN is trained to generate a pair of data $\mathbf{x}$ and $\mathbf{x}'$, which are two successive data of a time series. Input to G are a pair of state variables $\mathbf{s}$ and $\mathbf{s}'$, which generate $\mathbf{x}$ and $\mathbf{x}'$, respectively, and the other latent variable $\mathbf{z}$, which is common to both $\mathbf{x}$ and $\mathbf{x}'$. Then, the output is given as a pair of samples $(\mathbf{x}, \mathbf{x}') = G(\mathbf{z}, \mathbf{s}, \mathbf{s}')$. The subsequent state $\mathbf{s}'$ is given by the stochastic transition rule $T(\mathbf{s}'|\mathbf{s})$ in the state space, which is also acquired through the training. The goal of G is to generate a realistic pair of samples $\mathbf{x}$ and $\mathbf{x}'$ at two consecutive time points. Discriminator D is conversely trained to discriminate whether a pair $\mathbf{x}$ and $\mathbf{x}'$ is sampled from real time-series data $P(\mathbf{x}, \mathbf{x}')$ or generated by G. As a result, the objective function for training three networks (G, D, and T) is given by

$$V(G, D, T) = \mathbb{E}_{\mathbf{x},\mathbf{x}'\sim P(\mathbf{x},\mathbf{x}')} [\log D(\mathbf{x}, \mathbf{x}')] + \mathbb{E}_{\substack{\mathbf{z}\sim P(\mathbf{z}), \mathbf{s}\sim P(\mathbf{s}), \\ \mathbf{s}'\sim T(\mathbf{s}'|\mathbf{s})}} [\log(1 - D(G(\mathbf{z}, \mathbf{s}, \mathbf{s}')))].$$

$$\tag{3}$$

In addition, to enforce that the time development in time series from $\mathbf{x}$ to $\mathbf{x}'$ is expressed only by the transition of state variable from $\mathbf{s}$ to $\mathbf{s}'$ but never by the other variable $\mathbf{z}$, mutual information is introduced exactly as in InfoGAN. Here, the mutual information between $(\mathbf{s}, \mathbf{s}')$ and generated data $(\mathbf{x}, \mathbf{x}')$ from $(\mathbf{z}, \mathbf{s}, \mathbf{s}')$ by G is added to the objective function, which should be maximized in the training. Again, auxiliary probability distribution $Q(\mathbf{s}, \mathbf{s}'|\mathbf{x}, \mathbf{x}')$ of the input state value conditioned by generated data is introduced. Finally, the objective function for the training of four networks (G, D, T, and Q) is given by

$$\min_{G,T,Q} \max_{D} V(G, D, T, Q) - \lambda \mathbb{E}_{\substack{\mathbf{z}\sim P(\mathbf{z}), \mathbf{s}\sim P(\mathbf{s}), \mathbf{s}'\sim T(\mathbf{s}'|\mathbf{s}), \\ \mathbf{x},\mathbf{x}'\sim G(\mathbf{z},\mathbf{s},\mathbf{s}')}} [\log Q(\mathbf{s}, \mathbf{s}'|\mathbf{x}, \mathbf{x}')]. \tag{4}$$

Stochastic transition T in Causal InfoGAN [7] is given by Gaussian perturbation to the present state $\mathbf{s}$, and the next state is drawn as $\mathbf{s}' \sim N(\mathbf{s}, \boldsymbol{\sigma}(\mathbf{s}))$. For the

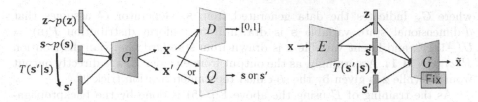

(a) First step for the generator training by
Causal InfoGAN

(b) Second step for the encoder training
by the proposed method

Fig. 1. Two steps of training to characterize time series data

simplicity, variance-covariance σ of the Gaussian is assumed as diagonal, and it is implemented by a simple layered neural network. Furthermore, $Q(\mathbf{s}, \mathbf{s}'|\mathbf{x}, \mathbf{x}')$ is given by a symmetric and decomposed form as $Q(\mathbf{s}, \mathbf{s}'|\mathbf{x}, \mathbf{x}') = Q(\mathbf{s}|\mathbf{x}) \cdot Q(\mathbf{s}'|\mathbf{x}')$.

3   Temporal Anomaly Detection Using an Encoder

This section describes the proposed method. First, an encoder attached to the obtained generator of the above Causal InfoGAN framework is described in Sect. 3.1. The goal is to infer and characterize the dynamics of the input time-series data. Then, a method is proposed to quantify the temporal anomaly from the inferred latent state in Sect. 3.2.

3.1   Encoder to Infer the Temporal State of the Input Data

Our method [14,15] introduces the encoder to use the latent space of the generator for anomaly detection. The approach is similar to f-AnoGAN [12], though our proposed loss function to be minimized in the encoder training is given alternatively by following Eq. (5) and (6).

The latent space of the generator in CIGAN is expected to be decomposed into state space $\mathbf{s}$, which represents a temporal evolution, and the complementary subspace $\mathbf{z}$ for the other features. Because of the independence between $\mathbf{s}$ and $\mathbf{z}$ forced by the training, a set of data $\mathbf{x}$ from one time series possess a common $\mathbf{z}$, and each data is given by a successive transition in $\mathbf{s}$. The encoder is trained to be an inverse mapping of generator G, which outputs $\mathbf{s}$ and $\mathbf{z}$ from data $\mathbf{x}$.

Two steps of training in the proposed method are shown in Fig. 1.

In the first step, generator G, discriminator D, and auxiliary probability distribution Q are trained by the data of the normal time series by the framework of CIGAN (Fig. 1(a)). Then, in the second step, encoder E is trained, while the obtained parameters of G are fixed (Fig. 1(b)). The loss function to be minimized during the training of the encoder is given by the following reconstruction error for input data $\mathbf{x}$ in L2 norm:

$$\mathcal{L}_\mathbf{X}(E) = \mathbb{E}_{\mathbf{s}' \sim T(\mathbf{s}'|\mathbf{s}), (\mathbf{s}, \mathbf{z}) \sim E(\mathbf{x}), \mathbf{x} \sim P(\mathbf{x})}[\|\mathbf{x} - G_\mathbf{x}(\mathbf{s}, \mathbf{s}', \mathbf{z})\|^2], \tag{5}$$

where G_x indicates the data generated from s. Generator G assumes that d-dimensional state variable s is drawn from uniform distribution $P(s) = U(-1,1)^d$, and latent variable z is drawn from standard Gaussian distribution $P(z) = N(0,1)$. Accordingly, as the output from encoder E, s is directly output from E, while z is given by the so-called reparameterization trick [6].

As the training of E using the above Eq. (5) is done by the backpropagation while keeping G fixed, the efficiency becomes low in general. Therefore, an alternative loss function is introduced, which forces composite function $E \circ G$ be the identity in the latent space $s \times z$. Furthermore, to enforce that a pair of generated samples (x and x') share the common z, the second term is added to the following loss function to be minimized:

$$\mathcal{L}_{SZ}(E) = \mathbb{E}_{\substack{(x,x') \sim G(s,s',z), s' \sim T(s'|s), \\ s \sim P(s), z \sim P(z)}} [\|(s,z) - E(x)\|^2 + \alpha \|z - E_Z(x')\|^2] , \quad (6)$$

where α is a non-negative parameter and E_Z indicates z output from E.

Finally, the training of encoder E uses both loss functions $\mathcal{L}_X$ and $\mathcal{L}_{SZ}$, alternately with a certain ratio.

3.2 Characterization of the Temporal Anomaly by the State Space

Encoder E trained by normal time-series data is used for the anomaly detection. In particular, the dynamics of data x is characterized by s inferred by E. The obtained transition rule T for s indicates a velocity field of a flow in the state space, and the deviation from the normal flow is detected as a temporal anomaly.

In Sect. 4, biological time-series data are analyzed by the proposed method. In this case, the time evolution of the normal population is obtained in the state space, and each point in the state space corresponds to a certain normal age distribution. The deviation from the normal age at each time step of data x is used to characterize and quantify the temporal anomaly of x. The detailed definition of the anomaly score for the case study is given in Sect. 4.4.

4 Detection of Phenotype Anomalies in a Biological Data

Proposed method is applied to a biological time series data. Normal data is defined as a wild type (WT) organism with a certain distribution, and phenotype anomaly detection is a target in reverse genetics. Data described in Sect. 4.1 is three dimensional time series data of a cell division process in an early embryonic development of a nematode, $C.$ $elegans$. After each essential gene is specifically silenced in a fertilized egg, a morphological anomaly observed during the development is considered to be caused by the malfunction of the silenced gene. Our model structure and the parameter settings for the training are given in Sect. 4.2. Then, the obtained state space is shown in Sect. 4.3, and the detected temporal anomaly is given in Sect. 4.4.

4.1   Three Dimensional Time Series Data of Cell Division

Caenorhabditis elegans (*C. elegans*) is a nematode, which has been extensively studied as a model organism of the multicellular animals. In particular, the development and differentiation process of all the cells, from a fertilized egg to an adult, has been revealed as the cell lineage. Related genetic regulations are also studied. Reverse genetics is an approach to discovering a gene function by analyzing the phenotype of a specifically manipulated gene sequence. RNA interference (RNAi) is one of these manipulation techniques, where RNA molecules inhibit a specific gene expression or translation.

Worm developmental dynamics database (WDDD) [8] is the public database provided by RIKEN, which contains the data of cell division dynamics in early embryos of *C. elegans*. Each essential embryonic gene is silenced by RNAi. Time series of three-dimensional differential contrast interference (DIC) microscopy for each embryo is provided, together with the nucleus regions obtained by image segmentation. One of 72 essential genes is knocked down in each RNAi embryo. DIC image is preprocessed into three-dimensional data of $55 \times 40 \times 40$ voxels, where each side length of a voxel is 5.0, 1.05, and 1.05 μm, respectively. Figure 2 shows an example of WT data during the two-cell stage, with time length 20, for this embryo. Temporal change of two nucleus regions is shown as sliced images stacked along z axis.

A total of 50 samples of WT embryos and 136 samples of RNAi embryos are obtained. A total of 45 WT samples are used for the training, while 5 samples are left for the test to set the threshold for the anomaly. In the following experiments, the data in the two-cell stage are used. Two cells are named AB and P_1, and AB will form an anterior part of a worm, while P_1 will be a posterior. In the two-cell stage, the axis from anterior to posterior (AP axis) can be identified, while the axis of ventral and dorsal, or the axis of left and right of the body, is still undefined. As a result, the normalization of the three-dimensional posture is impossible, as the rotation symmetry around AP axis remains. Therefore, for the experiments, three-dimensional DIC data at each time step are normalized in the position by the center and AP axis and then rotated by 30 degrees around the axis. Thus, 12 samples are generated from one original volume data sample. As the time length of the two-cell stage is approximately 20 time steps for WT, the total number of training samples becomes 10,452, as 45 (WT data) $\times$ time length per each embryo $\times$ 12 (rotations).

Related work was reported by Yang et al. [16] for the phenotype analysis. Although the same data on WDDD were used, the original parameters were defined in the preprocessing step into the volume data, while the present study uses the parameters in the database. They focused on the asymmetric division into two cells, and the anomaly was characterized by the principal component analysis on several handcrafted features.

4.2   Network Structure of the Model

Structure of each network of the proposed model is shown in Table 1. All convolutional layers in all networks are given by three-dimensional filters. Discriminator

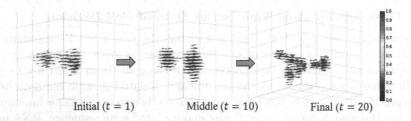

Initial ($t = 1$)   Middle ($t = 10$)   Final ($t = 20$)

Fig. 2. Example of nucleus regions in two-cell stage of a WT embryo. The color indicates the density by a value in $[0, 1]$ obtained by the reconstruction from the original pixel value in $\{0, 1\}$ in DIC depth images. Left: after the division from one cell ($t = 1$). Middle: round shapes of two nuclei. Right: before the division into four cells ($t = 20$).

Table 1. Network structure of the proposed model

D/Q	G
$\mathbf{x}, \mathbf{x'} \in R^{55 \times 40 \times 40 \times 2}$ for D and $\mathbf{x}$ for Q	$\mathbf{z} \in R^{32} \sim N(\mathbf{0}, \mathbf{1}), \mathbf{s} \in R^2 \sim U[-1, -1]^2, \mathbf{s'}$
5^3 Conv3D, out 32, stride 2, lReLU, SN	5^3 Deconv3D, out 128, stride 2, ReLU, BN
5^3 Conv3D, out 64, stride 2, lReLU, SN, Mnibatch-std	5^3 Deconv3D, out 64, stride 2, ReLU, BN
5^3 Conv3D, out 128, stride 2, lReLU, SN	5^3 Deconv3D, out 32, stride 2, ReLU, BN
fc. 4096 → 1 for D and fc. 4096 → 2 for Q	5^3 Deconv3D, out 2, stride 2, sigmoid

E
$\mathbf{x} \in R^{55 \times 40 \times 40 \times 1}$
5^3 Conv3D, out 32, stride 2, lReLU, BN
5^3 Conv3D, out 64, stride 2, lReLU, BN
5^3 Conv3D, out 128, stride 2, lReLU, BN
fc. 4096 → 32 for μ, fc. 4096 → 32 for σ and fc. 4096 → 2 for $\mathbf{s}$

D and auxiliary network Q share the layers, except the final fully connected layer. Transition rule T is given by the three-layered fully connected network with 100 hidden units, whose activation function is given by a rectified linear unit (ReLU). Adam optimization is used during the training. Spectral normalization (SN) [11] is used to train D and Q, and batch normalization (BN) [4] is used to train generator G, to improve the acquisition of the disentangled representation [10]. Furthermore, Minibatch-std [5] is used for the second layer of D and Q to maintain the data diversity.

The hyperparameters in the objective functions for the training are set to $\lambda = 1$ and $\alpha = 1$. The ratio of using two loss functions $\mathcal{L}_X$ and $\mathcal{L}_{SZ}$ in the encoder training is set to $50 : 1$ in each iteration.

4.3 Visualization of the Cell Division in the Obtained State Space

The latent space obtained through the proposed method using WT data as normal time-series data is visualized as follows. Figure 3 shows the generated

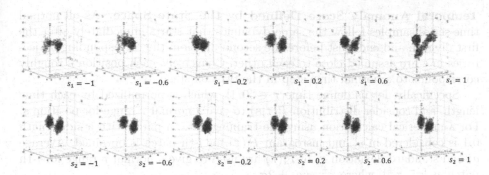

Fig. 3. Visualization of the acquired state space by the generated data. The upper figures are the data generated from $s_1 = -1, -0.6, ..., +1$ with fixed $s_2 = 0$ and $\mathbf{z} = \mathbf{0}$, which corresponds to the initial and to the final stage in the two-cell stage, from left to right. The lower figures are the data generated from $s_2 = -1, -0.6, ..., +1$ with fixed $s_1 = 0$ and $\mathbf{z} = \mathbf{0}$, and no obvious change is found.

data from latent space $\mathbf{s} \times \mathbf{z}$. Here, $\mathbf{z}$ is fixed at $\mathbf{0}$, while two-dimensional state value $\mathbf{s} = (s_1, s_2)$ is changed in $[-1, 1]^2$. Moreover, in Fig. 3, s_2 is fixed in the upper row, and s_1 is changed from -1 to $+1$ by 0.4. Then, a generated data sample changes from the initial to the final stage of two-cell stage, as shown in Fig. 2.

In contrast, s_1 is fixed in the lower row, and s_2 is changed from -1 to $+1$ by 0.4. Then, no clear difference is seen in the generated data. Thus, the time development seems mainly coded in s_1. Furthermore, no rotational change around AP axis is observed in state space $\mathbf{s}$ for the fixed $\mathbf{z}$.

4.4 Temporal Anomaly Detection Quantified by the State Space

A temporal anomaly in the two-cell stage, such as delayed growth, is detected as follows. Time-series data of an embryo are mapped by encoder E to state space $\mathbf{s}$, and the trajectory is used to characterize the dynamics. The deviation from the normal trajectory distribution is used to quantify the anomaly.

Feasibility Criteria Based on the Reconstruction Error. First, if the reconstruction of input data $\mathbf{x}$ by $G \circ E$ causes a large error, then the mapped point in latent space $\mathbf{s} \times \mathbf{z}$ is not appropriate to characterize the data. Therefore, a threshold is set for the reconstruction error in L2 norm: $\|\mathbf{x} - G \circ E(\mathbf{x})\|^2$. The error for a time series is defined as the average over all time steps and over 12 rotation angles. The threshold is set based on average m and standard deviation σ of 45 WT training samples as $m + 2\sigma$. The corresponding error per voxel is 0.077. All WT test samples are under the threshold, while some RNAi samples cause errors over the threshold and are detected as the morphological anomaly. Otherwise, the latent representation is used for a further analysis in the next step.

Temporal Anomaly Score Defined by the State Space. As all normal time-series samples follow the same dynamics that starts immediately after the first division and ends just before the second division, the corresponding trajectories in s are assumed close to each other. Conversely, each position s roughly corresponds to a normal time step in the two-cell stage.

Specifically, let us define time $\tau \in [0,1]$, which is normalized by each time length, and consider distribution $P(\tau|s)$ to give a normal τ range for position s. For a numerical calculation using the training data, a patch with a side length 0.1 is considered in s, and histogram $P_i(\tau)$ for i-th patch is obtained. Average a_i and standard deviation σ_i of $P_i(\tau)$ are used to give a normal τ range for i-th patch as $[\tau_i^-, \tau_i^+]$, where $\tau_i^\pm = a_i \pm 2\sigma_i$.

Then, the anomaly score of input data sequence $\{x(\tau)\}_\tau$ is defined as follows. If $x(\tau)$ is mapped onto i-th patch, the deviation of τ from the normal range $[\tau_i^-, \tau_i^+]$ is counted as the anomaly score at τ; $S_\tau \equiv \max(\tau - \tau_i^+, 0) + \max(\tau_i^- - \tau, 0)$. The positive value of the first term indicates that the time evolution is too fast, while the positive second term indicates that it is too slow. The total anomaly score for the input sequence is given by the average over τ and 12 rotation angles.

The threshold of the anomaly is again given by $m + 2\sigma$, based on average m and standard deviation σ of the scores of 45 WT training samples. Under the threshold of 0.008, 19 RNAi embryos are detected as abnormal. The highest score is 0.223 for RNAi embryo whose gene *mev-1* is silenced. The second highest score is 0.080 for RNAi embryo with silenced *hcp-3*, a gene known to play an important function in mitotic nuclear division. The fourth highest score is caused by silenced *knl-1*, a gene known to play a role in meiotic chromosome segregation. The function of other detected genes needs further study. More detailed dynamics of the above genes *mev-1* and *hcp-3* is shown as follows.

State Space Trajectory and the Anomaly Score. Figure 4 shows the trajectory in the state space of (a) a WT test sample and RNAi sample with silenced (b) *mev-1* and (c) *hcp-3*. In Fig. 4(a), the trajectory moves along s_1 until $t = 14$, and then it turns to a negative direction in s_2. The trajectory in (b) keep staying at the initial position for a long time. It fails to develop into the second cell division. The trajectory in (c) also stays long around the initial position before a large jump at $t = 14$ to enter a short subsequent period.

Figure 5 shows the deviation between physical time τ and the biological time in development, given by state s for the same three samples in Fig. 4. Horizontal axis is t, while the vertical bar indicates the normal time range $[\tau_i^-, \tau_i^+]$ inferred from s. Physical τ is shown by a red point. In Fig. 5(a) for WT, each red point is covered by a bar, which means a normal development. However, in Fig. 5(b), the biological time proceeds forward at the early period and then stays far behind without any growth. Figure 5(c) shows a slow growth until $t = 14$ and then a sudden rapid catch-up in the final two steps, as shown in Fig. 4(c).

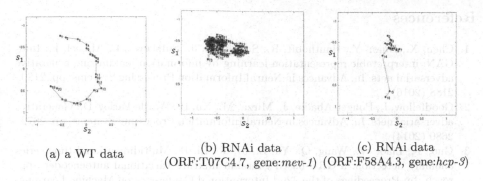

(a) a WT data

(b) RNAi data
(ORF:T07C4.7, gene:*mev-1*)

(c) RNAi data
(ORF:F58A4.3, gene:*hcp-3*)

Fig. 4. Trajectory in the state space. (a) WT test data and RNAi data with silenced (b) *mev-1* and (c) *hcp-3*.

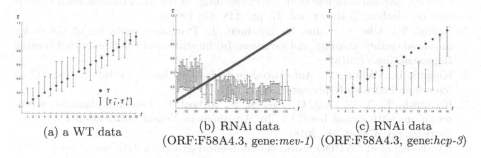

(a) a WT data

(b) RNAi data
(ORF:F58A4.3, gene:*mev-1*)

(c) RNAi data
(ORF:F58A4.3, gene:*hcp-3*)

Fig. 5. Temporal anomaly as a deviation between physical time τ, shown by a red dot, and biological time $[\tau_i^-, \tau_i^+]$, indicated by a vertical bar. Three data samples (a)–(c) are the same as in Fig. 4.

5   Summary

An anomaly detection method is proposed using a disentangled representation of deep generative models. In particular, temporal anomalies in time-series data are quantified by the acquired state-space representation based on Causal InfoGAN. The proposed method is applied to time series of three-dimensional data of cell division in the early embryo of *C. elegans*. The next step of the research includes the improvement of the disentangled latent representation for anomaly detection, and the extension of the biological studies with experimental verifications.

References

1. Chen, X., Duan, Y., Houthooft, R., Schulman, J., Sutskever, I., Abbeel, P.: Info-GAN: interpretable representation learning by information maximizing generative adversarial nets. In: Advances in Neural Information Processing Systems, pp. 2180–2188 (2016)
2. Goodfellow, I., Pouget-Abadie, J., Mirza, M., Xu, B., Warde-Farley, D.: Generative adversarial nets. In: Advances in Neural Information Processing Systems, pp. 2672–2680 (2014)
3. Guo, Y., Liao, W., Wang, Q., Yu, L., Ji, T., Li, P.: Multidimensional time series anomaly detection: a GRU-based gaussian mixture variational autoencoder approach. In: Proceedings of the 32nd International Conference on Machine Learning, vol. 95, pp. 97–112 (2018)
4. Ioffe, S., Szegedy., C.: Batch normalization: Accelerating deep network training by reducing internal covariate shift. In: Proceedings of the 32nd International Conference on Machine Learning, vol. 37, pp. 448–456 (2015)
5. Karras, T., Aila, T., Laine, S., Lehtinen, J.: Progressive growing of GANs for improved quality, stability, and variation. In: International Conference on Learning Representations (2018)
6. Kingma, D., Welling, M.: Auto-encoding variational bayes. In: International Conference on Learning Representations (2014)
7. Kurutach, T., T.A., Yang, G., Russell, S., Abbeel, P.: Learning plannable representations with causal InfoGAN. In: Advances in Neural Information Processing Systems, pp. 8747–8758 (2018)
8. Kyoda, K., et al.: WDDD: worm developmental dynamics database. Nucleic Acids Res. **41**, D732–D737 (2012)
9. Li, D., Chen, D., Jin, B., Shi, L., Goh, J., Ng, S.-K.: MAD-GAN: multivariate anomaly detection for time series data with generative adversarial networks. In: Tetko, I.V., Kůrková, V., Karpov, P., Theis, F. (eds.) ICANN 2019. LNCS, vol. 11730, pp. 703–716. Springer, Cham (2019). https://doi.org/10.1007/978-3-030-30490-4_56
10. Lin, Z., Thekumparampil, K.K., Fanti, G.C., Oh, S.: InfoGAN-CR: disentangling generative adversarial networks with contrastive regularizers. vol. abs/1906.06034 (2019)
11. Miyato, T., Kataoka, T., Koyama, M., Yoshida., Y.: Spectral normalization for generative adversarial networks. In: International Conference on Learning Representations (2018)
12. Schlegl, T., Seeböck, P., Waldstein, S.M., Langs, G., Schmidt-Erfurth., U.: f-AnoGAN: fast unsupervised anomaly detection with generative adversarial networks. In: Medical Image Analysis, vol. 54, pp. 30–44 (2019)
13. Schlegl, T., Seeböck, P., Waldstein, S.M., Schmidt-Erfurth, U., Langs, G.: Unsupervised anomaly detection with generative adversarial networks to guide marker discovery. In: Niethammer, M., et al. (eds.) IPMI 2017. LNCS, vol. 10265, pp. 146–157. Springer, Cham (2017). https://doi.org/10.1007/978-3-319-59050-9_12
14. Ueda, T., Seo, M., Nishikawa, I.: Data correction by a generative model with an encoder and its application to structure design. In: Kůrková, V., Manolopoulos, Y., Hammer, B., Iliadis, L., Maglogiannis, I. (eds.) ICANN 2018. LNCS, vol. 11141, pp. 403–413. Springer, Cham (2018). https://doi.org/10.1007/978-3-030-01424-7_40

15. Ueda, T., Seo, M., Tohsato, Y., Nishikawa, I.: Analysis of time series anomalies using causal InfoGAN and its application to biological data. In: Liu, Y., Wang, L., Zhao, L., Yu, Z. (eds.) ICNC-FSKD 2019. AISC, vol. 1074, pp. 609–617. Springer, Cham (2020). https://doi.org/10.1007/978-3-030-32456-8_67

16. Yang, S., et al.: Phenotype analysis method for identification of gene functions involved in asymmetric division of caenorhabditis elegans. J. Comput. Biol. **24**, 436–446 (2017)

17. Zenati, H., Romain, M., Foo, C.S., Lecouat, B., Chandrasekhar., V.: Adversarially learned anomaly detection. In: 2018 IEEE International Conference on Data Mining, pp. 727–736 (2018)

Inferring, Predicting, and Denoising Causal Wave Dynamics

Matthias Karlbauer[1]([✉]) [iD], Sebastian Otte[1] [iD], Hendrik P. A. Lensch[2],
Thomas Scholten[3], Volker Wulfmeyer[4], and Martin V. Butz[1] [iD]

[1] University of Tübingen – Neuro-Cognitive Modeling Group,
Sand 14, 72076 Tübingen, Germany
{matthias.karlbauer,martin.butz}@uni-tuebingen.de
[2] University of Tübingen – Computer Graphics,
Maria-von-Linden-Straße 6, 72076 Tübingen, Germany
[3] University of Tübingen – Soil Science and Geomorphology,
Rümelinstraße 19-23, 72070 Tübingen, Germany
[4] University of Hohenheim – Institute for Physics and Meteorology,
Garbenstraße 30, 70599 Stuttgart, Germany

Abstract. The novel DISTributed Artificial neural Network Architecture (DISTANA) is a generative, recurrent graph convolution neural network. It implements a grid or mesh of locally parameterizable laterally connected network modules. DISTANA is specifically designed to identify the causality behind spatially distributed, non-linear dynamical processes. We show that DISTANA is very well-suited to denoise data streams, given that re-occurring patterns are observed, significantly outperforming alternative approaches, such as temporal convolution networks and ConvLSTMs, on a complex spatial wave propagation benchmark. It produces stable and accurate closed-loop predictions even over hundreds of time steps. Moreover, it is able to effectively filter noise— an ability that can be improved further by applying denoising autoencoder principles or by actively tuning latent neural state activities retrospectively. Results confirm that DISTANA is ready to model real-world spatio-temporal dynamics such as brain imaging, supply networks, water flow, or soil and weather data patterns.

Keywords: Recurrent neural networks · Temporal convolution · Graph neural networks · Distributed sensor mesh · Noise filtering

1 Inroduction

Although sufficiently complex artificial neural networks (ANNs) are considered as universal function approximators, the past has shown that major advances

This work received funding from the DFG Cluster of Excellence "Machine Learning: New Perspectives for Science", EXC 2064/1, project number 390727645. Moreover, we thank the International Max Planck Research School for Intelligent Systems (IMPRS-IS) for supporting Matthias Karlbauer.

I. Farkaš et al. (Eds.): ICANN 2020, LNCS 12396, pp. 566–577, 2020.
https://doi.org/10.1007/978-3-030-61609-0_45

in the field of artificial intelligence were frequently grounded in specific ANN structures that were explicitly designed to solve a particular task, such as long short-term memories (LSTMs) for time series prediction, convolutional neural networks (CNNs) for image processing, or autoencoders (AEs) for data compression. This illustrates that—although theoretically any ANN can solve any desired task—a network model benefits considerably from being reasonably restricted in a way that constrains (and thus limits) the possibilities of approximating a desired process.

The process that is to be modeled here, is a two-dimensional circular wave expanding from a point source—a spatio-temporal learning problem that has been shown to be challenging for known ANN architectures. In [8], however, a novel distributed graph neural network (GNN) architecture was introduced, named DISTANA, that is specifically designed to learn these kinds of data appropriately. It was demonstrated that this architecture can accurately predict spatio-temporal processes over hundreds of closed loop steps into the future, while assuming that the underlying data has a dynamic graph-like structure.

GNNs raise new challenges as traditional convolution techniques are not directly applicable, but they also offer new possibilities as they explicitly facilitate the processing of irregularly distributed data patterns [13]. Accordingly, various promising GNNs have been proposed recently [3,12], which explicitly encode graph nodes (vertices) and node connections (edges), making them applicable to a wide range of problems. [15] offers a general survey on GNNs and distinguishes between convolutional GNNs, graph autoencoders, and spatio-temporal GNNs (called spatial-temporal in [15], STGNNs). DISTANA is a kind of STGNN and shares architectural principles with [6].

The contribution of this paper is the application of DISTANA in order to filter noise from an underlying dynamic, spatially distributed data stream without latency. To accomplish this, two techniques are investigated: (a) training models directly on noisy data and (b) applying active tuning [10], a retrospective, gradient based inference technique. Results are compared to convolutional LSTMs (ConvLSTMs) [16] and temporal convolution networks (TCNs) [1]. While TCNs have been proposed as being more suitable than recurrent neural networks (RNNs) in modeling time series data, ConvLSTM constitutes a convolution-gating LSTM architecture, which is able to perform systematic video predictions, including the dynamics in sequential satellite images of clouds. DISTANA models the wave benchmark more accurately in mid to low noise conditions and generalizes to larger extent. Furthermore, active tuning filters noise from distributed sensor meshes highly effectively, outperforming standard denoising approaches.

2   Methods

In this paper, we focus on modeling and, in particular, denoising a two-dimensional circular wave benchmark, which expands in space over time while being reflected at borders, as illustrated in Fig. 1. Wave dynamics are generated by a set of local differential equations as specified in [8].

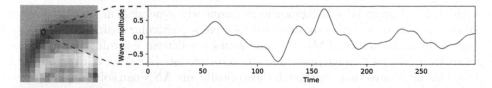

Fig. 1. Left: 16 × 16 data grid example, showing a circular wave around time step 55 propagating from bottom right to top left and being reflected at the borders. Right: the wave amplitude dynamics over time for one pixel in the 2D wave field.

For training, the standard MSE metric is used, whereas the dynamic time warping (DTW) distance [11] is used to evaluate and test the models. The DTW distance compares two sequences by finding the smallest number of transition operations to transfer one sequence into the other. When noise is added to the data (to be filtered away by the model), it is reported in terms of its signal to noise ratio (SNR), which is computed as $\text{SNR} = P_{\text{signal}}/P_{\text{noise}}$, where the power of the signal P_{signal} and of the noise P_{noise} are calculated as root mean square amplitudes (RMSA), using $\text{RMSA} = \sqrt{\frac{1}{T \cdot I \cdot J} \sum_t \sum_i \sum_j s_{tij}^2}$, where t denotes the time, i and j the position, and s the signal value.

Three different types of artificial neural network models were implemented. For each of these three types, two versions were tested: a small variant of roughly 300 parameters and a large variant with roughly 3 000 parameters. Numerous model complexities were compared. We report the best results throughout.

2.1 Convolutional LSTM (ConvLSTM)

Both ConvLSTM variants consist of two ConvLSTM layers [16]. The simple version, ConvLSTM2 with 324 parameters, projects the 16 × 16 × 1 input via the first layer on two feature maps (resulting in dimensionality 16 × 16 × 2) and subsequently via the second layer back to one output feature map. All kernels have a filter size of $k = 3$, use zero-padding and come with a stride of one. The complex version, ConvLSTM8 with 2 916 parameters, projects the input to eight feature maps and subsequently back to one output map. Code was taken and adapted from[1].

2.2 Temporal Convolution Network (TCN)

The two TCN variants have the same principal structure: an input layer projects to either two (TCN121, 320 parameters) or to nine (TCN191, 2 826 parameters) feature maps, which project their values back to one output value. A kernel filter size of $k = 3$ is used for the two spatial dimensions in combination with the standard dilation rate of $d = 1, 2, 4$ for the temporal dimension, resulting in a temporal horizon of 14 time steps (cf. [1]). Deeper networks with larger temporal horizon did not improve performance. Code was taken and adapted from [1].

---

[1] https://github.com/ndrplz/ConvLSTM_pytorch.

2.3 Our Spatio-Temporal Graph Neural Network (DISTANA)

DISTANA [8] assumes that the same dynamic principles apply at every spatial position. Accordingly, it models the data at each position in a regular sensor mesh with the identical network module. This module, which we call Prediction Kernel (PK), consists of a 4-neurons, tanh-activated fully connected layer (compressing one dynamic input value and eight lateral input values), followed by an LSTM layer with either four (DISTANA4, 200 parameters) or 24 (DISTANA24, 2 940 parameters) LSTM cells, followed by a 9-neurons tanh-activated fully connected layer (producing one dynamic output prediction and eight lateral outputs). Each PK predicts the dynamics of its assigned pixel (or sensor mesh point) in the next time step, given its previous hidden state, the predicted or measured sensor data, and the lateral information coming from the PKs in the direct eight-neighborhood (see Fig. 2). Standard LSTM cells are used [5]. However, no bias neurons are used to prevent spontaneous cell activation without external input.

More concretely, the DISTANA version considered here consist of a prediction kernel (PK) network, which is made up of the weight matrices $\mathbf{W}_{pre}^{DL}$, representing a dynamic- and lateral input preprocessing layer, the weight matrices of a regular LSTM layer (see [5]), and $\mathbf{W}_{post}^{DL}$, defining a dynamic- and lateral output postprocessing layer. DISTANA implements $k \in \mathbb{N}$ PK instances $\{p_1, p_2, \ldots, p_k\}$, where each one has a list of eight spatial neighbors $\mathbf{n}_i \in \mathbb{N}^8$. Each PK instance p_i receives dynamic input $\mathbf{d}_i \in \mathbb{R}^d$ and lateral input $\mathbf{l}_i \in \mathbb{R}^l$ from the eight neighboring PK instances, with $d, l \in \mathbb{N}$ being the dimensionality of dynamic- and lateral inputs, respectively. The LSTM layer in each PK instance contains $m \in \mathbb{N}$ cells with hidden- and cell states $\mathbf{h}_i$ and $\mathbf{c}_i \in \mathbb{R}^m$.

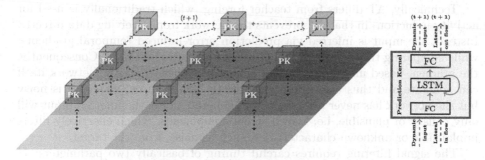

Fig. 2. Left: 3×3 sensor mesh grid visualizing a 2D wave propagating from top right to bottom left and showing the connection scheme of Prediction Kernels (PKs) that model the local dynamical process while communicating laterally. Right: exemplary prediction kernel, receiving and predicting dynamic and lateral information flow.

To perform the forward pass of PK instance p_i at time step t, the corresponding dynamic- and lateral inputs $\mathbf{d}_i^{t-1}, \mathbf{l}_i^{t-1}$, with $\mathbf{l}_i^{t-1} = \{\mathbf{l}_i | i \in \mathbf{n}_i\}$, along with the according LSTM hidden- and cell states $\mathbf{h}_i^{t-1}, \mathbf{c}_i^{t-1}$, are fed into the PK network to realize the following computations:

$$\mathbf{dl}_{\mathrm{pre}} = \tanh(\mathbf{W}_{\mathrm{pre}}^{DL}(\mathbf{d}_i^{t-1} \circ \mathbf{l}_i^{t-1})) \tag{1}$$

$$\mathbf{c}_i^t, \mathbf{h}_i^t = LSTM(\mathbf{dl}_{\mathrm{pre}}, \mathbf{c}_i^{t-1}, \mathbf{h}_i^{t-1}) \tag{2}$$

$$\mathbf{dl}_{\mathrm{post}} = \tanh(\mathbf{W}_{\mathrm{post}}^{DL}\mathbf{h}_i^t) \tag{3}$$

$$[\mathbf{d}_i^t | \mathbf{l}_i^t] = \mathbf{dl}_{\mathrm{post}}, \tag{4}$$

where vector concatenations are denoted by the $\circ$ operator. As depicted in Eq. 1 and 3, the lateral input and output is processed by a fully connected nonlinear layer, leading to a potentially different treatment of the lateral information coming from each direction. Although transitions between neighboring PKs should, in theory, be direction invariant, we give the model the freedom to develop unique transition weights. Experiments with shared perpendicular and diagonal weights did not improve performance (not shown).

2.4 Active Tuning

Active tuning (AT) is a technique that allows to use an already trained network for signal denoising, input reconstruction, or prediction stabilization, even if the training did not cover these tasks [10]. In this work, AT is used to filter noise by inducing reasonable activity into the network, meaning that a dynamic input to the PKs is inferred such that they reflect the current wave pattern of the dynamic process (see Algorithm 1).

Technically, AT differs from teacher forcing (which traditionally is used for activity induction) in that AT prevents the network from receiving data directly. Instead, the input is inferred via prediction error induced temporal gradients, while comparing the output of the network to some target signal. Consequently, the gradient-based inferred input can only take values which the network itself can generate and thus also interpret correctly. If the target sequence is noisy but the network has never been trained to generate noise, the inferred input will only consist of plausible, i.e. known signal components, which effectively filters implausible or unknown characteristics, such as noise, from the target.

The signal filtering requires careful tuning of basically two parameters: H as the history length, which indicates how many time steps into the past the

---

Algorithm 1. Active Tuning procedure

1: Initialize zero or random input vector $\mathbf{x}$.
2: Forward $\mathbf{x}$ through the network to obtain the network output vector $\mathbf{y}$.
3: Compute and apply gradients on $\mathbf{x}$ by comparing the network output vector $\mathbf{y}$ with the noisy target vector $\mathbf{t}$.
4: Repeat (2) and (3) until convergence or for c optimization cycles.

---

input vector **x** will be projected and optimized, and η as the learning rate, which weighs the update of **x** based on the obtained gradients. A third potential parameter is the number of optimization cycles c, that is, how often the optimization procedure is repeated. We set $c = 30$ in this work.

3   Experiments and Results

All models were trained for 200 epochs with 100 training sequences of length 40 each. Every model was trained ten times with different random seeds to obtain mean and standard deviation scores. A learning rate of 0.001 was used in combination with the ADAM optimizer [9], minimizing the MSE between network output and target. Different noise levels were added to the data and the signal to noise ratios (SNRs) $[0.25, 0.5, 1, 2, 4, 10, 100, 10^3, 10^5]$ were evaluated, where 0.25 is a particularly challenging case (the signal has only a quarter of the power of the noise) and 10^5 is considered as the noise-free case.

Model evaluations are based on the dynamic time warping (DTW) distance on 20 test sequences consisting of a spatial size of 16×16 pixels and 150 time steps. Either 30 teacher forcing steps or 30 active tuning steps are initially performed (to induce activity into the network), followed by 120 closed loop steps (to evaluate the actual model accuracy at continuing the spatio-temporal wave dynamics). The DTW distance metric is exclusively calculated over the 120 closed loop steps to measure the stability of each model when running detached from external data input. Note that all models were only trained on 40 time steps and, in consequence, are required to properly generalize over 150 time steps in order to reach a small test error. More noise-free experiments about comparing DISTANA to many more baseline approaches can be found in [8].

3.1   Training on Noisy Data – ConvLSTM Vs TCN Vs DISTANA

To quantify the different network model's denoising capabilities when being trained explicitly on noisy data, ten models of each variant were trained on the different SNRs specified above. We expect that an increasing SNR results in lower error rates, since in low noise cases (high SNR) a model does not have to additionally filter noise disturbances to encounter the actual signal.

Training Convergence. Two different convergence plots, showing the decreasing MSE error over time along with standard deviations for all models, are provided in Fig. 3. While the left convergence plot, depicting training on the challenging 0.25 SNR condition, clearly favorites the large ConvLSTM8 model over all others, both DISTANA variants outperform the ConvLSTM and TCN models on the noise-free condition, that is 10^5 SNR, as depicted in the right convergence plot.

A further analysis reasonably shows the expected trend that large SNRs (small noise levels) lead to lower and thus better training errors (see Fig. 4, left). The same plot also reveals how much the training approximation accuracy

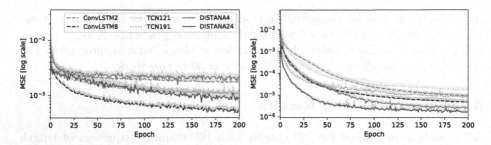

Fig. 3. Training convergence on different signal to noise ratios (left: 0.25, right: 10^5) for two versions of each of the compared network architectures ConvLSTM, TCN and DISTANA. Note the logarithmic y-axis and different y-axis scales.

of a certain model depends on the SNR, confirming the previous finding that ConvLSTM seems to be slightly better than other models for a low SNR (large noise) while DISTANA considerably reaches superior performance on low-noise conditions (high SNR).

DTW-Based Model Evaluation. A model evaluation based on the DTW distance is visualized in the right plot of Fig. 4. These results corroborate the findings from the training analyses and emphasize the GNN's superiority over the other two approaches even more clearly. With an order of magnitude less parameters, DISTANA4 reaches the same level of performance as the large ConvLSTM and TCN architectures, while, with an equal number of parameters, the GNN model produces significantly better results compared to ConvLSTM and TCN (note the logarithmic y-axis scale, making the performance differences even

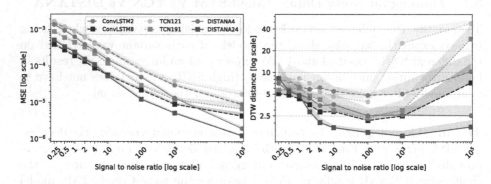

Fig. 4. Left: final training MSE scores over different SNRs for two versions—300 parameters (circular markers, bright color), 3 000 parameters (square markers, dark color)—of each of the three compared architectures ConvLSTM (blues, dashed), TCN (greens, dotted), DISTANA (reds, solid). Note the logarithmic scales on both x- and y-axis. Right: test accuracies, based on dynamic time warping (DTW) distance. (Color figure online)

clearer). Additional video material[2] shows that none of the models reaches satisfying results on the lowest SNR condition when trained directly on noisy data, which is noticeable in either a quick fading to zero or a chaotic wave activity; an issue that we approach in the following section.

3.2   Active Tuning

As mentioned beforehand (see Sect. 2.4), active tuning (AT) can be used, for example, to infer network inputs via gradients. Therefore, AT can replace teacher forcing (TF), where data are fed directly into the network to induce adequate activity into the model and thus to let it run in closed loop to produce future predictions.

Here, we compare DISTANA4's closed loop performance when initial activities are induced via TF or AT. DISTANA4 was chosen due to its small number of parameters while reaching comparably good performance; however, the results in principle can be generalized to any desired recurrent neural network model. TF and AT are compared in three conditions: (a) the SNR during training is larger than the SNR during testing, that is $SNR_{train} > SNR_{test}$, (b) $SNR_{train} = SNR_{test}$, and (c) $SNR_{train} < SNR_{test}$. The four SNRs $[0.25, 4, 100, 10^5]$ are compared (see Table 1).

Stability and Applicability Gains Through AT. As indicated by the blue-colored entries in Table 1, AT outperforms TF in 11/16 cases. In most cases,

Table 1. Dynamic time warping distances for models that are initialized with teacher forcing (TF) or active tuning (AT) and that have been trained and tested on different signal to noise ratios (SNR). Varied AT parameters η and H are reported for each model. Entries above the dashed line in each Train SNR block correspond to models that were tested on larger noise than they were trained on. Superior performances are emphasized in blue.

Test SNR	TF	AT	η	H	TF	AT	η	H
	Train SNR: 0.25				Train SNR: 4			
0.25	8.02 ± 1.01	7.11 ± 0.98	0.400	1	63.71 ± 2.36	5.78 ± 1.43	0.020	25
4.00	8.25 ± 1.01	7.78 ± 1.03	0.350	2	5.50 ± 1.37	5.26 ± 1.35	0.100	25
100	8.25 ± 1.02	7.94 ± 1.15	0.500	5	4.95 ± 1.28	5.08 ± 1.33	0.100	25
10^5	8.25 ± 1.02	7.94 ± 1.15	0.500	5	4.91 ± 1.29	5.01 ± 1.21	0.500	1
	Train SNR: 10^2				Train SNR: 10^5			
0.25	38.08 ± 12.19	3.58 ± 0.60	0.010	25	23.86 ± 0.91	8.26 ± 0.49	0.002	25
4.00	3.49 ± 0.39	3.00 ± 0.60	0.070	10	15.31 ± 1.27	4.96 ± 0.76	0.004	25
100	1.93 ± 0.17	2.09 ± 0.26	0.400	4	6.06 ± 0.57	4.52 ± 0.90	0.005	25
10^5	1.76 ± 0.18	1.79 ± 0.19	0.300	1	4.14 ± 0.47	4.25 ± 0.48	0.300	2

---

[2] https://youtu.be/j8xJnoo1wOo.

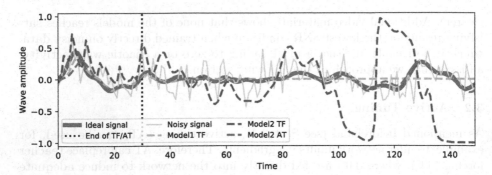

Fig. 5. Denoising a signal (light blue) with 0.25 SNR using either teacher forcing (TF) or active tuning (AT) to induce reasonable activity in the first 30 time steps. Model1 is trained on 0.25 SNR and tested with TF (orange, dashed). Model2 is trained on 100 SNR and tested with TF (dark green, dashed) and with AT (magenta, dashed). Ideal signal displayed in dark blue; all models are DISTANA4 architectures. (Color figure online)

however, the techniques do not differ significantly. Yet, in condition (c), DISTANA4 systematically benefits from being initialized through AT, that is if $SNR_{train} < SNR_{test}$. Referring to Table 1, these cases are above the dashed horizontal lines within each Train SNR block. In consequence, AT makes a model applicable to larger noise than it was trained on. Besides, using AT instead of TF never decreases the model performance significantly.

Figure 5 shows the wave activity at a single position in the two-dimensional wave grid and visualizes the filtering capabilities of the model in three scenarios: (a) Model1 TF, trained and evaluated on 0.25 SNR; initialized with TF, (b) Model2 TF trained on 100 SNR and evaluated on 0.25 SNR; initialized with TF, and (c) Model2 AT, trained on 100 SNR and evaluated on 0.25 SNR; initialized with AT. The same scenarios are visualized spatially in one particular time step in Fig. 6. While Model1 TF is accurate during TF, it quickly fades to zero activity in closed loop application; which is reasonable since the very high

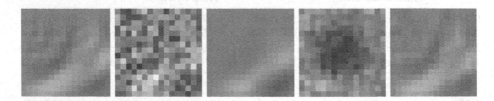

Fig. 6. 2D wave approximation in time step 45 provided by differently trained DISTANA4 models. From left to right: ideal wave (target), noisy wave with 0.25 SNR (to be filtered), DISTANA4 trained on 0.25 SNR and initialized with 30 steps teacher forcing, DISTANA4 trained on 100 SNR and initialized with 30 steps teacher forcing, DISTANA4 trained on 100 SNR and initialized with 30 active tuning steps.

training noise (0.25 SNR) forced it to developed a strong low-pass filter. Model2 TF already produces inaccurate predictions in the TF phase and subsequently is incapable of continuing the signal reasonably; the model cannot deal with the strong noise, which it has never encountered during training. However, the same model initialized with AT (Model2 AT) can be used to produce highly detailed and accurate predictions in closed loop application without fading to zero or oscillating chaotically. Previously mentioned video material emphasizes these findings.

The tuning parameters η and H were chosen carefully for each model. Two trends can be observed in Table 1. First, history length H requires to be longer when $SNR_{train} < SNR_{test}$. Second, tuning rate η correlates with the training noise, that is, small training noise (large SNR) requires small choices of η.

Drawback of Active Tuning. Although AT yields impressive results when used to induce reasonable dynamics into a model, it requires explicit hand crafting of the tuning rate η, history length H, and number of optimization cycles (left constant at 30 in this work). Additionally, AT comes with a massively increased computational cost when compared to TF, since instead of just forwarding an input through the network (TF), AT applies a local optimization procedure in every time step, which—depending on the chosen history length and optimization cycles—can slow down the activity induction process significantly.

4   Discussion

A spatio-temporal graph neural network (STGNN), DISTANA, designed to model and predict spatio-temporal processes—such as two-dimensional circular wave dynamics—has been compared to two state-of-the-art neural network structures: convolutional LSTMs (ConvLSTMs) and temporal convolution networks (TCNs). The results show that DISTANA yields more accurate predictions and is mostly more robust against noise. Furthermore, DISTANA was applied with active tuning (AT), which was used to successfully induce a stable state into the model and to replace the conventional teacher forcing (TF) procedure.

When trained on different signal to noise ratios (SNRs), the three architecture types differed in both train and test accuracy depending on the noise level. As reported in Sect. 3.1, ConvLSTM reached best results on extremely noisy data, while with decreasing noise, DISTANA was superior. This behavior might likely come from the very basic architectural differences between the two models: while ConvLSTM has a spatial focus, DISTANA has a temporal focus. More specifically, ConvLSTM first aggregates spatial input via the convolution operation and considers the temporal dimension solely on this aggregation. DISTANA, on the other hand, first accesses the very local data, that is one pixel, while spatial aggregation is done via lateral temporal information exchange between Prediction Kernels (PKs). This difference in processing order can explain ConvLSTM's slight advantage in highly noisy conditions (where information can be aggregated spatially), while DISTANA has the potential to very accurately approximate a specific dynamical process, once it is sufficiently interpretable. Our results do not confirm recent findings [4,7] which report TCNs as superior to recurrent neural networks in temporal information processing. In our experiments, TCN never reached top performance. Video material clearly shows the limits to which extent any explored architecture (even ConvLSTM) can factually model highly noisy data when explicitly trained on the particular noise level.

DISTANA was significantly less affected by overfitting (see Fig. 4). While the test accuracy of ConvLSTM and TCN decreased on small training noise conditions (high SNR), DISTANA did not follow this trend, which can be explained by DISTANA's generalization abilities. Apparently, DISTANA approximated the actual causal process with much smaller divergence in the training data vicinity, enabling it to properly switch from TF to closed loop application even in low-noise and noise-free training conditions.

We also applied DISTANA to the moving MNIST dataset [14]. DISTANA was not capable of identifying global characters and failed whenever a symbol touched the border and hence bounced off into the other direction. Due to DISTANA's local connection scheme, it is not able to model the abrupt changes in motion direction of pixels that are far away from the border. This issue will be addressed by extending the PK's neighborhood (e.g via skip connections) in future research.

Another essential finding of this work is that AT extends the applicability of any recurrent neural network model over the horizon of the training statistics. The traditionally applied TF procedure fails here because a neural network model used with TF for activity induction generally cannot handle direct input that has a smaller SNR compared to the SNR it was trained on. AT can bridge this gap by tuning the model states invariant to noise levels. The necessary selection of convenient tuning parameters η and H and the additional computational overhead may be negligible in the light of the rather dramatic performance gains.

Overall, the long prediction stability over hundreds of closed loop steps produced by DISTANA is in line with findings from other works on GNNs, such as [2], who used a GNN to model the behavior of physical entities moving through space over thousands of time steps.

5   Conclusion

In conclusion, our evaluations show that DISTANA—a spatio-temporal graph neural network (STGNN)—outperforms ConvLSTM and TCN to large extents and in various respects. Our findings thus suggest that GNNs should be further applied to modeling spatio-temporal processes, which promises increased generalization, denoising, and deep, closed-loop future prediction abilities. Moreover, our results imply that active tuning may replace teacher forcing for the initialization of the latent activities in generative, recurrent neural network architectures, enabling models to be applied to larger noise than they were originally trained on. Future research needs to focus on evaluating this potential using real-world data such as soil, traffic, brain-imaging or social network data, while first results of ongoing research demonstrate DISTANA's applicability to global weather data.

References

1. Bai, S., Kolter, J.Z., Koltun, V.: An empirical evaluation of generic convolutional and recurrent networks for sequence modeling. arXiv preprint arXiv:1803.01271 (2018)
2. Battaglia, P., Pascanu, R., Lai, M., Rezende, D.J., et al.: Interaction networks for learning about objects, relations and physics. In: Advances in Neural Information Processing Systems, pp. 4502–4510 (2016)
3. Battaglia, P.W., et al.: Relational inductive biases, deep learning, and graph networks. arXiv preprint arXiv:1806.01261 (2018)
4. Dauphin, Y.N., Fan, A., Auli, M., Grangier, D.: Language modeling with gated convolutional networks. In: Proceedings of the 34th International Conference on Machine Learning, vol. 70, pp. 933–941. JMLR. org (2017)
5. Hochreiter, S., Schmidhuber, J.: Long short-term memory. Neural Comput. 9(8), 1735–1780 (1997)
6. Jain, A., Zamir, A.R., Savarese, S., Saxena, A.: Structural-RNN: deep learning on spatio-temporal graphs. In: Proceedings of the IEEE Conference on Computer Vision and Pattern Recognition, pp. 5308–5317 (2016)
7. Kalchbrenner, N., Espeholt, L., Simonyan, K., Oord, A.V.D., Graves, A., Kavukcuoglu, K.: Neural machine translation in linear time. arXiv preprint arXiv:1610.10099 (2016)
8. Karlbauer, M., Otte, S., Lensch, H.P., Scholten, T., Wulfmeyer, V., Butz, M.V.: A distributed neural network architecture for robust non-linear spatio-temporal prediction. arXiv preprint arXiv:1912.11141
9. Kingma, D., Ba, J.: Adam: A method for stochastic optimization. In: International Conference on Learning Representations (2014)
10. Otte, S., Butz, M.V.: Active tuning: signal denoising, reconstruction, and prediction with temporal forward model gradients (2019). pCT/EP2019/069659, patent pending
11. Salvador, S., Chan, P.: Toward accurate dynamic time warping in linear time and space. Intell. Data Anal. 11(5), 561–580 (2007)
12. Scarselli, F., Gori, M., Tsoi, A.C., Hagenbuchner, M., Monfardini, G.: The graph neural network model. IEEE Trans. Neural Netw. 20(1), 61–80 (2008)
13. Shuman, D.I., Narang, S.K., Frossard, P., Ortega, A., Vandergheynst, P.: The emerging field of signal processing on graphs: extending high-dimensional data analysis to networks and other irregular domains. IEEE Signal Process. Mag. 30(3), 83–98 (2013)
14. Srivastava, N., Mansimov, E., Salakhudinov, R.: Unsupervised learning of video representations using LSTMs. In: International Conference on Machine Learning, pp. 843–852 (2015)
15. Wu, Z., Pan, S., Chen, F., Long, G., Zhang, C., Yu, P.S.: A comprehensive survey on graph neural networks. arXiv preprint arXiv:1901.00596 (2019)
16. Xingjian, S., Chen, Z., Wang, H., Yeung, D.Y., Wong, W.K., Woo, W.C.: Convolutional LSTM network: a machine learning approach for precipitation nowcasting. In: Advances in Neural Information Processing Systems, pp. 802–810 (2015)

PART-GAN: Privacy-Preserving Time-Series Sharing

Shuo Wang[1,2(✉)], Carsten Rudolph[1], Surya Nepal[2], Marthie Grobler[2],
and Shangyu Chen[3]

[1] Monash University, Melbourne, Australia
{shuo.wang,carsten.rudolph}@monash.edu
[2] CSIRO, Melbourne, Australia
{surya.nepal,marthie.grobler}@csiro.au
[3] University of Melbourne, Melbourne, Australia
shangyuc@student.unimelb.edu.au

Abstract. In this paper, we provide a practical privacy-preserving generative model for time series data augmentation and sharing, called PART-GAN. Our model enables the local data curator to provide a freely accessible public generative model derived from original data for cloud storage. Compared with existing approaches, PART-GAN has three key advantages: It enables the generation of an unlimited amount of synthetic time series data under the guidance of a given classification label and addresses the incomplete and temporal irregularity issues. It provides a robust privacy guarantee that satisfies differential privacy to time series data augmentation and sharing. It addresses the trade-offs between utility and privacy by applying optimization strategies. We evaluate and report the utility and efficacy of PART-GAN through extensive empirical evaluations of real-world health/medical datasets. Even at a higher level of privacy protection, our method outperforms GAN with ordinary perturbation. It achieves similar performance with GAN without perturbation in terms of inception score, machine learning score similarity, and distance-based evaluations.

Keywords: Generative model · Data sharing · Privacy-preserving · Deep learning · Differential privacy

1 Introduction

Multivariate time series data are ubiquitous in various fields of study from health and medical records to financial and meteorological observations. Time series data generally contain a large number of missing values due to the intermittent failures/faults of collection devices. Besides, the time intervals of the observations in time series are not always fixed. Current studies have started to synthesize time series data using both synthesizers and machine learning models to some degree of success, e.g., Generative Adversarial Network (GAN) [12–14].

© Springer Nature Switzerland AG 2020
I. Farkaš et al. (Eds.): ICANN 2020, LNCS 12396, pp. 578–593, 2020.
https://doi.org/10.1007/978-3-030-61609-0_46

GANs had brought the practical potential to relieve the data availability limitation and showed significant progress in generating authentic-looking data. However, it has been demonstrated that releasing only the generative distribution derived from generative models can reveal private information of the original training samples [2]. It is necessary to embed privacy-preserving mechanisms into the generative models to break privacy barriers that hamper data sharing.

In this paper, we propose a Privacy-preserving Augmentation and Releasing scheme for Time series data via GAN (PART-GAN), which adopts a robust differential privacy paradigm and incorporates three optimizing strategies to improve utility and feasibility. Our contributions can be summarized as follows:

(1) We propose the Conditional & Temporal - Generative Adversarial Network (CT-GAN) to generate new noisy and irregularly-sampled time series data. This augments the unbalanced time-series datasets for better classification performance. The generator and the discriminator are conditioned with the timestamps to capture the latent representations of the time series for naturally mimicking the time-series dynamics and according to a given label (e.g., arrhythmia classification).

(2) Based on CT-GAN, we propose a PART-GAN scheme that can be applied to produce an unlimited amount of synthetic privacy-sensitive time-series data for many participants to balance their local datasets for the deep neural network training. This is done in a robust privacy-preserving manner, integrated with differential privacy mechanisms and resulting in a better classification performance after data augmentation.

(3) To the best of our knowledge, PART-GAN is the first attempt to balance the utility and privacy trade-offs the privacy-preserving model releasing frameworks for time series data augmentation. To improve the utility, PART-GAN is incorporated with a combination of optimization strategies, e.g., weight pruning and grouping, generator selecting, and denoise mechanisms.

(4) We conduct extensive empirical evaluations using real-world medical time series data, e.g., EEG data and eICU data, to validate the efficacy of PART-GAN. We demonstrate PART-GAN's ability to effectively support augmentation tasks for medical time series data while providing theoretically guaranteed privacy protection and maintaining a reasonable (single-digit) privacy budget.

The next section describes the preliminary concepts. Sections 2 and 3 explain the system design and our optimization strategies. Section 4 describes our experimental results. Section 5 concludes the work as a whole.

2   PART-GAN Schemes

This section describes the idea of PART-GAN, a generic scheme for differentially private releasing of synthetic time series data using CT-GAN for time series mimicking.

2.1   CT-GAN Architecture

In this section, the CT-GAN framework, improved from ACGAN [16] and Conditional GAN (CGAN) [15], is proposed to model the temporal irregularity of the incomplete time series and guide the generation using a given classification. CT-GAN integrates timestamps as the conditional class (similar to [18]) using CGAN to generate irregular time-series sequence while composing with an auxiliary decoder to reconstruct class labels using ACGAN to guide the generation under a given label. We feed side information (timestamps) to the discriminator and the reconstructing side information (classification label). The discriminator D is modified to comprise an auxiliary decoder network that yields the class label for the training samples or a subsection of the latent variables from which the samples are generated. As shown in Fig. 1, the CT-GAN framework is composed of a generator network G to yield synthetic examples with the same distribution as that of real examples; and a discriminator neural network D to distinguish between real and synthetic samples.

In the CT-GAN, each generated sample has a corresponding class label $l \sim L$ and temporal timestamp $t \sim T$ as two kinds of conditional information, in addition to the noise $z \sim Z$. Z is a noise space used to seed the generative model. T and L is the space of timestamps and labels used to condition G and D. Let G generate a segment $x = <x_1, \ldots x_n>$ with n timestamps, similar with the size of x, $t = <t_1, \ldots t_n>$ is a sorted vector of timestamps sampled from T. G uses both x, l and t to mimic time series $x_{fake} = G(t, z, l)$. x represents a time series output from G or input to D. Samples of $z \in Z$ are sampled from a noise distribution $p_z(z)$. In our experiments, p_z is a simple Gaussian noise distribution with a mean equal to 0, and the standard deviation equals 1. Based on the time series in the training data and their associated conditional data, we can define a data distribution $p_{data}(x, t, l)$. The D generates both a probability distribution over fake or real and a probability distribution over the class labels, namely $P(S|X), P(C|X) = D(X)$. The objective function is composed of three parts: the log-likelihood of the corresponding fake or real source (LS), the log-likelihood of the corresponding class (LC), and the loss of temporal conditional (LT).

$$L_S = E[logP(S = real|X_{real})] - E[logP(S = fake|X_{fake})]$$
$$L_C = E[logP(C = l|X_{real})] - E[logP(C = l|X_{fake})] \tag{1}$$
$$L_T = E_{x \sim p_{data}(x)}[logD(x|t)] + E_{z \sim P_z(z)}[log(1 - D(G(z|t)))]$$

2.2   (ϵ, δ)-Differential Privacy

One variant of differential privacy is used in this work, i.e. (ϵ, δ)-differential privacy [5], which allows for the possibility that plain ϵ-differential privacy is broken with probability δ[1]. Formally,

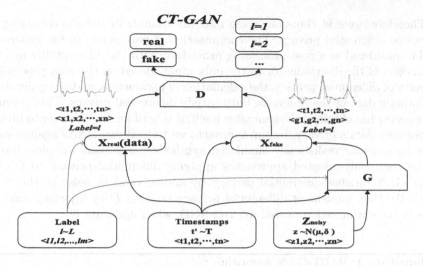

Fig. 1. Structure of CT-GAN.

Definition 1. (ϵ, δ)-*Differential privacy* [4]

Let $\epsilon > 0$ be a constant. A randomized mechanism $\mathcal{M}(\Delta)$ satisfies (ϵ, δ)-differential privacy if, for any two adjacent inputs d_1 and d_2 and for any subset of outputs S $(S \subset Range\ (F))$, there is:

$$Pr[\mathcal{M}(d_1) \in S] \le e^{\epsilon} Pr[\mathcal{M}(d_2) \in S] + \delta \tag{2}$$

The parameter $\epsilon > 0$ is called the privacy budget and it allows users to control the level of privacy. δ evaluates the violation of the ϵ-differential privacy, which allows for the possibility that plain ϵ-differential privacy is broken with probability δ. Given the deterministic function, differential privacy can be satisfied by adding random noise into the output of the deterministic function, where the scale of noise is decided by the sensitivity of Δf. The sensitivity reveals the maximum change in the query answers due to the change of a single database entry.

2.3 PART-GAN Scheme

This work aims to preserve privacy during the training procedure instead of adding random noise to the final parameters. Since GANs consist of both a generator G and a discriminator D, the direct approach is to add noise to the training procedures of both G and D. However, the minimax game formulation makes it hard to accurately obtain an evaluation of the privacy loss, causing large distortion in the generative models. As illustrated in Fig. 1, only the discriminator D directly accesses the real data. Therefore, it is reasonable to inject random noise only in training discriminator D, namely perturbing the training discriminator D is sufficient to protect privacy [1]. Besides, the architecture and number of parameters of discriminator D are small and straightforward. Thus, it is feasible to tightly estimate the privacy loss of perturbation in training D.

Therefore, we add Gaussian noise into the training of the discriminator to guarantee differential privacy. The computation of parameters of the generator can be considered as a post-processing procedure, with the differentially private parameters of the discriminator as the only input. Based on the post-processing property of differential privacy, the calculation of parameters, and the generation of synthetic data of the generator both satisfy differential privacy. Thus, even if the observer has obtained the generator itself, it is hard for the observer to invade the training data's privacy. In our approach, we trained two DNNs against each other to generate realistically simulated synthetic participant samples. Based on the commonly-adopted approaches applying differential privacy to DNNs, PART-GAN satisfies differential privacy by adding random noise to the SGD [1,21]. We then implement differential privacy training D by injecting random noise in the optimization procedure, i.e., SGD, when updating D.

Algorithm 1: PART-GAN Algorithm

   Output: Differentially private generator G.

1   Initialize discriminator and generator parameters θ_d^0, θ_g^0;
2   **while** θ_g *has not converge* $\mathcal{E}$ $\delta > \delta_0$ **do**
3   **for** $t=1$ *to* n_g **do**
4   //Single-shot Pruning Pre-Processing;
5   **for** $i=1$ *to* n_d **do**
6   //Parameter Grouping Optimization;
7   Sampling $\{x^{(j)}\}_{j=1}^m \backsim p_{data}$, $\{z^{(j)}\}_{j=1}^m \backsim p_z$, $\{t^{(j)}\}_{j=1}^m \backsim T, \eta \backsim [0,1]$;
8            $\{\hat{x}^{(j)}\}_{j=1}^m \leftarrow \eta x + (1-\eta)G(\{z^{(j)}\}_{j=1}^m)$;
9   Gradient $g_w(\hat{x}^{(j)}, z^{(j)}) \leftarrow \nabla_w[f_w(\hat{x}^{(j)}) - f_w(g_\theta(z^{(j)}))]$;
10           $\overline{g}_w = \frac{1}{m}\sum_{j=1}^m g_w(\hat{x}^{(j)}, z^{(j)})$;
11           $g_w' \leftarrow Clipping(\overline{g_w}, C) + \mathcal{N}(0, (\Delta f)^2 C^2 \mathcal{I})$;
12   Updating privacy accountant $\mathcal{A}$ with (σ, m_d, m);
13   Updating discriminator w with (w, g_w', α_d);
14   Sampling $\{z^{(j)}\}_{j=1}^m \backsim p_z$;
15      $\overline{g}_\theta = \frac{1}{m}\sum_{j=1}^m \nabla_\theta f_w(g_\theta(z^{(j)}))$;
16   Updating the generator θ with $(\theta, g_\theta, \alpha_g)$;
17   //Generator Selecting Optimization;
18   Cumulative privacy loss $\delta \leftarrow$ query $\mathcal{A}$ with ϵ_0;

We introduce the paradigm of PART-GAN in Algorithm 1. The inputs are as follows: α_d, α_g, the learning rate of the discriminator and generator; C, gradient clipping bound constant. n, the total number of training data points in each discriminator iteration; σ_n, noise scale; n_g, number of iterations of the generator; n_d, number of discriminator's iterations per generator iteration; m_d, number of discriminator's parameters; m, batch size for training GAN; (ϵ_0, δ_0), the overall privacy target; k the number of parameter groups. As illustrated, at every stage of the SGD, when the gradient $\nabla_\theta L(\theta; x_i)$ is calculated for a random subset of examples, the l_2-norm of gradients are clipped by a threshold C at first to bound the sensitivity by a constant C. Here, f_w is the function used as the loss function. We then obtain the average of these gradient values, followed by injecting random noise sampled from a Gaussian distribution that has a variance proportional to the gradient clipping to protect the privacy. Note that a privacy accountant A is adopted in this work, similar to [1], to track the cumulative privacy loss in each step. This progress is iterated until convergence or exceeding the privacy budget. Our empirical results illustrate that directly injecting noise into the training procedure of D encounters several challenges: (1) the utility of generated examples is limited and unrealistic; and (2) the differentially private GAN converges slower than the ordinary GAN, giving rise to unnecessary privacy loss. Therefore, we implement three optimization strategies to improve the training stability and utility of differentially private GAN and convergence rate. (1) **Single-Shot Pruning Pre-Processing.** We use a connection sensitivity definition to discover important connections in the neural network. In the training and perturbation, only the top k important connections are selected to be trained and perturbed while the rest will be skipped from these procedures and kept inactive. Based on the connection sensitivity, it is feasible to identify and prune unimportant connections in single-shot before training, resulting in a perturbation-free mask. (2) **Parameter Dynamic Grouping.** We aggregate parameters with small gradient values when their gradient values are similarly small and close, and the parameters have a similar trend of gradient value change, aiming to reduce the scale of noise introduced to satisfy differential privacy. During each training iteration, we first group the parameters into k groups $\{G_j\}_j^k = 1$, each G_j sharing similar clipping bound c_j. We then use the average clipping bounds in G_j to estimate c_j, followed by group-wise clipping and perturbation. (3) **Generator Selecting Optimization.** We save all the generative models, e.g., generator G, across all epochs followed by selecting generators that can produce training samples for the most accurate models in a differential privacy-preserving manner. Instead of directly adding noise to each gradient, we choose appropriate noisy data that was previously published and reuse it if it is close to the real gradient, which we want to perturb. The details for these improvements are illustrated in Sect. 3.

3 Optimizations

3.1 Single-Shot Pruning Optimization

As neural networks are usually overparameterized, comparable performance can be obtained by pruning the neural network into a smaller network while enhancing generalization [3]. Intuitively, the pre-processing goal is to propose an optimization that can build a sparse network while maintaining the accuracy of the network by selectively pruning redundant connections for a given task in a data-dependent way before training. We assume that besides the private datasets D_{pri} to train the model, a small amount of relevant public dataset D_{pub} is available in many settings, e.g., public human face dataset or public EEG or eICU database.

First, a weight-independent criterion is selected to measure and identify important (or sensitive) connections used for pruning. The neural network pruning can be formulated as an optimization problem. Given a dataset $D = \{(x_i, y_i)\}_{i=1}^n$, a desired pruning rate p (i.e., the number of non-zero weights), auxiliary indicator variables $c \in \{0,1\}^m$ representing the presence of each connection (e.g., the value of c_j indicates whether the connection j is active in the network or pruned), neural network pruning can be written as the following constrained optimization problem:

$$\underset{c,w}{Min} L(c \odot w; D) = \underset{c,w}{min} \frac{1}{n} \sum_{i=1}^{n} l(c \odot w; (x_i, y_i)) \tag{3}$$

$$s.t. w \in R^m, c \in \{0,1\}^m, \|c\|_0 < p$$

Here, $l(\Delta)$ is the standard loss function (e.g., cross-entropy loss), where $\odot$ is the Hadamard product, w is the set of parameters of the neural network, and m is the total number of parameters. This measure is used to separate the weight of the connection (w) from whether the connection is present or not (c) [11]. Then the importance of each connection can be decided by measuring its effect on the loss function. Specifically, to measure the effect of connection j on the loss, the difference in loss can be evaluated separately on $c_j = 1$ and $c_j = 0$. The effect of removing connection j, denoted by ΔL_j, can be measured by:

$$\Delta L_j(w; D) = L(1 \odot w; D) - L((1 - v_j) \odot w; D) \tag{4}$$

where 1 is the vector of dimension m and v_j is the indicator vector of element j. ΔL_j can be approximated by the derivative of L w.r.t. c_j , denote by $d_j(w; D)$. Consequently, the effect of connection j on the loss can be defined as [10,11]:

$$\Delta L_j(\mathbf{w}; D) \approx d_j(\mathbf{w}; D) = \frac{\partial L(\mathbf{c} \odot w; D)}{\partial c_j}\bigg|_{c_j=1}$$
$$= \lim_{\delta \to 0} \frac{L(\mathbf{c} \odot \mathbf{w}; D) - L((\mathbf{c} - \delta e_j) \odot \mathbf{w}; D)}{\delta}\bigg|_{c_j=1} \tag{5}$$

As an infinitesimal version of ΔL_j, $\partial L / \partial c_j$ can be figured out on one forward-backward pass using automatic differentiation for all j at once. Note that a higher magnitude of the derivatives essentially means that the connection c_j has a significant positive or negative effect on the loss [11]. Then, connection sensitivity cs for j can be defined as the normalized magnitude of the derivatives:

$$cs_j = \frac{|d_j(w; D)|}{\sum_{k=1}^{m} |d_k(w; D)|} \tag{6}$$

Neural network initialization [11] that guarantees the gradients to be in a reasonable range is adopted to relieve the impact of weights on the derivatives. The single-shot pruning-based optimization algorithm is described in Algorithm 2, in which a relevant public dataset is used to initialize and calculate the connection sensitivity of the model. This optimization is placed before the Algorithm 1 as the pre-processing, where the mask is used for gradient perturbation.

3.2   Parameter Dynamic Grouping

The common approach to satisfy differential privacy for SGD optimization is to directly add random noise to each gradient value. This straightforward way

---

Algorithm 2: Single-shot pruning-based optimization

Input: Loss function L, relevant public dataset D_{pub}, pruning rate k
Output: Perturbation-free mask

1   Construct random batch B with size $|B| = K$;
2   Calculate $\nabla L_B(x_t)$ and V_B; **while** $\|w^*\|_0 \leq k$ **do**
3      $w_0 \leftarrow VarianceScalingInitialization$;
4   // Sample a mini-batch from D_{pub}
5   **cs** $\leftarrow$ Calculate $cs_j \forall j \in \{1, \cdots, m\}$;
6   **c** $\leftarrow$ top k c_j according to DescendingSorting(**cs**);
7   Return **c**;

---

introduces great perturbation, especially for gradients with small values. To this end, grouping optimization [22,24] has been applied to aggregate parameters with small values to reduce the amount of introduced noise.

In this section, we use a dynamic grouping approach that can dynamically aggregate parameters with small gradient values when their gradient values are similarly small and close, and the parameters have a similar trend of gradient value change. According to the post-processing property of the differential privacy definition, no privacy is compromised when using the perturbed gradient values of previous iterations to predict the trend of gradient value change and estimated gradient value at the current iteration.

Formally, given perturbed gradient value set $\{g^a_{i-k}, g^a_{i-k+1}, \cdots, g^a_{i-1}\}$ at k previous iterations for one parameter a, the estimated gradient value gradient for a at a i_{th} iteration is predicted as $\overline{x}^a_i = \sum_{j=i-k}^{i-1} g^a_i / k$. The Pearson Correlation Coefficient is further used to represent the similarity of gradient value change trend for various parameters at the i_{th} iteration, based on the purebred gradient values at k previous iterations. Then, parameters with small predicted gradient value and high similarity will be aggregated together to generate groups. Finally, we treat each group as a single value and then perturb it with a Gaussian mechanism. Specifically, we determine the sum of gradient values for each group at first, then add Gaussian noise to perturb the sum. The average perturbed value is used as the perturbed gradient for each parameter in the group.

As demonstrated by the example in Fig. 2, there are three parameters at the current i^{th} iteration and perturbed gradient values. At least three iterations are used to estimate the gradient value and change trend at current iteration (circle in green colour). Given $\tau_1 = 20, \tau_2 = 0.5, \tau_3 = 10, k = 3$, the value of each circle is the perturbed gradient values and the estimated gradient ($\overline{x}^a_i$) for three parameters at the current iteration is $(10 + 12 + 18)/3 = 13.3$, $(6 + 10 + 13)/3 = 9.7$ and $(48 + 62 + 80)/3 = 63.3$, respectively. As $63.3 > 20$, θ_3 is set as a separate group. For parameter θ_1 and θ_2, their Pearson Correlation Coefficient with their k previous perturbed gradient set $[10, 12, 18]$ and $[6, 10, 13]$ is 0.9347. Since $0.9347 > 0.5$, and $13.7 - 9.7$ is smaller than 10, we can group the two parameters together.

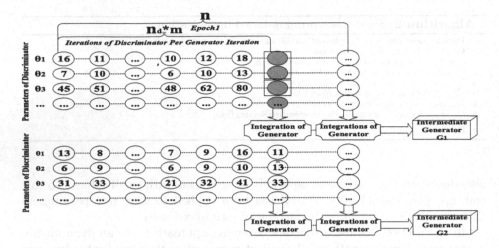

Fig. 2. The training progress of GAN.

3.3 Generator Selecting Optimization

As shown in Fig. 2, all the trained generators across all epochs, e.g., $G1, G2, ...,$ are archived as the GAN is trained. We apply targeted learning tasks to evaluate each intermediate generator. Specifically, we produce a batch of synthetic samples using each intermediate generative model and implement some specific machine learning algorithms, e.g., SVM, to build a prediction model based on these synthetic samples. We then test each prediction model using the original training samples to decide the accuracy of each prediction model. Based on the accuracy evaluation, we select these intermediate generators with better resulting accuracy to generalize the final generator.

To protect privacy in the generator selection, we apply the differentially private mechanism to perturb the selecting procedure. Specifically, to select a generator that can produce training samples for the most accurate machine learning models in a differential privacy-preserving manner, we use the standard "Report Noisy Max" subroutine [6]. For example, independent Laplace noise is injected to the accuracy of each prediction model, which is drawn from Laplace distribution $Lap(\Delta f/\epsilon)$ to achieve (ϵ, 0)-differential privacy. Here Δf is the sensitivity for queries.

4   Experimental Results

This section presents the result from empirical evaluations of the proposed PART-GAN over two benchmark datasets (EGG and eICU). These experiments aim to investigate the practical use of privacy-preserving GAN on synthetic data release: (1) Does PART-GAN enable the synthesization of realistic medical datasets, e.g., ICU data, with differential privacy perturbation? (2) Does the generated data retain satisfactory quality and utility for various data analysis tasks? (3) How do different optimization strategies affect the performance of PART-GAN?

4.1 Datasets and Settings

Datasets. In our experiments, we use two benchmark datasets:

EEG Database. We use the EEG signals from nine subjects provided by the Institute for Knowledge Discover[1]. The dataset contains data about the motor imagery of four different motor imagery tasks: the imagination of movement of the left hand (class 1), right hand (class 2), both feet (class 3), and tongue (class 4).

Philips eICU Database[2]. This dataset consists of about 200,000 patients from 208 care units across the United States, with a total of 224,026,866 entries divided into 33 tables. From this data, we focus on generating the four most frequently recorded, regularly-sampled variables measured by bedside monitors: oxygen saturation measured by pulse oximeter (SpO2), heart rate (HR), respiratory rate (RR) and mean arterial pressure (MAP).

Training and Architecture Setting. We use WGANs to further improve training stability, and train the network according to the setup described in [9], incorporating our perturbation mechanism and optimization strategies. We also scale the penalty term λ by the current critic difference $\tilde{W}(\mathbb{P}_r, \mathbb{P}_\theta)$ and use the one-sided penalty

$$P_1(\mathbb{P}_{\hat{x}}) = \lambda E_{\hat{x} \sim \mathbb{P}_{\hat{x}}}[max(0, (\|\nabla_{\hat{x}} D(\hat{x})\|_2 - 1)^2)]$$

The loss function for the critic is

$$L = -\tilde{W}(\mathbb{P}_r, \mathbb{P}_\theta) + max(0, \tilde{W}(\mathbb{P}_r, \mathbb{P}_\theta)) \times P_1(\mathbb{P}_{\hat{x}})$$

The λ is set at 10 [8]. Each stage is trained for 2000 epochs. Latent variables Z for the generator are sampled from $\mathcal{N}(0,1)$.

Here, the default parameters and threshold values were set as $\tau_1 = 20, \tau_2 = 0.5, \tau_3 = 10, k = 3, \eta = 0.002, \sigma_{EEG} = 0.561, \sigma_{eICU} = 0.598, K = 6$. The default values are used if no other values have been specified. Note that the experiments were performed on three classical differential privacy leakage levels, i.e., $(\epsilon, \delta) = \{Strong : (1, 10^{-5}); Weak : (4, 10^{-5}); VeryWeak : (15, 10^{-5})\}$. Each experiment was tested 10 times and the average result reported.

Metrics. The performance of the proposed PART-GAN is evaluated in terms of three different aspects: the data utility-based evaluation of the synthesis mechanism, the privacy-based evaluation of the perturbation mechanism, and the effectiveness of optimization. The detailed evaluation metrics are given as follows:

---

[1] http://www.bbci.de/competition/iv/#datasets.
[2] https://eicu-crd.mit.edu/.

(1) Data utility-related evaluation. The statistical distributions and cumulative distribution of each attribute are used to compare the statistical similarity between the original data and the corresponding attribute in perturbed/synthesized data. Also, the inception score (IS) [19] is adopted to evaluate the quality of data generated by GAN, $IS(G) = exp(\mathbb{E}_{x \sim G(z)} KL(Pr(y|x)||Pr(y)))$. The x is a sample generated by generator G, $Pr(y|x)$ is the conditional distribution of a pre-trained classifier to predict x's label y. A small entropy of $Pr(y|x)$ reveals that x is similar to a real sample. The marginal distribution of y is $Pr(y) = \int_x Pr(y|x = G(z))dz$. Note that baseline classifiers to predict $Pr(y|x)$ can be trained on an entire training set. The inception score $s(G)$ can describe both the quality and diversity of the synthetic data. However, since the inception score only relies on the final probabilities of the classifier, it is sensitive to noise and is not able to detect mode collapse. Thus, a pre-trained Deep4 model [20] is adopted as a replacement for the inception model. Besides, the correlation structure of attributes is used to compare the statistical similarity between the original data and the corresponding attribute in perturbed/synthesized data.

(2) Privacy-related evaluation. Distance-based metrics are widely used in many data privacy works. Euclidean distance can be used to evaluate how similar generated samples from the PART-GAN (PGS) are to the generated samples from ordinary GAN (OGS). By comparing the distances between OGS and PGS samples, we can investigate the distortion of generated samples from the perturbed generator. Here, we use the minimal distance (MD), i.e., Euclidean distance between a sample s of PGS to the sample closest to s in OGS. Optimally, the distribution of MD between samples of OGS and PGS should be equivalent to the distribution of MDs between only real samples with others than themselves. We calculate the distance after attribute-wise normalization because each attribute contributes equally to the distance after the normalization.

We compare PART-GAN performance with existing ordinary privacy-preserving GAN approaches [7,17,23,24] under differential privacy and ordinary GAN without perturbation using our evaluation metrics. (a) Original database. The baseline method for the data utility-related evaluations is to perform such evaluations on ordinary training samples, denoted by **original**. (b) Ordinary GAN approach without perturbation mechanism. To conduct the privacy-related evaluations, the synthetic samples generated from the ordinary GAN without perturbation mechanisms are used as the baseline datasets, denoted by **GAN**. (c) Regular GAN under differential privacy. To evaluate the improvements of our PART-GAN, the synthetic samples generated from the regular privacy-preserving GAN approaches under differential privacy are used as the baseline datasets, denoted by **DP-GAN** (e.g., commonly-adopted DP-SGD approaches [1,23,24]).

(3) The effectiveness of optimization strategies. We evaluate the impact of multi-folds optimization strategies on PART-GAN performance in terms of allowed iterations and Inception Score before and after applying optimization strategies.

4.2 Evaluation

In this section, a set of quantitative evaluations are conducted to evaluate the performance of PART-GAN, to address the second question: *Does the generated data retain satisfactory quality and utility for various data analysis tasks?*

Table 1. IS of original and synthetic data on MNIST/EEG/eICU dataset

Database	Model	$n(10^4)$	(ϵ, δ)	IS
MINIST/EEG/eICU	Original	5/200/300	–	$9.87 \pm 0.03/5.27 \pm 0.02/6.56 \pm 0.04$
	GAN	5/200/300	–	$8.98 \pm 0.03/4.01 + 0.02/5.42 \pm 0.04$
	DP-GAN	4/180/280	$(5/10/15, 10^{-5})$	$8.45 \pm 0.03/3.09 \pm 0.02/4.11 \pm 0.04$
	PART-GAN	4/180/280	$(5/10/15, 10^{-5})$	$8.77 \pm 0.03/3.89 \pm 0.02/5.07 \pm 0.04$

Inception Score Evaluation. Table 1 summarizes the Inception scores of original and synthetic data (generated by GAN with and without perturbation mechanism) for the EEG and eICU datasets. We found that PART-GAN enables us to synthesize data with Inception scores close to the original data, similar to ordinary GAN and better than DP-GAN. For EEG, the difference between the real data and the synthetic data by PART-GAN is less than 1.4, increasing from 3.09 to 3.89 compared to regular DP-GAN. For eICU, the difference between the real data and the synthetic data by PART-GAN is less than 1.5, increasing from 4.11 to 5.07 compared with regular DP-GAN.

Statistics and Cumulative Distribution Evaluation. The statistical distributions and cumulative distributions of specific sensitive attributes for original and synthetic data are demonstrated in Fig. 3, 4, 5 and 6.

Figures 3(a–b) and 4(a–b) are statistics of the sample label in the MNIST and EEG using ordinary GAN without perturbation, regular DP-GAN and our improved PART-GAN under various privacy-preserving level perturbation. We find that each label's statistics results using PART-GAN with the low-privacy setting are more realistic than regular GAN under the same setting.

Figures 5(a–b) and 6(a–b) show four cumulative distributions of the C3 of EEG attribute of EEG and the MAP attributes of the eICU dataset using ordinary GAN, regular DP-GAN, and PART-GAN under low and high privacy-preserving level perturbation. PART-GAN with the low-privacy setting produces a more realistic cumulative distribution and a wider range of values than others.

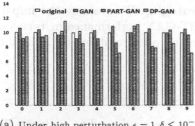
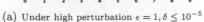
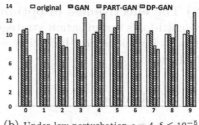

(a) Under high perturbation $\epsilon = 1, \delta \leq 10^{-5}$ (b) Under low perturbation $\epsilon = 4, \delta \leq 10^{-5}$

Fig. 3. Label distribution of the generated MNIST dataset via ordinary GAN, regular DP-GAN and PART-GAN. PART-GAN with the low-privacy (perturbation) setting are realistic as regular GAN under the same setting for the MNIST generation task.

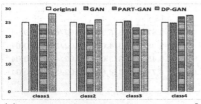
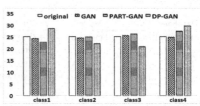

(a) Under high perturbation $\epsilon = 1, \delta \leq 10^{-5}$ (b) Under low perturbation $\epsilon = 4, \delta \leq 10^{-5}$

Fig. 4. Label distribution of the generated EEG dataset via ordinary GAN, regular DP-GAN and PART-GAN. PART-GAN with the low-privacy (perturbation) setting are realistic as regular GAN under the same setting for the EEG generation task.

In all cases, synthetic tables are statistically similar to the original table. PART-GAN with the high-privacy setting performs better than ordinary GAN. The optimization strategies show a better synthesis performance than both ordinary GAN and improved GAN without optimization.

At last, the efficiency of different optimization strategies on PART-GAN's performance is evaluated, to address the third question: *How do different optimization strategies affect the performance of PART-GAN?*

Table 2. Effect on allowed iterations #.

Itereations	# before	# after
MNIST	590	820
EGG	3300	4500
eICU	15000	22000

We first evaluate the optimization strategies on the number of allowed iterations given the same privacy constraints. We illustrate the maximum number of allowed iterations before and after applying optimization strategies, under the same privacy constraint. The number of allowed iterations is significantly increased by optimization strategies (from 3300 to 4500 for EGG and 15000 to 22000 for eICU), resulting in improved utility in the generators. Then, the effect of optimization strategies on the performance of PART-GAN is demonstrated in Table 2 for the EGG (labeled database) and eICU (unlabeled database), taking the Inception score as an example. It is clear that the performance of PART-GAN can be significantly improved by combining multi-fold optimization strategies.

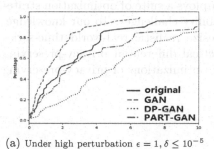
(a) Under high perturbation $\epsilon = 1, \delta \leq 10^{-5}$

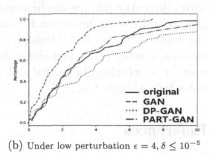
(b) Under low perturbation $\epsilon = 4, \delta \leq 10^{-5}$

Fig. 5. Cumulative distribution of attribute C3 for the generated EGG dataset via ordinary GAN, regular DP-GAN and PART-GAN. PART-GAN under low-privacy (perturbation) generates a more realistic cumulative distribution and a wider range of values than others for EGG generation task.

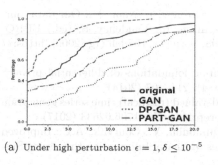
(a) Under high perturbation $\epsilon = 1, \delta \leq 10^{-5}$

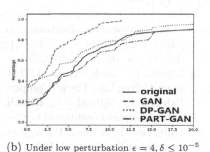
(b) Under low perturbation $\epsilon = 4, \delta \leq 10^{-5}$

Fig. 6. Cumulative distribution of attribute MAP for the eICU dataset by ordinary GAN, regular DP-GAN and PART-GAN. PART-GAN under low-privacy (perturbation) generates a more realistic cumulative distribution and a wider range of values than others for eICU generation task.

5   Conclusion

In this paper, we proposed PART-GAN, a generic scheme of publishing to synthesize time-series data in a privacy-preserving manner. Instead of releasing sanitized datasets, PART-GAN releases differentially private generative models, which can be used by analysts to synthesize an unlimited amount of data for arbitrary analysis tasks. To achieve this, PART-GAN uses a CT-GAN model for the generation of time series data with irregular sampling and under the guidance of a given classifier label. Then PART-GAN integrates the CT-GAN framework with differential privacy mechanisms and employs a suite of optimization strategies to address the utility and training stability challenges. To our knowledge, our method is the first attempt to synthesize realistic real-world time-series databases using GAN techniques in a practical differential privacy-preserving manner, combining the utility and stability optimizations of privacy-preserving GAN into a single task.

References

1. Abadi, M., et al.: Deep learning with differential privacy. In: Proceedings of the 2016 ACM SIGSAC Conference on Computer and Communications Security, pp. 308–318. ACM (2016)
2. Arjovsky, M., Chintala, S., Bottou, L.: Wasserstein GAN. arXiv preprint arXiv:1701.07875 (2017)
3. Arora, S., Ge, R., Neyshabur, B., Zhang, Y.: Stronger generalization bounds for deep nets via a compression approach. arXiv preprint arXiv:1802.05296 (2018)
4. Cynthia, D.: Differential privacy. In: Automata, Languages and Programming, pp. 1–12 (2006)
5. Dwork, C., Kenthapadi, K., McSherry, F., Mironov, I., Naor, M.: Our data, ourselves: privacy via distributed noise generation. In: Vaudenay, S. (ed.) EUROCRYPT 2006. LNCS, vol. 4004, pp. 486–503. Springer, Heidelberg (2006). https://doi.org/10.1007/11761679_29
6. Dwork, C., Roth, A., et al.: The algorithmic foundations of differential privacy. Found. Trends® Theor. Comput. Sci. 9(3–4), 211–407 (2014)
7. Esteban, C., Hyland, S.L., Rätsch, G.: Real-valued (medical) time series generation with recurrent conditional GANs. arXiv preprint arXiv:1706.02633 (2017)
8. Gulrajani, I., Ahmed, F., Arjovsky, M., Dumoulin, V., Courville, A.C.: Improved training of Wasserstein GANs. In: Advances in Neural Information Processing Systems, pp. 5767–5777 (2017)
9. Karras, T., Aila, T., Laine, S., Lehtinen, J.: Progressive growing of GANs for improved quality, stability, and variation. arXiv preprint arXiv:1710.10196 (2017)
10. Koh, P.W., Liang, P.: Understanding black-box predictions via influence functions. In: Proceedings of the 34th International Conference on Machine Learning, vol. 70, pp. 1885–1894. JMLR. org (2017)
11. Lee, N., Ajanthan, T., Torr, P.H.: SNIP: single-shot network pruning based on connection sensitivity. arXiv preprint arXiv:1810.02340 (2018)
12. Li, Y., Swersky, K., Zemel, R.: Generative moment matching networks. In: International Conference on Machine Learning, pp. 1718–1727 (2015)

13. Makhzani, A., Shlens, J., Jaitly, N., Goodfellow, I., Frey, B.: Adversarial autoencoders. arXiv preprint arXiv:1511.05644 (2015)
14. Mescheder, L., Nowozin, S., Geiger, A.: Adversarial variational bayes: unifying variational autoencoders and generative adversarial networks. arXiv preprint arXiv:1701.04722 (2017)
15. Mirza, M., Osindero, S.: Conditional generative adversarial nets. arXiv preprint arXiv:1411.1784 (2014)
16. Odena, A., Olah, C., Shlens, J.: Conditional image synthesis with auxiliary classifier GANs. In: Proceedings of the 34th International Conference on Machine Learning, vol. 70, pp. 2642–2651. JMLR. org (2017)
17. Park, N., Mohammadi, M., Gorde, K., Jajodia, S., Park, H., Kim, Y.: Data synthesis based on generative adversarial networks. Proc. VLDB Endow. 11(10), 1071–1083 (2018)
18. Ramponi, G., Protopapas, P., Brambilla, M., Janssen, R.: T-CGAN: conditional generative adversarial network for data augmentation in noisy time series with irregular sampling. arXiv preprint arXiv:1811.08295 (2018)
19. Salimans, T., Goodfellow, I., Zaremba, W., Cheung, V., Radford, A., Chen, X.: Improved techniques for training GANs. In: Advances in Neural Information Processing Systems, pp. 2234–2242 (2016)
20. Schirrmeister, R.T., et al.: Deep learning with convolutional neural networks for eeg decoding and visualization. Hum. Brain Mapp. 38(11), 5391–5420 (2017)
21. Song, S., Chaudhuri, K., Sarwate, A.D.: Stochastic gradient descent with differentially private updates. In: 2013 IEEE Global Conference on Signal and Information Processing (GlobalSIP), pp. 245–248. IEEE (2013)
22. Wang, Q., Zhang, Y., Lu, X., Wang, Z., Qin, Z., Ren, K.: Real-time and spatio-temporal crowd-sourced social network data publishing with differential privacy. IEEE Trans. Dependable Secure Comput. 15, 591–606 (2016)
23. Xie, L., Lin, K., Wang, S., Wang, F., Zhou, J.: Differentially private generative adversarial network. arXiv preprint arXiv:1802.06739 (2018)
24. Zhang, X., Ji, S., Wang, T.: Differentially private releasing via deep generative model. arXiv preprint arXiv:1801.01594 (2018)

EvoNet: A Neural Network for Predicting the Evolution of Dynamic Graphs

Changmin Wu[✉], Giannis Nikolentzos, and Michalis Vazirgiannis

LIX, Ecole Polytechnique, 91120 Palaiseau, France
{cwu,nikolentzos,mvazirg}@lix.polytechnique.fr

Abstract. Neural networks for structured data like graphs have been studied extensively in recent years. To date, the bulk of research activity has focused mainly on static graphs. However, most real-world networks are dynamic since their topology tends to change over time. Predicting the evolution of dynamic graphs is a task of high significance in the area of graph mining. Despite its practical importance, the task has not been explored in depth so far, mainly due to its challenging nature. In this paper, we propose a model that predicts the evolution of dynamic graphs. Specifically, we use a graph neural network along with a recurrent architecture to capture the temporal evolution patterns of dynamic graphs. Then, we employ a generative model which predicts the topology of the graph at the next time step and constructs a graph instance that corresponds to that topology. We evaluate the proposed model on several artificial datasets following common network evolving dynamics, as well as on real-world datasets. Results demonstrate the effectiveness of the proposed model.

Keywords: Dynamic graph · Topology prediction · Graph neural network

1 Introduction

Graph Neural Networks (GNNs) have emerged in recent years as an effective tool for analyzing graph-structured data [7,24]. These architectures bring the expressive power of deep learning into non-Euclidean data such as graphs, and have demonstrated convincing performance in several graph mining tasks, including graph classification [16], link prediction [27], and community detection [4]. So far, GNNs have been mainly applied to tasks that involve static graphs. However, most real-world networks are dynamic, i.e., nodes and edges are added and removed over time. Despite the success of GNNs in various applications, it is still not clear if these models are useful for learning in dynamic scenarios. Although some models have been applied to this type of data, most studies have focused on predicting a low-dimensional representation (i.e., embedding) of the graph for the next time step [8,12,17,19,21]. These representations can then be used in downstream tasks [8,12,15,19]. However, predicting the topology of the graph

© Springer Nature Switzerland AG 2020
I. Farkaš et al. (Eds.): ICANN 2020, LNCS 12396, pp. 594–606, 2020.
https://doi.org/10.1007/978-3-030-61609-0_47

(and not its low-dimensional representation) is a task that has not been properly addressed yet.

Graph generation, another important task in graph mining, has attracted a lot of attention from the deep learning community in recent years. The objective of this task is to generate graphs that exhibit specific properties, e.g., degree distribution, node triangle participation, community structure, etc. Traditionally, graphs are generated based on some network generation model such as the Erdős-Rényi model. These models focus on modeling one or more network properties, and neglect the others. Neural network approaches, on the other hand, can better capture the properties of graphs since they follow a supervised approach [3,9,26]. These architectures minimize a loss function such as the reconstruction error of the adjacency matrix or the value of a graph comparison algorithm.

Capitalizing on recent developments in neural networks for graph-structured data and graph generation, we propose in this paper, to the best of our knowledge, the first framework for predicting the evolution of the topology of networks in time. The proposed framework can be viewed as an encoder-predictor-decoder architecture. The "encoder" network takes a sequence of graphs as input and uses a GNN to produce a low-dimensional representation for each one of these graphs. These representations capture structural information about the input graphs. Then, the "predictor" network employs a recurrent architecture which predicts a representation for the future instance of the graph. The "decoder" network corresponds to a graph generation model which utilizes the predicted representation, and generates the topology of the graph for the next time step. The proposed model is evaluated over a series of experiments on synthetic and real-world datasets, and is compared against several baseline methods. To measure the effectiveness of the proposed model and the baselines, the generated graphs need to be compared with the ground-truth graph instances using some graph comparison algorithm. To this end, we use the Weisfeiler-Lehman subtree kernel which scales to very large graphs and has achieved state-of-the-art results on many graph datasets [22]. Results show that the proposed model yields good performance, and in most cases, outperforms the competing methods.

The rest of this paper is organized as follows. Section 2 provides an overview of the related work and elaborates our contribution. Section 3 introduces some preliminary concepts and definitions related to the graph generation problem, followed by a detailed presentation of the components of the proposed model. Section 4 evaluates the proposed model on several tasks. Finally, Sect. 5 concludes.

2   Related Work

Our work is related to random graph models. These models are very popular in graph theory and network science. The Erdős-Rényi model [6], the preferential attachment model [2], and the Kronecker graph model [10] are some typical examples of such models. To predict how a graph structure will evolve over time, the values of the parameters of these models can be estimated based on the corresponding values of the observed graph instances, and then the estimated values can be passed on to these models to generate graphs.

Other works along a similar direction include neural network models which combine GNNs with RNNs [14,19,21]. These models use GNNs to extract features from a graph and RNNs for sequence learning from the extracted features. Other similar approaches do not use GNNs, but they instead perform random walks or employ deep autoencoders [8,17]. All these works focus on predicting how the node representations or the graph representations will evolve over time. However, some applications require predicting the topology of the graph, and not just its low-dimensional representation. The proposed model constitutes the first step towards this objective.

3   EvoNet: A Neural Network for Predicting Graph Evolution

In this Section, we first introduce basic concepts from graph theory, and define our notation. We then present EvoNet, the proposed framework for predicting the evolution of graphs. Since the proposed model comprises of several components, we describe all these components in detail.

3.1   Preliminaries

Let $\mathcal{G} = (V, E)$ be an undirected, unweighted graph, where V is the set of nodes and E is the set of edges. We will denote by n the number of vertices and by m the number of edges. We define a permutation of the nodes of $\mathcal{G}$ as a bijective function $\pi : V \to V$, under which any graph property of G should be invariant. We are interested in the topology of a graph which is described by its adjacency matrix $A^\pi \in \mathbb{R}^{n \times n}$ with a specific ordering of the nodes π[1]. Each entry of the adjacency matrix is defined as $A^\pi_{ij} = \mathbb{1}_{(\pi(v_i), \pi(v_j)) \in E}$ where $v_i, v_j \in V$. In what follows, we consider the "topology", "structure" and "adjacency matrix" of a graph equivalent to each other.

In many real-world networks, besides the adjacency matrix that encodes connectivity information, nodes and/or edges are annotated with a feature vector, which we denote as $X \in \mathbb{R}^{n \times d}$ and $L \in \mathbb{R}^{m \times d'}$, respectively. Hence, a graph object can be also written in the form of a triplet $\mathcal{G} = (A, X, L)$. In this paper, we use this triplet to represent all graphs. If a graph does not contain node/edge attributes, we assign attributes to it based on local properties (e.g., degree, k-core number, number of triangles, etc.).

An evolving network is a graph whose topology changes as a function of time. Interestingly, almost all real-world networks evolve over time by adding and removing nodes and/or edges. For instance, in social networks, people make and lose friends over time, while there are people who join the network and others who leave the network. An evolving graph is a sequence of graphs $\{\mathcal{G}_0, \mathcal{G}_1, \ldots, \mathcal{G}_T\}$

---

[1] For simplicity, the ordering π will be omitted in what follows.

where $\mathcal{G}_t = (A_t, X_t, E_t)$ represents the state of the evolving graph at time step t. It should be noted that not only nodes and edges can evolve over time, but also node and edge attributes. However, in this paper, we keep attributes of each node and edge fixed, and we allow only the node and edge sets of the graphs to change as a function of time. The sequence can thus be written as $\{\mathcal{G}_t = (A_t, X, E)\}_{t \in [0,T]}$. We are often interested in predicting what "comes next" in a sequence, based on data encountered in previous time steps. In our setting, this is equivalent to predicting $\mathcal{G}_t$ based on the sequence $\{\mathcal{G}_k\}_{k<t}$. In sequential modeling, we usually do not take into account the whole sequence, but only those instances within a fixed small window of size w before $\mathcal{G}_t$, which we denote as $\{\mathcal{G}_{t-w}, \mathcal{G}_{t-w+1}, \ldots, \mathcal{G}_{t-1}\}$. We refer to these instances as the graph history. The problem is then to predict the topology of $\mathcal{G}_t$ given its history.

3.2 Proposed Architecture

The proposed architecture is very similar to a typical sequence learning framework. The main difference lies in the fact that instead of vectors, in our setting, the elements of the sequence correspond to graphs. The combinatorial nature of graph-structured data increases the complexity of the problem and calls for more sophisticated architectures than the ones employed in traditional sequence learning tasks. Specifically, the proposed model consists of three components: (1) a graph neural network (GNN) which generates a vector representation for each graph instance, (2) a recurrent neural network (RNN) for sequential learning, and (3) a graph generation model for predicting the graph topology at the next time step. This framework can also be viewed as an encoder-predictor-decoder model. The first two components correspond to an encoder network which maps the sequence of graphs into a sequence of vectors and another network that predicts a representation for the next in the sequence graph. The decoder network consists of the last component of the model, and transforms the above representation into a graph. Figure 1 illustrates the proposed model. In what follows, we present the above three components of EvoNet.

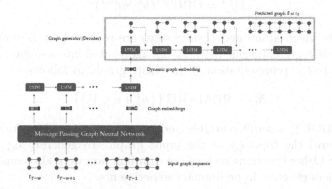

Fig. 1. Illustration of the proposed architecture

Encoding Graphs Using Graph Neural Networks. Graph Neural Networks (GNNs) have recently emerged as a dominant paradigm for performing machine learning tasks on graphs. Several GNN variants have been proposed in the past years. All these models employ some message passing procedure to update node representations. Specifically, each node updates its representation by aggregating the representations of its neighbors. After k iterations of the message passing procedure, each node obtains a feature vector which captures the structural information within its k-hop neighborhood. Then, GNNs compute a feature vector for the entire graph using some permutation invariant readout function such as summing the representations of all the nodes of the graph. As described below, the learning process can be divided into three phases: (1) aggregation, (2) update, and (3) readout.

Aggregation. In this phase, the network computes a message for each node of the graph. To compute that message for a node, the network aggregates the representations of its neighbors. Formally, at iteration step $l + 1$, a message vector m_v^{l+1} is computed from the representations of the neighbors $\mathcal{N}(v)$ of v:

$$m_v^{l+1} = \text{AGGREGATE}^{l+1}(\{h_w^l \mid w \in \mathcal{N}(v)\}) \tag{1}$$

where AGGREGATE is a permutation invariant function. Furthermore, for the network to be end-to-end trainable, this function needs to be differentiable. In our implementation, AGGREGATE is a multi-layer perceptron (MLP) followed by a sum function.

Update. The new representation h_v^{l+1} of v is then computed by combining its current feature vector h_v^l with the message vector m_v^{l+1}:

$$h_v^{l+1} = \text{UPDATE}^{l+1}(h_v^l, m_v^{l+1}) \tag{2}$$

The UPDATE function also needs to be differentiable. To combine the two feature vectors (i.e., h_v^l and m_v^{l+1}), we employ the Gated Recurrent Unit proposed in [13]:

$$h_v^{l+1} = \text{GRU}^{l+1}(h_v^l, m_v^{l+1}) \tag{3}$$

Readout. The *Aggregation* and *Update* steps are repeated for L iterations. The emerging node representations $\{h_v^L\}_{v \in V}$ are aggregated into a single vector which corresponds to the representation of the entire graph, as follows:

$$h_G = \text{READOUT}(\{h_v^L \mid v \in V\}) \tag{4}$$

where READOUT is a differentiable and permutation invariant function. This vector captures the topology of the input graph. To generate h_G, we utilize *Set2Set* [23]. Other functions such as the sum function were also considered, but were found less effective in preliminary experiments.

Predicting Graph Representations Using Recurrent Neural Networks.
Given an input sequence of graphs, we use the GNN described above to generate
a vector representation for each graph in the sequence. Then, to process this
sequence, we use a recurrent neural network (RNN). RNNs use their internal
state (i.e., memory) to preserve sequential information. These networks exhibit
temporal dynamic behavior, and can find correlations between sequential events.
Specifically, an RNN processes the input sequence in a series of time steps (i.e.,
one for each element in the sequence). For a given time step t, the hidden state
h_t at that time step is updated as:

$$h_{t+1} = f(h_t, x_{t+1}) \tag{5}$$

where f is a non-linear activation function. A generative RNN outputs a probability distribution over the next element of the sequence given its current state
h_t. RNNs can be trained to predict the next element (e.g., graph) in the sequence,
i.e., they can learn the conditional distribution $p(G_t|G_1, \ldots, G_{t-1})$. In our imple-
mentation, we use a Long Short-Term Memory (LSTM) network that reads
sequentially the vectors $\{h_{G_i}\}_{i\in[t-w,t-1]}$ produced by the GNN, and generates
a vector h_{G_t} that represents the embedding of G_t. The embedding incorporates
topological information and will serve as input to the graph generation module. The GNN component presented above can be seen as a form of an encoder
network. It takes as input a sequence of graphs and projects them into a low-
dimensional space. Then, this component takes the sequence of graph representations as input and predicts the representation of the graph at the next time
step.

Graph Generation. To generate a graph that corresponds to the evolution
of the current graph instance, we capitalize on a recently-proposed framework
for learning generative models of graphs [26]. This framework models a graph
in an autoregressive manner (i.e., a sequence of additions of new nodes and
edges) to capture the complex joint probability of all nodes and edges in the
graph. Formally, given a node ordering π, it considers a graph G as a sequence
of vectors:

$$S_G^\pi = (S_1^\pi, S_2^\pi, \ldots, S_{|V|}^\pi) \tag{6}$$

where $S_i^\pi = [a_{1,i}, \ldots, a_{i-1,i}] \in \{0,1\}^{i-1}$ is the adjacency vector between node
$\pi(i)$ and the nodes preceding it $(\{\pi(1), \ldots, \pi(i-1)\})$. We adapt this framework
to our supervised setting.

The objective of the generative model is to maximize the likelihood of the
observed graphs of the training set. Since a graph can be expressed as a sequence
of adjacency vectors (given a node ordering), we can consider instead the distribution $p(\hat{S}^\pi; \theta)$, which can be decomposed in an autoregressive manner into the
following product:

$$p(\hat{S}^\pi; \theta) = \prod_{i=1}^{|V|} p(\hat{S}_i^\pi | \hat{S}_{k:k<i}^\pi, \theta) = \prod_{i=1}^{|V|} \prod_{j=1}^{i-1} p(\hat{a}_{ji}^\pi | \hat{a}_{li:l<j}^\pi, \hat{S}_{k:k<i}^\pi, \theta) \tag{7}$$

This product can be parameterized by a neural network. Specifically, following [26], we use a hierarchical RNN consisting of two levels: (1) the graph-level RNN which maintains the state of the graph and generates new nodes and thus learns the distribution $p(\hat{S}_i^\pi | \hat{S}_{k:k<i}^\pi)$ and (2) the edge-level RNN which generates links between each generated node and previously-generated nodes and thus learns the distribution $p(\hat{a}_{ji}^\pi | \hat{a}_{li:l<j}^\pi)$. More formally, we have:

$$h_0 = h_{\mathcal{G}_T} \qquad h_i = RNN_1(h_{i-1}, \hat{S}_{i-1}^\pi)$$
$$m_{0,i} = h_i \qquad m_{j,i} = RNN_2(m_{j-1,i}, \hat{a}_{j-1,i}^\pi) \qquad (8)$$
$$p(\hat{a}_{j,i}^\pi = 1) = \sigma(m_{j,i}) \qquad \hat{a}_{j,i}^\pi \sim p$$

where h_i is the state vector of the graph-level RNN (i.e., RNN_1) that encodes the current state of the graph sequence and is initialized by $h_{\mathcal{G}_T}$, the predicted embedding of the graph at the next time step T. The output of the graph-level RNN corresponds to the initial state of the edge-level RNN (i.e., RNN_2). The resulting value is then squashed by a sigmoid function to produce the probability of existence of an edge $a_{\hat{j},i}$. In other words, the model learns the probability distribution of the existence of edges and a graph can then be sampled from this distribution, which will serve as the predicted topology for the next time step T.

To train the model, the cross-entropy loss between existence of each edge and its probability of existence is minimized:

$$L = \sum_{i=1}^{|V|} \sum_{j=1}^{i-1} a_{j,i}^\pi \big(1 - p(\hat{a}_{j,i}^\pi = 1)\big) + (1 - a_{j,i}^\pi) p(\hat{a}_{j,i}^\pi = 1) \qquad (9)$$

4   Experiments and Results

In this section, we evaluate the performance of EvoNet on synthetic and real-world datasets for predicting the evolution of graph topology, and we compare it against several baseline methods.

4.1   Datasets

We use both synthetic and real-world datasets. The synthetic datasets consist of sequences of graphs where there is a specific pattern on how each graph emerges from the previous graph instance, i.e., add/remove some graph structure at each time step. The patterns we experimented on are paths, cycles and ladders. The real-world datasets correspond to single graphs whose nodes incorporate temporal information, which we decompose into sequences of snapshots based on their timestamps. The size of the graphs in each sequence ranges from tens of nodes to several thousand of nodes. We experimented on Bitcoin trading datasets (Bitcoin Alpha, Bitcoin OTC), social network datasets (UCI-Forum, UCI-Message) and Email exchange datasets (EU-core, DNC). Details about these datasets are given in Table 1, and their descriptions can be found in [11] and [20].

Table 1. Statistics of the 6 real-world datasets used in our experiments.

	$|V|$	$|E|$	% Pos.Edges	Timespan	
				Begin	End
BTC-OTC	5,881	35,592	89%	2010-11-08	2016-01-25
BTC-Alpha	3,783	24,186	93%	2010-11-08	2016-01-22
UCI-Forum	899	33,720	—	2004-05-15	2004-10-26
UCI-Message	1,899	59,835	—	2004-04-15	2004-10-26
EU-Core	986	332,334	—	1970-01-01	1972-03-14
DNC	1,891	39,264	—	2013-09-16	2016-05-25

4.2 Baselines

We compare EvoNet against several random graph models: (1) the Erdős-Rényi model (ER, [6]), (2) the Stochastic Block model (SBM, [1]), (3) the Barabási–Albert model (BA, [2]), and (4) the Kronecker Graph model (Kron-fix, Kron-rand, [10]). These are the traditional methods to study the topology evolution of temporal graphs, by proposing a driven mechanism behind the evolution. To be precise, these models begin with an initial graph and a rule to connect new emerged nodes with existing ones, then gradually grow the initial graph to the expected size following this rule.

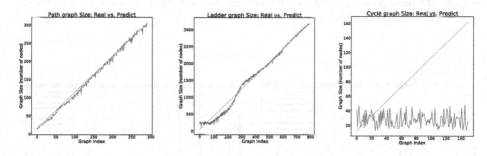

Fig. 2. Results of synthetic datasets. Comparison of graph size (path, ladder and cycle graphs from left to right): predicted size (blue) vs. real size (orange). (Color figure online)

4.3 Evaluation Metric and Experimental Setup

In general, it is very challenging to measure the performance of a graph generative model since it requires comparing two graphs to each other, a long-standing problem in mathematics and computer science [5]. We propose to use graph kernels to compare graphs to each other, and thus to evaluate the quality of the generated graphs. Graph kernels have emerged as one of the most effective tools for graph comparison in recent years [18]. A graph kernel is a symmetric positive semidefinite function which takes two graphs as input, and measures their similarity. In our experiments, we employ the Weisfeiler-Lehman subtree kernel which counts label-based subtree-patterns [22]. Note that we also normalize the kernel values, and thus the emerging values lie between 0 and 1.

As previously mentioned, each dataset corresponds to a sequence of graphs where each sequence represents the evolution of the topology of a single graph in 1000 time steps. We use the first 80% of these graph instances for training and the rest of them serve as our test set. The window size w is set equal to 10, which means that we feed 10 consecutive graph instances to the model and predict the topology of the instance that directly follows the last of these 10 input instances. Each graph of the test set along with its corresponding predicted graph is then passed on to the Weisfeiler-Lehman subtree kernel which measures their similarity and thus the performance of the model.

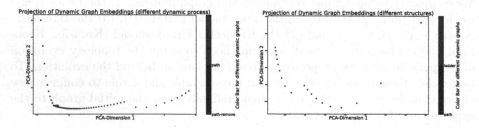

Fig. 3. 2D projection of dynamic embeddings learned from datasets with different structures or different dynamics

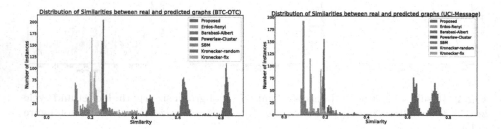

Fig. 4. Similarity histograms on BTC-OTC (left) and UCI-Message (right) datasets. Blue one is the result of EvoNet, which is compared against 6 random graph models.

The hyperparameters of EvoNet are chosen based on its performance on a validation set. The parameters of the random graph models are set under the principle that the generated graphs need to share similar properties with the ground-truth graphs. For instance, in the case of the Erdős-Rényi model, the probability of adding an edge between two nodes is set to a value such that the density of the generated graph is identical to that of the ground-truth graph. However, since the model should not have access to such information (e.g., density of the ground-truth graph), we use an MLP to predict this property based on past data (i.e., the number of nodes and edges of the previous graph instances). This is in par with how the proposed model computes the size of the graphs to be generated (i.e., using also an MLP).

4.4 Results

We next present the experimental results and compare the performance of EvoNet against that of the baselines.

Table 2. Statistics on the similarity distribution of different models.

Model/Stat.	BTC-OTC		BTC-ALPHA		UCI-Forum		UCI-Mesg		EU-Core		DNC	
	Mean	90%ile	Mean	90%ile	Mean	90%ile	Mean	90%ile	Mean	90%ile	Mean	90%ile
ER	0.28	0.40	0.22	0.32	0.15	0.16	0.16	0.26	0.06	0.09	0.82	1.00
SBM	0.21	0.30	0.18	0.27	0.10	0.10	0.13	0.22	0.03	0.05	0.84	1.00
BA	0.35	0.48	0.23	0.28	0.29	0.31	0.23	0.33	0.12	0.16	**0.85**	1.00
Power	0.35	0.48	0.23	0.28	0.29	0.31	0.23	0.33	0.12	0.16	0.85	1.00
Kron-Rand	0.62	0.64	0.44	0.47	0.59	0.62	0.62	0.65	0.60	0.65	0.01	0.02
Kron-Fix	0.21	0.23	0.08	0.11	0.44	0.47	0.18	0.20	0.53	0.55	0.01	0.06
EvoNet	**0.82**	**0.84**	**0.55**	**0.59**	**0.64**	**0.68**	**0.71**	**0.75**	**0.76**	**0.81**	0.83	1.00

Synthetic Datasets. Figure 2 illustrates the experimental results on the synthetic datasets. Since the graph structures contained in the synthetic datasets are fairly simple, it is easy for the model to generate graphs very similar to the ground-truth graphs (normalized kernel values > 0.9). Hence, instead of reporting the kernel values, we compare the size of the predicted graphs against that of the ground-truth graphs. The figures visualize the increase of graph size on real sequence (orange) and predicted sequence (blue). For path graphs, in spite of small variance, we have an accurate prediction on the graph size. For ladder graph, we observe a mismatch at the beginning of the sequence for small size graphs but then a coincidence of the two lines on large size graphs. This mismatch on small graphs may be due to a more complex structure in ladder graphs such as cycles, as supported by the results of cycle graph on the right figure, where we completely mispredict the size of cycle graphs. In fact, we fail to reconstruct the cycle structure in the prediction, with all the predicted graphs being path graphs. This failure could be related to the limitations of GNN mentioned in [25].

Dynamic Graph Embedding. It is also important to check whether, in our encode-decoder framework, the learned code, which we refer to as "dynamic graph embedding", is really meaningful. We design two experiments to verify the effectiveness of our embedding, with the help of synthetic graphs. In the first experiment, we take as input two sequences of graphs belonging to the same class but following different evolution dynamics. Specifically we took path graph and path graph with removal. In the second experiment, we control the evolution dynamic and vary the structures of graphs, where we use path graphs and ladder graphs following the same evolution of increasing size. The dynamic graph embeddings of different datasets learned from these experiments are recorded and visualized in Fig. 3. Each point represents the projections of embeddings of each graph in the sequence into a 2-dimensional space by Principle Component Analysis (PCA). As we can see from the figure, embeddings learned from different datasets, either with different dynamics or with different structures, are both well separated, which suggests that the embeddings are meaningful, and those from the same dataset form special patterns such as a line in the space, which suggests a temporal dependency between these embeddings as they are learned from sequential data.

Real-World Datasets. Finally, we analyze the performance of our model on the six real datasets. We obtain the similarities between each pair of real and predicted graphs in the sequence and draw a histogram to illustrate the distribution of similarities. Due to page limit, we choose to only show the histogram plot of BTC-OTC and UCI-Message datasets in Fig. 4. Among all the traditional random graph models, Kronecker graph model (with learnable parameter) performs the best, however on both datasets, our proposed method EvoNet (in blue) outperforms tremendously all other methods, with an average similarity of 0.82 on BTC-OTC dataset and 0.71 on UCI-Message dataset. Detailed statistics and results for other datasets can be found in Table 2, where we can find that our proposed model performs consistently better than the traditional methods. Overall, despite a failure in capturing some specific structures discovered in synthetic datasets, our experiments demonstrate the advantage of EvoNet over the traditional random graph models on predicting the evolution of dynamic graphs, especially for real world data with complex structures.

5   Conclusion

In this paper, we proposed EvoNet, a model that predicts the evolution of dynamic graphs, following an encoder-decoder framework. We also proposed an evaluation methodology for this task which capitalizes on the well-established family of graph kernels. Experiments show that the proposed model outperforms traditional random graph methods on both synthetic and real-world datasets.

References

1. Airoldi, E.M., Blei, D.M., Fienberg, S.E., Xing, E.P.: Mixed membership stochastic blockmodels. J. Mach. Learn. Res. **9**, 1981–2014 (2008)
2. Albert, R., Barabási, A.L.: Statistical mechanics of complex networks. Rev. Mod. Phys. **74**(1), 47 (2002)
3. Bojchevski, A., Shchur, O., Zügner, D., Günnemann, S.: Netgan: generating graphs via random walks. arXiv preprint arXiv:1803.00816 (2018)

4. Chen, Z., Li, X., Bruna, J.: Supervised community detection with line graph neural networks. arXiv preprint arXiv:1705.08415 (2017)
5. Conte, D., Foggia, P., Sansone, C., Vento, M.: Thirty years of graph matching in pattern recognition. Int. J. Pattern Recogn. Artif. Intell. 18(03), 265–298 (2004)
6. Erdős, P., Rényi, A.: On the evolution of random graphs. Publ. Math. Inst. Hung. Acad. Sci 5(1), 17–60 (1960)
7. Gilmer, J., Schoenholz, S.S., Riley, P.F., Vinyals, O., Dahl, G.E.: Neural message passing for quantum chemistry. In: Proceedings of the 34th International Conference on Machine Learning-Volume 70, pp. 1263–1272. JMLR. org (2017)
8. Goyal, P., Kamra, N., He, X., Liu, Y.: Dyngem: Deep embedding method for dynamic graphs. arXiv preprint arXiv:1805.11273 (2018)
9. Grover, A., Zweig, A., Ermon, S.: Graphite: iterative generative modeling of graphs. arXiv preprint arXiv:1803.10459 (2018)
10. Leskovec, J., Chakrabarti, D., Kleinberg, J., Faloutsos, C., Ghahramani, Z.: Kronecker graphs: an approach to modeling networks. J. Mach. Learn. Res. 11, 985–1042 (2010)
11. Leskovec, J., Krevl, A.: SNAP datasets: stanford large network dataset collection, June 2014. http://snap.stanford.edu/data
12. Li, C., Guo, X., Mei, Q.: Deepgraph: graph structure predicts network growth. arXiv preprint arXiv:1610.06251 (2016)
13. Li, Y., Tarlow, D., Brockschmidt, M., Zemel, R.: Gated graph sequence neural networks. arXiv preprint arXiv:1511.05493 (2015)
14. Manessi, F., Rozza, A., Manzo, M.: Dynamic graph convolutional networks. arXiv preprint arXiv:1704.06199 (2017)
15. Meng, C., Mouli, S.C., Ribeiro, B., Neville, J.: Subgraph pattern neural networks for high-order graph evolution prediction. In: Thirty-Second AAAI Conference on Artificial Intelligence (2018)
16. Morris, C., et al.: Weisfeiler and leman go neural: higher-order graph neural networks. Proceedings of the AAAI Conference on Artificial Intelligence vol. 33, pp. 4602–4609 (2019)
17. Nguyen, G.H., Lee, J.B., Rossi, R.A., Ahmed, N.K., Koh, E., Kim, S.: Continuous-time dynamic network embeddings. In: Companion Proceedings of the The Web Conference 2018, pp. 969–976. International World Wide Web Conferences Steering Committee (2018)
18. Nikolentzos, G., Siglidis, G., Vazirgiannis, M.: Graph Kernels: a Survey. arXiv preprint arXiv:1904.12218 (2019)
19. Pareja, A., et al.: Evolvegcn: evolving graph convolutional networks for dynamic graphs. arXiv preprint arXiv:1902.10191 (2019)
20. Rossi, R.A., Ahmed, N.K.: The network data repository with interactive graph analytics and visualization. In: AAAI (2015). http://networkrepository.com
21. Seo, Y., Defferrard, M., Vandergheynst, P., Bresson, X.: Structured sequence modeling with graph convolutional recurrent networks. In: Cheng, L., Leung, A.C.S., Ozawa, S. (eds.) ICONIP 2018. LNCS, vol. 11301, pp. 362–373. Springer, Cham (2018). https://doi.org/10.1007/978-3-030-04167-0_33
22. Shervashidze, N., Schweitzer, P., Leeuwen, E.J.V., Mehlhorn, K., Borgwardt, K.M.: Weisfeiler-lehman graph kernels. J. Mach. Learn. Res. 12, 2539–2561 (2011)
23. Vinyals, O., Bengio, S., Kudlur, M.: Order matters: sequence to sequence for sets. arXiv preprint arXiv:1511.06391 (2015)
24. Wu, Z., Pan, S., Chen, F., Long, G., Zhang, C., Yu, P.S.: A comprehensive survey on graph neural networks. arXiv preprint arXiv:1901.00596 (2019)

25. Xu, K., Hu, W., Leskovec, J., Jegelka, S.: How powerful are graph neural networks? arXiv preprint arXiv:1810.00826 (2018)
26. You, J., Ying, R., Ren, X., Hamilton, W.L., Leskovec, J.: Graphrnn: Generating realistic graphs with deep auto-regressive models. arXiv preprint arXiv:1802.08773 (2018)
27. Zhang, M., Chen, Y.: Link prediction based on graph neural networks. In: Advances in Neural Information Processing Systems, pp. 5165–5175 (2018)

Hybrid Neural-Symbolic Architectures

Facial Expression Recognition Method Based on a Part-Based Temporal Convolutional Network with a Graph-Structured Representation

Lei Zhong[1,2], Changmin Bai[1,2], Jianfeng Li[1,2(✉)], Tong Chen[1,2], and Shigang Li[1,3]

[1] School of Electronic and Information Engineering, Southwest University, Chongqing, China
1169501290@qq.com, 794091154@qq.com, {popqlee,c_tong}@swu.edu.cn,
shigangli@hiroshima-cu.ac.jp
[2] Chongqing Key Laboratory of Nonlinear Circuit and Intelligent Information Processing,
Southwest University, Chongqing, China
[3] Hiroshima City University, Hiroshima, Japan

Abstract. Facial expressions are controlled by facial muscles and can be regarded as appearance and shape variations in key parts. A key challenge in facial expression recognition is capturing effective information from a facial image. In this paper, we propose a basic graph contour that is based on key parts for facial expression recognition. Each node on the graph contour represents a landmark, and each edge represents the connection between the two selected nodes. To further investigate the graph representation and to make the graphs more distinctive, we use a Gabor filter to extract appearance variations around the graph nodes while applying an affine transformation to capture the shape variations from graphs without expression in graphs with expression. Then, to serve as an efficient network for processing in which the graph extracts the appearance and shape representations, we introduce the temporal convolutional network (TCN). Finally, we propose a part-based temporal convolutional network (PTCN) that emphasizes the key facial parts. The experimental results demonstrate that this method realizes significant improvements over state-of-the-art methods utilizing three widely used facial databases: Oulu-CASIA, CK+, and MMI.

Keywords: Facial expression recognition · TCN · Graph-structured representation

1 Introduction

In human-machine systems, biometrics, such as gaze, gesture, and facial expression, are always of increasing concern. Since facial expressions can provide a machine with direct feedback regarding human feelings, the recognition of facial expressions has been a hot topic of research for many years. In the early days, research on facial expression

L. Zhong and C. Bai have contributed equally.

© Springer Nature Switzerland AG 2020
I. Farkaš et al. (Eds.): ICANN 2020, LNCS 12396, pp. 609–620, 2020.
https://doi.org/10.1007/978-3-030-61609-0_48

recognition focused mainly on appearance variation analysis with LBP or a Gabor filter since the appearance variations among expressions are large. Then, people gradually determined that expression generation is a dynamic process. The geometric variation is also important in distinguishing among expressions. Many methods have been proposed that are based on the previous studies, such as the local binary patterns on three orthogonal planes (LBP-TOP) and expressionlets on a spatiotemporal manifold (STM-ExpLet). In this stage, studies focus mainly on feature extraction and efficient feature selection. After feature extraction and feature selection, traditional classification is used to recognize facial expressions. SVM is commonly used to process features. However, satisfactory results are difficult to obtain via the traditional classification method.

The recent success of deep learning has led to an increase in deep learning-based facial expression recognition methods. Yao et al. [1] constructed a CNN architecture, namely, HoloNet, that uses the concatenated rectified linear unit (CReLU) instead of the popular rectified linear unit (ReLU) to reduce the number of redundant filters and improve the non-saturated nonlinearity in the lower convolutional layers. Simultaneously, this model designs an inception-residual block that learns multiscale features that can explicitly capture variations in emotions. Liu et al. [2] proposed a 3D convolutional neural network with deformable action parts (3DCNN-DAP) model, which incorporates a deformable-part learning component into the 3D CNN framework to capture the expression features from motion. Zhang et al. [3] proposed a deep evolutional spatial-temporal network (composed of PHRNN and multi-scale-CNN (MSCNN)) that extracts the partial-whole, geometry-appearance, and dynamic-still information, thereby effectively improving the facial expression recognition performance. Among these approaches, many have not explicitly exploited the spatial relationship among the facial landmarks, which is important for understanding facial expressions. In addition, many have fed all facial expression images, which contain substantial amounts of useless information for facial expression, into neural networks.

Considering the previous research on appearance-geometry variation and the recent research on neural networks, we use a graph-structured presentation in this paper. Facial expressions are controlled by facial muscles and can be regarded as dynamic variations of facial muscle groups. If a facial muscle group deforms the skin of the face locally, the reflectance properties of the skin change [4]. Thus, the shape and appearance variations in facial key parts lead to various expressions. Typically, we use 49 facial landmarks to annotate the face (brows, eyes, nose, and mouth) [3]. Li et al. first proposed a graph representation for static-based expression recognition [5], which ignored the shape variation of expressions, and their processing was coarse because they did not divide the faces into patches to boost the facial expression recognition performance [6, 7]. In this paper, we build a graph representation of the shape and appearance variations in key facial parts and use a deep learning method to process the graph.

Our work differs from previous works in three main aspects: 1) We propose a graph-structured representation that considers both appearance and shape variations by tracking key parts (determined by the brows, eyes, nose, and mouth) from neutral to expression, and we use an affine transformation to describe each key part. 2) Since considering patches can boost the performance, we use a temporal convolutional network (TCN) to process the graph, and we propose a part-based temporal convolutional network (PTCN) for emphasizing the influences of key facial parts. 3) A comprehensive evaluation of three public datasets for facial expression recognition is conducted, and the results demonstrate that the proposed method outperforms previous methods.

2   Proposed Method

2.1   Basic Graph Contour

According to [8], the facial action coding system (FACS) encodes the movements of individual facial muscles during slightly differing instantaneous changes in facial appearance. Using FACS, nearly any anatomically possible facial expression can be deconstructed into the action units (AU) and temporal segments that produce the expression. For example, happiness can be represented by AU6 and AU12, and sadness can be represented by AU1, AU4 and AU15. AU1 represents raising the inner brow, AU4 represents lowering the brow, AU6 represents raising the cheek, AU12 represents pulling the corner lip, and AU15 represents depressing the corner lip. In addition, facial landmark points around facial components and facial contours cover most of the facial area of the action unit. Therefore, facial landmarks can accurately represent rigid and non-rigid facial deformations that are due to facial expressions.

First, we use the discriminative response map fitting (DRMF) method [9] to identify the facial landmarks, after which only 49 landmarks remain (Fig. 1). Based on the facial landmarks of the key parts, we construct a basic graph contour. As shown in Fig. 1, we first group the 49 facial feature points according to the distribution of the key facial parts (brows, eyes, nose, and mouth). Since the landmark locations in the face are caused by regular movements of the key parts, each landmark is closely related to the other landmarks that are on the same key part. These types of connections are regular and cannot be ignored; hence, we treat them as a single unit, which is similar to a sub-graph. To prove that the sub-graph contour is distinct for expression recognition, we calculate and normalize the distances between all facial landmarks and form a distance matrix. Figure 2 shows the part of the distance matrix that corresponds to the mouth section from the CK+ database. We find that subjects that have identical expressions are common, while a subject has large variations in the distance matrix if he/she is experiencing different emotions. However, the accuracy based on only the basic graph contour is low. To make it robust, we also add appearance and shape variations for facial expression recognition. To more effectively utilize both appearance information and shape information, we propose a graph representation that is based on the basic graph contour for facial expressions.

2.2   Graph Representation

Our proposed graph presentation is illustrated in Fig. 3. We use a Gabor filter to extract appearance variations around the graph nodes while applying an affine transformation to capture the shape variations from the graph without expression in the graph with expression.

Cells in the early visual cortex in humans can be modelled using Gabor filters [10], and there is evidence that during face perception, Gabor-like modelling is used to realize

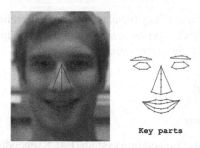

Key parts

Fig. 1. Basic graph contour that is based on key parts

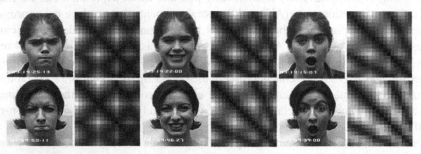

Fig. 2. Examples of distance matrices for the mouth section from the CK+ database. From left to right are (a) anger, (b) happiness, and (c) surprise. Bright squares correspond to higher values. Each image is of size 18 × 18 because the mouth has a total of 18 facial landmarks. The distance matrices differ among mouth shapes.

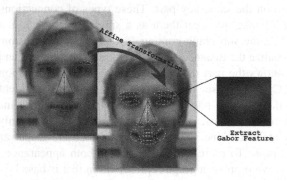

Affine Transformation

Extract
Gabor Feature

Fig. 3. We use a Gabor filter to extract appearance variations around the graph nodes while applying an affine transformation to capture the shape variations from the graph without expression in the graph with expression.

invariance to shading changes, such as those that occur when expressing emotions [11]. Therefore, to introduce the appearance representation into the graph, we use a Gabor filter to extract the appearance information near the facial landmarks and use this information to represent nodes on the graph. The formula that we used to generate the Gabor kernel function is as follows:

$$g(x, y; \lambda, \theta, \phi, \sigma, \gamma) = e^{-\frac{1}{2}\left[\left(\frac{x'}{\sigma}\right)^2 + \left(\frac{\gamma y'}{\sigma}\right)^2\right]} \cos\left(\left(\frac{2\pi \cdot x'}{\lambda} + \phi\right)\right) \tag{1}$$

The detailed parameter information is the same as in [5]. Finally, we use x_i ($i = 1, 2, \ldots, 49$) to represent the appearance feature vector in the graph.

As discussed previously, the shape variation in key parts also contributes to the facial expression. To increase the gap between graph contours that represent different expressions, we introduce another graph contour from the neutral expression as the initial contour of shape variation. When people make expressions, the landmarks shift from neutral to maximum, and the shape of each sub-graph changes. However, the shape of each sub-graph contour is a polygon, and it is difficult to illustrate the deformation; therefore, we divide it into multiple groups (the white ellipses in Fig. 3), and each group consists of two or three landmarks.

Then, we use an affine transformation to capture the variation in groups. We select the affine matrix that is obtained via the affine transformation as our shape representation for the graph. For each group, we use $\vec{\alpha}$ to represent the vector of group i in the neutral expression and $\vec{\beta}$ to represent the vector of group i in the maximum expression. The affine matrix can be calculated via Eq. 2.

$$\begin{bmatrix} \vec{\beta} \\ 1 \end{bmatrix} = \begin{bmatrix} A & \vec{b} \\ 0 \ldots 0 & 1 \end{bmatrix} \begin{bmatrix} \vec{\alpha} \\ 1 \end{bmatrix} \tag{2}$$

where $A = \begin{bmatrix} \cos\theta & \sin\theta \\ -\sin\theta & \cos\theta \end{bmatrix}$ and $\vec{b} = \begin{bmatrix} t_x \\ t_y \end{bmatrix}$. We obtain a 3×3 affine transformation matrix, delete the third row $[0, 0, 1]$, and line up the matrix to obtain a shape representation of the group. For each landmark, we obtain a transformation vector. We use $\vec{Y_i}$ ($i = 1, 2, \ldots, 49$) to represent the shape feature vector in the graph.

2.3 Neural Networks

In this section, we introduce neural networks for processing our proposed graph-structured representation from the previous section.

Prior to processing, we must fuse the appearance representation $\vec{X_i}$ and the shape representation $\vec{Y_i}$ ($i = 1, 2, \ldots, 49$) to form new nodes n_i ($i = 1, 2, \ldots, 49$). By comparing various combination methods, which include one-dimensional convolution, average multiplication, and cascade, we determine that the best performance is realized by cascade.

$$n_i = conv\left(\vec{X_i}, \vec{Y_i}\right)(i = 1, 2, \ldots, 49) \tag{3}$$

Recently, TCN has received substantial attention and has outperformed canonical recurrent networks such as long short-term memory (LSTM) and GRU across a diverse range of tasks and datasets [12]. TCN outperforms GRU and LSTM in terms of memory length. Therefore, we attempt to apply TCN to the processing of the facial graph. TCN uses a 1D fully convolutional network (FCN) architecture to produce an output of the same length as the input. Meanwhile, TCN uses causal convolutions to ensure that there is no leakage from the future into the past. For a 1D sequence n and a filter $f:\{0,...,k-1\}$, the dilated convolution operation F on element s is defined as:

$$F(s) = (n*_d f)(s) = \sum_{i=0}^{k-1} f(i) \cdot n_{s-d \cdot i} \tag{4}$$

where d is the dilation factor, k is the filter size, $*$ represents convolution, d s-$d \cdot i$ considers the direction of the past. Compared with LSTMs and GRUs, TCN has two main advantages: 1) TCN can realistically retain memory for longer than LSTM and GRU, and the entire frame design is simpler than that of LSTM. Thus, the feature from the front node can also be treated equally; and 2) TCN can change its receptive field size by using larger dilation factors, stacking additional convolutional layers, and increasing the filter size. Therefore, TCN can better control the model's memory size than GRU and LSTM, and it is more flexible for identifying suitable parameters for our task.

In [13], faces were divided into patches and these patches were concatenated as individual vectors. Then, the individual vectors and landmarks were fed together into a network for facial expression prediction. In addition, [6, 7] show that dividing faces into patches can boost the performance of facial expression recognition. The contributions of face areas differ among expressions. Therefore, the weights should differ among the facial patches. Benefiting from the ability of TCN to process a long input sequence and exhibit substantially longer memory, we propose a PTCN for static-based facial expressions. The texture and geometric information of the facial image are mainly represented on the critical facial areas, which can be well-mapped to our facial graph. According to the physical facial structure of the human face, we divide the facial graph into four subgraphs: eyebrows, eyes, nose and mouth. All facial expressions can be realized by these subgraphs. For example, surprise causes the eyes and mouth to open wide, and sadness can be decomposed to depressed lip corners and lowered eyebrows. To learn powerful features, the four parts of the expression graph are fed into four TCN subnets.

As discussed above, a facial expression can be regarded as an appearance and shape variation of key parts, which are fused to form the variations of local parts and of the whole face. Therefore, a key challenge is to effectively capture both local and global variations from facial images. The PTCN, which is illustrated in Fig. 4, is proposed based on this strategy: We divide the facial graph into four parts and feed them into four TCN subnets for extraction of one part of the low-level feature s (Eq. 5). Let S_k be the result and N_k be the input of each TCN subnet k (eyebrow: $N_1(n_1, n_2, \ldots, n_{10})$, eye: $N_2(n_{11}, n_{12}, \ldots, n_{22})$, nose: $N_3(n_{23}, n_{24}, \ldots, n_{31})$, and mouth: $N_4(n_{32}, n_{33}, \ldots, n_{49})$).

$$S_k = TCN(N_k) k \in [1, 4] \tag{5}$$

To extract the global high-level features, the features of the four parts are concatenated and fed into a TCN. S_{all} represents the concatenated features, and S represents the features from the final TCN.

$$S_{all} = con(S_1, S_2, S_3, S_4) \tag{6}$$

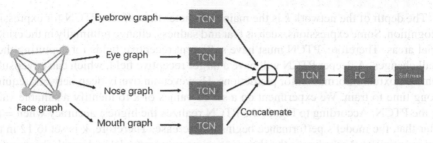

Fig. 4. Our proposed PTCN model for facial expression recognition. A facial graph is divided into four parts, and each part is fed into a TCN. Local features are concatenated from a lower TCN, while the global high-level features are formed in the upper layer.

$$S = TCN(S_{all}) \tag{7}$$

Finally, a fully connected layer and a softmax layer are used to estimate the facial expression.

$$Z = f(W_1 S + b_1) \tag{8}$$

$$y = softmax(W_2 Z + b_2) \tag{9}$$

Many parameters may affect the performance of the PTCN, such as the network depth, the filter size and the dilation factor. The use of a larger dilation factor and filter size and a deeper network enables the output at the top level to represent a wider range of inputs, which effectively expands the receptive field of a ConvNet. We select the same settings as in [12]. The filter size is 7, and the depth is 12, which can yield the best performance. The dilation factor increases exponentially with the depth of the network ($d = O(2^i)$ at level i of the network). In addition, the number of hidden units per layer is 25. The learning rate is 0.002, and we update all the weights after learning each sequence. The size of the facial expression database is small, which is a major impediment to the application of the deep learning method. We add a spatial dropout after each dilated convolution for regularization, and the dropout is set to 0.05.

3 Experiments

We evaluate the performance of our model on three widely used facial expression databases: the CK+ [14], Oulu-CASIA [15], and MMI [16] databases. A 10-fold cross-validation strategy is used.

3.1 Database Classification

First, according to [5], the Gabor kernel size of 3×3 and the Gabor feature vector average in eight directions yield the best performance. Therefore, we use these settings in the following experiment.

The depth of the network k is the main parameter that affects PTCN for expression recognition. Some expressions, such as fear and sadness, change minimally in the critical facial areas. Therefore, PTCN must have sufficient receptive fields for capturing these small changes. A deeper PTCN will have a larger receptive field, which can cover sufficient contextual information for predictions. However, an overly deep network requires a long time to train. We experiment on a set of values of k to identify a suitable value for the PTCN. According to Fig. 5, the PTCN realizes the highest accuracy when =12. After that, the model's performance begins to decrease. Therefore, k is set to 12 in the next experiment. According to the above experiments, our model realizes the best performance when the Gabor kernel size is 3×3, the Gabor feature vector is averaged in eight directions, and the structure is the PTCN. The PTCN is trained with the Adam optimizer [17] with a learning rate of 0.002 and a batch size of 64. All weights are initialized from a zero-centred normal distribution with a standard deviation of 0.2. We use these settings for comparison with state-of-the-art methods.

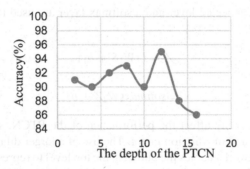

Fig. 5. Facial expression recognition accuracy of PTCN as a function of parameter k.

3.2 Results and Analysis

Tables 1, 2 and 3 compare the performance of our model with those of current state-of-the-art methods on three databases. For the Oulu-CASIA database, the previous best algorithm that is based on traditional methods for facial expression recognition is Atlases [18], which realizes 75.52% accuracy. Recently, Li et al. [5] first proposed a graph model that realizes the best performance. They realize 93.06% accuracy. According to Table 1, our proposed method realizes higher accuracy (96.1%) than the state-of-the-art methods. On the CK+ and MMI databases, our proposed model also outperforms the previous best methods. However, our method only marginally outperforms SOA on the CK+ database. This is because the samples in the CK+ database are of satisfactory quality and, hence, most methods can perform well on this dataset (above 95%); thus, it is difficult to realize a substantial breakthrough.

The experiments show that our three proposed networks all outperform other methods. This demonstrates the effectiveness of our graph model in modelling the appearance features and geometric features of facial expressions and proves that our graph representation is efficient. The proposed Graph-PTCN also outperforms Graph-TCN. This

Table 1. Comparison of different methods on the Oulu-CASIA database

Method	Descriptor	Accuracy
Zhao et al. [22]	LBP-TOP	6 classes: 68.13%
Liu et al. [23]	STM-ExpLet	6 classes: 74.59%
Guo et al. [18]	Atlases	6 classes: 75.52%
Zhao et al. [21]	PPDN	6 classes: 84.59%
Yu et al. [20]	DPCN	6 classes: 86.23%
Zhang et al. [3]	PHRNN-MSCNN	6 classes: 86.25%
Yang et al. [19]	DeRL	6 classes: 88.00%
Li et al. [5]	Static-based Graph	6 classes: 93.06%
Our method	**Graph-TCN**	**6 classes: 94.1%**
Our method	**Graph-PTCN**	**6 classes: 96.1%**

Table 2. Comparison of different methods on the CK+ database

Method	Descriptor	Accuracy
Cai et al. [24]	Island loss	7 classes: 94.35%
Zeng et al. [25]	DSAE	7 classes: 95.79%
Meng et al. [26]	multitask network	7 classes: 95.37%
Liu et al. [27]	(N+M)-tuplet clusters loss	7 classes: 97.10%
Yang et al. [19]	DeRL	7 classes: 97.30%
Li et al. [5]	Static-based Graph	7 classes: 98.27%
Our method	**Graph-TCN**	**7 classes: 97.4%**
Our method	**Graph-PTCN**	**7 classes: 98.9%**

Table 3. Comparison of different methods on the MMI database

Method	Descriptor	Accuracy
Zhao et al. [22]	LBP-TOP	6 classes: 59.51%
Liu et al. [23]	STM-ExpLet	6 classes: 75.12%
Zhong et al. [28]	CSPL	6 classes: 73.53%
Liu et. al [2]	3DCNN-DAP	6 classes: 63.4%
Hasani et al. [29]	3DCNN-LSTM+landmark	6 classes: 77.50%
Kim et al. [30]	CNN-LSTM	6 classes: 78.61%
Zhang et al. [3]	PHRNN-MSCNN	6 classes: 81.18%
Sun et al. [31]	Network ensemble	6 classes: 91.46%
Li et al. [5]	Static-based Graph	6 classes: 94.44%
Our method	**Graph-TCN**	**6 classes: 94.7%**
Our method	**Graph-PTCN**	**6 classes: 95.4%**

supports that dividing faces into patches can boost the performance of facial expression recognition. It also proves that PTCN can better capture both local and global variations from facial images, as PTCN considers the partial-whole and geometry-appearance features simultaneously.

4   Conclusions

In this paper, we presented a deep neural network for facial expression recognition that processes graph-structured representations of facial expressions. The variations in the areas around facial landmarks contain useful information for distinguishing expressions, while the entire facial image contains a substantial amount of useless information. Therefore, we utilized a Gabor filter to extract the appearance variations in the facial landmarks and used an affine transformation to extract the shape variations. Finally, we used PTCN to predict the expression. The experimental results obtained using three databases demonstrated that our model realized state-of-the-art performance.

Acknowledgments. This work was supported in part by the Fundamental Research Funds for the Central Universities (XDJK2020C016).

References

1. Yao, A., Cai, D., Hu, P., Wang, S., Sha, L., Chen, Y.: HoloNet: towards robust emotion recognition in the wild. In: ACM International Conference on Multimodal Interaction, pp. 472–478. ACM (2016)
2. Liu, M., Li, S., Shan, S., Wang, R., Chen, X.: Deeply learning deformable facial action parts model for dynamic expression analysis. In: Cremers, D., Reid, I., Saito, H., Yang, M.-H. (eds.) ACCV 2014. LNCS, vol. 9006, pp. 143–157. Springer, Cham (2015). https://doi.org/10.1007/978-3-319-16817-3_10
3. Zhang, K., Huang, Y., Du, Y., Wang, L.: Facial expression recognition based on deep evolutional spatial-temporal networks. IEEE Trans. Image Process. **26**(9), 4193–4203 (2017)
4. Angelopoulo, E., Molana, R., Daniilidis, K.: Multispectral skin color modeling. In: Proceedings of the 2001 IEEE Computer Society Conference on Computer Vision and Pattern Recognition, 2001. CVPR 2001, vol. 2, pp. II–II. IEEE (2001)
5. Zhong, L., Bai, C., Li, J., Chen, T., Li, S., Liu, Y.: A Graph-Structured Representation with BRNN for Static-based Facial Expression Recognition. In: 2019 14th IEEE International Conference on Automatic Face & Gesture Recognition (FG 2019), pp. 1–5. IEEE, May 2019
6. Wang, Y., Yu, H., Stevens, B., Liu, H.: Dynamic facial expression recognition using local patch and LBP-TOP. In: International Conference on Human System Interactions. IEEE (2015)
7. Happy, S.L., Routray, A.: Automatic facial expression recognition using features of salient facial patches. IEEE Transactions on Affective Computing **6**(1), 1–12 (2015)
8. http://www.cs.cmu.edu/afs/cs/project/face/www/facs.ht
9. Asthana, A., Zafeiriou, S., Cheng, S., Pantic, M.: Robust discriminative response map fitting with constrained local models. In: 2013 IEEE Conference on Computer Vision and Pattern Recognition (CVPR), pp. 3444–3451. IEEE, June 2013
10. Daugman, J.G.: Uncertainty relation for resolution in space, spatial frequency, and orientation optimized by two-dimensional visual cortical filters. JOSA A **2**(7), 1160–1169 (1985)

11. Cowen, A., Abdel-Ghaffar, S., Bishop, S.: Using structural and semantic voxel-wise encoding models to investigate face representation in human cortex. J. Vis. **15**(12), 422 (2015)
12. Bai, S., Kolter, J.Z., Koltun, V.: An empirical evaluation of generic convolutional and recurrent networks for sequence modeling (2018)
13. Zhang, W., Zhang, Y., Ma, L., Guan, J., Gong, S.: Multimodal learning for facial expression recognition. Pattern Recogn. **48**(10), 3191–3202 (2015)
14. Lucey, P., Cohn, J.F., Kanade, T., Saragih, J., Ambadar, Z., Matthews, I.: The extended cohn-kanade dataset (ck+): a complete dataset for action unit and emotion-specified expression. In: 2010 IEEE Computer Society Conference on Computer Vision and Pattern Recognition Workshops (CVPRW), pp. 94–101. IEEE, June 2010
15. Taini, M., Zhao, G., Li, S. Z., Pietikainen, M.: Facial expression recognition from near-infrared video sequences. In: 19th International Conference on Pattern Recognition, 2008. ICPR 2008, pp. 1–4. IEEE, December 2008
16. Valstar, M., Pantic, M.: Induced disgust, happiness and surprise: an addition to the mmi facial expression database. In Proceedings 3rd International Workshop on EMOTION (satellite of LREC): Corpora for Research on Emotion and Affect, p. 65, May 2010
17. Kingma, D.P., Ba, J.: Adam: a method for stochastic optimization. arXiv preprint arXiv:1414. 6980 (2014)
18. Guo, Y., Zhao, G., Pietikäinen, M.: Dynamic facial expression recognition using longitudinal facial expression atlases. In: Fitzgibbon, A., Lazebnik, S., Perona, P., Sato, Y., Schmid, C. (eds.) ECCV 2012. LNCS, vol. 7573, pp. 631–644. Springer, Heidelberg (2012). https://doi.org/10.1007/978-3-642-33709-3_45
19. Yang, H., Ciftci, U., Yin, L.: Facial expression recognition by de-expression residue learning. In: Proceedings of the IEEE Conference on Computer Vision and Pattern Recognition (2018)
20. Yu, Z., Liu, Q., Liu, G.: Deeper cascaded peak-piloted network for weak expression recognition. The Visual Computer **34**(12), 1691–1699 (2017). https://doi.org/10.1007/s00371-017-1443-0
21. Zhao, X., et al.: Peak-piloted deep network for facial expression recognition. In: Leibe, B., Matas, J., Sebe, N., Welling, M. (eds.) ECCV 2016. LNCS, vol. 9906, pp. 425–442. Springer, Cham (2016). https://doi.org/10.1007/978-3-319-46475-6_27
22. Zhao, G., Pietikainen, M.: Dynamic texture recognition using local binary patterns with an application to facial expressions. IEEE Trans. Pattern Anal. Mach. Intell. **29**(6), 915–928 (2007)
23. Liu, M., Shan, S., Wang, R., Chen, X.: Learning expressionlets on spatio-temporal manifold for dynamic facial expression recognition. In: 2014 IEEE Conference on Computer Vision and Pattern Recognition (CVPR), pp. 1749–1756. IEEE, June 2014
24. Cai, J., Meng, Z., Khan, A. S., Li, Z., O'Reilly, J., Tong, Y.: Island loss for learning discriminative features in facial expression recognition. In: 2018 13th IEEE International Conference on Automatic Face & Gesture Recognition (FG 2018), pp. 302–309. IEEE, May 2018
25. Zeng, N., Zhang, H., Song, B., Liu, W., Li, Y., Dobaie, A.M.: Facial expression recognition via learning deep sparse autoencoders. Neurocomputing **273**, 643–649 (2018)
26. Meng, Z., Liu, P., Cai, J., Han, S., Tong, Y.: Identity-aware convolutional neural network for facial expression recognition. In: 2017 12th IEEE International Conference on Automatic Face & Gesture Recognition (FG 2017), pp. 558–565. IEEE, May 2017
27. Liu, X., Kumar, B.V.K.V., You, J., Jia, P.: Adaptive deep metric learning for identity-aware facial expression recognition. In: IEEE Conference on Computer Vision and Pattern Recognition Workshops, pp. 522–531. IEEE Computer Society (2017)
28. Zhong, L., Liu, Q., Yang, P., Liu, B., Huang, J., Metaxas, D.N.: Learning active facial patches for expression analysis. In: 2012 IEEE Conference on Computer Vision and Pattern Recognition (CVPR), pp. 2562–2569. IEEE, June 2012

29. Hasani, B., Mahoor, M.H.: Facial expression recognition using enhanced deep 3D convolutional neural networks. In: 2017 IEEE Conference on Computer Vision and Pattern Recognition Workshops (CVPRW), pp. 2278–2288. IEEE, July 2017
30. Kim, D.H., Baddar, W., Jang, J., Ro, Y.M.: Multi-objective based spatio-temporal feature representation learning robust to expression intensity variations for facial expression recognition. IEEE Trans. Affect. **10**, 223–236 (2017)
31. Sun, N., Li, Q., Huan, R., Liu, J., Han, G.: Deep spatial-temporal feature fusion for facial expression recognition in static images. Pattern Recogn. Lett. **119**, 49–61 (2017)

Generating Facial Expressions Associated with Text

Lisa Graziani[1]([✉]), Stefano Melacci[2], and Marco Gori[2,3]

[1] DINFO, University of Florence, Florence, Italy
lisa.graziani@unifi.it
[2] DIISM, University of Siena, Siena, Italy
{mela,marco}@diism.unisi.it
[3] Maasai, Universitè Côte d'Azur, Inria, CNRS, I3S, Biot, France

Abstract. How will you react to the next post that you are going to read? In this paper we propose a learning system that is able to artificially alter the picture of a face in order to generate the emotion that is associated with a given input text. The face generation procedure is function of further information about the considered person, either given (topics of interest) or automatically estimated from the provided picture (age, sex). In particular, two Convolutional Networks are trained to predict age and sex, while two other Recurrent Neural Network-based models predict the topic and the dominant emotion in the input text. First Order Logic (FOL)-based functions are introduced to mix the outcome of the four neural models and to decide which emotion to generate, following the theory of T-Norms. Finally, the same theory is exploited to build a neural generative model of facial expressions, that is used create the final face. Experimental results are performed to assess the quality of the information extraction process and to show the outcome of the generative network.

Keywords: Facial expression generation · Logic rules · Topic prediction · Emotion detection

1 Introduction

The huge popularity of Generative Adversarial Networks (GANs) [6] has led to the development of a large number of approaches that are aimed at extending and refining the generative process, showing impressive results in the context of image-to-image translation [3,12,14,17]. Real-world applications based on generative models have spread out, especially in the case of smartphone applications that alter human faces [2,21]. In particular, several approaches have been proposed to change hair color [3], add glasses [13,16], change sex [3,13,16], get older or younger [3,13].

In this paper we propose a system that answers the question *how will a certain person react when reading a given post?* For example, we might want to see what would be the face of a famous Hollywood star or of a popular politician when he/she is reading a newspaper title or a Facebook post that is about

© Springer Nature Switzerland AG 2020
I. Farkaš et al. (Eds.): ICANN 2020, LNCS 12396, pp. 621–632, 2020.
https://doi.org/10.1007/978-3-030-61609-0_49

something that he/she cares of. Differently from most existing generation-based applications, the way the system alters the input face is the outcome of a decision process that is not user-selected and that involves the information extracted from the provided post (newspaper title, short-text, etc.), from the input face itself, or from other sources of knowledge. In other words, we bridge two processes, namely information extraction and image generation, with the purpose of creating a system that generates new data in function of the information that is either given or extracted from the input signals.

Not all the people would react at the same way reading the same content. For example, given a newspaper title that is about politics, a person who dislikes such topic will react differently compared to a person who likes it, while, on average, the female audience is less interested into posts that are about motors compared to males. Our system automatically extracts information about the sex and the expected age of the input person using Convolutional Neural Networks, while those details that cannot be grasped from the face picture are explicitly provided to the system. In particular, we consider the case of the topics of interest (or not-interest) of the considered person, that can be compared with the topics of the input post, automatically predicted by a Recurrent Neural Network-based pipeline. A similar pipeline detects the dominant emotion in the input text.

Differently from common approaches to emotion detection, our model learns to predict emotions from Facebook posts paired with reaction labels, bridging emotions and reactions by means of First Order Logic (FOL) formulas, following [10]. FOL is also used to mix the outcome of the four neural models, where a T-Norm-based module allows the system to handle the distribution of probabilities yielded by the four networks and to decide which emotion to generate. In order to create the final expression we exploited the widely used GANs [6], following the approach in [14] and its FOL-based instance [16]. In particular, our model includes a generator and a discriminator for each class of emotions, and it learns to translate pictures of "neutral" faces into pictures that are associated with target emotional states.

This paper is organized as follows. Section 2 describes the proposed system, including the FOL-based decision process (Sect. 2.1). Numerical and qualitative results are provided in Sect. 3, while Sect. 4 concludes the paper.

2   Model

The proposed model implements a generative procedure that is function of a given image of a person, and that alters the face region of such image. A short text is provided to the system (post, newspaper title, etc.), together with additional knowledge about the considered person. The system modifies the input face with the facial expression that the subject is expected to have after having read the short text (see Fig. 1). The system is composed of several modules that are described in what follows, distinguishing among the information extraction stages, the knowledge organization and image generation.

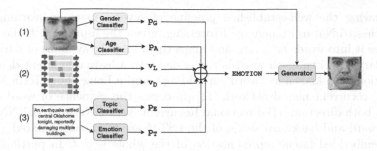

Fig. 1. The main computational blocks of the proposed system. Three different inputs are provided: (1) a picture of person; (2) information about the topics that the person likes or dislikes, paired with a degree that indicates how strongly each topic is either liked or not (the 7 sliders); (3) a short-text. The input data undergo an information extraction stage, whose outcome is a set of distribution of probabilities or set of scores over different attributes (p_G, p_A, v_L, v_D, p_E, p_T). A logic-based decisional process (the circled cross) yields the target emotion that the input person is expected to have when reading the short text. Finally, a Neural Network-based generator generates the target facial expression.

Gathering Information from the Input Image. The system processes a frontal-view image I of the target person with neutral expression. Several types of information could be extracted from the original visual input that, due to the variability of such input, might only be available in some input data and not visible in others (types of background, types of clothes, objects that the person is holding, etc.). In the context of this paper we focus on two features that are common to all the expected inputs since they are estimated by only looking at the face region, and that we can extract in a pretty accurate way: gender and age. The face is automatically localized, cropping the face region and rescaling it to 100×100 pixels (RGB). Then, it is fed to two Convolutional Neural Networks (CNNs) that act as classifiers of the *gender* and the *age* of the face in I. Both the classifiers yield predictions over two classes, distinguishing either between *male* and *female* and between *young* and *old*. The last layer of each network includes a softmax activation function, so the output of each network is composed of the probabilities of the target classes, that are $p_G \in [0, 1]^2$ in the case of the gender classifier and $p_A \in [0, 1]^2$ in the case of the age classifier.

Gathering Information from the Input Text. Another input that is provided to the system consists of a short text t, typically composed by a single sentence or just a few sentences, that might be, for example, a newspaper title or a post in a social network. We focus on the emotion-related information that is carried by such textual data and on its topic. From a very abstract perspective, the former is information that will have an important role in determining *how* the input subject is expected to react when reading the input text, while the latter is what allows the system to decide *if* the input subject is somewhat interested in the provided text (details in Subsect. 2.1).

Following the well-established pipeline of several machine learning-based approaches to Natural Language Processing, given the input text t, the system tokenizes it into words $t_0, \ldots, t_n$ and maps them into the symbols of a fixed-size vocabulary V. Then, each word is embedded into a learnable latent dense representation, also known as "word embedding", and a Long Short-Term Memory (LSTM) recurrent neural network [11] processes the sequence of word embeddings in both directions (Bidirectional Recurrent Neural Network (BRNN) [19]). The forward and backward states of the LSTM are then concatenated, producing an embedded latent representation of the whole text t. In particular, our system involves two instances of the described pipeline, computing two independent latent representations of t, namely $\hat{t}_T \in \mathbb{R}^{d_T}$ and $\hat{t}_E \in \mathbb{R}^{d_E}$, where d_T and d_E are the sizes of the embeddings. Two feed-forward networks with softmax activation function in the output layer process such representations. The first network processes $\hat{t}_T$, implementing a *topic classifier* that yields a probability distribution $p_T \in [0,1]^7$ over 7 topics: *fashion, motors, politics, religion, science, sport, technology*. The second network handles $\hat{t}_E$, and it implements an *emotion classifier* that outputs the probability distribution $p_E \in [0,1]^6$ over the six universal emotions: *anger, disgust, fear, happiness, sadness, surprise* [8,9].

Facebook is a precious mine of data paired with reaction labels[1], so that, for the purpose of our system, it seems natural to train a classifier to predict reactions (i.e., LOVE, HAHA, WOW, SAD, ANGRY) instead of universal emotions. However, in order to train the facial expression generator, there exist public datasets of faces labeled with emotions and not with Facebook reactions. It turns out that mapping reactions to emotions is sometimes ambiguous. For example, the reaction ANGRY might be the emotion *anger* or emotion *disgust*. In [10], it is shown that such mapping can be described by FOL formulas, that in the case of the previous example is $\forall x \in D$, $\text{ANGRY}(x) \Rightarrow anger(x) \vee disgust(x)$, where D is the set of all the training examples, being them supervised or not. We follow the ideas presented in [10], and these logic formulas are injected in the learning problem by converting them into T-Norms [5,7] and building a loss function that involves both the classic supervision-related information and logic. Supervisions might be about emotions or reactions, so that we can merge Facebook data with public datasets of text labeled with the emotions. Moreover, unsupervised text can be easily collected and used to optimize the logic-related portion of the loss.

Organizing the Input Knowledge. Further knowledge about the input subject is provided to the system, in order to better characterize the details of the considered person and to estimate the most appropriate facial expression to associate to the considered input text. Our system can be fed with information about how strongly the input subject likes or dislikes one of the aforementioned topics, modeling the strength of each liking/disliking attribute with a real value in $[0,1]$. In particular, 1 indicates a strong liking/disliking of a topic and 0 means that the person does not care at all. We end up with two vectors of scores, each of them in $[0,1]^7$ (since we have 7 topics). The first vector, v_L, collects the scores about how strongly the input subject likes the 7 topics, while the second

---

[1] We considered the most dominant reaction.

vector, v_D, collects the scores about how strongly he/she dislikes the 7 topics. Of course, we assume that if $v_L(k) > 0$ then $v_D(k) = 0$, and vice-versa, being $v_L(k)$ ($v_D(k)$) the k-th component of v_L (v_D). In other words, if the target person likes a topic, the disliking score is zero.[2] Notice that if no knowledge is provided, the two vectors are set to zeros (i.e., do not care).

Facial Expression Generation. A decision process (whose details are postponed to Subsect. 2.1) defines the target emotion to generate accordingly to the information collected by the modules described so far. A Neural Network-based generative model handles the face region from the input image I, and it generates an altered instance of the input face with an expression corresponding to the target emotion. Our model generates an RGB image at the resolution of 100×100 pixels that is rescaled and superimposed to the face area of I.[3] We notice that we do not have the use of training data in which each face in a neutral expression is paired with the same face in a non-neutral expression. For this reason, we exploited a variant of the UNsupervised Image-to-image Translation (UNIT) approach [14] and, in particular, a FOL implementation of it [16] that follows the same T-Norm-based formulation we used in the emotion classifier.

Our generator handles 7 domains, one for each emotion class plus the neutral class, and the notation x_i indicates an image associated with the i-th universal emotion ($i = 0, \ldots, 5$) or a neutral face ($i = N$). During the *training* stage, the model is given a tuple of 7 training images, one for each class (not necessarily belonging to the same subject). If $\bar{x}_{i \to j}$ is the fake image with emotion j generated from the input x_i, then the output data of the model consist of 19 generated pictures, that are $\bar{x}_{h \to h}$, $\bar{x}_{h \to N}$, for $h = 0, \ldots, 5$, and $\bar{x}_{N \to i}$, for $i = 0, \ldots, 5, N$. The reason why we need to generate 19 pictures is due to the constraints that we have to impose while training the model. Internally, the model is composed by 7 encoders and 7 decoders, as shown in Fig. 2. The encoders $e_i(x_i)$, $i = 0, \ldots, 5, N$ project their inputs onto a shared latent space Z. Notice that each encoder e_i only processes inputs of class i, i.e., x_i. Then, decoders $g_i(z)$, $i = 0, \ldots, 5, N$ are able to decode data from the shared space Z, generating fake pictures.

The encoder e_i and decoder g_i are feed-forward Neural Networks, and they act as VAE (Variational AutoEncoder) [4] for the i-th domain/class. Following [14], the weights of the last few layers of the encoders (that extract high-level representation of the input images) are shared, and the same sharing principle is also applied to the weights of the first few layers of the decoders (that decode high-level representations for reconstructing the input).

In order to learn the weights of the networks, 7 discriminators d_i ($i = 0, \ldots, 5, N$) are trained to distinguish the real images of class i from the ones that are artificially generated by the model. The learning criterion consists in trying to fool the discriminators, generating images that are not easily distinguishable

---

[2] In our GUI, this information is inserted by means of 7 sliders. For each topic k the user can define a value $v(k)$ between -5 and 5. If such value is positive, then $v_L(k)$ is set to $\frac{v(k)}{5}$ and $v_D(k) = 0$. Otherwise, $v_D(k)$ is set to $\frac{|v(k)|}{5}$ and $v_L(k) = 0$.

[3] The system averages the original and the generated pixels, weighing in a decreasing way the generated pixels while moving closer to the borders of the face area.

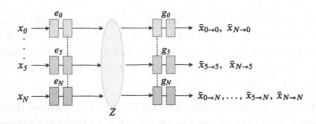

Fig. 2. Generative model – *training* stage. The input data consist of 7 training images, one for each emotion (plus neutral). The model is composed of 7 encoders e_i and 7 decoders g_i and a shared latent space Z. Each vertical rectangle indicates a group of layers of neurons (some of them are tied – dashed lines). Each decoder g_i, $i = 0, \ldots, 5$ outputs a pair of images (the regenerated x_i and the neutral-to-emotion translation), while g_N outputs the 7 neutral expressions generated from each input x_i.

from the fake ones, while improving the discriminators themselves, as in classic GANs. However, the model is also subject to a set of FOL-based constraints that ensure cycle-consistency (see [16] for more details). In this work, we adapted the FOL constraints to the case of emotion generation, taking care of handling the neutral class in a special way, since our final goal is to learn how to generate an emotion-related facial expression from a neutral face, and not to learn to convert each emotion into any other emotion. First of all we constrain the system to be able to re-generate the input,

$$\forall x_i \quad g_i(e_i(x_i)) = x_i, \tag{1}$$

where the equality operator expresses a pixel by pixel similarity between the images. We impose multiple cycle consistency constraints to the generation procedure, ensuring that when translating x_i from domain i to domain j and translating it back to domain i we get the exact same x_i (and not another image of class i). These constraints are needed to enforce the system to generate output images that are alterations of the input ones, and not new faces that have nothing to do with the inputs. In detail, for each i, a new image $\bar{x}_{N \to i}$ with emotion i is generated from the image with neutral expression x_N. Then, the system must be able to reconstruct x_N when $\bar{x}_{N \to i}$ is provided as input, and the same cycle consistency must be enforced in the case of an input image x_i that is translated into a neutral one $\bar{x}_{i \to N}$, and then translated back into x_i. Formally,

$$\forall x_N \quad g_N(e_i(\bar{x}_{N \to i})) = x_N, \quad \forall x_i \quad g_i(e_N(\bar{x}_{i \to N})) = x_i. \tag{2}$$

Finally, the discriminators must keep their capability of recognizing the real images from the generated ones. If $d_i(x)$ is a function in $[0, 1]$ that is closer to 1 when x is real and to 0 when it is fake, for each $h = 0, \ldots, 5$ we have

$$\forall x_h \quad d_h(x_h) \wedge \neg d_N(\bar{x}_{h \to N}), \quad \forall x_N \quad d_N(x_N) \wedge \neg d_h(\bar{x}_{N \to h}). \tag{3}$$

Once training has ended, we only need to keep e_N and g_h, $h = 0, \ldots, 5$, that is what the system needs to generate a facial expression from a neutral input.

2.1 Fuzzy Logic-Based Decision Process

The information that is either automatically extracted using neural models from the image I and from text t and the information that comes from the provided knowledge is encoded into the previously described vectors p_G, p_A, p_T, p_E, v_L and v_D. Such vectors are probability distributions over certain classes (p_G, p_A, p_T, p_E) or vector of independent probabilities (v_L, v_D), in both the cases each element is in $[0, 1]$. The system needs to take a decision on which emotion to generate, and we propose to integrate the outcome of the information extraction stages using FOL formulas and cast them into a fuzzy logic setting using T-Norms [5,7]. This choice allows us to exploit the uncertainty in the output of the neural networks and in the provided knowledge, and to naturally embed such uncertainty into the decision process, since we have no data from which we could learn how to mix the probabilities. However, the proposed rules are differentiable, so they could allow us to integrate learning also at this stage, if supervised data will become available for this task.

We introduce a set of FOL predicates that are about the information extracted from I and t and the knowledge in K, temporarily discarding emotion-related information. In detail, the FOL predicates are female(I), male(I), old(I), young(I), fashion(t), motors(t), politics(t), religion(t), science(t), sport(t), tech(t). Each element of the aforementioned vectors p_G, p_A, p_T is the truth degree of one of such predicates. For example, the first element of p_G is the truth degree of predicate female(I), while its second element is the truth degree of male(I), and so on. In the case of the target person-related knowledge, we use the following predicate names associated with the truth degrees in v_L: like_fashion(k), ...,like_tech(k). Similarly, the predicates dislike_fashion(k), ..., dislike_tech(k), are associated with the truth degrees in v_D.

We also introduce three special predicates that are related to the generation of a neutral face (i.e., the system does not alter the input face), neutral(I), to the generation of the most-dominant emotion in the input text, gen_emo(I) (that can be retrieved by $\arg\max p_E$), and the generation of a disgusted expression, gen_disgust(I). These predicates are not associated to pre-computed truth scores, but they participate to a set of FOL formulas that are evaluated to determine if these predicates are true (i.e., 1) or false (i.e., 0), so that the face expression generator will react accordingly. In this paper, we considered two categories of rules. The first category is inspired by the principle that if a person is interested in the topic of the input text, then he/she should react by showing the facial expression associated to the emotion that is detected in such text. If there is not a specific interest on such topic, then we can follow some commonly assumed statistical relations between being male/female/young/old and certain topics (for example, it is pretty frequent – not always the case – for male audience to have interest in motors, sports and not being interested in fashion; similarly, younger people might be less interested into politics than adults). Please consider that these rules are just simple examples, with no attempts to model realistic stereotypes, and our system is general with respect to them. The first category of rules includes (rules are intended to hold for $\forall I, \forall t, \forall k$),

1) `fashion`$(t) \land ($`female`$(I) \lor $`like_fashion`$(k)) \Rightarrow $`gen_emo`$(I)$
2) `fashion`$(t) \land $`male`$(I) \land \neg$`like_fashion`$(k) \Rightarrow $`neutral`$(I)$
3) `motors`$(t) \land ($`male`$(I) \lor $`like_motors`$(k)) \Rightarrow $`gen_emo`$(I)$
4) `motors`$(t) \land $`female`$(I) \land \neg$`like_motors`$(k) \Rightarrow $`neutral`$(I)$
5) `politics`$(t) \land [($`male`$(I) \land $`old`$(I)) \lor $`like_politics`$(k)] \Rightarrow $`gen_emo`$(I)$
6) `politics`$(t) \land [($`female`$(I) \lor $`young`$(I)) \land \neg$`like_politics`$(k)] \Rightarrow $`neutral`$(I)$
7) `religion`$(t) \land [($`female`$(I) \land $`old`$(I)) \lor $`like_religion`$(k)] \Rightarrow $`gen_emo`$(I)$
8) `religion`$(t) \land [($`male`$(I) \lor $`young`$(I)) \land \neg$`like_religion`$(k)] \Rightarrow $`neutral`$(I)$
9) `science`$(t) \land $`like_science`$(k) \Rightarrow $`gen_emo`$(I)$
10) `science`$(t) \land \neg$`like_science`$(k) \Rightarrow $`neutral`$(I)$
11) `sport`$(t) \land [($`male`$(I) \land $`young`$(I)) \lor $`like_sport`$(k)] \Rightarrow $`gen_emo`$(I)$
12) `sport`$(t) \land [($`female`$(I) \lor $`old`$(I)) \land \neg$`like_sport`$(k)] \Rightarrow $`neutral`$(I)$
13) `tech`$(t) \land ($`young`$(I) \lor $`like_tech`$(k)) \Rightarrow $`gen_emo`$(I)$
14) `tech`$(t) \land $`old`$(I) \land \neg$`like_tech`$(k) \Rightarrow $`neutral`$(I)$.

Notice that ¬`like_*` has nothing to do with disliking something, and it only means do-not-care about topic *. The second category of rules deals with cases in which a person does not like the topic of the input text. In this case, the system will generate a disgusted facial expression. Formally, we have,

15) `fashion`$(t) \land $`dislike_fashion`$(k) \Rightarrow $`gen_disgust`$(I)$
...
21) `tech`$(t) \land $`dislike_tech`$(k) \Rightarrow $`gen_disgust`$(I)$.

The premise of each rule is transformed into a polynomial using the product T-Norm [16], that can be evaluated generating a real value in $[0, 1]$. The system evaluates all the premises, finding the one that holds with a larger truth degree. The associated conclusion is set to true (i.e., 1) and the corresponding action is taken on the facial expression generation. Notice that if there is a strong uncertainty in the topic of the input text (max p_T is small, <0.55 in our experiments) then the rules are discarded and `gen_emo`(I) is directly set to true.

3   Experimental Results

We experimentally evaluated the quality of each of the modules that compose our system. In order to train these modules, we collected either popular datasets or data that we crawled from the web and semi-automatically labeled.

In detail, CelebA [15], an annotated face dataset with several celebrity images, was used to train the gender and age classifiers, and it was also used in the generation module. In the former case, we considered the images annotated with both gender and age information, that were preprocessed by localizing the face areas, cropping them and resizing such area to 100×100. We obtained almost 100,000 images of females and 70,000 of males, 40,000 of older people and 130,000 images of younger people. In each task we divided the data into training, validation and test sets (70%, 15%, 15% of the data, respectively – this is what we did in all the experiments of this paper), and we selected the optimal architecture by focussing on two-layer CNNs followed by max pooling layers and evaluating different filter sizes, number of filters, number of fully connected layers. The final models were composed by 32 and 64 filters of size 3×3, two fully connected layers with 516 hidden and 2 output neurons (number of classes). We obtained satisfying (micro) accuracies on the test splits, i.e., 97.3% for gender classification and 87.5% for age classification.

The topic classifier was trained in supervised manner on texts collected from Wikipedia. We automatically crawled Wikipedia pages from categories and sub-categories that matched (or were similar) to the selected 7 topics. We collected $\approx 200{,}000$ short texts (each of them composed of a sentence or up to two shorter sentences). We evaluated architectures with differently sized word embeddings and states of the BRNN, multiple fully connected layers and number of hidden units. After the validation stage, we selected word embeddings of size 200, BRNNs with a hidden state composed of 200 units and a single fully connected layer. In the Table 1 (top) we report the model accuracies, that are slightly below 80%, both in the micro and macro cases. The error analysis suggested that is mostly due to the fact that there is clearly some ambiguity in determining the topic of those texts that are about, for example, biographical information, that are indeed present in Wikipedia pages.

Table 1. Accuracies for topic classifier (top) and emotion classifier (bottom).

fashion	motors	politics	religion	science	sport	tech	micro acc.	macro acc.
0.782	0.684	0.741	0.645	0.775	0.879	0.704	0.779	0.774
anger	disgust	fear	happiness	sadness	surprise		micro acc.	macro acc.
0.394	0.608	0.662	0.732	0.607	0.238		0.598	0.540

The model we used for emotion classification from text shares the same overall structure of the just described topic classifier. However, in this case we used pre-trained word embeddings of size 300 (from the popular Google word2vec model), and 2 fully connected layers with 25 and 6 neurons respectively (we have 6 classes), as suggested in [10]. The model was trained using a large collection of unsupervised text together with data labeled with emotion classes (7,866 examples), taken from the following datasets: *AffectiveText*, *ISEAR* and *Fairy Tales* (see [10]). The model was also trained using Facebook posts that include reactions (95,624 examples), taken from the same dataset used in [10]. 100,000 Facebook posts with a small number of reactions were used in the trained process as unlabeled data (recall that the model is semi-supervised). In Table 1 (bottom) we report the results we obtained, that are in line with the ones of [10].

The face expression generator was trained using images of facial expressions, subdivided into the six universal emotions and the neutral class. We used several public datasets (ADFES [20], WSEFEP [18], MUG [1]), we also downloaded images from the web and collected faces from non-emotion-related datasets (CelebA [15]). Then, we classified these images using the emotion classifier we presented in [8] and we manually filtered out the cases in which the classifier was not confident (and the most evident cases in which the emotion class was inappropriate). All the images were cut around the face area and resized to 100×100 pixels (RGB). In Fig. 3 we show some samples generated by the final model.

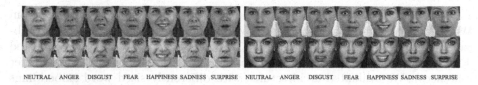

NEUTRAL   ANGER   DISGUST   FEAR   HAPPINESS   SADNESS   SURPRISE   NEUTRAL   ANGER   DISGUST   FEAR   HAPPINESS   SADNESS   SURPRISE

Fig. 3. Automatically generated faces (test data). The neutral faces are the input and the following columns are outputs of our model.

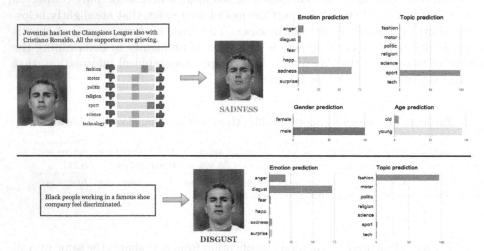

Fig. 4. Example showing some portions of our web interface. (Top-row) Left: input data, i.e., face image, text and additional knowledge. Middle: the generated image (*sadness*). Right: the histograms of the information extraction stage. The target person likes sport. The system is predicting that the topic of the post is sport, and the dominant emotion is sadness. For this reason, the final facial expression is sadness. (Bottom-row) We changed the input text. The subject likes fashion a bit, the text is classified as *disgust*, and that is the generated facial expression.

System Interface and Generations. We implemented a web interface from which the user can upload a picture or select preexisting templates.[4] The user can use 7 sliders to indicate how strongly the target person is interested/not-interested in the 7 topics. Finally, the post from which we want to estimate a facial expression is provided in a text area. The backend of the system consists of a TensorFlow implementation of the previously described neural models, with a Python server that is queried by the web interface.

In Fig. 4 (top-row) we report an example of generated reaction, showing portions of the web interface. The input text is about sport, the subject is both young and male and he also likes sport, so the rule with highest premise value is rule number 11 of Subsect. 2.1. The emotion predictor classifies the text with *sadness* ($\arg\max p_E$), so a sad expression is generated.

---

[4] https://sailab.diism.unisi.it/emoreact.

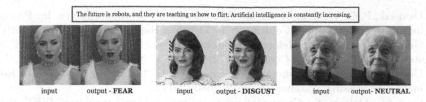

Fig. 5. An example of different reactions to the same post (image copyrights belong to their respective owners.)

In Fig. 4 (bottom-row) we show another example with the same person, but with a different input text. The predicted topic is fashion and the emotion predictor classifies the text as *disgust*. Since the subject is also a bit interested in fashion (fuzzy score, smaller than 1), the rule with high premise is rule number 1 of Subsect. 2.1, so a disgusted expression is generated. Figure 5 shows an example in which different people react in different ways to the same post, talking about technology. The first subject likes technology and the rule activated is rule number 13, which indicates to generate the emotion coming from the text, that is *fear*. The second person dislikes technology and the automatically selected rule is number 21 (that indicates to generate a disgusted expression). The third subject does not care about this topic and it is an old woman, so rule 14 indicates to keep a neutral expression.

4   Conclusions

We presented a Neural Network-based system that is capable of extracting information from a face picture and a short-text and of automatically generating the facial expression associated with the expected reaction of who is reading such short-text. The system massively uses T-Norm-based First Order Logic (FOL) constraints to train semi-supervised neural classifiers and to bridge their outputs. A constrained Generative Adversarial Network is used to transform a neutral expression into a target emotion.

Acknowledgements. This project has received funding from the European Union's Horizon 2020 research and innovation program under grant agreement No 825619.

References

1. Aifanti, N., Papachristou, C., Delopoulos, A.: The mug facial expression database. In: 11th International Workshop on Image Analysis for Multimedia Interactive Services WIAMIS 10, pp. 1–4. IEEE (2010)
2. Amin, M., Shah, B., Sharif, A., Tanveer, T., Kim, K.L., Anwar, S.: Android malware detection through generative adversarial networks. Trans. Emerg. Telecommun. Technol. (2019). https://doi.org/10.1002/ett.3675
3. Choi, Y., Choi, M., Kim, M., Ha, J.W., Kim, S., Choo, J.: Stargan: unified generative adversarial networks for multi-domain image-to-image translation. In: Proceedings of IEEE CVPR, pp. 8789–8797 (2018)

4. Diederik, P.K., Welling, M., et al.: Auto-encoding variational Bayes. In: Proceedings of the International Conference on Learning Representations (ICLR) (2014)
5. Gnecco, G., Gori, M., Melacci, S., Sanguineti, M.: Foundations of support constraint machines. Neural Comput. **27**(2), 388–480 (2015)
6. Goodfellow, I., et al.: Generative adversarial nets. In: Advances in Neural Information Processing Systems, pp. 2672–2680 (2014)
7. Gori, M., Melacci, S.: Constraint verification with kernel machines. IEEE Trans. Neural Netw. Learn. Syst. **24**(5), 825–831 (2013)
8. Graziani, L., Melacci, S., Gori, M.: The role of coherence in facial expression recognition. In: Ghidini, C., Magnini, B., Passerini, A., Traverso, P. (eds.) AI*IA 2018. LNCS (LNAI), vol. 11298, pp. 320–333. Springer, Cham (2018). https://doi.org/10.1007/978-3-030-03840-3_24
9. Graziani, L., Melacci, S., Gori, M.: Coherence constraints in facial expression recognition. Intelligenza Artificiale **13**(1), 79–92 (2019). https://doi.org/10.3233/IA-180015
10. Graziani, L., Melacci, S., Gori, M.: Jointly learning to detect emotions and predict Facebook reactions. In: Tetko, I.V., Kůrková, V., Karpov, P., Theis, F. (eds.) ICANN 2019. LNCS, vol. 11730, pp. 185–197. Springer, Cham (2019). https://doi.org/10.1007/978-3-030-30490-4_16
11. Hochreiter, S., Schmidhuber, J.: Long short-term memory. Neural Comput. **9**(8), 1735–1780 (1997)
12. Karras, T., Laine, S., Aila, T.: A style-based generator architecture for generative adversarial networks. In: Proceedings of the IEEE Conference on Computer Vision and Pattern Recognition, pp. 4401–4410 (2019)
13. Lample, G., Zeghidour, N., Usunier, N., Bordes, A., Denoyer, L., Ranzato, M.: Fader networks: manipulating images by sliding attributes. In: Advances in Neural Information Processing Systems, pp. 5967–5976 (2017)
14. Liu, M.Y., Breuel, T., Kautz, J.: Unsupervised image-to-image translation networks. In: Advances in Neural Information Processing Systems, pp. 700–708 (2017)
15. Liu, Z., Luo, P., Wang, X., Tang, X.: Deep learning face attributes in the wild. In: Proceedings of the IEEE International Conference on Computer Vision, pp. 3730–3738 (2015)
16. Marra, G., Giannini, F., Diligenti, M., Gori, M.: Constraint-based visual generation. In: Tetko, I.V., Kůrková, V., Karpov, P., Theis, F. (eds.) ICANN 2019. LNCS, vol. 11729, pp. 565–577. Springer, Cham (2019). https://doi.org/10.1007/978-3-030-30508-6_45
17. Mirza, M., Osindero, S.: Conditional generative adversarial nets. arXiv preprint arXiv:1411.1784 (2014)
18. Olszanowski, M., Pochwatko, G., Kuklinski, K., Scibor-Rylski, M., Lewinski, P., Ohme, R.K.: Warsaw set of emotional facial expression pictures: a validation study of facial display photographs. Front. Psychol. **5**, 1516 (2015)
19. Schuster, M., Paliwal, K.K.: Bidirectional recurrent neural networks. IEEE Trans. Signal Process. **45**(11), 2673–2681 (1997)
20. Van Der Schalk, J., Hawk, S.T., Fischer, A.H., Doosje, B.: Moving faces, looking places: validation of the Amsterdam dynamic facial expression set (ADFES). Emotion **11**(4), 907 (2011)
21. Vincent, J.: This app uses neural networks to put a smile on anybody's face. The Verge (2017).https://www.theverge.com/tldr/2017/1/27/14412814/faceapp-neural-networks-ai-smile-image-manipulation

Bilinear Fusion of Commonsense Knowledge with Attention-Based NLI Models

Amit Gajbhiye[✉], Thomas Winterbottom, Noura Al Moubayed,
and Steven Bradley

Department of Computer Science, Durham University, Durham, UK
{amit.gajbhiye,thomas.i.winterbottom,noura.al-moubayed,
s.p.bradley}@durham.ac.uk

Abstract. We consider the task of incorporating real-world common-sense knowledge into deep Natural Language Inference (NLI) models. Existing external knowledge incorporation methods are limited to lexical-level knowledge and lack generalization across NLI models, datasets, and commonsense knowledge sources. To address these issues, we propose a novel NLI model-independent neural framework, BiCAM. BiCAM incorporates real-world commonsense knowledge into NLI models. Combined with convolutional feature detectors and bilinear feature fusion, BiCAM provides a conceptually simple mechanism that generalizes well. Quantitative evaluations with two state-of-the-art NLI baselines on SNLI and SciTail datasets in conjunction with ConceptNet and Aristo Tuple KGs show that BiCAM considerably improves the accuracy the incorporated NLI baselines. For example, our BiECAM model, an instance of BiCAM, on the challenging SciTail dataset, improves the accuracy of incorporated baselines by 7.0% with ConceptNet, and 8.0% with Aristo Tuple KG.

Keywords: Natural Language Inference · Commonsense knowledge

1 Introduction

Natural Language Inference (NLI), also known as Recognizing Textual Entailment (RTE), is one of the key problems in the field of Natural Language Understanding (NLU). Popularised by a number of PASCAL RTE challenges, the task is formulated as a - "directional relationship between pairs of text expressions, denoted by T (the entailing Text) and H (the entailed "Hypothesis"). Text T, entails hypothesis H, if humans reading T would typically infer that H is most likely true." [4]. The task is very challenging as it requires an entailment system to acquire the linguistic knowledge (word meaning, syntactic structure and semantic interpretation), and also to understand commonsense knowledge.

In the context of artificial intelligence, commonsense knowledge is the set of background information about the everyday world, that an individual is expected to know or assume, and the ability to use it when appropriate [16]. Many complex

© Springer Nature Switzerland AG 2020
I. Farkaš et al. (Eds.): ICANN 2020, LNCS 12396, pp. 633–646, 2020.
https://doi.org/10.1007/978-3-030-61609-0_50

Table 1. SNLI example with commonsense triples (red) from ConceptNet KG.

p: Two young girls hang **tinsel** on a Christmas tree in a room with blue curtains. **(tinsel IsA decoration)**
h: Two girls are decorating their Christmas tree. **(tree RelatedTo christmas)**

NLU applications such as machine reading [21] achieved improved performance when supplied with commonsense knowledge.

Thus far, NLI research has not fully leveraged the additional information available via the use of commonsense knowledge. For example, state-of-the-art NLI models [2,11] are limited to incorporating only lexical-level external knowledge, such as synonym and hypernymy. However, NLI is a complex reasoning task, in addition to lexical-level external knowledge, the task requires real-world commonsense knowledge to reason inference. Table 1 shows examples from the SNLI dataset [1], where the commonsense knowledge is retrieved from the ConceptNet Knowledge Graph (KG) [19]. The common knowledge that, *tinsel IsA decoration* and *tree RelatedTo christmas* is useful to ascertain the inference relationship. Due to the lack of such common knowledge, state-of-the-art NLI models perform substantially worse for such premise-hypothesis pairs [9].

Incorporating external commonsense knowledge in deep neural NLI models is challenging. Existing models require considerable architectural changes with marginal performance gains [2]. Incorporating such knowledge implicitly by refining word embeddings using KGs may negatively affect model performance [20]. Moreover, the existing external knowledge-based NLI models do not generalize well, and lack extensive evaluation across NLI datasets and KGs [10].

This paper aims to mitigate the aforementioned limitations. We present BiCAM (**Bi**linear fusion of **C**ommonsense knowledge with **A**ttention-based NLI **M**odels) - a novel neural network framework that incorporates NLI models without any architectural changes to the model. The BiCAM is NLI model-independent framework that generalizes across NLI models, datasets and commonsense knowledge sources. In the proposed framework, we first formulate the heuristics to retrieve commonsense knowledge from the KGs. We then embed retrieved knowledge with Holographic Embeddings (HolE) [17], a KG embedding method to learn the embeddings of entities and relations in the KG. We learn the commonsense features from KG embeddings using a Convolutional Neural Network (CNN) based encoder. Finally, we use a state-of-the-art feature fusion technique, factorized bilinear pooling, to learn the joint representation of the learned commonsense features and the sentence features from the NLI model.

Evaluation results on two established NLI baselines ESIM [3] and decomposable attention model [18], in combination with ConceptNet [19] and Aristo Tuple [5] KGs demonstrate that BiCAM considerably improve the accuracy of all the incorporated baselines. For example, compared with ESIM baseline, BiCAM achieves 7% absolute improvement with ConceptNet and 8% absolute improvement with AristoTuple KG on SciTail dataset. We analyze the effect of incorporating the different number of commonsense features and find that syntactically and semantically complex sentences require more commonsense knowledge to reason inference. Further, we evaluate the impact of various feature fusion techniques and demonstrate the efficacy of bilinear feature fusion. Finally, we analyze the examples from SNLI test set, where ESIM and BiCAM succeed and fail.

In summary, the main contributions of this paper are: (1) We introduce the NLI model-independent neural framework, BiCAM, that generalizes across NLI models, datasets, and commonsense knowledge sources. (2) We devise an effective

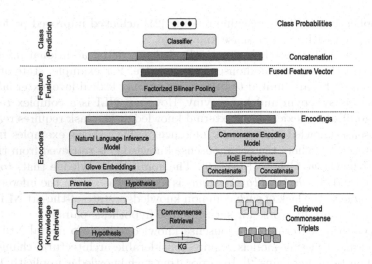

Fig. 1. A high-level view of our proposed architecture (BiCAM). The data (premise, hypothesis and the corresponding commonsense triples) flows from bottom to top. Premise and the corresponding triples are depicted in yellow, hypothesis and the corresponding triples are shown in purple. (Color figure online)

set of knowledge retrieval heuristics from KGs. (3) An extensive evaluation of the proposed approach with two established NLI baselines in combination with a general commonsense and (science) domain-specific KG on two NLI benchmarks.

2   Related Work

Leveraging commonsense knowledge in NLU systems has long been proposed [16], however, NLI neural models have only recently started utilising commonsense knowledge. KIM [2], is the state-of-the-art neural Knowledge-based Inference Model, that incorporates lexical-level semantic knowledge into the attention and composition components. Specifically, external lexical knowledge (such as synonym and antonym) extracted from the lexical database, WordNet [15], is used to form relation embeddings between premise-hypothesis words. The AdvEntuRe [11] framework train the decomposable attention model [18] with adversarial training examples generated by incorporating knowledge from linguistic resources such as WordNet, and with a sequence-to-sequence neural generator. However, lexical knowledge individually is insufficient to reason about the premise-hypothesis relationship. Intuitively, when a human judges a premise-hypothesis relationship, a full range of real-world commonsense knowledge, and not just the lexical knowledge, is necessary to come to a conclusion [16]. Therefore, we incorporate knowledge from and empirically evaluate BiCAM on the real-world commonsense KG, ConceptNet. We also evaluate BiCAM on the (science) domain-specific KG, Aristo Tuple.

NSnet [10] is a neural-symbolic entailment model, that integrates the connectionist, deep learning approach with the symbolic approach for the scientific entailment task. The model decomposes each of the hypotheses into various facts and verifies each sub-fact against the premises using decomposable attention model and against the Aristo Tuple KB using a structured scorer. An aggregator network then combines the predictions from the two modules to get the final entailment score. Word embeddings are refined by dynamically incorporating relevant background knowledge from external knowledge sources in [20]. Our approach differs in the manner and the level at which commonsense is incorporated. We fuse the commonsense features to the sentence encodings of the premise and hypothesis which we show achieves a better performance.

3   Methods

A high-level view of our proposed BiCAM framework is illustrated in Fig. 1. In this section, we discuss the individual BiCAM components and the uniquely structured framework.

3.1   Commonsense Knowledge Retrieval

To extract external commonsense knowledge we consider two KGs: ConceptNet, for general real-world commonsense knowledge and Aristo Tuple, for (science) domain-specific knowledge. The knowledge in these KGs is represented as a triple (*head, relation, tail*), where *head* and *tail* are the real-world entities and the *relation*, is a specific set of associations, describing the relation between entities. For example, (*tinsel IsA decoration*) is a triple in ConceptNet KG.

Retrieval and preparation of contextually specific and relevant information from knowledge graphs are complex and challenging tasks and is the crucial step in our model. We use a heuristic retrieval mechanism for knowledge retrieval. We find empirically that non-specific commonsense knowledge from the KGs degrades the model performance. Heuristic mechanism is fast and is effective in filtering irrelevant knowledge. We formulate the following heuristics and illustrate the triples retrieved by the application of each heuristic in Table 2.

Table 2. A step by step illustration of commonsense knowledge retrieval for a SNLI premise-hypothesis pair from ConceptNet. Step 4 shows the final set of triplets for the premise and hypothesis.

Step	Premise	Hypothesis
Input	A **white horse** is pulling a **cart** while a **man** stands and watches	An **animal** is walking **outside**
1.	('white', 'horse', 'pulling', 'cart', 'man', 'stands', 'watches')	('animal', 'walking', 'outside")
2.	(horse has-property white), (cart related-to horse)	(animal at-location outside)
3.	(horse is-a animal), (horse related-to animal), (horse at-location outside)	(animal related-to horse), (animal antonym man), (animal distinct-from man)
4.	(horse has-property white), (cart related-to horse) (horse is-a animal), (horse at-location outside)	(animal at-location outside), (animal related-to horse) (animal antonym man)

1. Stop words are removed from the premise and hypothesis.
2. To identify the relations between the words within the premise or hypothesis, we retrieve all triples involving each pair of words as head and tail.
3. To identify the relations from premise words to hypothesis words, we retrieve the triples with premise words as head and the words of hypothesis as tail. For hypothesis, we extract the relations from the hypothesis to premise.
4. The relation *RelatedTo* has the largest number of triples in ConceptNet. Although the relation communicates that the head and tail are related, it does not specify the specific relationship between them. To eschew the extracted commonsense knowledge from non-specific information and a higher number of triples with *RelatedTo* relation, we randomly select one triplet with *RelatedTo* relation, if multiple such triples are extracted. Additionally, we removed any duplicated triples from the final set of retrieved triples.
5. Finally, if the words of the premise and the hypothesis do not extract any commonsense knowledge by the application of above heuristics, we randomly select a word from them and extract a triple from one of the relations in (*entails, synonym, antonym*).

3.2   Encoders

Commonsense Encoding Model. The model learns the features from the retrieved commonsense triples. We provide a layer-by-layer description.

Embedding Layer. We learn the Holographic Embeddings (HolE) [17] of KG triples. Given a commonsense triple (h, r, t), HolE represents both the entities and relations as vectors in $\mathbb{R}^d$. First, HolE compose the head and tail into $\mathbf{h} \star \mathbf{t} \in \mathbb{R}^d$ using the circular correlation:

$$[\mathbf{h} \star \mathbf{t}]_i = \sum_{k=0}^{d-1} [\mathbf{h}]_k \odot [\mathbf{t}_{(k+i) \bmod d}] \tag{1}$$

where $\odot$ denotes the Hadamard product. The compositional vector obtained is then matched with the continuous representation of relation to score the commonsense triple using the scoring function defined as:

$$f_r(h, t) = \mathbf{r}^\mathrm{T}(\mathbf{h} \star \mathbf{t}) = \sum_{i=0}^{d-1} [\mathbf{r}]_i \sum_{k=0}^{d-1} [\mathbf{h}]_k \odot [\mathbf{t}]_{(k+i) \bmod i} \tag{2}$$

where $\mathbf{r} \in \mathbb{R}^d$ is the relation embedding. The score measures the plausibility of the commonsense triple. We train the HolE embeddings (Θ) using the pairwise ranking loss computed as:

$$\min_{\Theta} \sum_{i \in \Gamma_+} \sum_{j \in \Gamma_-} \max(0 \; \gamma + \sigma(\eta_j) - \sigma(\eta_i)) \tag{3}$$

where Γ_+ denotes the set of triples in the KG, Γ_- denotes the "negative" triples that are not observed in KG and $\gamma > 0$ specifies the width of margin, $\sigma(.)$ denotes the logistic function and η is the value of the scoring function.

For ConceptNet and Aristo Tuple, we train the HolE embeddings for the triples retrieved from the SNLI and SciTail vocabulary. We use AdaGrad [6] to optimize the objective in Eq. 3, via an extensive grid search over an initial learning rate of $(0.001, 0.01, 0.1)$, a margin of $(0.2, 1, 2, 10)$, mini-batch size $(50, 100, 150, 200)$ and entity embedding dimensions of $(50, 100, 150, 200)$. At each gradient step, we randomly generate 5 negative *tail* entities with respect to a positive triple. The learned HolE embeddings are evaluated on the triplet classification task. For SNLI/ConceptNet pair, the model achieves the highest accuracy of 64.0% with an embedding dimension of 150. For SciTail/ConceptNet and SciTail/Aristo Tuple pairs, HolE reported the top accuracy of 62.8% and 69.4% respectively at embedding dimension 100.

Encoding Layer. To learn the features over the pre-trained HolE embeddings, we employ a CNN-based neural model [13].

For each premise/hypothesis, let $T = (\tau_1, \tau_2, \ldots, \tau_m)$ be a sequence of length n created by joining the m retrieved triples from the KG. Each τ is of the form (h, r, t) and, hence, $n = 3m$. The sequence T, padded where necessary, and represented as:

$$T = (x_1, x_2, , x_3), (x_4, x_5, , x_6), \ldots, (x_{n-2}, x_{n-1}, x_n) \tag{4}$$

where, x_i is the i-th word in the sequence. Let $\mathbf{x}_i \in \mathbb{R}^d$ be the d-dimensional pre-trained HolE embedding corresponding to the i-th word. A sentence of length n is represented as a matrix $\mathbf{X} \in \mathbb{R}^{d \times n}$, by concatenating its word embeddings as columns, *i.e.*, $\mathbf{x}_i$ is the i-th column of $\mathbf{X}$. We apply a convolution operation with filter $\mathbf{W} \in \mathbb{R}^{d \times h}$, to a window of h words. The convolution operation learns a new feature map from the set of h words with the operation:

$$c = f(\mathbf{X} * \mathbf{W} + b) \in \mathbb{R}^{(\frac{n-h}{s})+1} \tag{5}$$

where, $b \in \mathbb{R}^{(\frac{n-h}{s})+1}$ is the bias term, s is the stride of convolution filter, and $f(\cdot)$ is the activation function, rectified linear unit in our experiments and $*$ denote convolution operation. The filter convolve over each window $(\mathbf{x}_{ih+1: (i+1)h})$ where $0 \leq i \leq n-1$ in $\mathbf{X}$. We set the h and s to 3 for the commonsense triples. Convolving the same filter with the 3-g beginning at every 3rd position in the triple sequence allows the features to be extracted from every triplet from the KG. We then apply a max-over-time pooling operation over the feature map and take the maximum value $\hat{c} = \max\{\mathbf{c}\}$ as a feature corresponding to this filter. Max pooling operation captures the most important feature for each feature map.

Above we detailed the process of extracting one feature from one filter. Multiple filters (with fixed window size and stride of 3) are employed to obtain multiple features. Each filter is considered as a linguistic feature detector that learns to recognize a specific feature from the commonsense triple. The output of the commonsense encoder is a l-dimensional vector to represent commonsense.

NLI Encoders. We incorporate BiCAM with two established NLI baselines: ESIM [3] and decomposable attention model [18].

Feature Fusion. We apply factorized bilinear pooling [22] to fuse the commonsense features and NLI sentence features. Let $\mathbf{p}$ and $\mathbf{h}$ be the NLI model generated encoding of premise and hypothesis. Also, let $\mathbf{p}_{cs}$ and $\mathbf{h}_{cs}$ denote the corresponding commonsense encoding generated by commonsense encoding model. We apply the factorized bilinear pooling defined as:

$$\mathbf{z}_p = \mathrm{SumPooling}(\widetilde{U}\mathbf{p} \odot \widetilde{V}\mathbf{p}_{cs}, k)$$
$$\mathbf{z}_h = \mathrm{SumPooling}(\widetilde{U}\mathbf{h} \odot \widetilde{V}\mathbf{h}_{cs}, k),$$

(6)

where $\mathrm{SumPooling}(x, k)$ denote a sum pooling over x with a one dimensional non-overlapped window of size k, $\widetilde{U}$ and $\widetilde{V}$ are projection matrices learned during training, $\odot$ is the Hadamard product and z is the fused feature vector. To prevent overfitting, we also added a dropout layer [8] after the element-wise multiplication of the projection matrices. Further, to allow the model to converge to a satisfactory local minimum, we append power normalization ($\mathbf{z} \leftarrow \mathrm{sign}(\mathbf{z})|\mathbf{z}|^{0.5}$) and l_2 normalization layers ($\mathbf{z} \leftarrow \mathbf{z}/\|\mathbf{z}\|$) after SumPooling layer [22]. The factorized bilinear pooling captures the complex association between the features from premise-hypothesis and the corresponding commonsense features. The pooling method is implemented as a feed-forward neural network.

Classification Layer. We classify the relationship between premise and hypothesis using a Multilayer Perceptron (MLP) classifier. The input to the MLP is the concatenation of sentence encodings ($\mathbf{p}$ and $\mathbf{h}$) obtained from NLI model and the corresponding encodings ($\mathbf{z_p}$ and $\mathbf{z_h}$) obtained from feature fusion layer. The MLP consists of two hidden layers with *tanh* activation and a softmax output layer to obtain the probability distribution for each class. The network is trained in an end-to-end manner using multi-class cross-entropy loss.

4 Experiments and Results

Our aim is to incorporate commonsense knowledge into NLI models in order to augment the reasoning capabilities. The method should generalize across different NLI datasets, models and KGs. We evaluate BiCAM using two attention-based NLI baselines on two benchmarks in combination with two KGs. We compare our models with both external knowledge-based and attention-based NLI models. We refer to BiCAM as BiDCAM, when the decomposable attention model is used as NLI baseline and BiECAM, when ESIM is used (see Fig. 1).

Datasets. We assess **BiCAMs** (BiDCAM and BiECAM) on **SNLI** (570 K examples) and **SciTail** (27 K examples) benchmarks. We consider **ConceptNet** for general commonsense, and **Aristo Tuple** for domain-specific knowledge.

Results on SNLI. Table 3 shows the results of the state-of-the-art external knowledge-based and attention-based NLI models in comparison to BiCAMs. We evaluate ConceptNet KG for commonsense knowledge for the SNLI dataset. The models, BiDCAM and BiECAM, improve the performance of their respective attention-based baselines (decomposable attention and ESIM models) by

+0.4% and +0.8%. BiCAMs also perform consistently better among the external knowledge-based and attention-based NLI models. BiECAM model achieves an accuracy of 88.8% competitive to the state-of-art external knowledge-based NLI models, ESIM+Syntactic Tree LSTM [3] and KIM [2] without any architectural changes to the underlying NLI models.

Table 3. NLI Models: Test accuracy. For our models, BiCAMs, the percentage in the parenthesis shows the performance improvement over the base models.

SNLI dataset	
NLI Model	Test Acc(%)
External knowledge-based baselines	
AdvEntuRe [11]	84.6
BiLSTM (E$_3$) [20]	86.5
ESIM (E$_3$) [20]	87.3
Char+CoVe-L [14]	88.1
ESIM + Syntactic TreeLSTM [3]	**88.6**
KIM [2]	**88.6**
Attention-based baselines	
CAM [7]	86.1
Decomposable Attention [18]	**86.3**
ESIM [3]	**88.0**
Our models	
BiDCAM + ConceptNet	**86.7 (+0.4%)**
BiECAM + ConceptNet	**88.8 (+0.8%)**
SciTail dataset	
NLI Model	Test Acc%)
External Knowledge-based baseline	
Majority classifier [10]	60.3
AdvEntuRe(seq2seq)[11]	76.9
Attention-based baseline	
ESIM [3]	**70.6**
Decomposable Attention [18]	**72.3**
CAM [7]	77.0
DGEM [12]	77.3
Our models	
BiDCAM + ConceptNet	**76.8 (+4.5%)**
BiDCAM + Aristo Tuple	**77.3 (+5.0%)**
BiECAM + ConceptNet	**77.6 (+7.0%)**
BiECAM + Aristo Tuple	**78.6 (+8.0%)**

Results on SciTail. The test accuracy of different NLI models on SciTail benchmark is summarised in Table 3. For SciTail, we study the performance of BiCAMs on the general commonsense ConceptNet KG as well as the (science) domain-targeted Aristo Tuple KG. All our models significantly outperform the incorporated baselines across both the KGs, achieving absolute improvements of up to 4.5% (BiDCAM + ConceptNet), 5% (BiDCAM + Aristo Tuple) on decomposable attention baseline and 7% (BiECAM + ConceptNet), 8% (BiECAM + Aristo Tuple) on ESIM baseline. This demonstrates our framework's ability to generalize well across a number of NLI models and different KGs. All our models perform competitively on attention-based baselines, CAM and DGEM. BiECAM + Aristo Tuple observes an accuracy improvement of 1.3% over the previous state-of-the-art DGEM model.

5   Analysis

5.1   Number of Commonsense Features

To investigate the effect of incorporating various numbers of commonsense features, we vary the number of triples input to the commonsense encoding model. Particularly, we are interested in answering the question: How many commonsense features are required for optimal model performance? Fig. 2 shows the results of the experiment.

For SNLI, the model BiECAM + ConceptNet achieves the highest accuracy (88.8%) using 7 triples. We observe a decrease in accuracy with increasing the number of triples. BiDCAM + ConceptNet follow the same trend, however, it attains the highest accuracy (86.7%) with the fewer number (5) of triples. The fewer number of triples required for BiCAMs to achieve their maximum accuracies on SNLI dataset, is attributed to the limited linguistic variation and short average length of stop-word filtered premise (7.35 for entails and neutral class) and hypothesis (3.61 for entails and 4.45 for neutral class) [12] of the SNLI dataset, which limit its ability to fully extract and exploit KG knowledge.

For SciTail, the BiCAMs, when evaluated using the general commonsense knowledge source ConceptNet, require a relatively high number of triplets (11

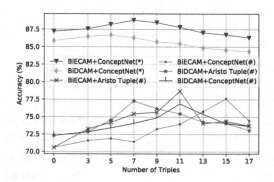

Fig. 2. Accuracy of BiCAMs with varying amount of commonsense triples. (*) denotes SNLI and (#) SciTail datasets.

and 15 resp.) to achieve their maximum accuracy. This is due to the higher syntactic and semantic complexity of SciTail, that needs more knowledge to reason inference. However, when evaluated with the domain-specific Aristo Tuple KG, the models achieve the highest accuracies with fewer (BiDCAM at 7 and BiECAM at 11) triples. The specialised scientific knowledge in Aristo Tuple improves the model performance with less external knowledge.

We observe that the BiCAMs, when trained on SciTail dataset, require a higher number of triples to attain maximum accuracy relative to when trained on the SNLI dataset. This can be attributed to the small training size of the SciTail dataset, which thus requires a higher number of triples to compensate for missing knowledge. We conclude that: (1) The commonsense features, when incorporated in the correct number, help reason the relationship between premise and hypothesis. (2) The number of commonsense features required depends on the syntax, semantics and size of the target dataset, as well as the domain of source KG.

5.2   Ablation Study

To evaluate the impact of factorized bilinear feature fusion, we perform an ablation study on BiECAM + Aristo Tuple, our best performing model on the SciTail dataset. Table 4 demonstrates the performance of various non-bilinear and bilinear pooling methods. We observe that factorized bilinear pooling significantly outperforms all the non-bilinear pooling methods. To ascertain that the performance gain is not due to the higher number of parameters in bilinear method, we stack fully connected layers (with 1200 units per layer, ReLU activation and dropout) to increase the parameters in non-bilinear methods. We observe that increasing the number of parameters does not increase the model accuracy. The high accuracy of factorized bilinear pooling may be attributed to the outer product between the NLI sentence and the commonsense feature vectors. Outer product allows each feature point in the two feature vectors to interact and capture associations between them. The joint representations created in such manner are more expressive than the representations created through concatenation or element-wise summation or multiplication.

Table 4. Ablation study. ($\odot$ implies Elementwise)

Fusion method	Acc(%)
Concat	74.6
FC + Concat	75.5
FC + FC + Concat	74.3
FC + $\odot$ Sum	72.5
FC + FC + $\odot$ Sum	73.3
FC + $\odot$ Product	76.4
FC + FC + $\odot$ Product	76.8
FC + $\odot$ Difference Concat	77.6
FC + $\odot$ Product	
Factorized Biliniear Pooling	**78.6**

Table 5. Qualitative analysis

BiECAM correct ESIM incorrect
p: Four boys are about to be **hit** by an approaching **wave**. *(wave RelatedTo crash)*
h: A giant **wave** is about to **crash** on some boys. *(crash IsA hit)*

BiECAM incorrect ESIM correct
p: A **red** truck is parked next to a burning **blue** building while a man in a **green** vest runs toward it. *(red Antonym blue), (blue Antonym green), (green Antonym red)*
h: The burning **blue** building smells of smoke. *(blue Antonym red), (blue Antonym green)*

For the commonsense encoder, our experiments with Recurrent Neural Networks (RNNs), LSTMs and BiLSTMs, considerably degraded the performance of the BiCAMs. This may be attributed to the inherent nature of RNNs, which learns the representations of words in the context of all previous words in the sequence. However, the set of triples input to the commonsense encoder is sequential within an individual triple. For example, in the set of triples - *(outside Antonym inside) and (table RelatedTo eating)*, the word *inside* is associated with the words in its own triple, *outside* and *Antonym*, but not with the words *table*, *RelatedTo* and *eating* of the second triple. RNNs, due to their inherent recurrent nature, learn the incorrect features from the part-sequential input of set of triples. In contrast, CNNs learns features independently of the position of words in the sequence. In the commonsense encoder, learning the features over the window of three words with a stride of three, allows the correct features to be learnt from the part-sequential set of input triples.

5.3 Qualitative Analysis

Table 5 highlights selected sentences from the SNLI test set showing correct and incorrect inference prediction example for both BiECAM and the baseline ESIM. For the first example, BiECAM has additional context for premise and hypothesis from the knowledge that *(wave RelatedTo crash)* and *(crash IsA hit)*, which helps the model to correctly predict the inference class. However, the specific knowledge, about the *wave* and the *crash* is not available to the baseline ESIM model and hence, it incorrectly predicts the inference class.

We observe that BiECAM fails to predict the correct inference class when noisy and irrelevant knowledge is retrieved from the KGs. For example, the last test case in Table 5, only retrieves the information that colors (such as red and blue) are antonyms of each other. The retrieved knowledge is irrelevant and is not completely correct, which does not help BiECAM.

6   Conclusions

We have introduced an NLI model-independent neural framework, BiCAM, that incorporates commonsense knowledge to augment the reasoning capabilities of NLI models. Combined with convolutional feature detectors and bilinear feature fusion, BiCAM provides a conceptually simple mechanism that generalizes across NLI models, datasets and KGs. Moreover, BiCAM can be easily applied to different NLI model and KG combinations. Evaluation results show that our BiCAM considerably improves the performance of all the NLI baselines it incorporates, and does so without any architectural change to the incorporated NLI model. BiCAM achieves state-of-the-art performance on SNLI with Concept-Net KG, outperforming existing state-of-the-art external knowledge-based NLI models. Particularly for the smaller, syntactically and semantically complex Sci-Tail dataset, commonsense knowledge incorporation via BiCAM achieves performance improvements of 7.0% with ConceptNet and 8.0% with Aristo Tuple KG. Further analysis shows that the sufficient number of commonsense features required depends upon the syntax, semantics and size of the target dataset, as well as the domain of source KG. We observe that retrieval and selection of commonsense knowledge relevant for inference is challenging. In future work, we plan to leverage contextual word embeddings for commonsense knowledge retrieval from KGs.

References

1. Bowman, S.R., Angeli, G., Potts, C., Manning, C.D.: A large annotated corpus for learning natural language inference. In: Proceedings of the 2015 Conference on EMNLP, pp. 632–642. ACL (2015)
2. Chen, Q., Zhu, X., Ling, Z.H., Inkpen, D., Wei, S.: Neural natural language inference models enhanced with external knowledge. In: Proceedings of the 56th Annual Meeting of the ACL (volume 1: Long Papers), pp. 2406–2417 (2018)
3. Chen, Q., Zhu, X., Ling, Z.H., Wei, S., Jiang, H., Inkpen, D.: Enhanced LSTM for natural language inference. In: Proceedings of the 55th Annual Meeting of the ACL, vol. 1, pp. 1657–1668 (2017)
4. Dagan, I., Roth, D., Sammons, M., Zanzotto, F.: Recognizing Textual Entailment. Morgan & Claypool Publishers, San Rafael (2013)
5. Dalvi, M.B., Tandon, N., Clark, P.: Domain-targeted, high precision knowledge extraction. Trans. ACL **5**, 233–246 (2017)
6. Duchi, J., Hazan, E., Singer, Y.: Adaptive subgradient methods for online learning and stochastic optimization. JMLR **12**(7), 2121–2159 (2011)
7. Gajbhiye, A., Jaf, S., Moubayed, N.A., Bradley, S., McGough, A.S.: Cam: a combined attention model for natural language inference. In: 2018 IEEE International Conference on Big Data (Big Data), pp. 1009–1014, December 2018
8. Gajbhiye, A., Jaf, S., Moubayed, N.A., McGough, A.S., Bradley, S.: An exploration of dropout with RNNs for natural language inference. In: Kůrková, V., Manolopoulos, Y., Hammer, B., Iliadis, L., Maglogiannis, I. (eds.) ICANN 2018. LNCS, vol. 11141, pp. 157–167. Springer, Cham (2018). https://doi.org/10.1007/978-3-030-01424-7_16

9. Glockner, M., Shwartz, V., Goldberg, Y.: Breaking NLI systems with sentences that require simple lexical inferences. In: Proceedings of the 56th Annual Meeting of the ACL (volume 2: Short Papers), pp. 650–655. ACL, Melbourne, July 2018)
10. Kang, D., Khot, T., Sabharwal, A., Clark, P.: Bridging knowledge gaps in neural entailment via symbolic models. In: Proceedings of the 2018 Conference on EMNLP, pp. 4940–4945. ACL, Brussels, October–November 2018
11. Kang, D., Khot, T., Sabharwal, A., Hovy, E.: AdvEntuRe: adversarial training for textual entailment with knowledge-guided examples. In: Proceedings of the 56th Annual Meeting of the ACL (volume 1), pp. 2418–2428. Acl, Melbourne, July 2018
12. Khot, T., Sabharwal, A., Clark, P.: Scitail: a textual entailment dataset from science question answering. In: Proceedings of the Thirty-Second AAAI Conference on Artificial Intelligence, 2–7 February 2018, New Orleans, Louisiana, USA (2018)
13. Kim, Y.: Convolutional neural networks for sentence classification. In: Proceedings of the 2014 Conference on EMNLP, pp. 1746–1751. ACL, Doha, Qatar, October 2014
14. McCann, B., Bradbury, J., Xiong, C., Socher, R.: Learned in translation: contextualized word vectors. In: Advances in NIPS, pp. 6294–6305 (2017)
15. Miller, G.A.: Wordnet: a lexical database for English. Communi. ACM **38**(11), 39–41 (1995)
16. Minsky, M.: The Society of Mind. Simon & Schuster Inc., NY, USA (1986)
17. Nickel, M., Rosasco, L., Poggio, T.: Holographic embeddings of knowledge graphs. In: Proceedings of the Thirtieth AAAI Conference on Artificial Intelligence, pp. 1955–1961. AAAI 2016. AAAI Press (2016)
18. Parikh, A., Täckström, O., Das, D., Uszkoreit, J.: A decomposable attention model for natural language inference. In: Proceedings of the 2016 Conference on EMNLP, pp. 2249–2255. ACL, Austin, Texas, November 2016
19. Speer, R., Chin, J., Havasi, C.: Conceptnet 5.5: an open multilingual graph of general knowledge (2017)
20. Weissenborn, D., Kočiský, T., Dyer, C.: Dynamic integration of background knowledge in neural NLU systems (2017). arXiv preprint arXiv:1706.02596
21. Yang, B., Mitchell, T.: Leveraging knowledge bases in LSTMs for improving machine reading. In: Proceedings of the 55th Annual Meeting of the ACL, pp. 1436–1446. ACL, Vancouver, Canada July 2017
22. Yu, Z., Yu, J., Fan, J., Tao, D.: Multi-modal factorized bilinear pooling with co-attention learning for visual question answering. In: Proceedings of the IEEE International Conference on Computer Vision, pp. 1821–1830 (2017)

Neural-Symbolic Relational Reasoning on Graph Models: Effective Link Inference and Computation from Knowledge Bases

Henrique Lemos[1]([envelope])[ID], Pedro Avelar[1][ID], Marcelo Prates[1][ID], Artur Garcez[2][ID], and Luís Lamb[1][ID]

[1] Institute of Informatics, UFRGS, Porto Alegre, Brazil
{hlsantos,morprates,phcavelar,lamb}@inf.ufrgs.br
[2] Department of Computer Science, City, University of London, London, UK
a.garcez@city.ac.uk

Abstract. The recent developments and growing interest in neural-symbolic models has shown that hybrid approaches can offer richer models for Artificial Intelligence. The integration of effective relational learning and reasoning methods is one of the key challenges in this direction, as neural learning and symbolic reasoning offer complementary characteristics that can benefit the development of AI systems. Relational labelling or link prediction on knowledge graphs has become one of the main problems in deep learning-based natural language processing research. Moreover, other fields which make use of neural-symbolic techniques may also benefit from such research endeavours. There have been several efforts towards the identification of missing facts from existing ones in knowledge graphs. Two lines of research try and predict knowledge relations between two entities by considering all known facts connecting them or several paths of facts connecting them. We propose a neural-symbolic graph neural network which applies learning over all the paths by feeding the model with the embedding of the minimal subset of the knowledge graph containing such paths. By learning to produce representations for entities and facts corresponding to word embeddings, we show how the model can be trained end-to-end to decode these representations and infer relations between entities in a multitask approach. Our contribution is two-fold: a neural-symbolic methodology leverages the resolution of relational inference in large graphs, and we also demonstrate that such neural-symbolic model is shown more effective than path-based approaches.

Keywords: Neural-symbolic computing · Graph neural networks · Relational learning

Supported by Coordenação de Aperfeiçoamento de Pessoal de Nível Superior - Brazil (CAPES) - Finance Code 001 and by CNPq - the Brazilian Research Coucil.

I. Farkaš et al. (Eds.): ICANN 2020, LNCS 12396, pp. 647–659, 2020.
https://doi.org/10.1007/978-3-030-61609-0_51

1   Introduction

Neural-symbolic computing has recently become one of the promising research subfields in artificial intelligence, with both academic researchers and companies such as IBM and Microsoft setting up agendas that foster the integrated use of connectionist learning and symbolic inference techniques [6,10,13,16]. Deep learning (DL) models are now well-established frameworks towards solving Natural Language Processing (NLP) tasks. In recent years, however, the need for improved explainability and interpretability in machine learning and AI, has called for the investigation of models which lend themselves to clear semantic analyses, which in turn suggest the use of neural-symbolic approaches [5,6,10].

In this work, we propose a neural-symbolic graph neural network (GNN) model to perform integrated relational learning and inference over large scale knowledge graphs. To show the effectiveness and generality of our approach, we solve the relevant task of reasoning and inference on link prediction. More specifically, we leverage the relational learning capabilities of graph neural networks, which lend themselves soundly to integrated learning and reasoning tasks, which one can claim is the *raison d'etre* of neural-symbolic models. The core concept of our neural-symbolic model is built upon a connectionist architecture modelled by multilayer perceptrons (MLP) and long-short term memories (LSTM) whose message-passing structure reflects the relational knowledge expressed by the graph itself.

In this context, knowledge bases (KBs) are understood as a repository of *facts* stated over pairs of *entities*. Facts can be described by 3-tuples (e_s, r, e_t) connecting a source entity e_s and a target entity e_t with a relation r. For example, the fact that *the LHR Airport serves the city of London* can be formalised as (LHR Airport, serves, London). Because KBs are often compiled from scraped data, they may be incomplete, with missing facts about the stored entities. This motivates the problem of link prediction, in which one learns to predict previously unknown facts between two entities given the existing ones in the KB. Traditionally, attempts to solve this problem have relied on accumulating information over all facts directly connecting two entities to predict a new one [2,12,17]. This approach is conceptually limited, as two entities can possibly be connected by *paths* of facts and these paths may store useful information which could also be exploited to predict new facts. The most obvious benefit from considering this kind of input is also that eventually there will be no direct relation between two entities in the KB and yet we may infer some relation between them [9,11,20]. A recent study has made an effort to take these paths into consideration, by processing each path connecting a source and a target entity via a RNN and accumulating their outputs to produce a prediction [4].

Our approach goes a step further by acknowledging that useful information can be lost when one does not take all paths into consideration *at the same time*. To overcome this issue, we propose a neural-symbolic graph neural network model which is able to feed on the minimal sub-graph containing all paths connecting a given source and target pair (fully described in Sect. 3). A GNN is an end-to-end differentiable DL model which feeds on graphs. It does so by assigning multidimensional embeddings[1] for each node and each edge in the graph and refining these embeddings over many iterations of a parameterised (and thus trainable) procedure of "message-passing". Techniques in the GNN family have enjoyed increased interest in the last years, with applications to generative models of source code [3], quantum chemistry [7] and urban planning [8].

The remainder of the paper is structured as follows. Next, we formalise the problem tackled in the paper and briefly discuss related work. In Sect. 3, describe our neural-symbolic model and how we trained it on link prediction. Finally, in Sect. 4 and Sect. 5, we analyse and compare our results to state-of-art techniques and point out directions for further research.

2 Preliminaries

The problem of link prediction can be formalised as follows. A Knowledge Base (KB) is a 4-tuple $\mathbf{KB} = (\mathcal{E}, \mathcal{T}, \mathcal{F}, \mathcal{R})$, where $\mathcal{E}$ is the set of entities, $\mathcal{T}$ is the set of entity types, $\mathcal{F}$ is the set of facts and $\mathcal{R}$ is the set of relations. Given a subset $\mathbf{KB}' = (\mathcal{E}', \mathcal{T}', \mathcal{F}', \mathcal{R}') \subseteq \mathbf{KB}$ of a knowledge base $\mathbf{KB} = (\mathcal{E}, \mathcal{T}, \mathcal{F}, \mathcal{R})$ and two entities $e_s, e_t \in \mathcal{E}'$, we want to predict a fact $f = (e_s, r, e_t)$ such that $f \notin \mathcal{F}'$ but $f \in \mathcal{F}$, that is, we want to use the (incomplete) information in $\mathbf{KB}'$ to recover facts from its superset $\mathbf{KB}$.

It should be noted that, in general, $\mathbf{KB}$ is not known. The motivation for link prediction is precisely the fact that knowledge bases are usually incomplete, so that our goal is to learn a procedure for enriching an input knowledge base into its (hypothetical) most complete form. In practice, for a given real-world knowledge base, there is no way for one to evaluate whether the output of a link predictor is correct, because the missing labels are not known. But one can still train such a model in a supervised way by training it on subsets of real-world knowledge graphs and forcing its outputs to match the removed data.

On the subject of link prediction, the *Universal Schema* [14] can be seen as the seminal approach, tackling the problem by enforcing the learning of latent feature embeddings for entity tuples and relations through matrix factorisation. This and other initial efforts rely solely on the set of facts directly connecting two entities in order to predict a new one [2,12,17]. This can be improved by taking *paths* of facts into consideration: apart from being directly connected by a set of facts, two entities can also be indirectly connected by a sequence of them (for example "the **LHR Airport** is located in **England** of which the capital is **London**"). Considering this approach, one may highlight the Path Ranking Algorithm (PRA) [9] and the Path-RNN [11]. One may also highlight the work of Das et al. [4] which enhanced the task of reasoning over chains of relations, previously performed by PRA and Path-RNN, by including representations also for the entities and for the entity types along the path, and by considering

---

[1] We use the words "embeddings" and "representations" depending on the context, but with the same meaning of real-valued projections of some object.

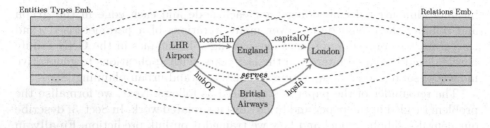

Fig. 1. A dummy example of how a knowledge graph between two entities (LHR Airport and London) is mapped into two lookup tables. Each relation is mapped into a unique relation embedding, while each entity may be mapped into several entity types (e.g. British Airways node), which are then fed to an aggregation function, such as mean or sum. Note that _capitalOf is an inverse relation, so it is read backwards.

multiple paths, combined via score pooling methods, to predict the missing relation between source and target entity. More recently, Yin et al. [20] tackled the same issue by encoding the paths with Gated Recurrent Units and by updating the embeddings multiple times along the entire path. These four methods were jointly evaluated on the dataset released by Das et al. [4] and the latter has achieved the best results so far. As we will see shortly, our approach extends the concept of learning over *paths* to learning over *graphs*. In this context, the evolution of approaches toward link prediction can be summarised as 1) learning over *edges*, 2) learning over *paths* and 3) learning over *graphs* (this paper).

The *Single-Model* introduced by Das et al. [4] is parameterised by three trainable components: the first is a table of representations (i.e. real-valued vectors) for each entity in the KB, the second is a table of representations for each relation in the KB, and the third is a Recurrent Neural Network (RNN) which will be fed with a sequence of facts $\pi = e_s, r_0, e_1, r_1, e_2, \ldots, r_n, e_t$ connecting a source entity e_s with a target entity e_t. The RNN's hidden state can be seen as a representation for the path π, which can be later decoded into a prediction for a new fact connecting e_s and e_t directly. At each timestep, the input for the RNN is a tuple (e_i, r_i) where e_i is the i-th entity in the path and r_i is the relation connecting it with the following entity. Because there is no relation later to e_t, the last input (e_t, r_{dummy}) contains a "dummy" relation:

$$\begin{aligned}
\mathbf{h}^{(0)} &\leftarrow f(\mathbf{h}^{(s)}, (e_s, r_0)) \\
\mathbf{h}^{(i+1)} &\leftarrow f(\mathbf{h}^{(i)}, (e_i, r_i)) \\
\mathbf{h}^{(last)} &\leftarrow f(\mathbf{h}^{(n)}, (e_t, r_{dummy}))
\end{aligned} \tag{1}$$

For each relation r, a similarity measure is computed between the representation for the path π, produced by the RNN, and the representation for r, which is learned. But because the RNN can only process each path separately, the authors propose finding different paths using random walks in the KB and score-pooling the outputs to accumulate their information.

The main enhancements of the *Single-Model*, compared to PRA and Path-RNN, are the addition of embeddings to represent the entities along the path, the inclusion of neural attention mechanisms (in terms of score-pooling) to reason over multiple paths and the ability to train one single model to predict several target relations. However, later work of Yin et al. [20] was able to improve the performance on the dataset provided by Das et al. [4]. Their strategy consisted in forcing the RNN (a Gated Recurrent Unit - GRU) to predict entities representations as outputs along the path, and to update these representations at each step of the path. One may also highlight the work of Xiong et al. [19] which defines a policy-based agent to reason over a KG according to a reward function – at each step the agent picks a relation to extend the KG it is interacting with. These two approaches understand the problem of link prediction as combining multiple paths connecting e_s to e_t, and learning their intermediate representations separately. By changing the perspective to a graph-view, one could expect a faster learning since relations and entities of different paths will be aware of each other when considered inside the same graph.

Only very recently link prediction tasks have been tackled by neural networks whose inputs are graphs. Outside of a KB scope, work of Zhang and Chen [21] has already demonstrated an unprecedented performance of GNNs on the binary link prediction task – with no edge features. Still, the R-GCN model [15] relies on a graph convolution architecture to perform link prediction on KGs: the R-GCN itself can be seen as an encoder, which takes the graph as an input and outputs a real-valued vector for each vertex $v_i \in \mathcal{V}$; then a decoding step (*DistMult* algorithm) scores 3-tuples through a function whose inputs are the real-valued vectors of the source entity and the target entity, and a learned diagonal matrix associated with the relation. The crucial difference of our model to the R-GCN is the statefulness: while their models learn functional applications over a neighbourhood, treating the node in the same way it treats its neighbours, our model uses LSTMs to process the abstractions learned in a way that the node uses its own state and its neighbourhood aggregation.

3 A Neural-Symbolic Model for Reasoning on Graphs

As stated before, our model goes one step further than previous approaches and trains a model to reason directly over *graphs* as opposed to *paths*. In this context, before we fully describe our model, it is important to clarify how the information in the KB is modelled as a graph. First of all, our model is not fed with the *entire* KB graph but with subsets thereof. Such a subset corresponds to the minimal subgraph containing all known paths connecting the source and target entities of interest (e_s, e_t). Entities correspond to *nodes* in our graph, while facts correspond to directed *edges*. Each edge is *labelled* with its corresponding relation, and each node is labelled with the set of entity types it belongs to. Also, because any two entities can be directly linked by more than one fact, we have *parallel edges*. In summary, our learning task is defined over a (node and edge)-labelled directed graph with parallel edges.

Over the course of its computation, our model will refine (real-valued vector) representations for each entity and for each fact in our graph. Because entities

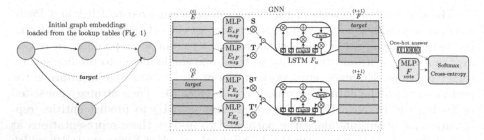

Fig. 2. Overall view of our model: the initial embeddings are loaded from the lookup tables – except the *target* relation embedding which is filled with zeros – and then fed to the GNN internal memory ($E^{(t)}$ and $F^{(t)}$). After t timesteps, we gather the updated *target* relation embedding and provide it as the input to a voting MLP, which will answer which relation is being represented by this embedding. The loss computed by Softmax Cross-entropy is then backpropagated throughout all the neural modules (MLP, GNN and embedding layer). Note that we omit the hidden and cell states and the unrolling of the two LSTMs inside the GNN to optimise readability.

(nodes) and facts (edges) are labelled, the initial representation for each of them must be initialised with the corresponding label – note that we also force a *fake* fact (edge) between e_s and e_t whose embedding is initialised with zeros. In this context, the first two trainable components of our model are two embedding layers, which can be conceptualised as two tables, the first one storing representations for entity types and the second one storing representations for relations. These representations will be used to initialise the representations for entities and facts. The reader should be reminded that each entity can belong to possibly many entity types at once. So, in our model, the initial representation for each entity is computed as an aggregation of the representations of all entity types it belongs to. As each fact is associated with a single relation, fact representations are simply initialised with the representation for their corresponding relations (Fig. 1). This process is described throughout lines 8–9 of Algorithm 1.

Then, the kernel of our model is a Graph Neural Network. As briefly mentioned above, a GNN can be seen as an end-to-end differentiable, message-passing algorithm between graph elements which is implemented with neural components. A GNN initially assigns (real-valued vector) representations for nodes and edges, and then iteratively refines these representations through many iterations of message-passing. In each message-passing iteration, the representation for each node is fed to an MLP which computes a representation for a "message" which will be sent to its neighbour elements. In the same way, another MLP computes representations for edge messages. These messages will be sent to neighbour elements in the graph: each node receives messages from all edges connected to it, while each edge receives two messages – one from its source and one from its target node. The set of messages received by each element is aggregated into a single vector – the matrices multiplications in Fig. 2) do not only aggregate the messages but also mask them with adjacency information so each node receives an aggregated message only from its neighbours. Finally, for each element, this vector is fed alongside with the current element's representation to an LSTM which updates it into a new representation. This process is described throughout lines 11–17 of Algorithm 1. Also, we avoided to provide a thorough description of how GNNs generally work in this paper, but interested readers may refer to Battaglia et al. [1] and to Wu et al. [18] for complete and up-to-date surveys of how GNNs work and have evolved along the last years.

The representations for entities and facts are updated by LSTMs. Concretely, we have an LSTM E_u to update entity embeddings and an LSTM F_u to update fact embeddings. One can see the representations for entities or facts as the *hidden states* of each one of these LSTMs. Lastly, from line 18 to 20 of Algorithm 1, we gather from the GNN the final embedding of the forced unknown fact and feed it to a *voting* MLP F_{vote}. This MLP can also be seen as a decoding function: it receives a fact embedding and extracts its label (relation). It outputs C logits, where C is the total amount of target relations. A *softmax* function is then applied to these logits in order to transform them into C probabilities – the most likely relation is to be considered as the predicted answer.

3.1 Experimental Setup

Our model architecture is structured as follows. We use embedding sizes of 64 for entity, fact and message representations. The message-computing MLPs $\mathcal{M}_{\mathcal{E}\rightarrow\mathcal{T}}, \mathcal{M}_{\mathcal{F}\rightarrow\mathcal{R}} : \mathbb{R}^{64} \rightarrow \mathbb{R}^{64}$ are three-layered with layer sizes $(64, 64, 64)$ and have ReLU nonlinearities as activations for all layers except for a linear activation in the last layer. The update functions $\underset{u}{E}, \underset{u}{F} : \mathbb{R}^{64}, \mathbb{R}^{64} \rightarrow \mathbb{R}^{64}, \mathbb{R}^{64}$ are implemented by layer-norm LSTM cells with ReLU activations. Finally, we define F_{vote} as a four-layered MLP with layer sizes $(64, 64, 64, 46 + 1)$ with ReLU non-linearities except for the last linear activated layer.

At the end of the pipeline depicted in Fig. 2, our model is trained to minimise the following loss $\mathcal{L}$:

$$\mathcal{L} = \frac{1}{B} \sum_{b=1}^{B} \left(-\sum_{c=1}^{C} y_{b,c} \log(\frac{e^{z_c}}{\sum_{c=1}^{C} e^{z_{b,c}}}) \right) \tag{2}$$

where B stands for the batch size and C for the number of target relations. Note that Eq. 2 just computes a softmax cross entropy over the C target relations for each instance, averaging over the batch.

Each model was trained for 2000 epochs, each one comprising 128 operations of stochastic gradient descent (Tensorflow's Adam optimiser with learning rate $= 2 \times 10^{-5}$) in batches of 10 instances each. We also set t_{max} to 25 to allow the GNN kernel to refine entities and relations embeddings throughout sufficient iterations

We ran our meta-model under three different configurations:

Algorithm 1. Neural-Symbolic Relation Predictor

1: **function** GNN$((\mathcal{E}, \mathcal{T}, \mathcal{F}, \mathcal{R}, \mathbf{M}_{\mathcal{E} \to \mathcal{T}}, \mathbf{M}_{\mathcal{F} \to \mathcal{R}}))$
2:
3:      // Compute binary adjacency matrix from facts to source & target entities
4:      $\mathbf{S}[i,j] \leftarrow \mathbb{1}(\exists e', r' | f_i = (e_j, r', e')) | \; \forall f_i \in \mathcal{F}$
5:      $\mathbf{T}[i,j] \leftarrow \mathbb{1}(\exists e' \exists r' | f_i = (e', r', e_j)) | \; \forall f_i \in \mathcal{F}$
6:
7:      // Gather facts & entity repr. from lookup tables (operator $\langle \rangle$ indicates any aggregation function - i.e. sum, mean, etc.)
8:      $\overset{(1)}{\mathbf{F}}[i] \leftarrow \mathbf{M}_{\mathcal{F} \to \mathcal{R}}(\mathcal{R}[i]) \; | \; \forall f_i \in \mathcal{F}$
9:      $\overset{(1)}{\mathbf{E}}[i] \leftarrow \langle \mathbf{M}_{\mathcal{E} \to \mathcal{T}}(\mathcal{T}[i,k]) | \forall k \in [0, mt] \rangle \; | \; \forall e_i \in \mathcal{E}$
10:
11:      // Run t_{max} message-passing iterations
12:      **for** $t = 1 \ldots t_{max}$ **do**
13:          // Refine entity repr. with messages from facts
14:          $\overset{(t+1)}{\mathbf{E}_h}, \overset{(t+1)}{\mathbf{E}} \underset{u}{\leftarrow} E(\mathbf{E}_h, \underset{msg}{\mathbf{S}^\mathsf{T} \times F_{E_s}(\overset{(t)}{\mathbf{F}})}, \underset{msg}{\mathbf{T}^\mathsf{T} \times F_{E_t}(\overset{(t)}{\mathbf{F}})})$
15:          // Refine fact repr. with messages from entities
16:          $\overset{(t+1)}{\mathbf{F}_h}, \overset{(t+1)}{\mathbf{F}} \underset{u}{\leftarrow} F(\mathbf{F}_h, \underset{msg}{\mathbf{S} \times E_{s_F}(\overset{(t)}{\mathbf{E}})}, \underset{msg}{\mathbf{T} \times E_{t_F}(\overset{(t)}{\mathbf{E}})})$

17:      // Translate the forced unknown fact (i=0) into logit probabilities of each relation
18:      $\mathbf{R_{logits}} \leftarrow F_{vote}\left(\overset{(t_{max})}{\mathbf{F}}[0] \right)$
19:      // Apply softmax cross-entropy to identify which is the most likely target relation
20:      prediction $\leftarrow$ argmax(softmax($\mathbf{R_{logits}}$))

- **GNN-Relation** – Only relations were considered, therefore there was only one table to store the embeddings – $\mathcal{M}_{\mathcal{F} \to \mathcal{R}}$ – and all entities were mapped into a single real-valued vector, which is also learned.
- **GNN-Mean** – Both entities and relations embeddings are mapped into separate tables, and to aggregate several entity types into one entity representation we used arithmetic mean.
- **GNN-Sum** – The same as **GNN-Mean** but using sum as the aggregation function over entity types.

During the training procedure, a faster loss decay was observed on **GNN-Mean** and **GNN-Sum**, which corroborates the importance of taking both entities and relations into account instead of considering only relations.

3.2 Benchmark Description

We trained and tested our model on the benchmark dataset released by Das et al. [4]. It comprises 3.22 M entity pairs and 51390 different types of relations coming either from Freebase or from ClueWeb. We were able to reduce

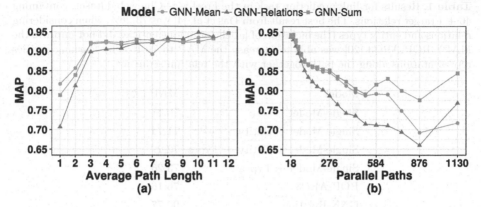

Fig. 3. Plot (a): each graph has many paths with different lengths (number of edges) connecting e_s to e_t. This plot shows how each of our models performs as the average path length between e_s and e_t increases. Plot (b): as the number of parallel paths between e_s and e_t increases, all of our models' performances decreases. There are many unique number of parallel edges, so we clustered them into 20 intervals and some of their max values are labelled in the x-axis.

the amount of relation types to 25737 due to our strategy of incorporating directional data into the graph itself – a relation and its reversed form, such as "/location/location/contains" and "_/location/location/contains", were mapped into a single index.

Instead of using an unique representation for each entity, in **GNN-Mean** and in **GNN-Sum** we chose to rely on entities types, as the dataset's distribution of entities is heavy tailed [4]. We gathered this mapping of entity to entity types from the vocabulary provided in the dataset which yielded a total of 2247 unique entity types. There are positive and negative instances for each one of one the 46 target relations, all the negative ones were mapped into a *null* relation target, thus resulting in 46 + 1 target relations left to be predicted. We used positive and negative instances from both *train* and *dev* files during training, we also forced our minibatch to be balanced by alternating positive and negative (*null* target relation) instances.

4 Analyses and Results

For each one of the testing instances, our model outputs a ranking over all target relations (in total 46 + 1 target relations), thus we followed previous works in this dataset and chose the Mean Average Precision (MAP) as our main evaluation metric. However, we restricted it to be MAP@5. The results are presented in Table 1 and demonstrate how well our models perform under this dataset. Even our simpler model – **GNN-Relation** – was able to achieve 90.77% of MAP over more than 2.1 M testing instances. Our best performance, however, came from the **GNN-Sum** model – increasing around 16% previous best result

Table 1. Results for link prediction task in the Freebase+Clueweb dataset, containing 46 + 1 target relations. The best result from Das et al. [4] was 73.26%, when considering relations and entity types (the inclusion of labels for unique entities did not improve the MAP). ROP_ARC3 [20] was able to increase the MAP to 76.16% by learning entities representations along the path together with the relation sequence.

Model	MAP (%)
Single-Model	70.11
Single-Model + Entity	71.74
Single-Model + Entity + Types	72.22
Single-Model + Types	73.26
ROP_ARC3	76.16
GNN-Relation	90.77
GNN-Mean	91.83
GNN-Sum	**92.32**

(ROP_ARC3) – which is somewhat expected, since *Single-Model* also achieved its best results when enhanced with relations and entities types embeddings – the latter combined via sum.

Despite the outstanding average results, our best model presented some variation in its results when analysed from specific target relations viewpoints. Table 2 shows the top and bottom three target relations, sorted according to average accuracy, a more strict metric than MAP. It is still unclear why there are some relations in which our model has some issues: both TPR and TNR below 75%. One possibility is that the negative and positive examples of such troublesome target relations are quite similar in their general labelled graph structure. Nevertheless, even the worst MAP (83.92%) is still higher than the average performance of previous path-based models.

Table 2. GNN-Sum: Top and bottom three results sorted according to Average Accuracy. Note that the Average Accuracy is closer to TNR due to imbalance between negative and positive testing examples in the dataset.

Target relation	MAP	TPR	TNR	Avg. Acc
/book/written_work/original_language	98.38	93.12	97.21	96.90
/film/film/directed_by	97.92	81.00	97.31	96.13
/music/genre/albums	97.59	87.50	95.90	95.25
/cvg/game_version/platform	85.03	89.93	68.55	70.13
/music/artist/origin	84.32	72.46	69.06	69.31
/people/person/religion	83.92	87.39	66.33	67.91

It is also remarkable that all of our models have no problem dealing with longer paths – amount of intermediate relations between e_s and e_t. In fact, Fig. 3(a) shows that as the Average Path Length increases all of our models tend to perform better. The most significant performance increase is seen on **GNN-Relation** which starts with very poor performance, due to very little information since relations types embeddings is all that it sees, but quickly stabilises its performance around 92.5% – after average path length equals to 5. The other two models also experiment an increase of performance but much less pronounced than the one **GNN-Relation** experiments. On the other hand, all of our models presented some level of performance decreasing when facing larger numbers of parallel paths between e_s and e_t (see Fig. 3(b)). That is, even though we change the perspective to a graph viewpoint (instead of single paths), our models are much more comfortable dealing with *long* graphs than with *wide* ones.

5   Conclusions and Future Work

The problem of link prediction in a Knowledge Base consists in automatising the discovery of new facts: i.e. learning to predict a missing labelled edge between two nodes. In this context, a *fact* is the connection between two *entities* through a *relation*. This problem arises in scraped structured data, which may miss facts about the existing entities, and also by knowledge bases which were augmented with unstructured data.

Recently, approaches for link prediction have evolved from learning over *edges* to learning over *paths*. In this paper, we go a step further and propose a neural-symbolic based model which learns directly over *graphs*, enabling reasoning over many paths at once. We achieve this by feeding the minimal subgraph containing all known paths between two entities to a GNN, a deep learning architecture which learns real-valued vector representations for nodes (entities) and edges (facts) in a graph. After the GNN learns a representation for the missing fact, we use a MLP to decode it, enabling us to predict the relation it represents.

Our results surpassed all previous path-based models in a dataset from Freebase+ClueWeb containing over 3 M entities – in the best scenario we increased the MAP metric by 16% over 46 + 1 target relations. However, there are two main points to be addressed in the future: (i) our model relies on matrix multiplications to produce embeddings' updates, and can be improved to deal with huge graphs; (ii) we currently update entities types and relations embeddings at the end of the pipeline, with the Softmax Cross-Entropy loss; Yin et al. [20] were able to improve previous models' results by updating entities representations along the entire path; in this sense our model could be adapted to perform updates in the same manner.

References

1. Battaglia, P., et al.: Relational inductive biases, deep learning, and graph networks (2018). arXiv preprint arXiv:1806.01261
2. Bordes, A., Usunier, N., García-Durán, A., Weston, J., Yakhnenko, O.: Translating embeddings for modeling multi-relational data. In: Proceedings of NIPS, pp. 2787–2795 (2013)
3. Brockschmidt, M., Allamanis, M., Gaunt, A.L., Polozov, O.: Generative code modeling with graphs (2018). arXiv preprint arXiv:1805.08490
4. Das, R., Neelakantan, A., Belanger, D., McCallum, A.: Chains of reasoning over entities, relations, and text using recurrent neural networks. In: Proceedings of EACL, vol. 2017, pp. 132–141 (2017)
5. Evans, R., Grefenstette, E.: Learning explanatory rules from noisy data. J. Artif. Intell. Res. **61**, 1–64 (2018)
6. d'Avila Garcez, A., Gori, M., Lamb, L., Serafini, L., Spranger, M., Tran, S.: Neural-symbolic computing: An effective methodology for principled integration of machine learning and reasoning. FLAP **6**(4), 611–632 (2019)
7. Gilmer, J., Schoenholz, S.S., Riley, P.F., Vinyals, O., Dahl, G.E.: Neural message passing for quantum chemistry. In: Proceeding of ICML, pp. 1263–1272 (2017)
8. Hu, J., Guo, C., Yang, B., Jensen, C.S., Chen, L.: Recurrent multi-graph neural networks for travel cost prediction (2018). arXiv preprint arXiv:1811.05157
9. Lao, N., Mitchell, T.M., Cohen, W.W.: Random walk inference and learning in a large scale knowledge base. In: Proceeding of EMNLP 2011, pp. 529–539 (2011)
10. Mao, J., Gan, C., Kohli, P., Tenenbaum, J.B., Wu, J.: The neuro-symbolic concept learner: Interpreting scenes, words, and sentences from natural supervision. In: ICLR 2019 (2019)
11. Neelakantan, A., Roth, B., McCallum, A.: Compositional vector space models for knowledge base completion. In: Proceedings of ACL, vol. 2015, pp. 156–166 (2015)
12. Nguyen, D.Q., Sirts, K., Qu, L., Johnson, M.: Stranse: a novel embedding model of entities and relationships in knowledge bases. In: NAACL HLT 2016, pp. 460–466 (2016). http://aclweb.org/anthology/N/N16/N16-1054.pdf
13. Raghavan, S.: 2020 AI predictions from IBM research (2019). https://www.ibm.com/blogs/research/2019/12/2020-ai-predictions/. Accessed 14 Jan 2020
14. Riedel, S., Yao, L., McCallum, A., Marlin, B.M.: Relation extraction with matrix factorization and universal schemas. In: NAACL-HLT, pp. 74–84 (2013). http://aclweb.org/anthology/N/N13/N13-1008.pdf
15. Schlichtkrull, M., Kipf, T.N., Bloem, P., van den Berg, R., Titov, I., Welling, M.: Modeling relational data with graph convolutional networks. In: Gangemi, A., et al. (eds.) ESWC 2018. LNCS, vol. 10843, pp. 593–607. Springer, Cham (2018). https://doi.org/10.1007/978-3-319-93417-4_38
16. Smolensky, P.: Next-generation architectures bridge gap between neural and symbolic representations with neural symbols (2019). https://www.microsoft.com/en-us/research/blog/next-generation-architectures-bridge-gap-between-neural-and-symbolic-representations-with-neural-symbols/. Accessed 14 Jan 2020
17. Socher, R., Chen, D., Manning, C.D., Ng, A.Y.: Reasoning with neural tensor networks for knowledge base completion. In: Proceeding of NIPS, pp. 926–934 (2013)
18. Wu, Z., Pan, S., Chen, F., Long, G., Zhang, C., Yu, P.S.: A comprehensive survey on graph neural networks. CoRR abs/1901.00596 (2019)

19. Xiong, W., Hoang, T., Wang, W.Y.: Deeppath: A reinforcement learning method for knowledge graph reasoning. In: Proceedings of EMNLP, vol. 2017, pp. 564–573 (2017)
20. Yin, W., Yaghoobzadeh, Y., Schütze, H.: Recurrent one-hop predictions for reasoning over knowledge graphs. In: Proceedings of COLING, vol. 2018, pp. 2369–2378 (2018)
21. Zhang, M., Chen, Y.: Link prediction based on graph neural networks. In: Proceeding of NIPS, pp. 5171–5181 (2018)

Tell Me Why You Feel That Way: Processing Compositional Dependency for Tree-LSTM Aspect Sentiment Triplet Extraction (TASTE)

Alexander Sutherland[1](✉), Suna Bensch[2], Thomas Hellström[2], Sven Magg[1], and Stefan Wermter[1]

[1] Department of Informatics, University of Hamburg,
Vogt-Koelln-Str. 30, 22527 Hamburg, Germany
{sutherland,magg,wermter}@informatik.uni-hamburg.de
[2] Department of Computing Science, Umeå University, Umeå, Sweden
{suna,thomash}@cs.umu.se

Abstract. Sentiment analysis has transitioned from classifying the sentiment of an entire sentence to providing the contextual information of what targets exist in a sentence, what sentiment the individual targets have, and what the causal words responsible for that sentiment are. However, this has led to elaborate requirements being placed on the datasets needed to train neural networks on the joint triplet task of determining an entity, its sentiment, and the causal words for that sentiment. Requiring this kind of data for training systems is problematic, as they suffer from stacking subjective annotations and domain over-fitting leading to poor model generalisation when applied in new contexts. These problems are also likely to be compounded as we attempt to jointly determine additional contextual elements in the future. To mitigate these problems, we present a hybrid neural-symbolic method utilising a Dependency Tree-LSTM's compositional sentiment parse structure and complementary symbolic rules to correctly extract target-sentiment-cause triplets from sentences without the need for triplet training data. We show that this method has the potential to perform in line with state-of-the-art approaches while also simplifying the data required and providing a degree of interpretability through the Tree-LSTM.

Keywords: Sentiment analysis · Tree-LSTM · Hybrid Neural-symbolic

1 Introduction

Sentiment Analysis (SA) has been described as a suitcase [1], where SA is composed of several smaller Natural Language Processing (NLP) tasks that need to be performed to acquire a contextual understanding of a predicted sentiment label. One of the most prevalent steps beyond sentence-level sentiment classification is Aspect-Based Sentiment Analysis (ABSA) [8]. In ABSA, targets in

I. Farkaš et al. (Eds.): ICANN 2020, LNCS 12396, pp. 660–671, 2020.
https://doi.org/10.1007/978-3-030-61609-0_52

sentences for a particular domain are determined and assigned specific sentiment labels that may differ from other targets in the same sentence. Jointly being able to determine a target and its sentiment is a necessary step towards being able to use that information in practical scenarios.

Extracting terms used to identify the cause or reason for a sentiment outcome in a sentence is sometimes called Opinion Term Extraction (OTE) [6]. The goal of OTE is to identify these causal words in a sentence and compare them to user annotations of what they consider to be the cause of a sentiment. OTE provides an idea of what words convey affective meaning. In recent works, ABSA and OTE have been combined [6] to create triplets of information describing a target, its sentiment, and the cause of that sentiment. This task, known as Aspect Sentiment Triplet Extraction (ASTE) [6], has the potential to provide a lot of contextual information to intelligent agents allowing them to not only know what is being spoken about but how an individual feels about it and what the cause of that feeling may be. With this information, the agent can either reinforce a certain behaviour based on the cause, if positive, or attempt to remedy a negative cause if possible. An example of such a triplet for the sentence "the food was excellent" would be ("the food", positive, "excellent") where "the food" is the target, the sentiment is positive, and "excellent" is the opinion term.

While predicting sentiment triplets is valuable, the method in which we acquire them for agents needs to be robust. Agents often find themselves in dynamic contexts provided by natural language when interacting with individuals in virtual and real-world environments. These context shifts are very problematic when doing triplet sentiment analysis, as the new targets or aspects that occur may not have been captured by the training data. Likewise, the process of having three subjective labels that have to be jointly predicted is difficult to learn and difficult to expand upon, as any new datasets would require annotators to make three subjective decisions regarding what substring constitutes a target, what the sentiment of that target is, and what the cause for that sentiment is.

These tasks have the possible flaw of introducing annotator bias and the alignment of triplet information introduces further bias. As an example, the original opinion terms were aligned with aspects by only two annotators [3] and we do not know how many annotators the opinion terms had. Across all of the papers used by the triplet dataset [6] this has resulted in 5 different degrees of subjective error for the individual tasks and alignments combined during training and evaluation. While these errors could be mitigated by naively relabelling the data set with triplets from scratch, it would not solve shortcomings in scenarios in which we would want additional context as quadruplet or more or would like to change into a new domain. Methods that require specific jointly annotated data do not scale well between domains. Therefore we propose leveraging a combination of symbolic information and neural processing to circumvent this.

As an alternative, we propose a hybrid neural-symbolic method for Tree Long-Short Term Memory (Tree-LSTM) Aspect Sentiment Triplet Extraction (TASTE) through the symbolic analysis of the compositional processing of a Dependency Tree-LSTM (DTLSTM) [11]. This approach has the benefit of not requiring domain-specific triplet training data but only requires sentiment annotations from the Stanford Sentiment Treebank (SST) [9]. This method scales between domains as it only relies on the compositional processing done by the DTLSTM and noun chunk identification as opposed to learning high-level relations at domain-level between labels. Furthermore, due to the structured recursive processing of the DTLSTM, we are granted a degree of interpretability through predictions over the dependency parse tree, allowing for common-sense reasoning as to why a certain target, sentiment, and causes were selected. We show that this method allows us to perform in line with state-of-the-art neural approaches under the correct circumstances while allowing for the aforementioned interpretability and simple output and behaviour modifications through symbolic rules.

2   Related Work

Sutherland *et al.* [10] provide a method of identifying targets and their sentiment based on the sentiment parse of a Tree-LSTM over a dependency parse tree. This is done by applying a set of symbolic rules to the neurally determined output of the Tree-LSTM for every node in the syntactic dependency parse tree, where each prediction is based on hidden states of the children of a node. This method relies upon the structure of dependency parses having verbs as the heads of affective substrings that contain targets, wherein the targets are children of the verb. In this paper, we extend the work of Sutherland *et al.* to identify more targets and include cause, also known as Opinion Term Extraction (OTE).

Using dependency trees is beneficial for ABSA and often involves symbolic operations on the dependencies. Wang *et al.* [12] present Recursive Neural Condition Random Fields (RNCRF) which utilise a recursive network to produce high-level representations based on the syntactic structure. They are then used to train conditional random fields to extract aspect-opinion pairs. Dai *et al.* [2] also trained a Bi-directional LSTM-Conditional Random Field (BiLSTM-CRF) which utilises additional unlabelled data together with the SemEval data [8] to determine aspect-opinion pairs.

Peng *et al.* [6] go so far as to actively construct the triplet dataset and use a two-stage model of first predicting the target and opinion together, and then use a Bidirectional LSTM to predict if the two are a valid pair in the second stage. This allows the system to utilise information from the opinion extraction when predicting targets to get a higher performance overall. In our work, we utilise the data provided by Peng *et al.* and symbolic rule-based principles from Sutherland *et al.* [10] to show that the task of ASTE can be performed comparatively under the right conditions with only access to standard sentiment data.

3   SemEval ASTE Dataset

We utilise the SemEval ASTE dataset [6] which is an extension of the SemEval ABSA dataset [8]. The SemEval ABSA task, proposed at the 2014 International Workshop on Semantic Evaluation (SemEval), is based on identifying targets of sentiment in sentences. The SemEval ABSA dataset was extended by Pontiki *et al.* [8] to include additional elements such as being able to identify the particular category a target may belong to or being able to perform ABSA in different languages. This dataset was used as the foundation to further deepen the analysis of sentiment by introducing *"opinion terms"* [12], what can be considered to be the reason or cause for a particular sentiment. The alignments between the aspects and the opinion terms are provided by Fan *et al.* [3].

This all culminated in the work of Peng *et al.* [6], wherein they introduce the SemEval ASTE dataset[1], consisting of identifying targets, classifying the sentiment towards those targets, and determining which words in a sentence were responsible for the sentiment towards a target, the *"opinion"*. We use this extended dataset, which has been provided by the authors to analyse how well our approach can extract sentiment triplets and to compare against other approaches. Each data-point consists of a sentence and each sentence can have multiple targets which are substrings in the sentence. Each target has a specific sentiment, with the labels positive, neutral, and negative, and an opinion term which consists of a substring in the sentence defined by annotators.

The dataset itself is split up into two domains restaurants and laptops: there are three versions of the restaurant dataset, denoted rest14, rest15, and rest16 based on the year the data was used in the SemEval challenge, and lap14 for the 2014 laptop ABSA data. The total number of viable targets for each version can be seen in Table 1.

4   Dependency Tree-LSTM

Our method is based on the compositional processing used by the Dependency Tree-LSTM (DTLSTM) [11], that was utilised for ABSA by Sutherland *et al.* [10], whose method functions as a basis for our approach. To extract our sentiment triplet we need to know the distribution of sentiment over a dependency tree. To do this, we pre-train a DTLSTM on the Stanford Sentiment Treebank (SST) [9] training data. What differentiates a DTLSTM and an LSTM is that it can take several inputs at each time-step and processes input based on the dependency tree parse structure of its input sentence. A DTLSTM has the weight matrices W and U, and a bias vector b similar to the LTSM it is based upon with the same sigmoidal activation function σ_g.

For a DTLSTM, a node j in a dependency tree possesses a set of dependent child nodes, denoted $C(j)$, which contains the indexes of children k, with each child possessing a hidden state h_k. An input word vector x_j is the vector corresponding to the word associated with j in the parse tree. The summed hidden states $\tilde{h}_j$ of the child nodes are the input to the input gate i_j. The DTLSTM has several forget vectors f_{jk} for each child k of node j. The DTLSTM has an output gate activation vector o_j, such as those possessed by an LSTM, and a memory cell vector u_j. The updated memory cell state vector c_j is the summed element-wise multiplication of i_j and u_j with the summed element-wise multiplications

---

[1] https://github.com/xuuuluuu/SemEval-Triplet-data.

of each child cell state c_k with f_{jk}. The hidden state h_j is the element-wise multiplication of o_j and $tanh(c_j)$. The equations for the DTLSTM, are defined by Tai *et al.* [11] and are as follows:

$$\tilde{h}_j = \sum_{k \in C(j)} h_k, \tag{1}$$

$$i_j = \sigma_g(W^{(i)}x_j + U^{(i)}\tilde{h}_j + b^{(i)}), \tag{2}$$

$$f_{jk} = \sigma_g(W^{(f)}x_j + U^{(f)}h_k + b^{(f)}), \tag{3}$$

$$o_j = \sigma_g(W^{(o)}x_j + U^{(o)}\tilde{h}_j + b^{(o)}), \tag{4}$$

$$u_j = \sigma_g(W^{(u)}x_j + U^{(u)}\tilde{h}_j + b^{(u)}), \tag{5}$$

$$c_j = i_j \odot u_j + \sum_{k \in C(j)} f_{jk} \odot c_k, \tag{6}$$

$$h_j = o_j \odot tanh(c_j). \tag{7}$$

Words in a sentence are represented as Word Embeddings from the pre-trained Common-Crawl 840 B data[2] before they are fed to the DTLSTM. To analyse sentiment for sentences according to a tree structure, we use the state of the art NLP library SpaCy [5] to extract dependency trees. We see when predicting over dependency trees that the sentiment that propagates through the tree can come from many different sources, such as nouns, adjectives, and sometimes the verb heads themselves [9]. The compositional structure also allows for the extraction of sub-trees as opposed to other approaches that only provide individual words.

5   Aspect Sentiment Triplet Extraction

To analyse how close the features utilised by our neural models are to the annotations provided by a user we have to determine what are viewed as salient features. We do this by observing two TASTE approaches that can allocate salience to words in a sentence when considering the sentiment.

5.1   Target Identification

Our method of identifying affective targets extends the method of Sutherland *et al.* [10] by changing the conditions under which targets are extracted. In the work of Sutherland *et al.*, targets are extracted when there exists a noun chunk, as identified by SpaCy, that has a verb as its head in the dependency tree. This provided both a target and the sub-tree it belongs to as defined by the children of the head verb.

We adjust this method by addressing cases where there is no verb or the verb is defined as an auxiliary verb, and therefore possesses the *"AUX"* dependency

---

[2] https://nlp.stanford.edu/projects/glove/.

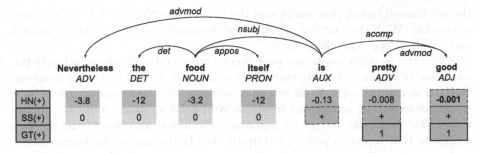

Fig. 1. An example of what kind of sentiment opinion terms are identified from a sentiment dependency parse for the positive sentiment (+) in an example sentence with the target "food" and the sentiment "positive" for our two methods: Highest Node (HN) and Sentiment Search (SS). The selected reason candidates for the respective methods, as represented by the dashed boxes, can be compared against the ground truth reasoning (GT) as provided by annotators. In this sentence, we see that HN identifies the word "good" as the reason, whereas SS identifies the substring "is pretty good", and annotators identified "pretty good" as the correct reason. The values in the HN row are the logarithmic softmax values for the positive sentiment class of the projection layer of the Tree-LSTM.

tag. The same basic algorithm is followed: for every verb or auxiliary verb in a sentence, if a noun chunk exists as a substring within the substring created from that parent's children and itself then that noun chunk is a viable target. Every target can only be associated with its closest parental verb but a parental verb may possess multiple noun chunks. In addition to this, we allow dependency trees that have noun chunks but no verbs to also be considered as targets. An example sentence where this would be relevant would be the sentence *"Good food."*, where *"food"* would become the target.

5.2 Target Sentiment Classification

Sutherland *et al.* [10] leveraged a method classifying the sentiment of a target by having the target inherit the sentiment of its parental verb in a trickle-down fashion. This is possible thanks to the DTLSM's compositional parsing and the fact that sentiment is propagated up through the dependency tree to the root of the sentence. We utilise the same method of sentiment prediction, by using the DTLSTM to predict a sentiment vector over the negative, neutral, and positive classes for every node in the dependency parse tree.

The DTLSTM is pre-trained on the SST [9] and retains the hyper-parameter set as reported by Tai *et al.* [11]. We use these hyper-parameters as the default in the implementation we adjusted for our approach[3], as we found adjustments to be insignificant and further optimisation of the architecture is outside of the scope of this paper. Similar to Sutherland *et al.* [10] and Peng *et al.* [6], we select

---

[3] https://github.com/ttpro1995/TreeLSTMSentiment.

the pre-trained model that performed the best on the SST validation data over ten epochs. With this, we can acquire a prediction for every sentiment class for every node in the dependency tree.

Once this is done we iterate over every target and each target inherits the sentiment of its parental verb, essentially trickling down the sentiment from the verb to the noun chunks. As an example, sentence *"the food is good"* would have a positive sentiment propagated from the word good up to the root *"is"*. As the target *"the food"* has *"is"* as its parental verb, it will also inherit the positive sentiment that has been propagated up to *"is"*. In the case of sentences or sub-sentences where there are no verbs, the noun of the noun chunk acts as the root of the sentence and is the receiver of the sentiment charge.

5.3   Target Opinion Term Extraction

We examine two different TASTE approaches for extracting cause from a sentiment dependency parse. The first approach, Highest Node (HN), is to recursively search the predictions of the sub-tree of a target from the parental node of the target and extract the node in its sub-tree with the highest logarithmic softmax activation level for the intended sentiment. This provides us with a single word from the dependency parse tree that is believed to be the most likely reason for the outcome sentiment. The benefit of this approach is that it is likely to reliably identify at least one word in the reason, as additional non-salient words are likely to reduce the activation level as opposed to increase it. Drawbacks are that reasons that require multiple words to understand, e.g. *"very good"* cannot be fully extracted. Another issue is that if a parental node is somewhat trending toward the sentiment, but not the primary cause, it may be picked instead.

The second approach, Sentiment Search (SS), allows for the extraction of this additional causation context, as we recursively search through the sub-tree of the parent node of a target and extract all nodes where the target sentiment is higher than the other classes. This allows for the selection of multiple reason words and the construction of multi-word substrings. So for the sentence *"The sushi was pretty good"* *"was"*, *"pretty"* and *"good"* would be extracted as reasons for the positive sentiment towards sushi.

The drawbacks of this method are that it can suffer from low precision, as it will pick up words that inherit positive sentiment as they propagate up the dependency tree, and that it cannot identify a reason if positive sentiment is not being properly propagated up the tree, i.e. nodes that incorrectly have a higher sentiment for neutral rather than positive. Examples of what both methods identify and the kind of features they look at can be seen in Fig. 1. The method used for recursively going through the affective dependency parse tree and picking out either HN or SS is defined in Algorithm 1, which recursively searches through the tree of nodes from the root in a depth first fashion to identify the SS and HN nodes.

Algorithm 1. RecursiveSearch

1: **if** $node_iSentiment$ **equals** $targetSentiment$ **then**
2:     $SSHypothesis.insert(nodeWord)$
3: **end if**
4: **if** $len(children(node_i))$ **is** 0 **then**
5:     **return** $node_iSentActivation$
6: **else**
7:     $highestActivation \leftarrow node_iSentActivation$
8:     $HNHypothesis \leftarrow nodeWord$
9:     **for** c **in** $children(node_i)$ **do**
10:         $temp \leftarrow RecursiveSearch(node_i)$
11:         **if** $temp \geq highestActivation$ **then**
12:             $highestActivation \leftarrow temp$
13:             $HNHypothesis \leftarrow childWord(c)$
14:         **end if**
15:     **end for**
16:     **return** $highestActivation$
17: **end if**

---

6   Evaluation

Google's Bilingual Evaluation Understudy (Google-BLEU or GLEU) [13] is used to measure distance between our extracted targets and what are designated as such in the dataset in addition to precision and recall. We choose to include GLEU as one of our measurements at extraction level, as we wish to take a more inclusive stance on what is considered to be correctly extracting a target or opinion term. For example, the sentence *"I loved the red cake"* may have a given target *"cake"*, however, the *"red cake"* or even *"the red cake"* are also equally valid targets for the positive sentiment in that sentence.

As such we consider a target or opinion term extracted if they are equal to or exist as a substring of the annotation or vice-versa. Therefore, we provide the GLEU to give an estimate on how far our extraction strays from the original label, as we believe collecting additional contextual information for a target is beneficial and that this metric also addresses that the annotations are subjective and not always objectively correct. When calculating GLEU for targets and SS we remove determiners and copula, as annotators did not deem these as part of the labels and removing them does not change the semantic meaning. For determiners we remove "the", "a", and "an". For copula we remove "is", "was", "were", and "are".

GLEU, as defined by Wu *et al.* [13] and as implemented in the NLTK python package [7], is calculated for a generated and reference sentence by calculating recall and precision for all sub-sequences of 1 to 4 tokens between the two sentences, where recall is the ratio of correct sub-sequences in the reference sentence and precision is the ratio of matching sub-sequences in the generated sentence. The GLEU score itself is the minimum of recall and precision, selecting the lowest value, with the lowest value being 0, indicating no matching sub-sequences and the highest possible value being 1, indicating a full match between all possible sub-sequences for both precision and recall. In this section, we present the cascading results of target identification, sentiment classification for that target, and the extraction of the opinion term for that target given its sentiment.

6.1   Target Identification Results

In Table 1 we present the results of target identification from sentences using the symbolic method specified in Sect. 5.1. We see that the laptop dataset is more difficult to extract targets from when compared to the restaurant datasets.

Table 1. Targets, precision, and recall for the identified targets over all of the datasets as provided by our symbolic extraction method. In addition to this, the average GLEU is provided to indicate how well the identified target tokens match the labelled ground truth tokens. A reference for the strength of the GLEU can be found in Table 4, where we show GLEU for labels against the entire sentence and single words.

	Targets	P	R	Avg. GLEU
14res	849	0.549	0.921	0.722
14lap	475	0.426	0.785	0.713
15res	426	0.461	0.920	0.731
16res	444	0.476	0.921	0.714

6.2   Targeted Sentiment Classification Results

Here we present the results of the targeted sentiment analysis after target identification, which can be seen in Table 2. In general, we see that sentiment performance between restaurants and laptops is fairly uniform, indicating that the sentiment propagation and reliance on parental verbs for classification does not differ with as large a margin as for the tasks of target identification and OTE.

Table 2. Overall sentiment accuracy for target sentiments over all of the datasets based on the targets that were identified.

	Accuracy
14res	0.740
14lap	0.719
15res	0.722
16res	0.778

6.3   Targeted Opinion Term Extraction Results

In this section, we show the results of OTE and triplet extraction. In Table 3 we see the results of applying **HN**, **SS** and merging the set of extracted terms for **HN & SS** for OTE. We also compare these results against GLEU for the entire sentence (**FULL**) to show that the extracted data is more semantically relevant. We see that SS can extract more opinion terms than HN, however, we also see in Table 4 that HN tends to give predictions closer to what is labelled by annotators. Interestingly, we see in Table 3 that there is a misalignment between extracted opinions and sentiment, otherwise, both rows would be mirrored by their "−3" counterparts. This implies that the system is extracting the correct target despite using the incorrect sentiment when recursively searching.

Table 3. F1-scores of the HN and SS methods for extracting opinion terms for the targets found in Table 1. Rows denoted with "−3" refer to when the sentiment and opinion term are correctly identified for a correctly extracted target in the previous step, thus successfully identifying a full triplet. As a triplet is generated for every found target, the F1-score is equivalent to the precision and recall under these conditions.

	14res	14lap	15res	16res
HN	0.482	0.398	0.515	0.503
SS	**0.625**	**0.488**	**0.633**	**0.615**
HN-3	0.420	0.315	0.450	0.447
SS-3	**0.547**	**0.386**	**0.547**	**0.543**

Table 4. GLEU scores at opinion level for our two different opinion targeting identification methods with the copula "is", "was", "s", "were", and "are" removed for the SS method. We include the full sentence score against the label to provide a contrast to the selection methods.

	14res		14lap		15res		16res	
	Avg. GLEU	σ	Avg. GLEU	σ	Avg. GLEU	σ	Avg. GLEU	σ
Full Sent	0.036	0.049	0.041	0.050	0.056	0.079	0.056	0.075
HN	**0.797**	0.342	**0.736**	0.376	**0.786**	0.344	**0.778**	0.349
SS	0.377	0.381	0.377	0.377	0.411	0.362	0.398	0.377

In Table 5, we see that recall values for SS and when HN & SS are in line with state of the art approaches, even beating them for 15rest, in-spite of our method only using one pre-trained model and not being trained on triplet data. However, our model is penalised for generating more targets than what are considered aspects of that domain by annotators. If our approach was not being penalised for the out-of-domain targets, then our recall would become our F1-score.

Table 5. Precision and recall scores for the correctly predicted triplets from each version of the restaurant and laptop dataset for our method against different benchmarks. TD stands for triplet data and denotes how much triplet training data is required to achieve the specified results. Methods with a "+" are the cascading results of models presented in the paper by Peng *et al.* [6]. TASTE* SS shows results of our SS method for cases with correct targets before triplet alignment based on Table 3.

	14res			14lap			15res			16res		
	TD	P	R	TD	P	R	TD	P	R	TD	P	R
RINANTE+	2669	0.376	0.340	1602	0.231	0.176	1161	0.294	0.269	1605	0.271	0.205
CMLA+	2669	0.401	0.466	1602	0.314	0.346	1161	0.344	0.376	1605	0.436	0.398
Peng *et al.* [6]	2669	**0.442**	**0.629**	1602	**0.404**	**0.472**	1161	**0.410**	0.547	1605	**0.468**	**0.630**
TASTE HN	0	0.225	0.379	0	0.128	0.248	0	0.203	0.416	0	0.208	0.417
TASTE SS	0	0.293	0.493	0	0.157	0.304	0	0.246	0.505	0	0.253	0.507
TASTE HN & SS	0	0.323	0.543	0	0.182	0.353	0	0.269	**0.552**	0	0.273	0.549
TASTE * SS	0	**0.547**	0.547	0	0.386	0.386	0	**0.547**	0.547	0	**0.543**	0.543

7 Discussion and Conclusion

We show in Table 5 that we can perform ASTE without the need for triplet data if we can be flexible with acquiring targets and opinion terms. This is at the cost of precision, as if we require an exact GLEU match with the annotations then the average accuracies shown in Table 3 will decrease, with HN dropping from 0.474 to 0.333 and SS more sharply declining from 0.590 to 0.151 as we approach a GLEU value of 1. The decline of SS being due to SS over-selecting tokens while HN will under-select tokens. However, in practice, the content will be largely the same, as the intended label still exists as a substring in the extracted opinion.

By interpreting DTLSTM output, our research aligns with recent work in interpretable AI for making decisions in AI systems understandable to humans [4]. Current algorithms can determine some sentiment but methods for detecting what the cause of a sentiment is or who is targeted by the sentiment are not thoroughly investigated. The application areas of interpretable AI are vast including being able to explain the reasons for recruitment decisions, credit check decisions or to mitigate bias but also for intelligent agents or robots to successfully function alongside humans. For instance, robots that only detect an unhappy human cannot act without knowing the cause of this unhappiness.

We present a method of extracting target-sentiment-cause triplets, TASTE, without the need for domain-specific or triplet training data. We show that this method can retrieve as many correct triplets as state-of-the-art methods that require prohibitive triplet data. We believe that this method is useful for intelligent agents, such as robots, that would have to be able to interpret contextual sentiment information on the fly in a dynamic context and domain.

Our approach can determine triplets regardless of how the context shifts, as targets are syntax-based and sentiment is learned compositionally, systems then having a selection of valid triplets that can be interpreted in a scenario. Furthermore, our system does not require the constant acquisition of new domains that require further triplet annotation collection, as our method learns hierarchical sentiment composition from the SST through the DTLSTM. In summary, our method allows for more domain independent ASTE that works in more dynamic contexts at the cost of precision.

Acknowledgements. This work has received funding from the European Union's Horizon 2020 research and innovation programme under the Marie Skłodowska-Curie grant agreement No 721619 for the SOCRATES project.

References

1. Cambria, E., Poria, S., Gelbukh, A., Thelwall, M.: Sentiment analysis is a big suitcase. IEEE Intell. Syst. **32**(6), 74–80 (2017)
2. Dai, H., Song, Y.: Neural aspect and opinion term extraction with mined rules as weak supervision. In: Proceedings of the 57th Annual Meeting of the Association for Computational Linguistics, pp. 5268–5277 (2019)
3. Fan, Z., Wu, Z., Dai, X., Huang, S., Chen, J.: Target-oriented opinion words extraction with target-fused neural sequence labeling. In: Proceedings of the 2019 Conference of the North American Chapter of the Association for Computational Linguistics: Human Language Technologies, volume 1 (Long and Short Papers), pp. 2509–2518 (2019)
4. Hellström, T., Bensch, S.: Understandable robots. Paladyn **9**(1), 110–123 (2018)
5. Honnibal, M., Montani, I.: Spacy 2: natural language understanding with bloom embeddings. Convolutional Neural Netw. Incremental Parsing. To appear **7** (2017)
6. Peng, H., Xu, L., Bing, L., Huang, F., Lu, W., Si, L.: Knowing what, how and why: a near complete solution for aspect-based sentiment analysis (2019). arXiv preprint arXiv:1911.01616
7. Perkins, J.: Python 3 Text Processing with NLTK 3 Cookbook. Packt Publishing Ltd, Birmingham (2014)
8. Pontiki, M., et al.: Semeval-2016 task 5: Aspect based sentiment analysis. In: Proceedings of the 10th International Workshop on Semantic Evaluation (SemEval-2016), pp. 19–30 (2016)
9. Socher, R., et al.: Recursive deep models for semantic compositionality over a sentiment treebank. In: Proceedings of the 2013 Conference on Empirical Methods in Natural Language Processing, pp. 1631–1642 (2013)
10. Sutherland, A., Magg, S., Wermter, S.: Leveraging recursive processing for neural-symbolic affect-target associations. In: 2019 International Joint Conference on Neural Networks (IJCNN), pp. 1–6. IEEE (2019)
11. Tai, K.S., Socher, R., Manning, C.D.: Improved semantic representations from tree-structured long short-term memory networks. In: Proceedings of the 53rd Annual Meeting of the Association for Computational Linguistics and the 7th International Joint Conference on Natural Language Processing (volume 1: Long Papers), pp. 1556–1566 (2015)
12. Wang, W., Pan, S.J., Dahlmeier, D., Xiao, X.: Recursive neural conditional random fields for aspect-based sentiment analysis. In: 2016 Conference on Empirical Methods in Natural Language Processing, pp. 616–626 (2016)
13. Wu, Y., et al.: Google's neural machine translation system: Bridging the gap between human and machine translation (2016). arXiv preprint arXiv:1609.08144

SOM-Based System for Sequence Chunking and Planning

Martin Takac[1,2(✉)], Alistair Knott[1,3], and Mark Sagar[1,4]

[1] Soul Machines, Ltd., Auckland, New Zealand
{martin.takac,alistair.knott,mark.sagar}@soulmachines.com
[2] Comenius University in Bratislava, Bratislava, Slovakia
[3] University of Otago, Dunedin, New Zealand
[4] University of Auckland, Auckland, New Zealand
https://www.soulmachines.com

Abstract. In this paper we present a connectionist architecture called C-block combining several powerful and cognitively relevant features. It can learn sequential dependencies in incoming data and predict probability distributions over possible next inputs, notice repeatedly occurring sequences, automatically detect sequence boundaries (based on surprise in prediction) and represent sequences declaratively as chunks/plans for future execution or replay. It can associate plans with reward, and also with their effects on the system state. It also supports plan inference from an observed sequence of behaviours: it can recognize possible plans, along with their likely intended effects and expected reward, and can revise these inferences as the sequence unfolds. Finally, it implements goal-driven behaviour, by finding and executing a plan that most effectively reduces the difference between the current system state and the agent's desired state (goal). C-block is based on modified self-organizing maps that allow fast learning, approximate queries and Bayesian inference.

Keywords: Sequence learning · Self-organizing maps · Planning

1 Introduction

In many domains of human action, it is important to learn *sequences* of items, and to represent these sequences declaratively. Sometimes these sequences are actions produced by the agent; in this case, the agent needs to find sequences that are useful, or rewarding. Sometimes, they are sequences of stimuli perceived in the world; in this case, the agent needs to identify frequently occurring stimuli. In either case, the items being sequenced can be of many different types: the sequences can be of motor actions, or perceived movements, or spoken words, or whole events.

There is good evidence that the brain makes use of a *general-purpose* circuit for learning to recognise, perform, and represent sequences, which is *replicated* for different cognitive faculties, that sequence different types of item. This idea is at the heart of many current general models of cognition, e.g., [1,3,7].

© Springer Nature Switzerland AG 2020
I. Farkaš et al. (Eds.): ICANN 2020, LNCS 12396, pp. 672–684, 2020.
https://doi.org/10.1007/978-3-030-61609-0_53

In this paper we present a connectionist model of such a circuit. We name it the 'C-block' circuit, where the 'C' stands for **chunking**. The process of chunking is the process of learning a *declarative* representation of a temporal sequence of items. The representation of a whole chunk can serve for *identification* (inferring what chunk is being generated after seeing its first few elements), or *generation* (where the chunk serves as a motor schema: a high-level representation of a sequence of actions, that guides generation of this sequence).

In many contexts, the elements of a temporal sequence can be thought of as actions that have an effect on the global state of the system, whatever that state is. Learned chunks then correspond to plans that take the system from one state to another. The planning component of C-block learns associations between chunks and their effects (potentially including an externally provided reward signal). This allows the C-block to operate in a goal-driven mode, wherein it selects a plan supposed to reduce as effectively as possible the differences between the system's current state and a desired goal state, or a plan most likely to bring about an expected reward. Plan selection is dynamic: each time a plan completes (or fails), the new current state is used to recompute a new difference between the current state and the goal state, and the plan which most effectively reduces this new difference is selected.

We have been successfully using C-block in BabyX [9]—a hyperrealistic virtual simulation of a human baby combining models of the facial motor system and models of basic neural systems involved in interactive behaviour and learning. Different C-block instances are used for sequencing of the baby's own motor movements, and for sequencing a wide variety of events she can perceive in the world, from low-level events involved in the production of facial expressions, to high-level events associated with utterances in a dialogue. In this paper we illustrate the operation of C-block on a simple artificial example of chunking sequences of letters into words.

2   The Architecture

The C-block consists of two components: a sequencer and a planner. The sequencer learns to predict the next element in a sequence, and in the process, learns declarative representations of whole sequences: that is, chunks. Chunk boundaries can be identified through two separate methods. One method implements the idea that chunk boundaries are associated with surprise [6]. The other method implements the idea that chunks are associated with reward states [4]. (We implement this by setting a 'chunk boundary' signal whenever a reward signal occurs.) At a chunk boundary, however it is identified, the planner learns a declarative representation of the preceding sequence, and associates this representation with the effect achieved by the whole sequence on a multidimensional system state, and with a reward signal (if one was provided).

The C-block circuit can operate in three different modes. In *observation mode* it receives a sequence of items, together with information about the global state and/or reward, and learns to represent chunks and their effects. At each moment, the circuit generates a Bayesian prediction about the most likely next item, and makes inferences about the plan that likely generated the sequence thus far, and the likely effect of this inferred plan. In *generation mode*, the C-block's predictions are used to actively influence the global state of the world, through motor actions.[1] Generation is goal-driven: the C-block begins with an active goal, then selects a plan that is expected to achieve this goal, then predicts a sequence of items that implement this plan. The third *collaboration mode* is a combination of observation and generation. The C-block begins by observing a fragment of a sequence, and makes inferences about the likely plan (and goal) that produced it, as usual. If there is a pause in the observed sequence, and the C-block is confident in its inference, it can adopt the inferred goal itself, and actively produce the rest of the sequence. This kind of cooperation is seen in infants at an early age.

2.1   Architecture of the Sequencer

At the core of the **sequencer** is a neural network trained to predict the next item in the incoming sequence. Because the next item is often a function of the recent items, neural networks for sequence learning usually use recurrent connections that enrich the immediate input with a *context*—an exponentially decaying encoding of the history of preceding elements. A seminal solution for this task is the simple recurrent network (SRN) [2], trained with back-propagation of error, and using a softmaxed output layer. As long as the output representation is localist, i.e. there is one neuron for each possible next element, the softmaxed output can be interpreted as a probability distribution and standard measures such as entropy or KL-divergence can be applied to it. The SRN trained on the next element prediction task is known to learn transition probabilities between elements [2]. A SRN can be augmented with a tonic input that drives the prediction and biases it towards a particular declaratively represented sequence. This tactic was used, for instance, in Reynolds *et al.*'s [8] model of event segmentation, where the tonic signal represented an event and significantly helped to stabilise the prediction of the event's elements.

In the C-block, we use a recurrent version of the **self-organising map (SOM)** [5] as the sequence-learning engine, rather than a SRN. The reason for that is twofold. First, backpropagation is slow and it takes many training epochs before the prediction reflects transition probabilities implicit in the training data. Second, the SRN operates in one direction only: it predicts the next element of the sequence from the immediate input, the recurrent context and the declarative representation of the chunk. We would like the system to also predict the likely chunk based on the fragment of the sequence seen so far.

The recurrent SOM implementing the sequencer network is shown in Fig. 1. A SOM basically learn declarative representations of common patterns on its

---

[1] This happens outside the C-block proper. 'Reafferent' representations of executed actions are passed back to the system as perceptual inputs at the next time step.

input media. Unlike networks trained with backprop, a trained SOM can operate with partial inputs, and reconstruct the missing ones. (Note that unlike a SRN, the sequencing SOM takes the 'next' item as one of its inputs.) A SOM basically implements an auto-associative memory over its inputs, by retrieving a best-matching stored weight vector for any partial or noisy input. We have significantly refined this ability with two modifications to the standard SOM:

1. Instead of using a simple Euclidean distance for finding the best match, we use a weighted Euclidean distance where differences in some parts of the vector can be emphasized, deemphasized, or even ignored (by setting the mixing weight to zero).
2. Instead of returning the weights of the best-matching neuron, we reconstruct the input as a combination of all weight vectors with mixing coefficients proportional to their degree of match. This effectively turns the SOM into a Bayesian probabilistic device computing the expected value of the input based on posterior probabilities that the input falls into categories represented by the neurons in the map (see the Appendix for details).

The SOM in Fig. 1 thus learns to associate the next item (Next) with the most recent item (Recent), the context representing the history of previous elements (Context) and the Tonic—declarative representation of the whole sequence. It can be queried to predict the next item based on the Tonic, Content and Recent, or to estimate Tonic based on the remaining parts of the input vector.

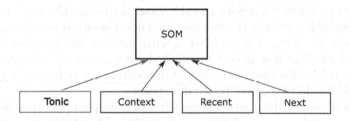

Fig. 1. The sequencing SOM: the C-block's sequence-learning device.

The Context is computed as an overlay/sum of localist representations of previous inputs (preceding the most recent item) exponentially decaying into the past. This implements a variant of the **merge SOM** [10].

To illustrate how this merge SOM-like recurrent architecture works, assume it is receiving a stream of letters, that spell people's names. Say the SOM has been trained on the word JAMES. When the first three letters (JAM) have been presented to the SOM, and the fourth letter E is then presented, the SOM's *Next* field will hold a localist representation of E. The *Recent* field will hold M (the previous input), and the *Context* field will hold representations of A and J, with the most recent of these most strongly represented.[2] When the letter E arrives,

---

[2] More formally, we can write this $A + c \cdot J + c^2 \cdot \text{prev}$, where 'prev' is whatever preceded J, and $c < 1$ is a decay coefficient, usually between 0.5–0.9.

the SOM is trained on the input fields as just described. Then its plasticity is turned off, and the input fields are updated. Then three things happen: the *Context* field is multiplied by c, and the contents of the *Recent* field are added to it; the letter in the *Next* field (E) is copied to the *Recent* field; and the mixing weight of the *Next* field in the Euclidean distance is set to zero, so that the network starts predicting the next element from its other inputs. Thanks to the localist representation in the next layer and the SOM reconstructing the input from its full activity (instead of just the best-matching neuron), the result can be interpreted as a probability distribution over possible next letters. In this case, if it is already trained, it will predict S, with some confidence.

Besides this basic next element prediction functionality, the SOM also has an input field where a representation of chunks can be learned: the *Tonic* input, shown in red in Fig. 1. As the name suggests, the contents of this field should have tonic, or persistent, activity, during sequential presentation of all elements of the chunk. In the letter sequencing example, chunks are names. Crucially, the circuit must have the capacity to *infer* possible chunks from an incomplete letter sequence. Since there can be several possible chunks consistent with the items presented so far, our *Tonic* input field holds an intermediate representation with *some* tonic properties, that is *underspecified* between alternative possible chunks.

In fact, our underspecified *Tonic* representation is the same kind of representation as that maintained in *Context* field: an overlaid combination of the items presented so far, but with the emphasis on the earliest, not the latest items. At the chunk boundary (based on an external signal or a mismatch in prediction), the chunk representation is reset and the *Tonic* field is simply set to hold a copy of the *Recent* field (which is the first item in a new chunk). If the chunk boundary occurs again, the *Tonic* will be filled in with the new *Recent*; otherwise it will be retained and the new *Recent* (multiplied with a decaying constant) will be overlaid on it.[3] In this way, the tonic and the context layers form complementary representations decaying in opposite directions.

We will illustrate the above scheme with an example of two words that start with the same subsequence: JOHN and JOSEPH. After both chunk representations have been successfully learned, they will both contain J as the most active item, O as the second most active and then decaying HN, or SEPH respectively. When a J is observed as the onset of a new sequence, the tonic representation will only contain J at that moment and will be consistent with both JOHN and JOSEPH (and any other chunk starting with J). The identity of the chunk will be progressively specified in a natural way as more items arrive. In a strict sense, the chunk representation is not tonic, because it is evolving in time, but because of its nature, there should be a high similarity between J, JO, JOH and JOHN.

The progressively specified *Tonic* representation supports the inference of fully-specified chunk representations in the other part of the C-block, the planner, which we will now describe.

---

[3] A similar approach to encoding chunks is used in [8], with the difference that they use a SRN instead of an SOM and their tonic representation follows a more complex update rule and is more noisy.

2.2   Architecture of the Planner

The complete C-block circuit is shown in Fig. 2, with the sequencer (Sequencing SOM) on the right, and the planner (Plan SOM) on the left. The planner is implemented by the same kind of modified SOM as the sequencer (with the weighted Euclidean distance for different parts of the input and option to either reconstruct from the best matching unit or from the full SOM activity). Its main function is to learn *declarative* representations of the chunks identified by the *Tonic* field of the sequencer, and to use these for goal-driven behaviour. Recall that representations of chunks are *gradually* constructed, item by item, in the sequencing SOM's *Tonic* field. The planner, by contrast, only learns its representations of chunks *at chunk boundaries*, when the representation of a chunk in the *Tonic* field is complete. Because of its autoassociative property, the trained plan SOM is able to reconstruct a full chunk representation from a fragment of an evolving sequence (either the best matching one or a mixture of several chunk representations proportional to their similarity with the fragment). In the letter sequencing example given above, if JO is presented, the activity in the plan SOM will be high in areas representing the names JOHN and JOSEPH and the retrieved tonic will reflect their mixture. But if the letter S is then presented, the plan SOM will update to a distribution highlighting only JOSEPH.

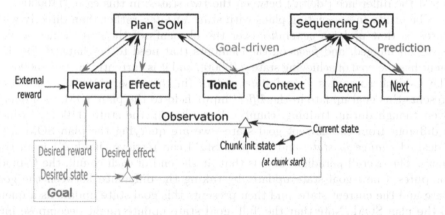

Fig. 2. The complete C-block, including the planner. During observation (black arrows), the system is trained to recognize the sequence and its outcome (reward and effect) from a fragment and predict its next element (purple arrows). In goal-driven mode (green arrows) it selects the best plan to achieve the goal and conditions the sequence generation on the tonic retrieved top-down from the planner. (Color figure online)

Associating Plans with Reward Values. The planner is more than just autoassociative memory for tonic chunk representations. It can also learn associations between chunks and their effects/outcomes. The simplest outcome is a scalar reward state, encoded in the *Reward* input field of the plan SOM. When a chunk boundary is reached, the plan SOM not only learns a declarative representation of the chunk encoded in the *Tonic* input field, but also learns *an* *association between this chunk and the current reward.* After training of this type, the plan SOM can be queried with a high reward value, to retrieve plans associated with high reward, and then select one of these to execute. We will describe this process in more detail below.

Plans as State Update Operations. The plan SOM can also represent chunks more semantically, as plans that have a particular effect *on the state of the world,* as represented by the agent. In the same way that the plan SOM associates a completed chunk with a reward value, it can also associate a completed chunk with a *state update* representation, in the *Effect* input field of the plan SOM.

In the C-block, our representation of 'state' is very general: it is an n-dimensional vector. We will discuss our conception of state in more detail below. We will begin by illustrating how plans can be associated with state updates.

Assume a simple state space with six dimensions, each occupied by either 1 or 0. Say the agent starts off in state [000011], and then performs a sequence of actions associated with a chunk $C1$, that leave it in the state [110011]. The plan SOM can learn to associate the chunk with a **state update operation**, that represents the *change in state* the chunk brings about. The change in state is just the difference ('delta') between the two states: in this case, [110000].

The utility in associating plans with state *updates*, rather than directly with states, is that updates *generalise* over the elements of the state which a plan leaves unchanged, and *focus* on the elements that need to be changed. Say the agent has the goal of achieving state [110000], and it is currently in state [000000]. The C-block computes a *goal state update* (in this case, [110000]), and then presents this goal update in the *Effect* input field to the plan SOM, as a query. Even though during training, chunk $C1$ resulted in the state [110011]—which is different from the current goal state—we are querying the plan SOM with a desired *change in state*, and the plan SOM can retrieve chunk $C1$ from this query. The overall paradigm here is that at the end of each chunk, the C-block computes a new goal state update, by taking the difference between the goal state and the current state, and then presents this goal state update as a query to the plan SOM. Note that the 'full' goal state update might decompose into several *separate* state updates, which are associated with distinct chunks. In this case, we have the equivalent of a partially ordered plan at the higher level, where some actions can be taken in an arbitrary order. For instance, say the plan SOM has learned two chunks, associated with updates [110000] and [001100]. If the agent is currently in state [000000], and desires to be in state [111100], both chunks will be (somewhat) activated, and can be performed in either order.

Attentional Modulation of Effect/State Inputs to the Plan SOM. Not every aspect of the current state is equally relevant to the agent at any given time. It needs to *attend* to different aspects of the state vector at different times. For instance, if it is thirsty, it might pay more attention to a state dimension encoding the presence/absence of water.

These attentional emphases can be neatly encoded by setting the coefficients in the weighted Euclidean distance in the SOM calculations on each individual dimension of the *Effect* input field to the plan SOM, that encodes a desired state update. Dimensions with a zero coefficient will be ignored in the selection of plans, while dimensions with high values will have a significant influence in selecting the next plan. The same mechanism can also be used to weight the contribution of the *Reward* input field (which is entirely neutral to state) against the more content-focussed contribution of the *Effect* field.

2.3 Operation of the C-Block in Observation and Generation Mode

We have already mentioned the difference between *observation* and goal-driven *generation* modes of operation of the C-block. More formally, the difference is charted in the arrows in Fig. 2 that depict the direction of information flow. The crucial issue is how the *Tonic* input shared by the plan SOM and sequencing SOM is activated.

Observation Mode. In observation mode (black arrows in Fig. 2), the tonic representation of the whole sequence is gradually constructed from the incoming inputs, as their overlay decaying into the future, and at each point is passed as a bottom-up input to the plan SOM for plan recognition. This SOM works as an autoassociator, retrieving the distribution over plans most likely to have produced the sequence seen so far.[4] This in turn is used by the sequencer alongside the context and the most recent element to predict the next element.

Generation Mode. In generation mode (green arrows in Fig. 2), the plan SOM is first queried with a goal state update, and reward, appropriately weighted by attentional coefficients, to evoke an activity pattern representing the probability distribution over plans. The winning plan is then selected from this distribution, and used to reconstruct a representation in the *Tonic* input. This is then used as a tonically active input to the sequencing SOM to produce a sequence of inputs.[5]

The plan terminates in one of the following ways:

- Surprise: plan terminates unexpectedly because of a mismatch in prediction.
- Plan completion: the 'end-of-sequence' signal is predicted.
- Goal reached: a good match is achieved between the goal (desired effect and/or reward along with their attention coefficients) and the actual effect and reward.

---

[4] The distribution is encoded by the SOM activity. We can pick the most active plan, or reconstruct its expected value based on the whole distribution (see Appendix for details).

[5] Actually, what is produced is a sequence of *probability distributions* over possible inputs, from each of which a 1-hot input is selected.

An inhibition-of-return (IOR) scheme operates on plans, to encourage selection of different plans. When a plan is selected, it receives a small amount of inhibition, that decays slowly over time. If two plans are equally activated by a given goal/reward state, this inhibition means that if one plan is picked, and fails, the other plan is likely to be picked next.

3 Experiments

3.1 Training Set

We demonstrate the C-block operation on sequences of letters that form words as chunks. In order to demonstrate fast learning, the network was exposed to each letter sequence only once. At the end of each sequence the system got an external chunk boundary signal (EoS) together with high reward value $r = 1$: JASON(EoS)ANDREW(EoS)LIAM(EoS)CAROLINE(EoS)KHURRAM(EoS) MARTIN(EoS)ALI(EoS)MARK(EoS)DAVID(EoS)NICOLAS(EoS)TIM(EoS) PAULA(EoS)PAULINE(EoS)ROB(EoS)SIMON(EoS)OLEG(EoS)XUEYUAN (EoS)RACHEL(EoS)GREG(EoS)KIERAN. We also maintained a representation of the 'current state' after each letter input. To simulate the effects brought about by whole chunks, we updated this state representation at the end of each word, to create an 'effect' input for the network, as described in Sect. 3.2.

3.2 Network Parameters

The sequencing SOM had 50×50 neurons. Tonic, Context, Recent, Next fields had 100 neurons each. Incoming letters in the Recent and Next parts were coded 1-hot in their first 26 components.[6] The plan SOM had 30×30 neurons. The Tonic and Effect parts of its input had 100 components each; the reward was scalar (1 component). The Effect input was computed as a difference between the system's state at the beginning and end of the chunk. We represented the effect of generating the words listed above with localist coding (counters) in the first 20 components of the system's state. Each time a generated sequence happened to correspond to one of the words, the respective counter was incremented. For example, generating JASON incremented the first component, ANDREW the second, etc. Both SOMs had a high learning rate (0.9) and a small Gaussian neighbourhood size ($\sigma = 0.6$). The decay coefficient was 0.6 for both Context and Tonic and 0.4 for plan IOR.

3.3 Sequence Prediction and Plan Recognition

We began by testing the trained system in 'observation mode'. We randomly shuffled the words in the training set and played them to the C-block's input

---

[6] The remaining 74 components were zero all the time. This was because we used the same parameters and network sizes across several applications, in some of which we needed more neurons to encode the input.

letter by letter. We then measured the match between the most strongly predicted letter and the actual next letter.[7] The prediction was correct in 94.1%
cases (80 out of 85). All 5 errors occurred at places with genuine ambiguity. For
instance, when presented with the sequence MAR, which appeared in training
both in MARK and MARTIN, it predicted K most strongly. If the test word happened to be MARTIN, then after seeing the next letter T, the C-block revised its
hypothesis about the chunk, and correctly predicted I as the next letter. Given
the Bayesian nature of our SOMs, both hypotheses K and T should have high
probability in the soft-reconstructed Next field. To verify this, we also computed
the Kullback-Leibler divergence (KLD) between the prediction in the Next field
and the actual input in the next step. Because the actual input is always 1-hot,
the KLD reduces to the negative log surprise $-\log_{26}(p)$ where p is the predicted
activity at the position of the actual next letter. If the system's predictions about
the next letter are accurate, we expect the mean value of surprise for all but the
first position to be close to zero.[8] Indeed, mean KLD excepting first letters of
words was 0.06 (SD=0.22).

Table 1. Success rate and the negative log surprise for predictions of the 'effect' of a
chunk after seeing its first N elements.

N	1	2	3	4	5+
Ratio	15/20	18/20	18/20	16/17	28/28
Proportion	75.0%	90.0%	90.0%	94.1%	100%
Surprise mean (SD)	0.34 (0.40)	0.14 (0.29)	0.14 (0.29)	0.12 (0.25)	0.10 (0.21)

We also explored whether the C-block can accurately identify whole words
(chunks) while their letters are arriving, and accurately predict the 'effect' of the
currently arriving word on the global state. To do this, we inspected the system's
predicted 'effect' field after each letter of each arriving word. We counted how
often this prediction was correct (see Table 1), and we computed negative log
surprise for the prediction after each letter (i.e. KLD with the effect that will
actually occur). On all these measures, we found good performance from the
earliest letters of words. Errors were again only found for ambiguous words.
This shows the C-block is able to correctly identify chunks and predict their
effects while they are still arriving.

3.4 Sequence Generation to Achieve Desired States

We then tested the model's ability to autonomously choose and generate
sequences for a composite desired effect. To do this, we configured the C-block

---

[7] We did this for all but the first position in a chunk, because C-block has no means
to predict the continuation of a chunk before it has started.
[8] Predicting the winner with probability $p = 1$ leads to KLD$= 0$. Flat predicted
distribution $p = 1/26$ leads to KLD$= 1$.

to 'want' to bring about a global state in which the effects associated with each word are all true, by setting the first 20 components in the 'Desired State' input to 1, and setting the attention coefficients for Effect to 1, and for Reward and Tonic to 0. We then ran the C-block in goal-driven generation mode. Because the C-block updates the difference between the desired state and the actual state at each chunk boundary, it was then able to execute all the plans without repetition (in random order). All words were generated with all letters at correct positions.

3.5   Sequence Generation to Achieve Reward States

We also tested the model when configured to 'replay rewarding plans'. To do this, we set the attention coefficients for Reward to 1, and for Effect and Tonic to 0 and set the Desired reward to 1; then we again ran the C-block in goal-driven mode. In this mode, the C-block first selected and generated the word most strongly associated with reward. On completion of this word, its inhibition-of-return mechanism led it to select a different word, and cycle through a varied sequence of words. All letters were again generated at correct positions.

3.6   Collaboration Mode

Finally, we tested the model in 'collaboration mode', by presenting it with the first two letters of a word and allowing it time to complete the intended word itself. The C-block did so correctly in all cases (except for ambiguous cases MARK/MARTIN and PAULA/PAULINE where it completed the first option).

4   Summary

The C-block is a network that can learn sequences, and learn to group particular sequences into chunks. In this paper, we have shown how the C-block can use these abilities both in perception, to predict sequences and upcoming states, and in action, to generate sequences based on higher-level goals. While most sequencing models in current AI use backprop-trained deep networks, SOM-based models have some interesting strengths of their own, which we have tried to emphasise here. For one thing, they can be configured to learn very rapidly, as in the experiments we report. They also have great versatility: because a SOM can operate flexibly with different patterns of input and output, the same network can be co-opted for a variety of sequence-related functions, both in perception and motor control.

A   Bayesian Inference in the SOM

In our version of SOM, the activity A_i of each unit is computed as

$$A_i = \frac{a_i}{\sum_{j=1}^{N} a_j}, \text{ where } a_i = exp\left(-c \cdot d^2(\boldsymbol{x}, \boldsymbol{w}_i)\right) \cdot m_i . \tag{1}$$

$d^2(\boldsymbol{x}, \boldsymbol{w}_i)$ is the squared Euclidean distance between the input $\boldsymbol{x}$ and the weight vector $\boldsymbol{w}_i$, a_i is the (unnormalized) activity of the i-th unit, m_i is the activation mask for the i-th unit. Activities A_i are normalized to sum to 1.

Comparing Eq. 1 with the standard Bayes' rule

$$p(h_i|d) = \frac{p(d|h_i) \cdot p(h_i)}{p(d)} = \frac{p(d|h_i) \cdot p(h_i)}{\sum_{j=1}^{N} p(d|h_j) \cdot p(h_j)} \tag{2}$$

we can interpret the activity of each unit as the posterior probability $p(h_i|d)$ of the *hypothesis* that the current SOM input (*data*) belongs to the class represented by the unit i. The Gaussian[9] term $\exp\left(-c \cdot d^2(\boldsymbol{w}_i, \boldsymbol{x})\right)$ corresponds to the likelihood $p(d|h_i)$. The mask m_i corresponds to the prior probability of the i-th hypothesis $p(h_i)$. The denominator $\sum_{j=1}^{N} a_j$ in the formula for normalized activities A_i is a total response of the map to the current input and corresponds to $\sum_{j=1}^{p}(d|h_j) \cdot p(h_j) = p(d)$, which is just the probability of the data itself. A very low total activity in the map indicates strange (or novel) input data.

By specifying coefficients m_i, we can choose different prior bias on the SOM, for example relative frequency of how often the i-th neuron became the best-matching unit in the past. All m_i equal to the same value would effectively mean a uniform prior and will have no influence.

Normalized activity of the whole SOM corresponds to the posterior probability distribution over all the hypotheses/neurons given the current input/data. We can reconstruct the most likely input either as the weights of the winner ('hard' output) or as an activity-weighted combination of the weights of all the neurons ('soft' output): $\boldsymbol{y} = \sum_{j=1}^{N} A_j \cdot \boldsymbol{w}_j$, which corresponds to the expected value of the input given the distribution.

References

1. Bar, M.: Predictions: a universal principle in the operation of the human brain. Philos. Trans. R. Soc. Series B **364**(1521), 1181–1182 (2009)
2. Elman, J.: Finding structure in time. Cogn. Sci. **14**, 179–211 (1990)
3. Friston, K.: The free-energy principle: a unified brain theory? Nature Rev. Neurosci. **11**, 127–138 (2010)
4. Graybiel, A.: The basal ganglia and chunking of action repertoire. Neurobiol. Learn. Mem. **70**(1–2), 119–136 (1998)
5. Kohonen, T.: Self-organized formation of topologically correct feature maps. Biol. Cybernet. **43**, 59–69 (1982)
6. Kurby, C., Zacks, J.: Segmentation in the perception and memory of events. Trends Cogn. Sci. **12**(2), 72–79 (2007)
7. Parr, T., Friston, K.: The anatomy of inference: Generative models and brain structure. Front. Comput. Neurosci. **12**, 90 (2018)
8. Reynolds, J., Zacks, J., Braver, T.: A computational model of event segmentation from perceptual prediction. Cogn. Sci. **31**, 613–643 (2007)

---

[9] c regulates the width of the Gaussian. We used $c = 30$ for sequencing SOM and varied $c = \{15, 25, 2\}$ for plan SOM predicting from Tonic, Reward and Effect respectively.

9. Sagar, M., Seymour, M., Henderson, A.: Creating connection with autonomous facial animation. Commun. ACM **59**(12), 82–91 (2016)
10. Strickert, M., Hammer, B.: Merge SOM for temporal data. Neurocomputing **64**, 39–71 (2005)

Image Processing

Bilinear Models for Machine Learning

Tayssir Doghri[✉], Leszek Szczecinski, Jacob Benesty, and Amar Mitiche

Institut National de la Recherche Scientifique, 800 de la Gauchetiere Ouest, Suite 6900, Montreal, QC H5A 1K6, Canada
{tayssir.doghri,leszek,benesty,mitiche}@emt.inrs.ca

Abstract. In this work we define and analyze the bilinear models which replace the conventional linear operation used in many building blocks of machine learning (ML). The main idea is to devise the ML algorithms which are adapted to the objects they treat. In the case of monochromatic images, we show that the bilinear operation exploits better the structure of the image than the conventional linear operation which ignores the spatial relationship between the pixels. This translates into significantly smaller number of parameters required to yield the same performance. We show numerical examples of classification in the MNIST data set.

Keywords: Classification · Bilinear forms · Machine learning

1 Introduction

The purpose of this work is to define and analyze the bilinear model for the use in ML, as well as, to propose the suitable learning algorithms. We focus on the simplest ML model defined through logistic regression (LR) composed of linear processing followed by a nonlinear activation function. Since the latter is a building block of many more advanced ML models such as neural networks, the first step is to understand the properties and learning algorithms in case of bilinear processing which replaces the linear one.

Our work is motivated by the fact that the typical ML tasks, such as classification, often use data which, when originally acquired, has a strong structural dependence between its elements. In particular, monochromatic images acquisition yields the structures which are naturally represented as matrices and there is often similarity/relationship between the pixels which are close to each others.

A common approach to deal with any data in ML is a vectorization which lists data elements in a predefined order, e.g., row by row. The obvious advantage is that the resulting vectors can be treated by generic ML algorithms like those described in [3].

On the other hand, the loss of structure is intuitively counterproductive and here we want to explore the possibility of using operations which are defined taking the data structure into account, e.g., the relationship between neighbour pixels. To this end, we propose to replace the linear operation, which weights and sums all the pixels in the image, with a sum of bilinear operators.

The advantage of such bilinear logistic regression (BLR) is that, by exploiting the input data in its original structure, we may directly access the useful information and

© Springer Nature Switzerland AG 2020
I. Farkaš et al. (Eds.): ICANN 2020, LNCS 12396, pp. 687–698, 2020.
https://doi.org/10.1007/978-3-030-61609-0_54

thus define the model using less parameters. More specifically, for an input image represented as a matrix $\mathbf{X} \in \mathbb{R}^{M \times N}$, the conventional linear operation first creates the vector $\mathbf{x} \in \mathbb{R}^{MN}$ which requires MN parameters of linear combiner, while a bilinear form requires $M + N$ parameters; the difference which becomes important for large M and N. When using the sum of L bilinear forms, the number of coefficients grows linearly with L. We show that exploiting the spatial structure of the image reduces significantly the number of coefficients required by the classifier, which also points to the overparametrization problem inherent in ML which is blind to the image structure.

1.1   Contribution and Related Work

The idea of bilinear structures to replace the generic linear vector-based processing is not entirely new. For example, it was already adopted in the context of acoustic signal processing to identify the response of the acoustic channel [2,5].

In the context of ML, the bilinear forms were also used to replace the linear processing in support vector machines (SVM) [10], to make classification based on LR for multi-channel medical data [8], in recommender systems [4] and for discriminant analysis [6].

The main difference with the previous work is that, [8] limited the considerations to rank-1 BLR and [4,6] use rank-1 bilinear form; here, we propose high-rank BLR; this is possible thanks to the algorithms we devise that rely on the alternate optimization. This stands in contrast to the approach adopted by [8] which defined the global optimization problem, which does not guarantee the convergence.

Our work is closest in the spirit to [2,5] which were mainly concerned with tracking of time-varying models, while we deal with static data for classification which allows us to devise new efficient alternate optimization algorithms for high-rank BLR.

1.2   Structure

This paper is organized as follows: Section 2 introduces the concept of bilinear model applied to logistic regression along with its interpretation, while the learning algorithm is shown in Sect. 3, where the regularization is also discussed. Section 4 generalizes softmax regression using bilinear forms to treat multiclass classification problems. The experimental results are presented as examples to illustrate the behaviour of the proposed models. We conclude the work in Sect. 5.

2   Bilinear Logistic Regression

Before talking about bilinear logistic regression (BLR), which is the focus of our work, it is convenient to re-discuss the conventional linear logistic regression (LLR).

2.1   Conventional Logistic Regression

The problem is defined as follows: from the observed features gathered in the vectors $\mathbf{x}_t$, indexed by t, we want to obtain the estimate of the posterior probability of the classes $C_t \in \{0, 1\}$ to which $\mathbf{x}_t$ belongs; that is, we want to find $y_t = \Pr\{C_t = 1 | \mathbf{x}_t\}$.[1]

---

[1] In this binary classification case, we have $\Pr\{C_t = 0 | \mathbf{x}_t\} = 1 - y_t$.

LLR refers to a model which approximates y_t using a non-linear function applied to a linear transformation of $\mathbf{x}_t$ [3]

$$y_t = f(z_t), \tag{1}$$
$$z_t = \mathbf{w}^\mathsf{T}\mathbf{x}_t, \tag{2}$$

where $\mathbf{w}$ contains the weights and $f(\cdot)$ is the *logistic function* defined as

$$f(z) = \frac{1}{1 + e^{-z}}. \tag{3}$$

Then, given the training data $\{(\mathbf{x}_t, c_t)\}_{t=1}^T$, where $c_t \in \{0, 1\}$ is the class of the vector $\mathbf{x}_t$ and T is the number of training examples, we want to find the most appropriate weights $\mathbf{w}$. This *learning* is done via optimization

$$\hat{\mathbf{w}} = \arg\min_{\mathbf{w}} J(\mathbf{w}), \tag{4}$$

$$J(\mathbf{w}) = V(\mathbf{w}) + \alpha R(\mathbf{w}), \tag{5}$$

where

$$V(\mathbf{w}) = -\frac{1}{T} \sum_{t=1}^T \left[c_t \log y_t + (1 - c_t) \log(1 - y_t) \right], \tag{6}$$

is the cross-entropy (or, the negated likelihood of the classes) which ensures adequacy of the model fit to the data, α is the regularization parameter, and $R(\mathbf{w})$ is the regularization function, often the squared norm of $\mathbf{w}$, i.e.,

$$R(\mathbf{w}) = \frac{1}{2} \|\mathbf{w}\|_2^2. \tag{7}$$

Since $J(\mathbf{w})$ is convex, the solution of (4) is unique and can be sought using the gradient which is calculated as

$$\nabla_{\mathbf{w}} J(\mathbf{w}) = \frac{1}{T} \sum_{t=1}^T (y_t - c_t)\mathbf{x}_t + \alpha\mathbf{w}. \tag{8}$$

In this most common approach to the LR, the features are represented as a vector $\mathbf{x}_t$ to simplify the calculations as shown above; any explicit relationship between the elements of $\mathbf{x}_t$ is deliberately ignored. In particular, and this is the focus of this work, if the features $\mathbf{x}_t$ are originally represented by a matrix $\mathbf{X}_t \in \mathbb{R}^{M \times N}$, which occurs naturally when $\mathbf{X}_t$ is a monochromatic image, the spatial information between the pixels in $\mathbf{X}_t$ is lost after vectorization of $\mathbf{X}_t$ into $\mathbf{x}_t$.

The vectorization not only removes the structure but makes the interpretation of the results less natural. In fact, it is much more convenient to represent the relationship (2) using a matrix notation

$$z_t = \langle \mathbf{W}, \mathbf{X}_t \rangle, \tag{9}$$

where $\langle \cdot, \cdot \rangle$ is the inner product of its arguments; $\mathbf{W}$ is a matricized version of $\mathbf{w}$ in (2) and may be seen as the spatial filter applied to the image represented by $\mathbf{X}_t$.

2.2 Bilinear Logistic Regression

While the matrix-based calculation of z_t in (9) provides the interpretation of the weights $\mathbf{W}$ in the domain of images, it is done merely by reorganization of the elements.

On the other hand, the relationship between the pixels is not accounted for. To address this issue we propose the bilinear processing defined as follows:

$$z_t = \sum_{l=1}^{L} \mathbf{a}_l^T \mathbf{X}_t \mathbf{b}_l, \tag{10}$$

where the left- and right-hand side elements of the bilinear transformation, $\mathbf{a}_l$ and $\mathbf{b}_l$, are gathered in matrices

$$\mathbf{A} = [\mathbf{a}_1, \dots, \mathbf{a}_L] \tag{11}$$
$$\mathbf{B} = [\mathbf{b}_1, \dots, \mathbf{b}_L]. \tag{12}$$

Indeed, we can now interpret the vectors $\mathbf{a}_l$ and $\mathbf{b}_l$ as filters acting, respectively, on the columns and rows of the image $\mathbf{X}$.

Two following observations are in order regarding the proposed BLR:

- For $L = \min\{M, N\}$, BLR defined in (10) is equivalent to the linear logistic regression (1) under suitable choice of $\mathbf{A}$ and $\mathbf{B}$; we demonstrate it in Sect. 2.3.
- For $L < \min\{M, N\}$, BLR introduces correlation between the pixels in the same columns and the same rows; this is shown in Sect. 2.4.

2.3 Equivalence Between LLR and BLR

To demonstrate the equivalence between (10) and (9), we rewrite the latter as

$$z = \langle \mathbf{W}, \mathbf{X} \rangle = \text{Tr}(\mathbf{W}^T \mathbf{X}), \tag{13}$$

where $\text{Tr}(\cdot)$ denotes the trace of a matrix and temporarily we removed the subindexing with t.

The matrix $\mathbf{W}$ may be decomposed using singular value decomposition (SVD) as follows:

$$\mathbf{W} = \mathbf{U}\mathbf{S}\mathbf{V}^T = \sum_{l=1}^{L} s_l \mathbf{u}_l \mathbf{v}_l^T, \tag{14}$$

where $\mathbf{U} = [\mathbf{u}_1, \cdots, \mathbf{u}_M] \in \mathbb{R}^{M \times M}$ and $\mathbf{V} = [\mathbf{v}_1, \cdots, \mathbf{v}_N] \in \mathbb{R}^{N \times N}$ are orthogonal matrices and $\mathbf{S} = \text{diag}(\mathbf{S}_1, \mathbf{0})$, $\mathbf{S}_1 = \text{diag}(s_1, \cdots, s_L)$.

Thus, we get

$$z = \text{Tr}\left[\left(\sum_{l=1}^{L} s_l \mathbf{u}_l \mathbf{v}_l^T\right)^T \mathbf{X}\right] = \sum_{l=1}^{L} s_l \mathbf{u}_l^T \mathbf{X} \mathbf{v}_l. \tag{15}$$

By setting $\mathbf{a}_l = \sqrt{s_l}\mathbf{u}_l$ and $\mathbf{b}_l = \sqrt{s_l}\mathbf{v}_l$, we obtain (10); we can also rewrite (14) as

$$\mathbf{W} = \sum_{l=1}^{L} \mathbf{a}_l \mathbf{b}_l^T. \tag{16}$$

2.4   Induced Conditional Dependence

The useful insight into the bilinear model we propose may be obtained looking at the implicit generative model underlying the classification principle of the linear logistic regression.

Namely, if we assume that the distribution of the features $\mathbf{x}$ conditioned on the class C is given by

$$p(\mathbf{x}|C = 1) \propto \exp(\mathbf{w}^{\mathsf{T}}\mathbf{x})g(\mathbf{x}), \tag{17}$$

where $g(\mathbf{x})$ is an arbitrary function independent of the class C, (1) follows, similarly as in [3, Ch. 4.2.1]. This relationship also means that, conditioned on the class C, we know the weight w_i and thus the features x_i are independent. This is equivalent to assuming that (1) implements a naive Bayes rule [7, Ch. 6.6.3].

This can be seen in the graphical representation of the probabilistic dependencies shown in Fig. 1, where we use the formalism of representing the dependence in Bayesian network via arrows connecting the parent (arrow's tail) and the child (arrow's head) [1, Ch. 3.3]. This also corresponds to the conditional probability.

Then, knowing C, "blocks" any path connecting the weights $w_{i,j}$ which are thus (conditionally) independent.

On the other hand, in the case of the BLR with $L = 1$ we can rewrite (16) as $\mathbf{W} = \mathbf{ab}^{\mathsf{T}}$, i.e., each term of the matrix $\mathbf{W}$ can be written as $w_{i,j} = a_i b_j$, where a_i and b_j are elements of the vectors $\mathbf{a}$ and $\mathbf{b}$. This relationships is shown in Fig. 1b and we see that knowing C does not block the paths between the weights $w_{i,j}$ and they remain connected through the elements of a_i and b_j. For example, there exist a path connecting $w_{1,1}$ and $w_{1,N}$ (via variable a_1) and which does not include C. We hasten to say that this merely says that the elements $w_{i,j}$ are not structurally independent, their independence can still be obtained with the appropriate choice of the values in the vectors $\mathbf{a}$ and $\mathbf{b}$.

We emphasize also that we do not need the generative models (17) to perform the classification. We rather use it in Fig. 1 to clarify the difference between the conventional LLR and the BLR. The most important conclusions is that while, the dependencies between the features (here, the pixels) are often imposed by a non-linear transformation of $\mathbf{x}$ (such as, e.g., squaring, see [7, Ch. 4.1]), here they are imposed by the hierarchical structure of the bilinear operation.

3   Model Training

Our objective is to learn the weights vectors $\mathbf{a}_l$ and $\mathbf{b}_l$ gathered in matrices $\mathbf{A}$ and $\mathbf{B}$ directly from the training set $\{(\mathbf{X}_t, c_t)\}_{t=1}^{T}$.

As in the conventional LLR, it will be done by optimization

$$[\hat{\mathbf{A}}, \hat{\mathbf{B}}] = \underset{\mathbf{A},\mathbf{B}}{\arg\min}\, J(\mathbf{A},\mathbf{B}), \tag{18}$$

$$J(\mathbf{A},\mathbf{B}) = V(\mathbf{A},\mathbf{B}) + \alpha R(\mathbf{A},\mathbf{B}), \tag{19}$$

where $V(\mathbf{A},\mathbf{B})$ is the bilinear version of the cross-entropy defined in (6) and the regularization term $R(\mathbf{A},\mathbf{B})$ plays the same role as $R(\mathbf{w})$ in (5). While it is not immediately

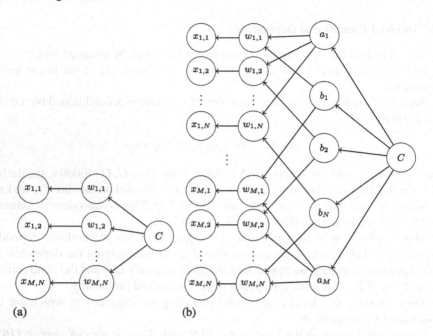

Fig. 1. The implicit generative model behind a) conventional logistic regression, and b) bilinear logistic regression for $L = 1$.

obvious how to choose this function, for the purpose of the discussion about training we assume it takes form similar to (7), namely

$$R(\mathbf{A}, \mathbf{B}) = \frac{1}{2} \sum_{l=1}^{L} \left(\|\mathbf{a}_l\|_2^2 + \|\mathbf{b}_l\|_2^2 \right). \qquad (20)$$

We note that i) the function (5), $J(\mathbf{w})$, was convex in $\mathbf{w}$ due to the linear relationship between z and $\mathbf{w}$ see (2), and ii) z in (10) is *not* linear in $\mathbf{a}_l$ and $\mathbf{b}_l$. Thus, the convexity of $J(\mathbf{A}, \mathbf{B})$ with respect to $\mathbf{a}_1, \ldots, \mathbf{a}_L, \mathbf{b}_1, \ldots, \mathbf{b}_L$ is not guaranteed and the direct use of the gradient methods should be discouraged.

On the other hand, we note that fixing all, but one, terms in $\mathbf{A}$ and $\mathbf{B}$, the optimization problems is transformed into the one we already dealt with in the case of LLR in Sect. 2.1.

This can be easily seen taking the gradient of the cost function with respect to $\mathbf{a}_l$ and $\mathbf{b}_l$:

$$\nabla_{\mathbf{a}_l} J(\mathbf{A}, \mathbf{B}) = \frac{1}{T} \sum_{t=1}^{T} (y_t - c_t) \mathbf{X}_t \mathbf{b}_l + \alpha \mathbf{a}_l, \qquad (21)$$

$$\nabla_{\mathbf{b}_l} J(\mathbf{A}, \mathbf{B}) = \frac{1}{T} \sum_{t=1}^{T} (y_t - c_t) \mathbf{a}_l^T \mathbf{X}_t + \alpha \mathbf{b}_l, \qquad (22)$$

which yields the equations similar to the one we show in (8).

Thus, the function $J(\mathbf{A}, \mathbf{B})$ is convex with respect to $\mathbf{a}_l$ or $\mathbf{b}_l$ if all other vectors are fixed. This suggests the use of alternate optimization procedure, where we optimize with respect to the vectors $\mathbf{a}_l$ or $\mathbf{b}_l$ one at the time, as described in Algorithm 1. Since each of the problems we solve is convex we can use the gradient-based methods as we did before; that is, we optimize with respect to $\mathbf{a}_l$ (lines 11-16 in Algorithm 1) then with respect to $\mathbf{b}_l$ (lines 17-22 in Algorithm 1).

The optimization is done in multiple steps denoted by $i = 1, \ldots, i_{max}$. The initialization of the weights (for $i = 1$) is important to speed-up the convergence.

First of all, for a given l, we want to learn the weights $\mathbf{a}_l$ and $\mathbf{b}_l$ knowing $\mathbf{a}_k, \mathbf{b}_k, k < l$ but assuming the null contribution from the weights $\mathbf{a}_k, \mathbf{b}_k, k > l$. In other words we treat each rank l as providing additional approximation level. This explains why $\mathbf{a}_l$ is initialized to zero. It is of course possible to initialize randomly all weights $\mathbf{a}_k$ and $\mathbf{b}_k$ but this slows down the convergence because, during training of $\mathbf{a}_l$ and $\mathbf{b}_l$, we are affected by the random values attributed to $\mathbf{a}_k, \mathbf{b}_k, k > l$.

Second, for a given rank l, since the vectors $\mathbf{a}_l$ and $\mathbf{b}_l$ affect z_t through multiplication, we cannot set them both to zero, as this would produce zero gradient, see (21) and (22); this explains the random initialization of $\mathbf{b}_l$ (line 3 of Algorithm 1). We also noted that the initial orthogonalization of the vectors $\mathbf{b}_l, l = 1, \ldots, L$ (lines 4-7 of Algorithm 1) improves the convergence rate. This approach is inspired by the SVD decomposition (14). We note however, that this is not a formal constraint on the solution. In fact, imposing such a constraint slightly deteriorates the performance.

The last comment to be made concerns the non-uniqueness of the solution which is due to the very structure (16), from which it is clear that any solution in the form $\left(\beta \mathbf{a}_l, \frac{1}{\beta} \mathbf{b}_l\right)$ yields exactly the same results, because the product in (16) cancels out any $\beta \neq 0$.

3.1   Regularization Strategies

The choice of the regularization function is often dictated by the simplicity of the resulting optimization procedure thus, the choice of (20) is justified by the simplicity of gradient calculation.

Taking into account the fact that the bilinear filtering approach is equivalent to the linear counterpart, see Sect. 2.3, it might be interesting to use the regularization function $R(\mathbf{A}, \mathbf{B})$ which is equivalent to the original LR problem (7); that is, using (16) we would define

$$R(\mathbf{A}, \mathbf{B}) = \frac{1}{2} \| \sum_{l=1}^{L} \mathbf{a}_l \mathbf{b}_l^{\mathsf{T}} \|_F^2 \tag{23}$$

where $\| \cdot \|_F^2$ is the Frobenius norm.

However, such a definition would lead to a burden in the calculation of the gradient $\nabla_{\mathbf{a}_l} R(\mathbf{A}, \mathbf{B})$ and $\nabla_{\mathbf{b}_l} R(\mathbf{A}, \mathbf{B})$, we thus opt for (20) or for

$$R(\mathbf{A}, \mathbf{B}) = \frac{1}{2} \sum_{l=1}^{L} \| \mathbf{a}_l \|_2^2 \| \mathbf{b}_l \|_2^2, \tag{24}$$

Algorithm 1: Training of BLR

---

1 Initialization:
2 $\mathbf{a}_l = 0, l = 1, \ldots, L$
3 $\mathbf{b}_l =$ drawn from a uniform distribution over [-1,1]
4 **for** $l = 2, \cdots, L$ **do**
5 $\quad$ $\mathbf{S}_{l-1} = \left[\frac{\mathbf{b}_1}{\|\mathbf{b}_1\|}, \cdots, \frac{\mathbf{b}_{l-1}}{\|\mathbf{b}_{l-1}\|} \right]$
6 $\quad$ $\mathbf{b}_l \leftarrow \mathbf{b}_l - \mathbf{S}_{l-1}(\mathbf{S}_{l-1}^T \mathbf{b}_l)$
7 **end**
8 Optimization:
9 **for** $i = 1, \cdots, i_{\max}$ **do**
10 $\quad$ **for** $l = 1, \cdots, L$ **do**
11 $\quad\quad$ **while** $\mathbf{a}_l$ not converged **do**
12 $\quad\quad\quad$ $\mathbf{g}_l = \nabla_{\mathbf{a}_l} J(\mathbf{A}, \mathbf{B})$
13 $\quad\quad\quad$ $\mathbf{D}_l = [0, \cdots, \mathbf{g}_l, \cdots, 0]$
14 $\quad\quad\quad$ $\hat{\eta} \approx \arg\min_\eta J(\mathbf{A} - \eta \mathbf{D}_l, \mathbf{B})$
15 $\quad\quad\quad$ $\mathbf{a}_l \leftarrow \mathbf{a}_l - \hat{\eta} \mathbf{g}_l$
16 $\quad\quad$ **end**
17 $\quad\quad$ **while** $\mathbf{b}_l$ not converged **do**
18 $\quad\quad\quad$ $\mathbf{g}_l = \nabla_{\mathbf{b}_l} J(\mathbf{A}, \mathbf{B})$
19 $\quad\quad\quad$ $\mathbf{D}_l = [0, \cdots, \mathbf{g}_l, \cdots, 0]$
20 $\quad\quad\quad$ $\hat{\eta} \approx \arg\min_\eta J(\mathbf{A}, \mathbf{B} - \eta \mathbf{D}_l)$
21 $\quad\quad\quad$ $\mathbf{b}_l \leftarrow \mathbf{b}_l - \hat{\eta} \mathbf{g}_l$
22 $\quad\quad$ **end**
23 $\quad$ **end**
24 **end**

---

which is actually equivalent to (23) for $L = 1$. Also, for $L = 1$, the sum-regularization (20) will yield the same solution as product-regularization (24).

This can be seen easily noting that, without any loss of generality, the solutions based on (24) may be forced to satisfy $\|\mathbf{a}_1\|_2 = \|\mathbf{b}_1\|_2$ (as said before Sect. 3.1, the product of terms is what matters, and it may be kept constant while normalizing). The same can be said about the sum-regularization (20) which is obviously minimized for $\|\mathbf{a}_1\|_2 = \|\mathbf{b}_1\|_2$. In other word, only the norm $\|\mathbf{a}_1\|_2 = \|\mathbf{b}_1\|_2$ affects the solutions for the sum-regularization and the product-regularization.

On the other hand, increasing the rank L such equivalence cannot be guaranteed.

Experiment 1. *To test the proposed approach, we consider MNIST dataset consisting of $M \times N$ grayscale images of handwritten digits going from 0 to 9 [9] with the size $M = N = 28$. Thus the LR requires $MN = 784$ weights to represent $\mathbf{w}$, while the BLR requires $L(M + N) = 56L$ weights to represent $\mathbf{A}$ and $\mathbf{B}$.*

We used the training set with different number of elements $T \in \{32, 128, 512, 1024, 4096, 8192\}$. The final classification accuracy was obtained from the testing set with size $T_{\text{test}} = 2000$. The product-regularization (24) was applied and the regularization parameter α was chosen using cross-validation on the validation set composed of $T_{\text{val}} = 2000$ elements.

The results of pairwise comparison of digits 8 *vs.* 9 *are shown in Fig.* 2 *and the comparison* 5 *vs.* 8 *is shown in Fig.* 3.

We can observe that i) for $L = 1$, *the BLR is consistently outperformed by the LLR; this is due to the equivalence of the regularization functions for* $L = 1$ *and smaller number of parameters in BLR, and ii) the gap in recognition accuracy is practically filled using* $L = 2$; *thus, with* 112 *coefficients required to represent* **A** *and* **B** *we obtain essentially the same performance as the conventional, LLR which requires approximately seven times more coefficients; this indicates that ignoring the structure of the image leads to the overparametrization of the solution.*

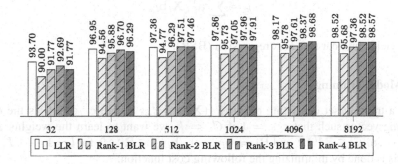

Fig. 2. Accuracy of LLR and rank-L BLR while performing classification of digits 8 and 9 with different training set size T on MNIST data set.

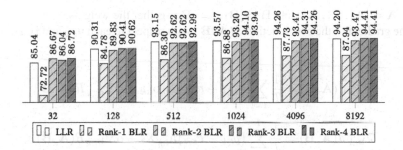

Fig. 3. Accuracy of LLR and rank-L BLR while performing classification of digits 5 and 8 with different training set size T on MNIST data set.

4   Generalisation to Multiclass Problem

The generalization of linear logistic regression that can perform multiclass classification is obtained via soft-max regression (SR): given K classes, we have to calculate the posterior probability for each class $C_t \in \{1, 2, \ldots, K\}$, i.e., $y_{t,k} = \Pr\{C_t = k | \mathbf{X}_t\}$, $k = 1, \ldots, K$. This is done using the following model:

$$y_{t,k} = \frac{\exp\left(z_{t,k}\right)}{\sum_{j=1}^{K} \exp\left(z_{t,j}\right)}, \tag{25}$$

where

$$z_{t,k} = \langle \mathbf{W}_k, \mathbf{X}_t \rangle, \tag{26}$$

and each $\mathbf{W}_k, k = 1, \ldots, K$ represents the weights corresponding to the class k. For $K = 2$, the indexing of the outputs with k may be avoided as we did when discussing binary classification with LLR.

Using the same arguments as before, we will replace the inner product (26) with its bilinear counterpart:

$$z_{t,k} = \sum_{l=1}^{L} \mathbf{a}_{l,k}^{\mathsf{T}} \mathbf{X}_t \mathbf{b}_{l,k}, \tag{27}$$

which yields bilinear soft-max regression (BSR).

4.1   Model Training

Given a training set consisting of pairs $\{(\mathbf{X}_t, \mathbf{c}_t)\}_{t=1}^{T}$ where $\mathbf{c}_t \in \mathbb{R}^K$ is the class-encoding vector such that $c_{t,k} = 1$ if $C_t = k$, we want to learn the weights $\mathbf{A}_l = [\mathbf{a}_{l,1}, \cdots, \mathbf{a}_{l,K}] \in \mathbb{R}^{M \times K}$ and $\mathbf{B}_l = [\mathbf{b}_{l,1}, \cdots, \mathbf{b}_{l,K}] \in \mathbb{R}^{N \times K}$ for $l = 1, \cdots, L$.

This is done by minimizing the following cost function:

$$J(\mathbf{A}, \mathbf{B}) = -\frac{1}{T} \sum_{t=1}^{T} \sum_{k=1}^{K} c_{t,k} \ln y_{t,k} + \alpha R(\mathbf{A}, \mathbf{B}), \tag{28}$$

where $\mathbf{A} = [\mathbf{A}_1, \ldots, \mathbf{A}_L]$ and $\mathbf{B} = [\mathbf{B}_1, \ldots, \mathbf{B}_L]$ gather the weights.

The gradient of the cost function $J(\mathbf{A}, \mathbf{B})$ with respect to each $\mathbf{a}_{l,k}$ and $\mathbf{b}_{l,k}$ is given by

$$\nabla_{\mathbf{a}_{l,k}} J(\mathbf{A}, \mathbf{B}) = \frac{1}{T} \sum_{t=1}^{T} (y_{t,k} - c_{t,k}) \mathbf{X}_t \mathbf{b}_{l,k} + \alpha \nabla_{\mathbf{a}_{l,k}} R(\mathbf{A}, \mathbf{B}), \tag{29}$$

$$\nabla_{\mathbf{b}_{l,k}} J(\mathbf{A}, \mathbf{B}) = \frac{1}{T} \sum_{t=1}^{T} (y_{t,k} - c_{t,k}) \mathbf{a}_{l,k}^{\mathsf{T}} \mathbf{X}_t + \alpha \nabla_{\mathbf{b}_{l,k}} R(\mathbf{A}, \mathbf{B}). \tag{30}$$

We optimize $J(\mathbf{A}, \mathbf{B})$ using gradient descent as described in Algorithm 2 which generalizes BLR training defined in Algorithm 1 to the BSR training.

Experiment 2. *The BSR algorithm was applied to the same MNIST data set as in Experiment 1 but using all $K = 10$ classes. The validation set and the testing set contain 10000 images.*

The classification accuracy is shown in Fig. 4 and the conclusions are in line with those we drew in Experiment 1. The main difference is that the rank of the bilinear representation must be increased up to $L = 3$ to obtain the results comparable with those yield by the linear soft-max regression (LSR). Thus, instead of $784K$ weights required in SR, BSR needs $168K$ weights.

Algorithm 2: Training of BSR

1 Initialization:
2 $\mathbf{A} = \mathbf{0}$
3 $\mathbf{B}$ = drawn from a uniform distribution over [-1,1]
4 **for** $k = 1, \cdots, K$ **do**
5 $\quad$ **for** $l = 2, \cdots, L$ **do**
6 $\quad\quad$ $\mathbf{S}_{l-1,k} = \left[\frac{\mathbf{b}_{1,k}}{\|\mathbf{b}_{1,k}\|}, \cdots, \frac{\mathbf{b}_{l-1,k}}{\|\mathbf{b}_{l-1,k}\|} \right]$
7 $\quad\quad$ $\mathbf{b}_{l,k} \leftarrow \mathbf{b}_{l,k} - \mathbf{S}_{l-1,k} (\mathbf{S}_{l-1,k}^{\mathsf{T}} \mathbf{b}_{l,k})$
8 $\quad$ **end**
9 **end**
10 Optimization:
11 **for** $i = 1, \cdots, i_{\max}$ **do**
12 $\quad$ **for** $l = 1, \cdots, L$ **do**
13 $\quad\quad$ **while** $\mathbf{A}_l$ not converged **do**
14 $\quad\quad\quad$ $\mathbf{G}_l = [\nabla_{\mathbf{a}_{l,1}} J(\mathbf{A}, \mathbf{B}), \cdots, \nabla_{\mathbf{a}_{l,K}} J(\mathbf{A}, \mathbf{B})]$
15 $\quad\quad\quad$ $\mathbf{D}_l = [\mathbf{0}, \cdots, \mathbf{G}_l, \cdots, \mathbf{0}]$
16 $\quad\quad\quad$ $\hat{\eta} \approx \arg\min_\eta J(\mathbf{A} - \eta\mathbf{D}_l, \mathbf{B})$
17 $\quad\quad\quad$ $\mathbf{A}_l \leftarrow \mathbf{A}_l - \hat{\eta}\mathbf{G}$
18 $\quad\quad$ **end**
19 $\quad\quad$ **while** $\mathbf{B}_l$ not converged **do**
20 $\quad\quad\quad$ $\mathbf{G}_l = [\nabla_{\mathbf{b}_{l,1}} J(\mathbf{A}, \mathbf{B}), \cdots, \nabla_{\mathbf{b}_{l,K}} J(\mathbf{A}, \mathbf{B})]$
21 $\quad\quad\quad$ $\mathbf{D}_l = [\mathbf{0}, \cdots, \mathbf{G}_l, \cdots, \mathbf{0}]$
22 $\quad\quad\quad$ $\hat{\eta} \approx \arg\min_\eta J(\mathbf{A}, \mathbf{B} - \eta\mathbf{D}_l)$
23 $\quad\quad\quad$ $\mathbf{B}_l \leftarrow \mathbf{B}_l - \hat{\eta}\mathbf{G}_l$
24 $\quad\quad$ **end**
25 $\quad$ **end**
26 **end**

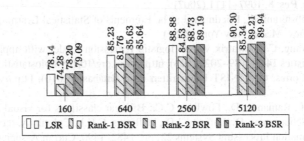

Fig. 4. Accuracy of LSR and Rank-L BSR while performing multiclass classification with different training set size T on MNIST data set.

5 Conclusions

In this work we introduced and analyzed the bilinear model to replace the linear operation used conventionally in the logistic regression. We also proposed a suitable optimization algorithm which exploits the convexity of the solution space; this allows us to obtain unique solution using gradient-based methods.

The solution was tested using MNIST data set of monochromatic images. We have shown that BLR can provide the same—and in some cases, better—performance as the conventional LLR which ignores the structure of the image. The results obtained using BLR require much less parameters which indicates that the overparametrization in the LLR is due to ignoring the correlation between the neighbourhood pixels.

References

1. Barber, D.: Bayesian Reasoning and Machine Learning. Cambridge University Press, London (2012)
2. Benesty, J., Paleologu, C., Ciochină, S.: On the identification of bilinear forms with the Wiener filter. IEEE Signal Process. Lett. **24**(5), 653–657 (2017). https://doi.org/10.1109/LSP.2017.2685461
3. Bishop, C.: Pattern Recognition and Machine Learning. Springer-Verlag, New York (2006)
4. Chu, W., Park, S.T.: Personalized recommendation on dynamic content using predictive bilinear models. In: Proceedings of the 18th International Conference on World Wide Web. p. 691–700. WWW'09, Association for Computing Machinery, New York, NY, USA (2009). https://doi.org/10.1145/1526709.1526802
5. Dogariu, L., Ciochina, S., Benesty, J., Paleologu, C.: System identification based on tensor decompositions: a trilinear approach. Symmetry **11**, 556 (2019). https://doi.org/10.3390/sym11040556
6. Dyrholm, M., Christoforou, C., Parra, L.C.: Bilinear discriminant component analysis. J. Mach. Learn. Res. **8**, 1097–1111 (2007)
7. Hastie, T., Tibshirani, R., Friedman, J.: The Elements of Statistical Learning. Springer Science & Business Media, New York (2009)
8. Hung, H., Wang, C.C.: Matrix variate logistic regression model with application to EEG data. Biostatistics **14**(1), 189–202 (2013). https://doi.org/10.1093/biostatistics/kxs023
9. LeCun, Y., Cortes, C.: MNIST handwritten digit database (2010), http://yann.lecun.com/exdb/mnist/
10. Pirsiavash, H., Ramanan, D., Fowlkes, C.C.: Bilinear classifiers for visual recognition. In: Bengio, Y., Schuurmans, D., Lafferty, J.D., Williams, C.K.I., Culotta, A. (eds.) Advances in Neural Information Processing Systems 22, pp. 1482–1490. Curran Associates, Inc. (2009), http://papers.nips.cc/paper/3789-bilinear-classifiers-for-visual-recognition.pdf

Enriched Feature Representation and Combination for Deep Saliency Detection

Lecheng Zhou and Xiaodong Gu$^{(\boxtimes)}$ ⓘ

Department of Electronic Engineering, Fudan University, Shanghai 200433, China
xdgu@fudan.edu.cn

Abstract. One of the most challenging issue in visual saliency detection is to discover and integrate meaningful features through deep neural networks. Saliency detection model should be carefully designed to extract sufficient features from different levels and reorganize them into the final prediction. In this paper, we propose an efficient saliency detection framework by introducing multi-scale representation and multi-level combination to deep convolutional neural networks. The main idea of our proposed model is to optimize intra-level feature extraction and inter-level feature combination, so that both saliency semantic and object details can be correctly preserved in final saliency maps. The model utilizes parallel dilated convolutions and pyramid pooling structures to enhance local details and acquire multi-scale feature representation. Feature maps of different resolutions are integrated by performing hierarchical combination in the encoder and decoder parts respectively. As a result, the model can better retain detail information during feature extraction and locate salient regions for saliency map recovery. Experimental results show that our model achieves state-of-the-art performance on several representative datasets.

Keywords: Visual saliency detection · Convolutional neural networks · Dilated convolution · Feature integration

1 Introduction

Visual saliency detection is receiving considerable attention these years with the rapid growth of image data to be processed. Motivated by the human attention selection mechanism, this biomimetic procedure can automatically derive the most critical information from images. Saliency detection has been considered as a preprocessing step and widely applied to many computer vision such as image retrieval [1], visual tracking [2], object recognition [3], image editing [4] and semantic segmentation [5]. The main challenge of saliency detection is to produce a precise saliency map, which presents exact saliency score for each pixel in the image. Though great efforts have been made to this field, existing models are still far from perfect as the definition of salient object is affected by complicated factors in various scenes, which are too difficult to be completely covered.

Earlier work [6–10] on saliency detection mostly relies on predefined rules for extracting and concatenating low-level features of an image. These bottom-up models

© Springer Nature Switzerland AG 2020
I. Farkaš et al. (Eds.): ICANN 2020, LNCS 12396, pp. 699–710, 2020.
https://doi.org/10.1007/978-3-030-61609-0_55

are light-weighted and achieve favorable performance on uncomplicated cases. However, handcrafted cues may suffer from poor semantic representation and confusing background, limiting these approaches to satisfying prediction. To enhance the representation ability of computational model for saliency features, later researches [11–13] utilize deep convolutional neural networks for feature extraction. Such methods segment the input image into patches and predict saliency scores for them separately, which break the integrity of objects and consume much time and space. Instead, the proposal of fully convolutional architecture [22] enables end-to-end computation model with saliency output of full resolution. Such approaches [14–21] based on fully convolution networks (FCN) have made a significant breakthrough on model performance, yet the details and contours of generated saliency maps still require further improvements, because of the information loss in high-level feature maps. Though recent saliency detection models [17, 20, 33] utilize multi-level features to improve the quality of saliency maps, they pay less attention to the representation and combination strategy from different feature levels.

Motivated by the abovementioned issues, we propose a novel saliency detection model, which focuses on mining and integrating more precise and sufficient feature representations. The main contributions of this work includes:

- We propose a multi-scale feature representation (MFR) module, which extracts effective saliency cues for the network. The module not only generates feature maps with various receptive field sizes, but also concatenate feature maps with different scales. It is proven that the MFR module enriches the detail information thus improves the overall performance for saliency detection.
- We propose a hierarchical combination strategy in our model, which enables features of different levels to be integrated. In the encoder part, low-level feature maps are injected to high-level layers for enhancing the detail information of the image during feature encoding. In the decoder part, high-level feature maps are fused to low-level layers as a progressive refinement for saliency prediction.
- Experimental results on five representative datasets prove the superior performance of our proposed model against other state-of-the-art approaches. Ablation studies also demonstrate the effectiveness of the proposed feature representation module and hierarchical combination structure.

We will introduce the detailed architecture of our proposed approach in Sect. 2. Section 3 provides comprehensive experiments on our model. Finally, a summary of this paper is presented in Sect. 4.

2   Proposed Model

2.1   Overview

Figure 1 illustrates the overall architecture of our proposed framework, which is based on a fully convolution network [22]. The network consists of eight multi-scale feature representation (MFR) module to achieve more detailed feature extraction and precise saliency map recovery. The hierarchical combination (HC) strategy for feature maps among different level of the network is also presented in the figure. These layer wise connections allow the network to have more complicated mappings for saliency prediction. The source input first goes through the image encoder to obtain high-level saliency cues of the image. During the process, low-level feature maps are down sampled and integrated with high-level feature maps. The high-level saliency representation is then decoded to the origin resolution to produce a saliency map. Each decoder receives additional feature maps from its corresponding encoder and former decoders to recursively generate the saliency prediction.

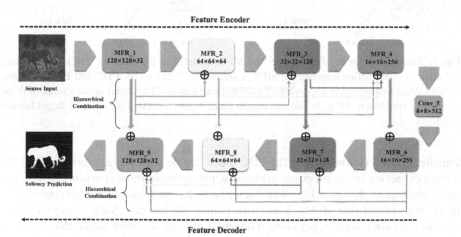

Fig. 1. The overall architecture of the proposed network. The model can be considered as a fully convolutional encoder-decoder network. Both of the encoder and decoder have four multi-scale feature representation (MFR) modules. The numbers in these modules represent the sizes of output feature maps. Features are integrated among these MFR modules through hierarchical combinations as the arrows show in the figure. Feature injections from different levels are distinguished by color.

We will next elaborate on the principles of different components in our proposed model.

2.2 Multi-scale Feature Representation Module

To explain the architectures of the proposed MFR module, we provide an example of two specific layers from the encoder network in Fig. 2. Each MFR module can be divided into two parts: a feature extraction mainstream and a side output branch. In the mainstream, we utilize two parallel dilated convolution (PDC) blocks with a pooling layer between them to perform feature extraction. A pyramid pooling is appended at the end of MFR module, to concatenate feature maps of different scales with the origin ones and double the output channels. The side output branch down samples the feature maps with pooling and 1 × 1 convolution layers to serve as additional inputs for other MFR modules. We will next explain the two main components, PDC block and pyramid pooling structure, applied in our MFR module.

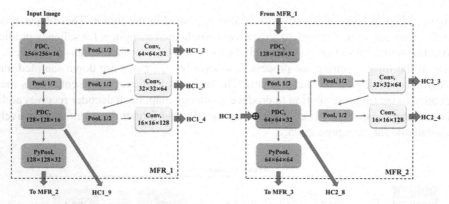

Fig. 2. Illustrations for the first and second MFR modules in the network. **HC1_2** represents hierarchical combination between the MFR_1 and MFR_2, and so on. **PDC** and **PyPool** means parallel dilated convolution and pyramid pooling, respectively. The detail architectures of these two blocks are shown in Fig. 3. The numbers in these blocks represent the sizes of output feature maps.

Parallel Dilated Convolution. The PDC block can be regarded as a primary unit for feature extraction in our proposed network, which contains three convolution branches and a shortcut as shown in Fig. 3(a). Each branch has two stacked dilated convolution layers with kernel size of 3 × 3 and a particular dilation rate. Such strategy enables synchronous convolution operations with small to large receptive fields, thus enriches the information extracted by the network. Feature maps from previous layers also go through a shortcut with 1 × 1 convolution and batch normalization for residual learning [23], thus improve the training performance. The feature maps generated by the three branches and the shortcut are added together as the final feature representation of PDC block.

Multi-scale Feature Generation. We utilize pyramid pooling [24] for generating and concatenating feature maps with multiple scales. The structure of pyramid pooling is illustrated in Fig. 3(b). Average pooling operations with different sampling rates (1, 1/2, 1/3 and 1/6 as suggested in [24]) are performed to the input feature maps respectively. An 1 × 1 convolution layer is utilized to reduce the dimension of each set of down sampled feature maps. These feature maps are up sampled to origin resolution through bilinear interpolation so that we can concatenate them with the origin input feature maps. As multi-scale pooling kernels cover feature map patches of different sizes, pyramid pooling structure serves as a powerful tool to enhance local to global contextual information for a certain level of feature.

2.3 Hierarchical Combination

To better preserve the information from different feature levels, a hierarchical combination strategy is utilized in our saliency prediction model. Figure 1 provides a general structure of our network with all the inter-level connections on it. We utilize altogether

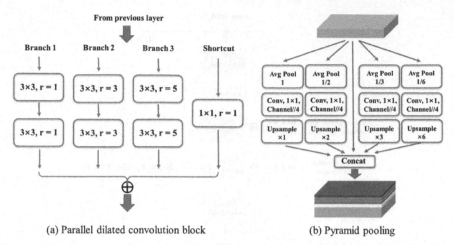

(a) Parallel dilated convolution block   (b) Pyramid pooling

Fig. 3. Illustrations for the structures of (a) parallel dilated convolution block and (b) pyramid pooling.

16 inter-level connections in our network including 6 encoder connections, 6 decoder connections and 4 encoder-decoder connections. Additional low-level feature maps can enrich the detail properties of the image in the encoder network. Meanwhile each decoder obtains shared saliency prediction from previous decoders, which can better locate salient regions and preserve object structures for final saliency maps.

Taking MFR_1 as an example, it generates three sets of feature maps with different scales HC_{1_2}, HC_{1_3} and HC_{1_4} respectively as side outputs. Three sets of 1/2 max pooling with 1×1 convolution layers are applied to compute large to small scales of feature for the following decoders. The module also provides cross connection HC_{1_9} as suggested in U-Net [25] architecture. HC_{1_9} is directly obtained by the output of the second DPC blocks, as it has the same dimension with feature representation in MFR_9 for efficient element wise addition.

2.4 General Representation for Saliency Prediction

As described before, the network can be divided into an encoder for feature extraction and a decoder for saliency map recovery. For encoder network, MFR in shallower level has more side outputs for hierarchical combination, meanwhile MFR in deeper level receives more feature maps from former ones. More specifically, the first PDC block in MFR takes the feature maps from previous level as input. Then a pooling layer decrease the size of output feature maps to 1/2. Before sent to the second PDC block, the feature maps will be added with all the injected features. For example, MFR_1 has no injected feature; MFR_3 has two injected features from MFR_1 and MRF_2, etc.

MFR for decoder network is slightly different from encoder, as it receive feature injections not only from previous MFR but also from the corresponding encoder. To give an example, the detailed structure of MFR_8 is illustrated in Fig. 4. As can be seen, decoder has an additional PDC blocks for feature injection from the encoder. Meanwhile

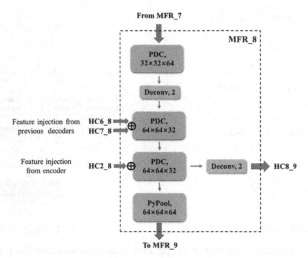

Fig. 4. The structure of MFR_8 for decoder network.

branch outputs with pooling and convolution layers are replaced by deconvolution layers for up sampling.

To sum up, the feature representation process of a certain feature level m in our network can be presented as follow:

$$\mathbf{F}_{en}^m = \Phi^m \left(\Psi_2^m \left(\Psi_1^m \left(\mathbf{F}_{en}^{m-1} \right) + \sum_{i=1}^{m-1} HC_{i\_m} \right) \right), \tag{1}$$

$$\mathbf{F}_{de}^m = \Phi^m \left(\Psi_3^m \left(\Psi_2^m \left(\Psi_1^m \left(\mathbf{F}_{de}^{m-1} \right) + \sum_{i=6}^{m-1} HC_{i\_m} \right) + HC_{[10-m]\_m} \right) \right), \tag{2}$$

where $\mathbf{F}_{en}$ and $\mathbf{F}_{de}$ are feature representations for encoder and decoder, respectively. Φ means multi-scale concatenation with pyramid pooling structure. Ψ is parallel dilated convolution operation in a PDC block. HC_{i_m} refers to feature injection from the ith to mth level in our network.

2.5 Implementation Details

Except for our proposed PDC blocks, we also utilize normal convolution block in our model, which consists of two stacked 3×3 convolution layers as mainstream and a 1×1 convolution layers as shortcut. The normal convolution block is applied when the size of feature map is smaller than 16×16, as dilated convolution would not acquire more information than trivial convolution in this situation. For example, Conv_5 is a normal convolution block between the encoder and decoder as illustrated in Fig. 1.

We use 1×1 convolution layer and Sigmoid function to generate 2-D saliency map ranged in [0, 1]. Binary cross entropy (BCE) loss and recursive supervision structure for decoders as suggested in [17] are applied to train our network.

Suggested by some related work [18, 20], we also adopt conditional random field (CRF) [26] as a selective smoothing process in our model. The CRF can further preserve object boundaries and remove small isolated regions in the saliency maps, thus improve the quality of final prediction.

The proposed model is implemented on open sourced Pytorch framework. The network is trained on a NVIDIA GeForce GTX1080Ti GPU with totally 120000 iterations. We apply step learning rate policy during training, initially set to 0.0001 and divided by 10 every 40000 iterations. Adam optimizer is utilized with weight decay set to 0.0001.

3 Experiments

3.1 Experiment Settings

Datasets. We choose the widely used **DUTS** [27] dataset for training our network. DUTS contains 10553 training images (DUTS-TR) and 5019 testing images (DUTS-TE) with pixel wise annotations, which is currently the largest dataset for saliency detection. Many of the images are of complex scenes with one or more salient objects. We also perform data augmentation by horizontal flipping. **ECSSD** [28] is a popular saliency testing set, which has 1000 images with semantically prominent objects. **PASCAL-S** [29] contains 850 images derived from PASCAL VOC dataset. **MSRA-B** [30] is another large dataset with 5,000 images of great structural diversity. **HKU-IS** [31] includes 4447 challenging images with many low contrast and multiple salient objects. **SED2** [32] has 100 images, and all of them have two salient objects.

Evaluation Metrics. We use precision-recall (P-R), F-measure (F_β) and mean absolute error (MAE) in our experiments for saliency evaluation.

P-R curve. A set of precision and recall rates is obtained through applying different binary thresholds ([0, 255]) to a particular saliency map. The overall performance of a saliency detection model can be evaluated through the P-R curve.

F-measure. It is calculated by the harmonic mean of precision and recall:

$$F_\beta = \frac{(1 + \beta^2)Precision \times Recall}{\beta^2 \times Precision + Recall}, \tag{3}$$

where β^2 is set to 0.3 as in most work. F_β refers to the largest F-measure obtained from the P-R curve, which represents the upper limit of a saliency prediction model.

MAE. It refers to the mean distance between the saliency map and its ground truth:

$$MAE = \frac{1}{W \times H} \sum_{x=1}^{W} \sum_{y=1}^{H} |SM(x, y) - GT(x, y)|. \tag{4}$$

3.2 Visual Comparison

We compare our model with other state-of-the-art approaches in our experiments, including a traditional method DRFI [10], and deep learning based methods MCDL [12], ELD [13], DS [14], DCL [18], RFCN [19], UCF [16], Amulet [17], NLDF [15], DSS [20] and DGRL [21].

For qualitatively comparisons, some saliency maps of different approaches are presented in Fig. 5. It is obvious that our saliency maps provide the most accurate prediction under various circumstances compared with other methods. Moreover, with the help of enriched feature representation, object details and contours are better preserved in our saliency maps, which also indicates the superiority of our model.

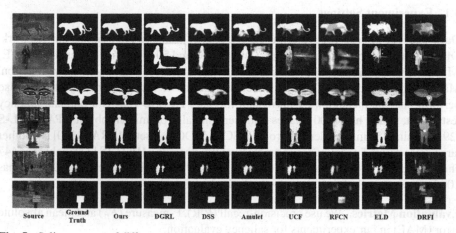

Fig. 5. Saliency maps of different approaches. Our results are displayed on the third column from the left, which are the closest to ground truths compared with other approaches.

3.3 Qualitative Comparisons

We also compute quantitative metrics of these approaches on six datasets. As can be seen from Table 1, our model achieves the best scores (for F_β higher is better and for MAE lower is better) on almost all these datasets.

The P-R curves on ECSSD, PASCAL-S and HKU-IS datasets are also illustrated in Fig. 6. It can be observed that P-R curves of our model are much closer to upper-right corners, which means a higher precision and recall among different binary thresholds. This indicates a better overall performance of our proposed model.

Table 1. Quantitative comparisons with state-of-the-art approaches. We report the results of both **Ours** (results without CRF) and **Ours⁺** (refined results with CRF), as many other approaches also utilize CRF for refinement, for fair comparison. The best and second best results are highlighted with bold and italic, respectively. Our model achieves better performance even without CRF refinement.

	ECSSD		PASCAL-S		HKU-IS		MSRA-B		DUTS-TE		SED2	
	F_β	MAE	F_β	MAE	F_β	MAE	F_β	MAE	F_β	MAE	F_β	MAE
DRFI	0.786	0.119	0.676	0.215	0.783	0.143	0.855	0.120	0.582	0.174	0.860	0.095
MCDL	0.821	0.101	0.726	0.145	0.780	0.092	0.872	0.062	0.672	0.106	0.793	0.120
ELD	0.868	0.079	0.778	0.123	0.886	0.072	0.912	0.043	0.738	0.093	–	–
DS	0.882	0.122	0.758	0.176	0.860	0.080	0.887	0.079	0.777	0.090	0.897	0.075
DCL	0.901	0.084	0.823	0.107	0.908	0.048	0.918	0.047	0.782	0.088	0.905	*0.062*
RFCN	0.897	0.106	0.830	0.118	0.898	0.079	0.920	0.065	0.784	0.091	0.898	0.076
NLDF	0.905	0.063	0.824	0.099	0.902	0.048	0.911	0.044	0.812	0.066	–	–
UCF	0.910	0.078	0.828	0.121	0.888	0.074	–	–	0.771	0.117	0.890	0.076
Amulet	0.914	0.061	0.837	0.098	0.900	0.052	–	–	0.778	0.085	0.901	0.070
DSS	0.909	0.063	0.833	0.096	0.910	0.041	*0.922*	0.045	0.825	0.057	0.897	0.075
DGRL	0.922	0.049	0.853	0.072	0.916	0.036	0.910	0.048	0.829	**0.050**	0.882	0.083
Ours	*0.923*	*0.044*	*0.859*	*0.064*	*0.918*	*0.036*	**0.924**	*0.041*	*0.841*	0.053	*0.913*	*0.062*
Ours⁺	**0.927**	**0.041**	**0.864**	**0.062**	**0.921**	**0.034**	**0.924**	**0.037**	**0.846**	*0.052*	**0.922**	**0.061**

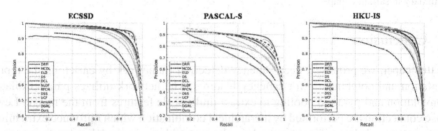

Fig. 6. P-R curves of different approaches on three datasets.

3.4 Ablation Analysis

For better demonstrating the effectiveness of the proposed feature representation and combination strategy, we have conducted ablation experiments on our model as in Table 2. The results indicates that the model performance is evidently improved by replacing the normal convolution with MFR module. Applying hierarchical combination strategy further optimizes the saliency prediction. Moreover, Fig. 7 provides visual comparisons between the results with and without enriched feature representation. Obviously, our proposed architecture greatly enhance the accuracy and details in saliency maps.

Table 2. Ablation results on our proposed model. '+ MFR' means using MFR module. '+ HC' means using hierarchical combination.

	ECSSD		PASCAL-S		HKU-IS	
	F_β	MAE	F_β	MAE	F_β	MAE
FCN	0.860	0.086	0.800	0.123	0.867	0.087
+ MFR	0.911	0.058	0.836	0.093	0.895	0.052
+ HC (our full model)	0.923	0.044	0.859	0.064	0.918	0.036

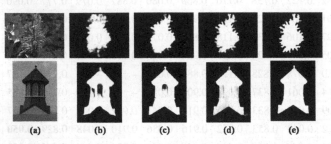

(a)   (b)   (c)   (d)   (e)

Fig. 7. Saliency maps for testing different components proposed in our paper. (a) Source input, (b) results from trivial FCN, (c) FCN with MFR modules, (d) our full model, (e) ground truth. As can be seen, our proposed model can preserve detail information and generate more precise boundary in saliency maps.

4   Conclusion

In this paper, we propose a deep saliency detection framework by enriching the representation and combination for saliency features. The network utilizes parallel dilated convolution and pyramid pooling to extract multi-scale features from the image. Level wise connection are performed by hierarchical combination which introduce extra information for each layer. Experimental results prove that our model outperforms other state-of-the-art approaches on several benchmark datasets. Further studies on our model demonstrate the effectiveness of our feature representation and combination strategy.

Acknowledgements. This work was supported in part by National Natural Science Foundation of China under grant 61771145 and 61371148.

References

1. Gao, Y., Wang, M., Tao, D., Ji, R., Dai, Q.: 3-D Object Retrieval and Recognition With Hypergraph Analysis. IEEE Trans. Image Process. **21**(9), 4290–4303 (2012)
2. Borji, A., Frintrop, S., Sihite, D.N., Itti, L.: Adaptive object tracking by learning background context. In: IEEE Computer Society Conference on Computer Vision and Pattern Recognition Workshops, pp. 23–30, Providence, RI (2012)

3. Wang, Z., Chen, T., Li, G., Xu, R., Lin, L.: Multi-label image recognition by recurrently discovering attentional regions. In: 16th IEEE International Conference on Computer Vision, pp. 464–472. IEEE Press, Venice (2017)
4. Zhang, G.X., Cheng, M.M., Hu, S.M., Martin, R.R.: A Shape-preserving Approach to Image Resizing. Comput. Graph. Forum **28**(7), 1897–1906 (2009)
5. Wei, Y., Feng, J., Liang, X., Cheng, M.M., Zhao, Y., Yan, S.: Object region mining with adversarial erasing: a simple classification to semantic segmentation approach. In: 30th IEEE Conference on Computer Vision and Pattern Recognition, pp. 6488–6496. IEEE Press, Honolulu (2017)
6. Itti, L., Koch, C., Niebur, E.: A Model of Saliency-based Visual Attention for Rapid Scene Analysis. IEEE Trans. Pattern Anal. Mach. Intell. **20**(11), 1254–1259 (1998)
7. Achanta, R., Hemami, S., Estrada, F., Susstrunk, S.: Frequency-tuned salient region detection. In: 22th IEEE Conference on Computer Vision and Pattern Recognition, pp. 1597–1604. IEEE Press, Miami (2009)
8. Cheng, M.M., Zhang, G.X., Mitra, N.J., Huang, X., Hu, S.M.: Global Contrast Based Salient Region Detection. IEEE Trans. Pattern Anal. Mach. Intell. **37**(3), 409–416 (2011)
9. Li, X., Lu, H., Zhang, L., Xiang, R., Yang, M.H.: Saliency detection via dense and sparse reconstruction. In: 26th IEEE Conference on Computer Vision and Pattern Recognition, pp. 2976–2983. IEEE Press, Portland (2013)
10. Jiang, H., Wang, J., Yuan, Z., Wu, Y., Zheng, N., Li, S.: Salient object detection: a discriminative regional feature integration approach. In: 26th IEEE Conference on Computer Vision and Pattern Recognition, pp. 2083–2090. IEEE Press, Portland (2013)
11. He, S., Lau, R.W.H., Liu, W., Huang, Z., Yang, Q.: SuperCNN: a superpixelwise convolutional neural network for salient object detection. Int. J. Comput. Vis. **115**(3), 330–344 (2015). https://doi.org/10.1007/s11263-015-0822-0
12. Zhao, R., Ouyang, W., Li, H., Wang, X.: Saliency detection by multi-context deep learning. In: 28th IEEE Conference on Computer Vision and Pattern Recognition, pp. 1265–1274. IEEE Press, Boston (2015)
13. Lee, G., Tai, Y.W., Kim, J.: Deep saliency with encoded low level distance map and high level features. In: 29th IEEE Conference on Computer Vision and Pattern Recognition, pp. 660–668. IEEE Press, Las Vegas (2016)
14. Li, X., Zhao, L., Wei, L., Yang, M.H.: DeepSaliency: multi-task deep neural network model for salient object detection. IEEE Trans. Image Process. **25**(8), 3919–3930 (2016)
15. Luo, Z., Mishra, A., Achkar, A., Eichel, J., Li, S.Z., Jodoin, P.M.: Non-local deep features for salient object detection. In: 30th IEEE Conference on Computer Vision and Pattern Recognition, pp. 6593–6601. IEEE Press, Honolulu (2017)
16. Zhang, P., Wang, D., Lu, H., Wang, H., Yin, B.: Learning uncertain convolutional features for accurate saliency detection. In: 16th IEEE International Conference on Computer Vision, pp. 212–221. IEEE Press, Venice (2017)
17. Zhang, P., Wang, D., Lu, H., Wang, H., Ruan, X.: Amulet: aggregating multi-level convolutional features for salient object detection. In: 16th IEEE International Conference on Computer Vision, pp. 202–211. IEEE Press, Venice (2017)
18. Li, G., Yu, Y.: Contrast-oriented deep neural networks for salient object detection. IEEE Trans. Neural Netw. Learn. Syst. **29**(12), 6038–6051 (2018)
19. Wang, L., Wang, L., Lu, H., Zhang, P., Ruan, X.: Salient object detection with recurrent fully convolutional networks. IEEE Trans. Pattern Anal. Mach. Intell. **41**(7), 1734–1746 (2019)
20. Hou, Q., Cheng, M.M., Hu, X., Borji, A., Tu, Z., Torr, P.H.S.: Deeply supervised salient object detection with short connections. IEEE Trans. Pattern Anal. Mach. Intell. **41**(4), 815–828 (2019)

21. Wang, T., et al.: Detect globally, refine locally: a novel approach to saliency detection. In: 31th IEEE Conference on Computer Vision and Pattern Recognition, pp. 3127–3135. IEEE Press, Salt Lake City (2018)

22. Long, J., Shelhamer, E., Darrell, T.: Fully convolutional networks for semantic segmentation. In: 28th IEEE Conference on Computer Vision and Pattern Recognition, pp. 3431–3440. IEEE Press, Boston (2015)

23. He, K., Zhang, X., Ren, S., Sun, J.: Deep residual learning for image recognition. In: 29th IEEE Conference on Computer Vision and Pattern Recognition, pp. 770–778. IEEE Press, Las Vegas (2016)

24. Zhao, H., Shi, J., Qi, X., Wang, X., Jia, J.: Pyramid scene parsing network. In: 30th IEEE Conference on Computer Vision and Pattern Recognition, pp. 6230–6239. IEEE Press, Honolulu (2017)

25. Ronneberger, O., Fischer, P., Brox, T.: U-Net: convolutional networks for biomedical image segmentation. In: Navab, N., Hornegger, J., Wells, W.M., Frangi, A.F. (eds.) MICCAI 2015. LNCS, vol. 9351, pp. 234–241. Springer, Cham (2015). https://doi.org/10.1007/978-3-319-24574-4_28

26. Krähenbühl, P., Koltun, V.: Efficient inference in fully connected CRFs with gaussian edge potentials. In: Advances in Neural Information Processing Systems (2011)

27. Wang, L., et al.: Learning to detect salient objects with image-level supervision. In: 29th IEEE Conference on Computer Vision and Pattern Recognition, pp. 3796–3805. IEEE Press, Honolulu (2017)

28. Yan, Q., Xu, L., Shi, J., Jia, J.: Hierarchical saliency detection. In: 26th IEEE Conference on Computer Vision and Pattern Recognition, pp. 1155–1162. IEEE Press, Portland (2013)

29. Li, Y., Hou, X., Koch, C., Rehg, J.M., Yuille, A.L.: The secrets of salient object segmentation. In: 27th IEEE Conference on Computer Vision and Pattern Recognition, pp. 280–287. IEEE Press, Columbus (2014)

30. Liu, T., Sun, J., Zheng, N., Tang, X., Shum, H.: Learning to detect a salient object. In: 20th IEEE Conference on Computer Vision and Pattern Recognition, pp. 353–367. IEEE Press, Minneapolis (2007)

31. Li, G., Yu, Y.: Visual saliency based on multiscale deep features. In: 27th IEEE Conference on Computer Vision and Pattern Recognition, pp. 5455–5463. IEEE Press, Boston (2015)

32. Alpert, S., Galun, M., Basri, R., Brandt, A.: Image segmentation by probabilistic bottom-up aggregation and cue integration. IEEE Trans. Pattern Anal. Mach. Intell. 34(2), 315–327 (2012)

33. Cornia, M., Baraldi, L., Serra, G., Cucchiara, R.: A deep multi-level network for saliency prediction. In: 23th International Conference on Pattern Recognition, pp. 3488–3493. Amsterdam (2016)

Spectral Graph Reasoning Network for Hyperspectral Image Classification

Huiling Wang[(⊠)] [iD]

Computing Sciences, Tampere University, Tampere, Finland
huiling.wang@tuni.fi

Abstract. Convolutional neural networks (CNNs) have achieved remarkable performance in hyperspectral image (HSI) classification over the last few years. Despite the progress that has been made, rich and informative spectral information of HSI has been largely underutilized by existing methods which employ convolutional kernels with limited size of receptive field in the spectral domain. To address this issue, we propose a spectral graph reasoning network (SGR) learning framework comprising two crucial modules: 1) a spectral decoupling module which unpacks and casts multiple spectral embeddings into a unified graph whose node corresponds to an individual spectral feature channel in the embedding space; the graph performs interpretable reasoning to aggregate and align spectral information to guide learning spectral-specific graph embeddings at multiple contextual levels 2) a spectral ensembling module explores the interactions and interdependencies across graph embedding hierarchy via a novel recurrent graph propagation mechanism. Experiments on two HSI datasets demonstrate that the proposed architecture can significantly improve the classification accuracy compared with the existing methods with a sizable margin.

1 Introduction

Hyperspectral image comprises hundreds of continuous spectral bands throughout the electromagnetic spectrum with high spectral resolution, which facilities the precise differentiation of chemical properties of scene materials remotely. Consequently hyperspectral images have been considered as a crucial data source in various fields, such as environmental monitoring, mining, agriculture, and land-cover mapping.

HSI classification involves assigning a categorical class label to each individual pixel location given the corresponding spectral feature. Various classification approaches have been proposed to address the hyperspectral image classification problem. Early approaches largely adopted traditional machine learning methods which were trained on hand-crafted features from HSI data to empirically encode the spectral information, *e.g.* SVM [13], KNN [18], dictionary learning [2], graphical model [21], extreme learning machine [16] and among others.

© Springer Nature Switzerland AG 2020
I. Farkaš et al. (Eds.): ICANN 2020, LNCS 12396, pp. 711–723, 2020.
https://doi.org/10.1007/978-3-030-61609-0_56

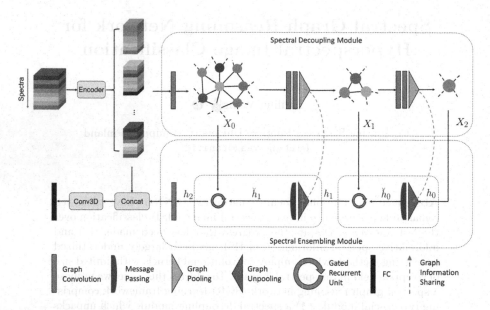

Fig. 1. Illustration of our proposed network architecture.

Other methods [28,29] also exploited both spectral and spatial information since utilizing only the spectral information regardless of the spatial correlation is difficult in accurately classifying different land-cover categories.

With the advent of new remote sensing instruments and increased temporal resolutions, the deluge of high dimensional HSI data is posing new challenges on the limited discriminative power of the empirically designed features and the traditional classification methods. Deep learning based HSI classification methods have been proposed inspired by its success in visual recognition of natural images. Those methods benefit from the strong representation capability and end-to-end learning. Chen *et al.* [4] developed the first deep neural networks (DNN) method which utilized stacked autoencoders to learn high-level features. Mou *et al.* [19] introduced a Recurrent Neural Network (RNN) based architecture. More powerful end-to-end Convolutional Neural Network (CNN) based architectures [3,8,11] have been proposed recently. Lee *et al.* [15] explored local contextual interactions by jointly exploiting local spatio-spectral relationships of neighboring pixels. Residual learning [9] was introduced by Song *et al.* [22] to build very deep network for extracting more discriminative feature representations for HSI classification. Li *et al.* [17] introduced a 3D-CNN architecture which was improved by He *et al.* [10] to jointly learn Multi-scale 2D spatial feature and 1D spectral feature from HSI data. Graph convolutional network (GCN) based approaches [20,26] have also been proposed which operated on graphs constructed in the *spatial* domain, aggregating and transforming feature information from the neighbors of every graph node given their relevance.

Despite of the significant improvements by the DNN based methods, they suffer from a number of inherent pitfalls. Specifically, all existing methods utilize convolutional kernels with limited size of receptive field to encode the very high dimensional and informative spectral domain. As a consequence, output constituting a certain new spectral channel is derived from only a fraction of all spectral channels which blocks information flow between distant spectra and fails to capture longer term contextual information. Furthermore, spectral domain normally contains abundant yet noisy information which can lead to spurious classifications due to this weakened representation based on local contexts.

In this paper, we propose a novel spectral graph reasoning network (SGR) to explicitly address the above issues. Specifically, we firstly unpack and cast multiple spectral embeddings into a unified graph with each node corresponding to an individual spectral embedding channel via a novel spectral decoupling module. Graph reasoning facilitates the interactions between spectra which in turn boosts the representational capacity of the network by discriminating the significance of different spectral bands. A spectral-specific graph embedding hierarchy is generated through the spectral decoupling module which encodes a hierarchical representation of the spectral information. Each level of the hierarchy carries different degrees of discriminative power for HSI classification. To the best of our knowledge, this is the first method to model and interpret HSI data using graph neural network in the spectral domain.

We further introduce a spectral ensembling module that correlates the multicontextual spectral-specific graph embeddings across the spectral hierarchy. This is achieved through a novel recurrent graph propagation mechanism which learns to map from a sequence of input graphs with varying size, each representing a state of transformed spectra with its intrinsic structure, to an ensembled spectral representation containing the key discriminative features from each contextual level to improve the classification accuracy.

2   Method

We propose a novel end-to-end spectral-specific graph representation learning framework for HSI classification, which comprises two core modules *i.e.* spectral decoupling module and spectral ensembling module, as illustrated in Fig. 1.

2.1   Graph Construction

We define a graph structure for mining correlations and constraints among spectral embedding channels. Specifically, we define an undirected graph $\mathcal{G} = (\mathcal{V}, \mathcal{E}, \mathcal{A})$. Given the feature map $X \in \mathbb{R}^{N \times H \times W}$ produced by the encoder network from an input HSI data volume centered at each pixel location, we seek to construct graph node set $\mathcal{V} = \{v_i\}_{i=1}^N$ and each node $v_i \in \mathcal{V}$ corresponds to a spectral feature from the embedding and the associated feature vector with $C = H \times W$ dimensions indicates $x_i \in \mathbb{R}^C$. The set of edges $\mathcal{E} = \{e_{ij}\}$ indicate the connection between nodes, and $\mathbf{A} = (e_{ij})_{N \times N}$ is the adjacency matrix, with

$a_{i,j} = 0$ if $(i,j) \notin \mathcal{E}$, and $a_{i,j} = 1$ if $(i,j) \in \mathcal{E}$. We adopt K-Nearest Neighbor Graph (KNN-Graph) construction [23–25,27] in which two vertices v_i and v_j are connected by an edge, if the distance between v_i and v_j is among the k-th smallest distances measured by cosine distance. The normalized graph Laplacian [6] is computed as $L = I_N - D^{-\frac{1}{2}} A D^{-\frac{1}{2}}$, where $D^{ii} = \sum_j A^{ij}$.

The spectral convolutions on graphs [7] can be formulated as the multiplication of input $x \in \mathbb{R}^n$ with operator g_θ in Fourier domain,

$$y = g_\theta(L) * x = U g_\theta(\Lambda) U^T x \tag{1}$$

where graph Fourier basis U is the matrix of the eigenvectors of the normalized graph Laplacian L such that $L = U\theta(\Lambda)U^T$ with Λ being its corresponding eigenvalues, and $U^T x$ represents the graph Fourier transform of x. To reduce the computational complexity, Kipf and Welling [12] stacked multiple localized graph convolutional layers with the first-order approximation of graph Laplacian,

$$Y = \tilde{D}^{-\frac{1}{2}} \tilde{A} \tilde{D}^{-\frac{1}{2}} X W \tag{2}$$

where $W \in \mathbb{R}^{M \times F}$ is the matrix of filter parameters, $\tilde{A}$ and $\tilde{D}$ are the normalized versions with $\tilde{A} = A + I_N$ and $\tilde{D}^{ii} = \sum_j \tilde{A}^{ij}$.

2.2 Spectral Decoupling

The spectral decoupling module aims to learn spectral-specific feature representation by reasoning within spectral embedding at multiple scales. Necessitated by the excessive information of the broad and noisy spectral domain, this module explores the long-range contextual dependencies in the original feature space to form multiple lower dimensional intermediate representations in order to capture the essence of the spectral information.

We adopt a graph pyramid of spectral features - at each scale of the graph pyramid, graph convolution (GCN) is applied to capture the interdependence of graph via message passing between the nodes of graphs, *i.e.* spectral features, as illustrated in Fig. 1. Assuming that filters in later layers of an encoder are responsive to various materials that make up the scanned scene, the proposed band GCN captures correlations and occurrences between more abstract characteristics in the scene like constituent materials. Graph pooling is applied to reduce the resolution of spectral features, whose result forms the input of the following graph convolution layer.

Graph pooling aims to enable down-sampling on graph data while preserving as much information as possible from the original graph. To this end, we employ a single neuron linear layer parameterized by W_θ, followed by a sigmoid function and top-k pooling. This is implemented as multiplying the input at lth layer $X^l \in \mathbb{R}^{N \times C}$ with $W_\theta^l \in \mathbb{R}^C$ followed by sigmoid operation, whose result is an 1D vector $\mathbf{s} \in \mathbb{R}^N$ measuring how much information of nodes can be retained when projected onto the direction W_θ^l. Graph coarsening can thus be done by selecting nodes with the largest scalar projection values on W_θ^l to form a new graph.

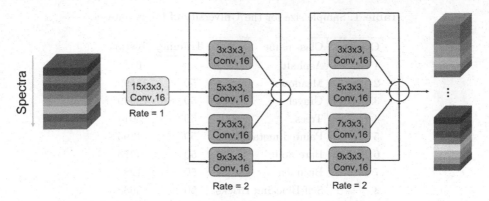

Fig. 2. Illustration of the encoder network.

The location of selected nodes in the original graph is recorded for graph unpooling operation. The feature of the selected nodes is adjusted by its projection values as $X^{l+1} = X^l \odot s$ where $\odot$ is the Hadamard product. Intuitively the selected nodes represent the "cluster centers" of spectral features and the edges measure the similarity between these clusters.

2.3 Spectral Ensembling

Once obtaining a pyramid of graph embeddings after graph pooling, *i.e.* $\mathcal{X} = \{X_1, X_2, \cdots, X_L\}$, with each level of the hierarchy encoding the key spectral-specific feature at a certain scale, we explore their interactions across the hierarchy via a novel recurrent spectral ensembling module. There are mainly two challenges in ensembling a sequence of multi-level graph embeddings. Firstly, interaction between graphs of different number of nodes is not as straightforward as grid-like data *e.g.* images and texts due to the lack of spatial locality and order information. Note, the number of nodes in the graph corresponds to the cardinality of spectral embeddings. Secondly, recall that each of the previous graph pooling layer selected some important nodes to form a new graph for high-level feature encoding, the nodes in the new graph might become isolated due to the related edges have been removed while removing nodes.

In order to address the above issues, we propose a recurrent message passing ensembling mechanism. Specifically, for every two neighboring graph embeddings, the smaller but higher level graph is firstly unpooled to match the size of the bigger yet lower level graph. Then two graphs are interacting in a way that higher level graph is used as the hidden state encoding historical information, transferring its graph embedding and node interdependency to guide the message passing within the lower level graph. Figure 1 illustrates the unrolled recurrent spectral ensembling where all the intermediate graph representations are processed as a sequence of input instances in the recurrent unit with shared weights.

Table 1. Sample size for the University of Pavia dataset.

Class no.	Class name	Training	Testing
1	Asphalt	50	6581
2	Meadows	50	18599
3	Gravel	50	2049
4	Trees	50	3014
5	Painted metal sheets	50	1295
6	Bare Soil	50	4979
7	Bitumen	50	1280
8	Self-Blocking Bricks	50	3632
9	Shadows	50	897
	Total	450	42776

Formally, indicating $\mathbf{h}_0 = X_L$, the graph unpooling layer l is defined as

$$\check{\mathbf{h}}_l = \text{MessagePassing}(f(0_{N \times C}, \mathbf{h}_l, \mathcal{I}), \mathcal{G}_{L-l}) \tag{3}$$

where $\mathcal{I}$ represents the set of indices of selected nodes in the corresponding graph pooling layer $L - l$ which reduced the number of graph nodes from N to k (due to top-k pooling), $\mathbf{h}_l \in \mathbb{R}^{k \times C}$ is the feature map of current graph, $0_{N \times C}$ is the empty feature matrix for the new graph, $f(\cdot)$ indicates the mapping operation distributing row vectors of $\mathbf{h}_l$ into $0_{N \times C}$ according to the corresponding indices in $\mathcal{I}$, $\mathcal{G}_{L-l}$ indicates the graph definition before graph pooling layer $L - l$ which consists of affinity matrix and edge weights, and MessagePassing defines the message passing process [12] as

$$\check{\mathbf{h}}_l^i = \sum_{j \in \mathcal{N}(i) \cup \{i\}} \Theta \cdot \mathbf{h}_l^j, \tag{4}$$

where neighboring node features are first transformed by the weight matrix Θ passed via $\mathcal{G}_{L-l}$. The potential isolation of upsampled nodes in the new graph due to the removed related edges is properly compensated by the message passing based on the original graph interdependency information.

Then the framework updates the hidden state based on spectral feature X_{L-l} and hidden state $\mathbf{h}_{l-1}$ from previous step via a gated mechanism similar to Gated Recurrent Unit (GRU) [5] as

$$
\begin{aligned}
\mathbf{z}_l &= \sigma\left(\mathbf{W}_z X_{L-l} + \mathbf{U}_z \check{\mathbf{h}}_{l-1}\right), \\
\mathbf{r}_l &= \sigma\left(\mathbf{W}_r X_{L-l} + \mathbf{U}_r \check{\mathbf{h}}_{l-1}\right), \\
\tilde{\mathbf{h}}_l &= \tanh\left(\mathbf{W}_o X_{L-l} + \mathbf{U}_o(\mathbf{r}_l \odot \check{\mathbf{h}}_{l-1})\right), \\
\mathbf{h}_l &= (1 - \mathbf{z}_l) \odot \check{\mathbf{h}}_{l-1} + \mathbf{z}_l \odot \tilde{\mathbf{h}}_l
\end{aligned}
\tag{5}
$$

Table 2. Sample size for the Indian Pines dataset

Class no.	Class name	Training	Testing
1	Alfalfa	40	6
2	Corn-notill	100	1328
3	Corn-mintill	100	730
4	Corn	100	137
5	Grass-pasture	100	383
6	Grass-trees	100	630
7	Grass-pasture-mowed	20	8
8	Hay-windrowed	100	378
9	Oats	15	5
10	Soybean-notill	100	872
11	Soybean-mintill	100	2355
12	Soybean-clean	100	493
13	Wheat	100	105
14	Woods	100	1165
15	Buildings-Grass-Trees-Drives	100	286
16	Stone-Steel-Towers	80	13
	Total	1355	8894

where $\sigma(\cdot)$ is the logistic sigmoid function, $\tanh(\cdot)$ is the hyperbolic tangent function, and $\odot$ is the Hadamard product. Interactions between all levels in the graph embedding hierarchy are enabled by encoding higher level contextual spectral information in the hidden states. The process is repeated L times according to the levels of hierarchy, and the final hidden state $\mathbf{h}_L$ goes through another GCN layer before being concatenated with the feature map from the encoder network for predicting the category label of the input HSI volume with a fully connected layer.

2.4 Encoder Network

We adopt a multi-path dilated 3D convolutional residual network to encode the original HSI data as illustrated in Fig. 2. Specifically, the encoder starts with a 3D convolutional layer with kernel size $15 \times 3 \times 3$ corresponding to the spectral dimension and two spatial dimensions respectively, which is followed by two multi-path ($3 \times 3 \times 3$, $5 \times 3 \times 3$, $7 \times 3 \times 3$ and $9 \times 3 \times 3$ kernels respectively) dilated (rate = 2) convolutional residual modules with identity shortcuts. Note that our proposed framework is agnostic to the utilized encoder network.

3   Experimental Results

We evaluate our method on two publicly available hyperspectral image datasets with four metrics including per-class accuracy, overall accuracy (OA), average

Table 3. Per-class accuracy, OA, AA (%), and Kappa coefficient achieved by different methods on the University of Pavia dataset.

Class no.	FCN [14]	MS 3D-CNN [10]	SS 3D-CNN [17]	3D-CNN [8]	SGR
1	61.98	92.47	91.98	91.86	**95.91**
2	72.16	94.22	93.88	90.55	**98.27**
3	12.90	86.38	81.46	85.89	**88.47**
4	39.52	92.63	94.98	93.65	**99.83**
5	99.46	98.57	**100.00**	98.59	99.91
6	41.78	80.45	74.34	70.49	**84.75**
7	50.49	83.60	84.94	84.66	**86.42**
8	67.99	90.30	86.92	88.58	**91.43**
9	97.55	97.43	**99.94**	98.82	98.24
OA	61.21	91.35	90.30	88.14	**94.37**
AA	60.42	90.67	89.82	89.23	**93.69**
Kappa	48.44	88.56	87.15	84.46	**91.26**

accuracy (AA), and Kappa coefficient. The network architecture of the proposed method SGR is identical for both datasets. Specifically, we use an architecture of $L = 2$ and the input HSI is sampled on 7×7 image patches in the spatial domain. We adopt stochastic gradient descent with momentum set to 0.9, weight decay of 0.0005, and with a batch size of 30. We initialize an equal learning rate for all trainable layers to 0.05, which is manually decreased by a factor of 10 when the validation error plateaus. The number of training epochs is set to 500. All the reported accuracies are calculated based on the average of five training sessions to obtain stable results.

3.1 Datasets

The University of Pavia dataset was captured with the ROSIS sensor in 2001 which consists of 610×340 pixels with a spatial resolution of $1.3\,m \times 1.3\,m$ and has 103 spectral channels in the wavelength range from 0.43 μm to 0.86 μm after removing noisy bands. This dataset includes 9 land-cover classes and the false color image and ground-truth map are shown in Fig. 3.

The Indian Pines dataset was captured with Airborne Visible/Infrared Imaging Spectrometer sensor comprising 145×145 pixels with a spatial resolution of $20\,m \times 20\,m$ and 220 spectral channels covering the range from 0.4 μm to 2.5 μm. This dataset includes 16 land-cover classes and the false color image and ground-truth map are shown in Fig. 4.

Table 1 and Table 2 provide information about all the classes of both datasets with their corresponding training and test samples respectively. During training, 90% of the training samples are used to learn the network parameters and 10% are used as validation set for tuning the hyperparameters.

Table 4. Per-class accuracy, OA, AA (%), and Kappa coefficient achieved by different methods on the Indian Pines dataset

Class no.	FCN [14]	SS 3D-CNN [17]	MS 3D-CNN [10]	3D-CNN [8]	SGR
1	6.7	80.00	**100.00**	30.77	99.56
2	64.81	76.41	77.52	70.90	**79.32**
3	74.67	78.06	79.36	76.12	**80.47**
4	59.21	76.65	80.85	77.46	**83.72**
5	92.19	92.16	96.43	90.96	**97.62**
6	97.66	99.13	99.84	96.86	**99.92**
7	47.56	40.00	**100.00**	48.48	100.00
8	97.04	99.87	**100.00**	97.70	100.0
9	16.95	58.82	**100.00**	71.43	100.00
10	78.71	76.75	79.84	70.07	**81.55**
11	76.59	80.09	82.50	77.83	**85.26**
12	65.23	78.03	76.56	68.31	**80.97**
13	98.51	97.65	99.53	95.57	**99.92**
14	94.88	94.64	97.34	96.12	**98.75**
15	70.75	73.96	85.53	71.70	**85.97**
16	49.33	89.66	**100.00**	78.79	100.00
OA	79.20	83.37	85.79	80.35	**87.83**
AA	68.17	80.74	90.96	76.19	**92.06**
Kappa	75.89	80.89	83.58	77.19	**85.42**

3.2 Classification Results

The University of Pavia Dataset. The quantitative results obtained by different approaches on the University of Pavia dataset are reported in Table 3. Our method outperforms the compared methods on 7 out of 9 categories and achieves the best overall results, *i.e.* OA, AA and Kappa. Generally, all other networks significantly outperform FCN [14]. One possible reason could be that FCN heavily squeezed the spectral dimension and utilized small 2D convolutional kernels in the spatial domain. 3D-CNN [8] adopted more 3D convolutional layers to perform simultaneous spatial-spectral convolution. Compared with [14], [8] used a large number of 3D filters per layer to improve the feature representation over the very high dimensional spectral domain which increases the accuracy by ~2%. [10] addresses the limitations of single scale 3D CNN architectures by introducing a multi-scale 3D CNN architecture, which improves the accuracy by ~1% compared to [8]. Nevertheless, none of the existing methods has explicitly performed reasoning among the spectral embedding channels in a global manner, but rather modeling the local context by convolutional kernels with limited size of receptive field. Our method bridges this gap by casting spectral embeddings into a unified graph whose node corresponds to an individual spectral feature in

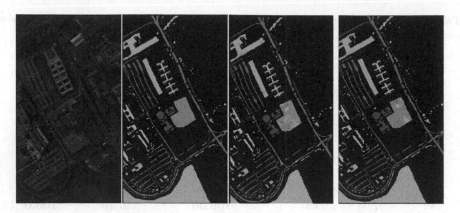

Fig. 3. The university of Pavia dataset: (a) False color image (b) Groundtruth map (c) Prediction of SSLSTMs [30] (d) Prediction of the proposed SPGAT

the embedding space and thus the interaction between graph nodes guides learning spectral-specific graph representations. Quantitative results shows that our method outperforms the best competing method [10] with a significant margin of 3.02%.

Figure 3 shows a visual comparison of our proposed SGR and the best competing method [10] on the University of Pavia dataset. The observation reveals that [10] suffers more mis-classifications than SGR in large semantically coherent regions, due to its weaker representation capability of encoding the discriminative spectral features with the presence of noise. The qualitative result that our SGR produces more accurate and coherent predictions.

The Indian Pines Dataset. Table 4 gives the quantitative results on the Indian Pines dataset, which shows that the proposed method obtains the best overall accuracy of 87.83%. Similar observations with the University of Pavia dataset can be found that all 3D CNN architectures outperform FCN [14] which adopts small 2D convolutional kernels as majority components. 3D CNN architectures generally explore the spatial-spectral contexts simultaneously and achieves better accuracy. Nevertheless, our proposed method has the advantage over the compared methods by exploring inter-spectral relations and learning a graph embedding hierarchy representation with each level emphasizing on specific spectral features exhibiting discriminative power toward the classification. Figure 4 shows a visual comparison of our proposed SGR and the second best method [10], which confirms that our SGR produces more accurate and coherent predictions.

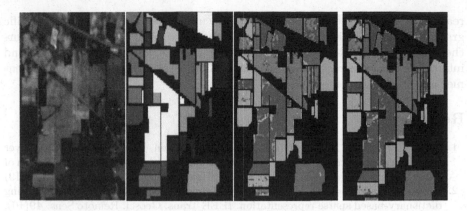

Fig. 4. Indian Pines dataset: (a) False color image (b) Groundtruth map (c) Prediction of LBMSELM [1] (d) Prediction of the proposed SPGAT

Table 5. OA achieved by different baselines on the University of Pavia dataset.

	Baseline-1	Baseline-2	Baseline-3	Baseline-4	SGR
OA	88.24	91.87	94.21	92.54	94.37

3.3 Ablation Study

We conduct ablation study on the University of Pavia dataset to quantitatively verify the effectiveness of the proposed architecture. The first baseline is applying a predicting layer (Conv3D-FC-Softmax) on top of the encoder network, *i.e.* Baseline-1. We also investigate spectral decoupling module with two different depth 1 and 3, dubbed as Baseline-2 and Baseline-3 respectively. To verify the contribution from spectral ensembling, we replace it with a naive graph upsampling and embedding summation operation, *i.e.* Baseline-4.

As shown in Table 5, a significant accuracy gain of 6.13% is achieved by our proposed spectral graph reasoning network, by comparing Baseline-1 and SGR. Adding one level of spectral coupling module improves the accuracy from 88.24% to 91.87%, which confirms its effectiveness. However, adding three levels slightly decreases the accuracy, *i.e.* a loss of 0.16% compared with SGR which has two levels. The possible reason is using the limited training samples for learning a more complex architecture. Furthermore, introducing the spectral ensembling module boosts the performance by 1.83%.

4   Conclusions

In this paper, we proposed a novel spectral graph reasoning network for hyperspectral image classification which has significantly advanced the state-of-the-art. At the core of our network architecture lies a new spectral feature reasoning and ensembling paradigm. We demonstrated that applying interpretable graph reasoning in the spectral feature domain enables learning a spectral-specific graph embedding which in turn improves the discriminative capability. We further proposed a spectral ensembling module that explores the interactions and interdependencies across the graph embedding hierarchy via a novel recurrent message propagation mechanism.

References

1. Cao, F., Yang, Z., Ren, J., Chen, W., Han, G., Shen, Y.: Local block multilayer sparse extreme learning machine for effective feature extraction and classification of hyperspectral images. IEEE Trans. Geosci. Remote Sens. **57**(8), 5580–5594 (2019)
2. Chen, Y., Nasrabadi, N.M., Tran, T.D.: Hyperspectral image classification using dictionary-based sparse representation. IEEE Trans. Geosci. Remote Sens. **49**(10), 3973–3985 (2011)
3. Chen, Y., Jiang, H., Li, C., Jia, X., Ghamisi, P.: Deep feature extraction and classification of hyperspectral images based on convolutional neural networks. IEEE Trans. Geosci. Remote Sens. **54**(10), 6232–6251 (2016)
4. Chen, Y., Lin, Z., Zhao, X., Wang, G., Gu, Y.: Deep learning-based classification of hyperspectral data. IEEE J. Sel. Top. Appl. Earth Obser. Remote sensing **7**(6), 2094–2107 (2014)
5. Cho, K., et al.: Learning phrase representations using RNN encoder-decoder for statistical machine translation. In: EMNLP, pp. 1724–1734. ACL (2014)
6. Chung, F.R., Graham, F.C.: Spectral graph theory. No. 92, American Mathematical Society (1997)
7. Defferrard, M., Bresson, X., Vandergheynst, P.: Convolutional neural networks on graphs with fast localized spectral filtering. In: Advances in Neural Information Processing Systems, pp. 3844–3852 (2016)
8. Hamida, A.B., Benoit, A., Lambert, P., Amar, C.B.: 3-d deep learning approach for remote sensing image classification. IEEE Trans. Geosci. Remote Sens. **56**(8), 4420–4434 (2018)
9. He, K., Zhang, X., Ren, S., Sun, J.: Deep residual learning for image recognition. In: Proceedings of the IEEE Conference on Computer Vision and Pattern Recognition, pp. 770–778 (2016)
10. He, M., Li, B., Chen, H.: Multi-scale 3D deep convolutional neural network for hyperspectral image classification. In: 2017 IEEE International Conference on Image Processing (ICIP), pp. 3904–3908. IEEE (2017)
11. Hu, X., Wang, X., Zhong, Y., Zhao, J., Luo, C., Wei, L.: SPNET: a spectral patching network for end-to-end hyperspectral image classification. In: IGARSS 2019–2019 IEEE International Geoscience and Remote Sensing Symposium, pp. 963–966. IEEE (2019)
12. Kipf, T.N., Welling, M.: Semi-supervised classification with graph convolutional networks. In: Proceedings of International Conference on Learning Representations (2017)
13. Kuo, B.C., Huang, C.S., Hung, C.C., Liu, Y.L., Chen, I.L.: Spatial information based support vector machine for hyperspectral image classification. In: 2010 IEEE International Geoscience and Remote Sensing Symposium, pp. 832–835. IEEE (2010)
14. Lee, H., Kwon, H.: Contextual deep CNN based hyperspectral classification. In: 2016 IEEE International Geoscience and Remote Sensing Symposium (IGARSS), pp. 3322–3325. IEEE (2016)

15. Lee, H., Kwon, H.: Going deeper with contextual CNN for hyperspectral image classification. IEEE Trans. Image Process. **26**(10), 4843–4855 (2017)
16. Li, W., Chen, C., Su, H., Du, Q.: Local binary patterns and extreme learning machine for hyperspectral imagery classification. IEEE Trans. Geosci. Remote Sens. **53**(7), 3681–3693 (2015)
17. Li, Y., Zhang, H., Shen, Q.: Spectral-spatial classification of hyperspectral imagery with 3D convolutional neural network. Remote Sens. **9**(1), 67 (2017)
18. Ma, L., Crawford, M.M., Tian, J.: Local manifold learning-based k-nearest-neighbor for hyperspectral image classification. IEEE Trans. Geosci. Remote Sens. **48**(11), 4099–4109 (2010)
19. Mou, L., Ghamisi, P., Zhu, X.X.: Deep recurrent neural networks for hyperspectral image classification. IEEE Trans. Geosci. Remote Sens. **55**(7), 3639–3655 (2017)
20. Qin, A., Shang, Z., Tian, J., Wang, Y., Zhang, T., Tang, Y.Y.: Spectral-spatial graph convolutional networks for semisupervised hyperspectral image classification. IEEE Geosci. Remote Sensing Lett. **16**(2), 241–245 (2019)
21. Shi, L., Zhang, L., Yang, J., Zhang, L., Li, P.: Supervised graph embedding for polarimetric SAR image classification. IEEE Geosci. Remote Sens. Lett. **10**(2), 216–220 (2012)
22. Song, W., Li, S., Fang, L., Lu, T.: Hyperspectral image classification with deep feature fusion network. IEEE Trans. Geosci. Remote Sens. **56**(6), 3173–3184 (2018)
23. Wang, H., Raiko, T., Lensu, L., Wang, T., Karhunen, J.: Semi-supervised domain adaptation for weakly labeled semantic video object segmentation. In: Lai, S.-H., Lepetit, V., Nishino, K., Sato, Y. (eds.) ACCV 2016. LNCS, vol. 10111, pp. 163–179. Springer, Cham (2017). https://doi.org/10.1007/978-3-319-54181-5_11
24. Wang, H., Wang, T.: Primary object discovery and segmentation in videos via graph-based transductive inference. Comput. Vis. Image Underst. **143**, 159–172 (2016)
25. Wang, H., Wang, T., Chen, K., Kämäräinen, J.K.: Cross-granularity graph inference for semantic video object segmentation. In: IJCAI, pp. 4544–4550 (2017)
26. Wang, T., Wang, G., Tan, K.E., Tan, D.: Spectral pyramid graph attention network for hyperspectral image classification. arXiv preprint arXiv:2001.07108 (2020)
27. Wang, T., Wang, H.: Graph transduction learning of object proposals for video object segmentation. In: Cremers, D., Reid, I., Saito, H., Yang, M.-H. (eds.) ACCV 2014. LNCS, vol. 9006, pp. 553–568. Springer, Cham (2015). https://doi.org/10.1007/978-3-319-16817-3_36
28. Zhang, L., Zhang, Q., Du, B., Huang, X., Tang, Y.Y., Tao, D.: Simultaneous spectral-spatial feature selection and extraction for hyperspectral images. IEEE Trans. Cybern. **48**(1), 16–28 (2016)
29. Zhong, Z., et al.: Discriminant tensor spectral-spatial feature extraction for hyperspectral image classification. IEEE Geosci. Remote Sens. Lett. **12**(5), 1028–1032 (2014)
30. Zhou, F., Hang, R., Liu, Q., Yuan, X.: Hyperspectral image classification using spectral-spatial LSTMs. Neurocomputing **328**, 39–47 (2019)

Salient Object Detection with Edge Recalibration

Zhenshan Tan, Yikai Hua, and Xiaodong Gu(✉)

Department of Electronic Engineering, Fudan University, Shanghai 200433, China
xdgu@fudan.edu.cn

Abstract. Salient Object Detection (SOD) based on Convolutional Neural Networks (CNNs) has been widely studied recently. How to maintain a complete and clear object boundary structure is still a key issue. Existing works with the utilization of edge information have already improved this issue to some extent. However, these methods extract boundary features indiscriminately, which may weaken useful edge information and mislead edge construction. To address this problem, we present an Edge Recalibration Network (ERN) model for image-based SOD to perform edge-guided features effectively. In a specific, a progressive Fully Convolutional neural Networks (FCNs) for SOD is adopted to incorporate multi-scale and multi-level features. Besides, to locate the edge position and preserve the boundary features accurately, we propose an edge enhancement module with pixel-wise semantic-edge integration and channel-wise feature recalibration. Based on pixelwise semantic-edge integration, the semantic features and boundary features are integrated into the holistic feature maps. Based on channel-wise feature recalibration, the boundary features selectively recalibrate salient semantic features on channel dimension, aiming to enhance useful features and suppress useless features, for the similarity of boundary features and salient semantic features. Experimental results on five popular benchmark datasets show that the proposed model ERN outperforms other state-of-the-art methods under different evaluation metrics.

Keywords: Salient object detection · Edge recalibration · Fully convolutional neural network

1 Introduction

The goal of Salient Object Detection (SOD) is to locate the attractive parts of images. SOD is one of the most important visual tasks and has various applications such as image captioning, visual tracking, object detection, visual question answering and image retrieval. Up to now, most of the state-of-the-art SOD methods are based on the deep learning models especially the convolutional neural networks, which can extract high-level semantic features better than traditional unsupervised stimuli-driven methods. However, the coarse boundary, caused by unconstrained boundary features, is still a key issue in SOD.

© Springer Nature Switzerland AG 2020
I. Farkaš et al. (Eds.): ICANN 2020, LNCS 12396, pp. 724–735, 2020.
https://doi.org/10.1007/978-3-030-61609-0_57

Early methods introduce additional hand-crafted models to preserve the boundaries of salient objects [1]. However, the extra postprocessing steps are time-consuming though they can improve the resulting saliency boundaries. Besides, attention modules and feature enhancement methods based on Fully Convolutional Networks (FCNs) [6–12] are also introduced to SOD. Several widely-used attention models include channel-wise attention [2,13], reverse attention [14] and pyramid feature attention [3,15,16]. Attention mechanism makes the deep network models focus on the affinities of semantic features and refine the local regions. Feature enhancement methods leverage guidance features such as recurrent model [13], multiple direction model [19] and boundary features [17,18] to refine the resulting saliency maps and the edges. Although the attention mechanism and feature enhancement module of previous researches improve the resulting saliency maps under different metrics, they do not consider the relevance between attention mechanism and edge guidance module. The indiscriminately harmful information may deteriorate the saliency maps especially the edges.

To address the above issue, we present an Edge Recalibration Network (ERN) to locate the edge and preserve the boundary features. In short, we make three major contributions as follows:

- We propose an edge recalibration fully convolutional network for accurate image-based salient object detection. The proposed model is able to embed the attention mechanism to the edge enhancement module, which generate high-quality saliency maps.
- We design an edge guidance block with pixel-wise semantic-edge integration and channel-wise feature recalibration. The pixel-wise semantic-edge integration incorporates semantic features with boundary features, and the channel-wise feature recalibration selectively recalibrates salient semantic features on channel dimension.
- The proposed method is compared with several methods on five widely applied testing datasets. Without any bells and whistles, new state-of-the-art results are achieved by the proposed edge recalibration network in this paper.

2 Edge Recalibration Network

In this paper, we propose a novel edge recalibration network, which contains the baseline network to capture multi-level and multi-scale saliency features and boundary features, along with an edge recalibration module to locate the saliency objects and recalibrate the salient edges. The overall architecture is shown in Fig. 1.

2.1 Baseline Network

As illustrated in Fig. 1, we adopt a widely-used U-net [4,5] structure as the baseline network. The main structure of U-net consists of a contracting path and an

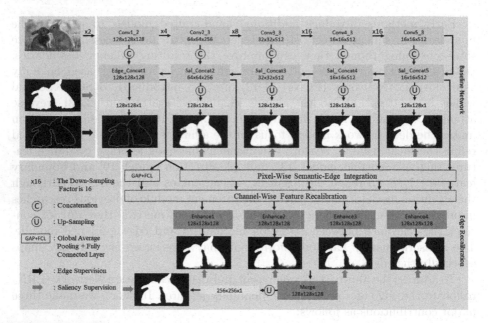

Fig. 1. Overall Architecture. Conv denotes the convolutional layers. Conv1_2, Conv2_3, Conv3_3, Conv4_3 and Conv5_3 denote the second or the third layer of the output layer in each convolutional block. Concat denotes the layer after concatenation. Enhance denotes the layer after the enhancement with edge recalibration. Merge denotes the layer after merging.

expanding path. The convolutional layer and the pooling layer in the contracting path extract the multi-level features from the images under multiple receptive fields. In the expanding path, the network reconstructs the features extracted from the contracting path through the up-sampling and convolutional layer to generate the output of the network. In addition, the multi-scale image features extracted in the contracting path will be combined with the up-sampling features of the symmetric convolutional module in the expanding path, and then used as the input features of the convolutional module. Because of the special combination of features, there is a certain symmetry between the contracting path and the expanding path. Benefitted from the special designment, the baseline network is able to extract multi-level features. Furthermore, the size of each feature map in U-net structure is down to up, which makes full use of multi-scale features.

Refer to the paper [20], the best down-sampling factor is less than 16 especially for the saliency detection. Therefore, different from the original U-net structure, we maintain the size of the last layer in the network backbone according to set the last down-sampling unchanged. In addition, different from the original U-net structure, we adopt an output side way supervision to constrain the saliency features and boundary features. As the shallow layers contain the low-level features such as edge and point, they are more likely designed for edge extraction. Therefore, the Conv1 is designed as the edge convolutional layer. On contrast, the deep convolutional layers contain high-level features such as semantic and aggregation of textures, which are proper for saliency supervision. Consequently, the layers from Conv2 to Conv3 are designed as the saliency convolutional layers. The resolution of the input image I is set to 256×256, then from the network backbone, we can obtain five contracting paths Conv1_2, Conv2_3, Conv3_3, Conv4_3 and Conv5_3. The feature maps of the five contracting paths can be denoted as:

$$C = \{C^1, C^2, C^3, C^4, C^5\} \tag{1}$$

where, C^i denotes the feature map of $i - th$ contracting path. As mentioned above, the U-net structure contains an expanding path, and their features can be denoted as:

$$E = \{E^1, E^2, E^3, E^4, E^5\} \tag{2}$$

where, E^i denotes the feature map of $i - th$ expanding path. In addition, as illustrated in Fig. 1, the output side paths of baseline network can be calculated by the sum of contracting paths and expanding path. Furthermore, the first output side path denotes the boundary features, and the other output side paths denote the saliency features. Therefore, on the one hand, the edge output side path of baseline network can be denoted as:

$$O^{Edge} = F^{out}(Concat(C^1, E^1); \Theta^{out}) \tag{3}$$

where, $Concat(*)$ denotes the operation of concatenation. $F^{out}(*; \Theta^{out})$ refers to the convolutional layer to change the channels to 1 and Θ is the parameters. On the other hand, the saliency output side path of baseline network can be denoted as:

$$O^{Sal_i} = Up(F^{out}(Concat(C^i, E^i); \Theta^{out})), i = 2, 3, 4, 5 \tag{4}$$

where, $Up(*)$ denotes the operation of up-sampling. Similar to previous methods, we adopt the bilinear interpolation as the up-sampling function. Besides, the ground truth of edge and saliency are also applied to supervise the output side path to improve the resulting saliency maps.

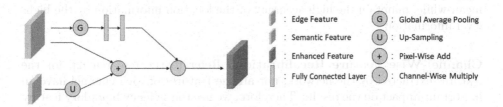

Fig. 2. The Framework of Edge Recalibration Module.

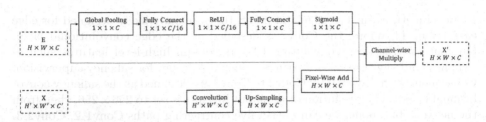

Fig. 3. The Sketch Map of Edge Recalibration Module. E denotes the edge feature map and X denotes the four saliency feature maps. X' denotes the edge recalibration feature map.

2.2   Edge Recalibration Module

The framework of edge recalibration module can be illustrated in Fig. 2, which includes the pixel-wise semantic-edge integration and the channel-wise feature recalibration. In consider of the complementarity between salient object boundary features and salient object features, the salient boundary features can be used for enhancing the salient object features, aiming to improve the performance of the network. As mentioned in Subsect. 2.1, the boundary features are extracted in shallow layer and the saliency features are extracted in deep layers. Compared with the deep layers, the information in shallow layer is disorganized, which is hard to filter out the useful information. Therefore, to recalibrate the edge, we combine attention mechanism and edge enhancement module. The sketch map of edge recalibration module is shown in Fig. 3.

Pixel-Wise Semantic-Edge Integration. According to the baseline network, the boundary features O^{Edge} and saliency features O^{Sal_i} can be obtained. Pixel-wise semantic-edge integration aims to incorporate boundary features O^{Edge} and semantic saliency features O^{Sal_i} on pixel dimension as follows:

$$F_{add}^i = Up(\varphi(Trans(O^{Sal_i}; \Theta))) + O^{Edge} \tag{5}$$

where, $Trans(*; \Theta)$ denotes the feature channel conversion convolutional function and Θ is the parameters. $\varphi(*)$ denotes ReLU function. The fusion features F_{add}^i improve the segmentation details of the salient object in the edge region, mean-while, maintain the high accuracy of the location information by the high-level information.

Channel-Wise Feature Recalibration. Refer to the research [2], for the features extracted by the network, not all the features of each channel have an important impact on the results. Therefore, we use the saliency boundary feature to recalibrate the channel dimension, and further enhance the saliency features. The experimental results verify the statement.

As illustrated in Fig. 2, besides the pixel-wise semantic-edge integration, the boundary features are also used as the input of the global average pooling layer to extract the global embedding information. Then, the extracted global information passes through two full connection layers to get channel recalibration weights. The weighted features of the channel dimension are used as the final output of the edge recalibration module.

As shown in Fig. 3, the size of the fusion features F^i_{add} and boundary features O^{Edge} is expressed as $H \times W \times C$, H. W and C are the height, width and channel of the feature maps. The size of channel-wise feature recalibration Z_c obtained from the boundary features O^{Edge} can be expressed as $1 \times 1 \times C$. The process of channel-wise feature recalibration Z_c can be denoted as:

$$Z_c = \sigma(f_2(\varphi(f_1(P^{avg}(O^{Edge}); \Theta_1)); \Theta_2)) \tag{6}$$

where, P^{avg} denotes global average pooling layer. $f_1(*; \Theta_1)$ and $f_2(*; \Theta_2)$ denote the fully connected layers, Θ_1 and Θ_2 denote the relevant parameters. $\sigma(*)$ denotes Sigmoid function. After that, Z_c and F^i_{add} can be fused as F^i_o:

$$F^i_o = Z_c \cdot F^i_{add} \tag{7}$$

where, the operator $\cdot$ represents the multiplication of channel wise. The final result can be denoted as:

$$\mathbb{Y} = F^{out}(Up(\sum_{i=2}^{5} F^i_o); \Theta^{out}) \tag{8}$$

Besides, the fully connected layers $f_1(*; \Theta_1)$ and $f_2(*; \Theta_2)$ are designed as the bottleneck structure, which can be shown in Fig. 3. The edge enhancement module uses full connection layer $f_1(*; \Theta_1)$ to reduce dimension of input features. Meanwhile, the full connection layer $f_2(*; \Theta_2)$ is used to generate channel recalibration weights for channel dimension weighting. Benefitted from the special design, the two fully connected layers can effectively reduce the large parameters produced by the traditional full connection layer. Therefore, the proposed edge recalibration module is lightweight, which only brings a small increase to the complexity and the computational costs of the overall network.

2.3   Loss Function

In this paper, the total loss function is divided into saliency loss function and edge loss function. To be fair, similar to other methods, we adopt cross-entropy loss function to supervise the results of each output, including outputs of baseline network, outputs of edge recalibration module and the final result. Cross-entropy loss function can be calculated as:

$$\mathbb{L}^{Sal} = -\frac{1}{M \times N} \sum_{i=1}^{M} \sum_{j=1}^{N} (\widehat{y}_{ij} \log y_{ij} + (1 - \widehat{y}_{ij}) \log(1 - y_{ij})) \tag{9}$$

where, y_{ij} and $\widehat{y}_{ij}$ denote the results of ERN and the ground truth at the location (i, j). y_{ij} can belong to O^{Sal_i}, F^i_o and $\mathbb{Y}$.

Motivated by the effective applications of IoU boundary loss [6], the edge loss can be calculated as:

$$\mathbb{L}^{Edge} = 1 - \frac{2|O^{Edge} \cap \widehat{O}^{Edge}|}{|O^{Edge}| + |\widehat{O}^{Edge}|} \tag{10}$$

where, O^{Edge} and $\widehat{O}^{Edge}$ denote the final edge saliency map and the edge ground truth and of ERN respectively. The total loss is shown as:

$$\mathbb{L} = \mathbb{L}^{Sal} + \mathbb{L}^{Edge} \tag{11}$$

3   Experimental Results

3.1   Datasets and Evaluation Metric

The performance of ERN is evaluated on five benchmark testing datasets: ECSSD, HKU-IS, PASCAL-S, DUT-OMRON and DUTS. ECSSD includes 1000 challenging complex images. HKU-IS has 4447 meaningful and complex semantic images. PASCAL-S has 850 images. DUT-OMRON contains 5168 difficult images and DUTS has 5019 images.

Similar to other methods, two widely-used metrics F-measure and Mean Absolute Error (MAE) are applied to evaluate ERN and other methods. F-measure can be calculated as:

$$F_\beta = \frac{(1 + \beta^2) Precision \times Recall}{\beta^2 \times Precision + Recall} \tag{12}$$

where, precision and recall denote the ratio of detected salient pixels in the predicted saliency map and the ground truth map respectively. β^2 is set to 0.3 as other methods do. MAE can be calculated as:

$$MAE = \frac{1}{M \times N} \sum_{i=1}^{M} \sum_{j=1}^{N} |y_{ij} - \widehat{y}_{ij}| \tag{13}$$

3.2   Implementation Details

ERN is trained on DUTS training dataset followed by [6,12]. The validation dataset is not used in this paper followed by [6]. We train ERN for 30 epochs, and cross-entropy loss is applied to supervise the results of the proposed ERN. During the process of training, the learning rate is set to 5e−5 and reduced to one tenth for every 12 epochs. The weights of the rest part in ERN are initialized randomly. In addition, to reduce the over-fitting, we set the weight decay to 5e−4. Different from previous methods, we do not use the data augmentation techniques.

Table 1. Ablation studies on five testing datasets. Baseline denotes the U-net structure with output side paths and ERM denotes the edge recalibration module.

Methods	ECSSD		HKU-IS		PASCAL-S		DUT-O		DUTS-Test	
	maxF	MAE	maxF	MAE	maxF	MAE	maxF	MAE	maxF	MAE
Baseline	0.845	0.111	0.830	0.102	0.754	0.145	0.682	0.144	0.737	0.122
ERM	**0.948**	**0.038**	**0.938**	**0.032**	**0.872**	**0.074**	**0.841**	**0.055**	**0.895**	**0.038**

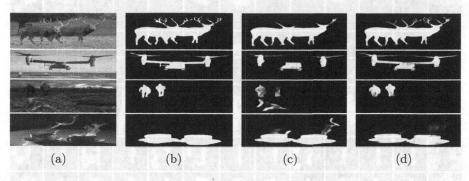

(a)　　　　　　　(b)　　　　　　　(c)　　　　　　　(d)

Fig. 4. Visual Comparison of Resulting Saliency Map with and without ERM. (a) Image. (b) Ground Truth. (c) Without ERM. (d) With ERM.

3.3　Ablation Studies

To demonstrate the effectiveness of the proposed each module in ERN, we train the U-net structure with output side path and the U-net structure with output side paths and edge recalibration module on the training dataset DUTS respectively. During the process of the comparison, the hyperparameters and the implementation details are unchanged.

As illustrated in Table 1, the scores of edge recalibration module added have significant improvement. In a specific, compared with the baseline network, edge recalibration module increases 12.2% and 65.8% under the metrics of max F-measure and MAE on ECSSD dataset. On HKU-IS dataset, ERM increases 13.0% and 68.6%, and on the PASCAL-S dataset, ERM increases 15.6% and 49.0%. On DUT-OMRON dataset, ERM increases 23.3% and 61.8%. On DUTS-test dataset, ERM increases 21.4% and 68.9%. The experimental results prove that the proposed edge recalibration module improve the resulting saliency maps with a huge leap. In addition, as shown in Fig. 4, ERM detects segmentation details more completely and filters out the noises and the interferences.

3.4　Comparison with State-of-the-Art Methods

We compare the proposed ERN method with ten state-of-the-art methods in recent three years: Amulet [10], UCF [15], NLDF [6], SRM [11], RAN [14], C2S [18], BMPM [19], HRSOD [16], DSS [8] and AFNet [12].

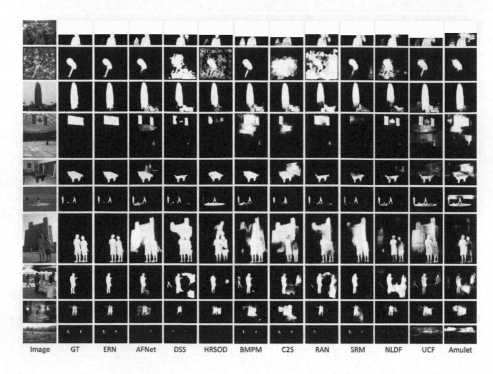

Image   GT   ERN   AFNet   DSS   HRSOD   BMPM   C2S   RAN   SRM   NLDF   UCF   Amulet

Fig. 5. Compared with State-of-the-art Methods.

Visual Comparison. As illustrated in Fig. 5, we compare ERN with other state-of-the-art methods. Obviously, the resulting saliency maps of ERN outperforms other methods, which are closer to the ground truth in visual. In a specific, (1) With the help of output side path in U-net structure, ERN constrains the obtained features and filters interference of images. (2) ERN recalibrates the object edges more accurate benefitted from the edge recalibration module. For instance, in the 9th rows of Fig. 5, ERN maintain the edge better such as the arms of the two persons. Similarly, in the 6, 7, 8, 10 rows of Fig. 5, ERN not only detects the saliency maps more accurate, but also obtains the better object edges. (3) By the aid of complementarity of saliency features and boundary features, ERN generates the resulting saliency maps more accurate and complete than other methods even though in the complex background (see Fig. 5 the 1, 2, 7–10 rows). (4) Benefitted from the complementarity of boundary features and saliency features, ERN is able to filter interference and noise in images (see Fig. 5 the 3, 4, 5 rows). (5) Compared with other methods, ERN highlights the useful salient object and suppresses the useless background better.

Quantitative Comparison. As illustrated in Table 2, ERN is compared with ten state-of-the-art methods on five widely-used and challenging testing datasets in terms of max F-measure and MAE. It can be found that the proposed ERN

Table 2. Comparing with state-of-the-art methods. The best three results are shown in Bold, italic and bold italic. The – denotes the authors do not provide the related data.

Methods	ECSSD		HKU-IS		PASCAL-S		DUT-O		DUTS-Test	
	maxF	MAE	maxF	MAE	maxF	MAE	maxF	MAE	maxF	MAE
Amulet [10]	0.868	0.058	0.854	0.052	0.763	0.098	0.647	0.098	0.737	0.085
UCF [15]	0.852	0.069	0.823	0.062	0.741	0.116	0.628	0.120	0.791	0.111
NLDF [6]	0.905	0.063	0.902	0.048	0.831	0.099	0.753	0.080	–	–
SRM [11]	0.892	0.056	0.874	0.046	0.845	0.084	0.707	0.069	0.846	0.058
RAN [14]	0.918	0.059	0.913	0.045	0.834	0.104	0.786	*0.062*	0.839	0.059
C2S [18]	0.910	0.054	0.896	0.048	0.761	0.089	0.757	0.071	0.807	0.062
BMPM [19]	*0.928*	*0.044*	*0.920*	0.038	*0.862*	*0.074*	*0.793*	0.064	*0.850*	*0.049*
HRSOD [16]	0.923	0.052	0.891	*0.037*	0.848	*0.079*	0.732	0.065	0.796	0.051
DSS [8]	0.915	0.052	0.913	0.039	0.830	0.080	0.770	0.063	–	–
AFNet [12]	*0.935*	*0.042*	*0.923*	*0.036*	*0.868*	**0.071**	*0.797*	*0.057*	*0.862*	*0.046*
ERN	**0.948**	**0.038**	**0.938**	**0.032**	**0.872**	*0.074*	**0.841**	**0.055**	**0.895**	**0.038**

model wins on most testing datasets and gets the best two results on all the testing datasets under the metrics, which verifies the effectiveness and accuracy of the proposed ERN model. To be specific, compared with the suboptimal method on ECSSD dataset, ERN increases 1.4% and 9.5% under max F-measure and MAE respectively. On HKU-IS dataset, ERN increases 1.6% and 11.1%. On PASCAL-S dataset, ERN increases 0.5% under the metric of max F-measure, and is close to the best result under MAE. On DUT-OMRON dataset, ERN increases 5.5% and 3.5% respectively. On DUTS-Test dataset, ERN increases

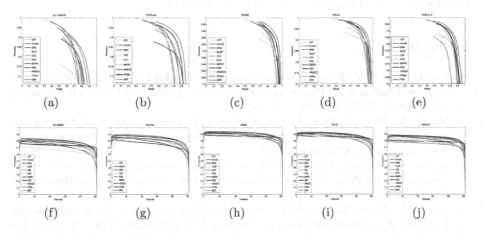

(a)   (b)   (c)   (d)   (e)

(f)   (g)   (h)   (i)   (j)

Fig. 6. Quantitative Comparisons. Quantitative comparisons of the proposed ERN model and ten state-of-the-art learning-based SOD approaches on five most applied test datasets. The first row are PR curves and the second row are the F-measure curves.

3.8% and 17.4% under the metrcis of max F-measure and MAE. Obviously, ERN significantly improves the resulting saliency maps compared with previous methods.

In addition, as shown in Fig. 6, the Precision-Recall curves and F-measure curves verify the statement. In a specific, on PR curves, ERN is overall superior to previous methods, which is closer to the upper right of the figure. On the F-measure curves, ERN also outperforms other methods.

4   Conclusion

In this paper, a novel Edge Recalibration Network is proposed for accurate salient object detection. By the aid of the proposed baseline network, ERN incorporate multi-scale features with multiple receptive fields. To locate the edge position and recalibrate boundary features, we propose an edge recalibration module with pixel-wise semantic-edge integration and channel-wise feature recalibration. With the help of pixel-wise semantic-edge integration, the fusion features improve the segmentation details of the salient object in the edge region, meanwhile, maintain the high accuracy of the location information by the high-level information. Benefitted from channel-wise feature recalibration, we recalibrate the channel dimension and further enhance the saliency features. Based on the edge recalibration module, the useful features are enhanced and the useless features are suppressed. Experimental results on five widely-used testing datasets show that ERN outperforms other methods under two standard metrics. The visual comparison verifies the results as well.

Acknowledgements. This work was supported in part by National Natural Science Foundation of China under grant 61771145 and 61371148.

References

1. Lee, G., Tai, Y.W., Kim, J.: Deep saliency with encoded low-level distance map and high-level features. In: Proceedings of Computer Vision and Pattern Recognition, pp. 660–668. IEEE, Las Vegas (2016)
2. Wang, W., Zhao, S., Shen, J.: Salient object detection with pyramid attention and salient edges. In: Proceedings of Computer Vision and Pattern Recognition. pp. 1448–1457. IEEE, California (2019)
3. Karen, S., Andrew, Z.: Very deep convolutional networks for large-scale image recognition. In: Proceedings of International Conference on Learning Representations, San Diego (2015)
4. He, K.M., Zhang, X., Ren, S.Q.: Deep residual learning for image recognition. In: Proceedings of Computer Vision and Pattern Recognition, pp. 770–778. IEEE, Las Vegas (2016)
5. Ronneberger, O., Fischer, P., Brox, T.: U-Net: convolutional networks for biomedical image segmentation. In: Navab, N., Hornegger, J., Wells, W.M., Frangi, A.F. (eds.) MICCAI 2015. LNCS, vol. 9351, pp. 234–241. Springer, Cham (2015). https://doi.org/10.1007/978-3-319-24574-4_28

6. Luo, Z., Mishra, A., Achkar, A.: Non-local deep features for salient object detection. In: Proceedings of Computer Vision and Pattern Recognition, pp. 6609–6617. IEEE, Hawaii (2017)

7. Zhao, T., Wu, X.: Pyramid feature attention network for saliency detection. In: Proceedings of the IEEE Conference on Computer Vision and Pattern Recognition, pp. 3085–3094. IEEE, California (2019)

8. Hou, Q., Cheng, M., Hu, X., Borji, A.: Deeply supervised salient object detection with short connections. IEEE Trans. Pattern Anal. Mach. Intell. (2019)

9. Wang, T., Zhang, L., Wang, S., Lu, H.: Detect globally, refine locally: a novel approach to saliency detection. In: Proceedings of Computer Vision and Pattern Recognition, pp. 3127–3135. IEEE, Salt Lake (2018)

10. Zhang, P., Wang, D., Lu, H., Wang, H.: Amulet: aggregating multi-level convolutional features for salient object detection. In: Proceedings of International Conference on Computer Vision, pp. 202–211. IEEE, Venice (2017)

11. Wang, T., Borji, A., Zhang, L.: A stagewise refinement model for detecting salient objects in images. In: Proceedings of International Conference on Computer Vision, pp. 4019–4028. IEEE, Venice (2017)

12. Feng, M., Lu, H., Ding, E.: Attentive feedback network for boundary-aware salient object detection. In: Proceedings of Computer Vision and Pattern Recognition, pp. 1623–1632. IEEE, California (2019)

13. Zhang, X., Wang, T., Qi, J., Lu, H., Wang, G.: Progressive attention guided recurrent network for salient object detection. In: Proceedings of Conference on Computer Vision and Pattern Recognition, pp. 714–722. IEEE, Salt Lake (2018)

14. Chen, S., Tan, X., Wang, B., Hu, X.: Reverse attention for salient object detection. In: Ferrari, V., Hebert, M., Sminchisescu, C., Weiss, Y. (eds.) ECCV 2018. LNCS, vol. 11213, pp. 236–252. Springer, Cham (2018). https://doi.org/10.1007/978-3-030-01240-3_15

15. Zhang, P., Wang, D., Lu, H., Wang H., Yin, B.: Learning uncertain convolutional features for accurate saliency detection. In: Proceedings of International Conference on Computer Vision, pp. 212–221. IEEE, Venice (2017)

16. Zeng, Y., Zhang, P.: Towards high-resolution salient object detection. In: Proceedings of International Conference on Computer Vision, pp. 7234–7243. IEEE, Seoul (2019)

17. Zhao, J., Liu, J., Fan, D., Cao, Y., Yang, J., Cheng, M.: EGNet: edge guidance network for salient object detection. In: Proceedings of Conference on Computer Vision, pp. 8779–8788. IEEE, Seoul (2019)

18. Li, X., Yang, F., Cheng, H., Liu, W., Shen, D.: Contour knowledge transfer for salient object detection. In: Ferrari, V., Hebert, M., Sminchisescu, C., Weiss, Y. (eds.) ECCV 2018. LNCS, vol. 11219, pp. 370–385. Springer, Cham (2018). https://doi.org/10.1007/978-3-030-01267-0_22

19. Zhang, L., Dai, J., Lu, H., He, Y., Wang, G.: A bi-directional message passing model for salient object detection. In: Proceedings of Computer Vision and Pattern Recognition. pp. 1741–1750. IEEE, Salt Lake (2018)

20. Li, Z., Peng, C., Yu, G., Sun, J.: Detnet: a backbone network for object detection. In: Proceedings of European Conference on Computer Vision. Springer, Munich (2018)

Multi-Scale Cross-Modal Spatial Attention Fusion for Multi-label Image Recognition

Junbing Li[1], Changqing Zhang[1(✉)], Xueman Wang[2], and Ling Du[2]

[1] College of Intelligence and Computing, Tianjin University, Tianjin 300350, China
{lijunbing,zhangchangqing}@tju.edu.cn
[2] School of Computer Science and Technology, Tiangong University,
Tianjin 300387, China
xuemanwang@tiangong.edu.cn, duling@tjpu.edu.cn

Abstract. Multi-label image recognition aims to jointly predict multiple tags for an image. Despite great progress achieved, there are still two limitations for existing methods: 1) can not accurately locate the object regions due to the lack of adequate supervision information or semantic guidance; 2) can not effectively identify the target categories of small-size object due to only employing the high-level feature of deep CNN. In this paper, we propose a Multi-Scale Cross-Modal Spatial Attention Fusion (MCSAF) network to accurately locate more informative regions by introducing a spatial attention module, and our model can effectively recognize target classes of different scales with multi-scale cross-modal feature fusion. Furthermore, we develop an adaptive graph convolutional network (Adaptive-GCN) to capture the complex correlations among labels in depth. Empirical studies on benchmark datasets validate the superiority of our proposed model over state-of-the-art methods.

Keywords: Multi-label image recognition · Multi-Scale · Spatial Attention · Cross-Modal · Adaptive-GCN

1 Introduction

Recognizing accurately multiple tags for an image is still a challenging task in computer vision, which can be applied to many fields such as image annotation [23], medical diagnosis classification [8] and human attribute recognition [14]. Compared with the task of predicting one single label for an image [5], the task of multi-label image recognition is more difficult due to the exponential label output space.

Apparently, there is a straightforward idea for multi-label classification to transform the multilabel problem into a set of binary classification tasks. However, this strategy ignores the underlying label correlations which can effectively reduce the label output space and improve the prediction accuracy in practice. It motivates another line of researches which focuses on effectively capturing

© Springer Nature Switzerland AG 2020
I. Farkaš et al. (Eds.): ICANN 2020, LNCS 12396, pp. 736–747, 2020.
https://doi.org/10.1007/978-3-030-61609-0_58

the interdependency among labels, including structured inference network [11], probabilistic graphical models [13], and Recurrent Neural Networks (RNNs) [19].

Recently, Some representative approaches implicitly model the label correlations by introducing the attention mechanisms [9,20,26]. Wang *et al.* [20] proposed a spatial transformer layer to locate important regions on the convolutional maps and employed LSTMs to explore the label correlation. Zhu *et al.* [26] developed the spatial regularization net to locate the object regions and further exploited label correlation of these regions by self-attention. Guo *et al.* [9] defined the attention consistency assumption and designed a two-branch network with an original image and its transformed image as inputs.

Despite the significant improvements achieved by previous attention-based methods, current approaches still exist some limitations, more concretely: 1) can not accurately locate the object regions due to the lack of adequate supervision information or semantic guidance; 2) can not effectively identify the target categories of small-size object due to only employing the high-level feature (*e.g.* the feature map from "conv5_x" layer of ResNet-101).

To address these two crucial problems, in this paper, we proposed a Multi-Scale Cross-Modal Spatial Attention Fusion (MCSAF) network for image multi-label recognition. The overview of MCSAF is illustrated in Fig. 1. On the one hand, we firstly introduce a spatial attention module to locate the more informative and important part in each feature map of different scale. Then, we adopt global average-pooling and max-pooling strategies to aggregate spatial attention information from different views, generating two types of vectors. These two types of vectors are added to generate a more efficient global feature descriptor. On the other hand, we extend graph convolutional network (GCN) [12] to Adaptive-GCN to capture the correlations among labels in depth and obtain label re-embeddings using label word embedding vectors as input. Finally, the two cross-modal representations, *i.e.* global feature descriptor and label re-embeddings, are efficiently fused by computing their correlation scores for multi-label prediction. Benefited from the semantic guidance of label re-embedding and cross-modal feature fusion, our MCSAF is able to accurately locate more informative object regions.

Moreover, inspired by the effectiveness of multi-scale deep CNN feature in object detection [1,16], we conduct cross-modal feature fusion on multiple global feature descriptors corresponding to feature maps with different scales and multiple label re-embeddings from different layers of Adaptive-GCN, which enables our MCSAF to accurately identify target objects of different sizes. The intuition is that lower network layer (*e.g.* "conv3_x" of ResNet-101) has smaller receptive fields so that it can identify small objects more accurately. On the contrary, higher layer (*e.g.* "conv5_x" of ResNet-101) is more suitable for the recognition of large objects. Therefore, the satisfactory multi-label classifiers at different output layers are combined to form a strong multi-scale multi-label classifier.

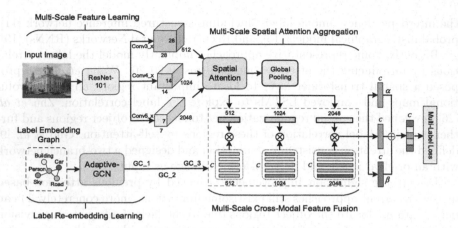

Fig. 1. Overview of our proposed MCSAF. MCSAF consists of four modules: (1) Image Multi-Scale Feature Learning, (2) Label Re-embedding Learning, (3) Multi-Scale Spatial Attention Aggregation and (4) Multi-Scale Cross-Modal Feature Fusion. The key of our model is to conduct both multi-scale spatial attention aggregation and multi-scale cross-modal feature fusion, which promotes the proposed MCSAF to accurately locate more informative regions and effectively recognize target objects of different sizes. Furthermore, we build an Adaptive-GCN to capture the complex label correlation in depth.

For clarification, the main contributions of this paper are summarized as follows:

- We propose a novel Multi-Scale Cross-Modal Spatial Attention Fusion (MCSAF) network for multi-label image recognition, which can accurately locate more informative object regions by introducing a spatial attention module and performing cross-modal feature fusion.
- We conduct cross-modal feature fusion on multiple global feature descriptors and multiple label re-embeddings (multi-scale cross-modal feature fusion), which promotes our model to accurately recognize target objects of different sizes.
- We further develop an Adaptive-GCN to exploit the label inter-dependency in depth, which updates the label correlation matrix adaptively with label embedding propagating by a graph convolution layer.
- Extensive experiments on benchmark datasets demonstrate the superiority of our proposed method over state-of-the-arts.

2   Our Method

In this section, we will methodically introduce our proposed MCSAF for multi-label image recognition. MCSAF consists of four modules: (1) Image Multi-Scale Feature Learning, (2) Label Re-embedding Learning, (3) Multi-Scale Spatial Attention Aggregation and (4) Multi-Scale Cross-Modal Feature Fusion. Firstly, we explain the way to obtain image multi-scale feature representation and label re-embedding matrix. Then, we describe the process of multi-scale spatial attention aggregation. Finally, multi-scale cross-modal feature fusion for multi-label prediction is illustrated in detail.

2.1 Image Multi-Scale Feature Learning

To obtain the consistency between the sizes of objects and receptive fields as far as possible, the feature map of lower and higher network layers should be effectively integrated. There are some different effective deep CNN structures [10,18] for image feature extraction. Following [2,26], we use ResNet-101 [10] as our base model, which consists of repetitive building blocks with different output dimensions. Specifically, we employ the output of "conv3_x", "conv4_x" and "conv5_x" layer as the multi-scale feature representation of our model. Let I denotes an image with the 448×448 resolution as input, we can obtain three feature maps with different scale from the "conv3_x", "conv4_x" and "conv5_x" layer by

$$F_i = f_{cnn}(I; \theta^i_{cnn}) \in \mathbb{R}^{D_i \times H_i \times W_i}, i \in \{1, 2, 3\}. \tag{1}$$

where F_1, F_2 and F_3 denote the feature map from "conv3_x", "conv4_x" and "conv5_x" layer, respectively. $D_1 \times H_1 \times W_1 = 512 \times 56 \times 56$, $D_2 \times H_2 \times W_2 = 1024 \times 28 \times 28$ and $D_3 \times H_3 \times W_3 = 2048 \times 14 \times 14$. We also consider $F_1(F_2, F_3)$ as $M_1(M_2, M_3)$ spatial locations and each one corresponds to a $D_1(D_2, D_3)$-dimensional visual feature vector, where $M_1 = H_1 \times W_1$, $M_2 = H_2 \times W_2$ and $M_3 = H_3 \times W_3$.

2.2 Adaptive-GCN for Label Re-embedding Learning

It is crucial to effectively capture the correlation among labels for the task of multi-label image recognition. In this work, we utilize the graph structure to model the correlations among labels. Specifically, inspired by the rapid development of Graph Convolutional Network (GCN) [12] in recent years, different from [4] which uses the original GCN directly, we propose an Adaptive-GCN for complex label correlation exploration. For clarification, we firstly introduce some preliminary knowledge of GCN, and then describe the proposed Adaptive-GCN in detail.

Preliminaries of GCN. Graph Convolutional Network (GCN) [12] updates the node (label) representation by propagating information between nodes (semantic label in our task). A graph convolution layer takes a feature matrix $X \in \mathbb{R}^{C \times d}$ with an adjacency matrix $A \in \mathbb{R}^{C \times C}$ as input, and outputs an updated feature matrix $Y \in \mathbb{R}^{C \times d'}$, where C, d and d' are the number of classes, the dimensionality of the original and updated node feature, respectively. Specifically, a graph convolution layer updates the node (label) representation by

$$Y = h(\widehat{A}XW), \tag{2}$$

where $\widehat{A} \in \mathbb{R}^{C \times C}$ is the normalized version of adjacency matrix A and $W \in \mathbb{R}^{d \times d'}$ is a transformation weight matrix to be learned, and $h(\cdot)$ denotes a non-linear activation function.

Adaptive-GCN. To explore the label semantic dependency in depth and bind to multi-scale feature from deep CNN more effectively, we propose an Adaptive-GCN for label re-embedding learning. The adaptiveness of our proposed Adaptive-GCN behaves in following two aspects: 1) the label correlation matrix (node adjacency matrix) is updated adaptively with label embedding propagating by a graph convolution layer; 2) the numbers of GCN layers and output dimensions are adaptive to match multi-scale visual features.

To be specific, Adaptive-GCN consists of three graph convolution layers of different output dimensions, which is determined by the dimensionality of multi-scale visual feature $F_1(F_2, F_3)$ on each spatial location. Each node (label) on the graph is associated with a word embedding vector obtained by the GloVe model [17] trained on the Wikipedia dataset. An adaptive graph convolution layer can be defined as

$$Y = h([X||A_a X]W),\tag{3}$$

where $A_a \in \mathbb{R}^{C \times C}$ is the adaptive label correlation matrix, and we express the degree of correlation between labels by computing cosine similarity of node features. That is, $A_a(i,j) = \cos(X_i, X_j)$. Operator $||$ denotes matrix concatenation along the feature direction. $W \in \mathbb{R}^{2d \times d'}$ is the learnable weight matrix and $h(\cdot)$ is the non-linear activation function.

In our Adaptive-GCN, the input label embedding matrix (in the first layer of Adaptive-GCN) is the original label word embedding feature matrix $X \in \mathbb{R}^{C \times d}$. As the label re-embedding learning by three graph convolution layers, we can obtain multiple label re-embedding matrixs $L_1 \in \mathbb{R}^{C \times D_1}$, $L_2 \in \mathbb{R}^{C \times D_2}$ and $L_3 \in \mathbb{R}^{C \times D_3}$ as output, where $D_1 = 512$, $D_2 = 1024$ and $D_3 = 2048$ denote the dimensionality of multi-scale visual feature F_1, F_2 and F_3 on each spatial location.

2.3   Multi-Scale Spatial Attention Aggregation

With the multi-scale feature maps from different layers of ResNet-101 [10] obtained, we introduce a spatial attention module [22] to focus on more informative regions for each feature map of different scale. For brevity, we firstly consider the spatial attention aggregation of single-scale feature (*e.g.* F_1). Specifically, we apply the average-pooling and max-pooling operations along the channel axis, generating two 2D maps: $F_1^{avg} \in \mathbb{R}^{1 \times H_1 \times W_1}$ and $F_1^{max} \in \mathbb{R}^{1 \times H_1 \times W_1}$. Then, these two 2D maps F_1^{avg} and F_1^{max} are concatenated and convolved by a standard convolution layer, producing the 2D spatial attention map. Accordingly, the spatial attention map is computed as:

$$\begin{aligned}M_s(F_1) &= \sigma(f^{7 \times 7}([AvgPool(F_1); MaxPool(F_1)]))\\&= \sigma(f^{7 \times 7}([F_1^{avg}; F_1^{max}])),\end{aligned}\tag{4}$$

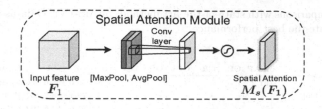

Fig. 2. The structure of spatial attention module.

where σ is the sigmoid activation function and $f^{7\times 7}$ denotes a convolution operation with the filter size of 7×7. Once the spatial attention map $M_s(F_1) \in \mathbb{R}^{1 \times H_1 \times W_1}$ obtained, we derive the spatial attention aggregation feature map by

$$F_1^s = F_1 \odot M_s(F_1), \tag{5}$$

where $\odot$ denotes element-wise multiplication. Furthermore, We can obtain the other two spatial attention aggregation feature maps F_2^s and F_3^s in the same way. Figure 2 illustrates the structure of introduced spatial attention module.

2.4 Multi-Scale Cross-Modal Feature Fusion

After obtaining the multi-scale spatial attention feature maps, global average-pooling and max-pooling operations are conducted to produce two types of vectors. Then, we add these two vectors to obtain multiple image-level feature vector of different dimension:

$$v_i = f_{GAP}(F_i^s) + f_{GMP}(F_i^s) \in \mathbb{R}^{D_i}, i \in \{1,2,3\}. \tag{6}$$

With the multi-scale global spatial attention feature vectors v_i and label re-embeddings L_i from different layers of Adaptive-GCN obtained, we further integrate the two cross-modal representations by computing their correlation scores for multi-label prediction. Specially, multiple cross-modal feature fusion scores are obtained by

$$\hat{y}_i = L_i v_i \in \mathbb{R}^C, i \in \{1,2,3\}. \tag{7}$$

To effectively balance the contribution of different scale cross-modal feature fusion, we set two equilibrium factors α and β on $\hat{y}_2$ and $\hat{y}_1$. Accordingly, the final multi-label prediction scores is obtained as $\hat{y} = \hat{y}_3 + \alpha\hat{y}_2 + \beta\hat{y}_1$. Assume that a training image with ground-truth labels $\mathbf{y} \in \mathbb{R}^C$, where $y^i = 1(0)$ indicates the ith label is (not) associated with this image. The proposed model is trained in the end-to-end manner by the cross-entropy classification loss as follows:

$$\mathcal{L} = \sum_{c=1}^{C} y^c \log(\sigma(\hat{y}^c)) + (1 - y^c) \log(1 - \sigma(\hat{y}^c)), \tag{8}$$

where σ is the sigmoid activation function.

Table 1. Comparisons with state-of-the-art methods on MS-COCO dataset. The values in bold indicate the best performance.

Methods	All							Top-3					
	mAP	CP	CR	CF1	OP	OR	OF1	CP	CR	CF1	OP	OR	OF1
CNN-RNN [19]	61.2	–	–	–	–	–	–	66.0	55.6	60.4	69.2	**66.4**	67.8
RNN-Attention [20]	–	–	–	–	–	–	–	79.1	58.7	67.4	84.0	63.0	72.0
Order-Free RNN [2]	–	–	–	–	–	–	–	71.6	54.8	62.1	74.2	62.2	67.7
SRN [26]	77.1	81.6	65.4	71.2	82.7	69.9	75.8	85.2	58.8	67.4	87.4	62.5	72.9
Multi-Evidence [7]	–	80.4	**70.2**	74.9	85.2	72.5	78.4	84.5	**62.2**	70.6	89.1	64.3	74.7
ACfs [9]	77.5	77.4	68.3	72.2	79.8	**73.1**	76.3	85.2	59.4	68.0	86.6	63.3	73.1
ResNet-101 (Baseline) [10]	77.3	80.2	66.7	72.8	83.9	70.8	76.8	84.1	59.4	69.7	89.1	62.8	73.6
MCSAF	**81.3**	**84.8**	67.8	**75.4**	**87.4**	71.9	**78.9**	**87.9**	61.0	**72.0**	91.4	64.2	**75.4**

3   Experiments

3.1   Implementation Details

We adopt ResNet-101 [10] as the feature extractor, which is pre-trained on ImageNet [5]. To get the label embedding vectors as the input of our Adaptive-GCN, we employ the GloVe model [17] trained on the Wikipedia and produce a 300-dimension vector for each label. Furthermore, we obtain the word embeddings of classes with multiple words by averaging their word embeddings. The Adaptive-GCN is composed of three graph convolution layers with output dimensionality of 512, 1024 and 2048. The input images are randomly cropped and resized into 448×448 with random horizontal flips for data augmentation. For optimization, SGD with momentum of 0.9 is used as the network optimizer. The initial learning rate is 0.0001, batch size is set 16 and weight decay is 10^{-4}.

3.2   Evaluation Metrics

Following [4,7,19,26], we report the overall precision, recall, F1 (OP, OR, OF1) and the per-class precision, recall, F1 (CP, CR, CF1) for performance evaluation. Particularly, to fairly compare with other methods [7,26], we also report the results of top-3 labels with highest confidences. In addition, the average precision (AP) for each label and mean average precision (mAP) over all categories are also employed for performance comparisons. For each image, the predicted labels with confidence greater than 0.5 are assigned as positive.

3.3   Experimental Results

Results on MS-COCO. MS-COCO [15] is a widely used benchmark dataset for multi-label image recognition. The training set consists of 82, 081 images and the validation set is composed of 40, 504 images. MS-COCO covers 80 common object categories with about 2.9 labels per image on average. As the ground truth labels of the test set are not available, the performance of all the methods are evaluated on the validation set.

Table 2. Comparisons with state-of-the-art methods in terms of AP and mAP on VOC 2007 dataset. The values in bold indicate the best performance.

Methods	Aero	Bike	Bird	Boat	Bottle	Bus	Car	Cat	Chair	Cow	Table	Dog	Horse	Motor	Person	Plant	Sheep	Sofa	Train	Tv	mAP
CNN-RNN [19]	96.7	83.1	94.2	92.8	61.2	82.1	89.1	94.2	64.2	83.6	70.0	92.4	91.7	84.2	93.7	59.8	93.2	75.3	**99.7**	78.6	84.0
RLSD [25]	96.4	92.7	93.8	94.1	71.2	92.5	94.2	95.7	74.3	90.0	74.2	95.4	96.2	92.1	97.9	66.9	93.5	73.7	97.5	87.6	88.5
FeV+LV [24]	97.9	97.0	96.6	94.6	73.6	93.9	96.5	95.5	73.7	90.3	82.8	95.4	97.7	95.9	98.6	77.6	88.7	78.0	98.3	89.0	90.6
HCP [21]	98.6	97.1	98.0	95.6	75.3	**94.7**	95.8	97.3	73.1	90.2	80.0	97.3	96.1	94.9	96.3	78.3	94.7	76.2	97.9	91.5	90.9
RNN-Attention [20]	98.6	97.4	96.3	96.2	75.2	92.4	96.5	97.1	76.5	92.0	**87.7**	96.8	97.5	93.8	98.5	**81.6**	93.7	82.8	98.6	89.3	91.9
Atten-Reinforce [3]	98.6	97.1	97.1	95.5	75.6	92.8	**96.8**	97.3	**78.3**	92.2	87.6	96.9	96.5	93.6	98.5	81.6	93.1	**83.2**	98.5	89.3	92.0
ResNet-101 (Baseline) [10]	99.5	97.7	97.8	96.4	65.7	91.8	96.1	97.6	74.2	80.9	85.0	**98.4**	96.5	95.9	98.4	70.1	88.3	80.2	98.9	89.2	89.9
MCSAF	**99.8**	**98.0**	**98.1**	**98.3**	76.7	93.2	95.9	**97.7**	77.2	**92.7**	87.0	97.8	**97.8**	95.4	98.5	76.2	**96.1**	80.7	98.9	**91.9**	**92.4**

Quantitative results of MS-COCO are presented in Table 1. We use the ResNet-101 [10] as baseline model and compare our proposed model with the state-of-the-art approaches, including CNN-RNN [19], RNN-Attention [20], Order-Free RNN [2], SRN [26], Multi-Evidence [7] and ACfs [9]. It is observed that our MCSAF performs much better than other state-of-the-arts in terms of almost all metrics, which validates the effectiveness and superiority of our proposed model.

Results on VOC 2007. PASCAL VOC 2007 [6] is another benchmark dataset for image multi-label classification, which contains 9,963 images with 20 object categories. The data is divided into training, validation and test sets. Following [3,20], we employ the *trainval* set to train our model, and evaluate the classification performance on the test set. We also use the ResNet-101 [10] as baseline model and compare our method with the existing state-of-the-art approaches: CNN-RNN [19], RLSD [25], FeV+LV [24], HCP [21], RNN-Attention [20] and Atten-Reinforce [3]. For comparison convenience, we report the results in terms of average precision (AP) and mean average precision (mAP).

As shown in Table 2, we provide the quantitative experimental results of different methods on the VOC 2007 dataset. It can be clearly seen that the proposed MCSAF outperforms the previous state-of-the-arts in terms of AP and mAP.

Table 3. Ablation studies for our model on different settings.

Architecture	MS-COCO					VOC
	All			Top-3		All
	mAP	CF1	OF1	CF1	OF1	mAP
The baseline (ResNet-101)	77.3	72.8	76.8	69.7	73.6	89.9
Ours (without Adaptive-GCN)	78.8	73.0	77.2	70.3	73.9	90.6
Ours (without multi-scale features)	79.6	73.6	77.5	71.0	74.2	91.2
Ours (without spatial attention)	80.5	74.2	78.1	71.6	74.8	91.9
Ours (MCSAF)	**81.3**	**75.4**	**78.9**	**72.0**	**75.4**	**92.4**

3.4   Ablation Studies

Effects of Different Modules for Our Model. To investigate the effects of employing different modules for our proposed MCSAF, we conduct ablation studies under the following settings: (1) Ours (without Adaptive-GCN): we apply the original Graph Convolutional Network (GCN) for label re-embedding learning; (2) Ours (without multi-scale features): the feature map from "conv5_x" layer of ResNet-101 is utilized instead of multi-scale features; (3) Ours (without spatial attention): the spatial attention module is not introduced for our model. To further validate the performance improvement from our model, we also report the result of the baseline (ResNet-101) as comparison. The experimental results are shown in Table 3, which indicates that employing different modules brings different degrees of performance gain, and validates the superiority of our proposed MCSAF on combinational design.

Effects of Different Scales Cross-Modal Feature Fusion. In this part, we investigate the effects using different scales feature maps and its corresponding label re-embeddings. Specifically, we apply the feature map from "conv5_x" layer of ResNet-101 passed through full connection layers as the baseline, and conduct experiments on only using the feature map from "conv5_x" layer of ResNet-101, the two scales feature maps from "conv4_x" and "conv5_x" layer and the multi-scale feature maps from "conv3_x", "conv4_x" and "conv5_x" layer. The comparison results are shown in Table 4. It can be observed that the proposed model with multi-scale cross-modal feature obtains better performance than that with single-scale cross-modal feature, which validates the superiority of multi-scale cross-modal feature fusion.

Table 4. Comparisons of different scales cross-modal feature fusion.

Architecture	MS-COCO					VOC
	All			Top-3		All
	mAP	CF1	OF1	CF1	OF1	mAP
The baseline	77.3	72.8	76.8	69.7	73.6	89.9
Only "conv5_x"	79.6	73.6	77.5	71.0	74.2	91.2
"conv5_x" + "conv4_x"	80.6	74.2	77.4	71.1	74.6	91.8
"conv5_x" + "conv4_x" + "conv3_x"	**81.3**	**75.4**	**78.9**	**72.0**	**75.4**	**92.4**

Effects of Different α and β. To balance the contribution of different scales cross-modal feature, we set two hyper-parameters α and β on $\hat{y}_2$ and $\hat{y}_1$. For parameter selection and analysis, we vary the values of α and β in a set of $\{0.1, 0.2, \ldots, 0.9, 1\}$ and choose the optimal value of α and β by cross-validations. As shown in Fig. 3, our model obtain the best performance on MS-COCO when α and β are 0.7 and 0.2, respectively. For VOC 2007, the optimal value of α and β are 0.6 and 0.4, respectively.

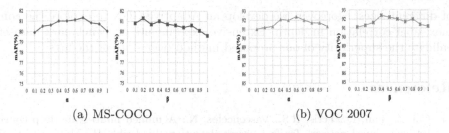

(a) MS-COCO   (b) VOC 2007

Fig. 3. Comparisons under different values of α and β.

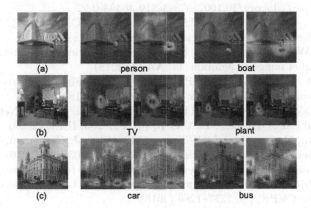

Fig. 4. Visualization and comparison of the high-layer feature map of ResNet-101 (on the left) with its corresponding spatial attention aggregation feature map (on the right).

3.5   Visualization Analysis

To validate the effectiveness of our proposed MCSAF on locating more imformative regions and recognizing target objects of smaller size, we visualize and compare the high-layer feature map from "conv5_x" of ResNet-101 with its corresponding spatial attention aggregation feature map. Figure 4 shows the visualization results of three sampled images on VOC 2007. In the first two lines of Fig. 4, we can clearly find that our MCSAF more exactly identify the target objects of small size than the baseline. In the last line of Fig. 4, we notice that there are more fine-grained differences between the "car" and "bus", and our proposed MCSAF is still able to accurately locate their corresponding imformative regions.

4   Conclusion

In this paper, we propose a novel Multi-Scale Cross-Modal Spatial Attention Fusion (MCSAF) network for multi-label image recognition. The key of our model is to conduct both multi-scale spatial attention aggregation and multi-scale cross-modal feature fusion, which promotes the proposed MCSAF to accurately locate more informative regions and effectively recognize target objects of different sizes. Moreover, we develop an Adaptive-GCN to explore the complex label correlation in depth. Extensive experiments on benchmark datasets validate the superiority of our proposed method over state-of-the-arts.

References

1. Cai, Z., Fan, Q., Feris, R.S., Vasconcelos, N.: A unified multi-scale deep convolutional neural network for fast object detection. In: Leibe, B., Matas, J., Sebe, N., Welling, M. (eds.) ECCV 2016. LNCS, vol. 9908, pp. 354–370. Springer, Cham (2016). https://doi.org/10.1007/978-3-319-46493-0_22
2. Chen, S.F., Chen, Y.C., Yeh, C.K., Wang, Y.C.F.: Order-free RNN with visual attention for multi-label classification. In: AAAI (2018)
3. Chen, T., Wang, Z., Li, G., Lin, L.: Recurrent attentional reinforcement learning for multi-label image recognition. In: AAAI (2018)
4. Chen, Z.M., Wei, X.S., Wang, P., Guo, Y.: Multi-label image recognition with graph convolutional networks. In: CVPR, pp. 5177–5186 (2019)
5. Deng, J., Dong, W., Socher, R., Li, L.J., Li, K., Fei-Fei, L.: ImageNet: a large-scale hierarchical image database. In: CVPR, pp. 248–255. IEEE (2009)
6. Everingham, M., Van Gool, L., Williams, C.K., Winn, J., Zisserman, A.: The pascal visual object classes (VOC) challenge. IJCV **88**(2), 303–338 (2010)
7. Ge, W., Yang, S., Yu, Y.: Multi-evidence filtering and fusion for multi-label classification, object detection and semantic segmentation based on weakly supervised learning. In: CVPR, pp. 1277–1286 (2018)
8. Ge, Z., Mahapatra, D., Sedai, S., Garnavi, R., Chakravorty, R.: Chest x-rays classification: a multi-label and fine-grained problem. arXiv preprint arXiv:1807.07247 (2018)
9. Guo, H., Zheng, K., Fan, X., Yu, H., Wang, S.: Visual attention consistency under image transforms for multi-label image classification. In: CVPR, pp. 729–739 (2019)
10. He, K., Zhang, X., Ren, S., Sun, J.: Deep residual learning for image recognition. In: CVPR, pp. 770–778 (2016)
11. Hu, H., Zhou, G.T., Deng, Z., Liao, Z., Mori, G.: Learning structured inference neural networks with label relations. In: CVPR, pp. 2960–2968 (2016)
12. Kipf, T.N., Welling, M.: Semi-supervised classification with graph convolutional networks. arXiv preprint arXiv:1609.02907 (2016)
13. Li, X., Zhao, F., Guo, Y.: Multi-label image classification with a probabilistic label enhancement model. In: UAI, vol. 1, p. 3 (2014)
14. Li, Y., Huang, C., Loy, C.C., Tang, X.: Human attribute recognition by deep hierarchical contexts. In: Leibe, B., Matas, J., Sebe, N., Welling, M. (eds.) ECCV 2016. LNCS, vol. 9910, pp. 684–700. Springer, Cham (2016). https://doi.org/10.1007/978-3-319-46466-4_41
15. Lin, T.Y., et al.: Microsoft COCO: common objects in context. In: Fleet, D., Pajdla, T., Schiele, B., Tuytelaars, T. (eds.) ECCV 2014. LNCS, vol. 8693, pp. 740–755. Springer, Cham (2014). https://doi.org/10.1007/978-3-319-10602-1_48
16. Liu, W., et al.: SSD: single shot multibox detector. In: Leibe, B., Matas, J., Sebe, N., Welling, M. (eds.) ECCV 2016. LNCS, vol. 9905, pp. 21–37. Springer, Cham (2016). https://doi.org/10.1007/978-3-319-46448-0_2
17. Pennington, J., Socher, R., Manning, C.: Glove: global vectors for word representation. In: EMNLP, pp. 1532–1543 (2014)

18. Szegedy, C., Vanhoucke, V., Ioffe, S., Shlens, J., Wojna, Z.: Rethinking the inception architecture for computer vision. In: CVPR, pp. 2818–2826 (2016)

19. Wang, J., Yang, Y., Mao, J., Huang, Z., Huang, C., Xu, W.: CNN-RNN: a unified framework for multi-label image classification. In: CVPR, pp. 2285–2294 (2016)

20. Wang, Z., Chen, T., Li, G., Xu, R., Lin, L.: Multi-label image recognition by recurrently discovering attentional regions. In: ICCV, pp. 464–472 (2017)

21. Wei, Y., et al.: HCP: a flexible CNN framework for multi-label image classification. TPAMI **38**(9), 1901–1907 (2015)

22. Woo, S., Park, J., Lee, J.-Y., Kweon, I.S.: CBAM: convolutional block attention module. In: Ferrari, V., Hebert, M., Sminchisescu, C., Weiss, Y. (eds.) ECCV 2018. LNCS, vol. 11211, pp. 3–19. Springer, Cham (2018). https://doi.org/10.1007/978-3-030-01234-2_1

23. Xue, X., Zhang, W., Zhang, J., Wu, B., Fan, J., Lu, Y.: Correlative multi-label multi-instance image annotation. In: ICCV, pp. 651–658. IEEE (2011)

24. Yang, H., Tianyi Zhou, J., Zhang, Y., Gao, B.B., Wu, J., Cai, J.: Exploit bounding box annotations for multi-label object recognition. In: CVPR, pp. 280–288 (2016)

25. Zhang, J., Wu, Q., Shen, C., Zhang, J., Lu, J.: Multilabel image classification with regional latent semantic dependencies. TMM **20**(10), 2801–2813 (2018)

26. Zhu, F., Li, H., Ouyang, W., Yu, N., Wang, X.: Learning spatial regularization with image-level supervisions for multi-label image classification. In: CVPR, pp. 5513–5522 (2017)

A New Efficient Finger-Vein Verification Based on Lightweight Neural Network Using Multiple Schemes

Haocong Zheng[1,2], Yongjian Hu[1,2]([✉]), Beibei Liu[1], Guang Chen[1,3], and Alex C. Kot[4]

[1] South China University of Technology, Guangzhou 510640, Guangdong, China
eeyjhu@scut.edu.cn
[2] Sino-Singapore International Joint Research Institute, Guangzhou 10700, Guangdong, China
[3] GRG Banking Equipment Co., Ltd., Guangzhou 510663, Guangdong, China
[4] Rapid-Rich Object Search (ROSE) Lab, Nanyang Technological University, Singapore 639798, Singapore

Abstract. Existing deep learning-based finger-vein algorithms tend to use large-scale neural networks. From the perspective of computational complexity, this is not conducive to practical applications. Besides, in our opinion, finger-vein images often have relatively simple textures and are small in image size, it is not economical to use large-scale neural networks. Inspired by the increasing accuracy of lightweight neural networks on ImageNet, we introduce the lightweight neural network ShuffleNet V2 as a backbone to construct a basic pipeline for finger-vein verification. To customize the network for this application, we propose schemes to improve it from the aspects including data input, network structure, and loss function design. Experimental results on three public databases have exhibited the excellence of the proposed model.

Keywords: Finger-vein verification · Lightweight neural network · ShuffleNet V2 · Data augmentation · Joint loss function

1 Introduction

Biometric features are widely used for authentication and identification applications. The most commonly used ones are the fingerprint, human face, voice, iris and finger-vein. Compared with other biometric features, the finger-vein has some prominent advantages. For example, the finger-vein is an internal biometric modality, and thus is much harder to copy and forge. On the other hand, the acquisition of finger-vein images is quick and friendly.

Supported in part by Sino-Singapore International Joint Research Institute (No. 206-A017023, No. 206-A018001), Science and Technology Foundation of Guangzhou Huangpu Development District under Grant 201902010028, and NTU-PKU JRI.

I. Farkaš et al. (Eds.): ICANN 2020, LNCS 12396, pp. 748–758, 2020.
https://doi.org/10.1007/978-3-030-61609-0_59

However, there are also some challenges for finger-vein verification. For example, the captured finger-vein images usually have low contrast and are easy to be affected by uneven illumination, temperature changes, 2D or 3D rotation, and other noise. Low-quality finger-vein images are difficult to classify correctly by employing manual feature extraction and matching methods. Compared with hand-crafted features, deep learning features extracted by convolutional neural networks (CNN) have proven to be more general and representative, and are being used in various computer vision tasks.

To use deep learning features for finger-vein verification, one needs to train the convolutional neural network with a huge amount of training data. Unfortunately, the size of public finger-vein databases is relatively small. As a result, the issue of creating training samples through data augmentation has attracted much attention. It is obvious that good recognition performance and satisfactory robustness can only be achieved by a deliberately designed and well trained neural network. Recent finger-vein studies mainly discuss these problems. For industrial applications, the computational complexity is also highly concerned.

Qiu et al. [1] proposed a region of interest (ROI) extraction method which is robust to light illumination and 3D rotation, but the performance is not satisfactory. Qin et al. [2] first designed a CNN to extract the vein patterns from any image region, and then recovered the missing finger-vein patterns in the binary image based on a fully convolutional network. They employed a template matching method for finger-vein verification. The whole process is too complex and time-consuming. Fang et al. [3] proposed a two-channel network to tackle the problem of lack of finger-vein data, and a two-stream network to overcome image displacement. The above two types of networks are integrated with a selective network to achieve good performance. Hu et al. [4] proposed the Finger-vein Network (FV-Net) to learn more discriminative features of finger-vein and addressed the misalignment problem like translation and rotation in vein imaging. Zeng et al. [5] proposed a new fully convolutional neural network (FCN) and integrated it with conditional random field to extract vein textures. The FCN takes the U-Net [6] as its basic structure and introduces deformable convolution and residual recurrent convolution to extract and retain deeper and more complex features. Hao et al. [7] proposed a multi-task neural network model algorithm to jointly carry out the ROI extraction task and the feature extraction task. By combining these two tasks, the quality of extracted vein features is improved.

In this article, we propose a lightweight deep learning model for finger-vein verification. We introduce a data augmentation scheme to mitigate the pressure of lack of training samples with brightness weakness, being partially cropped or rotated. We further modify a lightweight ShuffleNet V2 [8] to extract a more efficient feature map with a larger size. The label smoothing [9] and the joint loss function from [10] are also introduced for learning discriminative features. Experiments on databases including SDUMLA-HMT [11], FV-USM [12], and MMCBNU_6000 [13] have demonstrated that the proposed method is efficient and outperforms five current methods in literature.

2   The Basic Framework for Finger-Vein Verification

2.1   The Baseline

The pipeline of our basic model is shown in Fig. 1(a). We introduce the ShuffleNet V2 as the backbone network for our finger-vein verification task. In the training stage, we train the network with cross-entropy loss. In the inference stage, we compare the images by using the cosine similarity of features learned from the network. The cross-entropy loss is shown in Eq. (1).

$$L_S = -\sum_{i=1}^{M} p_i \log q_i \tag{1}$$

Where p is the truth probability distribution, q is the prediction probability distribution and M is the number of categories. Assume that the true label of the image is y. We let $p_i = 1$ if $i = y$ and $p_i = 0$ otherwise.

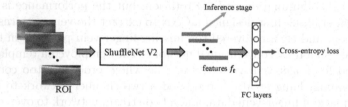

(a) Basic pipeline

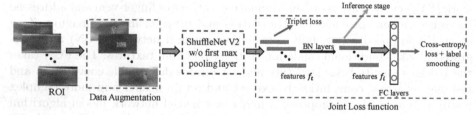

(b) Modified pipeline after using all schemes

Fig. 1. Basic pipeline and our proposed framework

2.2   Training and Inference

The training procedure employed is listed as follows.

1. We set the number of epochs to 500 and the batch size to 128. For each epoch, we randomly shuffle the images and normalize pixel value to [0, 1] as the input.

2. Finger-vein images are fed into the network to get the feature f_t. We obtain the prediction probability distribution by passing f_t through the fully connected layer and softmax function. After that, we calculate the cross-entropy loss based on the prediction probability distribution and the truth probability distribution, and update loss through backpropagation.

3. We adopt Adam optimizer and use Eq. (2) to determine the learning rate, where t is the number of epochs. We first adopt a gradual warmup strategy [14] to linearly increase the learning rate from 0 to the initial learning rate. Because at the beginning of network training, the network parameters are far away from the final solution. In this situation, using a large learning rate may result in model instability. With a warmup strategy, the model can become more stable. During training deep neural networks, it is usually helpful to drop the learning rate over time. Therefore we use a step decay learning rate schedule that drops the learning rate by a factor according to some predefined steps. The factor and the predefined steps are determined by manual tuning.

$$lr(t) = \begin{cases} \frac{t}{10} \times 3.5 \times 10^{-3}, & t \leq 10 \\ 3.5 \times 10^{-3}, & 10 < t \leq 180 \\ 7 \times 10^{-4}, & 180 < t \leq 300 \\ 1.4 \times 10^{-4}, & 300 < t \leq 360 \\ 2.8 \times 10^{-5}, & 360 < t \leq 500 \end{cases} \tag{2}$$

In our inference procedure, we normalize the input image to the value interval $[0, 1]$, and feed the normalized data to the trained network to get the features. During finger-vein verification, the cosine similarity between features is used directly for comparison.

3   Our Improvement Schemes

The basic model proposed above is an end-to-end algorithm. It is simple but the performance is not good. We improve it from several aspects including input data augmentation, network structure, and loss function design.

3.1   Input Data Augmentation

Deep learning model often needs a large training set. Unfortunately, there are not many databases available for finger-vein. For public finger-vein databases like SDUMLA-HMT, FV-USM, and MMCBNU_6000, the size of databases is still small. Meanwhile, some finger-vein images suffer from uneven brightness, missing textures, cropping, translation, rotation, and so on. To let the model learn about the invariance of vein pattern, we present a data augmentation scheme to simulate sample generation. The overall data augmentation pipeline is shown in Fig. 2.

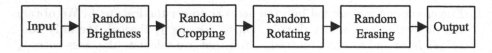

Fig. 2. Data augmentation pipeline

During the model training, the brightness of each input ROI image is randomly adjusted with a factor in a range of 0.7–1.3. Then, the ROI image is randomly cropped with a crop box of 0.9 times the original image size and resized back to the original image size. Next, the ROI image is randomly rotated by an angle between −3 and 3°. Finally, random erasing [15] is adopted. It can be seen that this data augmentation pipeline can greatly increase the number and varieties of training samples, making the model more robust against the mentioned disadvantages.

3.2   Network Improvement

ShuffleNet V2 network has been proven to achieve excellent performance in multiple computer vision tasks, including classification and object detection tasks. And the ShuffleNet V2 network is lightweight and efficient, so we take this network as the basic structure. However, the ShuffleNet V2 network was originally designed for 224 × 224 input images. If it is directly applied to the 128 × 64 ROI image, the output feature maps only have the size of 4 × 2. Apparently, that size is too small for the extraction of detailed features. Considering that a pooling layer would cause information missing, we remove the first max pooling layer so as to generate the feature map of size 8 × 4. This modification seems simple and straightforward, but the effect on performance improvement is enormous, as will be seen later. In fact, the output feature map with a larger size can better preserve the fine-grained features, which is especially important for finger-vein images. The modified network structure is shown in Table 1.

For model training, one serious problem would be raised due to lack of finger-vein training samples. If the weights are initialized by random initialization like Xavier, the network would hardly learn discriminative features from the limited data, and the final model would perform poorly. Therefore, we use the transfer learning concept and pre-train our backbone network on the ImageNet dataset. ImageNet is a large dataset that has a wide variety of objects. The massive data set ensures that the pre-trained network provides high generalization. Particularly, the shallow features learned by the pre-trained network, such as edges, textures, and curves, have excellent versatility. These shallow features also play an important role in finger-vein verification. Therefore, the pre-trained model can provide a useful starting point for the finger-vein verification task. The weights obtained are saved as the initial weights.

Table 1. The modified ShuffleNet V2 structure. The stage layer is constructed by repeatedly stacking the spatial down sampling unit and the basic unit proposed in [8].

Layer	Output size	Kernel size	Stride	Repeat	Output channels
Image	128×64	–	–	–	3
Conv1	64×32	3×3	2	1	24
Stage2	32×16	–	2	1	116
	32×16		1	7	
Stage3	16×8	–	2	1	232
	16×8		1	7	
Stage4	8×4	–	2	1	464
	8×4		1	3	
Conv5	8×4	1×1	1	1	1024
GlobaPool	1×1	8×4	–	–	–

3.3 Label Smoothing and Loss Function

We adopt the label smoothing to reduce overfitting. It changes the truth probability distribution to l_i as shown in Eq. (3), where ε is a small constant to encourage the model to be less confident on training set. Empirically, ε is set to be 0.1.

$$l_i = \begin{cases} \varepsilon/(M-1), i \neq y \\ 1 - \varepsilon, i = y \end{cases} \tag{3}$$

We define the loss after adding label smoothing L_{Sl} as follows

$$L_{Sl} = -\sum_{i=1}^{M} l_i \log q_i \tag{4}$$

The cross-entropy loss is suitable for feature separation of different categories but does not consider intra-class feature gathering. The learned features which are not compact within the intra class would reduce the performance of our finger-vein verification. On the other hand, the widely used triplet loss can effectively enhance the intra-class compactness in Euclidean space but can not provide globally optimal constraint. It would be more conducive for model training if these two loss functions are combined. However, the learning targets of these two loss functions are inconsistent. Cross-entropy loss mainly optimizes the cosine distance while triplet loss mainly optimizes the Euclidean distances. Luo et al. [10] proposed a simple way that added a batch normalization (BN) layer after features to solve the problem. It can help reduce the constraint between cross-entropy loss and triplet loss. Therefore, more discriminative features can be learned with the joint loss function. The triplet loss is shown in Eq. (5).

$$L_{Tri} = [d_p - d_n + \alpha]_+ \tag{5}$$

Where d_p and d_n are the Euclidean distances between positive and negative pairs. α is the margin of triplet loss. Empirically, α is set to 0.3. The triplet selection scheme is to randomly select P fingers, and each finger randomly selects K images to form a batch. For each image in the batch, it selects one image from different classes with the smallest Euclidean distance of the corresponding features and another image of the same class with the largest Euclidean distance to form a triplet. In our work, P is set to 32 and K to 4. The total loss function is $L = L_{Sl} + L_{Tri}$.

The modified pipeline is shown in Fig. 1(b). In the inference stage, the batch normalized feature f_i is used to measure the similarity.

4   Experiment and Analysis

In the training stage, we train the model on Ubuntu 18.04 system with a CPU E5-2683 v3@2.00 GHz and an NVIDIA Corporation GP102 (TITAN XP). In the test stage, the trained model runs on a Windows 10 system with a Ryzen 5 2500U@2.00 GHz. We conduct experiments on three public finger-vein databases which are SDUMLA-HMT, FV-USM, and MMCBNU_6000. The outline of the three databases are given in Table 2. Note that the ROI images are extracted using the method similar to the literature [16] to extract the ROI image. The difference is that we crop the outer rectangle of the whole finger area as the ROI and resize to 128×64. The extracted ROIs are shown in the second line of Fig. 3.

For the division of dataset, we randomly choose one half of the classes for training, and the remaining is only used for testing. For each class in the test set, half of the images are randomly selected as the gallery, and the remaining half is used as the probes. The probes and the samples in the gallery are used to construct the positive and negative sample pairs. We use the equal error rate (EER) to evaluate the performance of our finger-vein verification model. The EER is the ratio when the false acceptance rate and false rejection rate are equivalent. The lower the EER, the better the verification performance.

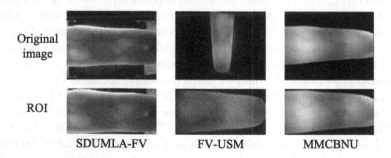

Fig. 3. Example images and their extracted ROIs from the three finger-vein databases

Table 2. The outline of three Finger-vein Databases

Databases	Subjects	Fingers per subject	Images per finger	Image size	Total images
SDUMLA-HMT	106	6	6	320 × 240	3816
FV-USM	123	4	12	640 × 480	5904
MMCBNU_6000	100	6	10	640 × 480	6000

4.1 Effect of Our Schemes on Model Performance

We use an ablation study to analyze the effect of our schemes on the input, network, and loss function. The results are shown in Table 3. Our data augmentation and the joint loss function can train the model well so it performs better than the baseline model. Next, the modified network further decreases the EERs due to the output of larger feature maps. Moreover, by using the pre-training, our model can further improve the performance. The additional use of label smoothing and joint loss function can make our model achieve the lowest EERs in all three databases. In summary, after applying all the schemes, the EERs of our finger-vein verification model decrease from 6.59%, 2.24%, 2.03% to 0.37%, 0.31%, and 0.05% in the order of SDUMLA-HMT, FV-USM, and MMCBNU_6000.

Table 3. Effect of our schemes on model performance (EER%)

Model	SDUMLA-HMT	FV-USM	MMCBNU_6000
Baseline	6.59	2.24	2.03
+Data augmentation	3.19	1.59	0.85
+Modified network	2.72	0.84	0.39
+Pre-trained	0.96	0.63	0.33
+Label smoothing	0.77	0.54	0.15
+Joint loss function	0.37	0.31	0.05

4.2 Effect of Backbone Network on Model Performance

We analyze the effect of different backbone networks on model performance. To investigate the effect in detail, we replace the backbone network with MobileNet V2 [17], ResNet18 [18], ResNet50 [18], and DenseNet121 [19] one by one under the same schemes such as data augmentation, ImageNet pretraining, label smoothing and joint loss function. As shown in Table 4, DenseNet121 and the modified ShuffleNet V2 achieve better results than the other networks. It is because both networks use a feature reuse structure, which can combine the advantages of low-level features and high-level features. Between them, our modified ShuffleNet V2 can better suit the finger-vein input size, so it gets the best results in the three public databases.

Table 4. Effect of different backbone networks on model performance (EER%)

Backbone	SDUMLA-HMT	FV-USM	MMCBNU_6000
MobileNet V2	0.82	0.48	0.21
ResNet-18	1.21	0.52	0.5
ResNet-50	0.80	0.45	0.21
DenseNet-121	0.73	0.33	0.14
Modified ShuffleNet V2	0.37	0.31	0.05

4.3 Comparison with Other Methods

The classical machine learning-based method DWP [1], and four state-of-the-art deep learning-based methods, Selective-network [3], FV-Net [4], FCN [5] and MTL [7] are selected for comparison. Tables 5 and 6 show that DWP runs the fastest in feature extraction and matching, but its performance is the worst among 6 methods. Our method is mainly compared with the four deep learning-based methods. FV-Net uses a modified VGGFace-Net as the backbone and the FLOPs (floating-point operations) are about 51 times of ours. Selective-network uses a lightweight neural network, but it needs to extract the mini-ROI as an additional input, and the average time spent on mini-ROI extraction is 50ms. FCN introduces deformable convolution and recursive convolution in the U-Net structure, which will result in some computational cost. And FCN uses multiple overlapping patches for prediction, which increases the FLOPs, it is the most time-consuming among all methods. MTL takes the original image as input. Since the original image has a large size, it will bring additional computational cost. Note that the FCN method and the MTL method have different input sizes for different databases, so the FLOPs are not fixed. It can be seen that our method can reach the lowest EERs in all three databases. In terms of FLOPs, the number of weights, and the average feature extracting time, our model performs the best. As for the average matching time, our model is slightly slower than Selective-network and MTL. On the whole, our model has the best overall performance.

Table 5. EER (%) of different methods

Methods	SDUMLA-HMT	FV-USM	MMCBNU_6000
DWP [1]	1.59	2.78	2.32
Selective-network [3]	0.47	–	0.30
FV-Net [4]	1.20	0.76	0.30
FCN [5]	5.827	–	0.364
MTL [7]	1.17	0.74	0.29
Proposed method	0.37	0.31	0.05

Table 6. Detailed comparison of different methods in the test stage

Methods	FLOPs	Number of weights	Average extracting time	Average matching time
DWP [1]	–	–	0.0175 ms	0.13 ms
Selective-network [3]	119.2M	6.04M	140 ms	0.18 ms
FV-Net [4]	4.88G	3.51M	684 ms	0.98 ms
FCN [5]	0.17–2.67T	193.22M	217 s	630 ms
MTL [7]	2.04–6.94G	13.16M	121 ms	0.19 ms
Proposed method	95.4M	1.26M	97 ms	0.20 ms

5   Conclusion

In this article, we have presented a method of using the lightweight neural network for finger-vein verification. We first introduced a baseline network, and then discussed the schemes of how to improve the model from several aspects including data augmentation, network modification and loss function design. The experiments validate the proposed framework. The test results on the three public databases have demonstrated that our method can significantly outperform one traditional method and well outperform four state-of-the-art CNN-based methods in terms of verification performance. Meanwhile, it needs less FLOPs and smaller memory than the four CNN-based methods.

References

1. Qiu, S., Liu, Y., Zhou, Y., Huang, J., Nie, Y.: Finger-vein recognition based on dual-sliding window localization and pseudo-elliptical transformer. Expert Syst. Appl. **64**, 618–632 (2016)
2. Qin, H., El-Yacoubi, M.A.: Deep representation-based feature extraction and recovering for finger-vein verification. IEEE Trans. Inf. Forensics Secur. **12**(8), 1816–1829 (2017)
3. Fang, Y., Wu, Q., Kang, W.: A novel finger-vein verification system based on two-stream convolutional network learning. Neurocomputing **290**, 100–107 (2018)
4. Hu, H., Kang, W., Lu, Y., Fang, Y., Liu, H., Zhao, J., Deng, F.: FV-Net: learning a finger-vein feature representation based on a CNN. In: 2018 24th International Conference on Pattern Recognition (ICPR), Beijing, China, pp. 3489–3494. IEEE (2018)
5. Zeng, J., et al.: Finger vein verification algorithm based on fully convolutional neural network and conditional random field. IEEE Access **8**, 65402–65419 (2020)
6. Ronneberger, O., Fischer, P., Brox, T.: U-Net: convolutional networks for biomedical image segmentation. In: Navab, N., Hornegger, J., Wells, W.M., Frangi, A.F. (eds.) MICCAI 2015. LNCS, vol. 9351, pp. 234–241. Springer, Cham (2015). https://doi.org/10.1007/978-3-319-24574-4_28

7. Hao, Z., Fang, P., Yang, H.: Finger vein recognition based on multi-task learning. In: Proceedings of the 2020 5th International Conference on Mathematics and Artificial Intelligence, Chengdu, China, pp. 133–140, ACM Digital (2020)
8. Ma, N., Zhang, X., Zheng, H.-T., Sun, J.: ShuffleNet V2: practical guidelines for efficient CNN architecture design. In: Ferrari, V., Hebert, M., Sminchisescu, C., Weiss, Y. (eds.) Computer Vision – ECCV 2018. LNCS, vol. 11218, pp. 122–138. Springer, Cham (2018). https://doi.org/10.1007/978-3-030-01264-9_8
9. Szegedy, C., Vanhoucke, V., Ioffe, S., Shlens, J., Wojna, Z.: Rethinking the inception architecture for computer vision. In: Proceedings of the IEEE Conference on Computer Vision and Pattern Recognition, Las Vegas, Nevada, USA, pp. 2818–2826, IEEE (2020)
10. Luo, H., Gu, Y., Liao, X., Lai, S., Jiang, W.: Bag of tricks and a strong baseline for deep person re-identification. In: Proceedings of the IEEE Conference on Computer Vision and Pattern Recognition Workshops, Long Beach, CA, USA. IEEE (2019)
11. Yin, Y., Liu, L., Sun, X.: SDUMLA-HMT: a multimodal biometric database. In: Sun, Z., Lai, J., Chen, X., Tan, T. (eds.) CCBR 2011. LNCS, vol. 7098, pp. 260–268. Springer, Heidelberg (2011). https://doi.org/10.1007/978-3-642-25449-9_33
12. Asaari, M.S.M., Suandi, S.A., Rosdi, B.A.: Fusion of band limited phase only correlation and width centroid contour distance for finger based biometrics. Expert Syst. Appl. **41**(7), 3367–3382 (2014)
13. Lu, Y., Xie, S. J., Yoon, S., Wang, Z., Park, D. S.: An available database for the re-search of finger vein recognition. In: 2013 6th International Congress on Image and Signal Processing (CISP), Hangzhou, China, vol. 1, pp. 410–415, IEEE (2013)
14. Goyal, P., et al.: Accurate, large minibatch SGD: training ImageNet in 1 hour. arXiv preprint arXiv:1706.02677 (2017)
15. Zhong, Z., Zheng, L., Kang, G., Li, S., Yang, Y.: Random erasing data augmentation. arXiv preprint arXiv:1708.04896 (2017)
16. Wang, M., Tang, D.: Region of interest extraction for finger vein images with less information losses. Multimed. Tools Appl. 1–13 (2016). https://doi.org/10.1007/s11042-016-4285-2
17. Sandler, M., Howard, A., Zhu, M., Zhmoginov, A., Chen, L. C.: Mobilenetv 2: inverted residuals and linear bottlenecks. In: Proceedings of the IEEE Conference on Computer Vision and Pattern Recognition, Salt Lake City, USA, pp. 4510–4520, IEEE (2018)
18. He, K., Zhang, X., Ren, S., Sun, J.: Deep residual learning for image recognition. In: Proceedings of the IEEE Conference on Computer Vision and Pattern Recognition, Las Vegas, Nevada, USA. pp. 770–778, IEEE (2016)
19. Huang, G., Liu, Z., Van Der Maaten, L., Weinberger, K. Q.: Densely connected convolutional networks. In: Proceedings of the IEEE Conference on Computer Vision and Pattern Recognition, Honolulu, Hawaii, USA, pp. 4700–4708, IEEE(2017)

Medical Image Processing

SU-Net: An Efficient Encoder-Decoder Model of Federated Learning for Brain Tumor Segmentation

Liping Yi, Jinsong Zhang, Rui Zhang, Jiaqi Shi, Gang Wang[(✉)], and Xiaoguang Liu

College of CS, TJ Key Lab of NDST, Nankai University, Tianjin, China
{yiliping,zhangjs,zhangruiann,shijq,wgzwp,liuxg}@nbjl.nankai.edu.cn

Abstract. Using deep learning for semantic segmentation of medical images is a popular topic of wise medical. The premise of training an efficient deep learning model is to have a large number of medical images with annotations. Most medical images are scattered in hospitals or research institutions, and professionals such as doctors always don't have enough time to label the images. Besides, due to the constraints of privacy protection regulations like GDPR, sharing data directly between multiple institutions is prohibited. To solve the obstacles above, we propose an efficient federated learning model SU-Net for brain tumor segmentation. We introduce inception module and dense block into standard U-Net to comprise our SU-Net with multi-scale receptive fields and information reusing. We conduct experiments on the LGG (Low-Grade Glioma) Segmentation dataset "Brain MRI Segmentation" in Kaggle. The results show that, in non-federated scenario, SU-Net achieves a AUC (Area Under Curve which measures classification accuracy) of 99.7% and a DSC (Dice Similarity Coefficient which measures segmentation accuracy) of 78.5%, which are remarkably higher than the state-of-the-art semantic segmentation model DeepLabv3+ and the classical model U-Net dedicated to semantic segmentation of medical images. In federated scenario, SU-Net still outperforms the baselines.

Keywords: Brain tumor segmentation · Federated learning · Privacy protection

1 Introduction

Recently, the use of deep learning methods to accurately segment lesions (such as brain tumors) in medical images is one of the research hot spots in wise medical. Precise segmentation of brain tumor contours is essential in radiotherapy

This work is partially supported by National Science Foundation of China (U1833114, 61872201, 61702521) and Science and Technology Development Plan of Tianjin (18ZXZNGX00140, 18ZXZNGX00200).

I. Farkaš et al. (Eds.): ICANN 2020, LNCS 12396, pp. 761–773, 2020.
https://doi.org/10.1007/978-3-030-61609-0_60

or surgical planning. Not only must the outline of brain tumor be outlined, but also the surrounding healthy tissues must be carefully excluded to avoid damaging functional parts such as language during surgery [9]. Therefore, training an efficient segmentation model is particularly important. The fundamental requirement for training such a high-efficiency model is a dataset with large amounts of independent and identically distributed annotated medical images.

At present, the main challenges faced in processing medical images involve: a) Medical images are mostly stored by medical institutions and individual patients, and the amount of medical images owned by a single institution or individual is relatively small. Due to the constrains of privacy protection and ethical issues, it is not realistic to directly share sensitive data, which leads to data island. b) Labeling medical images requires expertise and time, but professionals such as doctors don't have enough time to do this, so there are few medical images with complete annotations. c) Since the lesion areas in MRI images are relatively similar compared to the health areas, segmenting lesions in medical images is more difficult compared with natural images. d) There is obvious sample imbalance in medical images. Medical and natural images have different imaging principles, and medical images in different modalities (MRI, CT, etc.) have big differences in brightness, color, texture and so on. In addition, because of the differences in medical equipment and operations in different hospitals or research institutions, there are also large diversities in medical images with same modality. These make it impossible to simply treat medical images with natural images processing methods in computer vision. The above characteristics of medical images conform to the features of unbalanced and non-IID datasets in federated learning.

Federated learning can combine data from multiple institutions to train an efficient model commonly while keeping user data in local institution, which

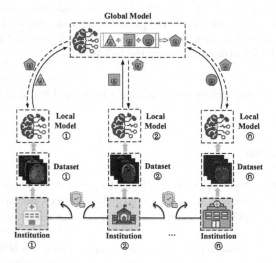

Fig. 1. Federated learning system for brain tumor segmentation.

effectively breaks data island. Hence, we adopt federated learning to train an efficient network of medical image segmentation by combining private data from multiple medical institutions. Figure 1 illustrates complete federated learning system for brain tumor segmentation.

The main contribution of this paper is that *we propose an efficient federated learning model SU-Net for brain tumor segmentation based on the encoder-decoder infrastructure of U-Net* [18]. SU-Net introduces inception module [21,22] and dense block [13] to increase the width and depth of network respectively. Figure 2 and Fig. 3 show the internal structure of inception module and dense block. From the perspective of width, inception module can extract features with different size of receptive field, which can improve classification accuracy. In terms of depth of network, short connections between layers in dense block are implemented by concatenation which allows the feature maps of previous layers can be reused in subsequent layers. Besides, we also propose to replace dropout layers in standard U-Net with batch normalization to further improve network performance.

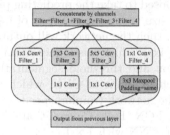

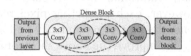

Fig. 2. Inception-v1 module.　　　　　　　　**Fig. 3.** Dense block.

We compare the performance of SU-Net with standard U-Net [18], FCN [15], DeepLabv3+ [7] in non-federated and federated scenarios. The experimental results show that it can achieve the state-of-the-art performance on public LGG (Low-Grade Glioma) Segmentation dataset of "Brain MRI Segmentation" in Kaggle [2,3,16].

2 Related Work

2.1 Federated Learning

Google proposed an efficient federated learning algorithm "FedAvg" (FederatedAveraging) [17] with server-client mode. The specific implementation processes are as follows: there are K clients in total, and C of them are randomly selected for participating each round's training. The server sends current state of global model to selected C clients. Each client performs local training based on the global model and its local data, then sends updates (encrypted gradient updates) to server. Server sums all the encrypted gradient updates and decrypts them. This process will be repeated until the global model converges. Furthermore, Google developed the first global product-level scalable large-scale mobile federated learning system TFF (TensorFlow Federated) based on tensorflow and FedAvg algorithms [1]. Google applied FedAvg algorithm into word predicting in mobile phone keyboard (Gboard) [11]. Applying federated learning to brain tumor segmentation was firstly stated in [20], but it focused on comparing multiple different distributed framework of federated learning and directly uses standard U-Net as training model. Unlike them, we pay more attention to proposing an efficient federated learning model for brain tumor segmentation.

2.2   Semantic Segmentation

In recent years, the advances made by deep learning in computer vision field have motivated researchers to focus on applying deep learning in medical image classification, localization and segmentation.

Ciresan et al. [8] and Sermane et al. [19] proposed to take the predicting pixel as the center point and select a patch of fixed size around it as input of CNN networks (such as AlexNet, VGG, GoogLeNet), then the network will output a binary classification result with the predicting pixel, which has higher accuracy than traditional methods such as edge detection and threshold segmentation. However, each predicting pixel requires a patch as input of CNN, which will generate a lot of redundancy and slows down the network training speed.

To improve the above shortcomings of CNN, FCN (Fully Convolutional Networks) [15] replaced all fully connected layers in CNN with 1×1 convolutional layers, and unsampling layers were added at the end of network to restore segmentation map which is consistent with input image size, achieving dense pixel-level prediction. Unlike CNN extracted patches as inputs, FCN took the entire image as input during each round of training, which improves the deficiency of CNN's large redundancy. Meanwhile, FCN used skip connection to fuse (sum) low-level features and high-level features, which improves the segmentation accuracy. FCN8s performs best among all versions of FCN.

U-Net [18] is another fully convolutional network with symmetrical down-sampling and unsampling layers, which likes letter "U", hence named U-Net. U-Net used skip connection to concatenate (not sum of FCN) high-level and low-level features, taking a more reasonable trade-off between classification and segmentation accuracy and achieving the state-of-the-art performance at that time. But the drawback of U-Net is its training speed: it takes 10 h to train 20–30 images on NVIDIA Titan GPU (6 GB). If U-Net is used as federated learning model directly, it will have an indirect negative impact on convergence speed of global model.

DeepLabv1 [4] proposed atrous convolution for sparse sampling, effectively extending receptive field without increase in parameter amount and calculation cost. DeepLabv2 [5] proposed ASPP (Atrous Spatial Pyramid Pooling) on the basis of v1 which uses multiple atrous convolution layers with different sampling rates to extract multi-scale features. DeepLabv3 [6] proposed two modes of network based on DeepLabv2: a) cascade mode and b) parallel mode. The latter was implemented by ASPP with batch normalization, which can achieve higher segmentation accuracy compared with the former. DeepLabv3+ [7] used an encoder-decoder structure similar to U-Net and adopted the parallel mode of DeepLab v3 in downloading layers. DeepLabv3+ achieves the state-of-the-art segmentation accuracy. However, DeepLab family has a common problem that they cannot segment sofas, chairs and objects with poor vision, which may be due to sparse sampling of atrous convolution, leading more detailed information lost.

3   Methods

In this section, we propose a more efficient federated learning model SU-Net (Strong U-Net) based on standard U-Net. We will discuss the advantages of SU-Net in detail from the perspective of increasing model width and depth.

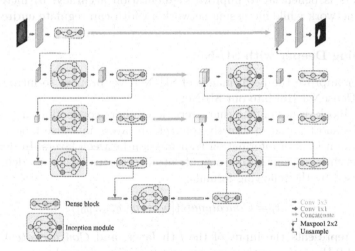

Fig. 4. The network architecture of SU-Net with inception module and dense block.

3.1   Going Wider with SU-Net

Inspired by ASPP in DeepLabv3+, we attempt to introduce inception-v1 module into standard U-Net and replace two convolutional layers of each depth in U-Net with inception modules. The outputs of previous maxpooling or unsampling layer will be directly regarded as the input of inception module in next depth. Figure 4 describes the locations of inception modules in SU-Net.

The structure of inception module is shown in Fig. 2 inception-v1 module adds four branches between two consecutive convolutional layers. The first branch involves a 1×1 convolution; the second branch is composed of a 1×1 convolution (reduce the number of filters in this branch to further save computation cost) and a 3×3 convolution; the third branch is a 1×1 convolution followed by a 5×5 convolution; the fourth branch consists of a 3×3 maxpooling layer with same padding and a 1×1 convolution in series. The four branches extract multi-scale information through filters with different receptive field sizes simultaneously inception-v1 module aggregates feature maps extracted from four separate branches through concatenation, thus the output feature map of inception module contains multi-scale and rich semantic information.

We insert inception modules after the outputs of last depth in standard U-Net, which can extract multi-scale information flowed from the nearest layers, reducing the loss of useful features. On the side, we also adds batch normalization (BN) after the output of inception module to prevent overfitting.

In theory, introducing inception module in our SU-Net has the following merits: a) extracting multi-scale information in downsampling layers is conductive to improve classification accuracy, and extracting multi-scale features in unsampling layers is beneficial to improve segmentation accuracy; b) increasing the depth of network while increasing network's width can regulate entire network.

3.2   Going Deeper with SU-Net

To further improve the performance of SU-Net, we propose to introduce dense block of DenseNet [13] into our SU-Net.

Dense block draws on the characteristic of short connection in ResNet [12], which uses short paths to directly connect all layers in dense block, to ensure the maximum level of information transmission between layers. In dense block, input of each layer comes from outputs of all previous layers, its definition can be expressed by the following formula:

$$x_l = Concatenate([y_{l-1}, y_{l-2}, ..., y_0])$$

where x_l represents the input of the l-th layer, and $Concatenate()$ fuses the outputs of 0-th to $(l-1)$-th layers by concatenating channels.

Figure 3 illustrates the structure of dense block. The first layer of dense block is bottleneck layer, a 1×1 convolution which can decrease the number of channels of input, thus reducing the number of parameters and calculation cost. There are k 3×3 convolutional layers followed by bottleneck layer, k is determined according to actual situation.

We add a dense block after inception module in each depth of SU-Net, which can relearn multi-scale features extracted from the last inception module, to promote the dissemination of useful information. Figure 4 depicts the positions of dense blocks in SU-Net. SU-Net modifies original dense block's inner structure by removing the bottleneck layer and placing three 3×3 convolutional layers in each dense block. This can evenly distribute the output feature maps' channels of previous inception module to three 3×3 convolutional layers. For example, if the number of channels of inception module's output is 60, then we set each 3×3 convolutional layer has 20 channels, finally the channels of dense block's output are also 60 due to concatenation.

In theory, the advantages of introducing dense blocks to SU-Net include: a) dense connections improve the efficiency of network information flow and gradient flow transmission, which alleviates gradient disappearance, and repeatedly learning information from previous layers is beneficial to improve network performance; b) dense blocks increase the depth of network which generates implicit deep supervision for entire network; c) dense blocks can effect the regularization and reduce the risk of falling into overfitting.

Adding inception modules can improve SU-Net's classification accuracy (AUC) efficiently due to extracted multi-scale information. Applying dense blocks will further improve segmentation accuracy (DSC) due to reused information. Hence, combining the two modules in SU-Net will improve the overall performance.

3.3   SU-Net with Four Cases

SU-Net improves standard U-Net from both width and depth. In order to explore the respective gain of introducing inception module and dense block, we discuss the following four cases with SU-Net:

- SU-Net-V1 (SU-V1): [inception module + BN] for downsampling and [BN] for unsampling.
- SU-Net-V2 (SU-V2): [inception module + BN] for both downsampling and unsampling.
- SU-Net-V3 (SU-V3): [inception module + BN + dense block + BN] for downsampling and only use [inception + BN] for unsampling.
- SU-Net-V4 (SU-V4): [inception module + BN + dense block + BN] for both downsampling and unsampling.

In theory, as both the width and depth are increased, SU-V4 has best classification accuracy (AUC) and segmentation accuracy (DSC), followed by SU-V3, SU-V2, SU-V1.

4   Experiments

We implement SU-Net based on Keras and evaluate the performance of SU-Net on LGG (Low-Grade Glioma) Segmentation dataset of "Brain MRI Segmentation" in Kaggle [2,3,16]. NVIDIA GTX1080Ti GPU (10G) Cards are used to train the models. We further verify the efficiency of SU-Net in non-federated and federated scenarios.

Dataset. LGG Segmentation dataset were originally acquired from The Cancer Image Archive (TCIA) [14]. It involves 3929 brain tumor images and corresponding FLAIR abnormal segmentation masks (size: 256×256) with 110 patients from

5 different institutions. The composition of this dataset is shown in Table 1. We divide each organization's sub-dataset into train, validation and test set with a ratio of approximately 8:1:1.

Table 1. LGG (Low-Grade Glioma) Segmentation dataset from 5 different institutions.

Institutions	Patients	Total	Train & Evaluation	Test
CS	16	358	320	38
DU	45	1878	1700	178
EZ	1	24	20	4
FG	14	640	600	40
HT	34	1029	900	129

Data Preprocessing. Brain MRI images in LGG Segmentation dataset are color maps with three channels of RGB. Since our purpose is to perform pixel level segmentation, i.e., predicting one pixel is 0 or 1, we gray all images to reduce their channels to one. We also normalize all images and map them to a normal distribution conforming to $\mathcal{N} \sim (0,1)$ so that gradients can be stabilized and quickly decreased, accelerating model convergence. In addition, since brain tumor images have high degree of similarity between tissues and grayed images have low contrast, we use histogram equalization to strengthen the brightest and darkest parts in images so that brain tumors will be more prominent in preprocessed images.

Data Augmentation. Limited by GPU memory, we adopt the method of extracting multiple patches as network input by overlapping to ensure our SU-Net can train images of any size. Whilst, the number of extracted patches is much more than the number of original images for training, which will effect data augmentation.

Training Settings. We refer to the sum of cross entropy of all pixels on the feature map as loss function, select standard SGD as optimizer and adopt fault learning rate (0.01).

Evaluation Metrics. We choose two evaluation metrics to measure the performance of our SU-Net: a) We use AUC (Area Under Curve) in binary classification problem to reflect classification accuracy of our model. b) We use DSC (Dice Similarity Coefficient) to describe segmentation accuracy, i.e., the similarity between predicted segmentation map and ground truth mask. DSC is commonly used for similarity calculations and defined as follows:

$$DSC(V_{pre.}, V_{mask}) = \frac{2\,|V_{pre.} \cap V_{mask}|}{|V_{pre.}| + |V_{mask}|} = \frac{2TP}{FP + 2TP + FN}$$

4.1 Evaluation in Non-federated Scenario

We firstly perform evaluation experiments in non-federated scenario on five institutions' sub-dataset. We choose FCN8s, standard U-Net and DeepLabv3+ as baselines. As mentioned above, we adopt overlap strategy to extract patches as network input for training. Besides, we fix epoch to be 100 and batch size to be 32. Different extracted patch size may affect network performance, so we compare model performance with 32×32, 64×64, and 128×128 patches. Since the minimum downsampling times of SU-Net and baselines are five, the size of extracted patches is at least 32×32. Because batch size is fixed at 32 in advance, if extracted patches' size is 256×256 (same as original image size in dataset), it will be impossible to train due to the constraints of GPU memory. Table 2 records the test results on institution CS's datasets, AUC and DSC are represented by the format of mean $\pm$ std. We mark the best values of each column with bold black and the overall best metrics with bold italic.

Table 2. Evaluation results of SU-Net and baselines on Dataset-CS. There are 358 brain MRI images in total, we randomly select 320 images for training and evaluation and the remained 38 images for testing. The total number of patches extracted during training is 32000 (320×100). AUC and DSC are expressed by mean (%) $\pm$ std (%).

Methods	Parameters	32×32 patch		64×64 patch		$128 \times \times 128$ patch	
		AUC	DSC	AUC	DSC	AUC	DSC
FCN	240.09M	94.1 ± 1.1	15.5 ± 2.5	93.9 ± 1.1	8.7 ± 1	84.6 ± 2	3 ± 0.3
U-Net	220.94M	93.1 ± 1.1	15.7 ± 2.4	96.5 ± 1.6	43.5 ± 11	97.4 ± 16.4	45.9 ± 16.4
DeepLabV3+	315.39M	53.6 ± 1.8	0.5 ± 0.9	54.4 ± 1.8	0.6 ± 1.3	78.2 ± 0.8	3.6 ± 0.8
SU-V1	80.66M	98.5 ± 0.4	45.8 ± 6	99.5 ± 0.1	69.9 ± 2.5	99.5 ± 5.6	73.7 ± 5.6
SU-V2	**12.51M**	98.3 ± 0.2	47.7 ± 8.3	99.6 ± 0.1	69.9 ± 3.1	99.5 ± 2	77 ± 2
SU-V3	76.08M	99 ± 0.6	52 ± 17.3	99.6 ± 0.1	68.3 ± 2.6	98.8 ± 15.3	62.6 ± 15.3
SU-V4	91.22M	**99.4 ± 0.6**	**64 ± 13.4**	*99.7 ± 0*	*78.5 ± 1.8*	**99.6 ± 2.2**	**77.2 ± 2.2**

Table 3. The AUC and DSC of SU-Net and baselines on the sub-datasets of four institution DU, EZ, FG, HT. Extracted patch size is 64×64. For each sub-dataset, the total number of patches extracted during training is (the number of training set) $\times 100$. AUC and DSC are expressed by mean (%) $\pm$ std (%).

Methods	Dataset-DU		Dataset-EZ		Dataset-FG		Dataset-HT	
	AUC	DSC	AUC	DSC	AUC	DSC	AUC	DSC
FCN	94.1 ± 0.5	12.2 ± 1.7	97.2 ± 0.4	2.1 ± 0.2	92.9 ± 0.2	6.4 ± 0.3	87.6 ± 4.1	2.1 ± 0.7
U-Net	94.1 ± 2.4	22.1 ± 7.8	94.4 ± 1	1.2 ± 2.4	96 ± 1.5	11.2 ± 5	97.9 ± 0.9	26.2 ± 15.9
DeepLabV3+	55.4 ± 2	0.5 ± 1	96.1 ± 4.5	31.8 ± 34.6	57.7 ± 1.9	0.3 ± 0.3	54.1 ± 1.8	0.2 ± 0.3
SU-V1	97.4 ± 0.4	51.5 ± 3.2	**99.9 ± 0**	73.6 ± 6.7	96.8 ± 2.1	50.7 ± 13	99 ± 0.2	49.8 ± 8.9
SU-V2	96.9 ± 1.5	44.4 ± 10.1	**99.9 ± 0**	77.2 ± 5.2	96.3 ± 2.1	51.3 ± 11.6	99.1 ± 0.4	51.1 ± 7.7
SU-V3	97.6 ± 0.9	48.9 ± 3.5	**99.9 ± 0**	**78.8 ± 2.4**	96.7 ± 0.6	58.5 ± 2.8	98.6 ± 0.7	46.1 ± 12.4
SU-V4	**97.6 ± 0.2**	**52.2 ± 2.4**	99.8 ± 0.1	62.1 ± 10.7	**96.8 ± 1**	**68.5 ± 8.8**	**99.2 ± 0.3**	51.3 ± 4.6

Parameter Capacity. For SU-Net, SU-V4 has the largest parameters (91.22 MB), but still 41% of U-Net. SU-V2 has the smallest parameter capacity of 12.51MB, which is 6% of U-Net, 5% of FCN and 4% of DeepLabv3+. Since AUC and DSC of any version of SU-Net are higher than baselines, parameter efficiency of SU-Net can be verified.

AUC and DSC. It can be seen from Table 2 that SU-V4 has both highest AUC and DSC regardless of the size of patches. And when the patch size is 64×64, SU-V4 achieved the best overall AUC and DSC. The AUC of SU-V4 is 6.18%, 3.32%, and 83.27% higher than FCN, U-Net, and DeepLabv3+ respectively. The DSC of SU-V4 is 9.02 times higher than FCN, 1.8 times higher than U-Net, and compared with DeepLabv3+, it has increased 130.83 times. The reasons for these results are that a) U-Net replaces directly summing a group of up-sampling layer and corresponding down-sampling layer in FCN with concatenation to reduce feature attenuation caused by summation, hence U-Net performs better than FCN; b) SU-V4 with multiple scale receptive fields and shorter connections between two consequent layers increases the depth and width of whole network simultaneously, which further improves overall performance compared with U-Net; c) ASPP module in DeepLabv3+ has similar effect with inception module in our SU-V4, whilst SU-V4 also applies dense blocks to further learn the output features of previous inception module repeatedly and therefore achieves better AUC and DSC.

For further verifying the state-of-the-art performance with SU-Net, we test same metrics of SU-Net and baselines on datasets of other four institutions. Since overall optimal metrics can be achieved on CS's dataset when patch size is 64×64, the default patch size will be 64×64 in subsequent experiments. Table 3 presents experimental results on other four institutions' datasets. We can observe that all versions of SU-Net achieve higher AUC and DSC than baselines on each institution's dataset. Based on experimental results of five institutions' datasets, SU-V4 has the state-of-the-art performance, followed by U-Net, FCN and DeepLabv3+. U-Net was originally dedicated to medical image segmentation and further improved FCN's shortcomings, so it shows better performance. However, since DeepLabv3+ was proposed for segmenting natural images such as urban landscapes, it does not show good performance on medical images in our experiments. Moreover, the effect of SU-V1, 2, 3 is marginally worse than SU-V4, hence SU-V4 is regarded as the final model of SU-Net in this paper.

Figure 5 illustrates segmentation visualization results on five institutions' datasets. We can see that SU-Net's segmentation results are always better than baselines on each institutions' dataset. Meanwhile, except for partial images in FG's dataset, each version of SU-Net can roughly segment the outline of brain tumors on remaining four datasets, especially SU-V4 can accurately segment brain tumor's position in entire image. For some visualized results of FG, even SU-Net can not accurately segment brain tumors. This may be due to the subtle pixel-level difference between brain tumors and surrounding brain tissues in grayed-out brain images. This can be improved by applying linear operators to further enhance the contrast between tumor and surrounding tissues.

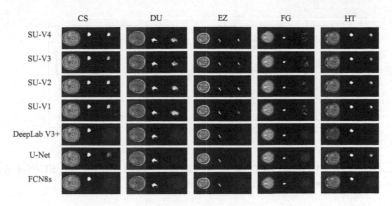

Fig. 5. The segmentation visualization results of FCN, U-Net, DeepLabv3+, SU-V1, SU-V2, SU-V3, SU-V4 on five institutions' datasets, each image from left to right consists of original image, ground truth, prediction.

Therefore, no matter from quantitative or qualitative perspective, SU-V4 can achieve the state-of-the-art performance. The SU-Net mentioned later refers to SU-V4 by default.

4.2 Evaluation in Federated Scenario

We further compare SU-Net with baselines in federated scenario. We adopt Google's TFF (TensorFlow Federated), an open source federated learning framework [10] for our experiments. We call its FL API to encapsulate SU-Net and baselines into federated learning models.

Since original dataset is provided by five real institutions' privacy data, we assume that there are a total of five clients participating in federated learning. Each client's training set still corresponds to training set of each institution, and test set of five clients (institutions) will be used to test the performance of final global model in federated learning.

To measure performance of SU-Net and baselines in federated learning, we fix the number of local model's epochs in one round to be 10, set local model's batch size as 32 and the category of communicating rounds as 1 to 10. Round is set as 10 in federated learning scenario, which is equal to epoch set with 100 in non-federated scenario.

Figure 6 describes experimental results in federated scenario. We can see that SU-Net still achieves best AUC and DSC compared to baselines in federated scenario. In addition, SU-Net's AUC (99.8%) and DSC (78.7%) in federated situation are slightly higher than in non-federated scenario, further indicating SU-Net has the state-of-the-art performance regardless of non-federated or federated scenario.

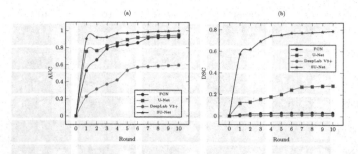

Fig. 6. Trends of AUC and DSC of FCN, U-Net, DeepLabv3+ and SU-Net with the number of communication rounds in federated learning.

5   Conclusion

This paper applies federated learning to brain tumor segmentation and propose an efficient federated learning model SU-Net for precise segmentation. SU-Net fuse the advantages of inception module and dense block to extract multi-scale features and reuse information from previous layers, promoting the transmission of information and gradient flows. Experimental results show that SU-Net achieves the state-of-the-art performance in both federated and non-federated scenarios. In future researches, we will further compress SU-Net and reduce its parameters to improve training efficiency during communication between clients and server in federated learning.

References

1. Bonawitz, K., et al.: Towards federated learning at scale: system design. In: Proceedings of SysML (2019)
2. Buda, M.: Brain MRI segmentation: Brain MRI images together with manual FLAIR abnormality segmentation masks (2019). https://www.kaggle.com/mateuszbuda/lgg-mri-segmentation
3. Buda, M., Saha, A., Mazurowski, M.A.: Association of genomic subtypes of lower-grade gliomas with shape features automatically extracted by a deep learning algorithm. Trans. Comput. Biol. Med. **109**, 218–225 (2019)
4. Chen, L.C., Papandreou, G., Kokkinos, I., Murphy, K., Yuille, A.L.: Semantic image segmentation with deep convolutional nets and fully connected CRFs. In: Proceedings of ICLR (2014)
5. Chen, L.C., Papandreou, G., Kokkinos, I., Murphy, K., Yuille, A.L.: DeepLab: semantic image segmentation with deep convolutional nets, atrous convolution, and fully connected CRFs. Trans. TPAMI **40**(4), 834–848 (2017)
6. Chen, L.C., Papandreou, G., Schroff, F., Adam, H.: Rethinking atrous convolution for semantic image segmentation. In: Proceedings of ECCV (2017)
7. Chen, L.C., Zhu, Y., Papandreou, G., Schroff, F., Adam, H.: Encoder-decoder with atrous separable convolution for semantic image segmentation. In: Proceedings of ECCV, pp. 801–818 (2018)

8. Ciresan, D., Giusti, A., Gambardella, L.M., Schmidhuber, J.: Deep neural networks segment neuronal membranes in electron microscopy images. In: Proceedings of NIPS, pp. 2843–2851 (2012)
9. Dong, H., Yang, G., Liu, F., Mo, Y., Guo, Y.: Automatic brain tumor detection and segmentation using U-net based fully convolutional networks. In: Valdés Hernández, M., González-Castro, V. (eds.) MIUA 2017. CCIS, vol. 723, pp. 506–517. Springer, Cham (2017). https://doi.org/10.1007/978-3-319-60964-5_44
10. Google: Tensorflow federated (2016). https://www.tensorflow.org/federated
11. Hard, A., et al.: Towards federated learning at scale: system design. arXiv preprint arXiv:1811.03604 (2018)
12. He, K., Zhang, X., Ren, S., Sun, J.: Deep residual learning for image recognition. In: Proceedings of CVPR, pp. 770–778 (2016)
13. Huang, G., Liu, Z., Van Der Maaten, L., Weinberger, K.Q.: Densely connected convolutional networks. In: Proceedings of CVPR, pp. 4700–4708 (2017)
14. Justin Kirby, C.K.: Tcga-lgg (2019). https://wiki.cancerimagingarchive.net/display/Public/TCGA-LGG
15. Long, J., Shelhamer, E., Darrell, T.: Fully convolutional networks for semantic segmentation. In: Proceedings of CVPR, pp. 3431–3440 (2015)
16. Mazurowski, M.A., et al.: Radiogenomics of lower-grade glioma: algorithmically-assessed tumor shape is associated with tumor genomic subtypes and patient outcomes in a multi-institutional study with The Cancer Genome Atlas data. J. Neurooncol. **133**(1), 27–35 (2017). https://doi.org/10.1007/s11060-017-2420-1
17. McMahan, H.B., Moore, E., Ramage, D., Hampson, S., et al.: Communication-efficient learning of deep networks from decentralized data. In: Proceedings of AIStats (2016)
18. Ronneberger, O., Fischer, P., Brox, T.: U-Net: convolutional networks for biomedical image segmentation. In: Navab, N., Hornegger, J., Wells, W.M., Frangi, A.F. (eds.) MICCAI 2015. LNCS, vol. 9351, pp. 234–241. Springer, Cham (2015). https://doi.org/10.1007/978-3-319-24574-4_28
19. Sermanet, P., Eigen, D., Zhang, X., Mathieu, M., Fergus, R., LeCun, Y.: OverFeat: integrated recognition, localization and detection using convolutional networks. In: Proceedings of ICLR (2013)
20. Sheller, M.J., Reina, G.A., Edwards, B., Martin, J., Bakas, S.: Multi-institutional deep learning modeling without sharing patient data: a feasibility study on brain tumor segmentation. In: Crimi, A., Bakas, S., Kuijf, H., Keyvan, F., Reyes, M., van Walsum, T. (eds.) BrainLes 2018. LNCS, vol. 11383, pp. 92–104. Springer, Cham (2019). https://doi.org/10.1007/978-3-030-11723-8_9
21. Szegedy, C., et al.: Going deeper with convolutions. In: Proceedings of CVPR, pp. 1–9 (2015)
22. Szegedy, C., Vanhoucke, V., Ioffe, S., Shlens, J., Wojna, Z.: Rethinking the inception architecture for computer vision. In: Proceedings of CVPR, pp. 2818–2826 (2016)

Synthesis of Registered Multimodal Medical Images with Lesions

Yili Qu[1(✉)], Wanqi Su[1], Xuan Lv[2], Chufu Deng[1], Ying Wang[1], Yutong Lu[1,2], Zhiguang Chen[1], and Nong Xiao[1,2]

[1] Sun Yat-sen University, Guangzhou, China
`quyli@mail3.sysu.edu.cn`, `yutong.lu@nscc-gz.cn`
[2] National University of Defense Technology, Changsha, China

Abstract. The collection and annotation of medical images data have always been a challenge in many data-driven medical image processing tasks, especially for registered multimodal medical images data. This can be effectively alleviated by utilizing the image synthesis technology. However, directly-synthesized medical images generated by current methods usually have unreasonable structures or contours and uncontrollable lesions. In this paper, we proposed a new method to synthesize registered multimodal medical images from a random normal distribution matrix based on the Generative Adversarial Networks. Besides, the corresponding lesions can be generated efficiently based on the selected lesion labels. We performed validation experiments on multiple public datasets to verify the effectiveness of synthetic lesions and the availability of synthetic data. The results show that our synthetic data can be used as pre-trained data or enhanced data in medical image intelligent processing tasks to greatly improve the generalization ability of the model.

Keywords: Image synthesis · Medical images · Multimodal · Lesions

1 Introduction

Intelligent medical image processing has attracted interest in the applications of deep learning (DL) in recent years. Medical images used for diagnosis are obtained in forms of different modalities by utilizing various imaging techniques. The common modalities include magnetic resonance imaging (MRI), computed tomography (CT), X-ray, etc. Some of them have different submodalities according to different settings during imaging, e.g. MRI has submodalities of T1, T2, etc. DL-based medical images studies expect large amounts of medical images data. However, the collection and annotation of medical images data remain challenging, especially for the registration of multimodal data. With the development of image synthesis technology, the synthesis of high-quality medical images has become a promising method to alleviate the scarcity of medical images data.

I. Farkaš et al. (Eds.): ICANN 2020, LNCS 12396, pp. 774–786, 2020.
https://doi.org/10.1007/978-3-030-61609-0_61

Medical images contain complex physiological structure information, and the normal method of synthesis is likely to produce unreasonable structures or contours. Moreover, it is difficult to ensure the registration when multimodal images are synthesized. Additionally, lesion information in medical images is an important basis for doctors to make the diagnosis and for medical image processing models to speculate and diagnose. Therefore, another challenge in synthesizing is to control the synthesis of lesions and generate corresponding lesion labels.

Generative Adversarial Networks (GAN) have been intensively studied in medical image segmentation [4], reconstruction [3], synthesis [2,10], translation [4,13] and super-resolution [14]. Recently, some studies have attempted to relieve medical data deficiency by synthesizing more diverse data, such as the synthesis of brain MRI [10], retina [2], and different body parts [15]. The brain MRI synthesis [10] utilized GAN to synthesize brain images and achieved image augmentation and anonymization. However, this method needs to collect additional labels for segmentation training, which restricted the application. In this study, tumor segmentation labels were firstly added to guide the lesions synthesis, but there were no additional constraints during the synthesis process, which means high uncertainty of the lesions synthesis. The retinal synthesis [2] achieved the random generation of vascular annotation images by variational Auto-Encoder (VAE) [9], and the color retinal images were synthesized with the generated vascular annotation images. The latest SkrGAN [15] made a single-modal image synthesis attempt, in line with our research, SkrGAN employed Sobel operator to extract sketches containing structural information from medical images for synthesis. However, similar to other studies, SkrGAN did not consider lesion information synthesis or the production of corresponding lesion labels, thus most of the synthesized data is not available.

To solve these problems, we designed a multimodal medical image synthesis framework, which accepts a random normal distribution matrix to synthesize a set of registered multimodal images with specified lesions. We conducted synthesis experiments on several public datasets to more comprehensively verify the effectiveness of synthetic data. Our main contributions are as follows:

- Compared with the state-of-the-art sketch extraction method, we proposed a more concise and clear structural map extraction method, which can directly extract anatomical structure from medical images without training.
- We proposed a method based on VAE and GAN to synthesize any number of diverse structural maps from normal distribution matrices.
- We proposed a new scheme for synthesizing multimodal medical images with lesions by adding lesion labels. The loss provided by the lesion processor guides the lesion generation according to label, and the loss provided by the modality translation network guides multimodal images to be registered.
- We employed synthetic data to train different medical image processing models. By evaluating the task performance of each model, we indirectly evaluated the quality of synthetic data and the effectiveness of synthetic lesions.

2 Method

Our method includes two stages. In the first stage, we extracted structural maps from MRI and further generate structural maps from random normal distribution matrices. In the second stage, A conditional generator was trained with the input of structural maps and lesion labels to synthesize MRI images of different modalities according to different conditions. Details of the model structure can be seen in our source code[1].

2.1 Structural Map Extraction and Generation

We designate the image that provides basic contour and structure information as a structural map. Medical images generated directly from random noise by GAN are usually in short of realistic structural information while structural maps can provide basic guidance for the synthesis of medical images. Therefore we extract structural maps directly from images and feed them to a generator for learning synthesis of structural maps.

Algorithm 1. Structural map extraction

Input: grayscale image x; pixel threshold α, β, γ; Gaussian kernel variance σ_1, σ_2.
Output: structural map s.

1: $s_1 = \text{reduce\_min}(\text{sobel}(x))$
2: $s_2 = \text{reduce\_max}(\text{sobel}(x))$
3: $s_1 = \text{gaussian\_blur}(s_1, \sigma_1)$
4: $s_2 = \text{gaussian\_blur}(s_2, \sigma_1)$
5: $s_1 = \text{mean}(s_1) - s_1$
6: $s_2 = s_2 - \text{mean}(s_2)$
7: $s_1 = ones \times (s_1 > \alpha)$
8: $s_2 = ones \times (s_2 > \alpha)$
9: $s = ones \times ((s_1 + s_2) > 0)$
10: $s = \text{gaussian\_blur}(s, \sigma_2)$
11: $s = ones \times ((s_1 + s_2) > \beta)$
12: $s = \text{medfilt}(s) \times (x > \gamma)$

Algorithm 2. Mask extraction

Input: grayscale image x; pixel threshold α; expanded pixel width p.
Output: mask m.

1: $m = 1.0 - ones \times (x > \alpha)$
2: $size = [x.width + p, x.length + p]$
3: $m = \text{resize}(m, size)$
4: $m = \text{crop\_padding}(m, p)$
5: $m = \text{medfilt}(m)$

---

[1] https://github.com/quyili/MultimodalMedicalImagesSynthesis.

Structural Map Extraction Method. The general structural maps such as retinal vascular maps [2] and brain segmentation labels [10] require additional data and training before extraction. Considering that the Sobel operator [12] in digital image processing field is widely used for edge extraction, we designed a structural map extraction method based on Sobel operator. As shown in Algorithm 1, gaussian_blur($\cdot$) is 3×3 Gaussian blur and medfilt($\cdot$) is 3×3 median filter function. The method is advanced for fast operation, no training, and no additional required data.

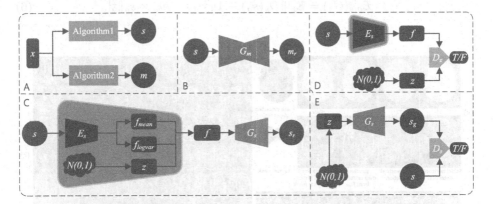

Fig. 1. Structural map generation training. x is an input real image, s is a structural map, m is a mask extract by Algorithm 2. E_s is a VAE encoder, which outputs the encode matrices f_{mean} and f_{logvar}. z is a random noise sampling from normal distribution $\mathcal{N}(0, 1^2)$ and f is a approximate normal distribution matrix. G_s is a VAE decoder, s_r is a reconstructed structural map, and s_g is a synthesis structural map. D_s and D_z are the discriminators. G_m is a mask generator and m_r is a generated mask. E_s, G_s, D_z, D_s are tuned on VGG11 [11], G_m is tuned on U-net [16]. E_s and all discriminators, including those described below, output two results in the last two layers. G_s is a reverse VGG11.

Structural Map Generation Training. The structural map generation training process is shown in Fig. 1, where $f = f_{mean} + \exp(0.5 \times f_{logvar}) \times z$. After training, the model can generate structural maps from random normal distribution matrices. And Fig. 2 shows examples of structural maps. The training losses in Fig. 1 are as follows, where $\mathbb{E}$ is the expectation operator, and $m_r = G_m(s)$, $s_r = G_s(f)$, $s_g = G_s(z)$, $m_g = G_m(s_g)$:

– Part B: Mask generation loss

$$\mathcal{L}_m(G_m) = \mathbb{E}_{m,s}[\|m - m_r\|_2^2]. \tag{1}$$

– Part C: Structural map reconstruction loss

$$\mathcal{L}_r(E_s, G_s) = \mathbb{E}_{s,f,m}[\|s - s_r\|_2^2 + \|m_r \times s_r\|_2^2]. \tag{2}$$

– Part D: Distribution encoding adversarial loss

$$\mathcal{L}_{d,z}(D_z) = \mathbb{E}_{s,z}[\|D_z(z) - 1\|_2^2 + \|D_z(f)\|_2^2], \tag{3}$$

$$\mathcal{L}_{g,z}(E_s) = \mathbb{E}_z[\|D_z(f) - 1\|_2^2]. \tag{4}$$

– Part E: Structural map decoding adversarial loss

$$\mathcal{L}_{d,s}(D_s) = \mathbb{E}_{s,z}[\|D_s(s) - 1\|_2^2 + \|D_s(s_g)\|_2^2], \tag{5}$$

$$\mathcal{L}_{g,s}(G_s) = \mathbb{E}_z[\|D_s(s_g) - 1\|_2^2 + +\|m_g \times s_g\|_2^2]. \tag{6}$$

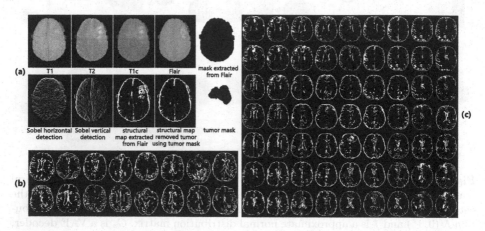

Fig. 2. Structural maps on BRATS2015. (a) The images produced by the structural map extraction method. (b) Randomly-synthesized structural maps. (c) Synthesized structural maps from sequence sampling on the normal distribution, where the output gradient effects are controlled by the gradient of the input.

Fusion of Structural Map and Noise. The structural map is a simple binary sparse matrix, which provides a limited amount of information. In DL training, adding noise is one of the most commonly used data augmentation methods. We define the equation $s' = s + z' \times (1 - m) \times (1 - s)$ to fuse random noise into the organ contour of the structural map, where $z' \sim \mathcal{U}(\alpha_1, \alpha_2)$, $\alpha_1 = 0.5, \alpha_2 = 0.6$ by default. m is a binary mask paired with the structural map s. As shown in Fig. 3, the final fusion structural map s' not only retains all the structure information, but also has rich random information. Moreover, it is closer to the expected medical image and thus easier to learn.

2.2   Multimodal Images Synthesis

As shown in Fig. 4, we use pre-trained G_s to obtain s_g, then fuse with noise, the fusion can concatenate with the specified lesion label l. When selecting a lesion label randomly, the label may indicate a lesion that out of the organ contour in structural map. For this reason, we use the corresponding mask to filter out these labels that out of contour. Next, G accepts the one-hot conditional matrix one_hot(i) and fusion input, and then decodes the input to generate the modality i image $x_{g,i}$. The lesion processor $G_{l,i}$ and the modality translation network G_t train completely in advance to provide the lesions generation guidance loss and the registration guidance loss for G.

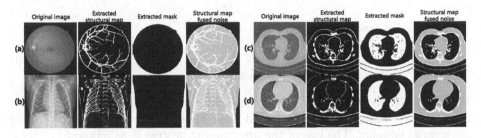

Fig. 3. Medical images and the corresponding maps. (a) DRIVE retinal images. (b) Kaggle Chest X-ray. (c) Kaggle Lung CT. (d) TC Lung CT.

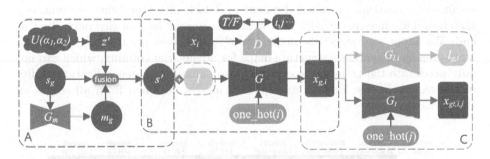

Fig. 4. Synthesis of multimodal images. Purple box A is the fusion process of structural map and random noise, gray box B is the core synthesis process, and yellow box C is the optional refinement process. $x_{g,i}$ is the image of modality i generated by generator G. $l_{g,i}$ is the lesion label of modality i generated by lesion processor $G_{l,i}$. $x_{gt,i,j}$ is the image of modality j translated from modality i by modality translation network G_t.

G and D are tuned on U-net and VGG11 respectively and then form a group of ACGAN [7] architecture. The loss items are as follows, where $d(x_i)$ and $c(x_i)$ are the true/false discrimination and category discrimination of the discriminator $D(x_i)$, $d(x_{g,i})$ and $c(x_{g,i})$ are the output of $D(x_{g,i})$, and concat() is the concatenate operation on feature map channel.

– Adversarial loss

$$\mathcal{L}_d(D) = \mathbb{E}_{x,s_g,l}[\sum_{i=0}(\|d(x_i) - 1\|_2^2 + \|d(x_{g,i})\|_2^2$$
$$+ \|c(x_i) - i\|_2^2 + \|c(x_{g,i}) - i\|_2^2)], \tag{7}$$

$$\mathcal{L}_g(G) = \mathbb{E}_{s_g,l}[\sum_{i=0}(\|d(x_{g,i}) - 1\|_2^2 + \|c(x_{g,i}) - i\|_2^2)]. \tag{8}$$

– Lesion generation guidance loss

$$\mathcal{L}_{les}(G) = \mathbb{E}_{s_g,l}[\sum_{i=0}(\|l - l_{g,i}\|_2^2)]. \tag{9}$$

– Registration guidance loss

$$\mathcal{L}_{reg}(G) = \mathbb{E}_{s_g,l}[\sum_{j=0}\sum_{i=0,i\neq j}(\|x_{g,i} - x_{gt,j,i}\|_2^2)]. \tag{10}$$

We can also use the real medical images and the structural maps extracted from the real images for self-supervised pre-training to accelerate the process of adversarial training. The loss of the pre-training process is as follows:

$$\mathcal{L}_{pre}(G) = \mathbb{E}_{s,l}[\sum_{i=0}(\|x_{g,i} - x_i\|_2^2 + \|x_{g,i} \times m_i - x_i \times m_i\|_2^2)]. \tag{11}$$

SkrGAN [15] employs real sketches and self-supervision loss for training, which results in overfitting on small datasets and lack of adaptability to synthesis sketches. This may eventually lead synthesis images lack of diversity. To this end, We adopt real structure maps for self-supervised pre-training and use a large number of synthesis structure maps for adversarial training, which can not only accelerate the training process but also enhance the generalization ability of the model. Figure 5 shows examples of images obtained from all stages on BRATS2015.

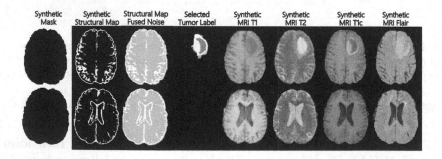

Fig. 5. Multimodal images synthesis on BRATS2015.

2.3   Lesion Processing and Translation Training

We perform lesion processing and translation training on real data before multimodal image synthesis. G_t, D_t have the same structure and adversarial loss with G, D. And G_t, D_t have the same cycle consistency loss CycleGAN [16]. U-net and SSD [6] are used for segmentation and detection as the lesion processor G_l. The loss of $G_{l,i}$ is the same in multimodal images synthesis stage, except that the real labels l_i is used.

3   Experiments

3.1   Datasets

BRATS2015[2] includes registered T1, T2, T1c, Flair, 274 3D MRIs per modality, and the corresponding tumor segmentation labels. **Kaggle Chest X-ray**[3] includes 5863 X-rays of chest. **Kaggle Lung CT**[4] includes 267 CTs of transverse from lung. **DRIVE**[5] includes 20 color fundus retinal photos and corresponding retinal vascular segmentation annotations in both training set and test set. **FIRE**[6] includes 268 color fundus retinal photos. **TC Lung CT**[7] includes 1470 3D CTs with detection label of 5 kinds of lesions. By filling the detection box, the detection label is converted into the lesion label image as the input of the model. We divided all 3D images to 2D slides. All images were normalized and scaled to $[512 \times 512]$.

Table 1. Ablation experiments on BRATS2015

Test	Noise	Structural map	$\mathcal{L}_{reg}$	Lesion label, $\mathcal{L}_{les}$	Filter lesion label	MS-SSIM
A	√	×	×	×	×	0.504
B	×	√	×	×	×	0.654
C	√	√	×	×	×	0.671
D	√	√	√	×	×	0.674
E	√	√	√	√	×	0.673
F	√	√	√	√	√	**0.686**

---

[2] https://www.smir.ch/BRATS/Start2015.
[3] https://www.kaggle.com/paultimothymooney/chest-xray-pneumonia.
[4] https://www.kaggle.com/kmader/finding-lungs-in-ct-data/data/.
[5] http://www.isi.uu.nl/Research/Databases/DRIVE/.
[6] https://projects.ics.forth.gr/cvrl/fire/.
[7] https://tianchi.aliyun.com/competition/entrance/231724/information.

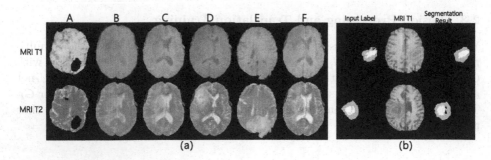

Fig. 6. (a) Synthetic MRIs of ablation experiments. (b) Segmentation results of synthetic MRI.

Table 2. Verification experiment of synthetic lesion effectiveness.

Training dataset	Test dataset	MSE↓	Dice score↑
Real	Real	0.027	0.915
Real	Synthetic	0.098	0.838

3.2 Experiments Settings

Each model was comprehensively trained more than 100 epochs until completely converged with a learning rate of 1e-5 and a batch size of 4. The loss was minimized using the Adam optimizer. We used multi-scale structural similarity (MS-SSIM) and FreshetInception distance (FID) [5] to assess the performance of synthetic medical images. Dice Score and mean square error (MSE) were used to evaluate the segmentation results. Sensitivity, Accuracy and area under the ROC curve (AUC) were used to assess vascular annotation results. The Mean Average Precision (mAP) was used to estimate the detection results. The performances were evaluated on 2D images. We adopted the best results after at least four effective training sessions.

Table 3. Evaluation of synthetic image quality (A).

Dataset	Metric	Ours	SkrGAN [15]	DCGAN [8,15]	ACGAN [7,15]	WGAN [1,15]	PGGAN [5,15]
Kaggle	MS-SSIM ↑	**0.597**	0.506	0.269	0.301	0.401	0.493
Chest X-ray	FID ↓	**102.5**	114.6	260.3	235.2	300.7	124.2
Kaggle	MS-SSIM ↑	**0.473**	0.359	0.199	0.235	0.277	0.328
Lung CT	FID ↓	**66.91**	79.97	285.0	222.5	349.1	91.89

3.3   Ablation Experiments on BRATS2015

Table 1 shows the settings and results of the ablation experiments of our method. Figure 6 (a) shows examples of synthetic images generated in ablation experiments. **A** no contour from structural map, the synthetic image conforms to the features of MRI, but not to the structural features of the brain. **B** was poorly trained due to the lack of a random sample. **C** registration effect seems unsatisfactory, especially the edge details. Lesions in **D** are random and exaggerated, which hardly match the input label. Obviously, the tumor in **E** is beyond the contours of the brain. **F** adopts our complete scheme and achieve the best synthesis quality. The results show that our method is helpful to improve the authenticity of the synthesized image. However, lesion labels need to be screened before input.

3.4   Evaluation of Lesion Effectiveness on BRATS2015

As shown in Table 2 and Fig. 6 (b), the segmentation model trained with real data can be used on the synthetic data, indicating that the distribution of synthetic data is very similar to that of real data, and the synthetic lesions and the real lesions are similar enough for the segmentation model to recognize the synthetic lesions. The results show that synthetic lesions are effective.

3.5   Evaluation of Synthetic Image Quality

Our method was quantitatively evaluated on multiple datasets and compared with state-of-the-art methods. As shown in Table 3, 4 and Fig. 7, the quality of the synthetic image input with structural map is much better than that of the synthetic image input with noise. The model generalizes better when the structural map is processed by fusion noise versus those processed without fusion noise or treated by binary inversion. Compared with the sketches of SkrGAN or noise input, our synthetic medical image achieves higher quality and seems more closer to the real image, which can be largely attributed to the structural map, self-supervised pre-training and lesion loss that we adopted.

3.6   Evaluation of Synthetic Data Availability

As shown in Table 5, we mixed real BRATS2015 training data with synthetic data in different amounts, then we used the mixed data for segmentation training, and finally evaluated the segmentation ability of the model on the real BRATS2015 test set. We set up three data mixing modes: random mixing, real data training first, and synthetic data training first. As reported in Table 5, our synthetic images can be used as pre-trained data or enhanced data to greatly improve the generalization ability of the model, and the performance of our synthetic data augmentation is much better than the usual data augmentation. We do not recommend using synthetic data completely for training or using synthetic data for supplementary training.

Table 4. Evaluation of synthetic image quality (B).

Dataset	Metric	Our tumor	Ours	SkrGAN*	Basic GAN
DRIVE+FIRE	MS-SSIM ↑	–	**0.607**	0.584	0.392
Color Fundus	FID ↓	–	**30.13**	37.91	227.41
BRATS2015	MS-SSIM ↑	0.692	**0.686**	0.653	0.504
MRI	FID ↓	20.15	**21.87**	28.76	124.53
TC Lung CT	MS-SSIM ↑	–	**0.676**	0.667	0.543
	FID ↓	–	**27.40**	29.81	113.65

*The reproduce SkrGAN trains on the inverse binary image of our real structure map.

Table 5. Synthetic data availability verification on BRATS2015 tumor segmentor.

Real	Synthetic	Enhanced	Mix	MSE↓	Dice score↑
×1	0	0	–	0.027	0.915
0	×1	0	–	0.294	0.708
×10%	×1	0	$\mathcal{S}$	0.036	0.906
×20%	×80%	0	$\mathcal{M}$	0.038	0.904
×80%	×20%	0	$\mathcal{M}$	0.028	0.914
×1	×20%	0	$\mathcal{M}$	0.025	0.921
×1	×50%	0	$\mathcal{M}$	**0.020**	**0.939**
×1	×1	0	$\mathcal{M}$	0.022	0.934
×1	0	×20%	$\mathcal{M}$	0.027	0.917
×1	0	×50%	$\mathcal{M}$	0.025	0.920
×1	0	×1	$\mathcal{M}$	0.026	0.919
×1	×1	0	$\mathcal{R}$	0.161	0.795
×1	×1	0	$\mathcal{S}$	**0.020**	**0.940**

$\mathcal{M}$: random mixing $\mathcal{S}$: synthetic first $\mathcal{R}$: real first

Table 6. Synthetic data availability verification on DRIVE vascular segmentor.

Training data	Test data	Sensitivity↑	Accuracy↑	AUC↑
Training set	Test set	0.7781	0.9477	0.9705
Training Set+2000 SkrGAN Synthetic Images	Test set	**0.8464**	0.9513	**0.9762**
Training Set+2000 SkrGAN* Synthetic Images	Test set	0.8297	0.9428	0.9732
Training Set+2000 Our Synthetic Images	Test Set	0.8416	**0.9518**	0.9749

*The reproduce SkrGAN trains on the inverse binary image of our real structure map.

As shown in Tables 6 and 7, We further tested the medical images in other medical images processing tasks with corresponding datasets. The results show that our synthetic data can also improve the generalization ability of the model in these tasks, which indicates that our synthetic data are available and the synthetic lesions are effective.

Table 7. Synthetic data availability verification on TC CT pulmonary nodule detector.

Training data	Test data	mAP↑
TC Lung CT training set	TC Lung CT Test Set	0.402
TC Lung CT Training Set + 20000 Synthetic Images	TC Lung CT Test Set	**0.410**

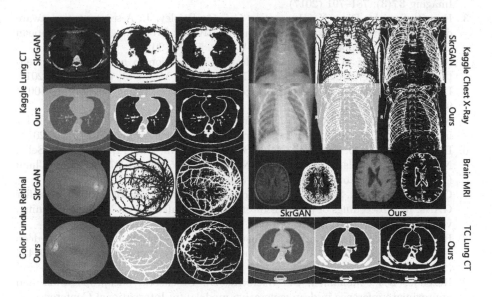

Fig. 7. Visual contrast of synthetic images. 'SkrGAN' lines are synthetic image of SkrGAN [15], the sketch and the sketch binary inversion image. 'Ours' lines are our synthetic images, the structural map fused noise and the original structural map.

4   Conclusion

In this paper, we proposed a clearer extraction method of medical image structural map based Sobel operator, which requires no training or additional labels, and takes advantage of VAE and GAN to learn the mapping between normal distribution and structure map distribution. The multimodal synthesis based on structural maps can synthesize the medical images that conform to the physiological structure. The well-designed lesion generation guidance loss and registration supervision loss ensure the synthesis of the specified lesion and multimodal registration. Experimental results on multiple datasets show that the synthetic lesions are effective, and the synthetic medical images can be used as pre-trained data or enhanced data to improve the performance of the model.

Acknowledgments. This work was supported by the National Key R&D Program of China Under Grant No. 2018YFB0203904; the Nature Science Foundation of China under Grant No. 61872392, No. U1611261, and No. U1811461; the Pearl River S&T Nova Program of Guangzhou under Grant No. 201906010008; and the Program for Guangdong Introducing Innovative and Entrepreneurial Teams under Grant No. 2016ZT06D211.

References

1. Arjovsky, M., Chintala, S., Bottou, L.: Wasserstein generative adversarial networks. In: International Conference on Machine Learning, pp. 214–223 (2017)
2. Costa, P., et al.: End-to-end adversarial retinal image synthesis. IEEE Trans. Med. Imaging **37**(3), 781–791 (2017)
3. Fan, Z., Sun, L., Ding, X., Huang, Y., Cai, C., Paisley, J.: A segmentation-aware deep fusion network for compressed sensing MRI. In: Proceedings of the European Conference on Computer Vision (ECCV), pp. 55–70 (2018)
4. Kamnitsas, K., et al.: Unsupervised domain adaptation in brain lesion segmentation with adversarial networks. In: Niethammer, M., et al. (eds.) IPMI 2017. LNCS, vol. 10265, pp. 597–609. Springer, Cham (2017). https://doi.org/10.1007/978-3-319-59050-9_47
5. Karras, T., Aila, T., Laine, S., Lehtinen, J.: Progressive growing of GANs for improved quality, stability, and variation. arXiv preprint arXiv:1710.10196 (2017)
6. Liu, W., et al.: SSD: single shot MultiBox detector. In: Leibe, B., Matas, J., Sebe, N., Welling, M. (eds.) ECCV 2016. LNCS, vol. 9905, pp. 21–37. Springer, Cham (2016). https://doi.org/10.1007/978-3-319-46448-0_2
7. Odena, A., Olah, C., Shlens, J.: Conditional image synthesis with auxiliary classifier GANs. In: Proceedings of the 34th International Conference on Machine Learning, vol. 70, pp. 2642–2651. JMLR.org (2017)
8. Radford, A., Metz, L., Chintala, S.: Unsupervised representation learning with deep convolutional generative adversarial networks. arXiv preprint arXiv:1511.06434 (2015)
9. Rezende, D.J., Mohamed, S., Wierstra, D.: Stochastic backpropagation and approximate inference in deep generative models. In: International Conference on Learning Representations, pp. 1278–1286 (2014)
10. Shin, H.-C., et al.: Medical image synthesis for data augmentation and anonymization using generative adversarial networks. In: Gooya, A., Goksel, O., Oguz, I., Burgos, N. (eds.) SASHIMI 2018. LNCS, vol. 11037, pp. 1–11. Springer, Cham (2018). https://doi.org/10.1007/978-3-030-00536-8_1
11. Simonyan, K., Zisserman, A.: Very deep convolutional networks for large-scale image recognition. arXiv preprint arXiv:1409.1556 (2014)
12. Sobel, I.: Camera models and machine perception. Ph.D. dissertation (1970)
13. Yi, X., Babyn, P.: Sharpness-aware low-dose CT denoising using conditional generative adversarial network. J. Digit. Imaging **31**(5), 655–669 (2018)
14. You, C., et al.: CT super-resolution GAN constrained by the identical, residual, and cycle learning ensemble (GAN-circle). IEEE Trans. Med. Imaging **39**(1), 188–203 (2019)
15. Zhang, T., et al.: SkrGAN: sketching-rendering unconditional generative adversarial networks for medical image synthesis. MICCAI 2019. LNCS, vol. 11767, pp. 777–785. Springer, Cham (2019). https://doi.org/10.1007/978-3-030-32251-9_85
16. Zhu, J.Y., Park, T., Isola, P., Efros, A.A.: Unpaired image-to-image translation using cycle-consistent adversarial networks. In: Proceedings of the IEEE International Conference on Computer Vision, pp. 2223–2232 (2017)

ACE-Net: Adaptive Context Extraction Network for Medical Image Segmentation

Tuo Leng[1](✉), Yu Wang[1], Ying Li[1], and Zhijie Wen[2]

[1] School of Computer Engineering and Science, Shanghai University, Shanghai, China
tleng@shu.edu.cn
[2] College of Sciences, Shanghai University, Shanghai, China

Abstract. It remains a challenging task to segment the medical images due to their diversity of structures. Although some state-of-the-art approaches have been proposed, the following two problems have not been fully explored: the redundant use of low-level features, and the lack of effective contextual modules to model long-range dependencies. In this paper, we propose a combination model based on ACE-Net of two newly proposed modules: The Joint Attention Upsample (JAU) module and Context Similarity Module (CSM). We extend skip connections by introducing an attention mechanism within the JAU module, followed by generating guidance information to weight low-level features using high-level features. We then introduce an affinity matrix into the CSM to optimize the long-range dependencies adaptively, which is based on a self-attention mechanism. Furthermore, our ACE-Net adaptively construct multi-scale contextual representations with multiple well-designed Context Similarity Modules (CSMs) which are been used in parallel in next process. Based on the evaluation on two public medical image datasets (EndoScene and RIM-ONE-R1), our network demonstrates significantly improvements of the segmentation performance of the model comparing to other similar methods, as the extraction on context information is more effectively and richer.

Keywords: Medical image segmentation · Deep learning · Adaptive context extraction network

1 Introduction

Image segmentation, aiming at assigning a category label for each pixel, is a crucial step in medical image analysis. Biomedical image segmentation can extract different tissues, organs, or pathologies based on specific tasks, which can support subsequent medical analysis, such as medical diagnosis, surgical planning and so on. In common practice, segmentation is performed manually by pathologists, which is time-consuming and tedious. However, the ever-increasing quantity and variety of medical images make manual segmentation impracticable in terms of cost and reproducibility. Therefore, there is a high demand for accuracy and

© Springer Nature Switzerland AG 2020
I. Farkaš et al. (Eds.): ICANN 2020, LNCS 12396, pp. 787–799, 2020.
https://doi.org/10.1007/978-3-030-61609-0_62

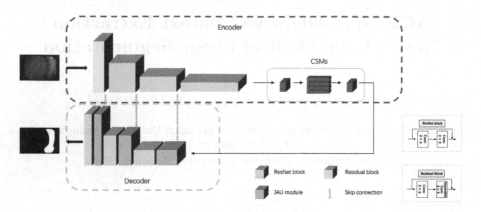

Fig. 1. Overview of Adaptive Context Extraction Network. The multi-scale context information is aggregated by CSMs, which contains multiple CSM in parallel. Based on JAU and decoder module, we obtain the mask as the segmentation prediction map.

reliable automatic segmentation methods that allow improvement of workflow efficiency in clinical scenarios, alleviating the workload of radiologists and other medical experts.

Recently, with the rapid development of convolutional neural networks (CNNs), a large number of methods based on CNNs keep emerging and refreshing the records of visual recognition tasks. The first end-to-end network model in the field of image segmentation is the fully convolutional network (FCN) [18]. In the FCN, the author first removed the fully connection layer from the CNNs and used bilinear interpolation to restore the image resolution, so that the model based on deep CNNs had end-to-end training ability for the first time. To solve the issue of detail loss in feature extraction to some extent, one of the most powerful models, called U-Net, was proposed [17], which is an encoder-decoder architecture deep convolutional network. The architecture of U-Net is composed of a contracting path, which collapses an input image into a set of high-level features, and an expanding path, in which high-level features are used to reconstruct a pixelwise segmentation mask at multiple upsampling steps. Moreover, U-Net introduced skip connections to retrieve detailed information by combining high-resolution features with the corresponding upsampled low-resolution features, and this structure shows great effectiveness in recovering fine-grained details of target objects and has been widely used in medical image segmentation.

Although the existing models have achieved good results in many segmentation tasks, there are still some problems to be solved. First, encoder-decoder-based networks with skip connections have achieved the most advanced performance in the field of medical image segmentation up to now, but these approaches lead to excessive and redundant use of computational resources and model parameters in that similar low-level features are repeatedly extracted by all models within the cascade. To address this issue, several variants of U-Net have emerged recently, among which Attention U-Net [15] and UNet++ [22] are the most famous methods. Attention U-Net uses a simple but effective module based on an attention mechanism, i.e., attention gates (AGs). Models trained with AGs can learn to suppress irrelevant regions in an input image while highlighting salient features useful for a specific task implicitly. In UNet++, a more powerful architecture was proposed, which is essentially a deeply supervised encoder-decoder network with a series of nested, dense skip pathways between sub-networks. By using the redesigned skip pathways, the semantic gap between the feature maps of the encoder and decoder sub-networks can be reduced. Second, because of the lack of effective context modules, long-range dependencies are not well modeled, which appears to be crucial to semantic segmentation performance. Recent works to solve this issue have aimed at aggregating multi-scale contextual information [1–3,21]. PSPNet [21] uses a novel context module called a pyramid pooling module to exploit the capability of global contextual information by aggregating different-region-based contexts. Unlike a pyramid pooling module, which aggregates multi-scale contextual information through pooling operations, Atrous Spatial Pyramid Pooling (ASPP) proposed in [2] is implemented by multiple dilated convolution blocks. Abundant experiments show that a context module is very effective in improving the performance of semantic segmentation. However, these multi-scale context modules are manually designed, lacking flexibility to model the multi-context representations. This leads to a failure to take full advantage of the long-range relationships, which is of pivotal importance in many medical imaging segmentation problems.

In summary, the three main contributions of this paper are the following. First, we propose a Context Similarity Module (CSM) to exact multi-scale context information through multiple feature-exaction branches, which contains separable atrous convolutions with different dilated rates. Second, we propose an upsampling module, i.e., the Joint Attention Upsample (JAU) module, based on the attention mechanism, which can aggregate low- and high-level feature information more effectively. By combining the above modules, the proposed Adaptive Context Extraction Network (ACE-Net) achieves state-of-the-art performance on two medical datasets.

2   Method

In this section, we first introduce the proposed Context Similarity Module (CSM) and Joint Attention Upsample (JAU) module in detail. Then, we describe the complete encoder-decoder network architecture, i.e., the Adaptive Context Extraction Network for medical image segmentation tasks. Figure 1 shows a flowchart of our proposed method, which is covered in detail in Sect. 2.3.

Context information has been proved to be essentially important for semantic segmentation tasks. In recent works [1,7,13,21], increasingly more articles introduce context-extraction modules and effectively boost the segmentation performance of their models. To extract the context information from high-level feature maps generated by the encoder module more effectively, we propose a novel module named the Context Similarity Module (CSM) that can extract multi-scale context information and long-range dependencies.

2.1   Context Similarity Module

The CSM is a key component in the proposed Adaptive Context Extraction Network (ACE-Net). As shown in Fig. 2, the proposed CSM mainly contains three branches. The first and second branches are used to generate a spatial affine matrix that contains region-to-region correlation. The CSM can not only extract long-range contextual information, but can also highlight features in the most important region with the spatial affine matrix. The third branch aims to process single-scale representation. Details follow.

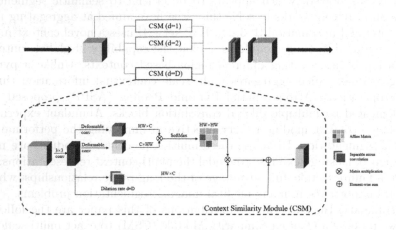

Fig. 2. Illustration of proposed Context Similarity Module. It contains three cascade branches, the first and second branches are used to code long-range information and the third branch is used to extract features from different scales.

Deformable Convolution: The recently proposed concept of deformable convolution [5,23] has caught our attention, which is capable of learning sampling locations adaptively. Deformable convolution was first proposed in DCNv1 [5], in which the offsets are learned by adding an additional convolutional layer to the standard convolution, which contributes to determining the sampling location. Last year, Zhu et al. proposed a revised version (DCNv2) of deformable convolution in [23]. The main improvement of DCNV2 compared with DCNV1 is to achieve more effective feature extraction by assigning different weights to each sampling point after offset correction. In particular, these weights are learnable, and they can adjust the sampled pixel's contribution so that the network can better focus on the inside of the object. The following equations represent a standard convolution operation, deformable convolution operation from DCNV1, and deformable convolution operation from DCNV2, respectively:

$$y[i] = \sum_{k}^{K} x[i + k] \cdot w[k], \tag{1}$$

$$y[i] = \sum_k^K x[i + k + \Delta k] \cdot w[k], \tag{2}$$

$$y[i] = \sum_k^K x[i + k + \Delta k] \cdot w[k] \cdot \Delta m_k, \tag{3}$$

where y indicates the output after convolution operation, i is the location, x is the input signal, Δk denotes offsets, Δm_k denotes the learnable modulation weights with a range of $[0,1]$, w denotes the filter with a length of k, and k enumerates K.

Affine Matrix: Since convolution operations would lead to a local receptive field, the features corresponding to the pixels with the same label may have some differences. These differences introduce intra-class inconsistency and affect recognition accuracy. To address this issue, we explore global contextual information by building associations among features with the attention mechanism, which is inspired by some recent works [9,14,16]. The proposed method could adaptively aggregate long-range contextual information and thus improve feature representation for medical image segmentation.

As illustrated in Fig. 2, given a feature map $X_0 \in R^{(H \times W \times C_0)}$, where H, W, C_0 represent the height, width and number of channels of the feature map respectively. First, we feed X_0 into a convolution layer and generate a new feature map X to filter out the irrelevant features, where $X \in R^{(H \times W \times C)}$ and $C < C_0$. In this work, we have $C = C_0/4$. For each pair of position (x_i, x_j) in the feature matrix X, a pixelwise similarity map $f(x_i, x_j) \in R^{(N \times N)}$ is computed and $N = H \times W$ here. Suggested by the non-local operation [7,19], we define f as a combination of dot-product and softmax:

$$f(x_i, x_j) = \frac{exp(\alpha(x_i)^T \beta(x_j))}{\sum_{j=1}^N exp(\alpha(x_i)^T \beta(x_j))}, \tag{4}$$

where $f(x_i, x_j)$ measures the jth position's impact on i^{th} position, and N is the number of pixels. $\alpha(x_i)$ and $\beta(x_j)$ are embedded layers implemented by deformable convolution. It can be inferred that f encodes the relationships of all positions between the original feature map and captured dense contextual information in detail. Meanwhile, we feed X to a separable dilated convolution layer to generate a new feature map $Y \in R^{(H \times W \times C)}$, and then we reshape it to $R^{(N \times C)}$. Furthermore, we multiply $f(x_i, x_j)$ by Y and perform an element-wise sum operation with feature map X as follows:

$$Z_i = \sum_{j=1}^N f(x_i, x_j) \cdot Y_j + X_i. \tag{5}$$

The resulting feature map Z is a sum of the relationship feature and the original feature, thus we believe that Z has a wide range of contextual views and detailed long-range context information. Then we concatenate the feature map Z generated by each CSM together with the original feature map X_0 to aggregate rich details and we get a feature map X_1. Finally, we feed X_1 into a 3×3 convolution layer to generate the final feature map which has the same shape as X_0.

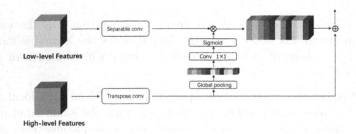

Fig. 3. Details of proposed Joint Attention Upsample module.

2.2   Joint Attention Upsample Module

In medical image segmentation, the precision of segmentation results is highly required, so gradually recovering the lost spatial details in the process of upsampling has become a research hotspot. Skip connection, introduced by U-Net [17], has been proved to be highly effective in numerous works. However, the problem of skip connections is that low-level feature maps are simply passed backwards, and we believe that there is a significant amount of redundancy in these feature maps, and naive skip connections cannot distinguish the more valuable and important parts of the information. Attention U-Net [15] can assign more weight coefficients to important regions to make the network more focused on specific local regions, which is implemented by incorporating attention-gates (AGs) into the standard U-Net architecture. In SE-Net [10], the two-dimensional (2D) feature map of each channel is squeezed into a scalar in the spatial dimension, which has a global perceptive field to some extent. Then, the correlation between the channels is explicitly modeled through two fully connected layers. Finally, the weight obtained is multiplied by the previous feature maps channel to channel to complete the re-calibration of the original feature maps. Last year, in PANet [12] a Global Attention Upsample (GAU) was proposed to deploy different-scale feature maps more effectively through a channel attention mechanism similar to SE block.

Inspired by PANet [12], we propose the JAU module to selectively combine low-level features with upsampled high-level features, which is depicted in Fig. 3. First, We feed the low-level features into a depthwise-separable convolutional layer to refine the features channel by channel without introducing too many parameters. At the same time, we perform global pooling on the high-level features to generate global context, which is of great significance to the subsequent feature screening. Then, a 1×1 convolutional layer with batch normalization is applied to the global feature to refine the channel-wise dependencies. Next, we feed the refined global context information into a sigmoid layer to make it in the interval [0, 1] on each channel, and then we multiply it by the low-level features. Finally, upsampled high-level features generated by the deconvolution layer are added to the weighted low-level features. The vector generated by the sigmoid layer indicates the importance of the channels, and it can be adaptively tuned to ignore less important channels and emphasize the important ones as the network learns.

2.3   Network Architecture

With the proposed CSM and JAU modules, we propose the ACE-Net as depicted in Fig. 1. We use pre-trained ResNet-34 as the feature-encoder module, which retains the first four feature-extracting blocks without the average pooling layer and the fully connected layers. The feature map generated by the encoder module is then fed into CSMs to gather dense contextual information, which can improve the precision of the dense classification task significantly. The finely extracted features are then fed into the decoder module, which is composed of JAU modules and residual blocks. In particular, the residual block we use here consists of a standard convolution block and a depth-separable convolution block. The adopted depthwise-separable convolution allows the reduction of the computational complexity, while the developed CSMs and JAU provide more effective context representations.

We treat the CSM as the center block between the encoder and decoder structure. The proposed CSM has multiple branches, and each branch can encode contextual information at a fixed scale through atrous convolution with the corresponding dilation rate. We believe that the proposed model is able to extract quite a wealth of contextual information by multiple CSMs in parallel, which is crucial for dense pixelwise classification tasks. Moreover, our CSMs and JAU can be integrated into existing networks easily and can improve the performance of existing networks significantly.

3   Experiments

To evaluate the proposed method, we carried out comprehensive experiments on two public medical datasets, covering polyp segmentation and optic disc segmentation.

3.1   Implementation Details

We implemented our method based on Pytorch. Following [4,7,20], we employed the "poly" learning rate policy: $lr = baselr * (1 - iter/(total\_iter))^{power}$, where power = 0.9, and the initial base learning rate is set to 0.001. The networks are trained for 300 epochs by adopting SGD with batch size 8, momentum 0.9, and weight decay 0.0005 for all three datasets. To reduce the risk of overfitting [11], we

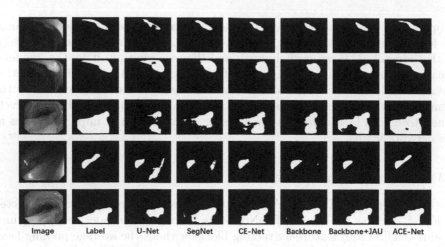

Image   Label   U-Net   SegNet   CE-Net   Backbone   Backbone+JAU   ACE-Net

Fig. 4. Polyp segmentation results of different methods. From left to right: raw images, groundtruth, U-Net, SegNet, CE-Net, Backbone, Backbone+JAU, and ACE-Net.

perform data augmentation in an ambitious way, including random flip, random rotation, elastic distortion, random brightness, random contrast, Gaussian blur, and median blur. All of our experiments were trained on a single GeForce RTX 2060 with 6 GB memory.

3.2 Polyp Segmentation

We first tested the proposed ACE-Net on the EndoScene dataset [6], which contains 912 images with at least one polyp in each image. We randomly selected 225 from the dataset as the test set. In addition, we split the remaining images into two parts, with 80% as the training set and all the rest as the validation set. We randomly sampled 3, 852 patches of size 256×256 from the training images and augmented them using the data-augmentation methods described above.

To facilitate better observation and objective performance evaluation of the proposed method, the following metrics were calculated: Dice similarity coefficient (DSC), accuracy (ACC), recall (Rec), and precision (Prec), which are defined as follows:

$$DSC = \frac{2|X \cap Y|}{|X| + |Y|},$$

$$ACC = \frac{TP + TN}{TP + FP + TN + FN},$$

$$Rec = \frac{TP}{TP + FN},$$

$$Prec = \frac{TP}{TP + FP},$$

where X denotes ground truth, Y denotes predicted result, and TP, TN, FP, and FN represent the number of true positives, true negatives, false positives, and false negatives, respectively.

Table 1. Performance comparison of polyp segmentation results on EndoScene dataset.

Method	DSC	Rec	Prec	ACC
U-Net	0.8729	0.8689	0.9242	0.9839
SegNet	0.8905	0.8817	0.9363	0.9853
CE-Net	0.9139	**0.8987**	0.9424	0.9882
Backbone	0.9011	0.8771	0.9464	0.9853
Backbone+JAU	0.9059	0.8619	0.9745	0.9881
ACE-Net	**0.9212**	0.8768	**0.9842**	**0.9896**
ACE-Net {1}	0.9124	0.8658	0.9782	0.9878
ACE-Net {1, 2}	0.9165	0.8711	0.9817	0.9892
ACE-Net {1, 2, 4}	**0.9212**	0.8768	**0.9842**	**0.9896**
ACE-Net {1, 2, 4, 8}	0.9150	0.8722	0.9769	0.9892

The detailed experimental results are presented in Table 1. To evaluate the performance of the proposed method, we compared it with several popular available methods, as listed in rows 1–3. Furthermore, to verify the effectiveness of the proposed JAU and CSM modules, we added two modules step by step and compared them with the backbone, as listed in rows 4–6. From Table 1, it can be seen that, compared with the backbone, backbone+JAU achieves better results, and this further confirms the effectiveness of the proposed JAU. Further, with the addition of JAU and CSM, it can be seen that the proposed ACE-Net has made consistent improvement in all indicators compared with the backbone and other existing models. This indicates that the proposed CSM can effectively aggregate multi-scale contextual information and improve the performance on segmentation tasks.

Moreover, we investigate the performance of ACE-Net with different settings of CSMs, as listed in rows 7–10. In Table 1, {1, 2, 4, 8} means that we choose 4 CSM modules, and their atrous rates are 1, 2, 4 and 8 respectively. Compared with the backbone, all settings improve the performance significantly, among which atrous rates of {1, 2, 4} achieve the best result with the DSC 0.9212. We can infer that the appropriate settings can aggregate context features more effectively for a particular dataset. Several examples for visual comparison of polyp segmentation are given in Fig. 4.

3.3   Optic Disc Segmentation

Then, we applied our model to the optic disc segmentation experiment. RIM-ONE dataset [8] consists of three releases, and the numbers of image are 169, 455 and 159 respectively. The images in the first (RIM-ONE-R1) and second (RIM-ONE-R2) releases have various sizes, while those in the third release (RIM-ONE-R3) have a fixed size of 2144 × 1424 pixels. The dataset we used in this paper is RIM-ONE-R1, which have five different expert annotations. We randomly selected 100 images for training and the rest 69 images for testing. In addition, we re-scale all the images to 256 × 256 in order to adapt to the input size of the network.

To evaluation metric we adopt is the overlapping error, which has been commonly used to evaluate the accuracy of optic disc segmentation:

$$E = 1 - \frac{Area(S \cap G)}{Area(S \cup G)},$$

where S and G denote the segmented and the manual ground truth optic disc respectively. Table 2 lists in detail the experimental results of the proposed method and other methods.

Table 2. Performance comparison of OD segmentation results on RIM-ONE-R1 dataset.

Method	Expert 1	Expert 2	Expert 3	Expert 4	Expert 5
U-Net	0.136	0.158	0.185	0.223	0.174
SegNet	0.147	0.179	0.162	0.187	0.164
CE-Net	0.096	0.105	0.104	0.123	0.098
ACE-Net	**0.088**	**0.097**	**0.101**	**0.116**	**0.089**

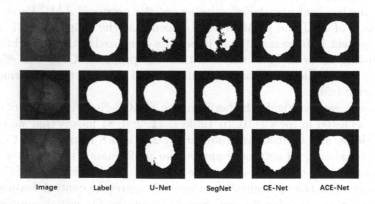

Image   Label   U-Net   SegNet   CE-Net   ACE-Net

Fig. 5. Optic disc segmentation results of different methods. From left to right: raw images, groundtruth, U-Net, SegNet, CE-Net, and ACE-Net

From the comparison shown in Table 2, we can see that the proposed ACE-Net outperforms the other methods in all indicators. The proposed ACE-Net is 0.7% lower in mean error than the second-place method (CE-Net), which was proposed in 2019. Several examples for visual comparison of optic disc segmentation results are given in Fig. 5. The images show that our method obtain more accurate segmentation results.

4 Conclusions

To promote the application of deep learning in the field of medical imaging, in this paper we introduce an end-to-end deep learning framework named ACE-Net for medical image segmentation. ACE-Net introduces a Context Similarity Module that generates an affine matrix to refine long-range dependencies and that is able to aggregate context information from multiple scales. Because of the excellent performance of skip connections in medical image segmentation, we introduce and extend skip connections to emphasize important information through an attention mechanism, which we believe can improve the effectiveness of subsequent feature extraction. Our experimental results show that the proposed method is able to improve medical image segmentation in different tasks, including polyp segmentation and optic disc segmentation. Furthermore, the proposed module can be embedded into any FCN-based semantic segmentation network, either in the Context Similarity Module or Joint Attention Upsample module. In this paper, our method is validated on 2D images, and its extension to 3D data is possible in future work.

Acknowledgments. This work was supported by the National Natural Science Foundation of China grants 11871328, 61976134, 11601315 and 11701357.

References

1. Chen, L.C., Papandreou, G., Kokkinos, I., Murphy, K., Yuille, A.L.: DeepLab: semantic image segmentation with deep convolutional nets, atrous convolution, and fully connected CRFs. IEEE Trans. Pattern Anal. Mach. Intell. **40**(4), 834–848 (2017). https://doi.org/10.1109/TPAMI.2017.2699184
2. Chen, L.C., Papandreou, G., Schroff, F., Adam, H.: Rethinking atrous convolution for semantic image segmentation. In: Computer Vision and Pattern Recognition (2017)
3. Chen, L.C., Zhu, Y., Papandreou, G., Schroff, F., Adam, H.: Encoder-decoder with atrous separable convolution for semantic image segmentation. In: Proceedings of the European Conference on Computer Vision, pp. 801–818 (2018)
4. Congcong, W., Cheikh, F.A., Beghdadi, A., Elle, O.J.: Adaptive context encoding module for semantic segmentation. In: Proceedings of the IEEE Conference on Computer Vision and Pattern Recognition (2019)

5. Dai, J., et al.: Deformable convolutional networks. In: Proceedings of the IEEE International Conference on Computer Vision, pp. 764–773 (2017). https://doi.org/10.1109/ICCV.2017.89

6. David, V., et al.: A benchmark for endoluminal scene segmentation of colonoscopy images. J. Healthcare Eng. 1–9 (2017)

7. Fu, J., Liu, J., Tian, H., Fang, Z., Lu, H.: Dual attention network for scene segmentation. In: Proceedings of the IEEE Conference on Computer Vision and Pattern Recognition, pp. 299–307 (2018)

8. Fumero, F., Alayon, S., Sanchez, J.L., Sigut, J., Gonzalez-Hernandez, M.: Rimone: an open retinal image database for optic nerve evaluation. In: 2011 24th International Symposium on Computer-Based Medical Systems (CBMS) (2011)

9. Guo, X., Yuan, Y.: Triple ANet: adaptive abnormal-aware attention network for WCE image classification. In: Shen, D., et al. (eds.) MICCAI 2019. LNCS, vol. 11764, pp. 293–301. Springer, Cham (2019). https://doi.org/10.1007/978-3-030-32239-7_33

10. Hu, J., Shen, L., Albanie, S., Sun, G., Wu, E.: Squeeze-and-excitation networks. In: Proceedings of the IEEE Conference on Computer Vision and Pattern Recognition, pp. 7132–7141 (2018). https://doi.org/10.1109/TPAMI.2019.2913372

11. Krizhevsky, A., Sutskever, I., Hinton, G.: Imagenet classification with deep convolutional neural networks. In: Advances in Neural Information Processing Systems 25, no. 2 (2012). https://doi.org/10.1145/3065386

12. Li, H., Xiong, P., An, J., Wang, L.: Pyramid attention network for semantic segmentation. arXiv preprint arXiv:1805.10180 (2018)

13. Liu, W., Rabinovich, A., Berg, A.C.: Parsenet: looking wider to see better. Computer Science (2015)

14. Mou, L., et al.: CS-Net: channel and spatial attention network for curvilinear structure segmentation. In: Shen, D., et al. (eds.) MICCAI 2019. LNCS, vol. 11764, pp. 721–730. Springer, Cham (2019). https://doi.org/10.1007/978-3-030-32239-7_80

15. Oktay, O., et al.: Attention u-net: learning where to look for the pancreas. arXiv preprint arXiv:1804.03999 (2018)

16. Qi, K., et al.: X-Net: brain stroke lesion segmentation based on depthwise separable convolution and long-range dependencies. In: Shen, D., et al. (eds.) MICCAI 2019. LNCS, vol. 11766, pp. 247–255. Springer, Cham (2019). https://doi.org/10.1007/978-3-030-32248-9_28

17. Ronneberger, O., Fischer, P., Brox, T.: U-Net: convolutional networks for biomedical image segmentation. In: Navab, N., Hornegger, J., Wells, W.M., Frangi, A.F. (eds.) MICCAI 2015. LNCS, vol. 9351, pp. 234–241. Springer, Cham (2015). https://doi.org/10.1007/978-3-319-24574-4_28

18. Shelhamer, E., Long, J., Darrell, T.: Fully convolutional networks for semantic segmentation. In: Proceedings of the IEEE Conference on Computer Vision and Pattern Recognition, pp. 3431–3440 (2015)

19. Wang, X., Girshick, R., Gupta, A., He, K.: Non-local neural networks. In: Proceedings of the IEEE Conference on Computer Vision and Pattern Recognition, pp. 7794–7803 (2018)

20. Zhang, H., et al.: Context encoding for semantic segmentation. In: Proceedings of the IEEE Conference on Computer Vision and Pattern Recognition (2018). https://doi.org/10.1109/CVPR.2018.00747

21. Zhao, H., Shi, J., Qi, X., Wang, X., Jia, J.: Pyramid scene parsing network. In: Computer Vision and Pattern Recognition, pp. 2881–2890 (2017). https://doi.org/10.1109/CVPR.2017.660

22. Zhou, Z., Rahman Siddiquee, M.M., Tajbakhsh, N., Liang, J.: UNet++: a nested U-Net architecture for medical image segmentation. In: Stoyanov, D., et al. (eds.) DLMIA/ML-CDS -2018. LNCS, vol. 11045, pp. 3–11. Springer, Cham (2018). https://doi.org/10.1007/978-3-030-00889-5_1

23. Zhu, X., Hu, H., Lin, S., Dai, J.: Deformable convnets v2: more deformable, better results. In: Proceedings of the IEEE Conference on Computer Vision and Pattern Recognition, pp. 9308–9316 (2019)

Wavelet U-Net for Medical Image Segmentation

Ying Li[1], Yu Wang[1], Tuo Leng[1(✉)], and Wen Zhijie[2]

[1] School of Computer Engineering and Science, Shanghai University,
Shanghai, China
tleng@shu.edu.cn
[2] College of Sciences, Shanghai University, Shanghai, China

Abstract. Biomedical image segmentation plays an increasingly important role in medical diagnosis. However, it remains a challenging task to segment the medical images due to their diversity of structures. Convolutional networks (CNNs) commonly uses pooling to enlarge the receptive field, which usually results in irreversible information loss. In order to solve this problem, we rethink the alternative method of pooling operation. In this paper, we embed the wavelet transform into the U-Net architecture to achieve the purpose of down-sampling and up-sampling which we called wavelet U-Net (WU-Net). Specifically, in the encoder module, we use discrete wavelet transform (DWT) to replace the pooling operation to reduce the resolution of the image, and use inverse wavelet transform (IWT) to gradually restore the resolution in the decoder module. Besides, we use Densely Cross-level Connection strategy to encourage feature re-use and to enhance the complementarity between cross-level information. Furthermore, in Attention Feature Fusion module (AFF), we introduce the channel attention mechanism to select useful feature maps, which can effectively improve the segmentation performance of the network. We evaluated this model on the digital retinal images for vessel extraction (DRIVE) dataset and the child heart and health study (CHASEDB1) dataset. The results show that the proposed method outperforms the classic U-Net method and other state-of-the-art methods on both datasets.

Keywords: Medical image segmentation · Deep learning · Wavelet transform · Attention mechanism

1 Introduction

Image segmentation, aiming at assigning a category label for each pixel, is a crucial step in medical image analysis. Biomedical image segmentation can extract different tissues, organs, or pathologies based on specific tasks, which can support subsequent medical analysis, such as medical diagnosis, surgical planning and so on.

© Springer Nature Switzerland AG 2020
I. Farkaš et al. (Eds.): ICANN 2020, LNCS 12396, pp. 800–810, 2020.
https://doi.org/10.1007/978-3-030-61609-0_63

Since the advent of convolutional neural networks (CNNs), many automatic segmentation methods have been emerging to improve the efficiency of clinical workflow. In 2014, the fully convolutional network (FCN) [22] was proposed. In the FCN, the authors first removed the fully connected layer from the CNNs and used bilinear interpolation to restore the image resolution, so that the model based on deep CNNs had end-to-end training ability for the first time. In addition, the author also optimized the segmentation results by integrating the output of multiple pooling layers, and achieved significant performance improvement.

Actually, CNNs in computer vision can be viewed as a nonlinear map from the input image to the target. In general, larger receptive field is helpful for improving fitting ability of CNNs and promoting accurate performance by taking more spatial context into account. In the traditional convolutional neural networks, the common methods to enlarge the receptive field are increasing the network depth, enlarging filter size and using pooling operation. But increasing the network depth or enlarging filter size can inevitably results in higher computational cost. In addition, it usually result in information loss because pooling increases the receptive field by directly reducing spacial resolution of feature maps.

To solve this problem, there are two common solutions: one is to use skip connection to merge low- and high-level features, which is very common in the networks based on encoder-decoder architectures; The other one is to use atrous convolution, which can enlarge receptive field without reducing the spatial resolution by inserting "zero holes" in convolutional filtering.

Encoder-Decoder-Based Methods: An encoder-decoder network is commonly composed of a contracting path and an expanding path. It is generally believed that the low-level feature maps contain more structural information, while the high-level feature maps contain more semantic information; thus, combining the two parts of information becomes a key problem. DeconvNet [18] and SegNet [2] use deconvolutional layers to recover the spatial resolution gradually by a well-designed unpooling operation. That same year, U-Net [21] is introduced as a method that is very effective and has a profound impact on subsequent research, called skip connection. Through skip connection, the low-level features in the contracting path can be combined with the high-level features in the expanding path, the detailed information gradually refined, and a satisfactory result finally obtained.

Atrous-Convolution-Based Methods: To resolve this contradiction between the receptive field and the resolution, in DeepLabs [4,5] atrous convolution is introduced, which can increase the receptive field without reducing the spatial resolution of the feature maps through different atrous rates. DeepLabs have achieved great success in natural image segmentation, especially DeepLabv3+ [6], which employs both skip connection and atrous convolution, thus reaching state-of-the-art performance on some benchmarks to date. Although atrous convolution is very effective in preserving detailed spatial information, the larger feature maps and larger convolution kernels make the network require greater computational resources.

Since IWT can reconstruct the image after wavelet transform without information loss, a lot of works have been thinking about how to embed the wavelet transform into CNNs in recent years. Travis Williams et al. [25] separate the image into different subbands with wavelet transform and fuse the learned low and high frequency features together, and then they improve the accuracy of image classification effectively by processing the combined feature mapping. In [8], the authors generalize both pooling layer and convolution layer to perform a spectral analysis with wavelet transform, which allow to utilize spectral information in texture classification. In [3], wavelet decomposition is introduced to replace pooling layer and increase the classification accuracy in MNIST dataset. That same year, Shin Fujieda et al. [9] integrate the high frequency subbands obtained by multistage wavelet transform into CNNs gradually as additional components, and achieve better accuracy than conventional CNNs with fewer parameters. [16] introduces discrete wavelet transform into the image segmentation task, but they simply decompose the feature maps in the encoder path and add the high frequency subbands to the decoding layer with the same resolution. Last year, the wavelet transform and inverse wavelet transform are embedded into CNNs in [15] and remarkable achievements have been made in many tasks, e.g., image denoising, single image super-resolution and object classification. Inspired by the above work, we embed the wavelet transform into the traditional CNNs and apply it to the segmentation task. To enlarge the receptive field, we replace the pooling operations by discrete wavelet transform (DWT) that both frequency and location information of feature maps can be captured, which is helpful for preserving detailed texture information. In the expanded path, we use inverse wavelet transform to gradually restore the resolution of feature maps. Due to invertibility of DWT, none of image information or intermediate features are lost by the proposed downsampling scheme.

This paper proposes a wavelet U-Net (WU-Net) model that greatly improves deep neural network's ability on medical image segmentation task. The main uniqueness of this model includes: (1) DWT and IWT are used to realize the down and up-sampling operation of the network, which can not only extract the features of the image effectively, but also recover the details of the image without information loss; (2) Densely Cross-level Connection strategy is used to encourage feature re-use and to enhance the complementarity between cross-level information; (3) propose an Attention Feature Fusion module to select useful feature map by applying channel attention mechanism.

2   Method

In this section, we will introduce the implementation details in the proposed WU-Net, e.g., discrete wavelet transform (DWT), inverse wavelet transform (IWT), Densely Cross-level Connection (DCC) and Attention Feature Fusion Module (AFF). Figure 1 shows a flowchart of our proposed method.

2.1 Network Architecture

Wavelet Transform: Wavelet theory involves representing general func-tions in terms of the simpler, fixed building block, which is referred to as a 'wavelet', at different scales and positions. The Discrete Wavelet Transform (DWT) can be regarded as a sequence of numbers which sample a certain continuous function [7, 20, 24].

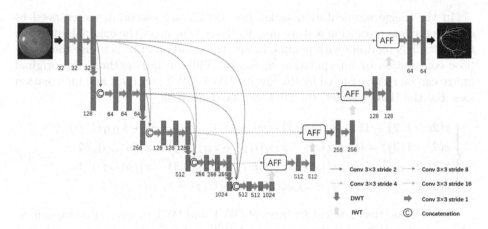

Fig. 1. Illustration of the proposed wavelet U-Net. It consists of two parts: the contracting and expanding subnetworks. The number of channels is annotated on the bottom of each block.

We briefly introduce main concepts of DWT (see [17] for a comprehensive introduction). The multi-resolution wavelet transform provides localized time-frequency analysis of signals and images. 2D DWT can filter images from both horizontal and vertical directions through four convolution filters to obtain four decomposed images. Taking Haar wavelet as an example, four filters are defined as

$$f_{LL} = \begin{bmatrix} 1 & 1 \\ 1 & 1 \end{bmatrix}, f_{LH} = \begin{bmatrix} -1 & -1 \\ 1 & 1 \end{bmatrix}, f_{HL} = \begin{bmatrix} -1 & 1 \\ -1 & 1 \end{bmatrix}, f_{HH} = \begin{bmatrix} 1 & -1 \\ -1 & 1 \end{bmatrix}, \quad (1)$$

where f_{LL} is the low-pass filter, and f_{LH}, f_{HL} and f_{HH} are the high-pass filters. From the above definition, we can find that f_{LL}, f_{LH}, f_{HL} and f_{HH} are orthogonal to each other and form a 4×4 invertible matrix. Consider an input image $x \in \mathbb{R}^{2M \times 2N}$, we can decompose it into four subband images x_{LL}, x_{LH}, x_{HL} and x_{HH} through the four convolutional filters above respectively. It is worth noting that in the wavelet transform, the convolution stride of the filter is set to 2, so the resolution of the four subband images we get is half of the original, that is, $\{x_{LL}, x_{LH}, x_{HL}, x_{HH}\} \in \mathbb{R}^{M \times N}$. In other words, DWT achieves the same purpose as pooling operation through four fixed filters with stride 2, that is, to reduce the spatial resolution of the image. According to the theory of Haar transform [10], the (i, j)-th value of x_{LL}, x_{LH}, x_{HL} and x_{HH} after 2D Haar transform can be written as

$$\begin{cases} x_{LL} = x(2i-1, 2j-1) + x(2i-1, 2j) + x(2i, 2j-1) + x(2i, 2j) \\ x_{LH} = -x(2i-1, 2j-1) - x(2i-1, 2j) + x(2i, 2j-1) + x(2i, 2j) \\ x_{HL} = -x(2i-1, 2j-1) + x(2i-1, 2j) - x(2i, 2j-1) + x(2i, 2j) \\ x_{HH} = x(2i-1, 2j-1) - x(2i-1, 2j) - x(2i, 2j-1) + x(2i, 2j) \end{cases} \quad (2)$$

In the image segmentation tasks, fine details are essential, so we need to enlarge the low-resolution feature map to the resolution of the original image. In the past CNN modules with pooling layers, the usual practice is to use the transpose convolution or interpolation methods. While in our method, the original image can be reconstructed by the inverse DWT (IWT) without any information loss. For the Haar wavelet, the IWT can be defined as

$$\begin{cases} x(2i-1, 2j-1) = ((x_{LL}(i,j) - x_{LH}(i,j) - x_{HL}(i,j) + x_{HH}(i,j))/4 \\ x(2i-1, 2j) = ((x_{LL}(i,j) - x_{LH}(i,j) + x_{HL}(i,j) - x_{HH}(i,j))/4 \\ x(2i, 2j-1) = ((x_{LL}(i,j) + x_{LH}(i,j) - x_{HL}(i,j) - x_{HH}(i,j))/4 \\ x(2i, 2j) = ((x_{LL}(i,j) + x_{LH}(i,j) + x_{HL}(i,j) + x_{HH}(i,j))/4 \end{cases} \quad (3)$$

Considering the excellent features of DWT and IWT in image decomposition and reconstruction, we attempt to use DWT and IWT to replace the pooling and unpooling operations in traditional CNN in our network, and optimize the network to be able to meet the task of medical image segmentation requiring extremely high accuracy. In a word, DWT is used in the encoder module to decompose the feature maps from fine to coarse resolution, while IWT is used in the corresponding decoder module to gradually reconstruct the feature maps from coarse to fine resolution.

Densely Cross-level Connection: For dense classification tasks like image segmentation, the semantic information of image seems to be particularly important that it is the basis of pixel classification. It is widely recognized that in a convolutional neural network, low-level feature maps (high-resolution) contain more image texture information, while high-level feature maps (low-resolution) encode more semantic information. In order to enhance CNN's ability of feature expression, a common practice is to deepen the network. But too many layers may encounter some problems, such as vanishing/exploding gradient. In the past few years, several approaches have been proposed to alleviate the problem of vanishing/exploding gradient, the most famous in which are ResNet [11] and DenseNet [13]. ResNet introduces a so-called identity shortcut connection to skip one or more layers and add their outputs. The emergence of ResNet makes extremely deep network models possible, greatly enhances the feature expression ability of the network. Since then, a number of variants of ResNet have emerged and continue to refresh the record of many computer vision tasks. DenseNet uses a more extreme form of shortcut connection. In a dense block, the features of each layer are passed on to all subsequent layers, and the features are fused by concatenation rather than summation in ResNet. However, this connection strategy is only used in the same downsampling level, thus lacking the information complementing ability between different downsampling levels. In CLCI-Net [26], the authors propose a CLF strategy in which the output of each downsampling layer is aggregated with all of the previous features before the downsampling operation. Inspired by above works, we use densely cross-level connection to fuse the features between the different layers, as shown in the Fig. 1. For each feature map before the downsampling operation, we use the 3×3 convolution with specific strides to downsample it and concatenate it with the corresponding feature map obtained by DWT. This strategy encourages feature re-use and enhances the complementarity between cross-level information.

Attention Feature Fusion Module: In medical image segmentation, the precision of segmentation results is highly required, so gradually recovering the lost spatial details in the process of upsampling has become a research hotspot. Skip connection, introduced by U-Net, has been proved to be highly effective in numerous works. However, the problem of skip connections is that low-level feature maps are simply passed backwards, and we believe that there is a significant amount of redundancy in these feature maps, and naive skip connections cannot distinguish the more valuable and important parts of the information. Attention U-Net [19] can assign more weight coefficients to important regions to make the network more focused on specific local regions, which is implemented by incorporating attention-gates (AGs) into the standard U-Net architecture. In SE-Net [12], the two-dimensional (2D) feature map of each channel is squeezed into a scalar in the spatial dimension, which has a global perceptive field to some extent. Then, the correlation between the channels is explicitly modeled through two fully connected layers. Finally, the weight obtained is multiplied by the previous feature maps channel to channel to complete the re-calibration of the original feature maps. Inspired by SENet, we introduce an Attention Feature Fusion Module (AFF) which applies channel attention mechanism to highlight more important features so that the network can extract more useful information. The details are shown in the Fig. 2.

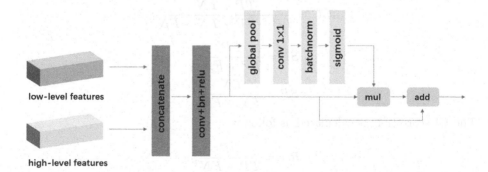

Fig. 2. Details of the proposed Attention Feature Fusion module.

3   Experiments

To evaluate the proposed method, we carried out comprehensive experiments on two public medical datasets, including the digital retinal images for vessel extraction (DRIVE) dataset and the child heart and health study (CHASEDB1) dataset.

3.1   Implementation Details

We implemented our method based on Pytorch. The networks are trained for 200 epochs by adopting Adam optimizer with batch size 64 for the dataset. Following [27], we employed "reduce learning rate on plateau" strategy, and set the learning rate as 0.01, 0.001, 0.0001 on epochs 0, 20 and 150 respectively. To reduce the risk of overfitting [14], we perform data augmentation in an ambitious way, including random flip, random rotation, elastic distortion, random brightness, random contrast, Gaussian blur, and median blur. All of our experiments were trained on a single GeForce RTX 2060 with 6 Gb memory.

3.2   Experiments on DRIVE

DRIVE [23] is a dataset for blood vessel segmentation from retina images. It includes 40 color retina images, from which 20 samples are used for training and the remaining 20 samples for testing. The original size of images is 565 × 584 pixels. The binary field of view (FOV) masks and segmentation ground truth are provided for each image in the dataset. To increase the number of training samples, we randomly sampled 5780 patches of size 64 × 64 pixels from the training images and augmented them with the data-augmentation methods described above. In both experiments, we directly input the test images into the network for evaluation.

To facilitate better observation and objective performance evaluation of the proposed method, the following metrics were calculated: accuracy (ACC), sensitivity (SE), and specificity (SP) which are defined as follows:

$$ACC = \frac{TP + TN}{TP + FP + TN + FN},$$

$$SE = \frac{TP}{TP + FN},$$

$$SP = \frac{TN}{TN + FP}.$$

The F1-score (F1) is calculated as follows:

$$Rec = \frac{TP}{TP + FN},$$

$$Prec = \frac{TP}{TP + FP},$$

$$F1 = \frac{2 \times recall \times precision}{recall + precision}.$$

where TP, TN, FP, and FN represent the number of true positives, true negatives, false positives, and false negatives respectively. To further evaluate the performance of different neural networks, we also calculated the area under receiver operating characteristics curve (AUC).

Table 1. Performance comparison of retinal vessel segmentation results on DRIVE.

Method	F1	SE	SP	ACC	AUC
U-Net	0.8142	0.7537	0.9820	0.9531	0.9755
Residual UNet [1]	0.8149	0.7726	0.9820	0.9553	0.9779
Recurrent UNet [1]	0.8155	0.7751	0.9816	0.9556	0.9782
R2U-Net [1]	0.8171	0.7792	0.9813	0.9556	0.9784
LadderNet [27]	0.8202	0.7856	0.9810	0.9561	0.9793
WU-Net	0.8243	0.8213	0.9837	0.9689	0.9869
Backbone	0.8213	0.8013	0.9858	0.9689	0.9864
Backbone+DCC	0.8220	0.8038	0.9857	0.9691	0.9867
Backbone+DCC+AFF	0.8243	0.8213	0.9837	0.9689	0.9869

A quantitative evaluation of the results which obtained on our experiments is presented in Table 1. To evaluate the performance of the proposed method, we compared it with several popular available methods, as listed in rows 2–7. The experiment results show that the proposed method is competitive with other state-of-the-art methods that WU-Net achieves the best results on almost all indicators. Furthermore, to verify the effectiveness of the proposed Densely Cross-level Connection (DCC) strategy and Attention Feature Fusion (AFF) module, we added them step by step and compared them with the backbone, as listed in rows 8–10. From Table 1, it can be seen that, compared with the backbone, backbone+DCC achieves better results, which confirms the effectiveness of the Densely Cross-level Connection strategy. Further, with the addition of DCC and AFF, it can be seen that the proposed WU-Net has made consistent improvement in F1-score, SE and AUC compared with the backbone and other existing models. This indicates that the proposed AFF can effectively select useful feature maps and improve the performance on segmentation tasks. Several examples for visual comparison of vessel segmentation are given in Fig. 3(a).

3.3   Experiments on CHASE DB1

Another experiment was carried out based on the CHASE DB1 dataset, which contains 28 images of the retina, and the size of each image is 996 × 960 pixels. Usually, the first 20 images were used for training and the other 8 images were used for testing. All the segmentation ground truth for 28 images is available in

Table 2. Performance comparison of retinal vessel segmentation results on DRIVE.

Method	F1	SE	SP	ACC	AUC
U–Net	0.7783	0.8288	0.9701	0.9578	0.9772
Residual UNet	0.7800	0.7726	0.9820	0.9553	0.9779
Recurrent UNet	0.7810	0.7459	0.9836	0.9622	0.9803
R2U–Net	0.7928	0.7756	0.9820	0.9634	0.9815
LadderNet	0.8031	0.7978	0.9818	0.9656	0.9839
WU–Net	0.8073	0.8291	0.9848	0.9751	0.9892

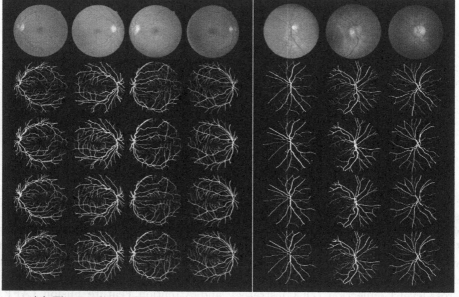

(a) The results on DRIVE dataset.   (b) The results on CHASE-DB1 dataset.

Fig. 3. The results on DRIVE and CHASE DB1 dataset. From top to bottom: raw images, groundtruth, U-Net, LadderNet and WU-Net.

CHASE DB1. We randomly sampled patches of size 64 × 64 from the training images and a total of 17400 patches were sampled for training.

Detailed results are presented in Table 2, which provides a quantitative evaluation of the experimental results obtained. From the comparison, it can be seen that the proposed WU-Net achieves 0.8073, 0.9751, and 0.9892 in F1-score, accuracy, and AUC, respectively, all better than achieved by other methods. The experimental results further proof that our method is competitive with other popular models. Several examples for visual comparison are given in Fig. 3(b).

4 Conclusions

In this paper, we use DWT as the downsampling operation to replace the pooling layer. Because we concatenate both low-frequency and high-frequency subbands together as input, the encoder module can reduce the spatial resolution and enlarge the receptive field without information loss. Due to the invertibility of DWT and its frequency and location property, the decoder module applies IWT can recover detailed textures and sharp structures from degraded observation effectively. In the encoder path, we introduce Densely Cross-level Connection to encourages feature re-use and enhances the complementarity between cross-level information, and the problem of vanishing or exploding gradient is alleviated to some extent. Furthermore, we introduce and extend skip connections to emphasize important information through channel attention mechanism, which we believe can improve the effectiveness of subsequent feature extraction. The experiments conducted on DRIVE dataset and CHASE-DB1 dataset show that all the designs improve the interpretability of U-Net, and the proposed WU-Net achieves the state-of-the-art performance compared with other mainstream models.

Acknowledgments. This work was supported by the National Natural Science Foundation of China grants 11871328, 61976134, 11601315 and 11701357.

References

1. Alom, M.Z., Hasan, M., Yakopcic, C., Taha, T.M., Asari, V.K.: Recurrent residual convolutional neural network based on U-net(R2U-Net) for medical image segmentation (2018)
2. Badrinarayanan, V., Kendall, A., Cipolla, R.: Segnet: a deep convolutional encoder-decoder architecture for scene segmentation. IEEE Trans. Pattern Anal. Mach. Intell. **39**(12), 2481–2495 (2017). https://doi.org/10.1109/TPAMI.2016.2644615
3. Chaabane, C.B., Mellouli, D., Hamdani, T.M., Alimi, A.M., Abraham, A.: Wavelet convolutional neural networks for handwritten digits recognition. In: Abraham, A., Muhuri, P.K., Muda, A.K., Gandhi, N. (eds.) HIS 2017. AISC, vol. 734, pp. 305–310. Springer, Cham (2018). https://doi.org/10.1007/978-3-319-76351-4_31
4. Chen, L.C., Papandreou, G., Kokkinos, I., Murphy, K., Yuille, A.L.: DeepLab: semantic image segmentation with deep convolutional nets, atrous convolution, and fully connected CRFs. IEEE Trans. Pattern Anal. Mach. Intell. **40**(4), 834–848 (2017). https://doi.org/10.1109/TPAMI.2017.2699184
5. Chen, L.C., Papandreou, G., Schroff, F., Adam, H.: Rethinking atrous convolution for semantic image segmentation. Computer Vision and Pattern Recognition (2017)
6. Chen, L.C., Zhu, Y., Papandreou, G., Schroff, F., Adam, H.: Encoder-decoder with atrous separable convolution for semantic image segmentation. In: Proceedings of the European Conference on Computer Vision, pp. 801–818 (2018)
7. Chui, C.K.: An Introduction to Wavelets. Academic Press, New York (1992)
8. Fujieda, S., Takayama, K., Hachisuka, T.: Wavelet convolutional neural networks for texture classification (2017)
9. Fujieda, S., Takayama, K., Hachisuka, T.: Wavelet convolutional neural networks (2018)

10. Mallat, M.S.: A theory for multiresolution signal decomposition: the wavelet representation. IEEE Trans. Pattern Anal. Mach. Intell. **11**, 674–693 (1989)
11. He, K., Zhang, X., Ren, S., Sun, J.: Deep residual learning for image recognition. In: Proceedings of the IEEE Conference on Computer Vision and Pattern Recognition, pp. 770–778 (2016)
12. Hu, J., Shen, L., Albanie, S., Sun, G., Wu, E.: Squeeze-and-excitation networks. In: Proceedings of the IEEE Conference on Computer Vision and Pattern Recognition, pp. 7132–7141 (2018). https://doi.org/10.1109/TPAMI.2019.2913372
13. Huang, G., Liu, Z., Laurens, V.D.M., Weinberger, K.Q.: Densely connected convolutional networks. In: Proceedings of the IEEE Conference on Computer Vision and Pattern Recognition, pp. 4700–4708 (2017). https://doi.org/10.1109/CVPR.2017.243
14. Krizhevsky, A., Sutskever, I., Hinton, G.: Imagenet classification with deep convolutional neural networks. In: Advances in Neural Information Processing Systems 25, no. 2 (2012). https://doi.org/10.1145/3065386
15. Liu, P., Zhang, H., Lian, W., Zuo, W.: Multi-level wavelet convolutional neural networks (2019)
16. Ma, L., Stückler, J., Wu, T., Cremers, D.: Detailed dense inference with convolutional neural networks via discrete wavelet transform (2018)
17. Mallat, S.: A wavelet tour of signal processing (2009)
18. Noh, H., Hong, S., Han, B.: Learning deconvolution network for semantic segmentation. In: Proceedings of the IEEE International Conference on Computer Vision, pp. 1520–1528 (2015)
19. Oktay, O., et al.: Attention u-net: learning where to look for the pancreas. arXiv preprint arXiv:1804.03999 (2018)
20. Rieder, P., Götze, J., Nossek, J.A.: Multiwavelet transforms based on several scaling functions (1994)
21. Ronneberger, O., Fischer, P., Brox, T.: U-Net: convolutional networks for biomedical image segmentation. In: Navab, N., Hornegger, J., Wells, W.M., Frangi, A.F. (eds.) MICCAI 2015. LNCS, vol. 9351, pp. 234–241. Springer, Cham (2015). https://doi.org/10.1007/978-3-319-24574-4_28
22. Shelhamer, E., Long, J., Darrell, T.: Fully convolutional networks for semantic segmentation. In: Proceedings of the IEEE Conference on Computer Vision and Pattern Recognition, pp. 3431–3440 (2015)
23. Staal, J., Abramoff, M., Niemeijer, M., Viergever, M., van Ginneken, B.: Ridge-based vessel segmentation in color images of the retina. IEEE Trans. Med. Imaging **23**(4), 501–509 (2004)
24. Strang, G., Strela, V.: Short wavelets and matrix dilation equations. IEEE Trans. Signal Process. **43**(1), 108–115 (1995)
25. Williams, T., Li, R.: Advanced image classification using wavelets and convolutional neural networks (2017). https://doi.org/10.1109/ICMLA.2016.0046
26. Yang, H., et al.: CLCI-Net: cross-level fusion and context inference networks for lesion segmentation of chronic stroke. In: Shen, D., et al. (eds.) MICCAI 2019. LNCS, vol. 11766, pp. 266–274. Springer, Cham (2019). https://doi.org/10.1007/978-3-030-32248-9_30
27. Zhuang, J.: Laddernet: multi-path networks based on u-net for medical image segmentation. arXiv preprint arXiv:1810.07810 (2018)

Recurrent Neural Networks

Character-Based LSTM-CRF with Semantic Features for Chinese Event Element Recognition

Wei Liu[1]([✉]), Yusen Wu[1], Lei Jiang[1], Jianfeng Fu[2], and Weimin Li[1]

[1] School of Computer Engineering and Science, Shanghai University,
Shanghai 200444, China
liuw@shu.edu.cn
[2] School of Mathematics and Information,
Shanghai Lixin University of Accounting and Finance, Shanghai 201620, China

Abstract. Event element recognition is a significant task in event-based information extraction. In this paper, we propose an event element recognition model based on character-level embedding with semantic features. By extracting character-level features, the proposed model can capture more information of words. Our results show that joint character Convolutional Neural Networks (CNN) and character Bi-directional Long Short-Term Memory Networks (Bi-LSTM) is superior to single character-level model. In addition, adding semantic features such as POS (part-of-speech) and DP (dependency parsing) tends to improve the effect of recognition. We evaluated different methods in CEC (Chinese Emergency Corpus), and the experimental results show that our model can achieve good performance, and the F value of element recognition was 77.17%.

Keywords: Event element recognition · Convolution neural network · Bi-LSTM · POS

1 Introduction

In the field of natural language processing, "Event" can be described as more dynamic, comprehensive structured knowledge than "concept" [1]. Event, as a knowledge representation paradigm, is more conform to the cognitive laws of individuals. Consequently, for machine cognition, it is increasingly important that extracting event information from natural language. Event extraction includes two main tasks: event recognition and event element recognition. The purpose of event recognition is to classify events, while event element recognition aims to recognize the event information and completing the corresponding events with time, place, person and other information. While some important events or activities happens, a host of relevant information will be posted on the Internet. In order to deal with these informations automatically, identifying information from the text become neccessary and important. At present, the work related to event recognition has been sufficient and achieved good results [2–4].

© Springer Nature Switzerland AG 2020
I. Farkaš et al. (Eds.): ICANN 2020, LNCS 12396, pp. 813–824, 2020.
https://doi.org/10.1007/978-3-030-61609-0_64

However, for the recognition of event elements, there is still a lack of research work to meet our expectations, which is the motivation of this paper.

Event element recognition is an event-centered recognition of related time, place, person, institutions and other entities, which can effectively help people understand the event. At present, there are two kinds of event elements recognition approaches: rule based and machine learning based. Rule based approaches focus on using pattern matching algorithms to recognize and extract designated types of event elements. For example, due to cross language problems, rule-based approaches tend to lead to poor robustness. Machine learning based approaches transform the task of event element recognition into a classification problem. The effectiveness of traditional machine learning methods depends on the selection and discovery of features, and the construction of classifiers. Although traditional machine learning based methods are easy to implement and explain, but they cannot mine deep semantic information of data.

In recent years, due to the excellent performance of deep learning in feature learning, a growing number of deep learning methods are applied to natural language processing. Currently, some researchers have made some attempts to apply deep learning in the field of event element recognition [5,6]. However, in most deep learning models, each word is treated as the basic semantic unit. For English, it is appropriate for each word to be processed as a smallest semantic unit, but not for Chinese. In Chinese, the information between characters is easily ignored when a word is used as a semantic unit. In addition, using different word segmentation tools may result in different word segmentation results, which will also affect the recognition effect of the model.

At present, although deep learning has been preliminarily used in many natural language processing tasks, but there is seldom research work on applying deep learning to event element recognition. Therefore, we propose a character-level model based on a Long Short-Term Memory and conditional random fields (LSTM-CRF) to identify event elements by extending the semantic information of words. In our model, the words in texts are converted into feature vectors containing word embedding and semantic features, and combined with character-level features. Then deep semantic information can be automatically mined by using network model. Experimental results show that the proposed model can achieve good performance in Chinese texts.

In summary, the contributions of this paper are as follows:

1. We construct a hybrid model constituted by Bi-LSTM and CNN to extract character-level features, which can capture more information hidden in words.
2. We analyze the effects of different semantic features on recognition task. On the basis, we propose a word representation method combining multi-dimensional semantic features, which can expand word semantic information and improve the recognition performance of the model.

The remainder of this paper is organized as follows. Section 2 introduces the related work of event element extraction. Section 3 introduces our model architecture in detail. Section 4 analyzes the experimental results. Finally, Sect. 5 concludes by summarizing our results and pointing our directions for future work.

2   Related Work

Event extraction is a hot spot in information extraction area, it aims to accurately identify the event and relevant person, time, place and other elements from Chinese text. It was widely used in information retrieval [7] and Question Answer System [8], and it is also one of the construction processes of knowledge graph [9]. There are two main types of methods: rule-based methods and machine learning methods.

Methods based on rules focus on a series of patterns to match the text for the purpose of event element recognition. Tan et al. [10] used multi-layer pattern matching to recognize event elements on ACE Chinese corpus. Patwardhan et al. [11] proposed an event extraction model that combined phrase and sentence context information. Kanhabua et al. [12] proposed a temporal language model to determine the time of text and increase the retrieval effectiveness by ordering the search results. Methods based on rules require language experts to participate in rule design, and there may be conflicts between different rules.

Methods based on traditional machine learning focus on the construction of classifier and selection of features. These methods transform the task of event element extraction into a classification problem, and usually have better robustness. Chieu et al. [13] firstly applied maximum entropy classifier for event element recognition. Fu et al. [14] proposed a feature weighting algorithm which improved the ReliefF feature selection in the classification algorithm. Zhang et al. [15] proposed an approach for time and location recognition based on improved k-means algorithm. Ma et al. [16] proposed a CFSFDP algorithm combining data preprocessing and reverse geocoding to realize the recognition of location elements. Traditional machine learning based methods require complex feature engineering, which don't adapt to different fields and applications.

In recent years, with the rapid development of deep learning technology, deep learning has also been applied to the field of event element recognition. Zhang et al. [5] proposed CEORM based on DBN to recognize object elements in Chinese Emergency Corpus. Zhang et al. [6] proposed a model based on Skip-Window Convolutional Neural Networks to recognize event triggers and arguments. Wu et al. [17] proposed character-word embedding based on attention to identify Chinese event arguments. Zhang et al. [18] applied a joint extraction model based on two-channel neural network, which can simultaneously extract event class and event elements relationships from text.

Although existing methods of event element recognition that based on deep learning have achieved a certain effect, the effect of character-level features and semantic features are ignored in the processing of Chinese text. In this paper we propose a hybrid model constituted by Bi-LSTM and CNN to extract character-level feature of words from Chinese texts, then combine word embedding and semantic features to automatically mine deep semantic information. The results of experiment show that our method outperforms the baseline methods, and demonstrate its effectiveness.

3   Proposed Model

In this section, we will introduce the structure of event element recognition model and details of each procedure.

The overall architecture of the model is shown in Fig. 1. Each word is represented as a long vector resulting from concatenating its word embedding with its character-level features that are extracted by using CNN and Bi-LSTM network. Then the word vector is fed to another Bi-LSTM network, which is connected to a Conditional Random Field (CRF) module that assigns each word to a specific event element type. Our model is mainly divided into three parts: data preprocessing, text vectorization and feature extraction. In the subsequent sections, we will describe the model in detail.

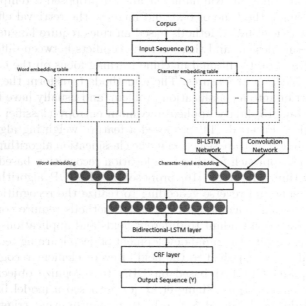

Fig. 1. The architecture of event element recognition model

3.1   Preprocessing System

The main function of Preprocessing System is to analyze and process files in corpus. In this paper, we use LTP [19] to segment sentences and obtain the semantic features of words such as POS (Parts of Speech), DP (Dependency Parsing). In our task, we define five types of annotation tags in text corpus according to element types: event trigger words, event object, event time, event participants and event location. We extract the type of elements in the corpus and label each word in the sentence as "DEN" (event trigger word), "OBJ" (event object), "TIM" (event time), "PAR" (event participants), "LOC" (event location), and "O" (not belongs to any type of event elements), then the tagged corpus will be used to train the deep classifier.

3.2 Word Representation

Word Embedding. Word embedding is the collective name for a set of language modeling and feature learning techniques in natural language processing (NLP) where words or phrases from the vocabulary are mapped to vectors of real numbers [20]. In our model, the word embedding is obtained by pretraining the open source corpus text. First, we preprocess the Sogou news data (http://www.sogou.com/labs/resource/ca.php), including special symbol filtering, word segmentation, delete stop words, etc. Then, we use word2vec to train 128-dimension word embedding and character embedding based on the preprocessed text obtained in the first step.

Character-Level Features. Although word-level representations can capture semantic information of words, they are unable to capture internal information between characters. For example, the Chinese idiom "望子成龙" (hold high hopes for one's child), the semantic meaning of this word "望子成龙" can be learned from its context. Due to the linguistic feature of Chinese, it also can be inferred from the meanings of its character "望" (expect), character "子" (children), character "成" (become) and character "龙" (dragon), and the semantic meanings of internal characters plays an important role in modeling semantic meanings of words. While character-level feature was concatenated as part of the word representation, more semantic information of words can be mined.

(1) Extracting Character feature with CNN
Convolution neural networks (CNN) are mostly used in computer vision to extract image features, but also suitable for natural language processing. In our model, the CNN structure based on maximum pooling layer is used to extract character feature from the word. For each word, we use different convolution kernels to extract a new feature vector from character embedding. Both sides of word are filled with some special padding character embedding on the basis of CNN window size. Figure 2 illustrates the aforementioned operation.

(2) Extracting Character feature with Bi-LSTM
Long Short-Term Memory Networks (LSTM) is a effective model for processing sequential data, which can be used to extract character-level representation of words [21]. In this paper, we use Bi-LSTM to extract the internal information between characters. The Bi-LSTM model process each word by means of character-by-character, the representation of each character use pre-training character embeddings. The output of the Bi-LSTM model will be character-level feature of the word.

Additional Semantic Feature. This paper use two different types of word feature abstraction layers (POS, DP) as supplement of word embedding. We describe them in detail below.

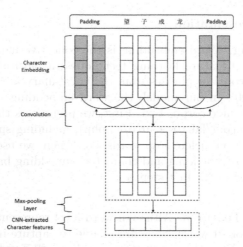

Fig. 2. A case of extracting character features from each word by using CNN

Parts of Speech (POS): POS is the basic semantic feature of words. In a sentence, the relationship between POS and event element words comforms to certain rules. For instance, nouns and pronouns can act as object elements in events, but adjectives usually are not used as object elements in events. In CEC[1], according to results of POS, event trigger words are usually verbs and gerunds. Therefore, using POS as part of semantic feature can improve recognition accuracy in theory. Dimension of POS feature vector is 29, which represent 29 kinds of POS. If the POS of any words matches the feature of the feature vector, the feature vector value of the word is 1, and the other 28 dimensions is 0.

Dependency Parsing (DP): DP reveals its syntactic structure by analyzing the relations between the components of language units, and advocates that the core verbs in the sentence are the central component affect other components. In CEC, we found that 62% of trigger words have subject-verb relationship in the sentence and 18% have verb-object relationship. The aim of DP is to get deep semantic information in sentences, which is transcend the constraints of syntactic rules of the sentences. Dimension of DP feature vector is 14, which represent 14 kinds of DP. If the DP of any words matches the feature of the feature vector, when in this dimension the feature vector value is 1, and the other 13 dimensions is 0.

3.3 Feature Extraction

In this section, we will discuss the detail of feature extraction model. Bi-LSTM-CRF expands Conditional Random Fields (CRF) layer on the basis of Bi-LSTM. The vector output from Bi-LSTM is used as the input of CRF. CRF has been

---

[1] CEC is a Chinese emergency corpus, its open source address is https://github.com/DaseLab/CEC-Corpus.

able to achieve superior performance in sequence annotation problem [22], so we use CRF as the last layer of the model. Bi-LSTM-CRF model can not only retain Bi-LSTM context information, but also enhances the constraints of synactic rules before and after labeling through CRF layer.

If $h = (h_1, h_2, ..., h_n)$ represents the output sequence of Bi-LSTM, h_i is the representation of the ith word in the sentence, $y = (y_1, y_2, ..., y_n)$ as candidate tag sequence is obtained through CRF probability model. The specific form of CRF probability model is:

$$P(y|h; W, b) = \frac{\prod_{i=1}^{n} \psi_i(y_{i-1}, y_i, h)}{\sum_{y' \in Y(h)} \prod_{i=1}^{n} \psi_i(y_{i-1}', y_i', h)} \tag{1}$$

$P(y|h; W, b)$ is the probability of marking the given input sequence h as sequence y. $\psi_i(y', y, z) = \exp(W_{y',y}^T z_i + b_{y',y})$, $W_{y',y}$ and $b_{y',y}$ represent the weight vector and bias transferred from label y' to label y. During CRF training, maximum likelihood estimation (MLE) is adopted to optimize it, calculate the log likelihood function by using formula 2:

$$L(W, b) = \sum_{i=1}^{n} \log P(y_i|h_i; W, b) \tag{2}$$

The goal of MLE is to adjust the relevant parameters W and b to maximize $L(W, b)$. When CRF is used for annotation, the candidate annotation sequence with the highest probability is selected as the final annotation result.

4   Experiments

4.1   Corpus and Hyperparameters

We use CEC 2.0 as experimental dataset. CEC is an event-based text corpus annotated by the Semantic Intelligence Laboratory of Shanghai University, collects 333 newspaper reports about earthquakes, fires, traffic accidents, terrorist attacks and food poisoning. CEC annotates events and event elements, and the relationships between events. CEC is available at https://github.com/DaseLab/CEC-Corpus. Statistics of event elements labeled exactly is shown in Table 1.

We extract texts in CEC as experiment corpus. The sentence length is different, so we need to even up the sentence (the number of words) as the same length. According to the distribution of sentence length, the value is set to 15. In addition, numbers of characters that make up different words are different, so we set the number of characters to 10. The number of words in the word embedding table is 7899, the number of characters in character embedding table is 2366, and dimensions of the vectors are both 128 dimensions. For this experiment, the corpus was divided into training set, test set and verification set at a ratio of 6:2:2.

Table 1. Quantitative statistics of event elements in CEC 2.0

Class	Trigger	Time	Location	Participants	Object	Sentences
Earthquakes	1001	261	313	439	277	1002
Fires	1216	274	361	493	481	1216
Traffic accidents	1189	352	440	783	605	1802
Terrorist attacks	823	207	197	519	177	823
Food poisoning	1112	301	236	699	301	1111
Total	5341	1395	1547	2933	1841	5954

In our model, we use Adam as the optimization method, with the leaning rate of 0.0008. In our character-level feature extraction model, the hidden state of Bi-LSTM has a dimension of 64 (for each direction), and CNN has 3 filters with the sizes of 2, 3, 4. Dropout is a technique that prevents neural network from over-fitting by randomly dropping some hidden layer neural nodes during training. In the whole network, the dropout parameter is set to 0.5. We use precision (P), recall (R) and F-measure (F) to evaluate the results. We run each model for 32 epochs and the model parameters with the best performance on the verification dataset is saved.

4.2   Experimental Results

In this paper, our model is a hybrid neural network based on Bi-LSTM-CRF, which uses Bi-LSTM and CNN to extract character-level features. It is necessary to analyze whether using Bi-LSTM or CNN can improve the recognition effect of the model. The experimental baseline is a Bi-LSTM-CRF model based on words, and the character-level feature extracted by Bi-LSTM and CNN were added to our model respectively. As shown in Table 2, parameter n is the feature amount for each filter in CNN, the hybrid model with 19 as parameter performed best in our experiment.

The experiment result shows that: 1) Single CNN or Bi-LSTM model to extract character-level feature can improve the model's performance; 2) Using hybrid model can perform better in our experiment, F-measure was increased by 1.67%; 3) The amount of CNN feature would affect the model recognition, so we need to adjust it according to different situation. The reason is that CNN and Bi-LSTM can extract semantic rules and semantic knowledge contained in the character embedding of words to assist the recognition of event elements, so as to achieve a better performance. For example, "斑马" (zebra) and "纯血马" (thoroughbred) are semantically related and contain common characters, "纯血马" may not be recognized by the baseline method because it does not appear in the corpus. In contrast, the character-level feature of "纯血马" extend the semantic representation of word, making it much closer to human judgements.

In order to investigate the impact of introducing different semantic feature layers on the model recognition performance, we design the following

Table 2. Comparison of recognition effect while adding different character-level extraction layers

Model	Precision (%)	Recall (%)	F-measure (%)
baseline	75.14	75.86	75.50
CNN+baseline	76.24	74.72	75.47
Bi-LSTM+baseline	76.05	75.57	75.81
Hybrid model ($n = 14$)	76.09	76.23	76.16
Hybrid model ($n = 15$)	76.34	76.09	76.21
Hybrid model ($n = 16$)	**77.17**	75.83	76.49
Hybrid model ($n = 17$)	76.03	76.34	76.19
Hybrid model ($n = 18$)	76.72	75.64	76.18
Hybrid model ($n = 19$)	76.32	**78.04**	**77.17**
Hybrid model ($n = 20$)	76.66	76.97	76.82
Hybrid model ($n = 21$)	76.05	76.90	76.47
Hybrid model ($n = 22$)	77.09	76.23	76.66

experiments by combining the semantic feature of POS and DP. For example, Word + POS means using both word representation and part-of-speech as input feature. As shown in Table 3, introducing difference semantic features can improve overall performance, but factors affecting the improvement are different. In future research, we will consider introducing more semantic feature layers to improve the model's performance.

Table 3. Comparison of recognition effect while different semantic feature layers overlapping

Word feature	Precision (%)	Recall (%)	F-measure (%)
Word embedding	74.01	75.97	74.98
Word + POS	75.71	75.94	75.83
Word + DP	75.59	76.90	76.24
Word + POS + DP	76.32	78.04	77.17

We compare our proposed model's results with other models shown in Table 4. In our previous work [23], we proposed a method based on event ontology, which complements and revises event elements by searching for event class constraints and non-taxonomic relations from event ontology. Zhang's method [15] was based on improved k-means algorithm. Khalifa [24] proposed a model for predicting a tag for each word by using word embedding and character-level features, where CNN was used to extract character-level features. Xu [21] proposed the character-based word embedding model, which used Bi-LSTM to train the character-level representation of words. Compare with the above methods, we use word embedding, character-level features and semantic features as the input of deep learning model, which can mine more semantic information. The experimental result shows that the recognition effect of our method perform better than other methods in Chinese text.

Table 4. Comparison of recognition effect in CEC corpus

Approach	Precision (%)	Recall (%)	F-measure (%)
Previous method [23]	74.75	75.2	74.97
Zhang's method [15]	72.0	73.71	72.85
Khalifa's method [24]	75.35	74.45	74.90
Xu's method [21]	76.41	75.25	75.83
Our method	76.32	78.04	77.17

We compare the F-measure of different methods for event elements recognition aim at different types of elements. As shown in Table 5, the recognition effect of object and participants are not as good as others elements. These are the main reasons: First, the features and lexical rules of participants words and object words are not obvious, and they may not act as event elements in some sentences. Second, participants words and object words appear frequently in datasets, which can easily result in mutual interference. Third, there may be multiple participants words and object words in some sentences, and we may not be able to identify all the elements in the event accurately.

Table 5. F-measure for event elements recognition

	Khalifa's method [24]	Xu's method [21]	Our method
Trigger	79.71	80.08	80.01
Object	62.07	63.58	65.69
Time	86.37	86.56	86.87
Participants	69.13	68.78	70.83
Location	72.62	72.87	76.78

As shown in Table 6, we calculated the average length of different event elements. We found that the average length of time words and location words are the largest, so our character-based model can extract more semantic information from time words and location words. This is one of the reasons why the recognition effect of time elements and location elements are better than object elements and participants elements.

Table 6. Average length of event elements

	Trigger	Object	Time	Participants	Location
Length	1.96	3.64	5.44	4.08	6.01

5 Conclusion

This paper propose an event element recognition model by using CNN and Bi-LSTM to extract character-level features as parts of word representation. Experimental results have shown that our model achieves good performance, both character-level CNN feature and character-level Bi-LSTM feature added to model can achieve better F-measure. Moreover, by analyzing the obtained results, we found that the number of CNN features has an effect on the recognition effect. The experimental results show that DP and POS feature of word can help to improve the effect of event element recognition. In future, we will attempt to combine the attention mechanism to optimize the character-based model, so as to achieve automatic annotation on event elements. As well, we will try to use transfer learning to alleviate the problem of insufficient event element annotated corpus.

Acknowledgments. This paper was supported by The National key Research and Development Program of China (No. 2017YFE0117500), The Ministry of Education in China Project of Humanities and Social Sciences for Youth Scholars (No. 19YJCZH031), The National Social Science Fund Major of China (No. 19ZDA301).

References

1. Zong-Tian, L., Meili, H., Wen, Z., Zhaoman, Z., Jianfeng, F.: Research on event-oriented ontology model. Comput. Sci. **36**(11), 189–192 (2009)
2. Zhang, Y., Liu, Z., Zhou, W., National Natural Science Foundation of China (NSFC): Event recognition based on deep learning in Chinese texts. PLoS ONE **11**(8), e0160147 (2016)
3. Han, S., Hao, X., Huang, H.: An event-extraction approach for business analysis from online Chinese news. Electron. Commer. Res. Appl. **28**, 244–260 (2018)
4. Michelioudakis, E., Artikis, A., Paliouras, G.: Semi-supervised online structure learning for composite event recognition. Mach. Learn. **108**(7), 1085–1110 (2019). https://doi.org/10.1007/s10994-019-05794-2
5. Zhang, Y., Liu, Z., Zhou, W., Zhang, Y.: Object recognition base on deep belief network. In: 2015 10th International Conference on Intelligent Systems and Knowledge Engineering (ISKE), pp. 268–273. IEEE (2015)
6. Zhang, Z., Xu, W., Chen, Q.: Joint event extraction based on skip-window convolutional neural networks. In: Lin, C.-Y., Xue, N., Zhao, D., Huang, X., Feng, Y. (eds.) ICCPOL/NLPCC -2016. LNCS (LNAI), vol. 10102, pp. 324–334. Springer, Cham (2016). https://doi.org/10.1007/978-3-319-50496-4_27
7. Glavaš, G., Šnajder, J.: Event graphs for information retrieval and multi-document summarization. Expert Syst. Appl. **41**(15), 6904–6916 (2014)

8. Liu, X., Huet, B.: Event-based cross media question answering. Multimedia Tools Appl. **75**(3), 1495–1508 (2014). https://doi.org/10.1007/s11042-014-2085-0

9. Zhang, H., Liu, X., Pan, H., Song, Y., Leung, C.W.K.: ASER: a large-scale eventuality knowledge graph. In: Proceedings of The Web Conference 2020, pp. 201–211 (2020)

10. Tan, H., Zhao, T., Zheng, J.: Identification of Chinese event and their argument roles. In: 2008 IEEE 8th International Conference on Computer and Information Technology Workshops, pp. 14–19. IEEE (2008)

11. Patwardhan, S., Riloff, E.: A unified model of phrasal and sentential evidence for information extraction. In: Proceedings of the 2009 Conference on Empirical Methods in Natural Language Processing: Volume 1, vol. 1, pp. 151–160. Association for Computational Linguistics (2009)

12. Kanhabua, N., Nørvåg, K.: Determining time of queries for re-ranking search results. In: Lalmas, M., Jose, J., Rauber, A., Sebastiani, F., Frommholz, I. (eds.) ECDL 2010. LNCS, vol. 6273, pp. 261–272. Springer, Heidelberg (2010). https://doi.org/10.1007/978-3-642-15464-5_27

13. Chieu, H.L., Ng, H.T.: Named entity recognition with a maximum entropy approach. In: Proceedings of the Seventh Conference on Natural Language Learning at HLT-NAACL 2003, vol. 4, pp. 160–163. Association for Computational Linguistics (2003)

14. Zong-tian, F.J.F.L., Jian-fang, L.W.S.: Feature weighting based event argument identification. Comput. Sci. **37**(3), 239–241 (2010)

15. Zhang, P., Liao, T.: Time and location recognition based on improved k-means algorithm. Comput. Knowl. Technol. **2017**(36), 82 (2017)

16. Ma, C., Shan, H., Ma, T., Zhu, L.: Research on important places identification method based on improved CFSFDP algorithm. Appl. Res. Comput. **34**(1), 136–140 (2017)

17. Wu, Y., Zhang, J.: Chinese event extraction based on attention and semantic features: a bidirectional circular neural network. Future Internet **10**(10), 95 (2018)

18. Zhang, J., Hong, Yu., Zhou, W., Yao, J., Zhang, M.: Interactive learning for joint event and relation extraction. Int. J. Mach. Learn. Cybernet. **11**(2), 449–461 (2019). https://doi.org/10.1007/s13042-019-00985-8

19. Che, W., Li, Z., Liu, T.: LTP: a Chinese language technology platform. In: Proceedings of the 23rd International Conference on Computational Linguistics: Demonstrations, pp. 13–16. Association for Computational Linguistics (2010)

20. Kiros, R., et al.: Skip-thought vectors. In: Advances in Neural Information Processing Systems, pp. 3294–3302 (2015)

21. Xu, K., Zhou, Z., Hao, T., Liu, W.: A bidirectional LSTM and conditional random fields approach to medical named entity recognition. In: Hassanien, A.E., Shaalan, K., Gaber, T., Tolba, M.F. (eds.) AISI 2017. AISC, vol. 639, pp. 355–365. Springer, Cham (2018). https://doi.org/10.1007/978-3-319-64861-3_33

22. Lafferty, J., McCallum, A., Pereira, F.C.: Conditional random fields: probabilistic models for segmenting and labeling sequence data. In: Proc ICML, pp. 282–289 (2001)

23. Wei, L., Feijing, L., Dong, W., Zongtian, L.: A text event elements extraction method based on event ontology. J. Chin. Inf. Process. **30**(4), 167–175 (2016)

24. Khalifa, M., Shaalan, K.: Character convolutions for Arabic named entity recognition with long short-term memory networks. Comput. Speech Lang. **58**, 335–346 (2019)

Sequence Prediction Using Spectral RNNs

Moritz Wolter[1,2(✉)], Jürgen Gall[1], and Angela Yao[3]

[1] Institute for Computer Science, University of Bonn, Bonn, Germany
{wolter,gall}@cs.uni-bonn.de
[2] Fraunhofer Center for Machine Learning and SCAI, Sankt Augustin, Germany
[3] School of Computing, National University of Singapore, Singapore, Singapore
ayao@comp.nus.edu.sg

Abstract. Fourier methods have a long and proven track record as an excellent tool in data processing. As memory and computational constraints gain importance in embedded and mobile applications, we propose to combine Fourier methods and recurrent neural network architectures. The short-time Fourier transform allows us to efficiently process multiple samples at a time. Additionally, weight reductions trough low pass filtering is possible. We predict time series data drawn from the chaotic Mackey-Glass differential equation and real-world power load and motion capture data. (Source code available at https://github.com/v0lta/Spectral-RNN).

Keywords: Sequence modelling · Frequency domain · Short time Fourier transform

1 Introduction

Deployment of machine learning methods in embedded and real-time scenarios leads to challenging memory and computational constraints. We propose to use the short time Fourier transform (STFT) to make sequential data forecasting using recurrent neural networks (RNNs) more efficient. The STFT windows the data and moves each window into the frequency domain. A subsequent recurrent network processes multi sample windows instead of single data points and therefore runs at a lower clock rate, which reduces the total number of RNN cell evaluations per time step. Additionally working in the frequency domain allows parameter reductions trough low-pass filtering. Combining both ideas reduces the computational footprint significantly. We hope this reduction will help deploying RNNs on VR-devices for human pose prediction or on embedded systems used for load forecasting and management.

We show in our work that it is possible to propagate gradients through the STFT *and* its inverse. This means that we can use time domain-based losses that match the (temporal) evaluation measures, but still apply the RNN in the frequency domain, which imparts several computation and learning benefits. Firstly, representations can often be more compact and informative in the frequency domain. The Fourier basis clusters the most important information in

© Springer Nature Switzerland AG 2020
I. Farkaš et al. (Eds.): ICANN 2020, LNCS 12396, pp. 825–837, 2020.
https://doi.org/10.1007/978-3-030-61609-0_65

the low-frequency coefficients. It conveniently allows us to integrate a low-pass filter to not only reduce the representation size but also remove undesirable noise effects that may otherwise corrupt the learning of the RNN.

One of the challenges of working with the Fourier transform is that it requires handling of complex numbers. While not yet mainstream, complex-valued representations have been integrated into deep convolutional architectures [25], RNNs [3,28,29] and Hopfield like networks [12]. Complex-valued networks require some additional overhead for book-keeping between the real and imaginary components of the weight matrices and vector states, but tend to be more parameter efficient. We compare fully complex and real valued-concatenation formulations.

Naively applying the RNN on a frame-by-frame basis does not always lead to smooth and coherent predictions [18]. When working with short time Fourier transformed (STFT) windows of data, smoothness can be built-in by design through low-pass filtering before the inverse short time Fourier transformation (iSTFT). Furthermore, by reducing the RNN's effective clockrate, we extend the memory capacity (which usually depends on the number of recurrent steps taken) and achieve computational gains.

In areas such as speech recognition [5] and audio processing [9], using the STFT is a common pre-processing step, e.g. as a part of deriving cepstral coefficients. In these areas, however, the interest is primarily for classification based on the spectrum coefficients and the complex phase is discarded, so there is no need for the inverse transform and the recovery of a temporal signal as output. We advocate the use of the forwards and inverse STFT directly before and after recurrent memory cells and propagate gradients through both the forwards and inverse transform. In summary,

- we propose a novel RNN architecture for analyzing temporal sequences using the STFT and its inverse.
- We investigate the effect of real and complex valued recurrent cells.
- We demonstrate how our windowed formulation of sequence prediction in the spectral domain, based on the reduction in data dimensionality and rate in RNN recursion can, significantly improve efficiency and reduce overall training and inference time.

2   Related Works

Prior to the popular growth of deep learning approaches, analyzing time series and sequence data in the spectral domain, i.e. via a Fourier transform was a standard approach [21]. In machine learning, Fourier analysis is mostly associated with signal-processing heavy domains such as speech recognition [5], biological signal processing [20], medical image [26] and audio-processing [9]. The Fourier transform has already been noted in the past for improving the computational efficiency of convolutional neural networks (CNNs) [4,22]. In CNNs, the efficiency comes from the duality of convolution and multiplication in space and frequency. Fast GPU implementations of convolution, e.g. in the NVIDIA cuDNN library [1] use Fourier transforms to speed up their processing. Such gains are especially relevant for convolutional neural networks in 2D [4,22] and even more so in 3D [27]. However, the improvement in computational efficiency for the STFT-RNN combination comes from reductions in data dimensionality and RNN clock rate recursion. The Fourier transform has been used in neural networks in various contexts [30]. Particularly notable are networks, which have Fourier-like units [11] that decompose time series into constituent bases. Fourier-based pooling has been explored for CNNs as an alternative to standard spatial max-pooling [23].

Various methods for adjusting the rate of RNN recurrency have been explored in the past. One example [17] introduces additional recurrent connections with time lags. Others apply different clock rates to different parts of the hidden layer [2,16], or apply recursion at multiple (time) scales and or hierarchies [7,24]. All of these approaches require changes to the basic RNN architecture. Our proposal, however, is a simple alternative which does not require adding any new structures or connections. Among others [19] approached mocap prediction using RNNs, while [18] applied a cosine transform CNN combination. In this paper we explore the combination of the complex valued windowed STFT and RNNs on mackey-glass, power-load and mocap time series data.

3 Short Time Fourier Transform

3.1 Forwards STFT

The Fourier transform maps a signal into the spectral or frequency domain by decomposing it into a linear combination of sinusoids. In its regular form the transform requires infinite support of the time signal to estimate the frequency response. For many real-world applications, however, including those which we wish to model with RNNs, this requirement is not only infeasible, but it may also be necessary to obtain insights into changes in the frequency spectrum as function of time or signal index. To do so, one can partition the signal into overlapping segments and approximate the Fourier transform of each segment separately. This is the core idea behind the short time Fourier transform (STFT), it determines a signal's frequency domain representation as it changes over time.

More formally, given a signal $\mathbf{x}$, we can partition it into segments of length T, extracted every S time steps. The STFT $\mathcal{F}_s$ of $\mathbf{x}$ is defined by [8] as the discrete Fourier transform of $\mathbf{x}$, $i.e.$

$$\mathbf{X}[\omega, Sm] = \mathcal{F}_s(\mathbf{x})$$
$$= \mathcal{F}(\mathbf{w}[Sm - l]\mathbf{x}[l]) = \sum_{l=-\infty}^{\infty} \mathbf{w}[Sm - l]\mathbf{x}[l]e^{-j\omega l} \tag{1}$$

where $\mathcal{F}$ denotes the classic discrete fast Fourier transform. Segments of $\mathbf{x}$ are multiplied with the windowing function $\mathbf{w}$ and transformed afterwards.

Historically, the shape and width of the window function has been selected by hand. To hand the task of window selection to the optimizer, we work with a truncated Gaussian window [14]

$$w[n] = \exp\left(-\frac{1}{2}\left(\frac{n - T/2}{\sigma T/2}\right)^2\right) \tag{2}$$

of size T and learn the standard deviation σ. The larger that σ is, the more the window function approaches a rectangular window; the smaller the sigma, the more extreme the edge tapering and as a result, the narrower the window width.

3.2   Inverse STFT

Supposing that we are given some frequency signal $\mathbf{X}$; the time signal $\hat{x}$ represented by $\mathbf{X}$ can be recovered with the inverse short time Fourier transform (iSTFT) $\mathcal{F}_s^{-1}$ and is defined by [8] as:

$$\hat{x}[n] = \mathcal{F}_s^{-1}(\mathbf{X}[n, Sm]) = \frac{\sum_{m=-\infty}^{\infty} \mathbf{w}[Sm - n]\hat{\mathbf{x}}_w[n, Sm]}{\sum_{m=-\infty}^{\infty} \mathbf{w}^2[Sm - n]} \tag{3}$$

where the signal $\hat{\mathbf{x}}_w$ is the inverse Fourier transform of $\mathbf{X}$:

$$\hat{\mathbf{x}}_w = \frac{1}{T}\sum_{l=-\infty}^{\infty} \mathbf{X}[l, Sm]e^{j\omega l} \tag{4}$$

and l indexing the frequency dimension of $\mathbf{X}_m$. Equation 3 reverses the effect of the windowing function, but implementations require careful treatment of the denominator to prevent division by near-zero values[1]. In Eq. 3, Sm generally evaluates to an integer smaller than the window size T and subsequent elements in the sum overlap, hence the alternative naming of it being an *"overlap and add"* method [13].

4   Complex Spectral Recurrent Neural Networks

4.1   Network Structure

We can now move RNN processing into the frequency domain by applying the STFT to the input signal x. If the output or projection of the final hidden vector is also a signal of the temporal domain, we can also apply the iSTFT to recover the output y. This can be summarized by the following set of RNN equations:

$$\mathbf{X}_\tau = \mathcal{F}(\{\mathbf{x}_{S\tau - T/2}, \dots, \mathbf{x}_{S\tau + T/2}\}) \tag{5}$$

$$\mathbf{z}_\tau = \mathbf{W}_c\mathbf{h}_{\tau-1} + \mathbf{V}_c\mathbf{X}_\tau + \mathbf{b}_c \tag{6}$$

$$\mathbf{h}_\tau = f_a(\mathbf{z}_\tau) \tag{7}$$

$$\mathbf{y}_\tau = \mathcal{F}^{-1}(\{\mathbf{W}_{pc}\mathbf{h}_0, \dots, \mathbf{W}_{pc}\mathbf{h}_\tau\}) \tag{8}$$

---

[1] We adopt the common strategy of adding a small tolerance $\epsilon = 0.001$.

where $\tau = [0, n_s]$, *i.e.* from zero to the total number of segments n_s. The output y_τ may be computed based on the available outputs $\{\mathbf{W}_p\mathbf{h}_0, \ldots, \mathbf{W}_p\mathbf{h}_\tau\}$ at step τ. Adding the STFT-iSTFT pair has two key implications. First of all, because $\mathbf{X}_\tau \in \mathbb{C}^{n_f \times 1}$ is a complex signal, the hidden state as well as subsequent weight matrices all become complex, *i.e.* $\mathbf{h}_\tau \in \mathbb{C}^{n_h \times 1}$, $\mathbf{W}_c \in \mathbb{C}^{n_h \times n_h}$, $\mathbf{V}_c \in \mathbb{C}^{n_h \times n_f}$, $\mathbf{b}_c \in \mathbb{C}^{n_h \times 1}$ and $\mathbf{W}_{pc} \in \mathbb{C}^{n_h \times n_f}$, where n_h is the hidden size of the network as before and n_f is the number of frequencies in the STFT.

The second implication to note is that the step index changes from frame t to τ, which means that the spectral RNN effectively covers S time steps of the standard RNN per step. This has significant bearing on the overall memory consumption as well as the computational cost, both of which influence the overall network training time. Considering only the multiplication of the state matrix $\mathbf{W}_c$ and the state vector $\mathbf{h}_\tau$, which is the most expensive operation, the basic RNN requires $N \cdot O(n_h^3)$ operations for N total time steps. When using the Fourier RNN with an FFT implementation of the STFT, one requires only

$$N/S \cdot (O(T \log T) + O(n_h^3)), \tag{9}$$

where the $T \log T$ term comes from the FFT operation. The architectural changes lead to larger input layers and fewer RNN iterations. $\mathbf{X}$ is higher dimensional than $\mathbf{x}$, but we save on overall computation if the step size is large enough which will make N/S much smaller than N. We can generalise the approach described above into:

$$\mathbf{X}_\tau = \mathcal{F}(\{\mathbf{x}_{S\tau-T/2}, \ldots, \mathbf{x}_{S\tau+T/2}\}) \tag{10}$$

$$\mathbf{h}_t = \text{RNN}_\mathbb{C}(\mathbf{X}_\tau, \mathbf{h}_{t-1}) \tag{11}$$

$$\mathbf{y}_t = \mathcal{F}^{-1}(\{\mathbf{W}_{pc}\mathbf{h}_0, \ldots, \mathbf{W}_{pc}\mathbf{h}_\tau\}), \tag{12}$$

where instead of the basic formulation outlined above, more sophisticated complex-valued RNN-architectures [3,28,29] represented by $\text{RNN}_\mathbb{C}$ may be substituted. We experiment with a complex-valued GRU, as proposed in [29]. An alternative to a complex approach is to concatenate the real and imaginary components into one (real-valued) hidden vector. The experimental section compares both methods in Table 2.

4.2 Loss Functions

In standard sequence prediction, the loss function applied is an L2 mean squared error, applied in the time domain:

$$\mathcal{L}_{mse}(\mathbf{y}_t, \mathbf{y}_{gt}) = \frac{1}{n_y} \sum_{l=0}^{n_y} (\mathbf{y}_t - \mathbf{y}_{gt})^2. \tag{13}$$

We experiment with a similar variation applied to the STFT coefficients applied in the frequency domain (see Table 2) but find that it performs on par but usually a little bit worse than the time-domain MSE. This is not surprising, as the evaluation measure applied is still in the time domain for sequence prediction so it works best to use the same function as the loss.

5   Mackey-Glass Chaotic Sequence Prediction

Initially we study our method by applying it to make predictions on the Mackey-Glass series [10]. The Mackey-Glass equation is a non-linear time-delay differential and defines a chaotic system that is semi-periodic: We first evaluate different aspects of our model on the chaotic Mackey-Glass time series [10]:

$$\frac{dx}{dt} = \frac{\beta x_\tau}{1 + x_\tau^n} - \gamma x, \tag{14}$$

with $\gamma = 0.1, \beta = 0.2$ and the power parameter to $n = 10$. x_τ denotes the value from τ time steps ago; we use a delay of $\tau = 17$ and simulate the equation in the interval $t \in [0, 512]$, using a forward Euler scheme with a time step of size 0.1. During the warm-up, when true values are not yet known, we use a uniform distribution and randomly draw values from $1 + U[-0.1, 0.1]$. An example of the time series can be found in Fig. 1; we split the signal in half, conditioning on the first half as input and predicting the second half.

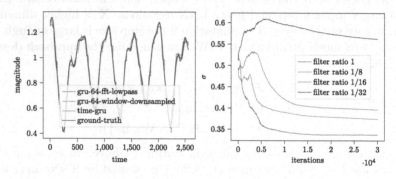

Fig. 1. Mackey-Glass series predictions for different RNN methods. As gradients flow through the STFT we can optimize the width of the gaussian σ. The learned window width for increasing degrees of low-pass filtering is shown here. Figure best viewed in colour.

5.1   Implementation Details

In all experiments, we use RNN architectures based on real [6] and complex [29] GRU-cells with a state size of 64 and a Gaussian window of width 128 initialized at $\sigma = 0.5$ unless otherwise stated. The learning rateas set intially to 0.001 and then reduced with a stair-wise exponential decay with a decay rate of 0.9 every 1000 steps. Training was stopped after 30k iterations. Our run-time measurements include ordinary differential equation simulation, RNN execution as well as back-propagation time.

5.2   Experimental Results and Ablation Studies

Fourier Transform Ablation. We first compare against two time-based networks: a standard GRU (time-GRU) and a windowed version (time-GRU-windowed) in which we reshape the input and process windows of data together instead of single scalars. This effectively sets the clock rate of the RNN to be per window rather than per time step. As comparison, we look at the STFT-GRU combination as described in Sect. 4.1 with a GRU-cell and a low-pass filtered version keeping only the first four coefficients (STFT-GRU-lowpass). Additionally we compare low-pass filtering to time windowed time domain downsampling (time-GRU-window-down). For all five networks, we use a fixed hidden-state size of 64. From Fig. 1, we observe that all five architecture variants are able to predict the overall time series trajectory. Results in Table 1 indicate that reducing the RNN clock rate through windowing and parameters through low pass filtering also improves prediction quality. In comparison to time domain downsampling, frequency-domain lowpass filtering allows us to reduce parameters more aggressively.

Table 1. Short time Fourier, Windowed and Time Domain results obtained using GRU cells of size 64. Windowed experiments process multiple samples of data without computing the STFT. Additionally we compare low-pass filtering the spectrum and downsampling the time domain windows. All models where trained for 30k iterations. We downsample and lowpass-filter with a factor of 1/32.

Net	Weights	mse	Training-time [min]
Time-GRU	13k	$3.8 \cdot 10^{-4}$	355
Time-GRU-window	29k	$6.9 \cdot 10^{-4}$	53
Time-GRU-window-down	13k	$12 \cdot 10^{-4}$	48
STFT-GRU	46k	$3.5 \cdot 10^{-4}$	57
STFT-GRU-lowpass	14k	$2.7 \cdot 10^{-4}$	56

Runtime. As discussed in Eq. 9, windowing reduces the computational load significantly. In Table 1, we see that the windowed experiments run much faster than the naive approach. The STFT networks are slightly slower, since the Fourier Transform adds a small amount of computational overhead.

The Window Function. Figure 1 shows the Gaussian width for multiple filtering scenarios. We observe a gradient signal on the window function. For more aggressive filtering the optimizer chooses a wider kernel.

Complex vs. Real Cell. We explore the effect of a complex valued cell in Table 2. We apply the complex GRU proposed in [29], and compare to a real valued GRU. We speculate that complex cells are better suited to process Fourier representations due to their complex nature. Our observations show that both

Table 2. Real and complex valued architecture comparison on the mackey-glass data, with increasing complex cell size. The complex architectures take longer to run but are more parameter efficient. The last row shows a complex RNN cell in STFT space without iSTFT backpropagation.

Net	Weights	mse	Training-time [min]
STFT-GRU-64	46k	$3.5 \cdot 10^{-4}$	57
STFT-cgRNN-32	23k	$2.1 \cdot 10^{-4}$	63
STFT-cgRNN-54	46k	$1.6 \cdot 10^{-4}$	63
STFT-cgRNN-64	58k	$1.1 \cdot 10^{-4}$	64
STFT-cgRNN-64-$\mathcal{L}_{\mathcal{C}}$	58k	$210 \cdot 10^{-4}$	64

cells solve the task, while the complex cell does so with fewer parameters at a higher computational cost. The increased parameter efficiency of the complex cell could indicate that complex arithmetic is better suited than real arithmetic four Frequency domain machine learning. However due to the increased run-time we proceed using the concatenation approach.

Time vs. Frequency mse. One may argue that propagating gradients through the iSTFT is unnecessary. We tested this setting and show a result in the bottom row of Table 2. In comparison to the accuracy of the otherwise equivalent complex network shown above the second horizontal line, computing the error on the Fourier coefficients performs significantly worse. We conclude that if our metric is in the time domain the loss needs to be there too. We therefore require gradient propagation through the STFT.

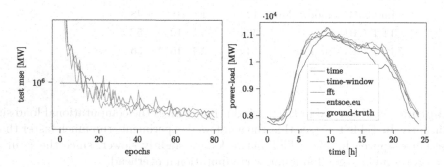

Fig. 2. Day ahead prediction results convergence (left) and prediction examples (right). We observe that all deep learning approaches beat the entsoe.eu baseline shown as the red line, which suggests that their approach could benefit from deep learning. (Color figure online)

6   Power Load Forecasting

6.1   Data

We apply our Fourier RNN to the problem of forecasting power consumption. We use the power load data of 36 EU countries from 2011 to 2019 as provided by the European Network of Transmission System Operators for Electricity. The data is partitioned into two groups; countries reporting with a 15 min frequency are used for day-ahead predictions, while those with hourly reports are used for longer-term predictions. For testing we hold back the German Tennet load recordings from 2015, all of Belgium's recordings of 2016, Austria's load of 2017 and finally the consumption of the German Ampiron grid in 2018.

6.2   Day-Ahead Prediction

We start with the task of day-ahead prediction; using 14 days of context, at 12:00, we are asked to predict 24 h of load from midnight onwards (00:00 until 24:00 o' clock at 12:00 o'clock on the previous day). We therefore forecast the load from noon until midnight on the prediction day plus the next day and ignore the values from the prediction day. We use the same network architecture as in the previous section. During training, the initial learning rate was set to 0.004 and exponentially decayed using a decay of 0.95 every epoch. We train for 80 epochs overall. We compare time domain, windowed time as well as windowed Fourier approaches. The window size was set to 96 which corresponds to 24 h of data at a sampling rate of 15 min per sample.

Table 3. 60 day ahead power load prediction using GRUs of size 64. We downsample and lowpass-filter with a factor of 1/4. We observe that windowing leads to large training and inference speed-ups. Our STFT approach performs better in the full spectrum case and with a reduced input-dimensionality.

Network	mse $[MW]^2$	Weights	Inference [ms]	Training-time [min]
Time-GRU	$261 \cdot 10^5$	13k	1360	1472
Time-GRU-window	$8.12 \cdot 10^5$	74k	9.25	15
Time-GRU-window-down	$8.05 \cdot 10^5$	28k	8.2	15
STFT-GRU	$7.62 \cdot 10^5$	136k	9.67	19
STFT-GRU-lowpass	$7.25 \cdot 10^5$	43k	9.69	18

In Fig. 2 we observe that all approaches we tried produce reasonable solutions and outperform the prediction produced by the European Network of Transmission System Operators for Electricity which suggests that their approach could benefit from deep learning (Fig. 2).

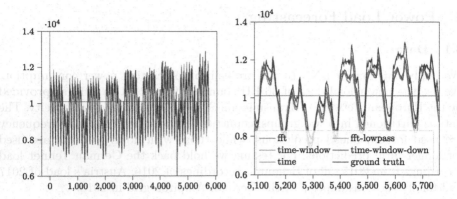

Fig. 3. A test set sample for showing the 60 day prediction results for all architectures under consideration. Close up for the last week of the 60 day prediction.

6.3 Long-Term Forecast

Next we consider the more challenging task of 60 day load prediction using 120 days of context. We use 12 load samples per day from all entenso-e member states from 2015 until 2019. We choose a window size of 120 samples or five days; all other parameters are left the same as the day-ahead prediction setting. Table 3 shows that the windowed methods are able to extract patterns, but the scalar-time domain approach failed. Additionally we observe that we do not require the full set of Fourier coefficients to construct useful predictions on the power-data set. The results are tabulated in Table 3. It turns out that the lower quarter of Fourier coefficients is enough, which allowed us to reduce the number of parameters considerably. Again we observe that Fourier low-pass filtering outperforms down-sampling and windowing.

7   Human Motion Forecasting

7.1   Dataset and Evaluation Measure

The Human3.6M data set [15] contains 3.6 million human poses of seven human actors each performing 15 different tasks sampled at 50 Hz. As in previous work [19] we test on the data from actor 5 and train on all others. We work in Cartesian coordinates and predict the absolute 3D-position of 17 joints per frame, which means that we model the skeleton joint movements as well as global translation.

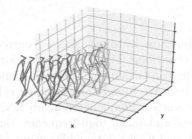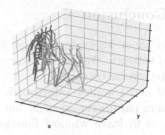

Fig. 4. Visualization of input and prediction results using a STFT-RNN combination and low pass filtering. Input is shown in red and blue, predictions in green and yellow. (Color figure online)

Table 4. 3D-Human motion forecast of 64 frames or approximately one second. Mean absolute error (mae) is measured in mm. Mean squared errors are reported in mm². We downsample and lowpass-filter with a factor of 1/4. Windowing runs much faster than the naive time domain approach. Among windowed approaches the STFT allows more aggressive input size reductions.

Network	mae [mm]	mse [mm]^2	Weights	Inference [ms]	Training-time [min]
Time-GRU [19]	75.44	$1.45 \cdot 10^4$	29M	115	129
Time-GRU-window	68.25	$1.47 \cdot 10^4$	33M	18	27
Time-GRU-window-down	70.22	$1.41 \cdot 10^4$	30M	18	27
STFT-GRU	67.88	$1.25 \cdot 10^4$	45M	25	38
STFT-GRU-lowpass	66.71	$1.30 \cdot 10^4$	32M	20	31

7.2 Implementation Details

We use standard GRU-cells with a state size of 3072. We move the data into the frequency domain by computing a short time Fourier transform over each joint dimension separately using a window size of 24. The learning rate was set initially to 0.001 which we reduced using an exponential stair wise decay every thousand iterations by a factor of 0.97. Training was stopped after 19k iterations.

7.3 Motion Forecasting Results

Prediction results using our STFT approach are shown in Fig. 4. The poses drawn in green and yellow are predictions conditioned on the pose sequences set in blue and red. We observe that the predictions look realistic and smooth. In our experiments low-pass filtering helped us to enforce smoothness in the predictions. Quantitative motion capture prediction results are shown in Table 4. We observe that all windowed approaches run approximately five times faster than the time domain approach during inference, a significant improvement. In terms of accuracy windowing does comparably well, while the STFT approach does better when the input sampling rate is reduced.

8   Conclusion

In this paper we explored frequency domain machine learning using a recurrent neural network. We have proposed to integrate the Short Time Fourier transform and the inverse transform into RNN architectures and evaluated the performance of real and complex valued cells in this setting. We found that complex cells are more parameter efficient, but run slightly longer. Frequency domain RNNs allow us to learn window function parameters and make high-frequency time sequence predictions for both synthetic and real-world data while using less computation time and memory. Low-pass filtering reduced network parameters and outperformed time-domain down-sampling in our experiments.

Acknowledgements. Work has been funded by the Deutsche Forschungsgemeinschaft (DFG, German Research Foundation) YA 447/2-1 and GA 1927/4-1 (FOR2535 Anticipating Human Behavior) as well as by the National Research Foundation of Singapore under its NRF Fellowship Programme [NRF-NRFFAI1-2019-0001].

References

1. NVIDIA Developer Fourier transforms in convolution. https://developer.nvidia.com/discover/convolution. Accessed 25 Mar 2020
2. Alpay, T., Heinrich, S., Wermter, S.: Learning multiple timescales in recurrent neural networks. In: Villa, A.E.P., Masulli, P., Pons Rivero, A.J. (eds.) ICANN 2016. LNCS, vol. 9886, pp. 132–139. Springer, Cham (2016). https://doi.org/10.1007/978-3-319-44778-0_16
3. Arjovsky, M., Shah, A., Bengio, Y.: Unitary evolution recurrent neural networks. In: ICML (2016)
4. Bengio, Y., LeCun, Y., et al.: Scaling learning algorithms towards AI. Large-scale Kernel Mach. **34**(5), 1–41 (2007)
5. Chan, W., Jaitly, N., Le, Q., Vinyals, O.: Listen, attend and spell: a neural network for large vocabulary conversational speech recognition. In: 2016 IEEE International Conference on Acoustics, Speech and Signal Processing (ICASSP), pp. 4960–4964. IEEE (2016)
6. Cho, K., et al.: Learning phrase representations using RNN encoder-decoder for statistical machine translation. In: EMNLP (2014)
7. Chung, J., Ahn, S., Bengio, Y.: Hierarchical multiscale recurrent neural networks. In: ICLR (2017)
8. D. Griffin, J.L.: Signal estimation from modified short-time Fourier transform. In: IEEE Transactions on Acoustics, Speech, and Signal Processing (1984)
9. Dieleman, S., Schrauwen, B.: End-to-end learning for music audio. In: 2014 IEEE International Conference on Acoustics, Speech and Signal Processing (ICASSP). IEEE (2014)
10. Gers, F.A., Eck, D., Schmidhuber, J.: Applying LSTM to time series predictable through time-window approaches. In: Tagliaferri, R., Marinaro, M. (eds.) Neural Nets WIRN Vietri-01, pp. 193–200. Springer, London (2002). https://doi.org/10.1007/978-1-4471-0219-9_20
11. Godfrey, L.B., Gashler, M.S.: Neural decomposition of time-series data for effective generalization. IEEE Trans. Neural Netw. Learn. Syst. **29**(7), 2973–2985 (2018). https://doi.org/10.1109/TNNLS.2017.2709324

12. Goto, H., Osana, Y.: Chaotic complex-valued associative memory with adaptive scaling factor independent of multi-values. In: Tetko, I.V., Kårková, V., Karpov, P., Theis, F. (eds.) ICANN 2019. LNCS, vol. 11727, pp. 76–86. Springer, Cham (2019). https://doi.org/10.1007/978-3-030-30487-4_6
13. Gröchenig, K.: Foundations of Time-frequency Analysis. Springer, Boston (2013). https://doi.org/10.1007/978-1-4612-0003-1
14. Harris, F.J.: On the use of windows for harmonic analysis with the discrete fourier transform. Proc. IEEE **66**(1), 51–83 (1978)
15. Ionescu, C., Papava, D., Olaru, V., Sminchisescu, C.: Human3.6m: large scale datasets and predictive methods for 3D human sensing in natural environments. IEEE Trans. Pattern Anal. Mach. Intell. **36**(7), 1325–1339 (2014)
16. Koutnik, J., Greff, K., Gomez, F., Schmidhuber, J.: A clockwork RNN. In: International Conference on Machine Learning, pp. 1863–1871 (2014)
17. Lin, T., Horne, B.G., Tino, P., Giles, C.L.: Learning long-term dependencies in NARX recurrent neural networks. IEEE Trans. Neural Netw. **7**(6), 1329–1338 (1996)
18. Mao, W., Liu, M., Salzmann, M., Li, H.: Learning trajectory dependencies for human motion prediction. In: Proccedings of the IEEE International Conference on Computer Vision, pp. 9489–9497 (2019)
19. Martinez, J., Black, M., Romero, J.: On human motion prediction using recurrent neural networks. In: CVPR (2017)
20. Minami, K., Nakajima, H., Toyoshima, T.: Real-time discrimination of ventricular tachyarrhythmia with fourier-transform neural network. IEEE Trans. Biomed. Eng. **46**(2), 179–185 (1999). https://doi.org/10.1109/10.740880
21. Pintelon, R., Schoukens, J.: System Identification: A Frequency Domain Approach. Wiley, Hoboken (2012)
22. Pratt, H., Williams, B., Coenen, F., Zheng, Y.: FCNN: fourier convolutional neural networks. In: Ceci, M., Hollmén, J., Todorovski, L., Vens, C., Džeroski, S. (eds.) ECML PKDD 2017. LNCS (LNAI), vol. 10534, pp. 786–798. Springer, Cham (2017). https://doi.org/10.1007/978-3-319-71249-9_47
23. Ryu, J., Yang, M.-H., Lim, J.: DFT-based transformation invariant pooling layer for visual classification. In: Ferrari, V., Hebert, M., Sminchisescu, C., Weiss, Y. (eds.) Computer Vision – ECCV 2018. LNCS, vol. 11218, pp. 89–104. Springer, Cham (2018). https://doi.org/10.1007/978-3-030-01264-9_6
24. Serban, I.V., et al.: Multiresolution recurrent neural networks: an application to dialogue response generation. In: Thirty-First AAAI Conference on Artificial Intelligence (2017)
25. Trabelsi, C., et al.: Deep complex networks. In: ICLR (2018)
26. Virtue, P., Yu, S., Lustig, M.: Better than real: complex-valued neural nets for MRI fingerprinting. In: ICIP (2017)
27. Wang, Z., Lan, Q., He, H., Zhang, C.: Winograd algorithm for 3D convolution neural networks. In: Lintas, A., Rovetta, S., Verschure, P.F.M.J., Villa, A.E.P. (eds.) ICANN 2017. LNCS, vol. 10614, pp. 609–616. Springer, Cham (2017). https://doi.org/10.1007/978-3-319-68612-7_69
28. Wisdom, S., Powers, T., Hershey, J., Le Roux, J., Atlas, L.: Full-capacity unitary recurrent neural networks. In: NIPS (2016)
29. Wolter, M., Yao, A.: Complex gated recurrent neural networks. In: NIPS (2018)
30. Zuo, W., Zhu, Y., Cai, L.: Fourier-neural-network-based learning control for a class of nonlinear systems with flexible components. IEEE Trans. Neural Netw. **20**(1), 139–151 (2008)

Attention Based Mechanism for Load Time Series Forecasting: AN-LSTM

Jatin Bedi[✉]

Department of CSIS, BITS Pilani, Pilani, India
jatin.bedi@pilani.bits-pilani.ac.in

Abstract. Smart grids collect high volumes of data that contain valuable information about energy consumption patterns. The data can be utilized for future strategies planning, including generation capacity and economic planning by forecasting the energy demand. In the recent years, deep learning has gained significant importance for energy load time-series forecasting applications. In this context, the current research work proposes an attention-based deep learning model to forecast energy demand. The proposed approach works by initially implementing an attention mechanism to extract relevant deriving segments of the input load series at each timestamp and assigns weights to them. Subsequently, the extracted segments are then fed to the long-short term memory network prediction model. In this way, the proposed model provides support for handling big-data temporal sequences by extracting complex hidden features of the data. The experimental evaluation of the proposed approach is conducted on the three seasonally segmented dataset of UT Chandigarh, India. Two popular performance measures (RMSE and MAPE) are used to compare the prediction results of the proposed approach with state-of-the-art prediction models (SVR and LSTM). The comparison results shows that the proposed approach outperforms other benchmark prediction models and has the lowest MAPE (7.11%).

Keywords: Energy load forecasting · Long short term memory network · Attention network · Time-series forecasting

1 Introduction

Every country in the world has seen significant technological developments in the recent decades. Some of these advancements come with a cost of increased electricity demand such as household automation, electric vehicles, smart healthcare appliances, agriculture machinery and many more [1, 2]. In addition to this, there exists some other critical factors [26] such as increasing population, economic growth and industrialization, which are actively contributing to the increasing electricity demand. While keeping all these factors in mind, ensuring a sufficient supply of energy to everyone is the primary concern of every nation. Hence, efficient energy demand forecasting tools and techniques are required for a number of reasons including transmission network optimization, future generation plants or capacity and economic planning.

© Springer Nature Switzerland AG 2020
I. Farkaš et al. (Eds.): ICANN 2020, LNCS 12396, pp. 838–849, 2020.
https://doi.org/10.1007/978-3-030-61609-0_66

Future demand estimation problem can be modelled as a time-series forecasting problem with demand observation at equal intervals of time [7]. Time-series forecasting models are based on estimating future values from the series of available historical observations [22]. Hence, historical demand observations data is pre-requisite for building efficient load forecasting models. Smart grids are the system that provides support for collecting high voluminous energy load demand data at different levels of granularity [10]. So far, several different types of energy load time-series forecasting models have been developed to forecast electricity demand by utilizing the historical demand observations data. Some of the significant contributions are stated as follows:

For many years, statistical models [8,11,13,18], such as Autoregressive (AR), Autoregressive Moving Average (ARMA), Autoregressive Integrated Moving Average (ARIMA) are baseline models for energy load demand forecasting. Later, machine learning models [12,21,24,25], such as Artificial Neural Networks (ANN), Support Vector Machine (SVM) and regression trees have shown great potential by providing improved prediction performance. However, these models are not suitable for handling temporal-dependencies of the time-series. In recent years, deep learning has emerged out as a powerful tool for time-series forecasting applications. Several deep learning models such as recurrent neural networks [6,15], convolutional neural networks [20,29] and deep belief networks [9,23] are widely adopted for prediction applications in different domains including transportation, healthcare, utility services and agriculture. Out of several available deep learning models, Recurrent Neural Network (RNN) models have gained immense importance in the time-series forecasting domain [15,27]. A large number of research studies have employed RNN models for the energy load demand forecasting. Among various RNN types, Long-Short Term Memory Network (LSTM) [7,28] models are most popular as they resolve the issues associated with basic RNN models such as vanishing and exploding gradient problem. Bandara et al. [5] presented an LSTM and multi-seasonal information based decomposition approach for time series forecasting. Kwon et al. [19] developed an climatic conditions coupled LSTM based approach for short-term load forecasting.

LSTM network introduced by Hochreiter and Schmidhuber [16] have been widely found to be very successful at handling temporal dependencies of the data. They do so by capturing relevant information in the form of memory cells. The architectural representation of the LSTM memory cell is given in Fig. 1. The main pillar to the cell are forget gate (f_t), input gate (i_t) and output gate (o_t) [4]. Based on the current scenario, the forget gate decides which information to be thrown away from the current cell state. The next step to decide the information to be added in the current cell state is taken care by the input gate. Finally, the output gate determines the output of the network based on the current state of forget and input gate. These cell states basically helps the LSTM model to keep track of long-term dependencies present in the time series data.

LSTM network models have been found to be very useful for prediction in time series domain [7]. In recent years, several LSTM based encoder-decoder network models have been introduced for time series prediction. However, these models are not suitable for handling long-term dependencies of the time series as most of these are based on extracting fixed-length feature sequences from the input data. Moreover, they suffer from the interpretability issues (determining the role of feature sequences to the task of prediction). In the current work, we introduce an attention-based LSTM model to assign weights to different partial sequences of the input time series and then utilize these weights for the case of time series prediction. Although these types of methods have shown great potential in natural language processing tasks [17,30], there are very few works which utilized this for the case of load time series prediction. The proposed attention based mechanism works by initially extracting different relevant segments of the input deriving series by using hidden state information and the uses them for input to the prediction model. More specifically, the seasonal based segmented information is combined with Attention-based LSTM model (AN-LSTM) for achieving the improved energy demand forecasting accuracy.

The rest of this paper is organized as follows: Section 2 explains the detailed step by step methodology of the proposed AN-LSTM approach. The experimental results of the proposed approach on the dataset of UT Chandigarh, India are detailed in Sect. 3. The conclusion of the paper is stated in Sect. 4.

2   Methodology

The overall architecture of the proposed approach is depicted in Fig. 1. The step by step working of each component (Fig. 1) is explained as follows:

2.1   Input Dataset

In this study, we have used the load demand dataset of Chandigarh, India to evaluate the performance of the proposed approach. The dataset is available for a period of five years (2013–2018) with a sampling rate of 15 min [7]. Chandigarh is a Union Territory (UT) in India and the capital of two neighbouring states (Punjab and Haryana). The average electricity demand of UT has rapidly grown to 2328 units in the year 2018–2019 [3] and is likely to be increasing faster. Central power generating stations are responsible for continuous power supply to UT Chandigarh as it does not have any own power generation units. The UT administration aims to provide "24 × 7" power to the citizens' of Chandigarh. So, stating future power requirements in advance is a major concern for the administration.

2.2   Data Preprocessing

One of the major contributing factor to the accurate knowledge extraction process is preprocessing of the input data [14,22]. It plays an important step in the process of data mining by removing irrelevant or redundant, noisy and unreliable information from the data. In the current scenario, the data preprocessing

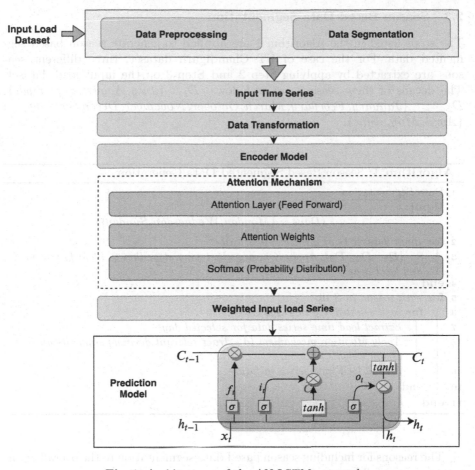

Fig. 1. Architecture of the AN-LSTM approach

stage is divided into three main parts: Initially all missing values in the data are filled by average of load demand value (for that day). Subsequently, the data transformation is implemented by dividing the electricity demand for each day into four time continuous interval namely I_1 *(00:00 am to 06:00 am)*, I_2 *(06:00 am to 12:00 pm)*, I_3 *(12:00 pm to 06:00 pm)*, I_4 *(06:00 pm to 12:00 am)*. Finally, the min-max data normalization (given by Eq. 1) is applied to linearly transform the data to a range of zero to one.

$$n' = \frac{n - min(n)}{max(n) - min(n)} \tag{1}$$

where n and n' denote the old and new normalized value of an input load-series feature respectively.

2.3   Season Based Data Segmentation

The steps listed in the Algorithm 1 are applied to generate season based segmented data. For the case of UT Chandigarh dataset, three different seasons are extracted by applying Step 2 and Step 3 on the input load dataset. The details of these seasons are as follows: D_1 : $\{July, August, September\}$, D_2 : $\{January, February, March, October, November, December\}$ D_3 : $\{April, May, June\}$.

Algorithm 1: Season Based Segmented Data Generation

---

1 Data Segmentation
   Input:
$$(Days = \{Monday, Wednesday, Sunday\})$$
2 **for** *input dataset D of UT Chandigarh* **do**
3 | S =[D_1, D_2, D_3]: *Apply K-means clustering algorithm to identify season and label it as S*
4 **end**
5 **for** *each season in S* **do**
6 | **for** *each selected day in* **Days** **do**
7 | | *Extract load time series data for selected day.*
8 | | *Apply attention mechanism to extract relevant deriving segments and assign weights to them.*
9 | | *Predict load time series in future.*
10 | **end**
11 **end**

The reasons for including season based data segmentation to the overall architecture are as follows:

– It allows to capture seasonal and day-wise flexibility, uncertainty and variability of the load demand time series.
– Including seasonal and timestamp information to the model allows capturing data dependencies at a deeper level by including more historic information to the model.
– The segmentation will provide support for less training time and is capable of working in a resource constrained environment.

2.4   Attention Based LSTM Network Model

Finally, for each of the selected three days ($Monday$: $weekday$, $Wednesday$: day $with$ $highest$ $variations$ in $load$ $demand$, $Sunday$: $weekend$) in the extracted seasons, the attention based LSTM network model are built. The step by step working of the AN-LSTM is explained as follows:

- **Step 1: Input load demand series**
  For the given input load series of the form

$$X = < x_1, x_2, \ldots x_n > \quad x_i : load\ demand\ at\ i^{th}\ timestamp \quad (2)$$

  Transform each value x_i to a vector form given by:

$$x_i = F(x_i) = < x_{i-d-1}, x_{i-d}, \ldots x_i > \in R^{nXd} \quad (3)$$

- **Step 2: Input to the Encoder model**
  For the transformed input series, the encoder model is applied to obtain a mapping of the form

$$h_t = encoder(h_{t-1}, x_t) \quad (4)$$

  In our case, we have implemented LSTM network model (encoder) to learn data dependencies. The overall working of the encoder model can be summarized with the help of following equations.

$$\left.\begin{aligned}
f_t &= \sigma(W_f[x_t.h_{t-1}] + b_f) \\
i_t &= \sigma(W_i[h_{t-1}.x_t.] + b_i) \\
o_t &= \sigma(W_o[h_{t-1}.x_t.] + b_0) \\
c_{t'} &= tanh(W_c[h_{t-1}.x_t.] + b_c) \\
c_t &= f_t \odot c_{t-1} \oplus i_t \odot c_{t'} \\
h_t &= o_t \odot tanh(c_t)
\end{aligned}\right\} \quad (5)$$

  where h_t denotes hidden state, x_t denotes current input vector, σ represents logistic sigmoid function, $\odot$ represents elements wise multiplication operator, W and b are weights and bias respectively.

- **Step 3: Attention Mechanism (Feed Forward Network)**
  The aim of this step is to focus on relevant deriving segments of the load time series and discard other irrelevant information. The attention mechanism forms its basis on the current hidden state (h_{t-1}) and cell state (c_{t-1}) of the encoder LSTM model. It is given as:

$$aw_t = V^T tanh(W_a[h_{t-1}, c_{t-1}] + W_x. \ x + b_a) \quad (6)$$

  where V, W_a, W_b and b_a are parameters (learnable) of the model. The next step in this sequence is to assign attention weights to the load sequences using Eq. 6.

$$Paw\_t = softmax(aw_t) \quad (7)$$

- **Step 4: Calculate hidden state vector for Prediction model based on the Attention Mechanism**
  The aim of this step is to enforce the prediction model to focus on the relevant portion of the input load sequence based on the attention weights. The attention mechanism achieves this by updating input series to the prediction model using the following two steps:

The new weighted input load sequences for input to the LSTM prediction model are calculated as:

$$\widetilde{x}_t = (Paw_t \,.\, x_t) \tag{8}$$

Finally, the hidden state at next time interval based on attention mechanism is given by:

$$h_t = LSTM(h_{t-1}, \widetilde{x}_t) \tag{9}$$

3   Experimental Results and Discussion

The experimental results of the proposed approach are evaluated on three different seasonal datasets of the UT Chandigarh, India. In order to ensure the reliability and prediction accuracy of the AN-LSTM model, the prediction results are compared to two popular time series prediction models namely Support Vector Regression (SVR) [22] and LSTM [16]. The evaluated measures employed to compare the performance are as follows:

– Mean Absolute Percentage Error (MAPE) [14]: It calculates the % deviation of predicted values from the real time values and is given as

$$MAPE = \frac{1}{n} \sum_{i=1}^{n} |\frac{A - \bar{A}}{A}| \times 100 \tag{10}$$

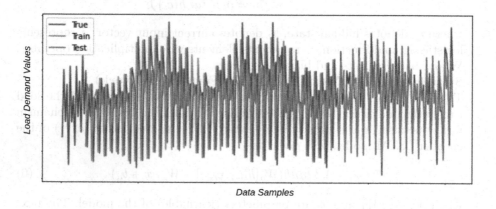

Fig. 2. Example prediction results using AN-LSTM model

– Root Mean Squared Error [14]: It signifies the residual error and is given as

$$RMSE = \sqrt{\frac{\sum_{i=1}^{n}(\bar{A} - A)^2}{n}} \tag{11}$$

where n represents the number of samples, A and $\bar{A}$ denotes the actual and predicted values respectively.

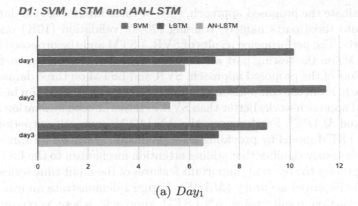

(a) Day_1

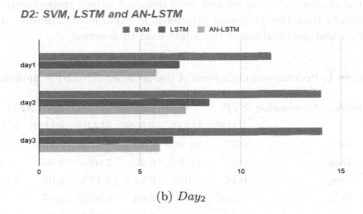

(b) Day_2

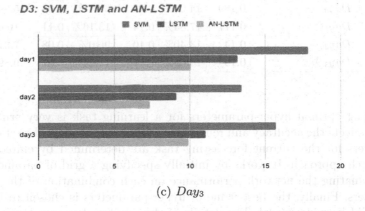

(c) Day_3

Fig. 3. Performance comparison of proposed approach with other baseline methods (in terms of MAPE (%))

To evaluate the proposed approach, each of three input seasonal datasets are divided into three parts namely, training (70%), validation (10%) and testing (20%) parts. The performance results of SVR, LSTM and the proposed approach (AN-LSTM) on the testing part are listed in Table 1. Figure 3 demonstrates the *MAPE* plots of the proposed approach, SVR and LSTM on three datasets of UT Chandigarh. From the comparison results (Table 1 and Fig. 3), it can be seen that the LSTM approach works better than SVR in terms of both evaluation measures (*RMSE* and *MAPE*). Furthermore, the AN-LSTM approach outperforms both SVR and LSTM model by providing least prediction errors for all three seasonal datasets. It clearly signifies that adding attention mechanism to the LSTM model allows capturing the relevant/important features of the input time series, thereby supporting improved accuracy (*MAPE*). Figure 2 demonstrate an example plot of the prediction results using AN-LSTM approach, where x-axis and y-axis denotes the number of samples and load demand values respectively. Figure 2 clearly depicts that the proposed approach is capable of handling non-linear complexities and fluctuations of the input load time series.

Table 1. Performance evaluation of the proposed AN-LSTM approach

Performance evaluation		SVR		LSTM		AN-LSTM	
		RMSE	MAPE	RMSE	MAPE	RMSE	MAPE
D_1	Day_1	0.17	10.18%	0.12	7.05%	0.10	5.85%
	Day_2	0.15	11.48%	0.10	7.08%	0.08	5.24%
	Day_3	0.16	9.10%	0.11	7.17%	0.09	6.56%
D_2	Day_1	0.168	11.51%	0.08	6.95%	0.07	5.81%
	Day_2	0.13	13.99%	0.09	8.41%	0.08	7.26%
	Day_3	0.189	14.04%	0.08	6.64%	0.08	5.99%
D_3	Day_1	0.177	17.84%	0.14	13.16%	0.11	10.07%
	Day_2	0.14	13.40%	0.10	9.10%	0.08	7.37%
	Day_3	0.19	15.68%	0.11	11.04%	0.07	9.89%

Finding optimal hyper-parameters for a learning task is very crucial as it directly affects the accuracy and reliability of a learning model. The set of hyper-parameters for the current forecasting task are determined by employing the grid search approach. It works by initially specifying a grid of parameters and then evaluating the network performance on each combination of the specified parameters. Finally, the best value of hyper-parameters is chosen to build the AN-LSTM learning model. The details of the significant parameters related to the proposed AN-LSTM model are as follows: the lag value (input window size) is set to value 16, the output window size parameter is set to value one, the number of LSTM layers varies from 2 to 8 (based on the seasonality factors), the number of hidden layers varies in the range (2–6), the number of neurons in hidden layers varies in the range (16–64), weight decay regularization, '*ReLu*' activation function and '*adam*' optimizer are used.

4   Conclusion

In this paper, we proposed an attention-based deep learning model to perform energy load demand forecasting over the UT Chandigarh time-series dataset. The approach comprises of three major stages. Firstly, the data clustering is applied to generate three season-based segmented datasets. Secondly, the attention mechanism is implemented to extract relevant deriving series segments from the seasonal input datasets. Thirdly, the LSTM network models are trained to forecast energy demand at the seasonal level by including only extracted appropriate segments for the current timestamp prediction. An extensive grid search based parameter search was conducted to determine the best parameters configuration. Finally, the performance comparison results of the proposed approach over the UT Chandigarh datasets showed that the AN-LSTM approach provides improved prediction accuracy as compared to the baseline SVR and LSTM prediction models. Hence, the proposed approach can be easily adopted for time-series prediction applications in other related fields including healthcare, transportation, agriculture, finance and so on.

References

1. Energy central. https://energycentral.com/c/ec/how-ai-and-automation-are-impacting-future-energy. Accessed 30 Feb 2020
2. International energy agency: digitalisation-and-energy. https://www.iea.org/reports/digitalisation-and-energy. Accessed 30 Feb 2020
3. Power ministry. https://powermin.nic.in/. Accessed 30 Feb 2020
4. Understanding LSTM networks. https://colah.github.io/posts/2015-08-Understanding-LSTMs/. Accessed 30 Jan 2020
5. Bandara, K., Bergmeir, C., Hewamalage, H.: LSTM-MSNet: leveraging forecasts on sets of related time series with multiple seasonal patterns. IEEE Trans. Neural Netw. Learn. Syst. (2020)
6. Bandara, K., Bergmeir, C., Smyl, S.: Forecasting across time series databases using recurrent neural networks on groups of similar series: a clustering approach. Expert Syst. Appl. **140**, 112896 (2020)
7. Bedi, J., Toshniwal, D.: Deep learning framework to forecast electricity demand. Appl. Energy **238**, 1312–1326 (2019)
8. Chandramowli, S., Lahr, M.L.: Forecasting new jersey's electricity demand using auto-regressive models. Available at SSRN 2258552 (2012)
9. Dedinec, A., Filiposka, S., Dedinec, A., Kocarev, L.: Deep belief network based electricity load forecasting: an analysis of Macedonian case. Energy **115**, 1688–1700 (2016)

10. Dey, A.N., Panigrahi, B.K., Kar, S.K.: Smartgrids/microgrids in India: a review on relevance, initiatives, policies, projects and challenges. In: Sharma, R., Mishra, M., Nayak, J., Naik, B., Pelusi, D. (eds.) Innovation in Electrical Power Engineering, Communication, and Computing Technology. LNEE, vol. 630, pp. 465–474. Springer, Singapore (2020). https://doi.org/10.1007/978-981-15-2305-2_37
11. Ekonomou, L.: Greek long-term energy consumption prediction using artificial neural networks. Energy **35**(2), 512–517 (2010)
12. Galicia, A., Talavera-Llames, R., Troncoso, A., Koprinska, I., Martínez-Álvarez, F.: Multi-step forecasting for big data time series based on ensemble learning. Knowl. Based Syst. **163**, 830–841 (2019)
13. González, V., Contreras, J., Bunn, D.W.: Forecasting power prices using a hybrid fundamental-econometric model. IEEE Trans. Pow. Syst. **27**(1), 363–372 (2011)
14. Goodfellow, I., Bengio, Y., Courville, A.: Deep Learning. MIT press, Cambridge (2016)
15. He, W.: Load forecasting via deep neural networks. Procedia Comput. Sci. **122**, 308–314 (2017)
16. Hochreiter, S., Schmidhuber, J.: Long short-term memory. Neural Comput. **9**(8), 1735–1780 (1997)
17. Hu, D.: An introductory survey on attention mechanisms in NLP problems. In: Bi, Y., Bhatia, R., Kapoor, S. (eds.) IntelliSys 2019. AISC, vol. 1038, pp. 432–448. Springer, Cham (2020). https://doi.org/10.1007/978-3-030-29513-4_31
18. Khashei, M., Bijari, M.: An artificial neural network (p, d, q) model for timeseries forecasting. Expert Syst. Appl. **37**(1), 479–489 (2010)
19. Kwon, B.S., Park, R.J., Song, K.B.: Short-term load forecasting based on deep neural networks using LSTM layer. J. Electr. Eng. Technol. (2020)
20. Lara-Benítez, P., Carranza-García, M., Luna-Romera, J.M., Riquelme, J.C.: Temporal convolutional networks applied to energy-related time series forecasting. Appl. Sci. **10**(7), 2322 (2020)
21. Liu, D., Chen, Q., Mori, K.: Time series forecasting method of building energy consumption using support vector regression. In: 2015 IEEE International Conference on Information and Automation, pp. 1628–1632. IEEE (2015)
22. Mining, H.J.K.M.D.: Concepts and techniques. Jiawei Han and Micheline Kamber 2 (2001)
23. Ouyang, T., He, Y., Li, H., Sun, Z., Baek, S.: Modeling and forecasting short-term power load with copula model and deep belief network. IEEE Trans. Emerg. Top. Comput. Intell. **3**(2), 127–136 (2019)
24. Prasad, R., Joseph, L., Deo, R.C.: Modeling and forecasting renewable energy resources for sustainable power generation: basic concepts and predictive model results. In: Singh, A. (ed.) Translating the Paris Agreement into Action in the Pacific. AGCR, vol. 68, pp. 59–79. Springer, Cham (2020). https://doi.org/10.1007/978-3-030-30211-5_3
25. Tso, G.K., Yau, K.K.: Predicting electricity energy consumption: a comparison of regression analysis, decision tree and neural networks. Energy **32**(9), 1761–1768 (2007)
26. Van Tran, N., Van Tran, Q., Do, L.T.T., Dinh, L.H., Do, H.T.T.: Trade off between environment, energy consumption and human development: do levels of economic development matter? Energy **173**, 483–493 (2019)
27. Wang, H., Lei, Z., Zhang, X., Zhou, B., Peng, J.: A review of deep learning for renewable energy forecasting. Energy Convers. Manage. **198**, 111799 (2019)

28. Yunpeng, L., Di, H., Junpeng, B., Yong, Q.: Multi-step ahead time series forecasting for different data patterns based on LSTM recurrent neural network. In: 2017 14th Web Information Systems and Applications Conference (WISA), pp. 305–310. IEEE (2017)
29. Zhang, X., He, K., Bao, Y.: Error-feedback stochastic configuration strategy on convolutional neural networks for time series forecasting. arXiv preprint arXiv:2002.00717 (2020)
30. Zhou, X., Wan, X., Xiao, J.: Attention-based LSTM network for cross-lingual sentiment classification. In: Proceedings of the 2016 Conference on Empirical Methods in Natural Language Processing, pp. 247–256 (2016)

DartsReNet: Exploring New RNN Cells in ReNet Architectures

Brian B. Moser[1,2]([✉]), Federico Raue[1]([✉]), Jörn Hees[1]([✉]),
and Andreas Dengel[1,2]([✉])

[1] German Research Center for Artificial Intelligence (DFKI),
Kaiserslautern, Germany
{brian.moser,federico.raue,joern.hees,andreas.dengel}@dfki.de
[2] TU Kaiserslautern, Kaiserslautern, Germany

Abstract. We present new Recurrent Neural Network (RNN) cells for image classification using a Neural Architecture Search (NAS) approach called DARTS. We are interested in the ReNet architecture, which is a RNN based approach presented as an alternative for convolutional and pooling steps. ReNet can be defined using any standard RNN cells, such as LSTM and GRU. One limitation is that standard RNN cells were designed for one dimensional sequential data and not for two dimensions like it is the case for image classification. We overcome this limitation by using DARTS to find new cell designs. We compare our results with ReNet that uses GRU and LSTM cells. Our found cells outperform the standard RNN cells on CIFAR-10 and SVHN. The improvements on SVHN indicate generalizability, as we derived the RNN cell designs from CIFAR-10 without performing a new cell search for SVHN. (The source code of our approach and experiments is available at https://github.com/LuckyOwl95/DartsReNet/.).

Keywords: DARTS · NAS · ReNet · RNN · CV

1 Introduction

Convolutional Neural Networks (CNNs) achieved state-of-the-art results on image classification, e.g., GoogLeNet, VGG, and ResNet [8,15,17]. The current trend of finding new architectures with better performances relies mainly on the basis of convolutional operations. Nevertheless, an alternative way is using Recurrent Neural Networks (RNNs) as a core element or in combination with CNNs. They have shown promising results for Computer Vision (CV) tasks, e.g., ReNet [18], MD-LSTM [7], PyraMiD-LSTM [16] or Optical Character Recognition related approaches [2]. RNN approaches have the advantage that they capture of capturing the global context. Nonetheless, RNNs are slower than CNNs because of their sequential nature, which is less parallelizable.

In general, finding suitable Neural Network architectures is an expensive human effort of trial and error until reaching a desirable performance (e.g. number of layers or the size of each layer). Nowadays, a new field has emerged called

© Springer Nature Switzerland AG 2020
I. Farkaš et al. (Eds.): ICANN 2020, LNCS 12396, pp. 850–861, 2020.
https://doi.org/10.1007/978-3-030-61609-0_67

Neural Architecture Search (NAS) [20], which is trying to automate the manual process of designing such architectures.

Recent works of manually designed state-of-the-art architectures showed that repetitions of fixed structures are favorable, e.g., Residual Blocks in ResNet [8] or Inception-Modules in GoogLeNet [17]. These structures are smaller-sized graphs and can be stacked to form a larger-scale network architecture. Across the NAS literature, they are called cells, and a cell-based approach tries to find them. For this work, we have a particular interest in DARTS, which is a cell-based NAS approach [12]. Moreover, DARTS is a differentiable architecture search, so it uses gradient descent to find such cells.

Although NAS approaches show mainly new architectures based on CNNs for CV tasks, there is only work on finding RNN cells for one dimensional sequential data, such as text prediction or speech recognition. We also observe that alternative RNN-based approaches for CV tasks are mostly considering standard RNN cells designs like LSTM or GRU [4,9]. Despite their effectiveness, it is unclear if they are optimal for an image-based domain since the original motivation of LSTM and GRU address one dimensional sequences.

In this work, we are interested in modifying the RNN cell design (which is the core element) in the ReNet model using DARTS. We further evaluated two more variants for search space: One is *Sigmoid* Weighting on the input sequence to weight the importance of a time step, and the other is Directional Weight Sharing, which uses the same weight matrix for both directions in a bidirectional RNN. The idea behind *Sigmoid* Weighting is to explore a new type of hard attention, specifically in the case of ReNet, and the idea behind Directional Weight Sharing is to save parameters. The resulting RNN cells are different from standard RNN cells, especially deeper and more sequential. We are able to outperform ReNet with standard RNN cells on the data sets CIFAR-10 and SVHN [11,13], as detailed in Sect. 4. Summarizing, our contributions are the following ones:

- We evaluated the DARTS approach in the ReNet model with new conditions not considered in the original paper. Thus, it is not searching RNN cells for sequential data like text, but finding an RNN cell for the visual domain.
- We compared the novel cells with GRU and LSTM in the ReNet architecture in two small-scale data sets. The new cells reached better results on CIFAR-10 and SVHN. We want to point out that we did the cell search on the CIFAR-10 data set but evaluated on CIFAR-10 and SVHN data sets.
- We added two more alternatives to the search space: *Sigmoid* Weighting and Directional Weight Sharing. Directional Weight Sharing achieved better results with fewer parameters on CIFAR-10 whereas the best performance for SVHN was achieved without a variant.

2   Background

This work relies on two crucial building blocks. The first is ReNet, which processes images or feature maps as a sequence. Hence, RNN cells can be applied to images or any feature maps. The second is DARTS. It finds cells, which are smaller-sized structures that are usable in a Neural Network, using gradient descent. Comparing to other NAS approaches (e.g., evolutionary methods or reinforcement learning), DARTS is fast to compute [1,14,20]. We combine both approaches to explore which RNN cells are suitable for image classification tasks.

2.1 ReNet

The ReNet layer is an RNN based alternative to convolution and pooling transformations[18]. The basic idea is to divide a given image into flattened patches and process the patches as a sequence to bidirectional RNNs, see Fig. 1.

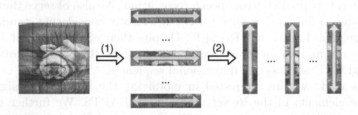

Fig. 1. Example of a ReNet layer. Initially, an image is split into several patches (i.e., $2 \times 2 \times 3$). Then, two bidirectional RNNs sweep over the image in the horizontal direction (1) and then in the vertical direction (2).

Let $I \in \mathbb{R}^{w \times h \times c}$ be an input, where h, w, and c are the width, height and number of channels, respectively. A ReNet layer with a window size of (w_p, h_p) creates a set of non-overlapping and flattened patches of I. Let $\mathbf{p}_{i,j}$ be the (i, j)-th patch of I. Let F and B denote the two directions of a bidirectional RNN, forward and backward. A bidirectional $RNN_H = \{RNN_H^F, RNN_H^B\}$ reads the sequence of flattened patches in the horizontal direction of the image. The initial hidden states are initially a zero vector $\mathbf{0}$. It creates a feature map

$$\mathbf{H} = \begin{bmatrix} \mathbf{h}^F \\ \mathbf{h}^B \end{bmatrix} \tag{1}$$

with the elements

$$\mathbf{h}_{i,j}^F = RNN_H^F \left(\mathbf{p}_{i,j}, \mathbf{h}_{i,j-1}^F \right) \text{ and}$$
$$\mathbf{h}_{i,j}^B = RNN_H^B \left(\mathbf{p}_{i,j}, \mathbf{h}_{i,j+1}^B \right) \tag{2}$$

with $i \in \{0, ..., h\}$ and $j \in \{0, ..., w\}$. Afterward, a second bidirectional $RNN_V = \{RNN_V^F, RNN_V^B\}$ processes the feature map $\mathbf{H}$ in a similar manner but in the vertical direction. The feature map $\mathbf{V}$ is the overall output of the ReNet layer.

Note that ReNet is agnostic to RNN cell definition (LSTM, GRU or any new development). Hence, it is suitable to use RNN cells derived by DARTS explained in the next section.

2.2   DARTS

DARTS is a cell-based NAS approach [12]. It is finding a cell design that can be used as components for a network architecture [14]. Like Residual Blocks in ResNet [8], a cell is a small graph representing a structure that is usable within a Neural Network. DARTS derives the cell with gradient descent in the Architecture Search Space.

We will explain two essential components of DARTS for developing a new RNN cell for ReNet: *cell definition* for RNNs and *cell search* based on the cell definition. *Cell definition* describes the sequence of operations within the RNN cell and the learnable elements (i.e., activation functions and connections to other internal components). *Cell search* performs gradient descent to explore the Architecture Search Space based on the *cell definition*.

Cell Definition. The next definitions follow the standard DARTS approach from the original paper for RNN cells. A *cell* is an acyclic, directed graph $G = (V, E)$ where each vertex $i \in V$ has exactly one ingoing edge $(j, i) \in E$ to a predecessor vertex $j \in V$. The edge is associated with an activation function f_i. We will denote the input of a vertex i with $\widetilde{\mathbf{x}}_{i,t}$. Vertex i receives the output of its predecessor as part of its input $\widetilde{\mathbf{x}}_{i,t}$. One vertex in this graph is the input vertex, which receives an input $\mathbf{x}_t$ independent from the *cell* itself (e.g., a flattened patch of an image). Thus, the input $\widetilde{\mathbf{x}}_{i,t}$ of i is defined as

$$\widetilde{\mathbf{x}}_{i,t} = \begin{cases} \begin{bmatrix} \mathbf{x}_t \\ \mathbf{h}_{t-1} \end{bmatrix} & \text{for } i = 0 \\ \mathbf{h}_{j,t-1} & \text{for } i > 0 \end{cases} \tag{3}$$

where j is denoting the predecessor vertex of i. The initial hidden states $\mathbf{h}_{i,0}$ are $\mathbf{0}$. Let $\mathcal{O}$ be a set of candidate activation functions, namely *Sigmoid*, *Tanh*, *ReLU*, and *Identity*. These are the common choices of activation functions in the NAS field. It calculates two vectors: update vector $\mathbf{c}_{i,t}$ and candidate values vector $\widetilde{\mathbf{h}}_{i,t}$:

$$\begin{pmatrix} \mathbf{c}_{i,t} \\ \widetilde{\mathbf{h}}_{i,t} \end{pmatrix} = \begin{pmatrix} \sigma \\ f_i \end{pmatrix} \mathbf{W}_i^T \, \widetilde{\mathbf{x}}_{i,t}, \tag{4}$$

with $\mathbf{W}_i$ as a learnable weight matrix and $f_i \in \mathcal{O}$, associated with an edge $e \in E$. The function and the predecessor vertex is found by DARTS during the *cell* search (described below in Section: *Cell Search*). An exception is given by the input vertex with $f_0 = Tanh$, also given by DARTS. The output of a vertex i is

$$\mathbf{h}_{i,t} = (1 - \mathbf{c}_{i,t}) \cdot \mathbf{h}_{i,t-1} + \mathbf{c}_{i,t} \cdot \widetilde{\mathbf{h}}_{i,t} \tag{5}$$

The addable value range for $\mathbf{h}_{i,t}$ is given by f_i since $\mathbf{c}_{i,t} \in [0, 1]$ determines the degree in which the old hidden state is updated. Thus, the value range addable to the hidden state is depending on $\widetilde{\mathbf{h}}_{i,t}$ that itself depends on f_i. The addable value range becomes important in the analysis part of this paper. The overall output h_t of the *cell* is given by

$$h_t = \mathbb{E}\left[h_{i,t} | i \in V \text{ and } i > 0\right]. \tag{6}$$

In order to apply the *cell* as a fully working RNN cell, we have to define for each vertex $i > 0$ the activation function f_i and its predecessor vertex j. This is done automatically by DARTS during the *cell* search described next.

Cell Search. The cell definition so far requires discrete choices of activation functions and predecessor vertices. DARTS initializes the graph (the cell) with all possible edges. Thus, for each vertex $i > 0$ exists one edge for each possible predecessor and activation function. We modify the cell definition from the section before by combining the outputs of all possible predecessors and all activation functions as weighted sums. This approach is called *continuous relaxation* by the authors. As a result, one can use gradient descent to determine the weights and with that the most beneficial predecessor and activation function for each vertex.

It comes with heavy computational costs because of all the connections but in comparison to other NAS approaches, this approach is reliably faster w.r.t. convergence [19]. The weighting of all possible paths are called architecture parameters and they are trained with standard optimizers like SGD. The following is the formal description of the idea. Let $i > 0$ be a vertex in the graph. In the following,

$$\varphi_{j,t}(g, \mathbf{x}) = \mathbf{h}_{j,t} \text{ with } g \in \mathcal{O}$$
$$\text{s.t. } f_j = g \text{ and } \widetilde{\mathbf{x}}_{j,t} = \mathbf{x} \tag{7}$$

is defined as the output $\mathbf{h}_{j,t}$ of vertex j under the condition that the activation function and input is given by g and $\mathbf{x}$, respectively. Instead of a single activation function f_i of the hidden state of predecessor j, DARTS is considering all activations with $\tilde{f}^{(j,i)}$. The function $\tilde{f}^{(j,i)}$ is a *softmax* weighted combination of all possible activation functions instead of a discrete choice. Thus, we can use it to compute gradients over all paths. More formally,

$$\tilde{f}^{(j,i)}(\mathbf{x}) = \sum_{f \in \mathcal{O}} \left[\frac{exp\left(\alpha_f^{(j,i)}\right)}{\sum_{g \in \mathcal{O}} exp\left(\alpha_g^{(j,i)}\right)} \right] \varphi_{i,t}(f, \mathbf{x}). \tag{8}$$

The variable $\alpha_f^{(j,i)}$ is a learnable parameter that represents the weight of an edge between i and j that is associated with the activation function $f \in \mathcal{O}$. The discrete activation function between i and any j after cell search is given by the most likely activation function

$$f^{(j,i)} = \arg\max_{f \in \mathcal{O}} \alpha_f^{(j,i)}. \tag{9}$$

The unique predecessor vertex for the final architecture is chosen by the highest probability value of the most likely activation functions among all vertices beforehand. Thus,

$$\tilde{\mathbf{x}}_{i,t} = \mathbf{h}_{j,t} \text{ and } f_i = f^{(j,i)}$$

$$\text{s.t. } j = \arg\max_{j<i} \left[\max_{f \in \mathcal{O}} \alpha_f^{(j,i)} \right]. \tag{10}$$

As a result, we find a suitable activation function and predecessor for each vertex. Thus, we have a fully working RNN cell that can be used. The objective for the search is given by the task, in our case minimizing the classification loss.

3   Methodology

In this section, we present the methods to find new RNN cells distinguishable from standard RNN formulations like LSTM or GRU. We present the network used to find these cells. Moreover, we explain the variants we explored. Additionally, we describe the training process and how we used the data sets for cell search and cell evaluation.

3.1   Cell Search and Network Architecture

We find new RNN cells using DARTS and ReNet, which translates an image into a sequence to apply RNN cells on images. Like mentioned in Sect. 2.1, an arbitrary RNN cell can be used within the ReNet layer. As a consequence, it is feasible to use DARTS to find new RNN cells specifically for the image-based domain, which has not been considered by the original DARTS paper. They have derived RNN cells for sequential data like text.

However, a cell found by DARTS and used by ReNet is only a component of a network for image classification. Since we use a cell-based NAS approach, the common way is to stack ReNet layers with the found RNN cells multiple times. Figure 2 shows the resulting network. It begins with three convolutional layers, followed by three ReNet layers (same number of layers as in the original paper of ReNet) with the RNN cells of DARTS. In the end, we use a single and fully connected layer to map the feature dimension to the number of classes. This architecture is fixed for all experiments.

The motivation behind the three convolution layers is that the original ReNet paper uses ConvZCA to whiten the input images [10,18]. We avoid this by using non-linear transformations of the input, realized by the convolution layers.

3.2   Variants

Besides "Vanilla ReNet" cell, we also examined two different variants. The first variant is a *Sigmoid Weighting* of the input. We calculated a learnable weighting factor for each patch in the input sequence and took the *Sigmoid* of this value to let the network choose how vital the patch is. Thus, each patch is multiplied with a value between zero and one. It is a type of soft attention.

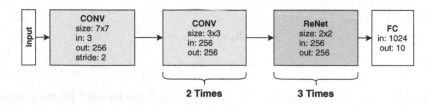

Fig. 2. The network architecture used for the experiments. It consists of three convolution layers in the beginning and three ReNet layers with window size of 2 after that. The last fully connected layer is used to map the features to the number of classes. We want to point out that the ReNet layer can be defined based on the selected RNN cell (i.e., LSTM, GRU or a cell derived by DARTS).

The second variant combines the weights of the bidirectional RNNs in a ReNet layer similar to "Directional Weight Sharing" proposed in ContextVP [3]. More formally, $RNN_V^F = RNN_V^B$ and $RNN_H^F = RNN_H^B$ for the same input, which reduces the number of parameters. We want to point out that even though the weights are the same, the direction still has an impact because the hidden states evolve differently during the time steps.

3.3 Training

All our experiments used the two data sets CIFAR-10 and SVHN, which have images of size $32 \times 32 \times 3$, and each data set contains ten classes [11,13]. The data sets were normalized to have zero mean and unit variance. We used horizontal flipping (with a probability of 50%) and random cropping of the original image with zero padding (size of four) and Cutout [6].

Cell search and evaluation are two different phases. Given the sets *Train*, *Validation* and *Test* of CIFAR-10. For the cell search, we divided the *Train* set s.t. $Train = train_{cs} \cup val_{cs}$, where cs stands for cell search. We used val_{cs} to determine the end of cell search by early stopping. During the cell search, we used two different Adam optimizers. One optimizer is for the network in Fig. 2 (i.e., convolution and fully connected layers) and for the RNN cell parameters mentioned in the cell definition (i.e., $\mathbf{W}_i \, \forall i \in V$ in Eq. 4). The other optimizer is for the architecture parameters in cell search step (i.e., $\alpha_f^{(j,i)} \, \forall i,j \in V$). The optimizing steps happen within the same batch. Thus, each optimizer works equally often. We repeated this procedure multiple times (ca. 10 per variant) since different weight initialization can lead to different cell designs.

After training, we derived the cells as described at the end of Sect. 2.2. Next, we re-initialized the weights of the network (i.e., $\mathbf{W}_i^T \, \forall i \in V$ and the weights of the convolution and fully connected layers) and trained it again on the complete *Train* set of CIFAR-10. We used the *Validation* and *Test* set of CIFAR-10 to determine the end of training and the final result of the found cell (cell evaluation). Likewise, we also evaluated the cell on SVHN. No cell search was applied here - also, no transfer learning of the weights. We used only the cell designs found during cell search on CIFAR-10. Therefore, the performance on SVHN does not explicitly benefit from the cell search.

4 Results and Analysis

This section presents DartsReNet cells that are beneficial for image classification along with a comparison to a standard RNN cell GRU. Like mentioned before, there are two phases: The cell search and the cell evaluation. Thus, this section is also divided into two sections to discuss the results of each phase.

4.1 Cell Search

Here we present the RNN cells found during the cell search on CIFAR-10 using DARTS. We will discuss each variant separately.

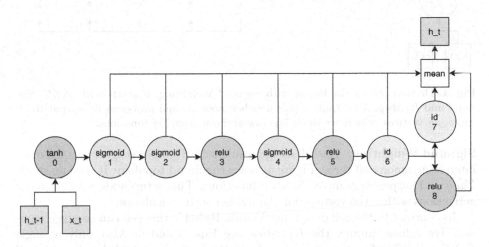

Fig. 3. Derived cell for the Vanilla ReNet. It uses two *Sigmoids* in the beginning, then alters between *ReLU* and *Sigmoid* until vertex 5. An *Identity* function follows and its output is processed through another *Identity* function and a *ReLU* in parallel.

Vanilla ReNet. The derived cell is mostly sequential and deep, see Fig. 3. The novel cell uses several *Sigmoid* activation functions, two *Identity* projections and *ReLU*. Surprisingly, it does not have any *Tanh* activation function as the original LSTM or GRU (except the fixed input vertex, set by DARTS), which would zero center the data.

The *Sigmoid* value can be inhibiting for the mean calculation. Consider Eq. 4, it holds that $c_{i,t} \in [0,1]$ and $h_{i,0} = \mathbf{0} \, \forall i \in V$. As a consequence of Eq. 5, the addable value range of $h_{i,t}$ depends only on the value range of $\tilde{h}_{i,t}$. Hence, if

$\widetilde{\mathbf{h}}_{i,t}$ is computed with $f_i = \sigma \Rightarrow \left(\mathbf{c}_{i,t} \cdot \widetilde{\mathbf{h}}_{i,t} \right) \in [0,1]$ since $\widetilde{\mathbf{h}}_{i,t} \in [0,1]$. Therefore, *Sigmoid* can add zero values to the mean calculation for $\mathbf{h}_t$, shrinking down the output, see Eq. 6. The cell also has the possibility to add negative values to the mean value because of the *Identity* functions. This is similar to the argumentation before: If $f_i = Identity$, then the value range of $\widetilde{\mathbf{h}}_{i,t}$ is in $[-\infty, \infty]$. Thus, negative values can be added to $\mathbf{h}_{i,t}$, see Eq. 5.

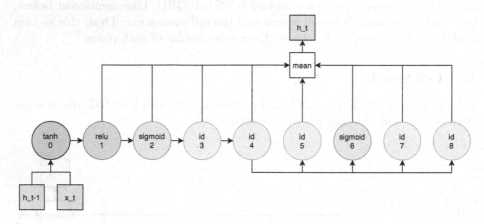

Fig. 4. Derived cell for the ReNet with Sigmoid Weighting. It starts with *ReLU*, *Sigmoid* and *Identity*. After that, it uses another *Identity* and processes its output to all successor vertices, which are three *Identity* and one *Sigmoid* functions.

Sigmoid Weighting. The cell design result with *Sigmoid* weighting is the most interesting among all three. Figure 4 shows the found topology. It uses no single *Tanh* and surprisingly many *Identity* functions. This setup adds a lot of linear activations within the vertices for the hidden state calculation.

In contrast to the cell design in "Vanilla ReNet", this cell can produce more negative values through the *Identities*, see Eqs. 5 and 6. Also, only a single *ReLU* activation function is used, right in the beginning. Additionally, this cell design uses many "wide" connections, starting at vertex 4. We mean with "wide" connections that more than one successor vertex use the vertex's output. Hence, this cell is not as deep as the cell for Vanilla ReNet, supporting the assumption that the depth might be too high.

Directional Weight Sharing. The ReNet layer with Directional Weight Sharing has the same outcome as the Vanilla ReNet: It does not use *Tanh*, and it is sequential. For both variants, the tendency is to go deeper instead of wider, like for CNNs in the recent development for image classification w.r.t. architecture [8,17]. The cell is visualized in Fig. 5.

An exciting aspect of this design is the lack of any single *Identity* function. In conclusion, the cell has no possibility to add negative values to the mean. Because of only two *Sigmoid*, the inhibitor effect is also lower than for the Vanilla ReNet cell.

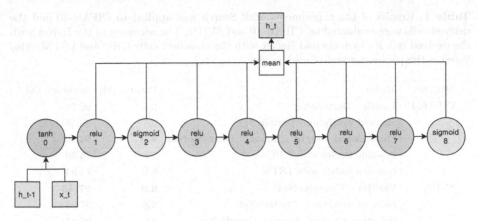

Fig. 5. Derived cell for the ReNet with Directional Weight Sharing. It uses a *ReLU* function in the beginning, followed by a *Sigmoid*. Then, five *ReLU* are used. The last vertex uses a *Sigmoid*. They are applied in one sequence without sharing the output to more than one successor vertex.

4.2   Cell Evaluation

The results of the cell evaluation are listed in Table 1 for both data sets. For Comparison, we also listed the results of ReNet with the standard RNN cells GRU and LSTM. In contrast to the original ReNet paper, we have used a different setup for the ReNet with the standard RNN cells to make a fair comparison feasible. First of all, the original paper has used no convolution layers in the beginning. Besides, the original paper has used the whitening technique ConvZCA for CIFAR-10, which has a considerable influence on the performance. According to the channel sizes, we used a fixed channel size of 256 for both data sets instead of 320 for CIFAR-10. Also, the original ReNet uses an additional fully connected layer for SVHN. Additionally, a fully connected layer of 4096 dimensions was used instead of 1024, which is the case for our architecture.

According to the new cells, all variants show better accuracy for all data sets. For CIFAR-10, the variant Directional Weight Sharing dominates. For SVHN, the Vanilla variant has the best accuracy. Because of the depth of the new cells, all variants have a higher parameter size w.r.t. GRU. An exception is the Directional Weight Sharing, which uses 0.8M fewer parameters than the baseline with GRU. Since the variants work like regularization to the training, one can see ascending accuracies among the variants for CIFAR-10. The regularization is also present for SVHN, where our Vanilla ReNet has the best performance. The complexity is high enough for Vanilla ReNet and additional regularization hurts the performance.

Table 1. Results of the experiments. Cell Search was applied to CIFAR-10 and the derived cells were evaluated on CIFAR-10 and SVHN. The accuracy of the ReNet with the derived cell, its variants and ReNet with the standard cells GRU and LSTM. Also listed is the parameter size of each model.

Data set	Model	Params [M]	Accuracy [%]
CIFAR-10	Vanilla - DartsReNet	6.8	90.26
	Sigmoid weighting - DartsReNet	6.8	90.56
	Directional weight sharing - DartsReNet	**4.0**	**91.00**
	Baseline ReNet with GRU	4.8	75.30
	Baseline ReNet with LSTM	6.0	74.94
SVHN	**Vanilla - DartsReNet**	**6.8**	**97.43**
	Sigmoid weighting - DartsReNet	6.8	97.04
	Directional weight sharing - DartsReNet	4.0	96.91
	Baseline ReNet with GRU	4.8	95.16
	Baseline ReNet with LSTM	6.0	94.10

5 Conclusion and Future Work

We wanted to examine alternative RNN cell designs for image classification other than standard formulations like LSTM or GRU. We achieved this by combining DARTS with ReNet. Moreover, we examined two different variants of RNN cells using this approach. Also, we compared the cells with a ReNet architecture with GRU and LSTM on CIFAR-10 and SVHN. We achieved better results by a large margin and the variant Directional Weight Sharing achieved this with 0.8M fewer parameters than GRU. Additionally, the RNN cell, found on CIFAR-10, is also evaluated on SVNH data set, where we were able to outperform the standard cells by at least 1%.

For the future, we are interested in evaluating our approach on ImageNet [5]. Also, this work only used NAS approaches to derive cells with a fixed network. However, it is possible to use it for the overall network design. Some other variants are also interesting for future investigation, like different ordering within a sequence or dropout parts of the image as learnable components.

Acknowledgement. This work was supported by the BMBF project DeFuseNN (Grant 01IW17002) and the NVIDIA AI Lab (NVAIL) program.

References

1. Baker, B., Gupta, O., Naik, N., Raskar, R.: Designing neural network architectures using reinforcement learning. arXiv preprint arXiv:1611.02167 (2016)
2. Breuel, T.M., Ul-Hasan, A., Al-Azawi, M.A., Shafait, F.: High-performance OCR for printed English and fraktur using LSTM networks. In: 2013 12th International Conference on Document Analysis and Recognition, pp. 683–687. IEEE (2013)

3. Byeon, W., Wang, Q., Srivastava, R.K., Koumoutsakos, P.: ContextVP: fully context-aware video prediction. In: Ferrari, V., Hebert, M., Sminchisescu, C., Weiss, Y. (eds.) ECCV 2018. LNCS, vol. 11220, pp. 781–797. Springer, Cham (2018). https://doi.org/10.1007/978-3-030-01270-0_46
4. Cho, K., et al.: Learning phrase representations using RNN encoder-decoder for statistical machine translation. arXiv preprint arXiv:1406.1078 (2014)
5. Deng, J., Dong, W., Socher, R., Li, L.J., Li, K., Fei-Fei, L.: ImageNet: a large-scale hierarchical image database. In: CVPR09 (2009)
6. DeVries, T., Taylor, G.W.: Improved regularization of convolutional neural networks with cutout. arXiv preprint arXiv:1708.04552 (2017)
7. Graves, A., Schmidhuber, J.: Offline handwriting recognition with multidimensional recurrent neural networks. In: Advances in Neural Information Processing Systems, pp. 545–552 (2009)
8. He, K., Zhang, X., Ren, S., Sun, J.: Deep residual learning for image recognition. In: Proceedings of the IEEE Conference on Computer Vision and Pattern Recognition, pp. 770–778 (2016)
9. Hochreiter, S., Schmidhuber, J.: Long short-term memory. Neural Comput. 9(8), 1735–1780 (1997)
10. Krizhevsky, A., Hinton, G., et al.: Learning Multiple Layers of Features from Tiny Images (2009)
11. Krizhevsky, A., Nair, V., Hinton, G.: Cifar-10 (Canadian institute for advanced research) (2009). http://www.cs.toronto.edu/~kriz/cifar.html
12. Liu, H., Simonyan, K., Yang, Y.: Darts: Differentiable architecture search. arXiv preprint arXiv:1806.09055 (2018)
13. Netzer, Y., Wang, T., Coates, A., Bissacco, A., Wu, B., Ng, A.Y.: Reading Digits in Natural Images with Unsupervised Feature Learning (2011)
14. Pham, H., Guan, M.Y., Zoph, B., Le, Q.V., Dean, J.: Efficient neural architecture search via parameter sharing. arXiv preprint arXiv:1802.03268 (2018)
15. Simonyan, K., Zisserman, A.: Very deep convolutional networks for large-scale image recognition. arXiv preprint arXiv:1409.1556 (2014)
16. Stollenga, M.F., Byeon, W., Liwicki, M., Schmidhuber, J.: Parallel multidimensional LSTM, with application to fast biomedical volumetric image segmentation. In: Advances in Neural Information Processing Systems, pp. 2998–3006 (2015)
17. Szegedy, C., et al.: Going deeper with convolutions. In: Proceedings of the IEEE Conference on Computer Vision and Pattern Recognition, pp. 1–9 (2015)
18. Visin, F., Kastner, K., Cho, K., Matteucci, M., Courville, A., Bengio, Y.: Renet: a recurrent neural network based alternative to convolutional networks. arXiv preprint arXiv:1505.00393 (2015)
19. Wistuba, M., Rawat, A., Pedapati, T.: A survey on neural architecture search. arXiv preprint arXiv:1905.01392 (2019)
20. Zoph, B., Le, Q.V.: Neural architecture search with reinforcement learning. arXiv preprint arXiv:1611.01578 (2016)

On Multi-modal Fusion for Freehand Gesture Recognition

Monika Schak[(✉)] and Alexander Gepperth[(✉)]

Fulda University of Applied Sciences, 36037 Fulda, Germany
{monika.schak,alexander.gepperth}@cs.hs-fulda.de

Abstract. We present a study of multi-modal freehand gesture recognition relying on three sensory modalities. The modalities are RGB images, depth data, and acceleration data from an IMD attached to the hand. Based on a new self-recorded dataset, we initially establish the ability of a deep Long Short-Term Memory (LSTM) network to correctly classify individual data streams from each modality. Notably, classifying the IMD stream alone generates very good results already. In addition, we investigate two different strategies of multi-modal fusion, since there is no agreement in the literature as to which strategy is preferable. Combining the modalities leads to better recognition performance. Most importantly, fusion considerably improves ahead-of-time classification, i.e., gesture class estimates before sequences are completed, for classes that are difficult to classify on their own.

Keywords: LSTM · Freehand gesture recognition · Multi-modal fusion · Ahead-of-time classification

1 Introduction

Freehand Gesture Recognition. The scientific context of this article is multi-modal freehand gesture recognition, see Fig. 1. This means classifying hand gestures that are extended in time (in contrast to hand poses, which are taken at a single point in time) into several distinct categories or classes.

Typical Sensors. To this effect, the hand is observed by one or more sensors, typical choices of which are RGB cameras, infrared cameras, depth sensors (using either stereo, time-of-flight, or structured-light technologies). Less commonly used types of sensors are IMDs (inertial measurement devices), which record accelerations, and by integration: velocities. IMDs are small, cheap, and reliable, but need to be physically attached to the hand, which is not always feasible in scenarios for hand gesture recognition.

Multi-modal Processing. Each sensor gives rise to a separate data stream, which is generally termed a *sensory modality*. Since all sensors measure physically distinct quantities, each sensory modality may contain unique and independent information. On the other hand, since all sensors observe the same thing (i.e.

I. Farkaš et al. (Eds.): ICANN 2020, LNCS 12396, pp. 862–873, 2020.
https://doi.org/10.1007/978-3-030-61609-0_68

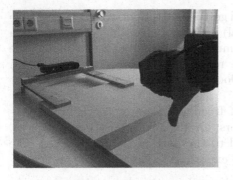
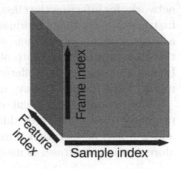

Fig. 1. Freehand gesture recognition as treated in this article. Left: experimental setup using an Orbbec Astra (RGB camera and depth sensor) and an IMD (inertial measurement device). The latter is attached to the hand using red tape and transmits its measurements via a serial cable. It will later be replaced by a more compact wireless version. Right: layout of the data used for training machine learning models. Each gesture represents a single data sample, which is composed of several successive frames, each of which is represented by a one-dimensional tensor (or feature vector), thus making the whole database of gestures a 3D structure.

the hand in our case), sensory modalities contain at least partially correlated information.

The goal of multi-modal information processing is, in general, to exploit the (partial) independency and complementarity of sensory modalities to obtain more precise and reliable observations.

Sequence Classification Terminology. The gesture recognition problem is a so-called sequence classification problem, where the basic entities to be classified are streams, or *sequences*, of sensory measurements or quantities derived from them. In the context of a database of sequences for training machine learning algorithms, we often denote a single sequence by the term *sample*. Sequence elements are generally called *frames*, which in our setting are one-dimensional tensors (or feature vectors) derived from sensory measurements. Please regard Fig. 1 (right) for a diagram of the basic data layout we use in this article.

Sequence Classification. Particular properties of sequence classification problems are that the individual frames become available one after the other (in contrast to image classification where all pixels are available at once) and that sequences need not have a common length. This requires machine learning strategies that are adapted to these requirements. A prominent example of this are LSTM neural networks [9], which are used for sequence classification in this study.

Overview. In our case, we try to obtain an estimate of the gesture's category by evaluating three sensory modalities: IMD (acceleration) data, RGB images, and depth images. Since each modality represents a temporally extended sequence of individual measurements, we use deep Long Short-Term Memory (LSTM) networks for inferring the class of the hand gesture that is performed. This article first investigates the individual (uni-modal) accuracy achievable when relying on a single modality only. Then, we examine multiple possibilities for combining the three modalities in order to obtain higher robustness or classification accuracy. Lastly, we perform two different types of look-ahead classification and the effect multi-modal fusion can have on it.

Additionally, we present a dataset of freehand gestures consisting of pre-processed data from three different sensors: an RGB camera, a depth camera, and a 6-axis acceleration sensor attached to the back of the user's hand. The aforementioned dataset is used for all the experiments described in this article.

Application Context. Such a system that allows the user to interact using freehand gestures, can, for example, be found in the scope of 3D object manipulation or augmented reality. To improve the ability of the before-mentioned system to correctly classify freehand gestures even as they vary due to different angles of the user towards the camera or entirely different users, we suggest the use of a classification system that combines the classification of multiple sensor streams into one joint classification result.

1.1 Related Work

Multi-sensory integration or fusion is a common concept in neurophysiological and psychological research [1,2] and has been confirmed by many experiments. An interesting fact is that, under certain circumstances, human brains perform the combination of several sensory modalities in a probabilistically well-founded fashion [7]: when assuming that each modality is corrupted by Gaussian noise of distinctive variance, each modality is apparently weighted by a factor that is inversely proportional to its noise variance, which implements the theoretically optimal (MAP) estimate in this situation. An overview of the probabilistic foundations of such set-ups is given in [8].

On the computational side, there are many studies of multi-modal gesture or activity recognition. There is no agreement on the best way to perform multi-modal fusion, rather a variety of possibilities whose advantages and difficulties depend on the dataset and particular task at hand. In [18], late fusion is applied on a dataset for human fall analysis consisting of four modalities (RGB, depth, skeleton, and acceleration). Here, the final score is produced by searching the maximum output score provided by single modality based classifiers.

Another approach [5] uses a collaborative representation classifier to combine the classification outcomes for two modalities (depth and acceleration) using Dempster-Shafer theory to improve human action recognition. A different fusion method at the classifier level is the non-linear combination method of using a Random Decision Forest [17].

A very commonly used technique for late fusion is softmax score fusion [11], where the outputs of multiple classifiers are transformed to probability scores by a softmax layer and then combined using sum rule, product rule, or max rule. An alternative technique is feature fusion [10], where features from fully-connected layers are combined and then fed to any classifier, e.g. linear support vector machines or kernel extreme learning machines.

Early fusion happens at the data level where incoming data from sensors is combined without further preprocessing [12]. Feature level fusion is another kind of early fusion, which first extracts features from raw data and then proceeds to fuse those features before classification [5] by using a collaborative representation classifier.

1.2 Goals and Contributions

Since there does not seem to be a consensus in the scientific literature about the best way to conduct multi-modal recognition tasks, this article makes the following novel and relevant contributions:

- We investigate the usefulness of wearable IMDs for gesture recognition, which are cheap and reliable.
- We conduct a computational case study of multi-modal (sequence) recognition, investigating and comparing several strategies for combining sensory modalities.
- We present a new result on ahead-of-time classification, showing that multi-modal fusion markedly improves the ability to correctly identify gestures before they are even completed.
- We publish a new publicly available benchmark for multi-modal freehand gesture recognition that contains 2.660 gestures from 7 classes that are observed with IMD, RGB and depth sensors.

2 Methods

2.1 Gesture Classes

We choose seven different free-hand gestures for our dataset. All of them can be performed with only one hand. The seven gestures are described as follows:

- **Agree:** Move the thumb up.
- **Disagree:** Move the thumb down.
- **Pinch Out:** Move the thumb and index finger together as if zooming out on a touch device.
- **Pinch In:** Move the thumb and index finger apart as if zooming in on a touch device.
- **Select:** Move the palm towards the camera.
- **Swipe Left:** Swipe from right to left with the whole hand.
- **Swipe Right:** Swipe from left to right with the whole hand.

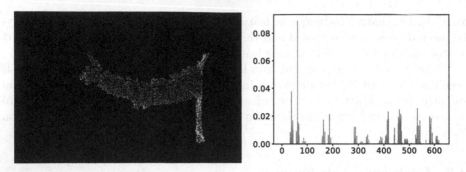

Fig. 2. Example of a point feature histogram (right) corresponding to one frame of a "Thumbs Up" gesture (left: point cloud from which the histogram was computed).

2.2 Dataset

The dataset contains 380 recordings of each of the 7 gesture classes, all coming from a single person, totaling to 2660 recordings. This is consistent with a scenario where a device is predominantly used by a single (or a few) individual(s) to whom it has been specifically adapted. This approach ensures that the conducted gestures are performed correctly and consistently across the dataset, and also that the variability of each gesture class is not excessive. Each gesture sample, irrespectively of its class, lasts for two seconds.

RGB Data. To record RGB data, we use one of the two streams provided by an Orbbec Astra 3D sensor. It simultaneously sends a stream of 800 × 600 RGB images and a stream of 640 × 480 depth images which are converted to point clouds. After cropping the images to obtain only the part of the image in which the hand is visible, we reduce the size of the images to 72 × 48 pixels. Afterwards, we calculate the histogram of oriented gradients (HOG) descriptor [6,13,19] for each image, using the OpenCV implementation [3]. We use the default parameters except for cell size which is set to be 8 × 8 pixels, and block size which is 16 × 16 pixels, giving a descriptor of 1440 entries. We set the frame rate such as to receive twelve images per gesture. Thus, a gesture is characterized by twelve HOG descriptors, each having a fixed size of 1440 values.

3D Data. To record 3D data, we use the stream of depth images/point clouds provided by an Orbbec Astra 3D sensor. During the two-second window for each gesture, we receive a total of six point clouds. Each of these point clouds is passed through the five steps of preprocessing:

- *Downsampling:* In the first step, we reduce the size of the point clouds to lower the computational costs. Therefore, we create a 3D-voxel grid over the input point cloud data. For every voxel, we calculate the centroid of all its points and use this to represent the voxel.
- *VoI Filtering:* In the second step, we use conditional removal to crop the point cloud to a defined volume of interest. Thus, removing background data and leaving just the area in which the hand is present.

- *Removing NaN:* Afterwards, we remove measurement errors by deleting all points whose x-, y-, or z-value is equal to NaN.
- *Computing Normals:* In the fourth step, we use approximations to infer the surface normals for all points in the point cloud.
- *Creating a Point Feature Histogram:* To get a descriptor of fixed length [15, 16], regardless of the size of the point clouds, that can be fed to the deep LSTM model, we decided on a representation with point feature histograms (PFH). These descriptors characterize the phenomenology of hand, palm, and fingers in a precise manner while remaining computationally feasible at the same time. PFH is based on the surface normals computed in step 4. In this step, we repeatedly select two points and compute their descriptor [4,14] which provides four values based on the length and relative orientation of the surface normals. Each of the four values is subdivided into five intervals, giving a total of 625 discrete possibilities. The result, therefore, is a 625-dimensional histogram for each point cloud. Lastly, we normalize the histogram so that all the 625 values total to 1.

We receive six frames for every gesture. Each frame consists of 625 values. Figure 2 shows the point feature histogram of one frame of one gesture (right) and the corresponding point cloud (left).

IMD Data. To record the acceleration data, we use a 6-axis acceleration sensor (JoyWarrior56FR1-WP) attached to the back of the user's hand. It can record 3-axis acceleration data and 3-axis yaw rates at a frequency 500 Hz, generating a 6-tuple at every measurement. To clean the rather noisy signals, we gather all $N = 100$ 6-tuples from each consecutive 200-millisecond window into a block and calculate statistical values for each entry of the 6-tuples: variance $\text{Var}(x)$, mean $\bar{x}$, and standard deviation $S(x)$, as shown in Eqs. 1–3.

$$\bar{x} = \frac{1}{N}\left(\sum_{i=1}^{N} x_i\right) = \frac{x_1 + x_2 + \cdots + x_N}{N} \tag{1}$$

$$\text{Var}(x) = \frac{1}{N}\sum_{i=1}^{N}(x_i - \bar{x})^2 \tag{2}$$

$$S(x) = \sqrt{\frac{1}{N-1}\sum_{i=1}^{N}(x_i - \bar{x})^2} \tag{3}$$

Thus, we receive ten frames for every gesture ($200ms \cdot 10$ frames $= 2s$). Each frame consists of 18 values: three statistical values for each of the six axes.

2.3   Fusion Methods

Since the three sensory modalities we are considering here have different numerical formats and arrive at different frequencies, we discard "early fusion" types of approaches (see Sect. 1.1) and focus on an analysis of the LSTM readout layer activities r^m for the last frame in each modality $m \in \mathcal{M} = \{\text{RGB}, 3\text{D}, \text{IMD}\}$. Since these are standard linear softmax layers (the same as the final layer of a standard DNN), they have **a)** as many entries as there are gesture classes, **b)** entries $r_i^m \in [0, 1]$ and **c)** entries normalized to 1: $\sum_i r_i^m = 1 \forall m \in \mathcal{M}$.

When denoting the decision for a certain class, in modality $m \in \mathcal{M}$ based on the last readout layer activity r^m, by $\mathcal{C}^m$, the following fusion strategies to obtain the fused class estimate $\mathcal{C}$ seem natural:

max-conf: use the most certain uni-modal class decision to obtain

$$x = \arg\max_{m \in \mathcal{M}} \left(\max_i r_i^m \right) \tag{4}$$

$$\mathcal{C} = \mathcal{C}^x \tag{5}$$

prob: treat the output layer activities as independent conditional probability distributions for a class i given the unimodal input sequence x^m. The probabilities are then given by $r_i^m = p^m(\mathcal{C}^m = i | x^m)$, and fusion is achieved by multiplication and renormalization using a constant C (this step can be skipped if we just want to infer the class of maximal probability):

$$\mathcal{C} = \arg\max_i \left(\frac{1}{C} \prod_{m \in \mathcal{M}} p(\mathcal{C}^m = i | x^m) \right) \tag{6}$$

$$= \arg\max_i \left(\prod_{m \in \mathcal{M}} r_i^m \right) \tag{7}$$

3 Experiments

3.1 Uni-Modal Baselines

To establish the initial ability of a deep LSTM network to correctly classify each of the modalities, we train LSTM classifiers separately for each modality. To make sure results are not affected by network architecture, we run multiple experiments per modality, varying different hyper-parameters: batch size, number of layers, and number of LSTM cells (neurons) per layer. Each training run is repeated five times with the same hyper-parameters. The results show test accuracies averaged over all 5 training runs. The recorded gestures from the database are randomly split into training and test groups with a proportion of 80:20 prior to training and subsequently used as training and test data in all uni-modal and multi-modal experiments.

IMD Data. We vary the batch size $b \in \{150, 250, 500, 1000\}$, the number of hidden layers $L = \{2, 3, 5\}$ and their size $S = \{150, 200, 250\}$. We use a fixed learning rate of $\epsilon = 0.001$ and a fixed number of iterations $I = 1.000$. Table 1 shows the results for the freehand gesture classification on acceleration data only. We observe that this modality can, just by itself, perform a reliable gesture classification.

Table 1. Classification results of IMD data: averaged accuracy (in percent) over five experiments.

BS	(L, S)								
	$(2, 150)$	$(2, 200)$	$(2, 250)$	$(3, 150)$	$(3, 200)$	$(3, 250)$	$(5, 150)$	$(5, 200)$	$(5, 250)$
150	98.12	**98.61**	97.26	97.28	97.97	97.89	96.84	97.29	97.33
250	97.89	97.74	97.63	98.27	98.04	98.01	97.63	97.82	98.12
500	98.38	98.35	98.42	97.82	97.97	94.89	98.12	97.14	98.57
1000	98.23	98.04	98.20	97.97	98.46	98.12	97.37	97.74	97.97

The average accuracy obtained across all experiments is 97.83%. As can be seen, an LSTM architecture with two hidden layers and 200 cells per layer $(L, S) = (2, 200)$ and a batch size $b = 150$ achieves the best results (98.61%). Table 4a shows the confusion matrix for the classifiers trained only on IMD data.

3D Data. We vary the batch size $b \in \{150, 250, 500, 1000\}$, the number of hidden layers $L = \{2, 3, 5\}$ and their size $S = \{150, 200, 250\}$ in the same way as for IMD data. We use a fixed learning rate of $\epsilon = 0.001$ and a fixed number of iterations $I = 5.000$. Table 2 shows the results for freehand gesture classification on 3D data alone. Preliminary experiments have shown that a smaller amount of fewer than 3.000 iterations leads to less accurate classification results.

The average accuracy obtained across all experiments is 86.92%. As can be seen, an LSTM architecture with two hidden layers and 200 cells per layer $(L, S) = (2, 200)$ and a batch size $b = 250$ can achieve the best results (93.61%). Table 4b shows the confusion matrix for the classifiers trained only on 3D data.

Table 2. Classification results of 3D data: averaged accuracy (in percent) over five experiments.

BS	(L, S)								
	$(2, 150)$	$(2, 200)$	$(2, 250)$	$(3, 150)$	$(3, 200)$	$(3, 250)$	$(5, 150)$	$(5, 200)$	$(5, 250)$
150	91.17	93.23	92.37	89.62	89.70	90.26	78.76	78.61	81.69
250	92.78	**93.61**	91.84	88.68	89.96	90.00	77.67	79.44	80.34
500	90.34	91.77	91.62	89.14	87.33	90.30	78.87	79.02	80.49
1000	90.60	91.54	92.14	89.55	88.95	90.34	77.93	79.21	80.41

RGB Data. We vary the batch size $b \in \{150, 250, 500, 1000\}$, the number of hidden layers $L = \{2, 3, 5\}$ and their size $S = \{150, 200, 250\}$, as we did for the IMD data and the 3D data. We use a fixed learning rate of $\epsilon = 0.001$ and a fixed number of iterations $I = 1.000$. Table 3 shows the results for the freehand gesture classification on the RGB data alone.

The average accuracy obtained across all experiments is 97.76%. As can be seen, an LSTM architecture with two hidden layers and 250 cells per layer

Table 3. Classification results of RGB data: Averaged accuracy (in percent) over five experiments.

BS	(L, S)								
	$(2, 150)$	$(2, 200)$	$(2, 250)$	$(3, 150)$	$(3, 200)$	$(3, 250)$	$(5, 150)$	$(5, 200)$	$(5, 250)$
150	98.87	99.00	**99.06**	98.93	98.74	98.75	97.49	98.50	98.56
250	98.37	98.81	99.00	97.25	97.81	98.05	96.55	97.75	96.30
500	97.93	98.31	98.31	96.37	97.56	97.37	98.31	94.55	95.49
1000	97.74	97.74	98.87	96.24	97.74	97.18	96.99	96.53	98.31

$(L, S) = (2, 250)$ and a batch size $b = 150$ can achieve the best results (99.06%). Table 4c shows the confusion matrix for the classifiers trained only on RGB data.

3.2 Multi-modal Fusion

Having established the uni-modal baselines, we pick the best architecture for each modality and compute class prediction accuracies on test data using the two fusion strategies outlined in Sect. 2.3.

Table 4. Confusion matrix for the uni-modal classifications. Rows display the actual gesture and columns show the predicted gesture.

IMD Data	3D Data	RGB Data

IMD Data

71	0	0	0	0	0	0
0	67	0	0	0	0	0
1	0	85	0	0	0	1
0	0	0	75	2	0	0
1	0	1	0	71	0	0
0	0	1	0	0	69	0
0	0	0	0	0	0	89

3D Data

60	4	1	0	1	3	2
1	64	2	0	0	0	0
1	1	82	1	0	0	0
1	0	7	68	1	0	0
1	0	5	1	66	0	0
2	0	1	0	5	62	0
1	0	0	0	0	2	86

RGB Data

71	0	0	0	0	0	0
0	66	0	0	1	0	0
0	0	83	2	0	0	0
1	0	2	74	0	0	0
0	0	0	0	73	0	0
0	0	0	0	0	70	0
0	0	0	0	0	0	89

Fusion Strategy: Max-conf. As a first step, we convert the predictions by using a softmax function to receive probabilities for each of the classes for every gesture. Then, using Eq. 4 and Eq. 5, we pick the most certain uni-modal class decision as our final prediction. Using this fusion strategy, we can improve our classification to achieving an accuracy of 100% by correctly classifying 532 out of 532 gestures.

Fusion Strategy: Prob. Same as for the max-conf fusion strategy, we convert the predictions by using a softmax function. Then, we use Eq. 7 to obtain a multi-modal probability, in which the highest probability determines the predicted class. Using this fusion strategy, we can improve our classification to an accuracy of 100% by correctly classifying all of the 532 gestures.

3.3 Ahead-of-Time Classification and Multi-modal Fusion

A feature of deep LSTM network classifiers is the possibility to read out class estimates ahead of time, i.e., before the sequence is complete. In reality, this enables technical systems to, e.g., anticipate a user's gesture command, thus realizing a more efficient and natural interaction. We compute the uni-modal ahead-of-time classification accuracies by simply making the LSTM output layer at a certain frame $f < F$ the basis of gesture class estimation, instead of using the last frame F. The same strategy is applicable for fusion: instead of fusing three output layer activities from the last sequence frame F according to Sect. 2.3, we fuse output layer activities evaluated at frames $f_m, m \in \mathcal{M} = \{RGB, 3D, IMD\}$. This is complicated by the fact that the three modalities have slightly unequal sequence lengths (12, 6 and 10 for RGB, 3D and IMD data). We therefore investigate the benefit of fusion for look-ahead classification for strong look-ahead ($f_{RGB} = 5, f_{3D} = 3$ and $f_{acc} = 4$) and moderate look-ahead ($f_{RGB} = 8, f_{3D} = 4$ and $f_{IMD} = 7$). The results are shown in Table 5. Since the results for uni-modal classification on IMD data are already very high, we investigate the effects of multi-modal fusion on look-ahead classification for $f_m, m \in \mathcal{M}_1 = \{RGB, 3D, IMD\}$ and $f_m, m \in \mathcal{M}_2 = \{RGB, 3D\}$.

Table 5. Effects of multi-modal fusion on look-ahead classification. Shown is the accuracy in % for uni-modal classification as well as fusing RGB and 3D data[1] and all three modalities[2] Respectively.

Look-ahead	Method						
	RGB	3D	IMD	Prob		Max-conf	
Strong: 50%	30.45	17.11	52.26	27.26[1]	27.26[2]	31.77[1]	42.48[2]
Moderate: 75%	62.97	37.78	93.05	70.49[1]	70.49[2]	60.71[1]	87.41[2]

As expected, the lower results of RGB and 3D data classification have a negative impact on the high results of IMD data classification. Fusion does not help in this case. On the other hand, looking at the effects of fusion on $\mathcal{M}_2$ shows that multi-modal fusion using the **prob** strategy improves the results for a moderate look-ahead. Using the **max-conf** strategy improves the results for a strong look-ahead. Therefore, a positive benefit of multi-sensory fusion can be observed on look-ahead classification for modalities that are more difficult to classify.

4 Discussion and Conclusion

Data Used in This Study. One might argue that the classification problem is a simple one since all recorded gestures come from the same person. On the other hand, this ensures that gestures are performed expertly and that any variability in the gestures is an intrinsic, structured one and not just caused by inexpert users performing gestures incorrectly. In the latter case, gesture classification may be hard for a human observer as well.

Assessment of Results. The presented results show, unsurprisingly, that fusing results from multiple modalities increases classification performance. This is however less spectacular since the results are already very satisfactory even without fusion. What makes multi-modal fusion worthwhile in this context is its impact on ahead-of-time classification accuracy which is significantly increased for moderate look-ahead where classification is attempted even though only 66% of a gesture has been observed.

Comparison of Fusion Schemes. The two presented fusion schemes are admittedly simplistic, but on the other hand, they are real-time capable since they do not incur a measurable computational overhead. Furthermore, fusing only the readout layer activities in the last frame for each modality is not as restrictive as it seems since LSTM networks retain information about states from past frames. One may, therefore, conclude that by fusing only at the last frame, one takes into account information from the whole sequence of multi-modal measurements. Based on this study, we can state that both investigated fusion schemes are equivalent.

Next Steps. As ahead-of-time classification has a high potential impact on user interaction, it would be an interesting theoretical study to modify the LSTM loss function such that early correct classifications are rewarded, thus actively enforcing ahead-of-time classification. Another conceptually important point is detecting outlier gestures that belong to no known class. This requires a learned, generative description of sequence data by, e.g., Hidden-Markov models.

References

1. Angelaki, D.E., Gu, Y., DeAngelis, G.C.: Multisensory integration: psychophysics, neurophysiology, and computation. Curr. Opinion Neurobiol. **19**(4), 452–458 (2009)
2. Beauchamp, M.S.: See me, hear me, touch me: multisensory integration in lateral occipital-temporal cortex. Curr. Opinion Neurobiol. **15**(2), 145–153 (2005)
3. Bradski, G.: The OpenCV library. Dr. Dobb's J. Softw. Tools (2000)
4. Caron, L.-C., Filliat, D., Gepperth, A.: Neural network fusion of color, depth and location for object instance recognition on a mobile robot. In: Agapito, L., Bronstein, M.M., Rother, C. (eds.) ECCV 2014. LNCS, vol. 8927, pp. 791–805. Springer, Cham (2015). https://doi.org/10.1007/978-3-319-16199-0_55
5. Chen, C., Jafari, R., Kehtarnavaz, N.: Improving human action recognition using fusion of depth camera and inertial sensors. IEEE Trans. Hum. Mach. Syst. **45** (2014). https://doi.org/10.1109/THMS.2014.2362520
6. Dalal, N., Triggs, B.: Histograms of oriented gradients for human detection. In: 2005 IEEE Computer Society Conference on Computer Vision and Pattern Recognition (CVPR 2005), vol. 1, pp. 886–893 (2005)
7. Ernst, M.O., Banks, M.S.: Humans integrate visual and haptic information in a statistically optimal fashion. Nature **415**(6870), 429–433 (2002)

8. Gepperth, A.R., Hecht, T., Gogate, M.: A generative learning approach to sensor fusion and change detection. Cogn. Comput. **8**(5), 806–817 (2016)
9. Graves, A., Jaitly, N.: Towards end-to-end speech recognition with recurrent neural networks. In: Xing, E.P., Jebara, T. (eds.) Proceedings of the 31st International Conference on Machine Learning, pp. 1764–1772. No. 2 in Proceedings of Machine Learning Research, PMLR, Bejing, China, 22–24 June 2014. http://proceedings.mlr.press/v32/graves14.html
10. Imran, J., Raman, B.: Evaluating fusion of RGB-D and inertial sensors for multi-modal human action recognition. J. Ambient Intell. Hum. Comput. February 2019. https://doi.org/10.1007/s12652-019-01239-9
11. Khaire, P., Kumar, P., Imran, J.: Combining CNN streams of RGB-D and skeletal data for human activity recognition. Pattern Recognit. Lett. **115**, 107–116 (2018)
12. Liu, K., Chen, C., Jafari, R., Kehtarnavaz, N.: Fusion of inertial and depth sensor data for robust hand gesture recognition. IEEE Sens. J. **14**(6), 1898–1903 (2014)
13. McConnell, R.: Method of and Apparatus for Pattern Recognition, January 1986
14. Rusu, R.B., Blodow, N., Marton, Z.C., Beetz, M.: Aligning point cloud views using persistent feature histograms. In: 2008 IEEE/RSJ International Conference on Intelligent Robots and Systems, pp. 3384–3391. IEEE (2008). https://doi.org/10.1109/IROS.2008.4650967
15. Sachara, F., Kopinski, T., Gepperth, A., Handmann, U.: Free-hand gesture recognition with 3D-CNNs for in-car infotainment control in real-time. In: 2017 IEEE 20th International Conference on Intelligent Transportation Systems (ITSC), pp. 959–964, October 2017. https://doi.org/10.1109/ITSC.2017.8317684
16. Sarkar, A., Gepperth, A., Handmann, U., Kopinski, T.: Dynamic hand gesture recognition for mobile systems using deep LSTM. In: Horain, P., Achard, C., Mallem, M. (eds.) IHCI 2017. LNCS, vol. 10688, pp. 19–31. Springer, Cham (2017). https://doi.org/10.1007/978-3-319-72038-8_3
17. Stein, S., McKenna, S.J.: Combining embedded accelerometers with computer vision for recognizing food preparation activities. In: Proceedings of the 2013 ACM International Joint Conference on Pervasive and Ubiquitous Computing, UbiComp 2013, pp. 729–738. Association for Computing Machinery, New York (2013). https://doi.org/10.1145/2493432.2493482
18. Tran, T., et al.: A multi-modal multi-view dataset for human fall analysis and preliminary investigation on modality. In: 2018 24th International Conference on Pattern Recognition (ICPR), pp. 1947–1952, August 2018. https://doi.org/10.1109/ICPR.2018.8546308
19. William, T., Freeman, M.R.: Orientation histograms for hand gesture recognition. Technical report TR94-03, MERL - Mitsubishi Electric Research Laboratories, Cambridge, MA 02139, December 1994. https://www.merl.com/publications/TR94-03/

Recurrent Neural Network Learning of Performance and Intrinsic Population Dynamics from Sparse Neural Data

Alessandro Salatiello[1,2](✉) and Martin A. Giese[1]

[1] Section for Computational Sensomotorics, Department of Cognitive Neurology,
Centre for Integrative Neuroscience and Hertie Institute for Clinical Brain Research,
University Clinic Tübingen, Tübingen, Germany
{alessandro.salatiello,martin.giese}@uni-tuebingen.de
[2] International Max Planck Research School for Intelligent Systems,
Tübingen, Germany

Abstract. Recurrent Neural Networks (RNNs) are popular models of brain function. The typical training strategy is to adjust their input-output behavior so that it matches that of the biological circuit of interest. Even though this strategy ensures that the biological and artificial networks perform the same computational task, it does not guarantee that their internal activity dynamics match. This suggests that the trained RNNs might end up performing the task employing a different internal computational mechanism. In this work, we introduce a novel training strategy that allows learning not only the input-output behavior of an RNN but also its internal network dynamics. We test the proposed method by training an RNN to simultaneously reproduce internal dynamics and output signals of a physiologically-inspired neural model of motor cortical and muscle activity dynamics. Remarkably, we show that the reproduction of the internal dynamics is successful even when the training algorithm relies on the activities of a small subset of neurons sampled from the biological network. Furthermore, we show that training the RNNs with this method significantly improves their generalization performance. Overall, our results suggest that the proposed method is suitable for building powerful functional RNN models, which automatically capture important computational properties of the biological circuit of interest from sparse neural recordings.

Keywords: Recurrent neural networks · Neural population dynamics · Full-FORCE learning · Motor control · Muscle synergies

1 Introduction

Recurrent Neural Networks (RNNs) are a common theoretical framework for the modeling of biological neural circuits. The rationale behind this choice is

Supported by: BMBF FKZ 01GQ1704, HFSP RGP0036/2016, KONSENS-NHE BW Stiftung NEU007/1, DFG GZ: KA 1258/15-1, and ERC 2019-SyG-RELEVANCE-856495.

I. Farkaš et al. (Eds.): ICANN 2020, LNCS 12396, pp. 874–886, 2020.
https://doi.org/10.1007/978-3-030-61609-0_69

that RNNs and biological neural systems share many essential properties. First, computations are performed through complex interactions between local units; second, these units act in a parallel and distributed fashion, and third, they communicate through recurrent connections [19].

Moreover, recent work [17] has re-emphasized the dynamical systems perspective of brain computation [16]. This has renewed interest in using RNNs, long known to be universal approximators of dynamical systems [6]. In brief, this perspective recognizes the intrinsic low-dimensionality of the activity patterns displayed by populations of neurons, and has been focusing on identifying and studying the low-dimensional projections of such patters, along with the *dynamic rules* that dictate their evolution in time [1,12].

RNNs have been used extensively in neuroscience [4] and have provided fundamental insights into the computational principles of different brain functions, including working memory [11], decision making [12], behavior timing [21], and motor control [9]. Nevertheless, the design of such networks and the determination of their parameters in a way that they capture the input-output behavior and the underlying internal computational mechanism of the biological circuit of interest remains an unsolved problem.

When there is a general understanding of the dynamics necessary to implement a specific function, RNNs can be designed by hand to generate the required dynamics (e.g. [11,13]). However, in most cases, this understanding is lacking, and the network design requires parameter training. The most popular training strategies fall into two categories: *task-based* (also referred to as *goal-driven*) and *activity-based* training (see [15] for a review).

The first strategy is to train the RNN to perform the (supposed) computational function of the target biological circuit (e.g. see [12]). This approach ensures that the biological and model network perform the same computational task. However, it does not guarantee that the RNN employs the same internal computational mechanism to perform the task. As a matter of fact, the population dynamics of the trained RNN frequently differ from those of the target biological network. The second strategy is to train the RNN to directly reproduce the recorded neuronal activity patterns (e.g. see [10]). The resulting models typically explain high fractions of the neural recordings' variance. However, in many cases, it remains unclear to which degree such networks perform the global underlying computational task.

In this paper, we introduce a novel training strategy that combines the strengths of the previously discussed approaches. Specifically, our training strategy makes it possible to train an RNN to perform the same computational task that a target biological network performs, while at the same time ensuring that the internal network dynamics are highly similar to those of the modeled neural system. This was accomplished by exploiting *full-FORCE learning* [5]. This algorithm has been shown to be effective for training RNNs to internally generate given target dynamics. In [5], the authors showed that when appropriately designed, such target dynamics can significantly improve RNN performance. However, the target dynamics used in this work were specified by rather simple *hint signals* (ramp and step functions), which were carefully designed to solve the task at hand and had no direct relationship with the activity patterns of real neurons.

Here, we extend this work and demonstrate that this training algorithm can be used to embed biologically-relevant dynamics in RNNs that perform biological functions, using sparse neural recordings. For this purpose, we first generate ground-truth data using a physiologically-inspired neural model. Then, we train an RNN to simultaneously reproduce both the input-output behavior and the internal dynamics of this model. Critically, we show that the RNNs trained with our method achieve superior generalization performance and are thus able to capture important computational properties of the target neural model.

2   Methods

2.1   Instructed-Delay Center-Out Reaching Task

To test the effectiveness of the proposed method, we applied it to learn a neural control model for the center-out reaching task [8], one of the most studied tasks in motor control. This task (Fig. 1A) requires reaching movements from a central starting position towards one of n_{tar} targets located at a fixed distance from it. First, participants are presented with a *Target Cue*, which indicates which target to reach to. Subsequently, after a variable delay period, they are instructed to perform the reach by an additional *Go Cue*. Variation of this delay period makes it possible to investigate the cortical dynamics associated with movement planning.

Studies in non-human primates have shown that concurrently recorded neurons in the motor cortex exhibit reproducible activity patterns during the different phases of the reach (see [17] for a review). In brief, during the delay period, the firing rates slowly transition from a baseline resting value to a steady-state value that varies with reach direction (Fig. 1B). Subsequently, after the Go Cue, the firing rates transition to an oscillatory regime that levels off before the target is reached (Fig. 1B). The dynamical systems perspective of the motor cortex [17] postulates that the activity observed during the delay period sets the initial state for subsequent autonomous oscillatory dynamics. Such dynamics generate control signals that are transmitted through lower motor centers to the muscles.

Furthermore, studies in both humans and non-human primates have recorded electromyographic signals (EMGs) from relevant upper-arm, shoulder and chest muscles, and have consistently observed multiphasic activity patterns during the movement phase of the reaching task. Such patterns can be explained by the superposition of few time-varying *muscle synergies* [7], which capture the coordinated activation of muscle groups.

2.2   Generation of Ground-Truth Data

In order to validate the proposed method, we generated ground-truth data using a custom biologically-inspired generative model. Such a model is able to reproduce the activity patterns typically observed in motor cortex and muscles during

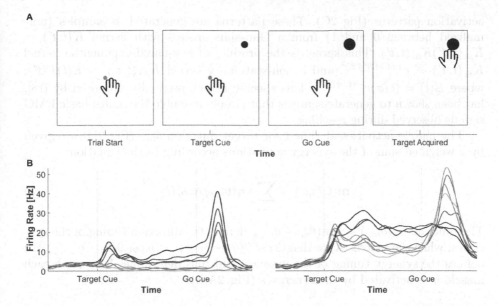

Fig. 1. Simulated task and typical motor cortical activation patterns. (A)
Center-out reaching task. Grey circle: starting position; black circle: target. **(B)** Firing
rates of two representative neurons in dorsal premotor cortex (PMd) during a 7-target
reaching task [3]; each trace represents the across-trial mean for one of the seven conditions. The data, retrieved from the online repository [2], were separately averaged
locked to Target Cue and Go Cue.

reaching movements. The model combines a Stability-Optimized Circuit (SOC)
network [9] for the generation of motor cortex-like activity, with a synergy-based
[7] model for the generation of multiphasic EMG-like activity.

Specifically, we first generated EMG-like patterns for $n_{tar} = 90$ target angles;
we then trained the SOC-network to generate the EMG patterns as stable solutions of its neural dynamics, starting from different initial conditions. Importantly, this type of network was shown to be able to autonomously generate
oscillatory activation patterns that closely resemble the ones observed in the
motor cortex during the movement phase of the reaching task.

Generation of EMG-like Patterns Through a Synergy-Based Model.
We generated time-varying EMG patterns only for the $t_{mov} = 500$ samples of the
movement phase of the reaching task. During the remaining period, each EMG
signal was set to a muscle-specific resting level. The model assumes the existence
of $n_{mus} = 8$ muscles that mainly actuate the directions $\theta_m = 0, \pi/4, ..., 7\pi/4$.
We assume that these muscles are driven by $n_{syn} = 4$ muscle synergies with
preferred directions $\theta_s = 0, \pi/2, ..., 3\pi/2$.

Each synergy is characterized by a time-dependent activity vector $\mathbf{s}_s(t)$
with n_{mus} components; this vector specifies muscle-specific and time-varying

activation patterns (Fig. 2C). These patterns are generated as samples (normalized between 0 and 1) from a Gaussian process with kernel $K(t, t') = K_{se}(t, t')K_{ns}(t, t')$. This kernel is the product of a squared-exponential kernel $K_{se}(t, t') = e^{-(t-t')^2/2\zeta^2}$ and a non-stationary kernel $K_{ns}(t, t') = E(t)E(t')$, where $E(t) = (t/\sigma)e^{-(t/\sigma)^2/4}$. This specific kernel, originally proposed by [18], has been shown to generate samples that closely resemble the multiphasic EMG signals observed during reaching.

The muscle activities at time t for target direction θ_{tar} (Fig. 2D) are given by a weighted sum of the synergy activations according to the equation:

$$\mathbf{m}(t, \theta_{tar}) = \sum_{s=1}^{n_{syn}} w_s(\theta_{tar})\mathbf{A}_s\mathbf{s}_s(t) \tag{1}$$

The function $w_s(\theta_{tar}) = [\cos(\theta_{tar} - \theta_s)]_+$ defines the direction tuning of the synergies, while the matrix $\mathbf{A}_s = \mathrm{diag}([\cos(.9(\theta_s - \theta_1))]_+, ..., [\cos(.9(\theta_s - \theta_{n_{mus}}))]_+)$ defines the synergy tuning of the muscles, and thus determines how much each muscle m is activated by the synergy s (Fig. 2A,B).

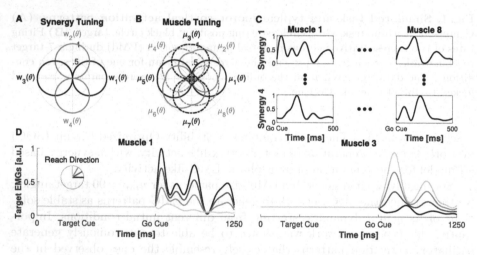

Fig. 2. Synergy-based generative model. (A) Direction tuning of muscle synergies $w_s(\theta_{tar})$. (B) Direction tuning of individual muscles, computed maximizing over time the muscle activities (i.e. $\mu_i(\theta_{tar}) = \max_t \mathbf{m}_i(t, \theta_{tar})$). (C) Synergies' activation patterns $\mathbf{s}_s(t)$. (D) Muscle activities (EMGs) of two representative muscles during reaches to four target directions. Traces are color-coded based on the target direction. Note the smooth modulation of EMGs' amplitude and shape as the reaching direction changes.

Generation of Motor-cortex-like Activity Patterns Through SOC Network.
SOC networks [9] are non-linear, rate-based recurrent networks that respect Dale's principle. The specific algorithm used to train these networks

renders their internal network dynamics remarkably similar to the activity patterns observed in the motor cortex during reaching movements. Since these networks generate motor-cortical-like data, in the remainder of the paper, we will refer to the trained SOC network as the *biological network*. In this section, we explain how we trained an SOC network of 500 neurons in order to generate the reach-related EMG signals (Fig. 2D).

The training comprises five steps (see [9] for details). First, we initialized the recurrent connectivity matrix $\mathbf{W}$ randomly, ensuring that its spectral radius was $R = 10$; this choice generates a strongly chaotic network behavior. Second, we made the network linearly stable by fine-tuning its inhibitory connections through an iterative algorithm, which minimizes the *smoothed spectral abscissa* of $\mathbf{W}$. Third, we found the four (orthogonal) initial conditions that generated the strongest transient responses in the network. These responses were arbitrarily associated with the *main target directions* $0, \pi/2, \pi, 3\pi/2$. Fourth, we linearly interpolated the four initial conditions on a quadrant-by-quadrant basis to generate initial conditions that are appropriate to reach to targets at intermediate angles. These directions define n_{tar} initial conditions, which all result in strongly oscillatory dynamics. Fifth, we learned by linear regression, across all the conditions, a single readout matrix that maps the activity of the network onto the EMG activity patterns $\mathbf{m}(t, \theta_{tar})$.

2.3 Learning of the RNN Model Using the Full-FORCE Algorithm

The goal of our work is to train rate-based RNNs to generate the multiphasic EMG-like signals produced by the biological network, while at the same time generating similar internal activation dynamics. If the training procedure is successful, we end up *embedding* the activation dynamics of the biological network in the trained RNNs. Therefore, in the remainder of the text, we will refer to these trained RNNs as *embedder networks*. These networks obey the dynamics:

$$\tau \frac{d\mathbf{x}(t)}{dt} = -\mathbf{x}(t) + \mathbf{J}H(\mathbf{x}(t)) + \mathbf{L}\mathbf{u}(t) \qquad (2)$$

The term $H(\mathbf{x}(t)) = \tanh(\mathbf{x}(t))$ represents the instantaneous firing rate as a function of the membrane potential vector $\mathbf{x}(t)$. The output signals that approximate the EMG-like signals $\mathbf{m}(t, \theta_{tar})$ are given by the vector $\mathbf{y}(t) = \mathbf{K}H(\mathbf{x}(t))$, where $\mathbf{K}$ is a read-out matrix.

The input signal vector $\mathbf{u}(t)$ has 12 dimensions and selects the relevant reaching direction. Its components are given by smooth ramping signals that ramp up between the Target Cue and the Go Cue, and then suddenly go back to zero to determine movement initiation. Their steady-state amplitudes, reached 40 ms before the Go Cue, code for reach direction. To determine such steady-state values, we used a procedure that mirrors the one we adopted to assign initial conditions to the biological network. Specifically, we first arbitrarily assigned 12-dimensional random vectors to each of the *main angles* $0, \pi/2, ..., 3\pi/2$, where their components were randomly drawn (with replacement) from the interval $[-0.6, 0.6]$. We then determined the amplitude components for intermediate angles by linearly interpolating the amplitudes associated to the main angles, on a quadrant-by-quadrant basis.

As training data, we used simulated EMG and neural activity data for reach directions 0, 8, 16, ..., 352°. As test data we used the corresponding data for reach directions 4, 12, ..., 356°, ensuring disjoint training and test sets. Importantly, the biological network generates data only for the movement phase of the reaching task, and we used only these data to embed the dynamics of the biological network in the embedder network. However, the embedder network had to generate the EMG signals and appropriate dynamics for the whole task, including the baseline and preparatory period. Critically, after training, also the embedder network produces the EMG signals through its autonomous dynamics, since the input signals $\mathbf{u(t)}$ return to zero right after the Go Cue to signal movement initiation.

Full-FORCE Learning Algorithm. We used the full-FORCE algorithm [5] to learn the recurrent weights $\mathbf{J}$ and the readout weights $\mathbf{K}$. This algorithm constructs an additional *auxiliary network* that receives a subset of the desired internal network activities as an additional input signal $\mathbf{u}_{hint}(t)$. In our case, this hint signal is defined by the firing rates of the neurons of the biological network we assume to be able to record from. The dynamics of the auxiliary network are given by:

$$\tau \frac{d\mathbf{x}^{D}(t)}{dt} = -\mathbf{x}^{D}(t) + \mathbf{J}^{D}H(\mathbf{x}^{D}(t)) + \mathbf{L}\mathbf{u}(t) + \mathbf{B}\mathbf{u}_{hint}(t) + \mathbf{C}\mathbf{m}(t, \theta_{tar}) \quad (3)$$

where $\mathbf{J}^{D}$, $\mathbf{L}$, $\mathbf{B}$, and $\mathbf{C}$ are fixed random matrices that are not trained. The role of the auxiliary network is to generate dynamics that are driven by the input variables $\mathbf{u}(t)$, $\mathbf{u}_{hint}(t)$ and $\mathbf{m}(t, \theta_{tar})^{1}$. The core idea of the algorithm is to train the recurrent weights $\mathbf{J}$ of the embedder network (2) so that this generates signals related to such input terms, through its recurrent dynamics. This can be achieved by minimizing the error function

$$Q(\mathbf{J}) = \langle |\mathbf{J}H(\mathbf{x}(t)) - \mathbf{J}^{D}H(\mathbf{x}^{D}(t)) - \mathbf{B}\mathbf{u}_{hint}(t) - \mathbf{C}\mathbf{m}(t, \theta_{tar})|^{2} \rangle \quad (4)$$

using a recursive least squares algorithm[2].

Embedding the Dynamics from Sparse Neuronal Samples. In real experiments, typically, one is able to record the activity of only a small fraction of neurons of the biological circuit of interest. It is thus important to assess whether one can efficiently *constrain* the dynamics of the embedder network using only the activities of small subsets of neurons sampled from the biological network. These 'recorded' neurons define the dimensionality of the additional input term

---

[1] These input terms are strong enough to suppress chaotic activity in the network [5].
[2] Following [5] we included an L2 regularization term for $\mathbf{J}$.

$\mathbf{u}_{hint}(t)^3$. Specifically, in our experiments, we constrain the embedder network dynamics using different percentages of neurons $\gamma = 0, 1, 2, 3, 10$, and 100 %, sampled from the biological network. Clearly, when $\gamma = 0\%$, we are effectively not embedding the dynamics. Furthermore, we investigated whether an embedder network of a size η smaller than the one of the biological network is still able to perform the task accurately and to learn its dynamics. For this purpose, we trained embedder networks of $\eta = 100, 200$, and 500 neurons.

2.4 Quantification of Embedder Network Performance

Features of Interest. To quantify how well the embedder network is able to reproduce the EMG signals, we computed the generalization error (GE), defined as the normalized reconstruction error on the test set, averaged across muscles and tasks. To quantify the similarity between the population activity dynamics of the biological (D_B) and embedder networks (D_E), we computed their singular vector canonical correlations (CC)[4] [14]. Moreover, as a baseline, we also computed the singular vector canonical correlations between the population dynamics of the biological network and those of an untrained RNN of 100 neurons with random connections (D_0).

Statistics. To measure the overall effect of embedding the dynamics on GE and CC, we fitted the linear regression models $GE = \beta_0 + \beta_1 EoD + \beta_2 \eta$ and $CC = \beta_0 + \beta_1 EoD + \beta_2 \eta$, where EoD is an indicator variable that takes on the value 1 whenever $\gamma > 0$. Note that η was included in the models since it is a potential confounder. Moreover, to quantify the effect of using different percentages of sampled neurons to embed the dynamics on GE and CC, we also fitted the linear regression models $GE = \beta_0 + \beta_1 \gamma + \beta_2 \eta$ and $CC = \beta_0 + \beta_1 \gamma + \beta_2 \eta$, considering only the networks with $\gamma > 0$. Finally, to summarize the results of the canonical correlation analysis, we also computed the *activation similarity index* (ASI), which is a normalized measure of the similarity between the activation dynamics of the biological network (D_B) and embedder network (D_E). This index is defined as

$$ASI_{D_E} = \frac{mCC(D_E, D_B) - mCC(D_0, D_B)}{1 - mCC(D_0, D_B)} \tag{5}$$

where $mCC(D_i, D_j)$ denotes the average CC between the activation dynamics D_i and D_j.

---

[3] To ensure a sufficiently strong effect on the embedder network, the hint signals were scaled by a factor of 5. In addition, the final 110 samples of such signals were replaced by a smooth decay to zero, modeled by spline interpolation. This ensured that the activities go back to zero at the end of the movement phase.

[4] We restricted our analysis to the first five singular vector canonical variables, which on average, captured >92% of the original data variance.

3   Results

Embedding the Dynamics Improves RNN Ability to Generalize. To assess how well the emebedder networks learned to perform the task, we measured their ability to approximate the EMG signals generated by the biological network for the test reach directions. Figure 3A shows representative EMGs generated by the biological and embedder networks, for different combinations of network size (η) and percentage of sampled neurons (γ). Figure 3B shows the average generalization error (GE) for all the trained embedder networks.

All the trained RNNs reproduced the target EMGs with relatively high accuracy ($GE \leq 32.25\%$), and their performance improved with embedder network size (η). Critically, the generalization error of the RNNs that were only trained to generate the appropriate input-output behavior was significantly higher than that of the RNNs that were also trained to internally generate the activation dynamics of the biological network ($p = 1.26 \times 10^{-35}$, Fig. 5A). Finally, GE decreases with γ ($p = 6.25 \times 10^{-4}$), although only by a small amount ($\beta_1 = -1.94 \times 10^{-2}$, Fig. 5B). Therefore, embedding the activation dynamics of the biological network improves the ability of the embedder networks to generalize.

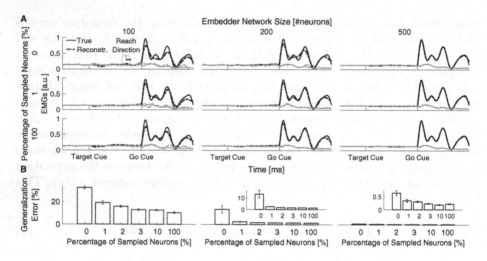

Fig. 3. Ground-truth and reconstructed EMGs. (A) Dashed lines: reconstructed EMGs of muscle 1 generated by embedder networks of different sizes, and trained using different percentages of ground-truth neurons; solid lines: respective ground-truth EMGs (generated by the biological network). **(B)** Generalization error averaged across muscles and reach directions. Insets: magnifications of the respective plots.

Embedding the Dynamics Increases RNN Activation Similarity. To quantify the similarity between the activation dynamics of biological and embedder networks, we computed their singular vector canonical correlations [14].

Figure 4A shows the firing rates of a representative unit across selected reach directions, for different combinations of η and γ. Note that when the RNN dynamics were *constrained* to be similar to those of the biological network ($\gamma > 0$), RNN units show activation patterns that resemble those observed in the motor cortex neurons during reaching: slow ramping activity during the preparatory phase followed by fast oscillations during the movement phase. Figure 4B shows the average activation similarity index (ASI) for all the trained embedder networks. Clearly, the ASI of the RNNs trained with $\gamma = 0$ approaches 0%; this suggests that untrained RNNs and RNNs trained to only reproduce the input-output behaviour of the biological network have activation dynamics that are comparatively similar to those of the biological network.

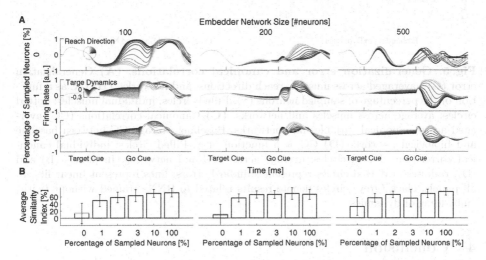

Fig. 4. Neural activities and activation similarities. (A) Firing rates of one representative neuron belonging to embedder networks of different sizes, and trained using different percentages of ground-truth neurons (γ). Traces are color-coded based on target direction. Inset: target firing rates specified by an example biological neuron. **(B)** ASI as a function of γ.

Critically, the canonical correlations (CC) of these input-output trained RNNs were significantly lower than those of the RNNs that were also trained with embedding of dynamics ($p = 1.87 \times 10^{-5}$, Fig. 5C). Importantly, CC do not significantly increase with γ ($p = 2.66 \times 10^{-1}$, Fig. 5D). This suggests that constraining the dynamics using the activation patterns of only 1% of neurons of the biological network is enough to have the RNN capture the dominant modes of shared variability. This finding is consistent with the results of a previous study on a population of neurons in the primary visual cortex [22]. Therefore, embedding the activation dynamics using a very small activity sample is enough to have the embedder network capture important response properties of the entire biological network.

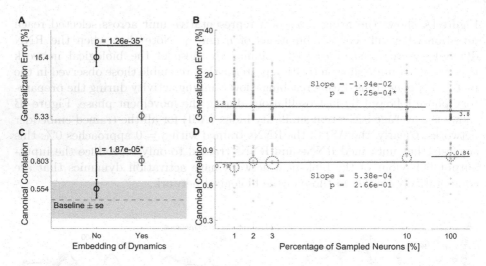

Fig. 5. Generalization error and canonical correlations. (A) Generalization error (GE) averaged across muscles, reach directions, and networks. **(B)** GE as a function of the percentage of sampled neurons (γ). Filled circles: individual muscles; dotted circles: average across muscles and networks. **(C)** Canonical correlations (CC) averaged across canonical variables and networks. Baseline: average CC between baseline and biological network. **(D)** CC as a function of γ. Filled circles: individual canonical correlation; dotted circles: average across CC and networks. In panels (B) and (D), radiuses of dotted circles represent standard errors; lines represent linear fits. In all panels, black (grey) circles denote results related to RNNs trained without (with) embedding of dynamics

4   Conclusion

A common strategy for the modeling of biological neural systems exploiting RNNs is the so-called *task-based* approach [19]. This method trains the RNNs to learn the mapping between the input and the output signals of the biological circuit of interest. However, the problem of identifying RNN parameters from input-output data is generally ill-posed, so that there can be manifolds of equivalent solutions in the parameters space. As a consequence, even though RNNs generally manage to approximate the input-output behavior accurately, the learned internal computations and activity dynamics might differ substantially from the ones of the target biological system [23].

In this work, we proposed a novel training strategy, which allows learning the input-output behavior of an RNN together with its internal network dynamics, based on sparse neural recordings. We tested the proposed method by training an RNN to simultaneously reproduce the internal dynamics and output signals of a physiologically-inspired neural model for the generation of the motor cortical and muscle activation dynamics typically observed during reaching movements.

Critically, we demonstrated our approach to be successful even in the presence of small samples of activation dynamics from the target neural model.

Furthermore, we showed that the RNNs trained with this approach achieved superior generalization performance. In sum, these results suggest that our method is suitable for the automatic generation of RNN models that capture critical computational properties of the neural circuit of interests. The resulting RNN models can then be further analyzed with methods from dynamical systems theory [20] in order to reverse engineer the computational principles of brain function.

References

1. Chaudhuri, R., Gercek, B., Pandey, B., Peyrache, A., Fiete, I.: The intrinsic attractor manifold and population dynamics of a canonical cognitive circuit across waking and sleep. Nat. Neurosci. **22**(9), 1512–1520 (2019)
2. Churchland, M.M.: Variance toolbox (2010). https://churchland.zuckermaninstitute.columbia.edu/content/code
3. Churchland, M.M., et al.: Stimulus onset quenches neural variability: a widespread cortical phenomenon. Nat. Neurosci. **13**(3), 369 (2010)
4. Dayan, P., Abbott, L.F.: Theoretical Neuroscience: Computational and Mathematical Modeling of Neural Systems. The MIT Press, Cambridge (2001)
5. DePasquale, B., Cueva, C.J., Rajan, K., Escola, G.S., Abbott, L.: Full-force: atarget-based method for training recurrent networks. PLoS ONE **13**(2) (2018)
6. Doya, K.: Universality of fully-connected recurrent neural networks. In: Proceedings of 1992 IEEE International Symposium on Circuits and Systems, pp. 2777–2780 (1992)
7. Flash, T., Hochner, B.: Motor primitives in vertebrates and invertebrates. Curr. Opinion Neurobiol. **15**(6), 660–666 (2005)
8. Georgopoulos, A.P., Kalaska, J.F., Massey, J.T.: Spatial trajectories and reaction times of aimed movements: effects of practice, uncertainty, and change in target location. J. Neurophysiol. **46**(4), 725–743 (1981)
9. Hennequin, G., Vogels, T.P., Gerstner, W.: Optimal control of transient dynamics in balanced networks supports generation of complex movements. Neuron **82**(6), 1394–1406 (2014)
10. Kim, C.M., Chow, C.C.: Learning recurrent dynamics in spiking networks. eLife **7**, e37124 (2018)
11. Machens, C.K., Romo, R., Brody, C.D.: Flexible control of mutual inhibition: a neural model of two-interval discrimination. Science **307**(5712), 1121–1124 (2005)
12. Mante, V., Sussillo, D., Shenoy, K.V., Newsome, W.T.: Context-dependent computation by recurrent dynamics in prefrontal cortex. Nature **503**(7474), 78–84 (2013)
13. Matsuoka, K.: Mechanisms of frequency and pattern control in the neural rhythm generators. Biol. Cybern. **56**(5–6), 345–353 (1987)
14. Raghu, M., Gilmer, J., Yosinski, J., Sohl-Dickstein, J.: SVCCA: singular vector canonical correlation analysis for deep learning dynamics and interpretability. In: Advances in Neural Information Processing Systems, pp. 6076–6085 (2017)
15. Saxena, S., Cunningham, J.P.: Towards the neural population doctrine. Curr. Opinion Neurobiol. **55**, 103–111 (2019)
16. Schoner, G., Kelso, J.: Dynamic pattern generation in behavioral and neural systems. Science **239**(4847), 1513–1520 (1988)
17. Shenoy, K.V., Sahani, M., Churchland, M.M.: Cortical control of arm movements: a dynamical systems perspective. Ann. Rev. Neurosci. **36**, 337–359 (2013)

18. Stroud, J.P., Porter, M.A., Hennequin, G., Vogels, T.P.: Motor primitives in space and time via targeted gain modulation in cortical networks. Nat. Neurosci. **21**(12), 1774–1783 (2018)
19. Sussillo, D.: Neural circuits as computational dynamical systems. Curr. Opinion neurobiol. **25**, 156–163 (2014)
20. Sussillo, D., Barak, O.: Opening the black box: low-dimensional dynamics in high-dimensional recurrent neural networks. Neural Comput. **25**(3), 626–649 (2013)
21. Wang, J., Narain, D., Hosseini, E.A., Jazayeri, M.: Flexible timing by temporal scaling of cortical responses. Nat. Neurosci. **21**(1), 102–110 (2018)
22. Williamson, R.C., et al.: Scaling properties of dimensionality reduction for neural populations and network models. PLoS Comput. Biol. **12**, e1005141 (2016)
23. Williamson, R.C., Doiron, B., Smith, M.A., Byron, M.Y.: Bridging large-scale neuronal recordings and large-scale network models using dimensionality reduction. Curr. Opinion Neurobiol. **55**, 40–47 (2019)

Author Index

Printed in the United States
By Bookmasters